BUSINESS JETS INTERNATIONAL 2017

VOLUME 1 – PRODUCTION

BUSINESS JETS INTERNATIONAL 2017

Steven Sowter and Barrie Towey

Thirty-Second Edition

VOLUME 1 – PRODUCTION

Published by:	Air-Britain
Sales Department:	Unit 1A, Munday Works Industrial Estate, 58-66 Morley Road, Tonbridge TN9 1RA
Sales e-mail:	sales@air-britain.co.uk
Membership Enquiries:	1 Rose Cottages, 179 Penn Road, Hazelmere, Bucks HP15 7NE, UK (email: membenquiry@air-britain.co.uk)
Web-site:	http://www.air-britain.co.uk

ISBN: 978-0-85130-499-1

Cover photographs:

Front cover:
Company publicity photo of an unidentified Challenger 350 over a Canadian coastline. (Bombardier Inc)

Back cover:

Top: Embraer Phenom 100E A6-EFC (50000369) appropriately-registered for the Etihad Flight College. (Embraer)

Centre: Gulfstream IV-SP N808MF (1448) on approach to Scottsdale-Municipal, Arizona. (Jarrod Wilkening)

Bottom: The first example of the Dassault Falcon 8X in test marks as F-WWQA (401). (Dassault Aviation)

Printed by Bell & Bain Ltd, Glasgow G46 7UQ

CONTENTS

INTRODUCTION

Welcome to the 32nd edition of *Business Jets International*, which follows the title's long-established annual format, but returning to the original size and placing the index and addenda into a second volume.

The prime purpose of the book continues to be the recording of the registration histories of all purpose-designed business jets, including Experimental and Non-Production types. Supplements also detail airliner variants that have been built or converted for corporate use and our traditional Grumman G159 Gulfstream listing.

Our unique master index shows all registrations known to have been allocated to business jets – in excess of 100,000 – in alpha-numeric order by country, with current registrations in bold print. Generic type designators and construction numbers help the location of aircraft in the production lists which form the main body of the book. In the case of Citation Is and IIs, the unit number is shown instead of the construction number, as those types are listed by unit number in their respective production lists. Sub-types and military designations can be identified in the main text. Preserved and similar extant aircraft are shown in normal type.

It has always been our policy to include and to distinguish marks that have not yet been fully allocated, for example those only reserved. To identify such marks we use the symbols *, ^ and + and also put unofficial marks within inverted commas. The full description of these symbols can be found within the Explanatory Notes.

The data in this issue of *Business Jets International* is correct to mid-May 2017 and our monthly magazine, Air-Britain News, can be used throughout the year to keep the book up-to-date. Non-subscribers to News will find details of subscriptions and Air-Britain membership at the back of this book or via www.air-britain.co.uk.

In a work of this nature, which can only ever be a snapshot in time, there are bound to be details which are not yet known to us, as well as some (hopefully few!) errors; the editorial team at the address below would welcome notification of any such errors or omissions. While we still have problems confirming the identities of aircraft that have been exported to certain countries, particularly Mexico and Venezuela (as is evidenced by the list of aircraft whose c/n is not yet known towards the back of the book), a growing problem is identifying the fates of military aircraft which have been retired from service. We would be delighted to hear from anyone who can assist us in this respect.

The 12 months since our last book have been challenging for business jet manufacturers, particularly those of small and mid-size aircraft. Analysts predict that this situation will last until at least 2020. The market for large-cabin aircraft fared better, so much so that Gulfstream Aerospace Corp felt confident enough to reserve registrations for 50 new G650s rather than its usual yearly batch of 24 or 25.

In this large-cabin sector, Bombardier's Global 7000 flew for the first time and 3 aircraft were engaged in certification test-flying at the time of writing. Similarly, Gulfstream's new G600 also made its first flight and both it and its G500 sister are now well into their certification programmes. Gulfstream announced that production of the G450 will cease when the G500 enters service. New G550s include 2 ordered by the Polish government. The first G650 on the Chinese register was delivered, joining the significant number of the type already operating in the country but registered elsewhere.

Dassault began delivering its Falcon 8X, with the first examples going to Greece, Brazil, the United Arab Emirates, India, the United Kingdom and Germany as well as the USA. Development of the Falcon 5X continued to be delayed – and Dassault suffered a number of cancelled orders as a result.

In other market segments, Gulfstream 150 and Cessna Citation Mustang production were both ended in the face of poor demand, and Learjet 45 and Citation X+ sales were so sluggish that their futures must also be in doubt. Deliveries of Citation Latitudes to NetJets continued apace but demand for the type from other customers does not appear to be huge!

Cessna's Citation Longitude made its first flight and at the time of writing 4 aircraft were involved in certification testing.

Embraer's Phenom 300 was the type delivered in the largest quantity for the 6th year in a row, with both NetJets and the now-merged Flexjet and Flight Options fleets continuing to receive new aircraft. Deliveries of the lighter Phenom 100 remained slow, however, although four aircraft were delivered to Etihad Flight College and the first machines for the United Kingdom Ministry of Defence have been noted at the factory in Brazil. Legacy 450 deliveries included four to Canada and one to Germany and Embraer began the process of moving production of both it and the larger Legacy 500 from Brazil to Melbourne in Florida.

HondaJet deliveries and production gathered momentum and included examples to Germany, Mexico and France. A third Pilatus PC-24 joined the flight-test programme.

The Manx, Maltese, Aruban, San Marino, Cayman and Bermudan registers continued to grow with the addition of business jets whose owners sought registers of convenience – with numerous examples of a change from one of these registers to another for whatever reason! A possibly surprising new country appearing in this book for the first time is the Cook Islands, where a Citation II is now registered.

As always, this book should be followed by our BizQR Quick Reference annual early next year.

May 2017

Address for correspondence:
Steven Sowter
78 Laburnum Road
Hayes, Middlesex UB3 4JZ
United Kingdom

email address: stevensowter2@aol.com

ACKNOWLEDGEMENTS

Business Jets International has been produced with the valued past and present assistance of, and from information provided by, the following companies and individuals, sadly some no longer with us:

Aerospatiale/EADS
Ascend Worldwide Ltd
Atlantic Aviation
Aviation Data Service of Wichita
Beech Aircraft Co
British Aerospace plc
Canadair Limited
Canadair Challenger Limited
Cessna Aircraft Co
Gulfstream Aerospace
Israeli Aircraft Industries
Jetnet LLC Utica NY
Lockheed Aircraft Co
Mitsubishi Aircraft Co
Raytheon Aircraft Co
Rockwell International
Sabreliner Corp

Barry Ambrose
Joseph Anckner
Steve Bailey
H W Barrett
Colin Berry
Bill Blanchard
Mike Brown
David C Buck
Peter Budden
B J Burt
Lyn Buttifant
Jim Cain
Russell Carter
Nick C Challoner
Chris Chatfield
Alan E Clark
Colin Clark
Dennis Clement
Paul Compton
Colin Darvill
John Davies
J F Elliott
Robert D Elliott
David England
Brian Gates
Wayne Gates
Ian Gibson
Jennifer Gradidge
S Graham
Nigel Green
Andrew Griffiths
Kay Hagby
Philip Hancock
Noam Hartoch
Richard Hill
Mike Holdstock
Gerry Hollands
Carolos Hopkins
Nigel Howarth
Heinz Kasmanhuber
John Kim
Bruce Leatherborrow
John MacMaster
Michael Magnusson
Stephen L Mart
J A Newton
Ole Nikolajsen
Justin Palmer
Pierre Parvaud
Nigel Prevett
Brian Print
Glyn Ramsden
Mark Reavey
Morian Reed
Doug Robinson
Terry Ross
Ian Sant
Don Schofield
Mike Schofield
Simon Scott-Kemball
D Sheldon
Peter Simmonds
Graham Slack
Terry Smith
Claude Soussi
Neville Spalding
David Thompson
Peter Thompson
Bob Underwood
Richard Urbeck
D F Walsh
Pete Watson

Plus the many regular contributors to the BIZ-JETS section of *Air-Britain News*. Due acknowledgement is also given to the monograph *Le Morane-Saulnier Paris MS760* by Pierre Parvaud and Pierre Gaillard published by *Le Trait d'Union* (the magazine of the French Branch of Air-Britain) and to the article in the Winter 1989 *Air-Britain Digest* by the same two authors on the HFB320 Hansa. We must also thank the Air-Britain Gulfstream specialist, Alain Jeneve, for his review of the Gulfstream I section. Thanks are also due to Brian Gates for supplying data on the Learjet AvCom fin conversions.

EXPLANATORY NOTES

The following abbreviations have been used in the text:

A/c	Aircraft	cx/canx	cancelled	ntu	not taken up
A/P	Airport	dbr	damaged beyond repair	r/o	rolled out
AFB	Air Force Base	dest	destroyed	TL	total landings
Avn	Aviation	exp	expired	TT	total time
b/u	broken up	ff	first flight	wfs	withdrawn from service
c/s	colour scheme	Inds	Industries	wfu	withdrawn from use
cvtd	converted	Inst	Institute	w/o	written off

+ following a set of marks is to bring to the readers attention a note which follows, sometimes on the next line, sometimes at the end of the listing.

* An asterisk following the last registration indicates that at the time of compilation these marks were only reserved.

^ Indicates marks which the owner/operator of the aircraft has requested. On many occasions such marks may never be taken up.

" " Quotation marks around a registration indicate that the marks were painted on the aircraft, either in error or for publicity purposes, but were not officially allocated.

( ) Brackets around a registration indicate that these marks were not taken up.

NOTE: when an aircraft has been sold to another country and the new marks are not known at the time of compilation, the country prefix only is shown. For Brazil and Mexico PT- and XA- are used even though they may eventually carry other prefixes for these countries.

BEECH 390 PREMIER I / IA*

C/n	Srs	Identities						
RB-1		N390RA	[rolled out 19Aug98; ff 23Dec98]		[wfu; cx 18Feb09]			
RB-2		N704T	[wfu; cx 23Feb09]					
RB-3		N390TC	[wfu; cx 18Feb09]					
RB-4		N842PM	N414TE					
RB-5		N155GD	N808V					
RB-6		N390R	N155RM	N391YS				
RB-7		N343PR	(N348PR)	SP-MRD				
RB-8		N460AS						
RB-9		N390EM	N60ME	XA-IAS	XA-ZUL	N21XP		
RB-10		N5010X	[w/o North Las Vegas, NV, 27May04; remains moved to Wichita/Mid-Continent, KS]					
RB-11		N5121P	N50PM	N50PN	(N50PQ)	[cx 17Feb17; wfu Wichita/Beech Field, KS]		
RB-12		N390TA	N390P	XA-TSN	N390BW	OE-FRJ	N881AA	[wfu Dunsfold, UK]
RB-13		N48TC						
RB-14		N969RE						
RB-15		N73WC	N335JB	N929SS				
RB-16		N151KD	N444SS	C-GYPV				
RB-17		N5017T	N88EL	N88ER				
RB-18		N88MM	N711AJ	LX-POO	N23WA	N833PS		
RB-19		N65TB	N16DK	N514AJ				
RB-20		N777MG	N777MQ	(N390BP)	YL-KSC			
RB-21		N390MB	PR-AMA	N390MB				
RB-22		N45NB	N45ND	N223F	N232F	N323CM		
RB-23		N109PM	N488PC	N488RC	VT-RAL	[w/o 19Mar08 Udaipur, India]		
RB-24		N5024J	(ZS-PRF)	ZS-PRM	N124BR	N903MT		
RB-25		N390CL	N808W	N719L	(N713L)	N719D		
RB-26		N390RB	(N390HR)	[w/o 07Jan03 Santo Domingo-Herrera Intl Airport, Dominican Republic]				
RB-27		N3216P	D-IFMC	(HB-...)	N264DL			
RB-28		N128RM	N128JL	N545G				
RB-29		N747BK	N110PR					
RB-30		N390BL	N84ML	N84FM				
RB-31		N3231K	ZS-AVM	N20VA				
RB-32		N5132D	PR-CIM	N1132D	PR-DFG			
RB-33		N50843	N677AS	N92SH				
RB-34		N390DP	N7JT	N390DP				
RB-35		N435K	D-IAGG	M-GDRS	D-ISKO			
RB-36		N1XT	N36XT	N390SM	(N29YW)			
RB-37		N452A	N567T					
RB-38		N972PF						
RB-39		N39KT	N390JK					
RB-40		N51140	PR-BER	N86RB	N390CE			
RB-41		N142HH	(N111HH)	N43HJ	OE-FMC	N882AA	[wfu Lasham, UK]	
RB-42		N390CK	N324AM	[cx 29Oct15; wfu]				
RB-43		N1EG						
RB-44		N5044X	N88MM					
RB-45		N809RM	N100WE					
RB-46		N460L	YL-KSG	N516GW				
RB-47		N5147Y	(N145SD)	N581SF	N5810F			
RB-48		N51480	D-IATT	HS-KAC				
RB-49		N5049U	N25MC					
RB-50		N344W	N390NS	D-ISXT	N523DR			
RB-51		N4251D	LX-LCG	N530PT				
RB-52		N605TC	N99WJ					
RB-53		N50453	N351CB	N351CW				
RB-54		N61754	ZS-MGK	N354RB				
RB-55		N390PL	N85PL					
RB-56		N390RC	PK-TWL	Indonesia A-9208				
RB-57		N457K	N488PC	VP-CRD	OE-FRC	D-IIMH	T7-OKA	
RB-58		N5158B	N34GN	C-FDAA				
RB-59		N701DF	N622JK					
RB-60		N6160D	LX-PRE	G-PREI	M-PREI			
RB-61		N61161	EC-IOZ	N39JC				
RB-62		N6162Z	N800CS	N808CS				
RB-63		N6163T	ZS-DDM	ZS-SRU				
RB-64		N6164U	LX-PMR	D-IKGT				
RB-65		N4395D	PR-GCA	N67FP				
RB-66		N50586	VP-BAE	N931BR	G-VONJ	ZS-SUW		
RB-67		N6167D	ZS-MGK	N167DP				
RB-68		N447TF	N50648	N133B	ZS-BDG			
RB-69		N205BC						
RB-70		N5070W	N731UG	(N391RB)	ZS-ABG	N70BR	N998PA	
RB-71		N4471P	N71KV					
RB-72		N5072X	N535BC	N535BR	ZS-SGS	ZS-MCO		
RB-73		N371CF	N371CE	N107WR	(N107YR)	F-GVBK		
RB-74		N61474	N902RD	(N9011P)	VP-CWW	N422HS	N144ST	N451KT
RB-75		N213PC	N213PQ					

BEECH 390 PREMIER I / IA*

C/n	Srs	Identities							
RB-76		N6076Y	N1XH						
RB-77		N6177A	TC-MHS	N32BR	OE-FKW	N889DT	N39RP		
RB-78		N390JW	N808SQ						
RB-79		N200PR	[w/o 07Apr04 Blackbushe, UK; remains to Air Salvage Int'l, Alton, Hants, UK 07Feb05]						
RB-80		N50280	N50PM	[w/o 17Dec13, Atlanta, GA]					
RB-81		N50468	N390P	N134SW					
RB-82		N61882	D-IBBB						
RB-83		N6183G	N88EL	N88EU	LY-HER	F-HBFA	G-HFAA	F-HLJP	N390AB
RB-84		N61784	PR-JRR						
RB-85		N4485B	N487DT						
RB-86		N390TA	N96NC	N110JD	N407MW				
RB-87		N6187Q	(B-8006)	N952GL	N952GM	N479MM			
RB-88		N4488F	G-OMJC	M-RKAY					
RB-89		N61589	D-IWWW						
RB-90		N32SG							
RB-91		N24YP	N24YD	N45NB					
RB-92		N62LW	N592HC						
RB-93		N322BJ							
RB-94		N6194N	ZS-PFE						
RB-95		N6195S	N24YP	N888LD	N390LM	N66LM			
RB-96		N535CD							
RB-97		N6197F	G-FRYL						
RB-98		N61998	N500CZ						
RB-99		N24YP	N24YR	N199RM					
RB-100		N122DS							
RB-101		N6201A	N101PN	N73PJ					
RB-102	*	N6182F	N3901A	N227FH	N200ST				
RB-103		N61930	N701KB	N781KB	N700KB	N730MS	N48KF		
RB-104		N5104G	N855JB						
RB-105		N5105A	N777JF						
RB-106		N61706	N20NL	[w/o Lewiston/Sharpe Farms, MO, 23Dec08; parted out by Dodson Int'l, Rantoul, KS]					
RB-107		N61717	N877W	N817W					
RB-108		N61908							
RB-109		N50078	D-IFMG						
RB-110		N701KB	N300SL						
RB-111		N6111F	N713AZ						
RB-112		N60322	N76HL						
RB-113		N11PM	N727KG	N113BR	N390PR	N657NG			
RB-114		N143CM							
RB-115		N6015Y	N72SJ	N193CS					
RB-116		N200LB							
RB-117		N6117G	N1SH						
RB-118		N6118C	B-8018	N390BR	(N30AJ)				
RB-119		N6119C	N1CR	N39DM	N84EA	N14EA	N901MT		
RB-120		N6120U	N311SL	UN-P1001	UP-P1001	D-IBBN	OH-ZET	RA-02787	
RB-121		N390GM	(N72DV)	N602DV	N520CH	N550CP			
RB-122		N3722Z	G-CJAG	PH-JCI	N810WT				
RB-123		N3723A	N112CM	N332CM					
RB-124		N6124W	N23SP						
RB-125		N3725F	N312SL	G-PHTO	VQ-BEP	LZ-PDM			
RB-126		N3726G	G-OEWD						
RB-127		N3727H	N18RF						
RB-128		N6128Y	VT-ANF						
RB-129		N6129U	N390JV						
RB-130		N5030V	N401PP						
RB-131		N36731	G-CJAH	OE-FWW	9H-FWW				
RB-132		N3332C	N9LV	(N48VC)					
RB-133		N3733J	(N545PT)	N575PT	N967F				
RB-134		N3734C	N84VA						
RB-135		N3735V	N390PT						
RB-136	*	N36636	N462CB						
RB-137	*	N6137U	N451MM	VH-TMA	ZS-SHC	(D-ISMV)	(D-IFAP)	N428CJ	
RB-138	*	N5118J	VP-BPO	M-VBPO	(N169DT)	N138SJ	N984CJ*		
RB-139	*	N3039G	N239RT	N239RF	PR-PRE				
RB-140	*	N3540R	N22VK						
RB-141	*	N3481V	N484AT	N784MA					
RB-142	*	N6142Y	(G-CJAI)	N646S	N767CS	N390ML			
RB-143	*	N61948	N727KG	N729KG	PK-ASB				
RB-144	*	N541RS							
RB-145	*	N37245	N42EL						
RB-146	*	N6146J	N1CR	M-YAIR	G-OOMC	[w/o Blackpool, UK, 12Mar15; cx 19Aug15]			
RB-147	*	N61678	ZS-KBS	N61678	N147FM				
RB-148	*	N6148Z	D-ISAR						
RB-149	*	N36979	F-HAST	OM-TAA					
RB-150	*	N6150Y	(N575PT)	C-FBPL					
RB-151	*	N37071	D-ICJA	N102SK	N103SK	(D-ICJA)			

BEECH 390 PREMIER I / IA*

C/n	Srs	Identities						
RB-152	*	N3732Y	HB-VOI	D-IGST				
RB-153	*	N36873	N888MN					
RB-154	*	N36964	(G-CJAJ)	XA-RRG	N176CR			
RB-155	*	N3725L						
RB-156	*	N3726T	N508RN					
RB-157	*	N6178X	N88EL					
RB-158	*	N36758	N727MH	N727ML				
RB-159	*	N37059	N146JF	N145JF	[stored Wichita/Beech Field, KS]			
RB-160	*	N36890	EC-KHH	N43GG				
RB-161	*	N71761	(N606JR)	N6JR	[w/o 27Jul10 Oshkosh, WI; parted out by Atlanta Air Salvage, Griffin, GA]			
RB-162	*	N608CW						
RB-163	*	N7163E	N72GD	(N59RK)	N46CK			
RB-164	*	N36864	D-IDBA					
RB-165	*	N7165X	N800FR	M-FROG				
RB-166	*	N36866						
RB-167	*	N71167	N404JM					
RB-168	*	N7268M	N64PM					
RB-169	*	N7269Z	N837JM	(N237JM)	PR-PRA			
RB-170	*	N7170Y	(N181JT)					
RB-171	*	N17CJ	N1XT					
RB-172	*	N7102U	G-EVRD	N390GM				
RB-173	*	N73736	N213PC	N213RQ	N329LN	N330AC		
RB-174	*	N71874	N855RM					
RB-175	*	N71865	VH-VHP	N59PA				
RB-176	*	N7176J	N906FM	N789DT	N563LC			
RB-177	*	N37019	(A6-RZA)	A6-RZJ	N37019	N527PM	N527PN	
RB-178	*	N3378M	N102CL					
RB-179	*	N7079N	N33PJ					
RB-180	*	N133CM	N133CQ	N835ZT				
RB-181	*	N7081V	VP-BBQ	M-VBBQ	UR-USB	OM-AMY		
RB-182	*	N7082V	N246DF	N999ZG	C-GMJJ			
RB-183	*	N994JR	N1J					
RB-184	*	N368CS	N368CC	I-GSAL	N368CC			
RB-185	*	N7085V	N502PM					
RB-186	*	N37086	N2HZ	N36HZ	N685LM			
RB-187	*	N7187J	HB-VOS	T7-NES				
RB-188	*	N7088S	N774KD					
RB-189	*	N7189J	VP-CFW	N255PX				
RB-190	*	N70890	N537RB					
RB-191	*	N7191K	N992SC					
RB-192	*	N7192M	N91BB	VT-RTR	[dbr by flood water, Chennai, India, 01Dec15]			
RB-193	*	N7193W	N408J	XA-BLE	N390BD			
RB-194	*	N7294E	N276RS	N678AM				
RB-195	*	N74065	A9C-RJA	A6-RZA	G-RIZA	G-ORXI	OM-GLE	
RB-196	*	N37346	D-IIMC	OE-FIM	LY-OJB	F-WTAS	F-HTTP	
RB-197	*	N7257U	(LX-VAZ)	N115WZ	N116WZ	N213VU		
RB-198	*	N7198H	C-FDMM	N7TX				
RB-199	*	N133CM	N716GS					
RB-200	*	N81HR						
RB-201	*	N801BP	I-DMSA	D-ISGE	N390GW	M-ARIE	(D-IRTY)	N603RS
RB-202	*	N202BP	VP-CAZ	[w/o nr Annemasse, France, 04Mar13]				
RB-203	*	N203BP						
RB-204	*	N204BP	RP-C390					
RB-205	*	N205GY	N801SA	N945LC				
RB-206	*	N306BP	N146JF	N146JE				
RB-207	*	N207AH						
RB-208	*	N208BP	N430GW	N777VG	[w/o Thomson, GA, 20Feb13]			
RB-209	*	N209BP	M-YSKY	G-IOMC				
RB-210	*	N210KP	PT-SBF					
RB-211	*	N701KB	N701KD	(D-IWAJ)	OE-FKK	N851TM		
RB-212	*	N42SC						
RB-213	*	N213BP	N952GL					
RB-214	*	N814BP	ZS-CBI					
RB-215	*	N215BR	OE-FAP	LZ-EVB				
RB-216	*	N3216G	YL-MLV	VQ-BDK				
RB-217	*	N3217P	C-GXMB	C-FSDB				
RB-218	*	N3K						
RB-219	*	N34859	VT-VRL					
RB-220	*	N34820	VP-BFU	N390RJ				
RB-221	*	N31921	D-ISAG					
RB-222	*	N32022	PT-CBA					
RB-223	*	N3203L	N427DB					
RB-224	*	N3204P	(PP-LUG)	PR-VPP				
RB-225	*	N3205W	VT-BKG	N3205W	VH-TGQ	N390K		
RB-226	*	N97JP	N26DK	(N677DC)	[w/o South Bend, IN, 17Mar13]			
RB-227	*	N166AN						

BEECH 390 PREMIER I / IA*

C/n	Srs	Identities					
RB-228	*	N3228M	F-HCJP	OO-JPC	G-RRIA	D-IEMO	
RB-229	*	N229RB	N50VM	(N50VH)			
RB-230	*	N3330S	F-HNCY				
RB-231	*	N390GS	PR-PRC				
RB-232	*	N208HP	N208MM				
RB-233	*	N233WC	SP-RDW				
RB-234	*	N367CS	N368CS				
RB-235	*	N33805	D-IIBE	UR-USA			
RB-236	*	N3186C	VT-UPN				
RB-237	*	N33837	PR-RRN	N373MM			
RB-238	*	N3198N	ZS-DDM				
RB-239	*	N3289H	VT-KBN				
RB-240	*	N3400Y	PR-RSN				
RB-241	*	N3241G	I-NGIR	N9930B			
RB-242	*	N390EU	N69SB	N99BC			
RB-243	*	N443BP	N111LP	N111LQ	VT-SSF		
RB-244	*	N3344T	N9CH	N808L			
RB-245	*	N3415A	I-AFOI				
RB-246	*	N3216L	PR-VMD				
RB-247	*	N3187G	N668Z				
RB-248	*	N3188V	N1899	N189K			
RB-249	*	N3194R	D-IAYL	[w/o 19Dec10 nr Samedan, Switzerland]			
RB-250	*	N3200X	N357PT	N390P	N815ST*		
RB-251	*	N3151W	N410SH				
RB-252	*	N3352W	N452AS	N111LP	N950JK		
RB-253	*	N3223G	N78HL	N70GY			
RB-254	*	N3354S	I-DMSB	N991ML			
RB-255	*	N3355D	C-GYMB	N255AG	N69YM	N853DC	
RB-256	*	N3396P	OM-VPB	RA-01809			
RB-257	*	N3197P	N701KB	N701KR	N70NL		
RB-258	*	N3298W	N826TG				
RB-259	*	N3395H	N42LG	C-GLIV	N72JT		
RB-260	*	N3400X	N952SP				
RB-261	*	N3441A	N199BP				
RB-262	*	N42LG	N262RB	SX-FCA			
RB-263	*	N42LG	N42LQ	(D-ISAS)	OE-FDB	UR-FDB	N514GW
RB-264	*	N264HB	N79CB				
RB-265	*	N6465W	ZS-AAM				
RB-266	*	N266AZ	N390MM				
RB-267	*	N64467	C-FJTN	N395DM			
RB-268	*	N63768	N33EM				
RB-269	*	N60669	F-GDRR	N858Q			
RB-270	*	N6470P	N124EK	N124GV	N323KM		
RB-271	*	N6471N	C-GYMB	C-FCTB			
RB-272	*	N64312	N23HD				
RB-273	*	N64373	N21FM				
RB-274	*	N6174Q	UP-P1002	RA-02797			
RB-275	*	N390P	C-FTIU	N937JR			
RB-276	*	N76EU	(SP-VVV)	N106PR			
RB-277	*	N6469X	N99MN				
RB-278	*	N6248J	N278AP	OY-FLW			
RB-279	*	N8079R	N775CM				
RB-280	*	N280EU	N722NB				
RB-281	*	N81491	N6JR				
RB-282	*	N282DF					
RB-283	*	N283HB	N707RK	N390HG			
RB-284	*	N8084U	M-MTRM	UR-NST	N110DC		
RB-285	*	N85EU	N285EB				
RB-286	*	N81516	TC-ANG	M-SFOZ	N480RE	N946MP	
RB-287	*	N287AP	UP-P1003	PR-DIA*			
RB-288	*	N8148U	N213PC				
RB-289	*	N289HB	N289BZ	C-FJTA	N390XX		
RB-290	*	N8110N	N986PB				
RB-291	*	N291EU	N26CS	HB-VTS			
RB-292	*	N8092F	UP-P1004				
RB-293	*	N8113Q	N390MG	[also wore fake serial 12-293]			XA-VWA
RB-294	*	N8144D	N51GM	(N440LK)			
RB-295	*	N295HB	N54VM	N84VM	ZS-ETN		

Production complete following the bankruptcy of Hawker Beechcraft Corp in 2012. The following aircraft also had marks assigned but were not completed:

RB-296	*	(N296AP)	
RB-297	*	(N297EU)	
RB-305	*	(N124EK)	(N305BP)

BEECH 390-2 PREMIER II

The Premier II would have been marketed as the Hawker 200 had it entered production.

C/n	Identities			
RD-1	N392X	[ff 13Mar10]	N200HA	[cx Nov15, wfu at Wichita/Beech Field, KS]
RD-2	N392P	N200HW	[ff 31May11; cx Oct15, wfu at Wichita/Beech Field, KS]	

Type did not enter production due to Hawker Beechcraft Corp's bankruptcy in 2012.

BEECHJET 400

* Denotes aircraft originally manufactured by Mitsubishi as MU300-2s and then converted to Beechjet 400 standard. The c/n shown in brackets in these cases is the old Mitsubishi c/n. C/n RJ-12 is the first pure Beechjet 400.

C/n	Series	Identities
*RJ-1 (A1001SA)	400	N64VM
*RJ-2 (A1002SA)	400	N103AD N402FB N369EA
*RJ-3 (A1003SA)	400	N508DM N203BA N49JN N63SN*
*RJ-4 (A1004SA)	400	N504DM N92RW (N401TJ) N8YM
*RJ-5 (A1005SA)	400	N77GA N54TK N933AC
*RJ-6 (A1006SA)	400	N106DM N18JN YV-737CP YV-738CP YV-838CP N406TS N111YJ
*RJ-7 (A1007SA)	400	N507DM N207BA N106VC N25BN N85BN N403JP N644JP
A1008SA	2	N411BW [reportedly w/o at unknown location in Mar97; to Dodson Avn, Rantoul, KS, Oct97, for spares use]
*RJ-9 (A1009SA)	400	N109DM N209BA (N248PA) N42SR N242SR N800FT N65RA
*RJ-10 (A1010SA)	400	N499DM N410BA I-ALSE N131AP [parted out Tulsa, OK]
*RJ-11 (A1011SA)	400	N114DM N111BA N72HG
RJ-12	400	N3112B N129DB N3112K N106CG [parted out by AvMATS, St Louis, MO]
RJ-13	400	N3113B (N400TN) N428JD [w/o 18Sep12 Macon/Downtown, GA] N468JD [parted out by Atlanta Air Salvage, Griffin, GA]
RJ-14	400	N3114B N208R N208D N58AU N672AT (N770TB) N599JL [parted out by White Inds, Bates City, MO]
RJ-15	400	N3115B N25W N25WA N73BL N73BE N902P N415CT N222YJ
RJ-16	400	N165F N512WP N803E (N440MP) [parted out by Dodson Int'l, Rantoul, KS]
RJ-17	400	N417BJ N877S N400T N94BJ N84BJ N486MJ N1CG N455FD N655CM
RJ-18	400	N3180T I-STAP N940GA ZS-NOD N595PT N824SS N418RM LV-COO
RJ-19	400	N3119W N800HM (N700HM) N880HM PJ-SOL N24BA N101CC N598JL [parted out by White Inds, Bates City, MO]
RJ-20	400	N3120Y I-ONDO (N20CV) N901P N455DW
RJ-21	400	N3121B N721FA [cx 27Aug12; parted out by MTW Aerospace, Montgomery, AL]
RJ-22	400	N3122B 9M-ATM N992GA (VR-BLG) I-INCZ OY-JAT N724AA N48CK N913SF N913MC (N315SA) N567BA
RJ-23	400	N3123T [rebuilt using parts of RK-11, following accident] (I-ALSU) N400GJ [wfu Lawrenceville, GA]
RJ-24	400	N3124M N510WS N512WS N800WW N800WV [cx 17Feb15; wfu]
RJ-25	400	N3025T I-MPIZ N125RJ I-OTTY N425BJ ZS-OUU N425BJ
RJ-26	400	N3026U N88WG N90SR N388DA N426MD N91MT N401GJ
RJ-27	400	N3127R N484CC (N427CW) N611TG
RJ-28	400	N31428 I-ACIF N48GA N700LP N51EB
RJ-29	400	N3129E N503EB N193TR (N597N) XA-OAC N129BT [parted out by Dodson Int'l, Rantoul, KS]
RJ-30	400	N3130T (N815BS) N486MJ N777FE
RJ-31	400	N545GM N5450M I-ALSI N5450M I-ALSI N114AP N499P [parted out by Dodson International, Rantoul, KS]
RJ-32	400	N31432 XA-RAR XB-UNO
RJ-33	400	N31733 (N233BJ) XA-JJA XA-BNG XA-JMM
RJ-34	400	N3134N I-ALSO N96WW (N41TJ) N80TS (N800TS) (N1X) N1TY N7EY N80TS
RJ-35	400	N3035T N85TT I-SAMI N71GA N737MM N137MM N1AG N46AG
RJ-36	400	N3236Q G-RSRS N3236Q G-MARS I-RDSF VR-BNV N52GA XA-OAC N555BY
RJ-37	400	N31437 LV-PAM LV-RCT N31437 ZS-ORW N31437
RJ-38	400	N3238K N147CC N447CC VT-OAM N438DA N52AL
RJ-39	400	N3239K N48SR N393BB N398BB
RJ-40	400	N3240M PK-ERA N3240M N400DW
RJ-41	400	N3141G (N441EE) (N270BJ) N241BJ [wfu Fergus Falls, MN; cx 10Feb12]
RJ-42	400	N3142E N31542 N400PL I-FTAL N735GA N444WB N442JC N40MA N418CT
RJ-43	400	N3143T N401CG N500DG N416CT
RJ-44	400	N3144A HB-VJE N3144A I-GCFA N22WJ I-TOPJ N110GA N922TR
RJ-45	400	N3145F N58AU N218RG N241TR
RJ-46	400	N1546T N146JB VT-TEL [cx 2012; instructional airframe, Hindustan University, Chennai, India]
RJ-47	400	N1547B (N900EF)
RJ-48	400	N1548D XB-JHE XC-LJS
RJ-49	400	N1549J N88UA
RJ-50	400	N1550Y G-OTMC N56GA N102MC N406GJ N8HQ
RJ-51	400	N1551B [converted to RK-1 (qv)]
RJ-52	400	N196KC (N196KQ) (N52EB) N196JH N930MG N324MM YV3153
RJ-53	400	N195KC N195KA N711EC N53EB N520WS
RJ-54	400	N1554R XB-FDH N418MG
RJ-55	400	N1555P (VH-...) N711FG N711FC N780GT N724HB PP-KIK
RJ-56	400	N1556W G-BSZP OK-UZI N70DE OK-RHM HA-YFK
RJ-57	400	N1557D N25BR [w/o 11Dec91 Lavender Mt, NW of Rome Airport, GA; cx Jun92]
RJ-58	400	N1558F XA-RNG XA-MII N258BJ N458HC (N750KP)
RJ-59	400	N1559U ZS-MHN N801YA [parted out Lanseria, South Africa, still marked as ZS-MHN; cx 14Dec16]
RJ-60	400	N1560T G-BRBZ N89GA N400FT XA-LEG N250KD N95RT N700WH
RJ-61	400	N1561B XA-RNE N701LP N461EA
RJ-62	400	N89KM N89KK N333RS N424BT
RJ-63	400	N848C
RJ-64	400	N1564B N195JH N215TP
RJ-65	400	N1565B N16MF CC-AQV

End of production from Japanese components; production continued with US-built components from c/n RK-1

BEECHJET 400A / HAWKER 400XP

C/n	Series	Identities
RK-1	400A	N1551B [converted from c/n RJ-51] N294FA N294AW (N401CW) N481CW [parted out by Alliance Air Parts, Oklahoma City, OK]
RK-2	400A	N1902W N272BC N272BQ N402CW N827SB
RK-3	400A	N400A XA-CLA N640AC N400VG N400VK N519RW
RK-4	400A	N147CC N147CG N400BE N777FL N771EL N494CW N222JE
RK-5	400A	N501BG (N405CW) N495CW N30XL
RK-6	400A	N56576 I-IPFC N3119H N600CC (N401FF) N401EE N406CW (N406ML) N480M N408M PR-ALY
RK-7	400A	VR-COG N416RP N631RP (N631RR) N401AB N9PW N848TC
RK-8	400A	N440DS
RK-9	400A	N8152H N315R (N150TF)
RK-10	400A	N2842B (D-CLSG) D-CEIS N488DB (N404FS)
RK-11	400A	N2843B N5680Z I-ALSU [w/o 27Nov91 Parma, Italy; remains to Dodson Av'n, Ottawa, KS – parts used to rebuild RJ-23 (N3123T) qv]
RK-12	T-1A	[built as Jayhawk c/n TT-1; for USAF]
RK-13	400A	N56BE N56BX N13GB N610EG N510TL
RK-14	400A	N28..B N81709 (F-GKCJ) F-GLYO (N414RK) N81TJ N916SB
RK-15	T-1A	[built as Jayhawk c/n TT-2; for USAF]
RK-16	400A	N8163G N71FE N46FE N416CW XA-MGM N16HD
RK-17	400A	N505EB N877S N877Z N417CW (N401LX) N857C
RK-18	400A	N5598Q N717DD N717DW N418CW (N402LX) TC-ASE N189GA ZS-MJD
RK-19	400A	N1901W N11GE (N8ME) N41ME N419CW (N403LX) N144AW ZP-BJB N312JS N286DW
RK-20	400A	N82628 I-UNSA N82628 N870P N703LP PR-MMG
RK-21	400A	(N401TC) N1904W N1881W N717VL N717VA N1920 (N1962) N2920 HK-4794 N763AJ
RK-22	400A	N56616 N51ML N85CR N422CW (N404LX) (N522KJ) N870BB [cx 15 Mar16; instructional airframe, Skedsmo High School, Norway]
RK-23	400A	N107BJ N200BL (N960AJ) N250AJ
RK-24	400A	N8073R [wfu; parted out by Dodson Intl, Rantoul, KS; cx 01Jul09]
RK-25	400A	N81918 (VR-CDA) D-CLBA N237SP
RK-26	400A	N8097V VH-BBJ VH-IMP N700GB N8097V N80DX (N80DE) HK-4446X HK-4446-W HK-4446-G
RK-27	400A	N10FL N10FQ N427CW (N405LX) N95GK
RK-28	400XT	N42SK N411SK PT-WLM (N902PC) N400NS N401NX (N401XT) N75TG
RK-29	400A	I-IPIZ N15693 I-IPIZ OY-JJE
RK-30	400A	N205R N430CW (N406LX) N494CC
RK-31	400A	N10J N10JX N431CW (N407LX) N850C
RK-32	400A	N999GP N998GP N553PF N432CW (N408LX) N932EA
RK-33	400A	N1878C N60B N197PF N197BE
RK-34	400A	N400A N700GM N74VF N232BJ N511JP N511JF N721SS N134FA N184AR
RK-35	400A	N81661 VH-BJD VH-LAW VH-BJD VH-LAW VH-BJD N435CW (N409LX) (N936EA) N492AM
RK-36	400A	XA-RZG N56327 N57B N156DH N155DH N568SD
RK-37	400A	(F-GLPD) N8014Q (F-GLOR) SE-DRS N998FF
RK-38	400A	N5685X N522EE N522EF N515MW YV363T
RK-39	400A	N400Q N34VP N70BJ (N97XP) N492P
RK-40	400A	N8252J N496EE N440CW (N410LX)
RK-41	400A	N8265Y I-FSJA N920SA N546BZ N101WR
RK-42	400A	N8253Y N442CW (N411LX) N443C N307MT
RK-43	400A	N56400 N45RK
RK-44	400XPR	N8249Y N404VP N908R N712GK N312GK
RK-45	400A	N56423 N490TN (N8051H) N445E (N600CC) N445CC N445CW (N412LX) N445PK
RK-46	400A	N8239E N515RY
RK-47	400A	N8053V N400FT N408PC N109CP [w/o 06Feb10 Washington/Dulles, VA – hangar collapsed]
RK-48	400A	N8060V N94HT N48SE
RK-49	400A	N8060Y N54HP N54HD (N349HP)
RK-50	400A	N80KM N750AB N450CW (N413LX) [cx 24Apr13; parted out by Anglin Aircraft Recovery Services, DE]
RK-51	400A	N8085T (N7113Z)
RK-52	400A	N709JB (N709EW) N709EL
RK-53	400A	N62KM N200GP N200GB N453CW (N414LX) N896C N593M
RK-54	400A	N80938 PT-WHG
RK-55	400A	N400Q N404CC N42AJ
RK-56	400A	N89KM N456CW (N415LX) N56FF XA-JAM XA-KJM XA-JPA
RK-57	400A	N8157H ZS-NZO N762BG N457CW (N416LX) N368EA
RK-58	400A	N56356 PT-WHC
RK-59	400A	N80544 N50KH N5PF N27JJ N895CP
RK-60	400A	N8260L (N794SM) N61SM N55SQ
RK-61	400A	N82378 G-RAHL N461CW (N417LX) N478DR N479DR
RK-62	400A	N8083N N462CW (N418LX) N5895K
RK-63	400A	N2792B N82412 PT-JQM N163RK N304JR
RK-64	400A	N8164M N53MS
RK-65	400A	N39HF (N97TT) (N81TT) PR-AEX PR-HAW*
RK-66	400A	N400A (N400DT) N400Y HB-VLM N6048F I-AVSS
RK-67	400A	N8167Y (N850RG) N467RG N429JG N699PM

BEECHJET 400A / HAWKER 400XP

C/n	Series	Identities
RK-68	400A	N8280J N295FA (N419LX) XA-PYN N900EF YV2452
RK-69	400A	N8169Q N877S N877J
RK-70	400A	C-FOPC N750T N73HM N79HM N826JH [w/o Atlanta/DeKalb-Peachtree 18Jun12; parted out by Atlanta Air Salvage, Griffin, GA; remains to Dodson Av'n, Rantoul, KS]
RK-71	400A	N82497 I-IFPC N777ND N73BL N402GS [parted out by Alliance Air Parts, Oklahoma City, OK]
RK-72	400A	N8210W N709JB (N72BJ) N910SH N428WE N82QD
RK-73	400A	N8070Q PT-WHB
RK-74	400A	N8146J N26JP N93XP
RK-75	400A	(N275PC) N82400 N125JG (PR-TGA) PR-TGM
RK-76	400A	N8166A N261JP
RK-77	400A	N8277Y PT-WHD
RK-78	400A	N8278Z N611PA [dbr in hangar collapse at Boca Raton, FL, 24Oct05; to Dodson Av'n, Rantoul, KS, for spares]
RK-79	400A	N8279G (N30SF) OH-RIF N8279G [cx 16Oct14; wfu]
RK-80	400A	N8180Q AP-BEX [w/o in hangar collapse at Lahore 06Jun04]
RK-81	400A	N8167G PT-WHE
RK-82	400A	N8282E PT-WHF [w/o Sao Jose dos Campos, Brazil, 15Jul08]
RK-83	400A	N8283C XA-SNP XA-MII N8283C N880MG
RK-84	400A	N8138M D-CHSW OE-GFB VQ-BNJ SP-TAT*
RK-85	400A	N8299Y N419MS N419MB LV-FWF
RK-86	400A	N1563V N777GC (N72PP) N757CE N20ZC (N202RA)
RK-87	400A	N1567L N702LP N87EB YV3106
RK-88	400A	N1549W N654AT N654AP N843RH
RK-89	400A	N1560G N94HE
RK-90	400A	N1570L N165HB N132WE N458SF
RK-91	400A	N1545N N296FA N491CW (N420LX) N511VB N400TB
RK-92	400A	N3240J N555KK N124PP
RK-93	400XT	N3038V N493CW (N421LX) N400XT N475BC [cx 21Apr16; wfu]
RK-94	400A	N3051S HB-VLN N585G N681WD N661WD
RK-95	400A	N3114X HS-UCM N747RR
RK-96	400A	N3196N N924JM N824JM N800GF N800GK N400XP [Hawker 400XPR development aircraft]
RK-97	400A	N3197Q VH-MGC
RK-98	400A	N3210X N400A N866BB N999JF N999YB
RK-99	400A	N3199Q N95FA N575RB
RK-100	400A	N1570B N400SH
RK-101	400A	N3221T ZS-JRO N400FT N490AM
RK-102	400A	N3232U N916GR N111FW
RK-103	400A	D-CIGM HB-VLW N103LP N403CW (N422LX) N12NV YVO157
RK-104	400A	N3224X LV-PLT LV-WPE N704SC PR-DOT N410ML
RK-105	400A	N3235U (N8252J) (N423LX) N127BW N124BV N105AX
RK-106	400A	N3246H N1HS N625W
RK-107	400A	N3227X N733MK N907JE
RK-108	400XT	N3218L N498CW N408CW (N424LX) (N408NX) [Nextant 400XT conversion, ff with Williams FJ44 engines 08Sep10] (N408XT) N404FL
RK-109	400A	N3269A N121EZ N491AM B-3905
RK-110	400A	N1090X N400VP (N400A) XA-FRO
RK-111	400A	N42SK N411SK N412WP N13SY N116SS PK-ELI
RK-112	400A	N3272L N94LH N112BJ
RK-113	400A	N3263N N400VG [w/o 17Apr99 Beckley, WV, cx Dec02]
RK-114	400A	N1084D N363K N698PW N855RA
RK-115	400A	N3265A (N369EA) N52AW N512F
RK-116	400A	N1116R
RK-117	400A	N1117S N97FB N97FF N12MG N12MQ N496AS N886EP (N886ER)
RK-118	400A	N1118Y LV-PMH LV-WTP
RK-119	400A	N1119C N456JG (N456NS) (N7981M) N450WH
RK-120	400A	N3261Y TC-MDJ N9146Z N159AK N702NV G-ERIE
RK-121	400A	N1121Z N419MS N473JE PR-IJE
RK-122	400A	N1102B PT-WJS
RK-123	400XT	N1123Z N110TG N740TA N203FL N410FL
RK-124	400A	N1124Z TC-MSA N124BG OE-GUK YU-BVA 4O-BVA
RK-125	400A	N1105U N400KP N400KL N939GP
RK-126	400A	N3226B N197SD XB-INI
RK-127	400A	N1127U N696TR N686TR N127UH
RK-128	400A	N1108Y N912SH N621VS N551JK
RK-129	400XT	N1129X N129MC N334SR N129WH N258AF
RK-130	400A	N1130B TC-NEO
RK-131	400A	N1083Z N305MD
RK-132	400XT	N1087Z N106KC N954TW N500PM
RK-133	400A	N1133T VP-BMR N133BP I-TOPB OY-JJD
RK-134	400A	N1094D N134BJ N134WF LV-CBJ
RK-135	400A	N1135A N135BJ
RK-136	400A	N1136Q N780TP N397CA N130WW
RK-137	400XT	N1117Z N400AJ N400XT N209BK
RK-138	400A	N40PL N48PL N400XA
RK-139	400A	N1099S VH-PNL VH-MZL VH-BZL
RK-140	400A	N1094N ZS-OCG A6-ELJ ZS-OCG A2-MCG A2-WIN ZS-TGT
RK-141	400A	N1027S N974JD N874JD N855FC N824DM N824D YV3173

BEECHJET 400A / HAWKER 400XP

C/n	Series	Identities							
RK-142	400A	N142BJ	(N223DK)	YV-943CP	N142BJ	N9WW			
RK-143	400A	N191NC	N191NQ	N824HG					
RK-144	400A	N134CM	PR-SKB						
RK-145	400A	N745TA	(N425LX)	N144JS					
RK-146	400XT	N146TA	N746TA	(N426LX)	(N456FL)	ZS-LMF			
RK-147	400A	N147BJ							
RK-148	400A	N1108T	TC-SMB	N663AJ	OE-GHM	C6-SAP			
RK-149	400A	N149TA	N749TA	(N427LX)	N499LX				
RK-150	400A	N1135U	N100AG	N100AW					
RK-151	400A	N1126V	PT-MAC	N115CD	N586SF	N196CT	N198CT	N548KK	
RK-152	400A	N2252Q	N97FB	YV-754CP	YV213T	N152SV	XB-TNY	XA-TYP	N615RB
RK-153	400A	N153BJ	N500HY						
RK-154	400A	N2354B	VH-BJC	VH-EXB	HS-ASC				
RK-155	400A	N2355T	N627RP	N631RP	N631PP	N567DK	PR-JPK	N502TC	
RK-156	400A	N2056E	N400PU	N156RK					
RK-157	400A	N397AT	N897AT	ZS-ONP	N897AT	N157WH			
RK-158	400A	N2358X	PT-MPL	N158SN	N475TC				
RK-159	400A	N2159P	N3337J	(N466TS)	N333YJ	N290TC			
RK-160	400A	N2360F	N54HP						
RK-161	400A	N761TA	N471CW	(N428LX)	N706RM				
RK-162	400A	N2362G	ZS-PDB	N2362G	OY-SIS	N520CH	OE-GMC	OK-PMI	
RK-163	400A	N2363A	XA-JET	N163BJ	I-TOPD				
RK-164	400A	N2164Z	TC-MDB	N2164Z	(N69LS)	N280AJ	(N717CH)	N188HA	
RK-165	400A	N2225Y	N224MC						
RK-166	400A	N2299T	N975CM	N93FT	N93FB				
RK-167	400A	N2267B	N711EC	N501BW					
RK-168	400A	N2168G	N768TA	(N429LX)	N679SJ	XC-LLZ	N679SJ	[parted out by Dodson Int'l, Rantoul, KS]	
RK-169	400A	N2329N	N757WS	PR-SRB					
RK-170	400A	N2289B	TC-MCX	TC-MSB	N70HT	PP-DDR			
RK-171	400A	N2201J	PT-WUF	N287CD	XA-LEG	N888BY	N693GS		
RK-172	400A	N2272K	N615HP	N200GP					
RK-173	400A	N2273Z	HK-4801						
RK-174	400A	N2204J	N174AB	HK-4645					
RK-175	400A	N175BJ							
RK-176	400A	N476BJ							
RK-177	400A	N2277G	N717CF	YV602T					
RK-178	400A	N708TA	(N478CW)	(N430LX)	N406LX				
RK-179	400A	N2279K	N75GF	N75GK	N400CT	OD-DTW			
RK-180	400XT	N709TA	(N480CW)	(N407LX)	OK-EAS				
RK-181	400A	N2235V	N314TL	N450TB					
RK-182	400A	N2322B	N234DK						
RK-183	400A	N710TA	(N432LX)	N488LX	N488KL				
RK-184	400A	N2314F	N141DR						
RK-185	400A	N2298L	N140GB	N148GB	(N450AT)	(N185FN)			
RK-186	400A	N712TA	(N433LX)	N12NV	N552CC				
RK-187	400A	N2298S	N400TE	PR-FOL					
RK-188	400A	N2298W	TC-VIN	N2298W	VP-CPH				
RK-189	400A	N715TA	(N434LX)	N440LN					
RK-190	400A	N2290F	TC-YRT	N2290F	N325JG	VT-RPG			
RK-191	400A	N2291T	N960JJ	N960JA	N367EA	N400HD	N1AG		
RK-192	400A	N492BJ	N272BC	N272BQ	N116AD	N116AP	[Hawker 400XPR development aircraft, first flew with Williams FJ44 engines 03May12]		
RK-193	400A	N13US	N914SH	N366EA	N193BJ				
RK-194	400A	N194BJ	N909ST	PK-ELX					
RK-195	400XT	N718TA	(N485CW)	(N435LX)	(N410LX)	N872MK			
RK-196	400A	N2283T	XA-MEX	N619GA	N619G				
RK-197	400A	N3197A	N214WM	N940VA					
RK-198	400A	N798TA	(N436LX)	N403WC	N168WC				
RK-199	400A	N739TA	N446M	N826JM					
RK-200	400A	N200NA	VP-CKK	N399RA					
RK-201	400A	N741TA	(N437LX)	N402FL					
RK-202	400A	N742TA	N438LX						
RK-203	400A	N2359W	B-3989	N2359W	VP-CHF	N203RK	N262PA	N203DF	
RK-204	400A	N2357K	I-ASER	N204KR	PP-SJJ				
RK-205	400A	N3030D	N143HM	(N17CM)	N400WF				
RK-206	400A	N3014R	N30046	N982AR					
RK-207	400A	N3015F	N717DD	N257CB					
RK-208	400A	N3101B	N890BH	HI-766SP	HI766	N766AB	N127SJ		
RK-209	400XT	N799TA	(N439LX)	N413LX	ES-CMK				
RK-210	400XT	N111CX	ZK-NXJ						
RK-211	400A	N3028U	TC-NNK	N3028U	N686SC				
RK-212	400A	N3029F	N299AW	N11UB	HK-4756				
RK-213	400A	N3033A	N175PS	N545TC					
RK-214	400A	N79EL							
RK-215	400A	N3038W	N515WA						
RK-216	400A	N3050P	N213BK						

BEECHJET 400A / HAWKER 400XP

C/n	Series	Identities							
RK-217	400A	N217MB	N385PB						
RK-218	400A	N3068M	N48MF	N426GF					
RK-219	400A	N3059H	N511JP	N80BL	N219SJ	4X-CPY			
RK-220	400A	N220BJ	N799SM	N499AS	N563RJ				
RK-221	400A	N221BJ	N18BR	N400KG	N400SF				
RK-222	400A	N748TA	N482CW	(N440LX)	N482RK	VH-YRC	VH-IPG	HS-EMM	N482RK
RK-223	400A	N3223R	N777FL	N877FL					
RK-224	400A	N3224N	N51NP	N642AC					
RK-225	400XT	N751TA	N415LX	N440LN	N400TC				
RK-226	400A	N3226Q	N59BR	N59BP	N750TA	(N416LX)			
RK-227	400A	N3197K	N362KM	N862KM	N497AS	YV3057			
RK-228	400A	N3228V	N12WF	(N12WQ)	N20PJ*				
RK-229	400A	N3129X	N515TJ						
RK-230	400XT	N753TA	(N441LX)	N417LX	(N431FL)	N722NK	N440XT		
RK-231	400A	N781TP	N615HP						
RK-232	400A	N2355N	N674SF	N674DJ					
RK-233	400A	N2293V	N233MW						
RK-234	400A	N783TA	(N442LX)	N418LX	N1PU				
RK-235	400A	N695BK	N560MT						
RK-236	400A	N2349V	N11WF	N106EA					
RK-237	400A	N784TA	N437CW	N443LX					
RK-238	400A	N23525	XA-DOS	XA-VRO	N96GA				
RK-239	400XT	N785TA	(N421LX)	N485FL	N868JL	VH-OVS			
RK-240	400A	N3240J	N749SS	N150TF	N393GH				
RK-241	400A	N3241Q	N993H	PR-DDS					
RK-242	400A	N2322B	N32AA	N32AJ	XA-LOA	N400VP			
RK-243	400A	N782TP							
RK-244	400XT	N428HR	N793TA	(N445LX)	N493LX	N188TS			
RK-245	400A	N3199Z	N744TA	(N446LX)	N424LX	HS-CKI	HS-BRM		
RK-246	400A	N500TH							
RK-247	400A	N40252	N20FL	N25XP	XB-MSZ				
RK-248	400XT	N786TA	N447LX	N226WC					
RK-249	400A	N4249K	N611WM	C9-CFM					
RK-250	400A	N2293V	N250HP						
RK-251	400A	N3106Y	N705LP	N495AS	N1853				
RK-252	400XT	N790TA	N490FL	G-FXAR					
RK-253	400A	N4053T	N90CU						
RK-254	400A	N3254P	TC-BYD	N254RK	HA-YFJ				
RK-255	400A	N988JG	N3255B	N960JJ	N400JJ	N960JJ	N402FB		
RK-256	400A	N3079S	N397AT	N387AT	N26PA	N602JC			
RK-257	400A	N739TA	N449LX	N618LT					
RK-258	400A	N40215	(PP-LUA)	PP-WRV					
RK-259	400A	N3259Z	XA-AFS	XA-UKU	N397MG				
RK-260	400XT	N787TA	(N450LX)	N727KG	N727KB				
RK-261	400A	N3261A	N51B						
RK-262	400A	N300GB							
RK-263	400A	N724MH	N724KW	N724CP					
RK-264	400XT	N792TA	(N451LX)	N428LX	N482MS				
RK-265	400A	N797TA	(N452LX)	N429LX	N498LX				
RK-266	400A	N3166Q	N41283	N10FL	N27XP				
RK-267	400A	N4467X	OY-JJO	N85HP					
RK-268	400XT	N789TA	(N453LX)	(N489FL)	ES-NXT				
RK-269	400A	N400MV	N400MR	N440RC					
RK-270	400A	N3231H	N800SD						
RK-271	400A	N743TA	(N454LX)	(N431LX)	N800GV				
RK-272	400A	N3237H	N701CP						
RK-273	400A	N731TA	(N483CW)	(N455LX)	(N433LX)	N725T	YV2839		
RK-274	400XT	N735TA	(N456LX)	N434LX	N402XT	[first production Nextant 400XT]			
RK-275	400A	N4275K	N426EA						
RK-276	400XT	N775TA	(N457LX)	N435LX	N427DJ	N253AF			
RK-277	400A	N4477X	(N566W)	N101CC					
RK-278	400A	N4378P	N823TT	N750AJ					
RK-279	400XT	N773TA	(N458LX)	N436LX	N436FL	G-FXKR			
RK-280	400A	N4480W	N26XP	N75KH	N275KH				
RK-281	400A	N4081L	XA-TDQ	N311JV					
RK-282	400A	N794TA	(N482LX)	(N459LX)	N88CA				
RK-283	400A	N4083N	N600SB	N404MS					
RK-284	400XT	N795TA	(N460LX)	N439LX	N439FL	N520TM			
RK-285	400A	N3185G	N149SB	N249SB	N249RM	N793TH*			
RK-286	400A	N400MV							
RK-287	400A	N4467E	N361AS	JA78MA					
RK-288	400A	N51VC	N848PF	N41FD					
RK-289	400XT	N796TA	(N461LX)	N440LX	N440FL	N530TM*			
RK-290	400A	N23263	N400QW	N204DH					
RK-291	400A	N3191L	N816DK						
RK-292	400XT	N899TA	N441LX	N444FL	N570TM*				

BEECHJET 400A / HAWKER 400XP

C/n	Series	Identities						
RK-293	400A	N4293K	EC-HTR	N293RK	XC-LMC	N293RK	OK-BEE	
RK-294	400A	N5094E	HS-TPD	[wfu Bangkok/Don Muang, Thailand; w/o in floods 2011; to Nilai University, Malaysia, as instructional airframe]				
RK-295	400XT	N898TA	(N463LX)	(N406FL)	OK-ESC	(SP-KTB)		
RK-296	400A	N311HS	N68JV	N937RV				
RK-297	400A	N699TA	N497CW	(N464LX)	N497RC			
RK-298	400A	N698TA	N445LX	YV2674	N445LX	XA-MSL		
RK-299	400A	N697TA	N446LX	YV453T	YV2736			
RK-300	400A	N4001M	VP-CVP	N401XR				
RK-301	400A	N696TA	(N465LX)	(N496LX)	XA-GOB			
RK-302	400A	N5002G	XA-TTS					
RK-303	400A	N695TA	N400HS	N400HD	SE-RBO	TC-IBO		
RK-304	400XT	N5004Y	N304SE	N527PM				
RK-305	400A	N693TA	N405CW	(N466LX)	N448LX	N705KU		
RK-306	400A	N4056V	YV-968CP	YV198T	YV2698			
RK-307	400A	N692TA	N407CW	(N467LX)	PT-TRA			
RK-308	400A	N51008	N400KP					
RK-309	400A	N3239A	I-VITH					
RK-310	400XT	N695TA	N410CW	(N468LX)	N451LX	N451FL		
RK-311	400A	N755TA	N711GD	N711GL	N311GL	N40SC		
RK-312	400A	N5012U	N75RL	(N312GS)				
RK-313	400A	N4483W	(PH-BBC)	PH-DTP	OK-IMO			
RK-314	400A	N5014G	N400HS	N92LP				
RK-315	400A	N3215J	N6MF	N720XP				
RK-316	400A	N3216X	XA-AFA					
RK-317	400A	N691TA	(N469LX)	N452LX	N452SB	N452FL		
RK-318	400A	N3185K	HB-VNE	OK-BII				
RK-319	400A	N689TA	N660CC					
RK-320	400A	N4469E	N717TG	(N290AR)				
RK-321	400A	N688TA	N379DR	XA-TYD				
RK-322	400A	N687TA	N800EL	N800EH	PT-FGV	SP-OHM*		
RK-323	400A	N5003G	N268PA	N369AK	N106KH			
RK-324	400A	N5024U	N755TA	(N470LX)	(N412FL)	N224FL	N224FD	
RK-325	400A	N272BC	N275BC	N408PC				
RK-326	400A	N749RH	N420DH	N440JR				
RK-327	400XT	N689TA	(N471LX)	N454LX	N454FL			
RK-328	400A	N5028J	N686TA	(N472LX)	N455LX	N423AK	(N70HB)	N424SK
RK-329	400A	N5129U	N580RJ	N580RK				
RK-330	400A	N4330B	(N450CB)	N33NL	N330TS			
RK-331	400A	N5031D	N12MG	N489BH	N744C	XA-ESR		
RK-332	400A	N5032H	XA-TWW					
RK-333	400A	N72FL	N903CG	N160RC				
RK-334	400XT	N5034J	N684TA	N484CW	(N473LX)	N442FL	N590TM	
RK-335	400A	N5015B	N400GR					
RK-336	400A	N5136T	(N706PL)	N706LP				
RK-337	400A	N5037L	N726PG					
RK-338	400A	N5038V	N116AD					
RK-339	400A	N4309N	N439CW	N400TL	N404LR			
RK-340	400A	N51540	N500LJ	N400XR				
RK-341	400A	N51241	N61GB					
RK-342	400A	N50552	N400A	N522EE	N522EL			
RK-343	400A	N4357H	N806GG	N106DD	OE-GTM	(SP-GHM)	I-PSCU	
RK-344	400A	N6144S	N99ZB					
RK-345	400XT	N4445Y	N425CW	(N474LX)	(N457LX)	N445FL	(N400XT)	OK-JFA
RK-346	400XT	N446CW	(N475LX)	N422FL	N569TM*			
RK-347	400A	N447CW	N108PJ	N168PJ	N498AS			
RK-348	400A	N448CW	N309AK	(N309BE)	N348BE			
RK-349	400A	N449CW	N975RR					
RK-350	400A	N61850	PR-MVB					
RK-351	400A	N6051C	N371CF	N387LS				
RK-352	400A	N6052U						
RK-353	400A	N400A	N353AE	XA-GAO				
RK-354	400XP	N5084U	N717EA	EC-KRS	EC-LIO	OY-OYO	OK-BMM	
RK-355	400XP	N6055K	N767SB	N400RY				
RK-356	400XP	N6056M	N400XP	N800GR	N800HT	N808HT	N217EC	
RK-357	400XP	N5057Z	N317PC					
RK-358	400XP	N5158D	N865AM					
RK-359	400XP	N61959	XA-UAW	XA-FAF				
RK-360	400XP	N6200D	N823ET					
RK-361	400XP	N61661	N25CU					
RK-362	400XP	N6162V	N362XP	Indonesia P-2034		Indonesia P-8001		
RK-363	400XP	N6193D	(N363XP)	N790SS				
RK-364	400XP	N394BB						
RK-365	400XT	N455CW	N459LX	N456FL				
RK-366	400XP	N466CW	N460LX	N466CW	OD-STW	HZ-ALS1		
RK-367	400XP	N404BL						

BEECHJET 400XP

C/n	Series	Identities					
RK-368	400XT	N448CW	N461LX	N427FL			
RK-369	400XP	N369XP	N624B	N917EA			
RK-370	400XP	N60270	(N470CW)	N72GH	N432MA		
RK-371	400XP	N371CW	N401CW	N824GB	N72NE		
RK-372	400XP	N6172V	N375DT				
RK-373	400XP	N373XP	N490JC				
RK-374	400XP	N374XP	N109NT	N25SJ			
RK-375	400XP	N375XP	XA-UCV				
RK-376	400XT	N476CW	N476LX	N426FL	G-SKBD		
RK-377	400XP	N477CW	N477LX	N477FL			
RK-378	400XP	N370FC					
RK-379	400XP	N979XP	PP-UQF	N379RK			
RK-380	400XP	N102QS	N402GJ				
RK-381	400XP	N106QS	N702CS	N381XP			
RK-382	400XP	N108QS	N408GJ				
RK-383	400XP	N115QS	PK-YGK				
RK-384	400XP	N84XP	N302TB				
RK-385	400XT	N116QS	N117XP	OK-PPP			
RK-386	400XP	N524LP	N502N	N300R	N330R		
RK-387	400XP	N478LX	N125DT	N130DT	N959CR		
RK-388	400XP	N479LX	N45LX	(N45LN)	N997RS	(N202TA)	
RK-389	400XP	N50727	N717DD	N28VM			
RK-390	400XP	N480LX	N975RD	PP-AML	N390SB		
RK-391	400XP	N117QS	N68GS				
RK-392	400XP	N36792	AP-BHQ				
RK-393	400XP	N118QS	N835TB				
RK-394	400XP	N119QS	N281TX	(N125GE)	4L-VIP	N281TX	N260JR
RK-395	400XP	N7600					
RK-396	400XP	N31496	XA-MEX	[dbr Telluride, CO, 23.12.15]			
RK-397	400XP	N36997	N479LX	N473FL			
RK-398	400XT	N483LX	N480LX	N480FL	N599TM		
RK-399	400XP	N700FA	N402CB	D2-EAH			
RK-400	400XP	N400XP	ZS-POT	VT-HBX			
RK-401	400XP	N36701	CS-DMA	N315SL	N140FM		
RK-402	400XP	N485LX	N61CP	OE-GSG	ZS-XPH		
RK-403	400XP	N36803	CS-DMB	N426CB	N732WB		
RK-404	400XP	N37204	CS-DMC	N404XP	N478DR		
RK-405	400XP	N481LX	N40ZH	N94LH			
RK-406	400XP	N140QS	VH-EIG				
RK-407	400XT	N36607	CS-DMD	N363EA	N800WC	N259AF	
RK-408	400XP	N37108	CS-DME	N260TX	N411SC	PK-...	
RK-409	400XP	N120QS	N412TS				
RK-410	400XP	N37310	CS-DMF	N259TX	B-95995		
RK-411	400XP	N611XP	N380JR				
RK-412	400XP	N37312	N412GJ				
RK-413	400XT	N482LX	HB-VPV	OK-RAH			
RK-414	400XP	N136QS	N401NW				
RK-415	400XP	N37115	XA-UFS	N102NS			
RK-416	400XP	N116XP	N900ST	N900SQ	XA-LMG	N13GG	XA-RFC
RK-417	400XP	N36907	CS-DMG	M-ABFO	N600WM		
RK-418	400XP	N618XP	N418GJ				
RK-419	400XP	N619XP	N279AK				
RK-420	400XP	N620XP	N877S	N400VK			
RK-421	400XP	N145QS	N145WC	N145QS	N152RJ	N345HC	
RK-422	400XP	N151QS	N290TX	PR-DIS			
RK-423	400XT	N223XP	N462LX	N429FL	G-FXCR		
RK-424	400XP	N24XP	N1JB	N24XP			
RK-425	400XP	N37325	CS-DMH	N261TX	N858EZ	N333EA	N287LS
RK-426	400XT	N26XP	N463LX	N465FL			
RK-427	400XP	N132QS	N116XP				
RK-428	400XP	N28XP	OE-GYR	EC-JPN	N544LF	PR-BLG	
RK-429	400XP	N29XP	N263PA	A2-DBK			
RK-430	400XP	N30XP	N990DF	PR-BED			
RK-431	400XP	N131QS	N311GF				
RK-432	400XP	N142QS	N741RD	N1JP			
RK-433	400XP	N125QS	N113XP	N310GF			
RK-434	400XP	N34XP	(N464LX)	XA-UEV	XC-BJG		
RK-435	400XP	N161QS	PP-SKI				
RK-436	400XP	N147QS	N436RK				
RK-437	400XP	N37337	CS-DMI	N276MM	PR-EKR		
RK-438	400XP	N162QS	N438BC				
RK-439	400XP	N166QS	N159AK	N159AL	PP-DSS		
RK-440	400XP	N152QS	N440WF				
RK-441	400XP	N130QS	N610PR	N43BD			
RK-442	400XP	N124QS	N442GJ				
RK-443	400XP	N36646	CS-DMJ	N258TX			

BEECHJET 400XP

C/n	Series	Identities					
RK-444	400XP	N465LX	N144XP	N702LP			
RK-445	400XP	N466LX	N45XP	N536V	PR-DIF		
RK-446	400XP	N46XP	N188JF				
RK-447	400XP	N467LX	(N467FL)	XA-AMY			
RK-448	400XP	N146QS	N212FH	OE-GAG	N400RB	PR-LBP	N448SC
RK-449	400XP	N133QS	N127BW				
RK-450	400XP	N650XP	N61VC				
RK-451	400XP	N51XP	N964JD				
RK-452	400XP	N36752	XA-UFR	N109NS			
RK-453	400XP	N464LX	ZS-AOT	ZS-JPS			
RK-454	400XP	N465LX	N454RJ				
RK-455	400XP	N466LX	N800HT	N915TB	N401XP	N401RL	
RK-456	400XP	N61256	LV-BEM				
RK-457	400XP	N6137Y	PR-MMS	N128TN			
RK-458	400XP	N50858	N339SM				
RK-459	400XP	N459XP	N517MD	XA-TEN			
RK-460	400XP	N460XP	N460KG	(N460JW)	N937RA*		
RK-461	400XP	N61XP	N101AR	N823HM			
RK-462	400XP	N462XP	N689AK	PR-WRR	N107CZ		
RK-463	400XT	N469LX	N469FL				
RK-464	400XP	N36764	CS-DMK	N262TX			
RK-465	400XP	N37165	CS-DML	N500XP	N99VS		
RK-466	400XP	N466XP	N610PR	PR-SCE			
RK-467	400XP	N122QS	N115XP				
RK-468	400XT	N468LX	N467FL				
RK-469	400XP	N37079	(CS-DMM)	N114QS	N114XP	N481MM	
RK-470	400XP	N470XP	PR-IND				
RK-471	400XP	N471LX	N471XP				
RK-472	400XP	N36632	CS-DMM	N416TM	N472EM		
RK-473	400XP	N149QS	N76GR				
RK-474	400XP	N474XP	N474ME	XA-UQJ			
RK-475	400XP	N61675	CS-DMN	N418TM			
RK-476	400XP	N36846	TC-STA				
RK-477	400XP	N477XP	(N2944M)	N477GJ			
RK-478	400XP	N470LX	N598DR				
RK-479	400XP	N479XP	PP-JCF				
RK-480	400XP	N36880	SU-ZBB	VQ-BIL	M-ABGM	SP-ATT*	
RK-481	400XP	N472LX	(N481GJ)				
RK-482	400XP	N482XP	N482GS				
RK-483	400XP	N139QS	(N275TX)	N483PA	OD-APA		
RK-484	400XP	N101QS	N29134				
RK-485	400XP	N485XP	[instructional airframe, Wichita Area Technical College National Center for Aviation Training, KS]				
RK-486	400XP	N123QS	N362EA				
RK-487	400XP	N487XP	G-EDCS	N487XP	XA-EGS		
RK-488	400XP	N719EL					
RK-489	400XP	N489XP	N489B				
RK-490	400XP	N153QS	N153Q	(PT-CBT)	PR-CBT	N615KZ	
RK-491	400XP	N491XP	N491HR				
RK-492	400XP	N138QS	(N500XP)	N840JM	N940JM		
RK-493	400XP	N493XP	CC-CRT				
RK-494	400XP	N72594	CS-DMO	XA-ETP			
RK-495	400XP	N495XP	N410CT	N419TM			
RK-496	400XP	N496XP	N410KD	PR-VHB			
RK-497	400XP	N497XP					
RK-498	400XP	N141QS	N276TX	N420BD			
RK-499	400XP	N499XP	I-GFVF	V5-WAW			
RK-500	400XP	N500XP	I-FDED				
RK-501	400XP	N501XP	F-HITM				
RK-502	400XP	N502XP	G-STOB	TC-KJA			
RK-503	400XP	N203XP	XA-FLX	N121GF	XA-FLX		
RK-504	400XP	N204XP	(N45LN)	N202TT			
RK-505	400XP	N505XP					
RK-506	400XP	N471LX	N415FL				
RK-507	400XP	N466LX	N507HB	N507WM			
RK-508	400XP	N70158	CS-DMP	N450TM			
RK-509	400XP	N154QS	N400MX				
RK-510	400XP	N510XP	N225SB				
RK-511	400XP	N511XP	VT-TVR				
RK-512	400XP	N37339	CS-DMQ	N408LH	YV564T		
RK-513	400XP	N513XP					
RK-514	400XP	N514XP	N416RX				
RK-515	400XP	N3735U	I-ALVC				
RK-516	400XP	N74116	CS-DMR	N460TM			
RK-517	400XP	N517XP	N420CT				
RK-518	400XP	N518XP	N473LX	N219DC	PP-MCO	N518TG	(PP-AAW) N54FB
RK-519	400XP	N72539	CS-DMS	N477TM			

BEECHJET 400XP

C/n	Series	Identities				
RK-520	400XP	N157QS	N999WW	PP-MFL		
RK-521	400XP	N521XP	EI-ICE	N521XP	PR-MGD	
RK-522	400XP	N522XP	(N385PB)	N522MB		
RK-523	400XT	N523XP	N425CT	N523AJ		
RK-524	400XP	N524XP	PR-OEC			
RK-525	400XP	N502CA				
RK-526	400XP	N7226P	AP-PAL			
RK-527	400XP	N527XP	(N527DF)	PK-ELV		
RK-528	400XP	N528XP	HA-YFH			
RK-529	400XP	N167QS	N918TT	N311HS		
RK-530	400XP	N530XP	OY-CJN	AP-KNM		
RK-531	400XP	N435CT				
RK-532	400XP	N532XP	CS-DMT	N481TM		
RK-533	400XP	N533HB	EC-KKD			
RK-534	400XP	N440CT				
RK-535	400XP	N445CT				
RK-536	400XP	N470CT				
RK-537	400XP	N537XP	N537DF			
RK-538	400XP	N538XP	CS-DMU	N482TM		
RK-539	400XP	N539XP	N300RC			
RK-540	400XP	N540RK	N777G			
RK-541	400XP	N32051	N474LX	N420FL		
RK-542	400XP	N542XP	N393BB			
RK-543	400XP	N731PS	N710RA			
RK-544	400XP	N480CT				
RK-545	400XP	N485CT				
RK-546	400XP	N490CT				
RK-547	400XP	N495CT				
RK-548	400XP	N548XP	TC-NEU	M-ILLA		
RK-549	400XP	N34249	CS-DMV	N483TM		
RK-550	400XP	N3500R	CS-DMW	N484TM		
RK-551	400XP	N551XP	(N551EU)	YV580T	N305SH	
RK-552	400XP	N552XP	N552EU	G-KLNR		
RK-553	400XP	N553XP	N975BD			
RK-554	400XP	N475LX	N465TM			
RK-555	400XP	N31975	CS-DMX	N487TM		
RK-556	400XP	N3186B	CS-DMY	N488TM		
RK-557	400XP	N557XP	YV457T	N457CP		
RK-558	400XP	N558XP				
RK-559	400XP	N3289R	CS-DMZ	N489TM		
RK-560	400XP	N560XP	N475TM			
RK-561	400XP	N3501M	CS-DOB	N496TM		
RK-562	400XP	N33062	B-77701			
RK-563	400XP	N63XP	(N475LX)			
RK-564	400XP	N564XP	N491TM			
RK-565	400XP	N565XP	N565EU	HZ-PM3	N565EU	PP-AAO
RK-566	400XP	N3206K	VT-GRG	N103DD	N100FN	
RK-567	400XP	N567XP				
RK-568	400XP	N3468D	(N141HB)	PP-JMS		
RK-569	400XP	N180QS	N3438			
RK-570	400XP	N570XP	N979CM			
RK-571	400XP	N979CM	N571TW	HZ-PM2	N571TW	XA-YCC
RK-572	400XP	N3502T	N365KM	N213RA		
RK-573	400XP	N573XP	N449TM			
RK-574	400XP	N175QS	XA-ABS			
RK-575	400XP	N575XP	N112WC			
RK-576	400XP	N576XP	N451TM			
RK-577	400XP	N577XP	N452TM			
RK-578	400XP	N179QS	N711P			
RK-579	400XP	N579XP	CN-TJD	N579XP	I-TOPX	
RK-580	400XP	N580XP	N492TM			
RK-581	400XP	N481LX	N453TM			
RK-582	400XP	N582XP	N493TM			
RK-583	400XP	N176QS	N583XP	AP-RBA		
RK-584	400XP	N3204Q	VH-NTX	N584SC	LV-CLF	
RK-585	400XP	N585XP	N456TM			
RK-586	400XP	N586XP	N480M			
RK-587	400XP	N587XP	HZ-SPAA			
RK-588	400XP	N588XP	HZ-SPAB			
RK-589	400XP	N589XP	HZ-SPAC			
RK-590	400XP	N3190C	N5031T			
RK-591	400XP	N591XP	HZ-SPAD			
RK-592	400XP	N492TM	N592XP	HZ-SPAE		
RK-593	400XP	N493TM	N593XP	YV471T		
RK-594	400XP	N594XP	HZ-SPAF			
RK-595	400XP	N595XP	N595EU	PR-BCK		

BEECHJET 400XP / JAYHAWK

C/n	Series	Identities		
RK-596	400XP	N596XP	N497TM	
RK-597	400XP	N597XP	N410LG	
RK-598	400XP	N598EU	N728EF	
RK-599	400XP	N599XP	N92AJ	PR-BPL
RK-600	400XP	N60XP	(N600ST)	N31ST
RK-601	400XP	N601XP	N498TM	
RK-602	400XP	N602XP	N499TM	
RK-603	400XP	N603XP	XA-DVH	
RK-604	400XP	N604XP	N93FT	
RK-605	400XP	N605XP	[aircraft registered but not built]	

Production complete

Nextant Aerospace are refurbishing Beechjet 400As and 400XPs and retro-fitting them with Williams FJ44 engines. The upgraded aircraft are renamed Nextant 400XT. Known conversions are labelled 400XT in the listings above.

T-1A JAYHAWK

C/n	Identities			
TT-1	N2886B	91-0077		
TT-2	N2887B	90-0412	N2887B	90-0412
TT-3	N2892B	90-0400		
TT-4	90-0405			
TT-5	N2876B	89-0284		
TT-6	N2872B	90-0404		
TT-7	N2896B	90-0401		
TT-8	N2868B	90-0402		
TT-9	90-0403			
TT-10	90-0407			
TT-11	90-0406			
TT-12	90-0408			
TT-13	90-0409			
TT-14	90-0410			
TT-15	90-0411			
TT-16	90-0413			
TT-17	91-0076			
TT-18	91-0075			
TT-19	91-0078			
TT-20	91-0079			
TT-21	91-0080			
TT-22	91-0081			
TT-23	91-0082			
TT-24	91-0083			
TT-25	91-0084			
TT-26	91-0085			
TT-27	91-0086			
TT-28	91-0087			
TT-29	91-0088			
TT-30	91-0089			
TT-31	91-0090			
TT-32	91-0091			
TT-33	91-0092			
TT-34	91-0093	[damaged 16Aug03 at Kessler AFB, MS; moved 10Mar05 to Aeronautical Systems Center, Wright Patterson AFB]		
TT-35	91-0094			
TT-36	91-0095			
TT-37	91-0096			
TT-38	91-0097			
TT-39	91-0098			
TT-40	91-0099			
TT-41	91-0100			
TT-42	91-0101			
TT-43	91-0102			
TT-44	92-0330			
TT-45	92-0331			
TT-46	92-0332			
TT-47	92-0333			
TT-48	92-0334			
TT-49	92-0335			
TT-50	92-0336			
TT-51	92-0337			
TT-52	92-0338			

JAYHAWK

C/n	Identities	
TT-53	92-0339	
TT-54	92-0340	
TT-55	92-0341	
TT-56	92-0342	
TT-57	92-0343	
TT-58	92-0344	
TT-59	92-0345	
TT-60	92-0346	
TT-61	92-0347	
TT-62	92-0348	
TT-63	92-0349	
TT-64	92-0350	
TT-65	92-0351	
TT-66	92-0352	
TT-67	92-0353	
TT-68	92-0354	
TT-69	92-0355	
TT-70	92-0356	
TT-71	92-0357	
TT-72	92-0358	
TT-73	92-0359	
TT-74	92-0360	
TT-75	92-0361	
TT-76	92-0362	
TT-77	92-0363	
TT-78	93-0621	
TT-79	93-0622	
TT-80	93-0623	
TT-81	93-0624	
TT-82	N2830B	93-0625
TT-83	93-0626	
TT-84	93-0627	
TT-85	93-0628	
TT-86	93-0629	
TT-87	93-0630	
TT-88	93-0631	
TT-89	93-0632	
TT-90	93-0633	[w/o May08; to National Museum of USAF, Wright-Patterson AFB, OH; loaned to Laughlin AFB Museum, TX]
TT-91	93-0634	
TT-92	93-0635	
TT-93	93-0636	
TT-94	93-0637	
TT-95	93-0638	
TT-96	93-0639	
TT-97	93-0640	
TT-98	93-0641	
TT-99	93-0642	
TT-100	93-0643	
TT-101	93-0644	
TT-102	93-0645	
TT-103	93-0646	
TT-104	93-0647	
TT-105	93-0648	
TT-106	93-0649	
TT-107	93-0650	
TT-108	93-0651	
TT-109	93-0652	
TT-110	93-0653	
TT-111	93-0654	
TT-112	93-0655	
TT-113	93-0656	
TT-114	94-0114	
TT-115	94-0115	
TT-116	94-0116	
TT-117	94-0117	
TT-118	94-0118	
TT-119	94-0119	
TT-120	94-0120	
TT-121	94-0121	
TT-122	94-0122	
TT-123	94-0123	
TT-124	94-0124	
TT-125	94-0125	
TT-126	94-0126	
TT-127	94-0127	
TT-128	94-0128	

JAYHAWK

C/n	Identities
TT-129	94-0129
TT-130	94-0130
TT-131	94-0131
TT-132	94-0132
TT-133	94-0133
TT-134	94-0134
TT-135	94-0135
TT-136	94-0136
TT-137	94-0137
TT-138	94-0138
TT-139	94-0139
TT-140	94-0140
TT-141	94-0141
TT-142	94-0142
TT-143	94-0143
TT-144	94-0144
TT-145	94-0145
TT-146	94-0146
TT-147	94-0147
TT-148	94-0148
TT-149	95-0040
TT-150	95-0041
TT-151	95-0042
TT-152	95-0043
TT-153	95-0044
TT-154	95-0045
TT-155	95-0046
TT-156	95-0047
TT-157	95-0048
TT-158	95-0049
TT-159	95-0050
TT-160	95-0051
TT-161	95-0052
TT-162	95-0053
TT-163	95-0054
TT-164	95-0055
TT-165	95-0056
TT-166	95-0057
TT-167	95-0058
TT-168	95-0059
TT-169	95-0060
TT-170	95-0061
TT-171	95-0062
TT-172	95-0063
TT-173	95-0064
TT-174	95-0065
TT-175	95-0066
TT-176	95-0067
TT-177	95-0068
TT-178	95-0069
TT-179	95-0070
TT-180	95-0071

Production complete

T400 JAYHAWK

C/n	Identities			
TX-1	N82884	Japan 41-5051	[code 051]	
TX-2	N82885	Japan 41-5052	[code 052]	
TX-3	N82886	Japan 41-5053	[code 053]	
TX-4	N3195K	Japan 41-5054	[code 054]	
TX-5	N3195Q	Japan 41-5055	[code 055]	
TX-6	N3195X	Japan 51-5056	[code 056]	
TX-7	N3228M	Japan 51-5057	[code 057]	
TX-8	N3228V	Japan 51-5058	[code 058]	
TX-9	N1069L	Japan 71-5059	[code 059]	
TX-10	"N3221Z"	N32212	Japan 01-5060	[code 060]
TX-11	N50561	Japan 21-5061	[code 061]	
TX-12	N50512	Japan 21-5062	[code 062]	
TX-13	N50543	Japan 41-5063	[code 063]	

Production complete

BRITISH AEROSPACE (RAYTHEON) 125 SERIES

The majority of the series 3, 400 and 700 aircraft which were exported to North America were allocated an additional number in the NA… range, and these numbers are quoted as the c/n. This practice was reintroduced on production 800 and 1000 series aircraft but has since ceased. The production list is in the normal c/n order, and a cross-reference of the two sets of numbers follows the production list.

Early-build aircraft were known as DH125s and then HS125s and subsequently BAe125s. 800 series aircraft above c/n 258208 and 1000 series aircraft above c/n 259024 are known by the nomenclature Corporate Jets BAe125. Following the sale of Corporate Jets by BAe to Raytheon, owner of Beechcraft, yet another nomenclature change took place to Hawker 800 (at c/n 258255) and Hawker 1000 (at c/n 259043).

UK B condition marks from G-5-501 onwards are only shown once against the airframe to which they were allocated, even though they would be re-used whenever that aircraft went to Chester for maintenance.

C/n	Series	Identities
25001	1	G-ARYA [ff 13Aug62; CofA exp 01Oct65; wfu Kelsterton College, UK; cockpit section to Mosquito Museum, London Colney UK Feb04]
25002	1	G-ARYB [CofA exp 22Jan68; wfu BAe Hatfield, UK; cx 04Mar69; to Midland Air Museum, Coventry, UK]
25003	1	G-ARYC [CofA exp 01Aug73; wfu Mosquito Museum, London Colney, UK]
25004	1/521	G-ASEC G-FIVE [wfu by Jun83; cx 14May85, used for spares – wings to c/n 25008]
25005	1	G-ASNU (D-CFKG) D-COMA G-ASNU [wfu by Dec82; impounded Lagos, Nigeria; cx 18Nov91]
25006	1	HB-VAG I-RACE [CofA exp Nov87; wfu]
25007	1	(G-ASSH) HB-VAH G-ASTY HB-VAH F-BKMF [w/o 05Jun66 Nice, France]
25008	1	G-ASSI 5N-AWD [wfu by Dec83, Luton, UK; to Staggenhoe Farm, Whitewell, Beds UK for use by emergency services in crash exercises 10Sep98]
25009	1	G-ATPC XW930 [wfu, scrapped Jordan's scrapyard, Portsmouth, UK by Jun97]
25010	1/522	G-ASSM 5N-AMK [wfu by Dec83; to Science Museum, Kensington, London, UK, painted as G-ASSM]
25011	T1	G-37-65 XS709 [code M] [wfu 20Jan11; to RAF Museum, Cosford, UK, 11Feb11]
25012	T1	XS710 [code O] 9259M [stored RAF Cosford, UK circa 1997]
25013	1A	G-ASSJ N125J N2426 N7125J N4646S N88MR [wfu prior to Jun82; parted out by White Inds, Bates City, MO]
25014	1A/522	G-ASSK N125G N734AK N621ST (N125WC) XA-JUZ N621ST [wfu by Dec82; b/u 1985]
25015	3B	VH-CAO (9M-AYI) VH-CAO (N750D) [Australian marks cx May91; stripped of re-usable parts by Dodson Av'n during 1998. Fuselage to Australian Air Museum at Sydney-Bankstown, moved to The Oaks, South West of Sydney, NSW by Jun05 to join c/n 25062 reportedly to restore one of the two to flying condition]
25016	1A	G-ASSL CF-RWA CF-OPC C-FOPC C6-BPC N4997E N222NG [b/u Fort Lauderdale Executive]
25017	1A/522	G-ASSH N3060 N3060F N306MP N123JB N495G N333M XA-RSR [wfu Fort Lauderdale Executive, FL; b/u]
25018	731	CF-DOM C-FDOM N125LM C-GXPT N125PT N118TS N218TJ (P4-ZAW) (XA-…) N218TJ
25019	1A	G-ASYX N1125G N1135K [w/o 25Feb66 Des Moines, IA]
25020	731	G-ASZM N167J N959KW N2KW N2KN N365DJ N711WM (N128TJ) N55RF [parted out following landing accident Seattle, WA Dec02; cx Aug 03]
25021	1A/522	G-ASZN N575DU N2504 N228G N228GL N125BT N125KC N711WJ N300HW [wfu; parted out by White Inds, Bates City, MO]
25022	1A/522	G-ASZO CF-SDA N505PA N100GB N50HH [w/o 02Aug86 Bedford, IN]
25023	731	G-ASZP N1125 N338 (N125BW) N125BM N58BT N284DB N584DB N62TJ (N89FF) ZS-PJE ZS-TBN
25024	T1	XS711 [code L] [wfu]
25025	1B	D-COME HB-VAR F-BOHU (F-OCGK) 5N-AWB [wfu by early 87]
25026	1A	G-5-11 G-ATAY N225KJ N225K N225LL N4400E (N40AD) [wfu by Apr86; used for spares early 86]
25027	1A	CF-SEN C-FSEN N227DH N125BH N777RN
25028	1B	Ghana G.511 (N48172) C-GLFI N48172 N50SS XA-ESQ N29977 [w/o 14Dec81 as XA-ESQ and parted out; last allocated US marks, N29977, were not worn; cx Apr91; remains to White Inds, Bates City, MO]
25029	1A/522	G-ATAZ N10122 N391DA N10D [wfu Mar04 Tulsa/Jones Field, OK; parted out by White Inds, Bates City, MO; cx 29Apr09]
25030	1A	G-ATBA N413GH N123VM (N97VM) XB-MBM XA-MBM XA-RDD [wfu Saltillo, Mexico]
25031	1A	G-ATBB N1923M N43WJ N79AE N105HS [wfu circa Oct05 Oklahoma City, OK]
25032	731	G-ATBC N65MK (N657K) N90WP N692FC N98TJ N942DS (N16GG) (9Q-…) [wfu Lanseria, South Africa]
25033	1A/522	G-ATBD N125G N1125G N111AG N111AD (N111AX) (N700AB) N63BL (N32HE) N125LC N125AL N125LL RP-C125 [wfu Lapu-Lapu City, Philippines]
25034	1A	CF-HLL C-FHLL [wfu Quebec City by Jun83, possibly following accident 18Apr83 at Gashe, PQ, Canada; fuselage noted at Montreal-St.Hubert Oct95; wings used on c/n 25027; cx Dec90]
25035	1A	G-ATCO N1515P N1515E N151SG (N57TS) [instructional airframe at Nehru College of Aeronautics & Applied Science, Kuniamuthur, India; cx 03Feb12]
25036	1A	CF-PQG C-FPQG N136DH [cx Jul95 as destroyed/scrapped]
25037	1A	G-ATFO D-CAFI N787X N26T N26TL (N26WJ) (N389DA) [b/u for spares; cx Jul92]
25038	731	G-ATCP N926G N125G (N900KC) N66KC (N15UB) N27RC N301CK (N417TF) (N28MM) N28M N42CK N806CB
25039	1A	CF-SIM C-FSIM N125TB N911AS [wfu to Sanford, FL; b/u & cx Sep03]
25040	T1	XS712 [code A] [wfu 20Jan11] N19CQ [to RJ Mitchell Aircraft Maintenance Academy, Humberside, UK, 20Feb15 as instructional airframe]

BAe 125

C/n	Series	Identities
25041	T1	XS713 [code C] [wfu 20Jan11; to RAF Shawbury as fire trainer]
25042	731	CF-ANL C-FANL N79TS (N42FD) N725WH [parted out by White Inds, Bates City, MO; cx 25Oct07]
25043	1A/522	G-ATGA N125J N1230V N3007 N300R N70HB N522BW N522ME N65TS (N165AG) [parted out by Dodson Int'l, Rantoul, KS circa Jan01]
25044	T1	XS726 [code T] 9273M [wfu RAF Cosford, UK circa 1997; to Everett Aero, Sproughton, UK, 2007, then to Newark Air Museum, Newark, UK, Sep14]
25045	T1	XS727 [code D] [wfu 20Jan11; preserved RAF Cranwell]
25046	1A/S-522	G-ATGS N48UC N4886 N125P N666AE N812TT N125AD LV-YGC [wfu Moron, Argentina]
25047	1A/522	G-ATGT N778SM N580WS N75CT N800DA (N717GF)
25048	T1	XS728 [code E] [wfu 20Jan11] N19CU [cx 23Jan15, b/u Kemble, UK]
25049	T1	XS729 [code G] 9275M [wfu 1996; to Everett Aero, Sproughton, UK, 2007; to Vilanova i la Geltru, Spain, as instructional airframe]
25050	T1	XS730 [code H] [wfu 20Jan11] N19UG [cx 23Jan15; to instructional airframe, Lufthansa Resource Technical Training, Kemble, UK]
25051	731	G-ATGU N9300 N9300C N125HD C6-BEY N77VK [wfu 18Dec85; cx Jan87, parted out]
25052	1A/522	G-ATIK N816M N816MC N812M N812N N388WM N125JR (N252MA) XB-JVL [impounded Jun01 Toluca, Mexico; wfu]
25053	1A/522	CF-IPG CF-IPJ C-FIPJ N4465N N125TB N254JT N250JT N25JT [cx 30Sep04, wfu at Monterrey/del Norte, Mexico]
25054	T1	XS714 [code P] 9246M [wfu; to RAF Manston, UK for fire training use]
25055	T1	XS731 [code J] [wfu 20Jan11] N19XY [cx 23Jan15, b/u Kemble, UK]
25056	T1	XS732 [code B] [wfu Jan91 due to fuselage corrosion; fuselage to Research Establishment, Fort Halstead, Kent, UK 27Mar91; TT 11,955.20, TL 9,067]
25057	1A/522	G-ATIL N188K N125AW [cx 02Apr86; b/u for spares Pontiac, MI]
25058	1A	D-COMI N9308Y N215G N470R N632PB N632PE (EC-...) [used for spares; cx Nov05; b/u]
25059	T1	XS733 [code Q] 9276M [wfu 1996; stored RAF Cosford, UK; to Everett Aero, Sproughton, UK, 2007]
25060	1A/522	G-ATIM N2601 N26011 N2728 N22DL N22DE XB-FIS XB-EAL XA-BOJ XA-HOU XB-CXZ N96SG [cx 25Aug09, parted out]
25061	T1	XS734 [code N] 9260M [stored RAF Cosford, UK circa 1997; to Everett Aero, Sproughton, UK, 2007]
25062	3B	VH-ECE [wfu 21Jul81; to Camden Airport Museum, NSW; TT 13936, TL 53882; derelict at The Oaks, NSW by May97]
25063	1B	HB-VAN G-BAXG G-ONPN 5N-ASZ [wfu 03Jun86 Southampton, UK; parted out]
25064	1A/522	G-ATKK N230H N125JG N33BK N222G XA-RYW N222G XB-GGK XA-TAL [w/o 09Jul99 Toluca A/P, Mexico]
25065	1A/522	G-ATKL N631SC N631SQ N1YE XA-KOF XC-ANL [instructional airframe CONALEP Apodaca, Monterrey, Mexico]
25066	731	G-ATKM N925CT N369JB (N374DH) N373DH (XA-...) N372RS XA-UEX
25067	1B/522	9J-RAN ZS-MAN 9J-SAS 9J-EPK Z-TBX ZS-MAN
25068	1A/522	XB-BEA XA-BEM XB-VUI XA-MIR XB-SBC [reported Oct89 with dual marks XA-MIR/XB-SBC] N5274U [parted out by Dodson Av'n, Rantoul, KS]
25069	3B	VH-ECF G-BAXL G-OBOB [w/o 31Jan90 Concordia, MO; parted out by White Inds, Bates City, MO]
25070	1A/522	G-ATKN N520M N214JR N2148R N84W N51V N470TS N333GZ [parted out by White Inds, Bates City, MO; cx 29Apr09]
25071	T1	XS735 [code R] [wfu; ground instructional airframe at RAF St Athan, UK May02]
25072	T1	XS736 [code S] [parted out RAF Cranwell, UK; remains to Everett Aero, Sproughton, UK, 2007; then to Winterbourne Gunner, UK]
25073	1A/522	G-ATLI N372CM N372GM N36MK [w/o 28Dec70 Boise, ID]
25074	1A/522	G-ATOV N400NW N400UW N300GB N411FB [parted out Lancaster, TX]
25075	731	G-ATLJ N666M CF-MDB C-FMDB N9124N N750GM N731BW N600EG XB-GAM [wfu Hermosillo, Mexico]
25076	T1	XS737 [code K] [wfu 20Jan11] N19EK [cx 23Jan15; to instructional airframe, Lufthansa Resource Technical Training, Kemble, UK]
25077	T1	XS738 [code U] 9274M [stored RAF Cosford, UK circa 1997; to RNAS Predannack fire training area by 2007]
25078	1A/522	G-ATLK N40DC N448DC N125NT (N770BC) (N16PJ) XA-DCS XA-RPT [wfu Saltillo, Mexico]
25079	731	G-ATLL N440DC N448DC N40DC N425DC N425FD N79TJ N425FD N942Y N942WN P4-AOC N963YA [instructional airframe, Tulsa Technical Center, Tulsa/R.L.Jones, OK]
25080	1A/522	VQ-ZIL 3D-AAB G-BDYE EI-BGW C-GLEO N23KL EC-EGT [wfu Jan93; parted out by Dodson Av'n, Rantoul, KS]
25081	T1	XS739 [code F] [wfu 20Jan11] N19UK [to RJ Mitchell Aircraft Maintenance Academy, Humberside, UK, 20Feb15 as instructional airframe]
25082	1A/522	G-ATNM N909B N2125 N125CA N1MY N17SL [wfu; cx Dec92; parted out by White Inds, Bates City, MO]
25083	1A/522	G-ATOW N16777 N435T N437T N533 N538 N50AS [wfu 1988; parted out by OK Aircraft, Gilroy, CA; cx Sep92]
25084	1A/522	G-ATNN N1125G N453CM N154TR N30EF N784AE (N745HG) N71BL N890RC N888CJ [wfu Santo Domingo/Herrera, Dominican Republic]
25085	1B/522	G-ATPD 5N-AGU G-ATPD [wfu circa Sep00 at Bournemouth A/P, UK, to fire training mid 2002; cx Dec03]
25086	1A/522	CF-DSC N3699T XA-COL [w/o 11Oct73 Acapulco, Mexico]
25087	731/S	G-ATOX CF-ALC C-FALC N66AM N330G
25088	1A/522	G-ATNO N1230B 5B-...
25089	1B/522	G-ATPB OO-SKJ 5N-ALH
25090	1B/S522	HB-VAT G-AWYE N102TW N429DA [cx 13May13; wfu]

BAe 125

C/n		Series	Identities
25091		1A/522	G-ATNP N1230G N20RG N90RG N65FC XA-RSP [wfu Fort Lauderdale Executive, FL; b/u]
25092		1B/522	G-ATPE [CofA exp 01Apr87; to Southampton Airport Fire Svce 1989; canx 14Mar90]
25093		1A/522	G-ATSN N77D N306L N3MF [w/o 26Jan79 Taos NM]
25094		1B/R522	G-ATWH HZ-BO1 G-ATWH G-YUGO [cx 29Mar93 as wfu; remains to Biggin Hill, UK circa 2000 for fire training]
25095		1A/522	G-ATSO N125Y CF-SHZ N1923G N5001G (N5012P) N80CC N61BL N25AW N831LC [w/o 16Mar91 nr San Diego, CA]
25096		1A/522	G-ATNR N235KC [w/o 21Nov66 Grand Bahama, Bahamas]
25097		1A/S522	G-ATSP LN-NPE N125V N12KW N21MF N89HB N67TS [b/u; cx Jan02]
25098		731	G-ATNS N10121 N666SC N57G N11AR N45SL N926LR N29CR YV-815CP (N77LJ) YV2416
25099		1B/522	HB-VAU 5N-AER N2246 N121AC [wfu; located at aircraft trades school Zaira, Nigeria]
25100		1A/522	G-ATNT N125J N952B N7SZ N104 N44TG N44TQ N6SS [cx 06Aug12; wfu]
25101		731/S	G-5-11 G-ATXE N142B N124BM XA-RCH XA-RUX N251LA N78AG XA-MBM
25102		1A/522	G-ATUU N756 N756M XB-AKW N3274Q [to spares Houston, TX circa 1995 (cx Feb96) marks N3274Q were never carried]
25103		1A/522	G-ATUV N533 N210M (N700UU) N601UU N60HU N402AC
25104		1A/522	G-ATUW N257H N140AK C-FMTC [derelict Nov97 Vancouver, Canada; hulk removed to Lakeland, FL circa Mar00]
25105		1B/522	(D-CKOW) D-CKCF G-AYRY HZ-FMA [reported wfu]
25106		1B/522	HZ-BIN G-AWUF 5N-ALY G-AWUF G-DJMJ G-OMCA G-BOCB [wfu 1994 Luton, UK; cx 22Feb95; cockpit to Sth.Yorks Aircraft Museum, Doncaster, UK]
25107		1A/522	G-ATUX N7125J N2426 C-GFCL N107BW N694JC XA-GOC XA-HFM XA-UBK
25108		731	G-ATUY N1025C N901TC N901TG N31B C-FTAM N11QD N25LA C-GTTS N46190 [wfu circa Sep04; parted out by White Inds, Bates City, MO, Jly05 still wearing C-GTTS]
25109		1A/S522	G-ATUZ N201H N4CR [wfu Phoenix/Williams Gateway, AZ]
25110		1A/522	G-5-11 G-ATZE N3125B N125E [w/o 30Jun83 Houston Hobby, TX]
25111		3A	G-ATYH N1041B N125GC C-GKRL N31AS N177GP N900CD [w/o 30May94 Waukegan Regional A/P, Waukegan, IL; parted out by White Inds, Bates City, MO]
25112		3A	G-ATYI N2525 N252V XB-AXP XA-LFU XB-FFV XA-SLR
25113		3B/RA	G-5-13 G-AVDX 5N-AVZ [noted semi-derelict Dec96 Lagos, Nigeria]
25114		3A	G-ATYJ N425K N44K N44KG N78RZ N25PM XA-SGP N114WD [parted out by Dodson Av'n, Rantoul, KS]
25115		731	G-ATYK N229P N333ME N333MF N317EM N111DT N180ML N21GN N429AC (N750WC) N249BW N249MW N420JC N48DD [w/o 09Mar01 Bridgeport, CT]
25116		3A	G-ATZN N93TC N136LK N345DA (N90SR) N345CT N726CC SX-BSS [wfu at Thessalonkia, Greece circa Jul01]
25117		3B	5N-AET 5N-AKT G-BSAA G-DBAL [cx 16Apr93; wfu]
25118		731	G-ATYL N743UT N45PM N731KC N300KC N227HF N14HH N118DA 9Q-CVF
25119		731	G-5-11 G-AVAD N213H N500XY [parted out; still current on USCAR]
25120		3B	G-AVGW [w/o 23Dec67 Luton, UK]
25121		731	G-AVAE N795J N307G N807G N200PB N200PF XA-SKZ XB-GHC N125TJ N125LK N685FF [parted out Spirit of St Louis a/p, MO; cx 15Sep07]
25122		3A	G-AVAF N12225 N555CB N255CB (N123AG) N123AC [parted out 1992, San Jose, CA; remains to OK Aircraft, Gilroy, CA; cx Nov01]
25123		3A	G-AVAG N700M N706M N77C N77CD N46TG N44PW N125FD [parted out by Dodson Int'l, Rantoul, KS circa Oct01; cx 18Apr17]
25124		3A	G-AVAH N125J N552N N912AS [wfu to Titusville/Cocoa Beach, FL]
25125		F3B	G-AVAI LN-NPA G-AVAI F-GFMP 5N-AAN (EL-AMJ) (EL-ELS) [to instructional airframe at Newcastle Aviation Academy, Newcastle UK]
25126		3B	G-5-11 G-AVDL N510X N66HA [w/o 13Aug89 Houston, TX – remains to Aviation Warehouse film prop facility, El Mirage, CA]
25127		F3B	G-AVPE G-5-623 G-KASS N125GK [w/o 26Jun06 Barcelona, Venezuela; parted out by White Inds, Bates City, MO]
25128		3B	G-AVOI F-GECR ZS-SMT [wfu at Lanseria, South Africa]
25129		3A	G-5-12 G-AVDM N521M [w/o 12Dec72 Findlay, OH]
25130		3B	G-5-14 G-AVRD HB-VAZ F-BSIM TR-LXO F-BSIM TR-LFB [cx; used for fire-fighting demonstrations, Musee de l'Air, Paris/Le Bourget, France]
25131		3B	G-5-11 G-AVRE F-BPMC G-FOUR I-RASO F-GFDB 3A-MDB F-GJDE 3A-MDE 7T-VVL
25132		3B	OY-DKP G-AZVS G-MRFB G-OCBA EI-WDC G-OCBA EI-WDC G-OCBA S9-PDH
25133		3B	G-AVRF G-ILLS VT-EQZ [instructional airframe, Flytech Aviation Academy, Hyderabad, India]
25134	NA700	3A/RA	G-5-11 G-AVHA N514V N514VA N338 N366MP N366BR N117TS N725DW N946FS N230TS [to Dodson International Parts May05]
25135		3B	G-5-14 HB-VAY G-AXPS [w/o 20Jul70 Edinburgh, UK]
25136	NA701	3A/RA	G-AVHB N501W N506N N505W N605W N700RG N700RD N700RG N125HS Brazil VU93-2113 [preserved Museo Aerospacial, Campo dos Afonsos, Brazil]
25137	NA702	3A/RA	G-5-11 G-AVJD CF-AAG CF-KCI C-FKCI N13MJ N813PR C-GMEA [parted out Arnoni Av'n, Houston, TX circa Sep00; cx Aug99]
25138		3B	(G-5-12) G-5-16 G-AVVA HB-VBN I-BOGI 5N-AVV [parted out Coventry, UK, 1997]
25139	NA703	3A/RA	G-5-11 G-AVOJ N612G N2G N22GE N140JS XB-JLY XB-KQB [instructional airframe at Patna, India]
25140		3B/RA	(G-5-16) G-5-17 G-AVVB G-DJLW C6-MED N140LF [parted out by Dodson Int'l, Rantoul, KS]
25141	NA704	3A/RA	G-5-12 G-AVOK N75C N55G N208H N14GD N14GQ (N90WP) N888WK C-GSKV N132RL [parted out by White Inds, Bates City, MO; cx 29Apr09]

BAe 125

C/n		Series	Identities
25142	NA705	731	G-AVOL N7055 N9040 N688CC N9040 N744CC N7440C N822CC N770DA (N60AM) N25MJ N705EA [parted out by White Inds, Bates City, MO; cx 29Apr09]
25143		3B/RA	G-5-18 G-AVXK D-CHTH G-AVXK 5N-AOG [wfu before Jun93; b/u for spares Hurn, UK]
25144		3B/RA	G-5-12 G-AVRG G-OHEA [cx Jun94; wfu to Cranfield Inst of Technology, Cranfield, UK, as instructional airframe]
25145		3B	G-5-20 G-AVXL LN-NPC G-AVXL I-SNAF [CofA exp 1983; derelict at Milan-Linate 1989; cx 1990]
25146	NA706	3A/RA	G-AVRH N77617 N214JR N214TC N711SW N214TC N114PC N21AR N999SA (N899SA) N777GA XA-ADR XB-JKG [wfu Monterrey del Norte, Mexico]
25147		3B/RA	G-5-14 PK-PJR PK-DJW [CofA expired 20Oct86; wfu; derelict near Jakarta-Halim Airport, Indonesia circa 99]
25148		3A/R	G-5-13 G-AVRI N8125J N450JD (N100TT) XB-ERN N814P (N819P) XA-TTH [stored Guadalajara, Mexico]
25149		3A/R	G-AVRJ N1125E N99SC N99GC N99KR [wfu 09Sep80; donated to Northrop University nr Los Angeles A/P, CA; cx Apr91; to Malaysian Institute of Aviation Technology, Dengkil nr Kuala Lumpur, 1998, painted as N1125E]
25150		F3A	G-5-13 G-AWMS N511BX VR-BKY VP-BKY N42AS [parted out by Alliance Air Parts, Oklahoma City, OK]
25151		3A/RA	G-AVTY N125F [wfu at Lima, Peru, circa 1997; fuselage to Collique, Peru, by Feb07]
25152		3A/RA	G-AVTZ CF-QNS C-FQNS N45793 N123RZ XA-IIT N28686 N50MJ N23CJ
25153		731	G-5-19 G-AVXM N30F N30FD N731G N336MB N676PC N88DJ N88DU [cx 27Aug13; wfu]
25154		3B/RA	G-5-11 EP-AHK G-AZCH [b/u Luton, UK Dec82 due to corrosion; TT 4261hrs, TL 4695, CofA exp 16Aug81; rear fuselage/fin used on c/n 25270; forward fuselage at Cheddington airstrip, Bucks, UK]
25155		3A/RA	G-AVXN N32F N466MP (N411MF) N999LF N333CJ N77BT N158AG [still painted as N77BT circa Dec00; wfu Titusville/Cocoa Beach, FL; b/u; cx Sep03]
25156		3A/RA	G-AVZJ N522M N10LN [b/u 1993 Lakeland, FL; fuselage remains only]
25157		3B/RA	D-CAMB VR-BGD G-GGAE G-JSAX [wfu Dec82; cx 10Jan86 – at Eastleigh, UK minus outer wings]
25158		3A/RA	G-AVZK XB-PUE (N702GA) XA-DAN
25159		731	G-5-19 G-AVZL CF-WOS C-FWOS N4767M N511WM N511WN N67TJ N600SV ZS-CNA
25160	NA707	3A/RA	G-5-15 G-AWKH N350NC N873D N873G N627CR SE-DHH N160AG
25161	NA708	3A/RA	G-AWKI N9149 N756N N75GN XA-RPT XA-DCS [wfu Saltillo, Mexico]
25162		3B/RC	Brazil VC93-2120 Brazil VU93-2120 [scrapped 2009]
25163	NA709	731	G-5-16 G-AWMV N208H N55G (N2G) [cx 28Jul14; wfu Fort Lauderdale Executive]
25164		3B/RC	Brazil EC93-2125 Brazil EU93-2125 Brazil XU93-2125
25165		3B/RC	Brazil VC93-2121 Brazil EU93-2121 [wfu]
25166		3B/RC	Brazil VC93-2122 Brazil VU93-2122 [w/o 19Jun79 Brasilia, Brazil]
25167		3B/RC	Brazil VC93-2123 Brazil VU93-2123
25168		3B/RC	Brazil VC93-2124 Brazil VU93-2124 [wfu]
25169		3A/RA	G-5-17 G-AWWL VH-BBJ N3AL G-AWWL N84TF (N9300P) N9300C N99SC (N711SC) N122AW N163AG [cx 24Jul08, b/u]
25170	NA710	3A/RA	G-AWMW N1259K N226G N228G N223G C-GKCO N500YB C-FMKF N322TP N814ER N314ER (N767LC) [parted out Rantoul, KS]
25171		F3B/RA	G-5-19 HB-VBT G-AXPU G-IBIS G-AXPU G-BXPU (N171AV) G-OPOL G-IFTC (N171AV) D2-FEZ
25172		F3B/RA	G-AXEG ZS-CAL G-AXEG ZS-CAL
25173	NA711	400A	G-AWMX N125J N3711L (N610HC) N711AQ N601JJ ZP-TDF ZP-TKO
25174	NA712	400A	G-AWMY N1199M N1199G N511WP N60JC N496G N7777B N712VS N713SS [parted out by White Inds, Bates City, MO circa Oct05]
25175	NA713	731	G-AWPC N217F YV-825CP N272B N773AA XB-MGM [w/o 04Nov13, shot down over Venezuela on suspected drug-running flight]
25176	NA714	731	G-AWPD CF-NER C-FNER N176TS N311JA N811JA N31EP YV299T
25177		400B	G-AWXN S Africa 02 [w/o 26May71 Devils Peak, S Africa]
25178		400B	G-AWXO 5N-BUA G-OOSP 5N-WMA XA-AEE XA-ULN XA-UOF
25179	NA715	731	G-AWPE N778S N200CC N400CC N800CB N800QB N22EH N629P N824TJ N284DB XA-GLS
25180	NA716	400A	G-AWPF N196KC N196KQ N888CR N400PH [w/o 05Dec87 Blue Grass Field, Lexington, KY]
25181		400B	(G-5-13) G-AXLU S Africa 01 [w/o 26May71 Devils Peak, S Africa]
25182		400B	G-AXLV S Africa 03 [w/o 26May71 Devils Peak, S Africa]
25183	NA717	731	G-5-18 G-AWXB N162A N162D N100HF N984HF [w/o 07Nov85 Sparta, TN]
25184		400B	G-AXLW S Africa 04 ZS-LPE [wfs – stored at Waterkloof AFB, South Africa]
25185	NA720	400A	G-AWXE N140C N4PN N7LG XA-GUB XB-DSQ XA-RMN XB-FRP XA-FRP XB-MSV [wfu Monterrey del Norte, Mexico]
25186	NA721	731	G-AWXF N125G N93BH N933 N40SK N666JT N668JT (N105EJ) N99CK HR-AMD N12YS (N999NM) N186NM N777GD N43TS
25187	NA718	731	G-AWXC N600L N600LP N600JA N900DS (N7WG) N16WG N50SL N141JL XA-SSV N250DH [cx 28Jul14; parted out by Arnoni Av'n, Houston, TX]
25188	NA719	731	G-AWXD N545S XB-IPX [wfu Queretaro, Mexico]
25189		400B	G-5-20 (G-AXFY) Malaysia FM1200 FM1801 M24-01 [wfu, to technical school at Alor Setar, Malaysia, wearing fake marks M24-02]
25190	NA722	400A	G-AXDO N1393 N75CS N75QS N75TJ N51MN N209NC N38TS (N280CH) XB-ILD [impounded at Portoviejo, Ecuador, Oct03 for drug-running] Ecuador FAE050
25191	NA723	731	G-AXDP N511YP N900KC N100T N723TS N401JR N444HH YV-1145CP YV1687 [dbr Caracas/Simon Bolivar 26Nov15]
25192	NA724	731	CF-SDH C-FSDH N724TS [wfu Houston/Hooks, TX]

BAe 125

C/n		Series	Identities
25193	NA725	400A	CF-CFL [w/o 11Nov69 Newfoundland, Canada]
25194		400B	G-AXDM [wfu & dismantled at Edinburgh, UK Sep03; to Farnborough, UK; cx as destroyed 13Nov03]
25195	NA726	731	G-AXDR N111MB N949CW N949CV N60B N60BD N731G N31VT YV-141CP N922RR N922GK [parted out by White Inds, Bates City, MO]
25196	NA727	731	G-AXDS N814M N114B N81RR N117RH N100RH XA-TNY
25197		400B	G-5-11 PP-EEM PT-LHK N97CS [b/u Fort Lauderdale Executive, FL, Aug12; parted out by Dodson Av'n, Rantoul, KS]
25198	NA728	731	G-AXJD N24CH N400KC N320JJ N410PA N32GM (N232JS) [parted out by Alliance Air Parts, Oklahoma City, OK]
25199		400B	G-AXLX HB-VBW G-AXLX (HB-VGU) HB-VBW N3118M (N905Y) [parted out 1994 by Dodson Avn, Ottawa, KS]
25200	NA729	400A	G-AXJE N702S N1C N702SS Brazil VU93-2118
25201	NA730	731	G-AXJF N220T N56BL N125MD N800JC N810MC N730TS N101HS N730TS N82CA N800WZ
25202	NA731	400A	G-AXJG N65LT N700CC N300LD (N125DC) N31TJ (N700PG) (N600DP) XA-JRF N336AC XB-MAR (XB-ASO) [wfu Cuernavaca, Mexico]
25203	NA732	400A	G-AXOA N500AG N73JH N44CN N21ES N100LR N109LR N2020 N70JC N732TS N400PR [preserved at 1940 Air Terminal Museum, Houston/ Hobby, TX]
25204	NA733	731	G-AXOB N380X N31GT (N125RT) N243JB ZS-PLC [cx; scrapped Sep15]
25205	NA734	731	G-AXOC N125J N111RB N621L N621S N6218 N99ST (N38TS) XA-GTC N20PJ XA-GTC
25206	NA735	400A	G-AXPX VP-BDH N125AJ N400AG N11SQ XA-ROJ N165AG N800GE
25207	NA736	400A	G-AXOD N30PR N30PP N112M (N400HF) N800AF N736LE [wfu; stored Cambridge, MD]
25208	NA737	400A	G-AXOE N2500W N65EC N65DW (N165AG) N643JL N400KD XA-YSM [impounded for drug-running Valencia, Venezuela, Sep07]
25209		400B	Malaysia FM1201 FM1802 M24-02 [wfu, to Malaysian Institute of Aviation Technology, Dengkil nr Kuala Lumpur, Malaysia]
25210	NA738	400A	G-AXOF N702D Brazil VU93-2117 Brazil XU93-2117 [wfu at Guaratingueta, Brazil, by May05]
25211	NA739	731	G-AXTR N125DH N820MC N820MG [cx Apr10, wfu]
25212	NA740	400A	G-AXTS N702P Brazil VU93-2114 [wfu 1998]
25213	NA741	400A	G-AXTT CF-CFL C-FCFL [w/o 09Dec77 Newfoundland, Canada]
25214	NA742	731	G-AXTU N40PC N60PC N60QA G-AXTU G-5-20 N731HS N12BN N12AE N369CS N569CS (N87DC) N74RT N843B [cx 23Mar15; wfu]
25215		403B	HB-VBZ G-BHFT 9M-SSB G-BHFT Z-VEC ZS-NPV D2-EXR [dbr 21Nov03 Luanda, Angola]
25216	NA743	400A	G-AXTV N9138 XC-GOB Mexico TP0206 Mexico TP108/XC-UJH N125JW HP-125JW HP-1128P N400D HK-3653X HK-3653 N400LC XA-...
25217		403B	G-5-14 G-AXYJ 9Q-CGM 9Q-CHD G-5-651 G-BRXR G-OLFR 5N-EAS
25218	NA744	400A	G-AXTW N575DU N575 (N382DA) N711BP N440BC [parted out]
25219		F400A	G-5-14 G-AYEP 4W-ACA 9K-AEA G-5-12 N5594U N292GA (N292RC) N128DR N219EC RA-02805 N219EC (ZS-OZU) D2-FFH N114AF [instructional airframe Sinclair University, Dayton, OH]
25220	NA745	731	G-AXYE N41BH N125AR N125AP N427DA N745TS N400XJ N700TR XB-LWC
25221	NA746	731	N42BH CF-BNK C-FBNK N468LM N62CH N74WF N103RR ZS-OIF
25222	NA747	731	G-AXYF N43BH N125EH N900EL N400FE N590CH N125NW P4-AOB N401AB [cx 21May13; to instructional airframe, Tulsa Technical Center, Tulsa/R.L.Jones, OK]]
25223		403B	G-5-15 G-AYIZ PJ-SLB F-BSSL G-AYIZ G-TACE [cx 09Jan90; wfu]
25224	NA748	731	G-AXYG N44BH N22DH N222RB N222RG N144PA N189B N199B N143CP N728KA N777SA YV-1111CP N748TS N601KK N748TS N62TW N77WD N748TS (N399JC)
25225	NA749	731	G-AXYH N45BH N81T N119CC N583CM N100HF N100HE N45NC N45NQ (N45ND) SE-DVS N498R N498RS XB-KKS N498RS XB-KNH XB-MZI
25226	NA750	400A	G-AXYI N46BH N300P N304P XA-DIW XB-CCM N3933A N20RG N251AB XA-RWN N131LA [cx 26Jan15; CofR expired]
25227		F403B	G-AYFM G-MKOA 5N-AMY N227MS N355AC XB-MYA
25228	NA751	731	N47BH N640M G-BCLR N640M G-BCLR N120GA N120GB N75RD N75RN N125GH N79B HC-BTT N400FR [cx 20Sep12; wfu]
25229	NA752	731	N48BH N914BD N61MS N61MX N731HS N700PL N700FA N602JR (N998PS)
25230	NA753	731	N49BH N400BH N840H N345GL N145GL
25231		731	D-CBVW G-BEME 5N-AQY G-BEME N125GC N707EZ N707SH (N125TJ) N832MR (N832MB) N831NW N831DF YV113T
25232	NA754	731	CF-TEC C-FTEC C-GVQR N62TF N125VC N125EC N60RE N711HL N227LT N228EA
25233	NA755	400A	N50BH N711SD N755GW (N5MW) XB-AXP XB-LXP XB-AXP N755WJ (N871MA) ZS-MEG [wfu Lanseria, South Africa]
25234	NA756	731	N51BH N701Z N7NP N100MT C-GFCD N40Y N400JK N624PD N624MP [instructional airframe, Lansing Technical College, MI]
25235		F403A	G-5-18 HB-VCE G-AYNR G-BKAJ G-5-19 N235AV N227LA N297JD N101UD N101UR N330AM
25236	NA757	731	N52BH N125BH N10C N154 (N44BH) N999RW N499SC N50NE (N745WG) N900WG XA-AGL
25237	NA761	400A	N56BH N125BH N1924L N500MA N580MA XA-RIL N814D [cx 01Apr13; wfu]
25238		F403B	G-AYER 9K-ACR G-AYER G-TOPF N125GC N808V VR-BKK VP-BKK G-36-1 VP-BKK [dbr in storm at Bournemouth, UK, 14Feb14]

BAe 125

C/n		Series	Identities								
25239	NA758	731	G-5-19	N53BH	N6709	N731MS	N800NP	YV586T			
25240		400B	G-5-11	G-AYLI	I-GJBO	VR-BKN	VR-BMB	[stripped of spares – to fire section at Stansted A/P,			
			UK circa Apr99; b/u there Sep03 and remains removed]								
25241	NA759	400A	G-5-20	N54BH	N6702	N702M	N702MA	N810CR	N127CM	N125CF	(N400MR)
			YV2315								
25242		403B	G-5-20	VH-TOM	G-BDKF	3D-ABZ	ZS-LME	[wfu; stored Waterkloof AFB, South Africa]			
25243		F400A	G-5-14	(G-AYOI)	PT-DTY	N243TS	VP-CTS	N4ES			
25244	NA760	400A	G-5-12	N55BH	N731X	N70LY	N456WH	YV-....			
25245	NA762	731	N57BH	N523M	N400GP	N125DH	[cx 28Aug14; CofR expired]				
25246		403B	G-AYOJ	9Q-COH	(G-5-16)	G-AYOJ	G-LORI	[derelict Nigeria for many years; cx 21Apr93]			
25247		403B	G-AYRR	9Q-CCF	G-5-672	G-AYRR	9Q-CSN	9Q-CPR			
25248		F403B	D-CFCF	G-5-707	G-BTUF	G-SHOP	(N792A)	G-SHOP	N792A	G-TCDI	N189RR
			YV-1122CP	(N119GH)	N189RR	N505LC					
25249		731	G-5-16	G-AZAF	N51993	N72HT	N72HA	N107AW	N125KC	N200KC	N200VT
			N711VT	N54JC	N154JC	(N303BX)	N27UM				
25250		731	G-AYOK	TR-LQU	G-AYOK	N20S	N24S	N300CC	N300QC	N125G	N125HG
			(N125SJ)	N7SJ	N888TJ	[cx 31Oct12; wfu]					
25251		400B	Argentina 5-T-30/0653			LV-AXZ	CX-BVD	[cx; wfu Monevideo, Uruguay]			
25252		400B	G-5-17	XX505	G-BAZB	N48US	P4-AMB	XA-RDD	[wfu; preserved Saltillo, Mexico]		
25253		F400A	G-5-18	OY-APM	G-BROD	N731HS	N3338	N50EB	N50FC	N610HC	XA-SKE
			N253MT	(N253CC)	N911RD	[parted out by White Inds, Bates City, MO]					
25254		F400B	G-AYLG	3D-AVL	G-AYLG	G-5-624	G-VJAY	VT-UBG	G-5-624	VT-UBG	[wfu;
			preserved by Kingfisher Airlines, India]								
25255		CC1A/F400A		XW788	G-BVTP	(N255TS)	N4QB				
25256		600B	G-AYBH	RP-C111	G-5-13	G-AYBH	Ireland IAC236		[w/o 27Nov79 Dublin, Ireland]		
25257		403B	G-5-19	G-BATA	9M-HLG	[wfu Jun93]					
25258		F600B	(G-AYRR)	G-AZHS	G-BFAN	VR-CJP	VP-CJP	G-OJPB	TL-ADK	9Q-CBC	[wfu
			Kinshasa/N'Djili, Democratic Republic of Congo]								
25259		400B	G-AZEK	S Africa 05	ZS-JBA	[b/u for spares following accident at Lanseria, South Africa; cx Mar03]					
25260		400B	G-AZEL	S Africa 06	ZS-JIH	D2-EFM	[b/u Lanseria, South Africa]				
25261	NA763	731	N58BH	(N91BH)	N246N	N46B	(N68BW)	N246N	N55B	N125MT	N62TC
			N19H	N1QH	6V-AIN						
25262	NA764	400A	N59BH	XB-CUX	N55RZ						
25263	NA765	731	N62BH	N125PA	N700BW	N708BW	N61MS	N68CB	N765TS		
25264		CC1A/F400A		XW789	G-BVTR	N264TS	N7171	(N264WD)	(N731WB)	(N264TS)	N93TS
			N178PC	[cx 14Mar12; wfu]							
25265	NA766	731	N63BH	N711YP	N711YR	N300LD	N200CC	N125MD	VH-PAB	N150SA	N854SM
			N854JC								
25266		CC1A/F400A		XW790	G-BVTS	(N266TS)	N135CK	N125CK			
25267	NA767	400A	N64BH	N92BH	N28GP	N28GE	N125CM	[parted out Oct94, Spirit of St Louis A/P, MO; cx			
			Jun95; remains to AvMATS, Paynesville, MO]								
25268		CC1A/F400A		XW791	G-BVTT	(N268TS)	N41953	[w/o 07Apr95 Santo Domingo-Herrera Intl Apt,			
			Dominican Republic; parted out by Arnoni Avn, Houston, TX circa Sep00]								
25269		400B	G-AZEM	S Africa 07	ZS-LPF	EX-269	AP-BGI	EX-500	[wfu Bishkek, Kyrgystan]		
25270		F403B	G-5-13	G-BBGU	G-BKBA	N270AV	N400GP	N440RD	[parted out by Dodson Int'l, Rantoul, KS]		
25271		400A	G-5-14	G-BABL	XX506	G-BABL	EC-CMU	N37516	N103CJ	N365DA	N400DP
			N70AP	N810HS	[parted out by AvMats, St Louis, MO, Jan04; cx]						
25272		F400A	G-5-15	G-BAZA	N4759D	N121VA	N121VF	N800JT	N63EM	[cx 16Feb17; wfu]	
25273	NA768	400A	G-5-20	N65BH	N125BH	N69KA	XA-DIN	N11FX	N7WC	XA-SFQ	N2155P
			XA-SFQ								
25274		403B	G-5-20	Brazil EU93-2119		Brazil IU93-2119		[wfu]			
25275	NA769	400A	N66BH	N872D	N972D	N125PP	N42BL	N369JH	N900AD	[cx 28Aug14; CofR	
			expired]								
25276	NA770	731	G-5-11	N67BH	N88GA	N300CF	N74B	N7170J	N38LB	N805WD	
25277		403B	G-5-11?	Brazil VU93-2126		Brazil XU93-2126		[scrapped 2009]			
25278	NA771	731	N68BH	CF-AOS	C-FAOS	N731H	VR-BVI	N298NM	N4WC	[wfu; used as fire trainer	
			at Miami a/p, FL]								
25279	NA772	400A	G-5-12	N69BH	XA-CUZ	[w/o 27Dec80 Cancun, Mexico]					
25280	NA773	731	N70BH	CF-PPN	C-FPPN	N32KB	[parted out Conroe, TX]				
25281	NA774	731	N71BH	N1BG	N18GX	N125DB	EI-BRG	N70338	N774EC	RA-02804	G-5-821
			RA-02804	N774TS							
25282	NA775	731	N72BH	N5V	N7HV	N17HV	N333DP	XA-EMA	N223RR		
25283	NA776	403A	N73BH	G-BACI	XA-LOV	XA-SGM	XB-GNF	XA-LOV	[wfu Monterrey del Norte, Mexico]		
25284	NA777	731	N74BH	N571CH	N571GH	N228GC	N125FM	N125MD	N101AD	(N425JF)	[w/o
			06May91 Shreveport, LA; cx Sep91 – fuselage at Tulsa, OK, circa Oct99]								
25285	NA778	731	N75BH	N555CB	N733K	C-GCEO	N2694C	N67EC	N89SR	N88AF	N778JA
25286	NA779	731	N76BH	N88SJ	N33CP	N84CP	N400WT	N408WT	N808CC	N731JR	N781JR
			(N989AB)	[cx 24Mar11, instructional airframe at Fanshawe College, London, Canada]							
25287	NA780	731	N78BH	N72HC	N65DL	N265DL	N800TG	9Q-CPF			
25288		403B	Brazil VU93-2127		[preserved Brasilia International a/p, Brazil]						
25289		403B	G-5-16	Brazil VU93-2128		[preserved TAM Museum, Sao Carlos, Brazil]					
25290		403B	Brazil VU93-2129		[w/o 08Sep87 Carajas, Brazil]						

Production complete

BAe 125 SERIES 600

C/n	Series	Identities
256001	FA	G-AZUF N82BH N711AG G-BEWW N711AG N82RP N82PP N444PE N444PD N700R N709R N561RP N61TS N773JC N699TS
256002	A	G-5-15 N79BH (N925BH) N631SC N631SQ N915JT N61SB N602MM XA-SLP
256003	A	N80BH CF-HSS C-FHSS N256FC N42TS N91KH N91KP [cx 29Oct13; wfu Fort Lauderdale Executive, FL]
256004	A	N81BH N94BD N94BB N19HH N19HE VR-BRS N4TS (N103RA) N399GA N5AH N600MK [submerged in lake at Athens Scuba Park, Athens, TX, 28May11 for use as diving training aid; cx 19Apr17]
256005	B	G-BART (G-BJXV) (G-BJUT) G-CYII EC-EAC N4253A [b/u for spares by Western A/C Parts; to White Inds, Bates City, MO; cx Jun95]
256006	FB	XX507 N606TS N21SA [w/o 21Feb05 Bromont, Canada; parted out Montgomery, AL; cx 17Jan08]
256007	A	N21BH N125BH N125KR N3007 N317TC [parted out Houston, TX; cx 14Jan08]
256008	FA	XX508 N256WJ
256009	A	N22BH N3PW N219ST (N210ST) N183RD "N183RM" N28TS
256010	A	N23BH N40PC [w/o 28Apr77 McLean, VA]
256011	A	N24BH N6001H N555CB N555GB VR-BGS N42622 N81D EC-EHF [parted out Oct94, Spirit of St Louis A/P, MO unmarked – remains to Dodson Int'l, Ottawa, KS, circa 1998; fuselage reported at Gary, IN, summer 2012]
256012	B	G-5-17 G-BAYT 5N-ALX G-BAYT G-BNDX G-BAYT EC-272 EC-EOQ N8000Z [parted out at Houston, TX circa 1995; cx Feb96; allocated marks N8000Z not worn]
256013	A	N25BH N25BE N505W (N65GB) N218AC N627HS N80TS VR-CDG 5N-YET
256014	A	N26BH N922CR N922GR N5SJ N47HW N47HV [parted out by Dodson Int'l, Parts, Rantoul, KS]
256015	FA	G-5-19 G-BBCL G-BJCB G-BBCL 9K-ACZ G-BBCL Ireland 239 G-BBCL G-5-11 (D-CCEX) G-BBCL N600AV N917K N777SA (N74TJ) (N615TJ) N777TK N700XJ N957MB
256016	A	N27BH N99SC XA-SAI [parted out by White Inds, Bates City, MO]
256017	B	G-5-18 G-BBAS PK-PJD N600WJ (N415BA) N225HR [parted out by White Inds, Bates City, MO]
256018	A	N28BH N500GD (N780SC) N880SC N125E N600AW N93TS N288MW XA-JRF N16GA XA-TNX XB-ADZ
256019	B	G-BARR HZ-AA1 G-FANN [cx 29Mar93, wfu; fuselage on fire dump Dunsfold, UK, still marked as HZ-AA1]
256020	A	N29BH (N501H) N125CU N334JR C-GDUP N334JR N5NG XA-NTE N5NG [derelict Monterrey, Mexico and scrapped; cx Sep00]
256021	A	G-5-11 HB-VDL C-GSTT N125HS N125JJ (N128JJ) N125JA XA-SNH N37SG C-GKHR N111UN N220TS 3D-BOS S9-DBG S9-PDG 9Q-COX
256022	A	N34BH N701Z N701A N1515P N757M N757P XA-XET N2114E [parted out by Arnoni Aviation, Houston, TX; marks N2114E not carried]
256023	A	N35BH N514V EC-121 EC-EGL N523MA N702HC [parted out by White Inds, Bates City, MO]
256024	A	G-BBMD N50GD G-BBMD G-BSHL G-OMGA YR-DVA (N731TC) N669SC N411GA [parted out by Arnoni Av'n, Houston, TX]
256025	A	N36BH C-GTPC N721LH [parted out by MTW Aerospace, Montgomery, AL]
256026	FA	N37BH G-5-16 N124GS N699SC N818TP XA-SWK N125NA N450TB XA-ATC
256027	FA	D-CJET G-5-585 D-CJET OE-GIA N693TJ N800NM N245RS
256028	A	G-5-12 VP-BDH C6-BDH C-GDHW XA-KUT [w/o 18Jan88 Houston-Hobby, TX; parted out by Dodson Av'n, Ottawa, KS]
256029	FB	G-BBRT PK-PJE PK-HMG N629TS N35WP
256030	B	G-BBEP G-BJOY G-BBEP 5N-ARD G-BBEP G-TOMI N217A [parted out by Arnoni Av'n, Houston, TX still marked as G-TOMI]
256031	B	G-5-14 9Q-CFW "9Q-CFG" 9Q-CGF 9Q-CJF
256032	A	N38BH N4BR (N14BR) G-DBOW C-GLBD N332TA EC-EAV N921RD N801BC N334PS [to Alberta Aviation Museum, Edmonton, Canada]
256033	B	F-BUYP G-DMAN HZ-YA1 N330G G-PJWB G-HALK N6033 XB-FMF N303MW N600HS N514AJ N514MH N514RD [wfu California City, CA]
256034	A	N39BH N90B N90BL N600FL N600SB EC-115 EC-EGS [used for spares Oct94 at Spirit of St Louis A/P, MO; fuselage to Elsberry, MO by Apr96]
256035	A	F-BKMC G-BETV G-SUFC VP-BCN "N635PA" N128YT [to White Inds, Bates City, MO, 18Jan05 for spares]
256036	B	(G-BBRT) [used for paint-spraying trials Chester, UK; aircraft not completed]
256037	B	(VH-ARJ) AN-BPR YN-BPR VH-NJA RP-C1600 VP-BBW (N16VT) N63810 N228MD [cx 30Aug12; wfu]
256038	A	N40BH N77C N77CU SE-DKF N199SG XA-ACN [cx; status?]
256039	B	G-BCCL G-BKBM N61TF N410AW G-BKBM EC-EAO EC-183 EC-EAO G-OMGB [wfu Oct94; TT 6,944 hrs; to spares at Houston, TX]
256040	A	N41BH C-GJCM N4224Y N125GS N601BA N621BA N16VT N287DL (N301JJ) N287DM TJ-...
256041	B	G-5-13 G-BCJU VR-CBD N450DA N888PM N273K N42TS N808RP N603TS [wfu Toluca, Mexico]
256042	B	G-BBRO G-BKBU G-5-505 5N-AWS [w/o 15Dec86 Casablanca, Morocco]
256043	B	G-BCUX [w/o 20Nov75 Dunsfold, UK]
256044	A	N42BH N600MB N46B (N46BE) C-GKCC N848W N992SF XA-CAH N9282Y N116DD N454DP N453DP [cx 10Sep12; wfu]
256045	FB	G-5-18 EC-CQT G-5-11 G-BGYR N508VM (N803LL) [cx 08May15; CofR expired]
256046	FA	N43BH N91HR (N401HR) N402HR N117EM XA-AGL N299BW N299GA N299TJ (N299DG) N299GS

BAe 125-600

C/n	Series	Identities
256047	A	G-5-16 "N44BH" (C-GBNS) "N4203S" N4203Y N400NW N400NE N600TT XA-JEQ N47EX N47WU XA-RYK N68GA 9Q-CYA 9Q-CAI
256048	A	G-5-15 HB-VDS G-BHIE YU-BME N6567G TC-COS N852GA [parted out by Arnoni Av'n, Houston, TX]
256049	B	G-BCXL ZS-JHL G-BCXL HZ-KA5 P4-VJR 5V-TTP
256050	B	G-5-12 5N-ANG G-BLOI 5N-AOL [wfu, believed scrapped in 1997]
256051	A	(N45BH) C-GBNS N22DL N5DL N35DL N601PS N601JJ N616PA N600AL N95TS N601JA 9Q-CFJ
256052	B	G-5-11 G-BDJE G-BKBH TR-LAU G-5-698 G-BKBH G-5-698 G-BKBH G-5-698 5N-NBC 5N-DNL G-5-698 5N-DNL G-BKBH [cx Jly99 wfu Southampton, UK]
256053	B	D-CFSK HC-BUR N125WJ N5NR N721RM
256054	B	G-5-17 G-BCXF 9K-AED "G-BKFS" G-BCXF 5N-YFS 5N-RNO [w/o May01, Lagos, Nigeria]
256055	A	G-5-19 G-BDOP N94B N94BF N777SA N100QR N100QP N125GS N20FM N111UN (N600GP) [cx 22Jan13; CofR expired]
256056	B	G-5-13 G-BDOA G-BKCD 5N-ARN G-BKCD G-OMGC [wfu Sep94; TT 6404 hrs; parted out at Houston, TX circa 1995]
256057	B	G-5-17 HZ-KA2 G-FFLT VR-BNW VP-BNW N602CF N11AF [parted out by Arnoni Av'n, Houston, TX]
256058	FA	G-5-18 G-BGKN N9043U N701Z N129BA (N429BA) (N658TS) N200XR N658TS N658KA N20FM [cx 16Mar16; CofR expired]
256059	B	G-5-19 HZ-DAC HZ-SJP G-BLUW ZF130 [stored St. Athan, UK, March 2002; wings and tail removed 21Oct02; fuselage to Farnborough, UK, by 24Oct02 for spares, then to Hanningfield Metals scrapyard, Stock, Essex, UK, 07Jan03; to Elektrowerkz nightclub, London EC1, UK, 2006; removed and scrapped 2008]
256060	B	G-5-12 HZ-MF1 G-BFIC 5N-AYK N660TC N422TK N422TR N395EJ [parted out by MTW Aerospace, Montgomery, AL]
256061	FA	G-5-14 G-BDOB N125HS N5253A N8253A N707WB N169B N189B N169B N331DC N701MS XA-EXL XB-EXC
256062	B	G-5-15 G-MFEU G-TMAS EC-319 EC-ERX G-TMAS 5N-MAY 5N-DOT [parted out]
256063	A	G-5-13 A6-RAK G-BSPH N484W EC-349 EC-ERJ 5N-OPT N9AZ YV345T YV2680
256064	A	G-5-17 HZ-AMM N105AS N666LC N500MA N580MA N600SN N125HF XA-MKY [wfu Monterrey del Norte, Mexico]
256065	A	G-5-16 G-BJCB XA-MAH N73JA N59JR VR-CSF V2-LSF N125SF N4SA N10SA
256066	FA	G-5-15 G-BDZH N32RP N800JP N600G (N700SM) XB-RYP
256067	A	G-BEIN N522X N522C N270MC N270MQ N1884 N67MR XA-SKH N822BL N822BD (N157RP) CX-CBS
256068	FA	G-5-20 G-BDZR N33RP N90WP G-5-16 N90WP N14GD N54GD N500R N501R N600AE [disappeared 11Sep14, believed stolen for drug-running]
256069	A	G-BEIO N350MH N600AG N369TS 5N-EMA [wfu Lagos, Nigeria]
256070	FA	G-5-11 G-BEDT N322CC G-5-15 N322CC N319MF (N411TC) N411TP N83TJ N365SB (N76TJ) N75GA
256071	A	G-5-14 G-BEES N91884 N571DU N571E N121SG N171TS [cx May04, parted out in Mexico]

Production complete

BAe 125 SERIES 700

C/n		Series	Identities
257001		A	G-BEFZ VR-HIM G-BEFZ N4555E N700SV N101SK N101XS N80KA N189GE N97TS VH-LYG N257AJ N193TA N701CW (N807CW) N425KG
257002	NA0201	A	G-5-20 N700HS N40WB N40GT N700NY N886GB VR-BNB G-IECL N701TS (N828SA) N530BL "N509SM"+ [+mispainted at Fort Lauderdale Int'l, FL, Jan10] N529SM N609AM [cx 19Feb16; wfu]
257003	NA0202	A	G-5-19 G-BERP N64688 N333ME N727TA N403BG XA-ULT
257004	NA0218	A	G-5-15 G-BGDM G-5-15 N37975 N222RB N700RJ N546BC N746BC N648WW N704CW N804CW N804FF N903SC M-JCPO [cx 23Jul14; b/u]
257005	NA0203	A	G-BERV N620M N104AE N828PJ
257006	NA0204	A	G-5-18 G-BERX N724B
257007		A	HB-VFA D-CADA G-5-721 D-CADA G-BUNL RA-02800 G-5-721 RA-02800 (N307TC) N257TH N257WJ N54WJ (N545SH) N49RJ
257008	NA0205	A	G-5-11 (G-BEWV) C-GYYZ N333PC N807TC N700FW N618KR RP-C8108 [wfu Manila, Philippines]
257009	NA0206	A	G-5-12 G-BEYC N813H (N20GT) N986H XA-SNN N701NW N818KC N828KC N706AM
257010		A	HZ-MMM LX-MJM G-5-631 N700WH N700ER N3399P (N339BW) (N41CC) N977CC N425RJ N424RJ N819WG N1ES N819WG XA-...
257011	NA0207	A	G-5-13 G-BFAJ N255CT (N255QT) N255TT N500FC N33RH N70X N7UV N816JM
257012	NA0208	A	G-5-14 G-BFBI N125HS N700HS N162A N700FS N622AB N622AD N37PL N38PA N41HF N449EB RA-02810
257013		A	G-CBBI N219JA N75ST N101HF N96FT N36FT P4-AOH P4-SKY N813VC
257014	NA0209	A	G-5-17 G-BFDW N46901 N120GA N60MS N453EP N586JR N74B N843CP N209TS
257015	NA0210	A	G-5-18 G-BFFL N37P SE-DPZ (N725WH) OY-JPJ N418RD P4-AOF N418RD
257016	NA0216	A	G-BFFH N72505 N800CB N23SB N23SK (N23SN) N999JF "N197FT" N98FT [cx 08Dec14; CofR expired]
257017	NA0211	A	G-5-19 G-BFFU N62MS N454EP N757M N757C (I-DRVM) I-DVMR HB-VLH RA-02806 N211WZ N411PA (N602JJ)
257018	NA0212	A	G-BFGU N733H N662JB N125CS (N125MJ) N425SD N118CD
257019	NA0213	A	G-BFGV N370M N370RR N339CA XA-UPE
257020		B	(G-BFTP) (G-BFVN) G-EFPT VR-BHE (N2634B) N125HM N818 N311JD N777EH
257021	NA0214	A	N34CH N900KC N1868M N1868S (N526JC) N926ZT N926TC N926MC
257022		A	(G-5-11) F-GASL G-5-17 N34RE N92RP N109AF N700WC RA-02809
257023	NA0215	A	G-BFLF N54555 N125GP N6JB N6UB N35LM N195XP N215RS
257024	NA0217	A	G-BFLG N94BD N94BE N7005 N7006 (N6960) N700RR
257025		B	G-5-12 G-BFPI VR-HIN G-BFPI N93TC N7782 N886S N205TW
257026	NA0219	A	G-BFMO N1230A N372BC N372BD N685FM N685EM N788WG N428AS N428FS N219TS N45BP [w/o 20Sep03 Beaumont, TX]
257027	NA0220	A	G-BFMP C-GPPS N705CC N725CC XA-SAU
257028		A	G-BFSO G-5-534 N700TL N603GY N7728 N899DM VP-COK N949EB [instructional airframe, Tulsa Technical Center, Tulsa/R.L.Jones, OK, then scrapped]
257029	NA0221	A	N465R N700PD (N248JH) N705JH C-GTOR
257030	NA0222	A	G-BFSI C-GSCL C-FFAB HB-VLJ C-GNAZ N18CC
257031		BA	G-BFSP G-PRMC G-BFSP G-5-701 D-CBAE G-BFSP G-5-701 N89TJ HB-VLA N703TS N703JN [wfu Fort Lauderdale Int'l, FL]
257032	NA0223	A	G-5-14 G-BFUE N700BA N353WC N853WC N154JS (N158JS) N154JD N720PT
257033	NA0224	A	N50JM N50TN N200GX N200GY XA-MJI N336AC XB-JYS XB-PAM
257034		A	G-5-14 G-BFXT N7007X N510HS G-PLGI N402GJ N34GG
257035	NA0225	A	G-5-16 N36NP SE-DPY N486MJ N995SK (N995SL) N995SA N137WR (N137WK) 9Q-...
257036	NA0226	A	G-5-17 N60JM N60TN N600HC N902RM N902PM N47TJ N42SR (N42SE) N7WC N1776E N102BP XA-UOW
257037		B	G-5-18 G-BFVI G-IFTE
257038	NA0227	A	G-5-19 N10CZ N81KA N216KH [cx 06Jun14; wfu]
257039	NA0228	A	G-5-11 N555CB N555CR N545GM [cx to Mexico 03Nov14 but had already been dbr at Roatan, Honduras, 15Dec13]
257040		B	HZ-RC1 G-OWEB EC-375 EC-413 EC-ETI N47TJ VR-BPE VP-BPE HB-VMD G-BYFO G-OWDB P4-LVF N67BL C6-IUE ZS-SYS
257041	NA0229	A	G-5-12 N700BB N400NW N400NU (N601UU) N700LS N825CT N820CT XA-BYP N820CT
257042	NA0230	A	G-5-13 N360X (N360DE) N881S N899AB XB-SMV
257043	NA0232	A	G-BFYV (N300LD) N900CC N500ZB N22EH N22KH N232TN (N331CG) [wfu Fort Lauderdale Int'l, FL, after wheels-up landing 1Nov06]
257044	NA0231	A	G-5-17 G-BFYH N35D N5735 N125G (N125GB) N225BJ
257045	NA0240	A	G-BFZJ N130BA N700HH N800E C6-SVA
257046		A	4W-ACE G-BKJV VH-JCC VH-LRH N7465T XA-LEG N746TS N55MT "N55TS" N746TS LV-ZRS N828AN N587VV N257AM N770AZ
257047	NA0233	A	G-BFZI C-GABX N79TS N79EH
257048	NA0234	A	G-5-16 N711YP N205BS N731DL N323JK [parted out by Alliance Air Parts, Oklahoma City, OK]
257049	NA0239	A	G-5-17 G-BGBL N33BK C-GKPM C-GNOW C-GOHJ
257050	NA0235	A	G-5-18 N700GB N10C
257051	NA0236	A	G-5-11 N700UK N14JA N64HA N236BN [dbr 20Dec00 Jackson, WY; parted out by Arnoni Av'n, Houston, TX]

BAe 125-700

C/n		Series	Identities
257052	NA0237	A	G-5-19 G-BGBJ N737X N697NP N511GP N511KA N700QA
257053	NA0238	A	G-5-20 N700AR N33CP N130MH N120MH N200JP ZS-SDU
257054		B	C6-BET G-BVJY RA-02802 G-BVJY G-NCFR G-OURB OD-HHF OD-BBF VP-CFI [wfu; b/u Bournemouth, UK; fuselage to Birchwood airfield, Yorks, UK]
257055		A	G-5-16 HZ-RC2 N876JC G-5-598 G-BOXI F-WZIG F-GHHG N46PL (N696JH) (N755TS) N47PB N347TC C6-...
257056	NA0241	A	G-5-13 N700NT N492CB N6VC N25MK N300BS (N388BS) XA-UCU N84GA XA-UCU N57EJ
257057	NA0242	A	G-5-14 N700UR N60HJ (N60HU) C-GPCC N125BW N701CF (N988GA) N418BA N241RT [cx 13Aug14; wfu Ontario, CA]
257058	NA0245	A	G-5-15 N125HS N700BA N354WC N854WC N750GM N8PL N810V N81QV VP-CLU RA-02775
257059	NA0243	A-II	G-5-17 N130BH N20S N20SK N702BA XA-JRF N104JG N9395Y N717AF XA-UQN N466MM
257060	NA0244	A	G-5-18 N130BG N1103 N1183 N230DP N414RF [to instructional airframe, North Valley Occupational Center, Los Angeles/Van Nuys, CA]
257061		A	G-5-19 G-BGGS G-OJOY N700SS N700SF N810GS XA-UEA (N730AA) N23RT C9-...
257062		B	G-5-16 HB-VGF G-5-708 HB-VGF G-5-708 N7062B G-5-708 (G-BWJX) RA-02809 N62EA N416RD EI-WJN 6V-AIM [w/o 05Sep15, crashed into Atlantic Ocean]
257063	NA0246	A	G-5-20 N130BB N79HC N700NW
257064		B/A	HZ-NAD HZ-OFC G-BMOS G-5-519 VH-JFT N395RD N48LB [parted out by AvMATS, St Louis, MO; cx 06Aug14]
257065	NA0247	A	G-5-11 N130BC N30PR N530TL (N530TE) N87AG N120JC N720JC (N247PJ)
257066	NA0248	A	G-5-13 G-BGSR C-GKCI C-FBMG N900CQ N900CP [cx 22May13; wfu Queretaro, Mexico]
257067		B	HZ-DA1 N9113J (N115RS) N360N N144DJ HB-VKJ N267TS N42TS
257068	NA0249	A	G-5-14 N130BD N31LG N799SC XB-FMK XA-FMK
257069	NA0250	A	G-5-15 N130BE N29GP N29GD N308DD (N900JG) (N54TJ) N418DM XB-SVV N464FG
257070		B	HB-VGG G-5-604 HB-VGG G-5-604 G-BWCR "G-JETG" G-BWCR G-DEZC P4-AMH [parted out Farnborough, UK, May11; cockpit section to Bombay Night Indian Restaurant, Brentry, Bristol, UK; fuselage to caravan site Birchington, UK]
257071	NA0251	A	G-5-17 N130BF N514B N396U N810CR N571CH CX-CIB
257072	NA0252	A	G-5-18 N700HS N900MR N401GN N513GP N895CC N237WR (N237RG) [w/o 10Nov15 on approach to Akron/Fulton, OH]
257073		B	G-5-12 G-BGTD N7788 (N59TJ) N701TA N210RK
257074	NA0253	A	G-5-19 N422X (N831CJ)
257075	NA0254	A	G-5-13 (G-BHKF) N125AM N125TR N124AR N125XX M-ALUN
257076		A	G-5-17 7Q-YJI MAAW-J1 G-5-524 G-BMWW G-5-571 XA-LML N111ZN N111ZS N180CH (N776TS) N111ZS
257077	NA0255	A	G-5-14 N125AJ N540B XA-SEN N770PJ [cx 26Nov14; wfu]
257078	NA0256	A	G-5-15 N125AK N571CH N455BK (N830LR)
257079	NA0268	A	G-5-16 XA-JIX N74JA (N74JE) N501MM XA-SON N111QJ
257080	NA0257	A	G-5-18 N125HS N611MC (N611EL)
257081	NA0258	A	G-5-19 (N125AM) N700CU N711CU N809M N812M N193RC N227MM [wfu Houston Intercontinental, TX]
257082		A	Ireland 238 (N98AF) XA-TCB N70HF N752CM [cx 21Jun16, CofR expired]
257083	NA0259	A	G-5-12 (N150RH) N125AH N100Y N128CS N941CE N125CJ
257084	NA0260	A	G-5-14 N130BK N202CH N965JC N184TB XB-IRZ XA-HXM XB-MWQ XB-NVE
257085		B	G-5-15 G-BHIO RP-C1714 N10TN
257086	NA0261	A	G-5-17 N125AL N277CT N500EF N983GT N999CY N700UJ
257087	NA0262	A	G-5-16 (N130BL) C-GKRS N3234S N404CB (N601JR) N908JE N988JE N350DH N711WM N3RC (N313RC) N396RC N561PS
257088		B	HZ-DA2 G-5-531 N29RP N222HL N224EA
257089	NA0263	A	G-5-18 N130BL N151AE (N130AE) N101FC (N263TN) N125RG N125EK
257090	NA0264	A	G-5-19 N299CT N88MX N264WC (N160WC) N161WC N724EA [parted out St Augustine, FL]
257091		B	G-BHLF G-OCAA VP-CLX C6-IUN
257092	NA0265	A	G-5-20 N733M N783M N91CM N299WB
257093	NA0266	A	G-5-11 G-BHMP C-GBRM N7UJ N86MD N497PT N804CS N212XX
257094		B	G-OBAE HB-VEK G-5-16 N49566 N80KM N713KM N713K D-CKIM (G-....) 9M-STR N415RD N483FG [cx 09Nov16; status?]
257095	NA0267	A	G-5-12 N125L N215G N352WC N852WC N427MD N745TH N36GS N267JE N829SE [ditched into Loreto Bay, Mexico, 05May11; status?]
257096	NA0276	A	G-5-14 XA-KEW [w/o 01May81 Monterrey, Mexico]
257097		B	(G-BHTJ) G-HHOI G-BRDI G-BHTJ RA-02801 G-5-810 RA-02801 [dbr Moscow/Vnukovo, Russia, 12Feb14]
257098	NA0269	A	G-5-15 N125Y N89PP N70SK N50HS XA-NTE N702NW N972LM N438PM (N61GF) XA-AMI
257099	NA0270	A	G-5-16 G-BHSK C-GDAO N621JH N621JA PK-CTC N52GA
257100		A	G-5-19 D-CLVW G-5-549 G-BNFW N858JR N801RA N925WC XA-...
257101	NA0272	A	G-5-17 (N700E) N89PP (N700E) N109JM N14SY N77D N89GN N700XF [cx 21May14; to Singapore as instructional airframe]
257102	NA0280	A	G-5-18 XA-KIS N700CN N700K N810M XA-TCR N280AJ N280VC N500FM
257103		B	G-5-12 G-BHSU G-LTEC VR-BOJ VP-BOJ YL-VIP YL-VIR G-GIRA OY-MFL [cx to Canada, parted out]

BAe 125-700

C/n		Series	Identities
257104	NA0273	A	G-5-20 N10PW N411SS N46TJ N110EJ (N4477X) N815TR
257105	NA0274	A	G-5-11 N125BA N125TA N44BB N700DE HB-VLL N560SB (OY-VIA) G-CFBP N700KL
257106	NA0275	A	G-5-13 N125V N661JB N664JB N404CE N404CF N125SJ (N550JP) XB-JND XB-OBS XA-OBS N459MM
257107		A	G-BHSV G-5-808 N90AR VR-CVD N71MA (N38HH) N85HH N900MD N880RG
257108	NA0278	A	G-5-14 XA-KON N45500 N6GG N6GQ N86WC N700FE N77SA N130AP N770CC N518RR
257109		B	G-BHSW VR-BPT VR-BTZ VP-BTZ VP-BOY OD-BOY
257110	NA0271	A	G-5-15 XA-KAC N277JW N177JW N154FJ
257111	NA0277	A	G-5-16 N125AF N324K N824K N500 N509 (N799FL) N509QC N972W
257112		B	D-CMVW G-5-536 G-BNBO G-5-553 9M-SSL (D-CLUB) G-SVLB RA-02850
257113	NA0279	A	G-5-17 N125AD N204R N204N N5511A N1VQ N90FF ZS-ICU
257114	NA0281	A	G-5-18 N125AN N533 C-GXYN N169TA N403DP N281BT N101LT
257115		A	HZ-DA3 G-5-502 G-BMIH 5N-AMX G-5-502 G-BMIH N125YY N333MS OD-MAS
257116	NA0282	A	G-5-19 N125AP N1982G N120YB N150YB C6-FSI
257117	NA0283	A	G-5-20 N125AS N90B (N90BN) N220FL N93CR N93GR N26SC
257118		A	(G-BIHZ) 5N-AVJ G-BWKL VP-BBH VP-CRA C-GNND N619TD N810KB
257119	NA0284	A	G-5-11 N125AE N326K N826K N125AR N125AP N10UC (N311MG)
257120	NA0285	A	G-5-13 N125AT N40CN (N14WJ) N130YB N445UC C6-JAG
257121	NA0286	A	G-5-14 N125AU N20FX N700SB N301PH (N156K) N150CA (N501MD) N83MD
257122	NA0287	A	G-5-15 N125U N77LP N299FB N3444H (N731GA) N564BR
257123	NA0288	A	G-5-16 N125AH N700BW N198GT XA-EFL
257124		B	HZ-DA4 OD-FNF OD-FAF VP-CFJ [wfu]
257125	NA0289	A	G-5-17 N125AJ N125CG N62WH N62WL N369G N27KL N302PC N802RC N70QB
257126	NA0290	A	G-5-18 N700AC N246VF N7WG N17WG N710AF XA-NSA N650TC
257127		B	G-TJCB OY-MPA (F-GNDB) F-GODB HB-VLC N795A XA-LUN
257128	NA0291	A	G-5-19 N125BC N126AR XA-MSH N45AF N947CE
257129	NA0292	A	G-5-20 N125AK (N256MA) N256EN N805M N728JW N748FB N48FB N241FB N966RJ
257130		A	G-DBBI G-CCAA G-BNVU N700FR G-5-588 N700FR G-RJRI RP-C235 N130TS N499GA N405DP N405TP N405DW [cx 10Dec14; CofR expired]
257131	NA0293	A	G-5-11 N700BA N80G N520M N52LC N7CT N7WG N700NB N996RP N296RG N406J
257132	NA0294	A	G-BIMY C-FIPG N925WC N925WG N925DP N188KA [cx 07Jan13; wfu]
257133		B	G-5-14 LV-PMM LV-ALW [w/o 11Apr85 Salta, Argentina]
257134	NA0295	A	G-5-13 N871D N371D N888SW N89MD N134NW (N134RT)
257135	NA0296	A	G-5-15 N490MP N31AS N28GP N28GG N700DA N100JF N10QJ N927LL
257136		B	G-BIRU G-5-545 OH-JET N136TN N318CD P4-AOE P4-XZX [scrapped Kemble, UK, Jun11]
257137	NA0297	A	G-5-16 N125BD N78CS (N78QS) N589UC N945CE
257138	NA0298	A	G-5-17 N125G N80K N298TS N298BP N917TF [cx to Mexico but crashed into Caribbean Sea still wearing N917TF while drug-running May15]
257139		B	G-5-18 (G-GAIL) G-BKAA G-MHIH RA-02803 G-5-875 RA-02803
257140	NA0299	A	G-5-19 N125BE VR-BHH N125BE N555RB N703JP N700NY N800LM [wfu Denton, TX]
257141	NA0300	A	G-5-20 N70PM N80PM N80PN N700SA N943CE
257142		B	G-5-12 G-BJDJ G-RCDI G-BJDJ P4-OBE RA-02802
257143	NA0325	A	G-5-20 N700HA N26H C-GOGM C-GQGM C-FCSS N30DV
257144	NA0326	A	G-5-11 N522M N70AR N94SA (N702TJ) N164WC N194WC N819DM ZS-SOI
257145	NA0339	A	G-5-18 N70FC N125BJ PT-ORJ N700SA N83HF [cx 02Jul14; wfu]
257146	NA0301	A	G-5-13 N700HB N711RL N713RL N744DC N421SZ N107LT N107ET
257147	NA0303	A	G-5-14 N125P N70PM N70PN N67PW N678W N900JT
257148	NA0304	A	G-5-17 N700BB N707DS C-GTDN N99JD N96PR N700NH N237DX
257149	NA0302	A	G-5-19 N700AA N700HA N290PC N795HE (N795HL) C-GEPF C-GLIG
257150	NA0305	A	G-5-11 N700HS N73G N730H N305TH 5N-BFC
257151		B	G-5-12 N161MM N161G N613MC (N613EL) N825MS RP-C8101
257152	NA0306	A	G-5-17 N700DD N270MH C-FEXB N400WP N800MP N141AL N141AE
257153	NA0313	A	G-BJOW XB-CXK N18G PK-CTA N419RD P4-AOD [w/o 02Jan06 Karkiv, Ukraine]
257154	NA0307	A	G-5-18 N700GG N270MC N270KA N888GN [cx 19Jan16; wfu]
257155	NA0308	A	G-5-19 N700KK N1620 C-GYPH N1843S N10CN N9999V N314RC
257156	NA0309	A	G-5-17 N15AG N700MK N529DM N526DM N309WM N95CM N57AY
257157	NA0310	A	G-5-20 N700LL N64GG N2640 N18SH (N168WU) N128WU N109BG
257158		A	G-5-14 G-BJWB N45KK XB-DZN N700VT XA-NEM N813NA
257159	NA0311	A	G-5-15 N91Y N50JR (N620CC) (N502R) VR-CKP N311NW N425WN N700LP ZS-WJW
257160		B	G-5-19 5N-AVK
257161	NA0323	A	G-5-17 N700RR C-GZZX N700RR N2630 N2830 VT-AAA [cx 2009, instructional airframe]
257162	NA0312	A	G-5-18 N700NN N1896T N1896F N176RS N500GS N412DP C-GLBJ N70HB
257163		B	G-5-12 7T-VCW
257164	NA0314	A	G-5-11 N152AE (N106AE) N53GH XA-ERM
257165	NA0315	A	G-5-14 N869KM N26ME
257166		B	G-5-18 F-BYFB F-GRON EC-HRQ RP-C5998

BAe 125-700

C/n		Series	Identities
257167	NA0316	A	G-5-15 N700PP N125BA N2989 N640PM N63PM N73PM N333NR (N501F) N18BA
257168	NA0317	A	G-5-20 N700SS N612MC (N612EL) N789BA
257169		B	G-5-21 (VH-SOA) VH-HSS "B-HSS" VR-HSS B-HSS 5N-MAZ [wfu Lanseria, South Africa]
257170	NA0318	A	G-5-14 N819M N80CL EI-RRR N114BA N356SR N431RC
257171	NA0319	A	G-5-15 N710BP (N168H) N120MH N128MH N319NW XB-MLC N319NW XA-JAI XA-TYG
257172		B	5H-SMZ G-BKFS 5H-SMZ G-5-568 5H-SMZ G-5-765 G-BKFS VT-MPA N355WJ ZS-CAG
257173	NA0320	A	G-5-17 N710BN N500LS N300LS N300HB N100LR (N100FF) N320GP N700HW N7490A
257174	NA0321	A	G-5-18 N710BL N469JR C-GTLG N165DL N65DL N65DU [parted out Houston, TX; cx 19Sep07]
257175		B	(C9-TTA) C9-TAC N770TJ VP-CEK VP-BEK G-MKSS RA-02804
257176	NA0322	A	G-5-20 N109G C-FCHT N322BC
257177	NA0324	A	G-5-11 N710BJ N711TG N2000T N1996F (N1996E) N69SB (N880CR) N507F N2KZ N944TB
257178		A	G-5-14 4W-ACM G-5-530 G-BMYX G-5-570 VH-LMP G-5-747 N700CJ N621S EI-COV N178WB N803BF N175MC N326TD
257179	NA0327	A	G-5-15 N810SC C-GAAA C-GSQC
257180	NA0328	A	G-5-16 N710BG N2HP N192A C-FEAE N910KS N917NY*
257181		CC3	G-5-16 ZD620 [wfu Mar15; preserved Bournemouth Aviation Museum, UK]
257182	NA0329	A	G-5-17 N710BF (N277CB) N1824T N18243 N756N N512GP N190WC 5N-DAO
257183	NA0330	CC3	G-5-20 N710BD G-5-20 ZD703 [wfu Mar15; parted out at Dunsfold,UK, Mar15-May16 then Biggin Hill, UK, May16-Jan17; scrapped]
257184		B	G-5-12 9K-AGA YI-AKG 9K-AGA G-OMGD SU-PIX G-88-03 SU-PIX G-36-2 SU-PIX RA-02808
257185	NA0331	A	G-5-12 N700BA N900BL XB-JTN
257186	NA0332	A	G-5-11 N710BC N400CH N400QH N16GS XA-STX N332WE 5N-MAO
257187		B	G-5-14 9K-AGB YI-AKH [dest 1991 during first Gulf War, Muthenna AFB, Iraq]
257188	NA0333	A	G-5-15 N523M N125DP (N301AS) (N301LX) N125AS N511LD RP-C5808
257189		B	G-BKHK (G-OBSM) G-OSAM N700BA N94B N81HH N8KG N45KG
257190		CC3	ZD621 [wfu Mar15; preserved RAF Northolt, UK]
257191	NA0336	A	G-5-17 N710BA N677RW (N477RW) N11TS VT-SRR N770HS (N778HS) XA-UKR [w/o 19Apr14 Saltillo, Mexico]
257192	NA0337	A	G-5-14 N125MT N2015M N201PM N300TW N300TK N818LD
257193	NA0338	A	G-5-15 N710BZ N710AG (N797EM) N797FA N350PL
257194		CC3	ZD704 G-5-870 ZD704 [damaged in hailstorm, possibly w/o, Kandahar, Afghanistan, Apr13; airfreighted back to UK]
257195	NA0334	A	G-5-18 N710BY N702M N93GC N46WC N46WQ TY-SAM [parted out Farnborough, UK, then scrapped Mar15]
257196		B	G-5-11 5N-AXO G-5-693 5N-AXO G-5-766 5N-AXO [w/o 17Jan96 Kano, Nigeria]
257197		A	G-5-12 N790Z N207PC N207RC N3GL (N2QL) 5N-BEX
257198	NA0335	A	G-5-18 N710BX N702E C-GJBJ [cx to USA but no N-number allocated; parted out?]
257199	NA0340	A	G-5-12 N710BW N702W VR-BKZ N921RD XA-SSY N23BJ N23EJ N804WJ N242AL XA-HOM N391TC XC-LNJ N83CV [cx 13Sep16, CofR expired]
257200		B	G-5-14 G-MSFY VR-BMD VP-BMD RA-02811
257201	NA0341	A	G-5-19 N710BV N2KW I-CIGH N700KG I-AZFB N646AM D2-EAI
257202	NA0342	A	G-5-17 N710BU N518S N65LC N8400E N93FR N230R (ZS-IPI) ZS-IPE
257203		B	G-5-14 5N-AXP [w/o 31Dec85 Kaduna, Nigeria]
257204	NA0343	A	G-5-15 N524M N949CE
257205		CC3	G-5-19 ZE395 [wfu Mar15; parted out Dunsfold, UK]]
257206	NA0344	A	G-5-16 N710BT N1C N502S C-FWCE C-GMBA N11YR XA-GIC N511RG N27BH N344BP
257207	NA0345	A	G-5-18 N710BS N774GF N686SG N686FG N21NY N21NT N913V "N313VR" N913V N700NP
257208	NA0346	A	N710BR G-5-19 (G-BLMJ) G-BLSM N501GF YV575T N501GF
257209		A	G-5-20 VR-BHW VP-BHW N127SR N805CD RP-C9808
257210	NA0347	A	N710BQ G-5-18 (G-BLMK) G-BLTP N502GF ZS-TBT
257211		CC3	ZE396 [wfu 26Feb15]
257212		B	G-5-12 G-RACL N81CH N81CN G-IJET G-5-659 OH-BAP G-5-659 OH-BAP LY-ASL LY-BSK VP-BMU RP-C602
257213		A	G-5-16 G-BLEK N213C N700NP (N703MJ) N700CE
257214		B	G-5-17 HZ-SJP G-UKCA G-OMID VR-BCF VP-BCF P4-CMP VP-CMP RA-02771
257215		B	G-5-20 VH-HSP VT-OBE [wfu Mumbai, India]

Production complete

BAe 125 SERIES 800 (HAWKER 800)

(1) * after the c/n indicates US assembled aircraft.

(2) 800SP/800XP2 aircraft are those which have been converted by the addition of Aviation Partners blended winglets and are noted in the series column

C/n	Series	Identities
258001	B	G-5-11 [ff 26May83] "N800BA" G-BKTF G-5-522 G-UWWB G-5-557 ZK-TCB N785CA OH-JOT N801CR N800RM (N928KH) N800JM
258002	B	(G-5-16) G-DCCC (VH-CCC) VH-III G-DCCC VH-NJM G-DCCC N800RY (N1169D) (N802CW) N882CW N15AX [parted out Wilmington, DE]
258003	SP	G-5-20 G-BKUW N800BA N800N N454JB N803TJ N803BA N583VC N803GE N803RK
258004	A	G-5-15 G-BLGZ N800EE N94BD (N98DD) N94SD XA-SEH XA-RET XA-TVI N84GA XA-KTY XC-LND XA-KTY
258005	A	(G-5-12) (G-5-19) G-5-15 G-BLJC N800GG (N219JA) N601UU N800FL
258006	A	G-5-17 N800WW N800S N70SK N861CE N886CW (N886GW) N800FH XA-JUL
258007	B	G-5-20 G-GAEL G-5-554 C-GKRL C-GYPH C-GWLL C-GWLE N258KT [parted out Roanoke, TX]
258008	A	G-5-11 N722CC N850LA N802WJ
258009	A	G-5-15 N400AL N408AL N45Y N48Y N298WB
258010	A	G-5-19 (G-BLKS) (G-OVIP) N84A N810BG N810CW (N800LX) N810BA [parted out by AvMATS, St Louis, MO; cx 06Jun14]
258011	A	G-5-20 N800VV N1BG N186G N811CW (N144AW) N820GA N801RM
258012	SP	G-5-18 N800TT N400NW N80BF N80BR N106JL N644JL N801CW (N801LX) N804MR XA-...
258013	B	G-5-14 G-OCCC N334 "N500RH" N300RB N802RM XB-VLM N305AG
258014	A	G-5-15 N800MM N294W N800BS N94WN N298AG N484AR
258015	A	G-5-17 G-BLPC C-FTLA C-GWFM C-GWEM N705BB [cx 29Mar17, wfu]
258016	SP	G-5-18 F-GESL N415PT N904SB N906SB N816CW N800VR
258017	A	G-5-16 N800LL N801G N801P (N801R) N217RM N888ZZ
258018	A	G-5-12 N800PP N818TG N350WC N350WG N601RS N36TJ N525CF N904JR
258019	A	G-5-12 VH-SGY VH-LKV N900MD G-5-704 N799SC N799S (N800NW) N7996 N880WW N614AJ N609RB
258020	SP	G-5-14 N800ZZ N270HC (N251TJ) 5N-QTS
258021	B	G-5-15 G-GEIL VR-CEJ G-RCEJ (N582CP) G-IFTF
258022	B	G-5-16 G-JJCB G-5-569 HZ-KSA EC-193 EC-ELK G-5-874 EC-ELK N4257R N822BL
258023	A	G-5-15 N810AA (N10AA) N1910H N1910J N47HW
258024	A	G-5-18 N811AA N800DP N802DC N802D N337RE
258025	B	G-5-14 3D-AVL G-5-742 G-BUIY N7C C-GMLR C-GGYT PR-LTA
258026	SP	G-5-18 N800HS N6TM N6TU N826CW N82SR
258027	A	G-5-12 N812AA (N100PM) N800PM (N553US) N553M N558M (N80CC) N880M XA-MER
258028	B	G-5-12 G-TSAM N85KH N277SS [cx 23Jan12; wfu]
258029	A	G-5-16 (N600TH) N813AA N600HS N77LA N800LR XA-UUV
258030	A	G-5-14 N600TH N6GG N10WF N91CH N616WG
258031	B	G-5-15 PT-ZAA PT-LHB
258032	A	G-5-11 N815AA N526M HZ-WBT5 N664LP
258033	A	G-5-19 N157H N57FF I-CASG N24RP N673TM N833CW (N802LX) N408MM N621WP
258034	B	G-5-12 G-HYGA G-5-595 G-HYGA G-5-595 N85DW N125HH [parted out Bangor, ME; cx 16Mar16]
258035	SP	G-5-20 N816AA N30F HB-VKM PT-ORH (N.....) HB-VKM PT-WIA N835TS N835CW N85MG (N85VC) XA-JMC XA-RLV
258036	A	G-5-18 N817AA N31F HB-VKN D-CFRC N621MT XA-ISH [w/o 27Oct03 near Tampico, Mexico]
258037	B	G-5-15 G-5-501 4W-ACN 7O-ADC M-HDAM M-DSML
258038	SP	G-5-20 N800TR N206PC N206WC N550RH D-CHEF C-GTNT C-FDDD
258039	A	G-5-19 N818AA N400TB N200KF N193TR N173TR N731TC [cx 06Feb17, parted out]
258040	B	G-5-15 VH-IXL G-5-697 I-IGNO N832MJ N832MR N713HC N718HC (N16CM)
258041	A	G-5-18 N819AA N71NP N626CG [parted out by Alberth Air Parts Ltd, TX]
258042	A	G-5-11 N820AA N20S N112K N804RM N904BW
258043	SP	G-5-12 (D-CAZH) N319AT N313CC N313CQ N937BC M-ISSY HA-YFI N800SN N829CR N821MP
258044	A	G-5-12 N821AA N72NP N833JP XA-UEH N645MS
258045	SP	G-5-16 N822AA N800TF N845CW (N803LX) N802SA (N593WH) [parted out Wilmington, DE; cx 29Dec15]
258046	A	G-5-20 N823AA N800BA N125SB
258047	A	G-5-11 N824AA N84BA N84FA N324SA XA-FGS
258048	A	G-5-16 G-BMMO (N125BA) C-GCIB N716DB N716BB
258049	A	G-5-19 N825AA N800EX N24SB N24SP N93CT N796CH
258050	SP	G-5-503 HZ-OFC G-BUCR I-OSLO N9LR G-ICFR G-OURA D-CLBC N65GD ZS-PAR M-SITM N80BF [cx 03Dec15; wfu]
258051	A	G-5-18 N826AA N889DH N888DH N258SR N851CW (N804LX) XA-ELM
258052	SP	G-5-20 N360BA N87EC N68DA N233KC N221HB C-FKGN C-GFHJ
258053	A	G-5-11 N361BA N5G N484RA N489SA [cx 22Oct14; wfu]
258054	A	G-5-15 N527M XB-NYM XA-UWF

BAe 125-800 (HAWKER 800)

C/n		Series	Identities
258055		A	G-5-504 N528M N508MM XA-UHI N855BC
258056		B	G-5-509 G-JETI M-JETI
258057		A	G-5-508 N362BA N300GN N800GN N614AF N614AP
258058		B	G-5-510 (ZK-EUR) ZK-EUI VH-NMR N125JW G-5-637 N125JW G-OMGG G-JJSI [parted out Kidlington 2015; fuselage to restaurant in Yorkshire, UK]
258059		SP	G-5-506 N363BA N400GN N355RB N255RB N355RB N686CP
258060		A	G-5-511 N364BA N686CF N330X N330DE N303SE [30Sep16]
258061		A	G-5-515 N365BA N161MM N611MM (N611CR) N861CW (N805LX) N412DA
258062		A	G-5-516 N366BA N961JC N862CW (N806LX) N245TX (N962DP) [parted out Wilmington, DE; cx 21Nov14]
258063		A	G-5-518 N367BA N684C N74ND N391TC XB-MTG
258064		B	G-5-514 Malawi MAAW-J1 N803BG RP-C8082
258065		A	G-5-520 N368BA N77CS N77CU N65FA N16GH [parted out by MTW Aerospace, Montgomery, AL]
258066		A	G-5-521 N369BA N75CS N55RF N244FL
258067		B	G-5-525 D-CEVW G-BUZX G-5-807 N801MM N801MB N801MM N867CW N801MM N867CW (N807LX) N469AL N469RJ
258068		B	G-5-539 HZ-SJP G-5-653 HZ-SJP G-5-738 G-BUIM N68GP N68HR N167DD N606
258069		SP	G-5-526 N519BA (N743UP) N746UP N364WC N160WC N517ST
258070		A	G-5-527 N520BA N528AC N255DV N255DA N998PA N798PA
258071		A	G-5-528 N521BA N890A N789LT N94JT [cx 03Feb17, wfu]
258072		SP	G-5-529 N522BA (N745UP) N747UP N164WC [dbr 04Dec15, Palm Springs, CA; cx 04Aug16]
258073		SP	G-5-532 D-CFVW G-BVBH N802MM VR-BSI VP-BSI N2236 N212RG (N214RG) N213RG
258074		A	G-5-541 ZK-MRM N800MD G-5-640 N800MD N800MN N300BW N850SM N103HT N518S RA-.....
258075		A	G-5-533 N518BA N189B N533P XA-GFB N3GU XA-RYM N460MM
258076		B	G-5-535 D-CGVW G-BVAS RA-02807 [w/o near Minsk, Belarus, 26Oct09]
258077		A	G-5-538 N523BA N509GP N877CW N897CW (N808LX)
258078		B	G-5-544 G-BNEH G-5-713 G-BNEH ZS-FSI OE-GHS YL-VIP G-88-01 YL-VIP [scrapped Kemble, UK, Sep11]
258079		B	G-5-542 G-GJCB G-BVHW SE-DRV 9M-DDW N800LL
258080		A	G-5-540 N524BA N800BP N800WH
258081		A	G-5-543 N525BA N650PM N700PM N196MC N196MG N800CJ
258082		A	G-5-548 ZK-RJI N499SC N90ME N601BA (N601BX) N800S XA-ASH
258083		A	G-5-546 N526BA (N800HS) N5C N8UP N852A (N805AF)
258084		A	G-5-547 N527BA N780A N877RP N884CF N24JG N124JG N323SL PR-WSW
258085		A	G-5-551 G-WBPR N285AL (N910VP) N457J
258086		A	G-5-550 N528BA N125BA N523WC N523WG (N523W)
258087		A	G-5-552 N529BA N800TR C-GAWH C-FIGO N6200H
258088		SP	G-5-563 (ZK-RHP) G-BOOA G-BTAB N757BL N800PZ
258089		A	G-5-555 N530BA N125JB N862CE N593HR N598HR
258090		SP	G-5-556 N531BA N2SG N2YG N410US N8090 N800FJ N800FN N900RL N901RL N901RP N414PE
258091		A	G-5-560 HB-VIK N165BA N1776H [parted out by Tulsa Turbine Engines & Aircraft LLC, OK; cx 08Nov16]
258092		A	G-5-558 N532BA N2MG N3007 N3008
258093		A	G-5-559 N533BA N331SC N800S (A6-HMK) N358LL N317CC N317CQ N2033
258094		B	G-5-576 D-CFAN (LN-BEP) LN-ESA HS-EMG
258095		A	G-5-561 N534BA N200LS (N500LL) C-FPCP C-GHXY N40255 ZS-OXY AP-BJL ZS-OXY [parted out Lanseria, South Africa]
258096		SP	G-5-562 N535BA N800UP N10TC N596SW N311JA N311JX N234GF N233GF N275RB
258097		B	G-5-567 HB-VIL N170BA N800BV N384AB
258098		A	G-5-564 N536BA N300LS N181FH
258099		A	G-5-565 (G-BNUB) N537BA C-FAAU OY-MCL N10YJ
258100	NA0401	A	G-5-566 N538BA N108CF N815CC N180NE
258101	NA0402	A	G-5-572 N539BA N1125 N757M
258102	NA0403	A	G-5-573 N540BA N89K (N89KT) N89NC N316EC N316CS N316GS N266JW
258103	NA0404	A	G-5-574 N541BA N916PT N494AT VP-CCH N801ST N13SY N12SY
258104	NA0405	A	G-5-575 N542BA N527AC N211JN
258105	NA0406	A	G-5-577 (N551BA) G-BNZW C-GKLB C-FSCI C-FSCY C-FSCI C-GCCU N813AC
258106		B	G-5-580 PK-WSJ PK-RGM (N107CF) N888SS G-OLDD RA-02806 [dbr 07Jul14, Moscow/ Vnukovo, Russia]
258107	NA0407	A	G-5-578 N552BA N70NE
258108	NA0408	A	G-5-579 N553BA N61CT N309G N703VZ N118GA
258109		B	(N554BA) G-5-581 5N-NPC
258110		B	(N555BA) G-5-584 D-CMIR N710A (N167SG) N422CS
258111	NA0409	SP	(N556BA) G-5-582 N554BA N800TR N375SC N875SC XA-TKQ N870CA N801LM
258112		A	G-5-583 Botswana OK-1/Z-1 G-5-664 PT-OBT N112NW N331DC N831DC N812GJ
258113	NA0410	A	G-5-587 N555BA N683E N683F
258114	NA0411	SP	G-5-586 N556BA N600LS N800EC (4X-COZ) N807MC
258115		B	G-5-599 (G-BPGR) Saudi Arabia 104 G-5-665 Saudi Arabia 104 G-5-599 G-TCAP P4-BOB 9H-BOB P4-JCC N666JC
258116		B	G-5-592 PT-LQP

BAe 125-800 (HAWKER 800)

C/n		Series	Identities								
258117	NA0412	A	G-5-589	N557BA	N825PS	N826CT	C-GBIS	N955DP			
258118		B	(G-5-590)	G-5-605	(G-BPGS)	Saudi Arabia 105		HZ-105			
258119	NA0413	SP	G-5-591	N558BA	N203R	N221RE	N239R	N166WC	N413HS		
258120		SP	G-5-606	G-POSN	HB-VLI	VT-EAU	N120AP	G-POSN	N120AP		
258121	NA0414	A	G-5-593	(N559BA)	G-BOTX	C-FRPP	N4361Q	N800WA			
258122	NA0415	A	G-5-594	N560BA	N800VC	N830BA	[parted out by AvMATS, St Louis, MO; cx 06Jun14]				
258123	NA0416	A	G-5-600	N561BA	N353WC	N353WG	C-GCGS				
258124	NA0417	A	G-5-596	N562BA	N800BA	N376SC	N876SC	N801NW	C-GCRP	C-GRGE	N824CW
			(N809LX)	N67JF	N620RM	N668JF					
258125	NA0418	A	G-5-601	N563BA	N802X	(N99DA)	N913SC				
258126	NA0419	SP	G-5-597	N564BA	(N82BL)	HZ-BL2	N196GA	N818WM	RA-02772		
258127	NA0420	A	G-5-602	N565BA	N803X	N3QG					
258128	NA0421	SP	G-5-603	N566BA	N804X	N40GS					
258129		A	G-5-622	N269X	USAF 88-0269		N94	N8029Z	XA-IZA	N956RA	
258130		B	G-5-620	G-FDSL	G-TPHK	G-BVFC	G-ETOM	D-CPAS	G-OSPG	G-DCTA	G-GRGA
			G-OGFS	G-GMMR							
258131		A	G-5-611	(N271X)	N270X	USAF 88-0270		N95	N8030F	N770SW	N595US
258132	NA0422	A	G-5-607	N567BA	N125TR	N222MS					
258133		B	G-5-616	G-GSAM	G-5-642	N800FK	G-JETK	N800FK	HP-1262	PT-WAU	N800FK
			PR-SOL	PP-ACP	N800FK	PP-ACP					
258134		A	G-5-634	(N270X)	N271X	USAF 88-0271		N96	N1061	N54ES	N953DP
258135	NA0423	A	G-5-608	N568BA	N801AB	N801RJ	(N241SM)	N204SM	N423SJ	N952DP	
258136	NA0424	A	G-5-609	N569BA	N452SM	I-SDFG	N80GJ	[cx 05Aug13; parted out by Atlanta Air Salvage,			
			Griffin, GA]								
258137	NA0425	A	G-5-610	N570BA	N733K	(N100MH)	N110MH	N800SE	[parted out by Dodson Int'l, KS]		
258138	NA0428	A	G-5-614	N582BA	N244JM	N384TC	N800FJ				
258139	NA0426	A	G-5-612	N580BA	N125BA	(VR-BPA)	VR-BLP	N47VC	N49VG	(N47TJ)	N795PH
			N726EP	N797EP	N218AD	N218PJ					
258140	NA0427	A	G-5-613	N581BA	N45Y	N856AF	N858XL	N326N			
258141	NA0429	A	G-5-615	N583BA	N72K	C-FGLF	N106GC	N73WF	N141MR		
258142	NA0430	A	G-5-617	N584BA	N1903P	N850BM	N149VB	N149VP	N50BN	N45GD	
258143		SP	G-5-656	5N-NPF	5N-AGZ	5N-BOO					
258144	NA0431	A	G-5-618	N585BA	N682B	N682D					
258145	NA0432	SP	G-5-619	N586BA	N540M	N805CW	N810LX	N22NF			
258146		B	G-5-629	(G-BPYD)	"HZ-109"	G-5-703	HZ-109				
258147	NA0433	A	G-5-621	N587BA	N919P	N9UP	N812AM				
258148		B	G-5-630	(G-BPYE)	HZ-110	Saudi Arabia 110		HZ-110			
258149		SP	G-5-635	G-FASL	N155T	N577T	YV2477				
258150	NA0434	A	G-5-625	N588BA	N77W	N432AC	N432AQ	XA-RCL	XC-LNG	XA-RCL	
258151		1000	G-EXLR	[prototype BAe125-1000; ff 16Jun90; last flight 10Jly92; wfu Nov93; shipped to Wichita, KS 27Sep95;							
			remains located in scrapyard, Wichita, KS circa Mar96; to Raytheon Svs hangar, Wichita, KS circa Sep99 to train South								
			Korean Hawker 800XP engineers]								
258152		B	G-5-626	HB-VHU	(N42US)	N800WG	XA-UVH	N549MF			
258153		B	G-5-627	HB-VHV							
258154		A	G-5-655	N272X	USAF 88-0272		N97	N359CF	N950DP		
258155		SP	G-5-628	N800BM	D-CBMW	N159RA	N238AJ	N300BL	(N800LV)	N711PE	N702PE
			N723LK								
258156		A	G-5-661	N273X	USAF 88-0273		N98	N355FA			
258157	NA0435	A	G-5-632	N589BA	N800BA	C-GMTR	N976SC				
258158		SP	G-5-667	N274X	USAF 88-0274		N99	N8064Q	N158TN	N800AF	
258159		1000	G-OPFC	[second prototype BAe125-1000; ff 25Nov90]				N10855	[used for ground tests; cx 05Sep03,		
			parted out by APPH Houston Inc, Houston, TX]								
258160	NA0436	A	G-5-633	N590BA	N354WC	N354WG	N369BG	N389BG	N160NW	N803JL	ZS-AOA
258161	NA0437	A	G-5-636	G-BPXW	C-FFTM	N17DD	XA-QPL				
258162	NA0438	A	G-5-638	N591BA	N753G	N800PA					
258163	NA0443	A	G-5-639	G-BRCZ	C-GMOL	C-FWCE	N360DE	N717MT			
258164		B	G-5-654	Botswana OK1		[code Z2]	Botswana OK2		G-OBLT	(VR-BND)	G-5-654
			Saudi Arabia 130		HZ-130						
258165		A	G-5-657	VR-BPG	ZS-BPG	VT-RAY	N324BG				
258166	NA0439	SP	G-5-641	N592BA	N74PC	N74PQ	C-GKPP	C-GFLZ	C-FXGO		
258167		A	G-5-662	N125AS	VR-CAS	VP-CAS	(N802SJ)	N825DA	N48AL	N257PL	
258168	NA0440	A	G-5-643	N593BA	N74NP	N295JR	N816BG				
258169		A	G-5-644	N47CG	N526AC	N255DV	C-FDKJ	N777VW			
258170	NA0441	A	G-5-645	N594BA	N75NP	N79NP	N24JG	XA-EXC			
258171	NA0442	A	G-5-646	N595BA	N754G	N4444J	N707PE	N729HZ	N729EZ	XA-HOM	
258172	NA0444	SP	G-5-647	N596BA	N290EC	N811AM					
258173	NA0447	SP	G-5-648	N599BA	N95AE	N82XP	C-FCRH	C-FCRF	C-GTAU	N41PJ	
258174	NA0445	A	G-5-649	N597BA	N174A	N174NW	N800QC	N119ML			
258175	NA0446	A	G-5-650	N598BA	(VR-BPB)	VR-BLQ	N204JC	HB-VMF	N175U	N2032	N591CF
258176		B	(N610BA)	G-5-652	HB-VJY	N176WA	XA-TPB	N176TL	XA-DAS	N176TL	
258177		A	G-5-668	PT-OJC	N411RA	N217AL	N5119	N52RZ			
258178	NA0449	SP	G-5-658	N611BA	D-CWIN	N800WT	N868WC	N178AX	N430BB	N463DD	
258179	NA0448	A	G-5-660	N610BA	N125BA	N60TC	N60TG	N904GP	N904GR		
258180		B	G-5-675	G-XRMC	G-BZNR	VP-BMH					
258181	NA0450	SP	G-5-663	N612BA	N355WC	N355WG	C-GAGU	C-GAGQ	N861CE	(N675RW)	C-FIQF
258182		B	G-5-676	(VR-B..)	G-PBWH	G-5-676	N128RS	N12F	N312LR	N212LR	

BAe 125-800 (HAWKER 800)

C/n		Series	Identities								
258183	NA0451	A	G-5-666	N613BA	N50PM	N90PM	N63PM	N599EC	CS-DNI	N883EJ	N731JR
			XA-GIC	N183FM	N800DN	4X-CZO					
258184		B	G-5-678	(PT-WAW)	PT-OSW						
258185	NA0452	A	G-5-669	N614BA	N207PC	(N207RC)	XA-SIV	N801CF			
258186		A	G-5-683	G-BSUL	VR-BPM	G-BSUL	N8186	N818G	N818MV	[w/o 31Jul08	
			Owatonna, MN]								
258187	NA0453	SP	G-5-670	N615BA	N60PM	N750RV	(N750PB)	(N242JG)	N4242	XA-LEX	
258188	NA0454	A	G-5-671	N616BA	N1910A	N191BA	N180EG	(N892BP)			
258189	NA0455	A	G-5-673	N617BA	N6JB	N6UB	N195KC	N25BB	N32PJ		
258190		B	G-5-684	G-BTAE	PT-OHB	PT-JAA					
258191	NA0456	A	G-5-674	N618BA	N152NS	N801P	(N730BG)				
258192		SP	G-5-691	TR-LDB	N192SJ	N38CZ	N801SA	RA-02773	[dbr 05Jun16, Chulman, Russia]		
258193	NA0457	A	G-5-677	N619BA	N300PM	N699EC	CS-DNH	N893EJ	C-GKGD	C-GDBC	
258194		B	G-5-692	PT-OTC							
258195	NA0458	A	G-5-679	N630BA	N800BA	N800GX	N100GX	N940HC	N941HC	N28ZF	
258196	NA0459	A	G-5-680	N631BA	N125TR	N511WM	N511WD	N929WG	N929WQ	N189TM	
258197		A	G-5-696	G-BTMG	G-OMGE	N150SB					
258198		B	G-5-694	PT-WAL							
258199	NA0460	SP	G-5-681	N632BA	N4402	N442MS					
258200	NA0461	A	G-5-682	N633BA	N461W	N722A	S2-AHS				
258201		B	G-5-699	(D-C...)	G-OCCI	G-BWSY	P4-AMF	N59DM	YV2837		
258202	NA0462	A	G-5-685	N634BA	N200GX	N800DR	N800DN	A6-MAA	N43PJ	N462MM	
258203	NA0463	A	G-5-686	N635BA	YV-735CP	N228G	N453TM	N805JL			
258204	NA0464	A	G-5-687	N636BA	N341AP	N57LN	N703SM				
258205	NA0465	A	G-5-689	N637BA	N805X	N939TT					
258206	NA0466	A	G-5-688	N638BA	(N800BJ)	PT-OMC	N638BA	N466CS	N466AE	N395HE	
258207	NA0467	A	G-5-690	N639BA	N600KC	(N48DD)	N2BG	N2QG	(N103BG)		
258208		SP	"G-5-670"	G-5-700	(PT-...)	G-BUID	TC-ANC	N208BG	N123HK		
258209	NA0468	A	G-5-695	N670BA	YV-800CP	N168BA	N693C	N410BT	N661JN	N9990S	TN-AJE
258210		B	G-5-705	G-RAAR	HB-VMI	VP-CSP					
258211		A	G-5-724	PT-OSB	N91DV	N151TC	N855GA				
258212		B	G-5-710	G-BUCP	D-CSRI	RP-C8008	(N323L)				
258213		B	G-5-709	D-CWBW	G-BURV	N10857	[cx 21Jly05; parted out Houston, TX]				
258214		B	G-5-706	VR-CCX	PT-OOI	[wfu Sao Paulo/Congonhas, Brazil]					
258215		U-125	G-5-727	G-JFCX	Japan 29-3041 [code 041]						
258216	NA0469	A	G-5-714	N671BA	N500J	N50QJ					
258217	NA0470	SP	G-5-715	N672BA	N600J	N60QJ	N125GB	N800SV			
258218	NA0471	SP	G-5-725	N673BA	N57PM	N118K	(N503RJ)	N118KL	N418CA		
258219		A	G-5-740	(9M-WCM)	9M-AZZ	N8881J					
258220	NA0472	A	G-5-728	N674BA	N58PM	N125AW	N999JF	XA-RAA			
258221	NA0473	SP	G-5-731	N675BA	N25W	N25WN	VP-BHB	N919SS	N406VC		
258222		B	G-5-745	G-VIPI							
258223	NA0474	A	G-5-733	N677BA	N800BA	N622AB	N622AD	N44HH	N23AN		
258224		SP	G-5-763	ZS-NJH	N827RH	N847RH	N618JL	N478PM	N810V	N65DL	
258225	NA0475	A	G-5-739	N682BA	N800BA	N800CJ	N935H				
258226		A	G-5-755	(9M-...)	G-BVCU	D-CSRB	RP-C1926	N709EA	N800MJ	PR-HFW	
258227		U-125	G-5-769	G-BUUW	Japan 39-3042 [code 042]						
258228		A	G-5-758	HB-VKV	N130LC	N889MB	XB-ORG				
258229		SP	G-5-744	N683BA	PT-OTH	N229RY	TC-TEK	N984HM	N304HE	N504HE	
258230		A	G-5-748	N678BA	N71MT	N800RG					
258231		A	G-5-750	N685BA	N75MT	ZS-PSE	5N-BMT				
258232		A	G-5-752	N686BA	N900KC	XA-NGS	XA-AEN	N723HH	C-FBUR		
258233		B	G-5-770	D-CAVW	F-WQCD	(VR-BQH)	VR-BTM	VP-BTM	G-BYHM	M-AZAG	N440A
258234		B	G-5-757	VR-CDE	YV-814CP	VR-CDE	VP-CDE	N65CE	(N160H)	N68AR	
258235		B	G-5-774	D-CBVW	G-BWVA	OY-RAA	N258SA	D-CWOL	(PH-WOL)	OY-RAA	
258236		A	G-5-764	N162BA	N80PM	N800TJ	(N39BL)	N58BL			
258237		A	G-5-775	D-CCVW	G-BWRN	9M-DRL	VP-BAW	N237RA	N250JE	N250MB	
258238		SP	G-5-767	N163BA	N70PM	N100AG	N188AF				
258239		A	G-5-768	N164BA	VR-BPN	N904H	N62TC	(N262CT)	N84CT	C-GMLR	C-GMFB
258240		B	G-5-772	G-BUWC	G-SHEA	HB-VLT	G-HCFR	G-CJAA	G-WYNE	XA-KVD	
258241		SP	G-5-777	N165BA	N125CJ	N94NB	N540BA	XA-CHA	N855MW		
258242		U-125	G-5-793	G-BVFE	Japan 49-3043 [code 043]			[w/o 06Apr16, crashed nr Kanoya Air Base, Japan]			
258243		SP	G-5-778	(G-BUWD)	G-SHEB	VH-XMO	C-GSCL	C-FLPH	C-FTVC	N732AA	
258244		SP	G-5-780	N166BA	N800CJ	N95NB	N530BA	N252DH	N252DT	N252DH	N252DT
			N862CE	N671RW	N671RR						
258245		U-125A	G-JHSX	Japan 52-3001 [code 001]							
258246		A	G-5-782	N387H	HB-VKW	ZS-ZEN					
258247		U-125A	G-5-813	G-BVRF	Japan 52-3002 [code 002]						
258248		A	G-5-784	N388H	N789LB	N260H					
258249		A	G-5-786	N933H	N326SU	(N826SU)	N500HF	N249SR	N117HH		
258250		U-125A	G-5-815	G-BVRG	Japan 52-3003 [code 003]						
258251		A	G-5-787	N937H	N194JS	N192JS	N171MD				
258252		A	G-5-788	N938H	XB-GCC	XA-GCC					
258253		A	G-5-790	N942H	N801CE	N3RC	N1310H				
258254		A	G-5-791	N943H	N2015M	N800NY	N770JT				
258255		SP	G-5-792	[first Hawker 800]		N946H	N127KC	N575MR	N339AV		

BAe 125-800 (HAWKER 800)

C/n	Series	Identities								
258256	SP	G-5-795	N947H	N256BC	(N256FS)	N613CF				
258257		G-5-796	N951H	N802DC	N415BJ	N304AT				
258258	B	G-5-798	G-BVJI	(N953H)	G-BVJI	N54SB	N910JD	N910JN	N258SP	N258MR
258259		G-5-799	N954H	(N966L)						
258260		G-5-800	N957H							
258261		G-5-802	N958H	PT-GAF						
258262		G-5-803	N959H	N521JK						
258263		G-5-804	N961H	N826GA	N826GC					
258264		G-5-806	N805H	HB-VLF	5N-BMR					
258265		G-5-809	N806H	HB-VLG	5N-BNE					
258266	XP	G-5-811	(N293H)	G-BVRW	(N293H)	N800XP	(N800GT)	N414XP	N800CC	
258267		G-5-812	N294H	N811CC	N980DC	N601VC	I-SIRF	VP-CAF	(D-CALI)	(D-CKAS)
		N910CF								
258268	U-125A	G-5-829	G-BVYV	Japan 62-3004		N809H	Japan 62-3004 [code 004]			
258269		G-5-814	N295H	N380X	N380DE	N302SE	N302EA			
258270	SP	G-5-816	N297H	N802CE	N838JL	N850SX				
258271		G-5-818	N298H	N803CE	N787CM	N489BM				
258272		G-5-819	N299H	N2426	N4426	N814ST				
258273		G-5-820	N803H	N967L	N258RA	N337WR				
258274		G-5-822	N804H	N2428	N4428	N41HF				
258275		G-5-823	N905H	N77TC	N7775	XA-RBV				
258276	SP	G-5-824	N667H	N126KC						
258277	XP	G-BVYW	N97SH	N333PC	(N339PC)	N339CC				
258278	XP	G-BVZK	N872AT							
258279	XP	G-BVZL	(N817H)	4X-CZM	N817H	N877DM	N880AF			
258280	XP	G-BWDC	N351SP	N351SB	N100LA	(N108LA)	N47HA			
258281	XP	G-BWDD	N914H	VH-ELJ	N281XP	N781TA	N832LX	N801WJ		
258282	XP	G-5-827	G-BWDW	N916H	PT-WHH	N782TA	(N811LX)	(N800LX)	N603MA	N622KR
258283	XP	G-5-828	G-BWGB	N918H	(N283XP)	4X-COV	N283BX	N82EA	C-FJHS	
258284	XP	G-5-830	G-BWGC	N919H	(PT-LTA)	PT-WNO	N919H	PR-DBB		
258285	XP2	G-5-831	G-BWGD	N808H	(N800XP)	N285XP				
258286	XP	G-5-832	G-BWGE	N807H	N501F	N304RJ	N504MF			
258287	XP2	G-5-833	N668H	(N287XP)	N801WB	XA-UFK	N564CC			
258288	U-125A	G-5-848	N816H	Japan 72-3005		[code 005]				
258289	XP2	G-5-834	N669H	N515GP	N863CE	N672RW	(N1957S)	N881AF		
258290	XP	G-5-835	N670H	N348MC	N250GM	4X-CLZ				
258291	XP	"G-5-837"	G-5-836	N672H	N291XP	N291SJ	N791TA	N833LX	N801SS	
258292	XP	G-5-838	N673H	N33BC						
258293	XP	G-5-839	N679H	N404CE	N150NC	N52484				
258294	XP2	G-5-840	N682H	N404BS	N632FW	N35CC				
258295	XP	G-5-841	N683H	VH-LAW	VH-LAT	VH-KEF	VH-EJL	VH-VRC	XA-LAU	
258296	XP2	G-5-842	N685H	N801JT	N707TA	(N812LX)	N934RD			
258297*	XP	[first US-assembed aircraft]			N297XP	N725TA	N725JA	N725TA	N843LX	N553BW
		N960TC								
258298	XP	G-5-843	N298XP	N880SP	N435JD					
258299	XP	G-5-844	N299XP	(N32BC)	N601DR	N87RB				
258300	XP	G-5-845	N689H	N800VF	N950PC	(N800NE)				
258301*	XP	N1105Z	PT-WMA	N800XZ	N800GK*					
258302	XP	G-5-847	N302XP	XA-RUY	XA-GIE	N302MT	XA-GIE	N302PJ		
258303	XP2	G-5-849	N303XP	N876H	N621CH	N4SA	N303DT	N104LR		
258304*	XP	N802JT	N5734							
258305	U-125A	G-5-864	N305XP	Japan 72-3006 [code 006]						
258306*	U-125A	N1103U	Japan 82-3007 [code 007]							
258307	XP2	G-5-850	N307XP	N109TD	N802WM	N307AD	N85CC			
258308	XP	G-5-851	N308XP	(N11WC)	N345BR	N875LP				
258309*	XP	N803JT	N5735	N92UP						
258310	XP2	G-5-852	N310XP	PT-WMG	N33VC	N97XP				
258311*	XP	N804JT	N800RD	N850J	N225RP					
258312	XP2	G-5-853	N312XP	PT-WMD	N251X	B-3998	N251X	N924JM	A6-ZZZ	5N-EXJ
258313*	XP	N2159X	N313XP	N84BA	N908VZ	N411VZ	N313MU	N721KY	(N721KE)	N969JJ
		N820JS								
258314	XP	G-5-854	N314XP	OM-SKY	N800NJ	XA-GMM	N316MF			
258315*	XP	N2169X	N9292X							
258316	XP	G-5-855	N316XP	N516GP	C-GDII	N215SP	N75HL			
258317*	XP	N2173X	N9NB	N520BA	N520JF					
258318	XP	G-5-856	N318XP	N1910H	N191GH					
258319*	XP	N2291X	C-FIPE	OD-TSW						
258320*	XP	N2322X	N720TA	(N813LX)	(N801LX)	XB-MCB				
258321	XP	G-5-857	N691H	N32BC	(N32BQ)	N291B				
258322*	XP2	N722TA	(N814LX)	N307RM						
258323	XP	G-5-858	N323XP	N877S	N877SL	N752CS				
258324	XP	G-5-860	N324XP	N303BC						
258325*	U-125A	N1112N	Japan 82-3008 [code 008]							
258326*	XP2	N326XP	N1897A	N897A						
258327	XP2	G-5-861	N327XP	N111ZN	N801HB	(N219DC)	N22GA	XA-URN	XA-JPF	XA-UYF
258328	XP	G-5-866	N328XP	VH-SGY	VH-SCY	A6-MAH	N91PS			

BAe 125-800 (HAWKER 800)

C/n	Series	Identities							
258329	XP2	G-5-862	N329XP	N901K	N903K	N825CP			
258330	XP2	G-5-869	N330XP	N139M	N86MN				
258331*	XP2	N10NB	N510BA	N160CT	N864CE	N673RW	(N859RP)	(N855ER)	XA-MJA
258332	XP2	G-5-865	N332XP	N36H	N53LB	N214TD			
258333*	U-125A	N3261Y	Japan 82-3009 [code 009]						
258334*	XP2	N334XP	N399JC	N80HD	N60HD	N800YY	N808YY		
258335	XP	G-5-867	N335XP	OY-RAC	OE-GHU	F-HREX			
258336*	XP	N336XP	N2286U	N745UP					
258337	XP	G-5-868	N337XP	[last to be assembled at Chester, UK – rolled out 22Apr97, ff 29Apr97, del to USA 08May97]					
		(9M-VVV)	N337XP	N733TA	(N815LX)	C-FDKL	N606JF		
US Production									
258338	XP	N838QS	N838WC	N951DP	PR-GPW*				
258339	XP2	N23395	SE-DVD	N14SA	N294CV				
258340	XP	N840QS	N840WC	N907MC					
258341	U-125A	N3251M	"N2351M"	Japan 92-3010 [code 010]					
258342	XP	N2320J	South Korea 258-342						
258343	XP	N1102U	South Korea 258-343						
258344	XP	N29GP	N29GZ	(N977GR)					
258345	XP	N1135A	D-CBMV	D-CBMW	(G-VONI)	OY-LKG	N100HL		
258346	XP	N23204	South Korea 258-346						
258347	XP	N1115G	N40PL	N409AV					
258348	U-125A	N2175W	Japan 92-3011 [code 011]						
258349	XP2	N723TA	VP-BHL	(N74WF)	N349GA	C-FEPC	N377JC	C-FYTZ	
258350	XP	N23207	South Korea 258-350						
258351	XP	N23208	South Korea 258-351						
258352	XP	N2321S	South Korea 258-352						
258353	XP	N2321V	South Korea 258-353						
258354	XP	N2G	N262G	N116JG	N789HA				
258355	XP	N855QS	N291TX	N830TM	N535RV*				
258356	XP	N550H	N55BA						
258357	XP	N2321Z	South Korea 258-357						
258358	XP2	N240B	D-CJET	OY-JBJ					
258359	XP	N25WX	P4-ALE	N359XP	N44UN				
258360	U-125A	N3189H	Japan 92-3012 [code 012]						
258361	XP	N861QS	N861WC	N999RZ	VP-CGG				
258362	XP	N862QS	N862WC	(N862JA)	N949JA				
258363	XP	N726TA	N816LX						
258364	XP	N728TA	(N817LX)	(N804LX)					
258365	XP2	N865SM	N243BA	N343SC					
258366	XP2	N1133N	(CS-MAI)	N894CA	VH-ZUH	VH-OVE			
258367	XP	N3263E	N367DM	OY-GIP	N704JM				
258368	XP2	N804AC	N804AQ	N248EC					
258369	XP	N800PC	N621WH	N800MA					
258370	U-125A	N23556	Japan 02-3013 [code 013]			[dbr by tsunami flood waters 11Mar11, Matsushima, Japan]			
258371	XP2	N848N							
258372	XP	N1251K	N372XP	LV-ZHY	N800GN	VH-VLI	N800GN		
258373	XP	N3270X	N168BF	(N808AL)					
258374	XP	N729TA	(N874CW)	(N818LX)	N805LX				
258375	XP	N875QS	N154RR						
258376	XP	N1640	N1645						
258377	XP2	N1251K	N984GC	[1,000th DH/HS/BAe/Raytheon 125 sale]				N993SA	N993SJ
258378	XP	N494RG	N442MA	N780DW					
258379	XP	N879QS	[w/o 28Aug06 Carson City, NV]			N879WC	[parted out Atlanta/DeKalb-Peachtree, GA; cx 18Apr17]		
258380	XP2	N8SP	N999JF	N101FC	N380PL				
258381	U-125A	N23566	Japan 02-3014 [code 014]						
258382	XP	N23451	SE-DYE	EI-WXP					
258383	XP	N730TA	(N819LX)	N806LX	XA-MLP	XA-STK			
258384	XP	N23455	TC-MDC	N23455	N955MC	G-LAOR	M-LAOR	VT-VAP	
258385	XP	N23466	SE-DYV	G-0502	SE-DYV	F-HCSL	M-HASL	S5-AFR	
258386	XP2	N23479	N61DF	N61DN	N715WG	N715WT	XA-FYN	N800CV	N803WJ*
258387	XP	N887QS	N282TX	N835TM					
258388	XP2	N23488	TC-OKN	N809TA	(N809TP)	N809BA	N110WS		
258389	XP	N23493	I-DDVA	YR-VPA	YL-MAR	[b/u Biggin Hill, UK, Mar12; cockpit section to Belgium as flight simulator]			
258390	XP	N23509	(N800SG)	N800FD	N850HS	N736MB*			
258391	XP	N391XP	N771SV	4X-CPS	N543LF				
258392	XP	N23569	"LX-BYG"	LX-GBY	G-0504	LX-GBY	F-HBOM	C-FMIX	
258393	XP	N893QS	N269TX	N840TM					
258394	XP	N394XP	N800DW	N800ER	N800TL				
258395	XP	N23577	PT-WVG	N800UW					
258396	XP	N23585	N21EL						
258397	XP	N752TA	(N887CW)	(N820LX)	(N752LX)	N852LX	XA-WNG		
258398	XP	N168HH	TC-VSC	LY-HCW					
258399	XP2	N899QS	CS-DNJ	N979JB	LY-LTC	[cx; status?]			

BAe 125-800 (HAWKER 800)

C/n	Series	Identities							
258400	XP	N404JC	N314TC						
258401	XP	N23592	Brazil EU93A-6050						
258402	XP	N729AT							
258403	XP	N23550	ZS-DCK	N25XP	N601RS	N111VG	N333MV		
258404	XP	N30289	VP-BCM	N404DB	N448JM	N930PT			
258405	XP	N405XP	N866RR	N866RB	D-CLBD	M-CLAA	N362AP	N258MS	
258406	XP	N754TA	(N821LX)	N821LX	ZS-EXG				
258407	U-125A	N30562	Japan 02-3015 [code 015]						
258408	XP	N30319	B-3990						
258409	XP	N30337	PT-WPF	N929AK	N929AL	(VP-LV.)	N929AL	VP-BSK	N827NS	XA-TPB
258410	XP2	N755TA	N322LA	N315BK	N885M	OD-EAS			
258411	XP2	N617TM	LV-CJG						
258412	XP	N30682	N990HC						
258413	XP2	N760TA	N813CW	(N822LX)	N807LX	XA-ELX			
258414	XP	N30742	N800XP	N800XM	EI-RNJ	N800XM			
258415	XP	N31016	TC-BHD	TC-STR	N800LR	N444MG	VT-VPA		
258416	XP	N816QS	N274TX	N895TM					
258417	XP	N747NG	N246V	N240V					
258418	XP	N31046	N806XM	(N516TM)	N516TH				
258419	XP	N419XP	N508BP	N559DM					
258420	XP2	N31340	N910JD	N89WA					
258421	XP	N31820	Brazil EU93A-6051						
258422	XP	N822QS	CS-DNM	VT-SRA					
258423	XP	N925JF	N388BS	N7NY	N99AP				
258424	XP	N1899K	YL-NST	[parted out Kemble, UK]					
258425	XP2	N825XP	N800VA	N59BR	N89BR	N438PM	N802CF		
258426	XP	N426XP	N27FL						
258427	U-125A	N31833	Japan 02-3016 [code 016]						
258428	XP	N772TA	N828CW	(N823LX)	(N808LX)	N842FL	N885LS	N718RR	
258429	XP	N88HD	N68HD	ZS-PKY	5N-BNM				
258430	XP	N31590	CS-DNK	N905MT	N905MG	YV572T			
258431	XP	N144HM	XA-TEM						
258432	XP	N432XP	N1650	N165L	N832CW	(N824LX)	N809LX	A6-SKA	A6-GAL
258433	XP	N833QS	N285TX	N822TM					
258434	XP	N40027	Brazil EU93A-6052						
258435	XP	N835QS	CS-DNN	ZS-MNU					
258436	XP	N836QS	N294TX	N845TM	N114BA				
258437	XP	N780TA	(N825LX)	N812LX	N800WJ				
258438	XP	N40113	VP-BHZ	N827SA	N481SC	N804TB			
258439	XP	N31596	CS-DNL	N497AG					
258440	XP	N40488	N801MB	N408RT	N8TA				
258441	XP	N800PE	N800PB	N370DE	N715LA				
258442	XP	N40202	PT-XDY	N442XP	N80PK				
258443	XP	N310AS	N489VC	N798KG					
258444	XP	N40489	EC-HJL	LX-ARC	C-GBAP	C-GXPG			
258445	U-125A	N40708	Japan 12-3017 [code 017]						
258446	XP	N529M	(N983EC)	N983CE					
258447	XP	N40310	Brazil EU93A-6053						
258448	XP	N41280	N532PJ	N19DD	N19DU	N15RY			
258449	XP	N41431	N365AT	N717KV					
258450	XP	N41441	D-CTAN	I-DLOH	LY-LTD				
258451	XP	N41534	N475HM						
258452	XPR	N852QS	N270TX	N252XJ	N899TM				
258453	XP	N802TA	N68CB						
258454	XP	N41093	N802TA	(N826LX)	N813LX	N854FL			
258455	XP	N803TA	(N827LX)	N803FL	N500XP	N517GW*			
258456	XP	N800EM	N41762	G-JMAX	(G-UJET)	M-MIDO	G-EGSS		
258457	XP	N41984	CS-DNO	N855TM	N925MP				
258458	XP	N42685	N228TM	(SE-RIS)	SE-RLX				
258459	XP	N43259	N939LE	N800WW	N800WP	N552ME			
258460	XP	N81SN	N810N	C-FHRD	N85PK	N460WF	9G-CTH	A2-MBG	ZS-MBA
258461	XP	N804TA	N881CW	N828LX	N846FL	N32KB			
258462	XP	N43230	LV-PIW	LV-ZTR					
258463	XPR	N863QS	N298TX	N298XJ	N818TM				
258464	XP	N41964	HZ-KSRA	N828NS	N810SC				
258465	XP	N43265	ZS-DDT	VT-RPL					
258466	XP	N805TA	N866CW	N829LX	N866CW	N829LX	LV-FPW		
258467	XP	N5732	N43310	N5732	N42FB	N804JM			
258468	XP	N43436	CS-DNT	N850DP					
258469	U-125A	N43079	Japan 12-3018 [code 018]						
258470	XP	N42830	B-3991						
258471	XP2	N43642	N5736	N513BE					
258472	XPR	N44722	N872QS	N292TX	N272XJ	N820TM	N423SG		
258473	XP	N73UP							
258474	XPR	N874QS	N283TX	N274XJ	N833TM				
258475	XP	N43675	HZ-KSRB	N829NS	VP-CMB	N220JJ			

BAe 125-800 (HAWKER 800)

C/n	Series	Identities								
258476	XP	N44676	N192NC	N830NS	VT-HCB	N830NS	XA-GGP			
258477	XP	N44767	OE-GEO	VP-BOO	G-CGHY	G-MAXP	ZS-DAD			
258478	XP2	N44648	N806TA	N800DR	N989ST					
258479	XP	N44779	CS-DNU	N860TM	VT-...					
258480	XP	N4403	(N73WW)							
258481	XP	N43926	HZ-KSRC							
258482	XPR	N43182	N882QS	N277TX	N285XJ	N808TM				
258483	XP	N44883	N807TA	N830LX	N830FL					
258484	XP	N84UP								
258485	XP	N44515	(HZ-KSRD)	A7-AAL	N485LT	N125XP				
258486	XPR	N886QS	N278TX	N278XJ	N806TM					
258487	XP	N51387	N3007							
258488	XP	N50788	N488HP	N719HG						
258489	XP	N28GP	N26GP	XA-HEL						
258490	XP	N50490	N327LJ	N985CE						
258491	XP	N51191	VP-BKB	N51191	XA-TYH	N544PS				
258492	XP	N51192	N800FJ	N800LF	C-GCIX					
258493	U-125A	N40933	Japan 22-3019 [code 019]							
258494	XP	N808TA	VP-BXP	M-HAWK	N55LB					
258495	XP	N51495	C-GGCH	5B-CKL	SX-FAR	M-OBLA				
258496	XPR	N125TM	N175TM	G-RDMV	EI-ECE	N80AG	[Hawker 800XPR development aircraft; ff 09Jul11]			
		(OY-JJC)	OY-JJA							
258497	XP	N51197	N825CT	N825QT						
258498	XP	N809TA	N11UL	LY-KLA						
258499	XP	N51099	CS-DNV	N265TX	ZS-ZIM					
258500	XP	N50600	C-FPCP	C-FPCE	N400CH	N167DF				
258501	XP	N5001S	B-3992							
258502	XP2	N4469B	XA-AET	N502HR	HK-4670					
258503	XP2	N802WM	N801WM	N134CM						
258504	XP	N5004B	TC-AHS	JY-AWG	YI-ASB					
258505	XP	N50005	N805QS	N835QS	N297TX	N865TM				
258506	XP	N50166	I-RONY	(N125JN)						
258507	XP	N507BW	C-GIBU	N5G	(N296G)	N22CP				
258508	XP2	N5008S	N800PE							
258509	XP	N4109E	N509XP	N313CC	N983CE	N162JB				
258510	XP	N810TA	N890CW	N831LX						
258511	XP	N5011J	CS-DNX	N264TX	N79TS					
258512	XP	N501CT	M-VITO							
258513	U-125A	N50513	Japan 22-3020 [code 020]							
258514	XP	N4021Z	D-CHEF	(M-CHEF)	M-OOUN	5N-IZY	N255LA	4X-CUZ		
258515	XP	N321EJ	N321MS							
258516	XP	N811TA	N896CW	(N832LX)	N817LX	N415JA				
258517	XP	N817QS	N293TX	N870TM						
258518	XP	N29B								
258519	XP2	N443M	N72FC							
258520	XP	N4469U	VP-CRS	OE-GEA	VP-CEA	JY-AW4	JY-AWD	JY-WJA	JY-AWD	YI-ASC
		JY-AWD								
258521	XP	N50521	HB-VNJ	N58521	VT-RAN	A6-ICU				
258522	XP	N812TA	N746UP	N18GU	(N284RP)					
258523	XP	N5023J	N824QS	N296TX	N875TM					
258524	XP	N4224H	N7374	(N73741)	(N666BC)	N872BC	N875BC	(N875WP)		
258525	XP	N4425R	B-3993							
258526	XP	N50626	B-3995	N526XP	N837RE	N837RF	N595PL	N595PD		
258527	XP2	N813TA	N56BE	XA-RAD						
258528	XP	N828QS	N286TX	N880TM						
258529	XP	N814TA	N259RH							
258530	XP	N890SP	C-FBBF	N76LV	XA-JMR					
258531	850XP	N4469F	N259SP	N622VL	VT-HBC	N259SP	N81SF	N81SJ	N400TJ	N627MZ
		N621SB								
258532	XP	N317CC								
258533	U-125A	N50733	JASDF 32-3021 [code 021]							
258534	XP	N815TA	(N833LX)	N818LX						
258535	XP	N51335	N853QS	N255DX						
258536	XP	N51336	B-3996	N102PA	OE-GCE					
258537	XP2	N100NG	N600NG	N650JS	XB-OAE					
258538	XP	N816TA	N25853	4X-CRY	N538LD	P4-SNT	N178BH			
258539	XP	N51239	VP-BKB	JY-AW5	JY-AWE					
258540	XP2	N50440	N700MG	N571CH						
258541	XP2	N50441	N800XP	OY-FCG	N541XP					
258542	XPR	N842QS	N284TX	N286XJ	N877TM					
258543	XP	N806TA	N843CW	(N834LX)	N819LX	(N766CH)	XA-GOI			
258544	XP	N799JC	D-CXNL							
258545	XP	N50445	N845QS	N279TX	N890TM					
258546	XP2	N50461	N108BP	N488VC	N470EM	N880YY				
258547	XP	N4469N	PR-OPP	N1161G						
258548	XP	N808TA	(N835LX)	N850JL	N860JL	A6-PHS	N116JK	9G-UHI	N256LA	

BAe 125-800 (HAWKER 800 / 850)

C/n	Series	Identities							
258549	XP	N51149	N155NS						
258550	XP	N793RC							
258551	XP	N44759	N190NC	N777DB	N85594	N800LQ			
258552	XP	N817TA	(N836LX)	N834LX	XA-NIC				
258553	XP	N51453	PR-LUG						
258554	XP	N50034	(5B-CKG)	XA-GTE	N258HH	XA-HHH			
258555	XP	N820TA	N300CQ						
258556	XP2	N51556	N800WY	N512JC					
258557	XP	N51457	N1630	N1638	N987CE				
258558	XP	N51058	N225PB						
258559	XP	N50459	N819AP	N819AB	PR-FAP	N223FA	(PR-CSP)	N977AV	
258560	XP	N50740	N877S	N8778					
258561	XP	N1630	N16300	I-ALHO	N561XP	N901SC			
258562	XP	N5062H	(N877S)	N802DC	N361LA				
258563	XP	N4469M	N981CE						
258564	XP	N864QS	N295TX	N885TM	N885TR				
258565	XP	N4465M	N240Z						
258566	XP	N4466Z	N664AC						
258567	XP	N50667	N74PC	N24SM					
258568	XP2	N4468K	N96FT	N716DB					
258569	XP	N4469X	N244LS	N906AS					
258570	XP	N50670	"N873QS"	N880QS	N553BW				
258571	XP	N4471N	RP-C8576						
258572	XP	N5072L	N80FB	N293S	C-GKPP				
258573	XP	N873QS	N873TX						
258574	850XP	N51274	N915AM	(N915MT)	N915AP				
258575	XP	N3215M	B-3997						
258576	XP	N867QS	N867TX						
258577	XP	N51027	N800UK						
258578	XP	N50378	N91HK	N81HK	N406TM				
258579	XP	N50309	PK-TVO						
258580	XP	N880QS	N1989D						
258581	XP	N50661	XA-ICF	N581GE	XA-JCT	N687AC	XA-BWB		
258582	850XP	N50182	(N170SK)	XA-JMS	VP-CFS	N48AM	N800EA		
258583	XP	N50983	XA-GLG	N1730M	N55XP				
258584	XP2	N51384	N884VC	N107CE					
258585	XP2	N50285	(N885VC)	N585VC					
258586	XP	N876QS	N876VR	N876TX					
258587	XP	N50657	N261PA	N703RK	(N778CC)	(N703RE)	N770CC		
258588	XP	N44888	N799S						
258589	850XP	N51289	N974JD	N874JD	[converted to prototype 850XP]			ZS-PCY	N810AF
258590	XP2	N50910	(N890VC)	(N590VC)	N733H	(N446TW)	N130YB		
258591	XP2	N61791	N380GG	N380GP	PK-EJR				
258592	XP	N892QS	N892VR	(N592VR)	N892TX				
258593	XP	N898QS	N174WC						
258594	XP2	N61904	N140GB	N323MP	VH-RIO				
258595	XP2	N61495	N76CS	N76CY	N512WC				
258596	XP	N896QS	N596XP	N804BH					
258597	XP	N895QS	N597XP	XA-TYK					
258598	XP2	N61198	(N800JA)	N92FT	(N92FL)	N988RS			
258599	XP	N51169	N59BR						
258600	850XP	N61500	N250SP	N908NR	M-GDRS	M-ARIE			
258601	XP	N61101	ZS-DDA	N68HB	XA-PBT				
258602	XP2	(N898QS)	N61702	N899SC	N401TM				
258603	XP	N803QS	(N803CW)	N893CW	N893FL	N878MB			
258604	XP	N60664	N8186	N565SK					
258605	XP	N61805	C-GJKI	C-GJKK					
258606	XP	N60506	N895QS	N895VR	N608TX				
258607	XP	N60507	N919RT	N500AZ	N118DL				
258608	XP2	N61708	N500BN	I-KREM					
258609	XP	N60159	N80HD	N80HX	M-ABDP	4X-CUT*			
258610	U-125A	N61320	Japan 42-3022 [code 022]						
258611	XP	N809QS	(N944PP)	N944BB					
258612	XP	(N896QS)	N50522	N711GD	N612XP	OM-OIG			
258613	850XP	N90FB							
258614	XP	N811QS	N810TX						
258615	XP	N61515	VP-CKN	N615XP	HS-CPH				
258616	XP	N61216	N88HD	N88HX	N900SS	N254SB			
258617	XP	N5117F	N617XP	N551VB	N557VB	P4-SEN			
258618	XP	(N895QS)	N896QS	N618XP	N82GK	G-IWDB	A6-MAB	N527WA	N447SP
258619	XP	N61719	N676JB						
258620	XP	N61920	N620XP	N77CS	N77CX	N77CS	N356SR		
258621	XP2	N61681	(N621XP)	N522EE	N522EF	N123KH			
258622	850XP	N622XP	N800EL	N850RG	N17TV				
258623	XP	N623XP	(N823CW)	N221PB					
258624	XP	N624XP	N866RR	N660HC	N757GS				

BAe 125-800 (HAWKER 800 / 850)

C/n	Series	Identities							
258625	XP	N625XP	N305JA	VP-BNK	M-UKHA				
258626	XP	N626XP	N25W	N945SL	XA-LAS				
258627	850XP	N627XP	N929AK						
258628	850XP	N628XP	XA-JET						
258629	U-25A	N61729	Japan 52-3023 [code 023]						
258630	XP	N630XP	N125ZZ	N599AK	N215BB				
258631	XP	N631XP	N74NP	N74NB	OD-MAF				
258632	XP2	N632XP	ZS-PZA	TY-VLT	5V-TTM				
258633	XP	N633XP	N800NS	ZS-PTP	A2-MCB				
258634	XP	N808BL	N851RG						
258635	XP	N635XP	N919SF	N45KN					
258636	XP	N636XP	N800CQ	(N775RB)	N438PM				
258637	XP2	N637XP	PP-ANA	N637XP	OY-JJC				
258638	XP	N638XP	XA-NTE						
258639	XP	N639XP	N95UP						
258640	XP	N640XP	N896QS						
258641	850XP	N641XP	N513ML	N104RF					
258642	XP	N642XP	N12PA	N279CF					
258643	XP	N883CW	(N843TS)	N33NL					
258644	850XP	N644XP	N484JC	HB-VCJ	XA-PYC				
258645	XP	N645XP	N733K	(N645XP)	N733L	N618AR	OY-OAA	HB-VOT	M-HSXP
258646	850XP	N646XP	N528BP	XA-EBF					
258647	XP	N847CW	(N837LX)	(N847FL)	N864DC				
258648	XP	N848CW	(N823LX)	N848FL	N483AM	N488AM			
258649	XP	N649XP	N800EM						
258650	850XP	N650XP	N50AE	N50AN	N821LB				
258651	850XP	N651XP	N470BC	N159FM					
258652	XP	N652XP	N241JS						
258653	XP	N653XP	N203TM	(N203TR)					
258654	XP	N654XP	N149SB						
258655	XP	N655XP	N535BC	N655XP	(N16SM)	N22SM			
258656	XP	N656XP	CS-DFX	N850VR	B-3915				
258657	XP	N657XP	(N857CW)	N839LX	N417TM				
258658	850XP	N658XP	(ZS-ARK)	5N-JMA	[wfu Chester, UK]				
258659	850XP	N659XP	5N-JMB						
258660	XP	N660XP	N800RC						
258661	XP	N661XP	N800WW						
258662	XP	N662XP	N305SC	N474CF					
258663	XP	N663XP	CS-DFY	N863GJ					
258664	XP	N664XP	CS-DFW	N808NA	XA-FSA				
258665	XP	N665XP	N689AM						
258666	XP	N876CW	N840LX	N840FL	(N926JR)	N923JR			
258667	XP	N667XP	N802DR	N405TM					
258668	XP	N668XP	N156NS						
258669	XP	N669XP	N520SP	N333PC					
258670	850XP	N670XP	N1776N	ZS-PZX	ZS-AOT				
258671	XP	N671XP	N184TB	N184TR					
258672	XP	N672XP	N1CA	N191CA	N120JC				
258673	XP	N673XP	CS-DFZ	N851VR	B-3917	N851VR	F-HPUR	N851VR	
258674	XP	N674XP	N841WS	G-OJWB	G-KLOE	N475RS			
258675	XP2	N675XP	N351TC	N66ZB					
258676	XP	N676XP	N676GH						
258677	XP2	N677XP	N850CT	M-CTEM	N840CE	N850FB			
258678	XP	N678XP	N9867						
258679	XP2	N679XP	N800AH	N800LA	[w/o in hangar collapse at Washington/Dulles, VA, 06Feb10; parted out by AvMATS, St Louis, MO]				
258680	XP	N680XP	N80E	N80EH	N426TM				
258681	XP	N681XP	N80J	N80JE	N119BG				
258682	XP	N682XP	4X-CRU	D-CLBG	N682DK	P4-PRT			
258683	XP	N61343	N832QS	N683TX*					
258684	850XP	N684DK							
258685	U-125A	N36685	Japan 62-3024		[code 024]				
258686	XP	N61746	CS-DRA	N851QS	N686TX				
258687	XP	N61987	N733A	N120YB					
258688	850XP	N688G	C-FMRI	N944KR					
258689	XP	N36689	F-HBFP						
258690	XP	N36690	CS-DRB	XA-RED					
258691	XP	N858QS	XA-ELR	XA-UYQ					
258692	XP	N37092	N700R	N90WP					
258693	XP	N693XP	N302PE	N322PE	N277RS				
258694	XP	N36894	N800R	N694FJ	N694ES				
258695	XP	N695XP	N39H	CC-AME	N515JM				
258696	XP2	N36896	N800PL						
258697	XP	N697XP	N530SM	N137LA	N133KS				
258698	XP	N860QS	N698TX						
258699	850XP	N699XP							

BAe 125-800 (HAWKER 800 / 850)

C/n	Series	Identities						
258700	XP2	N108DD	N212RG					
258701	XP	N501XP	N6NR					
258702	XP2	N841LX	N96SK	N966K	VP-BAS	XA-DAK		
258703	XP	N50553	N707JC	N707JQ				
258704	XP2	N614BG	N312KG	N898DD				
258705	XP	N815QS						
258706	XP	N706XP	N74GW					
258707	XP	N707XP	LV-PJL	LV-BBG				
258708	850XP	N799RM						
258709	XP	N709XP+	[+marks worn but not registered as such]				N821QS	N823TX*
258710	XP	N37010	G-CDLT	OD-EKF				
258711	XP	N37211	N1910A	N514SK*				
258712	XP	N36672	N18AQ	VH-MBP	VH-MEP	N713SC		
258713	850XP	N713XP	N199DF	XA-SJM	N110GD			
258714	XP	N61944	CS-DRC	N852QS	N874TX			
258715	850XP	N715XP	N715PH	XA-JBT	XA-JBG			
258716	XP	N716XP	VT-RBK	VT-ABG				
258717	850XP	N717XP	ZS-PPH					
258718	XP	N718XP	N718SJ					
258719	XP	N19XP	VP-BCW					
258720	XP	N36820	OM-USS	N720XP	N427TM			
258721	XP	N36621	CS-DRD	N853QS				
258722	XP	N37322	I-PZZR					
258723	850XP	N723XP	N627AK	M-YCEF	VH-RIU			
258724	850XP	N724XP	ZS-AFG	ZS-TNF				
258725	XPi	N30355	CS-DRE	N854QS	N854TX	N528MX		
258726	XP2	N726XP	N405LA					
258727	850XP	N787JC	XA-CHK					
258728	XPi	N728XP	N110DD	VP-CXP	N800WF			
258729	850XP	N729XP	N729AG	N232EH				
258730	XPi	N37060	CS-DRF	N855QS	N707BM			
258731	850XP	N37061	XA-UGO	XA-CHG	XA-LEY			
258732	XPi	N870QS	N872TX*					
258733	XPi	N333XP	HB-VOB	N280CB				
258734	XPi	N884QS						
258735	U-125A	N6135H	Japan 72-3025					
258736	XPi	N136XP	TC-TAV					
258737	850XP	N518M						
258738	XPi	N138XP	TC-ADO					
258739	XPi	N739XP	N499PA					
258740	XP2	N740XP	N824LX	(N824FL)				
258741	XPi	N36841	CS-DRG	N741VR				
258742	850XP	N742XP	TC-FIN	N742XP	N299JM	XA-RCE		
258743	XPi	N885QS	N743TX*					
258744	850XP	N744XP						
258745	850XP	N745XP	VT-FAF					
258746	XPi	N6046J	CS-DRH					
258747	850XP	N519M	N519MN	N100AG				
258748	850XP	N748XP	EC-JNY	TC-ILY	N451RS	OE-GMI		
258749	850XP	N36669	N50UG	XA-GBP				
258750	850XP	N950XP	N1776A	Mozambique FAM-002				
258751	850XP	N751MT						
258752	850XP	N752MT						
258753	850XP	N805M	N546MG	N544MG	XA-DAR			
258754	850XP	N37054	N754AE	N754AF	CC-AEN	N295JM		
258755	850XP	N575JR	VP-CDE					
258756	XPi	N37056	CS-DRI	N75GR				
258757	850XP	N757XP	N345MP	N437JD	N437JR	XA-OLA		
258758	850XP	N37158	N725CS	N858XP				
258759	850XP	N801RR	N426MJ					
258760	XPi	N37160	CS-DRJ	LY-LTA				
258761	850XP	N761XP						
258762	850XP	N762XP	N901SG	N801SG	PR-FAF	N71LG	PR-FNE	
258763	XPi	N871QS	N870TX*					
258764	850XP	N764XP	N522EE					
258765	XPi	N61285	CS-DRK	N868QS	N868TX	N705BB*		
258766	850XP	N542M						
258767	XPi	N767XP	(N143RL)	N825LX	N825FL	N429TM		
258768	850XP	N768XP	N850VP					
258769	850XP	N769XP	CC-CAB	N630GS				
258770	XPi	N36970	CS-DRL					
258771	XPi	N6171U	CS-DRM	N869QS	N877TX			
258772	XPi	N672XP	CS-DRN					
258773	XPi	N883QS	N773TX*					
258774	850XP	N774XP	N143RL	N820M	N774WF			
258775	XPi	N37105	CS-DRO	N875TX				

BAe 125-800 (HAWKER 800 / 850)

C/n	Series	Identities						
258776	850XP	N36726	N535BC	N776RS	(N2707)			
258777	850XP	N877XP	N900ST	N900SK	N694PD	N694BD	N201LS	
258778	850XP	N36578	OE-IPH	N36578	M-IRNE			
258779	XPi	N37179	CS-DRP	N779TX				
258780	850XP	N37070	VH-SGY					
258781	850XP	N37261	A6-ELC	N146DJ	N73SL			
258782	850XP	N782XP	(N706CW)	(N260G)	N126HY	N830		
258783	XPi	N37146	CS-DRQ	N783TX				
258784	850XP	N784XP	N76FC	N850RC	N850MS*			
258785	850XP	N785XP	N785VC					
258786	XPi	N36986	CS-DRR	N878TX				
258787	850XP	N72617	N851CC	(N815RK)				
258788	850XP	N891QS						
258789	850XP	N789XP	N850NS	N850EC				
258790	850XP	N790XP	TC-TKC					
258791	850XP	N70791	N255RB					
258792	850XP	N792XP	A6-TBF	OD-LEA				
258793	850XP	N793XP	TC-STB	M-CSTB	TC-SBL			
258794	850XP	N71794	VT-JHP					
258795	XPi	N37295	CS-DRS	N879TX				
258796	850XP	N796XP	N850KE	N858KE	C-GTUF			
258797	U-125A	N71907	Japan 82-3026		Japan 92-3026			
258798	850XP	N798XP	N850ZH	N850TM				
258799	850XP	N37009	HB-VOJ	XA-DAD	N452RS	N850EZ		
258800	850XP	N880XP	N865JT	N465VC	N269AA			
258801	850XP	N7101Z	(N906BL)	TC-DOY	N72LA			
258802	XPi	N7102Z	CS-DRT	N802TX				
258803	850XP	N853CC						
258804	850XP	N71904	OE-GRS	OD-SKY	[w/o 04Feb11 Sulamaniyah, Iraq]			
258805	850XP	N71025	EI-KJC	A6-AUJ	VT-SSN	RP-C850		
258806	850XP	N36826	N906BL					
258807	850XP	N36878	VH-MQY					
258808	850XP	N70708	TC-CLK	N220PK	N228PK	N850PE		
258809	850XP	N70409	I-TOPH					
258810	850XP	N71010	OE-GJA	G-CERX				
258811	850XP	N71881	LY-DSK	OE-GWP	LY-DSK			
258812	850XP	N812XP	D-CLBH	N359BC				
258813	850XP	N73793	OE-GRF	VQ-BVA				
258814	850XP	N70214	N189TA	VH-TNX	N85NX	C-GMGB	N669CC	
258815	850XP	N74155	VT-KNB					
258816	850XP	N74166	(N850ZH)	VP-COD	M-FRZN	M-ABGL	N816TR	PP-CNS
258817	850XP	N37170	N85HH					
258818	850XP	N403CT						
258819	850XP	N405CT	VT-ARR	N277SR				
258820		[Hawker 900XP c/n HA-0001]						
258821	XPi	N73721	CS-DRU					
258822	850XP	N822XP	N103AL	N915TB				
258823	850XP	N823XP	N150GF					
258824	U-125A	N60724	Japan 02-3027					
258825	XPi	N3725Z	CS-DRV					
258826	850XP	N826LX	PT-FPM					
258827	850XP	N7077S	G-HSXP					
258828	850XP	N7128T	C-GCGT					
258829	XPi	N73729	CS-DRW					
258830	850XP	N72520	N111ZN	HS-PEK				
258831	850XP	N676AH						
258832	850XP	N74142	SU-MAN					
258833	850XP	N72233	HS-CPG					
258834	XPi	N71934	CS-DRX					
258835	850XP	N7235R	VP-CMA	VT-AGP				
258836	850XP	N7236L	N773HR	TC-MAN				
258837	850XP	N662JN						
258838	850XP	N71938	VT-OBR					
258839		[Hawker 900XP c/n HA-0002]						
258840	XPi	N70040	CS-DRY					
258841	850XP	N70431	VP-BMM	N914CE	N159MN	N159MJ		
258842		[Hawker 900XP c/n HA-0003]						
258843	U-125A	N63600	Japan 12-3028					
258844	850XP	N71944	VH-RAM	VH-PNF	N230PA	PP-JFZ		
258845	850XP	N72645	TC-STD	M-CSTD	YL-KSD			
258846		[Hawker 900XP c/n HA-0004]						
258847	XPi	N74476	CS-DRZ					
258848	850XP	N827LX	N404TM					

Production continued as a mix of special-order Hawker 850XPs using the old-style 6-digit c/n sequence, Hawker 900XPs with c/ns starting HA- and Hawker 750s with c/ns starting HB-. The latter two models are shown in their own separate production lists.

BAe 125-800 (HAWKER 800 / 850)

C/n	Series	Identities				
258849 to 258851		[c/ns not used]				
258852	850XP	N7302P	C-GROG			
258853 to 258854		[c/ns not used]				
258855	850XP	N7255U	LX-OKR	F-GVIA	VP-BNW	
258856	850XP	N7256C	B-3901	N375BC		
258857		[c/n not used]				
258858	850XP	N71958	B-3902	N641RP		
258859	850XP	N859XP	OE-GNY	P4-WIN		
258860		[c/n not used]				
258861	850XP	N861ME	N850ME	N347JR		
258862 to 258871		[c/ns not used]				
258872	850XP	N872XP	TC-SHE			
258873		[c/n not used]				
258874	850XP	N874XP	TC-NUB	N841TC		
258875		[c/n not used]				
258876	850XP	N349AK	N349AS	N850EM	M-ARIA	N97KL
258877 to 258890		[c/ns not used]				
258891	850XP	N31991	(N315ML)	N315JL		
258892		[c/n not used]				
258893	850XP	N1620	N162G	N900WS		
258894		[c/n not used]				
258895	850XP	N3195F	HB-VOY	M-RACE	VH-BMW	
258896 to 258899		[c/ns not used]				
258900	850XP	N850HB	N440CX			
258901	850XP	N3201T	EI-GEM	N658DM	N107LT	
258902 to 258903		[c/ns not used]				
258904	850XP	N3204T	VT-BTA	N904JC	XA-IJC	
258905 to 258906		[c/ns not used]				
258907	850XP	N3207T	N448H	(N4424)		
258908		[c/n not used]				
258909	850XP	N3289N	VT-BTB	N997BX	XA-XXX	
258910 to 258911		[c/ns not used]				
258912	850XP	N32012	VT-BTC	N800CL		
258913 to 258914		[c/ns not used]				
258915	850XP	N3115Y	N383MR	T7-TUN		
258916 to 258920		[c/ns not used]				
258921	850XP	N32061	N888WY			
258922 to 258958		[c/ns not used]				
258959	850XP	N3400S				
258960		[c/n not used]				
258961	850XP	N3201P	N850KE			
258962		[c/n not used]				
258963	850XP	N3193B	N437WR	N963XP*		
258964 to 258976		[c/ns not used]				
258977	850XP	N977LC				
258978 to 258979		[c/ns not used]				
258980	850XP	N3188X	VT-FTL			
258981		[c/n not used]				
258982	850XP	N3482Y	P4-NUR	N982XP	Pakistan 101	
258983	850XP	N62783	N438WR			
258984	850XP	N63984	XA-KBA	N984MS	5N-SPL	

Production complete

HAWKER 900XP

The Hawker 900XP is a re-engined development of the Hawker 850XP.

C/n	Fuselage	Identities					
HA-0001	258820	N90XP	N170DC				
HA-0002	258839	N1776C					
HA-0003	258842	N903XP	A6-PJB	N330GW			
HA-0004	258846	N904XP	N351SP				
HA-0005	258849	N894QS					
HA-0006	258851	N71956	N96SK				
HA-0007	258853	N807HB	N77TC	N77CS			
HA-0008	258854	N900LD	N855FC				
HA-0009	258857	N809HB	N901K	N907PJ			
HA-0010	258860	N890QS					
HA-0011	258862	N211XP	C-GGMP	N297TX			
HA-0012	258863	N852CC	N526PS	N349JF			
HA-0013	258864	N113XP	N900R	N903R			
HA-0014	258865	N897QS					
HA-0015	258866	N915XP	C-GVMP				
HA-0016	258867	N575MA					
HA-0017	258868	N917XP	ZS-KBS	T7-KBS			
HA-0018	258869	N901RD	OK-HWK				
HA-0019	258870	N889QS	N899QS				
HA-0020	258871	N920XP	P4-ALA	N288KR	N900VA		
HA-0021	258873	N899QS	N889QS	N820LR			
HA-0022	258875	N922XP	N900PF	N900BF			
HA-0023	258877	N923XP	HZ-BIN				
HA-0024	258879	N924XP	N108PJ	N752AR			
HA-0025	258880	N33055	P4-ANG				
HA-0026	258881	N32926	ZS-SAH	M-SAPT	N838LJ	N703CD	
HA-0027	258882	N33527	N799AG				
HA-0028	258883	N31958	B-MBD	N25HA	XA-BNG		
HA-0029	258884	N700WY					
HA-0030	258885	N930XP	N630JS	N638JS*			
HA-0031	258886	N848QS					
HA-0032	258887	N932BC	ZS-SGJ	ZS-BOT	N762JP		
HA-0033	258888	N933XP	EC-KMT	N733DB	N581RS*		
HA-0034	258889	N31624	OK-KAZ	9H-KAZ			
HA-0035	258890	N33235	P4-PET	G-DLTC	N33235	N111MD	
HA-0036	258892	N34956	B-MBE	N130AB	XA-RGO		
HA-0037	258894	N865LS	N918JL				
HA-0038	258896	N34838	HB-VPJ	N900MJ			
HA-0039	258897	N580RJ					
HA-0040	258898	N16SM					
HA-0041	258899	N34441	G-ODUR				
HA-0042	258902	N888QS					
HA-0043	258903	N87PK					
HA-0044	258906	N944XP	VH-EVF	N881JC			
HA-0045	258908	N3285N	XA-AET				
HA-0046	258910	N31946	TC-KHA				
HA-0047	258911	N22VS					
HA-0048	258914	N34548	A6-RZB	A7-RZB	G-ORYX	(OE-GIS)	TT-ABF
HA-0049	258916	N31959	VH-ACE	N99GM	PP-HVD		
HA-0050	258918	N881QS					
HA-0051	258920	N951XP	CS-DGZ	TC-ACL	TC-ASH	[or TC-NRY, see also c/n HA-0092]	
HA-0052	258922	N104AG	(N952XP)	XA-KBL			
HA-0053	258924	N3193L	B-3903	N953XP			
HA-0054	258926	N878QS					
HA-0055	258928	N32185	N816SE	N919DW			
HA-0056	258927	N3386A	(D-BGRL)	I-BBGR			
HA-0057	258931	N900PE					
HA-0058	258933	N3088A	M-AJOR	N753BJ			
HA-0059	258935	N3400D	M-INOR	N272BW			
HA-0060	258937	N3260J	LY-FSK				
HA-0061	258939	N34451	VT-ICA				
HA-0062	258940	N32862	N900XP				
HA-0063	258942	N3363U	N288MB	N190HS			
HA-0064	258943	N31964	VH-NKD	N313ZP			
HA-0065	tbc	N365JR	N819JR				
HA-0066	tbc	N877QS					
HA-0067	tbc	N3217H	ZS-SGV	N309KR			
HA-0068	tbc	N3198C	XA-ESP				
HA-0069	tbc	N3198V	CS-DPA				
HA-0070	258955	N3207Y	N902BE	N131JR	N902BE		
HA-0071	258957	N3371D	(D-CAJA)	(M-ABCE)	PK-JBH		
HA-0072	258959	N33612	M-LCJP	5N-YYY			
HA-0073	258961	N3283V	M-ONAV				
HA-0074	258962	N3204W	I-MFAB				

HAWKER 900XP

C/n	Fuselage	Identities					
HA-0075	258966	N869QS	(N975XP)	N979TM	N979TB		
HA-0076	258968	N300R	N330R	N100R	N109R		
HA-0077	258970	N710HM	N702CS				
HA-0078	258972	N3378M	PP-ARG				
HA-0079	258975	N190SW					
HA-0080	258980	N31842	A6-HWK				
HA-0081	258978	N3217G	(N902BE)				
HA-0082	258979	N3222W	(N979TM)	N159M	N479M		
HA-0083	258981	N83XP	"M-HARP"+	[+marks worn but ntu]		M-NICO	N901AG
HA-0084	258984	N984XP	VP-CIS	N991PS			
HA-0085	258986	N985RM	EI-JJJ	VT-AJM			
HA-0086	258988	N986XP	TC-ENK				
HA-0087	258973	N87XP	N865JM	N451CG			
HA-0088	258989	N988AG	XA-DLV				
HA-0089	258990	N60089	PR-DBD	N416RR			
HA-0090	258985	N63890	F-HGBY	VP-CFS			
HA-0091	259101	N61391	CN-RBS				
HA-0092	259103	N64292	CS-DPJ	TC-TSH	TC-NRY	[or TC-ASH, see also c/n HA-0051]	
HA-0093	259106	N30VP					
HA-0094	258982	N301ML					
HA-0095	259113	N62895	(A6-HBC)	A7-RZD	VP-CBU	G-ORXX	N887PC
HA-0096	259107	N996XP	"LX-KSD"+	[+marks worn at factory but ntu; aircraft not delivered, parted out]			
HA-0097	259111	N62297	D2-EAA	P4-HBS	N375TW		
HA-0098	259112	N6198P	TC-CLG				
HA-0099	259115	N60099	M-LION				
HA-0100	259104	N125ML	VT-UPM				
HA-0101	259116	N15QB	N901MJ				
HA-0102	259109	N6452L	(ZS-HWK)	N955SE	N17EN*		
HA-0103	259120	N6403N	VT-BKL				
HA-0104	259124	N6434R	ZS-SME				
HA-0105	259125	N900FG	N900FU	N105XP	N21FX	N21FZ	N712BS
HA-0106	259118	N803D	N69FR				
HA-0107		N107XP	OE-GYP	N232EA			
HA-0108	259121	N6408F	VQ-BPH	N252DH			
HA-0109		[not built, order cancelled]					
HA-0110		N804D	N54VM				
HA-0111		[not built, order cancelled]					
HA-0112		N63812	G-OTAZ	N374HM			
HA-0113		N805D					
HA-0114		N62914	TC-MOH				
HA-0115		[not built, order cancelled]					
HA-0116		[not built, order cancelled]					
HA-0117		N117XP	N437JD				
HA-0118		[not built, order cancelled]					
HA-0119		(CS-DPK)	[not built, order cancelled]				
HA-0120		N60820	N239RT				
HA-0121		N6151C	M-JOLY	N524HA			
HA-0122		N859QS	(N869QS)	N122XP	[registered but not built]		
HA-0123		[not built, order cancelled]					
HA-0124		[not built, order cancelled]					
HA-0125		[not built, order cancelled]					
HA-0126		[not built, order cancelled]					
HA-0127		[not built, order cancelled]					
HA-0128		[not built, order cancelled]					
HA-0129		[not built, order cancelled]					
HA-0130		[not built, order cancelled]					
HA-0131		[not built, order cancelled]					
HA-0132		N857QS	N132XP	[registered but not built]			
HA-0133		[not built, order cancelled]					
HA-0134		[not built, order cancelled]					
HA-0135		[not built, order cancelled]					
HA-0136		[not built, order cancelled]					
HA-0137		[not built, order cancelled]					
HA-0138		[not built, order cancelled]					
HA-0139		[not built, order cancelled]					
HA-0140		N6340T	LX-KAT	G-KTIA	M-CKAY		
HA-0141		[not built, order cancelled]					
HA-0142		[not built, order cancelled]					
HA-0143		N6273X	G-OZAT	9H-ZAT	G-URTH	N900QC	
HA-0144		[not built, order cancelled]					
HA-0145		[not built, order cancelled]					
HA-0146		N146XP	N702A				
HA-0147		N147XP	N703A				
HA-0148		N148XP	OD-MIG				
HA-0149		N149XP	XA-XEL				
HA-0150		N950XP	N916JB				

HAWKER 900XP

C/n	Fuselage	Identities			
HA-0151		N6351Y	OM-USS	N154X	N377JC
HA-0152		N6452S	G-RGSG	N26XP	
HA-0153		N153XP	HZ-A8		
HA-0154		N154XP	N85PK		
HA-0155		N155XP	N80E	N337CC	
HA-0156		N156XP	N80J		
HA-0157		N157XP	N308GW		
HA-0158		N158XP	CN-TJS		
HA-0159		N6409A	HK-4758		
HA-0160		N160XP	N146JF		
HA-0161		N161XP	OE-GYB	9H-GYB	
HA-0162		N362XP			
HA-0163		N163XP	N459M	N879M	
HA-0164		N964XP	N835ZP	N100ZT	
HA-0165		N165XP	VT-LTA		
HA-0166		N166XP	N104AG	VP-CAG	N305KR
HA-0167		N167XP	B-3909		
HA-0168		N6368D	N50AE		
HA-0169		N81239	N51HH		
HA-0170		N970XP	TC-DMR		
HA-0171		N171XP	N754AE		
HA-0172		N972XP	N627TF		
HA-0173		N173XP	HZ-A9		
HA-0174		N174XP	N844JD		
HA-0175		N975XP	B-3912	N752SC	N234GF
HA-0176		N176XP	N75CS		
HA-0177		N977XP	9H-BOF	VP-CSD	N144UV
HA-0178		N178XP	N76CS		
HA-0179		N979XP	N571KG		
HA-0180		N980XP	OE-GOA	N36CD	
HA-0181		N181XP			
HA-0182		N82XP	YR-NAY		
HA-0183		N183XP	N118UF		
HA-0184		N184XP	D-CHGN	N184HA	N977HG
HA-0185		N985XP	VT-LTC		
HA-0186		N186XP	G-KLNE		
HA-0187		N187XP	VT-UDR		
HA-0188		N188XP	PK-JBB		
HA-0189		N189XP	N804AC		
HA-0190		N190XP	N1910H		
HA-0191		N191XP	N900ER		
HA-0192		N192XP	N192SA		
HA-0193		N193XP	N193BK		
HA-0194		N194XP	N638MA	5N-...	
HA-0195		N195XP	N979CF		
HA-0196		N396XP	N902MS		
HA-0197		N197XP	UP-HA001		
HA-0198		N198XP	LV-CTE		
HA-0199		N899XP	PP-WAV	N199FJ	
HA-0200		N888XP	PK-CAR		
HA-0201		N901XP	N536BW		
HA-0202		N902XP	N482MG		
HA-0203		N203XP	N251SP		
HA-0204		N204XP	CS-DSE		
HA-0205		N205XP	PR-DPD	N630AB	
HA-0206		N206XP	PT-MIA		
HA-0207		N907XP	PK-LRT		
HA-0208		N908XP	N515JM	XA-CAB	
HA-0209		N209XP	N900PF		
HA-0210		N910XP	M-ALBA	OE-GJL	N963JB
HA-0211		N211XP	N29GP		
HA-0212		N812XP	PK-LRU		
HA-0213		N903XP	N900LD		
HA-0214		(N214XP)	[aircraft built but not delivered; stored unmarked at Wichita/Beech Field, KS]		

Production complete. The following aircraft also had marks assigned in anticipation of being built:

HA-0215	(N915XP)
HA-0216	(N216XP)
HA-0217	(N217XP)
HA-0218	(N218XP)
HA-0219	(N219XP)
HA-0220	(N920XP)
HA-0221	(N221XP)

HAWKER 750

The Hawker 750 is a re-engined development of the Hawker 800XPi.

C/n	Fuselage	Identities					
HB-1	258850	N750HB	(N751NS)	B-MBF	N170FA	XA-MLA	
HB-2	258878	N752HB	(N752NS)	(N751NS)	N787FF	N626BS	
HB-3	258905	N752NS	N770GS				
HB-4	258913	N804HB	CS-DUA				
HB-5	258917	N31685	CS-DUB				
HB-6	258919	N3206V	(CS-DUA)	CS-DUC			
HB-7	258923	N3207V	(CS-DUB)	(N753NS)	VT-RSR		
HB-8	258925	N3198Z	CS-DUD	N809TX			
HB-9	258929	N3501Q	B-MBG	N750FA	XA-OAC	XA-UXZ	
HB-10	258930	N3210N	(N232AV)	XA-DPA			
HB-11	258932	N3211G	CS-DUE	N815TX			
HB-12	258934	N3212H	N750KH				
HB-13	258936	N3093T	B-MBH	N264TC			
HB-14	258938	N3194Q	(M-OANH)	N555RU	G-NLPA	G-TWIY	
HB-15	258941	N3215J	PR-NCJ	N40AG			
HB-16	tbc	N3216R	XA-AFS				
HB-17	tbc	N3217D	HZ-KSRD				
HB-18	tbc	N3418C	N750EL				
HB-19	tbc	N3491F	CS-DUF	N891TX			
HB-20	258960	N3220K	CS-DUG	N798TX			
HB-21	258964	N3201K	CS-DUH	N796TX			
HB-22	258967	N3222S	XA-AEM	XA-NXT	N232CS	XA-MAM	
HB-23	258969	N3433D	N751NS				
HB-24	258971	N3417F	(CS-DUI)	EC-KXS	9H-BSA		
HB-25	258974	N3285Q	B-MBI	N90SA	XA-EGE		
HB-26	258977	N3276L	N209HP				
HB-27	258976	N3497J	N666NF	M-INXS	G-ZIPR	F-HOSB	N341CW
HB-28	258983	N3488P	N752NS				
HB-29	258987	N3197K	N753NS				
HB-30	259110	N730HB	(C-GXMP)	VT-CMO			
HB-31	259102	N731TH	(C-GYMP)	N200RG			
HB-32	259105	N732HB	I-EPAM				
HB-33	259100	N63633	ES-PHR				
HB-34	259119	N760NS	N434HB	YR-MSS	OE-GBG	VP-BSX	
HB-35		N735XP	N750HM				
HB-36		[not built, order cancelled]					
HB-37		[not built, order cancelled]					
HB-38		[not built, order cancelled]					
HB-39		[not built, order cancelled]					
HB-40		[not built, order cancelled]					
HB-41		N62991	N219TF	N1986R			
HB-42		[not built, order cancelled]					
HB-43		N761NS	N743HB	N787CA	N259CA	N787CA	N307ST
HB-44		[not built, order cancelled]					
HB-45		[not built, order cancelled]					
HB-46		[not built, order cancelled]					
HB-47		[not built, order cancelled]					
HB-48		[not built, order cancelled]					
HB-49		[not built, order cancelled]					
HB-50		[not built, order cancelled]					
HB-51		[not built, order cancelled]					
HB-52		[not built, order cancelled]					
HB-53		[not built, order cancelled]					
HB-54		[not built, order cancelled]					
HB-55		[not built, order cancelled]					
HB-56		[not built, order cancelled]					
HB-57		[not built, order cancelled]					
HB-58		[not built, order cancelled]					
HB-59		[not built, order cancelled]					
HB-60		[not built, order cancelled]					
HB-61		[not built, order cancelled]					
HB-62		N762XP	N93KW				
HB-63		N6173K	N750SG				
HB-64		[not built, order cancelled]					
HB-65		N6405K	M-OLLE	VQ-BBQ			
HB-66		[not built, order cancelled]					
HB-67		N767HB	I-EDLO				
HB-68		N768HB	N605ML				
HB-69		N769HB	N750VM				
HB-70		N770HB	SP-CEO				
HB-71		N771HB	N599LP				
HB-72		N772HB	N327MP				
HB-73		N773HB	XA-JVG				
HB-74		N774HB	D-CFIC	HL7778			

Production complete

SERIES 1000 (BAe 1000) (HAWKER 1000)

C/n		Series	Identities								
259001		B	[built as c/n 258151]		G-EXLR	[ff 16Jun90; reported wfu Nov93; see c/n 258151]					
259002		B	[built as c/n 258159]		G-OPFC	N10855	[see c/n 258159; canx 05Sep03 as b/u]				
259003		B	G-5-702	G-ELRA	[built between c/ns 258195-6]			N503QS	(N503LR)	N261PA	
259004		B	G-LRBJ	G-5-779	VR-CPT	VP-CPT	M-ACPT				
259005	NA1000	A	G-BTTX	G-5-735	N1AB	N81AB	N410US	N505QS	N505LR	(N990TB)	N982LC
259006	NA1001	A	G-BTTG	N1000U	N100U	(N108U)	N850JA				
259007		B/A	G-BTSI	N84WA	N119PW	N119U					
259008		B/A	G-5-720	HZ-OFC	HZ-OFC2	N195L	D-CADA	N207TT			
259009	NA1002	A	G-5-716	G-BTYN	N229U	N168WU	XA-UTB				
259010	NA1009	A	G-5-722	(HZ-...)	N125CJ	N52SM					
259011	NA1003	A	G-5-717	G-BTYO	N14GD	N208R	N208L	XA-UVY			
259012		B/A	G-5-726	HZ-SJP2	N512QS	(N512HR)	N512LR	I-SRAF	VP-BMX		
259013	NA1004	A	G-5-711	G-BTYP	N125BA	N513QS	(N513RA)	N513LR			
259014	NA1005	A	G-5-712	G-BTYR	N680BA	N125CJ	N514QS	N514LR			
259015	NA1006	A	G-5-718	G-BTYS	N1000E	N515QS	N515LR				
259016		B/A	(D-BJET)	G-5-732	G-BULI	(5N-...)	G-5-732	N291H	N678SB	N707HD	
259017		B	G-5-719	ZS-NEW	ZS-AVL	N963H	N204R	N517QS	N517LR	A6-ELA	N517LR
			(N868GB)								
259018		B	G-5-741	5N-FGR	5N-DGN						
259019	NA1007	A	G-5-730	N125CA	N792H	N2SG	N600LS	N448CC	N730CJ		
259020	NA1008	A	G-5-723	N676BA	N520QS	N520LR	(N405FF)				
259021		B/A	G-5-736	G-BUKW	XA-GRB	N5794J	VR-CMZ	VP-CMZ	N137RP	N401FF	HB-VOQ
259022		B	G-5-734	VH-LMP							
259023	NA1010	A	G-5-729	(VH-...)	N679BA	N523QS	N523LR	XA-FRC			
259024		B	G-5-737	G-BUIX	N5ES	N263R	N524QS	N524LR	A6-ELB	N524LR	(G-WWDB)
			ZS-ABG	ZS-CFA	N524LR						
259025		B	G-5-759	(5N-...)	G-BVDL	N292H	N525QS	N501LR	N770RG		
259026		B	G-5-743	ZS-CCT	ZS-ACT	N9026	G-GDEZ	P4-MAF	G-GDEZ	F-HMED	
259027		B	G-5-746	5H-BLM	G-BVLO	N333RL	N333RU	N333RL			
259028		B	G-5-749	D-CBWW	N46WC	N46WE					
259029		B	G-5-751	G-BUNW	EK-B021+	EZ-B021					
259030		B/A	G-5-753	G-BUPL	G-DCCI	N530QS	N430LR	LN-SUU	HB-VOO	N271V	
			[cx 08Oct15; wfu]								
259031		B/A	G-5-754	G-BUUY	G-HJCB	N301PH	N301PE	N301PB	N777VC	N511BK	
259032		B/A	G-5-760	ZS-NHL	F-WQAU	G-BWCB	VR-CXX	VP-CXX	N401LS	N300LS	N850TC
			N850FC	XC-LNC	N850FC	N70PJ	XA-PAG				
259033		A	G-5-756	N684BA	N850BL	N533QS	N533LR				
259034		B	G-5-761	G-BUWX	N290H	N81HH	G-GMAB	F-....			
259035		A	G-5-773	N160BA	N535QS	N525LR	N567CL				
259036		A	G-5-762	N161BA	N1AB	N127RP	(N402FF)	N600MV	N767CJ		
259037		B	G-5-771	G-SCCC	G-SHEC	XA-TGK	XA-RGG	G-FINK	M-FINK	[wfu Southend]	
259038		A	G-5-776	N167BA	N125GM	N107RP	N403FF	N67WE			
259039		A	G-5-781	N169BA	N539QS	N539LR	N39QJ				
259040		A	G-5-783	N22UP	N540QS	N540LR	(N904H)				
259041		A	G-5-785	(N937H)	N936H	N541QS	N541LR				
259042		A	G-5-789	N941H	N542QS	N542LR	N888GJ				
259043			G-5-794	N948H	[first Hawker 1000]		(N543QS)	TC-AKH	(N881JT)	XA-RYB	N698DC
			(N117CP)	N8888H	(N626PM)						
259044			G-5-797	N956H	N544QS	N544LR					
259045			G-5-801	(N296H)	N545QS	(N545LR)	N207R	N207K			
259046			G-5-805	N962H	N546QS	N546LR					
259047			G-5-817	N296H	N547QS	N547LR					
259048			G-5-826	N802H	N548QS	N548LR					
259049			G-5-837	N679H	N549QS	N549LR	VP-B..				
259050			G-5-846	N550QS	N150LR						
259051			G-5-859	N551QS	N551LR	N880LT					
259052			G-5-863	N552QS	N552LR	N800WD					

Production complete

125 NA NUMBER DECODE

NA	C/n	NA	C/n	NA	C/n	NA	C/n	NA	C/n
NA700	25134	NA764	25262	NA0248	257066	NA0312	257162	NA0429	258141
NA701	25136	NA765	25263	NA0249	257068	NA0313	257153	NA0430	258142
NA702	25137	NA766	25265	NA0250	257069	NA0314	257164	NA0431	258144
NA703	25139	NA767	25267	NA0251	257071	NA0315	257165	NA0432	258145
NA704	25141	NA768	25273	NA0252	257072	NA0316	257167	NA0433	258147
NA705	25142	NA769	25275	NA0253	257074	NA0317	257168	NA0434	258150
NA706	25146	NA770	25276	NA0254	257075	NA0318	257170	NA0435	258157
NA707	25160	NA771	25278	NA0255	257077	NA0319	257171	NA0436	258160
NA708	25161	NA772	25279	NA0256	257078	NA0320	257173	NA0437	258161
NA709	25163	NA773	25280	NA0257	257080	NA0321	257174	NA0438	258162
NA710	25170	NA774	25281	NA0258	257081	NA0322	257176	NA0439	258166
NA711	25173	NA775	25282	NA0259	257083	NA0323	257161	NA0440	258168
NA712	25174	NA776	25283	NA0260	257084	NA0324	257177	NA0441	258170
NA713	25175	NA777	25284	NA0261	257086	NA0325	257143	NA0442	258171
NA714	25176	NA778	25285	NA0262	257087	NA0326	257144	NA0443	258163
NA715	25179	NA779	25286	NA0263	257089	NA0327	257179	NA0444	258172
NA716	25180	NA780	25287	NA0264	257090	NA0328	257180	NA0445	258174
NA717	25183	NA0201	257002	NA0265	257092	NA0329	257182	NA0446	258175
NA718	25187	NA0202	257003	NA0266	257093	NA0330	257183	NA0447	258173
NA719	25188	NA0203	257005	NA0267	257095	NA0331	257185	NA0448	258179
NA720	25185	NA0204	257006	NA0268	257079	NA0332	257186	NA0449	258178
NA721	25186	NA0205	257008	NA0269	257098	NA0333	257188	NA0450	258181
NA722	25190	NA0206	257009	NA0270	257099	NA0334	257195	NA0451	258183
NA723	25191	NA0207	257011	NA0271	257110	NA0335	257198	NA0452	258185
NA724	25192	NA0208	257012	NA0272	257101	NA0336	257191	NA0453	258187
NA725	25193	NA0209	257014	NA0273	257104	NA0337	257192	NA0454	258188
NA726	25195	NA0210	257015	NA0274	257105	NA0338	257193	NA0455	258189
NA727	25196	NA0211	257017	NA0275	257106	NA0339	257145	NA0456	258191
NA728	25198	NA0212	257018	NA0276	257096	NA0340	257199	NA0457	258193
NA729	25200	NA0213	257019	NA0277	257111	NA0341	257201	NA0458	258195
NA730	25201	NA0214	257021	NA0278	257108	NA0342	257202	NA0459	258196
NA731	25202	NA0215	257023	NA0279	257113	NA0343	257204	NA0460	258199
NA732	25203	NA0216	257016	NA0280	257102	NA0344	257206	NA0461	258200
NA733	25204	NA0217	257024	NA0281	257114	NA0345	257207	NA0462	258202
NA734	25205	NA0218	257004	NA0282	257116	NA0346	257208	NA0463	258203
NA735	25206	NA0219	257026	NA0283	257117	NA0347	257210	NA0464	258204
NA736	25207	NA0220	257027	NA0284	257119	NA0401	258100	NA0465	258205
NA737	25208	NA0221	257029	NA0285	257120	NA0402	258101	NA0466	258206
NA738	25210	NA0222	257030	NA0286	257121	NA0403	258102	NA0467	258207
NA739	25211	NA0223	257032	NA0287	257122	NA0404	258103	NA0468	258209
NA740	25212	NA0224	257033	NA0288	257123	NA0405	258104	NA0469	258216
NA741	25213	NA0225	257035	NA0289	257125	NA0406	258105	NA0470	258217
NA742	25214	NA0226	257036	NA0290	257126	NA0407	258107	NA0471	258218
NA743	25216	NA0227	257038	NA0291	257128	NA0408	258108	NA0472	258220
NA744	25218	NA0228	257039	NA0292	257129	NA0409	258111	NA0473	258221
NA745	25220	NA0229	257041	NA0293	257131	NA0410	258113	NA0474	258223
NA746	25221	NA0230	257042	NA0294	257132	NA0411	258114	NA0475	258225
NA747	25222	NA0231	257044	NA0295	257134	NA0412	258117	NA1000	259005
NA748	25224	NA0232	257043	NA0296	257135	NA0413	258119	NA1001	259006
NA749	25225	NA0233	257047	NA0297	257137	NA0414	258121	NA1002	259009
NA750	25226	NA0234	257048	NA0298	257138	NA0415	258122	NA1003	259011
NA751	25228	NA0235	257050	NA0299	257140	NA0416	258123	NA1004	259013
NA752	25229	NA0236	257051	NA0300	257141	NA0417	258124	NA1005	259014
NA753	25230	NA0237	257052	NA0301	257146	NA0418	258125	NA1006	259015
NA754	25232	NA0238	257053	NA0302	257149	NA0419	258126	NA1007	259019
NA755	25233	NA0239	257049	NA0303	257147	NA0420	258127	NA1008	259020
NA756	25234	NA0240	257045	NA0304	257148	NA0421	258128	NA1009	259010
NA757	25236	NA0241	257056	NA0305	257150	NA0422	258132	NA1010	259023
NA758	25239	NA0242	257057	NA0306	257152	NA0423	258135		
NA759	25241	NA0243	257059	NA0307	257154	NA0424	258136		
NA760	25244	NA0244	257060	NA0308	257155	NA0425	258137		
NA761	25237	NA0245	257058	NA0309	257156	NA0426	258139		
NA762	25245	NA0246	257063	NA0310	257157	NA0427	258140		
NA763	25261	NA0247	257065	NA0311	257159	NA0428	258138		

HAWKER 750 / 900XP FUSELAGE NUMBER DECODE

Airbus UK at Chester, in its capacity as Hawker Beechcraft's fuselage contractor, continues to use the old HS/BAe 6-digit numbering system for the fuselages it builds for the Hawker 750, 900XP and special-order 850XP. These are then given new aircraft c/ns by Hawker Beechcraft after arrival at Wichita/Beech Field. Tie-ups known to us are as follows:

Fuselage	C/n	Fuselage	C/n	Fuselage	C/n	Fuselage	C/n	Fuselage	C/n
258849	HA-0005	258889	HA-0034	258929	HB-9	258969	HB-23	259118	HA-0106
258850	HB-1	258890	HA-0035	258930	HB-10	258970	HA-0077	259119	HB-34
258851	HA-0006	258891	258891	258931	HA-0057	258971	HB-24	259120	HA-0103
258852	258852	258892	HA-0036	258932	HB-11	258972	HA-0078	259121	HA-0108
258853	HA-0007	258893	258893	258933	HA-0058	258973	HA-0087	259122	
258854	HA-0008	258894	HA-0037	258934	HB-12	258974	HB-25	259123	
258855	258855	258895	258895	258935	HA-0059	258975	HA-0079	259124	HA-0104
258856	258856	258896	HA-0038	258936	HB-13	258976	HB-27	259125	HA-0105
258857	HA-0009	258897	HA-0039	258937	HA-0060	258977	HB-26	259126	
258858	258858	258898	HA-0040	258938	HB-14	258978	HA-0081	259127	
258859	258859	258899	HA-0041	258939	HA-0061	258979	HA-0082	259128	
258860	HA-0010	258900	258900	258940	HA-0062	258980	HA-0080	259129	
258861	258861	258901	258901	258941	HB-15	258981	HA-0083		
258862	HA-0011	258902	HA-0042	258942	HA-0063	258982	HA-0094		
258863	HA-0012	258903	HA-0043	258943	HA-0064	258983	HB-28		
258864	HA-0013	258904	258904	258944	tba	258984	HA-0084		
258865	HA-0014	258905	HB-3	258945	tba	258985	HA-0090		
258866	HA-0015	258906	HA-0044	258946	tba	258986	HA-0085		
258867	HA-0016	258907	258907	258947	tba	258987	HB-29		
258868	HA-0017	258908	HA-0045	258948	tba	258988	HA-0086		
258869	HA-0018	258909	258909	258949	tba	258989	HA-0088		
258870	HA-0019	258910	HA-0046	258950	tba	258990	HA-0089		
258871	HA-0020	258911	HA-0047	258951	tba	259100	HB-33		
258872	258872	258912	258912	258952	tba	259101	HA-0091		
258873	HA-0021	258913	HB-4	258953	tba	259102	HB-31		
258874	258874	258914	HA-0048	258954	tba	259103	HA-0092		
258875	HA-0022	258915	258915	258955	HA-0070	259104	HA-0100		
258876	258876	258916	HA-0049	258956	tba	259105	HB-32		
258877	HA-0023	258917	HB-5	258957	HA-0071	259106	HA-0093		
258878	HB-2	258918	HA-0050	258958	258977	259107	HA-0096		
258879	HA-0024	258919	HB-6	258959	HA-0072	259108			
258880	HA-0025	258920	HA-0051	258960	HB-20	259109	HA-0102		
258881	HA-0026	258921	258921	258961	HA-0073	259110	HB-30		
258882	HA-0027	258922	HA-0052	258962	HA-0074	259111	HA-0097		
258883	HA-0028	258923	HB-7	258963	258980	259112	HA-0098		
258884	HA-0029	258924	HA-0053	258964	HB-21	259113	HA-0095		
258885	HA-0030	258925	HB-8	258965	258982	259114			
258886	HA-0031	258926	HA-0054	258966	HA-0075	259115	HA-0099		
258887	HA-0032	258927	HA-0056	258967	HB-22	259116	HA-0101		
258888	HA-0033	258928	HA-0055	258968	HA-0076	259117			

The fuselages numbered 258944 to 258954 inclusive and 258956 were used in the construction of Hawker 900XPs c/n HA-0065 to HA-0069 inclusive, Hawker 750s c/n HB-16 to HB-19 inclusive and Hawker 850XPs c/n 258959, 258961 and 258963 – but their tie-ups remain unknown at present.

Numbers 258991 to 259099 were not used to avoid any clash with the old BAe.125-1000 construction numbers.

HAWKER 4000

The Hawker 4000 was originally known as the Hawker Horizon.

C/n	Identities								
RC-1	N4000R	[ff 11Aug01; wfu Wichita/Beech Field, KS; cx 23Nov15]							
RC-2	N802HH	[ff 10May02]							
RC-3	N803HH	[wfu, cx 29Jun09]							
RC-4	N804HH	[ff 29Apr04]							
RC-5	N805HH	(N974JD)	[wfu; safety traing aid, Wichita/Beech Field, KS]						
RC-6	(N806HH)	N15QS	N607HB	[cx 31Jan14; wfu]					
RC-7	(N807HH)	N7007Q	N711GD	N700JE					
RC-8	(N808HH)	N803SA	N715CJ						
RC-9	(N809HH)	N119AK	N508CK						
RC-10	(N810HH)	N126ZZ	N7567T						
RC-11	N974JD	N119AK							
RC-12	N400MR	ZS-DTD	N400MR						
RC-13	N413HB	(ZS-PPR)	N440HB	XA-MMA					
RC-14	N514HB	VP-BCM	LV-CNW	VP-BCM	N169BG	N50GP*			
RC-15	N515HB	ZS-DDT	N115HB	XA-NOI					
RC-16	N455BP	(N988DT)	N699AK						
RC-17	N61407	N408U							
RC-18	N163DK	N163DE	N86LF						
RC-19	N419HB	N163DK	N190JE						
RC-20	N50QS	N420HB	N899AK						
RC-21	N621HB	(ZK-ABC)	A6-SHH	Pakistan HBC21		N23EA	A6-SHH	AP-SHH	N529AK
RC-22	N10QS	(N422HB)	N339RA	N639RA					
RC-23	N423HB	ZS-ZOT	N230JE						
RC-24	N35004	N995BE	N269LB	N400VR					
RC-25	N3185G	(VT-VIP)	N143RL						
RC-26	N3186N	VT-HJA							
RC-27	N3187N	(N36QS)	M-KENF						
RC-28	N25QS	N979TM							
RC-29	N14QS	N901SG	N77KV	N159MN					
RC-30	N830TS	(N921HA)	XA-OAC						
RC-31	N12QS	N78KN	N78KX	N31JE					
RC-32	N3502N	N984JC	(N24EA)	Pakistan EYE77		N786ZS	N729JF		
RC-33	N3433T	N440MB	N441MB	N614DJ					
RC-34	N3194F	M-PAUL	G-PROO						
RC-35	N986JC								
RC-36	N616EA	XA-UQZ	N360JE						
RC-37	N3197H	N33VC							
RC-38	N438HB	5N-NOC							
RC-39	N439HB	N71956							
RC-40	N40VK	XA-ATT	N40RQ						
RC-41	N41HV	(CS-DYA)	VT-VDM						
RC-42	N40QS	N542HB	(CS-DYB)	N349AK	N349AJ*				
RC-43	N60143	(CS-DYC)	B-3908	N2KL					
RC-44	N63744	(CS-DYD)	TC-NRN						
RC-45	N6005V	B-3907	N35NP	N51NP					
RC-46	N446HB	N223AF	LX-LOE						
RC-47	N447HB	N402SE							
RC-48	N448HB	XA-CHG	XA-UUG	N480JE					
RC-49	N449HB	B-3910							
RC-50	N950HB	N412TF	(N412TE)	N559AK					
RC-51	N451HB	M-ABDL	[cx 09May16; broken up]						
RC-52	N452HB	N339RA							
RC-53	N453HB	N453JE							
RC-54	N454HB	N837RE							
RC-55	N6455T	B-3906	N3663T						
RC-56	N984JC	N560RC	ZS-DDT						
RC-57	N457HB	VQ-BRI	OY-JJJ						
RC-58	N158HB	N900ST	N115EF						
RC-59	N459HB	N117DS	(LV-CWY)	(LV-FWC)	ZS-LOT				
RC-60	N460HB	N860AP							
RC-61	N461HB	N796RM							
RC-62	N8062L	N21FX							
RC-63	N6380H	(OE-HYN)	N46WC						
RC-64	N464HB	N446CC							
RC-65	N465HB	N243PC	N243PG						
RC-66	N466HB	5N-FGX							
RC-67	N467HB	N826GA							
RC-68	N68HB								
RC-69	N8139T	9H-BOA	(N454RR)	N621TF					
RC-70	N470HB	I-MPGA							
RC-71	N871HB	XA-BUD							
RC-72	N872HB	N713AK							

HAWKER 4000

C/n	Identities	
RC-73	N473HB	
RC-74	N474HB	N411TF
RC-75	N875HB	
RC-76	N476HB	AP-RRR

Production complete. The following aircraft also had marks assigned in anticipation of being built.

RC-77	(N477HB)
RC-78	(N478HB)
RC-79	(N179HB)

BOMBARDIER BD-100 CHALLENGER 300 / 350

The Challenger 300 was originally called the Continental.

C/n	Identities									
20001	C-GJCJ	[ff 14Aug01]		[converted to Challenger 350 prototype 2013]						
20002	C-GJCF	[cx 22Aug06, wfu]								
20003	C-GIPX	N303CZ								
20004	C-GJCV	OE-HPK	D-BFJE	N214SG						
20005	C-GIPZ	N850EJ	C-GIPZ							
20006	N5014F	N505FX	N505BX	VT-PIL						
20007	N506FX	XA-JGT	XA-UXW							
20008	C-GZDV	N507FX	N507BX	N508XJ						
20009	C-GZDY	N508FX	N306MF							
20010	C-GZEB	N41DP								
20011	C-GZED	N300LJ	(N311DB)	N17UC	N17UE	N228PK				
20012	C-GZEH	N509FX	PR-WSC	N862VP						
20013	C-GZEI	N315LJ	I-SDFC	N906G						
20014	C-GZEJ	N27MX	XA-JCP	M-OZZA	(M-DMCD)					
20015	C-GZEM	N115LJ	A6-SMS	N300SM	(N309SM)	A6-SAM	N300SM	PR-BSN	G-LEAZ	C-FLAV
20016	C-GZEO	N316LJ	N777VC	C-GFHR						
20017	C-GZEP	N510FX	M-EANS							
20018	C-GZER	N84ZC	N74ZC							
20019	C-GZES	N319RG	N60SB							
20020	C-GZET	N789MB	N828SK	(N630MT)	N905MT					
20021	C-GZDQ	N511FX	N31CA							
20022	C-GZDS	N512FX	HB-JFM	N565RX	N941JR					
20023	C-GZDV	N513FX	N514FX	M-YFLY	G-MRAP	N39ER	N575FD			
20024	C-GZDY	C-FAUZ	(N515FX)	N184R	XA-CHC					
20025	C-GZEB	N125LJ	EC-JEG	N375WB	N375RF	N497EC	N555GE			
20026	C-GZED	C-FDHV	N26FA	N604RF						
20027	C-GZEH	N448AS	N448CL	N596MC						
20028	C-GZEI	(N328RC)	C-FDIA	N328CC	N121LM					
20029	C-GZEJ	N129LJ	HB-JEC							
20030	C-GZEM	C-FDIH	N300BZ	N30BZ	N430SK					
20031	C-GZEO	N131LJ	N411ST	N411SF	N93NS					
20032	C-GZEP	C-FDIJ	N515FX	N520RP						
20033	C-GZER	C-FCMG	OE-HRR							
20034	C-GZES	C-FCXJ	ZS-ACT							
20035	C-GZET	N900WY								
20036	C-GZDQ	N516FX	N536XJ							
20037	C-GZDS	N885TW								
20038	C-GZDV	(ZS-SCT)	(ZS-ACT)	N517FX						
20039	C-GZDY	N139LJ	HB-JEU	OE-HNL	N847CA	PP-NOC	N724SJ	N727SJ		
20040	C-GZEB	N1967M	N234DP							
20041	C-GZED	N141LJ	VP-CLV	N1870G						
20042	C-GZEH	C-FDSR	A7-AAN	A7-CEC	N550LF	M-BTLT	(D-BHRN)	D-BTLT		
20043	C-FCZS	N143LJ	N818KC	XA-GXG						
20044	C-FDSZ	ZS-YES	N74WL	SP-ZSZ						
20045	N145LJ	N618R	N303WS							
20046	N518FX									
20047	C-FEUQ	OE-HPZ	N293KR	N557XJ						
20048	C-FDXU	A6-RJM	N348TS	N70CR						
20049	C-FFZI	N1980Z								
20050	C-FEPU	N350TG	A6-KNH	M-AKVI	M-MTOO					
20051	C-FCZN	C-FFLJ	N424TM	N400CH						
20052	C-FCZV	N606XT								
20053	C-GZDY	C-FGBP	N353PC							
20054	N302EM	N97SH	N1CF							
20055	C-GZEI	C-FFZE	N519FX							
20056	C-GZES	C-FGMR	N520FX							
20057	C-GDZQ	C-FGGF	N521FX							
20058	C-GZDV	C-FGJI	N300DG	(N380DG)						
20059	C-FDAH	C-FGNO	N620JF	N659JF	N304PS					
20060	C-GZEB	C-FGUT	N228N	(N372N)						
20061	C-GZEO	C-FGUD	N422CP	N422CR	N415NG					
20062	C-GZER	N888CN	N300MY							
20063	C-GZET	N363CL								
20064	C-GZDS	C-FGXW	N522FX							
20065	C-FFNT	4X-CPV	OE-HDD	RA-67224						
20066	C-FCZM	C-FGXK	N866TM							
20067	C-FCZS	C-FGZI	N304BC	N300BC						
20068	C-GZEM	C-FGZE	N303EM	N247FS						
20069	C-GZEP	C-FGZD	N987HP							
20070	C-FGYU	N78TC								
20071	C-FGFB	D-BTIM	N371TS	D-BSMI	9H-SMI					
20072	N724SC	N610SW								
20073	C-FHDN	N731DC	(N731BF)	N1RB						
20074	C-FHDE	N523FX								

BD-100 CHALLENGER 300

C/n	Identities							
20075	C-FHCY	N575WB	N487JA					
20076	C-FGBY	N54HA						
20077	C-FGCD	N304EM	N941SP					
20078	C-FGCE	"XA-FRO"	[painted in error at completion centre]	XA-FRD	M-NYJT	C-GNBN	N285KR	N578XJ
20079	C-FGCJ	D-BETA	OE-HOO					
20080	C-FGCL	N960CR						
20081	C-FGCN	N845UP	N845UR	N801PH				
20082	C-FGCV	N594CA						
20083	C-FGCW	N555DH	N31112	N1DH	N906TC	N903TC	N906TC	N300DH
20084	C-FGCX	XA-GPR	N552FX					
20085	C-FGCZ	N42GJ						
20086	C-FGVJ	N846UP	N846UR	N806PH				
20087	C-FGVK	N387PC	N924TC					
20088	C-FGVM	N130CH	N723JA	N727FJ	N31TF*			
20089	C-FGVS	N71FA	N605RF	N715JD				
20090	C-FGWB	N55HA	N300RL					
20091	C-FGWF	N391W						
20092	C-FGWL	N500AL	N300AV					
20093	C-FGWR	C-FDOL	C-FDOJ	N618KG				
20094	C-FGWW	I-CCCH	OE-HDU					
20095	C-FGWZ	N524FX						
20096	C-FHMI	C-GPCZ	G-MEGP	M-EVAN				
20097	C-FHMM	LX-PMA						
20098	C-FHMQ	N305EM	(N305EN)	N358RJ				
20099	C-FHMS	N991GS	N910CL					
20100	C-FHMZ	(N928MC)	VP-CAO	N456KT				
20101	C-FHNC	N306EM	N300FN					
20102	C-FHND	N555TF	N926AG	N128TS				
20103	C-FHNF	N926JR						
20104	C-FHNH	N125TM						
20105	C-FHNJ	N56HA	N788MM					
20106	C-FIDX	G-KALS						
20107	C-FIDZ	C-FGIL	C-FGIK	C-FEDG	C-FEDV	N394WJ		
20108	C-FIDU	N388WS	N365MC					
20109	C-FIDV	N955H						
20110	C-FIEA	C-GESO	N61TF					
20111	C-FIED	OE-HII						
20112	C-FIEE	N525FX						
20113	C-FIEM	N985FM						
20114	C-FIEP	C-FCSI						
20115	C-FIOB	N57HA	(N197JS)					
20116	C-FIOC	D-BADO						
20117	C-FIOE	N211TB	N202DH	N201MC				
20118	C-FIOG	N526FX						
20119	C-FIOH	N214RW	N214PW	N307BL	N963EC			
20120	C-FIOJ	N15GT						
20121	C-FIOK	N963RS	N963RB	N104FT	N729JM			
20122	C-FION	N5262						
20123	C-FIOO	N592SP	D-BFLY	M-BFLY	N723MC			
20124	C-FIOP	N527FX						
20125	C-FJQD	N528FX						
20126	C-FJQH	3B-SSD	VQ-BMJ	TC-AFF				
20127	C-FJQP	N297MC						
20128	C-FJQR	N529FX						
20129	C-FJQT	N660AL	N300LV					
20130	C-FJQX	N300KH						
20131	C-FJQZ	N390DB						
20132	C-FJRE	N518GS	N518GN	N517WZ				
20133	C-FJRG	3B-NGT	N433DC	M-OIWA	T7-AAB	S5-ADO	N712BH	
20134	C-FLCY	N600LS	N609LS					
20135	C-FLDD	9M-TAN	9M-TST					
20136	C-FLDK	TC-SCR	N37TL	SE-RMA				
20137	C-FLDO	N301TG	HB-JFO	M-ASRY	N318JS			
20138	C-FLDW	N247SS	N12SS	(N812SS)	TC-ISR	N238FJ	N81SF	
20139	C-FLDX	N610LS	N848CS					
20140	C-FLEC	VP-CDV						
20141	C-FLEJ	N341TS	LN-AIR	HB-JTB	T7-SIS	SP-SIS		
20142	C-FLEK	(N888UD)	N605UK	N228KT	N786FG			
20143	C-FLEN	N300FS	N593HR					
20144	C-FLQF	N629GB	N302PE					
20145	C-FLQG	D-BUBI						
20146	C-FLQH	N58HA						
20147	C-FLQM	(N600LS)	N480CB					
20148	C-FLQO	N530FX						
20149	C-FLQP	TC-KAR	N377RA	N377MD				

BD-100 CHALLENGER 300

C/n	Identities				
20150	C-FLQR	N531FX			
20151	C-FLQX	M-NEWT	N223TV		
20152	C-FLQY	N487F	N717JJ		
20153	C-FLQZ	N772JS			
20154	C-FMYA	N532FX			
20155	C-FMYB	OH-FLM	N375MH	N197JS	
20156	C-FMXX	N895BB			
20157	C-FMXW	N296SB	N300NB	N302LT*	
20158	C-FMXU	N797CB			
20159	C-FMXQ	LX-TQJ	N70RL	C-GHZD	N70RL
20160	C-FMXK	N533FX			
20161	C-FMXH	N534FX			
20162	C-FMWX	N888RT	N808RT	N825CT	
20163	C-FMWG	N58LC			
20164	C-FNUH	N782BJ			
20165	C-FOAE	N120GS	N818RC		
20166	C-FOAI	N166CL	N225AR	N697AH	
20167	C-FOAJ	N535FX			
20168	C-FOAQ	(PR-MDB)	PR-IDB	N777MS	
20169	C-FOAT	G-UYGB	A9C-DAR	C-FMHL	C-GMHV	SE-RMC
20170	C-FOMU	C-FOAU	N3975A		
20171	C-FPMQ	N536FX			
20172	C-FPMU	M-TAGB	D-BAVA	RA-67223	
20173	C-FOBJ	RA-67217			
20174	C-FOQR	VT-RAK			
20175	C-FOQW	5A-UAA			
20176	C-FORB	VP-BEK	N287KR	N81CR	
20177	C-FOSB	N896BB			
20178	C-FOSG	PP-BIR	N19DD		
20179	C-FOSM	D-BSKY	M-BSKY	OE-HEO	N716WW
20180	C-FOSQ	N269MJ			
20181	C-FOSW	TC-ARB			
20182	C-FOSX	C-GRCY			
20183	C-FOTF	N313DS			
20184	C-FPZZ	N384RV			
20185	C-FQCF	N329CH			
20186	C-FQEI	N725CF	N300GM	N330GM	N993MC	N874WD
20187	C-FQOA	N537FX	N155SL		
20188	C-FQOF	N414DH	N414DY	N503KJ	
20189	C-FQOI	G-KSFR			
20190	C-FQOK	(TC-THY)	N235AF	N335AF	
20191	C-FQOL	XA-LLA	N585LE		
20192	C-FQOM	C-FJCB	N86DQ		
20193	C-FQOQ	N794RC			
20194	C-FRQA	N194LE	N228Y	N228L	
20195	C-FRQC	N300AH	N632FW		
20196	C-FRQH	VT-JSE			
20197	C-FRQK	N480BA			
20198	C-FRQM	N202XT	N62MW		
20199	C-FRQN	N703VZ	N642DM		
20200	C-FRQP	OE-HVJ	N807JD	XA-ARO	
20201	C-FROY	N538FX			
20202	C-FSMO	N539FX	N360PA	N841TT	
20203	C-FSMW	LN-SOL	XA-DLA		
20204	C-FSNB	N552KF	N302R	N256GG	
20205	C-FSNP	N540FX			
20206	C-FSNQ	M-NOEL	D-BIVI	M-NOEL	D-BIVI	N763MT
20207	C-FSNU	N746E			
20208	C-FSLL	N729SB	PP-BIC		
20209	C-FSLR	(OH-ZIP)	N184BK		
20210	C-FSLU	N752M			
20211	C-FTKA	N541FX			
20212	C-FTKC	D-BAVB			
20213	C-FTKH	N300LJ	N537XJ		
20214	C-FTKG	OE-HVV	C-GDIK	N214BL	N166WC
20215	C-FTKK	N215BL	RP-C8215		
20216	C-FUBE	N97DK			
20217	C-FUBK	N542FX			
20218	C-FUBM	LX-VPG	TC-VPG		
20219	C-FUBO	LV-BSS			
20220	C-FUBP	N101UD	N205FP		
20221	C-FUBQ	D-BANN			
20222	C-FUBT	OE-HRM	N876DG		
20223	C-FUJA	N229BP			
20224	C-FUJE	N538XJ			
20225	C-FUJM	N7000C			

BD-100 CHALLENGER 300

C/n	Identities				
20226	C-FUJR	OE-HAP	N115LF		
20227	C-FUJT	OE-HAB	LV-GOK		
20228	C-FUJX	N30XC	N56BA		
20229	C-FURA	N147AG	N1013		
20230	C-FURB	N539XJ			
20231	C-FURC	N742E			
20232	C-FURD	OE-HAA	(D-BREA)	N320VA	XA-OVA
20233	C-FURF	TC-CMK	C-FURF	M-HSNT	
20234	C-FURH	N825TB			
20235	C-FVNB	RA-67221			
20236	C-FVNC	(I-STEF)	S5-ADE	N776BA	N553FX
20237	C-FVND	HB-JGQ			
20238	C-FVNF	N540XJ	C-FLDD		
20239	C-FVNI	N541XJ	N584D		
20240	C-FVNL	N544FX	N347K		
20241	C-FVNS	N801EL			
20242	C-FVNT	N542XJ	C-FKCI		
20243	C-FVLX	EC-LES	N243RC		
20244	C-FVLZ	N300BY	N301PE		
20245	C-FWUZ	N543XJ	C-FYUQ	C-GJEI	
20246	C-FWUT				
20247	C-FWUO	N402EF			
20248	C-FWUL	N544XJ	N217GH	N7NY	
20249	C-FWUK	N138CH	(N130CH)		
20250	C-FWUI	N999ND			
20251	C-FWUC	OY-EKS	OE-HPG		
20252	C-FWRE	CS-TFV			
20253	C-FWRG	N545XJ	N300GP		
20254	C-FWRX	N7100C			
20255	C-FWTK	VP-BJT	T7-GOB		
20256	C-FWTQ	VP-CPF			
20257	C-FWTY	C-FFBC	N905BA	C-FKXF	N905BA	N694PD
20258	C-FWVH	N672BP	N828SK		
20259	C-FXPB	N83JJ	N57SK		
20260	C-FXPI	(N546XJ)	C-GFCB		
20261	C-FXPL	OE-HDV	YR-TRC		
20262	C-FXPQ	N254DV	(N284DV)	N538SL	
20263	C-FXPR	N526AC	(N526AD)	N109MJ	
20264	C-FXPT	N40QG	N44QG	N300TU	
20265	C-FXPW	N265K			
20266	C-FYBG	N411ST	N423JG		
20267	C-FYBJ	N302K			
20268	C-FLDD	C-FYBZ	N1967M	N268CL	N270GP	N3LA*
20269	C-FYBM	N295SG	N508SN		
20270	C-FYBN	N800BD			
20271	C-FYBO	M-CLAB			
20272	C-FYBS	(D-BPWR)	D-BCLA	N551FX	
20273	C-FYBU	VT-JUA	N321GX		
20274	C-FYBV	OE-HCA			
20275	C-FZLX	D-BEKP			
20276	C-FZLY	OE-HMK	N626PS		
20277	C-FZLZ	M-ABCM	C-GRBA		
20278	C-GAKE	N545XJ			
20279	C-GAKF	N541XJ			
20280	C-GAKL	N546XJ			
20281	C-GAKN	N547XJ			
20282	C-GAKO	N710DL			
20283	C-GAKZ	N307EM	N707KG		
20284	C-GBZE	(OE-HEP)	M-EDOK	N284JC	TC-RZA
20285	C-GBZI	N808XT			
20286	C-GBZL	N272BC	N286EC		
20287	C-GBZV	N301MB	C-GVFX		
20288	C-GBXZ	F-HAKP	N430WC		
20289	C-GDTF	(OE-HIX)	N711NA	N711NK	
20290	C-GDTQ	N290CL			
20291	C-GDUH	N520CC			
20292	C-GDUJ	N725N			
20293	C-GEVU	N160SB			
20294	C-GEVW	(N845CA)	OE-HLL		
20295	C-GEVX	SP-CON	P4-AMR		
20296	C-GFIA	C-FDOL			
20297	C-GFIG	N612JN	N700BW		
20298	C-GFIH	N334EC			
20299	C-GFVL	N7670B			
20300	C-GFVN	N830EC			
20301	C-GFVT	N548XJ			

BD-100 CHALLENGER 300

C/n	Identities			
20302	C-GFUF	N545FX		
20303	C-GFUG	B-8106	N88RC	
20304	C-GFUI	N215DA		
20305	C-GFUM	N305CL	N160WC	
20306	C-GIIR	N877RF	N510AF	
20307	C-GIIU	N860SB	N860CS*	
20308	C-GIJP	N219RW	N214RW	
20309	C-GIJZ	N80HD		
20310	C-GJCO	B-8190	OE-HDC	
20311	C-GJCQ	B-8191	N863VP	PP-MQS
20312	C-GJCX	N300GM	N993JL	
20313	C-GJRG	N670CP		
20314	C-GJSO	M-LIFE	OE-HHH	
20315	C-GJSY	B-8233		
20316	C-GJUZ	N464GR	N463GR	
20317	C-GJVG	OE-HBA	RA-67250	
20318	C-GJVL	N583D		
20319	C-GJVO	N546FX	N1897A	
20320	C-GKIO	B-8192		
20321	C-GKIP	B-8193		
20322	C-GKIU	N549XJ		
20323	C-GKIV	N550XJ		
20324	C-GKIX	N551XJ		
20325	C-GKIY	PR-ADB		
20326	C-GKXH	N595CB		
20327	C-GKXK	N93LA		
20328	C-GKXL	N70FS	(N328CF)	
20329	C-GKXM	N552XJ		
20330	C-GKXN	N293HC		
20331	C-GLKX	N625EL	N115AN	
20332	C-GLKY	ZS-JDL	N332CG	
20333	C-GLKZ	N108LT		
20334	C-GLLF	OH-STP	OY-SPB	
20335	C-GLLJ	OE-HGL	N866BA	N1BC
20336	C-GLLY	N300KE		
20337	C-GMIC	N3337H	N3337J	
20338	C-GMIV	OE-HZP	N906BP	
20339	C-GMJY	PR-FMW		
20340	C-GMIQ	N300BZ		
20341	C-GMUV	N547FX		
20342	C-GMUW	N300RY	N548FX	
20343	C-GMUX	N311CJ	N406BJ	
20344	C-GMUY	N88HD		
20345	C-GMVD	N19UC	N17UC	
20346	C-GNPT	B-8115		
20347	C-GNPY	N399NC		
20348	C-GNPZ	XA-NTG		
20349	C-GNQA	N607RP		
20350	C-GNQD	B-8116		
20351	C-GNXF	N301JL		
20352	C-GNXH	N21FE		
20353	C-GNXK	N300CY	N200JB	
20354	C-GNXN	N354WG		
20355	C-GNXQ	N24FE		
20356	C-GOIE	VT-RSP	N782BA	
20357	C-GOIF	OE-HDT	OE-HDI	
20358	C-GOIH	N26FE		
20359	C-GOII	N334AF		
20360	C-GOIJ	N1CA		
20361	C-GOQJ	N28FE		
20362	C-GOQN	N1HP		
20363	C-GOZK	N167RD		
20364	C-GPDU	C-GSUT	C-GSUN	
20365	C-GPEQ	N313V		
20366	C-GPEV	N310VZ		
20367	C-GPEW	XB-NBJ	XA-EZI	
20368	C-GPFI	C-GPDQ		
20369	C-GPFU	N358MY	(N872BA)	C-FIOV
20370	C-GPGB	N26DE		
20371	C-GRJQ	N371HA		
20372	C-GRJU	N608RP		
20373	C-GRJV	N300EU		
20374	C-GRKJ	N549FX		
20375	C-GOVY	N91HK		
20376	C-GOWC	N1RH		
20377	C-GOWO	N377DP		

BD-100 CHALLENGER 300

C/n	Identities					
20378	C-GOWQ	N707JC				
20379	C-GOWY	N305WM				
20380	C-GOXA	N982JC	N60AD			
20381	C-GOXB	C-GUOO	C-FGGF			
20382	C-GOXD	N528YT				
20383	C-GOXG	ZS-JPO	N383GA			
20384	C-GOXM	C-FAJC				
20385	C-GOXN	N300KC				
20386	C-GOXR	N386JC				
20387	C-GOXU	PT-STU				
20388	C-GOXV	VP-CAG	N868LJ			
20389	C-GOXW	N302KC				
20390	C-GOXZ	N304KC				
20391	C-GOYD	N550FX				
20392	C-GOYG	N101UR	N101UD	N101UR	N947WK	N969AF*
20393	C-GOYL	N59KG				
20394	C-GOYO	PR-RBZ				
20395	C-GUGS	C-GVDS+	[+ marks assigned in error]	C-GUGS	C-GVLN	VT-APF
20396	C-GUGV	N567HB	N46VE			
20397	C-GUGY	N300CF	N939SG	N300NZ		
20398	C-GUHA	N300JE	N1901W			
20399	C-GUHE	N370EL				
20400	C-GOVY	C-GVVF	M-ARRH			
20401	C-GOWY	G-VCAN	S5-FUN	N401FN	N97SH	
20402	C-GOWQ	YR-NVY	D-BELO	N424AR		
20403	C-GOXA	LX-AVT				
20404	C-GOWC	C-GWEP	XA-RUA			
20405	C-GOXB	C-GVZL	CN-CTA			
20406	C-GOWO	N406CL				
20407	C-GOXD	N38BK				
20408	C-GUWH	N35FE				
20409	C-GUWP	[Challenger 350 development a/c]	N325PE			
20410	C-GOXM	N738E				
20411	C-GOXN	N37FE				
20412	C-GOXR	N39FE				
20413	C-GOXG	N2425				
20414	C-GOXW	N2428				
20415	C-GOXU	N415BE	N85BE			
20416	C-GOXV	C-FSXR				
20417	C-GOXZ	N585D				
20418	C-GOYD	N723JM				
20419	C-GUGY	D-BIGA	N980JC			
20420	C-GUGV	N420MP				
20421	C-GOYL	N690RB				
20422	C-GUHA	N422MP				
20423	C-GOYG	(D-BIGB)	N300AH	N992DC		
20424	C-GUGS	C-GWXH	TC-SPL			
20425	C-GOYO	C-GXVW	N425BD	N831FJ	N46WY	
20426	C-GOVY	N300AN	N813DH			
20427	C-GOWY	C-GYJZ	XA-VFV			
20428	C-GOWQ	N300ER				
20429	C-GUHE	N957DT				
20430	C-GOXB	C-GYFH	N300VC	N488VC		
20431	C-GOWC	N431EH	N10EH			
20432	C-GOXA	C-GDIL				
20433	C-GOXD	C-GSJK				
20434	C-GOWO	N235EF				
20435	C-GOXN	N796AC				
20436	C-GOXM	N300AY	N777SJ	N7778J		
20437	C-GUGS	N914GS				
20438	C-GOXR	N218KF				
20439	C-GOXV	N300DY	XA-BOM			
20440	C-GOXW	N300NC				
20441	C-GOXZ	N441CB	HK-5186*			
20442	C-GOXG	N300BU	N945AC			
20443	C-GOXU	N300LE	PR-YOU	[dbr in hangar collapse at Sao Paulo/Congonhas, Brazil, 08Jan15]		
20444	C-GOYD	N339PC	N278PC			
20445	C-GOYG	N300HQ				
20446	C-GOYL	N739E				
20447	C-GUGV	N300HK	N228Y			
20448	C-GUGY	N300CF	N773RC			
20449	C-GUHA	OE-HCZ				
20450	C-GOYO	N44MZ	N44M			
20451	C-GUHE	C-GZKH	C-GWWW			
20452	C-GOXB	D-BEAM				
20453	C-GOXD	N453FD				

BD-100 CHALLENGER 300 / 350

C/n	Identities		
20454	C-GOVY	N425XF	N425FX
20455	C-GOWQ	N325TG	
20456	C-GOWY	N43FE	
20457	C-GOXA	N812KC	

Production complete, replaced by the Challenger 350.

CHALLENGER 350

C/n	Identities				
20501	C-GYTX	N501BZ			
20502	C-GYTY	N762QS			
20503	C-GOXM	C-FEXI	N801KB		
20504	C-GOXN	OE-HRS			
20505	C-GOXR	N350KM			
20506	C-GOXW	N175DP			
20507	C-GUGC	N824DP			
20508	C-GOXG	SP-KHI			
20509	C-GOXZ	N411SF	N411ST		
20510	C-GOYL	N763QS			
20511	C-GUHE	N50LF			
20512	C-GOXV	N101UD			
20513	C-GOYO	9H-VCA			
20514	C-GOXU	9H-VCB			
20515	C-GOYD	N1987	N467MW	N515CH	N49SK
20516	C-GUGV	N414DH			
20517	C-GUGY	N764QS			
20518	C-GOVY	N358JM			
20519	C-GOXB	C-GJDR	C-GJDU		
20520	C-GOYG	N350GS	N768BL		
20521	C-GUHA	N572FX			
20522	C-GOWQ	N352JM			
20523	C-GOWY	N765QS			
20524	C-GOXA	(PT-PTR)	N10EF		
20525	C-GOXD	C-FJHO	OH-ADM		
20526	C-GOXM	N766QS			
20527	C-GOXR	N570FX			
20528	C-GOXW	C-FIZP	PT-PTR		
20529	C-GUGS	N6PG			
20530	C-GOWC	G-SCAR			
20531	C-GOWO	N350MB			
20532	C-GOXV	N7PG			
20533	C-GOXZ	N767QS			
20534	C-GUHE	N768QS			
20535	C-GOXB	9H-VCC			
20536	C-GOXN	N571FX			
20537	C-GOYL	(P4-AGL)	N718CG	N715CG	
20538	C-GOXB	9H-VCD			
20539	C-GOXU	N769QS			
20540	C-GOYD	9H-VCE			
20541	C-GOYO	9H-VCF			
20542	C-GUGV	PR-HNG			
20543	C-GUGY	N770QS			
20544	C-GOVY	CS-CHA			
20545	C-GOYG	9H-VCG			
20546	C-GUGS	9H-VCH			
20547	C-GOXA	OE-HUG			
20548	C-GOWC	N422CP			
20549	C-GOWO	C-FKKI	C-FFBC		
20550	C-GOWQ	9H-VCI			
20551	C-GOWY	N772QS			
20552	C-GOXM	N443DB			
20553	C-GOXR	CS-CHB			
20554	C-GUHA	N774QS			
20555	C-GUHE	N659NR			
20556	C-GOXD	ZS-JDL			
20557	C-GOXN	N775QS			
20558	C-GOXV	N776QS			
20559	C-GOXW	N559SA	N100SA		
20560	C-GOXZ	9H-VCJ			
20561	C-GOYD	N782QS			
20562	C-GOYO	N777QS			
20563	C-GOXU	N778QS			

BD-100 CHALLENGER 350

C/n	Identities			
20564	C-GOYL	N573FX		
20565	C-GUGY	N958CR		
20566	C-GOWO	N779QS		
20567	C-GOXB	N574FX		
20568	C-GOXG	N780QS		
20569	C-GOYG	N350VJ		
20570	C-GOVY	N781QS		
20571	C-GOWQ	C-FLOO	N350PH	
20572	C-GOXA	CS-CHC		
20573	C-GOXM	N351VJ		
20574	C-GUGS	N783QS		
20575	C-GUGV	N784QS		
20576	C-GUHA	N352VJ		
20577	C-GOWY	N575MW		
20578	C-GOXN	N575FX		
20579	C-GOXR	C-FKOC	N721PP	
20580	C-GUHE	N580SB	N509SB	
20581	C-GOXU	(D-BRCR)	M-OCNY	
20582	C-GOXV	N350RX		
20583	C-GOYL	D-BHGN		
20584	C-GUGY	CS-CHD		
20585	C-GOWO	N576FX		
20586	C-GOWQ	N586AL		
20587	C-GOXD	N587FA		
20588	C-GOXZ	M-SGJS		
20589	C-GOYD	N2XT		
20590	C-GOYG	N786QS		
20591	C-FLQZ	VT-JUI		
20592	C-GOVY	9H-VCK		
20593	C-GOWY	N277JH		
20594	C-GOXB	(N577FX)	N350AD	N424MP
20595	C-GOXG	N787QS		
20596	C-GOXR	P4-AGL		
20597	C-GOYO	N356JM		
20598	C-GOXA	C-FOEJ	N350EJ	N247JD
20599	C-GOXD	N599HA		
20600	C-GOXM	N272BC		
20601	C-GOXN	N578FX		
20602	C-GOXV	OY-SMS	N312EA	
20603	C-GOXW	N631RP		
20604	C-GOXZ	N686CB		
20605	C-GOYL	N350AJ	N350RM	
20606	C-GUGS	9H-VCL		
20607	C-GUGV	N788QS		
20608	C-GUHA	N305DL		
20609	C-GUHE	N353VJ		
20610	C-GOWQ	N979KC		
20611	C-GOWO	N350DA	N350PD	
20612	C-GOWY	N818NX		
20613	C-GOXU	N350EH	N724EH	
20614	C-GUGY	N354VJ		
20615	C-GOVY	C-FFBE		
20616	C-GOXM	N350FA	N123Q	
20617	C-GOYD	N789QS		
20618	C-GOYG	OE-HGG		
20619	C-GOYO	N350CX	N995CB	
20620	C-GOXA	C-FFIK		
20621	C-GOXB	M-TECH		
20622	C-GOXD	N678HB		
20623	C-GOXG	CS-CHE		
20624	C-GOXN	9H-VCM		
20625	C-GOXV	C-FTMF	N350KL	N351EC
20626	C-GOXW	ZS-CKA		
20627	C-GOXZ	N790QS		
20628	C-GOYL	9H-VCN		
20629	C-GOWQ	N791QS		
20630	C-GOXR	C-FALI		
20631	C-GUGS	N2HL		
20632	C-GUGV	N599JT		
20633	C-GUHA	C-FTMN	N350AV	N814AF
20634	C-GOWY	N792QS		
20635	C-GOXR	N131KR		
20636	C-GOXU	N793QS		
20637	C-GUHE	N355VJ		
20638	C-GOVY	N794QS		
20639	C-GOWO	N350DK	LN-STB	

BD-100 CHALLENGER 350

C/n	Identities		
20640	C-GOXA	N1350S	
20641	C-GOXM	N795QS	
20642	C-GOYO	9H-VCO	
20643	C-GOXB	C-FTVF	RA-67243
20644	C-GOXD	N255DV	
20645	C-GOYD	N170WC	
20646	C-GUGY	N796QS	
20647	C-GOXG	N579FX	
20648	C-GOXZ	N797QS	
20649	C-GOXR	N59978	B-98889*
20650	C-GOXW	G-CJOF	
20651	C-GUGS	N730QS	
20652	C-GOWQ	N580FX	
20653	C-GOXN	C-FUDA	RP-C7588*
20654	C-GOYG	N176WC	
20655	C-GUGV	N798QS	
20656	C-GOWY	N799QS	
20657	C-GOVY	N581FX	
20658	C-GOWO	N2926E	
20659	C-GOXA	N726QS	
20660	C-GOXU	N603GP	
20661	C-GOXV	N703VZ	
20662	C-GOYL	N727QS	
20663	C-GUHA	N725QS	
20664	C-GOXM	N522AC	
20665	C-GOYO	N350LM	N457WB
20666	C-GOXD	N728QS	
20667	C-GOYD	N729QS	
20668	C-GOXG	C-FEDG	
20669	C-GOWQ	C-FFIP	
20670	C-GOXB	HB-JLG	
20671	C-GOXZ	CS-CHF	
20672	C-GOYG	N672DE	
20673	C-GUGS		
20674	C-GUGY	N5161	
20675	C-GOWO	N883TW	
20676	C-GOXW	N179KC	
20677	C-GOYL	C-FVNM	N350XJ
20678	C-GOYO	N731QS	
20679	C-GUGV	N884BN	
20680	C-GUHA		
20681	C-GUHE		
20682	C-GOWQ	CS-CHG	
20683	C-GOXD		
20684	C-GOXG		
20685	C-GOXN		
20686	C-GOYD		
20687	C-GOXV		
20688	C-GOWY		
20689	C-GOVY		
20690	C-GOXA		
20691	C-GOXM		
20692	C-GOXR		
20693	C-GOXU		
20694	C-GOXZ		
20695	C-GOYG		
20696	C-GOYL		
20697	C-GUGY		
20698			
20699			
20700			
20701			
20702			
20703			
20704			
20705			
20706			
20707			
20708			
20709			
20710			
20711			
20712			
20713			
20714			
20715			

BD-100 CHALLENGER 350

C/n	Identities
20716	
20717	
20718	
20719	
20720	
20721	
20722	
20723	
20724	
20725	
20726	
20727	
20728	
20729	
20730	
20731	
20732	
20733	
20734	
20735	
20736	
20737	
20738	
20739	
20740	

BOMBARDIER BD-700 GLOBAL EXPRESS / GLOBAL 5000

C/n	Series	Identities
9001		C-FBGX [rolled out 26Aug96; ff 13Oct96; converted to RAF Airborne Stand-Off Radar test aircraft 2001; later converted to E-11A Battlefield Airborne Communications Node platform for USAF] N901GX USAF 11-9001
9002		C-FHGX N711MC N711MN N881WT
9003		C-FJGX C-FBDR 9M-CJG
9004		C-FKGX N1TK C-FKGX N1TK (N11TK) N115HK HB-JGO N617JN
9005		C-GEGX (VP-CPC) N700HX N613WF (N938WF) N618WF (F-GOVV)
9006		C-GCGY N1TM N906GX N161WC N420AG [modified for airborne laser test use]
9007		C-GCRW Malaysia M48-01 C-GCRW Malaysia M48-01 C-GCRW N907GX (C-....) EC-IUQ N801TK VH-LEP VH-LZP
9008		C-GDBG N9008 (N90005) N917R
9009		C-GDGO N816SR N816SQ N813SQ N998AM N980GG N988GG
9010		C-GDGQ N701WH (M-ABAK) N68005
9011		C-GDGW N700KJ VP-BJJ HB-IHQ D-AAHB
9012		C-GDGY N70PS (N70PX)
9013		C-GDXU HB-IUR C-GZSM LX-GEX D-AFAU
9014		C-GDXV N700GX C-FGGX N700GX (D-AFLW) C-FRGX XA-NGS N700GX
9015		C-GDXX N700KS N708KS HB-JEN N900LF VH-FMG
9016		C-GEIM N700AH N16GX N300ES N309ES EC-KVU G-GOYA
9017		C-GEIR VP-BDD HB-JER N295TX N90FX
9018		C-GEVO VP-BGG N84SD N818TS C-FOXA PR-VDR
9019		C-GEVU N600CC HL7576 N203JE N203JZ N149LP
9020		C-GEVV N700GK VP-BEN N81ZZ 9H-GBT (D-AGBT) F-HGBT CS-DTW N344JR N1JR
9021		C-GEYY N8VB
9022		C-GEYZ N700HG N622AB N226HD N393BZ N393BX
9023		C-GEZD N324SM ZS-KDR
9024		C-GEZF N700BH N288Z N287Z N9253V
9025		C-GEZJ N700AQ N616DC N816DC N322FA (PR-GEX) (PR-GBO) PR-HET*
9026		C-GEWV N70EW N78EW N843GX
9027		C-GEZX N305CC N304CC N850TR
9028		C-GEZY N117TF N717TF VP-BSE D-AFAM
9029		C-GEZZ HZ-AFA N929TS N5UU N418AB N829RA
9030		C-GFAD VP-BYY VP-CYY A6-CAG
9031		C-GFAE N700VN N724AF
9032		C-GFAK N700HE (N2T) G-52-26 G-CBNP OY-MSI
9033		C-GFAN N600AK
9034		C-GFAP N700HF JA005G N934SC
9035		C-GFAQ (D-AFLW) N817LS N711LS N818LS N838SC
9036		C-GFAT N777GX HB-ITG VP-BEM M-IIII 9H-III
9037		C-GFJQ N777SW N777VU N400GX [w/o in hangar collapse at Washington/Dulles, VA, 06Feb10]
9038		C-GFJR G-52-24 G-LOBL N738TS N20EG C-GSAP
9039		C-GFJS N700GT N90EW
9040		C-GFJT N22BH N228H N930EN
9041		C-GFKT N195WM N887WM N387WM (N802PF) N802CB
9042		C-GFKV N700WL N170SW
9043		C-GFKW N700BU N700ML N416BD N416BB (N880NE) PR-SIR N904BR
9044		C-GFKX N700BP I-MOVE OE-IGS D-AGEX*
9045		C-GFKY N17GX
9046		C-GFLS N700BV N1TS N517TT M-JNJL
9047		C-GFLU N410WW N373SB (PP-WSC) PR-HIC
9048		C-GFLW N700BY N4GX PR-OOF
9049		C-GFLX N471DG N949GP N471DG N949GP M-MDBD
9050		C-GFLZ N700FJ VP-COP N502JL M-AFMA
9051		C-GFWI N700DZ N421AL
9052		C-GFWP N700DQ N752DS N620K [w/o in hangar collapse at Washington/Dulles, VA, 06Feb10; parted out by Dodson Int'l, Rantoul, KS]
9053		C-GFWX N700LJ N53GX
9054		C-GFWY N700LA HB-IKZ N550LF M-RUAT N356AP N91FX
9055		C-GFWZ N449ML N540CH
9056		C-GCGY N700DU N421SZ N928SZ N670AG
9057		C-GGIR (TC-DHG) N700EX N18WF N18WY VP-BDU
9058		C-GGJA N700AD N79AD N79AY (TC-YIL)
9059		C-GGJF (VP-BXX) N700EG N18WF N18WZ N3PC N68JH
9060		C-GGJH "EC-FPI" [painted in error at completion centre] EC-IBD N542LF C-GJDU HL8229 N804TK C-GJDU M-ATAR
9061		C-GGJJ N16FX ZS-ESA (VP-C..) ZS-ESA N1AR
9062		C-GGJR N700CJ N801PN
9063		C-GGJS N700BD B-HMA (N733EY) N933EY N988EY*
9064		C-GGJU N700PL N264A N264A*
9065		C-GGKA N700CV N789TP N711SW (N711SQ) N704MF
9066		C-GGKC N898SC N708SC N823DF
9067		C-GGPZ N700BK N67RX N115TR
9068		C-GGQC N700BX (N889JC)
9069		C-GGQF N700LD N1868M N568M (N522KM) N163EG
9070		C-GGQG N700XR N34U N14FE N2FE
9071		C-GHDQ D-ADNB VP-CLY N888ZJ

BD-700 GLOBAL EXPRESS / GLOBAL 5000

C/n	Series	Identities								
9072		C-GHDV	N700LN	N983J						
9073		C-GHDW	N700XN	N338TP	N801KF					
9074		C-GHEA	N399GS	N2012C						
9075		C-GHEI	N316GS	N1812C	N1812U	N595E				
9076		C-GHER	N700XT	LX-VIP	VP-CGY	9H-GCM				
9077		C-GHET	N700XY	N100A	N200A	N520E	N365CJ			
9078		C-GHEZ	N700AH	N85D						
9079		C-GHFB	N700AP	(N217JC)	VH-VGX					
9080		C-GHFH	N283S	N125CH						
9081		C-GHGC	G-52-25	G-CBNR	G-52-25	C-GZTZ	F-GVML	D-AEGV	OE-IVG	
9082		C-GHYQ	N700AY	JA006G	N782SC					
9083		C-GHYT	N700AU	C-GKLF	VP-CEB	G-RBEN	CS-RBN			
9084		C-GHYX	N700GU	N2T	(N4LZ)	N908BX	N984TS	VP-COU	EC-KKN	LX-NYO
9085		C-GHZB	N700GQ	N404VL	N72XF					
9086		C-GHZC	HB-INJ	M-MNAA	M-MMAA	9H-STM	N288ZJ			
9087		C-GHZD	N700BQ	N360LA						
9088		C-GHZF	N15FX	C-FDLR	C-GNCB					
9089		C-GHZH	EC-IFS	N65WL						
9090		C-GIOD	N18TM							
9091		C-GIOJ	N700XM	N1FE						
9092		C-GIOK	N15FX	N799WW	N899WW	M-LWSA				
9093		C-GIOW	N17FX	C-GZVZ	VP-CDF	D-ACDF*				
9094		C-GIOX	(ZS-DAJ)	ZS-DLJ	OY-GLA	A6-EJB	EC-KJH	G-SENT	2-JFJC	
9095		C-GIPA	HB-IUJ	N97DQ						
9096		C-GIPC	Malaysia M52-01		C-GIPC	Malaysia M48-02				
9097		C-GIPD	N903TF	N908TE	N902MM	A6-MHA	M-ALSH			
9098		C-GIPF	N700CE	N149VB	N100VR	N1DS	9H-LLC	P4-MLC	CS-DVE	
9099		C-GIPJ	N700CU	C-GZKL	(ZS-DFN)	OE-IEL				
9100		C-GIXI	N700CX	N1SA	XA-PIL	N720CH				
9101		C-GIXJ	VP-BOK	N800TK	VH-VDX					
9102		C-GIXM	N700CY	HB-IGS	VP-CGS	D-AXTM				
9103		C-GIXO	N700CZ	N122BN						
9104		C-GJIU	N190WP	N889CP	N888ZP					
9105		C-GJIW	N700EC	N100A	N500E	N590E				
9106		C-GJIY	N816SG	N816SQ	N10E	OE-IRP				
9107	R-1	C-GJRG	United Kingdom ZJ690							
9108		C-GJRK	N700EK	N100ES	(N150ES)	N625SC	N625SG	N143KB		
9109		C-GJRL	N700DU	N700KS	N143MW					
9110		C-GJTH	N700EL	N14R	N906JW	(SP-WOY)	SP-WOI			
9111		C-GJTK	VT-DHA							
9112		C-GJTP	C-GBLX	OE-IKM	G-FAMT	N703CL	B-7699			
9113		C-GKCG	N920DS	N8762M	N8762W	N2MG				
9114		C-GKCM	N11EA	N1SL	N999YY	N999YA	VT-JSB	N91NG	N575WB	
9115		C-GKCN	(F-GOAK)	LX-PAK	N915AV	C-FNDF	VP-BEB	N915AV	VP-CCK	
9116		C-GKGZ	N700EW	N320GX						
9117		C-GKHC	N700EY	N917GL	N724MV					
9118		C-GKHE	N700EZ	N904DS						
9119		C-GKHF	N700FE	C-GZOW	XA-OVR	XA-OVG	XA-AYL			
9120		C-GKHG	N700FG	N887WS	(N910TS)	(D-AGTH)	(OE-IFH)	(N33NN)	G-GLBX	D-AACF*
9121		C-GKHH	N700FN	N711MC						
9122		C-GKHI	N700FQ	ZS-GJB	VP-BBK					
9123	R-1	C-FZVM	United Kingdom ZJ691							
9124		C-FZVN	N700GB							
9125		C-FZVS	N700FR	N711SX						
9126		C-FZVV	N60GX	C-GZPT	A7-AAM					
9127	5000	C-GERS	[prototype Global 5000 ff 07Mar03]							
9128		C-FZWB	N700FY	N18WF	(N38WF)	N613WF	N613WE			
9129		C-FZWF	N700FZ	N725LB	N103WG					
9130	5000	C-GLRM	4X-COI	HB-JFB						
9131	R-1	C-FZWW	United Kingdom ZJ692							
9132	R-1	C-FZXC	United Kingdom ZJ693							
9133		C-FZXE	G-XPRS	LX-AAA	N809SD	VH-CCV				
9134		C-FZXZ	A7-GEX	N452CS	N451CS	(N452CS)	N683GA			
9135	R-1	C-FZYL	United Kingdom ZJ694							
9136		C-GZPV	P4-AAA	M-YAAA	M-YFLY	T7-SSM				
9137		C-GZPW	C-GCDS							
9138		C-GZRA	N51SE							
9139		C-FYZP	OY-CVS	VQ-BAM	M-GLEX					
9140	5000	C-GAGQ	N140AE	N50DS						
9141		C-GAGS	VP-BOW	N286KR	N804AS	N629KD				
9142		C-GAGT	N700EW	VP-BSC	N442LF	N44GX				
9143		C-FAGU	VH-TGG	VH-TGQ	N777GZ	T7-ATL				
9144		C-FAGV	N6VB							
9145		C-FAHN	N914DT	HB-JEX	CS-DVI					
9146		C-FAHQ	EC-JIL							
9147		C-FAHX	P4-VVF	N489JB	N92FX					

BD-700 GLOBAL EXPRESS / GLOBAL EXPRESS XRS / GLOBAL 5000

C/n	Series	Identities							
9148		C-FAIO	N889JA						
9149	5000	C-FAIY	N356MS	N456MS	VT-BAJ				
9150		C-FAIV	N488CH						
9151		C-FBOC	N81UB	VQ-BHY	N598CH	N1LS			
9152	5000	C-FBPK	N605VF	N626DJ	N214MD				
9153		C-FBPJ	N454AJ	N120AK	TC-FRK				
9154	5000	C-FBPL	N555EF	N388RF	N3389H				
9155	5000	C-FBPT	N711LS	N717LS	N717MK				
9156	5000	C-FBPZ	N156DG	N1DG					
9157	5000	C-FBQD	VP-BAM	M-AQUA					
9158	5000	C-FCOG	N375G	(N858TS)	C-GPPI				
9159	XRS	C-FCOI	D-ATNR	OH-TNR	(D-AZNF)	OE-ITN	EI-ITN		
9160	5000	C-FCOJ	N47						
9161	5000	C-FCOK	N944AM	VP-BWB	N394HH*				
9162		C-FCOZ	N2T						
9163		C-FCPH	OY-ILG	N700FG	VH-FGJ				
9164	5000	C-FCSF	N376G	N37LP					
9165	XRS	C-FCSH	VP-BOS	M-ASRI					
9166	5000	C-FCSI	N166J	N1990C	M-YSAI				
9167	XRS	C-FCSL	N167GX	(OE-LNX)	HB-JGY	9H-AFP	VH-ZZH	N877AB	N123AB
9168	5000	C-FCSP	OE-INC						
9169	XRS	C-FCSR	G-XXRS						
9170	5000	C-FCSY	D-AAAZ	(VP-CKR)	OE-LAA	D-AAHI*			
9171	XRS	C-FCTE	VP-CGO						
9172	5000	C-FCTK	N729KF	N729KP	M-ANGO				
9173	XRS	C-FCUA	HB-JEY	VH-ZXH	[dbr by hangar fire, Indianapolis, IN, 07Nov10]	N744SD	[parted out by Red Aviation, Georgetown, TX]		
9174	5000	C-FCUF	HB-JRS						
9175	XRS	C-FCUG	N771TF	N117TF					
9176	5000	C-FCUK	N720WS	N907WS					
9177	XRS	C-FCUS	N528J	N528JR	[w/o in hangar collapse at Washington/Dulles, VA, 06Feb10; parted out by Challenger Spares & Support, Georgetown, TX]				
9178	5000	C-FCUX	C-GDPG						
9179	XRS	C-FCVC	HL7748	N905T					
9180	5000	C-FCVD	N818FH	N939AP					
9181	XRS	C-FEAB	N302AK	N382AK	N137BB				
9182	5000	C-FECA	N182GX	OE-IFG	M-AJWA	LV-GQE			
9183	XRS	C-FEAD	N821AM						
9184	XRS	C-FEAE	HL7749	N702DR					
9185	XRS	C-FEAG	N1955M	N185GX	N13JS				
9186	5000	C-FECI	P4-HER	OY-FIT	G-KBMM				
9187	XRS	C-FEAK	N540WY	N54SL	N11A				
9188	5000	C-FECN	F-HFBY	C-FFCD					
9189	XRS	C-FEAQ	LX-GJM	M-GYQM	T7-GQM				
9190	5000	C-FECX	N99XN	PR-XDN	M-RIDE				
9191	XRS	C-FEAZ	N91NG	N6D	N28ZD				
9192	5000	C-FECY	N700LK	N267BW					
9193	XRS	C-FEBG	VP-BVG						
9194	XRS	C-FEBH	N313RF						
9195	XRS	C-FEBL	N195GX	N4T					
9196	XRS	C-FEBQ	VP-CRC	G-CEYL					
9197	XRS	C-FEBS	LX-PAK						
9198	5000	C-FECZ	HB-JRR	VQ-BMM					
9199	XRS	C-FEBU	(N799TS)	N379G	PP-SGP*				
9200	XRS	C-FEBX	G-LXRS	N519CP					
9201	5000	C-FHPQ	N95ZZ	N205EL					
9202	XRS	C-FHPB	F-GVMV	N1415N	N1415				
9203	XRS	C-FHPG	N203XX	N200A	N210A	N688MC	N121RS		
9204	5000	C-FIHP	OE-IAK	LX-ZAK	N709RJ	VP-BSG			
9205	XRS	C-FIHL	N205EX	N100A	N102A	N1NE			
9206	5000	C-FIIB	N92ZZ	N343DF	N343DE				
9207	5000	C-FIIC	N723AB						
9208	XRS	C-FIHN	EC-KFS	OE-LUB					
9209	5000	C-FIIG	N171JJ	"M-BIJJ"+	[+ fake marks worn at Luton Jul08]	N171JJ	N828CC		
9210	XRS	C-FIOT	N190H	M-GBAL	N297SF				
9211	5000	C-FIPH	C-GXPR	[w/o Fox Harbour, Newfoundland, Canada 11Nov07; cx Mar08; parted out]					
9212	5000	C-FIPJ	N13JS	N166MK					
9213	XRS	C-FIOZ	(VP-CAH)	D-AEKT	(VH-ZXH)	VQ-BIS	M-VQBI		
9214	5000	C-FIPM	N93ZZ	VT-JSK					
9215	XRS	C-FIPC	N94ZZ	N18WF	N501MG				
9216	5000	C-FIPN	N900LS	(N530JM)	M-JSMN				
9217	5000	C-FIPP	N700LS	N709LS	N74DH				
9218	XRS	C-FIPF	N96ZZ	N86TW	C-GXBB				
9219	5000	C-FIPQ	N80ZZ	N611VT	SP-ZAK				
9220	XRS	C-FIPG	P4-CBA	C-GHSW	C-GMXP	C-FLMK			
9221	5000	C-FIPT	N10SL						

BD-700 GLOBAL EXPRESS XRS / GLOBAL 5000

C/n	Series	Identities					
9222	5000	C-FJNJ	N81ZZ	N45JE	N45UE	VP-CAK	
9223	XRS	C-FJML	N83ZZ	VP-BAH			
9224	5000	C-FJNQ	N224GX	N989RJ			
9225	XRS	C-FJMP	N36LG	N36EG	VH-CCX		
9226	5000	C-FJNX	A6-DHG	(N381MS)	N900TR		
9227	5000	C-FJNZ	(N200LS)	M-LLGC	M-SKSM		
9228	XRS	C-FJMQ	N87ZZ	N289Z	N288Z	N287Z	VT-SDK
9229	5000	C-FJOA	N84ZZ	YR-TIK			
9230	XRS	C-FJMV	A7-GEY	N57LE	ZS-AMP	VH-IQR	
9231	5000	C-FJOK	VP-CAU	G-TSLS	D-AOTL	G-TSLS	CS-TSL
9232	XRS	C-FJMX	D2-ANG				
9233	5000	C-FJOU	(A6-OWC)	N233FJ	C-GGLO		
9234	XRS	C-FLKZ	N234GX	(D-AANA)	OE-LAF	9H-FED	9H-COL N989SF
9235	XRS	C-FLLA	OE-LXR	N812SD	N980CC		
9236	XRS	C-FLLF	N624BP	N624BR			
9237	XRS	C-FLLH	(OE-LNY)	OH-PPS	OE-IRA		
9238	XRS	C-FLLN	HB-JGP				
9239	XRS	C-FLLO	N71ZZ	N421SZ	N928SZ		
9240	XRS	C-FLLV	N999YX	N999YY	N999YX		
9241	5000	C-FLKY	(G-LLGC)	N941TS	G-OCSA	G-CGFA	B-LRH
9242	XRS	C-FLTB	N942TS	(OH-PPS)	N942TS	N375G	
9243	5000	C-FLTH	OE-IMA	VP-CMA	N2900D		
9244	XRS	C-FLTI	C-FCNN	VP-CZK	N36MM		
9245	5000	C-FLTJ	N200ES	N247WE			
9246	XRS	C-FMFK	VP-BNX	N708RJ	C-GNRS		
9247	XRS	C-FMFN	N881TS				
9248	XRS	C-FMFO	N888GX				
9249	5000	C-FMGE	HB-JGN	9H-AFR	T7-TAA		
9250	XRS	C-FMGK	D-AKAZ	M-BTAR			
9251	XRS	C-FMKW	N73ZZ	OE-IGG			
9252	XRS	C-FMKZ	LX-FLY				
9253	XRS	C-FMLB	ZS-ZBB	VQ-BZB			
9254	XRS	C-FMLE	N754TS	VQ-BGS			
9255	5000	C-FMLI	N193LA	N199LA	N417CS		
9256	XRS	C-FMLQ	OE-ICN*	[aircraft built in 2007, still not delivered Apr17]			
9257	5000	C-FMLT	VP-CVU	5A-UAC			
9258	XRS	C-FMLV	N700ML	PR-MLJ			
9259	XRS	C-FMMH	N89ZZ	Botswana OK1			
9260	XRS	C-FMND	N74ZZ	ZS-XRS	SX-GJN	N651GS	SX-GJN N218AL
9261	5000	C-FMUI	N878HL				
9262	XRS	C-FMUN	N962TS	VT-STV	N433DC		
9263	5000	C-FMUO	VP-CSB				
9264	XRS	C-FNDN	C-GLUL	SE-RGB			
9265	5000	C-FNDK	N265DE	N501JT	N689WM		
9266	XRS	C-FNDO	N76ZZ	N104DA			
9267	XRS	C-FNDQ	N78ZZ	M-MMAS	OY-LUK	VP-CLP	
9268	XRS	C-FNDT	VQ-BJA	N713RJ	M-OGMC		
9269	5000	C-FNRP	OE-IBC				
9270	XRS	C-FNRR	VP-CNY				
9271	5000	C-FNSN	VP-CJC	N898WS			
9272	XRS	C-FNSV	VP-CVV	N15SD			
9273	5000	C-FNZZ	VP-BJN				
9274	XRS	C-FOAB	N974TS	G-EXRS	9H-SRT		
9275	5000	C-FOAD	N87ZZ	VH-KTG	N50XC	N137ZM	
9276	XRS	C-FOKD	VP-BJI				
9277	XRS	C-FOKF	N194WM				
9278	XRS	C-FOKH	N709DS				
9279	5000	C-FOKJ	N79ZZ	N468KL			
9280	XRS	C-FOVD	(D-AVIA)	OY-WIN	OE-IDO		
9281	XRS	C-FOVE	N981TS				
9282	5000	C-FOVG	N216PA	A6-FBQ			
9283	XRS	C-FOVH	VQ-BEB	M-YULI	N706RJ	T7-AAA	
9284	XRS	C-FOVK	N77UF				
9285	5000	C-FPFF	5A-UAB				
9286	XRS	C-FPGB	C-FHYL	OE-IPA	G-IDRO	LX-AMG	
9287	XRS	C-FPGD	N169DT	HB-JGE			
9288	5000	C-FPGI	N375WB				
9289	5000	C-FPQE	N26ZZ	VT-DBA	T7-FGL		
9290	XRS	C-FPQF	N774KK	N797KK			
9291	XRS	C-FPQG	OH-PPT	OE-IRN			
9292	XRS	C-FPQH	N837WM	N887WM			
9293	5000	C-FPQI	HZ-SJP	"HZ-BJP"	M-JANP		
9294	XRS	C-FQXW	M-CRVS	A7-CEF			
9295	5000	C-FQXX	B-LIM				
9296	XRS	C-FQXY	N96ZZ	N616DC			
9297	XRS	C-FQYB	VQ-BSC	N703RJ	VH-CCD		

BD-700 GLOBAL EXPRESS XRS / GLOBAL 5000

C/n	Series	Identities					
9298	5000	C-FQYD	N900GX				
9299	XRS	C-FQYE	N37ZZ	VH-LAW			
9300	XRS	C-FRJV	N709FG	N888ZG			
9301	5000	C-FRJY	(D-AMOS)	OE-IOO			
9302	5000	C-FRKL	N95ZZ	N352AF			
9303	XRS	C-FRKO	EC-LEB				
9304	XRS	C-FRKQ	N89MX	N3877			
9305	5000	C-FRMW	N815PA				
9306	XRS	C-FRNG	G-SHEF	LX-GXX			
9307	XRS	C-FRNJ	N528MP				
9308	5000	C-FSRX	N103ZZ				
9309	XRS	C-FSRY	G-CJME	G-IRAP			
9310	XRS	C-FSRZ	N38ZZ	VH-ZXH	VP-CKR		
9311	5000	C-FSSE	M-SALE	VH-DNK	VP-CES		
9312	XRS	C-FTIK	PP-VDR				
9313	6000	C-FTIO	[Global Vision Flight Deck test a/c; Global 6000 test a/c]				
9314	XRS	C-FTIQ	N807DC				
9315	5000	C-FTIR	B-LRW	T7-LRW			
9316	XRS	C-FTIS	N1328M	N1868M			
9317	XRS	C-FTUX	VT-HMA				
9318	5000	C-FTUY	TC-KRM				
9319	XRS	C-FTVF	OE-IRM	9H-IRA			
9320	XRS	C-FTVK	HB-JGH	N688MC	N283DM		
9321	5000	C-FTVN	VP-CWN				
9322	XRS	C-FTVO	XA-BUA	N717AL	N995ML		
9323	XRS	C-FUCV	OE-LGX	N679JB	F-HXRG		
9324	5000	C-FUCY	G-GRAN	M-GRAN			
9325	5000	C-FUCZ	N723HH	(N291SL)	N73SL	M-BRRB	N636JS
9326	XRS	C-FUDH	VH-OCV				
9327	XRS	C-FUDN	N105ZZ	N118WT			
9328	5000	C-FUOJ	N555HD				
9329	XRS	C-FUOK	9H-XRS	M-SIRI			
9330	5000	C-FUOL	N939ML	N700HM			
9331	XRS	C-FUOM	G-KANL	OY-LNA			
9332	XRS	C-FURP	(LX-GXR)	OH-TNF	(D-ATNF)	LX-TNF	N332JG	T7-SKA
9333	XRS	C-FUSI	G-SANL				
9334	5000	C-FUSR	G-PVEL	9H-PVL			
9335	XRS	C-FUTF	A6-BBD	VP-CTP			
9336	XRS	C-FUTL	(S5-ADE)	CS-DTG	G-OKKI	9H-OKI	
9337	5000	C-FUTT	N109ZZ	M-ATAK	N985EL		
9338	XRS	C-FVFW	N18WZ				
9339	XRS	C-FVGP	N112ZZ	C-GFRX	VQ-BNP	D-ABNP*	
9340	5000	C-FVGX	N340GF	N501JT	N426CF	N954L	(N962L)	N692L
9341	XRS	C-FVHE	VP-CNA				
9342	XRS	C-FVUI	N39ZZ	VQ-BKI			
9343	5000	C-FVUK	OY-SGC	N43GX			
9344	XRS	C-FVUP	VH-VLA	N360HP			
9345	XRS	C-FVUZ	N113ZZ	D-ACBO	A6-CBO		
9346	5000	C-FVVE	VH-LEP	P4-PIF			
9347	XRS	C-FWGB	N115ZZ	HB-JFY			
9348	XRS	C-FWGH	9H-BGL	D-ARKO			
9349	XRS	C-FWGP	(4X-CMB)	M-VANG	LX-ZED		
9350	5000	C-FWGV	9M-TAN				
9351	XRS	C-FWHF	G-OXRS	(PP-AHT)			
9352	XRS	C-FWIK	N868SC	C-GILQ	(M-YXRS)	N726AF	
9353	5000	C-FWZR	CS-EAM	OH-MAL	9H-FLN		
9354	XRS	C-FWZX	N92ZZ	N113CS	N923SG	N721FF	
9355	E-11A	C-FXAQ	N770AG	USAF 11-9355			
9356	5000	C-FXAY	N404NA				
9357	XRS	C-FXBF	N40ZZ	B-95959	N959GX		
9358	E-11A	C-FXIY	N760AG	USAF 11-9358			
9359	5000	C-FXJD	HB-JIH	A6-ACE			
9360	XRS	C-FXJM	EC-LJP	N863BA	EC-MNH		
9361	XRS	C-FXKE	N65ZZ	N579AT	VP-CYT		
9362	XRS	C-FXKK	B-8101	VP-CCN			
9363	5000	C-FXYK	RP-9363	[dbr Tacloban, Philippines, 17Jan15]			
9364	XRS	C-FXYS	C-GGOL	G-GABY			
9365	XRS	C-FXYY	N75ZZ	TC-YAA	TC-YYA		
9366	5000	C-FYGJ	N59ZZ	N700GR	N560U		
9367	XRS	C-FYGP	HB-JII				
9368	XRS	C-FYGX	VH-TGG				
9369	XRS	C-FYHT	VP-BEB	VH-SGA			
9370	5000	C-FYIG	A7-CED				
9371	XRS	C-FYIH	(CS-EAP)	M-UNIS			
9372	5000	C-FYIZ	VP-CGM				
9373	5000	C-FYJC	9H-OVB	HB-JRX			

BD-700 GLOBAL EXPRESS XRS / GLOBAL 5000 / GLOBAL 6000

C/n	Series	Identities					
9374	XRS	C-FYJD	G-FCFC	D-ATOM	VP-CJT	T7-JAT	
9375	XRS	C-FYMT	N121ZZ	N416BD			
9376	5000	C-FYMU	RA-67225				
9377	XRS	C-FYNI	(G-HVLD)	G-CGSJ			
9378	XRS	C-FYNQ	N211PB				
9379	5000	C-FYNV	VP-BSK	A7-TAT	N862BA	XA-JGT	
9380	XRS	C-FYOC	M-RSKL				
9381	6000	C-GBTY	N381GX	N885AQ*			
9382	5000	C-GBUA	(N119ZZ)	N15PX	(N15BX)	N954L*	
9383	5000	C-GBUI	N188J				
9384	XRS	C-GCKR	HL8230				
9385	XRS	C-GCLI	VQ-BRL	N393BV			
9386	5000	C-GCMJ	N968DS	N117MS			
9387	XRS	C-GCOX	B-8199	N789RR			
9388	XRS	C-GCPI	C-GDPF				
9389	5000	C-GCPV	C-GJCB				
9390	XRS	C-GCWQ	B-8266	N899CH			
9391	XRS	C-GCWU	VP-CHL				
9392	5000	C-GCWV	N782SF				
9393	XRS	C-GCWX	VQ-BIH	C-GKZW	VH-ICV		
9394	XRS	C-GCXE	VP-CBM	M-ULTI			
9395	5000	C-GDCF	Germany 9848		Germany 1401		
9396	XRS	C-GDCZ	VQ-BOK	N290KR	N497EC		
9397	XRS	C-GDEK	N169LL	C-FIPX			
9398	5000	C-GDEV	(B-8198)	N2707	N270F		
9399	XRS	C-GEHF	M-ARRJ	N871BA			
9400	5000	C-GEHK	N445DB				
9401	5000	C-GEHV	OE-III	M-IBID	9H-IBD		
9402	XRS	C-GEIM	N700WR	N1DS			
9403	XRS	C-GEUX	EC-LNM	N869BA	C-FTNB	P4-WNE	N700KS
9404	5000	C-GEVN	Germany 1402				
9405	5000	C-GEZJ	D-ACDE				
9406	XRS	C-GEZX	N268AA	M-SSSR	RA-67242		
9407	XRS	C-GFAE	C-GWHF				
9408	5000	C-GFAP	TC-MJA				
9409	XRS	C-GFKH	N368HK	S5-GMG	9H-ERO	M-DSUN	
9410	XRS	C-GFKJ	(VT-JSI)	N311NB			
9411	5000	C-GFKL	Germany 1403				
9412	XRS	C-GFKQ	B-8196				
9413	XRS	C-GGFJ	M-GLOB	G-GLOB			
9414	5000	[C-GGHN c/n changed to 9998 at customer's request]					
9415	XRS	C-GGHT	(B-LIZ)	B-KTL			
9416	XRS	C-GGIM	VP-CEO				
9417	5000	C-GGSA	Germany 1404				
9418	5000	C-GGSU	M-CCCP				
9419	XRS	C-GGUA	D-ARYR				
9420	XRS	C-GGUG	M-GSKY				
9421	5000	C-GHCE	A7-CEE				
9422	XRS	C-GHCS	HL8238				
9423	XRS	C-GHCZ	G-RAAA				
9424	5000	C-GHVB	4X-COF	India GB8001			
9425	5000	C-GHVN	B-KEZ				
9426	XRS	C-GHVO	P4-GMS				
9427	5000	C-GHVX	(D-APCA)	D-AOHS	OE-INL		
9428	XRS	C-GHWD	N979CB	N976CB	EC-MMD		
9429	XRS	C-GHXX	OE-LXX	9H-LXX			
9430	5000	C-GHXY	9H-VSM	P4-MMM	9H-MMM		
9431	5000	C-GHYK	4X-COH	India GB8002			
9432	6000	C-GIOC	VP-CWW				
9433	6000	C-GIOK	OY-LGI				
9434	6000	C-GIOW	M-MNAA	HZ-ATH			
9435	6000	C-GIOX	N797CT				
9436	6000	C-GISY	N302AK				
9437	6000	C-GITG	9H-AMF				
9438	6000	C-GIUD	"C-GUID"+	[+incorrect marks worn at completion centre]	(C-FBDR)	N88AA	
9439	6000	C-GIUP	N980GG				
9440	6000	C-GJFD	9H-VJB	9H-OPE			
9441	6000	C-GJFI	9H-VJA				
9442	6000	C-GJFQ	N112MY				
9443	6000	C-GJFW	M-AAAL				
9444	6000	C-GJGE	N1955M	N944GX	N688MC	N393BZ*	
9445	5000	C-GJJG	VP-CKM				
9446	5000	C-GJKA	VT-KJB				
9447	6000	C-GJKO	PP-GUL				
9448	6000	C-GJKZ	9H-VJC				
9449	5000	C-GJLH	N346L				

BD-700 GLOBAL 5000 / GLOBAL 6000

C/n	Series	Identities					
9450	6000	C-GJLY	M-NALE				
9451	6000	C-GKLC	N451GX	(N987JJ)	9H-NGX		
9452	6000	C-GKLX	N729KF				
9453	5000	C-GKMO	M-BLUE				
9454	5000	C-GKMU	N678RC				
9455	6000	C-GKNP	OE-IRT				
9456	6000	C-GKOH	F-GVMI				
9457	5000	C-GKOJ	M-IGWT	G-ISAN	N724MF		
9458	5000	C-GKOY	N168JH	C-GKOY	OY-GVI	9H-GVA	
9459	6000	C-GKUZ	N45GX				
9460	6000	C-GKVC	C-GPPX				
9461	5000	C-GKVL	M-SEAS				
9462	5000	C-GKVN	N565RS				
9463	6000	C-GKVO	N115MH				
9464	6000	C-GKYI	EC-LTF				
9465	5000	C-GKYK	N918TA	N918GL	N241EA*		
9466	6000	C-GKYL	S5-ZFL				
9467	6000	C-GKYN	N320GB	N203JE			
9468	5000	C-GKYO	N755RA				
9469	6000	C-GLEU	N46GX				
9470	6000	C-FHYL	C-GSDU	ZS-SYH	N683JB	OY-GVG	9H-GVG
9471	6000	C-GLFG	M-MYNA				
9472	6000	C-GLFK	(9H-VJC)	9H-VJD			
9473	6000	C-GLFN	N88GZ	B-8197			
9474	5000	C-GLUN	N702LK				
9475	6000	C-GLUP	N160QS				
9476	6000	C-GLUR	N118ZZ	N711LS			
9477	5000	C-GLUS	(N168HH)	B-98888			
9478	6000	C-GLKC	CS-GLA				
9479	6000	C-GLKH	(CS-GLA)	N141QS			
9480	5000	C-GMRX	N100QS				
9481	6000	C-GMSO	CS-GLB				
9482	6000	C-GMSU	M-DADA				
9483	5000	C-GMSY	N101QS				
9484	6000	C-GMTY	N162QS	N914BA			
9485	6000	C-GMWV	N142QS				
9486	5000	C-GMXH	M-SAID				
9487	6000	C-GMXY	(D-ALUK)	D-AGJP			
9488	6000	C-GMYE	B-8195				
9489	5000	C-GMYL	N2707				
9490	6000	C-GNGY	N612FG				
9491	6000	C-GNHB	N8762	N8762M			
9492	5000	C-GNHP	N286JS	(PR-IZB)			
9493	6000	C-GNKK	VT-SNG	[dbr by flood water Chennai, India, 01Dec15]			
9494	6000	C-GNKW	M-ABFQ	[cx to United Arab Emirates Armed Forces 31Jan17]			
9495	5000	C-GNZV	OE-LPZ				
9496	6000	C-GOAN	OE-IEO				
9497	6000	C-GOBF	HB-JFE				
9498	5000	C-GOCD	N130QS	N986BA	N130QS		
9499	6000	C-GODV	N143QS				
9500	6000	C-GOEB	F-GBOL				
9501	5000	C-GOIK	VP-CWQ				
9502	6000	C-GOIM	9H-VJE				
9503	6000	C-GOIP	9H-VJF				
9504	5000	C-GOIR	N933ML				
9505	6000	C-GOIS	VP-BOK				
9506	E-11A	C-GOUR	N9506G	USAF 12-9506			
9507	6000	C-GOUU	OE-IRS				
9508	5000	C-GOUX	N723HH				
9509	6000	C-GPIA	VP-CPT				
9510	6000	C-GPIW	B-8105				
9511	6000	C-GPKI	N806AS				
9512	6000	C-GPKX	N512BH	VP-BVM			
9513	5000	C-GPYF	C-FMPX				
9514	6000	C-GPYW	HB-JRM	CS-DPL			
9515	6000	C-GPYX	OH-TRA	N599CH			
9516	5000	C-GPZE	N41SH	M-IUNI			
9517	6000	C-GPZH	M-ABFR	[cx to United Arab Emirates Armed Forces 31Jan17]			
9518	6000	C-GRRI	(VP-BTD)	M-HAWK			
9519	6000	C-GRSF	N700LS				
9520	5000	C-GRSU	N443PR				
9521	6000	C-GRTU	EI-SSF	M-YSSF			
9522	6000	C-GRUK	N900LS				
9523	6000	C-GSKD	HB-JEH				
9524	6000	C-GSLW	N193LC	N193LA			
9525	6000	C-GSNB	M-AHAH	M-AHAR	M-AHAA		

BD-700 GLOBAL 5000 / GLOBAL 6000

C/n	Series	Identities				
9526	6000	C-GSNF	N526GX	VP-COJ	N526GX	
9527	6000	C-GSNG	VT-JSY			
9528	5000	C-GSYX	OE-IXX			
9529	6000	C-GSZB	N1812C			
9530	6000	C-GSZF	N805WB	N805WM		
9531	5000	C-GSZG	N103QS	(N176HT)	N176HS	
9532	6000	C-GTUA	VP-CJC			
9533	6000	C-GTUF	CS-GLC			
9534	5000	C-GTUO	A7-CEV			
9535	6000	C-GTUU	9H-CIO			
9536	5000	C-GTUV	N1368M			
9537	6000	C-GTVC	M-YFTA			
9538	6000	C-GTZN	CS-GLD			
9539	5000	C-GTZO	N50VC			
9540	6000	C-GTZS	VP-CZL			
9541	6000	C-GUAK	N41GX	(PR-IZB)	N8998K	PR-IZB*
9542	5000	C-GUAL	OE-ICA			
9543	6000	C-GUAN	N543GL			
9544	5000	C-GUDZ	OY-VIZ			
9545	6000	C-GUEL	M-RIZA	VP-CBD		
9546	6000	C-GUEO	N288DG			
9547	5000	C-GUEP	9H-TOR			
9548	6000	C-GUET	N548GX	N36LG		
9549	6000	C-GUEU	M-BMAL	9H-SMB		
9550	5000	C-GUEV	N627JW			
9551	6000	C-GUIF	N312AF			
9552	5000	C-GUIH	N500VJ			
9553	6000	C-GUIS	OH-MPL	S5-SAD		
9554	6000	C-GUIY	M-ARGO			
9555	5000	C-GUJK	N104QS			
9556	6000	C-GUJM	PP-FCC			
9557	6000	C-GUJP	N9099H			
9558	5000	C-GUOX	N468GH			
9559	6000	C-GUPK	(D-AABE)	(D-AABB)	LX-ABB	
9560	5000	C-GUPM	M-TYRA			
9561	6000	C-GUPB	N979CB			
9562	6000	C-GUPL	N562GX	(N14CK)	M-ABCC	
9563	5000	C-GUPN	N501VJ			
9564	6000	C-GUPF	XA-OVR			
9565	5000	C-GUSV	9H-VTA	N503VJ		
9566	5000	C-GUTG	9H-VTB			
9567	6000	C-GUTP	F-HFIP			
9568	6000	C-GUSX	VQ-BPG	N68889		
9569	5000	C-GUTN	N3338			
9570	6000	C-GUTE	9H-IGH			
9571	5000	C-GUSU	9H-VTC			
9572	6000	C-GVKL	N181CL			
9573	6000	C-GVGZ	N400BC			
9574	6000	C-GVKO	N533LM			
9575	6000	C-GVKH	N809PT	VP-BMG		
9576	6000	C-GVGY	M-YSKY			
9577	6000	C-GVRO	M-HOME	T7-OKY		
9578	5000	C-GVRU	9H-OMK			
9579	6000	C-GVRI	M-SAMA			
9580	6000	C-GVRY	9H-VJG			
9581	5000	C-GVRS	A7-CEI			
9582	6000	C-GVWV	PR-BPT			
9583	6000	C-GVXG	N116SF	N583JC		
9584	5000	C-GVXD	VP-CBF			
9585	6000	C-GVWR	9H-VJH			
9586	5000	C-GVXF	LX-RAK	N718RJ	M-MICS	
9587	6000	C-GVXB	N99ZM			
9588	6000	C-GWKV	N65XC	N60XC		
9589	5000	C-GWLK	N109QS			
9590	6000	C-GWNY	M-YVVF			
9591	6000	C-GWKY	N7777U			
9592	5000	C-GWLR	N110QS			
9593	6000	C-GWMY	9H-VJI			
9594	5000	C-GWKU	M-FINE			
9595	6000	C-GWKZ	M-IGWT			
9596	6000	C-GXBM	M-YULI			
9597	5000	C-GXAU	M-AGRI	M-BIGG		
9598	6000	C-GXAF	N145QS			
9599	6000	C-GXCE	N626JS			
9600	5000	C-GXBN	A6-RJC			
9601	6000	C-GXAZ	LX-NAD			

BD-700 GLOBAL 5000 / GLOBAL 6000

C/n	Series	Identities			
9602	5000	C-GXAH	CS-LAM		
9603	6000	C-GXCO	ZS-TDF		
9604	6000	C-GXCA	9H-VJJ		
9605	5000	C-GXBK	N50MG		
9606	6000	C-GXAN	N588LQ		
9607	6000	C-GWZR	N212LE	N212LF	
9608	5000	C-GXCD	N502VJ		
9609	6000	C-GXKK	OE-LII		
9610	5000	C-GXKV	N889ST		
9611	6000	C-GXKO	VP-CJK		
9612	6000	C-GXLG			
9613	5000	C-GXKG	N918TB		
9614	6000	C-GXLC	N878SC		
9615	6000	C-GXRC	N146QS		
9616	5000	C-GXRK	N616GX	N902MY	
9617	6000	C-GXRW	N244DS		
9618	5000	C-GXRD	N618GX	N667BB	
9619	6000	C-GXRA	9H-VJK		
9620	6000	C-GXRU	N620GX	N417LX	
9621	5000	C-GXZL	A6-RJD		
9622	6000	C-GXZD	N810TS		
9623	5000	C-GXZV	M-JGVJ		
9624	6000	C-GXZM	SE-RMT		
9625	6000	C-GXZG	I-PFLY		
9626	6000	C-GXZB	9H-VJL		
9627	5000	C-GXZR	HB-JRI		
9628	6000	C-GYOX	VP-CYA		
9629	5000	C-GYOH	N2QE		
9630	6000	C-GYRF	9H-VJM		
9631	6000	C-GYPW	ZS-OAK		
9632	6000	C-GYOV	N147QS		
9633	5000	C-GYOF	M-DANK	9H-AVA	
9634	6000	C-GYPX	N9634	N504R	
9635	6000	C-GZDY	VP-CFO		
9636	5000	C-GZEH	N83FF		
9637	6000	C-GZDS	(M-GABY)+	[+ntu marks worn at factory]	M-YOIL
9638	6000	C-GZEB	CS-GLE		
9639	5000	C-GZHO	M-KBSD		
9640	6000	C-GZGR	C-GHSW		
9641	6000	C-GZHG	N9641	N12G	
9642	5000	C-GZGP	C-FFIJ		
9643	6000	C-GZHU	N968EX	N88C	
9644	5000	C-GZGS	C-GJET	N880ZJ	
9645	6000	C-GZRU	N1955M		
9646	6000	C-GZRE	VQ-BCC		
9647	5000	C-GZRY	N625SC		
9648	6000	C-GZRA	N148QS		
9649	6000	C-GZRP	N70EW		
9650	5000	C-FBUH	N142HC		
9651	6000	C-FBVS	VT-AHI		
9652	6000	C-FBVG	VP-CEW		
9653	6000	C-FBUA	N9653	PR-FIS	
9654	6000	C-FBVL	VH-LEP		
9655	5000	C-FCZV	N5000P		
9656	6000	C-FCYX	N56GX	9H-AMZ	
9657	6000	C-FDIW	N150QS		
9658	5000	C-FCZS	VT-IBG		
9659	6000	C-FCYG	N9TJ		
9660	5000	C-FDHP	N111QS		
9661	6000	C-FCZN	(D-AMPX)	A7-TAA	
9662	6000	C-FDVX	9H-VJN		
9663	5000	C-FDUA	N970DX	N939GS	
9664	6000	C-FDXB	N600JV		
9665	6000	C-FDVO	9H-FCA		
9666	5000	C-FDSZ	VP-BCY		
9667	6000	C-FDXA	9H-VJY		
9668	5000	C-FDUV	N968GX	M-SAPT	
9669	6000	C-FEHT	9H-VJO		
9670	6000	C-FEMF	CS-GLF		
9671	5000	C-FEOF	N970NX		
9672	6000	C-FEHU	OE-IGL		
9673	6000	C-FEMN	N403PM	B-96999	
9674	5000	C-FEHG	N40TE		
9675	6000	C-FELO	N967NX	N529DB	
9676	5000	C-FFHW	3B-PGT		
9677	6000	C-FFMV	9H-VJP		

BD-700 GLOBAL 5000 / GLOBAL 6000

C/n	Series	Identities				
9678	6000	C-FFGZ	N968DW	M-MAXX		
9679	6000	C-FFLC	N401PM	N588ZJ		
9680	6000	C-FFMZ	VH-IEJ			
9681	5000	C-FFHA	VP-BGS			
9682	6000	C-FFLZ	N10HD			
9683	5000	C-FFGU	N402PM	M-RRRR	N683JC	M-CITI
9684	6000	C-FFWP	N588MM			
9685	6000	C-FFVM	N968DZ	N2020Q		
9686	6000	C-FFXS	VP-CAF			
9687	5000	C-FFVX	N968DX	C-FPQJ	M-CVGL	
9688	6000	C-FFVE	N688ZJ			
9689	6000	C-FGWV	N410MG	N410M*		
9690	5000	C-FGSU	M-AABG			
9691	6000	C-FGVS	9H-VJQ			
9692	6000	C-FGUD	LX-ZAK			
9693	5000	C-FGWF	9H-CMA	OE-IMA		
9694	6000	C-FGSS	N968BX	(N999HY)		
9695	6000	C-FHSX	EC-MKH			
9696	5000	C-FHNN	N898CC			
9697	6000	C-FHMG	N404PM	N566ZJ		
9698	6000	C-FHSN	N405PM			
9699	5000	C-FHND	N912MT			
9700	6000	C-FHMF	RA-67241			
9701	6000	C-FHPZ	9H-GFI			
9702	6000	C-FHMZ	N343DF			
9703	6000	C-FIEZ	9H-VJR			
9704	6000	C-FIFP	N161GF	M-RRRR		
9705	6000	C-FIIA	VP-CZJ			
9706	6000	C-FIFK	M-NAME			
9707	5000	C-FIHP	N968HX	N500QA		
9708	6000	C-FIEX	M-INER			
9709	6000	C-FIFN	N162GF	N116SF		
9710	5000	C-FIRT	N112QS			
9711	6000	C-FIPU	9H-VJS			
9712	6000	C-FIRK	B-3246			
9713	5000	C-FISO	B-7765			
9714	6000	C-FIPT	SE-RMY			
9715	5000	C-FIRG	VP-BLQ			
9716	6000	C-FJDZ	N788ZJ			
9717	5000	C-FJFJ	N412PB			
9718	6000	C-FJGK	CS-DVV			
9719	5000	C-FJDX	N165GF	N215TM		
9720	6000	C-FJGI	N163GF	N63KK*		
9721	6000	C-FJGX	9H-VJT			
9722	5000	C-FJEF	N113QS			
9723	6000	C-FJXR	D-ANMB			
9724	6000	C-FJWX	9H-VJU			
9725	6000	C-FJYB	9H-VJV			
9726	6000	C-FJXE	C-FLGZ			
9727	6000	C-FJXY				
9728	6000	C-FKFY	9H-VJW			
9729	6000	C-FKEX	N998ZX			
9730	6000	C-FKDN	(9H-VJX)	N151QS		
9731	6000	C-FKFO	N633EY			
9732	5000	C-FKDK	N114QS			
9733	6000	C-FKFS	N850MP			
9734	5000	C-FKRE	N115QS			
9735	6000	C-FKSN	N283JA	M-LLIN		
9736	6000	C-FKSB	N421SZ			
9737	5000	C-FKPY	N1226			
9738	6000	C-FKSF	9H-VJX			
9739	6000	C-FKRX	VQ-BEB			
9740	6000	C-FLGN	N988ZJ			
9741	6000	C-FLKU	N148L			
9742	6000	C-FLKC	M-MAVP			
9743	6000	C-FLGD	SE-RMZ			
9744	6000	C-FLHA	N426GA	N17JS		
9745	6000	C-FLKO	C-GJDR			
9746	6000	C-FLFT	9H-VJZ			
9747	6000	C-FLWV	OE-LML			
9748	6000	C-FLXD	F-HMBY			
9749	6000	C-FLVK	N770KF			
9750	6000	C-FLWX	9H-TNF			
9751	6000	C-FMFO	N18CZ			
9752	6000	C-FMCZ	C-FOEG			
9753	6000	C-FMHR				

BD-700 GLOBAL 5000 / GLOBAL 6000

C/n	Series	Identities			
9754	6000	C-FMCH	9H-LDN		
9755	5000	C-FMYG	F-HTTO		
9756	6000	C-FMZS	VT-SNT		
9757	6000	C-FMYD	CS-GLG		
9758	6000	C-FMYX	N758WT	N758JF*	
9759	6000	C-FNIR			
9760	6000	C-FNMC			
9761	6000	C-FNKX			
9762	6000	C-FNIL	M-TSLT		
9763	6000	C-FNLH			
9764	6000	C-FNXG	N246ZJ		
9765	6000	C-FNVR			
9766	6000	C-FNXK			
9767	6000	C-FODX	T7-RSP		
9768	5000	C-FOCF			
9769	6000	C-FODN			
9770	6000	C-FOHP			
9771	6000	C-FOHN			
9772	6000	C-FOTF			
9773	6000	C-FOSW			
9774	6000	C-FPUM			
9775	6000	C-FPSV			
9776	6000	C-FPSF			
9777	5000	C-FRFX			
9778	6000	C-FRCZ			
9779	6000	C-FRHZ			
9780	5000	C-FRZM			
9781	6000	C-FRYZ			
9782	5000	C-FRYO			
9783	6000	C-FSVZ			
9784	6000	C-FSRX			
9785	6000	C-FSYX			
9786	5000	C-FSZO			
9787	6000	C-FSYV			
9788	6000	C-FUBH			
9789	6000	C-FUBG			
9790	5000	C-FULD			
9791	6000	C-FUFA			
9792	6000	C-FUFT			
9793	6000	C-FUHF			
9794	6000	C-FUEZ			
9795	6000	C-FUFS			
9796	6000	C-FUGV			
9797	6000	C-FUEP			
9798	5000	C-FUPP			
9799					
9800					
9801					
9802					
9803					
9804					
9805					
9806					
9807					
9808					
9809					
9810					
9811					
9812					
9813					
9814					
9815					
9816					
9817					
9818					
9819					
9820					
9998	5000	C-GGHN	[c/n changed from 9414 at customer's request]		B-KMF

BD-700 GLOBAL 7000

C/n	Series	Identities	
70001		C-GLBO	[ff04Nov16, Toronto/Downsview]
70002		C-GBLB	[ff04Mar17, Toronto/Downsview]
70003		C-GLBX	[ff10May17, Toronto/Downsview]

CANADAIR CL600 CHALLENGER

C/n	Srs	Identities
1001		C-GCGR-X [ff 08Nov78; w/o 03Apr80 Mojave, CA, while flight testing]
1002	S	C-GCGS-X Canada 144612 code "X" [displayed Heritage Park, Air Command HQ, Winnipeg, Canada]
1003/3991	S	C-GCGT-X C-GCGT [wfu circa Feb06 to Canadian Aviation Museum, Rockcliffe, Canada for display]
1004	S	C-GXKQ N2677S N227CC N600BP N640TS N50PA [parted out]
1005	S	C-GBDH N600CL C-GBCC N444WA D-BJET N600CL N605TS N180CH N244AL [parted out by Dodson Int'l Parts, Rantoul, KS]
1006	S	C-GCSN N110KS HZ-AO4 C-GCSN Canada 144603 N296V N515BP (N6972Z) XB-ODO
1007	S	C-GBKC HZ-TAG C-GBKC Canada 144604 N600WJ (N799HF) (N607BH)
1008	S	C-GBEY (D-BBAD) Canada 144605 N380V N604SH
1009	S	C-GBFY N606CL C-GCVQ Canada 144606 N396V (N198SD)
1010	S	C-GCIB N909MG N802Q N7JM N2105
1011	S	C-GBHS N42137 N510PC N510PS N601JR N678ML N116RA N3RP [cx 25Jun15; parted out in South Africa]
1012	S	C-GBKE N600KC (N78499) N750PM N750BM N121VA N8KG N167SC N310PE N604AC VH-JPQ
1013	S	C-GBHZ N2428 N601SA N129BA N72SR N16RW
1014	S	C-GBLL-X N97941 HZ-TAG C-GBLL Canada 144607 N370V [w/o 02Feb05 Teterboro Airport, NJ]
1015	S	C-GBLN N37LB N604CL C-GBLN Canada 144608 N25V
1016	S	C-GWRT EI-GPA VR-BKJ N757MC N16TS N920RV (N812XL)
1017	S	C-GBPX N4247C N777XX C-GBPX Canada 144609 N270V M-CHLG N808CH
1018	S	C-GLWR N1812C N198CC N375PK N875PK N771WW N618AJ N618RL C6-SVB
1019	S	C-GLWT N9071M N603CL N600FF ZS-NER 3B-GFI N619TS
1020	S	C-GLWV N36LB N602CL N600MG N600PD N808TM N600BD N602AJ
1021	S	C-GLWX N914X N914XA N63HJ [canx 14Oct04 and parted out]
1022	S	C-GLWZ C-GOGO Canada 144610 N260V N600JJ
1023	S	C-GLXB N630M N680M N90UC (N610TS) N920DS (N333TS) N777GD N771GD [parted out by Dodson International Parts, Rantoul, KS]
1024	S	C-GLXD N637ML N567ML N326MM N810MT N811MT [parted out by Dodson Int'l Parts, Rantoul, KS]
1025	S	C-GLXF N2636N N111G N111J HB-ILH N888LW N620SB (OY-VIA) (OY-CKO) N711GA N399WB
1026	S	C-GLXH N507CC N507HC (N507WY) N694JC N694PG LV-CGL
1027	S	C-GLXK N420L N420TX (N456CG) N678CG N111FK N112FK N93BA N111JL [cx 03Feb17; parted out Wilmington, DE]
1028	S	C-GLXM HB-VHC N600ST 5B-CHX N600BZ YV-1111CP N858PJ
1029	S	C-GLXO HB-VGA D-BMTM (N205A) OH-WIH N600TN N722DJ
1030	S	C-GLXQ N1622 N604CL C-GCZU Canada 144611 (N196V) N60S N630BB N721ST ZS-SKC D2-SKC
1031	S	C-GLXS N620S
1032	S	C-GLXU N455SR N200CN N11AZ (N31DC) N1884 N70X N70XF
1033	S	C-GLXW N2642F VR-CKK N600YY N101SK N101ST N357RT N304TT (N518FS)
1034		C-GLXY N2634Y N153SR (N151SR) N209WF (N209WE) N481JT LV-YLB N134VS
1035	S	C-GLYA N122TY N122WF N64FC C-FEAQ (EI-BYD) VR-BLD N700CL N187AP N163EG N163ET
1036	S	C-GLYC C-GBOQ N80AT N88AT N66MF N900DP N900LG N275JP
1037		C-GLYE N805C [w/o 03Jan83 Sun Valley Friedman Memorial, ID]
1038	S	C-GLYH N8010X N1045X N65HJ N616DF N903DD [cx 19Apr17, CofR expired]
1039	S	C-GLYK N26640 N1868M N1868S N722HP N895CC N905MP N420PR*
1040	S	C-GLYM Canada 144601 [dbr McDill AFB, FL, 24May12]
1041	S	C-GLYO N733K N733CF N193DQ (N95DQ) N141TS N141RD
1042	S	C-GLWV N770CA N999SR N999TF (N939CG) N604MH N604SJ 4X-CZI
1043	S	C-GLWX N229GC C-GJPG C-FSXG N43NW N100QR (LV-CZU)
1044	S	C-GLWZ N541MM N205MM N55AR N800BT
1045	S	C-GLXB N55PG N900FC C-GBKB N247CK G-NREG [cx 15Feb15; parted out at Kemble, UK; fuselage used as film prop at Leavesden Studios, UK and White Waltham, UK]
1046	S	C-GLXD C-GTXV N46SR N246JL
1047	S	C-GLXH C-GBSZ N2741Q N601WW N818LS N555WD N556WD (N500EX) N315MK N249AJ
1048	S	C-GLXK N29687 N600TT N500LS N600LS N601LS (EI-BXN) C-FSIP C-GDDR
1049	S	C-GLXM N2720B HB-VFW N491DB N491TS N39RE N600CF N601CT
1050	S	C-GLXO N600MK N82CW N82CN N710HL N650TL
1051	S	C-GLXQ N27341 N20CX (N601CR) N601SR N91UC N27BH N505PM
1052	S	C-GLXS N3330M N3330L N110M N110TD N409KC N600LG N620AC "N168TS" N620AC N152TS N222LH N222LM
1053	S	C-GLYA HB-VHO N4424P N32BC N32BQ N397BE N415PT N54SK N54SU LV-BAS
1054	S	C-GLYC N80TF N7008 N9008 VR-CLI N602AS N660RM N217RM N915KH
1055		C-GLYE N2707T N1FE N55SR N271MB N643CR
1056	S	C-GLYH N26895 N600CC N600TE N712HL N1HZ N2HZ N777GA
1057	S	C-GLXU C-GBTK N605CL (VH-OZZ) N508CC N508HC XA-RAP XA-TIV XA-ISR N78SR N6MW
1058	S	C-GLXW N4000X N60HJ N658CF [cx 03Mar16; instructional airframe with Mohawk Valley Community College, Rome/Griffiss, NY]
1059	S	C-GLXY N227G N227GL (C-FRST) (C-GFCD) N3HB N103HB N403WY N396KM
1060	S	C-GLYK N29984 N22AZ N74JA
1061	S	C-GLYO N600JW VH-MXX VH-MCG N770JC N661TS N601KK (N661TS) (N604YZ) N696JB
1062	S	C-GLWV C-GBTT Malaysia M31-01 N4FE N62BL N68SD N95EB N444ET

CL600 CHALLENGER

C/n	Srs	Identities
1063	S	C-GLWX N31240+ N102ML PT-LXW N102ML XA-SOA N8260D (N74TJ) (N711AJ) (N88TJ) (N98TW) N409CC N457HL [+recorded for a while in error on FAA files as N32140]
1064	S	C-GLWZ C-GBUB Malaysia M31-02 N14FE N64GL N75B N100LR
1065	S	C-GLXB C-GBVE Canada 144602 N601WJ N287DL
1066	S	C-GLXD N67B N721SW N701QS N701GA N51TJ D-BSNA ZS-TCW
1067	S	C-GLXH "VR-CBP" C-GLXH C-GBZE N50928 N800AB N205EL N240AK M-IFES G-CIAU
1068	S	C-GLXK N215RL N938WH N160LC N604EF
1069	S	C-GLXM N203G N816PD I-LPHZ N74LM (N100LR) N500RH N788WG N818TH (N818E) N455BE N817CK N80CK
1070	S	C-GLXO N3237S HZ-MF1 N70DJ N24JK N670CL D-BUSY N600DP
1071	S	C-GLXQ N607CL N523B N588UC N121DF N127DF N671SR N711DB N220LC N600HA ZS-TSN
1072	S	C-GLXW N82A (N137FP) N331FP N125AC N10PN N302PC N329MP 9Q-CVA ZS-BGA
1073	S	C-GLXY N234RG N234MW N31WT (N331WT) N661JB N888KS VH-NKS N600BP (VR-BBP) (N512AC) N125AN (N600EC) N673TS N673YS (N673BH) N27BH RP-C5505
1074		C-GLYK N317FE N1FE N10FE HZ-SAA HZ-WT2 HZ-WBT1 HZ-RFM N800HH N674CW N674TB
1075	S	C-GLXO N600CP N2FE N25SR N751DB N450AJ (N458AJ) N240MC
1076	S	C-GLXK N8000 N7SP I-BLSM N601WW N87TR ZS-YAG
1077	S	C-GLXM N994TA (N778XX) C-GBZK N152SM N71M N500R N507R (N940DH) N300TK
1078	S	C-GLYO N600DL N600CF I-MRDV N53SR N1500 (N1504) VH-ZSU CC-ATA
1079	S	C-GLWV N46ES N125N N601Z N888FW N600RE N601SA N601CM [cx 14Mar2013, parted out by Pollard Spares LLC, Roanoke, TX]
1080	S	C-GLWX N800CC N3JL N300TW N677LM 9Q-CDR 9Q-CRD
1081	S	C-GLWZ N19HF (N54PA) (N681TS) N456DK N19DD N199D N19DD N199D ZS-ISA
1082	S	C-GLXB N3854B N600ST I-PTCT N700KK N777KK N777KZ N333KK N388DD [wfu Fort Lauderdale Executive, FL]
1083	S	C-GLXD N47ES N471SP N471SB N399FL
1084	S	C-GLXH N730TL (N10MZ) N175ST N550CW
1085	S	C-GLXQ N20G N20GX N600ST OE-HET LZ-YUM N807CH [cx 04Jun15; CofR expired]
1086		C-GLXS [marks reserved 29Mar83 but aircraft not completed – fuselage to Canadian Forces Fire Fighting Academy, CFB Borden]
1087		[aircraft not completed – fuselage to Canadian Forces Fire Fighting Academy, CFB Borden]
1088		[aircraft not completed – fuselage to Canadian Forces Fire Fighting Academy, CFB Borden]

Production complete

CANADAIR CL601 CHALLENGER

C/n **Identities**

3001 C-GBUU-X [ff 17Sep82] N601CL N601AG N789DR N74GR
3002 C-GBXH (N509PC) N4449F N273G N601SR N750GT N602CW N227PE N600NP [wfu Marco Island, FL, after landing accident 01Mar15]
3003 C-GLXU N500PC N500TB N500TD C-GESR N601CL (N680FA) VH-MXK
3004 C-GLXK N509PC N967L N501PC N45PH N45WL
3005 C-FAAL N601TX N783DM N958DP [cx 01May15; parted out Wilmington, DE]
3006 C-GLXY N372G (N3728) HB-IKX N372G (EI-TAM) P4-TAM N606BA ZS-ONL N256SD N601JG
3007 C-GLYE N711SR N711SX N711SZ N910KB N275MT
3008 C-GLYK N733A N783A N61AF (N999SW) N38SW N608CW N698CW (N600LX) N710GA N214FW [w/o 29Jan15, shot down by Venezuelan AF near Aruba on suspicion of drug-running]
3009 C-GLYO N373G N873G (N651AC) [w/o 28Nov04 Montrose, CO]
3010 C-GLWV C-GBLX N80CS N601UT N601SQ N601BD N411TJ N957DP
3011 C-GLWX C-GBYC N601AG N399WW N899WW N700MK N7788 N205EL N205EE N202PH N453GS [cx 12Dec15; parted out Wilmington, DE]
3012 C-GLXB N226GL N226G C-GMII VR-BMA N6165C XA-SHZ N603GJ N23BJ N23BN N878RM C-FKJM
3013 C-GLXD N601TG VR-BLA VP-BLA N124BC N633CW (N602LX) N213TS (N32WR)
3014 C-GLXH N14PN N292GA N698RS N698RT C-GDBF N807MM
3015 C-GLXM N374G XA-KIM XA-UXK
3016 C-GLWV N4562Q N1107Z N601CL VP-BIE N388DB N214MD N813TA N813WT*
3017 C-GLWX N778XX (HZ-AMA) HZ-SFS N778YY VR-CAR C-GJPG C-FBYJ A6-EJD JY-RY1 JY-RYA 2-MORO G-MORO [cx 05Apr17, wfu]
3018 C-GLWZ C-GBXW N779XX [w/o 07Feb85 Milan, Italy; cx May91; cockpit section conv to flight simulator and used by Flight Safety Intl at Montreal-Dorval, Canada]
3019 C-GLXB N375G N875G XA-SMS N5498G
3020 C-GLXO C-GCFI [parted out Addison, TX]
3021 C-GLXQ N5069P (N711SP) N711SJ N967L N503PC N966L N150MH [cx 20May15; parted out Georgetown, TX]
3022 C-GLXS C-GCFG
3023 C-GLXY N778YY N100WC N967L N501PC N524PC N601KF N601KE N601FJ AP-MIR
3024 C-GLYA N711ST HB-ILM N98CR N93CR N888AZ VP-COK N211LM
3025 C-GLWV N1620 N529DM N529D N363CR N997GC T7-GFA
3026 C-GLWX N5373U N927A N601GL N300S N80RP N716HP N810MT (N810MB) N307SC N601NP [parted out Gary, IN]
3027 C-GLWZ N5402X N17CN (N401NK) N627CW (N603LX) C-GPSI [cx Jul12; instructional airframe, Southern Alberta Institute of Technology, Calgary, Canada]
3028 C-GLXB C-FBEL C-FBEI [cx May12; instructional airframe, Ecole Nationale d'Aeronautique, Montreal-St Hubert, Canada]
3029 C-GLXD N5491V N1824T N629TS N773JC N629TS [cx 13Apr15; parted out Wilmington, DE]
3030 C-GLXH N611CL N34CD N39CD [parted out Chino, CA; cx 14May11]
3031 C-GLXK C-GCTB N607CL C-GCTB Germany 1201 VP-CCF N303BX (N631CF) N54JC (N181SM) G-LWDC 9H-IJK
3032 C-GLXM N779YY HZ-AK1 N7011H N111G N111GX N392FV N2000C N177FL
3033 C-GLXQ N601TJ HB-ILK VP-BBF M-MTPO [b/u Kemble, UK, Dec14; cx 20Jan16]
3034 C-GLXU N374BC N372BC N372BG N372PG N120MP C-GSAP C-GLOJ N747LV [cx 05Jan16; wfu]
3035 C-GLXW C-GCUN Canada 144613 [w/o 24Apr95 Shearwater AFB, Nova Scotia, Canada; scrapped CFB Greenwood, Canada]
3036 C-GLXY C-GCUP Canada 144614
3037 C-GLXB C-GCUR Canada 144615
3038 C-GLYA C-GCUT Canada 144616 [preserved Greenwood Military Aviation Museum, CFB Greenwood, Canada]
3039 C-GLYH C-GPGD C-GPCC N639CL N500PG N507PG N1ES
3040 C-GLYK N608CL Germany 1202 [final German AF flight 31May10] C-GJNG
3041 C-GLWV C-GRBC N610MS N600MS N169TA N169TD N418PP
3042 C-GLWX N613CL N900CC N333GJ N951RM N923SL
3043 C-GLWZ N609CL Germany 1203 C5-AFT
3044 C-GLXD N921K N125N N955DB N601GB (N801PA) LV-BPV N304CT
3045 C-GLXH N914BD N914BB N601RP OE-HCL N3045 N998JR N601PR
3046 C-GLXK C-GDBX B-4005 N601HJ N601TJ LX-AEN N46SR N228PK N600GA
3047 C-GLXM C-GBZQ B-4006 N602HJ N602TJ OE-HLE N824DH
3048 C-GLXO N35FP N601JM (N628WC) [cx 28Apr16; parted out Miami/Opa Locka, FL]
3049 C-GLXQ N610CL C-FQYT Germany 1204 C-FTDA
3050 C-GLXS (N9680N) N9680Z N62MS N62MU N95SR N601AE N802PA (N626JP) N528LJ N1219L
3051 C-GLWR N445AC N60MS N60MU N4415D N95SR N651CW (N604LX) N97SG [parted out by Dodson Int'l, Rantoul, KS]
3052 C-GLWT C-GDCQ B-4007 N603HJ (N601GF) N801GC VP-CRX N425WN N515LF
3053 C-GLWV N604CL Germany 1205 C-FDAH
3054 C-GLWX N605CL VH-MZL N54PR N601PR N601TP N601ZT N375PK N315SL N50TG N722HP N57MH N947KK
3055 C-GLWZ N100HG N608RP N601RC
3056 C-GLXB N612CL Germany 1206 C-FDAU C-GPAJ
3057 C-GLXD N19J 9J-RON (N602TS) N747TS N163WG
3058 C-GLXU N125PS
3059 C-GLXW N614CL Germany 1207 C-GDAX
3060 C-GLXY (N601SN) N601S

CL601 CHALLENGER

C/n	Identities									
3061	C-GLYO	N9708N	N999JR	N597FJ	N601AA	YV3221	YV3246			
3062	C-GLYK	N601HP	N601GT	N2183N	N628CM					
3063	C-GLYH	C-FURG	[instructional airframe Montreal/St Hubert, Canada]					C-FURB		
3064	C-GLYC	N566N	N356N	N224N	N224F	(N224HF)	N224U	(N424JM)	N664CW	(N606LX)
	N425SU									
3065	C-GLYA	N602CC	N1623	(N128PE)	N500PE	N601JP	"N603TS"	N601JP	(N54PA)	LX-GDC
	G-IMAC	[cx 16Apr15; wfu]								
3066	C-GLXQ	N609CL	N144SX	VR-CLE	VP-CLE	N105UP				

MODEL 601-3A

C/n	Identities									
5001	C-GDDP	[ff 28Sep86]		N245TT	N245TL	(N59FJ)	N604FJ	(N422PR)		
5002	C-GDEQ	N611CL	C-GDEQ	N611CL	N585UC	N43PR	N602TS			
5003	C-GDHP	N778XX	HB-IKT	N601FR						
5004	C-GDKO	N100KT	N180KT	N618DC	N504TS	XA-VDG				
5005	C-GLWR	N613CL	N101PK	HB-IKU	N14GD	N64FE	N902BW			
5006	C-GLWT	C-FLPC	C-GENA	N506TS	N220LC					
5007	C-GLWV	N60GG	N607CL	(N607CZ)	N17TE	N17TZ	N666CT			
5008	C-GLWX	N601CC	N601EG	N1M	N42EE					
5009	C-GLWZ	N399SW	N699CW	(N610LX)	N654CM					
5010	C-GLXB	N57HA	(N57HK)	N1812C	N181AP	N429WG	N601WG	XA-...		
5011	C-GLXD	N603CC	JA8283	N611MH	N602UK	VR-CIC	VP-CIC			
5012	C-GLXU	N107TB	N1868M	N500LR						
5013	C-GLXW	N711PD	I-CTPT	N604MC	N301MF	N950FB	N116LS			
5014	C-GLXY	N21CX	N31WH	N311G	N311GX	N888DH	(N714TS)	N514TS		
5015	C-GLXH	N601KR	N200DE	N514RB	N204JK					
5016	C-GLXQ	N604CC	N49UR	N622AB	(N622AD)	N868CE	C-GQWI	N325DA	N551SD	
5017	C-GLWX	N700KC	N202HG	N77058	N404HG					
5018	C-GLWV	N606CC	C-FBHX	9Q-CBS	C-FBHX	N601HH	N618DB	(D-AMTM)	N601GS	(N601DR)
	(N601GR)	N893AC	N828SK	N908DG						
5019	C-GLWT	N915BD	N915BB	(N247GA)	N237GA	N602BD	C-GJFQ	N575CF	C-GHGC	
5020	C-GLYA	C-FBKR	I-BEWW	C-GZHZ	N604CF	N39RE	N392JT			
5021	C-GLYC	N64F	N122WF	N48FU	(N305M)	N621CF	N620HF	N989BC		
5022	C-GLYK	N449ML	N449MC	VP-CJP	G-SAJP	VP-CJP	N655TH	N618RR		
5023	C-GLYO	N608CC	EI-LJG	N601CJ	N175ST	N623CW	(OE-...)	D-AAMA	G-JFJC	2-JFJC
	2-ODAY									
5024	C-GLYH	C-FCDF	B-4010	N604HJ	N601NB	N601DT	N712SD	N142RP	N628EF*	
5025	C-GLWR	C-FCGS	B-4011	N605HJ	N1TK	N11TK	N93DW	N1DW	N931DW	N660AF
	N139LJ									
5026	C-GLWT	N601WM	5N-APZ							
5027	C-GLWV	N244BH	N64BH	N421SZ	N420SZ	N420ST	N7PS			
5028	C-GLWX	N601TL	N601RL	(N601EA)	N161JG					
5029	C-GLWZ	C-FDAT	N602CC	VR-BMK	N67MR	N83LC	N594RJ	N375JP	N571NA	
5030	C-GLXB	N312CT	N816SQ	N816SP	N1HZ					
5031	C-GLXD	N900CL	N908CL	N721MC	N721MD	N64LE	(N710TP)			
5032	C-GLXF	N604CC	N667LC	N667CC	4X-COT	N601ER	N950SW	N684SW	LV-BYG	
5033	C-GLXH	VH-ASM	N32GG	N397J	(N397JQ)	N397Q	N144BS	N144BG	N797SA	
5034	C-GLXK	C-GIOH	[to Southern Alberta Institute of Technology, Calgary, as instructional airframe Nov09]							
5035	C-GLXU	N606CC	N333MG	N202W	HB-JRV	N635S	C5-NBB	N203AA		
5036	C-GLXW	N225N	N468KL	N468KE	N400DH					
5037	C-GLXY	N608CC	(JA8360)	N707GG	N353TC	N212LM	N710LM	5N-IGY	N253LA	
5038	C-GLXQ	C-GBJA	(N602CN)	N1271A	N78RP	(N220LC)	N78PP	N91KH		
5039	C-GLWX	N811BB	N811BP	N811BR	N765WT					
5040	C-GLWV	N652CN	N807Z	N898AK						
5041	C-GLWT	C-FETZ	G-FBMB	C-FTIE	N641CL	N352AF	N352AE	"N541TS"	N953FA	N170FL
	N601QA									
5042	C-GLYA	C-FEUV	HB-IKS	N28UA	HB-IKS					
5043	C-GLYC	N779YY	VR-COJ	N601BH	N601VH	N767MP*				
5044	C-GLYK	C-FFBY	I-NNUS	N901BM	VR-CMC	VP-CMC	VP-CBS			
5045	C-GLXS	C-FFSO	N616CC	N500GS	N601AF					
5046	C-GLXW	N6SG	N818TH	N818TY	N426PF	N426PE	N719UW	N423AK		
5047	C-GLXD	N140CH	N547FP	N900SS	N384MP	N507CZ	N517BB			
5048	C-GLXY	N2004G	N716RD	N907WS	N907WC					
5049	C-GLXF	N721EW	N721SW	N721BW	D-AGKG	N628VK	VR-CVK	VP-CVK	N888JA	B-MAI
	N368FJ									
5050	C-GLXK	N826JP	N831CJ	N881CJ	(N25GG)	N710VF	N651JP			
5051	C-GLXM	N1903G	N190GG	N300KC	N190SB	C-GQBQ				
5052	C-GLXO	N4PG	N652CW	N125ST	(N615SA)	XB-CAR				
5053	C-GLXU	N5PG	(N553CW)	N653CW	(N611LX)	N440KM				
5054	C-GLXB	N619FE	N3FE	N954BA						
5055	C-GLXH	N601HC	N46F	N460F	N219YY					

CL601 CHALLENGER

C/n	Identities
5056	C-GLXQ N614CC N153NS N525SD N545SD
5057	[Was to have been first CL601S with c/n 6001 but built as 601-3A] C-GLWR N900NM N830CB N830CD N733CF (N721KY) N91KY XA-...
5058	C-GLWZ N404SK N101SK N527JA
5059	C-GLWV XA-GEO XA-JFE XA-TTD C-GZNC N627KR C-FJNS C-FJNZ N408JC N403JC
5060	C-GLYO N5060H N630M ZS-NKD N506BA N573AC EC-JKT (D-ADLA) D-ARTE N117AA
5061	C-GLYH C-FHHD 9Q-CBS N661CL (N575MA) VP-BEJ
5062	C-GLWX N60FC N540W N548W N142B N727S N316BG N601ER [wfu Chino, CA]
5063	[Was to have been the second CL601S with c/n 6002 but built as 601-3A, last Cartierville-built airframe] C-GLXS N612CC N79AD N78AD N611JW N811JW N801FL (N315FX) N304FX N304BX N50DS N563TS XA-UEW N9771C
5064	[First Dorval-built airframe] C-GLXW C-FIOB VH-BRG N564TS N601EC N811NC
5065	C-GLXD N601BF N882C N103KB N800AJ
5066	C-GLXY N506TN N100KT N3PC N566TS N221LC N16KB
5067	C-GLXF N603CC 9A-CRO 9A-CRT N220TW HB-IUF VP-CFT G-OCFT
5068	C-GLXK N609CC N88WG JA8361 N602WA D-AOHP N113WA C-FNNT N66NT C-FNNS C-FLRP N360FF N360
5069	C-GLXM C-FIGR I-FIPP VR-BNF N655CN N324B C-GRTB N161PB LV-GDQ
5070	C-GLXO N980HC N780HC N305FX (D-AAFX) OY-CLD ZS-SGC
5071	C-GLWT+ N500PC (N5032H) TR-AAG [+shown in Canadian DoT files as C-FLWT in error]
5072	C-GLYC N609K N88HA [w/o 20Mar94 Bassett, NE; cx Apr95; remains to Executive Aircraft Corp, Wichita, KS; fuselage to Addison, TX, 2008]
5073	C-GLYK N60KR PK-HMK N5073 (VR-CKC) (N400KC) N803RR N70X
5074	C-GLXH N23SB VH-NSB VH-JEC
5075	C-GLXU N65357 N810D VR-CCV PT-OSA N601Z N409KC N607AX N625LR
5076	C-GLXB N5TM XA-GUA
5077	C-GLXQ N1622 N64YP N118MT
5078	C-GLWR N601MG N601MD N53DF N553DF N578FP N702RV N227WG
5079	C-GLWV C-FJDF VR-CCR VP-CCR N836CM
5080	C-GLYO C-FJGR N601DB N135BC N135BD N903TA N900H
5081	C-GLYH [also reported as C-GLXH] N619CC HL7202 N601ST
5082	C-GLWX C-GBJA N611NT N611GS N6BB N82FJ N794SB
5083	C-GLYA N189K N683UF N83UF
5084	C-GLWT [also reported as C-GLWZ] N399CF N622WM N622WZ N777GU
5085	C-GLXD C-FJPI N618CC D-ACTU D-ACTE I-DAGS PH-ABO M-YONE G-OWAY G-XRTV
5086	C-GLXS N353K N343K N343KA N601JE C-GIXI N723GH
5087	C-GLXW N601CC C-FLUT XA-RZD N587CC XA-ULQ XA-OHS N548CC [parted out by Dodson Int'l, Rantoul, KS]
5088	C-GLXH N601CD N601HC C-GPOT C-GPCS N613SB [dbr Chino, CA, 13Jun13; parted out by Alliance Air Parts, Oklahoma City, OK]
5089	C-GLXY N968L N516SM N360SL N360RL
5090	C-GLXF N601CB N404CB N818LS N818TH N400KC VP-CAM HB-ITK N621CF N226EC
5091	C-GLXM N915BD (N715BD) C-FTFC N366LP
5092	C-GLXQ [also reported as C-GLXO] C-FKIY HB-IKV N300CR N308CR N4JS
5093	C-GLYA N302EC N601CH N875H N375H N331DC N331DQ C-GGMP C-GMGB C-GFIG
5094	C-GLWT C-FKNN TC-OVA TC-DHB N675CF VP-BZT 5B-CKK N774PC N856JM
5095	C-GLYC N95FE N2FE N995BA
5096	C-GLYK C-FKTD HB-IKW C-GSQI N66NT N66NS C-FNNS C-FJJC
5097	C-GLXK C-FKVW XA-JJS XA-TLM N120PA N227CP
5098	C-GLXH N812GS N808G N329MD
5099	C-GLXU N509W N504M N801P N801R N601DW N203JE N203JD (N121GG) N112GG YV576T N787NM
5100	C-GLXB N510 N505M N225N N241N
5101	C-GLXQ N604CC N105BN (N108BN) N213GS N243JP
5102	C-GLWR C-FLYJ (HS-TDL) HS-TVA VR-CHK VP-CHK N604AC (N983CE) N494LC N241FB N241FR HZ-OHS
5103	C-GLWV N76CS N601BE
5104	C-GLYO N777XX VR-COJ VR-CEG N145ST (N233SG) 9M-SWG N233SG (N604TS) N212CT N720LM N111FK
5105	C-GLYH C-FMVQ OK-BYA Czech Republic 5105
5106	C-GLWX (N601PR) N106PR N523JM N996SR
5107	C-GLWZ N417CL N729HZ N211RG
5108	C-GLXD N428CL N224N N236N
5109	C-GLXS N439CL N721S N721G
5110	C-GLXU N392PT N308FX N308BX TC-MDG HZ-FJM
5111	C-GLXH C-GBJA N46SG N4SG N502F N502HE
5112	C-GLXF N112NC N109NC N404AB N604ME N605CK N800YY N199P
5113	C-GLXM N605CC N163M N163MR N733EY N733EX N128GB N770GE N116HL
5114	C-GLYA C-FOSK VR-BOA VP-BOA 2-MATO
5115	C-GLYC N25SB (N605AG) N1800C N604MB
5116	C-GLXW N841PC N1904P N436DM
5117	C-GLXY N606CC N80BF C-FBCR C-GAOB N9517 N601WY
5118	C-GLXK N824JK N24JK N900FN C-GZUM C-GZUQ N320SG
5119	C-GLXO VR-BNG VP-BNG N519DB C-GJDG N519DB N601FS C-FNEU N73ML
5120	C-GLWT N400TB (N500TB) N408TB PK-JKM

CL601 CHALLENGER

C/n	Identities							
5121	C-GLYK	N502PC	N702PC	XA-GCD	N328AM	N602NP		
5122	C-GLXS	N908CL	N7046J	N900CL	N65FF	XA-RYK		
5123	C-GLWR	N601UP	N147HH	N613PJ				
5124	C-GLXD	C-FBOM	C-GFCB	C-GFCD	N546LF	N939CC		
5125	C-GLWZ	C-FPIY	HB-IKY	N512BC	N604WB	(N14DP)	P4-EPI	VP-CEI	2-SEXY
5126	C-GLXU	N21CL	N21NY	N99UG	N650LG	N691CC		
5127	C-GLXB	N718P	N718R	N555LG	N550LG	N993SA		
5128	C-GLWX	C-FPOX	XA-GME	N321GE	N321GL	N307SC		
5129	C-GLXH	N129RH	(N603AF)	N129TF	VP-CRR	2-BLUE		
5130	C-GLXQ	N603KS	N601GB	VR-BQA	N601SR	N349JR	N405TC	
5131	C-GLWV	N602JB	N6JB	(N405DP)	XA-HMX	N377BD	XA-ICY	
5132	C-GLYO	N610DB	N289K					
5133	C-GLYH	N53DF	N121DF	N121FF	N486BG			
5134	C-GLXS	N43R	N43RK	N511WM	N511WN	N898EW	C-GPOC	N2369R

MODEL 601-3R

C/n	Identities									
5135	C-GLWR	N1902J	N1902P	N144MH						
5136	C-GLXW	N51GY	N20G	N20GX	N75EM					
5137	C-GLWZ	N137CL	N90AR	(OY-GSE)	N518JG					
5138	C-GLXF	N138CC	N85							
5139	C-GLXK	N139CD	N34CD	(N348D)	N902TA	(N612LX)	N639TS			
5140	C-GLXM	N1061D	N79AD	N79AN	N630AR	N680AR				
5141	C-GLXO	N312AT	N601ER	N601TM	N901TA	(N613LX)	N601JP	N358PJ		
5142	C-GLWT	C-FRGV	VR-CJJ	N330TP	(XA-...)	N22AQ	XA-MYN	XA-GDQ		
5143	C-GLYA	[built as CL604 prototype with c/n 5991 (qv)]								
5144	C-GLYC	N616CC	N347BA	N601CV	N621DJ					
5145	C-GLYK	C-GPGD	C-GDPF	N145LJ	N1DH					
5146	C-GLXW	C-FRQA	LX-MMB	N137MB	C-GWUG	N137MB	N96DS	N88NN	N825SG	
5147	C-GLWR	C-FRJX	XA-SOR	N514JR	XA-SOR					
5148	C-GLXD	N793CT	N792CT	N601DS						
5149	C-GLXY	N601GR	XA-GRB	N63ST	VP-BFS	VP-BZI	M-YBZI	T7-CCM		
5150	C-GLXU	N602CC	N601BW	N710AN						
5151	C-GLXB	C-GBJA	VR-BWB	VP-BWB	N333MX	C-GMMI	N360AP	N405AR		
5152	C-GLWX	N777XX	VR-COJ	VP-COJ	N605BA	N18RF	(N933PG)	N388PG	G-FBFI	N601FB
	(HB-JRX)	G-FBFI	G-CHAI	ZS-ANZ						
5153	C-GLXH	N601EB	VR-CHA	N604BA	OY-APM	N653AC	N115WF	[w/o Aspen, CO, 05Jan14]		
5154	C-GLXQ	N602DP	9M-TAN	N154BA	4X-COY	N601VF	C-FJLA	N601HW		
5155	C-GLWV	N342TC	N401RJ	C-FPDR	N808H	XA-OFM				
5156	C-GLYO	C-FSXH	VR-BAA	N255CC	N601TP					
5157	C-GLYH	N512DG	N471SP	N800KC	N808HG	5N-...				
5158	C-GLXS	C-FSYK	XA-ZTA	XA-MKY	XA-MKI	XA-JZL				
5159	C-GLWR	C-FTNN	EI-SXT	N159TS	C-GICI	N814PS	N659TS	N623BM	N615L	
5160	C-GLXW	N710HM	N94BA	N813VZ	N601MU					
5161	C-GLWZ	N994CT	(N997CT)	N190MP	N805DB	N807DD				
5162	C-GLXF	C-FTNE	VR-BCC	VP-BCC	N850FL	N850FB	N117RY	N949BC		
5163	C-GLXK	N709JM	N980HC	N224F	XA-ABF					
5164	C-GLXM	N715BG	N7008	N164CC	N431CB	XB-PMH	N113SR			
5165	C-GLXO	C-FTOH	VR-CPO	VP-CPO	C-GHCD	N165SC	N723HA	N723HH	XA-PTR	C-GURG
5166	C-GLWT	N618CC	9M-NSK	N601A	HB-IVS	N410AC	C-GXPZ	N61FF		
5167	C-GLYA	N151CC	N86							
5168	C-GLYC	C-GRPF								
5169	C-GLYK	N773A	N154NS	N620PJ						
5170	C-GL..	N166A	N888WS	N925DD	N441PJ					
5171	C-GLXW	N213MC	N614AF							
5172	C-GLXD	N601FS	C-FUND	N777YG	(N225JF)	N605JF				
5173	C-GLXY	N181JC	D-AKUE	N501KV						
5174	C-GLXU	N605CC	N477DM	N877DM	N47HR	N47HF	C-GHBV	4X-CMH	N28KA	(N386K)
	N276GR									
5175	C-GLXB	N601FR	N306FX	N306BX	N601KF	N800YB	N803TK	XA-UTL		
5176	C-GLWX	N142LL	ZS-CCT	N600DR	N600DH	N779AZ	N799AZ	C-GLSW		
5177	C-GLXH	N602MC	N757MC	N601UC	N227RH	N227RE	N895CC			
5178	C-GLXQ	(N602AN)	C-FWGE	CS-MAC	B-MAC	N888FJ				
5179	C-GLWV	(N604CC)	N608CC	N307FX	N307BX	N179TS	N168TS	N168LA	C-GDLI	
5180	C-GLYO	N518CL	5N-PAZ							
5181	C-GLYH	N602D	C-FCIB	C-FCID	N301KR	C-GOHG	N242CK			
5182	C-FVZC	HL7577								
5183	C-GLWR	N601HF	N55HF							
5184	C-GLXW	N605RP	N607RP	N607PH	N843GS					
5185	C-GLWZ	N611CC	N914X	N914Y	N991SH*					
5186	C-GLXF	N612CC	N9700X	N601AD						

CL601 CHALLENGER

C/n	Identities							
5187	C-GLXK	N601KJ	N511DD					
5188	C-GLXM	N614CC	HS-JJA	N575CF	N10FE	N2000C	N221BW	
5189	C-FXCK	PT-WLZ	C-GZWY	N203G	XA-IMY	N54VS		
5190	C-GLWT	N190EK	N87					
5191	C-GLYA	N191BE	N605T	N117W				
5192	C-GLYC	N354TC	N750LG					
5193	C-GLYK	N604D	VR-BCI	VP-BCI	(N601HJ)	VP-BIH	N11LK	VP-CLZ
5194	C-FXIP	EI-MAS	N601R	A9C-BXD	N539CS	N207JB		

CL601 production complete, replaced by CL604

Note: C/ns beginning 6001 were earmarked for the abortive CL601S programme

CANADAIR CL604 CHALLENGER

C/n	Identities
5991	C-GLYA [ff 18Sep94] C-FTBZ "N604CC"+ [+fake marks worn during 1994 NBAA Show at New Orleans/ Lakefront, LA] C-FTBZ [w/o 10Oct00 Wichita/Mid-Continent A/P, KS; parted out by Dodson Int'l, Rantoul, KS]
5301	C-FVUC N604CC N608CC N123KH N604BL
5302	C-GLXD C-GBJA N355CC N255CC
5303	C-GLXY C-FXKE HL7522 N604BD (OY-CLE) N609BD OY-TNF OE-INF (D-ARWE) (D-AKAT) N360PL
5304	C-GLXU C-FXHE I-MILK N604VM C-GITG N604VM (N604TS) N604CA
5305	C-GLXB N604B N747 N747Y N888DH
5306	C-GLWX N309FX N309BX N604AB N604WB
5307	C-GLXH C-FXUQ VR-BHA VP-BHA (N604BA) C-GIDG LX-FAZ G-UYAD N16DA N34FS
5308	C-GLYO N604KS N604TS N982J N713HC (N713HG)
5309	C-GLYH C-FXZS VR-BAC VP-BAC C-GHRK (N604LM) N666TR N666TF (N509TS) N814PS N609TS N770SW
5310	C-GLXS C-FCCP C-GPGD C-GPFC C-GWLI
5311	C-GLWR N225LY N604JS (N989DH) N604HS
5312	C-GLXW N604KC N312AM (N905SB)
5313	C-GLXD N605KC N312AT N906SB N3HB N712PR
5314	C-GLWZ N604CT VT-NGS
5315	C-GLXF N604LS N818LS N818TH
5316	C-GLXK N604BB N411BB N1848U N200UL N203TA N208R N484CR
5317	C-FYXC D-AMIM C-GGPK C-FNNT C-GYMM C-GKGN
5318	C-GLXO C-FYYH (TC-DHE) HB-IKQ HB-IVR ZS-LEO ZS-KEN
5319	C-GLWT N604KR N14R N14RU N100SA N2SA N5319 N27X M-LOOK
5320	C-GLXQ N605CC HZ-AFA2 N604MJ HZ-MEJ1
5321	C-GLYA C-FZDY PT-WXL C-FZPG N604CP N1CP N604CP XA-LUF XA-UWR
5322	C-GLXY N604CL 9A-CRO
5323	C-GLXU N604DS N623TS N604TC (N604TS)
5324	C-GLXB N601CC N667LC N667LQ N55LB N611AB
5325	C-GLWX N60CT N331TH N604JW [w/o 07Nov10 in hangar fire Indianapolis, IN; parted out by Dodson Int'l, Rantoul, KS]
5326	C-GLYC N908G N1903G
5327	C-GLYK N609CC HB-IKJ D-AJAB N146BA N838LJ
5328	C-GLXH N712DG ZS-AVL (A6-EJB) N328BX LN-BWG N604AZ XA-JCG
5329	C-GLWV N8MC N1GC N1QF N222MC (N222MZ)
5330	C-GLYO N812G
5331	C-GLYH N810D
5332	C-GLXS C-FZRR VP-BNF N606JL C-FNYU N606JL
5333	C-GLWR N603CC N811BB N600MS N991TW
5334	C-GLXU N604RC N43R
5335	C-GLXB C-FZVN VP-CAN N8206S N801P N604B N116JS*
5336	C-GLXW N310FX N310BX N212RR N2615S N675BP
5337	C-GLXD N270RA N990AK N302PC
5338	C-GLWZ N604PL N913JB N78RP N426CF N226CF N36VV
5339	C-GLXF C-GBJA N604CU C-GCNR
5340	C-GLXK N606CC N194WM N134WM
5341	C-GLXM C-GBJA N604SA N429WG
5342	C-GLXO N311FX N311BX N371JC N604AX VT-DBG
5343	C-GLWT C-GAUK C-GHKY N307KR C-GVXX N323SH
5344	C-GLXQ N344BA N604DH
5345	C-GLYA N345BA N600AM N2FD
5346	C-GLXS N604JP HZ-SJP3 M-KARN HZ-HSH
5347	C-GLXW C-GBDK PT-MKO N747TS N205EL N205EE (N154JC) N54JC
5348	C-GLWR N881TW N604NC D-AFAD
5349	C-GLXY N312FX N312BX N5349 N359V
5350	C-GLXU N331TP VQ-BRZ
5351	C-GLXB N374G N372G N3726
5352	C-GLWX C-GBKE 4X-COE N5352J N770BC N770BQ
5353	C-GLXH C-GRIO VH-LAM N758CC
5354	C-GLYC N604PM (N604AG) N604BM N11A N1101A
5355	C-GLWV N555WD
5356	C-GLYO N605PM (N605AG) N880CR N779WG 5N-BSP
5357	C-GLYH N604FS XA-AST XA-EVG
5358	C-GLXS C-GBRQ TC-DHE N127SB N127SR C-GJQN N127SR
5359	C-GLWR N497DM N597DA SX-KFA
5360	C-GLXW N606PM (N606AG) N14SR C-GZEK C-GHML M-VICA C-GHML N604WL
5361	C-GLXD N346BA N254AM N226SJ
5362	C-GLWZ N607PM N995MA JY-AW3 A6-AAH VP-CRK
5363	C-GLXF N964H N444CZ
5364	C-GLXK C-FBNS C-GDWF
5365	C-GLXM N604DC N618DC N280K N80DX
5366	C-GLXO N604DD Denmark C-066 N604DD RP-C1937 N604DD C-GJFC N906TF D-AFAI
5367	C-GCCZ EI-TAM VP-COJ N145DL C-FZOP N145DL N848CC N898CC N16YD
5368	C-GLXQ N368G N374G N3746 9H-MIR
5369	C-GCQB (D-AZPP) HB-IVP N247WF N247WE N248WE N605JA

CL604 CHALLENGER

C/n	Identities									
5370	C-GLXS	(N370CL)	N320CL	N755RV	VT-KAV	N370TS	VH-EVJ	N135D	N604WH	
5371	C-GLYK	N371CL	C-GGWH							
5372	C-GLWR	N314FX	(N413LV)	G-LVLV	A6-CPC	N604JC	N976AM			
5373	C-GCVZ	HB-ILL	N604LC	(9H-BRE)	T7-BRE					
5374	C-GLXU	N98FJ	N97FJ	N203						
5375	C-GLXB	N604HP	(D-ASTS)	XA-GRB	N352AP	M-ANNA				
5376	C-GLXW	N604CR	N604CC	N604CD	N604ZH	N1102B				
5377	C-GLXH	N315FX	N315BX	N604RB	N604RR	N610TM				
5378	C-GLYC	C-GDBZ	D-ASTS	D-AFAB						
5379	C-GLWV	N604CA	C-GQPA							
5380	C-GLYO	C-GDFA	N604DE	C-GEGM	Denmark C-080					
5381	C-GLYH	N900ES	(N909ES)	PR-TUB	N604MM					
5382	C-GLXS	N604HJ	M-OLOT							
5383	C-GLYK	N383DT	G-EMLI	M-EMLI	C-FGFG					
5384	C-GLXW	C-GDLH	HB-IVV	VP-BNS	N684TS					
5385	C-GLXD	N72NP	C-FCPI	N604SC	LV-FWZ					
5386	C-GLWZ	N315DG	N1DG	N37DG	N119GA	N203R	N800WC			
5387	C-GLXF	N316FX	N387CL	N999PX						
5388	C-GLXK	C-GDVM	4X-CMY	N488LW	N588AL					
5389	C-GLXM	N604JE	D-AUKE							
5390	C-GLXO	N604KG	ZS-DGB	(N200DE)	N541DE	N200DE				
5391	C-GLWT	N604PA	VP-BCA	N2409W	(N818SL)	N708SC	N788SC	N267BW	N267DW	N267DF
5392	C-GLXQ	C-GDZE	C-FLPC	C-FCDE	N596CH	N325JJ				
5393	C-GLYA	N355CC	N615TL	(VQ-BUX)	N645TL	VQ-BUX				
5394	C-GLXS	N604CH	HB-IVT	N141DL	N72WY	N350PR				
5395	C-GLYK	N606CC	N82CW	N82CN	N604LV					
5396	C-GLWR	N604SH	N273S	N604SH	N273S	C-GKTO				
5397	C-GLXY	N605PA	VP-BCB	HB-IIV	VP-BJH	A6-PJA	D-AFAA			
5398	C-GLXU	N597DM	N477DM	N577DA	(SX-TFA)	5N-JLS				
5399	C-GLXB	N604GM	N901SG	N604GF						
5400	C-GLWX	N604S	(N237G)	N237GA	N266GA	N60055	(N6550)	N400TJ		
5401	C-GLXH	N98FJ	N528GP	(N604GJ)	VT-MGF	M-AWAY	N243BA			
5402	C-GLYC	N603JM	RP-C5610	N15SP	N98AG	VP-BDX	N604CD	N888YC		
5403	C-GLWV	N604DC	D-ADND	G-JMCW	G-MPJM	G-MPTP	VP-CUP			
5404	C-GLYO	VP-BGO	M-SKZL	M-ADEL	N32UC					
5405	C-GLYH	N311BP	N811BP	N340AK						
5406	C-GLXS	N604MU	N604WW							
5407	C-GLWR	N317FX	N317BX	N604GG	LV-BNO	N548LF	VH-BLM	[wore fake marks N39DJP for film purposes at Archerfield, Australia, 18Jun14]		
5408	C-GLXW	N898R	N898AN	N604SA						
5409	C-GLXD	C-GETU	N401NK	N604M						
5410	C-GLWZ	N191BA	N199BA	N805VZ	(N410MU)	C-GFLU	N923KB			
5411	C-GLXF	N604JJ	PP-OSA	N604TS	N3PC	N66ZC	N66ZD	VH-VSZ		
5412	C-GLXK	N99FJ	N529GP	TS-IAM						
5413	C-GLXM	C-FSJR	C-FADU	(N802TK)	(N294KR)	N651LS				
5414	C-GLXO	N604AG	N90AG	[w/o 04Jan02 Birmingham A/P, UK]						
5415	C-GLWT	N318FX	VP-CAP	TC-SMZ	N295JL	5N-...				
5416	C-GLXQ	N604MG	N161MM	N161MN	N161MD	G-FTSL	D-AFAC			
5417	C-GLYA	N605MP	D-AETV	N791BR	C-GNRC					
5418	C-GLXS	N319FX	(N609CR)	N604CR	N529AK	A6-KBB	N309KB			
5419	C-GLYK	N500	N252DH	C-FKGY						
5420	C-GLWR	N603CC	VP-BCO	N604TS	C-GBKB	N549LF	(N614MJ)	N39RE	N39RN	
5421	C-GLXY	N200JP	N604JP	N604W	N38VS					
5422	C-GLXU	N605DC	D-ADNE	G-JMMD	G-MPCW	G-MPSP	AP-DOD	OE-IHK		
5423	C-GLXB	N238SW	N38SW	N38SV	N91MG	N5G				
5424	C-GLWX	N604CR	G-DAAC	N604GW						
5425	C-GLXH	N320FX	N604PC	VT-IBR						
5426	C-GLYC	N604JA	JY-ONE	N51VR	G-XONE					
5427	C-GLWV	N321FX	N902CG	USCG 02	[USCG type designation C-143A]			N902CG	N838DB	N828UM
5428	C-GLYO	N640CH	N300TW							
5429	C-GLYH	N604KM	Korea 701							
5430	C-GLXS	(N604MA)	C-GFOE	OY-MMM	D-AONE					
5431	C-GLWR	N276GC								
5432	C-GLXM	C-FDRS	C-GPGD							
5433	C-GLXD	N433FS	N181J	N777J						
5434	C-GLXY	N322FX	N322BX	N604AU						
5435	C-GLWZ	N604PN	OE-IYA	OE-INJ	M-AAAM					
5436	C-GLXF	N604LA	(N955CE)	N926SS						
5437	C-GLXK	N437FT	N17TE	N17TZ	N604AV					
5438	C-GLXM	N609CC	AP-GAK							
5439	C-GLXQ	N600ES	N300ES	N350ES	VH-URR					
5440	C-GLXU	N500PE	N208LT	N620TM						
5441	C-GLXB	N641CA	N1CA	N441CL	N33PA	N36HA	N604RM			
5442	C-GLWR	N604PS	G-POAJ	YL-WBD	HB-JRT	B-7696				
5443	C-GLWT	N605JA	JY-TWO	JY-IMK	M-CRCR	G-HOTY				
5444	C-GLWV	N604VF	N604AF							

CL604 CHALLENGER

C/n	Identities								
5445	C-GLWX	N604HD	N877H						
5446	C-GLWZ	N604CE	N156RC						
5447	C-GLYC	N323FX	N323BX	N1NA	N604PS				
5448	C-GLXD	N604CB	TC-DHH	VP-BHH	A9C-MRM				
5449	C-GLXF	N604GT	N604JR	VP-CCP	LX-SPK	D-AAAX			
5450	C-GLXH	N450DK	4X-CMZ	(N357AP)	M-ABGG				
5451	C-GLXK	N816CC	(N120MT)	N831ET	N604DF				
5452	C-GLXM	N452WU	OH-WIC						
5453	C-GLXO	N453AD	C-FHGC						
5454	C-GLXQ	N324FX	D-ARWE	[w/o Almaty, Kazakstan, 25Dec07]					
5455	C-GLXS	C-GCDS	C-GCDF	N604CW					
5456	C-GLXU	N456MS	VP-BNG	N604LE	VH-MXK	VH-ZZH	VH-VLC	N360SL	
5457	C-GLXW	N325FX	D-AKBH	EC-MIT	OE-IOY				
5458	C-GLXY	N458MS	C-GZPX						
5459	C-GLYA	N459MT	TC-TAN	Turkey TT4010					
5460	C-GLYH	N460WJ	VP-BMG	N698RS					
5461	C-GLYK	N832SC							
5462	C-GLYO	N462PG	D-AHLE	N604EP					
5463	C-GLXB	N463AG	D-AHEI	N777FF	(N777FN)				
5464	C-GLWR	N326FX	(N326BX)	(OE-IRJ)	I-IRCS	D-AMSC	[dbr 07Jan17, in-flight structural damage after being caught by Airbus A380 wake turbulence]		
5465	C-GLWT	C-GHIH	C-GLBB	N465AV	N604FS				
5466	C-GLWV	N327FX							
5467	C-GLWX	N467RD	G-REYS						
5468	C-GLWZ	C-GHRJ	Denmark C-168						
5469	C-GLYC	N469RC	N78SD	(N32FF)	N770FF				
5470	C-GLXD	N604DW	N604AC	N150BB					
5471	C-GLXF	N471MK	N604WS	N604DE	N604TB	N604MT			
5472	C-GLXH	C-GHRZ	Denmark C-172						
5473	C-GLXK	N604RP	N303KR	N579RS					
5474	C-GLXM	N328FX	C-FXPB	C-FXCN	C-FBEM	D-ADLD*			
5475	C-GLXO	N475AD	D-ASIE	YR-DIP	OE-IAH	N524LD			
5476	C-GLXQ	N329FX	N343K	A9C-BXH	M-SHLA	N604BA			
5477	C-GLXS	N477AT	A9C-BXB	M-ABEH	N477TX	N529KF			
5478	C-GLXU	N478BA	N604GR	N478U	N604PV				
5479	C-GLXW	N479KA	ZS-CMB	N604ST	N872BC				
5480	C-GLXY	N480LB	N121DF	N500M					
5481	C-GLYA	N481KW	N198DC	JY-AAD	M-AAAD	HZ-TFM	M-AAAD	JY-GRP	
5482	C-GLYH	N482BB	N322LA	N581TS					
5483	C-GLYK	N483BA	N483CC	N956PP					
5484	C-GLYO	N484GC	PT-XYW	N684TS	C-GWLL				
5485	C-GLXB	N485CL	"LX-RFBY"	LX-FBY	A9C-BXG	M-ABEI	N485TX	N82RL	
5486	C-GLWR	N486EJ	ZS-OSG	9J-ONE					
5487	C-GLWT	N330FX	I-AFMA	G-FABO					
5488	C-GLWV	N604D	N604CC	N870CM	N670CM	(N8570)	N604FM		
5489	C-GLWX	N489BA	N604BD	C-GGBL	C-FVSL	N490AJ	N230LC	C-GTJO	
5490	C-GLWZ	N604GD	N14GD	N14GU					
5491	C-GLYC	N331FX	N331PS	N331FX	N770MS				
5492	C-GLXD	N604SX	N711SX	N604SX	N604EM				
5493	C-GLXF	N604VK	LV-BHP						
5494	C-GLXH	N494JC	D-ANKE	HB-JRN	M-ALII	TC-TRB			
5495	C-GLXK	N495BA	N495BC	N495CE	N495DD				
5496	C-GLXM	N496DB	N604UP	N604TH	N604Z				
5497	C-GLXO	N604RT	N604LA						
5498	C-GLXQ	N598DA	N599DA	N333DS	N226MY				
5499	C-GLXS	N499KR	N999VK						
5500	C-GLXU	N225AR	N606GG	VP-CAS					
5501	C-GLXW	N501AJ	XA-SOL						
5502	C-GLXY	N502TF	D-ACTO	D-ACTU	HB-JRY	N598MT	N777DB		
5503	C-GLYA	N298DC	N503PC						
5504	C-GLYH	N71NP	N71NJ	N604RR					
5505	C-GLYK	N505JD	VP-BHS	N655TS	(D-ARTE)	G-OCSC	N664D		
5506	C-GLYO	C-GJFI	C-FHYL	C-FLCY	N1821U				
5507	C-GLXB	N53DF							
5508	C-GLWR	N528DK	P4-FAY	LZ-YUN	9H-MAL	A7-MHA	9H-MAJ		
5509	C-GLWT	N604BG	N112CF						
5510	C-GLWV	N511SC	B-7696	N610SA	VP-CHU	HB-JFZ	D-AFAB	N604TX	N100FL
5511	C-GLWX	N815PA	N815RA	N598WC	N598C	C-GLPP			
5512	C-GLWZ	(N626JW)	N512SH	N902AG					
5513	C-GLYC	N604NG	N729KF	N729KP	N604RB				
5514	C-GLXD	C-GJOE	N880ET						
5515	C-GLXF	N515DM	EI-IRE	G-CHVN	Denmark C-215				
5516	C-GLXH	N516DG	N1DG	N516DG	N118RH				
5517	C-GLXK	C-GJSO	N517RH	LN-SUN					
5518	C-GLXM	N8SP	N85PX						
5519	C-GLXO	N519MZ	P4-AVJ	N900UC					

CL604 CHALLENGER

C/n	Identities									
5520	C-GLXQ	C-GJTR	N520JR	XA-TVG	N116BJ	VP-CBR	A6-MBH	VP-CBR	VP-CST	2-NITE
5521	C-GLXS	N521RF	Australia A37-001							
5522	C-GLXU	N522FP	C-GKCB	(N.....)	4X-CMF	M-LRLR				
5523	C-GLXW	N552SC	B-7697	N523CL	LX-ZAV	OE-ICL	TC-ICK			
5524	C-GLXY	N251VG	N251CP	N601GT						
5525	C-GLYA	N525E	XA-JFE							
5526	C-GLYH	N804CB	N604CB	I-WISH	G-RCAV					
5527	C-GLYK	N554SC	(B-....)	XA-TZF						
5528	C-GLYO	N528DT	D-AJAG	G-JMMP	G-MPMP	TC-REA	EP-PUB	ZS-THB		
5529	C-GLXB	C-GJZB	HB-JRA							
5530	C-GLWR	C-GJZD	HB-JRB							
5531	C-GLWT	N168NQ								
5532	C-GLWV	N532DM	N432MC	YL-SKY						
5533	C-GLWX	N533DK	C-GKGR	Canada 144617						
5534	C-GLWZ	N534RF	Australia A37-002							
5535	C-GLYC	C-GKGS	Canada 144618							
5536	C-GLXD	N536MP	N25GG	N25ZG						
5537	C-GLXF	N537DR	N437MC							
5538	C-GLXH	N538RF	Australia A37-003							
5539	C-GLXK	N539AB	PP-BIA	VP-BDY	VP-CEO	CS-DTJ	HB-JFC	D-ATWO		
5540	C-GLXM	C-GKMU	HB-JRC							
5541	C-GLXO	N329FX	(D-AMHS)	D-ANGB						
5542	C-GLXQ	N876H	B-7766							
5543	C-GLXS	N332FX	(N605BA)							
5544	C-GLXU	N333FX	N604TS	N50DS	N544TS	N814PS				
5545	C-GLXW	N334FX	N6757M	N471RJ						
5546	C-GLXY	N335FX	N604BA	N459CS	N100AC					
5547	C-GLYA	N350ZE	N426PF							
5548	C-GLYH	N548LP	N416BD	N410BD	N604LL	N627AF				
5549	C-GLYK	N540JW	N2JW	(N26WK)	N604JE	C-FASD				
5550	C-GLYO	N250CC	N1987	N198D	N75KH					
5551	C-GLXB+	C-GLXF+	[+shown as C-GLXB in Transport Canada records but reported as C-GLXF while on production line]							
	N551BT	N604RS	N501PC							
5552	C-GLWR	N552CC	ZS-ALT	N552TS	VP-COP					
5553	C-GLWT	C-GZTU	HB-JRZ	P4-SAI	N728JP	C-GRLE				
5554	C-GLWV	N604KJ								
5555	C-GLWX	N555VV	N604HC	N604HM						
5556	C-GLWZ	N373G	N3736	C-GBBB						
5557	C-GLYC	C-FZSO	C-GAWH							
5558	C-GLXD	N604SR	N604KS	N508PC						
5559	C-GLXF	N559JA	N902MP	N7886						
5560	C-GLXH	N604CC	(N560TS)	N604BS						
5561	C-GLXK	N561CC	N604WF	VH-MZL	VH-VRE	N604LP				
5562	C-GLXM	N562BA	N562ME	M-EIRE	VP-COD	G-OCOD	N604VG			
5563	C-GLXO	N563BA	N300BC	N604BC						
5564	C-GLXQ	N564BA	N99KW	N79KW	C-GMIV					
5565	C-GLXS	N604KB	D-ABCD							
5566	C-GLXU	N604PA								
5567	C-GLXW	N567NT	C-FAOL	P4-TAT	RA-67216					
5568	C-GLXY	N604JC	N383MB	N456HK						
5569	C-GLYA	C-GZVZ	N604SB							
5570	C-GLYH	N604CL								
5571	C-GLYK	N604BA	N571BA	N907WS	N907WR					
5572	C-GLYO	N572MS	N400	(N472TS)	D-AIND	N790BR	N121RS	N283DM	N512NP	N401VE
5573	C-GLXB	N573BA	N573BC	N509GE	VH-VLZ					
5574	C-GLWR	N574F	N46F	A6-RDJ						
5575	C-GLWT	N529DM	N604HF	N950PG	N1VR*					
5576	C-GLWV	N1090X	C-GGBL							
5577	C-GLWX	N577CJ	C-FEUR	OO-KRC	LX-KRC	VH-LEF				
5578	C-GLWZ	N606RP	N604PH	XA-UXM	XA-ARK					
5579	C-GLYC	N110BP	C-FBCR							
5580	C-GLXD	C-FADG	XA-IGE	P4-CHV	G-OPRM					
5581	C-GLXF	N604MC	VP-CMS							
5582	C-GLXH	N604BB								
5583	C-GLXK	N121ET	A6-ASQ	(D-APJI)	N67ZS					
5584	C-GLXM	C-FAWU	N828KD							
5585	C-GLXO	N585BD	(D-ARTN)	OE-IMB	D-AAOK	SX-KMA	EI-KMA			
5586	C-GLXQ	N334FX								
5587	C-GLXS	N826JS	(N604UC)	N64UC						
5588	C-GLXU	N88								
5589	C-GLXW	N604SF	N22SF	N228E	OE-IPG	9H-IPG	N585PJ			
5590	C-GLXY	N721J	N420SK							
5591	C-GLYA	N604CD	G-OCSD	G-CGFD	CN-IAM					
5592	C-GLYH	N385CT								
5593	C-GLYK	N604SC	VP-BJM							
5594	C-GLYO	N594SF	N43SF	N438E	TC-CEA					

CL604 CHALLENGER

C/n	Identities							
5595	C-GLXB	C-FCOE	(D-AINI)	OE-INI	N351AP	TC-ASL		
5596	C-GLWR	C-FCSD	OY-SGM	RA-67222	N605AM			
5597	C-GLWT	N597JA	VP-CKR	VP-CHL	C-GMRL			
5598	C-GLWV	C-FDJN	OE-IGJ	M-MDDE	N959AM			
5599	C-GLWX	OE-IKP	HB-JFJ					
5600	C-GLWZ	N800BN	N810GT					
5601	C-GLXB	N44SF	N448E					
5602	C-GLXD	C-FDBJ	HB-JRW	LZ-YUP	D-AAAY			
5603	C-GLXF	N76SF	N768E	N349JR*				
5604	C-GLXH	N78RP	(N78RX)	B-LBL	M-AAEL			
5605	C-GLXK	C-FDUY	EC-JNV	N605CL	VP-BJE			
5606	C-GLXM	N606CC	N310TK	N810TK	(N730AS)			
5607	C-GLXO	N607LC	N954L	N610L				
5608	C-GLXQ	C-FDWU	G-DGET	M-TRIX	OE-IPD	M-SIMI		
5609	C-GLXS	C-FEFU	N604JC	D-ATTT				
5610	C-GLXU	C-FEFW	G-LGKO	M-ANGO	N801TK	N575AG		
5611	C-GLXW	C-FEIH	TC-ARD	(N361AP)				
5612	C-GLXY	C-FEPN	OE-IPK	G-VVPA	9H-VVP			
5613	C-GLYA	C-FEPR	HB-JEM	RA-67228				
5614	C-GLYH	N614JA	N614BA	[converted to prototype Boeing Maritime Surveillance Aircraft, ff 28Feb14]	N604TB			
5615	C-GLYK	N604SG	N904JK	N604CR				
5616	C-GLYO	C-FEXH	VP-CFD	LX-MDA	D-ANTR			
5617	C-GLXB	C-FEYU	G-PRKR	G-OCOM	M-OCOM			
5618	C-GLXF	C-FEYZ	VP-CMB	D-ASIX	OE-IAA	D-AMIB*		
5619	C-GLWT	N335FX	C-FIDT	VH-XNC	[converted to Search & Rescue aircraft for Australian government]			
5620	C-GLWV	C-FFGE	OE-IVE	VP-BST	M-YBST	G-MOCL		
5621	C-GLWX	C-FFHX	VP-CNK	VP-CBK	(N354AP)	N789SM		
5622	C-GLWZ	C-FFLA	B-LLL	VP-CCE	(N688NY)			
5623	C-GLYC	C-FFMQ	VP-CJB	N623HA	G-STCC	G-OCSH	N604AK	
5624	C-GLXD	C-FFMS	N604GD	OY-MKS	HB-JGR	9H-JGR		
5625	C-GLXF	C-FFQQ	VH-OCV	LZ-YUR	TC-MJB			
5626	C-GLXH	N807RH	VP-BSS	VP-BZM	OH-BZM	G-CGGU	N787LG	
5627	C-GLXK	N604DT						
5628	C-GLXM	C-FFZP	P4-ABC	(N30WJ)	TS-IBT	TS-INV	9H-INV	
5629	C-GLXO	C-FGBE	(D-AINX)	OE-INX	N356AP	(N317MG)	VT-ZST	
5630	C-GLXQ	C-FGBD	XA-SAD	N199GD				
5631	C-GLXS	N724MF	N345XB					
5632	C-GLXU	N604CG	D-AEUK					
5633	C-GLXW	N604CC						
5634	C-GLXY	N336FX	C-FKUL	VH-XND	[converted to Search & Rescue aircraft for Australian government]			
5635	C-GLYC	N604SL	N604EG	N604JJ				
5636	C-GLYH	N636HC	(N636TS)	OE-ITH				
5637	C-GLYK	N637TF						
5638	C-GLYO	N604MG	N604HT					
5639	C-GLXB	C-FGYI	VP-BJA	M-JSTA				
5640	C-GLXD	N640PN	N910J					
5641	C-GLWT	N641DA	A6-IFA					
5642	C-GLWV	N642JA	OH-WII					
5643	C-GLWX	N643CT	N793CT	N240WL*				
5644	C-GLWZ	C-FHCM	(D-AINY)	OE-INY	(N487LW)	(N297KR)	N395MH	N984DV
5645	C-GLYC	C-FHCL	4X-CUR	N865BA	N128RX			
5646	C-GLXD	N646JC	G-HARK	N438E				
5647	C-GLXF	N337FX	C-FMUS	VH-XNE	[converted to Search & Rescue aircraft for Australian government]			
5648	C-GLXH	C-FHDV	EC-JYT					
5649	C-GLXK	N649JA	P4-BTA	(D-ATWO)	UP-CL6001	T7-EAA		
5650	C-GLXM	C-FIEX	C-FRCI					
5651	C-GLXO	N651JC	HB-JRQ					
5652	C-GLXQ	N604CM	N225N					
5653	C-GLXS	C-FIMF	N720AS	XA-JEP				
5654	C-GLXU	N604MG	OE-IDG					
5655	C-GLXW	N604TF	N603L*					
5656	C-GLXY	C-FIXN	N338FX	C-FOGX	VH-XNF	[converted to Search & Rescue aircraft for Australian government]		
5657	C-GLYA	C-FIYA	VP-BNP	N352AP	C-GMBY			
5658	C-GLYH	N658JC	(OH-WIA)	(OH-NEM)	OH-MOL	N1218F		
5659	C-GLYK	C-FJCB	G-TAGA	HB-JRG				
5660	C-GLYO	N650KS	N848CC					
5661	C-GLXB	N224NS	N224N					
5662	C-GLWR	N652MC	N868CC					
5663	C-GLWT	N664JC	N604TB	N500PG				
5664	C-GLWV	C-FKDV	OE-IMK	N507FV	XA-PMS			
5665	C-GLWX	N665CT	N657CT					

Production complete

CANADAIR CL605 CHALLENGER

C/n	Identities						
5701	C-FGYM	[ff 23Jan06]	N605KS	N980SK	N2MG	N605KB	N545ZT*
5702	C-FIFK	N605CC	(N225AR)	A6-DNH	N170TY	N138DM	
5703	C-FLGN	VP-BML	N605WF				
5704	C-FLKC	(D-AIFB)	OE-IFB	M-FBVZ	LX-ZED	LX-AGA	
5705	C-GLXD	C-FLNZ	N933ML	M-AMRT	OE-IKZ		
5706	C-GLXF	C-FLSF	ZS-SDZ	G-TAGE	VT-AUV		
5707	C-GLXH	C-FLSJ	N605BA	OE-INS	(N486LW)	(N298KR)	N864BA N27AY
5708	C-GLXK	N605CB	C-GSTG				
5709	C-GLXM	C-GCSB	HB-JRP	9H-AFQ	N87878		
5710	C-GLXO	C-FMNL	C-GSAP	N710TS	G-OCSE	C-GFTL	
5711	C-GLXQ	C-FMNR	N529D	N529DM	N729DM	C-GVVY	
5712	C-GLXS	C-FMNW	(OE-IPR)	S5-ADA	N541LF	N605GN	
5713	C-GLXU	C-FMVQ	N604D	9H-AFC	N778BA		
5714	C-GLXW	C-FMVN	PP-SCB	N329TL			
5715	C-GLXY	C-FNIJ	(OE-IVB)	S5-ADB	CS-DTK	HB-JFA	D-AVPB
5716	C-GLYA	C-FNIN	N605JM	VP-CHH	M-GENT	B-LSB	N688SF
5717	C-GLYH	C-FSCI	N591CH	N569RS			
5718	C-GLYK	C-FNTM	N723HA	N571TS	N555NN	G-NAAL	N592CH N605KA
5719	C-FOBK	N339FX					
5720	C-FNUF	N720HG	N605HC				
5721	C-FNTP	N605HG	N4AS	(PR-RSI)	C-GURJ		
5722	C-FOGE	M-BIGG	SX-SHC				
5723	C-FOGI	N340FX					
5724	C-GLWX	C-FOMS	N17TE				
5725	C-FOMU	D-ACUA	OE-IMM				
5726	C-FOXU	N605JP	HB-JRE				
5727	C-FOXV	N400ES					
5728	C-FOYE	N605GG	A6-MBS	N78SD			
5729	C-FOBF	N540BA	N913TK*				
5730	C-FPWI	N605LD	TC-SAB				
5731	C-FPQT	M-RLIV					
5732	C-FPQV	(OE-III)	OY-GBB	P4-CEO			
5733	C-FPQW	N533TS	G-OCSF	G-CGFF	G-MACP	G-MACO	M-ALTI
5734	C-FPQY	G-NCCC	N683UF				
5735	C-FPQZ	N605DX	EZ-B022				
5736	C-FPSJ	HB-JGT	LV-GVH				
5737	C-FPSQ	N542BA					
5738	C-FPSV	N538TS	N605ZH				
5739	C-FQQE	N605AG	VP-CRS	A6-AAG			
5740	C-FQQG	N667LC	N667LQ	N605LC			
5741	C-FQQH	N741TS	N371G				
5742	C-FQQK	N341FX	N950RJ	N3FE			
5743	C-FQQO	OE-INN	(N291KR)	N859BA	N699ST		
5744	C-FQQS	N744JC	G-CFSC	M-NHOI			
5745	C-FQQW	OE-INP	N593CH	M-BASH			
5746	C-FQVE	C-GGBL	N4868	N469ED			
5747	C-FSIP	N605GL	TC-FIB				
5748	C-FSIQ	VP-BGM					
5749	C-FSIU	N749BA	OE-INU	N594CH	N729HZ		
5750	C-FSJH	VT-STV	N605AT	EZ-B023			
5751	C-FSJT	N605JA	P4-UNI	M-YUNI	9H-UNI	9H-MYU	
5752	C-FSJV	N342FX	N342F	N142J			
5753	C-FSJY	HB-JRN	N65HD	N605PA			
5754	C-FSKT	S5-ADD	LX-JNC				
5755	C-FSKX	N605GB	G-NYGB	C-FJNS			
5756	C-FTLB	D-ATYA	G-YAGT	9H-LDV			
5757	C-FTLH	S5-ADF					
5758	C-FTRY	OE-INT	N624EC	C-GVBY	G-KAHR	N307KR	N445BH
5759	C-FTRO	N605CJ	A7-RZC	9H-ALF	C-GRMZ		
5760	C-FTRQ	G-SJSS	N605DS				
5761	C-FTRM	N343FX	(N343HM)	N777QX			
5762	C-FTRF	9H-AFG	P4-SAT	N918SJ			
5763	C-FTQY	N605RJ	VQ-BZB	TC-CLH			
5764	C-FTQZ	OE-ISU					
5765	C-FUAU	N605FH	C-FYTZ	VQ-BDG	M-ASHI		
5766	C-FUAS	N605TX	N605GF				
5767	C-FUAK	N605FH	N605H	TC-CMK	M-ABJN		
5768	C-FUIT	LZ-BVD					
5769	C-FUIU	N769CC	N605MM				
5770	C-FUIV	VP-BES	(D2-EBR)	N299KR			
5771	C-FUVA	N548BA	N236WA				
5772	C-FUVC	C-FKMC	N858CV				
5773	C-FUVF	N344FX	N8888G	N605VV			
5774	C-FUVG	(LZ-BVF)	N68888				
5775	C-FUVH	N549BA					

CL605 CHALLENGER

C/n	Identities				
5776	C-FUUF	(N75NP)	VP-CLJ		
5777	C-FUUI	N878CC			
5778	C-FUUM	A9C-ACE			
5779	C-FUUQ	N520SC			
5780	C-FUUW	M-TOPI			
5781	C-FVOC	N605BL	M-VSSK	VP-COO	
5782	C-FVON	OE-INA	N339MH	N131KJ	
5783	C-FVOQ	A7-CEA			
5784	C-FVOZ	A7-CEB			
5785	C-FWQH	OH-ANS	9H-BOM		
5786	C-FWQL	C-FLMK	C-FLMY	N304HE	
5787	C-FWQM	VT-APL			
5788	C-FWQO	N605S			
5789	C-FWQV	N605BT	C-GBKB		
5790	C-FWQY	N605TA	N169TA	N189TA	N525SD
5791	C-FVMI	N899ST			
5792	C-FVMW	N605AB	N2JW		
5793	C-FXQG	N880HK			
5794	C-FXQH	M-ARIE	B-LSC	N446JB	N605L
5795	C-FXQJ	N605PS			
5796	C-FXQM	C-GHMW			
5797	C-FXQR	OE-IND	N366MH	N630AR	
5798	C-FXQX	N605RZ	A7-RZA	VP-CBV	D-AJAN	OE-IOS
5799	C-FYAY	P4-KMK	N818AC		
5800	C-FYAW	N605RC			
5801	C-FYAV	N605RP			
5802	C-FYAP	C-FBEL			
5803	C-FYAI	RA-67227			
5804	C-FYAB	N65PX			
5805	C-FXRD	LV-CCW			
5806	C-FYBK	N605FA	C-GJXK	B-3076	N605NS
5807	C-FYUD	VP-CIF			
5808	C-FYUH	OE-IPZ	N1220S	XC-LNS	XB-NWD
5809	C-FYUK	B-3561			
5810	C-FYUP	G-CGJA	M-AAES	N5810B	XA-LPZ
5811	C-FYUR	N513DL			
5812	C-FYUS	EI-WFI			
5813	C-FYUY	(VT-NKL)	M-ABCU	M-AIZB	T7-AAS
5814	C-FYTY	M-NOLA	N296KR	VH-LVH	
5815	C-FZLA	N605BX	N89		
5816	C-FZLB	N816CC	N15VC		
5817	C-FZLM	N605JK	N90		
5818	C-FZLR	N880CM			
5819	C-FZLS	N696HS			
5820	C-FZLU	B-3077			
5821	C-FZKY	N605MS	G-URRU	N775RP	
5822	C-GAIP	N605KR	A6-TLH	A9C-TLH	T7-BCH
5823	C-GAJG	PP-COA			
5824	C-GALP	M-AIRU	N304KR	(N920DS)	C-FXWT
5825	C-GANU	OE-INK			
5826	C-GBYG	B-LOL	M-MARI		
5827	C-GBYH	N605AZ	(HB-JRI)	G-OTAG	N688JH	M-AAAA
5828	C-GBYK	B-3566			
5829	C-GBYM	XA-GRB			
5830	C-GBYS	N1500			
5831	C-GDRJ	N859AG			
5832	C-GDRU	(VQ-BMJ)	N40XC	N926EC	
5833	C-GDRY	C-FGIL			
5834	C-GDSG	N634XJ	N66ZC		
5835	C-GDSO	N635XJ			
5836	C-GDSQ	N636XJ	M-TRBS		
5837	C-GEWI	A6-SAJ			
5838	C-GEWO	OE-IDV	M-KARI	N583TA	XA-KIM
5839	C-GEWV	N605FR	N807JD	N523AR	
5840	C-GEWX	M-HNOY	M-ACHO	T7-AOO	
5841	C-GEXB	M-ERCI	N633AB		
5842	C-GEXD	OE-INE	N290MH	N57MH	
5843	C-GEXY	(VP-CNK)	G-SFRI	M-SFRI	N652BL	LV-FWW
5844	C-GFJB	9M-ATM			
5845	C-GFJE	OE-ING	N692JB	N934TQ	HK-5193*
5846	C-GFJJ	(N878H)	N484JM		
5847	C-GFJO	VP-CSI	9H-ICS	N716JR	
5848	C-GFJQ	VT-MKJ			
5849	C-GFJT	OH-GVI	OE-IIX		
5850	C-GFJX	3B-RGT	N989BA	N39RE	
5851	C-GFUQ	N605AK	C-GNYZ	VP-BGO	

CL605 CHALLENGER

C/n	Identities				
5852	C-GFUY	OE-INH	N203MH	N267DW	
5853	C-GHZH	N515KS			
5854	C-GHZQ	C-FSJR			
5855	C-GHZU	N605CR	S5-ADK	(D-AZZA)	N855JC
5856	C-GIAB	M-AKAS	(D-ACAS)	D-AKAS	VP-BKA	9H-KAS
5857	C-GIAF	A7-CEG			
5858	C-GIVX	N605PW	N261PW		
5859	C-GJOJ	N605PX	N157NS		
5860	C-GJOK	N605JS			
5861	C-GJUR	C-FSEP			
5862	C-GJYV	N890CM	N670BP		
5863	C-GJXY	D-ABEY			
5864	C-GJYA	N605BB			
5865	C-GJYC	F-HMOB	N312HX		
5866	C-GJYE	A7-MBT	A6-ELD		
5867	C-GJYI	N605AJ	N372G		
5868	C-GJYK	(D-AKAS)	B-7761		
5869	C-GJYN	N825SA			
5870	C-GJYR	N605DJ	N373G		
5871	C-GJYS	B-7796			
5872	C-GKXO	G-LTSK			
5873	C-GKXP	N75NP			
5874	C-GKXQ	N86NP			
5875	C-GKXR	N605RK	N899KK		
5876	C-GKXS	VP-BGT	P4-BFM		
5877	C-GLNI	N99KW			
5878	C-GLMU	OE-INM	N423TX	N177FF	
5879	C-GLNF	M-ARKZ			
5880	C-GLNJ	N529DM			
5881	C-GLNP	C-FCIB			
5882	C-GLYV	N508MN	N207R		
5883	C-GLZB	M-SAPL	N955PM		
5884	C-GLZD	A6-MVD			
5885	C-GLZF	N1CP			
5886	C-GNCH	(M-CHAT)	P4-AIM	P4-AAG	
5887	C-GNDZ	AP-FFL	M-GINI	AP-FFL	
5888	C-GNEC	B-7768			
5889	C-GNRY	N705AM			
5890	C-GNSG	N605CM	N1CU		
5891	C-GNSI	N605JD	N22SF	N22QF	N605LP*
5892	C-GNSJ	M-AYRU			
5893	C-GNSM	N605BR	N43SF	N43QF	
5894	C-GNVF	N44SF	N44QF		
5895	C-GNVJ	N605NP	C-GJET		
5896	C-GNVQ	B-LVA			
5897	C-GNVR	N898DL			
5898	C-GNVU	B-LVB			
5899	C-GNVX	N605WV	HZ-ATG		
5900	C-GOVC	N76SF	N76QF		
5901	C-GOVF	N345FX			
5902	C-GOVG	N726MF	N736MG		
5903	C-GOVI	B-7769			
5904	C-GOVJ	G-LCDH	OE-IXI		
5905	C-GOVR	N97NP			
5906	C-GPUU	B-7763			
5907	C-GPUV	N567YX			
5908	C-GPVD	N530SC			
5909	C-GPVE	N605CL			
5910	C-GPVF	N1967M	N1969M		
5911	C-GRYI	N200LS			
5912	C-GRYM	N605AB	N156BF		
5913	C-GRYO	N600LS			
5914	C-GRYQ	M-WFAM	TC-KLN		
5915	C-GRYR	PR-FTR			
5916	C-GRYT	N732PA			
5917	C-GRYU	N605RT			
5918	C-GRYZ	VP-BOR	(D-AMOR)	5N-FGZ	
5919	C-GRZA	B-7799			
5920	C-GRZF	M-FRZN			
5921	C-GUAZ	C-GIIT			
5922	C-GUBA	A6-TSF	VP-BQN	T7-MHA	
5923	C-GUBC	N605LT			
5924	C-GUBD	RA-67238			
5925	C-GUBF	N605BA	N68UW		
5926	C-GUKT	D-ASHY			
5927	C-GUKS	N882CB	N712AG		

CL605 CHALLENGER

C/n	Identities				
5928	C-GUKU	VP-BMM	N325MH	N961TC	
5929	C-GUKV	M-BAEP			
5930	C-GUKW	N605DA			
5931	C-GUSJ	N817AF	N817AD		
5932	C-GURO	M-ABGS			
5933	C-GURP	CC-AMX			
5934	C-GURT	N630GA	N171CL		
5935	C-GURZ	N605BF	N605JM		
5936	C-GUSF	(D-ALIK)	M-ABGU	M-MSGG	
5937	C-GVEY	(D-AMUC)	PH-HWM		
5938	C-GVFF	N500PB	C-FEUR	C-FCDE	
5939	C-GVFH	N605AH	N605GS	M-AKER	9H-OWL
5940	C-GVFI	EI-TAT			
5941	C-GVFJ	M-JMIA			
5942	C-GVFK	N988JC	N4868		
5943	C-GVFN	C-FHYL	N227MH	N275GC	
5944	C-GVFO	XA-NDY			
5945	C-GVFP	N241EA	C-GKCP		
5946	C-GVVQ	(B-3365)			
5947	C-GVVU	C-FHRL			
5948	C-GVWE	C-FSCI			
5949	C-GVWF	N880CC			
5950	C-GVWI	(N605BE)	(D-ABIG)	N605BS	
5951	C-GWQJ	(N605BK)	N633WM		
5952	C-GWQL	N589MD			
5953	C-GWQM	M-SPBM			
5954	C-GWQQ	N605MX	N232MC		
5955	C-GWQR	Pakistan EYE77			
5956	C-GXNJ	N605BL	C-FGNI	TC-ABN	
5957	C-GXNK	N605AM	N905SA		
5958	C-GXNM	9H-JCD	N624MY		
5959	C-GXNO	N999MY			
5960	C-GXNU	N605MP	N717BN		
5961	C-GXVG	N903AG			
5962	C-GXVJ	M-SEVN			
5963	C-GXVK	HB-JSG			
5964	C-GXVM	TC-KLE			
5965	C-GXVR	N211GS	N213GS		
5966	C-GYLK	(9H-YES)	T7-YES		
5967	C-GYLO	Mexico 3911			
5968	C-GYLP	D-AZZA			
5969	C-GYLQ	Mexico AMT-208		Mexico ANX-1208	Mexico ANX-1202
5970	C-GYLY	9H-VFA			
5971	C-GYLZ	9H-VFB			
5972	C-GZJK	9H-VFC			
5973	C-GZJQ	9H-VFD			
5974	C-GZJR	9H-VFE			
5975	C-GZJV	N509MM	T7-DMA		
5976	C-GZJW	VP-BKM			
5977	C-FANH	9H-VFF			
5978	C-FAOF	9H-VFG			
5979	C-FAOU	9H-VFH			
5980	C-FAPO	C-FJRG	N605BD	G-RNJP	
5981	C-FAPQ	N605M	N46E		
5982	C-FAQB	C-FHYL			
5983	C-FAQD	N605ZK	G-RNFR		
5984	C-FAQY	9H-VFI			
5985	C-FAUR	N798RS			
5986	C-FAWU	C-FSJY			
5987	C-FAXN	9H-VFJ			
5988	C-FAYD	B-3028			

Production complete.

CANADAIR CL650 CHALLENGER

C/n	Identities				
6050	C-GZKL				
6051	C-GZSG	N650PP			
6052	C-FAQK	C-FNNI	N200QS`		
6053	C-FAUF	"N201QS"	[fake marks worn at factory]	C-FNOQ	N202QS
6054	C-FAUI	N205QS			
6055	C-FAZC	C-FNQH	N206QS		
6056	C-FAZO	C-FNZS	N208QS		
6057	C-FAZS	N209QS			
6058	C-FAKM	N211QS			
6059	C-FAMN	C-FNSJ	C-FJCB		
6060	C-FAPQ	N541BA			
6061	C-FAWU	N543BA			
6062	C-FAOF	N219QS			
6063	C-FAOU	XA-GRE			
6064	C-FAPO	N650JF	N5950E		
6065	C-FANH	N650AD	N650GK		
6066	C-FAQB	N212QS			
6067	C-FAQY	N858MY			
6068	C-FAQD	C-FSHJ	C-GZUM		
6069	C-FAUR	M-RAYS			
6070	C-FAXN	OE-IGA			
6071	C-FAYD	C-FTQK	I-DBLR		
6072	C-GZQA	N214QS			
6073	C-GZQJ	HB-JSF			
6074	C-GZQL	N650RL			
6075	C-GZQO	M-ARUB			
6076	C-GZQP	C-FTND	N650ZJ		
6077	C-FAQK	N216QS			
6078	C-FAMN	N505R			
6079	C-FAUF	CS-DOF			
6080	C-FAZC	N217QS			
6081	C-FAZO	N650JR			
6082	C-FAEH	N220QS			
6083	C-FAKM	N225QS			
6084	C-FAPQ	N544BA			
6085	C-FAUI	N547BA			
6086	C-FAWU	N841N			
6087	C-FAZS	OE-LDN			
6088	C-FAOU	OE-LAN			
6089	C-FAQB	M-DSTZ			
6090	C-FAQD	N43SF			
6091	C-FAOF	N894N			
6092	C-FAMN				
6093	C-FAQK	N506R			
6094	C-FAUR	N22SF			
6095	C-FAQY	N231QS			
6096	C-FAYD	N44SF^			
6097	C-FAZC	N234QS^			
6098	C-FAEH				
6099	C-FAMN	N76SF^			
6100	C-FAPQ				
6101	C-FAUI				
6102	C-FAXN				
6103	C-FAZO				
6104	C-FAKM				
6105	C-FAUF				
6106	C-FAWU				
6107	C-FAOF				
6108	C-FAOU				
6109	C-FAQB				
6110	C-FAQD				
6111	C-FAZS				
6112					
6113					
6114					
6115					
6116					
6117					
6118					
6119					
6120					
6121					
6122					
6123					
6124					

CL650 CHALLENGER

C/n	Identities
6125	
6126	
6127	
6128	
6129	
6130	
6131	
6132	
6133	
6134	
6135	
6136	
6137	
6138	
6139	
6140	

CESSNA CITATION AND CITATION I

This production list is presented in order of the Unit Number which was used and allocated by Cessna, rather than by the normally used c/n. A c/n-Unit Number cross-reference follows the production list.

Citation Eagle conversions are marked with an asterisk (*) alongside the unit number. Eagle II conversions are aircraft re-engined with Williams FJ44 engines and are shown in the text as such.

Unit No	C/n	Identities
	669	N500CC [ff 15Sep69; cx Jan78; scrapped]
	701	N501CC [first model 501, converted from model 500 c/n 670; ff 23Jan70; displayed in Smithsonian National Air & Space Museum, Washington, DC, Jun98-Jul00; to Kansas Aviation Museum, Wichita/McConnell AFB, KS; cx 03Nov09]
001	500-0001	(N510CC) N502CC N20SM N38SM N501RM N501KG N715JS N840SP N818RJ*
002*	500-0002	N8202Q CF-CPW C-FCPW ZS-ONE [wfu Pretoria/Wonderboom, South Africa]
003	500-0003	N503CC
004	500-0004	N504CC N500GS N500GE N5005 N505K (N22CA) [w/o 05Nov05 Houston-Hobby, TX]
005	500-0005	N505CC N501PC N981EE N815HC PT-OIG
006	500-0006	N506CC OE-FGP N506CC N506TF N500MX N506MX N506SR N500AD (N500AH) [cx May91; scrapped for spares]
007	500-0007	N507CC N500LF N555AJ [w/o 19Nov79 Denver, CO]
008	500-0008	N508CC HB-VCX N502CC N11TC N11QC ZP-TYO ZP-TYP PT-WBY
009	500-0009	N509CC N500JD N700JD N147DA N147DB (N147DA) N147WS N55FT
010	500-0010	N510CC XC-FIT XC-SCT XC-DGA XB-IKS N501SE XB-LVY
011*	500-0011	N511CC N227H N13UR N18UR N20FM C-GJEM N700VC
012	500-0012	N6563C N512CC XC-FIU N512CC [dismantled at Uvalde, TX; fuselage stored off-airport; cx 10Mar17]
013	500-0013	N513CC XC-FIV
014	500-0014	N514CC N6563C N766FT N900W N800W N18FM
015	500-0015	N515CC N5867 N58CC N979EE (N332GJ) N14JL PT-LPZ
016*	500-0016	N516CC N3JJ N15FS N711CR N7110K N9AX C-GPLN
017	500-0017	N517CC (N317AB) N500PB N508PB N49E N49EA N565SS [24Jan05 to Griffin, GA for parting out by Atlanta Air Salvage; fuselage to Italy as air ambulance training aid]
018	500-0018	N518CC N5Q N5QZ (N58AN) N978EE N222MS C-FDJQ N70841 C-FSKC [w/o 25Jly98 at Rawlings, WY, and scrapped]
019*	500-0019	N519CC USCG 519 N519CC N11DH N11DQ N256WN N111QP OB-S-1280 OB-1280 N397SC
020	500-0020	N520CC CF-BAX C-FBAX N556AT [scrapped for spares Jun87; canx Feb93]
021	500-0021	N521CC JA8421 N5B N550CC N208N (N133N) XA-JLV N7GJ [cx to Mexico but used as instructional airframe at Madrid, Colombia]
022	500-0022	N522CC N522JD N800JD C-GESZ [parted out Montreal/Saint Hubert, Canada; cx Mar97]
023	500-0023	N523CC N523JD N900JD I-ALBS N523CC N50FT N200QC [parted out 2008 Punta Gorda, FL]
024	500-0024	N524CC N524CA N33TH VH-ICN N94AJ
025	500-0025	N525CC D-IMAN N70703 N745US N976EE N220W N57LL
026	500-0026	N526CC N501GP [w/o 21Jan81 Bluefield, WV]
027	500-0027	N527CC N502GP N51B N777AN PT-OVK [cx, CofA expired; wfu Sorocaba Brazil]
028	500-0028	N528CC N10DG N103WV N284AM N133JM
029	500-0029	N529CC N31ST C-GDWN N424DA [cx 16Jan14; parted out]
030	500-0030	N530CC N52AN [cx 11Dec12; parted out]
031	500-0031	N531CC YU-BIA N81883 N666SA YV-646CP YV-939CP YV2245
032	500-0032	N532CC N536V C-GXFZ (N5364U) [w/o 26Sep84 Orillia A/P, Ontario, Canada]
033	500-0033	N533CC N533BF N65MA N58PL N20RT N20RF N990AL (N130AL) (N331GC)
034	500-0034	N534CC N25HC N980EE N500DN (N111FS) N11HJ N716LT
035	500-0035	N535CC N10108 YV-2479P N35SE XA-JOV XC-MMM
036	500-0036	N536CC OY-DVL SE-DEU D-IEXC N18HJ OO-LCM N50812 [parted out at Brussels, Belgium, still marked as OO-LCM]
037	500-0037	N537CC N109AL SE-DPL N109AL N407SC EC-GTS
038	500-0038	N538CC HB-VCU N2EL N81BA N777FC (N207L) N27L
039	500-0039	N539CC N555CC PT-OOK N118LA [to White Inds, Bates City, MO for parts Jly03]
040	500-0040	N540CC JA8422 N714US D-IKAN OY-ARP N2170J N600WM N98Q
041	500-0041	N541CC N541AG N50AS N50AM
042	500-0042	N542CC CF-BCL C-FBCL N [scrapped circa 1997]
043	500-0043	N543CC N104UA N34UT N5072L N5072E PT-KXZ N5072E N32DD N502RL N502RD (N96EJ) YV1152 [w/o 02Jul08, Maiquetia, Venezuela]
044	500-0044	N544CC N942B N712US N892CA VR-CWW N501WW OO-ATS PH-CTY N501WW N501VH ZS-DSA N28AR
045	500-0045	N545CC N4VF N6VF N7KH N11AQ N31MW N666ES N666BS N628BS (N628FS) [parted out by Atlanta Air Salvage, GA]
046	500-0046	N546CC N50SK N50SL N109AP N109BL N929CA N929RW PT-OTQ
047	500-0047	N547CC N180PF PT-WAB N7281Z (N60181) [cx to Venezuela 08Jan04; wfu Charallave, Venezuela, still wearing marks N7281Z]
048	500-0048	N548CC N727LE N727EE N11DH N5500S N44BW N67JR N911GM
049	500-0049	N549CC PP-FXB PT-FXB PT-LDH N25UT [parted out Montgomery, AL; cx 24Mar17]
050*	500-0050	N550CC N471MM N471MH N471HH N333PP VH-HKX (N565GW)
051	500-0051	N551CC N51BP (N51BR) (N61BP) N61BR N4646S VH-ICX VH-EMM VH-EGK [b/u Melbourne/Essendon, Australia, March13 still wearing marks VH-EMM]
052	500-0052	N552CC N52MA N52FP YV-2267P YV-2477P YV-2628P YV-881CP YV1316
053	500-0053	N553CC I-CITY N90WJ I-KUNA HB-VGO I-AEAL
054	500-0054	N554CC N54SK N98MB (N28U) (N54FT) XB-PBT
055	500-0055	N900KC N900MP N999SF N716CB [parted out Muskegon, MI, 2007; cx 11Mar13]
056*	500-0056	N556CC N777JM N500DB C-GCTD N360DA N956S N52FT N52ET N777JJ

CITATION I

Unit No	C/n	Identities
057	500-0057	N557CC PT-ILJ [w/o 03Jly97 Guanabara Bay/Rio-Santos Dumont A/p, Brazil; parted out by Dodson Av'n, Rantoul, KS]
058	500-0058	N558CC N11WC N11WQ N46RB C-GJLQ N6145Q YV-901CP YV1713
059	500-0059	N559CC N559BC N40RD N40PD N913RC N117TW N501DZ
060	500-0060	N560CC N712J N712G XA-SEN XA-PAZ N712G PT-OOL
061	500-0061	N561CC XC-GAD XC-ASA N490EA N52AJ N916RC [US Navy Squadron VT-8 colours, code 01 with legend "T-27A serial 061" where the Bu number would normally appear] ZS-DBS
062	500-0062	N562CC N4CH N4KH N334RC XB-ACS XB-MCN
063	500-0063	N563CC SE-DDE N70451 OO-RST N70MG [wfu Chino, CA]
064	500-0064	N564CC N27SF
065	500-0065	N565CC (N565TW)
066	500-0066	N566CC N66CC C-GQCC [cx to USA 22Apr05, no N-number allocated – parted out?]
067	500-0067	N567CC N3PC XB-DBA N5301J C-FADL N567EA (F-GIHT) (N949SA) N810RJ YV2982
068	500-0068	N568CC N568CM PT-LAY N53MJ N92FA XB-FDN XA-RYE XB-VGT XA-PPV
069	500-0069	N569CC PT-IQL N969SE N255RD C-FTMI N501ZD
070	500-0070	N570CC N500TD N600MT YV-707CP VR-CMO VP-CMO N227MK
071	500-0071	N571CC CF-BCM C-FBCM ZS-AMB D2-EDC D2-AJL D2-EDC V5-LOW V5-CAL
072	500-0072	N572CC N49R N491 XC-BEZ N590EA N103AJ PT-OYA N114LA N72DJ YV238T
073	500-0073	N573CC N720C (N881M) C-FKMC [parted out by White Inds, Bates City, MO; cx 22Dec06]
074	500-0074	N574CC N574W N8JG PT-OOF N500ML YV3030
075	500-0075	N575CC (N600TT) N575RD [parted out by White Inds, Bates City, MO; cx 29Apr10]
076	500-0076	N576CC N810SC N810SG C-GIAC N90CC N500CV N65WS ZS-PWT
077	500-0077	N577CC N342AP N869K ZS-OAM N147SC N28WL
078	500-0078	N578CC N2HD ZS-IYY TL-AAW N54531 N21TV N429RC N110CK N269RC
079	500-0079	N579CC D-INHH N31088 N40JF PT-LBN
080	500-0080	N580CC N50CC N419K C-GJAP N59019 N222KW N767PC N10JP N10UP ZS-NGR V5-OGL
081	500-0081	N581CC N5B HB-VDA I-PEGA (D-IEGA) YU-JET D-IECI
082	500-0082	N582CC EC-CCY HB-VGD N4434W N103JA N911JD N500CV N178HH N173HH N482RJ N428RJ C-GREK C-GTRL
083	500-0083	N583CC N10UC N10UQ N800KC CP-2131 N50602 CP-2131 N50602 [painted as "50602"] VR-CCP VR-BMT N50602 VR-BMO VR-CHH VP-CHH "VP-CRH" [painted in error] VP-CHH N31LW
084	500-0084	N584CC N10 N2 N25 N4 N7 N935GA XB-FPK XA-SMH [w/o 25Mar95 Vera Cruz, Mexico]
085	500-0085	N585CC N51MW N515AA (N64AJ) 5N-BCI ZS-PTT
086	500-0086	N586CC N503GP C-FMAN LX-YKH D-ICIA (PH-TEU)+ [+ntu marks worn at Rotterdam, Netherlands, Jun09] PH-TEV [cx Nov11, CofA expired; stored Teuge, Netherlands]
087	500-0087	N587CC N85AT (N64792) N700RY N500CP (N911A) (N911CJ) N633AT
088	500-0088	N588CC PH-CTA (OO-FAY) G-HOLL PH-CTA N170MD N251DD [wfu Ocurmare del Tuy, Venezuela]
089	500-0089	N589CC EC-EBR N39LH [parted out by Int'l Turbine Services, TX; cx May05]
090	500-0090	N590CC N590RB XB-EFR Mexico ETE-1329 Mexico 3929 [preserved Museo de Aviacion Militar, Santa Lucia AB, Mexico]
091	500-0091	N591CC N76RE (PT-LAW) N50PR C-FCHJ (N1899) N500AD PR-FMA
092	500-0092	N592CC Venezuela 0222
093	500-0093	N593CC PH-CTB OO-FBY N611SW G-OXEC G-OCPI N62BR YV317T [conv to Citation Long Wing]
094	500-0094	N594CC N94DE VR-CEB N80GB N96FB
095	500-0095	N595CC N2200R (N578WB) YV-15CP N4294A N500KP I-AMAW N950AM I-ARON [wfu Rome/Urbe, Italy]
096	500-0096	N596CC N222SL N202VS N202VV C-GXPT N202VV N837MA (N187AP) [cx 26Mar15; CofR expired]
097	501-0446	N597CC N14CF N63CF N888MJ A7-ASA N308JM RA-2400G
098	500-0098	N598CC PH-CTC G-BNVY PH-CTC N500GR N500GB [parted out by White Inds, Bates City, MO]
099	500-0099	N599CC N21CC [to spares circa 1999]
100	500-0100	N69566 HB-VDC D-ICPW OE-FNL HB-VDC OE-FNP D-IFAI N80AJ (N58BT)
101	500-0101	N601CC N12MB N101CD N1HM N6JL N6JU N15CC N15CQ C-GKCZ N666AG N370LN
102	500-0102	(N602CC) N800PL N400K N491BT N491PT
103	500-0103	(N603CC) N103CC PT-KIR C-GJVK
104	500-0104	(N604CC) N200KC N200KQ C-GPJW N40HP N3030C (N3330) N353PJ
105	500-0105	N105CC N105JJ N32W N234UM [w/o 26Feb01 Sault Ste Marie, MI; scrapped]
106	500-0106	N606CC ZS-RCC [b/u]
107	500-0107	(N607CC) N107CC N107SC C-GWVC N230JS N40RW N79RS
108	500-0108	N108CC EC-CGG [w/o 22Nov74 Barcelona, Spain]
109	500-0109	N44SA G-RAVY I-AMCU N221AM YV1677
110	500-0110	(N610CC) N500AB N154G (N52WS) N500Y N363K N368K N172MA XB-JDG XB-LSA
111	500-0111	N111CC N11A XA-SHO XA-SLQ [w/o 06Feb96 Ensenada A/P, Mexico]
112*	500-0112	N512CC VH-DRM N3LG C-GRJC N29858 N515DC N500TM [wfu Fort Lauderdale Executive, FL]
113	500-0113	(N613CC) N113CC N684HA N684H N500NJ [parted out by Alliance Air Parts, Oklahoma City, OK; cx 10Jan14]
114	500-0114	(N614CC) N999JB N899N (G-BNZP) I-AMCT N65SA N703RT
115	500-0115	YV-T-AFA YV-21CP [w/o 08Mar05 Charallave, Venezuela]
116	500-0116	N116CC EC-CJH D-IATC EC-HRH [instructional airframe at Berufskolleg fur Technik & Medien, Monchengladbach, Germany, Oct09]
117	500-0117	N617CC N90BA N161WC N442JB

CITATION I

Unit No	C/n	Identities
118	500-0118	(N618CC) N220CC N221CC N972JD (N10BF) N972GW N50MM [to spares circa 1999, fuselage to Aviation Fabrications Inc, MO who use it to demonstrate their range of Citation modifications]
119	500-0119	N619CC N111SU N11KA N95Q N501EJ
120	500-0120	(N620CC) N120CC N10DG N141DR N141DP N999TC (N500NX) N127BJ N712MB
121	500-0121	D-IANE N9871R N939SR OY-SUJ N3QE N661AC YV2892
122*	500-0122	N122CC CF-ENJ C-FENJ N122LM N122AP ZS-PFG
123*	500-0123	N123CC (PI-C7777) N523CC RP-C7777 RP-C102 N123CX N947CC VH-LJL ZK-LJL VH-ECD ZS-PMA
124	500-0124	N124CC N300HC N300HQ N303PC N8FC N92SM
125	500-0125	CF-CFP C-FCFP XA-SFE N108RL YV1475.
126	500-0126	(N626CC) HB-VDM D-IDWH N404MA N902DD [cx 06Apr15; wfu]
127	500-0127	N701AS N701AT N22DN N500R N580R [parted out by Total Aircraft Parts Inc, CT]
128	500-0128	D-INCC N53584 N40HL N501AR N3490L [parted out Montgomery, AL, 2007]
129	500-0129	D-IMLN N8114G N500SK
130*	500-0130	VH-CRM N4LG OY-ARW N4LG N130G ZS-MCP N800AB N130CE YV....
131	500-0131	D-IDAU N1045T N745DM (N725DM) N457CA PT-OJF [wfu Mojave, CA]
132	500-0132	(N632CC) N35LT N80CC (N10GR) N888JD N888GA N881CA N132BP N501RB N713SA (N992HG) YV2800
133	500-0133	N133CC F-BUYL OO-SEL N2070K N1270K PT-LXH
134	500-0134	N134CC PT-JMJ
135	500-0135	N135CC N135BC N900T N902T N975EE N111AM N220MT (N500EN) YV-717CP [modified with winglets] HK-3885 [reportedly crashed into mountains in NW Colombia 07Mar97]
136	500-0136	(N136CC) F-BUUL N136SA XA-JRV [instructional airframe at Trident Technical College, North Charleston, SC]
137	500-0137	N137CC N12MB N12ME ZS-MCU (N922BA)
138	500-0138	N3056R N138SA
139	500-0139	(N5353J) OE-FDP N3771U N15AW YV2498 N139FJ
140	500-0140	N140CC N300PX N111AT (N777SC) N977EE XA-EKO N135JW N2FA N4LK N4ZK N441TC N972AB
141	500-0141	N141CC XA-PIC XB-EWQ N727TK [cx 24Mar17, CofR expired]
142	500-0142	N142CC VH-UCC N650TF N200GM N69XW
143	500-0143	N143CC XC-GUQ XB-CXF N3W N14JZ N14T N787BA SE-DUZ N730RJ [parted out by Dodson Int'l, Rantoul, KS]
144	500-0144	(N644CC) N332H OH-CAR [w/o 19Nov87 Tuusula, Helsinki, Finland]
145	500-0145	N145CC N145FC N145TA (N415FC)
146	500-0146	N194AT N111ME
147	500-0147	N404G N494G N688CF YV2495
148	500-0148	(N100JC) N718VA N748VA N410GB N225DC LV-PMP LV-WXJ N989SC N500DB
149	500-0149	N4TL N4TE (N43TC) N100RG (N100FF) N149PJ ZS-TMG [parted out at Lanseria, Sth Africa, then preserved at Muldersdrift, Sth Africa]
150	500-0150	N150CC N5B VH-WRM N5LG OE-FAU N501JG (N78MC) N9V N914CD
151	500-0151	N151CC N6CD [cx Nov91; parted out by White Inds, Bates City, MO]
152	500-0152	N152CC (N194AT) I-FERN N53J N152CC XB-AMO N2782D XB-AMO
153	500-0153	9J-ADU N153WB N153JP N2RM
154	500-0154	C-GOCM N54MC PT-WFT C-GRFT
155	500-0155	(N655CC) N920W N5ZZ N88GJ (N188DR) N155MK [wfu Denton, TX]
156	500-0156	PT-KBR [cx, CofA expired; wfu]
157	500-0157	PH-CTD N190AB CS-DCA EC-HFY EC-HPQ
158	500-0158	N999CM N910Y N910N (N158TJ) OY-TAM N233DB
159	500-0159	N36MC N165BA N50AC N831CW N881JT N97DD N159KC
160	500-0160	N146BF (N146BE) N146JC N1951E N59TS C-GNSA [parted out by White Inds, Bates City, MO; cx 20Jul06]
161	500-0161	(C-GTEL) C-GHEC N161CC ZS-BTC A2-JDJ ZS-BTC [wfu Lanseria, South Africa]
162	500-0162	PT-JXS [w/o 16Mar75 Belem, Brazil]
163	500-0163	N192G (N94ZG) N8KH N54JV
164	500-0164	N164CC D-IHSV N4209K F-GEPL N382JP N334PS (N164GJ) N73MP
165	500-0165	N19M N19MQ G-PNNY VR-CSP VP-CSP N501LB (N501FF) OD-SAS [cx Mar08, CofA expired]
166	500-0166	N500WR N313JL (N29MW) N8DE N511AT [dbr Beverly, CA, 17Mar07; parted out Punta Gorda, FL; cx 01Nov12]
167	500-0167	PH-CTE N191AB N246RR N801KT YV-2821P YV1432
168	500-0168	N91BA N918A N135BK N135MA N891CA (N46JA)
169	500-0169	N20FL N19CM XC-CON XC-BOC XA-SJW N676CW (N676WE) N75GM C-GTNG [w/o 13Oct16, crashed nr Kelowna, Canada]
170*	500-0170	N60MS N90237 N818R N66LE [parted out by Dodson Av'n, Rantoul, KS]
171	500-0171	N171CC YV-370CP N728US PT-LIX (PP-LEM)
172	500-0172	N172CC PT-KIU [w/o 12Nov76 Aracatuba, Brazil]
173	500-0173	N77CP N59CL N500EL [parted out by White Inds Inc, Bates City, MO]
174*	500-0174	N26HC N21NA N211DB N14MH N931CA N19AJ N16LG N15JH
175	500-0175	N175CC XA-HOO XB-CCO XA-SIG N175CC N1DK [w/o 06Jan98 Pittsburgh-Allegheny County A/P, PA]
176	500-0176	G-BCII G-TEFH N150TT
177	500-0177	PH-CTF N192AB N888XL N883XL N431LC
178	500-0178	D-IKFJ I-FBCK (HB-VJP) HB-VKK EC-IBA [w/o 02Aug12 nr Santiago de Compostela, Spain]
179	500-0179	N444J N111KR N427DM (N997S) EI-BYM N179EA PT-OMT
180	500-0180	N180CC I-AMBR N31079 SE-DDO HB-VFH N31079 PT-LAZ N61MJ N772C N500ET
181	500-0181	N181CC PT-KPA [cx by 2000 last permit 1996; reported wfu]

CITATION I

Unit No	C/n	Identities
182	500-0182	D-IABC N525GA C-FNOC N590EA N13HJ OO-DCM N23W N900TA [parted out by White Inds, Bates City, MO; cx 24Mar17]
183	500-0183	N183CC (VH-FRM) N1VC (N721CC) N1880S N112CP N151AS [parted out Montgomery, AL; cx 24Aug07]
184	500-0184	N77RC N71RC N67SF N67BE N67BF N184NA N550LT
185	500-0185	N22EH N22FH N500JB N500WP N500AZ C-GIAD N500AZ ZP-TZH N141SA
186	500-0186	N186MW N186SC (N501WL) N186CP [parted out by Preferred Airparts, OH]
187	500-0187	(HB-VDR) (TI-ACB) N187MW N20VP (N75KC) N99MC N345KC N99BC (N95TJ) N5FW N130DW YV3217
188	500-0188	N5223J PT-KPB N505AZ
189	500-0189	XC-GOV XA-SJV N189CC N500HH [b/u; cx Jan01]
190	500-0190	N190CC (N424RD) N99BC N99MC N500HK N602BC N434UM [parted out; cx 29May09]
191	500-0191	N5600M N448EC N23WK N155CA N701BR LV-YRB
192	500-0192	N4TK N508S N220S N100JJ I-AMCY (N70WA)
193	500-0193	XC-GOW XA-SQZ N293S OY-JAI
194	500-0194	D-IMSM OY-ASR N310U PT-LAX N991SA (N728RX) N194TS N501DG+ [+ flew as N501DG between Oct02 and Apr04 without officially being registered as such] N225RD YV2737
195	500-0195	N14JA N100AC N100AQ N440EZ N500LJ N502BE [parted out by White Inds, Bates City, MO]
196	500-0196	N74FC C-GENJ N499BA (N969ZS) (N711FW) N270PM [cx 26Aug13; wfu]
197	500-0197	XC-GOX XA-SRB N297S N95VE N1TW N95VE N316MW
198	500-0198	G-BCKM G-JETE N9UJ N700MP N997CA XB-IJW XB-IUW XB-TRN
199	500-0199	N199SP C-FGAT XA-ASR XB-JVK N199JK
200	500-0200	N520CC N200MW N250AA N96G N96EA CS-DBM N102VP (YV-1071CP) [wfu Fort Worth/Meacham, TX] N590RJ*
201	500-0201	XC-GUO N690EA (F-GIHU) N690EA F-GRCH C-GLAA N221DA
202	500-0202	N202MW N240AA N500JK N500VK N500WJ N550RS
203	500-0203	N95DR (N724CC) N101HF N101HB CC-PZM (N51099) [parted out]
204	500-0204	C-GBCK N204Y TG-OZO N204Y N928RD [parted out]
205	500-0205	N520N (N541NC) N700CW [w/o 01Apr83 Eagle Pass, TX]
206	500-0206	N33NH N946CC VH-LGL N771HR [w/o 30Jun07 Conway, AR]
207	500-0207	N92BA N929A N39J N107SF N501TL
208	500-0208	N82JT N22JG (N520SC) N501AT (N508CC) N515WE N770AF
209	500-0209	N209MW (N919AT) N800AV EC-HFA [to parts use circa Feb05 by Atlanta Air Salvage, Griffin, GA]
210	500-0210	TR-LTI N9011R N210MT N716GA YV-625CP [modified with winglets, removed on resale in USA] N501TK XB-TRY XB-NXX
211	500-0211	N990CB N999CB N999CV [parted out by White Inds, Bates City, MO, 2000]
212*	500-0212	N1LB N222LB N223LB N223AS N223MC N92B N74LL
213	500-0213	N62HB N355H N741JB N73WC N100UF N100UH N101HG (N213CE) XA-AEI
214	500-0214	N214CC N371HH (N371W) N214CA N709TB N601GN XB-NKT
215	500-0215	N215CC YV-T-000 YV-55CP YV2030
216	500-0216	(N216CC) N314TC N99CK N199CK (N612CA) YV1686
217	500-0217	N217CC N500GA N560GA N625GA XA-ODC N2201U XA-SOX N217S N55GR YV2620
218	500-0218	(N218CC) N4AC N271AC (N271MF) YV3029
219	500-0219	N219CC N25CS N101KK (N161KK) N408CA PT-LIY [w/o 01Dec02 Marilia, Brazil]
220	500-0220	N5220J N93WD N932HA G-BOGA G-OBEL N619EA G-ORHE [cx 24Jul08, CofA expired]
221	500-0221	N221CC XC-GUH N24AJ
222	500-0222	N222CC N636SC N52PM [cx 10Jul13; wfu]
223	500-0223	N223CC N444LP N444KV N400SA OH-COC N223P I-CLAD
224	500-0224	(N224CC) N77RE N3ZD N5FG N145CM N697MB ZS-ISA ZS-SGT
225	500-0225	N5225J N5B PH-SAW OO-GPN D-IDFD VH-FSQ VH-OIL RP-C1500 [w/o 01Feb97 Mount Balakukan, Mindanao Island, Philippines]
226	500-0226	N5226J JA8418 N100AD PT-LTI
227	500-0227	(N227CC) G-BCRM N423RD C-GMMO N227HP (N776JS) N227GM TI-AZX N916DJ
228	500-0228	(N228CC) N6365C N769K [parted out by White Inds, Bates City, MO]
229	500-0229	N22FM [w/o 26Apr83 Wichita, KS]
230	500-0230	N5230J N230CC HB-VEH I-PLLL N92AJ N24S (N300TB) N299TB N200CG
231	500-0231	(N5231J) N99TD N2TN C-GMAT N500SJ N501GB
232	500-0232	N5232J N500PB N126R N999AM (N971AB) N804TS
233	500-0233	N5233J N233CC N233VM N223S N228S N233JJ
234	500-0234	(N5234J) PH-CTG N70CA
235	500-0235	N5235J N235CC N12AM (SE-RKZ) [to Sweden as instructional airframe; cx 17Dec09]
236	500-0236	N5236J N236CC N24PA N2801L N801L N801K N600SR N337TV N236TS N1X N742K N320RG N70SW
237	500-0237	(N5237J) N14TT VH-FSA [w/o 20Feb84 Proserpine, Queensland, Australia]
238	500-0238	(N5238J) N3Q N3QZ OO-IBI N68AG N53FT VP-CON N409S
239	500-0239	(N5239J) N239CC N6034F PT-LOS [parted out by Dodson Av'n, Rantoul, KS]
240	500-0240	N5240J N240CC N234AT
241	500-0241	(N9AT) N5241J XA-DAJ N9060Y XB-EPN N288SP N610ED [w/o nr Derby, KS, 18Oct13]
242	500-0242	N5242J RP-C1964 N888JL (N884DR) (N888PA) [wfu, stored Wichita/Mid-Continent, KS]
243	500-0243	N5243J XC-GOY XC-BEN XA-SQY N53AJ N243SH
244	500-0244	(N5244J) (SE-DMM) SE-DDM N244WJ N400BH N91LS (N91BS) N46RD N516AB PT-OQD
245	500-0245	N5245J (TI-AHE) TI-AHH XC-BUR N2019V 9M-FAZ (N245MG) (N245BC) D-IAJJ 9H-AJJ
246	500-0246	(N5246J) N50WM N227VG PT-LQR
247	500-0247	(N5247J) N4110S N9065J XA-JUA C-GMAJ [parted out Addison, TX]
248	500-0248	(N5248J) N75PX (N70PB) N111BB
249	500-0249	N5249J N27PA N411DR PT-LPF (N789DD) N501SE N1GG HA-JET

CITATION I

Unit No	C/n	Identities
250	500-0250	(N5250J) N250CC N25PA N25CK XA-JEL N444RP C-GRJQ N160JS (N413KA) (N200BA) N251P N251MG YV3095.
251	500-0251	N5251J I-COKE (HB-VGI) N500LP XC-QEO XC-ASB N790EA PT-OMS
252	500-0252	N5252J N10PS N200WN C-GZXA N244WJ N501JC N622AT
253	500-0253	N5253J YV-T-MMM YV-19P YV-07P N722US N8TG N592WP
254	500-0254	N5254J N26PA C-GJTX N29991 N79DD [w/o 24Sep90 San Luis Obispo, CA]
255	500-0255	N5255J D-INCI N37643 N877BP N885CA XA-SAM XB-HND N907RT N752CK
256	500-0256	N256CC SE-DDN N83TF N73TF N456GB N73HB PT-OZT N131SB N676DG
257	500-0257	N5257J N75MN N75FN N75GW ZS-PXD
258	500-0258	(N5258J) TI-AFB N80639 (N76AM) N66GE N886CA N125DS N246JJ*
259	500-0259	N5259J N410ND JA8247 RP-C1299 N259DH
260	500-0260	(N5260J) N260CC OK-FKA N50RD ZS-OGS N260RD ZS-OGS A6-ESJ N202HM
261	500-0261	N5261J N261CC N55HF N55LF N711SE N711SF (N124DH) N58TC XB-MGS
262	500-0262	N5262J N44JF N111MU N110AF N110AB (N642CT) ZS-BFS ZS-LMH
263	500-0263	N126KR (N126KP) N819H (N90WA) I-DUMA N263AL VH-AQR VH-AQS VH-ZMD [wfu Melbourne/Essendon]
264	500-0264	N5264J N205FM F-GLJA G-BWFL G-OEJA G-JTNC G-BWFL
265	500-0265	N5265J N504GP XA-VYF N38MH LV-ZPU N501SC N595DC YV....
266	500-0266	N5266J N5TK N751CC N424AD N7543H (N40RF) N11MN
267	500-0267	N5267J N28PA N1UT N626P OY-CPK N70704 N41SH (N4090P) N401RD [parted out by Dodson Av'n, Rantoul, KS, circa 2000]
268	500-0268	N5268J ZS-JKR 3D-ACR VH-NEW A6-RKH N900G
269	500-0269	N5269J (D-IKUC) D-ICCC (PH-CTW) SP-KBM
270	500-0270	N5270J N712J N712N N72BC N68CB N4238X G-SWET G-OSCA N501DR N915RP N970RP
271	500-0271	N5271J N168RL N4403 N53FB PT-LQG [cx Dec97, fate not known]
272	500-0272	N5272J N505GP N30SB N30JN N89AJ [parted out by White Inds, MO; cx 29Apr09]
273	500-0273	N5273J N273RC XA-LEO XB-OBE XA-RUR XB-GBF
274	500-0274	(N5274J) N111TH N140H XA-IIX N111TH XB-ETE N225BC N70TF N5LK
275	500-0275	(N5275J) N600SR N40MM (N38MM) N352WC N352WG N102HF N71HB ZP-TZY N275GK (N275MB) (N275BH) N411TN
276	500-0276	(N5276J) N276CC N100CM N473LP N473LR SE-DEG (N340TB) N29EB SE-DEG YU-SEG SE-DEG [instructional airframe Linkopings, Sweden]
277	500-0277	(N5277J) N277CC N67MP N67MA N652ND N662CC N662CG [wfu Addison, TX; cx 14Jan16]
278	500-0278	(N5278J) N278CC N278SP (N278SR) ZS-LYB N278SP XB-FQO XB-UAG N103PL VP-BBE (SE-RDA) N103PL OY-PCW EC-JXC
279	500-0279	(N5279J) D-IMEN OY-AJV SE-DEX N70454 VH-NMW N120S N501KG N700LW N425JS N138HB
280	500-0280	(N5280J) N280CC N100HP N102AD N814ER [w/o 01Feb06 Greensboro, NC; parted out by Dodson Int'l, Rantoul, KS]
281	500-0281	N5281J N49R N72WC N144JP (N721TB) N62TW N70TS
282	500-0282	(N5282J) N282CC N26WD N520RB N501SS N501CW N510RC HB-VNU N282SA [stored Zurich, Switzerland, still wearing marks HB-VNU]
283	500-0283	N5283J N10UC N18AF VH-ANQ [w/o 11May90 Mt Emerald, Cairns, QLD, Australia]
284	500-0284	(N5284J) N284CC YV-43CP N8508Z N37DW PT-LOG
285	500-0285	N5285J (N285CC) N2U N86SS N113SH [w/o 04Mar08 nr Oklahoma City/Wiley Post, OK]
286	500-0286	N5286J N286CC 5N-APN [wfu Lagos, Nigeria]
287	500-0287	(N5287J) N287CC N73LL N57MB OY-CGO N31LH PT-WHZ N287AB VP-BGE [crashed on approach to Biggin Hill, England, 30Mar08; w/o]
288	500-0288	(N5288J) N288CC D-IDWN OY-ASD N9013S N5TR (N502BA) N1DA
289	500-0289	N5289J YV-50CP N5591A XA-KAH N939KS OE-FAN [w/o 24Feb04 Cagliari, Italy]
290	500-0290	(N5290J) N290CC D-ICFA N4246Y N826RD N88AF (N390S) N896MA N896MB N400RM
291	500-0291	N5291J ZS-JOO N291DS OE-FGN N291JK
292*	500-0292	N5292J N10FM N255LJ C-FSUN N18BG SE-DDX N501RL N501HK N333JH XB-ESG XA-MMS
293	501-0643	(N5293J) N8RF N54CM N54TS [Sierra Stallion conversion with Williams FJ44-2A engines, ff 14Jun06] C-GQPJ N449RP
294	500-0294	N5294J HL7226 (N501LG) N924AS SE-DVB OY-VIP OE-FCM N468PD [parted out by Dodson Av'n, Rantoul, KS]
295	500-0295	N5295J EP-PAO EP-KIA N2274B N44HC N10FG XB-NYV
296	500-0296	(N5296J) N98DM N882CA ZS-NHF (N245BC) N296BF XA-BET
297	500-0297	N5297J (N818CD) YV-62CP N48DA N38SA
298	500-0298	N5298J N900GC N570MC YV561T YV3209
299	500-0299	N5299J HB-VEO N3JJ N66TR N55AK ZS-MGH N5133K YV-940CP PT-OZX N80364 (OY-EBD) OY-TKI N80364 [wfu Doncaster/Robin Hood, UK]
300	500-0300	(N5300J) OE-FAP (N500CX) [parted out by Dodson Av'n, Ottawa, KS, following accident 06Oct84 in Greece; cx Jun90]
301	500-0301	N5301J EP-PAP N81MJ N747WA OE-FNG N305S
302	500-0302	N5302J N302CE N469PW (N777QE) N710VL
303	500-0303	(N5303J) N19M N19U C-GDWS N8DX [w/o 24Mar17, crashed into house Marietta, GA]
304	500-0304	N5304J N304CC N5253A N5253E N70U N10UH [cx Jun05, parted out then used for fire training at San Antonio, TX]
305	500-0305	(N5305J) N305BB N805BB C-GMLC N137WC N100AM
306	500-0306	N5306J N36CJ N36SJ N606KK N606KR (N747BL)
307	500-0307	N5307J N2607 N2613 N777SL
308	500-0308	(N5308J) N308CC N38CJ N70TG N6525J (F-GIRS) F-GMLH F-GSMC F-HDMB 3B-...

CITATION I

Unit No	C/n	Identities
309	500-0309	N5309J (N1GB) N1JN N1UG N1382C N57LC SE-DKM N791MA N88NW N83NW
310	500-0310	(N5310J) N510CC N1851T N1851N N820FJ N820 XA-STT N998AA N222VV N941JC N900CC YV2696
311	500-0311	N5311J N818CD OH-COL N501RL N39RE SE-DRT (OY-VIP) LN-AAF I-RAGW
312	F500-0312	N5312J N33ME (N233ME) N33MQ N82AT F-GJDG EC-KGE F-HBMS EC-LZP
313	500-0313	(N5313J) N76GT XA-KUJ XB-DYF XA-SDS N313BA HB-VLE D-ISKM N513JK [cx 06Aug15; derelict at Friedrichshafen, Germany, still wearing D-ISKM]
314	500-0314	N5314J (N314CC) N501SC N100UF N180UF N66ES N668S N500NT
315	500-0315	N5315J N55SK N55SH SE-DRZ N694PW [parted out by Alliance Air Parts, Oklahoma City, OK]
316	500-0316	N5316J N398RP N97SK N711MT (N127CJ) YV....
317	500-0317	N53MJ D-ICCA N37489 C-GPCO N317VP YV-1133CP YV233T YV2753
318	500-0318	N5318J N518CC N944B VR-COM VP-COM
319	500-0319	N5319J HZ-NCI N5319J N22LH D-ICUW N94MA "F-GKIL" F-GKID
320	500-0320	(N5320J) N320CC N341CC N299WV N341CC I-NORT N74WA N70WA I-....
321	500-0321	N5321J JA8438 [cx Sep96, wfu; To Japan Newspaper Museum, Yokohama, Japan then to Asahi Shimbun Newspaper headquarters, Japan]
322	500-0322	N5322J N1AP N108MC
323	500-0323	N5323J N300PB N474L N523CC N307EW (N268GM) N388GM N386SC LV-CDI
324	500-0324	(N5324J) N324C N52TC N324JC (N721HW)
325	500-0325	(N5325J) N25CJ N50TR N60MP PT-OSD
326	500-0326	N5326J N45LC G-UESS [w/o 08Dec83 Stornoway, Scotland]
327	500-0327	N5327J HL7277 S Korea 5327 S Korea 70327 N399PA RP-C3958
328	500-0328	(N5328J) N328CC (N571K) PT-LSF N168AS XB-IXE
329	500-0329	N5329J ZS-JOK N5329J XC-IPP XC-PPM N4999H OY-CEV N810JT [cx 22Mar17, parted out]
330	500-0330	(N5330J) N330CC (N82CF) I-JESE N270BH (N237JP) N141SG N800CJ N812MG
331	500-0331	(N5331J) N331CC N86RE N96RE N40AC LN-NAT EC-500 EC-FUM LN-NAT G-LOFT [wfu Caernarfon, UK]
332	500-0332	N5332J LV-PUY LV-LZR N332SE
333	500-0333	(N5333J) N275AL VH-SOU
334	500-0334	N5334J N500DD N44RD (N527TA) ZS-MPI N334JC [canx Apr98 as scrapped]
335	500-0335	N5335J ZP-PNB ZP-PUP N2937L PT-LDI
336	500-0336	(N5336J) N336CC YV-O-MAC-1 [w/o Jun79 Caracas, Venezuela]
337	500-0337	N5337J N873D N22MB (F-GNAB) N17KD N615DS
338	500-0338	N5338J (N868D) HB-VEX N8499B N3300M N92LA N97LA N73WC (N404JW) N41HL XB-OIQ
339	500-0339	(N5339J) G-JEAN N707US N300EC G-JEAN G-DJAE [wfu; parted out by Dodson Av'n, Rantoul, KS]
340	500-0340	(N5340J) N2630 (N2610) N505AM HB-VIV VR-BTQ ZS-MBS N340DN PT-WOD (N340RL) N26NS N344RJ [instructional airframe, Saskatchewan Indian Institute of Technology, Saskatoon, Canada].
341	500-0341	(N5341J) N2650 N505JC C-GVKL C-FDMB N383SC LV-BPW
342	500-0342	(N5342J) N530TL N711TE N501DR N501LH
343	500-0343	(N5343J) N525AC C-FRHL N91D HB-VJR N91DZ C-FOSM N501JF
344	500-0344	(N5344J) N632SC HB-VHI VR-BLV VP-BLV CX-CCT
345	500-0345	(N5345J) N23ND N410NA N410N VR-BUB N345TL N747RL (N747KL) XA-TOF XB-CSI
346	500-0346	N5346J D-IJON N4234K (N99WB) N82SE N56DV PT-LUA
347	500-0347	(N5347J) N500XY N876WB V5-ACE
348	500-0348	(N5348J) N300HC N301HC C-GCLQ N712KM (N517RJ)
349	500-0349	(N5349J) N888AC (N988AC) N888GZ VH-HVM VH-HVH N501DA
350	501-0027	N5350J N350CC N10EH N54DS JA8380 N783KK
351	501-0001	N5351J N51CJ N506TF [converted to Sierra Stallion] (N15FJ) Mexico 3933
352	501-0261	N5352J N52CC N7NE N501VP YV2502
353	501-0002	N5353J OE-FPO N165CB XA-LUN N39301 N501WJ (N501WK) N88TB HP-1797
354	501-0263	N5354J N948N N501BE (N501BF) [cx 31Aug15; wfu]
355	501-0003	N5355J N55CJ N781L N81EB
356	501-0004	N5356J N88JJ N86JJ N142DA
357	501-0005	N5357J N661AA N665JB N143EP N284RJ N455FD N501SV
358	501-0006	(N5358J) N358CC N121JW N121UW (N1236P) N5016P N93TJ I-ERJA N501GR
359	501-0264	(N5359J) 9J-AEJ N353WB N27WW N403AA
360	501-0007	N5360J N222WA
361	500-0361	N5361J D-IKPW N5361J C-GOIL N5361J N90EB F-GKIR N501MX
362	501-0008	N5362J N362CC N6HT (N501DB) N900PS N909PS
363	500-0354	(N5363J) G-BEIZ N51GA G-CCCL G-TJHI N354RC N694LM HL8037
364	501-0011	N36842 (N1UB) N36JG N770MH N650AC N1UM N130SP N501
365	501-0267	N36846 G-DJBB D-IAEV N944TG N565VV N565V
366	500-0356	N5366J N36848 Argentina AE-185 LQ-CLW
367	501-0009	N36850 N67CC N715EK (N715JM) N505BC N505RJ
368	501-0269	N5368J N36854 YV-120CP N120RD N545GA (N545G) XB-GVY N501JJ
369	501-0012	N36858 N190K N999RB N99XY N99GC N8P N8PJ HI-527 HI-527SP N4196T N501GS N15FJ N449DT [Eagle II conversion]
370	501-0010	N36859 N7WF EP-PBC N7WF (N500MD) VH-POZ EC-EDN
371	501-0014	N36860 N22TP N888FL N645TS N505AH
372	501-0013	N36861 (N622SS) VR-BJK N501TJ [parted out by Dodson Int'l, Rantoul, KS]
373	501-0015	N36862 N1823B N18328 XA-MAL N4446P N454AC
374	501-0270	N36863 N300WK N893CA N105JM N501ST

CITATION I

Unit No	C/n	Identities
375	501-0016	N36864 N517A C-GHOS N501DL N38DA (N58DT) N58BT N38DA (N38DL) N255TS N17TJ N45TL
376	501-0017	N36869 N877C N100WJ N501AT
377	500-0358	N36870 (EP-PAQ) N82MJ SE-DEP I-UUNY
378	501-0018	N36871 N378CC N18BG N550TG N501GR N228AK N228AJ N228FS N228ES XB-JXG
379	501-0272	N36872 N5072L N700JR N700JA N44MK
380	501-0020	N36873 N32JJ N123EB (N60GG) N100GG
381	501-0041	N36880 N50MC N173SK N120ES [w/o 24Apr95 San Salvador Intl A/P, wreckage parted out by Dodson Av'n, Ottawa, KS; cx 24Apr15]
382	501-0273	N36881 (I-CCCB) XA-HEV N46106 D-IDPD N333PD N333PE N501MD (N273DA) N501JF (N501EM) N302TS N302AJ N110JA N301DR
383	501-0019	N36882 (N301MC) N501SP (N5EM) [dbr Mexicali, Mexico, 03Dec06; cx 04Mar14]
384	501-0021	N36883 (YV-135CP) YV-166CP XA-IEM N121SJ N203LH ZS-MGL N151SP
385	501-0022	N36884 N385CC N11DH N110H (N995AU) N10GE [w/o 21May85 Harrison Airport, AR]
386	501-0023	N36885 N56MC N56MT (N501FB) N56MK N14TM
387	501-0024	N36886 (N10CA) N1CA N711NR Z-WSY N724EA N70BG
388	501-0032	N36887 N388CJ N33AA N377KC N690MC N550T N550L N85WP N642BJ (N501SK) N307D
389	501-0025	N36888 N389CC N21BS N20RM
390*	501-0030	N36890 N301MC N301MG N100CJ C-GSLL N96BA N911MM (N911MU) N655AT
391	501-0026	N36891 N92C N92CC N92BL N610BD
392	500-0364	N36892 HB-VFF N221AC (N221JB) N20WP N40DA G-OKSP G-ORJB N501E SE-RGN SX-FDB [dbr Athens, Greece, 12Aug10]
393	501-0275	N36893 YV-159CP N31AJ ZS-MPN (N41AJ) N40AJ N23AJ N500WJ
394	501-0028	N36895 N1234X N501PV
395	501-0031	N36896 N395SC XA-SDI N510AJ LV-BFM
396	500-0370	N36897 SE-DEY D-IMCE HA-JEB OE-FML
397	501-0262	N36898 YV-O-SID-3 YV-79CP N9712T LN-AFC N50WJ N794EZ (N58T) N20CC N20CZ YV593T
398	501-0050	N36901 N20SP N880CM N750LA N59MA
399	500-0367	N36906 YV-52CP YV1541 YV2254
400	501-0033	N36908 N400GB N300PB (N715DG) N517BA (N101HC) N411DS N411ME N700LW C-GQJK N91PE [cx 15Jul13]
401	501-0034	N36911 N444MW N444MV N501CP
402	501-0278	N36912 G-BFAR ZS-LPH G-BFAR A6-SMH G-BFAR A6-SMH G-BFAR G-DANI N104AB N53RG N129AP N124NB N124NS N322ST
403	501-0039	N36914 N403CC N800DC N800BH N432DG N808BC N507DS N141M N212AT N501SP
404	501-0035	N36915 (N800M) N500WN N112MC N25MH (N35K) N35JF N501DD
405	501-0046	N36916 N405CC N5VP [parted out by Dodson Int'l, Rantoul, KS]
406	501-0036	N36918 N406CJ N36CC HI-493 N360MC N2904
407	501-0279	N36919 SE-DEZ (N371GP) (N371GA) N371GP N43BG SE-DEZ N66HD SE-DEZ PH-DEZ
408	501-0037	N36922 N10J N19J N234JW N501U LV-CGO
409	501-0038	N36923 N315S (N315P) N501JG (N510NY) N501NY
410	501-0042	N87185 N773FR I-TOSC (N120DP) N420AM I-AROM [w/o Rome-Ciampino, Italy, 09Sep05]
411	501-0029	N87253 (N411CJ) N411WC (N411RJ) N816LL N31JM (N45AQ) XA-TKY [w/o 06Oct10 Gulf of Mexico nr Coatzacoalcos, Mexico]
412	501-0040	N87258 N85FS I-KWYJ N501E N21EP LV-BPZ
413	501-0047	N87496 HB-VFI N1021T N550T N550U N9ZB
414	501-0048	N87510 N414CC (I-DAEP) I-OTEL
415	501-0280	N98449 YU-BKZ T9-BKA N212M
416	501-0045	N98468 N833 N833JL N22EL
417	501-0043	N98510 N10NL N16NL
418	501-0053	N98528 N59PC YV-253P YV-253CP N14EA N52TL
419	501-0054	N98563 N2BT N501EA
420	501-0049	N98586 N2ZC (N36WS) (N347DA) OY-SVL ZS-CWD
421	501-0062	N98599 D-IBWB N208W N900DM N980DM N501MR
422	501-0051	N98601 N422CC N150TJ N303CB N422DA N501A
423	501-0281	N36943 LV-PZI LV-MGB N501SJ N501CB
424	501-0044	N98675 N5TC N944JD (N122LG) N131SY N50US N600RM F-HFRA
425	501-0055	N98682 N552MD N400PC N400PG N145DF N145AJ N223LC [w/o 18Aug08, crashed into Caribbean Sea]
426	501-0056	N98688 (N426CC) (N501SF) N55WH CC-CTE N56WE
427	501-0052	N98715 N900MC N677JM (N13DL) N5DL N13DL
428	501-0282	(N98718) N36949 XC-PMX XA-SQX N82AJ [Eagle II conversion]
429	501-0283	N98749 C-GPTC N204CA
430	501-0057	N98751 N500JC N505BG N577VM N577JT
431	501-0059	N2079A N431CC N13RC ZS-EHL N16HL N501AJ
432	501-0066	N2098A D-IHEY N501BG N501CX C-GHRX N945AA VR-CTB VP-CTB N501CD
433	501-0284	N2131A N115K N409AC VR-BBY N788SS N284PC N729PX N45AF [Eagle II conversion]
434	501-0058	N2627A N44MC N444AG N36GC N32MJ N65RA (N400PG) N501FT N211EF N211X N501EZ [w/o 02Dec98 Grannis, AR]
435	501-0060	N2741A N435CC N500ZC N5737 N573L N11TM N129ZM N528RM
436	501-0061	N2757A N436CC N34DL N1401L N202CF SE-RBZ EC-KGX
437	501-0064	N2768A (N33KW) N9TK N96DS N12WH
438	501-0068	N2841A N438CC N9GT N50GT N68EA N363TD N299K
439	501-0285	N2887A N100BX N13ST

CITATION I

Unit No	C/n	Identities									
440	501-0065	N2888A	N33WW								
441	501-0069	N2906A	N501EF	N636N							
442	501-0067	N2959A	SE-DEO	D-IGMB	HB-VJB	VR-BLW	HB-VJB				
443	501-0063	N2991A	N305M	N408MM	N408MW	F-GESZ	N501BA	N555KW	(XA-...)		
444	501-0070	N3062A	(N444CW)	N78AB	N21HJ	N96G	N96GT	N70VP	HC-BTQ	(N277RW)	N628ZG
		N45MM	YV3025								
445	501-0286	N3104M	N445CC	I-ROST	(N789AA)	N381BJ					
446	501-0071	N3105M	N501SR	N501KR	N501KB	N509P	YV-697CP	YV232T	N666TS	(B-M..)	N501SJ
447	501-0072	N3110M	N1HA	N17HA							
448*	501-0073	N3117M	N100SV	N299RP	(N840MC)	N70FJ	[w/o Hailey, ID 15Mar03; cx Jul03]				
449	501-0074	N3118M	YV-232CP	N888DS	N717RB	N28GC	N552AJ				
450	501-0075	N3120M	N773LP	N773LR	N325BC	(N325PM)	N51ET	N713JD			
451	501-0076	N3122M	N451CJ	N315MR	N315MP	N150RM					
452	501-0077	(N3124M)	N15PR	N42HM	N678JD	(N678JG)	I-FRAI	N501AZ			
453	501-0078	(N3127M)	N13BT	ZS-MZO	N13BT	N501EK	N25MB	(N501VB)	N12VB		
454	500-0369	N3132M	C-GVER	N46253	[parted out circa 06Jly05 Bates City, MO as C-GVER]						
455	500-0374	N3141M	C-GRQA	N501SS	(N501BB)	(N505BB)					
456	501-0079	N3144M	N555EW	N33CX	VP-CFF	D-ICAM	N250GM	N79FT	N791JF		
457	501-0080	N3145M	N51CC	N51CG	N347DA	N37LA	N800BF	N888PN			
458	501-0081	N3146M	N12DE	N12CQ	N12CV						
459	501-0289	N3147M	LV-PAT	LV-MMR	N501NA	N1KC	(N501SK)	N501NZ	N82DT		
460	501-0082	N3150M	N460CC	N84CF	C-GEVF	N6RF	(N386DA)	XB-ERX	N5WF	N501AB	
461	500-0378	N3156M	C-GBNE	[to instructional airframe Stephenson Technical College, Winnipeg, Canada]							
462	501-0083	N3158M	N462CC	N5YP	N420PC	N420RC	(N83TJ)	N101LD	N910G		
463	501-0084	N3160M	(N463CJ)	(N11JC)	G-CITI	VR-CDM	VP-CDM	G-CITI	EC-ISP		
464	501-0098	N3161M	N44RD	N144AR	(N144AB)	HB-VIC	N92BE				
465	501-0093	N3163M	N88CF	N31RC	N623LB	N501RM	N501AD				
466	501-0090	N3165M	XC-CIR	N41JP	N3GN						
467	501-0099	N3170A	I-FLYA	(N216RL)	N216RJ	[wfu Sarasota, FL, still wearing I-FLYA]					
468	501-0101	N3170M	C-GDDM	N100TW	N106EA	(N501GS)	(N323JB)	N501KM			
469	501-0095	N3172M	N612DS	XA-AGA							
470	500-0386	N3173M	LV-PAX	LQ-MRM							
471	501-0089	(N3175M)	N471H	N106WV	N588CA	VH-LJG	VH-CCJ	VH-MMC	VH-CSP	[wfu Brisbane/Archer Field, Australia]	
472	501-0292	N3180M	YV-O-MTC-2		YV-2295P	N456R	N339HP				
473	501-0088	(N3181A)	N473CC	N31MT	N22TS	N22TY	N86MT	N23YZ	(N23TZ)	N3WT	
474	501-0087	(N3183M)	N501SE	C-GVVT	(N22508)	N501SJ	N501BB				
475	501-0085	N3189M	N575CC	N475CC	N34AA	N25DD	N707W	N70ZW	XA-...		
476	501-0091	N3194M	(N887DM)	(N55BE)	N33BE	N39BE	(JA8361)	I-OMEP	N2158U	HB-VKY	N2158U
477	501-0086	N3195M	N8LG	N88CF	(N711AE)	N583MP	N32SX	N501CW	N501JP	N11SQ	
		(N864TT)	N554T	N11SQ	(N554T)	EC-INJ	T7-TLM				
478	501-0092	N3197M	(HB-VGD)	N112WC	(N78BT)	LV-PLM	LV-WOI	N501X	N303A		
479	501-0097	N3198M	N479CC	N479JS	N501RS	N251CF	N251CB				
480	501-0096	N3202A	N660AA	(N480CC)	N660KC	N501HS					
481	501-0293	N3202M	Ecuador ANE-201		HC-BVP	N850MA	N597CS	N995JP			
482	501-0107	N3204M	(N333BG)	(N33VV)	N1UL	N107CC	N501LS	N54TB	3A-MTB	(N75471)	EC-GJF
483	501-0294	N3205M	N2LN	N38TM	N8EH	N80SL					
484	500-0387	N3206M	N484KA	N504D	N877RJ*						
485	501-0100	(N3207M)	N485CC	N41ST	(N26MW)	C-GSUN	C-GSUM	N54FT	[cx 19Jan17 to Angolan Air Force, new serial nyk]		
486	501-0102	(N2646X)	N486CC	(N223RE)	I-AIRV	N501CG	N45FS	[Eagle II conversion]		VH-FCS	
487	501-0120	N2646Y	N487HR	N487LS	OY-CPW	N71LP					
488	501-0094	(N2646Z)	N488CC	N103PC	N59CC	N159LC	C-FBDS	C-FBDQ			
489	500-0392	N26461	I-FLYB	D-ISSS	3D-IER	4O-OOO	OM-VOV	YU-TPC			
490	501-0103	(N2647U)	N49WC	N611AT	(N906EA)	ZS-PHP					
491	501-0109	(N2647Y)	N30RL	N30RE	N567WB	LV-BXH					
492	501-0104	(N2647Z)	N312GK	N81CC	N29CA	N33HC	N998EA				
493	501-0105	N2648X	(N231LC)								
494	501-0297	(N2648Y)	VH-SWC	N32DA	N35LD	N41GT	[Stallion conversion, FJ44 engines]				
495	501-0108	(N2648Z)	(N56CJ)	N777AJ	N777GG	N707GG					
496	501-0110	(N26481)	N15NY	[w/o 02Aug79 Akron, OH]							
497	501-0119	(N26486)	N35AA	N35TM	N53RC	N77GJ	N53EZ	N13KD			
498	501-0111	N2649D	N140WC	(N333RB)	N777FE	I-FOMN	N94SL	N59WP	N79BK	N357TX	N501PJ
499	501-0112	N2649E	(N900LL)	N350M	N14TV	(N84TV)	N74PM	(N74PN)	N112EB	N224GP	LV-FWX
500	501-0127	N2649H	N500K	N88BM	N96SK	N86SK	N117DJ	N529KT			
501	501-0106	(N2649J)	(N1234F)	OE-FYF	D-IANE	N793AA	(D-ISKY)				
502	501-0113	(N2649S)	(N515CC)	N502CC	N200ES	N502CC					
503	501-0114	N2649Y	N673LP	N673LR	N485RP	N711HL	(N725RH)	N811HL	[to White Inds, MO 17Feb05 for spares]		
504	501-0118	N2649Z	I-DECI	N61572	N311ME	XB-TMG					
505	501-0126	N26492	N505SP	N505JH							
506	501-0117	N26493	LV-PDW	LV-MZG	N91AP						
507	501-0115	N26494	N501GF	(N26540)	N501GK	N95RE	N728MC	N5ZN			
508	501-0122	(N26495)	N275CC	N275CQ	N400DB	N501HC	(N501MD)	N501MB			
509	501-0116	(N26496)	N500XX	N7CJ	N7QJ	(N90MT)	N7TK				
510	501-0239	N26497	LV-PDZ	LV-MYN	N164CB	OE-FMS	N501TB				

CITATION I

Unit No	C/n	Identities
511	501-0298	N26498 (PH-JOB) I-GERA OE-FIW N65M VR-CMS N501D N118RT
512	501-0129	(N26499) (N50WP) N70WP PT-LQQ N501JD
513	501-0123	N2650C N513CC N627L N627E
514	501-0249	N2650M RP-C237 N4263X ZS-LOW N133DM G-OHLA I-DIDY N249AS N851BC XA-OAC N40MA (N82MP) N117MA
515	501-0124	N2650N N95RE OE-FFK [w/o 26Oct88 nr Salzburg, Austria]
516	501-0134	N2650S N501LW N501EM N841CW N121EZ YV3009
517	501-0130	(N2650V) N148JB N148JS (N726BB) (N300RN) N102HS N505CF
518	501-0131	N2650X N490WC YV-301P N301PP YV-2605P N133SC (N501NP)
519	501-0135	N2650Y N77TW N711GL N49MP N63CG N501WL
520	501-0136	(N26502) N66AT N66AG N800TW N511HC
521	501-0137	N26503 N46SC N14VA
522	501-0128	(N26504) N522CC N900MM N501CF
523	501-0121	N26506 D-IANO HB-VID D-IANO OE-FHW [wfu Linz, Austria]
524	501-0142	N26507 HB-VHA N310AF N880M I-SATV YV-688CP N197FS (N123PL) N15FJ N67BE N142FJ N174CF
525*	501-0138	(N26509) 8P-BAR 8P-BAB C-GBTB N501CE N74FH Mexico 3934
526	501-0139	N2651B N526CC N1LQ (N3UG) N108JL N888BH N501AF
527	501-0132	N2651G N50US N91WZ N717JL N39HH
528	501-0133	N2651J (N955WP) N51WP N700SP N554T
529	501-0140	(N2651R) (N99TD) N96TD N96CF OE-FDM 9A-CHC [parted out by Atlanta Air Salvage, Griffin, GA]
530	500-0395	N2651S XA-JEX XB-JFV
531	501-0125	(N2651Y) (N2DP) (N501DP) N45MC N96TC N69EP N125EA
532	501-0141	N26510 N166CB VR-BJN N841MA N501GG N501DR Mexico 3931 [retro-fitted with Williams FJ44 engines]
533	500-0396	N26514 (XA-JEW) XC-GTO
534	501-0156	N26517 N123FG N44FM N829MB
535	501-0143	N26523 D-IGGK OY-ONE N501MG 4X-CMG N520BH N501WJ
536	501-0144	N2652U N270SF N270NF OE-FMK
537	501-0159	N2652Y D-IGLU N666JJ N308AT N1AT N8189J N80CJ N80HA
538	501-0145	N2652Z (ZS-KGF) VH-LCL N2652Z [w/o 22Apr90 Norfolk Island while regd VH-LCL; hulk to Dodson Av'n, Ottawa, KS still marked as VH-LCL for parts use; US marks cx Jly94]
539	501-0163	N1354G (I-AGIK) I-CIGB D-IGGG
540	500-0403	N1710E G-BPCP [w/o 01Oct80 Jersey, Channel Is, UK]
541	501-0147	N1728E N254TW CP-2105 N392DA N27TS N551MS
542	501-0148	N1758E (OO-ECT) N167CB N700ER N500DL I-GJMA N148EA N148ED XB-KHL N113CA
543	501-0149	(N1772E) N104CF N97FD (N721CG) N96FP N72VJ
544*	501-0302	(N1779E) (G-BHIW) XA-JFE XB-ELU XA-RLE XA-JCE N301EL N801EL N7EN
545*	501-0146	(N1782E) N545CC N54MH N61CD N1VU N194RC N53BB N804ST N36KJ*
546	501-0151	(N1820E) N269MD N269CM N2690M N797SF N797SE
547	501-0152	(N1874E) N547CC N501FM N501ED N40FJ N48FJ N15CV (N15UJ) VP-CMA VP-CCD N15CY
548	501-0153	(N1930E) N105CF (N118AT) N99CK (N484CS)
549	501-0160	N1951E (N58BD) N60PR C-GAAA N999PW
550	501-0161	N1955E OY-CYD N5UM XB-FXO XB-GRE N501FP N96MB N967B
551	501-0303	(N1958E) N6563C OH-CIT OY-FFC SE-DVA N301JJ N610GD N370TP N303RH N393PJ
552	501-0162	N1959E N455H N55H N44SW N446V N501DP
553	501-0157	N2052A (N88BR) N16VG
554	500-0399	N2069A YU-BML T9-SBA E7-SBA
555	501-0175	N2072A EI-BJN VR-BKP VP-BKP VP-BVK N23VK
556	501-0158	N2611Y N1MX N501WB
557	501-0165	N2612N (N20KW) N557CC N165NA N501RC
558	501-0154	N2613C N80MF CC-CWW N154SC
559	501-0166	N2614C N476X I-CIPA (N30AF) OY-INI N166FA
560	500-0404	N2614H G-BHTT G-ZAPI N789DD N789DK LV-BID
561	501-0185	N2614K N653DR N72787 N111RB N1CR N501LL N505BG N585BG
562	501-0150	N2616G N95MJ N73FW N405PC [w/o 02Apr01 Depere, WI]
563	501-0167	(N2616L) N563CC N323CB N38RT N900TW N723JM N501FJ
564	501-0155	N2617B (N108CT) N110TV N110TP N800DW VR-CJB VP-CJB N299D N321TS N347MH (N38MQ)
565	500-0401	N2617K N2651 I-FARN
566	501-0169	N2617U D-IBWG C-GFEE
567	501-0183	N6777V ZS-KPA CS-AYY (N8NC)
568	501-0168	(N6777X) N39LL PT-LNV N168EA N601WT N328NA
569	501-0188	N6778C N1JB N93JM N61DT N251CT N525PV
570	501-0164	(N6778L) N570CC N223GC N750LA N50DS N170JS N286PC
571	501-0193	N6778T N164CB XA-LIM N39300 N45MK N89MF N199DJ
572	501-0173	(N6778V) OE-FPH N25GT N91MS N91TE
573	501-0170	(N6778Y) N501HP G-GENE G-MTLE N170EA N610TT N610GG
574	501-0171	N67780 VH-BNK N171WJ
575	501-0184	N67786 N90CF N433MM N501VC N318DN
576	501-0187	N6779D N576CC (N414CB) N21EH N23EH (N576CC) N137GK (N600DH) N900DH N900DL N713AL N7MC N70CG (N614DD)
577	501-0176	N6779L N44LC N49LC (VR-CIA) VR-CFG VP-CFG N96DA XB-LYY
578	501-0177	N6779P (N999RB) N22SD N501DG N501NC N501GW N457CS N98AV
579	501-0174	N6779Y N20GT N721US N702NC N702NY (N174CF) N50JG N454DQ N1AG N921BE

CITATION I

Unit No	C/n	Identities
580	501-0178	N67799 LV-PML N4246A N83ND G-FLVU G-VUEM [w/o 19Nov10 Birmingham, UK; crash remains to AAIB Farnborough, UK, 22Nov10]
581	501-0186	(N6780A) N95EW N37HW N999WS
582	501-0189	N6780C N80SF VH-FUM
583	501-0182	N6780J N360DJ I-PALP N535GA (N125CA) D-ISIS VP-CAP N220HM
584	501-0190	(N6780M) N584CC N333MS N393DA N40AW N723JR
585	501-0191	N6780Y N98ME N64RT N164RT
586	500-0410	N6780Z XC-GAW
587	500-0408	N67805 XA-LUD XB-DVF
588	501-0181	N6781C N250SP N250SR N501KK XB-PMR
589	501-0179	(N6781D) N589CJ N414CB HB-VLD N718SA (N406RH) LV-CFH
590	501-0192	(N6781G) N190K N650BC
591	501-0194	N6781L N28JG N65WW
592	501-0222	N6781R N25HS N690DM N690WY
593	501-0180	(N6781T) (N593CC) N695CC N593DS N9NE N180VP N650MW N510NJ LV-BHJ
594	501-0197	N6781Z N100SN N324L
595	501-0195	N67814 N161CB N7111H N109DC (N123KD) N109DC N123KD
596	500-0409	N67815 XC-FEZ
597	501-0196	N6782B (N597JV) N575SR N311TP (N311TT)
598	500-0412	N6782F XA-LUV XB-GDJ
599	501-0172	(N6782P) N907KH HI-581SP N110JB
600	501-0311	(N6782T) SE-DES OY-JEY N311VP
601	501-0199	N6782X N501MM N441JT N62RG N7SV N91HG
602	501-0198	N67822 (N602CC) N105TW N500LE N500LH N198VP N800DT ZK-NBR ZK-NDT VH-NOU
603	500-0406	N67829 SE-DET OY-FFB
604	501-0231	N6783C N55WG N29HE N501BP D-IAWU N452TS [w/o Trier, Germany, 12Jan14]
605	501-0200	N6783L 7Q-YTL N47TL LV-CQP
606	501-0201	N6783U N801L N130JS N123SF N55BM N417RC N417RQ N78CN N953SL N953HC
607	501-0202	N6783V N520RP N607CJ (XA-PEV) XA-BOA N202VP N477KM N501G
608	500-0413	N6783X (PT-LBZ) PT-LCC
609	501-0203	N67830 D-IAEC [w/o 31May87 Blankensee A/P, Lubeck, Germany]
610	501-0207	N67839 N968DM (N207CF) OE-FYC VP-BHO N207JF D-IABG
611	501-0204	N6784L (N123HP) N345N (N345HB) N367HB N282JG
612	501-0208	N6784P N54MJ I-LAWN N208EA N82P N5942P [parted out by Alliance Air Parts, Oklahoma City, OK]
613	501-0205	N6784T PT-LVB N6784T (N501DA) N528RM (N501DL) VH-VPM
614	501-0209	N6784X N56MJ N501CR N111DT N36FD N98RG N70NB
615	501-0206	N6784Y N501HM N795MA OE-FBA N314EB N943LL N943RC N528DS
616	501-0210	N67848 N32FM YU-MDV N1008
617	501-0211	N6785C N617CC [cx Jun96, parted out by Dodson International Parts, Rantoul, KS]
618	501-0213	N6785D I-AUNY
619	501-0212	N6785L N67GM N70AA N2243 N243EE
620	501-0314	N6887M N56MC N56LW
621	501-0214	N6887R N567L I-JUST (N794WB) N3312T N2296S N2298S (N340AC) N241MH N241BF
622	501-0215	N1354G N50MM ZS-LXT N215NA
623	501-0217	N1710E N623RM N600SS N500TW N7MZ
624	501-0216	N1758E N57MJ (N65T) N57TW TG-RIF TG-RIE
625	501-0219	N1772E N25CJ N678DG N625CH N625J N58BT N501BW N12RN N18RN N510GA N56PB
626	501-0218	N1958E I-KODE N218AM N218JG
627	501-0223	N1959E N18HC (N26HA)
628	501-0220	N2052A N628CH N100CH N100QH N100LX
629	500-0415	N2072A JA8474 N50KR N53RD
630	501-0224	N2611Y N630CE N456CE N825PS
631	501-0228	N2612N (N999CB) N501CM JA8284 N228EA XA-SEY N665MM
632	501-0260	N2613C N224RP N500GA N7UF N41LE N501RG
633	501-0225	N2614C N49BL TG-MIL TG-KIT N412SE N5411 N501NZ
634	501-0227	(N2614Y) N2614H N374GS N47CF N83DM
635	501-0226	(N2615D) N29AC N226VP N501JM
636	501-0229	(N2615L) N636CC N57MC N57FC
637	501-0232	(N2616G) N2616C N853KB N35TL VR-CHF VR-CAT VP-CAT EC-LPP
638	501-0230	(N2617B) N2616G N653F N5RL G-ICED N505CC HB-VLB 9A-DVR N999MS
639	501-0234	N2617B N61PR N711RP PT-LIZ N643RT N77PA N77PX N123PL N125PL N123PL
640	501-0237	(N2617K) N640BS N237SC N831CB N29UF N420PC N712VF (N712VE) N420PC
641	501-0235	N2617U (N31CF) (N13BN)
642	501-0236	N26227 N711VF C-GQJJ N109C
643	501-0221	(N26228) N643MC N217RR N389JP HB-VKD N555HR N221EB N107GM N106GM (N643VP) N501HG XB-LVL
644	501-0240	N26232 N13BK N711BT OY-JET N62864 N77UB N501DY N238BG
645	500-0411	N6784Y G-BIZZ G-NCMT SE-DLZ
646	501-0242	N2623B N40PL N500BK N71L
647	501-0241	(N2624L) N174CB N207G C-GSTR N101RR
648	501-0243	N2624Z N43SP N5DL XB-SHA
649	501-0238	N2626A N238JS I-DVAL (N501EZ) N995PA N737RJ
650	501-0244	N2626J N650CJ (N711VF) N701VF N418R N244SL N176FB N501T (N501HD) N501MF
651	501-0317	N2626Z 5N-AVL (N317JQ) N706DC N51FT

CITATION I

Unit No	C/n	Identities									
652	501-0245	N26263	(N678DG)	ZS-LDO	A2-AGM	ZS-ACE					
653	501-0233	N26264	5N-AVM	N18860	N501Q	[stored dismantled Columbia, MO]					
654	501-0246	N2627N	N85RS	N26LC	OE-FHH	LZ-TBP					
655	501-0247	N2627U	(N24CH)	[w/o 12Nov82 Wichita, KS]							
656	500-0418	N2628B	ZS-LDV								
657	501-0252	N2628Z	N825HL	N574CC	I-TOIO	OY-JJN					
658	501-0254	N2629Z	N84CF	N66BK	(N84GF)						
659	501-0256	N2631N	D-ILLL	I-PAPE	N256P						
660	501-0257	N2631V	(N992NW)	N500NW	OE-FLY	N12NM	N570D	N501WX			
661	501-0255	N661TV	N661TW	N501MR	N707WF	G-SBEC	N400LX	N901NB	N501X		
662	501-0248	N2633N	N7700T	(N711EG)	[w/o Franklin, NC, 15Mar12]						
663	501-0250	N77FD									
664	501-0258	N664CC	N900RB	N900RD	N87FL	VR-BHI	VP-BHI	N16KW	N599BR	N810LG	
665	501-0319	N124KC	N60EW								
666	501-0251	N30BK	N945BC	N400LX	N501RG	N501WD	N581PJ				
667	501-0320	N2649D	ZS-LHP	3D-ADH	N70467	N401G	C-GPTI	C-GTOL			
668	501-0321	OE-FHP	N321VP	N550MH	N170MK	N510SJ	N986DS	N301MY			
669	501-0322	N2663J	N374GS	N314GS	(N669DM)	(N769EW)	N527EW	N526HA*			
670	501-0253	N2650Y	N501JE	(N1SH)	C-GKPC	[dbr Stella Maris, Bahamas, 15Feb14; parted out]				N501JE	
671	501-0323	N2651B	N55HL	N501RF	N501LE	(N142AL)	N505BB				
672	501-0324	N2651J	JA8493								
673	501-0325	N1710E	(D-IFGP)	N501LM	N64BH						
674	501-0259	N1758E	(N77111)	(N261WB)	N261WR	N261WD	VR-BJW	N501MS	D-IEIR	(N225WT)	S5-CMM
675	501-0675	N8900M	N501MT	N593BW							
676	501-0676	N1958E	N676CC	(N76JY)							
677	501-0677	(N1958E)	N727MC	(N184SC)	C-GAAA	N54CG	N74HR				
678	501-0678	N2052A	N3FE	N678CF	PT-ODC	(N26AA)					
679	501-0679	N2611Y	N200GF	N679CC	N2611Y	VR-BLF	VP-BLF	N73SK	(N501HH)	4L-MPX	
680	501-0680	N2614C	PT-LFR	PP-EIF							
681	501-0681	N2616G	N82LS	N427SS	N889SH						
682	501-0682	N2617B	N3951	N19GB	N55TK	N682DC	N682HC	N682BF			
683	501-0683	N501BK	N501FR	N170HL	(N49TA)	N96LC	N702RT				
684	501-0684	N3683G	N501TP								
685	501-0685	N5346C	N400SR	N501TB	(N243AB)	N501EG	XB-IXT				
686	501-0686	N6763M	N750PP	N118K							
687	501-0687	N321FM	N154CC	N361DB	N361DE						
688	501-0688	D-IMRX	[w/o 16Feb06 Northern Iraq]								
689	501-0689	N46MT	N689CC	(N88MT)	N88MM	N75TJ	N88MM	N288MM	C-FNHZ		

Production complete

CITATION 500 UNIT NUMBER CROSS-REFERENCE

Note: From c/n 500-0001 to 500-0349 unit numbers match the last three digits of the c/n, then the tie-ups are as follows:

C/n	Unit	C/n	Unit	C/n	Unit	C/n	Unit	C/n	Unit	C/n	Unit
500-0354	363	500-0367	399	500-0386	470	500-0399	554	500-0408	587	500-0412	598
500-0356	366	500-0369	454	500-0387	484	500-0401	565	500-0409	596	500-0413	608
500-0358	377	500-0370	396	500-0392	489	500-0403	540	500-0410	586	500-0415	629
500-0361	361	500-0374	455	500-0395	530	500-0404	560	500-0411	645	500-0418	656
500-0364	392	500-0378	461	500-0396	533	500-0406	603				

CITATION I CONVERSIONS

The following a/c have been converted from Model 500s to Model 501s (and, in one example, back again):

500-0097 to 501-0446
500-0293 to 501-0643
500-0350 to 501-0027
500-0351 to 501-0261
500-0352 to 501-0263
500-0353 to 501-0264
500-0355 to 501-0267
500-0357 to 501-0269
500-0359 to 501-0270
500-0360 to 501-0272
500-0361 to 501-0265 to 500-0361
500-0362 to 501-0275
500-0363 to 501-0273
500-0365 to 501-0262
500-0366 to 501-0285
500-0368 to 501-0278
500-0371 to 501-0279
500-0372 to 501-0281
500-0373 to 501-0280
500-0375 to 501-0289
500-0376 to 501-0282
500-0377 to 501-0283
500-0379 to 501-0284
500-0381 to 501-0286
500-0383 to 501-0292
500-0389 to 501-0293
500-0391 to 501-0294
500-0393 to 501-0239
500-0394 to 501-0297
500-0397 to 501-0303
500-0398 to 501-0298
500-0400 to 501-0249
500-0402 to 501-0302
500-0405 to 501-0311
500-0414 to 501-0314
500-0416 to 501-0260
500-0417 to 501-0317
500-0476 to 501-0063
500-0667 to 501-0320

CITATION 501 UNIT NUMBER CROSS-REFERENCE

C/n	Unit	C/n	Unit	C/n	Unit	C/n	Unit	C/n	Unit
501-0001	351	501-0064	437	501-0127	500	501-0190	584	501-0253	670
501-0002	353	501-0065	440	501-0128	522	501-0191	585	501-0254	658
501-0003	355	501-0066	432	501-0129	512	501-0192	590	501-0255	661
501-0004	356	501-0067	442	501-0130	517	501-0193	571	501-0256	659
501-0005	357	501-0068	438	501-0131	518	501-0194	591	501-0257	660
501-0006	358	501-0069	441	501-0132	527	501-0195	595	501-0258	664
501-0007	360	501-0070	444	501-0133	528	501-0196	597	501-0259	674
501-0008	362	501-0071	446	501-0134	516	501-0197	594	501-0260	632
501-0009	367	501-0072	447	501-0135	519	501-0198	602	501-0261	352
501-0010	370	501-0073	448	501-0136	520	501-0199	601	501-0262	397
501-0011	364	501-0074	449	501-0137	521	501-0200	605	501-0263	354
501-0012	369	501-0075	450	501-0138	525	501-0201	606	501-0264	359
501-0013	372	501-0076	451	501-0139	526	501-0202	607	501-0267	365
501-0014	371	501-0077	452	501-0140	529	501-0203	609	501-0269	368
501-0015	373	501-0078	453	501-0141	532	501-0204	611	501-0270	374
501-0016	375	501-0079	456	501-0142	524	501-0205	613	501-0272	379
501-0017	376	501-0080	457	501-0143	535	501-0206	615	501-0273	382
501-0018	378	501-0081	458	501-0144	536	501-0207	610	501-0275	393
501-0019	383	501-0082	460	501-0145	538	501-0208	612	501-0278	402
501-0020	380	501-0083	462	501-0146	545	501-0209	614	501-0279	407
501-0021	384	501-0084	463	501-0147	541	501-0210	616	501-0280	415
501-0022	385	501-0085	475	501-0148	542	501-0211	617	501-0281	423
501-0023	386	501-0086	477	501-0149	543	501-0212	619	501-0282	428
501-0024	387	501-0087	474	501-0150	562	501-0213	618	501-0283	429
501-0025	389	501-0088	473	501-0151	546	501-0214	621	501-0284	433
501-0026	391	501-0089	471	501-0152	547	501-0215	622	501-0285	439
501-0027	350	501-0090	466	501-0153	548	501-0216	624	501-0286	445
501-0028	394	501-0091	476	501-0154	558	501-0217	623	501-0289	459
501-0029	411	501-0092	478	501-0155	564	501-0218	626	501-0292	472
501-0030	390	501-0093	465	501-0156	534	501-0219	625	501-0293	481
501-0031	395	501-0094	488	501-0157	553	501-0220	628	501-0294	483
501-0032	388	501-0095	469	501-0158	556	501-0221	643	501-0297	494
501-0033	400	501-0096	480	501-0159	537	501-0222	592	501-0298	511
501-0034	401	501-0097	479	501-0160	549	501-0223	627	501-0302	544
501-0035	404	501-0098	464	501-0161	550	501-0224	630	501-0303	551
501-0036	406	501-0099	467	501-0162	552	501-0225	633	501-0311	600
501-0037	408	501-0100	485	501-0163	539	501-0226	635	501-0314	620
501-0038	409	501-0101	468	501-0164	570	501-0227	634	501-0317	651
501-0039	403	501-0102	486	501-0165	557	501-0228	631	501-0319	665
501-0040	412	501-0103	490	501-0166	559	501-0229	636	501-0320	667
501-0041	381	501-0104	492	501-0167	563	501-0230	638	501-0321	668
501-0042	410	501-0105	493	501-0168	568	501-0231	604	501-0322	669
501-0043	417	501-0106	501	501-0169	566	501-0232	637	501-0323	671
501-0044	424	501-0107	482	501-0170	573	501-0233	653	501-0324	672
501-0045	416	501-0108	495	501-0171	574	501-0234	639	501-0325	673
501-0046	405	501-0109	491	501-0172	599	501-0235	641	501-0446	097
501-0047	413	501-0110	496	501-0173	572	501-0236	642	501-0643	293
501-0048	414	501-0111	498	501-0174	579	501-0237	640	501-0675	675
501-0049	420	501-0112	499	501-0175	555	501-0238	649	501-0676	676
501-0050	398	501-0113	502	501-0176	577	501-0239	510	501-0677	677
501-0051	422	501-0114	503	501-0177	578	501-0240	644	501-0678	678
501-0052	427	501-0115	507	501-0178	580	501-0241	647	501-0679	679
501-0053	418	501-0116	509	501-0179	589	501-0242	646	501-0680	680
501-0054	419	501-0117	506	501-0180	593	501-0243	648	501-0681	681
501-0055	425	501-0118	504	501-0181	588	501-0244	650	501-0682	682
501-0056	426	501-0119	497	501-0182	583	501-0245	652	501-0683	683
501-0057	430	501-0120	487	501-0183	567	501-0246	654	501-0684	684
501-0058	434	501-0121	523	501-0184	575	501-0247	655	501-0685	685
501-0059	431	501-0122	508	501-0185	561	501-0248	662	501-0686	686
501-0060	435	501-0123	513	501-0186	581	501-0249	514	501-0687	687
501-0061	436	501-0124	515	501-0187	576	501-0250	663	501-0688	688
501-0062	421	501-0125	531	501-0188	569	501-0251	666	501-0689	689
501-0063	443	501-0126	505	501-0189	582	501-0252	657		

CESSNA 510 CITATION MUSTANG

C/n	Identities					
712	N27369	[ff 23Apr05; c/n originally quoted as E510-712001]				
0001	N510CE	[ff 29Aug05]		N510ND	N91FP	
0002	N510KS	[ff 27Jan06]	N199ML			
0003	N403CM	[ff 15Jun06]				
0004	N404CM					
0005	N600DE					
0006	N245MU					
0007	N510FF	N4FF				
0008	N396DM	LV-FKG				
0009	N910SY					
0010	N654EA	N24YY	N49MW	LY-VJB	N401DE	
0011	N2243W	(VH-SJP)	ZK-LCA			
0012	N443HC	N510DG				
0013	N50HS	(N565VV)	N1VV			
0014	N510VV	(N307TC)				
0015	N406CM					
0016	N416CM					
0017	N17MU	N510WC				
0018	N827DK	N2GS				
0019	N2427N	OK-PPC	OE-FCP			
0020	N24329					
0021	N80HQ	(N12TR)				
0022	N4089Y	OY-LPU	N575TP			
0023	N888TF	N75AP				
0024	N75ES					
0025	N325RR	PH-ORJ	G-LFPT	N510DW		
0026	N1693L	N83EM				
0027	N4092E	N327CM	G-FBLK			
0028	N54PV	N611MW				
0029	N4059H	N45SP	VH-NEQ			
0030	N725JB					
0031	N528DM					
0032	N4107D	N814WS				
0033	N4110T	VH-CCJ	VH-SJP	ZK-PGA	N533VP	C-GNTL
0034	N4155B	XA-JRT				
0035	N4202M	D-ISRM				
0036	N510GH	N999JD				
0037	N33NP	PR-TNP				
0038	N4115W	N821ND	C-GNTZ			
0039	N4159Z	XB-RYE	XA-RYE	N163TC		
0040	N4009F	OE-FID	D-IFID*			
0041	N4021E	PP-NNN				
0042	N591ES	C-GMMU				
0043	N4030W	PP-MIS	N89GR			
0044	XA-BAT	N366FW	OE-FCB			
0045	N761JP	(D-IJKP)	YR-RUS	N510CF	(N1199V)	
0046	N946CM	PP-MTG	N85TG			
0047	N22EM					
0048	D-IEGO	OE-FWF				
0049	N13616	9A-CSG	YU-SPM	OE-FWD	D-IFWD*	
0050	PH-TXI	G-OAMB	PH-TXI	EC-LZS		
0051	N510JH	N510JM				
0052	G-LEAI	F-HGIO				
0053	EC-KNL	OE-FTR	OK-FTR			
0054	N1749L	ZK-MUS	ZK-MOT	N510NZ		
0055	N551WH					
0056	PT-FLO					
0057	PR-MCL					
0058	PR-XSX					
0059	N40770	XA-VMX				
0060	N212C	ZS-CTF	N510J	PP-LDW		
0061	N1EL					
0062	N6183Q	PR-BSA				
0063	PR-DRI					
0064	N13ZM	N60CP				
0065	N61706	OE-FFB				
0066	N902LG					
0067	N967CM	G-FBNK	HB-VWS	G-FBNK		
0068	N968CM	G-FLBK				
0069	N6193S	T7-VIG	D-IUNQ			
0070	N235SS	VH-YDZ	ZK-YDZ			
0071	N921TX					
0072	G-LEAA					
0073	G-LEAB	N648JW				

CESSNA 510 CITATION MUSTANG

C/n	Identities				
0074	N510LL				
0075	N4084A	G-LEAC			
0076	N4085A	G-NGEL	N301GT		
0077	N774AR				
0078	N724DL	(N884MF)			
0079	ZS-JDM	N816CW			
0080	N4086L	PR-MPM	N305AK		
0081	OE-FHA				
0082	OE-FLR	D-IKOE			
0083	N510GJ				
0084	PR-RDM				
0085	PR-VDL				
0086	N808RD				
0087	N6200C	(PP-PMR)	(PR-FMP)	PR-SBH	
0088	N6197D	(PH-TXA)			
0089	N63223	M-USTG			
0090	N6324L	ZS-LKG	4X-DFZ	T7-DFZ	
0091	N6196M	ZS-KPM			
0092	N6325U	ZS-DIY	ZS-JIK		
0093	N6332K	ZS-DFI			
0094	N510SA				
0095	N6203C	N102DS			
0096	N40049	N996CM	G-FBKA	N258WC	N963FF
0097	N97HT	N214HT	N544MF		
0098	N510BW				
0099	PP-WGS				
0100	N6202W	HS-IOO			
0101	PP-EVG				
0102	N903JP				
0103	N923JP				
0104	OE-FWH				
0105	N245DR	(N61EP)	N1RS		
0106	N4076J	(OE-FWW)	OE-FMY	G-SCCA	
0107	N710EB	N568VA	N588VA		
0108	N939JC	F-HADT			
0109	N510MW				
0110	N66ES				
0111	(PH-TXB)	PH-TXA			
0112	N801GE	YV2864			
0113	N853JL	C-GDJG	N587AG		
0114	N510PT	F-HJPH			
0115	N69AY				
0116	OE-FMZ	OK-AML			
0117	N62076	HS-VIP			
0118	N510MB	N831MF			
0119	PR-NRN				
0120	N4041T	N1RD	N72DA		
0121	N60CP	N510K			
0122	N230BF	CS-DPV			
0123	PT-TOP				
0124	N510AZ				
0125	OO-PRM				
0126	N826CM	G-FBKB			
0127	N627CM	G-FBKC			
0128	N178SF				
0129	PR-FAC				
0130	N40753	G-FBLI	N630DB		
0131	(PH-TXC)	N510TX			
0132	LX-FGL	[suffered in-flight structural damage 16Apr13 en route Antwerp – Luxembourg; cx Mar14; parted out Linz, Austria]			
0133	(PH-TXB)	N6206W	N17RP		
0134	ZS-AFD				
0135	N5223F	JA510M	N200KP	N918ST	
0136	C-FDSH	C-GWCL	N333QV		
0137	ZS-MUS				
0138	N309MT				
0139	N921PP	ZP-BJE			
0140	N987CM				
0141	N141BG	LZ-AMA	F-GRET		
0142	N609TC	PR-CPT			
0143	N510BA				
0144	N5044V	EI-SFA	OE-FZA		
0145	N6207Z	EI-SFB	OE-FZB		
0146	N4082U	N914GW			
0147	PT-FLC				
0148	N700YY				
0149	F-HDPY				

CESSNA 510 CITATION MUSTANG

C/n	Identities				
0150	N220DK				
0151	N738DC	(N33AC)	C-FPCE		
0152	N4085D	EC-LAF	EC-LDK		
0153	N4085S	N442LV			
0154	N510SV	PP-RGL			
0155	N4085Z	N510KB			
0156	G-MICE	ZS-SIO	OE-FDT		
0157	G-KLNW				
0158	N271CS				
0159	N510LF				
0160	I-FITO				
0161	G-ZJET	F-HEND			
0162	(N4RH)	N620WB			
0163	CS-DPN	F-HDPN			
0164	N251MC				
0165	N81WL				
0166	N870HY	XA-UMS			
0167	N638AH				
0168	N510GG				
0169	HB-VWL	F-GLOS	G-FBKJ		
0170	N426LF	C-GXOP	N68NP		
0171	N510PS	OY-JSW	C-FIPN		
0172	N510K	N510WP	N610PT		
0173	N510CJ				
0174	N40049	XA-ULO			
0175	N4009F	N42WZ			
0176	N417GR				
0177	N247DR				
0178	N5020J	N662CC			
0179	N520JM				
0180	N884TM				
0181	N59VM				
0182	M-USTG	F-GISH	G-FBKK		
0183	N3QE				
0184	N123AD	N128AD			
0185	I-MCAS	OE-FNP			
0186	N4076J	S5-CMT	ES-LCC	OE-FPP	
0187	N453DW	N552M			
0188	N878SP	N878MM			
0189	SP-KHK				
0190	N4095H	T7-HOT	I-INCH	G-SSLM	N613ML
0191	N509DM	N123TF	N133TF		
0192	N4107D	LX-FGC	M-IFFY		
0193	N530AG	(N533AG)	PP-MTT	N510AK	
0194	LX-RSQ	F-HERE			
0195	N41227	N52338	PR-HOT		
0196	N41297	EI-SFC	OE-FZC		
0197	N4149W	PP-PRV			
0198	N995AU				
0199	N4202M	N978PC	N979PC		
0200	N15GJ				
0201	N352AS	N91CH			
0202	N510MD				
0203	N76GP				
0204	N1245				
0205	N4047W	C-GBPL	N34ST		
0206	N620CM				
0207	N101FU				
0208	N510DH				
0209	N209CJ	N888GS			
0210	N54NG				
0211	N369PA	C-FBCI	C-FHFV	N510BE	
0212	N32FM				
0213	N59LW	2-MUST			
0214	VH-EJT				
0215	N603WS				
0216	EI-SFD	OE-FZD			
0217	EI-SFE	OE-FZE			
0218	N949JB				
0219	N625TX				
0220	N510DP				
0221	C-GDLL				
0222	F-GMTJ				
0223	N520KC				
0224	C-GROP	N88CH			
0225	N52733	SU-BQF			

CESSNA 510 CITATION MUSTANG

C/n	Identities				
0226	N73AH				
0227	N377RV				
0228	N823M				
0229	N7876C				
0230	N230BF	N7711B			
0231	PR-MDE				
0232	N4082Y	C-GRRD			
0233	N301AJ				
0234	N530AJ				
0235	EC-LCX				
0236	N778JE				
0237	N918WA				
0238	N960PT				
0239	N4085C	N914G			
0240	N510TW				
0241	N270MK	G-GILB			
0242	N530RM	N580RM			
0243	N520BE	N243MS	N61MR		
0244	N700GD	N510VP	N244CE		
0245	N774ST				
0246	N510EG	RP-C718			
0247	N60GS	N247VP	(N510KA)	XB-JRS	N649JR
0248	N369GC				
0249	N510BD				
0250	N85VR	(D-IGEL)	N510JL		
0251	N510KZ				
0252	N40864	OK-LEO	F-HBIR		
0253	N54CF				
0254	N30NF	N38NF			
0255	N4088T	N5274G	SU-BQG		
0256	N991BB				
0257	N257CM				
0258	N5274K	SU-BQH			
0259	N4021E	(D-IMMH)	M-MHDH	F-HSHB	
0260	N4030W	OO-ACO			
0261	N52498	PP-DLC			
0262	(D-ICMH)	M-MHBW	D-IEEN	F-HPHD	F-HIBF
0263	N362B	N808LS			
0264	N4058A	OE-FAJ	N264CJ	N72SR	
0265	LV-CBO				
0266	YR-DAD	N166CJ	YV3148		
0267	N5274M	SU-BQI			
0268	OK-MYS				
0269	VH-PWX				
0270	OM-AES	OK-KUK			
0271	N324DR				
0272	OK-AJA	I-SKYT			
0273	N40938	N786AF			
0274	N713MD	D-IEMG			
0275	N510EE				
0276	N76BF	N763F	PP-PFD		
0277	N105J				
0278	N278MS	PR-XPI			
0279	N127FJ	C-GWWW	N82824		
0280	PR-ROD	N510BR	N747KS		
0281	YR-DAE	N181CJ	OE-FTS		
0282	N876AM				
0283	G-XAVB				
0284	N520BE				
0285	M-COOL				
0286	N4059H	N52905	B-8888		
0287	N4073S	XB-JPR	N287LA		
0288	N4074M	N9002D	PP-MID	N9002D	N323PG
0289	N4074Z	9A-DWD	OK-OBR		
0290	N4075L	N510HW	JA12NT	N72NT	
0291	N4075Z	N39EG			
0292	N40753	N578CM			
0293	N293MM				
0294	N4077P	N5251F	VH-SQW		
0295	C-FSTX	N246RE	2-MSTG		
0296	D-ISIO	N296VP	N495JK		
0297	N4078L	(D-IWHA)	N168TY		
0298	N4078M	C-GTTS	C-FPYP		
0299	N510DT	N61LF	4X-CMA		
0300	N40780	ZK-MUS	VH-MSU		
0301	N4079L	N301DN	N210PM		

CESSNA 510 CITATION MUSTANG

C/n	Identities					
0302	N4079S	N9168Y	N479DC			
0303	ZS-YES	PH-JAY	OE-FBD			
0304	N919MB	N510LM				
0305	N1956A					
0306	N146EP	D-IJHO				
0307	N307SH	N215NJ	N872G			
0308	N4082U	N91639	N56PZ			
0309	N9161X	N72AG				
0310	N4083J	N91MB				
0311	N4084A	(EI-...)	N510BK			
0312	N9008U	TC-TAI				
0313	N4085C	N514DD				
0314	N1618L	N223PW				
0315	N4085S	OE-FHK				
0316	N4085Y	N9023F	PJ-DOM			
0317	N4085Z	OO-RAM	N317VR	N850JD	N510WG	
0318	N40851	N318CM	N426NS	N426N		
0319	N40854	N90082	TC-TAJ			
0320	N9160T	N510HS				
0321	(D-ISIO)	N136MC	JA001Z			
0322	N8MY					
0323	N510KM					
0324	N4087B	N324HS	XA-EGL			
0325	N4087F	N325HS				
0326	N40878	N9048K	RP-C7979	N326CM	HI949	
0327	N4088P	N46RC	N951CM			
0328	N4088U	PR-IER	N328CL			
0329	N4088Z	N484VB				
0330	I-STCB	TC-DOU				
0331	N510AT					
0332	N4078H	N229JR	(EC-...)	N278MW	N820JT	N820UT
0333	N262DA	N282DA				
0334	N40339	I-STCA	G-FBKE			
0335	F-GTFB					
0336	N510BT					
0337	(C-....)	N928KG	N337CM			
0338	N40595	C-FMCL	C-FMNL	N935AC		
0339	N428P	N5510	N813CZ	N999XP		
0340	M-OUSE					
0341	HB-VWZ					
0342	N578CT	5H-LUX				
0343	N90298	VH-SQY				
0344	N771ES					
0345	N1744Z					
0346	N4115W	N9166N	G-FBKD	F-HKIL		
0347	N9043L	VH-SQJ	ZK-JAK	ZK-VXM		
0348	N678MB					
0349	OE-FRM	OE-FZG				
0350	N350HS					
0351	N262DA	N351V	N771KB			
0352	N929ST					
0353	N544JB					
0354	F-HECG	F-HOUR	G-FBKH			
0355	EC-LJC					
0356	N91665	TC-AGR				
0357	N480CM	N795T				
0358	N90573	VH-VSQ				
0359	N4075X	N510PX				
0360	N40753	I-STCC	G-FBKF			
0361	N40770	I-STCD	G-FBKG			
0362	N4078A	N878PR				
0363	N4078T	N363MU	VH-MHO			
0364	N35HC					
0365	N4080M	N91703	N829BC	N849BC		
0366	N40805	D-IFER				
0367	N4081C	N367CM	N677TW			
0368	N4081M	EC-LNZ	OK-LNZ	CS-DTY	N368TF	N188GS
0369	N4082Y	N369MU	(N373CC)			
0370	N4085A	N333HS				
0371	N4085D	N10TR	N371VP			
0372	N4085S	N295PJ				
0373	N4085Z	N542RK				
0374	N40854	N761PA				
0375	N4086L	D-ICCP				
0376	N40863	N360KE				
0377	N40864	N668JP				

CESSNA 510 CITATION MUSTANG

C/n	Identities				
0378	N4087B	N378CM			
0379	N40878	N379CZ	N610JL		
0380	N4088T	N778LC	N778BC		
0381	N4009F	N264CA	N26WF		
0382	N4021E	N382MU			
0383	N40339	N92958	N111JM		
0384	N40366	N72VK			
0385	N40595	N87WC			
0386	N4076J	I-STCE	HB-VPM	N386TA	D-IZMM
0387	N40938	VH-KXM			
0388	N4095H	F-HICM			
0389	N40049	N885RS			
0390	N4030W	N61HH	N390CM	N503BB	G-JJET
0391	N4107D	N248TA	N2Q	N524SM	
0392	N4110T	N874PW			
0393	N4115W	N393CM	N61HH		
0394	N4042H	N394CM			
0395	N4058A	N789TS			
0396	N4076A	N62WM			
0397	N41227	N397CM			
0398	N41297	VH-KJG	ZK-RJZ		
0399	N4149W	PP-IMP			
0400	N4155B	N826AG			
0401	N4159Z	PT-AMU			
0402	N4202M	PP-WEB			
0403	N4041T	N759SB			
0404	N40456	N404CZ			
0405	N4047W	N93564	ZS-MTG	F-HAHA	
0406	N40512	N862GS			
0407	N4059H	N511TP	N265GA*		
0408	N4073S	N662BM			
0409	N4074M	G-RNER			
0410	N4074Z	N575SF	D-IRIZ		
0411	N4075L	N54DT	N510FF		
0412	N4075X	N171AA			
0413	N40753	N678AB	(D-IPRO)	F-HSHA	
0414	N4076Z	N510EM			
0415	N4077P	N117PS			
0416	N40770	N416MU	N86WH		
0417	N4078A	N45VP			
0418	N4078L	N100TP			
0419	N4078M	N486GS			
0420	N4078T	N26DV	N510FD		
0421	N40780	N891NY			
0422	N4079L	PR-FRZ			
0423	N4079S	N427RC			
0424	N4080M	D-IRUN			
0425	N40805	N910GF			
0426	N4081C	N435HB	N484HB		
0427	N4081M	N747NL	N77TZ		
0428	N4082H	N428SK	JA123F		
0429	N4082U	N422TG			
0430	N4082Y	PP-JCG			
0431	N4083J	N94731	N802JD		
0432	N4084A	N194ER			
0433	N4085A	N9474L	YR-TRQ		
0434	N4085C	N94749	N171UT		
0435	N4085D	N94811	N812J		
0436	N4085S	N94817	N997T		
0437	N4085Y	N94818	N704TP		
0438	N4085Z	N9488B	VT-IAM		
0439	N40851	N75RN			
0440	N40854	N94970	N16GS	N510JK	
0441	N4086H	N570LT			
0442	N4086L	N363BS			
0443	N40863	N717ET			
0444	N40864	N800FZ			
0445	N4087B	N445MU	N416DM		
0446	N4087F	N422RR	D-ISXT		
0447	N40878	N510MT			
0448	N4088P	N94979	B-9813	N448WT	
0449	N4088T	N254TB			
0450	N4088U	N234P			
0451	N4088Z	G-FFFC			
0452	N4089Y	N155MM			
0453	N4084A	N912JD			

CESSNA 510 CITATION MUSTANG

C/n	Identities			
0454	N4085S	B-0408	N454MF	N66D
0455	N4086H	CC-ANR		
0456	N4087B	N7QF		
0457	N40339	LV-FVY		
0458	N4078H	N733CF		
0459	N4110T	N2WG		
0460	N4074Z	N545CM		
0461	N4078T	C-GCCU		
0462	N40805	N42LJ		
0463	N4081M	N53MU	N88WG*	
0464	N4084A	[test marks also reported as N4085S]	N464KF	
0465	N40851	N65MU	N465WG	
0466	N40864	N890LG		
0467	N4088P	N19CA	N19RP	
0468	N4009F	N510HM		
0469	N40339	N510ER		
0470	N4058A	N208BM		
0471	N4092E	D-ISSS		
0472	N4059H	N227JA		
0473	N4075X	N884ML		
0474	N4078A	N530RM		
0475	N40780	G-ERLI		
0476	N4081M	N884K		
0477	N4085A	N227CS	C-FEPA	
0478	N510MH			
0479	N313AQ			

Production complete

CESSNA 525 CITATIONJET

C/n	Identities									
702	N525CJ	[prototype; ff 29Apr91 – cx Mar99 re-engineered to serve as the Cessna 525A Citation Jet CJ-2 prototype with c/n 708 q.v.]								
0001	N525CC	[ff 20Nov91; pre-production prototype]				N444RH	"N444RF"	N444RH	N800VT	N800VL
	N525VP	N525GV	N133GL							
0002	N1326B	N25CJ	N137AL	N46JW	N54BP	(VH-VCJ)	VH-SIY			
0003	N1326D	N44FJ	N45FJ	[Citation M2 development aircraft]						
0004	N1326G	N4YA	N24CJ	N7CC	N7CQ					
0005	N1326H	(N1326D)	N56K	N58KJ	N521PF					
0006	N1326P	N106CJ								
0007	(N1327E)	N525KN								
0008	N1327G	C-GDKI	N525FD	(PP-CMN)	PP-MLA					
0009	N1327J	(N529CC)								
0010	(N1327K)	N210CJ	ZS-MVX	N525JV	N48GG	N626TM				
0011	(N1327N)	N525AL	N929JT							
0012	(N1327Z)	N12PA	N86LA	[retro-fitted with winglets by Tamarack Aerospace Group]						
0013	N1328A	N550T	N550TF	N511EC						
0014	N1328D	N70TR	N620TC							
0015	(N1328K)	N115CJ	PT-MPE							
0016	N1328M	N216CJ	D-IKOP	HA-KAR						
0017	(N1328Q)	N525AE	N28PT							
0018	(N1328X)	N525MC	N525LH							
0019	(N1328Y)	N19CJ	N63HB	(N525SP)	N525KA					
0020	N1329D	"OO-LFU"	N1329D	OE-FGD	N220JL					
0021	(N1329G)	N793CJ								
0022	N1329N	G-BVCM	G-THNX	YU-BST						
0023	(N1329T)	N525RF	N525RP							
0024	N13291	F-GNCJ	N525DJ	F-HAOA	D-IAOA	F-HEQA	N155EC			
0025	(N1330D)	N9LR	D-IOBO	D-IBBA	G-CGXM	N33NM				
0026	(N1330G)	N525FS	N286CW	(N214LX)	N602CA					
0027	N1330N	N825GA	N861PD	N861RD	N700CJ					
0028	N1330S	G-OICE	(N25EA)	G-OHAT	G-GRGG	N665DP	N7RL	N525WH	PR-JNW	
0029	N13308	D-IWHL	(N525KT)	OK-PBS						
0030	N1331X	"PT-MPE"	N177RE	(N93KV)	N53KV					
0031	(N13312)	(N131CJ)	N31CJ	N831S	N215RB					
0032	(N13313)	N532CJ	N95DJ	N32VP	N900DS					
0033	N1354G	ZS-NHE	N526CA	N472SW	N116AP	N501KR				
0034	N1772E	N96G	N9GU	N333VS	N525WR					
0035	N1779E	N525HS								
0036	N1782E	N525MB								
0037	N1820E	HB-VKB	EC-IAB	HB-VKB	OO-IDE					
0038	N1874E	N135MM	N600HR							
0039	N1958E	N39CJ								
0040	N1959E	D-ISCH	VP-CCC	N525AJ	OE-FMU					
0041	N2098A	N525GG	HB-VJQ	D-IAMM	F-HADA	N565JP	N565JF	N25MB	N86TG	
0042	N26105	N96GD	PH-MGT	D-IBWA						
0043	N2616L	N525PL								
0044	N2617K	XA-SKW	N55DG	D-IDBW	EC-KKE	HB-VPF	[retro-fitted with Tamarack winglets]			
0045	N2617P	N525AP	LV-AMB							
0046	N26174	N123JN	N127SG							
0047	N2621U	N47TH	(N47VP)	N47FH						
0048	N2621Z	N500HC	N525NA	N484J						
0049	N2633Y	N49CJ	N349SF	N4HK						
0050	N2634E	N70KW	N205BN							
0051	N2637R	N800HS	N808HS	N726SC						
0052	N26379	N252CJ	N52PK							
0053	N2638A	N53CJ	N66ES	N60ES	(N603JC)	N3WB	N654WW			
0054	N2638U	N54CJ	N851DB							
0055	N2639Y	N923AR	N570DM							
0056	N2646X	N56NZ	JA8420	N525KK	PP-BSP					
0057	N525DG	N585DG	N131PL							
0058	N2647Y	N525CK	N526CK	N525F	N509SE	N525LX				
0059	N2647Z	N71GW	N816FC	N818FC						
0060	N2648Y	XA-SOU	XA-TRI	N525WW						
0061	N26481	N61CJ	N525PS							
0062	N26486	C-FRVE	C-GINT	C-FPWB						
0063	N2649J	N55SK								
0064	N2649S	D-IHEB								
0065	N2649Y	N5259Y	EC-704	EC-FZP	N525GC					
0066	N26495	N420CH	N545ES	N823ES	N545ES	N824ES				
0067	N26499	N594JB	N525TF							
0068	N2650V	N68CJ	N303LC	N888KU	N522AJ					
0069	N26502	N169CJ	N20FL	N20VL						
0070	N26504	(N70HW)	D-ISGW							
0071	N26509	N940SW								
0072	N2651R	(TG-FIL)	TG-RIF							

CITATIONJET

C/n	Identities							
0073	N2656G	(D-IHEB)	N77794	(N780AJ)	N780AB			
0074	N26581	N511TC						
0075	N5076K	N719L	N719D	N775TB				
0076	N5079V	N80TF	N4TF	N805VC				
0077	N50820	N1000E	N1999E	(N9410P)				
0078	N5085E	N525CH						
0079	N5086W	N179CJ	N525WB					
0080	N5090A	N80CJ	N33DT					
0081	N5090V	N181JT	N525HA					
0082	N5090Y	D-IHHS	N525LW					
0083	N5091J	N34TC	(N121CP)	(N421CP)	(N50PL)			
0084	(N5092D)	D-ITSV	G-CITJ	N306EC	YV549T	YV3184		
0085	N5093D	VR-CDN	PT-MJC					
0086	(N5093L)	PT-MIL						
0087	(N5093Y)	N175PS	(N717DA)	N926CH	N100CH	N100CQ	N606HC	
0088	(N50938)	N188CJ	N722SG					
0089	N5135K	N189CJ	N920MS	N202BG	EC-KSB	N600HS	T7-MND	D-IMND*
0090	N5136J	N8288R	(N525KF)	LZ-DIN				
0091	N5138F	N295DS						
0092	N51396	N525AS	N523AS	N534TX	(N534LL)	N801PJ	N800DT	
0093	N5151S	I-IDAG	N525CM					
0094	(N51522)	N94MZ						
0095	N5153K	N61SH	N525JV					
0096	N5153X	(EC-...)	D-ICEE					
0097	(N5153Z)	N234WS	N130MR	[w/o 26Mar00 nr Buda, TX; to White Inds, Bates City, MO for spares]				
0098	N5156D	N511AC	N980VP	(HZ-NJ4)				
0099	N5156V	N525SC	N525CP	N526CP	N525VC*			
0100	N51564	N525CC	(N808HS)	N800HS	VH-CIT	VH-KXL		
0101	(N5157E)	F-GPFC	OM-OPR					
0102	N52038	N202CJ	TC-CRO	LX-LOV	HB-VWP	F-HGPG		
0103	N5204D	(N203CJ)	D-IVHA	OE-FLG				
0104	N5207A	N606MM	N608MM					
0105	N52081	N305CJ	(D-IAFD)	G-EDCJ	N10R			
0106	N5211A	N21VC	(N444H)					
0107	N5211F	N525WC						
0108	N5211Q	N108CJ						
0109	N52113	N37DG	N393N	C-GDWS	C-GSXX			
0110	N5213S	N195ME						
0111	N52136	N776DF	N28RK					
0112	N5214J	N1006F	VT-OPJ					
0113	N5214K	N111AM	G-SEAJ	N555BG				
0114	N5214L	N96GM	N294CW	(N215LX)				
0115	N52141	OO-PHI						
0116	N5201M	N41EB	N216CW	(N202LX)	N323JA	N10S		
0117	N5203J	N217CJ	(N349CB)	N26CB	N26QB			
0118	N5203S	N52178	(N61TF)	N118AZ	D-IRWR			
0119	(N5264E)	N47TH	N466F	PT-FBM				
0120	N5264M	PT-WGD	(N665AJ)	N525CZ	PR-VGD			
0121	N5264S	TC-EMA	D-ICSS					
0122	N5264U	N102AF	N41YP	N471MD				
0123	(N52642)	N5223P	D-IRKE					
0124	N5090A	N525JH	VP-CWW	(ZS-BSS)	OE-FRR	N91RB		
0125	N5090V	N525PE	N525PT					
0126	N5090Y	N1264V	N14TV	D-IFUP	VP-CFP	D-IHGW	D-IMPC	D-IAHG
0127	N5091J	N127CJ	N63LB	N63LF	N6UB			
0128	N5092D	N535LR	N818EE	N323EZ				
0129	N5093D	N52642	N229CJ	C-GPOS				
0130	N5093L	N416KC	N418KC					
0131	N5093Y	(N577SD)	N577SV	N281CW	(N203LX)	N800AJ	N41EA	N21TK
0132	N50938	N132AH	(N132RP)					
0133	N52038	EC-261	EC-GIE	N133KT	[parted out Roanoke, TX, still wearing EC-GIE]			
0134	N5204B	N234CJ	N525JM	(N525TL)				
0135	N5207A	N888RA						
0136	N52081	N525KL	[w/o 09Dec99 Branson-Point Lookout, MO]					
0137	N5211A	N810SS	(N525SE)					
0138	N5211F	VH-MOJ	VH-DAA					
0139	N52457	N76AE	N36RG					
0140	N5246Z	N725L	N111BF					
0141	N5250E	N774CA	N237DG	N525TA	N525JJ	N725CF	N545RW	
0142	N5068R	N815MC	N5068R	N815MC	N789DR*			
0143	N51993	D-IOMP	D-IALL	EC-KJV	9A-JSB			
0144	N5200R	D-IDAG	N525BQ					
0145	N52141	N145CJ	N424TV					
0146	N5100J	N1329G	(OE-FGG)					
0147	N52178	N996JR	[w/o 22Jul03 Penn Cove, WA]					
0148	N52144	N148CJ	XB-ATH	N300DL	C-GLBT	N908JP		

CITATIONJET

C/n	Identities									
0149	N5218R	N67GH	(N57GH)	(N67GU)	N77215	[w/o 12 Jan07 Van Nuys, CA]				
0150	N5090V	ZS-NUW	N8341C							
0151	N5086W	N1015B	9A-CGH	(9A-CAD)	(N151TT)	N7EN	N400RL	N28DM	N242GB	N562PC
0152	N5112K	N152KC	N152KV							
0153	N5090V	N551G	N551Q	(N525EF)	VP-CNF	G-PWNS	N153MR	N36TX		
0154	N51246	N401LG	N401EG	N254CW	(N204LX)	N520DF				
0155	N5132T	N155CJ	I-EDEM	N61SG						
0156	N156ML									
0157	N51817	N1115V	N57HC	N54HC						
0158	N5093D	N749CP	N800RL	N800RK	N695PA					
0159	N51872	N131RG	N351BC							
0160	N5076J	N66AM								
0161	N5076K	N525BT	(N39GA)							
0162	N5122X	N1XT	N525JW	(N39GA)						
0163	N5138F	N51CD	VH-CDG							
0164	N51444	D-ICGT	N204J							
0165	N5148B	D-IJYP	(OY-FCE)	D-IHCW	N525P					
0166	N5148N	N343PJ	F-GRRM	N252JK						
0167	N5151S	(N4EF)	N1EF	N525RA						
0168	N51522	D-IRON								
0169	N5153K	N68CJ	N230LL	N53KN						
0170	N5153X	N170BG	N170MU							
0171	N5153Z	N97VF								
0172	N5156B	N172CJ	D-IAVB	N350GM	VP-CTA	D-IFUP	OO-CEJ			
0173	N51564	N970SU	N129RP	N209RP						
0174	N5157E	N817CJ	N417C	(N417Q)	N66BE					
0175	N175CP	N41PG								
0176	N5161J	PT-WLX	[w/o 16Sep05 Rio de Janeiro-Santos Dumont, Brazil]							
0177	N5163C	N1280A	(RP-C717)	G-OCSB	G-OWRC	F-HASC	OE-FWM	D-ITRA		
0178	N525RC									
0179	N5166U	N377GS	N877GS	N608DB						
0180	N5168F	N123AV	(N133AV)	VP-BDS						
0181	N5180K	N181CJ	N88LD	SE-RIO	D-IVPD					
0182	N5183U	(N740JB)	N177JB	N177JF						
0183	N5185J	(N97CJ)	N399G							
0184	N5185V	N525J								
0185	N5187B	N51176	N1241N	(RP-C8288)	N83TR	N13FH	PR-HAP			
0186	N51246	N186CJ	N92ND							
0187	N5130J	N696ST	PR-AEG							
0188	N51342	(D-IVID)	D-IVIN	OE-FMA						
0189	N189CM									
0190	N51396	N41NK	N701TF	N708TF	N701TP	N79MX				
0191	N5145P	N525BF	(N525BL)	C-FIMA	N15LV	PR-CLB				
0192	N51444	N84FG								
0193	N5132T	N193CJ	D-ILCB	HB-VOX	D-IPOD					
0194	N5148B	N81RA	(N194VP)	I-DEAC	N22JM	N600MC				
0195	N5138F	N525DC	(N525ST)							
0196	N5135A	D-IURH	N250GM	N525LP						
0197	N5151S	N525KH	EC-HIN							
0198	N51522	N315MR	N198RG	N805KK						
0199	N5153K	N1216K	9A-CAD	N524AF	N525DY	N299CW	(N205LX)			
0200	N5153Z	N1276J	N226B	N525LK						
0201	N5156D	N525HV								
0202	N5120U	N202CJ	N747AC							
0203	N5122X	N525GP	N33FW							
0204	N5133E	N1293G	(N323LM)	B-4108	B-7027					
0205	N5156V	N550MC	N275CW	N206LX	(N205NP)	N525DU				
0206	N5136J	N17VB	(N45PF)							
0207	N51872	N31SG	N26RL	(N100WQ)						
0208	N5153X	N208JV	N211GM							
0209	N5162W	D-ILAT	N550BD	N580BD						
0210	N5157E	N210CJ	N999EB	XA-CAH	N28CK					
0211	D-IMMD	N525HJ	N1WW	N335MB						
0212	N51176	N67VW	N800NB							
0213	N5168F	N525WM	N486TT	N486CC						
0214	N51743	D-IFAN	N130NM	N130LM						
0215	N5166U	N28GA	N28QA							
0216	N5183V	N18GA	N18QA							
0217	N5202D	(5Y-TCI)	D-IEWS	OE-FMT	N525GJ					
0218	N51881	N64LF	N288CW	(N207LX)	N713SD					
0219	N5197A	N219CJ	N648HE							
0220	N220CJ	C-GHPP	N25MX	PR-HIP	N911Q					
0221	N5203S	D-IWIL								
0222	N52038	N111LR	[w/o 04Apr98 Roswell, GA]							
0223	N5211Q	D-IGAS	OY-INV	OM-HLZ	OE-FKH	N223JF				
0224	N52038	N224CJ								

CITATIONJET

C/n	Identities					
0225	N5211F	N525RM				
0226	N5214J	N1216N	TC-LIM	OE-FSS		
0227	N5214K	N741CC				
0228	N5216A	N668VP	N668VB	N669DB	N525CP	
0229	N5218R	D-IHOL	LX-TRA	LX-FOX	F-GXRK	N65AH
0230	N5218T	N323LM	N934AM	(N904AM)	N242BS	
0231	N5223D	N606JR	N606MG	[also wore fake serial 97-0231]		N5255B
0232	N5223Y	N525PF	N525PB	N525GB	C-GABE	
0233	N5235G	N233CJ	N53CG	PR-CAN		
0234	N900P	N950P	(N91GH)			
0235	N5246Z	VP-BZZ	I-ESAI	LX-GCA	F-HIVA	
0236	D-ISWA					
0237	N237CJ	N61YP	[w/o on approach to Elk City, OK, 03Feb14; parted out by Alliance Air Parts, Oklahoma City, OK]			
0238	N5203S	PT-WQI				
0239	N5188N	(PT-WQJ)	PT-XJS	N525VG	N525HY	
0240	N525GM	N524SF				
0241	N52081	N241WS	N207BS	N209BS	N110FD	N307BS
0242	N242LJ	(N27FB)	PP-SDY			
0243	CC-PVJ	CC-CVO	CC-PVJ	CC-CVO	N494BA	PR-OJL
0244	N66ES	N68BS	N525ET	YV533T	YV3182	
0245	N5214J	N33CJ	G-SFCJ	N961RA	N67AZ	
0246	N525EC	N525WF				
0247	N533JF	(N538JF)	N247CW	(N208LX)	N241EP	N609SM
0248	N248CJ	N300FC				
0249	N5214L	N909M	(N909F)			
0250	N250CJ	HB-VMT	F-HMJC	OO-JDK		
0251	N50ET	N1JB	N86JB	N616BM	PR-DCE	
0252	(N5223P)	N740JV	VP-CIS	N252RV		
0253	N5223P	N8940	N894Q	N253CW	(N209LX)	
0254	N5183V	OE-FGI				
0255	N514DS					
0256	(N196DR)	N196HA	C-GPCT			
0257	N9003	N116DK	N26DK	N561BC		
0258	N5203J	N108CR	OY-SML			
0259	N5235G	PT-MSP				
0260	N5197A	D-IGZA	N260AM			
0261	N31HD	(N61CV)				
0262	N52457	N262BK				
0263	N263CT					
0264	(D-IKHV)	VP-CHV	EC-HBC	D-IPCS	N550CM	N531BR
0265	N198JH					
0266	N52081	N266CJ				
0267	N5201J	PT-XMM				
0268	N850DG	N529NM	C-GSRG			
0269	N5219T	N607DB				
0270	N5194J	N525HC				
0271	N860DD	N860DB	HB-VNK	G-OSOH	G-LUBB	
0272	N4GA	N4QP				
0273	(N525HC)	N911NP				
0274	PT-XDB					
0275	N700GW	N42AA	(N174GM)	N69WH		
0276	N800GW	N187MC				
0277	N277CJ	OY-JMC	9A-JIM			
0278	N5145V	N1127K	N100SM	N901CJ	N525HX	
0279	D-IGME	SP-DLV				
0280	N5151D	PT-XAC				
0281	N5154J	N1280S	N41NK	N500TL	N508TL	VH-APJ
0282	N625PG					
0283	N95BS	PP-IZA				
0284	N256JB					
0285	N55PZ	N55PX	PR-SMJ			
0286	N51666	D-ICEY	D-INFS			
0287	N73PM	C-GBPM	N52KX			
0288	N288AG	RP-C525				
0289	D-ISHW	N553EJ	PR-SKW			
0290	N808WA	N97SK				
0291	N51744	F-GPLF	OE-FEM	HB-VPI	(PH-EEJ)	N249CA
0292	N117W	N171W	N525CU	OE-FCW		
0293	N1127K	[crash-landed in Romania 31Jan01; rebuilt]				
0294	N294AT					
0295	N5209E	N295CM	(PT-MTU)	OE-FJU	YU-MTU	
0296	N296DC					
0297	N316MJ	VP-CAD	N600GK			
0298	G-RSCJ	N55CJ				
0299	N525BE	N711BE	N711BX	[w/o 18Jan16 nr Cedar Fort, UT]		
0300	N300CQ	N881KS	PT-STK			

CITATIONJET / CJ1

C/n	Identities									
0301	N27CJ	N270J	N291CW	N915ST						
0302	N302CJ	N326B	C-GSYM							
0303	N51612	D-IMMI	RA-67172							
0304	N1128G	EC-HBX	N154RA	N525TX	(N444L)	N605HP	N525TX	N747AH	N678RT	
0305	N826HS	RA-67428								
0306	(N525BE)	N4RH	N525DY							
0307	N114FW	(N114FG)								
0308	N72SG	N525DR	N373AF							
0309	D-IBMS	EC-LCM								
0310	D-IVBG	D-IIJS	OK-SLA	D-IERF						
0311	N523BT	N270J	N27CJ							
0312	F-GTMD	CN-TLB								
0313	N525MP	N525MR	N525MF							
0314	N5154J	N428PC	N525DM	N525LJ						
0315	(D-IIRR)	D-IAME	S5-BAY	OE-FMI						
0316	N5136J	N187DL	N316EJ	N458MT	PR-BSK					
0317	N51444	N317CJ	N51GS							
0318	N5145P	N525DP								
0319	N5148N	PT-FNP								
0320	N150BV	N30AQ								
0321	D-IAAS	PH-ECI	N79AJ							
0322	N52LT	LX-YSL	F-HCPB	D-IGGW*						
0323	N900GW									
0324	(N428PC)	N5163C	G-IUAN	N525SY						
0325	N464C	N764C	N115BB							
0326	N5183U	N23KG	N226CW	(N211LX)	N188TW	N616PR				
0327	N398EP	LV-AXN	N780HS*							
0328	N328CJ									
0329	XA-DGP	XB-DGA								
0330	N5153K	N330CJ	N331MS	N38SC						
0331	N888RK	N9UG	PH-KOM	OE-FGK						
0332	N5161J	OO-FNL	(N332VP)	N511BP						
0333	N5185J	N99CJ								
0334	N51872	N44FE	N525M							
0335	N5156D	N335CJ	N335CT	N467F	N620JC	N525XD				
0336	N51564	N105P	PR-EGF							
0337	N5241Z	PT-FJA								
0338	N51575	N525RL	N977DM	N907DK						
0339	N5225K	N339B	N239CW	(N212LX)	N841TC	N810CM	N265BF			
0340	N5165T	N392RG								
0341	N341AR									
0342	N5216A	N342AC	N9180K	N918CW	N49TH	N56K	N613JG			
0343	N5244F	D-IURS								
0344	N77VR	N77VZ	N77VG							
0345	N5185V	G-ZIZI	D-ILUG*							
0346	N5153J	N5136J	PP-CRS							
0347	N5145P	N1133G	I-DAGF	D-IARI						
0348	N348KH	N248CW	(N213LX)	N8288R						
0349	D-ICWB	RA-67431								
0350	N51444	HP-1410HT	HP-1410	N1348T	N1848T	N720GM	CC-ADB			
0351	N5246Z	VP-BRJ	LX-SUP	F-HGOL	OK-DSJ					
0352	N5185V	N99JB	N31JB	N573CM						
0353	N5211Q	D-ICOL	(LN-FDB)	N237CJ	N275P					
0354	N5225K	N821P	(D-IMMP)	OE-FCA	I-CABD					
0355	N51396	N205FH	N312SB	N312SE	N525TK	N501CJ				
0356	N5213S	PP-YOF	N865VP	PP-JJZ						
0357	N5214J	N357JV	N194MG							
0358	N51564	G-HMMV	M-PARK	N358HA						
0359	F-GTRY									

CJ1

C/n	Identities						
0360	N5156D	N31CJ	N525CD				
0361	N5183U	N361RB	N128CS	LV-CKT			
0362	N5214L	N362CJ	N362PE	N362FL	N31WE		
0363	N5161J	N525AS	N523TS				
0364	N5211F	N525DL	N525DE	C-FTKX	VP-CHE	N364WT	PP-WTR
0365	N5130J	N651CJ					
0366	N5223Y	D-IRMA	N850GM	D-IRMA	N173CA	N376RS	
0367	N51872	N525MD	N525FT	(N525CY)	N615AK		
0368	N5185J	N820CE	N525FN				
0369	N5200U	N629DM	N161SM	N525AW			

CJ1

C/n	Identities					
0370	N5145P	N525MW				
0371	N5165T	N175SB	HZ-BL1	N175SB		
0372	N372CP	N345MG				
0373	N415CS	(N352HC)	N315HC			
0374	N12GS	N12GY				
0375	N5225K	N375KH	HB-VNL	N600XT		
0376	N52352	N802JH	C-GTRG	N814DM		
0377	N5241Z	N15C	N900BT	N900BQ	T7-ACA	
0378	N5135K	N525CP	N203BG			
0379	N5188A	I-IMMI				
0380	N5228Z	N381CJ	N525GB	N83DC	B-3669	
0381	N5185J	N856BB	N855BB	(N476JD)		
0382	N5124F	N525LF				
0383	N5231S	N600AL				
0384	N5148B	PP-JET	N684SC	SP-...		
0385	N5136J	N1326P	N417C	N417Q		
0386	N51993	N45MH	N386RF	N211JH		
0387	N51564	N7715X	N7715Y	N724FS	N33SW	N122HW
0388	N5162W	N525MH	N525LB	N520GB		
0389	N5156D	N389CJ	D-IDAS	D-IDAZ		
0390	N51396	N100PF				
0391	N5130J	LX-IIH	HB-VWO			
0392	N5165T	N392SM				
0393	D-IBIT	OM-HLY	OE-FFK	D-IXXX		
0394	N5132T	N64PM	N64PZ	S5-BAJ	N101PJ	PR-LVF
0395	N5183U	(N525AJ)	N525AR	N507HP		
0396	N51575	D-IMAC	D-IKCS	EC-MPN		
0397	N5163C	I-RVRP				
0398	N5183V	N398CJ	C-GMTI			
0399	N5135A	(VP-CTN)	D-ITAN			
0400	N5120U	(C-GPWM)	N525EZ	N526EZ	(N88798)	F-GMDL	N51C
0401	N51246	D-IFFI	N142EA	N44CK		
0402	N525ML	N585ML				
0403	N51817	PT-PRR	N223CF			
0404	N5145P	N88AD	(N746JB)			
0405	N5125J	N121EB	N7895Q			
0406	N5124F	N72JW				
0407	N51872	N525JL				
0408	N5156D	N408GR	PP-JBS			
0409	N5212M	N657RB	(N334DB)	N530AG	N530AQ	N525BW
0410	N52144	N4108E				
0411	N51575	N525RF	N535RF	D-ILIF	N411VR	
0412	N5161J	N82AE				
0413	N5185J	N525RK				
0414	N5223P	N726TM	(N26DV)			
0415	N5250E	N26SW	EC-ISS	D-IUWE	HB-VOD	PR-HJH
0416	N80C	N8UC	N186TW			
0417	N5203B	D-IEAI	PH-SOL	N91BB		
0418	N51444	N300BV				
0419	N7NE	N7XE				
0420	N5183U	N96SK	N86SK	N726CL	CC-AOC	N555DH
0421	D-ILME	OE-FET				
0422	N51881	N125DJ	N927CC	N422VP	N525LA	
0423	N5201J	N62SH	N292SG	G-OEBJ	G-ORAN	F-HFMA	N525MX
0424	N5231S	N28SW	N711WG			
0425	N5188A	N335J	C-FWBK	C-GZLM	N85VR	
0426	N5197A	N426ED				
0427	N5202D	N128GW	N525LM			
0428	N5203J	PR-ABV				
0429	N429PK	EC-IVJ				
0430	N52081	N430GR	PR-ARB			
0431	N51993	N431YD	ZS-PWU	N347BC		
0432	N51342	N94AL				
0433	N5223D	N102PT	[w/o 01Feb08 nr Augusta, ME]			
0434	N5226B	N860DD	N860DB			
0435	N5244F	N525AD	G-CJAD	D-IAWU		
0436	N5141F	EC-HVQ				
0437	N5185V	N717NA	G-HEBJ	N489HC	(N489JC)	
0438	N51942	N103CS	N325DM	N525RY		
0439	N5200Z	N395SD	N54CG			
0440	N5233J	C-GPWM	N440CJ	N525NT	(N525JT)	
0441	N5200R	PR-ARA				
0442	N5187Z	D-IFIS	D-ILLY	VH-TFW		
0443	N5136J	N443CJ	N77DB			
0444	N52136	N525BR	(N525WS)			
0445	N445CJ	N207BS				

CJ1

C/n	Identities						
0446	N5211A	N246GS					
0447	N5120U	N116CS	N952SP	N525LE			
0448	N448JC	EC-JFD	N448EA	F-GMMC	HB-VWW	N88ME	N655CK
0449	N5153K	N1259Y	(JA-001T)	JA525A			
0450	N5156D	I-BOAT	OE-FVJ				
0451	N5135A	N165CA	N911MM				
0452	N52178	N107GM	(N107PK)	N585PK	N585MC		
0453	N5211Q	N103CS	N80VP	N902RD	N929VC	N928VC	N869CB
0454	N5225K	N541CJ	N101U				
0455	N5183V	N75FC	(N15SS)	(N900TW)			
0456	N5185J	PR-LJM					
0457	N118CS	N774GE					
0458	N5188A	LX-MSP	N525NP	PR-BJM			
0459	N459NA						
0460	N5185V	D-IMMM	[rebuilt after accident 12Mar04 Florence, Italy]				N57EC
0461	N5207A	N200SL					
0462	N5197A	N965LC	N965EC	N86RL			
0463	N5200U	N1284D	Chile 361				
0464	N1284P	Chile 362					
0465	N1285P	Chile 363					
0466	N5200Z	N119CS	D-INCS				
0467	N5157E	N620BB					
0468	N468RW						
0469	N52038	N122CS	N520RM				
0470	N901GW						
0471	N768R	N471CJ	B-3668				
0472	N124CS	N525KM					
0473	N5201M	LX-MRC	HB-VOR	F-HJAV			
0474	N31CJ						
0475	N52113	N475CJ	XA-TTG	N88LS			
0476	N476CJ	N50ET	N74PG	D-IRSB			
0477	N5216A	D-INOC	D-IDIG	OE-FOI	OM-OLI	OM-TAB	
0478	N5233J	N869GR	(PR-GRN)	N869GS			
0479	N5200R	N525BP					
0480	N5223Y	N888SF	(N66FH)	OE-FIX	N103SK	OE-FIX	
0481	N5204D	N4DF	N795BM	N796BM	N30VR		
0482	N5211Q	PR-EXP	N482EA				
0483	N5250E	PR-EOB					
0484	N5211F	N484CJ	F-HALO	RA-67433			
0485	N52136	N674JM	N672JM				
0486	N5211A	N334BD	EC-JIU				
0487	N5200U	N243LS	CC-CMS	N191PP	PP-LJR	N487WF	N487CJ
0488	N5218R	N525WH	N488SR				
0489	N5218T	N489ED	N489CB				
0490	N52141	N130CS	(N130MH)	N120CS	N525PJ	N120CS	N907YB
0491	N5244F	N491CJ	N491LT	N926CC	N442CJ		
0492	N5226B	N492CJ	N888PS	N888PY	N213JT		
0493	N5203J	N65CK	N95CK	(N220JM)	(N315N)	CC-ADN	
0494	N71HR	D-ITIP					
0495	N5246Z	OY-RGG	OO-STE	SP-AST			
0496	N5223P	N382EM	PR-TRT				
0497	N5235G	N132CS	N525JJ				
0498	N5223K	N498YY	N5201J	N498YY			
0499	N5200Z	HB-VNP	F-HHSC	D-IBAK			
0500	N525CJ	N111GJ	N44VS				
0501	(N501CJ)	N41LF					
0502	N51881	N133CS	SE-RGX				
0503	N904DP	N909DP	(N818ER)				
0504	N52081	N665CH	N9915Z				
0505	N502TN	(F-HBSC)					
0506	N242ML						
0507	N5263U	Chile 364					
0508	N5225K	N508CJ	EC-JSH	F-HBSC	N918AM		
0509	N993GL						
0510	N5058J	N1DM	N971DM	(N278CA)	G-EDCK	N814SP	
0511	N5212M	ZK-TBM	N326JK				
0512	N411MY	(LN-FDC)	PR-GNL				
0513	N52591	N513RV	(N439PW)				
0514	N52136	N514RV	PH-FIS				
0515	N52141	N132CS	N551FP				
0516	N5060K	EC-IRB	N525CF	D-INER	N518RC		
0517	N52626	D-IFDH	N517CJ				
0518	D-ILLL	D-IETZ	F-HAGH				
0519	N926TF	D-IAMF	HB-VPD	T7-SCR			
0520	N135CS	N520CJ	N847JJ	N847JL	N152WR	N525H	
0521	N5066U	N521CJ	VH-ANE	VH-YNE			

CJ1/CJ1+

C/n	Identities					
0522	N138CS	N125CS	(N525BA)	N92AJ	N525RN	T7-FMS
0523	N51246	F-HAJD				
0524	N5202D	N524CJ	N759R	N770BX	N3WB	N525RL	N545JS
0525	N123S					
0526	N5163C	(SP-KCL)	N526LC	SP-KCL	VP-CJI	
0527	N5211Q	N527CJ	N15BV	N358K	N278K	
0528	N50612	N528CJ	G-GEBJ	M-DINO	N716SN	(LV-FUE)	LV-FWT
0529	N50820	N151CS	N151EW			
0530	N5244F	N430JH	N430JF			
0531	N5211A	N333J	N525FC			
0532	N32BG	N323G	PP-INT			
0533	N5180K	(D-IPMM)	D-IPMI	F-GPEB	9A-FNR	YU-FNR
0534	N52113	N1269B	JA100C	N534NA	N814LG	
0535	N5090A	N535CJ	JA525Y			
0536	N52369	[re-serialled 525-0600 q.v]				
0537	N5261R	N837AC	N839AC	N678RF	N425WH	
0538	N51564	N525AM				
0539	N152CS	OE-FRF	N90MT			
0540	N5172M	N40CJ				
0541	N458SM	N739LN				
0542	N5125J	N500CW	PR-MFJ			
0543	N5200U	N43NW				
0544	OE-FUJ	HB-VOG	M-OLLY	[retro-fitted with Tamarack winglets]		
0545	N545TG					
0546	N5188N	N981LB	C-GHSB			
0547	N5211Q	N547ST	N547TW			
0548	N5216A	N153CS	N257MV	PP-PIM		
0549	N51995	N549CJ	JA525J			
0550	N5112K	N1288P	SP-KKA	C-GDEK		
0551	N5105F	N1279A	B-3644			
0552	N51564	N1279V	B-3645			
0553	N51612	N902GW				
0554	N5157E	N1290N	B-3647			
0555	N5214L	N1287B	B-3648			
0556	N93LS					
0557	N5250E	N1287F	B-3649			
0558	N51993	N1288N	B-3650			

CJ1+

C/n	Identities						
0600	N525AD	(N55KT)	N919MC	[built from 525-0536; ff 08Oct04; received FAA type certificate 20Jun05]			
0601	N52626	N601CJ	N29ET	N620JW			
0602	N5248V	N602CJ	N46JV	N74UK	D-ISJM	N47LV	LV-GVQ
0603	N51143	N805CJ					
0604	N5183U	N122LM	[retro-fitted with Tamarack winglets]				
0605	N5188A	N800PF					
0606	N51896	N713WH	PR-FSB				
0607	N5218T	N59JN	N58JN				
0608	N52229	N970RP	N4017L	N915RP	N878J		
0609	N5161J	N50VC	M-TEAM				
0610	N51817	N35TK	N43MS				
0611	N52645	D-ICEY					
0612	N5155G	N525RZ	3A-MSR				
0613	N5112K	N1309V	PH-CMW				
0614	N51564	(OE-FMU)	D-IMMG	OE-FMD			
0615	N5095N	N65EM	(CS-DPU)	D-IAIB			
0616	N999EB	N525PC					
0617	N18TG	N1TG	N116LJ	D-IWPS	N617VP	B-9641	
0618	N618KA	XA-HPR					
0619	N1317Y	VT-NAB					
0620	N620CJ	N5UD					
0621	N52475	N621AD					
0622	N5270K	N622SL					
0623	N5124F	HB-VOF	N427AZ				
0624	N5141F	D-IOWA					
0625	N5236L	N625CJ	(VH-ODJ)	D-IEPR	N852L	B-0420	
0626	N5117U	N626CV					
0627	N5264N	N627MW					
0628	N52433	T7-FRA	G-TFRA				
0629	N56KP						
0630	N50054	N711C					
0631	N5206T	YV2331	N631EC	C-FUTL			

CJ1+

C/n	Identities							
0632	N50715	N1314H	CC-PGK	CC-CSA	JY-AWF	CC-CSA	N1314H	PR-EMX
0633	N5163K	(N28FM)	N43BH					
0634	N5196U	N634CJ	OE-FSR					
0635	N5241R	(N525JN)	N817BT	N817BF				
0636	N5066U	C-GTRG	N636VP	(LN-FDA)	XA-SML	N212RH		
0637	N51993	N637CJ	N779RB	C-GWGZ				
0638	N51342	VH-MYE						
0639	N5201M	(D-ICPO)	D-IMPC					
0640	N5076L	N34DZ						
0641	N5214K	C-GIRL						
0642	N5151D	N466AE	D-ICAO					
0643	N5228Z	N380CR	N380BR	N643RF	N72AC			
0644	N50321	N902DP	EC-LDE	D-ITXT*				
0645	OE-FPO	N788MP	(D-ILHF)	B-9629				
0646	N5154J	A7-CJI	N646VP					
0647	N1895C	N1865C						
0648	N5152X	G-CJDB						
0649	N51806	N794PF						
0650	N51511	HB-VWF	F-HRCA					
0651	N5267D	N24BC	N886EM	N448LL				
0652	N5148B	N41159	RA-67705					
0653	N52526	N7715X	XB-MTR					
0654	N52691	N94HL						
0655	N51612	N1367D	B-7777					
0656	N5069E	N388FW						
0657	"N52594"+	[+test marks as quoted, but already in use on a Cessna 182]	N65BK	C-GJOL	N484SE			
0658	N907WL							
0659	N5266F	N659CJ	OE-FNA	LZ-FNA				
0660	N5057F	N197RJ	PR-OUD					
0661	N5244F	N613AL	LN-RYG	(G-STPZ)	F-HKRA			
0662	N5267G	N607TN						
0663	N5244W	N297RJ	PR-GFS					
0664	N664CJ	N88QC	N88QG	D-ILHE				
0665	N5037F	N665CJ	HB-VOV	D-IOBB				
0666	N5076K	N7277	T9-SMS	E7-SMS				
0667	N5061P	N629DR	PP-WBP					
0668	N52613	N557HP						
0669	N5200R	N224BA						
0670	N5161J	VH-LDH	VH-JSO					
0671	N5053R	N525AJ	SE-RIX	D-IZZZ				
0672	N52071	N858SD	N853SD					
0673	N5241Z	N525AJ						
0674	N5061F	N4123S	N324BD					
0675	N5270E	N41196	(D-ILHA)	D-ILHB				
0676	N5120U	N903GW						
0677	N5245D	N413CQ	(N418CQ)	D-IHKW				
0678	N5250E	N528CB						
0679	N5076K	N525GE						
0680	N5061P	N680KH	(N895CB)					
0681	N5266F	N904GW						
0682	N5245U	N905GW						
0683	N5053R	N397RJ	N70GM					
0684	N5207A	D-IAMS	D-IBTI					
0685	N50612	N994JG	[converted to prototype Citation M2; ff as such 09Mar12]	N732M				
0686	N50549	N980MB	HL8201					
0687	"N50904"+	[+test marks as quoted, but already in use on a Cessna 150J]	N687CJ	N535WT				
0688	N5270E	N2259D	HL8283					
0689	N5263D	N101LD						
0690	N52627	HB-VWM						
0691	N52623	N4RH	N691CJ	HL8202				
0692	N5266F	N929MM						
0693	N5214K	CN-TJE						
0694	N52609	(D-ILHB)	D-ILHD					
0695	N5201M	D-ILHC						
0696	N51684	(D-ILHD)	D-ILHA					
0697	N5057F	N595DM	N585DM					
0698	N5148N	N619TC						
0699	N5266F	N699CJ						
0700	N51342	N884JG						
0701	N5250P	N805P						

Production complete, replaced by the Citation M2

Note: In 1993-94, Cessna developed a military jet trainer from the Model 525 for the US JPATS contract evaluation. It was given the model number 526 and used many 525 parts, although the complete aircraft bore no actual resemblance to the CitationJet. For the record, two prototypes were built, N526JT c/n 704, ff 20Dec93, and N526JP c/n 705, ff 02Mar94.

CESSNA 525 CITATION M2

C/n	Identities			

CITATION M2

0800	N40049	[ff 23Aug13]		N800CZ
0801	N4009F	N123TF		
0802	N4021E	N46EW		
0803	N4030W	N186DL		
0804	N40339	N600VM		
0805	N40366	N958MG		
0806	N4042H	N778LC	N778EC	N104LW
0807	N4058A	N480WB		
0808	N40595	N525HL		
0809	N4076A	N133TJ		
0810	N4076J	N260TT		
0811	N4078H	N1TG	N70LH	
0812	N4092E	N71FB		
0813	N40938	N94972	N1RD	
0814	N4095H	N371SF		
0815	N4107D	N525MM		
0816	N4110T	N30BP		
0817	N40512	N318JH		
0818	N4059H	N123AD		
0819	N4073S	N525JD		
0820	N4074M	N525PZ	N625PZ	
0821	N4074Z	N194SF	N77KN	
0822	N4075L	N822CC	N28FD	
0823	N4075X	N4ST	N888TF	N889TF
0824	N40753	N824MT	JA525M	
0825	N4076Z	N825MT		
0826	N4077P	N525TG		
0827	N40770	N525HQ		
0828	N4078A	N828MT	N316CW	N930AP
0829	N4078L	N5L	N6PS	
0830	N4078M	N63YA		
0831	N4078T	N71SY		
0832	N40780	N661BP		
0833	N4079L	N265DA	N262DA	
0834	N4079S	N834FW	ZS-FCW	
0835	N4080M	N30NS		
0836	N40805	N42AL		
0837	N4081C	N427KP		
0838	N4081M	N575TM		
0839	N4081C	N575RE		
0840	N4082U	N304SG	N525LS	
0841	N4082Y	PR-FRC		
0842	N4083J	(LX-FDJ)	N5KJ	
0843	N4085C	PR-FHI		
0844	N4085D	N94980	N844MM	
0845	N4085Y	PP-PRB		
0846	N4085Z	PR-RIY		
0847	N40851	N248SE		
0848	N40854	G-CMTO		
0849	N4086L	PP-OEG		
0850	N40863	N855ED		
0851	N40864	T7-FOZ		
0852	N4087F	N214RT	[dbr Orlando International, parted out]	
0853	N40878	N525CG		
0854	N40049	N696MM	D-IQXX	
0855	N4009F	N277JB		
0856	N4021E	VH-WMY		
0857	N4030W	OY-MUS	N621JA	
0858	N40366	C-FBCI		
0859	N4042H	M-CARA		
0860	N4058A	N408RK		
0861	N40595	N1WW	N861CG	
0862	N4076A	N862MT	HB-VPH	
0863	N4076J	N990FV		
0864	N4092E	LX-FDJ	M-RENT	
0865	N40938	N865MT		
0866	N4095H	N866ST		
0867	N4107D	N970MM		
0868	N40512	N907LW		
0869	N4059H	N725CG		
0870	N4073S	N135RU		
0871	N4074M	N819R		
0872	N4075L	N525GL		

CESSNA 525 CITATION M2

C/n	Identities		
0873	N4075X	N842AW	
0874	N40753	I-MCAM	
0875	N4076Z	N875MT	N741WY
0876	N4077P	N876MS	
0877	N40770	N921XT	
0878	N4078A	N878MT	N487CB
0879	N4078L	N188SB	
0880	N40780	N4997	
0881	N4079L	N915DH	
0882	N4079S	N52KH	N882MZ
0883	N4080M	N883MT	
0884	N4081C	N813FM	
0885	N4082H	N880WC	
0886	N4082U	N886MT	N986PR
0887	N4082Y	N887SB	
0888	N4083J	N888MQ	N1482B
0889	N4085A	N95KL	
0890	N4085C	N890MT	
0891	N4085D	N52ZG	
0892	N4085S	OY-RAW	G-ORAW
0893	N4085Y	N893A	N219GR
0894	N4085Z	N689HC	
0895	N40854	N927AA	
0896	N4086H	N96MU	N858DP
0897	N4086L	N97MU	N106MJ
0898	N40863	N898DV	N26DV
0899	N4087B	C-GTTS	
0900	N4087F	N525AU	
0901	N40878	N901GG	
0902	N4088T	N902MZ	
0903	N4088U	N154RP	N903TA*
0904	N4088Z	N904MT	N5FL
0905	N4089Y	N905MZ	(PP-JDF)
0906	N40049	N906MT	N906RR
0907	N4021E	N907MT	N219HF
0908	N4030W	N525KH	
0909	N40366	N329CS	N2U
0910	N4042H	N780DC	
0911	N40595	YU-MPC	
0912	N4076A	(PR-CYJ)	N7132C
0913	N4076J	N715TT	
0914	N4078H	N264YU	
0915	N40938	LV-GMQ	
0916	N4095H	I-FVAB	
0917	N4107D	N917AP	
0918	N4110T	F-HBTV	
0919	N40512	N919MZ	N19RC
0920	N4073S	N920MZ	N655WE
0921	N4074M	N650VM	
0922	N4074Z	N54RE	
0923	N4075L	LV-GQT	
0924	N40753	N522WP	
0925	N4076Z	PR-HFT	
0926	N4077P	N460RM	
0927	N40770	N2KH	
0928	N4078L	G-OREZ	
0929	N4078M	SP-KOW	
0930	N4078T	N525FM	
0931	N4079L	PP-CTT	
0932	N4079S	N684PS	
0933	N4080M	N933RG	
0934	N40805	(SP-RUS)	N934CW
0935	N4081C	LV-GUL	
0936	N4082H	LV-GUF	
0937	N4082U	N20160	N16GS
0938	N4082Y	N90PZ	
0939	N4083J	N522KL	
0940	N4084A	N125RK	HL8219
0941	N4085C	N313SP	
0942	N4085D	N287CB	
0943	N4085S	N90519	RP-C5606
0944	N4085Y	N944KK	
0945	N40854	N68KK	
0946	N4086H	D-ICCB	
0947	N4086L	N20537	
0948	N40863	N420JB	N711JB

CESSNA 525 CITATION M2

C/n	Identities	
0949	N40864	
0950	N4087B	N101JW
0951	N4087F	N829BC
0952	N40878	N116ML
0953	N4088P	N20483
0954	N4088T	
0955	N4088U	
0956	N4088Z	N63TR
0957	N4089Y	
0958	N40049	
0959	N4004F	
0960	N4021E	
0961	N4030W	
0962	N40339	
0963	N40366	
0964	N4042H	
0965	N4058A	
0966	N40595	
0967	N4076A	
0968	N4076J	
0969	N4078H	
0970		
0971		
0972		
0973		
0974		
0975		
0976		
0977		
0978		
0979		
0980		
0981		
0982		
0983		
0984		
0985		
0986		
0987		
0988		
0989		
0990		

CESSNA 525A CITATIONJET CJ2

C/n	Identities								
708	N2CJ	[ff 27Apr99 McConnell AFB, Wichita, KS – converted from original C525 prototype c/n 702 qv]							
	N244CJ	[test-bed for Williams FJ44-4A engine used on the CJ4, ff 02Apr07; cx Nov10, wfu]							
0001	N525AZ	N529PC							
0002	N5252	N765CT	N400WD						
0003	N5148N	N132CJ	N525DT						
0004	N52136	N142CJ	N200KP	N692JM	(N699JM)	N308GT	N7773A	PP-GSM	N713JL
0005	N5235G	N552CJ	N372CT	OY-LLA	I-LALL	9H-ALL			
0006	N5204D	(N411PB)	N411GC	N800WC	N245SP				
0007	N5213S	N7CC	(N8CQ)	N525CC	N257AR	PR-RAQ	N410JL		
0008	N52141	N900EB	N901EB						
0009	N5235G	N525LC	F-HAPP	M-AJDM	N457MD	(N860SC)			
0010	N5194J	N121CP	N25MB						
0011	N51881	N567JP	OE-FLP	[w/o Milan/Linate, Italy, 13Oct14]					
0012	N525MP	N525MA							
0013	N5201M	N4115Q	N8940	N894C	(N177RE)				
0014	N110MG	N110MQ	N18TF						
0015	N125DG	N606XG	N629PA	F-HASF	N610SF				
0016	N5207A	N306CJ	(N547AC)						
0017	N5162W	N172CJ	HB-VOE	LX-VOE	OE-FXE				
0018	N5148N	N96G	N96NJ	N307LJ					
0019	N51942	N57GH	N67GH	S5-BBB	F-GXRL	N5YD			
0020	N52141	N904AM	N323LM	N823L					
0021	N525TG	[cx 16Sep09, corrosion damage]							
0022	N5165T	N217W	(N117W)	N630TF					
0023	N5135K	N525PF							
0024	N5216A	N525TJ	N915MP						
0025	N51396	N550T	N550TB						
0026	N5203S	N126CJ	D-IMYA	D-IHAP	EK-52526	EP-MNZ			
0027	N5194J	N420CH	N420EH						
0028	N5218T	(N592DR)	D-IBBB	N592DR					
0029	N5132T	N92CJ	D-IKJS	OE-FRS					
0030	N5223Y	N302DM	D-ISJP						
0031	N5204D	N312CJ	VP-BFC	M-XONE	G-SONE				
0032	N5250E	D-IOBU	D-IOBO	D-IGIT	N525ME				
0033	N163PB	HB-VNO	(D-IETZ)	EC-JJU	F-HMSG				
0034	N5211F	D-IJOA							
0035	N51564	N288G							
0036	N5246Z	(D-IJOA)	D-IEVX	[w/o 08Oct01 Milan-Linate A/P, Italy]					
0037	N5221Y	N401LG							
0038	N5235G	I-IMMG	N800GF						
0039	N5223P	N842HS	(N525L)	N900HA					
0040	N525HB	N525VP							
0041	N43ND	D-IHHN	N505RM						
0042	N52352	PR-JET	N954AK*						
0043	N52002	N432CJ	D-IEKU						
0044	N5241Z	PR-JST							
0045	N5214L	N3ST	N525H	N219CM					
0046	N51246	N40RL	N46JW	N46NT	N707LL				
0047	N5148N	N2250G	N225GG	VT-TAX					
0048	N5183U	PT-FTC							
0049	N51575	D-IEFD	OE-FHB	M-CTLX	9A-JSC				
0050	N525DL								
0051	N6M	(N606MM)	N6JR	N415SL	G-OCJZ				
0052	N51881	D-ISCH							
0053	N5194J	PT-FTE							
0054	N5161J	(EI-OPM)	D-IAAS	PH-ECL	OO-SKA	VH-ZGP	N528CJ	N417MH	
0055	N5163C	N207BS	N525ZZ						
0056	N5202D	N743JG							
0057	N57EJ	[w/o 07Oct02 Plainville, CT; canx 08Mar05]							
0058	N52035	N811RC	N525KT						
0059	N59CJ	N917SL							
0060	N6877L	N57HC	N525RW	N854FM					
0061	N5214J	PR-TOP	N272HT						
0062	N5125J	N30HD	N82BB						
0063	N5135A	N263CJ	N5208F	VH-MOR					
0064	N513SK	EC-IEB	I-OMRA	N746CX	N20JK				
0065	N5136J	N225EL	N225WW	N55KT					
0066	N51396	N741PC							
0067	N5141F	N525PM	M-PMCN						
0068	N51444	N69FH	N69AH	N315MC	N124H				
0069	N51564	N757CP							
0070	N5157E	D-ILAM							
0071	N51575	N34RL	N701SF						
0072	N5120U	N65PZ	(N65PX)	N65BZ	N77ND				

CJ2

C/n	Identities							
0073	N5165T	I-LVNB	N295					
0074	N5125J	N222NF						
0075	N51246	HP-1461	N52AG	PR-REG				
0076	N5156D	N1277E						
0077	N5148N	N377GS	N346US					
0078	N5162W	N113BG						
0079	N51872	N117W	N717HA					
0080	N5135K	N525EZ	N525TK	F-HEKO	N788JB	N746JS		
0081	N51342	N414FW						
0082	N5183V	N282CJ	OE-FGL	G-CGSB	N58KY	LX-JCL		
0083	N975DM	N975DN	G-EDCL	G-CJTV	N716JS			
0084	N525DG	N523DG	N512TB	N207MM				
0085	N5185J	N85JV						
0086	N5132T	N520JM	N759R	N823DT	N67SB	N970ZG		
0087	N474PC							
0088	N569DM							
0089	OY-JET	[crashed into sea 15May05 off Atlantic City-Bader Field, NJ; repaired]					N525SA	PR-WOB
0090	N475DH							
0091	N8940	N431MC	(N548ME)	N518ME				
0092	N21RA							
0093	N5216A	N96SK	N93PE	N98PE	N954RM	N327MC		
0094	N942CJ	VH-RJB						
0095	N5221Y	I-DEUM						
0096	N5223D	N96CJ	JA525G	N96NA				
0097	N97CJ							
0098	N5223Y	N57HG	N57HC	N57HG	HI1005			
0099	N5223P	N444RH	N777HN	N747HN	CC-AES	N180YA		
0100	N170TM							
0101	N1255J	(N533JF)	N125BJ					
0102	N888KL	D-IWIR						
0103	N5218R	N800VT	N869AC					
0104	N80C							
0105	N13M	N91A	N878JP					
0106	N5148B	D-IUAC	OE-FUX					
0107	N525WD							
0108	N5136J	D-ICMS						
0109	N692JM	N301EL	N22LX	N109VP	C-GVSN	N707EL		
0110	N451AJ							
0111	N219FL	N971TB	[w/o in hangar fire 12Sep07 Danbury, CT]					
0112	N51575	N525U	N701TF	N620GB	N112VP	N920NL		
0113	N525VV	G-OCJT	M-WMWM					
0114	N726RP							
0115	N115CJ							
0116	N5233J	N711BE	N411BE	N46BE				
0117	N5214K	PT-FTG						
0118	N5163C	N464C	N971TB	N971TE	N718AL			
0119	N525DV	PP-CML	N119CJ					
0120	N5130J	N144EM	N220JD	N35CT				
0121	N121YD	N5YD	YV2152					
0122	N5135A	N224WD	N1901					
0123	N5203S	N37BG	PT-ASX					
0124	N27CJ	N523BT						
0125	N52038	N125CE	N525CC	N525CG	D-IBJJ			
0126	N534CJ	N999WE	VT-MON					
0127	N5211A	N12GS	N112GS					
0128	N5204D	N525CK						
0129	N129SG	N98DH	N715JS					
0130	N51396	N525JD	N550KR	N1962				
0131	N51564	N20GP	N340SP	N109AP				
0132	N5211F	N75PP	D-ITOP	N500SD				
0133	N251KD							
0134	N323SK							
0135	N5211Q	N4RP	(N114RP)	N70KW				
0136	N5141F	N345CJ						
0137	N717VB	N921AP						
0138	N722TS							
0139	N5228Z	N526HV	N365TB					
0140	N140DA							
0141	N51872	PT-FTR	N141JV	N6ZE				
0142	N5207A	OE-FPS	F-HMBG					
0143	D-ISUN							
0144	N144YD							
0145	N7GZ	N192MG*						
0146	N1220W							
0147	N5188W	VP-BJR	D-IVVA	N876UC	N876UD			
0148	N5132T	N148FB						

CJ2

C/n	Identities							
0149	N90CJ							
0150	N525GM	OE-FRA	N720SL	N750SL				
0151	N122SM	D-ISCO	SP-KKB*					
0152	N123JW	N128JW	N791JK					
0153	N5233P	N500SV	N153CJ					
0154	N5091J	N708GP						
0155	N5180C	N105PT	EC-KES					
0156	N522KN	N256CJ	JA525B					
0157	N5270E	N88KC	N913DC					
0158	N158CJ	SP-KCK						
0159	N5026	N74GL						
0160	N525KR	N525KP						
0161	N5100J	N28MH	N28NH	N525FF				
0162	N335JJ							
0163	N5151D	ZS-CJT	VT-NJB					
0164	N164CJ	OO-DDA						
0165	N5243K	N30AD						
0166	N5218R	D-IAMO	9A-JSD					
0167	N51806	D-ILDL						
0168	N767W	D-IHRA	JY-FMK	D-IHRA	N311HA	(PR-HBO)	PR-HBH	
0169	N5262W	F-GPUJ	N2796					
0170	N915RJ	C6-LVU	N170VP	C6-EVU	VT-BJA	N170MR		
0171	N271CJ	(F-GPSS)	CC-CHE					
0172	N179DV	N706TF	N525PB	N526PB	N388KT*			
0173	N525MR							
0174	N5076K	D-IDMH	N613LB	N745JS				
0175	N525SM							
0176	N100JS	N319R	OE-FYH	VT-TAY	OE-FYP	N525LR	N812PJ	
0177	N55KT	N25LZ						
0178	N52655	N7715X	N80AX	N44FJ	N103CL			
0179	N179FZ	OO-FLN	N237MP					
0180	N604LJ							
0181	N5218T	N93AK	N93AQ	N525CE				
0182	N777CJ	N219CQ						
0183	N283CJ	N183TX						
0184	N357J	N1QL	(N357J)	N184CD				
0185	N5257V	N65CK	N65CR	PR-TAP				
0186	N5247U	N350BV						
0187	N187MG	N252PC	N956HC					
0188	N5138J	N188JR	N837AC	N505BG				
0189	N5124F	N777DY	N189MS					
0190	N5141F	N680JB	G-OODM	N646TG	SE-RIN			
0191	N776LB	G-TBEA	M-TBEA					
0192	N688DB	(N688DP)	N193PP					
0193	N5183U	D-IKAL	F-HAMG					
0194	N806MN	N194SJ	[w/o Santa Monica, CA, 29Sep13]					
0195	N51942	D-IMAX						
0196	N5166T	D-INOB						
0197	N197CJ	OO-SKY						
0198	N5162W	N57FL						
0199	N5152X	I-GOSF	LN-AVA	N248RF				
0200	N5203S	F-GZUJ	CS-DGQ	LX-DGQ	N200FT			
0201	N888GL							
0202	N202CJ	N719WP	G-EEBJ	G-MROO	SE-RKS	G-ZEUZ		
0203	N736LB	OE-FSG	N460RV					
0204	"N5188W"+	[+marks as quoted, already current at the time on a homebuilt]					OE-FCY	OK-FCY
0205	N5241Z	N205YY						
0206	N29MR	OO-CIV						
0207	N5117U	N1267B	VT-JSP	N740JS				
0208	N400HT							
0209	N5085E	OY-UCA						
0210	N5214K	N280DM	N28DM	OE-FCU	N721SC			
0211	N515EV							
0212	N5226B	N104PC	N702FM					
0213	N5244W	N213CJ	(OE-FJR)	ES-LUX	G-EDCM	N714JS		
0214	N51511	N1DM	N7QM	F-HMPR				
0215	N748RE	N748RF	N420CR					
0216	N51246	OY-GGR	EC-JMS	N188JB	N788JS			
0217	N5211F	N67GH	N167GH	N771EM	TG-BEA			
0218	D-IPVD							
0219	N5247U	F-HEOL	N72JS					
0220	N800RL	N880RL	N75HF	N680SB				
0221	N5153K	N27VQ	YV305T	N27VQ				
0222	N778MA	VT-DOV						
0223	D-IWAN	OK-PBT						
0224	N5264N	N424CJ	N576SC					

CJ2 / CJ2+

C/n	Identities				
0225	N67BC	N67CC			
0226	N5266F	N526DV	PR-CNP	N526DV	
0227	N5174W	N761KG	N450TR	N795DE*	
0228	N5154J	PR-NTX			
0229	N5223P	SX-SMH	OE-FVB	OO-OSD	OE-FAG
0230	N5136J	D-IGRO			
0231	N5211A	D-IWIN	N484CT	N484CE	N406LA*
0232	N5245D	[re-serialled 525A0300 q.v. below]			
0233	N5236L	D-IBBE	D-IOHL		
0234	N313CR				
0235	N235KS	C-FTRM	N71EA	VT-BIP	
0236	N5259Y	TC-VYN	VH-IYG		
0237	N5263U	N333BD			
0238	N5117U	N1290Y	N228FS	N227FS	N777AG
0239	N5120U	(OE-FEB)	OE-FIN	OM-OPE	OM-FTS
0240	N5194B	N77VR	(N109TW)		
0241	N52081	N777QP	PR-CFC	N742JS	
0242	N5073G	PH-JNE	N962RA		
0243	N5165T	N551WM			
0244	N52086	N13087	JA525C		

CJ2+

C/n	Identities						
0300	N5245D	[converted from 525A0232 ff 3.4.05, certificated 03Oct05]	N432MA	N486TT	(N486TL)	(N466TT)	N490RM
0301	N52609	N301PG	N525HD				
0302	N52690	N302CJ	N6M	N302CJ	N832MG		
0303	N5260M	N85JE	OY-GLO	N525RU	PR-RHG	N525AY	
0304	N52699	N912GW					
0305	N5213S	N660S					
0306	N5180K	N306JR	N358WC				
0307	N5239J	N674AS	N583SB				
0308	N5188N	N308CJ	N110FD				
0309	N309CJ	M-TSGP	N309CJ				
0310	N5267G	N926JJ					
0311	N5211A	N1317X	JA001T				
0312	N5000R	N786AC	(D-IPAC)				
0313	N5157E	D-IBBS					
0314	N5096S	N1DM	N791DM	N747JJ	(N311DB)		
0315	N5094D	N1414P					
0316	N5165T	PR-NNP	N275ML	N48JM			
0317	N9UD	PR-HAL					
0318	N5268V	N525TA	YV289T	YV2844			
0319	N967TC	N967TG					
0320	N5188A	F-ONYY	(OO-STH)				
0321	N13195	OE-FII	OM-BJB				
0322	N51575	(LX-WGR)	F-GMIR	D-IMHA			
0323	N5132T	N65CK					
0324	N5228Z	N586ED	N586FD				
0325	N437JD	N487JD	PP-BBS				
0326	N5223P	OE-FXX	N207BG				
0327	N5226B	N525RF					
0328	N52352	D-IBCT					
0329	N5147B	N525PH	N697DC*				
0330	N5231S	D-IFLY	D-IFEY	N525DR			
0331	N5148B	OY-REN	HB-VPC				
0332	N50282	D-IOBU	D-IOBO	D-IOBC	N725AT		
0333	N929BC	N939BC	LV-GWZ				
0334	N52699	G-HCSA					
0335	N525LD						
0336	N336CJ	N15YD					
0337	N5063P	N525XD	PP-MEO				
0338	N722SM						
0339	N500NB	N54SL					
0340	N5086W	D-IFIS	SX-GVA	9H-ZRH			
0341	N5064Q	N241CJ	HB-VOL	LX-VOL	OE-FXM		
0342	N18TD	N178WG	N615WP				
0343	N5108G	D-IFDN	(D-IHTM)	HB-VER			
0344	N5200Z	N45MH					
0345	N5153K	N9180K	PR-NGT				
0346	N525EP	N585EP					
0347	N5262X	M-ICRO	D-IPCH				

CJ2+

C/n	Identities				
0348	N5076J	S5-BAS	D-ISJA		
0349	N52609	N535TV	N535JF		
0350	N5260Y	N117W	N114W		
0351	N909MN				
0352	N51896	N525HG			
0353	N929VC				
0354	N5101J	OE-FOA			
0355	N5079V	D-IWBL	F-HRSC		
0356	N5197A	N617CB	PR-FSA		
0357	N50820	N624PL	D-IVVB	D-IKBO	
0358	N5061F	D-IEFA	N584SB		
0359	N52682	N12742	JA359C		
0360	N52655	N13474	G-HGRC	G-SYGC	G-PEER
0361	N5157E	N361JR	(N322PD)	N322DP	
0362	N51564	OE-FGB	N147WE		
0363	N5197M	D-IETZ	N363VP		
0364	N5090V	D-ITOR			
0365	N50736	OE-FLA	N209AM		
0366	N366CJ	N999QE	N612JD		
0367	N367CJ	D-IAKN			
0368	N5032K	N93AK			
0369	N5181U	OE-FLB	N530DW	N500VA	N525KY
0370	N51993	N370JJ	N370RP		
0371	N51160	N574BB	N933MW		
0372	N5103J	OY-NDP			
0373	N5270E	N41174	VT-BRT		
0374	N5108G	N245RA			
0375	N51055	OE-FOE	HB-VPE		
0376	N51444	PR-JVF			
0377	N5211F	N950DB	N153TJ		
0378	N5214J	N41184	VT-VID		
0379	N5270J	N896P			
0380	N5168Y	N5192U	JA021R	N5192U	
0381	N52627	EC-KOI	N538CF		
0382	N5241Z	N129CK	D-IPAD*		
0383	N5120U	HB-VWA			
0384	N5218R	N118CJ			
0385	N50820	HB-VOP	N630PA	PR-AIC	
0386	N5270P	N2040E	JA516J		
0387	N5268M	N111JW	N525RG	C-GVCQ	
0388	N5267T	G-CROO	N525NG		
0389	N5153K	M-PSAC	D-ITMA		
0390	N52639	OE-FKO			
0391	"N52391"+	[+test marks as quoted, already current at the time on a Cessna T-50]	N2151Q	JA391C	
0392	N52081	PR-ARS	N606AK		
0393	N51896	N775TF			
0394	N5152X	C-FITC			
0395	N5154J	XA-UJY			
0396	N5162W	N400CV			
0397	N5148B	G-ODAG	G-TWOP		
0398	N5270K	OE-FNB	LZ-FNB		
0399	N5048U	N810PF			
0400	N5235G	D-IMMM			
0401	N5094D	YU-VER	ZS-SOM	N595CH	
0402	N5263U	N2224G	VT-PSB		
0403	N5103J	N250BL	PR-AGC	N525AL	
0404	N5103J	N85ER	N404CF	N70FA	
0405	N5180C	N405CJ	N413FC		
0406	N5072X	PR-WAT	N775AT		
0407	N5225K	N407CJ	N59JN		
0408	N5248V	G-NMRM	OH-SWI		
0409	N5270J	D-IPCC	N409VP		
0410	N5165P	N2297X	VT-BPS		
0411	N5211F	YU-BUU	N411CJ		
0412	N5141F	9A-DWA			
0413	N52086	N19KT	N935BB		
0414	N5165T	N208BG			
0415	N5225K	OE-FHC			
0416	N51396	N108KJ			
0417	N5090A	PR-RJN			
0418	N5265N	N677SL	N642WW		
0419	N52655	N785MT			
0420	N5130J	N10AU	N10GU	N420CX	
0421	N5265B	N379R			
0422	N5117U	N757EM	HB-VPB	ZS-PDZ	
0423	N51817	N806CJ	S5-BAR	N525JN	

CJ2+

C/n	Identities					
0424	N5136J	N41212	N285JE	N285FW		
0425	N5155G	N2044S	N96SW			
0426	N426CJ	N476JD				
0427	N5066U	I-CALZ	OE-FCZ			
0428	N51396	SP-DLB	(D-IANP)	D-INDA	N428JF	
0429	N5048U	D-ISCV				
0430	N5076L	N2046D	(VT-BJC)	N501KE		
0431	N5163C	OO-ACC				
0432	N5093D	N10WZ				
0433	N5183V	N433CJ	D-IJKP	OE-FPM		
0434	N5200R	9A-CLN	F-HCCP	N434CF		
0435	N52081	VP-BRL	SE-RKM			
0436	N5257V	N2051A	(VT-BJD)	7T-VNF		
0437	N5165T	OE-FPK				
0438	N5026Q	N438TA	EI-ECR			
0439	N52141	N125WT	N923GS			
0440	N52086	PR-KYK				
0441	N50522	N440CJ	N127FJ			
0442	N52655	N2064M	N494TB			
0443	N52645	D-IDAS	OH-SWJ			
0444	N5235G	N20669	D-IWWP	OY-JSW		
0445	N50282	N145SF	N503AS			
0446	N5068F	N2067E	N446CJ	LN-BAC	N446TA	2-GOLF
0447	N5265B	N447CJ	N312SB	D-IDWC		
0448	N52446	N360PK	N368PK	N507AS		
0449	N5211F	N525EG				
0450	N5180K	N926PY				
0451	N5245L	N451FP				
0452	N5090A	N721ES				
0453	N5161J	N484CW	N238RM			
0454	N5057F	N234CJ				
0455	N50054	YR-TOY	N455VP	OK-MAR		
0456	N5136J	C-GTRG				
0457	N5268V	ZS-PAJ	T7-APP			
0458	N52235	N6245J	N674JM	ZS-DIY		
0459	N5180C	D-IEVB	N459VP			
0460	N5257V	N525AP	N314BK*			
0461	N5267G	N461CJ	N792CB			
0462	N5197A	OK-ILA	OK-ILC	F-HIJD		
0463	N5207A	(N234CJ)	PP-KYK			
0464	N5185J	N64LW				
0465	N5000R	N380AR	N380CR	N237PT		
0466	N5214L	N466CJ				
0467	N5090V	N525HL	N467CJ	N540AS		
0468	N5090A	N461CQ	N580AS			
0469	N469CJ	N997SS	N469VP	N469LH		
0470	N5206T	(D-IWWP)	N6033R	VT-TVM		
0471	N5241Z	PP-CIT	N369KL			
0472	N5157E	PP-FRI				
0473	N52369	G-CGUZ	N473CJ	N981WA		
0474	N50522	N74JE				
0475	N5263D	N858SD	N358K			
0476	N5245D	N821PP				
0477	N52114	N477CJ	N22LX			
0478	N5270P	N478CJ	N595DM			
0479	N5130J	M-ICRO				
0480	N52059	N5VU				
0481	N5264A	N518AR	N481VP	N715DL		
0482	N5202D	(XA-TTC)	XA-UPZ			
0483	N5223Y	N188MP				
0484	N5265N	N639TC				
0485	N50625	G-POWG	OO-KOR			
0486	N5214L	(D-IOBC)	D-IOBU	D-IOBO		
0487	N5264N	D-IPCC				
0488	N5120U	N1895C	N1875C*			
0489	N51743	N53SF	N533F			
0490	N5214K	N82KA	N490VP			
0491	N50756	N535CM	N535VP	XA-TTQ		
0492	N5155G	N278KP	C-FCEU			
0493	N51869	N493CJ				
0494	N5212M	N573BC	N525RL			
0495	N5218T	OO-AMR				
0496	N52446	M-IWPS	D-IWPS			
0497	N5245L	N30ST				
0498	N5269X	D-IMGW				
0499	N5269Z	D-IFLY	OE-FLA			

CJ2+

C/n	Identities				
0500	N5235G	N6061U	N5235G	D-ILIB	D-IVVB
0501	N5109W	G-DAGS	D-IENE		
0502	N5030U	D-IMAH			
0503	N5264M	C-FASW			
0504	N50321	N889SW			
0505	N50543	PT-STM	N364BC		
0506	N5145V	N375DS	(N759R)	G-LFBD	
0507	N5061P	N78RK			
0508	N5247U	C-GZAS			
0509	N5040E	PR-KRT			
0510	N50736	C-GASR			
0511	N5125J	N242AS	C-FIAS		
0512	N5096S	N138GT	N38GT		
0513	N5241R	N759R	N759G		
0514	N5202D	N106CH			
0515	N5223Y	(C-FASP)	PR-MSZ		
0516	N5214K	N575DM	N525DM		
0517	N5270J	N327PD	N517PD		
0518	N51038	D-IVIV			
0519	N5101J	N242AS	C-FASP		
0520	N5264S	N520SL	VT-RKA	N525EW	
0521	N5188A	N545DL	TC-CJA		
0522	N675AB				
0523	N51246	PT-FLB			
0524	N5261R	C-FASR			

Production complete

CESSNA 525B CITATIONJET CJ3

C/n	Identities									
711	N3CJ	[ff 17Apr03]								
0001	N753CJ	[ff 08Aug03]		(N929SF)	N53SF	N535F	N887RB			
0002	N763CJ	N62SH	(N68SH)							
0003	N52059	N103CJ	N432LW	(N627BB)						
0004	N5207A	N1308L	N6525B							
0005	N5270E	N105CJ	N748CX							
0006	N5227G	N1278D	N417C	N525DE						
0007	N5239J	N7CC								
0008	N52627	N51HF	N946RM							
0009	N51806	N777NJ	N5GU							
0010	N5097H	N917RG								
0011	N110MG	N585PK	D-CELE	N551CF	N823LT					
0012	N5093D	N172DH	M-UPCO	N312VP	N525U					
0013	N5228Z	N831V	F-HBPP							
0014	N114CJ	N300ET	(N525JV)	N525BY						
0015	N5163K	N4RH	N747KR	N747KE						
0016	N50820	N200GM	(D-CORA)	S5-BAW	9H-JRF	SE-RLP				
0017	N614B									
0018	N51896	N52ET								
0019	N79LB	N11LB	N319VP							
0020	N52038	N899RR	N33UM							
0021	N5073G	N325RC								
0022	N5109W	N528CE	N487TT							
0023	N51055	N77M	N15C							
0024	N5221Y	N525GM	(N525GN)	N525GY						
0025	N5201J	N7NE	(N71NE)	N7NQ	N179WC					
0026	N162EC									
0027	"N5188W"+	[+marks as quoted, already current on a homebuilt]					N1287D	ZK-TBM	VH-ARZ	P2-MEH
0028	N5085E	PR-SPO	N50LV	N52RS						
0029	N726AG									
0030	N5145P	N401CS	N786JS							
0031	N303CJ	N103DS								
0032	N52433	N137BG								
0033	N5243K	N404CS	N783JS							
0034	N52446	N65VM								
0035	N51511	N93JW								
0036	N5244F	N405CS	N779JS							
0037	N52653	C-FXTC	N37VP	N71F						
0038	N51942	N100RC	N100RQ	N159JS						
0039	N526DG	N525DG	N706RT							
0040	N52369	N550T	N540VP	N518GH	N2020					
0041	N525PC	N3CT								
0042	N5163K	N69FH	N909EC	N42VP	N721MA	N573BB				
0043	N5183V	N406CS	N780JS							
0044	N144AL									
0045	N5221Y	N408CS	N781JS							
0046	N5124F	N860DD	N46VR	N52WK						
0047	N50820	PR-EBD	N347TX	N725HS*						
0048	N853JL	N92MA	N67JR							
0049	N628CB									
0050	N409CS	N784JS								
0051	N5148N	N525L								
0052	N999SM									
0053	N53NW									
0054	N5200U	N535GH	N500TS							
0055	N5151D	N4GA								
0056	N5093L	N156TW	N748RM	N11TH						
0057	N5239J	N999LB	N999UB	N733CJ						
0058	N5066U	N885BT								
0059	N412CS	N782JS								
0060	N5250P	N125DG								
0061	N361TL									
0062	N5269A	XC-GDC								
0063	N5226B	N123CJ	N128CJ	N611CS						
0064	N5263S	N1CH	N63CJ							
0065	N5269J	N105CQ	LN-HOT	N255RA						
0066	N362JM	N6243M	N602MJ							
0067	N51160	N96MR	OM-LBG	N67CX	N310EG					
0068	N5269Z	N51JJ	N245VP							
0069	N5231S	N3UD	N535DT							
0070	N51055	N279DV	N279D							
0071	N51511	N531CM								
0072	N5214L	N107CQ	N8106V	N808JN						
0073	N51995	N899MA	(N550RB)	N575HP						

CJ3

C/n	Identities				
0074	N5221Y	N742AR			
0075	N528JC	D-CJAK	N390TG	N233FT	
0076	N5207A	N1KA	N181KA		
0077	N52433	N7877T			
0078	N525DR	VH-MIF	N523CB		
0079	N52081	N835DM	N25CK	N79VP	C-GTSX
0080	N52352	N380CJ	N451GP		
0081	N52457	N868EM	N522NJ	N525EE	
0082	N413CS	N785JS			
0083	N5166T	N13001	HS-MCL		
0084	N51744	N841AM			
0085	N51881	D-CLAT	N885LA		
0086	N51993	D-CKJS	(D-CDIG)	D-CVHM	D-CFXJ	N4S
0087	N687DS				
0088	N5264U	N525MP			
0089	N5076J	N525EZ	[w/o in hangar fire 12Sep07 Danbury, CT]		
0090	N5197A	N417CS	N90CZ		
0091	N5214J	N219L	N219F	XA-ACR	
0092	N52653	N852SP			
0093	N5259Y	N93PE			
0094	N83TF				
0095	N5214K	N100JS	N100JZ	N423BB	
0096	N5270J	LX-GAP	3A-MRG	N816FC	
0097	N5216A	N888RK	N131MJ		
0098	N5270E	N87VM			
0099	N777NJ				
0100	N50820	N77M	(N563M)	N85GT	
0101	N52113	D-CTEC	PP-AVX	N511VP	CS-DVH
0102	N5213S	N812JM	N3JM	N812JM	N45BE
0103	N5188N	(N103CJ)	N417KM	N221LC	N443PW
0104	N5192E	N5216A	N560PJ	N590PJ	N525GT	(N525GB)
0105	N5135K	N247MV	N651SD		
0106	N5218T	N106JT			
0107	N709PG	D-COBO	D-CEMS		
0108	N5218T	N418CS			
0109	N5145J	N1255J	(N927CC)		
0110	N51246	N28MH			
0111	N5101J	N96PD	N96PB		
0112	N731WH				
0113	N5263U	N55GP			
0114	N52234	N114CJ	N901MV	(D-CELE)	N96G
0115	N5207A	N420CS	N51EM		
0116	N5244W	ZS-CJT	N80EP		
0117	N5212M	F-GRUJ	N656SM		
0118	N51143	C-GSSC	N532LW		
0119	N5257V	D-CNOB	SE-RMB		
0120	N5211A	D-CEFD			
0121	N52229	N423CS			
0122	N12GS				
0123	N73EM	N73EL	N515TX		
0124	N5203S	PR-ALC			
0125	N5194J	OE-GPO	C-FNCB		
0126	N5030U	N621GA	N525KD		
0127	N5268A	N107PT			
0128	N17CN	PR-BIR			
0129	N629EE	PR-ALV			
0130	(N910BH)	N329CJ			
0131	N5057E	N331CJ	N30UD	AP-PFL	AP-ESL
0132	N5058J	N425CS	N516KM		
0133	N5031E	N233MM	N3WS		
0134	N52691	N41ND			
0135	N5059X	OE-GRA			
0136	N5073G	PT-TJS			
0137	N51042	N550MX			
0138	N51942	N356MR	N591MB	N591ME	N745FJ
0139	N52059	N93CW	(N979TX)	G-RGBY	N139CJ
0140	N51612	N42AA	N15PG		
0141	N50756	N238SW			
0142	N28DM				
0143	N5185V	N320BP			
0144	N51055	(C-FXFJ)	N847NG		
0145	N332SB	C-FFCM	N999JA		
0146	CS-DIY	D-CCCG*			
0147	N5168Y	OO-FPC	N147TA		
0148	N52397	N148CJ	M-ELON	M-ELOW	N523LM	N300MV
0149	N5261R	N123CJ			

CJ3

C/n	Identities						
0150	N52626	N317BR	OE-GHG	N562PA	(N562PZ)		
0151	N52086	N420CH					
0152	N5262B	N427CS	N825AV				
0153	N5145P	N28FR	G-ODCM	N55FP			
0154	D-CRAH	N53KJ					
0155	N831FC	N222VR					
0156	N5145V	F-GVUJ					
0157	N5096S	N157JL					
0158	N5180K	(OO-FPD)	OO-FPE				
0159	N50275	N565JP					
0160	N5201J	VP-BUG	M-ASRY	M-ABDN	C-GZAM		
0161	N5268M	D-CMHS					
0162	N503LC	M-YEDC	G-YEDC				
0163	N5267K	N80HB	N80HE				
0164	N5125J	N1314V	N500AS	[cx 10Oct14 – status?]			
0165	N5267T	N428CS					
0166	N5061W	N7814					
0167	N450BV						
0168	N970DM						
0169	N5250P	D-CUBA					
0170	N50543	N996PE					
0171	N5172M	N727YB					
0172	N51780	N535DL					
0173	N5228J	OO-LIE	LX-WEB				
0174	N174SJ						
0175	N149WW						
0176	N5188N	(F-HAFC)	F-GYFC	N108LA			
0177	N5037F	N429CS					
0178	N5203S	F-GSGL					
0179	N5211A	N179CJ	G-OMBI	HB-VTJ			
0180	N5185J	N360CK					
0181	N5239J	N143JT					
0182	N5243K	N535CM	N533CM				
0183	N5062S	N4115H	A6-SAB	F-HBER	SE-RMJ		
0184	N52639	N914FF	N213F				
0185	N5076K	N430CS	N501DJ				
0186	N186CJ	N111JW	N491JL	N491J			
0187	N5076P	PR-MRG	[w/o Sao Paulo/Congonhas, Brazil, 11Nov12; parted out by Dodson Int'l, Rantoul, KS]				N508EA
0188	N541WG	N757PC					
0189	N5197A	N525CF					
0190	N5036Q	N81ER	N190VP	N286N*			
0191	N52626	N379DB					
0192	N5214L	XA-AVX					
0193	N5262B	N1382N	(SX-EDP)	SX-PAP	YU-BTN		
0194	N52645	OY-WWW					
0195	N5202D	N400GG	N400TG				
0196	N396CJ	VH-ANE	VH-NNE				
0197	N5262X	D-CUUU	OO-FYS				
0198	N52069	"VP-BJR"+	[+marks worn at factory]	VP-BRJ	OY-TSA		
0199	N51817	PR-CVC					
0200	N5073G	OO-EDV					
0201	N5260Y	C-FANJ	N211VR	N525NY	N115SM		
0202	N51896	N7CH	(N267CH)	N925EM			
0203	N50776	N328RC					
0204	N5066F	N5WN					
0205	N52682	N428BR					
0206	N52086	C-GPMW					
0207	N5262W	N856BB					
0208	N5180K	N414KD	N8880D				
0209	N5228Z	HB-VOW	N80EA				
0210	N52114	N1DM	N771DM				
0211	N51396	ZS-DPP					
0212	N52235	N711BE	N379B				
0213	N5188A	N527HV					
0214	N52433	N92MS					
0215	N5201J	D-CTEC	OE-GBO	D-CMAN			
0216	N5250E	HB-VWB	N216CJ	N688CK	N831HS		
0217	N52690	D-CASH	OM-VPT	N651TW			
0218	N5201M	N7725D	PR-PLU				
0219	N5243K	OE-GRZ	OE-GBC				
0220	N52136	(D-CJVC)	D-COWB				
0221	N15ZZ						
0222	N5061W	OE-GRU					
0223	N5117U	N229CN	N7773J*				
0224	N5250P	F-HCIC					
0225	N5296X	N27UB	N10TS	N615KJ			

CJ3

C/n	Identities				
0226	N50543	N880MR			
0227	N5211A	LX-DCA	N327TX		
0228	N5000R	N431CS			
0229	N5185J	N826CS			
0230	N5068F	F-GSMG	LX-NCG		
0231	N5247U	OE-GJF	G-TSJF	N539KH	
0232	N52682	D-CPAO	G-PAOL		
0233	N5194J	N956GA			
0234	N5214K	EC-KQO			
0235	N5174W	CS-DGW			
0236	N5151D	N308GT			
0237	N50736	N525WL			
0238	N5062S	N525EZ	M-OODY	N525CR	
0239	N5076P	PR-SCF			
0240	N51160	N240CJ	N75JK	(N204WP)	N4WP*
0241	N5226B	N241KA	N241CJ		
0242	N5227G	N899NH	N242KV		
0243	N5101J	C6-LUV	N528BS		
0244	N5076L	N432CS			
0245	N50776	PR-TBL			
0246	N5266F	N246CZ	N795BM	N800CU	
0247	N5244F	N377GA	J8-JET		
0248	N5109W	N839DM			
0249	N5163C	N608SG			
0250	N5245U	N403CH	N403ND		
0251	N5026Q	N220LC	(N37JK)	N716MB	
0252	N5093L	N941AM	N99RE		
0253	N5270M	N38M	N38MV	PR-SHC	
0254	N5214J	N307PE			
0255	N5181U	M-BIRD	D-CHAT	OE-GJP	
0256	N52627	N6M	N256CJ	N114CL	N256CJ	N145SF
0257	N5197A	N433CS	N32AC		
0258	N5262W	F-HAGA	(D-CFRA)	N99AG	
0259	N5180K	N724CV	UP-CS301		
0260	N5096S	N23BV			
0261	N5223Y	N100DW	N80F	N80FK	
0262	N5218T	N812HF	C-FNFS		
0263	N5270M	N888PS	N934CT		
0264	N5244W	F-GSCR			
0265	N5262B	N227JP	N265DW	N52MW	N52MN
0266	N5218R	N41203	EI-MJC	N330KM	PP-RCA
0267	N5163K	N500WD	N500WJ	N358JJ	
0268	N434CS	N151KD	C-GPLT	N767XT	
0269	N5194B	OM-OPA	D-CDLC	N411TJ	
0270	N5091J	N58JV	N824DM		
0271	N52144	N39GG			
0272	N52352	HB-VWC	N272CJ	N903MC	
0273	N5228Z	N79JS	N798S	N902SS	
0274	N5201J	N436CS	N436EP		
0275	N52690	OE-GNA			
0276	N5214K	N70NF			
0277	N5213K	N2074H	OE-GET	N369GM	PR-MTQ
0278	N50736	N2111W	PR-ADL		
0279	N51160	N279CJ	N2CP		
0280	N5197A	N150MJ	M-MIKE		
0281	N5174W	LX-JET	D-CIAU*		
0282	N5151D	N437CS	N578CJ		
0283	N51872	N283RA			
0284	N5076K	N835CB			
0285	N5093L	N11UD	PT-OOO		
0286	N5066F	D-CPMI	N286VP	N525TK	
0287	N5062S	D-CURA	OO-PAR		
0288	N5076P	D-CWIR	N288VP	N721MA	N525MC
0289	N5226B	N4RP	N204RP	N516TX	
0290	N5101J	N125PL			
0291	N50776	PH-FJK			
0292	N5241Z	N329BH			
0293	N52145	N28GA	C-GSLW		
0294	N52229	N108WQ	N106WQ	N294CC	
0295	N5207V	N525EZ	N295VP	N525NE	
0296	N5216A	N296CJ	N296PM	C-GVSN	N885EM
0297	N52457	N196MR	PP-MPP	N297KH	
0298	N5061P	N567HB	N298CJ		
0299	N5032K	N299CS	N611TK	N299VR	C-FBRP
0300	N52059	F-GVVB			
0301	N5058J	N110JC	N256DV	N256DA	N373AG

CJ3

C/n	Identities					
0302	N51881	N302CZ	(N88QC)	N18GA		
0303	N5112K	N724BP	N724PB			
0304	N5061F	N20AU				
0305	N5120U	N800FM	N404PG			
0306	N5250E	N525H	N949LL	N567RB		
0307	N5181U	N815LP	XA-ALT			
0308	N5260Y	N27EW	XA-TTC			
0309	N5218R	N41226	TC-GUR	N627V	TC-GUR	N309TX
0310	N5163K	PR-RBO	N175RD			
0311	N5194B	M-MHMH	N409DJ			
0312	N5091J	N312CJ	OE-GPK			
0313	N52144	N123CZ				
0314	N52352	OE-GPD	N369MN			
0315	N5228Z	N315CJ				
0316	N52690	N316BD				
0317	N52613	(CS-EAA)	N880PF	N883PF	(N883PP)	N317VP N95TX
0318	N5226B	OE-GMZ	N518CJ	N323AD		
0319	N50736	N52WC				
0320	N5124F	UR-PME	(D-CLXG)	N320RH	N321SD	
0321	N52038	N438CS	N5GQ	PR-HMV		
0322	N5108G	UR-DWH	N322PJ	N915MC		
0323	N5030U	N6132U	UP-CS302			
0324	N5267T	PR-MON				
0325	N5260M	N510RC	N325CJ	N571BB		
0326	N439CS	N480CC				
0327	N5185V	N527DV	N778BS*			
0328	N51038	N994MP	N421MP			
0329	N5270P	N528DV				
0330	N5066F	D-CAST				
0331	N5079V	(D-CIOL)	N819CW			
0332	N434CS	N91GT				
0333	N5221Y	N525CJ	C-GMLR	N76LW		
0334	N5206T	D-CCBH				
0335	N5065S	N335CJ	N929BC	N928BC	N410PT	
0336	N52627	N336CJ	N466F			
0337	N50820	N38M	N38MX	PR-VNA		
0338	N5200U	N338CZ	N109TW			
0339	N5245D	(D-CAVB)	D-CBVB	OE-GVB	N70FC	
0340	N5130J	N111KJ				
0341	N5062S	N808XR	N808SD			
0342	N52639	N885JF				
0343	N5076J	(N91GT)	OM-SYN	N18650		
0344	N5270E	N47NT				
0345	N5257V	N345NT	N345LT			
0346	N5090Y	N299LS	N346CZ	N710PT		
0347	N5057F	N5MQ				
0348	N5194J	OE-GIE				
0349	N5181U	D-CJET				
0350	N5201J	PR-BHV				
0351	N5197M	N330PK				
0352	N52691	VP-CCX	N906MC			
0353	N5031E	N509SB	N509SD	N971TB		
0354	N5061F	N354CJ	N10TR			
0355	N5268V	N3043F	N480JH	N430JH		
0356	N52457	N820NC				
0357	N5066F	N777HN	N177HN			
0358	N5059X	N529DV				
0359	N5037F	N777EW	N359CJ	N1LF		
0360	N5072X	N360TD				
0361	N5263S	UR-DWL	N361EV	M-MSVI		
0362	N5045W	PR-RMT	N362TA	OK-KIN		
0363	N5103J	N710GD	N700GD			
0364	N5109R	N982BZ				
0365	N52113	N501T	N550T			
0366	N5154J	N861HA				
0367	N5247U	D-CDTZ	D-CJOS			
0368	N5040E	N723SG				
0369	N50736	N777LB				
0370	N5260U	N351AJ				
0371	N5148N	N924TC	N924TD			
0372	N5241Z	N892AB	N356DC			
0373	N5060K	N65LW				
0374	N5156D	N59WG				
0375	N5196U	(PT-MPP)	N863DD	N860DD		
0376	N5066F	(PP-CMP)	N386SF			
0377	N5061F	N88GA				

CJ3 / CJ3+

C/n	Identities			
0378	N5117U	D-CHIO	D-CSCA	
0379	N51342	N379SM		
0380	N5157E	N181EA	N568CM	
0381	N5201M	N6062M	N77NT	
0382	N52229	N6061Z	N73EM	
0383	N52235	N383CJ	(N383JR)	
0384	N5223D	N6060S	N919SV	
0385	N5262B	N370MR		
0386	N5270K	PR-DRP	N406FB	
0387	N5270M	N216TM		
0388	N51666	N81110	N81ER	
0389	N5214J	N56WN	PT-GMU	
0390	N52626	PT-GBF		
0391	N50715	N1MG	[also wore fake serial 12-391]	N973CG
0392	N5093L	N392RS	N392MG	
0393	N5037F	N513PN	N393VP	N500WD
0394	N5260U	PR-JRV		
0395	N5151D	N196JH		
0396	N5203J	N730GA	N438SP	
0397	N5245D	N787EV		
0398	N5162W	N895CB		
0399	N5063P	N128WT		
0400	N51780	N54FL		
0401	N51806	N988MM		
0402	N52114	N73AD		
0403	N5270P	N578WZ		
0404	N5236L	N525GK		
0405	N5214J	N405CZ	PR-EDB	
0406	N52613	N559HF	N406TX	
0407	N5265B	N38HD		
0408	N52038	(D-COBC)	N906GW	
0409	N52655	N32PM	N363AL	
0410	N52690	N525TH		
0411	N5246Z	N435CM	N535CM	N538CM
0412	N5069E	N412AR	N518AR	
0413	N5265N	N278KP		
0414	N5214L	D-COBC	D-COBO	
0415	N5095N	N523DV		

CJ3+

C/n	Identities			
0451	N5257V	N30CJ	[r/o 29May14, ff 28Jul14]	N531AJ
0452	N5100J	N51GZ		
0453	N5061W	N1MF		
0454	N52653	N160BR		
0455	N5223X	N80VM		
0456	N5174W	N95LL		
0457	N5264M	N426NS		
0458	N5241R	N543PD		
0459	N52690	N989RS		
0460	N5196U	N778LC	N460TX	N6BB
0461	N5223D	N766LF		
0462	N50715	N84WC		
0463	N5214J	N865MK		
0464	N5000R	N550BW		
0465	N5166U	N525CW		
0466	N5181U	N504PS		
0467	N5194B	N816BL		
0468	N52639	N468CJ	N468EC	
0469	N5216A	N528HV	N458PC	
0470	N5206T	(D-CUGF)	N309TW	
0471	N5266F	N285ER	N85ER	
0472	N5180C	N225TJ		
0473	N5267D	N491AM		
0474	N5076P	N474CC	N525GM	
0475	N5124F	N122WY		
0476	N5093D	N223GB		
0477	N5145U	N872J		
0478	N5267G	N212GB	N304TC	
0479	N5165P	D-CUGF		
0480	N5201J	PP-MRX	N480JM	N145CG
0481	N5270J	N888TF		

CJ3+

C/n	Identities			
0482	N52114	N327RD	N327PD	
0483	N5058J	N327JA		
0484	N52690	N494CJ+	[+ marks allocated in error for one day only]	N484CJ
0485	N5214L	N485CZ		
0486	N5100J	N19537	N486JR	
0487	N5265S	N93MW		
0488	N5097H	N725TM		
0489	N5157E	C-FASY		
0490	N5166U	N858CB		
0491	N52699	N85VM		
0492	N52639	N1141C		
0493	N5200Z	N302JK		
0494	N5268V	N248PM		
0495	N5076J	N953XT		
0496	N5244F	LX-GCA		
0497	N5101J	N477RJ		
0498	N5233J	D-CHIP		
0499	N5156D	N997DM		
0500	N5188N	N20695		
0501	N5204D	N702CW		
0502	N5267J	N765JW		
0503	N5183V	N503KK		
0504	N5257C	N803BC		
0505	51575	OO-FPF		
0506	N5141F	N95VM		
0507	N5296X	N905RL		
0508	N5100J	N501LL		
0509	N5066U	N17QC		
0510	N5239J	N510CZ		
0511	N5268V	N525ML		
0512	N51780	N86CG		
0513	N52691	N721DJ		
0514	N52086			
0515	N5058J	N3SJ		
0516	N51612			
0517	N5094D	N825MD		
0518	N52690			
0519	N51942	N341SF		
0520	N5264S	N409RK		
0521	N51072			
0522	N5267J			
0523				
0524				
0525				
0526				
0527				
0528				
0529				
0530				
0531				
0532				
0533				
0534				
0535				
0536				
0537				
0538				
0539				
0540				

CESSNA 525C CITATIONJET CJ4

C/n	Identities						
714001	N4CJ	[ff 05May08]					
0001	N525NG	[ff 19Aug08]		N14CJ			
0002	N525KS	[ff 02Dec08]		N747HS	N747KR	(N747HR)	XA-MKA
0003	N52141	N525NB	N990H	N233VP	XA-GZZ		
0004	N5269Z	N525CZ	N88QC				
0005	N5211Q	N941KN	N941KD				
0006	N615PL						
0007	N5061W	N1DM	N6QM	N407CJ	N525EM		
0008	N5130J	N868HC					
0009	N5245L	N100JS	(N100JZ)	M-AZIA			
0010	N52229	N96PD	N787JJ				
0011	N52653	N429MR					
0012	N4M						
0013	N52609	N105AD					
0014	N5201M	N627RP	N627RR				
0015	N5155G	N1CH	N181CH				
0016	N5101J	N518TT					
0017	N51995	N80HB					
0018	N5228Z	N926TF					
0019	N52655	N80F					
0020	N5270K	N2250G					
0021	N51564	N817CJ	N417C				
0022	N5216A	N450CM					
0023	N50231	N219L					
0024	N51780	N424CJ	N87FL				
0025	N52645	XA-LPK					
0026	N5200R	N588MM	(N426VP)	XA-UTG			
0027	N5267G	N545JF					
0028	N51396	N428CJ	N909EC	N907SF			
0029	N5218T	N481AM					
0030	N5105F	N460PK	N360PK				
0031	N50275	N631TJ					
0032	N5263U	N740AK					
0033	N50715	N94JW					
0034	N5136J	N577TH					
0035	N52352	N163M					
0036	N5221Y	N436RV	PR-VON	N80CH	N548AJ	PR-MRE*	
0037	N52178	N80LD	N82LD				
0038	N5253S	XA-HOF	N438TA				
0039	N5093D	N38M	N38MJ	N3RC	N390TA		
0040	N5093Y	N181CN					
0041	N51872	N718MV					
0042	N5228J	N442RR	PR-RAR	N42VP			
0043	N50282	D-CEVB	OE-GWB	N543TX			
0044	N5153K	D-CEFA	N544TX				
0045	N5200Z	N8GQ					
0046	N5260Y	N446CJ					
0047	N5076L	N220BA					
0048	N51744	N126PG					
0049	N5154J	N816DV	N716DV				
0050	N5244W	PR-NJR					
0051	N51055	N999WC					
0052	N5135K	N279DV					
0053	N5207V	N322SB					
0054	N5269A	XA-UQG					
0055	N51038	D-CMOM	OE-GXB	N455TX	N581HC		
0056	N5079V	(PP-CFO)	PR-GML				
0057	N5267T	PT-MPP	N57CJ				
0058	N5185V	D-CHRA	(D-CEFE)				
0059	N5069E	PP-CMP	N59CJ				
0060	N51143	N4B	N357BV				
0061	N5181U	N44GL					
0062	N5197M	N503TF					
0063	N5076K	N5254C					
0064	N5263D	ZS-AML	N43LJ				
0065	N5048U	N329CF	N339CF				
0066	N5112K	N67GH					
0067	N51160	N545GH					
0068	N5162X	N7NE					
0069	N5163K	N569CJ	C-GDSH				
0070	N5180K	N929BC					
0071	N5200U	N181HB	N44FJ				
0072	N52144	N65CD	PR-VZN	N614SB	[w/o 29Dec16, crashed into Lake Erie, OK]		
0073	N5026Q	M-NSJS	N473SC	HK-5120			

CJ4

C/n	Identities				
0074	N5061W	N74CJ	N869KA	N795HC	
0075	N5073F	N765DF			
0076	N5101J	N277C	N300KK		
0077	N5135A	N400ET			
0078	N51564	N59JM	C-FXTC		
0079	N51612	N79HM			
0080	N5188N	N271MP			
0081	N52086	N851AC	N511AC		
0082	N5211Q	N482CJ	N82KA		
0083	N5236L	C-FANJ			
0084	N52397	N719L			
0085	N5239J	N1BL	N585VP	N485CJ	OK-ILA
0086	N5243K	N525KR			
0087	N52609	N87ED	N586ED		
0088	N5260M	N95FP			
0089	N5268M	C-FIMP	C-FMCI	N989CJ	D-CDUS*
0090	N50275	PP-WMA			
0091	N52623	N271CQ	(N752KP)		
0092	N51511	N2004D	5N-DIA		
0093	N5188A	D-CBCT			
0094	N5244F	N800RL			
0095	N52613	N770LE			
0096	N5000R	N5253Z	N525EZ		
0097	N5268A	N98CH			
0098	N5174W	N511TK	N611TK		
0099	N5201J	N1440W			
0100	N5095N	OE-GTI			
0101	N5094D	N1DM	N1WX		
0102	N51396	N1BL			
0103	N52178	PR-MJM			
0104	N5168Y	N34LA			
0105	N5250P	N460RG			
0106	N5228J	(D-COJS)	D-CCJS	M-FLYI	
0107	N50282	N573AB	N721MA		
0108	N5153K	D-CKNA			
0109	N5148N	N827BT	N817BT		
0110	N5241Z	N9542G	N747LA		
0111	N5156D	N38M	N826BM		
0112	N52699	ZK-PGA	ZK-OCB		
0113	N5267D	N95CT			
0114	N52591	F-HGLO	N114CJ		
0115	N5076L	F-HATG			
0116	N51744	N525KB	HB-VPA	N116TA	
0117	N5188N	N713WD	N218MB		
0118	N51942	D-CWIR			
0119	N51881	N45FS	N500SV		
0120	N5068R	N513NN	RP-C7513		
0121	N5245U	N606MC			
0122	N5254Y	N339KC			
0123	N5244W	N43KA			
0124	N51055	D-CVHA	D-CWIT		
0125	N5269A	N888KG			
0126	N5048U	N255MV			
0127	N5112K	N636DS			
0128	N51160	N47PB			
0129	N5152X	N129CJ			
0130	N5163K	N622GB	N620GB		
0131	N5000R	N892AB	N431TX		
0132	N50275	M-OBIL			
0133	N50549	N133CJ	N577RT		
0134	N5067U	N94FP	G-SDRY		
0135	N5068F	N55MZ			
0136	N5072X	N55BW			
0137	N5076K	N137JQ			
0138	N51072	N79JS			
0139	N5203S	N6064A	N810GW		
0140	N5166U	C-FLBS			
0141	N5161J	N953FF			
0142	N52136	N589GB	YV3333		
0143	N5045W	M-SSYS			
0144	N5262W	D-CHRB			
0145	N5058J	N899NB	N899NH		
0146	N5091J	N146CJ	N950RG		
0147	N51143	N133RC	N100RC		
0148	N5181U	N601FM			
0149	N5204D	N627RP			

CJ4

C/n	Identities				
0150	N5086W	N938LN			
0151	N5097H	N65DD			
0152	N51042	N152CZ	N111LP		
0153	N5197M	D-CHRC	N453TX	VP-BIB	
0154	N5212M	N154GV	JA008G		
0155	N5153K	N525KJ			
0156	N51744	N485HB	N435HB		
0157	N50282	(D-CCTS)	N4751	N925AK	
0158	N51575	C-GLUV			
0159	N51612	N159CJ			
0160	N52369	N189MM	N18MM		
0161	N52081	D-CJUG	D-CDUS	EC-MOQ	
0162	N51444	N1886X			
0163	N5130J	N448CJ			
0164	N5157E	F-ONCP			
0165	N5197A	N300BB			
0166	N52397	N1492J	N166TX	N525PB	
0167	N5109W	N167H	N886CA	N843CA	N888LB
0168	N522EP	N525EP			
0169	N5244W	N701AL			
0170	N5264S	N329SH	N525SJ		
0171	N194SS	9M-SSS			
0172	N52235	N292ST			
0173	N52626	N173NL	N754RL		
0174	N5270P	LX-GJM			
0175	N52613	N414KU			
0176	N5163K	N38M			
0177	N51072	D-CEFE			
0178	N5161J	N41KN			
0179	N5045W	N179GV	JA009G		
0180	N5204D	N910SS			
0181	N5226B	N986ST			
0182	N5141F	N22UB			
0183	N5270E	N888RK			
0184	N5066U	N389AL	N53SF		
0185	N5165T	N185GV	JA010G		
0186	N52682	N709CB			
0187	N5148N	N187CJ	N309CQ		
0188	N51511	N225CJ	M-SIXT		
0189	N52059	N679TC			
0190	N52699	N32PM			
0191	N5192E	CC-AOR			
0192	N51342	N492CA	N492CJ	N419CE	
0193	N5241Z	N193CF	N437MR		
0194	N51564	N329SH			
0195	N5211F	N159H			
0196	N51984	N326PZ	N525PZ	[w/o 16Jan17 Howell, MI]	
0197	N5244F	M-NTOS			
0198	N5061P	N449BZ			
0199	N51869	C-FSTX			
0200	N5135A	ZJ-THC			
0201	N5227G	N604DR			
0202	N5136J	N207RT			
0203	N51038	N759R			
0204	N51780	N100Y			
0205	N5076K	N415KA			
0206	N5207V	N939AM			
0207	N5246Z	N207CJ			
0208	N5265N	N601JL			
0209	N51942	N888KJ			
0210	N52645	N10AU			
0211	N5117U	N57HC			
0212	N51143	N254AB			
0213	N5130J	N213CJ	N727KG		
0214	N5000R	N2286B			
0215	N5194B	N215CJ			
0216	N5180C	N159WG			
0217	N5270E	N217CJ			
0218	N5148N	(D-CBRO)	D-CBTA		
0219	N5147B	N12SS			
0220	N5152X	N220GV			
0221	N52609	HB-VTA			
0222	N5168Y	N996TX	N967TC		
0223	N51995	N69ME			
0224	N5270M	N900BT			
0225	N5201M	N318SB			

CJ4

C/n	Identities			
0226	N5214J	N658AG		
0227	N52653	N267JL		
0228	N5221Y	N918CW		
0229	N5211Q	N522HV		
0230	N523HV			
0231	N5245U	(D-CEUS)	N71485	N511HS
0232	N5264U	XA-HOF		
0233	N50820	D-CEUS		
0234	N5079V			
0235	N52613	N1895C		
0236	N5095N	N11XK	N11AK	
0237	N5163K	N237GV		
0238	N52369	N238TD		
0239	N5109W	N787EP		
0240	N5218T	N97KT		
0241	N5245L			
0242	N5124F	N542CF	N591SF	
0243	N5264E			
0244	N5103J	N244MG		
0245	N51511	N245MG		
0246	N5268E	N278DK	[wears pseudo-USAF colours with fake serial 17-246 and code MG]	N1MG*
0247	N5264N	(N247CZ)+	[+ ntu marks worn at Wichita factory] N525PZ	
0248	N51038	N329LH		
0249	N5266F	N999CB		
0250	N5165P			
0251	N5262W			
0252	N5090A	N881CW		
0253	N5270K			
0254	N5207V			
0255	N5235G			
0256	N52639			
0257	N5233J			
0258	N5246Z			
0259	N5265N			
0260	N5257V			
0261	N52653			
0262	N5117U			
0263	N5161J			
0264	N5221Y			
0265				
0266				
0267				
0268				
0269				
0270				
0271				
0272				
0273				
0274				
0275				
0276				
0277				
0278				
0279				
0280				

CESSNA CITATION II/BRAVO

This production list is presented in order of the Unit Number which was used and allocated by Cessna, rather than by the normally-used c/n. A c/n-Unit Number cross-reference follows the production list.

Unit No	C/n	Identities
	686	N550CC [ff 31Jan77; cvtd to S550 standards;cx Apr91 presumed wfu]
001	550-0001	(N98751) (N551CC) N5050J N560CC [converted to Model 560; canx 11Apr05; scrapped 2016]
002	551-0027	N98753 N552CC N44GT N552CC N522CC N46PJ
003	550-0003	N98784 N553CJ YV-19CP N19CP N199Q N19CP
004	F550-0004	N98786 C-GPAW N312GA F-GNCP [cx 09Dec13; b/u]
005	550-0005	N98817 OE-GKP N77ND [w/o 30Sep05 70 miles North of Fairbanks, AK; wreck parted out by White Inds, Bates City, MO]
006	550-0006	N98820 N2 N6 N152GA N725RH N550LA
007	550-0007	N98830 N300PB (N447FM) N650WC N650WG (N550TY) N127JJ N127CL
008	550-0008	N98840 N575W OE-GIW (N108AJ) N550JF N70X N70XA G-VUEZ "M-VUEZ"+ [+fake marks worn at Doncaster/Robin Hood Oct12] N70XA
009	550-0009	N98853 N744SW N744DC N656PS
010	550-0010	N98858 OE-GEP N550PL N806C PT-LPK
011	550-0021	N98871 N296AB (N171CB) N900LJ N52RF (N252RF) N529F N15H
012	550-0011	(N99876) Venezuela 0002
013	550-0012	N3208M N513CC C-GHOL N11FH N586CP N586GR N51FK
014	551-0002	N3210M YV-140CP N20FM N700AS XA-SLD N39ML N502CL LV-CEN
015	550-0014	N3212M N702R N780GT (N94FS) N780CF
016	550-0013	N3216M YV-151CP N3952B N21SW N21SV PT-LML [w/o 15Aug87 Criciuma, Brazil: wreck parted out by Dodson Av'n, Rantoul, KS; cx Aug97]
017	550-0016	N3221M N276AL (N216VP) HC-BTJ N204MC N116LA YV....
018	551-0007	N3223M YV-169CP (N169CP) YV-169CP YV-05CP N60FJ N42MJ [parted out by Marklyn Jet Parts, TX]
019	550-0018	(N3225M) N752CC [wfu]
020	551-0006	N3227A YV-06CP YV-O-CVG-2 Venezuela 1967
021	550-0017	N3230M VH-MAY P2-RDZ N771ST N744AT
022	550-0019	N3232M N1851T N1851D (HI-530) HI-534 HI-534CA N1851D (N200GP) N900AF N7RC [w/o 26Apr95 Walkers Cay, Bahamas; cx Oct95 – remains to Dodson Avn, KS]
023	551-0071	N3236M PH-HES OO-RJT PH-HES N4578F N79CD N790D N551DS N551HH
024	551-0003	N3237M YV-205CP N4445N N72RC I-MESK [wfu Nairobi. Kenya]
025	550-0025	N3239M (EP-KID) EP-KIC N9014S N664JB N664J N78PH N78PR 9H-ACR OY-GMC N551DA
026	550-0026	N3240M N256W (N2231B) N30AV
027	550-0027	N3245M N527CC G-BFRM N222DE N222D N127PM N795JK
028	550-0028	(N3246M) (G-BFLY) OE-GAU N501BL N888MW N100CX (F-GHUA) 5Y-HAB N310AV N551CZ (N370CD) [retro-fitted with Williams FJ44 engines]
029	550-0029	(N3247M) G-JEEN N502AL N718VA N202PB N7CC N550TJ N524MA
030	550-0030	(N3249M) G-DJBI G-FERY G-MSLY N64CA VR-CSS N507AB N501KC (N200G) N601KK N4TS N16TS
031	550-0031	N3250M RP-C550 RP-C296 N22GA N9DC C6-MAS
032	550-0032	N3251M N810SC N810SG N55BP N66ES N50US N905EM N112JS N232CW
033	550-0033	(N3252M) TR-LYE N59MJ N755CM N46DA F-GPLT F-WPLT LX-GDL LX-JET LX-GDL G-CEUO N300GH N550CT*
034	550-0034	N3258M N771A N697A N60CC N922SL
035	550-0219	(N3261M) N108WG HB-VGK N4457A N108WG VH-ORE N12AC YV-606CP N550RP N550PM N10JA N321KR [parted out by Alliance Air Parts, Oklahoma City, OK]
036	550-0036	(N3262M) N58AN N5Q (N54DA) N36CE N711BP (N789RR) N789BR N336MA
037	550-0037	(N3268M) N37HG N361DJ XA-SDV (N551NA) N535MA N829NL N237CW (N37GA) N622PG
038	550-0038	(N3271M) N526AC N526AG C-FLDO N642CC (N842CC) N550JC
039	550-0039	(N3273M) G-BJHH EI-BJL N78FA ZP-TYO N848D N33PB
040	550-0040	(N3274M) N220CC N277CJ N900LC HK-3607X N554BA N550SC (N551GA) N545GA N554MB
041	550-0024	N3276M N533M N85MG N313CK XA-SJZ N313CK N413CK N404RP
042	550-0035	N3278M N8417B N50XX N333X N74G (N50GG) N15JA [parted out by MTW Aerospace, AL]
043	550-0041	N3279M N8418B N341AG N985BA N177HH OE-GCI D-CHSA HA-KAE
044	550-0042	N3283M N666RC N57MB N66AT C-FPEL C-FLBC N41GA
045	550-0045	N3284M N4CH N4CR 5N-AMR [w/o 21May91 private airstrip Bauchi, Nigeria]
046	550-0043	N3285M N6Q VR-CCI N801JP N112SH N551RM
047	550-0044	N3286M N3526 N550HM N300TW N308TW (N452AJ)
048	550-0048	N3288M N534M N161BH N384DA N10BF N19ER
049	551-0010	N3291M YV-137CP N55AL D-ICAC F-HMTE
050	550-0046	(N3292M) C-GRHC
051	551-0095	N3296M N1AP N66LB G-HOTL N999WA N49TJ N314CK N200TJ (N127TA) C-GAMW N627TA N400PC N402TJ N48DK
052	F550-0050	(N3298M) N102FC N362DJ D-CJJJ N250CF F-ODUT F-GMCI N342AJ
053	550-0053	(N3300M) N4VF N53VP N53KB TC-NKB N550EC N519AA YV....
054	550-0054	(N3301M) N501AA VH-WGJ VH-OYW VH-PSM [cx; wfu]
055	550-0055	(N3308M) N55CC N2JZ (N1466K) N10EG
056	550-0047	N3313M (N66VM) OB-M-1171 N66VM N44AS
057	550-0075	N3314M N55BH N58BH C-GSFA N710MT N910MT PR-LIG

CITATION II

Unit No	C/n	Identities
058	550-0068	N3319M N558CC N558CB N402ST N1WB N91VB (N406CJ)
059	550-0242	N1955E N551BC
060	550-0051	N1958E C-GJAP C-GBCB N678CA ZS-RKV
061	550-0263	N1959E D-IMTM (N458N) N13VP [w/o 20May02 Oklahoma-Wiley Post,OK: b/u for spares by Dodson Int'l Parts circa Oct02; but cx to Italy 20Dec04]
062	551-0017	N2052A N1UH (N33FW) N53WF N811VC N811VG
063	550-0069	N2069A F-GBPL 3A-MWA HZ-AAA HZ-ALJ N550CE OE-GIN (N269AJ) N551JF N550AB C-FFCL N712PD N550MN
064	550-0070	N2072A N564CC N108DB N777FL N550KA N892PB YV3051 [w/o Charallave 16Aug16]
065	550-0065	N4191G N55SX ZS-RCS N144GA [parted out by Dodson Int'l, Rantoul, KS]
066	550-0071	N4308G C-GDPD N404BF (N404BV) CS-DCI (OY-GMB) OY-GMK (D-CIRR) OE-GAD SE-RIM
067	550-0052	N4620G (OO-LFX) OY-ASV N90MJ N534MW N67TM PH-CTZ N550DR N302SJ
068	F550-0073	N4621G F-GBTL VP-CTJ G-JBIZ
069	550-0074	N4754G N48ND (N86JM) LN-AAI N386MA (N551GN) (N10GN) D-CIFA LX-THS N174DR
070	550-0056	N5342J N752RT N444FJ N89D
071	550-0058	N5348J N71CJ N100HB
072	550-0072	(N2661H) N360N N36QN (N700EA) N969MT N551SR N770JM N778JM N905CW [parted out by White Inds, Bates City, MO]
073	550-0057	(N2661N) VH-WNZ VH-FOJ E5-TCM
074	550-0338	(N2661P) (D-ICWB) (N71RL) N22RJ HB-VGE N28968 N550DW N500GM N500QM N900SE N900MF N992AS
075	550-0060	N26610 (N550KR) N75KR N98BE N315CK OE-GIL ZA-AMA
076	551-0015	N26613 YV-213CP YV-2671P YV2073 YV2662
077	550-0061	(N26614) N456N N458N
078	550-0062	(N26615) (N77SF) C-GDLR [cx 07Feb13; wfu]
079	551-0117	(N26616) C-GHYD N11AB OO-SKS N551AD 4X-CZD
080	550-0064	N26617 YV-36CP N64TF (N550TJ)
081	550-0066	N26619 (N3031) N3032 N733H N783H N10JP (N410JP) N19HU N360RP N425GT
082	550-0077	(N2662A) N582CC N578W XA-PIJ XA-AGN XA-GAA
083	550-0078	(N2662B) N31KW N71FM N78GA C-GPTR (N277A) N533MA N432NM
084	551-0122	(N2662F) N10LR N922EH
085	550-0090	N2662Z N4110S N4110C N410NA N290VP (N818RJ)
086	550-0371	(N26621) N551MC C-GCJN N585DM N550LS
087	550-0079	(N26622) N930BS (N26DA) N789SS N33RH N232DM YV3124
088	550-0089	(N26623) N88MJ (N44JX) (N444WJ) N43RW N81CC N800RR (N111DT) N61SS
089	550-0080	(N26624) G-BFLY HB-VGR N22511 N45ME ZP-BMG
090	550-0081	N26626 I-FBCT N254AM I-AROO N394AM I-GGLC
091	550-0082	N26627 G-BMCL N21DA N49U
092	551-0024	N26628 N2CA [w/o 18Dec82 Mountain View, MO]
093	550-0084	N26229 N222LB N808DM N156N N226N N226L N521WM (N467MW) N391AN N84NP N550SS
094	550-0067	N2663B N81TC N74TC N867CW N267CW N267BB
095	551-0018	N2663F N455DM N666AJ N556CC LN-AAD N387MA D-IEAR
096	550-0086	N2663G N414GC (N93CW) N43SA XC-JCY+ [+marks worn when flying Mexican Customs missions] N43SA [wfu]
097	551-0132	N2663J (C-FCFP) C-GTBR N78GA SE-DYR N170AR N551MW
098	551-0133	N2663N G-JRCT N222TG I-JESA HB-VDO F-GJOD
099	550-0076	(N2663X) LN-HOT VH-LSW VH-TFY VH-XDD P2-MBD VH-QQZ
100	550-0085	(N2663Y) OY-GKC N57AJ OE-GBA EI-MED G-IMED N143TW G-IMED
101	550-0094	(N26630) G-JETA G-RDBS G-JETA [wfu Doncaster/Robin Hood, UK]
102	550-0095	N26631 N400DT N100UF N550CG LV-CTT
103	550-0096	N26632 N550EW N30UC N87SF N96NF [parted out by Dodson Int'l, KS] N552NC*
104	550-0097	N26634 N404G N404E N202CE N999GR C-GRQC N207AP N550ME
105	550-0098	(N26635) N17S N212H N211JS N211MT
106	550-0374	N26638 YV-147CP YV-1478P (N772AC) YV-678CP N477A (N999LL) N695TA
107	551-0021	N26639 N107BB N307AJ N551CF N55LS N1HA
108	551-0141	N2664F (N108CT) N95CC N210MJ N888RF N888HW N100SC N388MA CC-CWZ N451DA (N636MA) N311TT N451DA
109	550-0099	N2664L N109JC
110	550-0100	N2664T (N801L) N801G N2S C-FKHD N140DA C-GLMK
111	550-0101	(N2664U) N91MJ (N42BM) [w/o 31Dec95 Marco Island Airport, FL]
112	550-0102	N2664Y VH-WNP VH-JCG VH-JPG VH-OYC VH-INT N2664Y
113	550-0376	N26640 N313BT N30FJ N30EJ N73ST
114	F550-0092	(N26643) N89B N89Q F-GFPO N89Q F-GNLF N567CA N550GZ
115	551-0026	(N26648) N551R N12TV N25NH N32PB N612VR
116	550-0105	N26649 N116CC D-CNCP I-MTNT N105BA N550LH
117	550-0106	N2665A Argentina AE-129 LQ-TFM AE-129 (N83MA) N37CR N308CK N820MC (N820MQ)
118	551-0149	N2665D N550CB N225AD N225FM N550JS (N715PS) N5WT N255WT N451MP
119	550-0108	(N2665F) N4TL N4EK (N65SA) VP-CBE N36NA N690EW
120	550-0109	N2665N N753CC [w/o Oklahoma City, OK, 21Dec12]
121	550-0091	(N2665S) N527AC N527AG N601BC
122	550-0110	(N2665Y) N222SG N122G N550SF

CITATION II

Unit No	C/n	Identities
123	550-0111	N26652 N3R N34WP (N3184Z) N123VP HP-7JH
124	550-0112	(N26656) (C-GDPE) C-GDPF N550PS N3FA N213CF YV2317
125	550-0113	N2666A N227PC C-GDMF C-FIMP N90DA N550KD
126	550-0114	N2745G (N89B) N55HF N88HF N83HF (N900BM) N991BM N819KR
127	550-0115	N2745L N127SC SE-DDY OY-CCU SE-DDY
128	550-0116	N2745M HZ-AAA HZ-AA1 PT-LGM N413CA N669MA N575BW N94PL
129	550-0117	N2745R N575FM N150HR N150HE N550RB N490DC
130	550-0162	N2745T VH-UOH N550KP N1UA N85HD N85HE
131	550-0118	N2745X LV-PHH N131ET N999BL N162DW EC-743 EC-FIL N118EA N138J N650BP N143BL
132	551-0163	N27457 N80BS D-IGRC ZS-ARG
133	550-0378	N2746B YV-299CP N3999H OH-CAT D-CIFA SE-RIK PH-SVZ
134	550-0121	N2746C N655PC OB-M-1195 OB-1195 N850BA N51FT N896MA N899MA N121HL
135	550-0122	N2746E N135CC N70GM C-FCEL G-OSMC HB-VKH N221GA C-GCUL N89GA
136	550-0123	N2746F (CC-CGX) N36CJ N81TF SE-DEV LN-NEA SE-DEV LN-NLA N748DC N948DC N550NT
137	550-0124	N2746U LN-VIP N4557W N57MK N57MF N124CR N109GA (N789DD)
138	550-0125	N2746Z N5500F N320S N125RR 5N-NPF
139	551-0169	(N2747R) OE-GHP N26863 N82RP N82RZ N50HW N700YM N14RM
140	550-0103	N2747U XA-JEZ N90MA
141	551-0171	N26178 (9V-PUW) ZS-PMC 5R-MHF N26178 N551NC
142	550-0184	N2619M N80DR N813DH N200NC (N20TV)
143	550-0127	N2631N N29TC (N29TG) N550TJ G-GAUL G-ESTA N550TJ [parted out by Dodson Int'l, Rantoul, KS]
144	550-0128	N2631V N536M N220LA YU-BPU RC-BPU 9A-BPU F-WLEF EI-CIR N60AR EI-CIR F-GJOB
145	550-0129	N2632Y N537M N129TC N122MM N122HM (N550RD) N237WC
146	550-0104	N2633N CC-ECN Chile E-301 CC-CLC
147	550-0132	N2633Y G-CJHH N13627 N500VB (N330MG) PT-LLU
148	550-0133	N2634Y G-BHBH C-GRIO N228CC N198NS YV3185
149	551-0179	N2635D HZ-AAI HZ-ZTC N203BE N127BU
150	551-0029	N26369 (G-BHGH) N168CB N551PL N500ER D-ICUR N450GM N35403 [w/o 01Jan05 Ainsworth, TX; parted out]
151	551-0180	N8520J (D-CACS) N852WR D-ICAB N166MA (N729MJ) N222VV D-IHAG
152	551-0181	N2638A N56GT N137CF N29B N565VV (N61442) N551GE
153	550-0138	N2646X XC-SCT [cx; status?]
154	550-0139	N2646Y ZS-KOO N222MJ PT-LJA N39FA PT-ORD (PT-WQG) OY-ELY 9H-LEO
155	550-0140	N2646Z N55WL (N45WL)
156	550-0141	N26461 VH-ING VH-INX VH-EJY
157	550-0142	N2648Z PT-LCR N387SC N550TJ YV....
158	550-0143	N2649D N100VV N550TT PT-LQW (N660AC) N150RD N50JP N507EC [wfu Fort Lauderdale Executive, FL]
159	550-0144	N2649E RP-C689 N418MA [w/o 18Nov03 Mineral Wells, TX] N97315
160	550-0145	N2653R N444JJ VH-TFQ P2-MBN P2-TAA [w/o 30Aug10 Misima Island, Papua New Guinea]
161	550-0146	N26610 N580AV (N611RR) N501LC N941JM
162	551-0036	N2661P N162CC N160D N317SM N3170B N889FA VH-JMM RP-C....
163	551-0191	N222AG N550CP (N771R) N107SB D-IVOB N127KR N386AM YV470T
164	550-0149	N116K N116KC
165	550-0150	N2668A N1SV
166	550-0279	(N88838) N566CC N886AT N566CC N550KA
167	550-0152	N88840 (N107) RP-C581 N88840 N550CA VH-FYP
168	550-0153	(N88842) N27BA N278A N50HS N50HE N27MH N37MH
169	550-0130	(N88845) N77RC N778C N630CC
170	550-0381	(N88848) N170CC N155PT N155BT (N49VP) N391BC N391KC N381VP
171	550-0154	(N8777N) G-DJBE G-EJET G-JETJ N80AX YV600T
172	550-0382	(N98715) YV-300CP N551TT N852SP N852SB N852HA
173	550-0383	(N98718) N551AB N561AS [cx 22Apr13; CofR expired]
174	551-0031	(N98749) N6565C YV-301CP N75TG N5T N5TQ EC-JTH (N25AQ) T7-XXV (PR-EVC) N25AQ
175	550-0155	N6566C (YV-209CP) YV-298CP N65TF N31RC N155TJ N168AM N215CW (N155FF) C-FNCT
176	550-0156	N98784 N6567C (N31F) N205SG N205SC EC-IAX
177	551-0201	N177CJ C-GGSP N550JB N550GB D-ISEC EC-MCF
178	550-0175	N10JK C-FWWW C-GHWW N550CU N1FM N75WL [parted out by Alliance Air Parts, Oklahoma City, OK]
179	550-0165	N98871 3D-ACQ ZS-LHU N976GA
180	550-0166	N88731 PH-MBX N166CF N166VP N367JC N867JC
181	551-0205	N88732 N999AU XA-KIQ N3951Z N342DA HB-VIO N828SS (N175TN) N69AH
182	550-0167	N88737 N100CJ N717DT YV182T YV3161
183	550-0158	N88738 (N662AA) N423D N550AJ N2JW N49HS N258CW N769H [parted out by White Inds, Bates City, MO]
184	550-0168	N88740 (VH-ICT) VH-TNP VH-LJK N785CA VH-LJK N68GA ZS-NII
185	550-0169	(N88743) N185CC N6001L XC-JDA+ [+marks worn when flying Mexican Customs missions] N6001L [wfu]
186	550-0170	N88791 N550TP N550TR N37BM N500CV N508CV N550DA YV3111
187	550-0172	N88795 (N28MM) N72MM N88JJ N78CS N412P N800TV SE-RCZ M-LEFB

CITATION II

Unit No	C/n	Identities									
188	550-0171	(N88797)	(C-GDPE)	N43D	N934H	(N984H)	N333CG	EI-BYN	(N171VP)	N19AJ	N1TY
189	550-0234	N88798	N511WC	C-FLPD	N65DA	N173AA	(N353HA)				
190	551-0214	N8881N	N107T	N163DA	N178HH	N9SS	N800CU	N71KG			
191	551-0215	N88822	(N36NW)	N286G	N169JM	(N169DA)	N550HP	(N151PR)	N500PX	N551CL	
192	550-0179	N88824	N60MM	N673LP	N673LR						
193	550-0180	N88825	N320V	N77WD	N77WU	N3030C	(N303GC)	(N89TA)	N3030T	N219MS	
		(N619MS)									
194	550-0181	N88826	RP-C653	N550GP	N50US	N50VS					
195	550-0182	N88830	(F-BKFB)	F-GCSZ	N78TF	F-GEFB	N30XX	N165MC	(F-....)	N107CF	
		F-HACA	[cx to Denmark 09Apr09 but no Danish marks allocated]								
196	551-0050	N98403	N1823B	N196HA	N196HR	N228AK	N228MH				
197	550-0186	N98418	N80AW	YV-187CP	N80AW	N676CM					
198	550-0187	N98432	N303X	N143DA	N6WU	N57CE	N57CK	C-GHOM	N598CA	N111GJ	
199	550-0218	N98436	N45EP	PT-LPP	(N250DR)						
200	551-0223	N98468	(N200MR)	N550LP	LN-AFG	5B-CIS	LN-AAC	N754AA	YV-2567P	(N28GZ)	
		YV1776									
201	550-0174	(N98510)	N201CC	N666WW	N87PT						
202	550-0151	(N98528)	N35HC	N495CM							
203	550-0176	N98563	N552TF	N900TF	(N900TE)	N900TJ	N83SF	N83SE	(N24TR)	N61MA	
204	551-0023	N98599	N155TA	N34DL	PT-LME	[w/o 23Jly03 Sorocaba, Brazil]					
205	550-0189	N98601	D-CAAT	HB-VGP	D-CCCF						
206	550-0183	N98630	(XC-DUF)	HB-VGS	G-JMDW	G-CGOA					
207	550-0188	N98675	VH-SWL	HB-VIZ	N38NA	N280PM					
208	550-0147	N98682	N155JK	N80GM							
209	550-0190	N98715	F-BTEL	F-GZLC	F-BTEL	F-GZLC	EC-JON				
210	550-0083	N98718	N54CC	N200VT	YV3228						
211	550-0164	N164CC	N7YP	(N24PT)	N916RC	N721DR	[cx 12Sep13; wfu]				
212	551-0033	N88692	D-IJHM	[w/o 19May82 Kassel, Germany]							
213	550-0191	N88707	C-GWCR	C-GWCJ	N550PA	YV2968					
214	550-0192	N88716	N44ZP	YV-900CP	N192DW	N941BB					
215	550-0249	N88718	N829JM	(N401U)	N201U	PT-LZO	(N48NA)	N39GA	N456AB	N456TX	
216	550-0159	(N88721)	N45ZP	N188SF	C-GAPT	N444GB	N550PW				
217	550-0194	N88723	N91B	C6-PCA	N519RJ						
218	550-0205	(N88727)	N30JD	XB-SGT							
219	550-0196	N6798Y	N68DS	N1212H	N800EC	N88ML	N400DK	HB-VLS	N196JS	N104WV	
220	550-0197	N6798Z	(N30F)	N44FC	HB-VIT	N510JC					
221	550-0198	(N67980)	XC-DOK	XA-SQV							
222	550-0199	N67983	N586RE	[wfu Gainesville, FL]							
223	550-0260	N67986	N32JJ	N82JJ	N8CF	N6HF					
224	551-0245	N67988	N224CC	LN-AAE	[w/o 15Nov89 Mt Langfjelltind, nr Bardufoss, Norway]						
225	550-0200	N67989	(G-BHVA)	N34SS	N28S	N287	N28S	N284	N810MC	(N810MG)	
		N797SF	N606KK	N804RC							
226	550-0206	N6799C	XC-DUF	XA-SQW	N280TA	N726HA					
227	550-0201	N6799E	N334AM	N566TX	N1GH						
228	550-0185	N6799L	N815GK	N600EZ	N370AC	N511DR	N511DL	N317HC	N550RT	N154RK	
229	550-0157	N6799T	N550K	N101BX	N257CW	N535PC	N61HT				
230	550-0202	N6799Y	N590RB	N10CF	(N5GA)	N175VB	N550NE	N704DA			
231	550-0203	N67990	N12JA	N62HA	N766AE	(N766AF)	(N857BT)	YV252T			
232	550-0209	N67997	N121C	N101KK	(N877GB)	N444G					
233	550-0238	N67999	N97S	N204CF							
234	550-0207	N6800C	(N95CC)	N163CB	N60BB	N1823C	HB-VJH	N207BA	N196RJ	N229BM	
235	550-0135	N6800J	VH-KDI	N39142	ZS-LLO	N555BC	TF-JET	N555BC	N550BP	YV-888CP	
		YV2103									
236	550-0214	N6800S	N13BJ	N44WF	N75Z	N75ZA	YV205T	YV2443			
237	550-0222	N6800Z	N17RG	PT-LNC							
238	550-0215	N68003	N500WP	(N400MT)	N40MT	N550MJ					
239	550-0204	(N6801H)	N820	N200JR	(N300PR)	N815CE	YV474T				
240	550-0216	N6801L	N240AR	(N911NJ)	N550PG	(N304TH)	XB-NXR				
241	550-0208	N6801P	N54RC	N222WL	[parted out, cx Mar91]						
242	550-0223	N6801Q	N900BA	N901RM	N701RM	N400PC	N81TJ	N239CD	N550WL		
243	550-0284	N6801R	I-ARIB	OY-JEV							
244	550-0211	N6801T	XA-LOT	N611CF	N77PH	N77PR					
245	550-0212	(N6801V)	N245CC	[cx 22Feb17, CofR expired]							
246	551-0038	N6801Z	D-IBPF	N550DA	N103M	N551BB	YU-BTT				
247	550-0210	N68018	N762PF	(N177CM)	N3PC	N37WP	(N3184V)	N19VP	XA-SDN	XA-KMX	
		N850PM	XA-PAA								
248	550-0220	N6802S	N95CC	N275CC	N288CC	HI-500	HI-500SP	HI-500CT	N80513	(N962HA)	N4CS
		N4ZS	N123RF	N614SJ	YV3229						
249	550-0193	N6802T	(N47RP)	XC-FOO	XC-ROO	N2160N	N492ST	N72FL	N260J	N485AK	
		PP-CST									
250	550-0213	N6802X	N420P	N421TX	N550HB	N213CC					
251	550-0224	N6802Y	YV-O-MTC	YV-O-MTC-20		Venezuela 2222					
252	550-0228	N6802Z	(N702BC)	5N-AWJ	N96CS	VH-EXM	N334ED	N334RJ			
253	550-0221	N68026	N253W	N95AX	N31GA						
254	550-0227	N68027	N254CC	(N71CG)	PT-LND	N227DR	XA-GMP				
255	550-0229	N6803E	N550JM	OY-GRC	N50FC	C-FGAT	N229MC				

CITATION II

Unit No	C/n	Identities
256	550-0239	N6803L 8P-BAR N4720T N66MC
257	550-0235	(N6803T) N67SG I-PNCA D-CNCA*
258	550-0225	(N6803Y) (N34SS) N258CC PT-LTJ
259	550-0195	N68032 N60JD (N41CK) N61CK N343CM [cx 19Apr17, CofR expired]
260	550-0236	N68033 N611ER N611CR N711VR LN-AAD N823NA N550G [cx 26Aug15; wfu]
261	550-0248	N6804C N550SA N233ST N125RG
262	550-0226	N6804F N29WS N300JK N550RG N772HP N872RT N872RD YV2596
263	550-0217	N6804L N88DD N66DD N66DN N340DA I-CIGA N217SA
264	550-0237	N6804M 3D-ACT ZS-NHO N41WJ XA-LFJ
265	550-0230	(N6804N) (G-OTKI) N3254G N270RA N141DA N550EK N550WB N558WB PR-NFT
266	551-0285	N6804S (N550RL) N551SR ZS-MLN N551HK Venda VDF-030 ZS-MLN
267	551-0046	N6804Y C-GDDC N34YL N81GD N518MV
268	550-0241	N6804Z N10FN N268J (N32TJ) XC-BCS N241FT XA-TQL N241FT VH-EUV P2-EUV
269	550-0390	N6805T N58GG (N500EE) N500AE N135BC N136BC VT-VPS N14RZ N717LC
270	550-0250	N68599 N9LR N33GK N250VP
271	550-0231	N6860A N28RF (N221BW) N671B N88TB N140DR N148DR N41SM N922RV
272	551-0289	N6860C N98GC N666JT N551BW PT-LJF
273	550-0243	N6860L TI-APZ VR-BHG N1333Z XA-POR XA-REN N214MD N67SF
274	550-0307	N6860R N37BM N550VW YV3259
275	550-0254	N6860S N171CB XA-TEL (N828SH) N112SA N888RT N888RL
276	550-0247	N6860T (N18DD) N928DS PT-LJJ (N85NA) [dbr Manhuacu, Brazil, 07Oct11; wreck dumped at Belo Horizonte/Pampulha, Brazil]
277	551-0035	N6860U N277HM N277JM
278	551-0039	N6860Y ECT-023 EC-DOH N71LP N550TA N551GF
279	550-0245	N68607 N505GP N388SB
280	550-0257	N68609 XC-HEQ XA-SQQ N187TA N53RG F-HCRT
281	550-0303	N6861D (N281AM) N160VE N40FJ N4JS N450CC XB-GLZ
282	550-0246	N6861E N72TC N78TC N69ME (N396DA) N68ME N35BP N551TK N550BP [w/o 04Jun07 Lake Michigan nr Milwaukee, MI]
283	550-0255	N6861L I-DEAF N28GA I-JESO D-CIAO
284	550-0232	N6861P N929DS N797CW
285	550-0258	N6861S N172CB (N550DD) N550CM N463C N550FB N258JS N550PR N424TG N752GS [cx 12Aug14; parted out by Atlanta Air Salvage, Griffin, GA]
286	550-0256	N6861X N3300L N550SM N550BM N75HS N75TP N55TP N111AF
287	550-0251	N68615 PK-WSO PK-TRV N550HF N20FB XA-GYA XB-NCR
288	550-0261	N68616 N40GS C-FLDM N41JP C-FLDM (N261VP) N261SS N50AZ N551WL
289	550-0259	N68617 VH-KDP N810JT OY-BZT
290	551-0304	N6862C G-DJHH G-TIFF N7028U N702KH N304KT N999MK N551NH
291	550-0393	N6862D N12GK I-FLYD N228AM I-GGLB
292	550-0264	N6862L N550KC N777WY N771WY N610JC
293	550-0265	N6862Q (N314MC) (N265QS) CN-TKK N16PL
294	550-0252	N6862R N507GP N6JL N6JU N525JA
295	550-0253	N68621 N23ND N18ND N31DA N75EC N202TS N953FT N157DW N127JM
296	550-0266	N68622 N296CC N296PH N296CF OE-GEC N15NA N825JW N825JV N550TT N550TP N330DK
297	550-0267	N68624 N932LM N15Y (N194JM) N502BG XA-OAC N910RB
298	550-0268	N68625 N298CJ N500EX N500FX N38TT
299	550-0289	N68629 D-CBAT OE-GST N550MD N820FJ N820SA N22HP C-FTIL C-FTMS VH-JMK P2-JMK VH-JMK P2-MRM
300	551-0313	N6863B OE-GLS N270CF YV-2426P YV1820
301	551-0051	N6863C (D-IHAT) D-ICTA
302	550-0269	N6863G N74MG N760 N28RC N1MM N28RC N1MM N550HJ N550TR
303	550-0271	N6863J (N303EC) N555EW N655EW N550CA N303J PT-ORO N167MA N729MJ N1NL N320JT
304	550-0290	N6863L VH-JBH OE-GCH N290BA N217LG N312NC
305	550-0285	N6863T N20CN N20CF (N17PL) N40PL N989TW N989TV C-GQCC
306	550-0286	N68631 N306SC SE-DLY N78BA N2GG N2GQ
307	550-0272	N68633 9M-WAN VH-JPK HB-VKX VR-BVV VP-BVV SE-DVV Sweden 103001 SE-DVV YU-BVV N550SM N247JM
308	550-0273	N68637 N217FS N121KM
309	550-0277	N6864B N44LF (N550MT) N550WJ N550BJ YV2332 Venezuela 1113
310	550-0274	N6864C ZS-LDK N14GA HB-VKT VP-CCM EC-HJD N75GA XB-JLJ N2057H
311	551-0323	N6864L (N990Y) N819Y N555RT
312	551-0056	N6864X (N312CC) I-GAMB N214AM I-NIAR N36WJ N826RT
313	550-0280	N6864Y N280MH N864D N300TC N7SN C-GKAU
314	550-0281	N6864Z N31RK N33EK
315	550-0282	N68644 G-JETC G-JCFR G-JETC [b/u Southend, Essex, UK, Jan13; fuselage to Bedworth, Warks, UK, 2013, then to Hangar Number 4 Restaurant, Warrington, UK, as customer attraction 2014]
316	550-0283	(N68646) N316CC N316H N316CF N316CC TC-BAY N124GA N225J N257DW
317	550-0287	N68648 N444MM N65LC N67LC N920E YV-909CP N550RL N771AA (N221JS) N527DS YV2788
318	550-0276	N68649 C-GGFW N53FT [parted out by White Inds, Bates City, MO]
319	550-0288	N6865C G-JETB N4564P G-JETB G-MAMA G-JETB (G-OXEH) [w/o 26May93 Eastleigh, Southampton, UK]

CITATION II

Unit No	C/n	Identities
320	550-0291	N6887T ZP-PNB ZP-TNB N550CD N41C N1AF N40MA N262Y [w/o 01Oct10 Manteo, NC; parted out by Atlanta Air Salvage, Griffin, GA]
321	550-0292	N6887X N114EL (N63FS) C-FTOM C-FTOC C-GTDK C-GREK N554GR
322	550-0293	N6887Y [w/o 19Dec92 Billings, MT; cx May93]
323	550-0294	N68872 PH-HET N323CJ PT-LPN
324	550-0298	N68873 N74KV N431DS D-ILCC N888FG
325	550-0295	N68876 N483G N800LA N345JR (N295EA) N339MC N48KH
326	550-0296	N6888C G-BJIR G-DWJM [b/u Staverton, UK, Apr12; fuselage to Southend, UK, then to Milton Hall Primary School, Westcliff-on-Sea, UK, Mar16]
327	550-0304	N6888D N208TC N369DA (N70PH) N42PH
328	550-0299	N6888L N538M HB-VIR N511AB
329	550-0302	N6888T N329CC N441T N133BC N33BC N792MA (SE-RCX) SE-RCY [to instructional airframe, Stockholm/Skavsta, Sweden]
330	550-0306	N6888X N303EC N550MT N341CW N296CW N206AG VH-NSB N539CC [cx 04Dec15; wfu]
331	550-0396	N6888Z N8AD N99DE N99CN N289CP (N289CR)
332	550-0300	N68881 YV-162CP YV2246
333	550-0310	N68887 N130TC (N779DD) (N730TC) N779DD N7798D N530P LV-CFS
334	551-0059	N68888 N114DS N59FA N59FY N59DY CC-ARV
335	550-0312	N6889E N58H N61HA N61CF YV-1055CP YV255T
336	550-0313	N6889K (N393HC) N393RC N246NW N960CP N32TM N32TK N941JP
337	550-0311	N6889L N43TC N43TE N44TC N121CP N2RC N211SP N300GC
338	550-0398	N6889T VH-BRX N101DD I-KESO (N550SC) N398S PH-CTX N610ED N707LM
339	550-0318	N6889Y N642BB PT-LJT PT-WJZ
340	550-0315	N6889Z N90JD N618DB N59GU SE-RBK (LN-AWF) N833JP
341	550-0308	N68891 3D-AVH N30SA (F-GIRS) N15XM
342	550-0399	(N6890C) N66MS N165RD N765RD*
343	550-0320	(N6890D) N343CC N300GM N800SB N800EL N800VJ N3MB N57MB N204PM
344	551-0351	(N6890E) N7FD N612CC N27U N322CS N5TR
345	550-0319	N6890G N8BX N26SC N26CT N76CK N78CK
346	550-0316	N5428G N828B N143RW N42KC N129TS N741JC N26HH
347	550-0321	N5430G N321SE TC-COY N321GN VP-CCO YU-FCS PH-MKL D-COMK 6V-AIQ F-HJAX
348	551-0355	N5451G N551AS I-ALPG F-HHHH T7-JET
349	550-0327	N5474G N74JA N74JN PT-LLT
350	550-0400	N5492G N350CC N888EB N53CC [w/o 02Oct89 Roxboro, NC; cx Jul90]
351	550-0323	(N5703C) OE-GCP TC-FAL TC-FMB TC-YZB (N323AM) VP-CLD N550LD
352	550-0324	N5873C N171LE I-JESJ N23W HB-VLQ F-HBMB OM-PTT 9H-PIK
353	551-0359	N67983 (N551SE) N142TJ N740JB 5Y-WEC [not delivered; safety training aid still wearing N740JB at Wichita/Mid-Continent, KS, May17]
354	551-0360	N67988 G-BJIL N550MD C-GSCR N24CJ N551EA
355	551-0361	N6799C LV-PNB LV-APL LQ-APL
356	550-0275	N6799L N550JR N550CP N555DS
357	550-0301	N6799T China 091 B-4103 B-7024
358	550-0333	N67990 PT-LCW N313CE N123GM N365WA
359	550-0305	N67999 China 090 B-4105 B-7026 [w/o 28Mar11 Xinjiang Uygur Region, China]
360	550-0329	N6800C (N49N) N491N N949SA N939SA
361	550-0334	N6800S N92LT N404KS N755BP N44FR
362	550-0297	N68003 China 092 B-4104 B-7025
363	551-0369	N696A N999GP N998GP N68BK N778JC
364	550-0401	N6825X N242WT (N551GC) N550KT N552BG
365	550-0335	N6829Y N1847B N1847P N51PS N667CG N204AB N235TS N187JN YV3188
366	550-0402	N6830X N700LB N717PC N57SF N624RL
367	550-0336	N6830Z N90Z
368	550-0337	N6802S N727C N75F (N78BA) N54HJ (N54HC) N406SS N3FW N93AJ
369	550-0326	N6802T N12FC PT-OAF (N983AJ) N390AJ (N390JP) YV589T
370	550-0339	N6802Y VH-KTK VH-SCD VH-EEE
371	550-0403	N68027 N101RL N637EH N362CP N404BS Venezuela 0403
372	550-0332	N6803L N372CC N1880F N12CQ N120Q C-FFCC
373	550-0341	N68032 C-GJAP N182U C-FDYL N141JC (N367EA)
374	550-0340	N6804F N374FC N219SC N219CS N219SC N235DB ZP-TWN N38DD N601AT
375	551-0378	N6804L G-BJVP N4581Y (N43D) N115VH N6EL (F-OGUO) (F-OGVA) N322MA
376	550-0345	N6804Y N312DC N3GT N30CZ N267TG N267TC (N782NA) (N50NA) N982NA (N982LC)
377	551-0060	N6805T N465D N46SD N458HW (N458H) (N60HW) N59GB
378	550-0344	(N6806Y) N6806X N532M PT-LKR N550GM C-GVGM N550GM
379	550-0357	N6808C N632SC N29G HB-VJA N29FA PT-OAG
380	550-0347	N6826U ZS-LEE VH-ZLE
381	550-0348	N381CC I-VIKI N550CA C-GSCX XA-RIV
382	550-0346	N550CF N106SP N106SR
383	550-0349	N6801L N8FD N870PT (N221LC) N600ST N600SZ N525LC N61CS
384	550-0350	N86SG N111LJ
385	550-0405	YV-276CP YV-604P YV-778CP YV1813
386	550-0351	N99KW I-ALKA (N167WE) N351CJ
387	551-0388	N68321 N711WM [w/o 06Nov86; no details known; cx Nov87]
388	550-0354	N121CG N121C VR-CJR VP-CJR SE-RBD S5-BBG
389	550-0358	N6801Q Myanmar 4400

CITATION II

Unit No	C/n	Identities								
390	550-0356	N6801Z	PT-OER	N133WA	N21UA					
391	550-0343	(N1214D)	G-MINE	N721US	N20GT	N56FB	A6-SMS	G-ORCE	N789TT	
392	551-0393	N1214H	(N18CC)	N122SP						
393	550-0352	(N1214J)	(N140DV)	N140V	(N72B)	I-ALKB	N352AM	VT-EUN	N352DA	N550WJ
394	550-0363	N1214S	(N777NJ)	N444CC	HK-3400X	N363SP	N741T	(N46NR)		
395	551-0396	(N1214Z)	N395CC	N39K	N39KY	N45GA	LV-WXD			
396	550-0362	N12142	N396M	(N440PJ)						
397	550-0353	(N12149)	G-GAIL	N3251H	N922RA	N922RT	LN-AAB	N922RT	N477KM	N353FT
		YV2959								
398	550-0406	(N1215A)	N398CC	C-GHKY	N551CE	C-FTAM	N781SC	LV-ZPD	N815MA	[w/o 04Jan09
		Wilmington, NC]								
399	550-0366	N1215G	N200E	N2008	N773LP	N55FM	(N614GA)	N110LD		
400	551-0400	(N67983)	N550WR	N95CT	N280JS	D-IMME				
401	550-0407	(N1215S)	N600CR	(N767TR)	N758S	(N950FC)	N55MV	YV2619		
402	550-0368	(N12155)	N94ME	N94MF	N718CK					
403	550-0364	N12157	N100AC	N550AV	C-GLTG	N180FW	N10VT	N420KH		
404	550-0365	(N12159)	N712J	N100AG	N100AY	N129DV	N122WW			
405	550-0367	(N1216A)	N95CC	N17LK	N17LV	N3MB	N45ML	LV-FWA*		
406	550-0408	N1216H	N400TX	N110WA	N82ML	[parted out by Alliance Air Parts, Oklahoma City, OK]				
407	550-0409	N1216J	N22T	HI-496	(N22TZ)	HI-496SP	N7153X	VR-CIT	N102HB	
408	550-0410	N1216K	(N258P)	N46MK	N46MF	C-GNWM				
409	550-0411	N1216N	N200YM	C-FMPP	N550KW	[cx 29Aug12; wfu; parts used in rebuild of VH-ZLE c/n 550-0347]]				
410	550-0412	N1216Q	N410CC	N830VL	N223J	N450KD	[cx 23Nov15; wfu]			
411	550-0355	(N1216Z)	N122CG	N125CJ	N440TX	N500BR	N355DF	N52LT		
412	551-0412	N12160	G-OMCL	N413VP	OY-PDN	EC-KJR				
413	550-0414	N12162	N342CC	(N414VP)	N814AM	N503BG	N983AG			
414	550-0415	N12164	D-CNCI	OH-CUT	N1949B	N1949M	F-GJYD	EC-KJJ	9H-TRT	EC-MAM
415	550-0416	N12167	N416CC							
416	550-0417	N1217D	ZS-LHW	N17DM	N303SD					
417	550-0418	N1217H	N550J	N418CG	N214JT					
418	550-0419	N1217N	G-JETD	VH-JVS	G-WYLX	G-DCFR	G-FJET			
419	550-0420	N1217P	N200RT	N200RN	(N10PX)	I-AGSM	N555KT	N585KT		
420	550-0421	N1217S	N67HW	N510GP						
421	551-0421	N1217V	N421CJ	OO-RJE	SE-DEF	OE-GES	N550RD	D-IAWA	3A-MRB	G-LUXY
		9H-MXP								
422	550-0423	N12171	N45MC	C-GUUU	C-FCCC	N248HA	N15WT			
423	550-0424	(N12173)	N18CC	N46A	(N469)	N24AJ	N555DH	N271CG	N551BP	N435UM
		C-FHLG								
424	550-0425	N1218A	(LN-FOX)	Spain U.20-1/01-405						
425	550-0426	N1218F	N404SB	N434SB	(N426SP)					
426	550-0427	N1218K	N923RL	PT-LHY	N527EA	N840MC	N840MQ	N711CC	YV2855	
427	550-0428	(N1218P)	N7004	N7864J	N107WV	N97BG	N550PF			
428	551-0428	N1218S	(N70HC)	(N147RP)	[w/o 22Dec99 Crisp County-Cordele, GA; cx Jun00]					
429	550-0430	N1218T	N264A	N1278	HB-VLY	N567S	N56FT	XB-AGV		
430	551-0431	N1218V	N21EH	N218H	N900TN	N59CC	(N431JC)	N4MM	N4NM	N551GS
431	550-0369	N1218Y	(N342CC)	N324CC	N431CB	N55MT	N725BA	N725BF	N725FL	N181EB
432	550-0433	N1219D	I-KIWI	N131GA	N7ZU	C-GMJN				
433	550-0434	(N1219G)	N1109	N1178	(N515M)	N152JC	(N152JQ)	(D-CVAU)	N53FP	
434	550-0435	(N1219N)	N434CC	N20CL	N390DA	N674G				
435	550-0436	N1219P	N711Z	N717DM	N717TR					
436	551-0436	N1219Z	N235KK	N437CF	N11SS	N102DR				
437	550-0438	N12190	(N555TD)	N437CC	N643TD	N100CH	N686RC			
438	550-0432	(N12191)	N432CC	I-ASAZ	N76AS	(N258TT)				
439	550-0439	N1220A	ZS-LHT	N550RS	HK-3191X	N550RS	N511WS	N1250V		
440	550-0440	(N1220D)	N31F	N31FT	N120TC	OY-CYV				
441	550-0441	N1220J	N50LM	N56PC	VR-CCE	HB-VKS	N221GA	G-RVHT	N80LA	G-JETO
		(CN-...)	N476RS							
442	550-0442	(N1220N)	N32F	N53M	N943LL	N442MR	N442ME	N668AJ		
443	550-0443	N1220S	N777FE	N777FB	OY-CYT	D-CGAS	EC-IMF			
444	550-0444	(N1248G)	N67MP	(N67ME)	N47SW	N71GA	C-FMJM	C6-...		
445	550-0445	N1248K	(N666WW)	N453S						
446	550-0446	N1248N	Spain U.20-2/01-406							
447	550-0447	"N1248K"	N12482	(N447CJ)	HB-VIS	G-JBIS	N550HT			
448	550-0448	N1249B	N964JC	N964J	N309AT	N82GA	N93DW	(N39HD)	N938W	N994CF
		N994CE								
449	550-0449	N1249H	(YV-1107)	YV-2338P	Venezuela 1107		YV-2338P			
450	550-0450	N1249K	N15EA	N505RP	N899RJ					
451	550-0451	N1249P								
452	550-0452	(N1249T)	N452CJ	N150DM	N707WF	N707PE	N707PF			
453	550-0453	N1249V	N962JC	N962J						
454	550-0454	N1216K	(N258P)	N12490	N93BD	N938D	(N250KD)	N905MH		
455	550-0455	N1250B	(YV-04CP)	N90SF	PT-MMO					
456	550-0456	N1250C	(N456CM)	N549CC	N24RF	N20RF	C-GMPQ	N283DF		
457	550-0457	N1250L	N220CC	N457CF	N63TM	OY-TMA	N122HK			
458	550-0458	N1250P	N458CC	(N458DS)	XA-SET	N25MK	N664SS	LV-BCO		
459	550-0459	N12500	N15TW	N15TV	N315ES	N604PJ				

CITATION II

Unit No	C/n	Identities								
460	550-0460	N12505	N818TP	N818TB	(PT-...)	N6523A	PT-OKP			
461	550-0461	N12507	N22FM							
462	550-0462	N12508	N509TC	N67JW	XA-LTH	XB-LTH	N501DK	N550AL	N62TL	(N550DK)
463	551-0463	N1251B	N121JW	(N131EL)	YV-05C	YV-713CP	YV1563			
464	550-0464	N1251D	XC-HEP	XA-SQR	N117TA	N822HA				
465	550-0465	N1251H	N206TC	N68JW	HB-VIU	N784A	N387HA	N551WJ	N90PT	
466	550-0466	N1251K	HI-420	(N1251K)	HI-420	N1251K	I-TNTR	N412MA	N10LY	
467	550-0467	N1251N	N1883	N64PM	N64CM	YV-810CP	YV2166			
468	550-0468	(N1251P)	N468CJ	D-CBEL	N123FH	N120JP				
469	550-0469	N1251V	G-BKSR	VR-BIZ	HB-VIP	N123SR	N50N	[crashed 18Oct01 Bolzano A/P Italy; cx Nov01]		
		(OY-ERY)	N50N	(I-....)	(OY-...)	N420SS	N550GT			
470	550-0470	N1251Z	N10RU	F-GFJL	N10RU	N202SW	N60FT			
471	550-0471	N12510	N797WC	N787WC	N92B	(N623KC)	N271AG	N770TB	N1HE	
472	550-0472	N12511	HZ-AFP	N12511	N492MA	N492AT	[w/o 24Jan07 Butler, PA; parted out]			
473	550-0473	N12513	HZ-AFQ	N12513	N484MA	XB-HZF	N70224	XB-IZK	XC-LLL	
474	550-0474	N12514	ZS-LIG							
475	550-0475	N1252B	N870MH	N475WA	N475HC					
476	551-0476	N1252D								
477	550-0477	N1252J	N1515P	N151JC	N648WW	N649WW	N47TW	(N477JR)	N269JR	N269JD
		N344KK	(N846L)	YV210T	YV2932					
478	550-0478	N1252N	N4FE	N57BC	N214RW	N17WC	N32SM			
479	550-0479	N1252P	N999RC	PT-OOM	N45NS	N68TS	N600HW			
480	550-0480	(N12522)	N72K	N72U	YU-BPL	SL-BAC	S5-BAC	N335CC	N380MS	ZS-OIE
481	550-0481	N1253D	N550MW	D-IADD	N531A	CC-LLM	N481VP	N97EM	N97FM	
482	550-0482	N1253G	N62GC	N62WG	N594G	N99DY	N550WR			
483	550-0483	(N1253K)	N141AB	N483AS	N83AG	N147PS	N483SC	N412PE	N17FS	N17VP
		N729TA	N917BB							
484	550-0484	N1253N	N84EA	N501GG						
485	550-0485	N1253P	N474SP	N74SP	N485A	PT-WBV	N727C	PR-LJJ		
486	550-0486	N1253Y	A4O-SC	N410CS	(N35PN)	XA-AAK	XA-ATA	CC-AHQ		
487	550-0487	N12532	(N487CC)	N444BL	N550DW					
488	550-0488	N12536	N84EB	C-FCSS	N990MM	N990MR				
489	550-0489	N12539	N63CC	N15RL	(N801TA)	N489SS	N121MJ			
490	550-0490	N1254C	N490CC	(N490CD)	J8-JTS					
491	550-0491	(N1254D)	I-AVRM	D-CVRM	[stored Rome/Ciampino, Italy]					
492	550-0492	(N1254G)	I-AVGM	D-CVGM	[stored Rome/Ciampino, Italy]					
493	550-0493	N1254P	(N258P)	N84AW	N84GC					
494	550-0494	N1254X	XC-JBR+	[+marks worn when flying Mexican Customs missions]						
495	550-0495	(N1254Y)	N495CC	JA8495	N505GL	PT-LLQ	(N400MC)	N10TC		
496	551-0496	(N12543)	N232CC	N8008F	N999GH	LX-PRS	LN-ACX	OE-FAD	9A-DOF	
497	550-0497	(N12549)	N1257B	XC-JBQ+	[+marks worn when flying Mexican Customs missions]					N1257B
		[stored Conroe, TX]								
498	550-0498	(N1255D)	N550CJ	N1823B	N78FK	N772SB				
499	550-0499	(N1255G)	N550PT	PT-LIV						
500	551-0500	N1255J	N90RC	N501MC	N9CR	N568PC				
501	550-0501	N12549								
502	550-0502	N1255D	Turkey 12-001		Turkey 84-007		Turkey 007			
503	550-0503	N1255G	Turkey 12-002		Turkey 84-008		Turkey 008			
504	550-0504	(N1255J)	N979C	N979G	N72SL	XA-TQA				
505	550-0505	N1255K	XC-JAY+	[+marks worn when flying Mexican Customs missions]					N1255K	[stored Conroe, TX]

Unit numbers 506 to 549 not used (506 to 531 built as S550s c/n 0001 to 0026 – qv)

Unit No	C/n	Identities								
550	550-0550	N1299N	PT-LOC	N550FM	HK-4128W	N550FM	N177RJ			
551	550-0551	N487LD	N600AT							
552	551-0552	OE-FPA	D-IADV							
553	550-0553	N553CC	N46MT	XA-ODC	(N555SL)	N5XR	N553MJ			
554	550-0554	N1297Y	ZS-NAT	N2140L	N40FC	(N40WE)	N40YC	N700JR	(N705JT)	N750SL
		N758SL								
555	550-0555	N1297Z	(EI-BUN)	EI-BUY	D-IRKE	N93BA	N560CB	N104HW	[parted out by Dodson Int'l,	
		Rantoul, KS]								
556	551-0556	(N12979)	N200GF	N513WT						
557	550-0557	N1298C	N711NV							
558	550-0558	(N1298G)	N209G	N558VP	N558AG	LV-WJN				
559	550-0559	(N1298H)	G-BNSC	VR-CHB	D-ICHE	OO-MMP	N409ST			
560	550-0560	N1298J	ZS-LNP	N560AJ	D-IMMF	N550GX	(YV....)			
561	550-0561	N1298K	I-SALV	N916WJ	PT-OYP	(N234RA)	C-GYCJ	[canx 14Oct03 as sold in USA; to Dodsons Intl		
		Parts following accident 12Nov02 Sandspit, BC, Canada]								
562	550-0562	(N1298N)	D-CBAT	N562CD	PT-OJT	N813A	N54RM	N45FS		
563	550-0563	N1298P	G-THCL	N518N						
564	550-0564	N1298X	PH-MCX	(N87683)	N564VP	C-GBCF	N674CA	D-CASH	[w/o 19Feb96 nr Freilassing,	
		Salzburg, Austria]								
565	550-0565	N1298Y	N565CJ	N88BM	N565JS	N565NC	N568ST			
566	550-0566	(N1299B)	N15SP	N15SN	N900PB					
567	550-0567	(N1299H)	N321F	N41BH	N926RM	N191TF	N315RS*			
568	550-0568	N1299K	N988RS	N83KE	N47SM					

CITATION II

Unit No	C/n	Identities								
569	550-0569	N1299P	G-JFRS	G-OSNB	5Y-TWE	ZS-SCX	C-GQYL			
570	550-0570	(N1299T)	N2KH	N570VP	N570WD	N270CW	(N189WW)	(N550AZ)		
571	550-0571	N12990	N90JJ	(N278S)						
572	551-0572	N12992	N193SS	N719EH	D-IRUP					
573	550-0573	(N12993)	C-FJOE	N944AF	PT-OKM	N155AC	YV2831			
574	551-0574	N12998	N60GL	N60GF	OE-FBS	N22AA	N1RV			
575	550-0575	N12999	N910G	N46BA	N337RE	N387RE				
576	550-0576	(N1300G)	N576CC	N438SP	N675SS	(N183JN)	(PR-PBV)	PR-MGT		
577	550-0577	(N1300J)	N557CC	N100CX	N120HC	N827JB	N8344M			
578	550-0578	N1300N	PT-LQJ	N54NS	N203PM	N15DF				
579	550-0579	(N13001)	N579L	N750TB						
580	550-0580	(N13006)	N912BD	N18NA						
581	550-0581	(N13007)	N905LC	N805LC						
582	550-0582	(N1301A)	Colombia FAC1211							
583	550-0583	N1301B	N62WA	(N583VP)	N12L	N12LW	N22PC	(N22PQ)	(N228G)	
584	550-0584	N1301D	N550WW	N550WV	N25QT	N25QF	N979WC			
585	550-0585	N1301K	C-GTCI	N94AF	N79SE	N89SE	N65AR	N585PS	VP-CRA	N585RA
586	550-0586	N1301N	F-GGGA							
587	550-0587	N1301S	ZS-MBX	N550SM	N1301S	N18HJ				
588	550-0588	N1301V	N255CC	N92BD	(N747RT)	N633RT				
589	550-0589	N1301Z	N679BC	N787JD	N589SJ	N12LD	N92LD	N86UR		
590	550-0590	C-GBCA	N673CA	N88NM	XA-UGG	XB-OFK	N941SC	N64DY		
591	551-0591	C-GBCE	N672CA	N1AT	N608JR					
592	550-0592	N1302N	Spain U.20-3/01-407							
593	550-0593	N1302V	N26621	XC-JBT+	[+marks worn when flying Mexican Customs missions]					N26621
		[stored Conroe, TX]								
594	550-0594	N1302X	N2531K							
595	550-0595	N2734K	XC-JCV+	[+marks worn when flying Mexican Customs missions]						
596	550-0596	N96TD	D-CAWA	EC-HGI						
597	550-0597	N13027	G-SSOZ	G-MRTC	N24EP	N400LX	N400EX	N213JS		
598	550-0598	N13028	(PT-...)	XC-ROO	N7WY	N888XL				
599	550-0599	G-SYKS	N599FW	VR-BPF	VR-BYE	N571BC				
600	550-0600	N1303H	PT-LSR	N415AJ						
601	550-0601	(N1303M)	G-ELOT	G-OCDB	G-CBTU	N42NA	N501RL			
602	550-0602	N2663Y	XC-JAZ+	[+marks worn when flying Mexican Customs missions]					N2663Y	[stored Conroe, TX]
603	550-0603	N603CJ	C-GMSM	N560AB	N550TW					
604	550-0604	N821G	N30WE	LV-WIT	N64VP	N827JB	N887SA	N904SJ		
605	550-0605	N26494	[stored Conroe, TX]							
606	550-0606	N770BB	N602AT							
607	550-0607	N26496	XC-JCW+	[+marks worn when flying Mexican Customs missions]					N26496	[stored Conroe, TX]
608	550-0608	N12419	PT-LTL	(N675DM)	N608VP	N608AM	N990M			
609	550-0609	(N1242A)	N609TC	D-CHOP	N344A	F-GLTK				
610	550-0610	N1242B	"M-JMF"	9M-JMF	(9M-UEM)	9M-NSA	N610BL	N610JB	YV2875	
611	550-0611	(N1242K)	F-GGGT							
612	550-0612	N1244V	N300AK	N380AK	(N534M)	N578M	YV3274			
613	550-0613	N1250P	PT-OAC	N664AJ						
614	551-0614	(N1251P or N1251V)		D-ILAN	N26HG					
615	550-0615	N12522	N88HF	N87CF	CS-AYS	N615EA	N577VM	N577VN	N803SC	
616	550-0616	(N1253K)	N55LS	(D-IAFA)	PT-OVV	N611NM	(PP-ONA)	PR-OLB		
617	551-0617	(N1253Y)	N617CM	D-ILTC	N450GM	N747JB	N881SA	N40EP	(N551GK)	
618	550-0618	N1254C	PT-LXG	PP-ESC						
619	550-0619	(N1254D)	N170TC	(N619BA)	N550BD	XA-LRL	N15FJ	N522FJ	N552FJ	N67BE
620	550-0620	N1254G	PT-LYA	N250GM	N508DW	(N508AJ)	N477JE	(N391DH)	N391DT	
621	550-0621	N12543	ZS-MLS	N502SU	OY-RDD	N102PA	N99TK			
622	550-0622	(N1255J)	N326EW	N826EW	HB-VKP	LX-VAZ	F-HAJV			
623	550-0623	(N1255L)	N89LS	PR-VIR	PR-VLJ*					
624	550-0624	N1255Y	PT-LYS	N662AJ	N65DV					
625	550-0625	(N12554)	PT-LYN	N625EA	N6846T	(F-HCCN)	F-HBFK			
626	550-0626	(N1256G)	N117GS	N626VP	LV-PLR	LV-WOZ	N466SS			
627	550-0627	(N1256N)	N17FL	N650WC	N804BC	N494GP				
628	550-0628	(N1256P)	N183AJ	N183AB	Ecuador IGM-628					
629	550-0629	N1256T	D-CHVB	[w/o 25Jan95 Allendorf, Germany; cx Mar95]						
630	550-0630	N1257K	PH-CSA	N220AB	N198DF	N198ND	PP-CMG	N18GY		
631	550-0631	(N1257M)	N631CC	XA-RUD	XA-ICP	N631EA	N631TS			
632	550-0632	N12570	5N-AYA	Nigeria NAF050		Nigeria NAF960				
633	550-0633	N12576	PT-OSK	N388FA	N7AB	N550AB				
634	550-0634	(N1258B)	PH-MDX	N550SB	SE-DVT	F-HDGT	EC-LBO			
635	550-0635	N1258H	PT-OAA	N550NS	(N622EX)	N622VH	(N214CP)	N277JE	N550HW	N760M
636	550-0636	N1258M	N4EW	N50NF	YV565T					
637	550-0637	(N1258U)	YV-376CP	YV2286						
638	550-0638	(N12582)	N500RR	N1717L	N255TC					
639	550-0639	(N1259B)	N22RG	N62RG	N100DS					
640	550-0640	(N1259K)	N1308V	PT-ODL						
641	550-0641	(N1259N)	N1309A	PT-OOA	N1309A	PT-WON	N395HE	(N391DT)	N895HE	N996AC
642	550-0642	(N1259R)	N1309K	XA-JRF	XA-SEX	XB-IKY	XB-TTT			
643	550-0643	(N1259S)	N13091	PT-ODW	N643MC	N747CR	G-EJEL			

CITATION II

Unit No	C/n	Identities
644	550-0644	(N1259Y) (N13092 or N1310B) XC-PGM
645	550-0645	(N1259Z) N1310C PT-ODZ
646	550-0646	(N12593) (N1310G) N9VF N562RM
647	550-0647	(N12596) N647CC N205BE N140MD N800MT N604DS YV603T
648	550-0648	N1260G (N1310Q) XC-PGP [instructional airframe, Instituto Politecnico Nacional Centro de Estudios Cientifico y Tecnologicos, Mexico City, Mexico]
649	550-0649	(N1310Z) I-ATSE N4320P N44LC N44LQ HB-VMH N649DA G-SOVA VH-VDF
650	550-0650	(N1311A) PK-WSG+ [+ marks worn but not officially reg'd] N28RC N824CT N823CT C-GBBX N38MR N50CZ N569GB XB-BRT XB-ODN
651	550-0651	(N1131K) N24E
652	550-0652	(N1311P) N3262M XC-HJF+ [+marks worn when flying Mexican Customs missions]
653	550-0653	N36854 N30RL
654	550-0654	N36886 XA-RZB XB-BON XB-LWN
655	550-0655	N37201 XC-LHH+ [+marks worn when flying Mexican Customs missions]
656	550-0656	N30GR
657	550-0657	N3986G CC-DGA
658	550-0658	N550MZ RP-C1180 N137PA RP-C5538
659	550-0659	N4614N XC-HGZ+[+marks worn when flying Mexican Customs missions]
660	550-0660	N5233J D-CMJS 5B-CIQ N550JF D-CILL N160SP N827DP [w/o 03Aug08 Reading, PA; parted out by AvMATS, St Louis, MO] N825LH [cx 27Jun11]
661	550-0661	N5252C N550RA N847HS N3444B N3444P XA-AFU N550AR VT-CLB
662	550-0662	N5294C N911CB N911QB N623DS N623JL XA-UME
663	550-0663	N5314J XC-JCX+ [+marks worn when flying Mexican Customs missions]
664	550-0664	N5315J N67LH XA-RYR N70PC N45BE N427TP
665	550-0665	N5348J N665MC N998BC
666	550-0666	(N5703C) N5408G XC-JBS+ [+marks worn when flying Mexican Customs missions]
667	550-0667	EC-621 EC-FDL N668EA VR-CWM VP-CWM N167EA N107EE
668	550-0668	N668CM N1879W (N866VP) XA-TVH N48PJ
669	550-0669	N6170C N98TJ N6170C N846HS N677GS VH-CFO P2-SOS VH-VBK N881JG N425WY
670	550-0670	N6637G XC-JCZ+ [+marks worn when flying Mexican Customs missions]
671	550-0671	(N6761L) 9M-TAA N671EA G-BWOM G-VUEA [cx 15Sep14; wfu Cambridge, UK]
672	550-0672	N6763C PT-OMB N550PF G-OTIS (N394MA) OY-VIS SE-RHP G-IBZA F-HBZA
673	550-0673	N6763L XC-HHA+ [+marks worn when flying Mexican Customs missions] [w/o Greenwood, SC, 17Nov12]
674	550-0674	(N6770S) (N550FB) N1883M N1888M N45TP N65TP N910HM N918HM N690AN XB-ACS
675	550-0675	N6773P PT-OJK N275BD PT-WKQ
676	550-0676	N67741 PT-OJG
677	550-0677	N6775C XC-HJC+ [+marks worn when flying Mexican Customs missions]
678	550-0678	N6775U EC-777 EC-FES SE-RCI EC-KBZ
679	550-0679	(N6776P) I-FJTO N250GM N622EX N782ST (N64JY)
680	550-0680	N6776T XC-HJE+ [+marks worn when flying Mexican Customs missions]
681	550-0681	(N6776Y) N1200N XC-LHA+ [+marks worn when flying Mexican Customs missions]
682	550-0682	N682CM YV-662CP N682CJ N90BL N90BY N73HH
683	550-0683	YV-701CP YV1192
684	550-0684	N6778L C-FJXN
685	550-0685	C-FJWZ
686	550-0686	C-FKCE
687	550-0687	N6778Y C-FKDX
688	550-0688	C-FKEB
689	550-0689	N12001 XA-JPA XA-JYO N689VP
690	550-0690	N6780C OE-GLZ VH-VLZ M-AGGY (D-CAAB) [dbr 11Dec15, Oyonnax/Arbent, France]
691	550-0691	N910H C-GAPD C-GAPV N600JB
692	550-0692	N692TT N75RJ N814LC
693	550-0693	VR-BTR VP-BTR N594WP
694	550-0694	N694CM N550KE N807MB
695	550-0695	N6782T N695VP N870WC N7851M N77DD N153TH N466SG
696	550-0696	N29PF N67PC N67NC N696VP (N74EH)
697	550-0697	N6851C ZS-NFL N697EA HB-VMP D-CHEP N697BA LV-BRE
698	550-0698	N12003 YV-911CP N550RM VT-CLC
699	550-0699	C-FKLB
700	550-0700	C-FJCZ
701	550-0701	C-FLZA
702	550-0702	C-FMFM
703	550-0703	N308A [parted out by Alliance Air Parts, Oklahoma City, OK] N157A
704	550-0704	N704CD (N197GH) N197HF (N187HF) N197PR
705	550-0705	N521TM
706	550-0706	7Q-YLF N706NA N168ES
707	550-0707	N1202T RP-C4654 (SE-DYY) N707EA OE-GDM HS-RBL OE-GRD SX-FDA
708	550-0708	N12022 N720WC N923JH
709	550-0709	N1203D N709CC N12RN N18RN N85KC N709VP N709RS VT-SGT N425ST
710	550-0710	N1203N ZP-TCA N510VP N90BJ N678GS
711	550-0711	N1203S N711CN N58LC XB-ZZZ N711ZC N53DD
712	550-0712	(N12030) PH-LAB
713	550-0713	N12033 N293PC N95HE N283CW N400EC
714	550-0714	N12035 N593EM G-SPUR

CITATION II / BRAVO

Unit No	C/n	Identities								
715	550-0715	N1204A	PT-OTN	N715AB	LV-PNL	LV-YHC	LQ-YHC			
716	550-0716	N1205A	N4VR	(N800KC)	VR-CTE	VP-CTE	VP-CTF	N550TL	XB-OGJ	
717	550-0717	(N1205M)	XA-TCM	N600GH	TC-SES	Sweden 103002		SE-RBM	OE-GBC	F-HBMR
718	550-0718	N12060	XA-FIR	N142GA	N129ED	N550HM				
719	550-0719	N12068	(N550BG)	YV1504	YV2766	Venezuela 1603				
720	550-0720	(N1207A)	N720CC	XA-SMV	N72WE	N848HS	N260TB	N550MW		
721	550-0721	N1207B	N721CC	YV3023						
722	550-0722	N1207C	XA-SMT	N1886G	N220LE	PP-JAS	N722CJ			
723	550-0723	N1207D	N5NE	(N888NA)	N777JE	PR-SNV				
724	550-0724	N1207F	LV-PGU	LV-WEJ						
725	550-0725	N1207Z	N222FA	N725CC						
726	550-0726	N1209T	XT-AOK	N918GA	VP-CMD	N726BM	N726AM	XA-CSM		
727	550-0727	(N1209X)	N727CM	N521BH	LV-ZNR	N232JS	N550DG	N550KR	VT-CLD	
728	550-0728	(N1210N)	N728CC	LV-PHN	LV-WJO					
729	550-0729	N1210V	VR-CBM	VP-CBM	N38NA					
730	550-0730	N1211M	N730BR	(N730VP)	N2NT	N773VP	(N650JP)	N501JP	XA-WWG	XA-UPX
731	550-0731	N12117	N550BP	XC-SST						
732	550-0732	N1213S	N101AF	N902DK	N36WL	N232KS				
733	550-0733	N1213Z	C-GFCI	N4347F	N550VR	N550TR	N44SW	N37HF	YV....	
734	550-0734	[first Bravo model]		(N1214J)	N550BB	[cx 05Apr17, CofR expired]				

Production continued as Citation Bravo

CITATION BRAVO

C/n	Identities						
550-0801	N5135K	N801BB	[parted out by MTW Aerospace, Montgomery, AL]				
550-0802	N5135R	N802CB	N550HH				
550-0803	N52113	N550FB	N141HL	N251CF	N251CM	N63TK	
550-0804	N5214J	N804CB	N550BC	(N41VY)			
550-0805	N5214K	N108RF	N4AT				
550-0806	N52141	N300PY	C-GKUT	N100RJ			
550-0807	N52144	C-FANS	C-GPGA	C-FJDS			
550-0808	N5216A	N1299B	SE-DVZ	YU-BSM	M-SGCR		
550-0809	N800AK	N300AK	N380AK	(N35KT)	[parted out by Alliance Air Parts, Oklahoma City, OK]		
550-0810	N5218T	VH-MGC	VH-XCJ	VH-XBP			
550-0811	N5221Y	PT-MMV					
550-0812	N5223P	C-FJBO	N808MV	N238EJ			
550-0813	N5096S	N813CB	N100KU	YV611T			
550-0814	N5093L	PT-WNH	N303CS	C-GOKO			
550-0815	N51038	N126TF					
550-0816	N5225K	C-FMCI	N550HK				
550-0817	N5076J	N817CB	(YV....)	N123GF	N550RZ		
550-0818	N5097H	LV-PMV	LV-WYH	N818AJ	N300CS	YV521T	
550-0819	N5092D	N1259B	N15CV	N15CN	N324JT		
550-0820	N5117U	N820CB	N302CS	N774KD	N779KD	N924CB	
550-0821	N5093Y	N77797	N225WT	N129LT			
550-0822	N5214L	N550TG	N822CB	N52MW	N2029E	N725DS	
550-0823	N50715	(N823CB)	N25FS				
550-0824	N5121N	N824CB	N26AP				
550-0825	N5060P	N25HV	(N45HV)	N305CS	N717TF	N717RA	N717CH
550-0826	N51072	N595PC					
550-0827	N51042	D-CCAB					
550-0828	N5058J	N6FR	[parted out by MTW Aerospace, Montgomery, AL]				
550-0829	N5096S	N829CB					
550-0830	N5076J	(N550KE)	N830KE	N717CB			
550-0831	N5145P	N331PR					
550-0832	N5148B	PT-WSO	N832UJ	N77VZ	N109DC		
550-0833	N5145P	PT-WVC	N833PA	PR-FEP			
550-0834	N834CB	D-CALL	N811GG	[parted out by Team Aero, KS]			
550-0835	N835CB	N198SL	(N835VP)	(N10PZ)	N226PC		
550-0836	N51872	N122NC	N122NB				
550-0837	N5185J	OE-GPS					
550-0838	N49FW	N49KW	N813JD				
550-0839	N839DW	N101FG	N101ND	N80PT			
550-0840	N5086W	N442SW	N773CA	N256PH	N64RT		
550-0841	N5086W	N841WS	N841W	N999CX	[dbr in hailstorm 24Jul16, Colorado Springs, CO]		
550-0842	N86AJ	N842CB	N621KR	N621KM			
550-0843	N5079V	N627L	AP-BHE				
550-0844	N550KL						
550-0845	N51817	N550WS					
550-0846	N5101J	N517AF					
550-0847	N5076K	N133AV	N304CS	N544PS	N584PS	(N550JN)	

CITATION BRAVO

Unit No C/n	Identities							
550-0848	N997HT	N550J						
550-0849	(N849CB)	N51143	N541JG	N246CB	N315N	N623N	N71LU	N560JA
550-0850	N5073G	N551G	N551V	N125PK				
550-0851	N7NN	N711KT						
550-0852	N5076J	VH-FGK	[w/o Lismore, Australia, 05Sep15]			N674ND	[parted out by Dodson Int'l, KS]	
550-0853	N5086W	N398LS						
550-0854	N5188A	N550KH	N550KJ	XB-FIR				
550-0855	N132LF	N232JR	XB-LVV	XA-LVV				
550-0856	N820JM	N300GF	N300GP	N426JK	N103CX			
550-0857	N51246	VP-CNM	VP-CCP	N984BK	N1NL			
550-0858	N1273Q	N100WT						
550-0859	N551KH	(N550KH)	I-BENN	G-SDEP	N800WT			
550-0860	N860JH	(N860J)	N844DR	N220DH				
550-0861	N861BB	N26CB	N26CV	N577MC				
550-0862	N442SW	N1962J	N888HS	N1967J	N467HS			
550-0863	N704JW	N709JW	N577VM					
550-0864	N864CB	OE-GTZ	D-CCWD	HB-VOH	TJ-ROA			
550-0865	N505X	D-CPPP	OE-GRM	OM-ATS				
550-0866	N866CB	D-CHZF						
550-0867	N161TM							
550-0868	N5117U	N627BC						
550-0869	N98RX	N499WM						
550-0870	N50612	VP-CED	M-ISKY					
550-0871	N5108G	N871CB	I-GIWW	D-CIWW	N1Q	N76RB		
550-0872	N5093L	OE-GKK	5N-IZZ	G-SPRE				
550-0873	N5109R	PT-XSX						
550-0874	N5194B	D-CHAN	LX-EJH	D-CHMC	N237MB			
550-0875	N51055	TG-BAC	N800AB	N877SD	N7CP			
550-0876	N5135A	N876CB	5Y-MNG					
550-0877	N5085J	N21SL						
550-0878	N5135K	VH-ZLT						
550-0879	N5000R	N4M	N35ET					
550-0880	N5112K	N7YA						
550-0881	N5105F	N546MT	(N312RD)	N306CS	N546MT	N306CS	N108MV	
550-0882	N5068R	N488A	N12MA	N438SP	VH-VFP	N882WF		
550-0883	N469DE							
550-0884	N5090Y	N602BW	N1318Y	N361DB	VP-CGL	D-CSWM	N50W	
550-0885	N5109W	N820JM	N88AJ					
550-0886	N550KH	N500TS	N139RN					
550-0887	N887BB	XA-ABE						
550-0888	N550BF	N162TJ	(N218G)					
550-0889	N619JM	N360HS	N368HS					
550-0890	N1961S							
550-0891	N5093L	N82MA	N86PC					
550-0892	N22GR	(N84CF)						
550-0893	N5073G	N333EB						
550-0894	N51160	N550TE	N107EG	N413ST	N413CR			
550-0895	N199BB	N87GS	N17FS					
550-0896	N121L	N58WV	N157WW					
550-0897	N5079V	EI-GHP	G-GHPG	N897SC	LV-CVC			
550-0898	N550GH	N149HC						
550-0899	N5076K	N899DC	N535SW	N235BS				
550-0900	N327LJ	N327LN	N214TJ	N138CA				
550-0901	N5058J	N857AA						
550-0902	N5095N	N770JM	N770UM	N688JD	N898BA			
550-0903	N51055	N14HB	N903VP	PR-ERP	N551ZD			
550-0904	N5093Y	N904BB						
550-0905	N5101J	N505AG						
550-0906	N5166T	C-GLCE	N850GM	D-CSSS	HB-VNZ	N906MS		
550-0907	N5155G	N316MA	HB-VMM	SX-BMK				
550-0908	N5264M	N242SW	(N208FC)					
550-0909	N5076J	N706CP	(N909CA)	C-GDSH	N40KW	N44KW	N391BC	
550-0910	N5207V	N574M						
550-0911	N52655	N575M	[parted out by Alliance Air Parts, Oklahoma City, OK]					
550-0912	N5117U	N588AC						
550-0913	N5096S	N232BC	N66MT	N66MQ				
550-0914	N5105F	N897MC	N499GS	N399GS	N858RM			
550-0915	N51143	N915BB	N346CM	N348CM				
550-0916	N5265N	N555BK						
550-0917	N5100J	EI-DAB	(SE-RBY)	G-IDAB	G-MHIS	N127RG		
550-0918	N5109R	N45VM						
550-0919	N52601	N100Y	(N919TX)	N565AR				
550-0920	N5109W	N63LB	N854JA					
550-0921	N5073G	N40MF						
550-0922	N51896	I-FJTB	OE-GAH	N508UJ	N365EG			
550-0923	N51160	N676BB	N676PB	N23YC				

CITATION BRAVO

C/n	Identities								
550-0924	N5090Y	XT-COK	N550VC	YU-BZZ					
550-0925	N5090V	N1305C	5N-DUK	N550PF	N10UH				
550-0926	N5154J	N72PB	N100Z	N144Z					
550-0927	N5061P	PH-DYE	G-OPEM	G-IPLY					
550-0928	N5000R	PH-DYN	(N928DA)	N928CB	N129RP				
550-0929	N5086W	N552SM	N81AU*						
550-0930	N5066U	PP-ORM							
550-0931	N233DW	C-FAMJ							
550-0932	N5103J	G-MIRO	I-MTVB	5Y-BYD	9H-PAL				
550-0933	N5262X	N417KW	N325WP						
550-0934	N5260Y	N200AS							
550-0935	N5264A	EI-PAL	G-IPAL	G-IPAC	G-YPRS	HS-EMT			
550-0936	N5101J	N550TM							
550-0937	N51666	N440CE							
550-0938	N51038	N5VN	EC-HRO	LX-VVR	N938AM				
550-0939	N5076K	(N939BB)	VP-BNS	N48NS	[parted out Wichita/Mid-Continent, KS]				
550-0940	N5263S	G-FIRM	N125JJ						
550-0941	N5093Y	N900SS	N878AG	4X-CPW	N796MA				
550-0942	N5095N	N72SG	N265TS	ZS-BVO					
550-0943	N5117U	N706CP	YV-2711P	YV266T	YV3086				
550-0944	N5267J	N723RE	(TG-PIB)	N813AK	N263WC*				
550-0945	N5109R	N585KS							
550-0946	N52229	HB-VMX							
550-0947	N947CB	N514BC	XA-UQO						
550-0948	N5264E	N49FW	N48FW						
550-0949	N550KG	N45NS	N49NS	N550WB	N200NS				
550-0950	N555HM								
550-0951	N5076J	TC-TPE	N51KR	LN-SUV	G-CGEI				
550-0952	N5268V	N952CH	N749FF	N749FB	N811JA				
550-0953	N50612	N953GM	C-GZEK	N550WG	VH-CCJ				
550-0954	N5079V	PP-OAA							
550-0955	N50715	HB-VMW	EC-KHP						
550-0956	N51666	N572PB	N800VA						
550-0957	N51780	N957PH	G-IKOS						
550-0958	N5168Y	N333BD	N833BD	N404RK	D2-EPI				
550-0959	N5172M	N418KW	N511JP	N418KW					
550-0960	N52229	N960CB	TC-MKA						
550-0961	N5181U	N961BB	HK-4250X	HK-4250	N641L	HK-4597X	HK-4597	N960SC	N82P
550-0962	N5212M	N797TE							
550-0963	N52114	N24QT	N24QF	N990TC					
550-0964	N52234	HB-VMY	N550TA	N497MN					
550-0965	N52086	N741PP	N965BB	N741PP	N256CC	XA-USS			
550-0966	N51806	N36PT							
550-0967	N52397	N967CB	N432RJ						
550-0968	N51612	N551G							
550-0969	N5228J	N401KC	N119LC						
550-0970	N5243K	N367BP	N78MD						
550-0971	N5239J	N717KQ	N717GK						
550-0972	N52462	PH-HMA	S5-BBL						
550-0973	N5245U	N129PB							
550-0974	N307CS	N307MS	OE-GAL						
550-0975	N975HM	5Y-MSR							
550-0976	N5168Y	N308CS	N308MS	OE-GML	N8892D	HS-MED			
550-0977	N5172M	N309CS	(OE-GLM)	OE-GLG	[w/o Vienna 03Sep15]				
550-0978	N52475	N696CM	N95AN						
550-0979	N5147B	N311CS							
550-0980	N51666	N312CS	N146CT	N67JB					
550-0981	N5093L	N313CS	N800MT						
550-0982	N5260U	C-GDSH	C-GVIJ	C-FMOS	C-FMOI	N156GW			
550-0983	N51055	XA-SDI							
550-0984	N5227G	VH-HVM	(N984VP)						
550-0985	N5269J	G-FCDB	G-EHGW	N410TG					
550-0986	N52690	N986PA	N45NF	N458F	XB-DBT				
550-0987	N51780	N987GR	N471WR	N500VA	N500VT	N998TS			
550-0988	N5174W	N32FJ	I-FJTC	(D-CFTC)	OE-GVR	E7-FRA	N524XA	(N275TA)	
550-0989	N5270E	XA-LOF	XA-FUM						
550-0990	N5154J	N990JM	N448RL						
550-0991	N5270J	N4190A	N628CB	N628GB					
550-0992	N52086	N777NG	G-EKWS	D-COFY	EC-KKO				
550-0993	N5244W	N721T							
550-0994	N580SH	C-GLGB	C-GGQF	C-GUJP					
550-0995	N550PD	5Y-SIR							
550-0996	N5270P	CC-LLM	Chile C-53						
550-0997	N5192E	N67BK							
550-0998	N5165P	OE-GHP	(D-CGHP)	D-CELI					
550-0999	N5270E	XA-UVA	XB-UVA	XA-GEN					

CITATION BRAVO

C/n	Identities					
550-1000	N5194B	N121CN				
550-1001	N26CB					
550-1002	N52397	N101JL				
550-1003	N51743	N777UU	Pakistan 1003			
550-1004	N314CS	N114VP	N355DF	LV-CZD		
550-1005	N5247U	CS-DHA	N366EA	N847JJ	(N847JA)	N589HH
550-1006	N5212M	N106BB	N992HE			
550-1007	N51995	N717CB	N67PC	N67PV	N117VP	N664DF
550-1008	N5181U	N40435	D2-ECE			
550-1009	N5155G	CS-DHB	(LV-CZH)	N363CA		
550-1010	N5228J	N316CS	N116VP	N544PS	N116VP	
550-1011	N51780	C-FRST	N1000E			
550-1012	N20AU	N20RU	XA-GPO			
550-1013	N5166U	CS-DHC	N371EA	N886YS		
550-1014	N52475	N610CB				
550-1015	N5253S	N81ER	N81LR	N140TF	PR-PAB	
550-1016	N926ED	N926EC	N958GC			
550-1017	N51666	CS-DHD	N406CA	D-CYKP		
550-1018	N5259Y	SU-HEC	(D-CEFM)	OO-IIG	G-JBLZ	
550-1019	N5231S	N317CS	N117VP	N799JL	N519VP	(N14CG)
550-1020	N5166T	N212BH	N219LC	N495MH	N447SF	
550-1021	N5174W	N49KW				
550-1022	N5168Y	CS-DHE	SE-DJH	LN-IDD		
550-1023	N4405	C-FEVC	N353MC			
550-1024	N5254Y	N550FP	A2-BCL	N238JP		
550-1025	N5172M	CS-DHF	N712BG	N712BD		
550-1026	N5180K	N552CB	N438SP	N488SB		
550-1027	N52691	OO-FYG	N328SB	N299RK		
550-1028	N442LW	N442LV	C-FYUL	C-GWUL	N831HS	N851HS
550-1029	N5270J	N318CS	N118VP	N550AR	N550BJ*	
550-1030	N52397	N322GT				
550-1031	N525PE					
550-1032	N5223X	N880CM	N910N	N31AD	N127ZA	
550-1033	N52114	N933BB	N701VV			
550-1034	N52086	CS-DHG	N802CA			
550-1035	N585TH	YV2825				
550-1036	N319CS	N119VP	LV-CTF			
550-1037	N5180C	N1258B	YU-BTB	D-CKLS*		
550-1038	N551VB	(N551VP)	SE-RBY	RA-.....		
550-1039	N320CS	N711HA	N511HA	OE-GRB	N139JA	D-CESA
550-1040	N52446	N12378	OK-VSZ	OM-ATN		
550-1041	N5206T	N412ET	N7725D	N7765D	N31JB	XA-UTI
550-1042	N51869	G-ORDB	G-OJMW	M-WOOD	2-WOOD	
550-1043	N52235	CS-DHH	N490CA			
550-1044	N52369	N141AB	PR-HCA			
550-1045	N52690	PP-BMG				
550-1046	N300GF	N900GF				
550-1047	N5231S	N889B				
550-1048	N5253S	CS-DHI	N484CA			
550-1049	N5267G	N249CB	N299HS	YU-BSG	[w/o 15Jul10 Brac, Croatia]	
550-1050	N5268E	N105BX	A9C-BXC	D-CMIX	OY-EVO	
550-1051	N5155G	N251CB	N745CC	VH-EYJ		
550-1052	N322CS	N152VP	CP-2790			
550-1053	N57MC	N57ME				
550-1054	N5239J	N254CB	N600ST	5R-MGX		
550-1055	N896CG					
550-1056	N52601	N45678	N5852K			
550-1057	N5245U	N714RM				
550-1058	N52691	VH-SCC				
550-1059	N324CS	N159VP	N693SV	ZS-SUA		
550-1060	N669B	N927MM				
550-1061	N5267K	N325CS	N161VP	PP-LCE		
550-1062	N662CB					
550-1063	N5268V	N96TM	N151TM	N6TM	(N166TM)	N335RJ
550-1064	N823PM					
550-1065	N326CS	N175CW	N896MA			
550-1066	N573M					
550-1067	N5085E	N6TM	N114TM	N44SW		
550-1068	N668CB					
550-1069	N5093Y	OE-GLL				
550-1070	N5296X	N327CS	XA-CAP			
550-1071	N5090A	N104FL	XB-MNV			
550-1072	N5148B	N143BP	YV2877			
550-1073	N899B					
550-1074	N328CS	N404LS				
550-1075	N5162W	N275BB	N8701L	N87011	N26T	N26TY

CITATION BRAVO

C/n	Identities						
550-1076	N51872	N359GW	N550TT	VT-IBS			
550-1077	N329CS	N107VP	N336SC				
550-1078	N442NR	N807CT					
550-1079	N5268E	C-FRNG	N1271B	N444EA			
550-1080	N132MT	YV3183					
550-1081	N332CS	N181VP	N193PC				
550-1082	N5180C	CS-DHJ	N510CA	N550MK	N550ML		
550-1083	N5201M	I-PABL	G-PABL	G-PJDS	N778TB		
550-1084	N52141	N338CS	N184VP	HI915			
550-1085	N5068R	N339CS	N633PC				
550-1086	N52446	N58HK	G-OMRH	N623AR	N5171M	Argentina AE-186	
550-1087	N5265B	[test marks not confirmed]			N151FD	N876BB	
550-1088	N153SG	N158SG	N188VP	5Y-CCB			
550-1089	N334CS	(N186VP)	N189VP				
550-1090	N51038	CS-DHK	N514CA	N942EB			
550-1091	N335CS						
550-1092	N52645	CS-DHL	N92VR				
550-1093	N5263D	CS-DHM	N93VR				
550-1094	N5109W	N308DT					
550-1095	N336CS	(N195VP)	LV-CQV				
550-1096	N52626	N877B	N707HP	VT-BNF			
550-1097	N5148B	N337CS	N85SC	C-FWQM			
550-1098	N5132T	CS-DHN	N363WC				
550-1099	N5180C	CS-DHO	N595VR	XA-MXN			
550-1100	N5203S	N110BR	G-WAIN	N110VR			
550-1101	N5264U	N342CS	C-FMCG				
550-1102	N5214L	N1276A	AP-BHD				
550-1103	N50612	LZ-ABV	N1276Z	LZ-ABV	HS-PSL		
550-1104	N52144	CS-DHP	N504VR				
550-1105	N5117U	N332MT					
550-1106	N341CS	N106VP	HI925				
550-1107	N51744	TC-AHE					
550-1108	N5181U	N717VL	N717VF	PR-BVO			
550-1109	N5212M	N1281A	CS-DHQ	N109VR	N603DW		
550-1110	N877B	LV-CED					
550-1111	N5165P	OK-ACH	[w/o 14Feb10 nr Dresden, Germany]				
550-1112	N5202D	N47NM					
550-1113	N5218R	N724EH	N724EB	N569CC			
550-1114	N5223Y	N1298Y	CS-DHR	N114VR			
550-1115	N5223X	N4002Y	HZ-133				
550-1116	N52457	N4060Y	HZ-134				
550-1117	N52591	OO-FPB	N550HJ				
550-1118	N550CY	PR-SCP					
550-1119	N51072	N630JS	N230JS	N63NW	N1SU	N830TA	C-GBZF
550-1120	N5109W	N112BR	LV-BEU				
550-1121	N5061W	N1309B	9M-ZAB*				
550-1122	N5211Q	N984GB	OE-GEN	LZ-GEN	N396PB	PR-GPE	
550-1123	N5212M	N106FT	N675SS				
550-1124	N5076K	N417JD	N417JP	N410PS			
550-1125	N5262X	VH-YXY	N28SP				
550-1126	N5233J	N12993	HZ-135				
550-1127	N52623	N1298P	HZ-136				
550-1128	N5296X	N23AJ	PR-MGB				
550-1129	N52059	N60LW	M-BRVO	G-XJCJ			
550-1130	N5125J	D-CSMB					
550-1131	N5227G	N110TP					
550-1132	N5165P	N338B					
550-1133	N5201M	N579M					
550-1134	N5068R	N412ET	N412BT				
550-1135	N5180C	D2-GES					
550-1136	N51743	N998SR	OE-GMV	LZ-GMV			

Production complete

CITATION 550 UNIT NUMBER CROSS-REFERENCE

C/n	Unit	C/n	Unit	C/n	Unit	C/n	Unit	C/n	Unit	C/n	Unit
550-0001	001	550-0082	091	550-0170	186	550-0249	215	550-0332	372	550-0430	429
550-0003	003	550-0083	210	550-0171	188	550-0250	270	550-0333	358	550-0432	438
550-0004	004	550-0084	093	550-0172	187	550-0251	287	550-0334	361	550-0433	432
550-0005	005	550-0085	100	550-0174	201	550-0252	294	550-0335	365	550-0434	433
550-0006	006	550-0086	096	550-0175	178	550-0253	295	550-0336	367	550-0435	434
550-0007	007	550-0089	088	550-0176	203	550-0254	275	550-0337	368	550-0436	435
550-0008	008	550-0090	085	550-0179	192	550-0255	283	550-0338	074	550-0438	437
550-0009	009	550-0091	121	550-0180	193	550-0256	286	550-0339	370	550-0439	439
550-0010	010	550-0092	114	550-0181	194	550-0257	280	550-0340	374	550-0440	440
550-0011	012	550-0094	101	550-0182	195	550-0258	285	550-0341	373	550-0441	441
550-0012	013	550-0095	102	550-0183	206	550-0259	289	550-0343	391	550-0442	442
550-0013	016	550-0096	103	550-0184	142	550-0260	223	550-0344	378	550-0443	443
550-0014	015	550-0097	104	550-0185	228	550-0261	288	550-0345	376	550-0444	444
550-0016	017	550-0098	105	550-0186	197	550-0262	282	550-0346	382	550-0445	445
550-0017	021	550-0099	109	550-0187	198	550-0263	061	550-0347	380	550-0446	446
550-0018	019	550-0100	110	550-0188	207	550-0264	292	550-0348	381	550-0447	447
550-0019	022	550-0101	111	550-0189	205	550-0265	293	550-0349	383	550-0448	448
550-0021	011	550-0102	112	550-0190	209	550-0266	296	550-0350	384	550-0449	449
550-0024	041	550-0103	140	550-0191	213	550-0267	297	550-0351	386	550-0450	450
550-0025	025	550-0104	146	550-0192	214	550-0268	298	550-0352	393	550-0451	451
550-0026	026	550-0105	116	550-0193	249	550-0269	302	550-0353	397	550-0452	452
550-0027	027	550-0106	117	550-0194	217	550-0271	303	550-0354	388	550-0453	453
550-0028	028	550-0108	119	550-0195	259	550-0272	307	550-0355	411	550-0454	454
550-0029	029	550-0109	120	550-0196	219	550-0273	308	550-0356	390	550-0455	455
550-0030	030	550-0110	122	550-0197	220	550-0274	310	550-0357	379	550-0456	456
550-0031	031	550-0111	123	550-0198	221	550-0275	356	550-0358	389	550-0457	457
550-0032	032	550-0112	124	550-0199	222	550-0276	318	550-0362	396	550-0458	458
550-0033	033	550-0113	125	550-0200	225	550-0277	309	550-0363	394	550-0459	459
550-0034	034	550-0114	126	550-0201	227	550-0279	166	550-0364	403	550-0460	460
550-0035	042	550-0115	127	550-0202	230	550-0280	313	550-0365	404	550-0461	461
550-0036	036	550-0116	128	550-0203	231	550-0281	314	550-0366	399	550-0462	462
550-0037	037	550-0117	129	550-0204	239	550-0282	315	550-0367	405	550-0464	464
550-0038	038	550-0118	131	550-0205	218	550-0283	316	550-0368	402	550-0465	465
550-0039	039	550-0121	134	550-0206	226	550-0284	243	550-0369	431	550-0466	466
550-0040	040	550-0122	135	550-0207	234	550-0285	305	550-0370	076	550-0467	467
550-0041	043	550-0123	136	550-0208	241	550-0286	306	550-0371	086	550-0468	468
550-0042	044	550-0124	137	550-0209	232	550-0287	317	550-0374	106	550-0469	469
550-0043	046	550-0125	138	550-0210	247	550-0288	319	550-0376	113	550-0470	470
550-0044	047	550-0127	143	550-0211	244	550-0289	299	550-0378	133	550-0471	471
550-0045	045	550-0128	144	550-0212	245	550-0290	304	550-0381	170	550-0472	472
550-0046	050	550-0129	145	550-0213	250	550-0291	320	550-0382	172	550-0473	473
550-0047	056	550-0130	169	550-0214	236	550-0292	321	550-0383	173	550-0474	474
550-0048	048	550-0132	147	550-0215	238	550-0293	322	550-0390	269	550-0475	475
550-0050	052	550-0133	148	550-0216	240	550-0294	323	550-0393	291	550-0476	476
550-0051	060	550-0135	235	550-0217	263	550-0295	325	550-0396	331	550-0477	477
550-0052	067	550-0138	153	550-0218	199	550-0296	326	550-0398	338	550-0478	478
550-0053	053	550-0139	154	550-0219	035	550-0297	362	550-0399	342	550-0479	479
550-0054	054	550-0140	155	550-0220	248	550-0298	324	550-0400	350	550-0480	480
550-0055	055	550-0141	156	550-0221	253	550-0299	328	550-0401	364	550-0482	482
550-0056	070	550-0142	157	550-0222	237	550-0300	332	550-0402	366	550-0483	483
550-0057	073	550-0143	158	550-0223	242	550-0301	357	550-0403	371	550-0484	484
550-0058	071	550-0144	159	550-0224	251	550-0302	329	550-0405	385	550-0485	485
550-0060	075	550-0145	160	550-0225	258	550-0303	281	550-0406	398	550-0486	486
550-0061	077	550-0146	161	550-0226	262	550-0304	327	550-0407	401	550-0487	487
550-0062	078	550-0147	208	550-0227	254	550-0305	359	550-0408	406	550-0488	488
550-0064	080	550-0149	164	550-0228	252	550-0306	330	550-0409	407	550-0489	489
550-0065	065	550-0150	165	550-0229	255	550-0307	274	550-0410	408	550-0490	490
550-0066	081	550-0151	202	550-0230	265	550-0308	341	550-0411	409	550-0491	491
550-0067	094	550-0152	167	550-0231	271	550-0310	333	550-0412	410	550-0492	492
550-0068	058	550-0153	168	550-0232	284	550-0311	337	550-0414	413	550-0493	493
550-0069	063	550-0154	171	550-0234	189	550-0312	335	550-0415	414	550-0494	494
550-0070	064	550-0155	175	550-0235	257	550-0313	336	550-0416	415	550-0495	495
550-0071	066	550-0156	176	550-0236	260	550-0315	340	550-0417	416	550-0497	497
550-0072	072	550-0157	229	550-0237	264	550-0316	346	550-0418	417	550-0498	498
550-0073	068	550-0158	183	550-0238	233	550-0318	339	550-0419	418	550-0499	499
550-0074	069	550-0159	216	550-0239	256	550-0319	345	550-0420	419	550-0501	501
550-0075	057	550-0162	130	550-0241	268	550-0320	343	550-0421	420	550-0502	502
550-0076	099	550-0164	211	550-0242	059	550-0321	347	550-0423	422	550-0503	503
550-0077	082	550-0165	179	550-0243	273	550-0323	351	550-0424	423	550-0504	504
550-0078	083	550-0166	180	550-0245	279	550-0324	352	550-0425	424	550-0505	505
550-0079	087	550-0167	182	550-0246	282	550-0326	369	550-0426	425		
550-0080	089	550-0168	184	550-0247	276	550-0327	349	550-0427	426		
550-0081	090	550-0169	185	550-0248	261	550-0329	360	550-0428	427		

Note: From c/n 550-0550 onwards, unit number and c/n are the same.

CITATION 551 UNIT NUMBER CROSS-REFERENCE

C/n	Unit	C/n	Unit	C/n	Unit	C/n	Unit	C/n	Unit	C/n	Unit
551-0001	–	551-0027	002	551-0059	334	551-0171	141	551-0289	272	551-0393	392
551-0002	014	551-0029	150	551-0060	377	551-0179	149	551-0304	290	551-0396	395
551-0003	024	551-0031	174	551-0071	023	551-0180	151	551-0313	300	551-0400	400
551-0006	020	551-0033	212	551-0095	051	551-0181	152	551-0323	311	551-0412	412
551-0007	018	551-0035	277	551-0117	079	551-0191	163	551-0351	344	551-0421	421
551-0010	049	551-0036	162	551-0122	084	551-0201	177	551-0355	348	551-0428	428
551-0017	062	551-0038	246	551-0132	097	551-0205	181	551-0359	353	551-0431	430
551-0018	095	551-0039	278	551-0133	098	551-0214	190	551-0360	354	551-0436	436
551-0021	107	551-0046	267	551-0141	108	551-0215	191	551-0361	355	551-0463	463
551-0023	204	551-0050	196	551-0149	118	551-0223	200	551-0369	363	551-0481	481
551-0024	092	551-0051	301	551-0163	132	551-0245	224	551-0378	375	551-0496	496
551-0026	115	551-0056	312	551-0169	139	551-0285	266	551-0388	387		

Note: From c/n 551-0550 onwards, unit number and c/n are the same.

CITATION CONVERSIONS

The following Citations have been converted from 550 to 551 or 551 to 550:

550-0002 to 551-0027
550-0020 to 551-0071
550-0030 to 551-0077
550-0040 to 551-0085 to 550-0040
550-0044 to 551-0092 to 550-0044
550-0049 to 551-0095
550-0059 to 551-0122
550-0063 to 551-0117
550-0074 to 551-0109 to 550-0074
550-0084 to 551-0129 to 550-0084
550-0087 to 551-0132
550-0088 to 551-0133
550-0092 to 551-0146
550-0093 to 551-0141
550-0098 to 551-0140 to 550-0098
550-0100 to 551-0143 to 550-0100
550-0107 to 551-0149
550-0118 to 551-0162 to 550-0118
550-0126 to 551-0169
550-0128 to 551-0174 to 550-0128
550-0131 to 551-0201
550-0134 to 551-0179
550-0136 to 551-0180
550-0137 to 551-0181
550-0139 to 551-0184
550-0148 to 551-0191
550-0160 to 551-0171
550-0161 to 551-0205
550-0163 to 551-0214
550-0177 to 551-0223 to 550-0177 to 551-0223
550-0178 to 551-0245
550-0240 to 551-0285
550-0244 to 551-0289
550-0246 to 551-0296
550-0249 to 551-0236 to 550-0249
550-0253 to 551-0308 to 550-0253
550-0262 to 551-0304
550-0266 to 551-0309 to 550-0266
550-0268 to 551-0311
550-0270 to 551-0313
550-0278 to 551-0323
550-0298 to 551-0335
550-0299 to 551-0339 to 550-0299
550-0306 to 551-0341
550-0313 to 551-0345 to 550-0313
550-0314 to 551-0396
550-0317 to 551-0355
550-0322 to 551-0351
550-0328 to 551-0360
550-0331 to 551-0369
550-0342 to 551-0378
550-0353 to 551-0398 to 550-0353
550-0359 to 551-0400
550-0373 to 551-0018
550-0397 to 551-0059
550-0413 to 551-0413
550-0420 to 551-0419
550-0422 to 551-0422
550-0429 to 551-0428
550-0435 to 551-0434
550-0437 to 551-0436
550-0450 to 551-0450
550-0452 to 551-0452
550-0476 to 551-0476
550-0459 to 551-0459
550-0460 to 551-0460 to 550-0460
550-0463 to 551-0463
550-0475 to 551-0475 to 550-0475
550-0476 to 551-0476 to 550-0476
550-0481 to 551-0481 to 550-0481
550-0485 to 551-0485 to 550-0485
550-0487 to 551-0487 to 550-0487
550-0490 to 551-0491 to 550-0490
550-0496 to 551-0496
550-0559 to 551-0559
550-0572 to 551-0572
550-0574 to 551-0575
550-0584 to 551-0584
550-0591 to 551-0591
550-0604 to 551-0604 to 550-0604
550-0617 to 551-0617
551-0004 to 550-00031
551-0005 to 550-0013
551-0008 to 550-0219
551-0009 to 550-0263 to 551-0009 to 550-0263
551-0014 to 550-0068
551-0012 to 550-0242
551-0016 to 550-0338 to 551-0016 to 550-0338
551-0018 to 550-0373
551-0019 to 550-0371
551-0020 to 550-0374
551-0022 to 550-0376
551-0025 to 550-0378
551-0026 to 550-0377 to 551-0026
551-0029 to 550-0379 to 551-0029
551-0030 to 550-0383
551-0032 to 550-0382
551-0047 to 550-0390
551-0048 to 550-0307
551-0049 to 550-0381
551-0050 to 550-0385 to 551-0050
551-0052 to 550-0228
551-0053 to 550-0399
551-0055 to 550-0400
551-0057 to 550-0402
551-0058 to 550-0403
551-0059 to 550-0397 to 551-0059
551-0062 to 550-0406
551-0065 to 550-0396
551-0066 to 550-0401
551-0077 to 550-0030
551-0084 to 550-0039
551-0109 to 550-0074
551-0296 to 550-0246
551-0311 to 550-0268
551-0335 to 550-0298
551-0341 to 550-0306
551-0345 to 550-0313
551-0351 to 550-0322
551-0419 to 550-0420
551-0445 to 550-0445
551-0496 to 550-0496 to 551-0496
551-0551 to 550-0551
551-0555 to 550-0555
551-0557 to 550-0557
551-0559 to 550-0559
551-0560 to 550-0560
551-0567 to 550-0567
551-0584 to 550-0584

CESSNA S550 CITATION II

C/n	Unit No	Identities
0001	(0506)	(N1255L) N95CC (N969MC) (N36H) N969MC N969MQ N151DD N86BA (N550VS)
0002	(0507)	(N1255Y) (N507CC) N507CJ N111VP N211VP CC-CWW
0003	(0508)	(N12554) (N21AG) N847G N847C N847G [parted out by White Industries, Bates City, MO]
0004	(0509)	N1256B N830CB N554CA N72AM N178DA
0005	(0510)	(N1256G) N666LN N123FF
0006	(0511)	(N1256N) N101EC N71FM N71EM N27MH (N66EA) N29EA N65DT N181G
0007	(0512)	(N1256P) N51JH N573CC TC-SAM N30CX CS-DCE OO-MMJ CS-DCE OO-SKP EC-LQF
0008	(0513)	(N1256T) N40PL SE-DKI N204A (N40KM) N600KM [dbr Nov11; cx 24Sep12; parted out by Air Care Inc, Warsaw, IN]
0009	(0514)	N1256Z N550A N165JB N819EK
0010	(0515)	(N1257K) N651CC N49MJ N47MJ XA-INF XA-INK N747RL N747KL N422MJ N550F N829TG
0011	(0516)	(N1257M) N68SK N211QS N25GZ T7-IGO
0012	(0517)	(N12570) N550TB N550RV N777GG YV570T.
0013	(0518)	(N12576) (N518AS) N277AL N389L N561PS N551PS N84LG
0014	(0519)	(N12583) N32JJ N32TJ N214QS N777AM N84EC
0015	(0520)	(N1258U) C-GMTV N600EA
0016	(0521)	(N1259B) (N99VC) N85MP N557CS
0017	(0522)	(N1259G) (N47LP) N1259G N88G (N1259G) (N188G) N88GD N86PC N413CT
0018	(0523)	(N1259K) N501NB N814CC N1AF N145DF N627X N614JK
0019	(0524)	(N1259M) N15TT N519CJ N29AU N119EA (N600VE) N550TB N670JD N670DD
0020	(0525)	(N1259R) N550AS N550JT YV....
0021	(0526)	(N1259S) N593M N693M N320DG N945ER
0022	(0527)	(N1259Y) N258P N360M N460M N50NB
0023	(0528)	(N1259Z) N420CC N94RT N293RT N500ZB
0024	(0529)	(N12593) PT-LGI N34NS N790AL
0025	(0530)	(N12596) PT-LGJ [w/o 06Sep88 Rio-Santos Dumont, Brazil]
0026	(0531)	(N1260G) N19AF (N126LP) N24PH N24PF N32TX N33610
0027		N1260K D-CBUS N27EA N27FP N5WC C-GSSK N4HK N112BR
0028		(N1260L) HB-VHH S5-BAX 9H-MCM
0029		(N1260N) N185SF N608LB HB-VMJ N257JC C-FBDS
0030		(N1260V) N7007V N7007Q (N999GL) N999HC N509RP
0031		(N12605) N531CC N50DS N54WJ N50BK [w/o 13Aug02 Big Bear, CA]
0032		(N1261A) N532CC N532CF N232QS CS-DNA N232WC N48BV
0033		(N1261K) (G-BLSG) G-BLXN N550ST N531CM N581CM N256CP
0034		(N1261M) OE-GAP N34CJ N59EC N610GD N220BP
0035		(N1261P) N712S N711JG N711JN XA-THO N834DC
0036		(N12615) N95CC N36H N36HR N27B N63JG N63JU N63CR C-FRGY C-FOBQ N308GL
0037		(N12616) C-GERC N72WC N573BB N578BB N12S
0038		N3D N1982U N100KP (N801CC) N214PN N406CT
0039		N22UL YV3226
0040		(N1269D) C-FEMA [instructional airframe, Stevenson Aviation & Aerospace Training Centre, Portage La Prairie, Canada]
0041		(N1269E) N772M N592M N692M N74BJ N74LM [retro-fitted with Williams FJ44 engines] ZS-BEN N767G
0042		(N1269J) N250AL N250AF N241DS
0043		(N1269N) N101EG (N727NA) (N727AL) N727NA N727EF
0044		(N1269P) N92ME
0045		N1269Y YU-BOE BH-BIH T9-BIH N97CC N750JM
0046		(N12690) N553CC N760NB N103VF N198ST N63RS
0047		N12695 I-CEFI N16RP
0048		N1270D N797TJ N999TJ N705SP
0049		N1270K B-4101
0050		N1270S B-4102
0051		N1270Y N251QS CS-DNB N132WC N77PA N311AF
0052		N12703 N4TL N4TU (N552CF) N27SD N27GD N57BJ
0053		N12705 N75BL N253QS N1223N N393E
0054		N12709 N717LS N57MB N999CB N599CB N812HA
0055		N1271A N374GS N374GC N87FL N417RC N408CT
0056		(N1271B) C-GERL N550F N52FT
0057		N1271D N1UL N1UH N1UL N57CJ N800HW
0058		N1271E N633EE N936BR
0059		(N1271N) PT-LHD N36NS N829JC N329JC (N904VA) N531PM N329JC N71WH
0060		(N1271T) N85AB N588CT N314G N260QS N442KM
0061		(N12712) N540JB N46A (N464) N53JM N200LX N811RG N45NC
0062		N12715 I-AVVM D-CVVM
0063		(N12717) VH-EMO
0064		(N1272G) N2000X N200CX (N990HP) N45H N200CX N200CV N575SG (N557MG)
0065		(N1272N) N7118A N612ST (N900RG) (N909RG) N995DC N90FJ XB-PAX
0066		N1272P N711MD N699MM
0067		(N1272V) N550FS C-GMAV N70AF N789MA (N67VP) "EW94228" HC-BTY N550HA N900DM N828AF N917GP
0068		N1272Z N404G N4049 N7070A

S550 CITATION II

C/n	Unit No	Identities								
0069		(N12720)	N43VS							
0070		(N12722)	N570CC	N570RC	XB-EEP	N550SG				
0071		(N12727)	N571CC	N1865M	YV....					
0072		(N1273A)	(N572CC)	N1273A	N186MT	N686MC	TC-NMC	N62NS	N627HS	
0073		(N1273E)	N1958N	[parted out by White Industries, Bates City, MO]						
0074		N1273J	N550LC	N22EH	N274QS	N274PG	N74JE	N74GZ		
0075		(N1273N)	N554CC	N882KB	N882RB	(N275VP)				
0076		(N1273Q)	N95CC	C-GQMH	N89TD	N52CK	N25DY	VH-JLU		
0077		(N1273R)	N747CP	(N747GP)	N277QS	CS-DNC	N202WC	N999EA	N999QH	
0078		N1273X	ZS-CAR							
0079		(N1273Z)	N1000W	N100QW	N97AJ	N97LB	(N27TB)	5N-BEL	N578GG	
0080		N12730	C-GTDO	N581EA	(N269MT)	XA-TMI	N260BS	XA-VGF	N712MG	
0081		(N1274B)	N168HC	N550KM	PR-MCN	N404KK	YV2692			
0082		N1274D	N97TJ	N9KH	N282QS	N27TB				
0083		N1274K	N511BB	N511BR	OE-GNS	N511BR	N883PF	N683PF	N688AT	
0084		N1274N	PT-LJL	N584TR						
0085		N1274P	N683MB	N683CF	N54AM	(N285CF)	N220CA	N8BG	N143BP	N550BT
		YV3125								
0086		(N1274X)	N586CC	N900RB	N86QS	4X-COO	OB-1792-T	OB-1792	N11SU	D-CJJJ
		VH-SQM								
0087		N1274Z	N21EG	ZS-DES						
0088		(N12744)	N825HL	N288QS	N127RC	(N557TC)	N67FT			
0089		N12745	(N289CC)	N134GB	VT-RHM	VT-ETG				
0090		N12746	N777GF	N320S	N76FC	(N4BP)	N97BP	(N50BM)	N113VP	XA-AEZ
		N113VP	N499RC							
0091		(N12747)	N595CC	N595CM	N241LA	N477LC+	[+ marks reserved in error]			N476LC
0092		(N1275A)	N92QS	N923S	N489GM					
0093		N1275B	N593CC	N33DS	N93QS	N400RE	N629RA	YV3019		
0094		(N1275D)	N594CC	(N347CP)	F-OHAH	N560AJ	N6LL	N1H	N19ZA	
0095		N1275H	N200NK	N200NV	N345CC	N409CT	XB-MYO			
0096		(N1275N)	N95CC	N29X	N29XA	[w/o 05Mar89 Poughskeepsie, NY]				
0097		N1290B	N97QS	N828WB	N551BE	N551RF	N302MB	YV3310		
0098		N1290E	N98QS	CS-DDA	N598WC	N598KW				
0099		N1290G	N44GT	N299QS	N777FD	YV2469				
0100		(N1290N)	N3000W	(N616GB)	N300QW	N550SJ	N941RJ*			
0101		(N1290Y)	N101QS	C-FABF						
0102		N1290Z	N287MC	N285MC						
0103		N12900	N103QS	N22HP	[w/o 03May07 Dillon, MT]					
0104		N12903	N224KC	[retro-fitted with Williams FJ44 engines]						
0105		(N12907)	N105BG	(N1058G)	N623BG					
0106		(N12909)	N106QS	N666TR	N9072U					
0107		N1291E	N474L	N713DH	N550HT	C-GBGC	N553SD	YV2988		
0108		(N1291K)	N108QS	N316MH	N192RS	N132GS				
0109		N1291P	N509CC	N1GC	N7QC	N38EC	N61TL	N75MC	(N50SL)	N501VE
		YV3231								
0110		N1291V	N45GP	(N116LD)	N550WD					
0111		(N1291Y)	N111QS	(N777HN)	N57KF	HP-18BLM				
0112		(N12910)	N112QS	A2-MCB	ZS-PSG					
0113		(N12911)	N553CC	PT-LJQ						
0114		N1292A	PT-LKS							
0115		(N1292B)	N505CC	N520RP	C-FDDD	C-GWBF	N92JT	N92JC	N724JK	
0116		N1292K	N125CG	N550HC						
0117		N1292N	PT-LKT	[w/o 01Dec92 Sao Paulo-Congonhas, Brazil]						
0118		N12920	N600TF	N820FJ	N820F	VH-IWU	N118AJ	N110LH	N721LR	4X-COZ
0119		(N12922)	N261WR	N261WD	N700SW	N700SV	(N500LH)	N11TS	N11TR	N11TS
		N63HA	N616TG							
0120		N12924	N1283M	N716DB	N716DD	(N716QW)				
0121		(N12925)	D-CLOU	N23NM	(N20NM)	N711XR	N550JE	YV3218		
0122		N12929	I-TALG	N122WS	N163C	N163J				
0123		N1293A	N121CG	N609MT*						
0124		(N1293E)	N1867W	N52CK	N550JC	N554T	N555WV	N123TL		
0125		N1293G	N122CG	N97CT	(N552SM)	N125QA	YV3152			
0126		N1293K	N126QS	(N127RC)	ZS-EDA					
0127		N1293N	N14UM	(N127CF)	PT-OSL	N14UM	N674JM	N874JM	N97SK	N431MS
0128		N1293V	N911BB	N370M	N550CZ					
0129		N1293X	N87TH	N480CC	N488CC	N323JR				
0130		(N1293Z)	N130CC	N302PC	N550PL	N552SD	N552SE	YV....		
0131		N12934	D-CHJH	N87BA						
0132		(N1294D)	N533CC	N91ME	N91ML	N394HA				
0133		(N1294K)	G-VKRS	N7047K	I-ZAMP	N133VP	N431WM	N133VP	YV2853	
0134		N1294M	N134QS	D-CFAI	SE-DYO	OY-GMJ	N66HD	SE-DYO	N51DA	
0135		(N1294N)	OE-GPD	D-CIAO	N2235	VT-KMB				
0136		(N1294P)	[converted on line to prototype Citation V c/n 560-0001]							
0137		(N12945)	D-CNCA	HB-VKA	N100TB	PT-WIB				
0138		(N1295A)	N538CC	N305PC	N138QS	N713HH	(N501BE)	N552BE	N20CS	ZS-CWG
0139		(N1295B)	N906SB	N706SB	N39TF	N881A				

S550 CITATION II

C/n	Unit No	Identities							
0140		(N1295G)	C-GLCR	N575EW					
0141		(N1295J)	N907SB	N707SB	N26JJ	N550AJ			
0142		(N1295M)	N542CC	C-FALI	C-GCRG	N701BG			
0143		(N1295N)	N143QS	N1VA	N458PE	CC-CWZ			
0144		(N1295P)	D-CNCB	N6516V	N543SC	VQ-BFT	N543SC		
0145		(N1295Y)	(PH-HMC)	(PH-HMA)	PH-RMA	N145VP	4X-CPT	N900LM	
0146		(N1296B)	(G-JBCA)	N1296B	N81SH	N815H	YV327T	YV2671	
0147		N1296N	OO-OSA	CS-DDV	N659AS				
0148		N1296Z	ZS-IDC	N170RD	D-CSFD	N550BG	(SE-RCY)	(SE-RCX)	M-BULL
0149		N149QS	C-GMGB	N816V	N810V	N43RC	N777AX		
0150		(N1297B)	N150CJ	N107RC					
0151		(N2634E)	N151QS	N151Q	N550SP	N88NW			
0152		N26369	N848G	N843G	N987CJ				
0153		(N2637R)	N153QS	N242LA	N476LC+	[+ marks reserved in error]			N477LC
0154		N26379	PT-LQI	N910DS	N660AJ	N550DS			
0155		(N2638A)	N155QS	N155GB	N550DL	[retro-fiited with winglets and Williams FJ44 engines]			
0156		(N2638U)	N156QS	N766NB	(N400AJ)	N901PV	N63JT		
0157		N2639N	N157QS	N157BM	N802Q				
0158		(N2639Y)	N158QS	N301QS	N158QS	N66EH	N886RP	N889RP	N550EZ
0159		(N2646X)	N50GT	N289CC	N9GT	N9GY	YV3040		
0160		N2642Z	N550GT	PT-OSM	N121WF	YV3098			

Production complete

CESSNA 552 CITATION (T-47A)

C/n	Identities			
0001	N552CC	N12855	162755	[w/o 20Jly93 in hangar fire Forbes Field, Topeka, KS]
0002	N12756	162756	[w/o 20Jly93 in hangar fire Forbes Field, Topeka, KS]	
0003	N12557	162757	[w/o 20Jly93 in hangar fire Forbes Field, Topeka, KS]	
0004	N12058	162758	[w/o 20Jly93 in hangar fire Forbes Field, Topeka, KS; cx Sep93]	
0005	N12859	162759	[w/o 20Jly93 in hangar fire Forbes Field, Topeka, KS; cx Sep93]	
0006	N12660	162760	[w/o 20Jly93 in hangar fire Forbes Field, Topeka, KS; cx Sep93]	
0007	N12761	162761	[w/o 20Jly93 in hangar fire Forbes Field, Topeka, KS; cx Sep93]	
0008	N12762	162762	[w/o 20Jly93 in hangar fire Forbes Field, Topeka, KS; cx Sep93]	
0009	N12763	162763	[w/o 20Jly93 in hangar fire Forbes Field, Topeka, KS; cx Sep93]	
0010	N12564	162764	[w/o 20Jly93 in hangar fire Forbes Field, Topeka, KS; cx Sep93]	
0011	N12065	162765	[w/o 20Jly93 in hangar fire Forbes Field, Topeka, KS; cx Sep93]	
0012	N12566	162766	[in compound outside Columbus State Community College hangar at Columbus Bolton Field, OH as N12566]	
0013	N12967	162767	[w/o 20Jly93 in hangar fire Forbes Field, Topeka, KS; cx Sep93]	
0014	N12568	162768	[cx 03Nov09, scrapped]	
0015	N12269	162769	[w/o 20Jly93 in hangar fire Forbes Field, Topeka, KS; cx Sep93]	

Production complete

CESSNA 560 CITATION V/ULTRA/ENCORE

C/n	Identities									
707	N5079V	N560VU	[Citation Ultra Encore prototype, c/n 0424 reworked qv; cx Nov10, wfu]							
550-0001	N560CC	[Model 550 aircraft cvtd to 560 standard]								
560-0001	(N1294P)	N560CV	N1217V	N561VP	[cvtd on production line from c/n S550-0136]					
0002	N1209T	N562CV	N90PG	N101HB	N560VP	N560CZ				
0003	(N1209X or N1216A)		N563CV	SY-AAP	Seychelles SY-001		S7-AAP	Seychelles SY-001		N560BA
	N560ER	N413LC	N561CF							
0004	(N1210N or N1216J)		N189H							
0005	(N1210V or N1216K)		N953F							
0006	(N1211M or N1216N)		N962JC	N566VP	N570MH	N269TA	N569TA			
0007	(N12117 or N1216Q)		N964JC	(N57VP)	N717MB	N763D	N933SP	(N560C)		
0008	(N1213S or N1216Z)		N561B							
0009	(N1213Z or N12160)		N456FB	VH-HEY	N77HN	N77HU	N77NR	N37NR	N91CV	N636AS*
0010	(N1214J or N12162)		N205PC	N205BC	N643RT	N560JM				
0011	(N1214Z or N1217H)		N700TF	N913BJ						
0012	N1217N	N560ME	N560RR							
0013	(N1217P)	N560WH								
0014	N1217S	N1MC	N88TJ	N12ST	(N650ST)	N900SM				
0015	N12171	N800DL	N560MR	N580MR	N480DG					
0016	N12173	N68HC	N68HQ	N462B						
0017	(N1218P or N1223A)		N89BM	N560H	C-FPJT	N560JZ				
0018	(N1218Y or N12249)		N164DW	N114CP	N500FZ					
0019	(N1219D or N1226X)		N99WR	OE-GRW	N61TW	N643RT				
0020	(N1219G or N1228N)		N520CV	N560HC	N560HG	N7867T				
0021	N1228V	N682D	C-FDLT	N560DC	N669AJ	N410DW	N83EP			
0022	(N1228Y)	N211MA	N574BB	N574BP						
0023	(N12283)	OE-GDP	VR-CTL	N560JM	N31RC	N345MB	N3FA			
0024	(N12284)	N501QS	N4CS	N560FN	N140U	N3509R				
0025	(N12285)	CNA-NV								
0026	(N12286)	N560LC	N49MJ	N350RD	N380RD					
0027	(N12289)	N560JR	N20CC	(N20YC)	N560JR	N531MB	N531MF	N625WA	(N540PA)	
0028	(N1229A)	N6FE	N6FZ	N757CK	N753MB					
0029	(N1229C)	N590A								
0030	(N1229D)	N560W	XB-MTS	N570BJ	N40HT					
0031	N1229F	D-CHDE	N198MM	N520BP						
0032	N1229M	G-DBII	N96MT	N96MY	N560BC					
0033	N1229N	I-ATSB	N4333W	C-GAPC						
0034	(N1229Q)	N895LD	N401MC	N560PY	ZP-BTP					
0035	N1229Z	N36H	N561EJ							
0036	(N12295 or N2663B)		(N107CF)	(N107CR)	HZ-ZTC	N532MA	(N560EJ)	N200MM	N50EL	
0037	(N12297 or N2663X)		N17LK	N416HF	N560GG					
0038	(N12298 or N2663Y)		N301QS	N2296S	N212BW	N560CV				
0039	(N1230A or N26630)		CNA-NW							
0040	(N1230G or N2664U)		N12403	N71NK	N91NK	N91NL	N560CF			
0041	N26643	VH-NTH	N400KS							
0042	(N26648)	N42CV	D-CAWU	N142GA	N500SX	N560BF				
0043	(N2665F)	N991PC	[w/o 30Dec95 Eagle River Airport, WI; cx May96; to White Inds, Bates City, MO, for spares]							
0044	N2665S	N111VP	N331CC	N560JL						
0045	N2665Y	PT-LZQ	N560WF	N560WJ						
0046	(N26656)	G-CZAR	G-CJAE	N846MA	JA118N					
0047	N2666A	N500FK	N560WW							
0048	N2667X	N4TL	N74TL	N57CE	N57CN	N870AJ	N220CM	N240CM	N561PF	
0049	(N2672X)	N560EL	N812SH							
0050	(N26771)	(N208BC)	N208PC	N208BC	N501CW	YV2655				
0051	N2680A	N599SC	N599SG	N314RW	N318RW					
0052	N2680D	N500LE	N500UB	N777RB						
0053	(N2680X)	N53CV	I-NYCE	N111CF	C-GCUW	C-FACO	C-FACC	C-GNGV	N560LW	
0054	(N26804)	N531F	N100SC	N100SY	(N748DC)					
0055	N2681F	HB-VJZ	N282RH	(N21JJ)	(N560CP)	N200CP	(N201CP)	N209CP	N715PS	N55EA
0056	N2682F	N78AM	(N56EP)	N560AE	N406VJ					
0057	(N2683L)	N560BL	N561BC	N561TS	N553SC	LV-CRL				
0058	(N2686Y)	F-GKGL	N62GA	N710LC						
0059	(N2687L)	F-GKHL	G-PPLC	A7-AKA						
0060	(N2689B)	N2697Y	N90MF	PT-FTB						
0061	(N2697X)	N2701J	D-CNCI	N46GA	N603HC					
0062	N2716G	ZS-MVV	N560EA	EC-411	EC-GLM	N500UJ	(N405RH)	(N328SB)		
0063	(N2701J)	N7FE	(N7FZ)	N68CK	N63FF					
0064	N2717X	(ZS-MYN)	ZS-MVZ	N45GA	OE-GPC	OY-NUD	N560AG	N560CC		
0065	N2721F	N77711	N560JV	N608CT						
0066	(N27216)	N60S	N501JS	N810BE	(N382AG)					
0067	N2722F	N45BA	JA119N							
0068	N2722H	(N40PL)	N711GF	N712GF	N246NW	N560LM	N569LM			
0069	(N2724R)	D-CNCP	N65229	N70TG	N357WC	N857WC	N367JC			

CITATION V

C/n	Identities								
0070	(N2725A)	F-GJXX	N570VP	5H-ETG					
0071	(N2725X)	N271CA							
0071A	N2728N	N45RC							
0072	N2726J	(N72FE)	(N91FA)	N572CV	N72CT	(N772KC)	JA120N		
0073	(N2726X)	N100WP							
0074	N2727F	N27WW	N174JS	N593MD	C-GBNX				
0075	(N2745L)	N75CV	N617PD	(N619PD)	N817PD				
0076	(N2745M)	N777FE	N777FH	N777FN	N94NB	N623KC	N217GL		
0077	N2745R	G-BSVL	C-GNND	N42NA	HB-VLV	[w/o 20Dec01 Zurich A/P, Switzerland]			
0078	N2748B	SE-DLI	OY-CKT	D-CSUN	PH-ILA	OY-CKT	N797MM		
0079	(N2746C)	N560GL	N224GP	N575CF					
0080	N2746E	JA8576	(N803EA)	N5JU	N300CH				
0081	(N2746F)	OE-GID	N560HP	N318CT					
0082	(N2746U)	N950WA	C-FETJ	N247DG					
0083	(N2747R)	N22LP	N568WC	N577XW					
0084	(N2747U)	N16NM	C-GHEC	N51C	XB-IML				
0085	(N2748F)	N591M	N891M	N85VP	N599LP	N599LR	LV-COV		
0086	(N2748V)	SE-DPG	N560CX	N560CJ	N218SE	N560CJ			
0087	N2749B	5N-IMR	N167WE	N600BW	N60QB				
0088	(N6783X)	OE-GSW	D-CMCM	OK-SLS					
0089	N67830	ZS-MPT	N54DD						
0090	(N67839)	N30PC	N30PQ	LV-AHX					
0091	N6784P	(N18SK)	N56GT	N3GT	(N8GY)	N32PB	N103BG	N604NB	YV3178
0092	N6784X	XA-RTT	XB-RTT	N719RM					
0092A	N6784Y	N906SB	N592VP	(N713HH)					
0093	(N6785C)	F-GKJL	N93EA	YV2686					
0094	N6785D	N1823S	(N594VP)	N340DR	N1827S	N94VP			
0095	N6788P	N707CV	N404G						
0096	N67890	(N96JJ)	N10TD						
0097	(N6790L)	N898CB	YV....						
0098	(N6790P)	(N18SK)	N59DF						
0099	(N67905)	OE-GPA	D-CDUW	N560GM	N565EJ				
0100	(N6792A)	PH-PBM	N560WE	N560AF					
0101	(N67980)	N101CV	N560EC	N560DM	N560EP	N560PW			
0102	(N67988)	VR-BUL	VP-BUL	N560BA	N555PG				
0103	(N67989)	N98E	YV616T						
0104	(N6799L)	(N560CT)	N400CT	(N416H)	N815CM	(N907EA)			
0105	(N6800C)	N105CV	LN-AAA	N147VC	N149VG	N560MH	(N800WT)		
0106	N6801H	(HB-V..)	(N560PT)	N60SH	N525RD				
0107	(N6801L)	N78NP	N560RJ	N365EA					
0108	(N6801P)	N8HJ	VH-NHJ	N777KY	N73ME	N73MN	N573BB	(N573BP)	N579BB
0109	(N6801Q)	N6801V	N2	N27	N109VP	N480RL			
0109A	(N68018)	N907SB	N560RS	(N22YP)	N4MM	N387MM			
0110	(N6802S)	N560LC	N832CB	N832QB	N26DY	N95TD			
0111	(N6802T)	(N91AN)	OE-GAA	[cx Oct14; status?]					
0112	(N68027)	N4110S	N145MK	N560G					
0113	N6803L	N26	N4	N113VP	N555FD				
0114	(N6803T)	OE-GPS	D-CZAR	PH-ILI	OY-CKJ	N401MM	N506RL		
0115	N6803Y	I-NEWY	N91YC	N87JK					
0116	N68032	N901RM	N49NS	N561PA					
0117	(N6804F)	D-CMEI	N21LM						
0118	N6804L	XA-RXO	XA-SKX	N118DF	N626SL	N900PS			
0119	(N6804N)	F-GLIM	N119CV	N450MM					
0120	(N6804Y or N6806X)		N120CV	N1824S	N560PS	(N994CF)	N129MC		
0121	N6808C	PT-MTG	N898GF	N821VP	N960CD	N560WR			
0122	(N6808Z)	N261WR	N510MT	N561MT					
0123	(N6809G)	N611ST	(N321VP)	N583CW	N92TE				
0124	(N6809T)	D-CBIG	N124VP	OB-1626	N7513D	N823WB	N560VS	N563TM	
0125	N6809V	OE-GCC	C-GMAE	N560RT					
0126	N68097	LV-PFN	LV-RED						
0127	(N6810L)	N64HA	N127VP	(C-....)	N127VP	XB-JHD	N150GP		
0128	(N6810N)	N19MK	N19ME	N85KC	N504BW	N154JK			
0129	(N6811F)	N22AF							
0130	(N6811T)	N130CV	N14VF	(N19VF)	PR-CCV				
0131	(N6811X)	N131CV	PT-ORE	N223JV					
0132	N6811Z	HZ-SFA	N226JV	N521LF					
0133	(N68118)	N77HF	N88HF	N93DW	N560PK				
0134	N6812D	YV-811CP	YV1022						
0135	(N6812L or N6871L)		N560BB	N560RL	N19HU				
0136	(N6812Z or N6872T)		(N136CV)	N501T	N772AA	N999AD	N560PA		
0137	(N560RB)	N6874Z	N7338	N733H	N193G	N137JC			
0138	(N68746)	(OY-JET)	OY-FFV	N511WV	N561SR				
0139	(N68753)	N561A	N75F	(N75FV)	N59NH	N77JD			
0140	(N6876Q)	N562E	N75G	(N75GV)	N24JD	N329PV			
0141	N6876S	N141AQ	N564TB						
0142	N6876Z	PT-OLV	N7220L	PT-WPC	N560FA	N560GT	N64FT		

CITATION V

C/n	Identities									
0143	N6877C	N65HA	(N543VP)	N744WW	N10TB	N734DB				
0144	N6877G	N2000X	N500VC							
0145	(N6877L)	N57MK	N57ML	D-CFLY	PH-ILZ	N308MM	N50US			
0146	(N6877Q)	N2000M	N500AT	[w/o 16Feb05 Pueblo, CO; cx]						
0147	(N6877R)	N27SD	XA-RKX	N125RH	N410J	N147RJ	(N880EF)	N508KD		
0148	N68770	N92HW	N560FB	N115K						
0149	(N68786)	N565JW	N61GK							
0150	(N6879L)	D-CTAN	(N560ED)	N191VF	N191VE					
0151	N6881Q	ZS-NDU	V5-CDM	N6881Q						
0152	N6882R	ZS-NDX								
0153	N6804Y	N502T	N502F	(N153VP)	N1SN	SE-DYZ	OO-SKV	EC-LEP		
0154	N6805T	N503T	(N503F)	(N154SV)	N154VP	N96MB	N432TX			
0155	N6872T	N40WP	N155VP	N630TK						
0156	(F-GLIM)	N6885L	XA-RKH	N560L	N75B					
0157	N6885V	N5734	N5704	N502TS	N88WC	N157TF				
0158	(N6885Y)	N601AB	N801AB	N560RP						
0159	(N68854)	N68MA	D-CLEO	G-JOPT	N18CV					
0160	N6886X	ZS-NDT	N458CK	N54TP						
0161	N68860	Spain TR.20-01/403-11								
0162	N68864	[painted as N6864 for a short while end 1991]				XA-SDT	N388RD	XB-PEM	XB-OGQ	
0163	N68869	N529X	N953C	(N163L)	N97JL	N104LR	N904LR	(N904SR)		
0164	(N6887T)	N164CV	N392BS	N570EJ	N830JB					
0165	(N6887X)	N910V	C-GAPD	N24HX						
0166	N68872	ZS-NDW	N166JV	HB-VMV	N203M	N17TX				
0167	(N68873)	N20CN	(N167WE)	N211DG	N311DG	N560JT	N580JT	N922KG		
0168	(N68876)	N168CV	N168EA							
0169	N6888C	N80AB								
0170	N6888L	N170CV	N814CM	(N417H)	LV-CAK					
0171	(N6888T)	N5735	N573F	N567F						
0172	(N6888X)	N172CV	N560BP	(N560BD)						
0173	N68881	N918BD	N247CN							
0174	N6889E	N563C	N164TC	N560JD						
0175	(N564D)	N1279Z	N49LD	N43LD	YV463T					
0176	N12798	PT-OOR	N176VP	PT-WOM	N661AJ	N83ZA				
0177	N12799	VR-CNS	D-CHHS	N242AC	N650CM					
0178	N1280A	N531CC	N500PX	N997EA						
0179	(N179CJ)	N1280D	N865M	N885M	N65RL					
0180	N1280K	N550WW	N558WW							
0181	N1280R	N181SG								
0182	(N1280S)	N560RA	N920PM	C-FCRH	C-FEPG	N561WF				
0183	N12807	N83RR	N83RE	Spain TR.20-03						
0184	N1281A	N873DB	N410DM							
0185	N1281K	N29WE	N29WF	N989TW	N939TW					
0186	N1281N	N583M	(N586CC)	N583N	N586CC	N47PW				
0187	N12812	N60GL	N80GE	N922AC						
0188	N12813	(N188CJ)	N64PM	N395R	N62CR	N180HL				
0189	N12815	N189CV	N62HA	N63JG						
0190	N12816	LV-PGC	LV-VFY	N555WF	N303CB	(N214LS)	N404LN	N650JS	N200NG	N655JS
0191	N12817	PT-ORT	N2JW	N45KB	C-FBCW	[retro-fitted with cargo door by Sierra Industries, Uvalde, TX; cx to USA 07Feb13 but no US marks assigned – status?]				
0192	(N1282D)	D-CEWR	N713HH	N238JC	N3444B	N621CD	[parted out by Alliance Air Parts, Oklahoma City, OK]			
0193	N1282K	Spain TR.20-02/403-12								
0194	(N1282M)	N194CV	N352WC	(N352WQ)	N852WC	N413CK	N413GK	N628CK	N700LP	
0195	N1282N	PT-ORC								
0196	N12824	N196CV	XA-SEJ	N560JS	N4JS	(N560JS)	N357AZ	N560RW		
0197	N12826	N197CV	(EI-DUN)	XA-SJC	N21LG					
0198	N1283F	N135BC	N560RG	N560BG	(N198VP)	N598CW	N198CV	N550DC		
0199	(N1283K)	N63HA	N7895Q	N4895Q	N500DW	N560PH				
0200	N1283M	OE-GDA	YR-TIC	YR-SMD						
0201	N1283N	ZS-NGM	N98GA	SU-EWA	N255RM	YV3268				
0202	N1283V	(N202CV)	ZS-NGL	N1283V	N815LT					
0203	N1283X	(N203CV)	ZS-NHC	N7700L	N9700T					
0204	N1283Y	N1000W	YV483T							
0205	N12838	F-GLYC	N205VP	N1AK	N11AK	N771A				
0206	N1284A	N560TX	N900E							
0207	(N1284B)	N207CV	N52SN	N780BF	N560CK	N320CB				
0208	(N1284D)	N208CV	N892SB	N88G	N208VP	(N758PM)				
0209	(N1284F)	N209CV								
0210	N1284N	N20MK	N420DM	N277RC						
0211	(N1284P)	N250SP	N250SR							
0212	N1284X	TC-LAA	TC-ARI	TC-LAA						
0213	N12845	PT-OTS								
0214	(N1285D)	OE-GCP	N938GR	N618VH						
0215	(N1285G)	PT-OTT	N23NS	N315EJ	N75DH					
0216	N1285N	TC-LAB	TC-BOR	TC-LAB						
0217	N1285P	N602AB	N802AB							

CITATION V / ULTRA

C/n	Identities									
0218	N1285V	XA-SIT	N218BR	N218DF	N5T	N5GE	N561AC	N901LB		
0219	N12850	N318MM	N318MN	N229VP	N515RW	LV-CNJ				
0220	N12852	N23UD	N23UB	N73KH	N70KH*					
0221	(N1286A)	N24UD	N24UB	N701DK	N626RB					
0222	N1286C	N456SW	N767LD							
0223	N1286N	N575PC	N93AG	N500MG	N223VP	N593CW	N223CV	N560MG		
0224	N1287B	N224CV	N523KW	N528KW	(N47TW)					
0225	N1287C	(N1865S)	N1823S	N525CW	N225CV	N545PL	N969GB			
0226	N1287D	N893CM	N226CV							
0227	N1287F	(N227CV)	LV-PGR	LV-WDR						
0228	N1287G	N228CV	XA-SLA	N87GA	N560MM					
0229	N1287K	XA-SNX	N98GA	N193SB	N193SE					
0230	N1287N	YV-169CP	N169CP	N394AJ	N384AJ					
0231	N1287Y	N501E	N12CQ							
0232	(N12879)	N502E	C-GJYL							
0233	N1288A	Pakistan 0233								
0234	N1288B	N234AQ								
0235	N1288D	N22RG	N52RG	N129PJ	N560MM	N335EJ	N92BF	N633SA	N608BC	
0236	N1288N	N506E	N840CT	M-EMCT	N840CT					
0237	N1288P	N593M	N893M	N237VP						
0238	N238CV	N1288T	N46WB	(N95HW)	N194SA					
0239	N1288Y	N239CV	N1GC	N93CV	(N560RB)					
0240	N1289G	N91ME	N966JM	N55CH	N387A					
0241	N1289N	N241CV	ZS-NGS							
0242	N1289Y	N242CV	N605AT	N826AC						
0243	N12890	N39N	D-CAMS	N243VP	[wfu; fuselage stored Wichita/Mid-Continent]					
0244	(N12895)	(N244CV)	N60RD	N701NB	C-GBNE					
0245	N12896	N615AT	(N508DW)	N508KD	N43RC	N824CK	N423HK			
0246	N1290N	N5060P	LV-PHD	LV-WGY						
0247	N12907	N94TX	N750ML							
0248	N12909	N248CV	N226N	(N229N)	(N123NW)	(N226U)	N50DR	N749TT		
0249	N1291K	N10CN	N733M	N2000X						
0250	(N1291K)	(N250CV)	N1291Y	N205CM	4X-CMC					
0251	N12910	LV-PGZ	LV-WGO	N625AC	(N621AC)					
0252	N12911	N252CV	N44GT	N252CV	N8996					
0253	N1292B	N253CV	N46MT	N20LT	N553CW	N858ME				
0254	N12921	N560GB	(N561GB)	N568GB	N710MT	N710ML				
0255	N12922	N255CV	ZS-NHD	N255WA	N355EJ	N61KM	N229JS			
0256	N12929	N22KW	N52KW	N356EJ	N356SA					
0257	N1293E	N155PT								
0258	N1293Y	PT-OZB	N60NS	PP-ISJ	ZP-BWW					
0259	N1293Z	N37WP	N56GA	N559BM						

CITATION ULTRA

0260	N1294B	N260CV	C-GPAW	N888RE	N888RT	N883RT	N180FW	N69VT	N863JB	
0261	N1294K	N261CV	XB-PYC	N261UH	N305QS	N135WC				
0262	N1294N	N262CV	N444GG							
0263	N12945	N979C	N560GS							
0264	N1295A	N5250K	N264CV	N264U	N294RT					
0265	N1295P	N5270K	LV-PHJ	LV-WIJ	N86CE	[w/o 24Jan06 Carlsbad, CA]				
0266	N1295G	N456JW	N458JW	N269JR	N288JR	N306QS	N350WC			
0267	N1295J	N96NB	N197JH	N267VP	N267WG					
0268	N1295M	"N5270M"	(XA-...)	N12012	N269CM	N750FL				
0269	N1295N	N331EC	N357EC	C-GRCC	C-GRQQ					
0270	N1295Y	N68HC	N68HQ	N159JH	(N259JH)	N4FC	N394CK	N404MU	N888PA	C6-AIP
0271	N1296N	PH-VLG	N49TT	HB-VNB	CS-DTA	N560TP				
0272	N5094B	N220JT	N372EJ	N672SA	N790PS	N15SL				
0273	N5095N	N910PC	N61JB	N861CE	(N861CF)	N521LL	N77MA			
0274	N5096S	N751CF	N511DR	(N511DP)	N137LA	(N137LX)	N560HD			
0275	(N5097H)+	N1297V	D-CVHA	(N560LW)	N560LT	N717D				
0276	N5100J	N183AJ	N376QS	N376WC	N145KK	[dbr 07Jun16 Gainesville, FL; parted out by Dodson Int'l, KS]				
0277	(N5101J)+	D-CFOX	N804WA	N308QS	N130WC	N560BG	N525JZ			
0278	N5103J	N2HJ	VH-FHJ	N560EM	N180B					
0279	(N51038)+	(N331EC)	N361EC	N594M	N190K					
0280	(N51042)+	PH-MDC	HB-VNA							
0281	(N5105F)+	N511ST	N281VP	N716SX	N560HW					
0282	N51055	D-CBEN	N282VR	YV3225						
0283	(N51072)+	N560JC	N1CH	N560JC	N568JC					
0284	N5108G	N966SW	(N369TC)							
0285	(N5109R)+	N285CV	N147VC	N285CC						
0286	(N5109W)+	N286CV	N57MB	N31NS						
0287	(N5112K)+	N287CV	N117CC	N117MR	N863RD	N774SP				
0288	N5141F	N522JA								

CITATION ULTRA

C/n	Identities								
0289	N51444	LV-PHY	LV-WLS						
0290	N5145P	N97BH							
0291	N5148B	N744R	N470DP						
0292	N5148N	N1295N	HL7501						
0293	N51575	N293QS	N131WC	N50CV	N136JD				
0294	N5161J	N1295Y	HL7502						
0295	(N5162W)+	N295CV	N61HA	N80LP	N80EP	N295BM	N903BH	N510JN	
0296	(N5163C)+	N560LC							
0297	N5165T	N1296N	HL7503						
0298	N5166U	N200CK	N25CV	N112CW	N656JG				
0299	N5168F	(N550TM)	VT-EUX						
0300	N51743	N1297V	HL7504						
0301	N5180K	(HB-V..)	VR-BQB	N560AG	HB-VOC	N168BG			
0302	(N5223Y)	N560CE	I-NYSE	N560CE	N580CE	N302EJ	(N602SA)	N901AB	
0303	N5225K	(N560BD)	(D-CAFB)	N560BJ	N190JH	N190JK			
0304	N5226B	N47VC	N401KH	C-GWWU					
0305	N5228Z	LV-PLE	LV-WMT	N284HS					
0306	N5231S	N49MJ	N306TR	N753BD	(N753BB)	(N753GL)	N753GJ		
0307	N5233J	N307QS	N139WC	N51FK	N535GR				
0308	N5235G	PT-WFD	N492CG						
0309	N52352	N212BD	N560RN	N615HR					
0310	N5241Z	N410CV	N868JT	N228PC	N228PG				
0311	(N5244F)	N311QS	(N211WC)	N531VP	N421LT	N469ES			
0312	(N52457)	N312QS	N521VP	(N127JW)					
0313	N5246Z	N313CV							
0314	N5250E	N314CV	C-FYMM	C-FYMT	N561DA				
0315	(N5250K)	N315QS	(N215WC)	N515VP	N220LC	N105BG			
0316	(N5251Y)	N12RN	N120QM						
0317	(N52526)	N317QS	N217WC	N818BL	N818BF				
0318	N5261R	N1273R	N877RF	N877RB	N910HM				
0319	N52613	N1319D	N52613	LV-WOE	N2RC				
0320	N5262B	N46WB	(N28ET)	VR-CCV	VP-CCV	N320VP	VH-SMF	VH-MXJ	VH-OHE
0321	N5262W	N320QS	N220WC	N560AV					
0322	N5262X	"ZS-NNV"	ZS-NVV	N850BA	N300QS	N300WC	N607HM	N560JS	
0323	(N5097H)	N323QS	N808AC						
0324	N5100J	N55LC	N55LQ	N342QS	N152WC	N853CR			
0325	(N5101J)	N96AT	N313QS	N140WC	N566KB				
0326	N5103J	N583M	(N711Z)	N200SC	N220SC	(N902AV)			
0327	(N51038)	N327QS	(N101EC)	C-GKZJ	N80JH				
0328	(N5104Z)	N554R	N554EJ	(N554UJ)	N984GA	N926NC			
0329	N5105F	N330QS	N302WC						
0330	(N51055)	N351WC	N851WC	N330VP					
0331	N51072	N331QS	N231WC	[parted out by Dodson Int'l, Rantoul, KS]					
0332	(N5108G)	N332LC	N332AR	VH-SJP	VH-MMC				
0333	(N5109R)	N333QS	(N397WC)	YV2798					
0334	N5109W	N4TL	N905LC						
0335	N335QS	N301WC	VH-WFE						
0336	N5265B	N336QS	(N128WC)	N690ES					
0337	N5265N	N108LJ							
0338	N52645	N592M	N338R						
0339	N339QS	N539VP	YV516T						
0340	N5267T	N21CV							
0341	N341QS	N541VP	N560HL						
0342	N5267T	(N14VF)	XA-RDM	N86CW	(N82CW)	N86CV			
0343	N5268A	N343CV	N60AE	N303QS	N325WC	N327VP			
0344	N5268M	N344QS	N126WC	N501JG					
0345	N5268E	N345CV	N75Z	(N560NS)	N64LV				
0346	N5269A	N346CC	C-GFCL	C-FNTM	N399AF	M-NEVA			
0347	N5268V	N72FC	N72FE	N106SP	N50LD	N50LQ			
0348	N52682	N348QS	(N399WC)	N980AG					
0349	N5151S	N1127P	JA001A						
0350	N51522	N645M	N250JH	N991L	N2500N	Colombia FAC5760			
0351	N5153K	N699CC	N560DM	C-GAWR	C-GAWU	N151VP	N31CV		
0352	N5153X	N352QS	(N133WC)	(N106EC)	C-GKZD	N215H			
0353	N51564	N353CV	N1873	N187S	N353Z	N20SM	N53SM		
0354	N5157E	N4200K							
0355	N51575	N355CV	N67GW	N67GU	HK-4304	N560MV	HK-4304		
0356	N5153Z	N354QS	(N130WC)	PR-BEE					
0357	N5148N	N81SH	N347QS	N110WC	ZP-BZH				
0358	N5163C	N358CV	N12TV	(N12TU)	N30TV	N284CP			
0359	N5166U	ZS-SMB	N416BA						
0360	N5168F	N6780A	N62WA	N62WD					
0361	N5156B	N361QS	N560VP	N217MW					
0362	N5183U	OE-GMI	PH-ILO	N831MM	N998TW				
0363	N5180K	N59KG	N59KC	C-GUWT	N213SW*				
0364	N5260Y	N991PC	N560A	N51ND					

CITATION ULTRA

C/n	Identities							
0365	N5235G	N7547P	N375CM	N712L	N2500D	Peru 721	N2500D	Colombia FAC5763
0366	N52352	SX-DCI	(N361CA)	N131RR				
0367	N5161J	N367QS	N395WC	N747GV	XA-...			
0368	N5194J	N343CC	N348CC	N555KT				
0369	N52113	N5200	N520G	N5200	N680GW	N210CM		
0370	N5262B	N607RJ	N749DC	N560MF				
0371	N5262X	N371CV	N315CS					
0372	N52601	N372CV	N76CK	N372QS	N372WC	N592MA		
0373	N373QS	(N113EC)	C-GKZC					
0374	N5214L	N7728T	N166KB	N163L	Colombia FAC5761		N1066W	Colombia FAC5761
0375	N375QS	N575VP	XA-SEB	N478SB				
0376	N5097H	VR-BCY	N1217H	N713DH	N600LF	N600EF	N554T	N554TS
0377	N5264A	N377RA	N450RA	N377QS	N377WC	N537VP	N100SN	N560HS
0378	N5090A	N350WC	N850WC	(N378VP)	N808TH	HP-3010	HP-3010HTB	
0379	N5101J	C-GWCR	N560RF	N560PE				
0380	N5103J	N380CV	N190KL	N147SB	N827DP	N380CF		
0381	N2762J	N857BL	N214L	N5373D	Columbia FAC5764			
0382	N382QS	N582VP	N560TX					
0383	N51038	N57ST	N63TM	N631M	N579BJ	(N241KP)		
0384	N5231S	N196SA	(N86DD)	N950TC	N331MW			
0385	N5109R	N333WM	(N833WM)	N444DN				
0386	N7274A	N720SJ	N615L	N2500B	Columbia FAC5762			
0387	N5108G	US Army 95-0123		[UC-35A]				
0388	N5269A	N92SS						
0389	N5092B	PT-WRR	N389JV	N118RK	(N118RY)	N118RW		
0390	N5093L	N390CV	C-GMGB	N390VP	N560SE	C-GNLQ	N217TH	
0391	N5092D	N391CV	N92DE	YV2940				
0392	N5124F	US Army 95-0124		[UC-35A]				
0393	N5156V	N393QS	(N116WC)	(N126EC)	C-FCBQ			
0394	N5093Y	N394QS	(N127EC)	C-GKZK	[stored Scottsdale, AZ]			
0395	N5093Y	(N395QS)	N19MK	(N19MU)	N15SK	N324LM		
0396	N50938	N396QS	N596VP	ZK-AWK	N3937E	ZK-AWK	N396VP	LV-CTX
0397	N50715	PT-WKS	N397AF	N560RC	N44LV			
0398	N5061W	ZS-NUZ	ZS-TSB					
0399	N51881	N97NB	N560WD	(N560DW)	N969DW	N322VA		
0400	N51942	N916CS	N916CG	N42ND	N443EA			
0401	N5197A	N401CV	VP-CSN	OY-KLG	[b/u Dusseldorf Jul16]			
0402	N5200U	N302QS	(N122WC)	N691ES				
0403	N5201J	N1202D	JA01TM	N403SC	N5150K	N14RP		
0404	N5201M	US Army 96-0107		[UC-35A]				
0405	N5202D	PT-WMQ	N137FA	N45TP	N45TE	N616TD		
0406	N5203S	PT-WMZ						
0407	N5204D	N1218Y	F-OHRU	N560RK				
0408	N5207A	PT-WOA	N560NS	N304QS	N408JT	YV1018		
0409	N52081	PT-WVH	(N409VP)	N390BA	C-FKBC			
0410	N5211A	US Army 96-0108		[UC-35A]				
0411	N5226B	PT-WNE	N38NS	N731TR				
0412	N5228Z	PT-WNF	(N412EA)	N412CW	N513EF	N17PL	N38MR	
0413	N5233J	N413CV	VP-CKM	N8041R	N561JS			
0414	N5235G	ZS-CDS	SE-RGY	PJ-TOM				
0415	N52457	US Army 96-0109		[UC-35A]				
0416	N5109R	N19PV	N713DH	N713DA	N416VP	N561CC		
0417	N5090A	N1248B	RP-C8818	N560TJ	VH-XTT	N525BA	N560RV	
0418	N5112K	N318QS	(N128EC)	C-GCFL				
0419	N5233J	EC-GOV						
0420	N51942	US Army 96-0110		[UC-35A]				
0421	N322QS	(N138EC)	C-GKZG	N555LG				
0422	N20SB	N5XP	N58RG	N59TF	N297CP			
0423	N5073G	N324QS	N523VP	N528VM	C-GKHD			
0424	(N324QS)	N424CV	[cx Sep97 cvtd to prototype Citation Ultra Encore with c/n 707 in the Cessna prototype series]					
0425	N325QS	(N139EC)	C-GKZH	C-GHCW				
0426	N5101J	US Army 96-0111		[UC-35A]				
0427	N5105F	N11LC	N11LQ	N573AB	N891FV			
0428	N328QS	N140EC	C-GKZQ	N117JL				
0429	N392QS	(N146EC)	C-FLBQ	N650NV	N560NV*			
0430	N433CV	C-GLIM	N560TA					
0431	N5076K	PT-WZW	N431JV	N560JP	N76TF			
0432	N51143	N356WC	N856CW	N564TJ				
0433	N5231S	N33LX	N88EX	XA-CDF	N660SB	N840AA		
0434	N334QS	(N148EC)	C-GKZO					
0435	N52352	N410NA	N5263					
0436	N5086W	N36LX	N86EX	N96FC	N560BJ	N97TE	N605PR	
0437	N337QS	(N149EC)	C-GKZR					
0438	N5207A	(PT-WQE)	N438MC	N228FS	N459MB			
0439	N50612	(N39LX)	VP-CSC	N6NY				
0440	N5076K	PT-WSN	N400MC	N560HB	N910TF	N910TR		

CITATION ULTRA

C/n	Identities							
0441	N314QS	(N151EC)	C-GMXD					
0442	N5226B	N23UD	N152JH	N752JH	N888SV	N778FW	N323NE	
0443	N5228Z	N24UD	N568RL	N561CM	N317JM	N818RU		
0444	N343QS	(N153EC)	C-GKZT					
0445	N5000R	N345QS	(N156EC)	C-GKZP				
0446	N51038	HB-VLZ	9H-VLZ	[wfu Dusseldorf, Germany]				
0447	N5108G	N51246	N261WR					
0448	N5100J	C-GSUN	C-GSUM	N4ZL				
0449	N5120U	N560BP	N555WF	N555WK	N75WP			
0450	N51246	PT-XCF						
0451	N5124F	N351QS	(N160EC)	C-GKZA	CP-2823			
0452	N5130J	US Army 97-0101		[UC-35A]				
0453	N5132T	N453CV	N400LX	N60KM				
0454	N5135K	TC-ROT	N1216Z	TC-ROT	N454RT	N63GB	C-GOOB	
0455	N51396	N358QS	(N161EC)	C-FUBQ				
0456	N51444	US Army 97-0102		[UC-35A]				
0457	N51564	N59HA	VP-CMS	G-GRGS	HB-VNW	N5UU		
0458	N5161J	LV-PNR	LV-YMA	N458DA				
0459	N5162W	N79PM	N76WR	N776WR				
0460	N5157E	N360QS	(N163EC)	C-GKZS	N303HC			
0461	N5185V	XA-ICO	N461VP	N61TL	N765WG			
0462	N5183U	US Army 97-0103		[UC-35A]				
0463	N50612	N56K	N58KJ	N48LC	N48LQ	D-CEMG	N463EA	N114KN
0464	N420DM	N53PE						
0465	N5086W	N465CV	N848G					
0466	N366QS	(N224WC)	N981AG					
0467	N5096S	ZS-OFM	N98NA	N20CC				
0468	N51042	US Army 97-0104		[UC-35A]				
0469	N5183V	N701CR	N7010R	N469DN				
0470	N44FG	N290BB						
0471	N5188A	N371QS	(N164EC)	C-GKZB				
0472	N5097H	US Army 97-0105		[UC-35A]				
0473	N5093D	N9LR	N473SB	N1CF	N716S			
0474	N51160	N474CV	XA-TKZ	N474VP	N321GG	N474PE		
0475	N374QS	N374WC	YV504T					
0476	N150S	N941RM						
0477	N5085E	N50GP	N560FF					
0478	N5095N	N70BR	N111JW	N458NC				
0479	N5125J	N379QS	N743DB	N811MB	YV3170			
0480	N51246	N71JJ	N560VR	N566VR				
0481	N5153K	C-GXCO	C-GXCG					
0482	N5156D	N44LC	N44LQ					
0483	N383QS	(N166EC)	C-GKZE	N212LP				
0484	N5125J	C-GYMM	C-FWHH	[wfu; to instructional airframe, South Alberta Institute of Technology, Calgary, Canada]				
0485	N998SA							
0486	N386QS	(N168EC)	C-FIBQ					
0487	N50820	N46MW	N43KW	N51EF				
0488	N12688	N555WF	N555WL					
0489	N66U							
0490	N390QS	N390WC	N565NC	N629EP				
0491	N51564	N404MM	N484MM					
0492	N5152X	N492CV	C-GDSH	N41VP	N41VR	N85EB		
0493	N391QS	(N173EC)	C-GKZF	N93HA				
0494	N5166T	N80GR	N86GR	N452AJ	N977DM			
0495	US Army 98-0006		[UC-35A]					
0496	N395QS	(N175EC)	C-GKZL	N496JH				
0497	N5161J	TC-MET	N497EA	OE-GCD	G-OBCC	N560EM		
0498	(N24QT)	N26QT	N26QL					
0499	N556BG							
0500	N500CU	N35TF	N960CR	N860CR				
0501	N51896	US Army 98-0007		[UC-35A]				
0502	N1298X	D2-EBA						
0503	N52059	(ZS-FCB)	VP-BDB	N204BG				
0504	N504CC							
0505	N52229	US Army 98-0008		[UC-35A]				
0506	N50820	G-RIBV	G-OGRG	EC-JFT				
0507	N5095N	N1129L	N994HP	N238JP	N998GB			
0508	N5085E	US Army 98-0009		[UC-35A]				
0509	N309QS	N509VE	YV3223					
0510	N399QS	(N176EC)	C-GKZM					
0511	N200NK	YV2110						
0512	N29WE	N10AU	N10RU					
0513	N5061W	US Army 98-0010		[UC-35A]				
0514	N340QS	N850MA						
0515	N51042	VH-PSU						
0516	N316QS	N316WH	YV3103					

CITATION ULTRA / ENCORE

C/n	Identities									
0517	N5145V	G-OTGT	N424HH	OE-GCB	N767KC					
0518	N51817	N1295B	JA02AA	N581SC	N93FS					
0519	N319QS	(N177EC)	C-GKZN	N100GY	N909LB					
0520	N51072	N620AT	N101KP							
0521	N5086W	N521CV	N22LC	N22LQ	N560AT	N265CM				
0522	N398QS	N795AJ	YV3190							
0523	N332QS	N166MC								
0524	N5091J	US Marines 165740		[UC-35C]						
0525	N5093Y	N593M	N777WY							
0526	N326QS	YV534T	YV3128							
0527	N51396	N627AT	N102KP	N12LD						
0528	N52WF									
0529	N5097H	US Marines 165741		[UC-35C]						
0530	N353QS	(N560PM)	N331BR							
0531	N397QS	[w/o 02May02 Leaky, TX; by Jan05 remains at Lancaster TX]								
0532	N5268V	N5209E	US Army 99-0100		[UC-35A]					
0533	N591M	XA-GSS								
0534	N5112K	US Army 99-0101		[UC-35A]						
0535	N5267D	N1247V	N57MK	(N57ML)	N403ET					
0536	N363QS	N701GP	ZS-FLJ							
0537	N5181U	G-TTFN	OO-CLX	SE-RLU						
0538	N51143	US Army 99-0102		[UC-35A]						

CITATION ENCORE

C/n	Identities									
0539	N5108G	N539CE	N303CP							
0540	N540CV	N154JS	N158JS							
0541	N51780	N541CV	(N486BG)	N812DC	C-FXSS					
0542	N5093L	N542CE	(N120SB)	N12MW	N12MY	I-CMCC	N430AM			
0543	N51995	N543LE	N1UM							
0544	N901DK	N701DK	D-CASA	N544VP	C-FTJC					
0545	N5091J	US Army 99-0103		[UC-35B]						
0546	N5151D	N368BE								
0547	N51995	N68MA	N906AS	N908AS	N610GD					
0548	N5097H	US Army 99-0104		[UC-35B]						
0549	N5090A	N713DH	N486BG	N11TS	N33TS	N560CS				
0550	N51072	N865M	N3865M	N563M						
0551	N52670	N560RG	N86SK	N927PK						
0552	N5154J	N55HV	N552HV							
0553	N5145V	G-KDMA	VH-YUL							
0554	N5154J	N747RL	N749RL	N8486	N554VP					
0555	N5155G	N154JH	YV-....							
0556	N5165P	N539WA	N556VP	N707W						
0557	N221CE	N557PG								
0558	N5174W	N560RV	N558V	N558CG	(D-CEBM)	N558GG	N558AK	N558NC	N80SN	N568TX
0559	N5192E	N359EJ	(N659SA)	N359EC	N444RF					
0560	N5180C	N560JW								
0561	N5197M	N120SB	N511TH	(N60AE)						
0562	N5180K	N60NF	N911UM							
0563	N51995	N59KG	N56KG							
0564	N5241R	N7895Q	N660LT	N5601T						
0565	N5211A	US Army 00-1051		[UC-35A]						
0566	N5000R	N560BL	C-FAMI	N560FP						
0567	N5268A	US Marines 165938		[UC-35C]	[w/o 10Mar04 NAS Miramar, CA]					
0568	N52639	N155JH	N582WP							
0569	N52433	(N600LF)	N1315C	N600LF	D-CEBM	N569P	N564M			
0570	N5262W	US Marines 165939		[UC-35C]						
0571	N5244W	N3616								
0572	N174JS									
0573	N162TF	C-FALI	C-FRKI	C-FRKL	N804BG	N804BC				
0574	N52526	US Army 00-1052		[UC-35A]						
0575	N5257C	N156JH	N912DP							
0576	N51072	N200JR	N280JR	C-GTGO	N560H					
0577	N5207V	US Army 00-1053		[UC-35A]						
0578	N5264N	D-CAUW								
0579	N5259Y	N579CE	N977DT							
0580	N5267G	N580CE	N1871R	N486SB	[w/o Upland, CA, 24Jun06]					
0581	N5269Z	N157JH	N560JE							
0582	N52229	N843HS	N560CX							
0583	N52591	N583CE								
0584	N5296X	N7HB	N90HB	N428SJ	N232JS					
0585	N5254Y	N221VP	(N585VP)	N832R						
0586	N52691	N201SU								
0587	N5270K	N120SB	(N587K)	N4TL						

CITATION ENCORE

C/n	Identities						
0588	N5243K	C-GJEI	C-FQYB	N560GT			
0589	N5151D	US Army 01-0301		[UC-35A]			
0590	N5166T	OE-GPH	N403SR	N21H			
0591	N591DK						
0592	N5180C	US Marines 166374		[UC-35D]			
0593	N5260M	N121LS	N300AK	N308AK	N554SD	N243SL	
0594	N52446	N560MR					
0595	N560TE	N595KW					
0596	N52235	N844HS	N507PD				
0597	N51869	N597KC	JA002A				
0598	N5250P	N800QS	N806WC	N757TR			
0599	N52690	N288HL					
0600	N52369	PR-LAM	N915DK	N56FS			
0601	N5239J	N801QS	N108VR				
0602	N5206T	N9CN					
0603	(N66W)	N5236L	N603CV	N313HC	N89PR		
0604	N911CB	N998JL					
0605	N5257C	N605CE	N250AL				
0606	N5245U	N802QS	N606CE	N91AG	N166ST		
0607	N5270K	ZS-UCH	SE-RGZ	N254DR			
0608	N52059	N608CE					
0609	N5269Z	N847HS	N242AC	N203NM			
0610	N52699	N804QS	N804VR				
0611	N98AC	N98AQ	N560CH	N568CH	N611MR	N611MP	
0612	N5260U	N89MD					
0613	N44SH	N448H	N25QT	N25QA	N189WT		
0614	N5296X	N806QS	N614VR*				
0615	N510BG	N152JH					
0616	N52114	N616CE	N80GR				
0617	N5207A	N807QS					
0618	N51995	N933PB					
0619	N52135	N808QS					
0620	N101WY						
0621	N102WY						
0622	N5197A	N560KL	N743DB				
0623	N51993	N977MR					
0624	N5257V	N1242K	N500MG	N93CL	N2U	N53ST	
0625	N810QS						
0626	N41VP						
0627	N5260M	N191VB	N191VF				
0628	N812QS						
0629	N844QS						
0630	N5180K	US Marines 166474 [UC-35C]					
0631	N813QS	N813OS	N560HC				
0632	N5228J	N6521F	N109WS	N105TD			
0633	N866QS	(N860Q)	N427CD	C-FTOM	N560BL		
0634	(N911CB)	N5254Y	N90NB				
0635	N5257C	N535CE	N5WT				
0636	N83TF	N83TK	N636SE	[w/o Cresco, IA, 19Jul06]			
0637	N5073G	CS-DIG	(PR-ALL)	LN-IDB			
0638	N5263S	(N814QS)	N1269P	N23YZ	N560ET		
0639	N5214L	N639CV	N24GF	(N2QE)			
0640	N640CE	N800BW					
0641	N5270J	N67GW	N1967G				
0642	N642LF	N379BC					
0643	N5264N	N960JH	(N990JH)	(N960BM)	C-FTJF		
0644	N5270K	N814QS	N95NB	N93NB	N644VP	N988PG	
0645	N5269A	N299DH	[parted out by Alliance Air Parts, Oklahoma City, OK; cx 17May16]				
0646	N5260U	N846QS	N535BP				
0647	N647CE	C-GDSH	C-FYUL	N230JK			
0648	N5248V	N820QS	C-GTOG	C-FVEJ	N648VP	C-FAMI	C-GIJP
0649	N5267T	US Army 03-0016		[UC-35B]			
0650	N5260Y	N820QS					
0651	US Marines 166500		N5156D	US Marines 166500		[UC-35D]	
0652	N652NR	YR-ELV	LN-IDC				
0653	N5265N	PR-SCR					
0654	N52653	N654CE					
0655	N825QS						
0656	N656Z						
0657	N5214L	N778BC	N450MQ				
0658	N52234	N560RM					
0659	N191KL	N721NB					
0660	N5264M	N844TM					
0661	N5162W	N591CF	N682CE				
0662	N5212M	N560CR	N338MC	N560LF			
0663	N5266F	N357BE					

CITATION ENCORE / ENCORE+

C/n	Identities					
0664	N5151D	N664CE				
0665	N5200R	OE-GEJ	YR-RPG	M-FRED	OM-ATM	N504U
0666	N51160	N700JR	N708JR			
0667	N52462	US Army 03-0726		[UC-35B]		
0668	N5214L	N560TG	(N560TP)	N45TP		
0669	N5216A	N834QS				
0670	N5243K	N670CE	N611CS	N560JT	N962KC	
0671	N52457	N600BW				
0672	N5253G	US Navy 166712		[UC-35D]		
0673	N5245U	N96NB	N98NB	N673VP	N682DG	
0674	N52601	N552TC	N552CN			
0675	N29QC					
0676	N227WS	C-FSNC				
0677	N5079V	US Navy 166713		[UC-35D]		
0678	N5203J	N399HS	N177JE			
0679	US Marines 166714		[UC-35D]			
0680	N5245L	N595MA	N595JJ	N958GB		
0681	N5265B	N681CE				
0682	N5204D	US Navy 166715*		[UC-35D]		
0683	N51042	F-HLIM				
0684	N5161J	N684CE	N684BM	(N827TV)	N370TC	N774SB
0685	N5086W	N837QS				
0686	N5188A	[c.f. c/n 0751 below]				
0687	N5207V	XA-UEF	XC-LNN			
0688	N5248B	N254AD				
0689	N52059	XC-GDT				
0690	N5218T	N839QS				
0691	N5241Z	N300PX	N500PX	N560PX	N960M	
0692	N5166T	N40166	N999CB	N852AC		
0693	N5076K	US Navy 166766		[UC-35D]		
0694	N5079V	N4018S	JA560Y			
0695	N5172M	N695V	N345NF			
0696	N50715	US Navy 166767		[UC-35D]		
0697	N5093D	N697CE	LV-CBB			
0698	N5216A	N809QS				
0699	N52462	N560HM				
0700	N5268E	N700NK				
0701	N113US					
0702	N702AM	C-GRYC	C-GRFC			
0703	N52144	VH-VPL	VH-VRL			
0704	N5248V	PR-GQG	N866VP			
0705	N52639	C-FYMM				
0706	N802QS					
0707	N13092	(HL7778)				

CITATION ENCORE+

0751	N560CC	[Encore+ prototype, believed to originally be c/n 560-0686, ff 22Mar06 Cedar Rapids, IA]	N560KW			
0752	N5112K	N752CE				
0753	N5095N	N753CE	N120SB	C-FACC	C-FACO	
0754	N5100J	(N960JH)	N990JH			
0755	N5218R	N56TE				
0756	N52645	N545BP				
0757	N52141	YV2389	N657RH	N868CW		
0758	N62WA	N83WA	N793BC			
0759	N387SV	N229N				
0760	N5245L	PR-CTB	N760WF	C-GKUR		
0761	N5036Q	N560DL				
0762	N68HC	N68NC	N24QT	N24QA		
0763	N50612	N926CE				
0764	N5174W	N764CE	LN-AKA	N64SV		
0765	N5245U	N713WD	(N719WD)	N587MV	(N589MV)	N946TS
0766	N766CE	N15CV	N15QV	N164RA*		
0767	N5247U	I-ZACK				
0768	N5085E	N179RP	EC-KKB	EC-KOV	N562CL	
0769	N5241Z	N769CS				
0770	N5093Y	EC-KKK	N770VR	C-GRYC		
0771	N237BG	N765F				
0772	N5244F	N772CS				
0773	N5207A	M-ANSL	SE-RIT	N560RH		
0774	N774CC	N422JT	N404SP	N853AC		
0775	N5211Q	N803QS				
0776	N5223D	N814QS				
0777	N5216A	N777EN	N475JC			

CITATION ENCORE+

C/n	Identities					
0778	N5223X	N818QS				
0779	N5185V	N787CW	N779RK			
0780	N780CE	N560CL				
0781	N781CE	C-GDSH	C-GPLS	N380LV	YV546T	N555JA
0782	N826QS					
0783	N5091J	N560CH				
0784	N830QS					
0785	N5257C	N203WS				
0786	N819QS					
0787	N887CS					
0788	N5259Y	N788CE	N468CE	N468CF	N717VL	
0789	N822QS					
0790	N843QS					
0791	N5079V	N507CR	N44GT	N44GF		
0792	N831QS					
0793	N793CS	N416BS				
0794	N823QS					
0795	N51942	N114EB				
0796	N829QS					
0797	N846QS					
0798	N5214L	N808PL				
0799	N841QS					
0800	N5097H	N800CV	N101CP	LQ-CVO		
0801	N827QS					
0802	N52136	N866TC				
0803	N5247U	N865M	N803CJ	(N69LD)	N49LD	
0804	N5030U	N804CV				
0805	N5188A	N571AP				
0806	N5196U	D-CAPB				
0807	N5064M	N807CE	VH-MXD			
0808	N5152X	N360HS	N681ZL			
0809	N5097H	N610BK	N196JP	D-CAWR		
0810	N5204D	N810CV	N337CC	N657DM		
0811	N50736	[test marks also reported as N5073G]			N811WE	
0812	N5268A	N812CV	C-GAWU	N812VP	N917TL	
0813	N51942	N100U	N813CJ	N505RH		
0814	N5200Z	D-CIFM	N814TX	OE-GDM		
0815	N488JD	N815CJ	N2426	N272P	C-FNDF	
0816	N5135K	[aircraft scrapped before completion]				
0817	[aircraft scrapped before completion]					
0818	[aircraft not built]					
0819	[aircraft not built]					
0820	(D-CNSC)	[aircraft not built]				
0821	[aircraft not built]					
0822	[aircraft not built]					
0823	N823CE	[aircraft registered but not built; cx 05Apr17]				

Production complete

+ after a registration indicates test marks not fully confirmed

CESSNA 560XL CITATION EXCEL/XLS/XLS+

C/n	Identities									
706	N560XL	[ff 29Feb96]								
5001	N561XL	[cx Jan11; b/u]								
5002	N5060K	N562XL	N12L	N750BA						
5003	N5165T	N563XL	(PT-WZO)	PT-FPP	N814BR					
5004	N5148N	OE-GAP	N504VP	N504BM	Pakistan J-754					
5005	N51575	N208PC	SE-RBB	N166MB	N77UW					
5006	N5141F	N8005	N569MK							
5007	N5200R	N83RR	N97VN	OE-GTK	I-CDBS	N70TH				
5008	N5204D	N207PC	SE-RBC	N944AH						
5009	N52113	N398RS								
5010	N52178	N27XL	VT-CLA							
5011	N52141	N560L								
5012	N52144	N561DA	I-JETS	N560CE						
5013	N5216A	N1243C	N1PB	N191PB	N977SD					
5014	N5221Y	N60GL	(N58KJ)	N56K	N1SN	N10SN	(N16SN)	N989TW	N531MB	N108RR
5015	N5223D	N523KW	N560HN							
5016	N615RG									
5017	N517XL	N157AE	N600BJ	N500PX	(N300PX)	N865CE	N580AW			
5018	N5250E	ZS-FCB	N223AM	N410MT	N500SX*					
5019	N980DK	N990DK	N380PK							
5020	N5246Z	PT-XCL	(N61850)	N18JE						
5021	N5244F	D-CMIC	N560GM	N862CE	N862CF	N909LA				
5022	N522XL	HZ-FYZ	D-CSFD							
5023	N51933	N822MJ	N236LD	N236LB	N3444B					
5024	N654EL	N622PC	N622PL	N556WF						
5025	N534CC	N584CC	LV-BMH	LQ-BMH						
5026	N5201M	N17UC	(N17UG)	C-GJRB	N697FF	N357MJ				
5027	N5202D	N560GB	N560GP	N560ML						
5028	N5203J	N528XL	CS-DDB	OO-MLG						
5029	N5203S	(PT-...)	SE-DYX	OE-GYX	N96TE					
5030	N52038	N1228N	N899BC	N17AN						
5031	N531BJ	N560BT								
5032	N165JB	N108EK	N140U							
5033	N5211Q	N456JW	XA-UVA	N50LD						
5034	N52113	PP-RAA								
5035	N5213S	N35XL	N4JS	N4KS						
5036	N52136	N884BB	N36XL	N884BB	N910CS	N317ML	N526SM	N528SM	N705WL	
5037	N5214J	D-CIII	OE-GTI	(D-CGTI)	D-CADY	N900WL				
5038	N5214K	N404BT	N590AK							
5039	N39JV	N88WU	N87WU							
5040	N5214L	N54HA	N840CC							
5041	N52141	N1XL	N39RC							
5042	N52178	N42XL	SU-EWC	N418CK	N413CK	N418CK	N842A			
5043	N5218R	PT-XIB								
5044	N5218T	N544XL								
5045	N5221Y	PP-JFM								
5046	N5223D	N966MT	A9C-BXA	N83GG	[cx Dec10; b/u]					
5047	N5223P	C-FCEL	N838RT	N888RT	N838RT	N847A				
5048	N868JB	N548XL	VP-CAI							
5049	N5223Y	N24PH	N24PY	N680VR	N560VR	N305LX	N907WT			
5050	N5225K	N184G	N88HP							
5051	N5226B	N1324B	SX-DCM	TC-TMO						
5052	N5228Z	N990MF								
5053	N5231S	I-BENT	N620GS	N991RW						
5054	N5233J	N1306V	N80X							
5055	N488CP	(N560KN)								
5056	N51993	D-CVHB	EC-IRU	N688AG	SE-RBX	OH-RBX				
5057	N52457	N350RD	N240B	N53WF						
5058	N5235G	N555WF	N555WE	HB-VNC	S5-BBD	OE-GGK				
5059	N55HA	N55HX	N580BC							
5060	N5201J	PT-WYU								
5061	N5200R	HB-VMO	OE-GUN							
5062	N5197A	N22KW	N23LM	N97EM						
5063	N5200U	N56HA	N56HX	N71LU						
5064	N5194J	N2JW	N555WF	N586SF	N386SF	N227MC				
5065	N5204D	N100SC	N112CW							
5066	N134SW	HB-VMU	N192RW							
5067	N42PA	HB-VMZ	OE-GPZ	N864CC	N309BT	N202CW				
5068	N52081	N57HA	N57HX	N56LP	OK-AST					
5069	N5201M	N404SB	N189WW							
5070	N5207A	VP-CNM	N507VP	N789CN	HB-VOU	N832JS				
5071	N51881	N671QS	N579MH							
5072	N52178	N565AB	N565BA	N180FW	N51VT					
5073	N5214K	D-CDBW	N79EA	N121TL	N121TE	N560DR				

CITATION EXCEL

C/n	Identities						
5074	N636GS	N466LM	4X-CPU	N574AV	N66LM	N958AP	
5075	N558R	N568R	CC-ARA				
5076	N521RA	N55VW					
5077	N51575	N221LC	N46VE	N76VE	XA-PLA	N960HD	
5078	N5203J	C-FPWC	N560HJ	SE-RHJ			
5079	N5218T	ZS-OHZ					
5080	N52141	N90CF	N475PD	N475CW*			
5081	N4000K						
5082	N145SM	N469RS					
5083	N52144	N520G	N520Q	XA-SID			
5084	N5211A	N684QS	N384WC	N12ND			
5085	N52113	N85XL	N883PF	N803PF	5Y-WHB		
5086	N51817	N62GB	N269JR	N394WJ	N957BJ		
5087	N5165T	PT-MSK					
5088	N52081	VP-BSD	G-WCIN	EC-KOL			
5089	N51942	N868JB	N868J	N21MA	N560GC		
5090	N51246	N690QS	N590VP				
5091	N5183V	N560CH	N83SD	N170SD			
5092	N5125J	N692QS	C-GYMC				
5093	N5203S	N19MK	N19MZ	N903DK	N210VS		
5094	N1094L						
5095	N5135A	N95XL	PR-LPG				
5096	N5202D	C-GCXL	N328PF				
5097	N5226B	C-GLMI	N597TX	N900TV			
5098	N5244F	N200PF	N502BC				
5099	N58XL	N58HA	N58HX				
5100	N51444	N510XL	N49MJ	N49MU	N100CJ		
5101	N5216A	N88845	N81SH				
5102	N5153K	N997CB	N560KC				
5103	N5218R	N68HC	N68HG				
5104	N5223D	(F-HACD)	LX-JCD	(F-GXXX)	N104XL	N717CD	
5105	N5185V	PR-RAA	PP-JGV				
5106	N5221Y	N506AM	HB-VND	G-ELOA	N316GK	N712GK	
5107	N51342	N560DA	I-NYNY	N300SJ	N833JS		
5108	N562DB	N562DD					
5109	N324LX	(N324LE)	N561GR	N58LC	N458LC	N58LQ	
5110	N5200Z	PH-RSA					
5111	N5141F	N532CC	(N530CC)	N522CC	N380M		
5112	N52457	N1129E	ZS-CCW				
5113	N52178	OE-GME	N810JB				
5114	N5223P	N20SB	N717MB	N38HG	N877RW		
5115	N5157E	N20WE	VT-ARA				
5116	N5246Z	N498AB					
5117	N5233J	N202RL					
5118	N5214L	N1241K	B-7019				
5119	N5197A	N357WC	N75HU				
5120	N5211Q	PR-AAA					
5121	N5223Y	N560CG					
5122	N5211F	N67TW	N673W	(N373MJ)	(N317JM)		
5123	N5201J	N699BC	N59EC				
5124	N5207A	N24NG	N883SC				
5125	N5214K	N4JB					
5126	N626QS	N39FW					
5127	N560KT	N560FH					
5128	N5228Z	PH-CJI					
5129	N5214J	N359WC	N94LA	N680AT	N560AT		
5130	N52113	N630QS	N29ZR				
5131	N52136	N631QS	N131VP	5R-AHF			
5132	N5225K	N632QS	N513VP	LV-CBK			
5133	N23NG	N359CC	N510FS				
5134	(N5250E)	N52352	N561BP	LV-BRX			
5135	N5200U	N135ET	LV-ZXW	N885BB			
5136	N52639	N4005G	VP-CWM	N560JP	N522RA	N100YB	
5137	N637QS	N300WC	LV-CCG	N785DW			
5138	N5265N	N704JW	N924JE	N138HW			
5139	N639QS	N239WC	N560HX				
5140	N52655	N884B					
5141	N52235	N17AN	N701CR	N901CR			
5142	N5093D	N705SG					
5143	N5096S	N1836S	N966JM	N150BL			
5144	N5108G	C-GOEL	N713DF	N713DH	N52MW	N560TS	N552SC
5145	N52645	N645QS	N645Q	N507D	N94JJ		
5146	N291DV						
5147	N52059	N24UD					
5148	N52234	N777FH	N200SC	XA-UTD			
5149	N627XL						

CITATION EXCEL

C/n	Identities							
5150	N5100J	N650QS	N150WC	LV-CCF	N817LF			
5151	N5147B	N79PF	C-GHCB	N560KS				
5152	N5101J	N652QS	(N650RJ)	N888RP	N124KF			
5153	N5105F	N916CS	N816CS					
5154	N51160	N154XL	HB-VNI	OE-GXL				
5155	N5095N	N1837S						
5156	N5155G	N2ZC						
5157	N5163G	N40577	OH-ONE	OE-GCA				
5158	N5151D	N917EE	N615EC					
5159	N5163K	C-GMNC	N336MA	N326MA				
5160	N51869	N595A	N903FH	N901FH	N902FH			
5161	N404MM	N405MM	G-VECT	N561HH	[parted out by MTW Aerospace, Montgomery, AL]			
5162	N51511	N168BG	N600BS					
5163	N5166T	N63LX	N68LX	N591MA				
5164	N5166U	N64LX	N84LX	N837JS				
5165	N5109W	N665QS	N190PR					
5166	N52059	N5068R	N580RC	N580EE				
5167	N5188N	N250SM	G-REDS	B-9429				
5168	N565DR	N780CS	VT-SWC	M-TIME	N562SC	N155FS	(N919WG)	N77DZ*
5169	N923PC	OE-GPN	C-GKXS					
5170	N670QS	N261GC						
5171	N5236L	SU-EWB	N632BL	N1219M				
5172	N5086W	HB-VNH	N105RJ	I-BEDT	SE-RKD	N562P		
5173	N51743	N5173F	N560JF					
5174	N5223X	N624AT	N624WP					
5175	N52114	N625AT						
5176	N676QS	N452M						
5177	N5061P	N841DW						
5178	N562TS	(N258TT)						
5179	N51984	N512DR	N86TW	N188WS	(N186WS)	N834JS*		
5180	N52235	N868JB	N868J	N845JS				
5181	N681QS	N696M	N604SN					
5182	N5058J	N98RX	N563CH	N712GC	N712CG			
5183	N5090V	G-CFRA	G-IAMS	OK-CAA				
5184	N5061W	N184XL	N531RC	N531RQ	N727PJ			
5185	N51042	G-SIRS						
5186	N186XL	N836JS						
5187	N687QS	C-FKHJ						
5188	N688QS	N647MK						
5189	N5073G	OY-GKC	OO-SAV	N560ZF	B-9465			
5190	N51038	N560S	G-XLSB	N104LV				
5191	N5090A	N767BS						
5192	N50820	N119LP	N192XL	N164AS	N176DL			
5193	N811ST	N968BS						
5194	N694QS	N708M						
5195	N51143	D-CVHI	D-CINI	(D-CJOY)	N237NA	N800AM		
5196	N51038	XA-ICO	N905AC					
5197	N697QS	N697SD						
5198	N552MA	N560NY	N86WU					
5199	N699QS	N950MA						
5200	N5109R	C-GXCO	N950BA	N842JS				
5201	N5096S	N533CC	N523CC	N828CK	(N760RE)	N760ED		
5202	N5095N	N50XL	N82KW	N600CF				
5203	N603QS	N137BW						
5204	N604QS	(N604VR)	N604SD					
5205	N5100J	N503CS	N525VP	N503CS	(N502VP)	N503QF		
5206	N5101J	N821DG	N921DG	N206CX	N561CE			
5207	N5076J	N62GB	N62GR	N592CF				
5208	N5109W	XA-TKZ						
5209	N5093Y	N501XL	(PH-DYX)	HB-VNS	S5-BDC	5R-HMR		
5210	N610QS							
5211	N5076K	PR-VRD	N399PV					
5212	N5090Y	N560DP						
5213	N5108G	N1130G	(D-CASH)	N24EP	N928CB			
5214	N57KW	N75EB						
5215	N50612	N560TH	N5091J	VP-CPC	N560TH	M-CEXL	S5-BDG	N560SJ
5216	N5103J	CS-DNY	N926HL					
5217	N5079V	(OY-LEG)	OY-EKC	SE-RCL	HB-VWJ	N550DU	ZP-BOG	
5218	N218AM	P4-ALM	VP-CFM	T7-FAY	N902CA	N46CF		
5219	N5079H	N877RF	N871RF					
5220	N5112K	N318MM						
5221	N5094D	CS-DNW	N551QS	N605VR				
5222	N2HB	N560JP	N426CH					
5223	N5068R	PR-EMS						
5224	N5093L	N146EP	N595G					
5225	N5117U	N351WC	N351CG					

CITATION EXCEL

C/n	Identities								
5226	N5196U	N350WC	N562WD	N411KQ					
5227	N5197M	N627QS							
5228	N5000R	EI-PAX	G-IPAX						
5229	N5105F	N504CS	N529VP	YV508T	N560CR				
5230	N5085E	G-NETA	OO-PGG						
5231	N231XL	N417JD	N511DN	N153SG	N876RA				
5232	N451W	N34WP	N9U						
5233	N233XL								
5234	N5076J	C-FCXL	N804PF						
5235	N5086W	CS-DNZ	N300AK						
5236	N51072	N236LD	S5-BAZ	S5-ICR	D-CICR*				
5237	N5061W	N751PL	N751PE	N838JS					
5238	N5061P	N238SM							
5239	N239XL	N626AT	N192W						
5240	N51055	N640QS							
5241	N5090V	N100AR							
5242	N51042	TC-LMA	G-LDFM	N560FS					
5243	N5093D	N567CH	N243CH	(D-CSLX)	OK-SLX				
5244	N51743	N5090A	N244XL	N898MC	N898PP				
5245	N50820	N245J	N1MM						
5246	N646QS								
5247	N51038	N7RL	N57RL	G-CIEL					
5248	N5109R	HB-VNR	OO-FPA	(N414XL)	N28XL	XA-HTL			
5249	N5096S	N80LP	N429JS	9H-...					
5250	N5095N	N25NG	N56FE	N90HH	N115TL				
5251	N651QS								
5252	N5145V	N505CS	(N552VP)	N501UP					
5253	N5154J	N72SG	(N62SG)	N73SG	C-FTIL	N600PY			
5254	N631RP	N681RP	N626TN						
5255	N52081	N60AG	N15TF	N716LD					
5256	N5194B	N4107V	PR-GAM						
5257	N5196U	CS-DFM	N770CK						
5258	N52334	C-GWII	PH-DRK	LX-VMF					
5259	N52526	G-XLMB	G-XLGB	N26SJ	VT-AVV				
5260	N527SC	N711HA	N711VH	N712BG	N450AJ				
5261	N5091J	N75TP	N57TP	C-FLFE					
5262	N662QS								
5263	N663QS								
5264	N5066U	N664QS							
5265	N5100J	OE-GPA	N5535	G-PEPE	N248SF				
5266	N5245D	G-CBRG	N562SC	N21GD					
5267	N5246Z	N506CS	V5-NDB						
5268	N668QS								
5269	N51160	HB-VAA	Switzerland T-784						
5270	N5058J	N356WC	N300DA						
5271	N5103J	LN-SUX	G-CGMF						
5272	N5079V	N1326A							
5273	N5073G	N1268D	N617PD	N143CG					
5274	N5060K	PR-ACC	N753JL						
5275	N675QS	N675VR*							
5276	N276A	N556LS							
5277	N5076K	N560CM	N695QE						
5278	N16GS	N176GS	N95CC	N278XL					
5279	N679QS								
5280	N621QS	N561LS							
5281	N68AA	N142AA							
5282	N5094D	N507CS	N528VP	YV540T					
5283	N5097H	CS-DFN	N1122K						
5284	N5109W	N560DE	(OO-VIZ)	N560JP	C-GUPC	N284VP	C-FMOS	C-FMOC	N325ND
5285	N5112K	N285XL	N422AB	N58FE	N45NS				
5286	N51143	N622QS							
5287	N118ST	YV2975							
5288	N5117U	SX-DCE	N560RS	N927BR					
5289	N5105F	PR-NBR	N44EJ	N1980M					
5290	N691QS								
5291	N5086W	N829JC	N829JQ	N397BC					
5292	N5101J	N666MX	N848JS	N886CP					
5293	N695QS								
5294	N5068R	N508CS	(N294VP)	N500UP					
5295	N50820	N641QS							
5296	N696QS								
5297	N51612	N821DG	(N721DG)	N1871R	C-GRCC				
5298	N5061P	C-GSEC	C-FBXL						
5299	N623QS								
5300	N5085E	N613GY	N613KS	(N618KS)	N829LC				
5301	N601QS								

CITATION EXCEL

C/n	Identities				
5302	(N118ST)	N624QS			
5303	N1867M				
5304	N636QS	N636EJ			
5305	N628QS				
5306	N629QS				
5307	N51072	XA-DRM	N894MA		
5308	N608QS				
5309	N5093D	N309XL	C-GMKZ		
5310	N509CS	N502UP			
5311	N5090A	N712KC	N560JP	N560PD	
5312	N612QS				
5313	N562XL	[first Citation XLS; re-serialled 560-5501 q.v.]			
5314	N5000R	CS-DFO	N91GY		
5315	N5095N	CS-DFP	OE-GRI		
5316	N5096S	D-CWWW	OE-GCG		
5317	N5269J	N57WP			
5318	N51743	N102FS	OO-FTS		
5319	N625QS				
5320	N5194J	N66W	N151KV	N847JS	
5321	N605QS				
5322	N5196U	N1838S	N183JS	N183YS	
5323	N606QS	N606Q	N560RS	N561RW	N440ML
5324	N511CS	(N324VP)	N504UP		
5325	N52397	N568DM	N48NA	N560FM	
5326	N512CS	(N326VP)	N503UP		
5327	N175WS	N178WS	YV3147		
5328	N514CS	N818BL			
5329	N848DM				
5330	N638QS	(N638Q)	N395WJ		
5331	N643QS	N6430S	N946TC	N510HF	
5332	N727YB	N710MT			
5333	N533XL	N2			
5334	N5093L	CS-DFQ	N552QS		
5335	N515CS	N335XL	N500XL		
5336	N5165P	N336XL	(N404PK)	(N336BC)	
5337	N51942	N198DF	N560JP	N79BC	YR-RPR	N17ED
5338	N5094D	N606QS			
5339	N51143	OE-GNW	HA-JED		
5340	N50820	N607QS			
5341	N5061W	N3			
5342	N5223P	N7337F	N777JV	N228Y	N228L	N342BL
5343	N5145V	G-WINA	N969XX	N843JS	
5344	N51055	I-CMAL	N1NA		
5345	N616QS				
5346	N517CS	N346XL			
5347	N47HF				
5348	N470SK				
5349	N676BB	N670BB	N447MJ		
5350	N5270M	N325FN	LV-AIW	N325FN	N562HC
5351	N5101J	N53XL	N1HS	N71HS	N560AW
5352	N5245D	ZS-IDC	ZS-FO	N846JS	
5353	N678QS	N5250E	EC-ISQ		
5354	N518CS	(N71RL)	N178BR		
5355	N659QS	N5200Z	CS-DFR	N168MC	
5356	N5101J	N519CS	XA-UAF	N562CC	N839JS
5357	N5161J	N567MC			
5358	N5235G	N635QS			
5359	N659QS				
5360	N5079V	N615QS			
5361	N52397	N361XL	VP-CGG	G-CFGL	N112AB	N561JL
5362	N521CS	N506UP			
5363	N638QS				
5364	N522CS	(N364VP)	N880P		
5365	N667QS				
5366	N5216A	N585PC	N555WF	N555WZ	(N560WF)
5367	N677QS				
5368	N5094D	N12686	VT-CSP		
5369	N5197A	N678QS	N504PK	N504LV	
5370	N5270P	N770JM	N421LT		
5371	N371P	PR-OUR			
5372	N5091J	CS-DFS	N553QS		

CITATION XLS

C/n	Identities							
5501	N562XL	[converted from c/n 560-5313]			N633RP	N683RP	N883RP	
5502	N52144	N502XL	N502EG					
5503	N503XS	N732JR	N553VP	XA-AEA				
5504	N5223Y	N111GU						
5505	N901DK							
5506	N618QS							
5507	N523CS	N270PR						
5508	N72SG							
5509	N617QS							
5510	N52352	N41118	N357EC	N941KA				
5511	N52609	N670MW						
5512	N52433	CS-DFT	N898MP	N669CC	N283MM			
5513	N196SB							
5514	N5086W	N143DH	N611MR					
5515	N5157E	N4118K	N361EC	N110PG	N715MS			
5516	N540CS	N719TT						
5517	N52639	PR-RAV	N778BC	N475JC	N478JC	N106SP	N106SJ	(N456HC)
5518	N52699	N602QS						
5519	N52655	N43HF						
5520	N5269A	CS-DFU	N554QS					
5521	N541CS	HI955						
5522	N51872	N609QS						
5523	N542CS	N900KD						
5524	N5267G	N546CS						
5525	N5264A	N370BA	N624GF					
5526	N5194B	N633QS						
5527	N5254Y	N713DH	(N712DH)	N321CL				
5528	N5296X	N579BJ	N456SL	HB-VON	N715MM	N613BB		
5529	N5262X	OE-GEG	SE-RIZ					
5530	N5270J	N4107W	N491N	N2Q				
5531	N52229	N560JG	N748W					
5532	N5270E	N562DB	N562LD					
5533	N711NK	N711NR	N917EE	N104PC	N913KZ			
5534	N5165P	N424HH	N3750N					
5535	N5141F	PT-ORM	N535TF	N54TJ				
5536	N25XL	D-CHSP	G-XLTV					
5537	N5152X	I-TAKA						
5538	N5163C	N538XL	OE-GCM	D-CMMI	N789KG			
5539	N52178	N4007J	B-3642					
5540	N5090Y	N4008S	B-3643					
5541	N5201J	N560JC	LV-BCS	N63FT				
5542	N5267K	N547CS	N507UP					
5543	N5165T	CS-DFV	N555QS					
5544	N5268M	PP-BRS	N754V	PP-SBR	N137TN	N900XL		
5545	N5269J	N45XL	N560TV					
5546	N51881	N549CS	N508UP					
5547	N5156D	N647QS						
5548	N5168Y	N611QS						
5549	N51780	CS-DXA	N39GA	N727MH	N527EE			
5550	N200JR	N632BL	N682BL	N21FR				
5551	N550CS	N509UP						
5552	N5231S	PP-MDB						
5553	N5103J	N12778	CS-DXB	N556QS				
5554	N5166U	JY-AW1	EC-JZK	G-CIFJ	N255RC			
5555	N51869	(D-CLDI)	D-CAAA	M-CESA	LV-FQD			
5556	N385MG	C-GSLC						
5557	N5197M	N551CS	N5NR					
5558	N52609	N634QS						
5559	N5093L	N1281N	CS-DXC	N557QS				
5560	N51984	N553CS	N264SC	N560CR	(N1PB)	N97TE		
5561	N5296X	N642QS						
5562	N5109R	N619QS						
5563	N5226B	N45NF	(N457F)	N563CS				
5564	N560TM	EC-JVF	OE-GAC	LX-NAT	N724GT			
5565	N5196U	N370M	N560MU					
5566	N52113	N70XL						
5567	N5213S	(D-CKLI)	D-CBBB	M-CESB	N567KS	N870SB		
5568	N5197A	N6779D	CS-DXD	N558QS				
5569	D-CTLX	OE-GHB						
5570	N10VQ	N155RW						
5571	N5211F	N24PH						
5572	N5194B	N554CS	N510UP					
5573	N51881	(OE-GAL)	D-CTTT					

CITATION XLS

C/n	Identities						
5574	N5090A	N648QS					
5575	N5267J	N75XL	N851AC				
5576	N5245U	HB-VNY	CS-DPZ	N707MT	N394AG		
5577	N5267K	N556CS	N758CP				
5578	N5261R	N1299H	CS-DXE	N578VR	N78XL		
5579	N5253S	N2HB	PP-RST				
5580	N614QS						
5581	N5153K	N577PS					
5582	N644QS						
5583	N5076J	PR-CON					
5584	N51342	G-CDOL	I-CDOL				
5585	N51396	(D-CTLX)	N558CS	N560BA	N560TW		
5586	N5145V	N1299K	CS-DXF				
5587	N5135A	N806MN	N808MN				
5588	N643QS						
5589	N5262W	N842DW	N500PX				
5590	N5197M	N590XL	N103PG	N101PG	N559VP		
5591	N771DE						
5592	N52639	N586SF					
5593	N5152X	N559CS	N593XL	EC-JXI	D-CCEA	D-CGMR	
5594	N5180C	N4017R	(VT-XLS)	VT-JSS			
5595	N5135K	CS-DXG					
5596	N5181U	N82GM	N1HS	N96XL	N906AC		
5597	N5228J	N562CS	N780CC	N711LV			
5598	N5264A	N12990	PK-ILA	PK-RJT			
5599	N613QS						
5600	N51780	N560PL	N228PC				
5601	N5268M	N563CS	N563XL	N867W			
5602	N52235	N499HS					
5603	N5244W	N868XL					
5604	N562DB	N562DL	N134FM				
5605	N5101J	OB-1824					
5606	N566F						
5607	N52038	N7HB	(N560HB)	N301HB	PR-XLS		
5608	N5103J	LN-XLS	SX-ADK	G-GXLS			
5609	N5162W	N442LW	N442LU	N90BL	N845MB*		
5610	N52613	LX-GDX	G-OMEA				
5611	N654QS						
5612	N5141F	N564CS	N926DR	N441BP			
5613	N5265B	N613XL	G-PKRG	G-CXLS			
5614	N5206T	N45PK	N614XL	N484SF	N560LD		
5615	N5266F	CS-DXH					
5616	N5267T	N678QS					
5617	N5201J	N563XP	[XLS+ prototype]				
5618	N52136	N618XL	C-GRPB	PH-JND	XA-LAP		
5619	N5246Z	PR-LFT					
5620	N5264E	D-CAIR					
5621	N52682	N1300J	CS-DXI				
5622	N52691	N561MK	N55CH				
5623	N5244F	D-CDDD	N562VP				
5624	N5267K	N1312K	SE-RCM				
5625	N5245D	N916CS	N913CS				
5626	N5197M	N68GW	N515CP				
5627	N51396	CS-DXJ					
5628	N51038	N890LE					
5629	N5261R	N560VH	N1897A	N1397A	5N-BOQ	N560PM	N312DB
5630	N51612	D-CEEE					
5631	N51042	SX-SMR	G-ECAI	N631JD			
5632	N5262W	N632XL					
5633	N5185J	N13218	CS-DXK				
5634	N51612	D-CFFF	N634VP	N823DT			
5635	N51806	N1312T	N573AB	N493RP	N486TT		
5636	N657QS						
5637	N5225K	N568CS	N511UP				
5638	N4086L	N64LX	N737D				
5639	N5152X	XA-MMX	N639VP	N212CE			
5640	"N5188W"+	[+Marks current on a homebuilt]			N1319X	CS-DXL	
5641	N51342	PH-JNX	D-CCSG	YU-SMK	N641TX		
5642	N5181U	N642XL	D-CRUW	HB-VOM	OE-GKE		
5643	N683QS						
5644	N52626	PR-TRJ					
5645	N5223X	N88SF	D-COBI				
5646	N5223P	N921MW					
5647	N660QS						
5648	N5109W	N1320P	N711HA				
5649	N5155G	SP-KCS					

CITATION XLS

C/n	Identities					
5650	N685QS					
5651	N5228J	N673QS				
5652	N5183V	N226JT	N876UC			
5653	N5257C	N698QS				
5654	N5264S	N682QS				
5655	N5161J	N655QS				
5656	N52369	N35SE	N40HC			
5657	N693QS					
5658	N5135A	A9C-BXI	HZ-BSA	HZ-KME1	HZ-SAAD	N818UD
5659	N689QS					
5660	N5247U	N602MA	S5-BAV	N560LS		
5661	N686QS					
5662	N5211Q	SX-DCD	N362CA	N894KS		
5663	N5268E	N672QS				
5664	N5241R	N600QS				
5665	N52601	N658QS				
5666	N51780	LN-EXL	EI-XLS	N68MY		
5667	N5192E	XA-UGQ	N128AW	D-CKHG		
5668	N5183U	(I-LAST)	(I-AGLS)	OE-GZK		
5669	N5202D	N633RP	N637RP	N357TW	N353TW	
5670	N52655	N670XL	(D-CCWD)	D-CAJK	N936EA	
5671	N5269Z	N55NG				
5672	(N656QS)	N5207V	C-FTXL			
5673	N5269J	VH-XCJ	VH-XCU			
5674	N51160	D-CHHH	9H-VMK			
5675	N5266F	G-OXLS	N189HE	N560DT		
5676	N5265N	A9C-BXJ	N560RB	N612AC		
5677	N5180K	N661QS				
5678	N52613	N702AC	N513SK	(N513XX)	N513CC	
5679	N5263S	N1230F	A6-GJB	N679CF	(N560PS)	Peru EP-861
5680	N52690	N571CS	N512UP			
5681	N5221Y	C-GPAW				
5682	N50549	F-GVYC				
5683	N5256Z	N1130X	CS-DXM			
5684	N5061P	N669TT				
5685	N5259Y	N11963	CS-DXN			
5686	N5061W	N86XL	C-FNXL	N892SB		
5687	N5068F	N533CC	N588CC			
5688	N50639	D-CVHB	N469ED	N489ED		
5689	N50275	N669QS				
5690	N5130J	(VP-BWC)	N560FC	M-BWFC	N690XL	
5691	N5264E	C-FWXL	C-FYUL			
5692	N5026Q	N1198V	CS-DXO			
5693	N5069E	TC-LNS	N693EA	N631HH		
5694	N5072X	N717NB				
5695	N5166T	OE-GSR	N859AE	N528AC		
5696	N5105F	LV-BIB	N569VP	PR-HOF	N629BT	
5697	N5136J	N594QS				
5698	N5091J	G-XBEL	N698VP	N75HF		
5699	N5148N	G-RSXL	N699XL	N177E		
5700	N52235	ES-SKY	N813DH	N713DH	N916DK	
5701	N5264U	N414AA	A6-GJC	N570CF	OE-GGP	
5702	N1275T	CS-DXP				
5703	N5250E	N560MF	5N-BJS			
5704	N1281R	CS-DXQ				
5705	N50736	N574CS	N705TX	N514UP		
5706	N592QS					
5707	N5253S	N534CC	N580HC			
5708	N576QS					
5709	N5227G	XA-UHQ				
5710	N5254Y	N1312T	5A-DRK			
5711	N51744	N1315D	(VT-...)	N560TD		
5712	N595QS	G-LEAX				
5713	N51881	N614EP	N854AN			
5714	N599QS					
5715	N32KM					
5716	N38KW					
5717	N52369	C-GAWR	N886BH			
5718	N399SF	N913CL				
5719	N5236L	N12UD	D-CMMP	N75PS		
5720	N52397	N121KL				
5721	N588QS					
5722	N5165T	D-CLLL	(TC-OHY)	TC-LLL		
5723	N5260M	D-CVVV	OK-IRI	9H-IRI	OE-GGF	9H-GGF
5724	N5263U	G-OROO	VT-AON			
5725	N5260U	N725XL				

CITATION XLS

C/n	Identities					
5726	N50054	N577CS	(N726XL)	N515UP		
5727	N5192E	VH-NGH	LX-INS	SE-RMR		
5728	N5264A	N946PC	N811MB			
5729	N5264N	C-GKEG	C-GTOG	N560DW		
5730	N575QS					
5731	N51995	I-CMAB				
5732	N656QS					
5733	N51143	OO-AIE	N735XL			
5734	N411EC					
5735	N577QS					
5736	N52229	N777LX				
5737	N404MM	N454MM				
5738	N590QS					
5739	N52623	"PR-FJU"+	[+marks worn at factory]	PR-FJA	N3410A	
5740	N166RD					
5741	N580QS					
5742	N5221Y	N911EK	N597BJ			
5743	N52613	N806AD				
5744	N5063P	N2003J	PR-MMV	N560QG	D-CHDJ	
5745	N5067U	PH-ANO				
5746	N50715	N8000U				
5747	N5040E	N47XL	C-FSXL			
5748	N5246Z	N585QS	CS-DXR			
5749	N5076L	N169SM	OE-GBR	D-CEBM*		
5750	N5095N	PR-ANP				
5751	N8701L					
5752	N412AB					
5753	N52653	EC-KPB				
5754	N51042	N578QS	CS-DXS			
5755	N51038	OE-GEH	LX-SEH			
5756	N5265B	OE-GSP	G-ZENT			
5757	N51246	OY-CKK	N57VP	N401AS		
5758	N5241R	N758XL	N178JC			
5759	N575NR	N959CC				
5760	N50756	YU-SPA	OE-GHA	G-LXWD		
5761	N5156D	N2060V	B-3666			
5762	N51780	D-CRON				
5763	N51869	OE-GSZ	N258PC	N855SC		
5764	N51666	EC-KPE	OE-GOL			
5765	N5233J	CS-DXT				
5766	N5155G	N2065X	B-3667			
5767	N5059X	CC-CDE	N767XL	N999CX		
5768	N5064Q	N75TP	N768TX			
5769	N5066U	N1387E	TC-DAG			
5770	N5030U	"G-SOVM"+	[+marks worn at factory]	G-OSVM	M-SNAP	M-XJOB	N311MB
5771	N5068R	XA-UJP	PP-CTU			
5772	N5076J	OE-GVL	YU-SVL			
5773	N5109R	N579QS				
5774	N5263S	N357MP	N828DR			
5775	N50522	CS-DXU				
5776	N51342	XA-VGR	N776VP	N499MD		
5777	N5069E	SE-RIL				
5778	N52141	PR-TEN				
5779	N5085E	N579CL	TC-LAC			
5780	N5204D	C-GFCL	N400LV			
5781	N51984	PH-MHM	OO-SLM			
5782	N5145P	CS-DXV				
5783	N52113	N783XL	VT-VDD			
5784	N5264M	D-CCVD				
5785	N5260U	G-KPEI	N721RN			
5786	N5267D	D-CNNN	M-CESC	N786TX	N786TT	
5787	N5145V	CS-DXW				
5788	N5259Y	D-CWWW	D-CLIC	(D-CFLO)	G-XSTV	
5789	N5211Q	CS-DXX				
5790	N5223D	D-CZZZ	M-CESD	N790TX		
5791	N5268A	CS-DXY				
5792	N5200Z	PH-DRS	N777AT	PP-IVA		
5793	N5264A	G-FCAP	YR-DPH	N413SK		
5794	N576CS	N513UP				
5795	N52229	N595CL	TC-LAD			
5796	N5268E	CS-DXZ				
5797	N52061	D-CAWU				
5798	N5157E	CS-DQA				
5799	N50321	N771PM				
5800	N578CS	N560ES				
5801	N5267J	I-CMAD	OE-GDA			

CITATION XLS / XLS+

C/n	Identities				
5802	N5263D	N731BP			
5803	N50715	CS-DQB			
5804	N52626	N41233	PK-BKS		
5805	N587QS				
5806	N51612	N67PK	N67PC	N67PR	
5807	N579CS	SE-RGS	YU-SPB		
5808	N5060K	N2067V	5A-DRL		
5809	N5203J	N145PK			
5810	N589QS				
5811	N5086W	(D-CSYB)	OE-GKM		
5812	N583QS				
5813	N52591	XA-UKQ	N813TX	N835JS	
5814	N5161J	(D-CMIC)	D-CNOC		
5815	N580CS	N728EC	N629EC		
5816	N5108G	N41237	VT-BSL		
5817	N581CS	N239TC			
5818	N565QS				
5819	N5267G	XA-DST			
5820	N574QS				
5821	N51038	N2116N	N673MG		
5822	N5228J	(G-XMAR)	(OE-GEM)	PP-ADD	
5823	N5264N	PP-PRR	N533ES	N806DE	N315VE*
5824	N5090V	N2087K	TC-DLZ		
5825	N566QS				
5826	N5000R	OE-GWV			
5827	N573QS				
5828	N52235	N21076	B-9330		
5829	N568QS				
5830	N51995	N2112X	5N-BMM	[dbr Port Harcourt, Nigeria, 14Jul11; parted out by Dodson Av'n, Rantoul, KS]	

CITATION XLS+

6001						
6002	N51806	N502XL	(D-CRUW)	D-CAWM		
6003	N5040E	N563XL	OO-CEH			
6004	N5253S	N343CC				
6005	N52609	N575JC	N562DB	N285FA		
6006	N5200U	N508MV	N412CC	N808W	N952RB	
6007	N892Z					
6008	N5130J	N748RE	N748RB	N717FH	N717EH	
6009	N560DG	N427MM				
6010	N33LX					
6011	N68HC	N68HQ	N458FS			
6012	N595S	PP-VYV				
6013	N5061W	N2011Z	OE-GGG			
6014	N5094D	N868JB	D-CFLY			
6015	N5211A	N488JD				
6016	N51666	N906DK				
6017	N52653	N7877D	OE-GNP			
6018	N51780	N881VP				
6019	N5233J	N193SB	N299DB			
6020	N5103J	N310BN	N620VP	OE-GWS		
6021	N5223X	(HB-VWE)	HB-VWD	(N941AA)	D-CEHM	
6022	N52691	(HB-VWG)	HB-VWE	N622XL	N423LM	N990DW
6023	N5085E	N623CL	7T-VCX			
6024	N50321	SP-ARK	M-AKAL			
6025	N5153K	OO-EBE	LX-EBE			
6026	N52639	LX-FGB	N560AR			
6027	N5076J	(D-CHAM)	D-CXLS			
6028	N5059X	N712DH	N7TM			
6029	N5037F	N826AG	OE-GWH			
6030	N5241R	N560GB				
6031	N51342	N853JA	N95NB			
6032	N5250P	N932XL	N743JA	(N713AG)	N76SN*	
6033	N5223Y	YR-GCI	N888RT			
6034	N5218T	PR-RMC	N634BE	N600WF*		
6035	N949LL	N635CJ	PK-DPD			
6036	N5105F	OE-GES				
6037	N50275	YU-BZM	N637TX	N576SA*		
6038	N5202D	N563WD	N560TE			
6039	N50756	D-CCWD				
6040	N5100J	TC-TSY				
6041	N5147B	(D-CDCC)	N100U	N417JD		
6042	N5261R	N2370S	CN-AMJ			

CITATION XLS+

C/n	Identities				
6043	N51806	PT-FPG			
6044	N221AM	I-GGLA	G-GGLA	I-GGEA	
6045	N5072X	I-CNDG			
6046	N5248V	PR-RTS	N646RH		
6047	N5096S	N2384K	CN-AMK		
6048	N5192E	N61442	TC-DAK		
6049	N5270M	(D-CDCD)	N900FS	N90FD	
6050	N50612	N565AP	N565AB	N595AB	N713DH RP-C8568
6051	N5157E	N912EL	PR-JSR	N651TK	D-CKHK
6052	N52626	N332BN	N332BM	N427PM	
6053	N52433	N2401X	N53XL	N883PF	
6054	N50715	N54XL	N98MD	N25CK	
6055	N5264U	N2009A	TC-SSH	VP-CSS	
6056	N51896	N156XL			
6057	N5037F	N868RB	N305LX		
6058	N5262W	N58XL	N155SM		
6059	N5262Z	N268CM			
6060	N51160	OK-XLS			
6061	N5269A	N61XL	PP-JSR	N316TF	
6062	N5254Y	(D-CDCE)	N916CS		
6063	N51042	(D-CDCF)	N533CC		
6064	N5231S	(N583CS)	N664AF		
6065	N5068R	XA-LOS			
6066	N5162W	PR-AFA	[w/o on approach to Santos, Brazil, 13Aug14]		
6067	N5212M	N30423	5N-HAR		
6068	N5067U	PR-AJP	N82GT		
6069	N51869	N814PE			
6070	N5085E	N534CC			
6071	N5223X	N907CR	N507CR	N607VP	N6TM
6072	N52136	N43TJ	N72XL		
6073	N5268M	VP-BJR			
6074	N5227G	N96NB			
6075	N5223J	YR-TYA			
6076	N5218R	N487JA	N487AV		
6077	N52230	(OO-OIL)	PH-PKD	N566VP	N824HH
6078	N50639	B-LCT	RP-C1290		
6079	N5165T	N716JN	N79XL	Turkey EM-805	
6080	N50944	XA-URQ			
6081	N5211A	N789HU			
6082	N51817	(N282XL)	D-CEFO		
6083	N51612	N599CS	N216BG		
6084	N5226B	PP-SFY			
6085	N5194B	N1SU	N52MW		
6086	N5248V	N26XL			
6087	N5096S	N52FE			
6088	N5241R	N270BC			
6089	N52690	D-CBEN			
6090	N5086W	N690XS	N54FE		
6091	N5063P	N865M			
6092	N5145V	N564CH			
6093	N5151D	D-CSEB			
6094	N5203J	N82KW			
6095	N5061P	N475JC	N476JC		
6096	N50820	N27XL			
6097	N5064Q	(PH-EER)	(PH-HRA)	PH-HRM	
6098	N5076J	N98XL	N681WA		
6099	N5245D	N5901D	N732JR		
6100	N5036Q	N167JN			
6101	N5132T	N301L			
6102	N51942	D-CSUN			
6103	N51881	N807AD			
6104	N5068R	N800KV			
6105	N5076P	N299RR	PR-TAQ		
6106	N5248V	G-EPGI	VT-BIR		
6107	N5192E	N965LC			
6108	N5064M	CS-DTX	LX-MMB		
6109	N52141	OY-GKC	D-CPOS		
6110	N5200R	N768LP	N768LR	N110XL	N60S
6111	N5213S	N790ZK			
6112	N5067U	N676BB	N149KW		
6113	N51817	N1401L			
6114	N5211F	LV-CYL			
6115	N52081	N613JT	N613WM		
6116	N5268E	G-EYUP	N1985H		
6117	N51984	PR-OFF			
6118	N50522	N532MT			

CITATION XLS+

C/n	Identities				
6119	N52475	G-DEIA			
6120	N5257V	N224JV	N224JW		
6121	N5227G	D-CPMI			
6122	N5228Z	N764JA	N44GT		
6123	N5226B	D-CAAA			
6124	N5194B	N768LP			
6125	N5066U	D-CBBB			
6126	N5065S	D-CCLA	N626SG		
6127	N5100J	D-CNNN			
6128	N50820	D-CZZZ			
6129	N5064Q	N600CB			
6130	N5076J	N918RZ			
6131	N52601	N242JT			
6132	N5225K	N278HN	C-GOSO		
6133	N5212M	N920CG	N133XL	N26T	
6134	N52645	D-CQQQ			
6135	N5265N	N539CC	N539WA		
6136	N5062S	YU-SPC			
6137	N5214L	D-CUUU			
6138	N5264N	N188ST	(PK-RGE)	N15TF	
6139	N5120U	G-CHUI			
6140	N51743	UR-UQA	(D-CZEC)	D-CECH	
6141	N5132T	N100SC			
6142	N5245D	N42XL	N512AB		
6143	N5180K	N7671G	TC-KIP		
6144	N5200U	N144XL	N985BC	N1BC	N144XL
6145	N52144	PR-RCN			
6146	N5026Q	N54SB	N838CT		
6147	N5207A	RP-C6038			
6148	N5031E	G-OJER			
6149	N5154J	N237EE			
6150	N5135K	N660AS			
6151	N5207V	N151XL			
6152	N5105F	PP-BBL			
6153	N5263U	EC-LYL			
6154	N52623	N897SS	N997SS		
6155	N5226B	PR-TUC			
6156	N5194B	N1088R			
6157	N52601	N157XL			
6158	N5093Y	PP-WEE	N715DR		
6159	N5231S	N106ST			
6160	N5259Y	N303ST			
6161	N5141F	B-9823			
6162	N5090A	OO-XLS			
6163	N5109R	N63XL	PR-VTO		
6164	N5263D	N838CC			
6165	N52645	D-CAHO			
6166	N5180K	D-CDDD			
6167	N5260Y	XA-TVG			
6168	N5148N	D-CVHB			
6169	N52645	XA-UTZ	XA-VGR		
6170	N52691	D-CFFF			
6171	N5218T	N617SA	7T-VNC		
6172	N52446	N1865K			
6173	N5245L	D-CGAA			
6174	N5296X	N921CG			
6175	N5269Z	N165DS			
6176	N5036Q	N51245	N3104R	B-3266	
6177	N5124F	N3103L	B-3299		
6178	N5165P	D-CIFM			
6179	N5235G	N101ER			
6180	N51055	N420PL			
6181	N5125J	N491JL			
6182	N5066F	N31031	B-10GC		
6183	N5262B	N175TP	N75TP	N183XL	N85HA
6184	N5236L	N3101N	N3JM		
6185	N5200U	SE-RHD			
6186	N52136	N560JV	N560GJ		
6187	N5245D	D-CLHS			
6188	N5200Z	N3103D	RP-C6188		
6189	N561JV	N5267T	N168GW	N68GW	
6190	N5213S	N212HF			
6191	N5147B	N701KB	N701KR	N560VA	
6192	N5221Y	N746PC			
6193	N562JV	N5163C	M-YXLS	OO-VMF	
6194	N5248V	N255SM			

CITATION XLS+

C/n	Identities				
6195	N563JV	N5268V	N679LG		
6196	N51995	N130WE			
6197	N5085E	(D-CSCT)	N197XL	N510RC	
6198	N52457	G-RSXP			
6199	N5214K	N199XL	YU-RDA		
6200	N5125J	N404MM			
6201	N5223P	N1907M			
6202	N5270K	G-XLSR			
6203	N51160	N623SA			
6204	N50549	N777HN			
6205	N5261R	N62WA			
6206	N5257V	N19539	N7148J	D-CJUH	D-CJUG
6207	N5264M	N7146T	N1492J		
6208	N5265B	N7146D	N80SN		
6209	N51612	YU-PNK			
6210	N5267T	N967VG	N827DP		
6211	N5213S	N564HV			
6212	N5262W	N560N			
6213	N5090A	N71278	N559HF		
6214	N5266F	N701KB			
6215	N5045W	N994LA			
6216	N5211A	N175TP	N75TP		
6217	N5105F	N714WA			
6218	N5135K	N178LC	(N778LC)		
6219	N5072X	N346CC			
6220	N50776	YU-PMK			
6221	N5262Z	N221XL			
6222	N52626	N718QQ			
6223	N5037F	N20762	RP-C....		
6224	N5247U				
6225	N5061W				
6226	N5059X	YU-PZM			
6227	N5172M				
6228	N5090Y	N75CV	N15CV		
6229	N5148N	OE-GTE			
6230	N5200Z	N2052U	7T-VNM		
6231	N5267T	N5097H			
6232	N5270E				
6233	N51160				
6234	N50549				
6235					
6236					
6237					
6238					
6239					
6240					
6241					
6242					
6243					
6244					
6245					
6246					
6247					
6248					
6249					
6250					
6251					
6252					
6253					
6254					
6255					
6256					
6257					
6258					
6259					
6260					

CESSNA 650 CITATION III

C/n	Identities
696	N650CC [ff 30May79 cx Nov89; wfu]
697	N650 [converted to Citation VII standards 1991; used as GMA3007 turbofan testbed for Citation X programme 1992; b/u circa 2001; front section used for training purposes, rear to scrapyard at Wichita Mid-Continent, KS]
0001	N651CC N1AP (N651AP) N654CC N651CC N651CG N345SK N945SK
0002	N652CC N5000C (N650BG) N650AS
0003	N653CC HZ-AAA N187CP N92LA OY-CCG N166MC N411SL CC-AGR
0004	(N654AR) N654GC N650GT N650LA LV-FVT
0005	N137S N439H N693BA N700RY [wfu Oberpfaffenhofen, Germany, Aug08; cx 14May15]
0006	N656CC N44HS (N306QS) N58RW N1TS N650TS N39RE N27TS N128GB N129GB
0007	(N13047) (N3Q) N657CC N929DS C-FLTL (N20EA) N52SY N719HG N650MG XA-UND N117BG
0008	(N13049) N618CC N10TC N84TJ N84WU N926CB N926CR N777XS
0009	(N1305C) N933DB N933SH [parted out by Alliance Air Parts, OK]
0010	(N1305N) N2UP N2EP (N610VP) OK-NKN N650LW [parted out Roanoke, TX]
0011	N1305U (C-GWPA) (N90LA) N91LA N17TE N17TN N311CW N362TW
0012	N1305V N15VF OE-GCO HA-JEN
0013	(N13052) N119EL (N13QS) N313QS N377JE N770GF N25TG
0014	(N1306B) (N664RB) N650CJ C-GHOO OE-GCN (N855DH) OY-EDP
0015	(N1306F) N83CT N369G N15QS N766MH
0016	N1306V N720ML N720ME N555DH (N45US) N32MG N316CW N21LL [wfu]
0017	N1307A C-GHLM N900CM N900QM (N650BP) N651BP
0018	(N1307C) N715BC N275WN N650SB N650KK
0019	(N1307D) (N44BH) N30CJ N333RL N833RL XA-TBA N650JL N650MS N707MS N71LU N970GW
0020	N1307G XA-VIT N488JT N10PN N650WB N420GT (N341MB) YV609T
0021	N2624M N2604 N650SS N460CP N94GH
0022	N650J PR-DIO
0023	N889G C-GHKY N658MA VR-CCC N38DD N650CG
0024	N1UP N1UH N624VP N643CR N95SR N650SL N422BC
0025	N10PX N200RT (N376HW) (N277HG) N700RR N650VP N625VP N16FE (N522GS) N16SU
0026	(N656CC) [damaged on production line early 1984 and not completed; fuselage used as test frame]
0027	N375SC N875SC N650NY N433LF N993LC
0028	N148C N328QS LN-NLC N38ED N650BW PP-USA
0029	(N30CJ) N600GH N70TT (N81TT) N89AC N409SF N67FS
0030	N650SC SE-DHL N650SC N380CW N51EM N651EM
0031	N631CC N1ZC N7ZG
0032	N54WC N38WP N3184Z N332FW XA-HVP (N632VP) XA-PRO
0033	(N1309A) CC-ECE Chile E-302 [w/o 09Jly92 4km from runway 20 Concepcion, Chile]
0034	N80CC N34QS N777LF (N45US) N650GH N650SF
0035	N650MD N400JD N408JD XA-GJC
0036	N700CS (N700RD) N20RD N36CD N43TC (N143RC) XA-TGA N650BS N651CV
0037	N411BB N37CD VH-OZI N37VP I-GASD (D-CLDF) D-CVAI C-GTKI
0038	N366G N366GE N373DJ XB-PGC
0039	N81TC N39WP N171L XA-KMX N71NT PP-NPC
0040	N82TC VR-BJY HB-VIY N650WE
0041	N55BH
0042	N142AB N342QS N342AS C-GPOP
0043	(N1310B) OY-GKL N643CC N953JF
0044	(N234HM) N650M (D-CRRR) N129PJ N126MT
0045	N84G N67SF N67SE N669W N689W
0046	N658CC N57TT N650TT C-FBNA
0047	N1102 (N1109) N650CN N33BC N33BQ N711VH N711VZ N706HB
0048	N98BD N98DD N986M N650MM (A6-GAN) VP-CGK A6-CGK A7-CGK N122TA
0049	(N1311A) C-FJOE PJ-MAR PT-LSN N30AF (N650AN)
0050	(N1311K) N44M N44MU N51JV
0051	(N1311P) N910F N651BH N777MX
0052	N20MW XA-SDU
0053	N367G N306PA
0054	(N1312D) N1103 N1183 (N26RG) N17AN N47AN (N224PG)
0055	N173LP N173LR N515VC N16AS N652CV N125RH N105RH
0056	N273LP (N273LB) N760EW N397CS N56JV N78AP N641MS
0057	N368G N101YC (N101PC) N400PC N31TJ N400PC N955HG N278TJ*
0058	N88DD N70DJ (N282PC) (N292PC) (N650JS) N143PL N72EP [dbr in hangar collapse at Atlanta/Paulding County, GA, 02Mar12; parted out by Team Aero LLC, Olathe, KS]
0059	N1313G PT-LHA N660AA N370TP
0060	(N1313J) HB-VHW N848US TC-CAO N660TJ N220TW N220TV OY-JPJ
0061	(N1313T) N137M (N129TC) N137X N650TP N650TC N450RS N440PC N400PC N939RT
0062	N626CC C-GHGK N388DA N19FR N342HM N650CN N475M N84PH N84JH*
0063	N13138 N41ST N72LE N650AT N651AT
0064	(N1314H) N801CC N650TC N444CW
0065	(N1314T) N500E C-FIMO
0066	(N1314V) N138M N138V N650CD N496RA (N156DT)
0067	(N1314X) N210F N9AX N232CF N232CE
0068	(N1314X) N273W N985M N9KL N650AJ XA-TMZ
0069	(N13142) N910M XB-GRN N455JD

CITATION III

C/n	Identities
0070	(N1315A) N149C N370QS N370TG LN-NLD OY-NLA N38ED OY-NLA
0071	(N1315B) N334H N297DD N97DD XA-VYM
0072	(N1315C) N277W N651CN N72ST N139MY
0073	(N1315D) N650JA N673JS N85DA XA-LEY N849AC
0074	(N1315G) (N555EW) N234YP N194DC N93CL N81SF N949SA
0075	N1315T N16AJ N85MS
0076	N1315V N376SC N876SC HB-VJT N731GA XA-SEP N424LB XA-PVR N760LB
0077	(N1315Y) N677CC N701AG VR-BGB (N42NA) TC-EES TC-SIS (N701AG) N800GM
0078	(N13150) N652CC PK-TRJ PK-WSE N650WJ N50DS (XA-...) N650WL N650KB
0079	(N1316A) N66ME N290SC N288CC N59CD N217RR N211RR N69VC N217RJ N650RB (N96SS) N96SN
0080	N1316E N69LD C-FDJC N802DB
0081	(N1316N) PT-LGT (N881BA) N910DP N910DF
0082	(N13162) N651AP N1AP N81AP N82VP N4VF N4VY N825JW N825UW
0083	N13166 N944H N944CA TC-TOP N2NR N5NR N677LM N650HG
0084	(N13168) N85AW N431CB (N431CQ) N650CB
0085	N1317G JA8249 N650DA I-CIST [w/o 04Nov00 Rome-Ciampino A/P, Italy; parted out by White Inds, Bates City MO circa Oct01]
0086	(N1317X) PT-LHC
0087	(N1317Y) N988H N988HL N687VP C-FQCY N680BC N37VP PP-AIO PR-MPF
0088	(N13170) PT-LGZ N290AS N590AS N650TA
0089	(N13175) N653CC N650JC N86WP N86VP (N229J) N15ZT
0090	(N1318A) N694CC N1823S N651TC N850MC N1DH N555DH N651PW N650JA
0091	N1318E N68HC N58HC PT-LUE
0092	(N1318L) N692CC N692BE
0093	(N1318M) (N693CC) N773M N93VP N222GT CS-DND N196SG N196SD LV-CQK
0094	(N1318P) N5114 N6114 N94VP N94TJ 5B-CSM N650SP N651RS N650SP N926HC N699MG N438AD
0095	(N1318Q) N5115 N6115 (N95VP) N882KB N883KB N941KA N650PF N650KP
0096	(N1318X) N5116 N96VP N700SW N702SW N629RM N629MD
0097	(N1318Y) N697MC N725WH N697MC [w/o 27Oct07 Atlantic City, NJ; parted out by White Inds, Bates City, MO]
0098	(N13189) N399W N389W N54HC N398CW N398DL (TI-BFY) TI-BFT
0099	N1319B (N555EW) N26SD N403CB XA-PYN N994U XA-AEB
0100	(N1319D) N200LH N200LL N202JK
0101	N1319M N847G C-GPEA N330TJ N650HR XB-GXV XA-LTH N9NL VH-SPJ
0102	(N1319X) (N406M) N406MM N406LM N24237 PP-FMA
0103	(N13194) (N407M) N407MM N407LM N2411A (N907RM)
0104	N13195 I-BETV N650CF C-FLMJ C-GOXB C-FORJ N82FD YV....
0105	(N1320B) N655CC N15TT N48TT N67BG I-FEEV [w/o nr Rome/Ciampino, Italy, 07Feb09]
0106	(N1320K) N106CC N650CE N725RH (N404LN)
0107	(N1320P) N8000U N650MP N650JG N397CW N397DR
0108	(N1320U) N650Z C5-MAC
0109	(N1320V) (N650AT) N20AT N134M (N134MJ) (N649AF) N109ST N106ST VH-SBU N353HA
0110	(N1320X) N76D N303PC N304PC
0111	(N13204) N500CM N381CW (N381EM) (N650RJ)
0112	N1321A N60BE N93DK N598C N598AW N500JS
0113	N1321C N10ST N872EC (N650AF) N652JM N393CW N393JC
0114	(N1321J) N7000G N651AF N650DA N650DD
0115	N1321K PT-LJC N1419J N541S
0116	(N1321L) N78D (N78DL) N788BA C-FJJC C-FJJG N928PS
0117	N1321N F-GGAL
0118	(N13210) N6000J N118CD N770MP N770MR N79KF N727TX
0119	(N13217) VR-BJS HB-VIN N100WH EC-EQX N96AF 8P-KAM N770AF N147PS N147TA N650HM N888KG N181MG
0120	N13218 N143AB (N818TP) (N650AF) I-SALG N650AF N1223N N30NM N907DF
0121	(N1322D) D-CATP N1322D N121AG N24VB N818DE
0122	(N1322K) EC-EAS N650TT (N650MT) N65WL N122EJ N515MB
0123	(N1322X) N624CC N434H N59FT (N491SS) (N14NB)
0124	(N1322Y) N95CC N7HV N650HC N776GM
0125	(N13222) EC-EAP N650AF N170HL N178HL
0126	(N1323A) N55HF N65HF XA-RZQ N65HF N311MA N101PG N131PG (N127CA)
0127	N1323D N723BH N92TX (N18PV) N95TJ N95UJ+ [+ marks worn at 2002 NBAA but not officially registered] N700MH
0128	(N1323K) N628CC N125Q LV-CAE
0129	(N1323N) N61BE (N309TA) PT-LUO N125N N330MB N989PT
0130	(N1323Q) N227LA N227BA N543SC N159M N159MR N130TS (N130RK) N603HC N603HP N918BH N901RH
0131	(N1323R) CC-ECL Chile E-303 Chile 303 CC-ANT
0132	N1323V N24KT N49SM N727AW YV619T
0133	N1323X N633CC N133LE N133LH ZK-NLJ N133LE N250CM N213HP
0134	(N1323Y) N75RD N75RN N27SD N123SL N1239L D-CARE (PH-EVY) PH-MSX N6707L [parted out]
0135	(N1324B) N5109 N135AF VP-CAR N702SS
0136	(N1324D) N841G N60AF N779AZ N779AF N650DF N3170B
0137	(N1324G) N874G N4Y
0138	(N1324R) N828G N650JV N35PN N717JM

CITATION III

C/n	Identities
0139	(N13242) N4EG N96CP N650AH
0140	(N1325D) N95CC N290SC N220CC N90CN (N650SS) N4FC N1400M
0141	N1325E N110TM TC-CMY N21WJ N140TS
0142	(N1325L) N142CC N20RD D-CRHR (N492BA) HA-JEO
0143	N1325X N143WR N11NZ N28S N312CF N40FC
0144	N1325Y N644CC VH-KTI N644CC N650KM N2605 PK-TSM N2605 N384CW N384EM
0145	N1325Z C-GCFP N650AF N29AU N385CW N385EM [w/o in Venezuela 18Feb08]
0146	N13256 N646CC XA-PIP N650FC
0147	N13259 OE-GNK N148N N141M N456AF N94BJ N151DR
0148	N1326A N55SC N55SQ N50PH N50EJ N7HF N92RP N413MH*
0149	N1326B N649CC N139M N139N (CS-DNE) D-CBPL HA-AXA OE-GAE D-CSAO HA-JEP
0150	N1326D N150F N61CK XA-RIB
0151	N1326G G-MLEE N91D PK-KIG N660AF N321AR N797VS
0152	(N1326H) (N4EG) N650AE (N152VP) N627R N327R N260VP N255VP (N260VP) N605SA N404BY
0153	N1326K N95CC N653CC N47CM N777ZC N1DH N2DH N845FW N308MR
0154	(N1326P) N154CC N696HC N650CH
0155	N13264 N788NB N97AL
0156	N13267 N68SK N38SK XA-ARS N209A N74VF N650CC [cx 02Jul15; parted out by Dodson Int'l, Rantoul, KS]
0157	N1327A N657CC N516SM N10JP N650RP
0158	N1327B N658CJ N121AT N135HC N735HC (N745EA) N721ST VH-SSZ
0159	N13113 N683MB N267TG N359CW YV3213
0160	N1312D N95CC N24UM N831CB N830CB (N830GB) N33UL N650PT N220CM
0161	(N1312K) N161CC I-ATSA N500AE N510SD
0162	N1312Q N202RB N275GC N660Q N85WT
0163	N1312T N137M (N137MR) N163AF N749CP N163JM
0164	N1312V N138M N138MR N164AF N364CW N162DS YV3279
0165	N1312X XA-FCP XC-PGN (N650GJ)
0166	N1313J PT-LTB
0167	N667CC N532CC (N532C) N832CC N88DJ N25EG
0168	N1314H N175J
0169	N169CC N88JJ N749DC N73HM N650PT
0170	N1314V N95CC N170CC N32JJ XA-RIE N476AC (YV....) N476AC
0171	N1354G PT-LVF PR-ITN
0172	(N1772E) N672CC N934H [cx Oct10; b/u]
0173	(N1779E) N843G N173VP
0174	(N1782E) N674CC D-CLUE
0175	(N175J) N1820E N235KK N835KK N175SR
0176	N176L N1874E N1526L N2TF N48TF N176AF N504RP
0177	N1930E JA8367 N707HJ N834H XB-OBM XA-UVV XB-OSP
0178	N1958E N95CC N178CC JA8378 N178CC N603AT TC-RAM N650BA N57CE N605DS N896RJ N427RR
0179	N1959E N679CC XA-RMY N35FC N63GC N287CD
0180	N2098A N768NB N498CS
0181	N2131A (N181CC) PT-OBX N743CC N650DR N857DN
0182	N26105 N682CC N491JB YV527T
0183	N2614Y EI-SNN N820FJ (N820F) (N376CW)
0184	N2615D N95CC N1128B N11288 (N650DW)
0185	N2615L N708CT N708CF N185VP VR-BMG N650HS N533CC N538CC (N650MG) 4X-CMR N521BH N468ES
0186	N2616L PT-OAK N186VP N386CW XA-UIS
0187	N2617K N187CM N500RP (N55PC) N70PT (N78PT) D-CAYK N39VP LN-AAA D-CRRR N226EM 4X-CZA
0188	N2617P N587S N650FP XA-PMH
0189	N26174 XA-RGS
0190	(N2621U) N142B N190JJ N350CD N260VP D-CCEU HA-JEC CN-TKD
0191	(N2621Z) N191CM N59B TC-KLS N650TJ N650SG
0192	N2622C N15TT N15TZ LN-AAU N78EM D-CREY SX-FDK
0193	N2622Z N95CC N95CM N55HF N55HD N650CC N2DH N91KK
0194	N26228 N111VW N2606 N831GA N831VP
0195	N26233 N411BB N411BP C-GAPT N800MC N140WH
0196	(N2625C) N196CM N896EC N534H
0197	N2625Y N95CC N197CC (N197VP) N797T N800R N840R N100R N50QN N111F
0198	N2624L (N650GA) N198CM N553AC (N650BW) XA-INF N650BC XA-XGX
0199	(N2626X) (N900JD) N65KB N890MC N527CP N400RE N193JC
0200	[Built as Citation VI (qv)]
0201	[Built as Citation VI (qv)]
0202	[Built as Citation VI (qv)]
0203	N26271 N95CC (N203CD) N4612 (N4612S) N4612Z N350M N350MQ VT-IPA
0204	N2630B XA-RZK (N691DE) N811JT N108WV
0205	N2630N PT-OMU
0206	N2630U PT-OKV N39H N826RP N610RP N119ES

Production complete

CESSNA 650 CITATION VI

Note: The Citation VI was to have used model number 660 but in the end used 650 in common with the Citation III and VII

C/n	Identities							
0200	(N2626Z)	N650CM	PT-OMV	[w/o 23Mar94 25 miles NW Bogota, Colombia]				
0201	(N26264)	N40PH	N347BG	N1419J	XA-GMG	N777AL		
0202	N2627A	(N202CV)	PT-OJO	N202TJ	N65BP	UP-CS401		
0203	[Built as Citation III qv]							
0204	[Built as Citation III qv]							
0205	[Built as Citation III qv]							
0206	[Built as Citation III qv]							
0207	(N2632Y or N6812D)		N207CC	N334WC	N107CG	N818SE		
0208	N6812L	N91TG	I-TALW	N500FR				
0209	(N6812Z)	N650L	N198DF	N198D	N902VP	N930MG	N830MG	
0210	(N6868P)	N610CM	VR-CVP	N7059U	N733H	N783H	N891SH	
0211	N6820T	N335WC	N333WC	(N59CC)	N211CC	N211CQ	N650CE	XB-ELJ
0212	(N6820Y)	N805GT	N972VZ	N651AR	D-CCSD			
0213	(N6823L)	N900JD	N900UD	PR-KKA				
0214	N68231	N95CC	N95CM	TC-CEY	N771JB	N7777B	N7717B	
0215	(N900JD)	(N6824G)	N215CM	N650KC	N650GC			
0216	N68269	I-BLUB	(D-CCUB)	HA-JES	CN-TKX			
0217	(N6828S)	N217CM	PH-MEX	5Y-YAH	9H-PLM			
0218	N6829X	XA-GAN	N218CC	XA-MTZ	XA-ACH	XC-CFE		
0219	N6829Z	N219CC	G-HNRY	(N211MA)	N650TS	XB-GTT		
0220	N6830T	B-4106	B-7022	[preserved in museum, Beijing, China]				
0221	N1301A	B-4107	B-7023	[w/o 02Sep02 Xichang, China]				
0222	N222CD	N733K	N738K	N780GT	N333AH			
0223	N1301D	N111Y	N111YW					
0224	N224CD	N1UP	(N7UL)					
0225	N1301Z	(N225CV)	N606AT	XB-MXK				
0226	N1302A	N400JH	XA-GPS					
0227	N1302C	(N227CV)	N2UP	(N2UX)				
0228	N1302V	N228CM	XA-SLB					
0229	N1302X	TC-ANT	Turkey TT2020		Turkey OR-0177			
0230	N1305N	N616AT	N660PA					
0231	N13052	LV-WHY	N67SF	N400WK	(N650FA)			
0232	N1303A	F-GKJS	N517MT	(N512MT)	N711LV	N711LT		
0233	N1303H	CC-DAC						
0234	N1306V+	N334CM	TC-SBH	N733AU	N733A	(N735A)	XA-GBM	
0235	(N1307A)	N1303V	N235CM	N235SV				
0236	(N1307C)	N1303M	N600JD	N600UD	N184GP			
0237	(N1307D)	N1306B	N650MC	(N656LE)	N650W			
0238	N1304B	(N9UC)	N19UC	N19QC	(N13QG)	(N650QF)		
0239	N1304G	N17UC	N17QC	N68ED	XB-OJA			
0240	N51143	PH-MFX	D-CAKE	PH-MFX				
0241	N5202D	(N651JM)	N666JM	N651JM	N651EJ			

Production complete

CESSNA 650 CITATION VII

Note: The Citation VII was to have used model number 670 but in the end used 650 in common with the Citation III and VI

C/n	Identities								
7001	N1259B	N701CD	N111RF	N404JF	N701HA	N682RS			
7002	N1259K	N702CM	N95CC	N19SV					
7003	N1259N	N1AP	N17AP	N888TX	(N650RJ)				
7004	N1259R	N708CT	N913SQ	N174VP	N144CA				
7005	N1259S	N200LH							
7006	(N1259Y)	N966H	N966K	(N706VP)	TC-KOC	OE-GCH	N650MK	PR-VII	
7007	N1259Z	N944H	N944L	N28TX					
7008	N12593	(N708CM)	N95CC	N901SB	N902SB	N909SB	N16KB	N678EQ	PR-RVW
7009	N12596	(N709CM)	N93TX	N709VP	N711NB	N97FS	N575HA		
7010	N1260G	N1S	(N1902)	N317MZ	N150JP	(N403BL)	N406CJ		
7011	N1260N	N5111	(N6111)	N700VP	SE-DVY	VH-DHN			
7012	N1260V	N712CM	N5112	N5144	N317MB	N817MB			
7013	N12605	N5113	N5118	(N713VP)	N2NT	N15LN			
7014	N1261A	N864EC	(N865EC)	(N714VP)	N375E	XA-EMY			
7015	N1261K	N5115	N5119	(N715VP)	(N317MX)	N317MQ	N817MQ	N750CK	
7016	N1261M	N18SK	N68SK	N650RP	N650CP	N710BB			
7017	(N1261M)	N775M							
7018	(N1261P)	N5114	N5174	N718VP	N119RM	N623PM	(N51LN)		
7019	N12616	XA-TCZ	XA-TRE	N105GV	XA-GAV	XB-RUA			
7020	N1262A	N95CC	N700RR	N832CB					
7021	N1262B	PT-MGS							
7022	N1262E	N722CM	N902RM	N902F	[2000th Citation]				
7023	N1262G	N6110	XA-JFC						
7024	N1262Z	Turkey 93-7024		[code ETI-024]		Turkey 93-004			
7025	N1263B	N442WT	N442WJ	N68BC	XA-RTS	XA-UHO	XA-RRQ	XA-GIT	N125TN
7026	N1263G	Turkey 93-7026		[code ETI-026]		Turkey 93-005			
7027	N1263P	N500	N657ER	N900MN	N622PM				
7028	(N1263V)	N728CM	XA-SPQ	N569RS	XB-RSC				
7029	(N1263Y)	N95CM	XA-SOK	N650RL	N444KE	JY-RYN	[wfu, stored Zurich, Switzerland]		
7030	N12632	N1263Z	N8JC	(N703VP)	N95CC	N782CC			
7031	N12636	N40N	N4QN						
7032	N12637	XA-XIS	N32FJ						
7033	N1264B	PT-OVU							
7034	N1264E	XA-SWM	N4360S	VP-CDW	N650K	N583SD			
7035	N1264M	VR-CIM	N3273H	PT-WLC	N95RX	N757MB	N650AT		
7036	N1264P	N95CC	N95HF	N77HF					
7037	(N1264V)	N737CC	N95TX	N787CV					
7038	N12642	N399W	N398W	PR-PTL	N156BA	N398W	PR-JAP		
7039	N12643	D-CACM	OY-GGG	D-CBIZ	N521RF				
7040	N1265B	N504T							
7041	N1265C	N430SA	(N449SA)						
7042	N1265K	N657T							
7043	N1265P	N78D	N78DL	TC-ATC	N650DH	N44M	N44MQ		
7044	N1265U	N7005	N650CJ						
7045	N12652	N95CM	CC-PGL	CC-CPS	N745VP	CS-DGR			
7046	N51160	N746CM	N746BR	N747TX	N703RB	(N328BT)	N270AB	N785AJ	
7047	N5117U+	N647CM	N1828S	N198TX	N650DD	N650KD	N650RA		
7048	N51176	N18GB							
7049	N5120U	N749CM	N900FL	N750FB	N182PA	N73UC	N937TC	N458RM	
7050	N5121N	N6150B	N33GK	N83GK	N650CZ				
7051	N51817	(N95CC)	N965JC	N77LX					
7052	N5183U	N752CM	N24NB	N24KT					
7053	(N5183V)	N344AS	N650AS	N650AB	N123SL	N128SL	N650AT	XB-JCM	
7054	N5185J	(N754CM)	PT-WFC	N7243U	LV-WTN	LQ-WTN			
7055	N5185V	N755CM	N317M	N317MZ	N817MZ	D-CMPI	N611NS	C-GOSI	
7056	N52144	N6781C	N60PL	N444EX	N325RD				
7057	N5216A	N157CM	N653EJ	N361EE	N808VA	N597AF			
7058	N52178	N625CC	N98XS						
7059	N5218R	(N95CC)	N4EG	N76PR	N144MH	N14DG	N625G	N963U	N650PJ
7060	N5218T	N55SC							
7061	N5221Y	N903SB	N908SB	N202CW	N102CE	N132CE			
7062	N5262Z	N876G	(N337GM)						
7063	N52623	N95CC	N877G	[dbr Fort Lauderdale Executive 28Dec11; parted out by AvMATS, St Louis, MO]					
7064	N52626	HB-VLP	N5117	N5112	N82GM	N901LK			
7065	N52627	(N765W)	N650W	N96MT	N650UA				
7066	N5263D	N766CG	N669W	N161SD					
7067	(N5263S)	N51143	N502T	C-FTOR					
7068	N51160	N111HZ	N111BZ	N7AB					
7069	N5117U	(N769CM)	XA-TMX	N191JT	XA-CTK	N478PA			
7070	N51176	N95CM	N22RG	N322RG	(N770VP)	N654EJ	OY-CKE	N556RA	CS-DVN
7071	N5120U	HS-DCG	N1130N	HS-DCG	HS-LNG				
7072	N5141F	(N8494C)	N35HS	N77SF					
7073	N51444	N1867M	N1887M	XA-UAM	PK-YRL	PK-RJB	PK-RSO		
7074	N5183V	PT-WLY	N32AJ	YV552T	YV3263				

CITATION VII

C/n	Identities							
7075	N52613	N12295	N711GF					
7076	N5213S	N286MC	N53HA*					
7077	N5203J	N877CM	N532JF	(N582JF)	VP-CGE	N603HD	N603HC	N650HW
7078	N5079V	N78BR	N84NG					
7079	N779QS	(N132WC)	N779VP	Spain U.21-01		[code 01-408]		
7080	N780QS	CS-DNF	S5-BBA	YU-BTM	HA-KAP			
7081	N781QS	CS-DNG	N8VX	XA-FRI	N650RF			
7082	N5086W	N782QS	(N133WC)	N782VP	N2RF	N91KC	N773HA	N181BR*
7083	N50820	PT-WQH	[w/o 10Nov15 between Brasilia and Sao Paulo, Brazil]					
7084	N5094D	TC-KON	N1127G	TC-KON				
7085	N5112K	N785QS	(N136WC)	N785CC	D-CLDF			
7086	N51342	N860W						
7087	N5163C	N787QS	(N139WC)	N149WC	N43FC			
7088	N5073G	N449SA	N440SA	XA-UGX	XA-PYN	N650PD	N657CJ	
7089	N5117U	N789QS	N789VP	VH-VRC	N789VP	N87SF		
7090	N790QS	N790VP	(D-CVII)	T7-VII	D-CWII	9H-WII		
7091	N791QS	N791VP	TC-STO					
7092	N792QS	(N792VP)	N792CC	C-GCIX	C-FSBC			
7093	N793QS	CS-DNE	OY-CLP					
7094	N794QS	N794VP	D-CVII	N650WT				
7095	N795QS	N795VP	VH-LYM					
7096	N5162W	N796QS	N287MC	N513TS				
7097	N797QS	N797CC						
7098	N5212M	N798QS	N601AB	(N612AB)	N621AB	N1254C	(N777MS)	N303PC
7099	N5141F	PT-XFG	N17NN					
7100	N710QS	N710VP						
7101	N5157E	N602AB	(N621AB)	N612AB	N650JL	N602DS*		
7102	N5223X	D-CNCJ	OE-GMG					
7103	N713QS	N713VP	LV-FQW					
7104	N5148B	VH-ING						
7105	N715QS	N118MM	(N56BP)					
7106	N5188A	N716QS	N71NK	N33RL	N7WF			
7107	N559AM	N652CC						
7108	N202AV							
7109	N5269A	N709QS	[w/o Dec99 in ground accident Wichita A/P, KS; cx Feb11]					
7110	N52235	(N12909)	RP-C650	N657JW	OE-GLS			
7111	N5172M	N256W	N226W	PR-AJG	N815TK	PT-RMB		
7112	N5174W	N257W	(N267W)	N269TA				
7113	N5192E	PP-JRA	N650JB	N737MM				
7114	N5194B	N68BR	N926CB					
7115	N5267K	N314SL	(N848FP)	N845FP	N845BB			
7116	N5268M	N175DP	N653CC					
7117	N5263D	N33D	N135HC	PH-MYX	D-CEAC*			
7118	N5264U	N33L	N840BM					
7119	N5152X	N651CC						

Production complete

+ indicates test marks not fully confirmed

CESSNA 680 CITATION SOVEREIGN

C/n	Identities					
709	N680CS	[ff 27Feb02]				
0001	N681CS	N605CS	[ff 27Jun02; fitted with experimental winglets 2013]	HI985		
0002	N682CS	N747RL	N747RC	N682SV	N168PX	
0003	N52114	N103SV	N602CS	N683SV		
0004	N5233J	XA-GMO	XA-CIA	N680DR	N1027P*	
0005	N52229	N105SV	OE-GMM			
0006	N5264U	N409GB	N499GB			
0007	N52081	N604CS	(N687VP)	PP-SGM		
0008	N900EB					
0009	N682DB					
0010	N5135A	N301QS				
0011	N5135K	N338QS				
0012	N970RC	N61DF	N680VP	VH-ZEK		
0013	N5136J	N346QS				
0014	N5270K	XA-HIT				
0015	N272MH	CC-ALZ				
0016	N616CS	(D-CNIC)	(N21FR)	XA-RTS		
0017	N5248V	N757EG	(N121LS)	N446RT	N448RT	C-GJAE
0018	N79PG	N889DF				
0019	N5188N	N63TM				
0020	N5245U	N914SP	N7777B	N77773	N198SB	
0021	N5200Z	N1276L	N621SV	N174TM	N988TM	N95TE*
0022	N1901	N110LE				
0023	N52235	N44SH				
0024	N5241R	N565A	N304AC			
0025	N52475	N680AR	N121GG			
0026	N5260Y	SU-EWD				
0027	N5264S	N532CC	N522CC	VH-EXA	N827DC	N966JM
0028	N5264E	N865EC				
0029	N5183V	N349QS				
0030	N680PH	N86LF	N808WC	N200Y		
0031	N5223P	N156PH				
0032	N51575	N52433	N132SV	C-FDHD		
0033	N52114	ZS-JDL	D-CAFE	OE-GEM		
0034	N5260U	N2426	N211CC			
0035	N5155G	N157PH				
0036	N5108G	N350QS				
0037	N5130J	N631RP	N681RP	N126AA	N637SV	
0038	N456SM					
0039	N39SV	N680SB	VP-CFP	N184G	N755LL	
0040	N5241R	N785RC	N781RC	N884HJ		
0041	N5200U	N789H				
0042	N5090V	N29WE				
0043	N5233J	N718MN	XA-GAN			
0044	N52623	N680SW	N680CG			
0045	N5203S	N145BL	Chile 304	Chile E-304		
0046	N5260M	N2428	N2478			
0047	N5267G	N737KB	N544KB	ZS-SUM		
0048	N52601	N777UT				
0049	N5058J	N158PH				
0050	N5257V	D-CVHA	N685VP	XA-CAR		
0051	N362QS					
0052	N5203J	N12925	N19MK	N19MQ	LV-CIQ	
0053	N5076K	N53HS	XA-FUD			
0054	N5168Y	N2425	N2475			
0055	N5147B	OE-GNB	N333MG	N334MG	(N680FH)	N10TS
0056	N747CC	(N5YH)	N680SV	VT-VED	N915FG	
0057	N51872	N365QS				
0058	N5060K	N121TL	ZK-JTH	N121TL	N339B	
0059	N5214J	N4017X	SE-RFH			
0060	N5207A	N51246	PR-SUN	(N68GA)	N420KM	
0061	N51575	N606CS	XA-CRS			
0062	N364QS					
0063	N5148B	N608CS	N655MM			
0064	N5214L	C-GNEQ	N413CK			
0065	N901G	N901S				
0066	N5223D	OE-GUP	D-CUPI	OE-GBY	N307LS	
0067	N5203S	(OY-JET)	OY-WET			
0068	N68HC	(N68HQ)	C-GSUN	N422ML		
0069	N5166U	N1315Y	PR-SOV	(N209CR)	N720HW	
0070	N51869	N927LT	N978BE			
0071	N5061P	C-GJKI	C-FRKI			
0072	N5254Y	VH-EXG				
0073	N5264S	N368QS				

CESSNA 680 CITATION SOVEREIGN

C/n	Identities					
0074	N5105F	N391KK				
0075	N5163C	N1312V	A6-GJA	D-CLIF	N680GT	N250AT
0076	N5270M	N121LS	N111NB			
0077	N961TC	N933SC				
0078	N51872	N678SV	(OO-SIN)	N680SE		
0079	N5172M	N680HC	D-CHEC			
0080	N5090V	OE-GLP	N345PF	N106SP		
0081	N369QS					
0082	N7402					
0083	N50612	N44M	N44MV	N672PP	N652PP*	
0084	N5250E	N4087B	N63LX	N137WH	N717MB	
0085	N5202D	N1ZC				
0086	N5090Y	N227DH	N86LQ	N73UC		
0087	N5093Y	(N666BK)	EC-JYG	N680EV		
0088	N305QS					
0089	N380QS					
0090	N868GM	(N84LF)	PR-RCB	N595AB		
0091	N5200R	N595SY	PP-ACV			
0092	N51444	N610CS	(N692VP)	N95CC	CC-AQY	
0093	N5245U	N204RP	(N4RP)	N497KK	N131GM	
0094	N5263D	G-SVSB	N94SV	N201RC	N694TX	5Y-PAA
0095	N5136J	N711NK	(N711NL)	N363AP		
0096	N5200Z	N16GS	N214LV			
0097	N381QS					
0098	N52178	N202DF	N475BC			
0099	N370QS					
0100	N5120U	C-GAGU				
0101	N51072	N696HC	N686HC	N153SG		
0102	N617CS	N680WC				
0103	N378QS					
0104	N51872	N680GG	(G-GALI)	N928JK		
0105	N389QS	N305EJ	N105HC	N284J		
0106	N51869	N83SD				
0107	N5235G	N531RC	N531FC			
0108	N680VR	N680PG				
0109	N900JD	N394CK	N680HH*			
0110	N384QS					
0111	N282DR					
0112	N52446	N829JC	N329JC	N401MW		
0113	N388QS					
0114	N5223D	N11084	SE-RFI	D-CCFF	N614TX	N399QS
0115	N5250P	N385QS				
0116	N5225K	N308QS				
0117	N5094D	N681SV	EC-KKC	N680CF		
0118	N52653	(N2UJ)	SU-SMA	N261NA		
0119	N5260M	N387QS				
0120	N52038	N621CS				
0121	N5188N	N822DS	C-GTOG			
0122	N52526	N122SV	N468SA	N63CR	N899JF	
0123	N52582	N396BB				
0124	N5233J	N622CS	D-CHRE			
0125	N5053R	N666FH	D-CBAY			
0126	N5270M	N359QS				
0127	N51038	N111Y				
0128	N5062S	N228RH				
0129	N50522	VH-EXQ	N1314T	VH-EXQ		
0130	N52178	N307QS				
0131	N5000R	N624CS	(N131SV)	N247TA		
0132	N5090A	PR-SPR	N132SV	C-FDNA		
0133	N5060K	(LN-TIH)	LN-SSS	N256DC		
0134	N5076K	N323QS				
0135	N5172M	N229LC	N138BG			
0136	N5093D	N320TM	N101FC			
0137	N5093L	N192CN	N37VP	XA-FLM		
0138	N51984	M-AGIC	N477RT			
0139	N52081	OK-UNI				
0140	N313QS					
0141	N230LC	N905WS				
0142	N51817	N685CS	D-CHRD			
0143	N5257C	N1318X	G-XBLU	N483TW		
0144	N397QS					
0145	N5117U	OE-GVO	G-GEVO	N145WF	PT-TNE	N680PB
0146	N599GB	N680DC				
0147	N52462	N1TG	N11GU			
0148	N51072	N515TB	N112MV			
0149	N5030U	N389QS				

CESSNA 680 CITATION SOVEREIGN

C/n	Identities					
0150	D-CHDC					
0151	N5204D	N681LF	N175WS	N271PH		
0152	N52113	N152SV	N930MG			
0153	N5223P	OE-GTT	D-CGTT	D-CATE	D-COST	N680UT
0154	N52234	N888SF				
0155	N5040E	N357QS				
0156	N5235G	D-CHIP	D-CHIL	D-CYOU	N611NJ	
0157	N5226B	C-FCPR				
0158	N158SV	C-GKEG	C-FMFN			
0159	N51872	TC-IST	N159TF	N793KK		
0160	N51869	N317QS				
0161	N5268V	G-NSJS	N161SV	N14DG	N650JC	
0162	N5218T	D-CMES	N710MS			
0163	N5267J	N1RF				
0164	N52627	N300QS	N334QS			
0165	N5268A	N629CS	XA-XDC			
0166	N5086W	N1FJ	N75SJ			
0167	N5180C	SU-SMB	N262NA			
0168	N5094D	N442LW	N442EW			
0169	N5263D	N320QS				
0170	N5268E	N630CS	N250CM			
0171	N5093D	(D-CLLS)	VP-CMH	N680BD	PR-BCO	
0172	N5045W	N633RP	N441GT*			
0173	N52475	N1315G	JA680C			
0174	N5212M	TC-TKN	N910AC			
0175	N52144	D-CCJS	N175VP	PR-SVG	N680TG	N791JP
0176	N5072X	N701CR				
0177	N52446	N338TM				
0178	N5163K	EC-KMK	D-CLEO	N178RH		
0179	N5200Z	N2UJ	(A6-DPD)	HB-JIL	M-ARIA	OO-KIN
0180	N5124F	N376QS				
0181	N5174W	N751BG				
0182	N5194B	PR-HLW				
0183	N5130J	LN-SOV				
0184	N5231S	PP-BST				
0185	N50275	PH-CIJ	D-CEIS			
0186	N5135K	"OE-GAC"+	[+marks worn at factory]		OE-GAK	XA-UJP
0187	N5135A	N377QS				
0188	N51881	N626CS				
0189	N5245D	G-CJCC	N884RS	N333KG		
0190	N52352	ZS-SAP				
0191	N5136J	N339QS				
0192	N680RC	N680AT*				
0193	N5257V	ZS-JDL	N289KR			
0194	N52526	N680CM				
0195	N5207V	N973AC	C-GSOC			
0196	N5203S	N311QS				
0197	N5061F	N631CS	N7HB	N67HB	N716GC	N151YD
0198	N51072	G-SVGN	M-SVGN			
0199	N50655	N806MN	N12LE			
0200	N51564	N100KZ	OE-GKZ	N830GS		
0201	N5223P	N372QS				
0202	N5197M	VP-CAV	PR-JJA	N927AC		
0203	N50282	N203DN				
0204	N51511	SX-BMI	N6EQ	PR-SVR	N382SC	N99EF
0205	N5112K	N1406S	SE-RFJ	N799MJ		
0206	N5269Z	N606SV	N120SB	XA-CDF		
0207	N50612	N306QS				
0208	N50549	N68EU				
0209	N5090Y	N1388J	ZS-DRS	N1388J	N310LV	
0210	N52059	N680GR				
0211	N5058J	N2208L	N402SF			
0212	N52369	PH-RID	N622TX			
0213	N52397	G-TLFK	SP-EAR	(N467PC)		
0214	N5188W	N342QS				
0215	N5093Y	OH-WIA	EC-MLV			
0216	N5100J	G-SIRJ	N997C			
0217	N52446	PR-BNP				
0218	N51881	N444A	N218SV	N712GC		
0219	N5061F	N843DW	N683SL			
0220	N5109R	N315QS				
0221	N5096S	N401PG				
0222	N632CS	N7403				
0223	N5206T	N223SV	C-GSOE			
0224	N5166T	ZS-IDC	N998G			
0225	N5135K	N341QS				

CESSNA 680 CITATION SOVEREIGN

C/n	Identities					
0226	N5135A	VP-CRH	D-CAHH	N226VP	N680NY	
0227	N5105F	N631CB				
0228	N5264U	N41199	SE-RFK	N221LC		
0229	N5147B	N61KT	JA04AA			
0230	N5261R	N375QS				
0231	N5264S	N570RZ	XA-GIM			
0232	N51444	TC-ATP				
0233	N5036Q	N208MF				
0234	N5057F	G-CFGB				
0235	N50054	N361QS				
0236	N633CS	N680LN	N12F			
0237	N51042	N21NR	PR-EGS	N405JD	PP-UTC	N101CF
0238	N5064Q	N28WE	C-FLFI	N80FW		
0239	N51143	N680RP	N636BC			
0240	N52623	N396QS				
0241	N5246Z	N2157D	PR-BRS	(N745BD)	N745DB	PR-BBP
0242	N52178	N324QS				
0243	N51896	N520G				
0244	N634CS	N955KC	N680BF			
0245	N5221Y	N382QS				
0246	N5162W	SU-SMC				
0247	N5185J	N9661S	N777DY			
0248	N5269Z	N312QS	N95SJ			
0249	N50275	N456CJ	N219LC			
0250	N5231S	N680JG	VH-VPL			
0251	N5201M	C-GDCP				
0252	N5296X	PR-SMK				
0253	N51869	LX-DEC				
0254	N5194J	ZS-AKG				
0255	N5206T	(N681MR)	N680PA	N860SM		
0256	N5068R	N631RP	N201RC			
0257	N5045W	N188TL				
0258	N51744	N21654	N702AB			
0259	N5212M	N310QS	PR-AGP			
0260	N5031E	PP-AAD				
0261	N5227G	N261SV	N261AH			
0262	N5257C	N262SV	N84EE	VH-PYN		
0263	N51072	N263SV	N41225	TC-TVA	N263TA	
0264	N5065S	N68SL				
0265	N5203S	M-ISLE	N265SV	OK-JUR	N265SV	
0266	N5154J	N696HC	N686HC	N138KV		
0267	N51564	PR-RTJ	N753MS			
0268	N5197M	N6GU				
0269	N51511	SU-BRF				
0270	N52699	N41221	SU-SMD			
0271	N5132T	OO-ALX				
0272	N5063P	N2465N	TC-RED			
0273	N5145P	N6242R	CN-TLA			
0274	N5267D	N41222	SU-SME			
0275	N635CS	N72UK				
0276	N5223D	G-CPRR				
0277	N5094D	N88JJ				
0278	N5201J	N278SV	N259CK			
0279	N5264A	OK-EMA				
0280	N5064Q	HB-JIG	N680G			
0281	N5145V	N149JS				
0282	N5203J	OE-GJM	N582CJ	N868EM		
0283	N52369	(SU-SMF)	N680AK			
0284	N5109R	N284RP	Mexico 3930			
0285	N5264S	N61855	JY-AWH	N680AJ		
0286	N5036Q	N715WE				
0287	N5262W	N681HS				
0288	N5267J	N288JA	JA68CE			
0289	N5247U	N680FD				
0290	N5270J	N9022D	TC-ICT			
0291	N5268E	N682HS				
0292	N5223P	N292CS	N8608			
0293	N5166T	PT-FIS	N578AN	D2-EPL		
0294	N51444	N122PH				
0295	N5135A	SU-BRG				
0296	N52178	N446RT				
0297	N5125J	N6026T	B-9300			
0298	N5026Q	N60286	B-9301			
0299	N5172M	N60280	B-9329			
0300	N5188N	PR-FOR				
0301	N5103J	N688JG				

CESSNA 680 CITATION SOVEREIGN / SOVEREIGN+

C/n	Identities				
0302	N5183V	LX-GSP			
0303	N5117U	LV-CFQ			
0304	N5076P	N19MK			
0305	N5245U	D-CWIN	N81NT		
0306	N5093L	N3099			
0307	N5032K	(PP-JSR)	N9021H	N115WZ	N370M
0308	N5145P	N21NG			
0309	N5192E	I-TAOS			
0310	N5244F	N680MB	N622PC		
0311	N5264E	N16GS	N59TF		
0312	N52627	PR-WDM	N77778	N7777B	
0313	N5270E	N288HK			
0314	N5183U	N724RM			
0315	N50054	N468CE			
0316	N5235G	N316MJ	B-KTS	N680BA	N215WS
0317	N5066U	N18WE			
0318	N5065S	XA-ICO			
0319	N5100J	N680AB	D-CAWB		
0320	N5147B	N67TW	N320TX		
0321	N50612	N103HB	PP-SVG		
0322	N50776	M-DMMH	D-CMDH		
0323	N5180C	N102CE			
0324	N52699	OK-UGJ			
0325	N5125J	N708BG			
0326	N51042	UR-LDB	N326TF	PH-JTJ	
0327	N52639	N327SV			
0328	N5185J	N682AB	D-CAWS		
0329	N52234	N610F	N61DF		
0330	N5085E	C-GREQ	N630TX	N521BU	
0331	N5145P	N568VA			
0332	N51995	N227SE	N333MG		
0333	N5218R	N542CC			
0334	N5231S	N777GD	B-9630		
0335	N5261R	C-GUPC			
0336	N5267G	N201PG	N101PG		
0337	N5267J	N555MB	C-GAWU	C-GAWR	
0338	N5073G	N680HB	N20H		
0339	N52433	N339ES			
0340	N5057F	N680LK	N24PR		
0341	N5259Y	N341ES			
0342	N5204D	N342CC	5N-EMS		
0343	N5086W	N680SG	TC-NTA		
0344	N5136J	N344GL	TC-OYD		
0345	N52352	C-FJRX			
0346	N51478	M-IMOR	N346EC	N3ZC	
0347	N50612	N971MD	N831GA		
0348	N5165T	N81EA			
0349	N5172M	N680RB			

CITATION SOVEREIGN+

0501	N681GF		
0502	N682SS	N354JR	
0503	N52627	N503SV	
0504	N5270E	N504SV	N680HA
0505	N5183U	N505SV	N259CA
0506	N50054	N989H	N990H
0507	N52639	N507SV	N507SF
0508	N5165P	N508SV	N885M
0509	N50360	N16YF	
0510	N5032K	N510WD	N294GM
0511	N5124F	N511SV	N742AW
0512	N5185J	N38WE	N356WA
0513	N52234	N513SV	N680SC
0514	N5085E	N683AB	D-CARO
0515	N5145P	N680MC	
0516	N51995	N311BN	N310BN
0517	N5103J	N517SV	N425PQ
0518	N518SV	N68VC	N68HC
0519	N5216A	N179PG	
0520	N5262Z	N680SV	N54DT
0521	N5066U	N680KJ	
0522	N5065S	XA-GME	
0523	N5225K	N523SV	N105CD

CESSNA 680 CITATION SOVEREIGN+

C/n	Identities			
0524	N51872	N671MD		
0525	N5218R	PH-CTR		
0526	N5165T	N680NA	JA680N	
0527	N5172M	N23NG		
0528	N5090Y	N17EE		
0529	N5203J	N314TM		
0530	N5206T	PH-HGT		
0531	N52682	PH-RLG		
0532	N52113	N101EF		
0533	N5135A	N533SV	C-GSOV	C-GLMI
0534	N52086	(D-CORA)	PP-JMT	
0535	N5228Z	N684AB	D-CAWX	
0536	N5227G	N30884	RP-C2910	N719MC
0537	N50820	N3088R	PP-LBM	
0538	N5223P	N956MB		
0539	N5059X	N442LW		
0540	N5268M	N578AB		
0541	N52229	N541SV	N224JV	
0542	N5093L	C-GREQ		
0543	N5152X	C-GLVE		
0544	N5203S	N544SV	N715GB	
0545	N5262W	N680RH		
0546	N5090A	N47SB		
0547	N50054	N4RP	N547TX*	
0548	N5065S	N711FS		
0549	N5263D	N516CM		
0550	N52352	N15KJ		
0551	N5228J	N551DN		
0552	N52691	N5264N	C-FMCI	
0553	N5296X	N660HC		
0554	N5269Z	N606KG		
0555	N5076L	N999CA		
0556	N51896	N45NF		
0557	N5262Z	N557SV		
0558	N5263S	OK-JRT		
0559	N5064Q	N7136K	JA45YD	
0560	N50736	N680TR		
0561	N5203S	N7148N	PP-UQN	
0562	N50054	N9053N	N785RC	
0563	N52475	N90525	N799LG	
0564	N5183U	PH-MDG		
0565	N5057F	N665CF	N67TW	
0566	N5060K	PR-SLE		
0567	N5202D	N16CP		
0568	N5069E	N237BG		
0569	N50275	N569CG		
0570	N5154J	N492CV	N492CA	
0571	N52136	N27EP		
0572	N5259Y			
0573	N5162W			
0574	N5243K	N179PF		
0575	N5136J			
0576	N5068F			
0577				
0578				
0579				
0580				
0581				
0582				
0583				
0584				
0585				
0586				
0587				
0588				
0589				
0590				
0591				
0592				
0593				
0594				
0595				

CESSNA 680A CITATION LATITUDE

C/n	Identities				
E68A-719001	N3765L	[ff 18Feb14]			
0001	N681CL				
0002	N682A				
0003	N683CL	N444A			
0004	N50275	N684CL	[r/o 29.1.15, first production model]	N50275	N717FH
0005	N5154J	N685CL			
0006	N5194J	N632BL			
0007	N52234	N275BS			
0008	N5103J	N328N			
0009	N52691	N985BC			
0010	N5218T	N388JR	N8JR		
0011	N52446	N80LD			
0012	N50776	N680CT			
0013	N5268A	N613CL			
0014	N5239J	N11TR			
0015	N5211Q	N550QS	CS-LAS		
0016	N5268E	N684DB			
0017	N5262Z	M-MJLD			
0018	N5243K	N968AG	TC-TVH		
0019	N5073G	N61JD			
0020	N5040E	N920CL			
0021	N52627	N621LA	TC-GRS		
0022	N52086	N868MJ			
0023	N5228Z	N996UA			
0024	N5148B	N868MJ	N763JA		
0025	N5188A	N58WE			
0026	N51806	N626LA			
0027	N52038	CS-LAT	N551QS	CS-LAU	
0028	N5059X	N992AB	N892AB		
0029	N5073F	N778SC			
0030	N5093Y	N680DJ			
0031	N5196U	N399DH			
0032	N5068F	XA-GGS			
0033	N5174W	N558R			
0034	N5241R	N576BB	N676BB		
0035	N5268M	N255VG			
0036	N5093L	N318SM			
0037	N5181U	N501QS			
0038	N51072	N940JF			
0039	N5235G	N151PL	N751PL		
0040	N5161J	N503QS			
0041	N5086W	N504QS			
0042	N5064M	N505QS			
0043	N5192E	N506QS			
0044	N5248V	N507QS			
0045	N5061P	N512QS			
0046	N5267G	N513QS			
0047	N51869	CS-LTA			
0048	N5223Y	(PR-SLE)	N428FX		
0049	N52144	N378TM			
0050	N5026Q	CS-LTB			
0051	N5223D	N816JC			
0052	N50715	N514QS			
0053	N515QS				
0054	N519QS				
0055	N519LM				
0056	N520QS				
0057	N52457	N968UD			
0058	N521QS				
0059	N5076L	N28GP			
0060	N522QS				
0061	N523QS				
0062	N524QS				
0063	N525QS				
0064	N120CL				
0065	N121CL				
0066	N200BF				
0067	N518KB				
0068	N526QS				
0069	N527QS				
0070	(CS-LTC)	N537QS	N687TX		
0071	N516ST				
0072	N530QS				
0073	N532QS				
0074	N533QS				

CESSNA 680A CITATION LATITUDE

C/n	Identities	
0075	N5188A	F-HSAO
0076	N289AR	N674PP
0077	N673PP	
0078	N535QS	
0079	N536QS	
0080	N5053R	
0081	N538QS	
0082	N539QS	
0083	N540QS	
0084	N541QS	
0085	N778LC	
0086	N710CR	
0087	N537QS	
0088	N67PC	
0089		
0090		
0091	N542QS	
0092	N543QS	
0093	N544QS	
0094		
0095	N545QS	
0096	N547QS	
0097		
0098		
0099		
0100		
0101		
0102		
0103		
0104		
0105		
0106		
0107		
0108		
0109		
0110		
0111		
0112		
0113		
0114		
0115		
0116		
0117		
0118		
0119		
0120		

CESSNA 700 CITATION LONGITUDE

C/n	Identities	
E700-741001	N9722L	[ff 08Oct16, Wichita/Beech Field, KS]
000001	N701GL	[ff 19Nov16, Wichita/Beech Field, KS]
000002	N702GL	[ff 17Mar17, Wichita/Beech Field, KS]
000003	N703DL	[ff 06May17, Wichita/Beech Field, KS]
000004	N704CL	
000005		
000006		
000007	N5261R	
000008	N5093Y	
000009	N5174W	
000010	N5135A	
000011	N5196U	
000012		
000013		
000014		
000015		
000016		
000017		
000018		
000019		
000020		
000021		
000022		
000023		
000024		
000025		
000026		
000027		
000028		
000029		
000030		

CESSNA 750 CITATION X

WL alongside the c/n indicates the aircraft has been fitted with winglets.

C/n		Identities							
703	WL	N750CX	[ff 21Dec93; ff with winglets 25Sep07]						
0001		N751CX	[ff 27Sep94]		TC-ATV	N754SE	HB-JGU	XA-USA	XA-GMG
0002		N752CX	N902QS	(N752VP)	C-FPUI	N902VP	HI1010		
0003		N5223D	N1AP	N200AP	(N300AT)	(N300VP)	PT-MMN		
0004	WL	N5223P	N754CX	(N96UD)	N597U	N62VE	PR-LUZ	HB-JLL	N199CF
0005		N5263S	N99BB	N1JM					
0006		N5263U	N76D	N484T	N484H	N706VP	N706XJ		
0007	WL	N52655	N750EC						
0008		N5266F	N1014X	N353WC	N853WC	N708VP	N750CW	N751WJ	
0009	WL	N5223Y	N96TX	N909QS	(N109VP)	N978DB			
0010		N5225K	N5112	N5112S	N808CZ	PR-CTA	N417NZ	PP-LAR	
0011		N5122X	N944H	N944D	N960KC	N845TX			
0012		N52136	N966H	N912QS	N712VP	VH-RCA	N712TX	[wfu Wichita/Mid-Continent, KS, still wearing marks VH-RCA]	
0013		N5241Z	N5113	N5113S	LV-BRJ	N405LS			
0014		N5244F	N757T	(N14VP)	N478PM				
0015		N5085E	N715CX	N326SU	N915QS	N715VP	VH-XCJ		
0016		N5263U	N206PC	N521FP					
0017	WL	N51072	N5114	N5144	N619AT	N347WS			
0018		N5091J	N95CC	N5115	N199WT	N287TG			
0019		N5109W	N5116	N199XP					
0020		N5125J	N95CM	N8JC	N8JQ	C-FJIC			
0021		N5131M	(N164M)	N138A	N630M	N61KB	N49FW	VP-CFP	
0022		N51313	(N5116)	N52639	(N722CX)	N10JM	OH-CXO	(N750AG)	N750VP
0023	WL	N5000R	N923QS	N923VP	N725DT				
0024		N52682	N164M	N5125J	N924EJ	N504SU	N942QS	N942QB	N201HR
0025		N50612	N750RL	[2500th Citation built]		N760BP	N444BC		
0026	WL	N5066U	N926QS	N926VP	N926VR				
0027	WL	N5068R	N354WC	N854WC	N27VP	N733FL			
0028		N5058J	N728CX	N100FF	PR-FNP	N228CF	[cx 29Sep14; wfu]		
0029		N5090V	N500RP	N500FP	(N992QS)	N929EJ	N945QS	N729VP	
0030		N5095N	N355WC	N369B	[w/o 29May08 Kearney, NE; parted out by Dodson Av'n, Rantoul, KS]				
0031	WL	N5061W	N22RG						
0032		N932QS	(N214BM)	N214WT					
0033		N5093D	N710AW	N808GG					
0034		N934QS	N34VP	N34VR	N752WJ				
0035		N5071M	N97DK	N96DK	N60ES				
0036		N5085E	N936QS	N541CX					
0037		N51160	N75HS						
0038		N51176	(N938QS)	N739CX	N938EJ	N938CC	(N788CW)	N700LX	N710FL
0039	WL	N51055	N98TX	N750LM	N22NG	N32NG	N736FL	N26BT	
0040		N52136	N68LP	N68LF	N740VP	N40KW	N110PK		
0041		N5066U	(N95CC)	(N22NG)	N98TX	C-GIWD	C-GIWZ		
0042		N5090A	N95CM	N915RB					
0043		N5090Y	N943QS	N943EL					
0044		N5103J	N96RX						
0045		N5109R	N45BR	N621FP					
0046		N5109W	N746CX	N946EJ	N749DX	N749P			
0047		N5091J	N947QS	(N752EL)	N947EL				
0048		N5135A	N84PJ	P4-MAA					
0049		N5153K	N949QS	N517CF					
0050		N5156D	N950QS	N750VR	N720CC	N950TX	XA-...		
0051		N5058J	N750J	(N1419J)	N119RM	(N119PM)			
0052		N5000R	N712JC	N681WD	PR-LAT				
0053		N5061P	N795HG	(N795HC)	N53VP	N753XJ			
0054	WL	N45ST	N450T	N610HC					
0055		N5068R	N955QS	N955VR					
0056	WL	N5105F	PP-JQM	N156VP					
0057	WL	N505MA	N74VF						
0058		N5120U	N758CX	(N87N)	(N750XB)				
0059	WL	N5108G	N751BH	N750RB					
0060		N5090Y	N95CM	N98CX	PR-JAQ				
0061		N5109R	N961QS	N751EL	N104PC				
0062		N724CC	N301HR						
0063	WL	N51038	N750JB	N999GY					
0064		N964QS	N964EJ	N931QS	N964EL	XA-TVA			
0065		N5163C	(N965QS)	N750JJ	N514X				
0066		N750GM							
0067		N967QS	N767XJ						
0068		N5100J	N377SF	N750PT	N751AA				
0069		N51055	N100FR	N96TX					
0070		N970QS	N790XJ						

CITATION X

C/n		Identities							
0071		N971QS	N771XJ	(N710TX)	N864MM				
0072		XA-VER	N72FD	N777CX					
0073		(N532JF)	N999CX	N269JR	N706LX	N716FL			
0074		N774CZ	N2418Y	N2418N	N2418F	N7418F	N703LX	N713FL	
0075		N5196U	G-HERS	(SE-DZX)	N21HE	N21HQ	P4-AND		
0076		N5197M	N400RB	N702LX	N702FL				
0077		N977QS	N797XJ	(N977TX)	N110CX				
0078		N51160	N199NP	(N711HE)	N121HE	N711HE	N711HQ	N707LX	N730FL
0079		N979QS	N979EL	N125DT					
0080		N5165T	ZS-SAB	(N178AT)	PT-PTL	N703DM			
0081		N810X	N1BS						
0082	WL	N82BG	(N242LT)	N705LX	N712FL				
0083		N983QS	(N256TX)	N783XJ					
0084		N984QS	(N253TX)	N784XJ					
0085		(N985QS)	N5103J	D-BTEN	D-BEAR				
0086		N5124F	N888CN	N986QS	(N986VR)	N860TX			
0087		N987QS	N87VR	N100MA					
0088		N5130J	N88EJ	N712WB					
0089	WL	N989QS	(N251TX)	N989VR	N900KM				
0090		N5132T	N1932P	N193ZP	C-GCUL	C-FSDS			
0091		N5061P	N991EJ	N991CX	(N791CW)	N704LX	N721FL		
0092		N5066U	PT-WUM						
0093		N993QS	N71RP	N114VW	N793XJ				
0094		N51038	N750XX	N84EA					
0095		N415FW	N19DD	N95CX	N104RP				
0096		N585M							
0097		N5060K	(N81SN)	VP-CYK	C-FTEL	C-GIGT	C-GMNC	N92TH	
0098		N5090V	N998EJ	N998CX	(N798CW)				
0099		N5090A	N442WT	N442WJ	N93TX	HI1001			
0100		N5100J	N104CT	(N104UT)	N170HL	N612EM			
0101		N901QS	N881G	N711VT	N711VJ				
0102		N51995	N901QS	N102VR					
0103		N5260Y	N96TX	N750HS	N737FL				
0104		N5147B	N5T	N750NA					
0105		N905QS	N905VR						
0106		N52642	N106CX	N955GH					
0107		N5086W	N107CX	(N332CM)	N520CM	N307RX	N107CX	D-BEEP	
0108	WL	N51744	N908QS	(N249TX)	N908VR	C-GAUH	C-GTCI		
0109		N900EJ	N750PT	N708LX	N708FL				
0110	WL	N910QS	(N255TX)	N910VP					
0111		N5264A	N750BP						
0112		N51072	N1107Z	N173WF	(N910RL)	PR-GRD	N194SR		
0113		N913QS	(N913VR)	N913TX					
0114		N50820	N114CX	N701LX	N732FL				
0115		N5085E	OH-PPI	ES-ELI					
0116		N916QS							
0117		N50612	N426CM						
0118	WL	N5266F	N753BD	PR-XDY	C-FTLH				
0119		N5223X	XA-FMX	XA-SAR	N187CR				
0120		N920QS	(N920VR)	N920TX					
0121		N51042	N358WC	N93LA	N910E				
0122		N800W	N577JC						
0123		N51038	N900QS	N703TX					
0124		N924QS	(N248TX)	XA-MIL					
0125		N5061W	N444CX	N977AE	N977AF				
0126		N5076K	N962QS	N962TX*					
0127		N52639	N15TT	N15TZ					
0128		N5145V	N67CX	N1873	N610CG				
0129		N929QS	N929TX*						
0130		N930QS	N903TX						
0131		N5155G	N131CX	C-GAPT					
0132		N51055	N627R	N75TX					
0133		N933QS	N932TX						
0134		N51780	CS-DCT	[impounded at Caracas-La Carlotta, Venezuela, 24Oct04]	(YV1969)	Venezuela 1060			
		YV2470	Venezuela 1060	(YV2818)	[wfu Caracas/Miranda]				
0135		N935QS							
0136		N5058J	N799TG	N1DH	N8TU	XA-BAE			
0137		N937QS	N937VR						
0138		N5241Z	N138SP						
0139		N5196U	N26MJ						
0140		N5112K	D-BLUE	CS-DGO	PT-TBR	CS-DVB	N750RT	N601DL	
0141		N5068R	N941QS	N941TX					
0142		N5172M	N700SW						
0143	WL	N51744	N825GA	N751AJ	(N884JL)	N13SY			
0144		N944QS	N944TX						
0145	WL	N5174W	N145CX	(N745CW)	N709LX	N709FL	N751GB*		

CITATION X

C/n		Identities								
0146		N5152X	N750DM	N751MM						
0147	WL	N5085E	N147CX	(N787CW)	N2AZ					
0148		N700LH								
0149		N52601	N948QS							
0150		N51896	TC-VZR	N750MD	N750TX					
0151		N951QS								
0152		N51744	OH-PPJ	N934BD	N750GS					
0153		N953QS								
0154		N5206T	N8JC							
0155		N551AM	N73ME							
0156		N956QS	N956TX*							
0157		N52081	B-7021							
0158		N958QS								
0159		N5245D	N1128V	N7600G	N7600L*					
0160		N960QS	N957TX	N3RC						
0161		N5245L	I-KETO	N280DM	N232CF					
0162		N903QS								
0163		N5253S	N610GR	N618GR	N675CS					
0164		N964QS	N964VR							
0165		N5257V	N15RL							
0166		N966QS								
0167		N5117U	N802W	N4165Y	N721VT	N610RT	N610RW			
0168		N52653	N1288B	N123SL						
0169		N5248V	N68LP	N563BA						
0170	WL	N5060K	N90NF							
0171		N51160	(B-....)	N399W						
0172	WL	N5066U	N750NS	N750WR						
0173		N5093D	N173CX	N749DX	D2-EZR					
0174		N5270M	N174CX	N87SL	N174CH	N699MG				
0175		N975QS								
0176		N51806	N1AP							
0177		N177EL	N3B	N125TH						
0178		N5152X	N275NM	N750BL						
0179		N5147B	OE-HFE	HB-JEZ	N719XJ					
0180		N51511	N353WC							
0181		N181BR	N600AW							
0182		N982QS								
0183		N938QS								
0184		N51896	I-JETX	HS-CDY						
0185		N5223X	N7SB	N185CX	N45ST	N185CX	N370EK	N750DD	N750HC	
0186		N5188N	N970SK							
0187		N978QS								
0188		N5163K	C-FTEN	N750EA						
0189		N51984	N93S							
0190		N990QS								
0191		N5267G	N354WC							
0192		N51817	N5FF	N750XX						
0193		N939QS								
0194		N5192E	N194CX	G-CDCX	N194VP	ZS-MRH	N194B	N19DD	N199D	N125RH
0195		N5241R	N946QS							
0196		N996QS								
0197	WL	N585T								
0198		N998QS								
0199	WL	N5245L	N484T							
0200		N952QS	N952TX							
0201		N907QS								
0202		N300JD	N202KC							
0203		N999QS								
0204		N5197M	N22NG	XA-KYE	[dbr Toluca 27Aug15; parted out]			N481XV*		
0205		N5181U	N4005T	C-GSUX	N700RH					
0206		N906QS								
0207		N5152X	N751GM	N49PW						
0208		N997QS								
0209		N52229	N7SB							
0210		N51666	N904QS							
0211	WL	N5247U	N954QS	N954Q	N65ST	N686T				
0212		N51744	N4101Z	N69SB	OY-LKS	LN-HST	SE-RIC	C-FWRX		
0213		N50715	N9NG	N399LF*						
0214		N5154J	OE-HGG	N44PR						
0215		N215CX	VH-TEN	N546MD						
0216		N51817	N1268F	N882KB						
0217		N5166T	N217CX	(N221AL)	N217AL	N717XJ				
0218		N5223X	D-BLDI							
0219		N5192E	D-BKLI	N288CX	[w/o on approach to Egelsbach, Germany, 01Mar12]					
0220		N52613	N48HF							
0221		N51042	N256W	XA-FJM						

CITATION X

C/n		Identities						
0222		N5166U	N222CX	(N850PT)	N750PT	N722XJ		
0223		N52526	N918QS					
0224		N919QS						
0225		N52526	N5223D	N921QS	N5223D	N215RX	N827SL	
0226		N5262X	N226CX	N257AL	N726XJ			
0227		N5267J	P4-LJG	M-DKDI	OH-DDI	EI-TEN	(D-BTAG)	D-BAVG
0228		N5269Z	N228BD	N228DB				
0229		N5268A	N229CE					
0230		N750WM	N10XT					
0231		N5109R	N432AC	N527NP				
0232		N5120U	N232CX	OE-HAC	EI-LEO			
0233		N51612	N442WT	N442WP	(N233VP)	N228WH		
0234		N52526	PP-AAA	N750WS				
0235		N400JD	N480JD					
0236	WL	N5246Z	N53HF	N349RR	N5FF			
0237		N5228J	N5197M	PR-MJC	LV-CEP	PR-XXI*	[impounded in Brazil]	
0238		N5183U	N238CX	N78SL				
0239		N5268V	N500N	N50QN	N910DP			
0240		N51666	N40CX	N1962J				
0241		N5197M	N921QS					
0242		N5194J	N1289G	9M-ATM	9M-VAM	M-MOON		
0243	WL	N5214J	N373AB					
0244		N52655	N750GF					
0245		N5269A	N200CQ	N200CV				
0246	WL	N5214K	C-GSEC	C-GSEO	N812KD	N15SD	N409CC	C-GAXX
0247		N5257C	N751PT	N747XJ				
0248	WL	N5268A	N1298G	N48VE	(N750CR)	N750ME		
0249		N5109R	N49VE	N265RX				
0250		N52526	N752PT	N750XJ				
0251	WL	N5096S	N251CX	VP-CFZ	M-ABGR	N17XR		
0252		N5000R	N252CX	G-CEDK				
0253		N5268V	N253CX					
0254	WL	N52627	N254CX	M-ARCH	N999TJ	N751EM		
0255		N51666	N712KC					
0256		N5268A	N753PT	N756XJ	D-BUZZ			
0257		N5090A	N754PT	N757XJ				
0258		N5264N	N755PT	N758XJ				
0259		N52114	OE-HAL	D-BOOC				
0260		N5260Y	N260CX	N760PT	N760XJ			
0261	WL	N5079V	OE-HJA	HB-JFD	T7-TAN			
0262		N5093D	N262CX	SX-ECI				
0263		N52609	N750DX					
0264		N52462	N764PT	N764XJ				
0265		N5262Z	N765PT	N765XJ				
0266		N5201M	N355WC	N355PX				
0267	WL	N5267G	N17CX	N92MK				
0268		N5262W	CC-CPS					
0269		N5066F	N769PT	N769XJ				
0270		N5165P	N270CX	N570PT	N770XJ			
0271		N271CX	(M-KAZZ)	P4-BUS	N250BC	N896RJ		
0272		N5200R	N772PT	N772XJ				
0273	WL	N5132T	OE-HUB					
0274		N5109W	N874PT	N774XJ				
0275	WL	N5141F	N4119S	N104CT	N1HS	N115HS		
0276		N51743	N776PT	N776XJ	N752GM	N347RL		
0277	WL	N52178	(OE-HEC)	[ntu marks worn at completion centre]	UP-CS501	VP-CEG	M-BEST	
0278		N5203J	N778PT	N778XJ				
0279		N5031E	N879PT	N779XJ	N720CC			
0280		N5163C	N780PT	N780XJ				
0281	WL	N50639	G-CTEN	N281VP	N9192W			
0282		N5064M	N282CX	N782PT	N782XJ			
0283		N5221Y	N711VT	N711VP	N610RT			
0284		N52178	N784PT	N784XJ	N750HH			
0285		N5060K	N940QS					
0286	WL	N5245L	N786XJ					
0287	WL	N5183V	N787XJ	XA-FGL				
0288		N928QS						
0289		N52457	N789XJ					
0290		N5032K	N927QS					
0291		N5125J	N2068G	M-PRVT				
0292		N51743	N792XJ					
0293		N5090A	N922QS					
0294		N5168Y	N794XJ					
0295		N5264E	N795XJ					
0296		N914QS						
0297	WL	N5268M	N797XJ	N797CX				

CITATION X / CITATION X+

C/n		Identities			
0298		N52114	N20768	HS-KCS	
0299		N925QS	N299CX		
0300		N50639	(N800XJ)	OE-HAK	[cx; impounded at Minsk-1, Belarus, 20Oct11]
0301	WL	N5156D	N92CX	N92RX	
0302		N5245L	N750JT		
0303	WL	N5244F	N442WT	N442WE	N845FP
0304	WL	N5109W	PP-JMJ		
0305	WL	N5239J	N305CX	C-FNRG	
0306	WL	N5032K	N110NB		
0307	WL	N52601	N98FG		
0308	WL	N51666	N308CX	N795HG	
0309	WL	N5225K	N411NB		
0310	WL	N5165P	N359TJ	N953TJ	
0311	WL	N51246	G-OTEN	N950M	
0312	WL	N5246Z	N858TH		
0313	WL	N5053R	PH-PKX	(LX-ITS)	OO-PKX

Replaced in production by the Citation X+, a stretched (by 15") variant with upgraded engines and avionics and winglets fitted as standard.

E750-716001	N750CT	[ff 17Jan12]			
0501	N751CT				
0502	N5233J	N502NX	[r/o 15Apr13]	N68ES	N287SL*
0503	N52141	N900JD	N503CX		
0504	N5200R	N750GB			
0505	N5064M	N15TT	N15TN	N750PT	
0506	N5192E	N586M			
0507	N5248V	N900JD			
0508	N5163C	N747RX			
0509	N51817	N509CX			
0510	N5201J	N555QB	N510CX		
0511	N5136J	N511CX	N752TX		
0512	N5148B	N512CX			
0513	N52609	(PP-OAS)	N680KG		
0514	N5201M	N442WT			
0515	N5073F	N300JD			
0516	N50756	N516CX	N555QB		
0517	N5094D	N745RP			
0518	N5201M	C-FTLS			
0519	N5263D	[test marks also reported as N52144]		N500CG	
0520	N5026Q	N520CX			
0521	N5207A	N71273	N3B		
0522	N5172M	N7145D	N504WV		
0523	N5090Y	CC-ARU			
0524	N50612	N387SL			
0525	N5200R	N487SL			
0526	N5180K	N587SL			
0527	N5066F	N255FP			
0528	N5108G				
0529	N51246				
0530	N52535				
0531	N50543				
0532	N5145V				
0533					
0534					
0535					
0536					
0537					
0538					
0539					
0540					

CIRRUS VISION SF50

A 6-passenger "personal jet" powered by a single Williams FJ-33 engine.

C/n	Identities	
0001	N280CJ	[ff03Jul08, Duluth, MN]
0002	N250CV	[ff24Mar14, Duluth, MN]
0003	N251CV	
0004	N252CV	N459PB*
0005	N253CV	[ff 05May16, Duluth, MN]
0006	N9ZN	N1WA
0007	N9943H	
0008	N730FA	
0009	N17CX	N124MW
0010	N52CV	
0011	N519AB	
0012	N234HS*	
0013	N7776W	
0014		
0015		
0016		
0017		
0018		
0019		
0020		
0021		
0022		
0023		
0024		
0025		
0026		
0027		
0028		
0029		
0030		
0031		
0032		
0033		
0034		
0035		
0036		
0037		
0038		
0039		
0039		
0040		

DASSAULT FALCON 10 / 100

C/n	Series	Identities
01	10	F-WFAL [ff 01Dec70] [w/o 31Oct72 Romorantin, France]
02	10	F-WTAL [ff 15Oct71] F-ZJTA France 02/F-ZACB [wfu; preserved at Aeroscopia museum, Toulouse-Blagnac, France]
03	10	F-WSQN [ff 14Oct72] F-BSQN [CofA expired Apr81, wfu, cx 1988]
1	10	F-WSQU [ff 30Apr73] F-BSQU PH-ILT F-WJLH F-BJLH N333FJ [parted out by Alliance Air Parts, Oklahoma City, OK]
2	10	F-WJMM N10FJ N103JM C-GRIS [cx 29Sep11, wfu]
3	10	F-WJMJ N100FJ N731FJ N661GL (N10PN) N52TJ (N149DG) [wfu, cx 06Aug08]
4	10	F-WJMK N101FJ XB-SII EC-353 EC-FTV XA-SYY N888FJ [parted out by White Inds, Bates City, MO]
5	100	F-WLCT F-BVPR F-V10F F-WVPR F-BVPR [cx 19Oct15; scrapped]
6	10	F-WJML N102FJ N600BT (N110FJ) N10AG N139DD C-GRDT N54H N999MH N32BL N32VC N59CC N77JW [parted out by Dodson Int'l Parts, Rantoul, KS; cx 26Sep16]
7	10	F-WJMN VR-BFF F-BXAG HB-VDE I-LUBE HB-VKE D-CASH HB-VKE N769SC [parted out by White Inds, Bates City, MO]
8	10	F-WJMN N104FJ N21ES N21ET N21EK N88ME N108KC
9	10	F-WJMM N103FJ N10TX N149TJ N510CL N189JW [cx 15Sep14; wfu]
10	10	F-WJMJ N105FJ N253K [w/o 30Jan80 Chicago, IL; remains to White Inds, Bates City, MO, for spares]
11	10	F-WJMK N106FJ N23ES N23ET (N23ED) N942C N452DP (N190DB) N211TJ (N11WC) N419WC N858SP
12	10	F-WJML N107FJ N3100X N10F (N76TJ)
13	10	F-WLCS N108FJ N734S N210FJ N72EU N10JZ N777SN N15TX [b/u for spares 1992; cx Feb93]
14	10	F-WJMK SE-DEL N59TJ (N50B) N333KE
15	10	F-WJMM N109FJ N60MB [w/o 03Apr77 Denver, CO]
16	10	F-WLCT N110FJ N48TT F-GELA N416AS N416HC N127WL [wfu Scottsdale, AZ]
17	10	F-WLCS OH-FFB VH-FFB N29966 N27DA N33HL F-GHDZ EC-949 F-GNDZ [cx 09Jan17, wfu]
18	10	F-WJMJ N111FJ N78MD N48MS (N74TJ) N1TJ N80CC N1TJ N241RS [parted out by Dodson Int'l Parts, Rantoul, KS; canx Feb06]
19	10	F-WLCU N112FJ N30JM (N30JH) (N36KA) N36JM N937J F-GJFZ 3A-MGT [while regd and painted as 3A-MGT used call sign C-GORI at 1995 NBAA] LX-TRG N600HL [parted out by Alliance Air Parts, Oklahoma City, OK]
20	10	F-WLCV N113FJ N42G
21	10	F-WJMK (HB-VDT) 3D-ACB N40WJ N60ND N40ND [parted out by Alliance Air Parts, Oklahoma City, OK]
22	10	F-WLCX N114FJ N44JC N48JC F-GJLL VP-BBV M-GACB
23	10	F-WLCY N115FJ N73B N310FJ N91MH N20WP N90LC XA-GPA C-GRBP
24	10	F-WJML N116FJ N1924V F-GBTI N301JJ N991RV N230RS N69GB [cx; parted out by Dodson Int'l Parts, Rantoul, KS]
25	10	F-WJMJ N117FJ N40N N83RG N22EH N83RG N60FC N600GM N719AL N177BC C-GJET N725CJ
26	10	F-WJMK N118FJ N592DC N707AM N720DF
27	10	F-WLCX SE-DDF OK-EEH N38DA XA-AAY
28	10	F-WJML N119FJ N130B N813AV N500DS N42EH (N655DB)
29	10	F-WJMM N120FJ N234U N66MF N332J N999F N404JW [parted out by Alliance Air Parts, Oklahoma City, OK]
30	10	F-WLCT N121FJ N294W N30FJ N156X N3WZ N191MC N171MC [w/o 24Jan96 Romulus, MI, as N191MC; to White Inds, Bates City, MO, for spares]
31	10	F-WLCU N122FJ N2MP N27C N50TC N81P (N952TC) (N29AA) N27AJ
32	MER	France 32
33	10	F-WJMJ N123FJ N881P (N246N) N900UC F-GHFO N54WJ (N18BG) TC-ORM N20373 C-FBVF N33BV (N933TS) [parted out by Alliance Air Parts, Oklahoma City, OK]
34	10	F-WLCS N124FJ N110M N220M N18SK
35	10	F-WLCV N125FJ N54V N777JJ N83TJ N726MR N17WG N73LR
36	10	F-WJMJ HB-VDD N10UN N224CC N894CA N676PC N76AF XA-MMM
37	10	F-WJML C-GFCS N39515 N123VV N123TG N347K N48JC N72GW N945MC [b/u for spares by Air Salvage, Griffin, GA cx Feb04]
38	10	F-WJMM N127FJ N20ES N20ET N20EE F-GBRF [wfu]
39	MER	F-WPUX France 39 [w/o 30Jan80 Toul-Rosieres, France]
40	10	F-WJMN N128FJ N10XX N15SJ XA-LIO N11697 [parted out by Dodson Int'l Parts, Rantoul, KS]
41	10	F-WLCS N129FJ N1HM N50DM N53DB F-GKLV N61TJ N116DD N34TJ
42	10	F-WLCU N126FJ N18X (N9147F) N100UB N282T
43	10	F-WJMN N135FJ N1515P N510CP (F-GHFI) F-GIQP N17TJ [wfu Alton, IL, 2005; used for paint trials]
44	10	F-WJMJ N130FJ N205X N62TJ N277SF N244TJ (N90AB) C-FZOP
45	10	F-WJML N131FJ N120HC N110CG C-FTEN N444CR PR-EGB
46	10	F-WLCT N134FJ N911RF N815LC (N908SB) N908RF N401JW
47	10	F-WLCY N132FJ YV-07CP PJ-AYA YV-221CP YV-101CP N3914L N101GZ N91LA N90LA N79PB (N190MD) F-GJGB [w/o 30Sep93 Besancon, France]
48	10	F-WJMM N133FJ N720ML N720ME N333SR F-WGTF F-GHRV LX-EPA N20LW
49	10	F-WLCV N136FJ (N490A) N49AS N449A N26EN N700TT PT-LMO N67LC [parted out by Dodson International, Rantoul, KS]
50	10	F-WLCS VH-MEI (ZK-WNL) N133FJ PT-OHM N411SC N299DB N299DP [cx 14Oct16, wfu]
51	10	F-WJML N137FJ N51BP N909TF N683WS

FALCON 10

C/n	Series	Identities
52	10	F-WLCX N138FJ N342G N52TJ N8100E N860E N711TF (N117RR) N828KW [cx 05Aug11, scrapped]
53	10	F-WLCS N139FJ N8100E N810US N125EM (N890E) N891CQ I-LCJG N53WA HI-836SP N824LA [parted out by Alliance Air Parts, Oklahoma City, OK]
54	10	F-WPUU N140FJ (XA-SAR) N464AC N4875 N53SN N54FJ VR-BFW VP-BFW N561D N110LA N791CP N61HX [parted out by Marklyn Jet Parts, Dallas, TX]
55	10	F-WPUV N141FJ N55FJ N702NC N702NG N700AL (N700PD)
56	10	F-WPUY HB-VDX OY-FRM N56WJ N16DD N56WJ N297PF (XA-...) N297FF [parted out by Alliance Air Parts, Oklahoma City, OK]
57	10	F-WJMJ N142FJ N142V N50TB (N50YJ) N10YJ (N6366W) [w/o 30Jun97 White Plains, NY; parted out by White Inds, Bates City, MO]
58	10	F-WJMM N143FJ N76FJ N58AS N458A N500FF (F-GHJL) N170CS [cx 29Oct07 after cracks found in fuselage]
59	10	F-WJMN N144FJ N300GN N300A N302A N633WW N52JA
60	10	F-WJML N145FJ N77GT N810E SE-DKD N69WJ N769BH [parted out by White Inds, Bates City, MO]
61	10	F-WPUV D-CBMB F-WZGD (F-BIPF) F-BFDG 3D-ART [w/o 03Oct86 Magoebaskloof, Transvaal, S Africa]
62	10	F-WJMM N146FJ N12LB N6VG [parted out by Alliance Air Parts, Oklahoma City, OK]
63	10	F-WLCX N147FJ PT-KTO N70TS N876MA N976M [parted out by Alliance Air Parts, Oklahoma City, OK]
64	10	F-WLCT N148FJ N100BG N721DP N500DE N718CA N444WJ [parted out by White Inds, Bates City, MO]
65	10	F-WJMJ N149FJ XB-BAK N21DB (F-GJMA) N66CF [cx 11Jun13; CofR expired]
66	10	F-WJMN N150FJ N50RL YV-70CP N63TS [parted out by AvMATS, St Louis, MO; cx 27Jun11]
67	10	F-WLCU N151FJ D-COME N427CJ YV2474
68	10	F-WLCV N152FJ N7NP (N7NL) N11DH N91DH N80MP F-GFPF [wfu]
69	10	F-WJML N153FJ N43CC N3RC F-GELE N7TJ N711JC N530TC [cx 15Jun15; CofR expired]
70	10	F-WJMM HB-VEG F-WQCO VR-BCH VP-BCH N349JC
71	10	F-WJMM D-CMAN N229JB (N728SA) (N203PV) N190H (N202PV) N341DB N220KS
72	10	F-WLCX N154FJ N10TB N31SJ N50TY ZS-FOX
73	10	F-WNGL N155FJ N88AT C-GDCO N130FJ YV-601CP N130FJ VR-BNT N378C N362PT (N810MK)
74	10	F-WJMJ N156FJ N30TH N34TH N518S N108MR N5JY N55FJ [displayed at Aerospace Museum of California, Sacramento/McClellan, CA]
75	10	F-WNGM N157FJ N12U N937D (N75MH) N97TJ N796SF N97DD N97DX N71TS [cx Mar06, b/u]
76	10	F-WPUU F-BYCC N727TS N528JD N528JL
77	10	F-WNGN N158FJ N82MD N301HC N53TS N107TB N607TC N915FB
78	10	F-WLCT N159FJ N83MD (N83MF) N784CE N178TJ N199SA C-FEXD
79	10	F-WPXB F-BPXB N160FJ N73B N692US
80	10	F-WPXD N161FJ N48R F-GMJS N1080Q N39RE (N320GP) N577RT N4RT (N803RA) N567RA
81	10	F-WPXF N162FJ N700BD N81TX [cx 07Dec16, wfu]
82	10	F-WPXE N168FJ N97MC N602NC N101HS [parted out by Alliance Air Parts, Oklahoma City, OK]
83	10	F-WPXG N163FJ N5GD XA-FIU N83EA N67TJ N76MB N724AS [cx 12Oct11, parted out Oshawa, Canada]
84	10	F-WPXH N164FJ N8447A JA8447 N8447A N526D N6PA N192MC (N100TW) N106TW
85	10	F-WPXI N165FJ N85JM (N95DW) (OE-...) [w/o 17Feb93 Aurillac, France; to White Inds, Bates City, MO, for spares 1993]
86	10	F-WPXJ N166FJ N410WW N411WW N50TE [w/o at McCall, ID, 18Dec1992; to White Inds, Bates City, MO, for spares]
87	10	F-WPXK N167FJ (N200AF) N662D N682D C-FBSS N80TS N99BL N549AS C-FNND N156BF N156BE N515LP [parted out by Alliance Air Parts, Oklahoma City, OK]
88	10	F-WPXL N169FJ N3600X (F-GKCD) F-GHER N71M
89	10	F-WPXM D-CADB F-WZGF I-CAIC 3X-GCI HB-VIG I-EJIC HB-VKF D-CENT TC-AND (N888WJ) N23TJ
90	10	F-WNGD N170FJ N14U N12TX [parted out by White Inds, Bates City, MO, Jun06]
91	10	F-WJMJ D-CBAG N790US N23VP [parted out by Alliance Air Parts, Oklahoma City, OK]
92	10	F-WNGM N172FJ (N61BP) N1PB (N58B) F-GHLT N95TJ N724DS N824DS
93	10	F-WNGN F-BYCV N40180 (N98TW) [parted out by White Inds, Bates City, MO; cx 01Feb13]
94	10	F-WNGO N171FJ N54RS N13BK N54DR
95	10	F-WPXD N173FJ PT-ASJ [w/o 17Feb89 nr Rio-Santos Dumont, Brazil]
96	10	F-WNGD N174FJ XA-SAR OE-GLG I-LCJT N174FJ N96TJ N115TD
97	10	F-WPXF N175FJ N6FJ
98	10	F-WPXG D-CBUR [w/o 08Aug96 near Offenburg, Germany]
99	10	F-WPXH N176FJ N10TJ (N65HS) N656PC N500GM N67JW F-GKBC N63BA N923HB (N923HE) N715JC
100	10	F-WPXI N177FJ N10FJ YV-17CP (N217CP) N100FJ XA-MGM XA-UKD XA-UML C-GSXJ
101	MER	F-WPXJ France 101
102	10	F-WPXK N178FJ N61BP N908TF
103	10	F-WPXL F-GBMH N103TJ N339TG N103TJ N9TE N26TJ N63XG N68XG N316GB
104	10	F-WPUU N179FJ N90DM VR-BHJ N4557P N913V N913VL N800SB N100CU

FALCON 10

C/n	Series	Identities
105	10	F-WPUV N180FJ N942B N71TJ N711MT N16DD N16WJ N804JJ
106	10	F-WPUX N181FJ N1JN N10FJ N730PV (N918PC) N902PC N913VS N103MM N20CF
107	10	F-WPUY N182FJ XB-ZRB XB-CAM XB-FWX XC-ZRB N160TJ N100T N91BP N907TF N907DW
108	10	F-WPUZ (HZ-KAI) HZ-AKI F-WZGF F-BIPC N246FJ N11DH N91DH N88LD (F-GFJK) F-GJHK [w/o 26Mar92 Brest, France; scrapped Mar93]
109	10	F-WNGD N183FJ N77NR C6-BEN N69EC N89EC N840GL YV2806
110	10	F-WNGO N184FJ N90MH N901MH I-SHIP N712US N104DD N43US N653FJ
111	10	F-WNGO N185FJ N8200E N820CE N10HE N289CA
112	10	F-WPXD N186FJ N12XX N12MB N598JC [parted out by White Inds, Bates City, MO; cx 29Apr09]
113	10	F-WPXE (I-SHOP) I-CHOC HB-VIW (F-GFHG) F-GFHH LX-DPA VP-BGD N220PA (N716JC) (N168DN) (N210MJ) [cx 1Jul14; parted out at Pompano Air Park, FL]
114	10	F-WPXF N187FJ N200YM N100YM N807F N15TM N555DH N108TG N982MC [cx 03Feb10, scrapped]
115	10	F-WPXH N188FJ N511S N211SR N420JD F-GGAR I-ITPR N115WA N636SC N169LS
116	10	F-WNGL N189FJ N4DS (N927DS) N925DS N525RC F-GJMA [w/o 27Sep96 Madrid/Barajas, Spain; cx 20Feb17]
117	10	F-WPXG N190FJ N23DS N923DS N18MX [cx 11Jul16; parted out Wilmington, DE]
118	10	F-WPXI HZ-AMA HZ-NOT HZ-AO2 N848MP I-DNOR F-GJJL HB-VJN F-GIJG N41TJ (N97RJ) N118AD N100FJ
119	10	F-WPXK N191FJ N257W N257V N119SJ C-GNDJ [parted out Oshawa, Canada]
120	10	F-WPXM N192FJ N20ES N359V N369V N100WG N402JW N710JC N631KA CN-TLD
121	10	F-WPUU (HB-VFS) HB-VFT F-GDLR N381MF [parted out by Dodson Int'l, Rantoul, KS]
122	10	F-WPUV N193FJ N22ES N312A N312AT OE-GSC N911UN (N104KW) [parted out by White Inds, Bates City, MO]
123	10	F-WPUX N194FJ N23ES N312AT N312AM N312AN N50TK N25FF SE-DKC N23WJ N110TP N689WC N54JE
124	10	F-WPUY F-GBTC [w/o 15Jan86 nr Chalon-Vatry, France]
125	10	F-WNGD N195FJ N400SP N100CK XA-SAR N269SW [cx 13May15; CofR expired]
126	10	F-WNGM (N196FJ) I-CHIC F-WZGS I-CHIC HB-VIX (F-GFHH) F-GFHG N26WJ N36WJ PR-CDF
127	10	F-WZGG F-GCTT I-CALC N8GA (N7RZ) ZS-SEB
128	10	F-WNGO N197FJ N1871R N79HA N79PB N99MC N99BC N175BC N228SJ P4-AVN CN-TKN
129	MER	F-WZGA France 129
130	10	F-WZGB I-SFRA (N777ND) N921GS N432EZ N454DP
131	10	F-WZGC N196FJ N654PC (D-CAJC) HB-VME N133EP C-FSXX
132	10	F-WZGD N198FJ N500GS N580GS SE-DKB N250MA TC-ATI [dbr Nov94 Le Bourget A/P, Paris, France; cx Mar95] N9258U [fuselage with White Inds, Bates City, MO by Apr96; cx 29Oct07]
133	MER	F-WZGE F-ZGTI France 133
134	10	F-WZGF N202FJ N900T N509TC VH-MCX VH-WJW [cx Sep11; instructional airframe, Cairns Aviation Skills Centre, Cairns, Australia]
135	10	F-WZGG N199FJ N835F N969F N707CX N245SP N707CX N272DN
136	10	F-WZGH I-MUDE F-WZGS F-GFMD [wfu]
137	10	F-WZGI N200FJ N837F C-GTVO [cx to USA 24May05, no N-number allocated – parted out?]
138	10	F-WZGJ N203FJ N30TH N100BG (N942M) F-GGVR N236DJ C-GNVT [w/o 14Jan01 Kuujuaq, Quebec]
139	10	F-WZGK N204FJ N10AH (N810J) (N610J) (N110J) (N803SR) N110J (N518RJ) [wfu Fort Lauderdale Executive, FL]
140	10	F-WZGL N205FJ N70WC N88WL F-GHDX 5Y-CAX
141	10	F-WZGM N206FJ (N10AH) N900D N77SF N7781 [parted out by Alliance Air Parts, Oklahoma City, OK]
142	10	F-WZGN N207FJ N10HK N11DH N5LP N174B
143	MER	F-WZGO France 143
144	10	F-WZGP N208FJ N1TC (N79FJ) N101TF (N144HE) N502BG N502PG
145	10	F-WZGQ N209FJ N244A
146	10	F-WZGR N211FJ F-GHVK (N17ZU) N461AS XA-CEG N110GF XA-CEG XA-UJG N957EC
147	10	F-WZGS N212FJ N12TX F-GHPL N125GA N212FJ [parted out by Dodson Int'l Parts, Rantoul, KS]
148	10	F-WZGT N213FJ N103PJ N79TJ ZS-BDC
149	10	F-WZGU N214FJ N711FJ (N830SR) N711EJ C6-LPV N149BL
150	10	F-WZGV N215FJ N212N N212NC (HB-V..) N99WA 9Q-CCA ZS-FGS
151	10	F-WZGX N217FJ N26CP OE-GAG N4581R N27AC N256W N256V RP-C9999 N256V
152	10	F-WZGY N216FJ N8463 JA8463 N8463 F-GDRN SE-DPK N152WJ N999LL (N999AH) N9TE
153	10	F-WZGZ N218FJ N344A N81P N81PX N600TW
154	10	F-WZGA N219FJ PT-LCO N777FJ N149HP [parted out by White Inds, Bates City, MO]
155	10	F-WZGC (N220FJ) D-CIEL N725PA F-GTOD
156	10	F-WZGE N221FJ N618S SE-DEK ZS-SEA
157	10	F-WZGF N222FJ (N900AR) N101EF N80GP F-GFBG N157EA N64AM N703JS (N157JA) (N814AA) (N450CT) N76AM [cx 15Apr16; to Singapore as instructional airframe]
158	10	F-WZGI N223FJ N81LB N220SC N790FH N700FH

FALCON 10 / 100

C/n	Series	Identities
159	10	F-WZGJ N224FJ N224RP N224BP (N88TB) N10WE N707DC N707AM
160	10	F-WZGK N225FJ N223HS N31TM F-GFFP LX-JCG (ZS-SEB) N160FJ PR-FDE
161	10	F-WZGM N230FJ N30CN N50SL I-CREM F-WWZK I-CREM G-ECJI (F-GOJI) M-ECJI
162	10	F-WZGN N226FJ N664JB N796MA N47RK (N162TJ) (N713G) N170MK N602DM N425JR
163	10	F-WZGP N227FJ N151WC N163F F-GJRN (N2CH) N163CH N163AV (N73TJ) N983CC N83JJ N50HT N163MJ
164	10	F-WZGQ N228FJ N222MU
165	10	F-WZGR N229FJ N111WW N56LP N707CG [cx Oct05; parted out by Dodson Int'l Parts, Rantoul, KS]
166	10	F-WZGS N232FJ N94MC (F-GIPH) F-GJFB N94MG N747AC N21CL (N166SS) N211EC
167	10	F-WZGT N233FJ N39K 5V-TAE 5V-MBG 5V-TAE N167AC N516SM N82CG N111WW N111WH
168	10	F-WZGU N234FJ N175BL N43EC C-GSXC
169	10	F-WZGV N235FJ VH-DJT N725P F-GHFB (N107AF) PT-WSF
170	10	F-WZGX N236FJ N821LG [w/o 22Feb86 Westchester, PA]
171	10	F-WZGY N237FJ N30TB N26ES PT-OIC N42US
172	10	F-WZGZ N238FJ YV-99CP N172CP N10NC
173	10	F-WZGA N239FJ N72BB N441DM N211CN N555SR N554SR 9A-CRL N8LT
174	10	F-WZGE N240FJ N5ES N402ES RP-C1911
175	10	F-WZGF N241FJ XA-LOK N12EP C6-NPV N175CJ
176	10	F-WZGI N242FJ HK-2968X HK-2968 N179AG N66HH N231JH
177	10	F-WZGJ N243FJ N533CS F-GFGB N101VJ N100ND
178	10	F-WZGK N244FJ N10QD N79BP N87TH (N210MJ)
179	10	F-WZGL I-DJMA (F-GGRA) F-GERO N100RR N3PW N777RF
180	10	F-WZGM N245FJ N593DC N398DC N25MC N211JL
181	10	F-WZGC N247FJ N87GT N151GS (N151DC) F-GJHG N138DM N204WS
182	10	F-WZGN N248FJ N111MU N809F C-GOJC
183	100	F-WZGO N249FJ N82CR N183SR SE-DLB N100HV
184	10	F-WZGP N250FJ N346P N4AC (C-....) N725DM N825DM
185	MER	F-WZGQ France 185 F-WQBJ France 185
186	10	F-WZGB N251FJ N2426 N2426G N63TJ N420PC N186TJ N555DH N555DZ [cx 24Mar17, CofR expired]
187	10	F-WZGR N252FJ N2427F "N2427N" N81TJ N303PL N555DH N1DH (N600AP) N5CA
188	10	F-WZGS N253FJ N188DH N64F D-CLLL HB-VJM I-TFLY N84TJ
189	10	F-WZGT N254FJ N605T N60SL N600PB N812KC N189JM N155PX
190	10	F-WZGU N255FJ N1887S N36BG N190L C-FBNW
191	10	F-WZGV N256FJ N700DK [w/o 23Sep85 Palwaukee, IL]
192	100	F-WZGX N258FJ N100FJ N121FJ [w/o 15Oct87 Sacramento, CA]
193	100	F-WZGY N259FJ N3BY OH-AMB (N30TN) EC-HVV
194	100	F-WZGZ N260FJ N100FJ N61FC F-GIPH
195	100	F-WZGA N261FJ N561NC N5736 N10NL (N10NV) N95WJ TS-IAM F-WWZL TS-IAM N1993
196	100	F-WZGB N262FJ N581NC N5734 N573J N125CA C-FICA
197	100	F-WZGC F-GEDB F-WEDB F-GEDB N888G N52N N197MJ
198	100	F-WZGF N263FJ N551NC N5738 N100RB N1PB N91PB N25ST
199	100	F-WZGG N264FJ N330MC (N1CN) N39TH PT-OXB N886MJ N486MJ N96VR N60HM N655PE
200	100	F-WZGG N265FJ N662D (N682D) N80BL N808L N1JW
201	100	F-WZGH N266FJ N8494 JA8494 N30TH (F-GKPZ) F-GKCC N100NW N844F
202	100	F-WZGD F-GDSA 3D-ADR N80WJ N202DN [w/o 09Dec01 Lawrence A/P, KS. To White Inds, Bates City, MO, for spares]
203	100	F-WZGJ N267FJ VR-CLA N100CT XA-TBL N45JB N54FH F-WQBM I-FJDC F-GPGL
204	100	F-WZGK N268FJ N101EU F-WGTG XA-TAB XA-UDP C-FFEV
205	100	F-WZGL N269FJ N700DW N606AM
206	100	F-WZGM N270FJ N100FJ N367F N46MK
207	100	F-WZGN N271FJ N711MT F-GKPB (N107US) N207US N456CM N55DG N456CM N55DG ZS-JLK
208	100	F-WZGO F-GELS I-OANN N71M F-WQBJ F-GSLZ
209	100	F-WZGP N272FJ N312AT (N312AR) HB-VKR OY-PHN EC-KPP 9H-SSG
210	100	F-WZGR N273FJ N312AM N812AM N85WN N35WN N110PP N210EM VP-BAF [w/o Samedan, Switzerland, 12Feb09]
211	100	F-WZGT F-GELT (N446BM)
212	100	F-WZGU CN-TNA F-WWZM CN-TNA CN-ANZ CN-MNZ
213	100	F-WZGV N274FJ ZK-MAZ F-GKAE F-WKAE N711HF
214	100	F-WZGX N275FJ N147G N147GX
215	100	F-WZGY F-GHPB N550FJ
216	100	F-WZGZ N276FJ N100H VH-JDW 9M-ATM N999WJ SE-DYB N707CX
217	100	F-WZGA N277FJ N100FJ N100WG F-GIFL N68GT N214RV
218	100	F-WZGB F-GHSK TC-ARK N218BA N130DS N303FZ [dbr Jeffersonville, IN, 23Mar11; parted out by Alliance Air Parts, Oklahoma City, OK]
219	100	F-WZGC N123FJ N2649 PT-ORS N219JW N485AS
220	100	F-WZGD N124FJ N368F N326EW N326LW N702NC N569DW N220CV
221	100	F-WZGH OE-GHA F-GPFD TR-...

FALCON 10 / 100

C/n	Series	Identities								
222	100	F-WZGF	N125FJ	N100CK	N98VR	N100YP				
223	100	F-WZGG	N126FJ	PT-LVD						
224	100	F-WZGH	N128FJ	(PT-...)	C-FREE	N135FJ	SE-DVP	F-WWZN	SE-DVP	N100TM
		N35CD								
225	100	F-WZGI	N127FJ	PT-LXJ	N225CC	(N814PJ)				
226	100	F-WZGJ	N130FJ	XA-RLX	N121AT					

Production complete

DASSAULT FALCON 20 / 200

Notes: "European Line Numbers" are quoted alongside the c/n where appropriate. These were numbers allocated by Dassault for administrative purposes but do from time to time get quoted as the c/n on its own, or jointly with the actual c/n.
Aircraft converted as part of the TFE-731 re-engining programme are known as 20-5s; known conversions are shown in the series column. Aircraft with TFE-731-5A engines (the earlier conversion) retain the series number in the designation, eg 20C-5 (c/n 24), while later conversions which use the TFE-731-5B engines (as also used in the Falcon 900B) do not retain the series letter; we have however retained this so that readers can be aware of the original model type.
Was known as the CC117 while in Canadian military service

C/n	Series	Identities
01	20	F-WLKB [ff 04May63] F-BLKB F-WLKB [last flt 06Feb76; used as mock-up for Guardian trials: donated to Musee de L'Air, Le Bourget, Paris, France]
1/401	20C	F-WMSH [ff 01Jan65] F-BMSH F-WMSH France 1/F-ZACV [wfu 31Dec81; TT 6,248 hrs, with 13,329 landings; to Bordeaux-Merignac Museum as F-WMSH]
2/402	20C	F-WMSS F-BMSS [canx Jan04 as wfu; to Musee de l'Air et de l'Espace site at Le Bourget, France on 02Mar05]
3/403	20C	F-WMKG F-BMSX VR-BCG HB-VAV N92MH N301R [wfu Oscoda, MI]
4	20C	F-WMKF N801F N116JD N121GW [w/o 18May78 Memphis, TN]
5	20C	F-WMKI N804F N747W F-GJPR N295TW [cx 03May16; wfu Addison, TX]
6	20C	F-WMKH F-BMKH N805F N20JM N21JM (N21DT) C-GOQG N65311 N497 N750SS EC-EDC
7	20C	F-WMKK N807F N607S N740L CF-GWI N777FA N20GH N12GH N110CE N93CP N600JC XA-ACI N666BT [canx 28Jly05; b/u]
8	20C	F-WMKJ N806F N1500 N150CG N1500 N190BD N612GA N277RA
9	20C	F-WMKI N809F N366G N3668 C-GSKA LV-PLC LV-WMF N611GA [wfu; cx 24Dec08]
10	20C	F-WMKK N810F N111M [cx Aug87; parted out by AvMATS, Paynesville, MO]
11	20C	F-WMKH N808F CF-SRZ N2200M N220CM N30CC N30CQ N4351M N4351N N409PC OO-DDD N983AJ N216CA [wfu at Addison, TX]
12	20C	F-WMKI N803F N221B N51SF LN-AAB [cx Mar89; to USA, no marks allocated; b/u for spares Jul89 Memphis, TN]
13	20C	F-WMKH F-BOEF TR-LOL F-BOEF D-CILL F-BTCY N977TW [wfu Addison, TX]
14	20C	F-WMKJ N804F CF-DML N22DL N22HC N91JF N41MH [wfu Chino, CA]
15	20C	F-WMKK N806F N622R N1502 N151CG N1501 [wfu at Detroit-Willow Run by Nov03; cx 15Aug13]
16	20DC	F-WNGL N807F N354H N10FE N122CA N120AF N216TW N216SA [parted out by Dodson Av'n, Rantoul, KS]
17	20C	F-WMKF N802F N545C N5450 N5C N5CE N55TH N234CA [wfu at Addison, TX]
18	20C	F-WNGM N840F N803LC D-COLO N777JF N9DM N210RS [wfu 1996 for spares]
19	20C	F-WNGN N841F N500PC N500PX N41PC (N41PD) C-GKHA [b/u for spares Mar04 at Ottawa-Rockcliffe, Canada]
20	20DC	F-WMKJ N842F N367G N367GA N5FE (N146FE) (N25FR) N903FR G-FRAJ
21	20C	F-WMKI N843F N3444G N370 (N500NU) N500EW N91TS XA-SWC N20LT C-FTUT N50446 [wfu Addison, TX]
22/404	20C	F-WMKK F-BMKK France 22/F-ZACS [wfu Bonneuil-en-France, nr Le Bourget, France]
23	20C	F-WNGL F-BNKX N844F N424JX N15CC N256EN N256MA (N582G) Venezuela 5761 [stored El Libertador, Venezuela]
24	20C-5	F-WNGM N845F N297AR N30JM (N13FE) N2255Q N738RH N60SM N60SN N703SC N20YA N25TX N204JP N1M N240TJ (N794SB) N240CK
25/405	20C	F-WNGN F-BOON HB-VCO F-BSYF N813AA TG-GGA N813AA [wfu Detroit-Willow Run, MI; parted out]
26	20C	F-WNGO N846F N802F N11827 N819AA [wfu Detroit-Willow Run, MI; cx 28Aug14]
27	20C-5	F-WMKJ N847F N677SW N33TP N174GA N326VW N481FL
28	20C	F-WMKG N848F N367EJ N10WA N573EJ YV-78CP N50CA (N280RC) (N126JM) N50CA C-GEAQ N333AV [at Montreal – Saint Hubert Aeronautical College]
29	20C	F-WMKI N849F N368G N368L C-GSKC LV-PLD? LV-WMM [parted out Buenos Aires/San Fernando]
30	20CF	F-WMKF N804F N368EJ YV-126CP N368EJ N407PC CS-ATD F-GPIM N514SA N123RA
31	20C	F-WNGM N806F N34C N814AA N828AA N131MV [wfu Laredo, TX]
32	20C	F-WNGL N805F N418S N218S 5B-CGB TL-AJK F-GIVT N232TW
33	20C	F-WNGO N807F N369EJ N888AR [w/o 07Aug76 Acapulco, Mexico]
34	20C	F-WMKJ N808F N369G N3690 C-GSKS LV-PHV LV-WLH [w/o 07Feb97 in mountains near Salta, Argentina]
35	20C	F-WMKG N809F (N1777R) N809P 9M-BCR [wfu by 2005; for sale in stripped down state for static use]
36	20C	F-WMKI N810F N900P N711BC N644X N85N OE-GUS N818AA [wfu Detroit-Willow Run, MI]
37/406	20C	F-WMKF (HB-VWW) HB-VAP (N7922) (N11WA) [w/o 01Oct77 Goose Bay, Canada; parts used in rebuild of c/n 28]
38	20C	F-WMKF N842F N1107M N957TH [wfu 1987; cx Jan93; remains to Elberry, MO]
39	20C	F-WNGM N843F N5555U N6565A N50MM N910U XA-LOB XB-EDU XA-RMA [wfu Toluca, Mexico]
40	20C	F-WNGL N870F CF-BFM N19BC N354H N354WC N854WC N65LC N65LE C-GSKQ N240TW
41/407	20F-5B	F-WNGL (S Africa 431) F-BOED LN-FOI Norway 041 [ECM Aircraft]
42	20C	F-WNGO N871F N1503 N7824M [w/o 16Jan74 Fort Worth, TX]

FALCON 20 / 200

C/n	Series	Identities
43	20C	F-WMKJ N872F N990L [w/o 03Mar75 Dallas, TX]
44	20C	F-WNGN N873F N355WB N355WC N355WG N692G N76TS N377BT (N773HS) N800PP (N120EN) [parted out Chino, CA; cx 08Dec14]
45	20C	F-WMKI N876F N147X N159FC N90JF N202KH N175GA N589DC
46	20DC	F-WMKG CF-ESO N23555 N7FE (N144FE) N46VG EC-EHC [wfu; instructional airframe Fuenlabrada, Spain]
47	20C	F-WNGM N875F N1846 [w/o 13Mar68 Parkersburg, WV]
48	20C-5	F-WMKG N878F N910Y N91CV (N23NQ) N23ND N541FL
49/408	20C	F-WNGN France 49/F-RAFJ F-TEOA France 49/F-RHFA [code 120-FA; preserved Villacoublay, France]
50	20DC	F-WMGO N879F N804F N565A N6FE (N145FE) N56VG EC-EDO N699TW
51	20C	F-WMKJ N880F N880P N218US N425JF N425JA [scrapped for spares Aug91; cx Oct94]
52	20C	F-WNGN N881F N72ET N85DB N825TC D-CLBR UR-CLG [wfu Paderborn, Germany]
53/417	20C	F-WNGO F-BNRE LN-FOD Norway 053 [ECM Aircraft]
54	20C-5	F-WMKI N886F N200P N2005 N10726 N54SN N100HG (N205TS) (N103RA) N380RA N405JW D2-JMM
55/410	20C	F-WNGO VR-BCJ HB-VBS EC-EHD N550AL CCCP-01100 UR-EFA N520FD N830AA [wfu at Detroit-Willow Run, MI; cx 25Nov14]
56	20C	F-WNGM N882F N671SR N100SR N185S N932S (OO-PPP) OO-OOO N388AJ N560RA [b/u for parts at Detroit-Willow Run, MI circa May05]
57	20C	F-WNGO N883F N499MJ N678BM N677BM N3JJ N76RY N711KG N812AA [cx 24Apr09; to Saudi Arabia as instructional airframe]
58	20C	F-WNGL N884F N600KC F-BTQZ HB-VDG N2954T [scrapped for spares 1987 Van Nuys, CA]
59	20DC	F-WNGO N971F N263MW N710MW N710MR N710MT N227GC N227CC N202TA N72BB N771LD N159MV N900RA
60	20C	F-WMKJ N885F N805F [w/o 05Jly71 Boca Raton, FL]
61	20C	F-WMKI N887F N299NW N20NY
62/409	20C	F-WMKJ F-BOLX LN-FOE (N17401) [w/o 12Dec73 Norwich, UK; used by Federal Express for spares, marks N17401 were reserved after the w/o]
63/411	20C	F-WMKI PH-LPS D-CBNA [w/o 04Aug01 Narssarssuaq, Greenland]
64	20C	F-WMKG N889F N806F N200JW N916AN N513AN N513AG N425JF
65	20C	F-WNGN N890F N383RF (N393RF) N393F N777WJ N777WL N1U N5052U C-GSKN N165TW [w/o Jamestown, NY, 21Dec08]
66	20C	F-WNGL N891F N401AB N581SS N109RK N181RB N766NW N830RA N814ER
67/414	20C	F-WJMN F-BOOA F-BTML N821AA N826AA
68	20C-5	F-WMKJ N892F N577S N458SW N521FL
69	20C	F-WMKF N893F N176NP N176BN N31LT [Parted out by March Aviation, Naples, FL then scrapped]
70	20C	F-WMKH N966F N647JP (N647SA) N78JR (N400NL) [wfu 20Mar89; b/u for spares Mojave, CA (TT 4,326 hrs); remains to Aviation Warehouse film prop yard, El Mirage, CA]
71	20C	F-WNGM N967F N807F N807PA N33SC N818SH N818CP (N293GT) N195AS N209CA [wfu at Addison, TX]
72/413	20C	F-WNGO HB-VAW N1270F N99KT VH-DWA N725P F-GJCC (N172MV) [wfu by Sep04 Middletown, OH]
73/419	20C	F-WJML VH-BIZ (F-BRHB) F-WMKG 9Q-CKZ (OO-RJX) (OO-ADA) LX-AAA LN-AAA [cx Dec89; scrapped for spares May89 Memphis, TN]
74	20C-5	F-WMKG N968F N1851T N1MB N57HH N800MC N800PA N800DC N702DM N702DD N522DD N8TP N221BR [cx 06May15; wfu]
75	20C	F-WNGL N969F N100V N256MA N2568 N800DC N77QM UR-EFB N217CA N962AA
76	20C	F-WMKF N970F N937GC N776DS F-GGFO F-GJDB
77/429	20C	F-WNGO I-RIED (F-GJBR) F-GHDN F-WGTF F-GHSG N613GA N844SL [wfu by Sep04 Toledo, OH still wearing N613GA; fuselage to Pontiac, MI by Oct05 for parts; cx 03Oct07]
78/412	20C	F-WNGM Australia A11-078 VH-JSX N6555C [canx 10Nov04 for parts; b/u]
79/415	20C	F-WMKH F-BNRH France 79/F-ZACT
80	20C	F-WMKI N972F N115K N356WB N356WC N356JB N76MB N24TW N925BE [fuselage noted 28Aug05 on trailer Pontiac, MI]
81	20C	F-WNGN N973F N799G N661JB N661J N747T N93RS N810RA [wfu Oscoda, MI; cx 18Nov14]
82/418	20C	F-WJMM Canada 20501 Canada 117501 G-FRAS
83	20C	F-WJMJ N974F N805CC N80506 N22JW N12WP N1TC N55ME N68JK N20PL (N82SR) N283SA
84	20C	F-WJMK N975F N530L N1FE (N150FE) N9FE [exhibited in Federal Express HQ, Memphis, TN]
85/425	20C	F-WMKH Australia A11-085 VH-JSY N6555L [cx 30Apr15; wfu Spirit of St Louis, MO]
86	20C	F-WMKI N976F N808F N622R (G-BBEK) F-BUYI G-BBEK (HB-VDW) F-WRGQ France 86/F-ZACG [wfu; to Musee Europeen de l'Aviation de Chasse, Montelimar, France]
87/424	20C	F-WJMJ Canada 20502 Canada 117502 G-FRAT
88	20C	F-WNGN N977F N130B N665P N665B N41CD N617GA [parted out by White Inds, Bates City, MO]
89	20C	F-WMKG N978F N345BM N71CP N505AJ [cx 30Jul12; b/u]
90/426	20C	F-WNGL Australia A11-090 VH-JSZ VH-CIR PK-CIR [wfu by Dec04 Jakarta-Soekarno, Indonesia]
91	20C-5	F-WMKJ N979F N115TW N25DB N8WN (N91MH) N777DC N20UA (N200SS)
92/421	20C	F-WJMM Canada 20503 Canada 117503 C-GWPB [in use as instructional airframe at BC Institute of Technology, Vancouver, Canada; wore marks "N9747I" in 2000 for film "Josie & The Pussycats"]
93/435	20C	F-WMKF F-RAFN F-RBQA France 93/F-RAFN France 93/F-RAEC France 93/F-RAED [code 65-ED] [wfu Chateaudun, France]
94/428	20C	F-WNGO I-ATMO F-ODSK CS-ATE F-GLNL N614GA N566YT N461FL

FALCON 20 / 200

C/n	Series	Identities
95	20C	F-WNGO N980F N802F N664P (OO-EEF) N664B N950RA N995CK
96	20C	F-WNGM N981F N511S N5RT N89SC F-GERT France 96/F-ZACB
97/422	20C	F-WJMJ Canada 20504 Canada 117504 G-FRAU
98/434	20C	F-WNGN TU-VAD OY-AZT N408PC OO-RRR N781AJ N980R N998CK
99	20C	F-WJMK N982F N921ML
100	20C	F-WJMN N983F N605RP N200FT I-VEPA N179GA [w/o 08Apr03 Mississippi River landing at St Louis-Lambert, MO; parted out by Dodson Int'l Parts, Rantoul, KS]
101	20C	F-WMKJ N984F N342K N342F N97WJ
102	20C	F-WMKI N985F N223B N53SF N710EC (N710EG) N710WB N403JW N204AN
103/423	20C	F-WMKH Canada 20505 Canada 117505 [ECM Aircraft] G-FRAV F-GPAA
104/454	20C	F-WJMK (OT-JFA) F-BOXV France 104/F-ZACW
105	20C	F-WNGL N986F N243K N77GR N97FJ N460MC [b/u for spares Jly87 Memphis, TN; cx Mar89; remains to Spirit of St.Louis A/P, MO circa Jan02]
106	20C	F-WJMM N987F F-GBPG N9300M N31V EC-EKK
107	20C	F-WMKJ N988F N965BC N155NK N330PC N213LS N107J
108/430	20DC	F-WNGO (D-CDAS) D-CBAT N5CA N4FE (N147FE) N26VG N101ZE N108R [wfu Oscoda, MI] N808CK
109/427	20C	F-WNGM Canada 20506 Canada 117506 [ECM Aircraft] C-FIGD [biofuel test aircraft]
110	20C	F-WMKG N989F CF-WRA C-FWRA VH-FWO [b/u for spares Oct88 Memphis, TN; cx Feb89]
111	20C	F-WMKI N990F N111AC N990F N111AM N111BP (XC-HIX) [cx 17Oct14; preserved Arkansas Air Museum, Fayetteville, AR]
112	20C	F-WJMJ N991F N2989 N830MF N200CX (HB-V..) CS-ATF UR-CCD UR-NIK [parted out by Atlanta Air Salvage, Griffin, GA]
113	20C-5	F-WNGL N993F PP-FOH PT-FOH (N713PE) N100WK N333WF N315PA N500HK (N731RG) F-WTFF N731F N129JE N129JF N400PC N400PG N22WJ N531FL
114/420	20C	F-WJMM Canada 20507 Canada 117507 [ECM Aircraft] G-FRAW
115/432	20SNA	F-WJML France 115/F-UGWL France F-UKJG [code 339-JG; stored Chateaudun, France by Jun02]
116	20C-5	F-WMKJ N994F HB-VJD OO-JBB F-WGTH (F-GPNG) F-GLMM F-WLMM F-GLMM N770FG
117	20C-5	F-WMKH N995F N171PF N421ZC TS-IRS HB-VKC EC-855 EC-FJP F-GLMD N207JS
118	20C	F-WMKG N996F N512T F-GGKE N820AA [wfu at Detroit-Willow Run, MI]
119/431	20C	F-WJMK I-SNAV F-GHFP N20FJ
120	20C-5	F-WMKI N4340F N410US N205FJ (F-GKAF) F-GICF N20AF N647JP N820CK
121	20C	F-WJMJ N4341F N242LB N813PA N813P N1199M N25CP N500BG N121DJ [parted out by Dodson Av'n, Rantoul, KS]
122	20C-5	F-WNGL N4342F N779P N335WR N335WJ N32PB N900LC N33QS N302TT N511FL
123	20C	F-WNGM N4343F N513T N45MR N223TW
124/433	20C	F-WJMJ France 124/F-ZACC [instructional airframe Toussus-le-Noble, France]
125	20C-5B	F-WJMN N4344F N6810J N812PA LN-FOE Norway 0125 [ECM Aircraft]
126/438	20C	F-WMKH HB-VBL PH-BAG N1047T N10VG N102ZE N126R [wfu Detroit-Willow Run, MI circa Oct01]
127	20C	F-WNGN N4345F N50AD XB-EPB XA-REY XB-GCR XB-HRA
128/436	20C	F-WMKJ 5A-DAF YN-BZH C-GNAA EC-551 EC-FAM N228CK N70CK
129	20C	F-WJMM N4346F N1823F N1823A N666DA N68TS PT-WUV N119LA PR-SUL
130	20C	F-WMKJ N4347F N514T XA-SCL (N130MV) (N130TJ) N722KS [canx 21Apr04; b/u; by Oct04 fuselage dumped at Ontario CA]
131/437	20C	F-WJMK France 131/F-ZACD [wfu Chateaudun, France]
132	20DC	F-WMKG N4348F N560L N2FE (N149FE) (N23FR) N902FR G-FFRA
133	20C	F-WNGO N4349F N894F VR-BKR F-GJLA N133FJ N200JE [dbr 21Jan04 Pueblo, CO; to Dodson Intl Parts for parts]
134	20C	F-WMKH N4350F N895F N897DM N897D I-NLAE [w/o 25Sep91 Kiel-Holtenau, Germany]
135	20C-5	F-WMKI N4351F N6820J N40XY N9999E N194MC N800DW N4MB [parted out by Dodson Int'l, Rantoul, KS]
136/439	20C	F-WJMJ HB-VBM 9K-ACQ F-GCGU HB-VBM SP-FCP LX-IAL N20MY RA-09007 [w/o 20May05 Moscow-Sheremetyevo, Russia]
137	20C	F-WLLK F-BLLK F-WLLK N4352F N8999A N777PV N200GT [parted out by AvMATS, St Louis, MO; cx 27Jun11]]
138/440	20C	F-WLCS D-CALL D-CGJH (G-BAOA) F-BUIC France 138/F-ZACR
139	20C	F-WNGM N4353F N334JR N926LR N1868M N1868N N23PL N900WB N235CA [wfu Addison, TX]
140	20C	F-WNGN N4354F N4350M N3350M N160WC N314AE N165WC [Volpar PW305 conversion; ff 05Feb91] [wfu 1994 Detroit-Willow Run, MI; b/u for spares by Active Aero cx Aug03]
141/441	20C-5	F-WMKF F-BPIO F-BIHY (UR-BCA) UR-CCB UR-SBS [cx; wfu Rotterdam, Netherlands]
142	20C-5	F-WJMM N4355F N100S N1BF N298W N777WJ N511T N511TA N43SM N220RT (N205FJ) XA-RNB N300BA
143/442	20C	F-WMKH 5A-DAG
144	20C	F-WJMJ N4356F N888L N888JR N800LS (N200WF) N800KR N911RG N385AC N960AA
145/443	20C	F-WNGN F-BPJB OO-PJB F-GCGY France 145/F-ZACU
146	20CF	F-WJMN N4357F N964M N777EG N11TC C-FCDS N182GA N345FH N299RA [cx Oct10; wfu]
147/444	20CF	F-WLCH PH-ILF (D-CORT) (D-CCNA) N41154 N183GA [w/o 08Apr03 Toledo, OH]
148	20C	F-WMKG N4358F N120HC N126HC N657MC N888WS N148WC N148TW
149	20C	F-WNGO N4359F N1818S (N4359F) N568Q EC-263 EC-EQP

FALCON 20 / 200

C/n	Series	Identities
150/445	20C	F-WMKH HB-VBO (N95591) N8227V N777XX N679RE N123RE (VR-C..) TG-RBW HC-BSS
151	20DC	F-WMKI N4360F N810F N810PA N3FE (N148FE) (N24FR) N904FR G-FRAL
152/446	20DC	F-WJMJ CN-MBG CN-ANN
153	20C	F-WLCT N4361F N70MD N207CA
154/447	20C	F-WLCV France 154/F-RAFK [w/o 22Jan76 nr Villacoublay, France]
155	20C	F-WJMK N4362F N500Y N205SC N212C (N205SE) N404R N68BC N68BP
156/448	20C	F-WMKI 7T-VRE [w/o 30May81 Bamako, Mali]
157	20C	F-WJMM N4363F N166RS Canada 117508 C-GRSD-X C-GRSD N5096F [wfu]
158/449	20C	F-WMKJ D-CMAX N450MA N158TW
159	20C	F-WMKJ N4364F N5RC N411CC N96WC N96RT XA-ICG XA-PCC N67AX XA-PCC
160/450	20C	F-WMKG I-DKET F-GHBT N48BT N100UF N301TT [cx 27Jun11; parted out]
161	20C	F-WMKF N4365F N93CD N19BD N93FH N21NC N10PP N10RZ N503RV N620RB [parted out by Alliance Air Parts, Oklahoma City, OK]
162/451	20C	F-WNGO OO-WTB D-CBBT HB-VED F-ODOK OO-DOK (F-GFLL) F-GFUN N162CT N911DG (N389AC) [cx 25Nov13; wfu]
163	20D	F-WNGM N4366F (N500HD) N500FE N500LD N178GA N258PE N471FL
164	20C	F-WJMN N4367F N654E N164NW [cx 23Apr13; CofR expired]
165/452	20C	F-WJMJ CN-MBH CNA-NM [ECM Aircraft]
166	20C-5	F-WLCS N4368F N33D N33DY N71TJ N201BR
167/453	20C	F-WMKG France 167/F-RAFL France 167/F-RAEB [code 65-EB; wore full "reg'n"; wfu; preserved Espaces Aero Lyon Corbas museum, Lyon, France]
168	20C-5	F-WLCX N4369F N100KW N108NC N300FJ N731RG N112CT N514JJ N168DJ
169	20C	F-WNGN N4370F XC-SEY XC-MIC
170/455	20C	F-WPUV I-EKET F-GHPA RA-09004 [cx; to scrapyard, Geneva, Switzerland, 14Mar06]
171	20D-5	F-WMKG N4371F N570L N900JL (F-GHRE) F-GICB N217AJ LV-BRZ
172/456	20C	F-WNGM F-BRHB I-LIAB [cx, C of A expired]
173	20D	F-WLCU F-BLCU N70PA N729S PK-TRI
174/457	20C	F-WNGL TL-AAY TL-KAZ (HB-VER) F-WSHT HZ-KA3 HZ-NES (D-CFAI) N174BD [wfu parted out at Fayetteville, AR circa Oct05]
175	20D-5	F-WMKF N4373F N866MM F-BUFG D-COFG F-ODHA F-GBMS I-CAIB N4246R N688MC N116BK HB-VJW SU-OAE 5A-DKQ [parted out by Atlanta Air Salvage, Griffin, GA Sep08]
176/458	20C-5	F-WMKG I-SNAM F-WGTM F-GHDT F-WQBM EC-JJH N179CJ [parted out by Dodson Int'l, Rantoul, KS]
177	20D	F-WMKI N4374F N6701 N14FG N41BP N82PJ [cx 14Oct11; wfu]
178/459	20C	F-WPXF OH-FFA G-FRBA [cx 06Dec11; CofA expired]
179	20D	F-WNGO N4375F N10LB N12LB N12MF N17JT XA-ACA N341PF XA-PVM XB-NOR
180/460	20C-5	F-WMKF OY-BDS I-GOBJ F-GVJR F-OVJR [w/o 15Mar06 Kiel, Germany]
181	20D	F-WNGL N4376F N836UC N966L N200GH N200GL N817JS N5225G [cx 06May13; wfu]
182/461	20C	F-WNGN HB-VCB F-WTDJ I-ROBM F-WVFV F-BVFV France 182/F-ZJTA France 182/F-UKJA [preserved Canopee museum, Chateaudun, France]
183	20D	F-WLCY N4377F N2979 EC-EFR RA-09003 [wfu at Moscow/Domodedovo by Aug07]
184/462	20D	F-WRQQ F-BTMF D-COMF F-GAPC OE-GCJ EC-HCX
185/467	20D-5	F-WMKF I-IRIF N3WN N147X N813LS N818LS N653MF [parted out by Alliance Air Parts, Oklahoma City, OK]
186/463	20SNA	F-WPXL France 463/F-UGWM [code 339-WM] France 463/F-UKJE [code 339-JE; stored Chateaudun, France by Jun02]
187	20D	F-WLCV N4379F N40AC N750R N811AA
188/464	20C	F-WJMK F-BRPK France 188/F-ZACX
189	20D	F-WPUU N4380F N950L N47JF N47JE N444BF EC-EFI [w/o 11Oct87 off Keflavik, Iceland]
190/465	20SNA	F-WNGN Libya 002 5A-DCO
191	20D-5	F-WPUX N4381F N910L N200DE N200CG N800CF OE-GCR N20HF [parted out by Alliance Air Parts, Oklahoma City, OK]
192	20DF	F-WPUY N4382F N920L N57JF N910W N192R N192CK
193	20D	F-WMKG N4383F N930L N37JF N400DB 9Q-CTT N219CA [wfu Addison,TX]
194	20DF	F-WPUZ N4384F N100M N555RA N297W N287W [w/o 11Feb88 Akron, OH; b/u Jun89; cx Jun92; parted out by AvMATS, Paynesville, MO]
195	20D	F-WPXD N4385F N200SR N186S N191C N500GM N43JK N195MP N822AA
196	20D	F-WPXE N4386F N811PA N701MG N369WR N216BG N79AE N255RK N196TS (N141JF) (N142JF) [cx Oct10; wfu]
197	20D	F-WPXF N4387F N399SW C-GTAK N5098F [cx 21May13; CofR expired]
198/466	20D	F-WNGO VR-BDK (N14FE) N74196 (XC-GAM) XC-BIN XA-SQS N520TJ N339TG N724DS
199	20DC	F-WMKH N4388F N8FE [wfu Aug83; displayed National Air & Space (Smithsonian) Museum, Steven F. Udvar-Hazy Center, Washington-Dulles, VA]
200	20D	F-WMKJ N4389F N550MC N44MC N44CC N48CC N38CC YV-200C HC-BUP YV-876C N12AR [b/u Ontario, CA, May03 still marked as YV-876C cx Jun03; fuselage still present 2009]
201/469	20D	F-WLCY D-CELL "D-CEUU" D-CELL I-DRIB [wfu by 2004 Rome-Ciampino, Italy]
202	20D-5	F-WNGM N4391F N814PA N33L N33LV N48TJ N9TE N29TE N9TE N365CD N100FT N604PT
203	20D	F-WPXH N4378F N1857B N20BE N911WT OE-GDR N36P N821AA [parted out by Dodson Av'n, Rantoul, KS]
204	20DC	F-WMKI N4392F N26FE N120FS EC-113 EC-EGM N204TW

FALCON 20 / 200

C/n	Series	Identities
205	20D	F-WPXF N4393F N21W N82A N4LH (N426CC) N815AA N915SA N585AC N961AA
206	20D	F-WLCS N4394F N815AC N632PB N801SC N28RK (N410FJ) [crashed into sea off Bahamas 17Dec09, w/o; cx 13Jun11]]
207	20DC	F-WMKF N4395F N27FE N908FR G-FRAP
208/468	20D	F-WPXD HB-VCA VH-BRR N300JJ N125CA [w/o 29Jun89 Cartersville, GA]
209	20DC	F-WLCX N4396F N28FE N909FR G-FRAR
210	20DC	F-WNGL N4397F N29FE N66VG EC-ECB [w/o 30Sep87 Las Palmas, Canary Islands, Spain]
211	20DC	F-WJMK N4398F N30FE Portugal 8101 Portugal 17101 N618GA N764LA N120RA
212	20DC	F-WPXG N4399F N31FE N212R [wfu Oscoda, MI]
213	20DC	F-WJMM N4390F N32FE N905FR G-FRAK (N213FC)
214	20DC	F-WNGO N4400F N33FE N906FR G-FRAO
215	20DC	F-WLCS N4401F N34FE Portugal 8102 Portugal 17102 N619GA N510BM [wfu for parts use; fuselage at Pontiac, MI by Oct05; canx Jan06 as b/u]
216	20DC	F-WLCT N4402F N9FE Venezuela 5840 [stored El Libertador, Venezuela]
217	20DC	F-WLCY N4403F N35FE Portugal 8103 Portugal 17103 [wfu; preserved Museo do Ar, Sintra, Portugal]
218	20DC	F-WMKJ N4372F N36FE N86VG OO-STE N86VG EC-EEU N218CA
219/470	20D	F-WPXH EC-BVV Spain TM.11-3/401-04 Spain TM.11-3/45-04 Spain TM.11-3/408-11 Spain TM.11-3/47-23
220	20DC	F-WPUU N4404F N24FE N36VG OO-STF EC-EDL "EC-EDC"+ [+ reported painted as EC-EDC for at least one flight (to Luton, UK) during 1987] N220CA [wfu Addison, TX]
221	20DC	F-WPUV N4406F N25FE N300NL EC-165 EC-EIV N221TW
222/471	20D	F-WNGL EC-BXV Spain TM.11-2/401-03 Spain TM.11-2/45-03 Spain TM.11-2/47-22
223	20DC	F-WPUX N4407F N22FE (N904FR) N900FR G-60-01 G-FRAH
224	20DC	F-WPUY N4408F N23FE N907FR G-FRAM 9M-FRA
225/472	20D	F-WPXD TR-KHA TR-LRU F-BOFH OH-FFJ N125MJ N37WT N332FE N338DB (N30AD) N102AD C-FONX N5098H [parted out Milwaukee, WI]
226	20DC	F-WPXI F-WSQK N4409F N21FE N226R N226CK
227	20DC	F-WMKG N4410F N14FE N24EV N227R N227CK
228/473	20D	F-WNGL ZS-LAL ZS-LLG 3D-LLG C-GWSA HB-VEZ 5N-AYM OE-GRU N823AA [cx 06May15, CofR expired]
229	20DC	F-WJMJ N4411F N15FE N25EV N229R N229CK
230	20DC	F-WJML N4412F N16FE N26EV N230RA [wfu Oscoda, MI]
231/474	20D	F-WPXE HB-VCG [w/o 20Feb72 nr St Moritz, Switzerland]
232	20DC	F-WJMN N4413F N17FE N27EV N232RA [w/o 15Feb89 Bingham, NY; cx Mar91]
233	20DC	F-WLCV N4414F N18FE N76VG I-TIAG N817AA [parted out by Dodson Av'n, Rantoul, KS]
234/475	20D	F-WLCU (D-CIBM) D-COLL I-LIAC [cx, C of A expired]
235	20DC	F-WPXJ N4415F N20FE Venezuela 0442 [stored El Libertador, Venezuela]
236	20D	F-WPXK (N4416F) CF-JES C-FJES N375PK N375BK YR-DSA N128AP N618GH N936NW N236TW
237/476	20D-5	F-WPXF (D-CHCH) (D-CALM) D-CITY N4227Y VR-CBT VR-BKH HB-VJV EC-JDV UR-MOA N119TA
238/477	20C	F-WRQP France 238/F-RAFM France 238/F-RAED France 238/F-RAEE France 238/F-RAFM France 238/F-RAEE [code 65-EE; wfu; instructional airframe Toussus-le-Noble, France]
239	20F	F-WPXM N4417F N10MT C-GBFL N134CJ I-AGEC PH-OMC N39WJ N697BH N239CD N239BD N300BP [cx 08Jul13; wfu; parted out Denton, TX]
240/478	20E-5	F-WLCX I-SNAG N240AT HB-VMN F-GYCA T7-ALM
241/479	20E	F-WRQP SE-DCO N48AD HZ-HE4 HZ-PL7 I-FLYK N241JC [cx 25Jun07, wfu]
242	20F	F-WPUZ N4418F N800CF (N320FJ) N2622M N911TR N66WB YR-DSB N129AP (N711RT) "N4RT" (N242RJ) N513AC (N242MA)
243/480	20F	F-WMKH OH-FFW [w/o 01Mar72 nr Montreal, Canada; remains to Sunstream Avn, Chicago-DuPage A/P, MI, gone by Jun95]
244	20F	F-WMKI N4420F N20FJ N11LB N226G N61LL VR-BJB [w/o 15Jan88 Lugano, Switzerland; remains to Dodson Avn, Ottawa, KS]
245/481	20E	F-WLCS SX-ABA F-BUIX HB-VDP HB-VDY EL-VDY [parted out by Dodson Int'l Parts, Rantoul, KS circa Oct98]
246/482	20F	F-WJMK F-BSTR (F-GLMT) N970GA [b/u for spares at White Inds. Bates City, MO]
247	20E	F-WPXE N4419F N730S VH-FAX N730S N67JR N95JR N70PL N247PL
248/483	20F	F-WRQV OH-FFV N37JJ XB-AQU XB-OEM XB-VRM XC-HIX XB-NET
249	20F	F-WJMM N4421F N11AK N777JF N451DP N431FL
250	20F	F-WMKF N4422F N111AM XA-HEW N223BG
251/484	20E	F-WRQR EP-VAP EP-FIE EP-IPA Iran 0110
252/485	20E	F-WRQP I-GIAZ France 252/F-ZACA
253/486	20E	F-WRQS EC-BZV Spain T.11-1/401-02 Spain T.11-1/45-02 Spain T.11-1/47-21
254	20F	F-WNGO N4423F CF-YPB C-FYPB G-FRAC F-GPAB [cx 19Oct15; scrapped]
255/487	20E	F-WRQP Jordan 122 HB-VDZ N2724K VH-HIF VH-MIQ N721J F-GHLN [w/o 20Jan95 Paris-Le Bourget A/P, France]
256	20F	F-WNGL N4416F N3RC C-GNTZ F-GKME UR-CCA N368DS N868DS N15SL N651SD N733JB
257	20F-5	F-WMKH N4425F N781W N300CC C-GNTL (F-GJPI) F-GKDD HB-VKO N18HN [wfu; cx 05Dec15]
258	20F	F-WNGM N4426F N20JM N544X N20AE N300SF N380SF N68UP
259	20F	F-WLCT N4418F N212H N45WH N45WN SE-DHK F-GIFP N569BW N569DW N569D [cx Mar11; to Finland as instructional airframe]
260/488	20E	F-WMKJ France 260/F-RAEA [code 65-EA; wfu Chateaudun, France]

FALCON 20 / 200

C/n	Series	Identities
261	20F-5	F-WLCU N4368F N200WK
262	20F-5	F-WJMK N4427F N720ML N750ME VH-WLH N501AS C-GTLU F-GHVR (N.....) D2-ESV (OO-MDN) (OO-RYB) N795AB N189RB
263/489	20E	F-WMKJ HB-VCR (PH-LEN) F-BSBU France 263/F-ZACY
264	20F	F-WJMN N4428F N373KC N777V N773V (N86BL) F-GJJS CS-ATG N264TN XA-III XA-NCC
265	20F	F-WLCX N4429F N606RP N265MP
266/490	20EF	F-WRQR PH-ILX N4115B N184GA [w/o 13Jun00 Peterborough, Canada; to White Inds, Bates City, MO for parts use circa Jan01]
267/491	20E	F-WRQZ I-REAL N731G N627JG N267H N129JE [parted out by Alliance Air Parts, Oklahoma City, OK]
268/492	20E	F-WNGN France 268/F-RAEB France 268/F-RAFK France 268/F-RAEF [code 65-EF; wfu Chateaudun, France]
269	20F	F-WPUX N4430F N1902W N501F XA-NAY XA-DUC
270	20DC	F-WPUZ N4435F N37FE (N907FR) N901FR G-FRAI
271/493	20E	F-WNGN 7T-VRP (F-GHPO) F-GKDB [cx to Switzerland 08Mar05 but no Swiss marks allocated; b/u, fueslage used as cabin trainer]
272	20F	F-WMKF N4431F N20FJ N732S N888RF N913MK N813MK (N803MM) XA-TAN (N272FA) N272JP N885BH N20FE N770RR N224WE
273	20F-5	F-WPUU N4432F N212T N212TC N212TG 5N-EPN F-WQBK N596DA N720JC N632KA CN-TNM
274	20F-5	F-WJMM N4433F N370WT N121WT N256M N26LA (D-CHEF) N260MB N100AS
275	20E	F-WMKH N4434F N661JB N9FB VR-BRJ SX-DKI N999EQ (N999BG) N200CP
276/494	20E	F-WNGL Belgium CM-01
277/501	20E	F-WPXD Pakistan J-753
278/495	20E-5	F-WNGM Belgium CM-02 F-WQBN Belgium CM-02
279/502	20E	F-WMKJ I-FKET F-GHFQ N279AL F-GROC N854GA D-CLBE UR-CLE
280/503	20E	F-WPXK I-EDIS N910FR G-FRAE F-GPAD
281/496	20F	F-WRQR D-CORF N20CG LN-AAC N70830 N347K N281JJ N341K N341KA N116GB [wfu Easton MD; cx 18May12]
282	20E	F-WMKG N4436F N131JA N282JJ N282C XC-DIP XB-IYK XC-HID [code PF-203]
283/497	20E	F-WRQX EP-AGX [w/o 21Nov74 Kermanshah, Iran]
284	20E	F-WPXM N4437F N132JA N284JJ N98RH N444FJ N441FA XA-BCC N441FA N284CE N501MD (N801MD) N201GF [cx 28Oct16, wfu]
285/504	20EF	F-WRQT A4O-AA A4O-GA PH-WMS VR-CCF PH-WMS N285AP N285TW
286/498	20E	F-WRQU EP-AGY Iran 15-2234
287	20E	F-WMKF N4438F YV-T-AVA YV-38CP XB-ALO XA-SAG XC-PFJ/PF-239 XC-QER [instructional airframe, Universidad Nacional en Queretano, Queretaro, Mexico]
288/499	20E	F-WRQZ F-BUYE France 288/F-ZACV
289	20F	F-WMKG N4439F N20FJ N54J N54JJ N1HF N40994 N211HF N105TW N75TJ N450CP [parted out]
290	20E	F-WMKH N4440F N133JA I-TIAL N816AA [instructional airframe, Doha, Qatar]
291/505	20E	F-WRQT France 291/F-RAEC France 291/F-RCAP France 291/F-RAEG [code 65-EG; wfu Mar07, stored Chateaudun, France]
292	20F-5B	F-WMKI N4441F N733S N510WS 9M-LLJ
293	20E-5	F-WMKJ N4442F N2615 N2613 HZ-PL1 HB-VJX OY-CKY F-WQBN F-GOBZ I-GOBZ F-WQVA RA-09005 UR-CLF N570ZD
294/506	20E-5B	F-WRQT F-BVPM SU-AXN
295/500	20E	F-WRQQ I-EDIM N911FR G-FRAF
296/507	20F-5	F-WRQP HB-VDB D2-EBB J5-GAS N4960S N214JP N297CK N19TX N20TX N220LA
297	20E	F-WMKF N4443F (N370EU) N121EU PK-TIR "N297AG" CS-DCK
298	20E	F-WMKG N4444F N86W N98LB OE-GNN N827AA
299	20F	F-WMKI (N734S) N21FJ N456SR N90CN N585UC F-GJSF TC-EZE (N669AC) N299JC
300/508	20E	F-WRQP I-EDIF (F-GIBT) (F-GEJX) F-GGMM N300FJ (N953DC) N600WD
301/509	20E	F-WNGL EP-AKC
302/510	20E	F-WRQP D-COMM OE-GDP N84V F-WQBM F-GOPM
303	20F	F-WMKH N4445F N27R [w/o 12Nov76 Naples, FL]
304/511	20E	F-WRQP G-BCYF G-FRAD 9M-BDK G-FRAD
305	20F-5	F-WMKJ N4446F N16R N56SL VR-CDB N282U N34CW N715WS
306/512	20E	F-WRQS (HB-VDY) (HB-VDO) D-CGSO VH-HFJ (N725P) N76662 N205WM N205WP
307/513	20E-5	F-WRQT HB-VDV I-GCAL OE-GLL F-GKIS F-GYPB F-GYMC CS-DPW F-HJYL [cx to USA but no N-number allocated]
308	20F	F-WMKF N4447F N668P N668S N37RM SE-DKA N81AJ N453SB N458SB
309/514	20SNA	F-WRQT TR-LUW France 309/F-RAFU France 309/F-UGWP [code 339-WP; named L'Etoile du Berger] [w/o 02Dec91 Villacoublay, France]
310	20F	F-WMKH N4450F (N370ME) N121AM N831HG N31FJ N724JC N20WK
311/515	20F-5	F-WRQS F-BVPN [cx to USA but no N-number allocated]
312	20F	F-WMKH N4448F N2605 N619MW N1971R N132AP N741MR N791SY [parted out by Dodson Int'l, Rantoul, KS]
313	20F-5B	F-WMKJ N4449F N220FJ N744CC N56CC N560R I-PERF F-GHCR N212PB N183TS N184TS N339RK [parted out by Alliance Air Parts, Oklahoma City, OK]
314/516	20E	F-WNGL D-COTT F-GDLU N314TW
315/517	20E-5	F-WRQP F-BVPQ OO-VPQ F-GDLO F-SEBI F-GSXF D-CLBB UR-CLD N204ED (N208MD) [parted out by Dodson Int'l, Rantoul, KS]
316	20F-5	F-WMKF N4451F N734S N242CT N424XT

FALCON 20 / 200

C/n	Series	Identities
317	20F	F-WMKG N4452F N31CM N99E N92K N88FE HB-VEV N939CK
318/518	20E	F-WRQT (EP-VAS) EP-VSP EP-FIG Iran 15-2235
319	20F-5	F-WMKF N4453F N730V N44NT C-GNTM N70LG N77LA N205K N724CP N520TC
320/519	20E	F-WRQS EP-AHV EP-FIF
321	20F-5	F-WJMJ N4454F N2525 N702SC N244CA N20FM (PH-BPS) N104SB PH-BPS [cx Jun10; CofA expired]
322	20F	F-WMKH N4455F N1971R N999DC N94GW N464M N300CV YV2723
323/520	20E	F-WRQS HB-VEB I-FCIM OE-GLF XU-008 [instructional airframe, Singapore/Seletar]
324	20F	F-WMKF N4456F N444SC N324TC N312K N373DN
325	20F	F-WMKG N4457F N100GN N400GN (N400GX) (N700GN) VH-RRC N7WG N599RR N555TF (N325MC) N877JG
326/521	20E	F-WRQQ PH-ILY TC-CEN TC-GGG
327	20F	F-WMKI N4458F N3H N2H N96L VH-NMN N900DB N25WG XA-HHF XA-ABF N327BC XA-MSA XA-UPO
328/522	20F	F-WMKJ (N4459F) YK-ASA [crashed Damascus, Syria, 19Oct08; rebuilt at Le Bourget, France, 2010]
329/523	20E	F-WRQV D-CMET
330	20F	F-WNGM N4460F N300AL C-GNTY N770MC (N227LA) N30FT
331/524	20F	F-WRQS YK-ASB
332/525	20E	F-WRQP EC-CTV Spain TM.11-4/401-05 Spain TM.11-4/45-01 Spain TM.11-4/408-12 Spain TM.11-4/47-24
333/526	20E	F-WNGL Iran 5-2801 Iran 15-2233 [w/o 09Jan06 Aidinlou, NW Iran]
334/527	20E	F-WRQU EP-FIC [w/o 03Mar14 nr Kish Island, Iran]
335	20F	F-WMKF N4459F N901TC N903SB D-CFAI N335AJ N707JC (N707JZ) (N301FC) N335TW
336/528	20E	F-WRQP Iran 5-2802 [wfu Tehran, Iran]
337/529	20F	F-WRQR YI-AHH Iran 5-9014
338/530	20E	F-WMKG EP-FID
339	20F-5	F-WMKH N4461F N200GN N100GN N200GN (N200GX) N131DB (N402NC) N22FS N19MX SE-DSA N38TJ N239CD
340/531	20E	F-WRQX Iran 5-2803 Iran 803
341	20F-5B	F-WMKF N4462F N20FJ N66GA N511WP N511WR N78BC N311JS VR-CDT F-OHCJ F-GYSL [cx 11Dec13, b/u]
342/532	20F	F-WRQP YI-AHI J2-KAC France 342/F-RAEC France 342/F-RAEG France 342/F-RAEC [code 65-EC]
343/533	20F	F-WRQR YI-AHJ Iran 5-9015
344/534	20F-5	F-WRQP A6-HEM A6-EXA N344FJ (N731F) N731AS (N731AE) N227WE N227WL [parted out by Alliance Air Parts, Oklahoma City, OK]
345	20F	F-WMKI N4463F N678BM F-GHMD N133AP OH-FPC UR-NOA N345FJ UR-NOA
346/535	20E	F-WRQP Iran 5-2804 [wfu Tehran, Iran]
347	20F	F-WMKF N4464F N744CC N298CK N347HS N20VF N711FJ N211FJ N730RA
348/536	20E	F-WRQR Iran 5-4039 Iran 5-3020 [w/o 03Mar97 Ardabil, Iran]
349	20F	F-WMKG N4465F N273K N66NT N767AC N767AG N287SA N220WE (N159RA)
350/537	20E	F-WRQS Iran 5-4040 Iran 5-3021
351/538	20F	F-WMKJ Iran 5-9001 [reportedly destroyed Feb91, no other details known]
352	20F-5	F-WMKF N4466F N920G N184WW
353/539	20F	F-WRQP Iran 5-9002 [reportedly destroyed Jan91, no other details known]
354/540	20F	F-WRQR Iran 5-9003 Iran 5-9016
355	20F-5	F-WMKF N4467F N20FJ N27AC N344G N550M N63PM N61PM N200MK N712ME N803WC N335MC N632PB
356	20F	F-WMKG N4468F N27R N27RX G-FRAB F-GPAE N111F N11UF N69SW N621JS [cx 16Sep13; wfu; parted out Denton, TX]
357	20F-5	F-WMKI N4469F N435T N435TP N342K N342KF N357PS M-ABCD N370AG VH-PNY
358/541	20F-5B	F-WRQS SU-AZJ F-WRQY SU-AZJ
359/542	20F	F-WRQR (N64769) HZ-TAG HZ-AO1 N64769 N647JP N35RZ N50SL (N508L) N369CA N369CE OH-WIP N829TS N359BR
360	20F	F-WMKJ N1010F N901YP N905SB N911SB F-GJEA N165PA N865VP N390AG N349MR N766RA
361/543	20F-5	F-WMKF SU-AYD
362	20G	(F-WZAS) F-WATF F-WDFJ F-GDFJ F-WDFJ [wfu Istres, France circa Sep00; preserved as 'gate guardian' Martignas-sur-Jalle, France]
363/544	20F-5	F-WRQV HZ-DC2 N363FJ N3VF N9TE N78MB (N68BC)
364	20F	F-WMKI N1013F N235U N285U OE-GCS N285U XA-FLM N134PA XB-KBW XA-FLG
365	20F	F-WMKJ N1018F N777TX N50BH N50BV [cx 11Mar13; wfu]
366	20F	F-WMKG N1020F N83V N300CT N100AC N100AQ N404DH
367/545	20F	F-WRQR EP-SEA
368	20F-5	F-WMKI N1036F N800CF N200DE N800CF VH-NCF N83D I-FIPE N110TJ F-GHTK N110TJ N65TS N107LW N23A N15H N987AB N913SH
369	20F	F-WRQP N1037F N20SR (N414JC) N415JW N509WP N420J N138FJ N138FN N887DR
370	20F	F-WMKG N1038F HL7234 N370HF N269SR N20WN
371	HU25C	F-WMKJ N1039F USCG 2141
372/546	20F	F-WRQV ST-PRS
373	20F-5	F-WMKI N1041F N53DS N922DS N91Y (N620CC) N610CC N620CC N399FG C-FSJI

FALCON 20 / 200

C/n	Series	Identities
374	HU25A	F-WRQP N1045F USCG 2101
375/547	20F	F-WRQR F-GBMD France 375/F-ZACZ
376	20F-5B	F-WRQS N103F N2624M N2614 N2616H N1892S N1897S N367BL
377/548	20F-5	F-WRQP D-CCMB N30FT N5VJ N377RP N600CD
378	20F-5	F-WRQT N107F (N662PP) N662P (N6621) N305AR N500JD N97SJ N378DB
379	20F-5	F-WMKF N130F (N37AH) (N33AJ) N33AH F-GGBL N62570 N892SB N892S (N724JS) XA-RHA N205ZZ [cx 06Feb17, parted out]
380	20F-5	F-WMKI N136F N8BX N1BX N9654N N922ML (N288MM) N289MM N3848U I-ULJA N380CJ VH-FAI
381/549	20F-5	F-WRQS (I-LAFA) D-CCDB N20TZ N20T N85TZ N602LP N840DP
382	20F	F-WMKG N138F HP-1A N138F N138E N382E N10AZ N453SB N459SB
383/550	20F-5	F-WRQR D-CONU 5N-AYO HB-VJS N900CH N908CH N706SB [dbr Scottsdale, AZ, 18Jan16; parted out by Alliance Air Parts, Oklahoma City, OK]
384/551	20F-5	F-WRQU OO-PSD N384JK N120CG N120TF N120DE N82TN N384PS
385	20F-5	F-WJMJ N139F N118R G-FRAA N120WH N87TN N385FJ ZS-KGS
386	HU25A	F-WJMK N149F USCG 2102
387	20F	F-WJML N162F N56CC N676DW N387CE N676DW N384K N650MG
388	20F-5	F-WJMM N169F N90GS N920CF F-WTFE N731RG N756 N502BG N579DN
389/552	20F	F-WRQV I-CMUT UR-KKA [b/u Geneva, Switzerland, Sep12; fuselage to GVA airport fire training area]
390	HU25C	F-WJMN N173F USCG 2104 [wfu; preserved USCGAS Astoria, OR]
391	20F	F-WLCS N175F N376SC N876SC VH-HPF N503F N995PT N990PT N550PT N420DP N420CL N420GL TR-LGZ
392/553	20F	F-WRQT D-CALL N328EW N326EW N326LW (N392FJ) N713MC
393	20F	F-WLCT N176F N21NL N76TA N809F XA-REY XA-PUE XB-FVH XC-FVH XC-SON XC-FVH XC-GDH
394	HU25A	F-WMKF N178F USCG 2103
395/554	20F	F-WRQX (HZ-AKI) OD-PAL (N395BB) [parted out by White Inds, Bates City, MO, circa Oct98]
396	20F-5	F-WMKG N179F N881J N711GL N711WV N811WV N711KU
397/555	20F	F-WRQP F-GBTM F-WBTM F-GBTM
398	HU25A	F-WMKF N183F USCG 2105 [wfu; preserved as 'gate guardian' Corpus Christi, TX]
399	20F-5	F-WMKI N184F N881G N70NE N70NF N70U N21FE N728JC N633KA
400/556	20F	F-WRQR RP-C1980 [w/o 24Apr96 at Davao City, Philippines; parted out by White Inds, Bates City, MO]
401	200	F-WZAH F-GATF (F-WDHA) N200FJ N207FJ F-GATF VR-BJJ F-GATF VR-BJJ F-GEXF Chile 301 code VP-1 N699GA N501KC [cx 13May15, CofR expired]
402	HU25A	F-WJMJ N187F USCG 2106 [wfu AMARC Davis-Monthan, AZ 04Jul95; park code AC410007] N771LD [parted out by Dodson Int'l, Rantoul, KS]
403	20F	F-WJMK N189F N15AT N108BG N960TX (N175BC) N722SF [preserved in flying condition, Spirit of Flight Center museum, Erie, CO]
404	20F	F-WJMK N404F N28C N313K
405	HU25A	F-WMKI N405F USCG 2108 [wfu AMARC Davis-Monthan, AZ 10Aug01; park code AC410016]
406/557	20F	F-WMKF G-BGOP N800FF
407	HU25A	F-WJMJ N406F USCG 2109
408	20F-5	F-WRQS (PK-CAJ) PK-CAG (N508TC) N408PA N757CX N200FJ
409	HU25A	F-WMKJ N407F USCG 2107 [wfu AMARC Davis-Monthan, AZ 04Sep01; park code AC410018]
410	20F-5B	F-WRQT N200CP N200J N410SB N410AZ
411	HU25A	F-WMKG N408F USCG 2110 N524NA
412	20F-5	F-WMKI N409F N85V N85VE N2FU N12FU N620A N97TD
413	HU25A	F-WJMK N410F USCG 2111 [wfu; placed into Atlantic Ocean 6 miles off N.Carolina coast to create new reef 04May05]
414	20F-5B	F-WJML N412F N1881Q
415	HU25A	F-WLCV N413F USCG 2112 [wfu]
416	20F	F-WLCT N415F N416F N88NT N9VG N416F N725JG N19TD
417	HU25A	F-WJMM N416F N416FJ USCG 2113 N417MD [stored Sacramento/McClellan, CA, still wearing USCG serial 2113]
418	HU25A	F-WJMN N417F USCG 2114 [wfu; to instructional airframe, North Valley Occupational Center, Los Angeles/Van Nuys, CA]
419	HU25A	F-WMKJ N419F USCG 2115 [wfu AMARC Davis-Monthan, AZ 04Sep01; park code AC410017]
420	HU25A	F-WMKG N420F USCG 2116 [wfu AMARC Davis-Monthan, AZ 25Apr94; park code AC410005]
421	HU25A	F-WMKI N422F USCG 2117 (N107AV) [wfu; stored Sacramento/McClellan, CA]
422	20F	F-WRQU (N422F) F-ZJTJ France 422/F-RCAL France 422/F-RAEH [code 65-EH]
423	HU25B	F-WJMJ N423F USCG 2118 [preserved Aerospace Museum of California, Sacramento/McClellan, CA]
424	HU25A	F-WMKF N424F USCG 2119 [damaged in storms Nov93 Mobile, AL; wfu AMARC Davis-Monthan, AZ, circa Jan94; park code AC410002]
425	HU25A	F-WMKG N425F USCG 2120
426	20F-5B	F-WJMK N427F N123WH N555PT N416RM I-BAEL HB-VNM N426ST
427	20F	F-WRQV 5N-AYN I-ACTL N42WJ [wfu Chino, CA]
428	20F-5B	F-WMKI N426F N98R I-FLYF N98R N148MC N93MC N98AS N373MG N378MG
429	20F-5B	F-WMKF VR-BHL HB-VHY N4286A N149MC N702CA N331DM
430	20F-5	F-WMKG N428F N660P N243FJ
431	HU25A	F-WMKJ N429F USCG 2121 [wfu; preserved New England Air Museum, Windsor Locks/Bradley, CT]
432	20F-5B	F-WJMK N430F N667P N237PT N855DG N355DG N4TB N760RA
433	HU25B	F-WJML N432F USCG 2122 [wfu AMARC Davis-Monthan, AZ 07Sep01; park code AC410020]
434	20F	F-WRQP Peru 300/OB-1433 [w/o 18Jun10 Chiclayo, Peru]
435	HU25A	F-WJMM N433F USCG 2123 [damaged in storms Nov93 Mobile, AL; wfu AMARC Davis-Monthan, AZ, circa Jan94; park code AC410003]
436	20F-5	F-WJMN N434F N181CB N436MP N8000U N436RB N70PL

FALCON 20 / 200

C/n	Series	Identities
437	HU25A	F-WMKG N435F USCG 2124 [wfu AMARC Davis-Monthan, AZ; park code AC410022]
438	20F-5	F-WMKI N442F N263K N256A N258A N438SJ
439	HU25B	F-WMKJ N443F USCG 2125 [AMARC Davis-Monthan, AZ; park code AC410023] N523NA N448TB N523NA N448TB
440	20F	F-WRQQ N452F N5152 N768J (N768V) VR-CAR N32TC N32TE N7000G N205JC N581FL
441	HU25A	F-WJMK N445F USCG 2126 [wfu AMARC, Davis-Monthan, AZ; park code AC410021]
442	20F-5	F-WJML N446F VH-FJZ N203TA I-SREG N747CX
443	HU25A	F-WMKG N447F USCG 2127 [wfu AMARC Davis-Monthan, AZ, circa Jul91; park code AC410001] USCG 2127 [returned to USCG service by Jan08]
444	20F-5B	F-WJMJ N453F N665P N244FJ LV-BIY
445	HU25A	F-WJMM N449F USCG 2128 N513YF [parted out by Dodson Int'l, Rantoul, KS]
446	20F	F-WJMN N454F N31WT N901SB N904SB N270RA N446D N81P
447	HU25A	F-WLCS N455F USCG 2129 N525NA
448	20G	F-WJMK France 48/F-ZWVF
449	20F	F-WLCT N457F N39TT N73MR N166RA
450	HU25A	F-WMKG N458F USCG 2130 [wfu AMARC Davis-Monthan, AZ, 25Apr94; park code AC410004] N513XF [parted out by Dodson Int'l, Rantoul, KS]
451	20F	F-WRQR F-ZJTS France 339/F-UGWN [code 339-WN] France 339/F-UKJC [code 339-JC] [wfu Chateaudun, France]
452	HU25A	F-WMKI N459F USCG 2131
453	20F	F-WJMK N460F N25S N189MM N520AW
454	HU25A	F-WJML N461F USCG 2132 [wfu AMARC Davis-Monthan, AZ 06Sep01; park code AC410019]
455	20F-5	F-WRQS F-GKAL N555SR N404HR
456	HU25A	F-WJMJ N462F USCG 2133 [preserved Cape Cod Air Station, MA]
457	20F-5	F-WJMM N463F N4351M N4362M N47LP
458	HU25B	F-WJMN N465F USCG 2134
459	HU25A	F-WMKJ N466F USCG 2135
460	HU25B	F-WJML N467F USCG 2136 [preserved Elizabeth City USCGAS, NC]
461	20F	F-WMKG N469F N747V N353CP OH-WIF N221H
462	HU25A	F-WMKI N470F USCG 2137 [wfu AMARC Davis-Monthan, AZ 10Apr95; park code AC410008] N513VF [parted out by Dodson Int'l, Rantoul, KS]
463	20F	F-WJMJ N471F N134JA N132EP C-GZOX
464	HU25A	F-WJMK N472F USCG 2138 [wfu AMARC Davis-Monthan, AZ 13Apr95; park code AC410009] N513UT [parted out by Dodson Int'l, Rantoul, KS]
465	20G	France 65/F-ZJTS
466	HU25C	F-WJML N473F USCG 2139 [wfu AMARG Davis-Monthan, AZ 20Oct10] N513ZF [parted out by Dodson Int'l, Rantoul, KS]
467	HU25A	F-WJMM N474F USCG 2140 [wfu]
468	20F	F-WMKG Pakistan J-468
469	20F	F-WMKI Pakistan J-469
470	20F-5	F-WJMJ N477F N607RP N470G N500NH N470FJ
471	20F-5	F-WJMK N478F N44JC N44JQ N911DT (N611DT) N2BW XC-HIX
472	20G	France 72
473	20F	F-WRQT F-GEJR 3A-MGR 3A-MJV N473SH 3A-MJV N473SH N393S N404FZ
474	20F-5	F-WMKF F-GFFS I-ACCG F-WGTG N211HF N1HF N998BM
475	20F	F-WJML Spain T.11-5/45-05 N475EZ XA-YUR
476	20F	F-WJMM France 76/F-ZJTD Venezuela 1650 YV2919
477	20G	France 77
478	20F-5	F-WJMN N161WT N181WT N300RT N39RP C-GBCI
479	200	F-WPUU N200FJ (N200FX) N200WD (N200FJ) N200LS N400WT (N60DD) (N200SA) N349MG N240RS N7KC N767AG HB-...
480	20G	France 80/F-ZJSA
481	20F-5B	F-WLCS N502F N250RA OH-WIN N599ZM [parted out by Alliance Air Parts, Oklahoma City, OK]
482	200	F-WPUZ F-WDSB F-GDSB SE-DDZ F-WGDZ VR-CCL VP-CCL (N94TJ)
483	20F	F-WRQQ France 483/F-UKJI [code 339-JI]
484	200	F-WPUV N202FJ N28U N357CL N422MU N24JG N425RJ N690EC
485	20F-5	F-WLCT N161EU N997TT (N23SJ) N22FW N485FW
486	20F-5	F-WLCV F-GEFS N6VF N852E
487	200	F-WZZB (N206FJ) F-GDSD "I-WDSD" I-SOBE N137TA (N387FJ) XB-NCM XB-NVT
488	200	F-WZZF HB-VHS N682JB N123CC N2HW C-GTNT N146CF N200NP N488KF
489	200	F-WPUX N203FJ (N109FC) N109NC N109NQ N200RT (TC-...) N7654F TC-DEM N489TK N489BB N613BS N613PB XA-...
490	200	F-WPUY N204FJ N14EN N806F N2TF N95JT N200RT (N208RT) HC-BVH N917JC N917JG PH-APV N490SJ M-JETT
491	200	F-WZZA N205FJ N200FJ N120FJ VH-PDJ VH-HPJ N491MB N343MG N843MG N500RR N25HU
492	200	F-WPUV VR-BHZ N805C N803F N412AB N492CC
493	200	F-WZZC N208FJ N901SB N1847B VH-ECG ZS-SOS ZS-JVS [wfu Lanseria, South Africa]
494	200	F-WZZD N209FJ N85LB LV-PFM LV-BAI N49US N204DD EC-HEG N200FJ RA-2058G
495	200	F-WZZE N210FJ (N290BC) VH-BGL N522C N48FU N48HU N800HM C-GSCL C-GSCR N800EG N1D N109TT [parted out by Alliance Air Parts, Oklahoma City, OK]
496	200	F-WZZC VR-BHY F-GFAY I-LXOT (F-GGAR) F-OGSR F-WGSR Chile 302 CC-PES N496RT N227TA N256JC N202AR
497	200	F-WZZA N212FJ N720HC N20CL
498	200	F-WPUV N215FJ N200ET N422D N422L N69EC

FALCON 20 / 200

C/n	Series	Identities								
499	200	F-WZZJ	N213FJ	N565A	N14CJ	N200CU				
500	200	F-WPUU	N214FJ	N595DC	C-GMPO	C-GRPM	N734DB	N777TE	[cx 22Apr13; CofR expired]	
501	200	F-WZZD	I-MAFU	F-WWGP	F-GOJT	N200TJ	N57TT	N214AS	HI1014	
502	200	F-WPUU	N216FJ	N5732	N573E	N232F	N64YP	N64YR	HB-VNG	VP-CCP
		C6-MIV	(N64YR)	N502SV	C6-AAA					
503	200	F-WPUY	N218FJ	N300HA	N50MW	(N50MX)				
504	200	F-WPUX	N217FJ	N902SB	N702SB	VH-CPE	(N504CL)	N504FJ	XB-OAP	
505	200	F-WZZA	N221FJ	ZK-MAY	VH-NGF	XA-SKO	N221FJ	N45JB	M-DEJB	C-FGOY
506	200	F-WPUZ	I-CNEF	N147TA	XA-MAM					
507	200	F-WPUV	N220FJ	N200FJ	(N122FJ)	C-FCEH	N79MB	N50MG	N50LG	N22HS
		XB-SJA								
508	200	F-WPUU	N219FJ	N1851T	XA-RKE	N777FC				
509	200	F-WPUX	N222FJ	(N8495B)	JA8270	N70TH	N200WY	(N277AT)	PR-SMT	N202AT
		N270MF	(N721JJ)							
510	200	F-WPUY	N223FJ	N79PM	N515DB	N510LF	N36DA	N84MJ	[parted out by Pollard Spares,	
		Roanoke, TX]								
511	200	F-WWGR	F-OGSI	F-WGTF	F-OLET	(F-GNMF)	VT-TTA	F-WQBK	EC-JBH	M-ENTA
512	200	F-WPUU	N224FJ	N45WH	N999TH	N767PJ				
513	200	F-WPUV	N225FJ	XB-ECR	XA-ECR	N881JT	(N200UP)	(N10UU)	N5UU	N5UQ
		N618GH	[parted out by Dodson Av'n, Rantoul, KS]							
514	200	F-WWGP	(F-GJIS)	F-OHES	PT-OQG	N531WB	(N81AG)	N87AG	N322RR	
515	200	F-WWGO	VR-CCQ	VR-CHC	F-GOBE	XA-PFM	N181RK			

Production complete

DASSAULT FALCON 50

* Denotes Falcon 50EX

C/n	Identities
1	F-WAMD [ff 07Nov76] "F-BAMD"+ [+ marks worn at 1977 Paris Air Show] F-WNDB F-BNDB F-WNDB F-BNDB F-WNDB [wfu fuselage to Conservatoire de l'Air et de l'Espace d'Aquitaine, Merignac, France, circa Oct99]
2	F-WINR F-BINR France 2/F-RAFJ F-BINR F-GSER N50BL
3	F-WFJC F-GBIZ N50FJ N50EJ N880F N8805 N728LW
4	F-WZHA N110FJ N50FJ YV-452CP YV-O-SATA-12 YV-462CP YV2165
5	(F-WZHB) (F-GBRF) France 5/F-RAFI France 5/F-ZWVA
6	F-WZHB N50FB N1871R N815CA 9XR-NN [w/o 06Apr94 Kigali, Rwanda]
7	F-WZHA HZ-AKI HZ-AO3 N8516Z N26LB N5DL N50HE F-WQBN France 7
8	F-WZHC N50FE N50PG N409ER (N408ER) (N119HB) (N119HT) N119PH N508EJ N550CL N550CE [parted out by AvMATS, St Louis, MO]
9	F-WZHD I-SAFP XA-LOH (HB-IED) VR-CBR "N100WJ" F-GGCP TR-LGY [parted out by Pollard Spares, Roanoke, TX]
10	F-WZHD N50FG N65B N420CL
11	F-WZHE N50FH N501NC N5739 F-GGVB F-HADH
12	F-WZHC CN-ANO
13	F-WZHF N50FK N150BG (N150NW) N150TX
14	F-WZHG N50FL N233U N283U N9X N955E N917SB N880TD
15	F-WZHM PH-ILR N350JS (N595CW) [cx 03Feb17; parted out Wilmington, DE]
16	F-WZHH (N50FM) D-BIRD D-BFAR F-WQBL (F-GYBM) F-HBBM F-WQBL F-HBBM N516CJ
17	F-WZHI 5A-DGI TY-BBM HB-IEB N4679T N3456F N349K N349KS N727S N517CW (N550LX) N9TE N114TD
18	F-WZHJ N50FN N187S N720M N1102A N82RP N82LP N518EJ (N525MA) (N10UG) N963JF [parted out by Alliance Air Parts, Oklahoma City, OK]
19	F-WZHB N50FM N63A N253L N519CW (N551LX) N519EM
20	F-WZHK N50FR C6-BER N63537 N590CW (N552LX) N590RA [parted out by Marklyn Jet Parts, TX]
21	F-WZHN (9K-ACQ) 9K-AEE N299W (F-GJKT) F-GHGT N70AF N77CE N770E N56LT
22	F-WZHF N50FS N203BT N866FP XA-SFP XA-AVE XA-TUH N220JP N50FL Venezuela 0018 YV1083
23	F-WZHG (D-BBAD) D-BBWK PH-ILD N725PA N821BS N523CW (N553LX) N523PB [parted out Wilmington, DE]
24	F-WZHL N51FJ N817M N200RT N280RT N929T
25	F-WZHI Yugoslavia 72101/YU-BPZ [carried both marks] YU-BPZ "N34S"+ [+marks worn but ntu] N502EZ N753JC N877DF N977KG
26	F-WZHA N52FJ N190MC N190MQ
27	F-WZHN HB-IEU F-WGTG France 27/F-RAFK France 27/F-ZWMM
28	F-WZHE N53FJ N131WT PH-LEM N47UF N800FM N752JC
29	F-WZHB I-SAFR F-WGTH CS-TMF N534MA N290TJ N529CW N529MM C-GRGE N309SF
30	F-WZHD I-SNAC (YV-553CP) I-SNAC F-WQFZ France 30
31	F-WZHC (N54FJ) I-KIDO N211CN N145W N145WF N105EJ XA-AAS N931CC (N931EJ) N890FH N292FH N987RC N250RJ N468AM N921EW N921ED
32	F-WZHJ VR-BTT N80TR N717LA N717LF XA-UWJ N717LF
33	F-WZHA N56FJ N8100E N8300E
34	F-WZHH HB-IEV F-WEFS France 34/F-RAFL France 34/F-ZWMT
35	F-WZHF N57FJ N800BD N907M N350AF XA-FVK N35YP
36	F-WZHJ N54FJ N345PA N450AF N59GS F-WWHZ F-ZWTA F-ZJTL France 36
37	F-WZHM (I-CAIK) I-SAME F-GMCU F-HAIR [w/o Paris-Le Bourget, France, 13Aug10; b/u Sep12]
38	F-WZHK N58FJ N993 N505CL N500FJ N951DJ
39	F-WZHL N59FJ N754S N326FB N850EP
40	F-WZHG 9K-AEF N90005 N50GF N1PR N695ST N150JT N156DB N47NS
41	F-WZHI N60FJ N546EX (N760DL) N76FD (N76FB) N352JS (N541FJ) (N841FJ) N888MF N888ME N956DP N950FJ
42	F-WZHE N61FJ N82MP D-BDWO OE-HCS OO-LFT (N250UC) N442AM ZS-LBB N185BA N405DC N167BD N167BR
43	F-WZHO Yugoslavia 72102 YU-BNA
44	F-WZHA N62FJ N150JP N50LT N44MK N285CP YV2346 (N485VL) N144PA [parted out Roanoke, TX]
45	F-WZHF N63FJ N731F N9BX N569BW
46	F-WZHK N64FJ N908EF N911RF N725LB N728LB N347K N547K N777ZL
47	F-WZHP N65FJ N150WC N23AC N23AQ N1BX (N81CH) (N601CH) N37ER N60HX N791CP*
48	F-WZHK HB-IET I-ERDN N134AP N247EM (N2478) N247BC C-FBVF
49	F-WZHL N66FJ N43ES N43BE N978W N650AL N800DW N805DW
50	F-WZHQ N67FJ N747 N747Y XA-GCH N406SA
51	F-WZHR N70FJ N52DC N52DQ F-GMGA N113WA N551CW (N554LX) (N551S) N524S
52	F-WZHV F-BMER F-WZHV JY-HAH N18G N86AK N163WW N900KE
53	F-WZHS N150JT (N77SW) N45SJ (N50SJ) N22T N22TZ N90AM N53FJ N22YP N53FJ YV1128
54	F-WZHT N71FJ N450X (N50EF) N204DD N202DD N392U N130A (OY-GDA) LX-GED N589KM N100DV N51MJ N400KE N954DP N954SG
55	F-WZHU N73FJ N839F (N30N) N1CN N332MC N332MQ N625CR N300CR N96UH N200UP N504WE N12QP
56	F-WZHR F-WDFE F-GDFE N112FJ N84HP (N844J) C-FCRH C-FFGI
57	F-WZHC HB-IER N57B N138F N138E N505TC
58	F-WZHA N72FJ N744X N50KR N451CF [cx 13Sep12]
59	F-WZHB N75FJ N31DM N31V N900JB N910CN

FALCON 50

C/n	Identities
60	F-WZHD JY-HZH N900W (N50RG) N560EJ CS-DFJ N105WC
61	F-WZHI HB-IES VP-CRF [wfu Basle, Switzerland]
62	F-WZHE N77FJ N292BC N50FH N562EJ (CS-DFK) N230BT [parted out Roanoke, TX]
63	F-WZHF N78FJ N841F HB-IAL VR-CGP N48GP C-FKCI N63FJ YV1129
64	F-WZHH N79FJ N418S N300A N731DD N496PT N496ED
65	F-WZHT N50FJ N90FJ N65HS D-BFFB N50LV N1EV F-GPPF
66	F-WZHP (PH-SDL) F-WZHP N500BL N50BL N4413N (VR-B..) 9U-BTB N789JC [trialled with spiroid wingtip devices then fitted with winglets] N711HT
67	F-WZHG N76FJ HB-IEP Switzerland T-783 N260ER
68	F-WZHQ 5A-DCM
69	F-WZHJ N80FJ N650X (N69VJ) N909VJ
70	F-WZHL N81FJ N230S N130K (N651SB) N699SC N300ES N306ES N700MP
71	F-WZHF YI-ALB J2-KBA N352WB
72	F-WZHM N82FJ N1181G [w/o 12May85 Lake Geneva, WI; remains to Clarkesville, MO]
73	F-WPXE HZ-SAB F-WGTG VR-CCQ N48TW N15TW (N15TA) N573CW (N556LX) N67JF [cx 18Aug16, parted out Wilmington, DE]
74	F-WZHA N83FJ
75	F-WZHH N95FJ N45ES N45BE N850CA N78LT N850BW
76	F-WZHB N84FJ N85MD N410WW N411WW N450CL
77	F-WZHC N85FJ N366F N992 N77NT N78LF N680KT
78	F-WPXF F-ODEO TR-LAI F-GEOY France 78/F-RAFJ France 78/F-ZWMO
79	F-WZHE N86FJ N60CN (N881K) (N79FJ) N56LN
80	F-WZHN N87FJ XB-OEM XA-FTC N4154G XA-GFC N80WE N50SJ N50BZ N50XJ N711RA
81	F-WZHA N89FJ N718DW N504CX [converted to Falcon 50-4]
82	F-WZHG N88FJ N293BC RP-C754 (N767W) (N40F) N511GG N450KP N150BP N582EJ N613PD [cx 01Feb17, parted out Wilmington, DE]
83	F-WZHJ N88U N881M N50HD N50XY
84	F-WZHK N2711B F-WZHK Spain T.16-1/401-09 Spain T.16-1/45-20 N503EZ N500JD N700JD
85	F-WZHO N90FJ N50FJ N40TH N254DV N82ST N107CV
86	F-WPXD N94FJ N238U F-GKDR HB-IAT N150UC N86JC N960S
87	F-WZHS N91FJ N283K N55NT C-GLRP C-GOIL C-GOIH N87FJ PR-FJL
88	F-WZHU N92FJ XA-OVR N188FJ F-WQCP VR-CRT VP-CRT N588FJ F-WQBK F-GYOL LZ-OIO F-GYOL (D-CHIC) N943RL N510GT
89	F-WZHV N93FJ N212K N212KM N890GA N400PC (N400LC) N120TJ N97BZ N589EJ CS-DFI N156WC TR-LGV
90	F-WZHX N290W N298W N600AS (N650AS) N4351M N925GS N963JN
91	F-WZHY (ZS-BFB) ZS-BMB ZS-CAS
92	F-WZHZ N97FJ N85A N40CN (N881J) N929ML T7-FGD N92CJ
93	F-WZHB N98FJ N844X N868BT
94	F-WZHC N99FJ N82NC N212JP XA-MVR (XA-AFG) XA-TVQ N504PA [converted to Falcon 50-4] N946TC
95	F-WPXD VR-CBL N3950N N331MC C-GSSS TC-KAM F-WQBJ N29YY N70FL N95FJ N101ET N903JS
96	F-WPXE N4AC C-FMFL
97	F-WZHL (N101FJ) C-FSCL N33GG N33GQ LZ-OII N597FJ C-FPDO N850MC N412PG C-GMLO C-GMLR
98	F-WPXF VR-CBO N39461 N50MK (N50ML) N600WG
99	F-WZHM (N96FJ) C-FMYB N816M N292PC
100	F-WZHN N102FJ N14CG N450AK
101	F-WPXH YI-ALC Iran 5-9012 EP-TFA
102	F-WZHO N103FJ N50BX (N50WB) N350WB
103	F-WZHQ N104FJ N83MP N370KP N303PM
104	F-WZHR N105FJ N90AE F-GFGQ F-WWHK N50VG SE-DVG N351JS LX-UAE F-GUAE HB-IGR N725PA N49KR N452CF
105	F-WZHS N106FJ N80CN (N881L) N100EG (N214GA) N990MM
106	F-WZHT N96FJ N50BF N9300C N74TS [cx 26Jan17, parted out Wilmington, DE]
107	F-WPXK (ZS-LJM) LX-RVR VR-BUC VP-BUC F-WQBM F-GIQZ VP-BCZ F-GTCD F-WQBM N253SJ F-GLSJ N108BK
108	F-WZHM N101FJ N350X N150K N399GG
109	F-WZHV N109FJ N280BC N280BG N5107
110	F-WPXG 5N-ARE VR-BJA N77TE N84TN
111	F-WZHZ N297W F-GKTV VR-CDF N50AH F-GMOT [b/u Geneva, Switzerland, Aug12]
112	F-WZHA N107FJ N144AD N193TR N652AL N216WD
113	F-WZHB N108FJ N186S N394U N35RZ N75RZ N450DR N900JB N654CP
114	F-WPXM ST-PSR
115	F-WZHC N111FJ N777MJ N50TC N522GS (N369CA) N569CA N569CC N502JB N950S N850BA N70BR
116	F-WZHD N112FJ N781B N69R F-GIDC N70AF XA-SOL XB-SOL N678MA
117	F-WPXI HB-ITH N50TG N124HM N50J N896DA (N896TW)
118	F-WZHF N113FJ N784B (N183B) N784B [w/o 10Nov85 on approach to Teterboro A/P, NJ]
119	F-WZHN N114FJ N83FC N57DC XA-SSS N168JC TS-JBT N929WT
120	F-WPXJ YI-ALD Iran 5-9011 EP-TFI
121	F-WZHO N115FJ N9311 N824R N121FJ N51FE N150MJ
122	F-WZHG YI-ALE Iran 5-9013
123	F-WZHH (F-GDSC) VH-SFJ N211EF F-GPSA N5123
124	F-WZHA N116FJ N711TU N6666R N500RE N600JM N25JM VP-BFM N50MV N987F

FALCON 50

C/n	Identities									
125	F-WZHB	N118FJ	N711KT	I-DENR	HB-IBQ	TS-JAM	N102TF	N250MJ		
126	F-WZHI	N119FJ	(YV-269CP)	N9312	N931G	N52DC	N52DQ	N200RT	(N986PA)	N650TC
	N838BB	N838FL*								
127	F-WZHD	N121FJ	N1896T	N1896F	N129JE	N48KR	N453CF	N154LA		
128	F-WZHF	N122FJ	N9313	N733E	N223DD	N42NA				
129	F-WZHQ	N123FJ	N1903W	N4903W	N99JD	N751JC	N634KA			
130	F-WZHR	N124FJ	N9314	N630L	N988T	C-GSRS	P4-BAK	N315SC		
131	F-WPXD	HZ-BB2	I-ADAG	(F-GPLH)	F-WGTF	F-GOAL	N750BR	N950CC		
132	F-WPXF	I-EDIK	France 132							
133	F-WPXH	HB-IEA	HZ-AKI	HB-IEA	ZS-CAQ					
134	F-WPXK	HB-IEC	VR-CLD	VP-CLD	F-GOGL	VP-BCD	F-GUDP	F-WQBN	N134FJ	F-GOCT
	(OY-CKH)	F-HALM								
135	F-WZHA	N125FJ	N293BC	N121BZ						
136	F-WZHB	N126FJ	N204HC	(N500HC)	N50HC	VR-BLL	N6550W	YV-455CP	YV1495	N136FJ
	XB-YJA									
137	F-WZHC	N127FJ	N50FJ	(N119FJ)	C-GTPL	N119FJ	N117SF	C-FJUH	N137FA	
138	F-WPXD	N75G	N941CC	I-CAFB	N138NW	VR-CEZ	VP-CEZ	N380TJ	N138AV	N903CS
139	F-WZHD	N128FJ	N96CE	N1S	N7GX					
140	F-WPXH	VR-BHX	(F-GJTR)	F-WGTF	I-MMEA	N303JW	N750DF	N914JH	N510MP	
141	F-WZHE	N129FJ	N16R	(N222MC)	N86MC	N96NX	N924WJ			
142	F-WZHK	N132FJ	N4350M	N860BA						
143	F-WZHI	N130FJ	N77CP	N444PE						
144	F-WZHL	N133FJ	N70FL	VR-BZE	VP-BZE	N544RA	(LX-FTJ)	N7011	N950BD	
145	F-WPXE	F-GEXE	A6-ZKM	I-CAFC	N50KD					
146	F-WZHA	N131FJ	N747	N7228K	XA-DUQ	N430AC	N957LJ			
147	F-WPXG	HB-IED	F-WPXG	VR-BKG	VP-BKG	N526CC	N844NX	N1CG	N50SQ	
148	F-WZHB	N134FJ	N81R	N81U	YR-FNA	N28KB	N254NA	N50LQ	N770JD	
149	F-WZHJ	N135FJ	N1904W	F-GHAQ	N149MD	N1971R	N198M	N198MR	N950CL	
150	F-WZHC	N136FJ	HB-IAE	N8200E	N8400E					
151	F-WPXD	Italy (MM151)		Italy MM62020		F-WQBM	I-DARK	F-GPGS	TR-...	
152	F-WZHD	N137FJ	N1841F	N75W	N75WE	N152FJ				
153	F-WZHE	N138FJ	N50FJ	N16CP	N50HM	N50HN				
154	F-WZHA	N139FJ	N320K	N920K	N404R	N404E	N154PA	N117AJ		
155	F-WPXH	Italy MM62021		F-WQBM	I-RODJ	F-GTHS	F-GKGO	TR-CHB		
156	F-WZHF	N140FJ	N5733	N4MB	N4MR	N377HW	N500RE	N156RE		
157	F-WPXG	N141FJ	N312A	N341M	N911HB	N901MK	N15FX	N19FX	N345SK	N89TD
158	F-WZHH	N142FJ	N54YR	N54YP	N15VX					
159	F-WZHC	LX-NUR	I-LXAG	VR-CWI	VP-CWI	HB-ISD	N839RM	N343PM	VH-FOL	
160	F-WZHI	N143FJ	N48R	N487F	N4VF	N82CA				
161	F-WZHA	N144FJ	N863BD	N800BD	TC-EYE	N301JJ	N770MP	N766HK		
162	F-WZHB	N145FJ	N90R	C-GYPJ	N244AD	N750JC	N750LQ	N954AM		
163	F-WZHA	N146FJ	N50FJ	(N165FJ)	N185FJ	N5VF	N5VH	N85HP	(N854W)	N521DC
164	F-WZHD	N164FJ	HB-IAM	N164MA	N164GB	(N132MS)				
165	F-WZHF	HZ-SM3	LX-FMR	HB-JSR	F-GXTM					
166	F-WZHE	N165FJ	N500AF	(N3115U)	N500AE	N316PA	N5VF	N80BC*		
167	F-WZHG	N166FJ	N186HG	N2T	N2FQ					
168	F-WZHH	N167FJ	N711SC	N48GL	XA-RXZ	N48GL	VR-CQZ	N48GL	(N420JP)	N514MB
169	F-WPXD	I-SNAB	F-GUAJ	F-HISI						
170	F-WZHI	N169FJ	N293K	N500AF	N508AF	N504YP	[converted to Falcon 50-4]			
171	F-WZHJ	N170FJ	N171FJ	N40AS	(N650AS)	N750H	N1CG			
172	F-WZHK	N170FJ	N98R	N9000F	N256A					
173	F-WZHL	N172FJ	(JA....)	PT-LJI	N544CM	N37KJ				
174	F-WPXE	HB-IAG	N79PF	N565A	N8KG	N988SB	N50FX			
175	F-WZHM	N177FJ	N50FJ	N334MC	N330MC	N200RT	(VR-B..)	N530AR	N50FX	M-AGER
	N200V	N20GP								
176	F-WZHN	N178FJ	VH-PDJ	N157SP	N95GC	I-DEGF	VR-CFI	C-FNNC	N568VA	N711T
	N777XY	N777UV								
177	F-WPXF	9Q-CGK	9Q-CPK	(N68BA)	ZS-PFB	N14NE	XA-UCN	XA-TAB	N177MJ	
178	F-WZHO	N179FJ	N239R	N59PM	N634H	T7-AWO				
179	F-WZHP	N180FJ	HL7386	N222MC	N212Q	N232PR	N500TS	N508TS		
180	F-WWHC	I-POLE	N45FG	N2254S	N50SF	N626HJ				
181	F-WWHA	N181FJ	N345AP	N367TP	N93AX	N600CH	N26WJ			
182	F-WWHB	N182FJ	N250AS	N713SN	N116GB	N227GJ				
183	F-WWHF	I-CAFD								
184	F-WWHD	N183FJ	N50FJ	N89FC	N25MB	N25ME	N633W	VP-CDG		
185	F-WWHE	N184FJ	C-GDCO	N23SY	N238Y	F-GKBZ	LX-THS	F-HFMB	T7-DFX	
186	F-WWHH	N278FJ	N450K	N25SJ	N107A	(N16NK)				
187	F-WWHG	N279FJ	N4CP	N4QP	VH-PPF	N187PN	N133NM*			
188	F-WWHA	N280FJ	N50FJ	PT-WAN	LV-WXV	N160AF	XA-ALA	N188FJ		
189	F-WWHB	N281FJ	N50WG	N55SN	N51V	N51VT	N51V			
190	F-WWHG	I-CAFE	CS-TMJ	F-GXMC						
191	F-WWHD	N282FJ	N950F							
192	F-WWHE	N283FJ	N212T	N96LT	N96UT	N96UJ				
193	F-WWHH	Italy MM62026		Italy CSX62026		Italy MM62026				
194	F-WWHM	N284FJ	N10AT	N10LT	N95PH	N194K	N28PH			
195	F-WWHK	Portugal 7401		Portugal 17401						

FALCON 50

C/n	Identities									
196	F-WWHD	N285FJ	N8575J	JA8575	N71TH	D-BNTH	VP-BSA	N388TC	N196FJ	N56CL
	N566L									
197	F-WWHA	N286FJ	N50FJ	N500KJ	N404JF	N57MK				
198	F-WWHC	Portugal 7402		Portugal 17402						
199	F-WWHB	N287FJ	N291BC	N290MX						
200	F-WWHE	N288FJ	N664P	N664B	N595JS	N749CP	N769CP	N62DT		
201	F-WWHA	N289FJ	N41TH	N54DA	N553M	N504ST	N526SM			
202	F-WWHB	N290FJ	N212N	N97LT	N97UT	N202CP	N750MC	N512JB		
203	F-WWHA	I-CSGA	C-GNCA	N203NC						
204	F-WWHD	F-GKAR	VR-CGP	VP-CGP	EC-GPN	EC-HHS	(F-HDCB)	N725PA	F-HDCB	N147GB
	N319GB									
205	F-WWHD	N291FJ	N57EL	N59EL	N52JJ	N348K	(N848K)	N504MK	N314AM	
206	F-WWHB	VR-BMF	VP-BMF	N801DL	N607BF	N607RJ				
207	F-WWHC	N292FJ	N55BP	N50CS	N396EG	N275HH	N192RS			
208	F-WWHP	I-CSGB	VR-CCQ	C-GWEI	N50AE	N50HC	N90HC			
209	F-WWHE	N293FJ	N59CF	N59CH	EC-168	EC-FPG	N1902W	N96DS	VP-BSL	N358MH
210	F-WWHL	F-GICN	XA-TXB	N411GC	N803AC					
211	F-WWHR	Italy MM62029								
212	F-WWHH	N294FJ	N50FJ	N30TH	N40TH	N85WN	LX-APG	UR-CCF	[destroyed by shellfire,	
	Donetsk, Ukraine, 2014]									
213	F-WWHW	N295FJ	XA-RVV	N991LB	2-NYAW					
214	F WWHX	N296FJ	N55AS	(N214FJ)	N265G					
215	F-WWHT	N297FJ	XA-SIM	D-BOOK	(D-BOOI)	HB-JSV	F-GOLV	9H-MSL		
216	F-WWHZ	N298FJ	N180AR	N56SN	N84NW	N722FS	(N270FX)	N650JS		
217	F-WWHV	N122FJ	N5732	N573AC	N573TR	N825JW				
218	F-WWHA	N50NK	N218WA	D-BERT	N750FJ	N703TM	N979JC			
219	F-WWHS	N129FJ	YV-450CP	YV1496	N256JC	(N509MD)	N98DH			
220	F-WWHG	N131FJ	N75RD	N100RR	N528JR	N50FF	N557LZ	N800TA		
221	F-WWHL	Portugal 7403		Portugal 17403						
222	F-WWHM	D-BELL	OE-HIT	N722MK						
223	F-WWHN	N132FJ	N633L	N840FJ	N451CL					
224	F-WWHO	N133FJ	VR-CNV	XA-SDK	XA-BEG	N800BD	N87TN	N258FV		
225	F-WWHP	N134FJ	N50FJ	N32TC	N428CC					
226	F-WWHC	N119AM	F-WQBN	VP-BBD	CS-DPO	SX-CRC	TN-AJN			
227	F-WWHE	N226FJ	N50FJ	(N227FJ)	N1848U	N630SR	N37LC	(N37LQ)	C-GGFP	N365DF
228	F-WWHR	(F-GNFS)	F-GNFF	VR-BJJ	F-GJEK	F-WWHR	N313GH	VR-CAE	C-GAZU	N228FJ
229	F-WWHH	N114FJ	C-GMII	C-GMID	N550WM					
230	F-WWHD	F-GNGL	HB-IAV	3B-NSY	OY-LIN	F-OMON	N506BA	N930JG		
231	F-WWHA	N228FJ	(VR-B..)	XA-SIF	N10PQ	N10PP	N199FG			
232	F-WWHT	F-WNLR	F-GNLR	N244FJ	N45NC	N45NQ	N100KP	N108KP	ZS-MGS	
233	F-WWHB	(N233FJ)	N232FJ	N48HB	N318GA	(N919GA)				
234	F-WWHC	N233FJ	PT-AAF	PR-WYW						
235	F-WWHM	F-GKRU	(UR-ACA)	UR-CCC	[destroyed by shellfire, Donetsk, Ukraine, 2014]					
236	F-WWHD	N234FJ	N50FJ	N70FJ	XA-HGF	N195SV	N196SV	XA-HHF	N725PA	N347K
	N50FJ	N394AJ	N497SB	N497SP						
237	F-WWHE	N237FJ	N2425	(N5425)	N94BJ	N74BJ	N89BM	N85TN		
238	F-WWHF	N238FJ	N50FJ	XA-LRA	N796A	N238DL	SE-DVL	N970S		
239	F-WWHG	N239FJ	N200SG							
240	F-WWHH	F-GNMO	(N40SK)	N780F	N33TY	N34TY	(N200BN)	N398AC	(N798AC)	N550JP
241	F-WWHF	F-OKSI	N233BC	N86TN						
242	F-WWHA	N241FJ	XA-SPM	N599SC	N9000F	N733M	N733N	N733K	N28US	
243	F-WWHM	N243FJ	N742R	N62HM	N576LC					
244	F-WWHK	N243FJ	N50FJ	N95HC	N954ME					
245	F-WWHL	N240FJ	N720ML	N720ME	N530DG	N827CT				
246	F-WWHF	N246FJ	TC-YSR	F-GTJF	3C-LGE					
247	F-WWHP	N247FJ	N740R	N520AF						
248	F-WWHB	N249FJ	N25UD	N25UB	N67PW					
249	F-WWHN	N248FJ	(XA-DMS)	N663MN	SE-DVK	N247CJ	N980S			
250	F-WWHR	N250FJ	N696HC	N696HQ	N277JW	N917JC	N917JG	N111WW		
251*	F-WOND	[ff 10Apr96]	(F-GOND)	VR-CLN	VP-CLN	(F-GIVD)	N870	N565	N171TG	
252	F-WWHE	(N313GH)	N93GH	N50FJ	XA-TDD	N52FJ	XA-RUY	N959DM		
253*	F-WWHA	N253EX	PT-WSC	N85F	N3VF					
254*	F-WWHB	N50FJ	N50AE	N345AP	N94PC	N67MT				
255*	F-WWHC	N255CM	N50MG	N60ME						
256*	F-WWHD	VP-CBT	N600N							
257*	F-WWHE	F-OKSY	N925BC	ZS-LAC						
258*	F-WWHF	F-WQHU	VP-BST	N48G	N726JG	PR-GJS				
259*	F-WWHG	VP-CHG	N373RS	N373RR						
260*	F-WWHK	N586CS	N777							
261*	F-WWHL	N140RT	(N97FJ)	N73GH						
262*	F-WWHM	N262EX	N1896T	C-GOFJ						
263*	F-WWHN	N8550A	N503PC	N503PQ	N725DM*					
264*	F-WWHO	F-GVDN	C6-BHD	N900CH	C-GWFM	C-GWFK				
265*	F-WWHP	N9550A	N501PC	N838DB	N868DB					
266*	F-WWHQ	VP-BPA	N50NM	(N266EC)						
267*	F-WWHR	(D-BETI)	F-OHFO	D-BETI						

FALCON 50

C/n	Identities									
268*	F-WWHS	EC-GTR	CS-TMS	PH-JNL	F-WQBL	N268FJ	F-WQBL	G-ITIH	G-DASO	M-DASO
	G-DASA	N133JA								
269*	F-WWHT	F-GPBG	F-GJBZ	N52RF						
270*	F-WWHU	N270EX	N148M	C-GJLB						
271*	F-WWHV	TC-BHO	N30FE	N30FT	N865PC					
272*	F-WWHW	N272EX	N50FJ	C-GMII	N272F	C-GKCI	C-FZYB	N695JB		
273*	F-WWHX	N158M	N198M							
274*	F-WWHY	N138M	N80GP	N299DB	N205JA					
275*	F-WWHA	F-GODP	N56LC	N44LC	N44EQ	N75FJ	N52YP			
276*	F-WWHB	N159M	N128M	N789ME	N96UT					
277*	F-WWHC	N368M	N198M	N192F	N818KF					
278*	F-WWHD	VP-CFI	N623QW	C-GXBB	M-SNSS	N421AE	N732AM			
279*	F-WWHE	N181MC	N928WK	N411SK	N58HL					
280*	F-WWHF	N50FJ	N1829S	N3BM						
281*	F-WWHG	N17AN	C-GNET	N463JD						
282*	F-WWHH	N191MC								
283*	F-WWHK	VP-CEF	VP-BEF	N283FJ	N223HD	(N868NB)	N248BT			
284*	F-WWHL	N904SB	N703AW	N900SS	N900BB*					
285*	F-WWHM	N901TF								
286*	F-WWHN	(F-GKIN)	VP-BMI	N286ZT	VP-BEA	N286ZT	[retro-fitted with winglets]			
287*	F-WWHO	ZS-ONG								
288*	F-WWHP	N288EX	N33TY	N83TY	(N89TY)					
289*	F-WWHQ	N214DV	N315DV	(N589FJ)	M-GPIK	F-HUNT	Bolivia FAB-002			
290*	F-WWHR	N44SK	N42SK	(N660AH)	(N302WY)	N50HM	N68YB			
291*	F-WWHS	N294EX	XA-GMD	XA-UDW	N291FJ					
292*	F-WWHT	N292EX	N38WP	XA-KMX						
293*	F-WWHU	N293EX	N195SV							
294*	F-WWHV	N39WP								
295*	F-WWHW	I-FJDN	P4-JET	9H-AVE						
296*	F-WWHX	N296EX	N50FJ	N23FM						
297*	F-WWHY	N119AG	F-WQBJ	OE-HHH	F-HCDD					
298*	F-WWHZ	N615SR								
299*	F-WWHA	N299EX	PP-PMV	N299MV	N299PR					
300*	F-WWHB	N344CM	N749CP	N549CP	N214FT					
301*	F-WWHC	N301EX	N476MK	N504MS	N353H	N715CB				
302*	F-WWHD	N302FJ	N45NC	N115RL	N115RN	C-FFTR				
303*	F-WWHE	N902TF								
304*	F-WWHF	N918JM	N909JM							
305*	F-WWHG	TC-BNT	F-WQBK	N302BG	N102BG	N102BQ	N710BG	N710BQ	N114HC	
306*	F-WWHH	LX-AKI	F-HCEF	N306FJ	9H-CGH					
307*	F-WWHK	N950H								
308*	F-WWHL	N902SB	N719DW	N50PC						
309*	F-WWHM	N903SB	N37WX							
310*	F-WWHN	N310EX	N50FJ	N310EX	N50FQ	N50SN				
311*	F-WWHO	N507AS	VP-CBF	N136MV						
312*	F-WWHP	N26WP								
313*	F-WWHR	G-JPSI	F-WQBM	N921EC	N225HD	N50CZ				
314*	F-WWHT	N314EX	N55LC	N55LQ	N311BP					
315*	F-WWHU	N668P	PH-LSV	LX-LXL	F-GVMF	S5-TSV				
316*	F-WWHV	N316EX	N696HC	N696HQ	N1838S	N4911				
317*	F-WWHW	N1839S	N607SG	N500RE						
318*	F-WWHX	N416KC	N410KC	N771HM						
319*	F-WWHY	N319EX	N50FJ	(N319EX)	N85CL	N85DN	XA-PRR	XA-UVS		
320*	F-WWHZ	N662P	N500AF	M-VGIN	M-CFLY					
321*	F-WWHA	N321EX	N900CM	N556HD						
322*	F-WWHB	N5322								
323*	F-WWHC	N323EX	N500N	N50QN	N500R	N500GR	N500LY			
324*	F-WWHD	N324EX	F-WWHD	LX-IRE	N150RJ					
325*	F-WWHE	N325EX	N146AS							
326*	F-WWHF	N37LC	N33LC	N33EQ	N850EN					
327*	F-WWHG	N327EX	N188DM	N1978G						
328*	F-WWHH	N328EX	N308DM	N223F	N918RD					
329*	F-WWHK	N329EX	(N50FJ)	N98AC						
330*	F-WWHL	N330EX	N115SK	N115MF						
331*	F-WWHM	N331EX	(N331SE)	N1839S	N963U					
332*	F-WWHN	N332EX	N280BC	N280BD						
333*	F-WWHO	N334EX	N701WC	N701WQ	N54YR					
334*	F-WWHP	N335EX	OE-HPS	F-HDPB						
335*	F-WWHQ	N535EX	C-GMII	C-GMIU	N505BL	PP-NOB	[retro-fitted with winglets]			
336*	F-WWHR	N224HD	N50FJ							
337*	F-WWHS	N50FJ	N89NC	N988GC						
338*	F-WWHT	N338FJ	N883RA	N883RW	(PP-AAH)	(N137LR)	N513SK	PP-LVY*		
339*	F-WWHU	5B-CKN	I-PBRA							
340*	F-WWHV	N340EX	N109CQ	N733G						
341*	F-WWHW	I-ZUGR	G-KPTN							
342*	F-WWHX	N342EX	N649TT							
343*	F-WWHY	N343EX	N733M							

FALCON 50

C/n	Identities				
344*	F-WWHZ	N344EX	N50YP		
345*	F-WWHA	VP-BMP	M-NICK	M-CICO	
346*	F-WWHB	N346EX	F-HAPM	HB-IGV	
347*	F-WWHC	F-HAPN			
348*	F-WWHD	N905SB	P4-SNS	F-GLSA	[w/o Moscow/Vnukovo 20Oct14]
349*	F-WWHE	N906SB	N30JC	N575JC	
350*	F-WWHF	N350DV	N214DV		
351*	F-WWHH	N158M	N191CP		
352*	F-WWHK	N1836S	N180NL		

Production complete

DASSAULT FALCON 900

C/n	Series	Identities								
1	B	F-WIDE	[ff 21Sep84]		F-GIDE	[converted to prototype 900B]			F-HOCI	G-HMEI
		(F-GOEI)								
2		F-WFJC	F-GFJC	France 2/F-RAFP						
3		F-WWFA	N403FJ	N327K	N991RF	N728GH	N345KM			
4		F-WWFC	(HB-...)	VR-BJX	F-WWFA	France 4/F-RAFQ				
5	B	F-WWFB	N404FJ	VH-BGF	F-GGRH	N905TS	PT-WQM	N905FJ	(D-ACDC)	G-HMEV
		(F-GOEV)	N905FJ							
6	B	F-WWFD	N405FJ	N80F	N885	[cx 19Dec16; wfu]				
7	B	F-WWFG	TR-LCJ	3B-XLA	F-GMOH	[cx 16Mar17; wfu]				
8	B	F-WWFE	N406FJ	N5731	N316SS					
9		F-WWFJ	(PH-ILC)	HB-IAB	C6-BHN	N900TR	N193TR	N232CL		
10	B	F-WWFF	N407FJ	N900FJ	(N910FJ)	N26LB	N96LB	N5MC	N349K	N349H
		N403HR	N91MS							
11		F-WWFK	LX-AER	F-WEFX	UN-09002	F-GLGY	N251SJ	F-GKHJ		
12	B	F-WWFH	N408FJ	N991AS	N77CE	N8VF				
13	B	F-WWFI	N409FJ	N328K	(N75V)	(N75W)	N75V	N61TS	N297AP	
14		F-WWFL	N410FJ	N900SB	N906SB	N324SR	VP-BLP	N44EG	(N47EG)	N900CZ
		(PR-IMP)	PP-IPR							
15		F-WWFM	HB-IAK	XA-RGB	(N115FJ)	N999EH				
16	B	F-WWFN	N412FJ	(N187HG)	N187H	VR-CTA	N619BD	VP-CBD	N64BD	N900SF
17	B	F-WWFO	N411FJ	N944AD	N790JC	N884BB				
18		F-WWFA	N413FJ	N72PS	N72PX	N900YB				
19		F-WWFB	N414FJ	N900SJ	N45SJ	N1L				
20		F-WWFC	N415FJ	(N711T)	N999PM	N70FJ	N911RF	N256DV	N920DB	N900LP
21	B	F-WWFJ	(HZ-R4A)	HZ-AFT						
22	B	F-WWFD	N416FJ	N54DC	OE-ICF	N988AK				
23		F-WWFK	I-BEAU							
24		F-WWFE	N417FJ	N901B	N67WB	N93GR	N93CR	N93GR	N202WR	
25	B	F-WWFF	N418FJ	N70EW	N75EW	N660BD	N615MS	N615ME	N922LJ	
26	B	F-WWFM	HB-IAC	SX-ECH	N900RN	VP-CJF	YR-CJF	N926CJ		
27	B	F-WWFH	N419FJ	N90EW	N91EW	N5VJ	N15VJ	N777XY		
28		F-WWFK	N420FJ	N85D	N86MC	N1S	N696JM			
29		F-WWFA	N421FJ	C-GTCP	N19VF					
30		F-WWFL	HB-IAF	F-WGTH	(F-GIRZ)	I-DIES	(PH-ERB)	PH-EBR	M-EBRB	N707FJ
31	B	F-WWFB	N422FJ	N900FJ	N910JW					
32	B	F-WWFG	N423FJ	VH-BGV	F-GJBT	N800BL	N500BL	N10MZ	N18MZ	
33	B	F-WWFC	N424FJ	N298W	F-GHEA	N9138Y	N901SB	N931SB	N203CW	TY-AOM
		5V-TTS								
34	B	F-WWFD	N425FJ	N8100E	N8200E					
35		F-WWFC	HB-IAD	F-GLMU	PP-PPA	F-GNDK	PH-OLI	N139AL	F-HJJB	N82MF
36	B	F-WWFE	N426FJ	N96PM	N91MK	N922JW				
37	B	F-WWFN	N427FJ	N45SJ	N41SJ	VH-FCP	VH-ACE	N394WJ	N377HW	
38		F-WWFE	Spain T.18-1/45-40							
39	B	F-WWFF	N428FJ	(N900BF)	N1818S	N181BS	N5733	N573J	N239AX	
40	B	F-WWFH	N429FJ	N904M	N145W	N369BG	(N389BG)	(N940SJ)	N924S	N839RM
		N900MK								
41		F-WWFI	N430FJ	N404F	N404FF	N76FD				
42	B	F-WWFJ	N431FJ	N900FJ	N42FJ	N117TF	N901BB	N990BB		
43	B	F-WWFC	I-MTDE	N288Z	N388Z	(N692SH)	N693SH	N410KA	[retro-fitted with winglets]	
		N504PA								
44	B	F-WWFA	N432FJ	N914J	N914JL	HB-IBY	N100UP			
45	B	F-WWFB	N433FJ	N64BE	N298W	(N798W)	N670JD			
46		F-WWFD	N434FJ	N329K	N779SG	N46FJ	TR-AFJ			
47		F-WWFA	A6-ZKM	F-WQBJ	(F-GOFC)	F-GNMF	F-WQBK	N678CH	LV-CRI	N687HS
48	B	F-WWFM	N435FJ	N900MJ	N233KC					
49		F-WWFD	VR-BLB	VP-BLB	N920SA					
50	B	F-WWFH	N436FJ	N330K	N900TA	(N711WK)	N950SF			
51	B	F-WWFG	N437FJ	N59LB	N26LB	(N50RG)	N9RG	N528JR	N328JR	VP-BMB
		N51FJ	(N888TD)	N74TD						
52		F-WWFC	5N-FGO	5N-BOH	(N367TA)					
53		F-WWFN	N438FJ	JA8570						
54		F-WWFC	(LX-IMN)	I-FICV	F-GKAY	N954FJ	F-GZME	9H-SVA	N754MM	
55	B	F-WWFO	N439FJ	C-FJES	N495GA	N404R	N704R	(N955FJ)	C-GSMR	N117SF
56		F-WWFB	N440FJ	JA8571						
57	B	F-WWFK	N441FJ	N900WK	C-FCRH					
58	B	F-WWFE	OE-ILS	HB-IGL	N116RW					
59	B	F-WWFD	N442FJ	N32B	TR-AFR					
60		F-WWFG	N443FJ	N900FJ	N91TH	N900VL	N860ST	N990LT		
61	B	F-WWFB	VR-CSA	HZ-AB2	HZ-AFZ					
62	B	F-WWFJ	F-GIVR	N62FJ	F-WQBL	F-GSCN	F-WQBJ	LX-LFB	OO-LFQ	LX-LFB
		VP-CAX	9H-WLD	CS-DTV	TT-DIT					
63		F-WWFF	N445FJ	N90TH	N127EM	N75W	N311JA	N211JA	N583JF	
64		F-WWFH	N446FJ	Malaysia M37-01						
65		F-WWFM	N447FJ	N216FP	N216FB	N990MC	(N990MQ)	N988T		
66		F-WWFE	F-GJPM	CS-TMK	CS-TFN	P4-BFF				

FALCON 900

C/n	Series	Identities								
67	B	F-WWFD	N448FJ	N900MA	N900MG	T7-OSB				
68	B	F-WWFL	N449FJ	N900HC	N900HE	N900HW	N610RL			
69		F-WWFD	I-SNAX	F-WQBM	HB-JSP	F-GPGK				
70		F-WWFN	N450FJ	Australia A26-070		VH-VIW	N105BK			
71	B	F-WWFB	N451FJ	(N900BF)	PK-TRP	N280BC	N280BQ	N642JC	N1PR	N711FJ
72		F-WWFF	VR-BLM	VP-BLM						
73		F-WWFA	N452FJ	Australia A26-073		VH-WII	N109BK	Spain T.18-5/45-44		
74		F-WWFF	N453FJ	Australia A26-074		VH-WIZ	N108BK	Spain T.18-4/45-43		
75		F-WWFC	N458FJ	C-FWSC	HB-IAI	N60RE	N60TL	C-GOIL		
76		F-WWFE	N454FJ	Australia A26-076		VH-WIZ	N106BK	N54SK	HZ-DME	N48WS
77		F-WWFG	N455FJ	Australia A26-077		VH-WIM	N107BK	Spain T.18-3/45-42		
78	B	F-WWFH	N456FJ	N332MC	C-GSSS	N522KM	LX-GES	F-GVMO	G-FLCN	
79	B	F-WWFM	N457FJ	N900FJ	N901FJ	N6BX	N6PX	N952GD	N800DW	
80	B	F-WWFA	N459FJ	N914BD	N914DD	N882SS				
81		F-WWFL	7T-VPA	N81GN	I-TLCM	N33GG	N484FM			
82		F-WWFM	7T-VPB	N82GP	(N561CM)	N649TT	N699BG			
83	B	F-WWFG	N460FJ	N900WG	N900NE	N361K				
84		F-WWFD	A6-AUH	F-WQBM	ST-PSA					
85		F-WWFC	N461FJ	N74FS						
86		F-WWFE	A6-UAE	F-GVAE	HB-JEI	OE-IOD	N904RS	C-FXOO		
87	B	F-WWFA	N462FJ	N33GG	N402FG	VQ-BZZ	C-FDOW			
88	B	F-WWFH	VR-BLT	F-GNDA	N987QK	N987GK	N122A			
89		F-WWFB	I-NUMI	F-HKMO						
90		F-WWFG	Spain T.18-2/45-41							
91		F-WWFH	A7-AAD	N91WF	CS-DFA	N991EJ	CS-DFH			
92		F-WWFL	N463FJ	PT-OEX						
93	B	F-WWFM	EC-617	EC-FEN	N900Q	N780SP	[retro-fitted with winglets]			
94		F-WWFC	A7-AAE	N94WA	CS-DFB	N889TD	N889TR	N960CL		
95	B	F-WWFO	N464FJ	N478A	N343MG	N898TS				
96		F-WWFF	F-GHTD	F-WWFF	5N-OIL	5N-FGE	Nigeria NAF961			
97	B	F-WWFA	EC-765	EC-FFO	XA-SJX	(N900DU)	N902NC	N595PL		
98	B	F-WWFM	N465FJ	N900FJ	(N903FJ)	N59CF	N590F			
99		F-WWFE	ZS-NAN							
100		F-WWFN	YK-ASC							
101	B	F-WWFO	N466FJ	D-ALME	VP-CAB	N101FJ	N56CL	N568L	N900YY	
102		F-WWFK	N467FJ	N906WK	N906CM					
103	B	F-WWFL	F-GHYB	F-WWFJ	V5-NAM					
104	B	F-WWFA	N468FJ	N104FJ	N881G	N900CS	N945TM	N610CX		
105	B	F-WWFD	N469FJ	N8572	JA8572	N71TH	F-GTGJ	F-WQBJ	F-GTGJ	CN-TFU
		N767CF	N405EJ	N225KS	N974BK	(N979BK)	N562BC*			
106	B	F-WWFL	F-GKDI	9M-BAN	F-GJRH	N332EC	N333EC	EC-JVR		
107	B	F-WWFJ	N470FJ	XA-GTR	N823BJ	N23BJ	N71GK			
108	B	F-WWFN	N471FJ	N334MC	N511WM	N229HD	(N108FJ)	YV2039	N108FJ	
109	B	F-WWFB	G-BTIB	Belgium CD-01						
110	B	F-WWFH	OY-CKK	F-GHGO	N110FJ	C-GJPG	C-GJPT	N900EJ	N999EA	
111	B	F-WWFH	N472FJ	N8BX	TS-JSM					
112	B	F-WWFM	N473FJ	N246AG	N248AG	N908JB	N900KL			
113	B	F-WWFB	HZ-SAB2	N612NL	N525MH					
114	B	F-WWFC	N474FJ	XA-SIM	N114GS	XA-FSB	XA-RFB			
115	B	F-WWFL	EC-235	EC-FPI	LX-TAG	HB-IBG	LX-MEL	I-FLYS	F-GSNK	N115FJ
		N900JS								
116	B	F-WWFO	N475FJ	N900FJ	N5VF	N5VN	N82RP	N782RP		
117	B	F-WWFA	N476FJ	N70TH	N900WF	(N995P)	N2111P	N111P		
118	B	F-WWFB	F-GNFI	RA-09000						
119	B	F-WWFD	N477FJ	N22T	N22FW					
120	B	F-WWFN	VR-BNJ	VP-BNJ	F-GRAX	F-WQBM	CS-DLA	F-GXDZ	C-FWKX	
121	B	F-WWFE	N478FJ	9M-BAB	HB-IFQ	RP-C9121				
122	B	F-WWFF	N479FJ	XA-SGW	N612BH	N247CJ				
123	B	F-WWFL	RA-09001							
124	B	F-WWFG	N480FJ	VR-BWS	VP-BWS	N14NA				
125	B	F-WWFL	F-GPAX	F-WWFL	VR-BSK	VP-BSK	RP-C7808	N978PW	N976PW	N85KB
126	B	F-WWFM	N481FJ	N900FJ	N733A	N733HL	N910CS	N94NA	N3HB	
127	B	F-WWFC	N482FJ	N654CN	N390F	N909AS	N963RS	N964RS	XA-VAL	
128	B	F-WWFM	N128FJ	N999PM	(N999PN)	N11LK	N98NX	N404BC		
129	B	F-WWFD	N483FJ	XA-VTO	N909VT	XA-VTO	N83TD			
130	B	F-WWFC	F-GOAB	F-WWFB	VR-CID	VP-CID	F-WQBN	F-GKBQ	G-HAAM	A6-SAC
		HZ-SPAL	F-WHLV	F-GKOM						
131	B	F-WWFH	N131FJ	N900FJ	N158JA	XA-TJG	N900VT	N900KD	N900D	
132	B	F-WWFI	N132FJ	N707WB	N767WB					
133	B	F-WWFH	F-GODE	HZ-OFC3	N395L	N5UU	N813TS	YV2040		
134	B	F-WWFA	N134FJ	N88YF	N322CP	N775GM				
135	B	F-WWFJ	VR-BPW	VP-BPW	F-GYCP	CS-DTP				
136	B	F-WWFE	N137FJ	N1818S	N187S	(N1836S)	N609SG	YV2726		
137	B	F-WWFF	N139FJ	XA-GAE	N99DQ	(N98DQ)	N35RZ			
138	B	F-WWF.	VR-BHJ	VP-BHJ	VH-FHR	C-FGFI	N346SK	N345SK		
139	B	F-WWFG	N140FJ	N523AC	(N523AG)	N900SX				

FALCON 900

C/n	Series	Identities								
140	B	F-WWFL	VR-CES	N70HS	N900UT	M-RURU	N140FJ			
141	B	F-WWFK	N141FJ	XA-OVR	XA-OVA	C-GHML	M-SAIR			
142	B	F-WWFN	N142FJ	N10AT	F-WSMF	F-GSMF	TC-CAG	F-HAAP	N103DT	VP-BPC
		N100FF	F-GXRM	N211WG						
143	B	F-WWFH	F-GNMR	ZS-ZBB	VP-BZB	CS-DDI	PH-LCG	N24FJ		
144	B	F-WWFO	N144FJ	N453JS	N512JY	N111	N111MU			
145	B	F-WWFK	VR-CGB	VP-CGB	F-GOFX					
146	B	F-WWFF	N146FJ	N216FP	N881P	N4MB	N81SV	N900KR	N326LF	
147	B	F-WWFG	N147FJ	N900FJ	(N901FJ)	OE-IMI	N147FJ	XA-ISR	N195CR	N990JA*
148	B	F-WWFD	N148FJ	N522AC	N900DV	N900VG	(N900VH)	N148FJ		
149	B	F-WWFH	VR-BPI	VP-BPI	ZS-DAV	N88879	N924S			
150	B	F-WWFC	N150FJ	N335MC	HB-IUW					
151	B	F-WWFK	G-OPWH	EC-HHK	N908CA	N906KW*				
152	B	F-WWFJ	N337MC	N660EG	N902M	N902MK	N18FX	N544CM		
153	B	F-WWFK	N153FJ	N57EL	N67EL					
154	B	F-WWFL	VR-BJA	VP-BJA	F-WQBJ	VP-BGF	F-WQBK	F-GVBF	LX-LFA	I-TCGR
155	B	F-WWFM	N2056	N730SA	N814M	N155FJ	N900TG	N939SS		
156	B	F-WWFA	N202FJ	HL7301	N910Q	N918MV				
157	B	F-WWFB	N157FJ	N1868M	N1868S	N626EK	N62NW			
158	B	F-WWFC	N158FJ	N900FJ	N404VL	N404VC	N721HM			
159	B	F-WWFD	P4-NAN	N263PW	LX-NAN	F-WQBL	LX-NAN	LX-COS	CS-DPE	M-JMMM
		D2-ANT								
160	B	F-WWFE	N176CF	N506BA						
161	B	F-WWFF	F-GSAB	VP-CTT	G-GSEB	PH-ILC	N161PE	N874VT		
162	B	F-WWFJ	N162FJ	N611JW	N1726M	[retro-fitted with winglets]				
163	B	F-WWFM	N163FJ	F-WWFM	(PH-EFA)	(F-GSAD)	VP-BEH	VP-CGP	N25MB	N82SV
		N600ME								
164	B	F-WWFC	G-MLTI	F-WQBM	VP-CFL	VP-CDA	N454AJ			
165	B	F-WWFD	G-EVES	VP-BEC	N183WW					
166	B	F-WWFG	N166FJ	N900FJ	F-GLHI	N995SK	N711WV			
167	B	F-WWFO	F-GUEQ	3C-ONM						
168	B	F-WWFA	N167FJ	XA-TEL						
169	C	F-WWFP	F-GRDP	VP-BGC	EC-KFA	N727GW				
170	B	F-WWFR	VP-BKA	N900DA	N900TR	N901TX	XA-QKY			
171	B	F-WWFW	TC-AKK	VP-CAB						
172	B	F-WWFD	N177FJ	N352AF	N352AE	N910SD				
173	B	F-WWFI	PH-LBA	VP-BFH	M-FASH					
174	B	F-WWFK	N138FA	N138F	XA-FXL	N167BS	N167BD			
175	B	F-WWFN	CS-TMQ	PH-NDK						
176	B	F-WWFW	N900SM	N909PM						
177	B	F-WWFY	N886DC							
178	B	F-WWFF	N179FJ	XA-APE	N10AZ					
179	C	F-WWFQ	N900FJ	N900DW	N902DW					
180	C	F-WWFX	N90TH							
181	C	F-WWFZ	HB-IUY	N833AV	EC-JNZ	F-WHLV	F-GXMF	ZS-JCC		
182	C	F-WWFB	N168HT	EC-JBB						
183	C	F-WWFK	N900CC	(N900WP)	N900RX					
184	C	F-WWFP	N129KJ	N184FJ	N247FR					
185	C	F-WWFF	HB-IGT	VH-PPD						
186	C	F-WWFJ	N900LC							
187	C	F-WWFO	N181FJ	N901SS	N900BK					
188	C	F-WWFZ	PH-EDM	F-HDSD	VH-OAA					
189	C	F-WWFD	N189FJ	C-GMND	N144FH					
190	C	F-WWFI	N900NB	N906NB	N468GH	N500JD				
191	C	F-WWFM	N31D	N48KZ						
192	C	F-WWFQ	N192FJ	PR-SEA	N192LW	VH-LAW	VH-LAL	VH-LUL	N820M	
193	C	F-WWFV	N193FJ	(VP-CGR)	F-WQBL	VP-BCX	N917BC			
194	C	F-WWFZ	OO-ACT	PH-STB						
195	C	F-WWFB	N195FJ	N100ED	(N100EQ)	N666TR	N666DJ	N655TC		
196	C	F-WWFH	N196FJ	N501DB						
197	C	F-WWFQ	N197FJ	F-WWFQ	(LX-MAM)	LX-GJL				
198	C	F-WWFR	N198FJ	C-GAZU						
199	C	F-WWFA	N199FJ	N900KJ						
200	C	F-WWFG	N207FJ	N404ST	N404TR	N144BS				
201	C	F-WWFA	N210FJ	LX-FTA	N888LG					
202	C	F-WWFF	VP-BMV	UR-CRD	M-TSKW					

Production complete

DASSAULT FALCON 900DX

C/n	Identities				
601	F-WWFA	[ff 13May05]		HB-JSW	A6-RTS
602	F-WWFB	N950JB			
603	F-WWFC	OO-VMI			
604	F-WWFD	OE-IDX	G-TAGF	C-GFLU	
605	F-WWFE	N605FJ	N453JS	M-OEPL	N89FC
606	F-WWFF	D-AUCR			
607	F-WWFI	(N607DX)	N907DX	C-GPOT	
608	F-WWFN	N50LB			
609	F-WWFO	VP-BNS	F-GRCV	M-WING	F-HTMS	N900VL
610	F-WWFI	VP-CIT	OD-MIK		
611	F-WWFP	N886BB	N890BB		
612	F-WWFJ	HB-JSU	M-MNDD	HB-JSU	
613	F-WWFQ	B-8021			
614	F-WWFS	VP-CHA	G-TAGK	M-GSIR	
615	F-WWFX	LX-AFD	N232SF		
616	F-WWFM	A6-SMS	F-HATB	SX-ZHT	VP-CBT
617	F-WWFH	OE-ISM	TC-SHU		
618	F-WWFO	N416KC			
619	F-WWVB	LX-SVW	LX-SAB		
620	F-WWFI	N620DX			
621	F-WWFA	N16FX	N790T		
622	F-WWFO	M-DADI	D-ADDI*		
623	F-WWFA	D-AMIG	G-ECHB		
624	F-WWFY	N14FX	N906D		
625	F-WWFS	[status?]			

Production complete

DASSAULT FALCON 900EX / 900LX

* after the c/n indicates 900EX EASy cockpit-configured aircraft
+ after the c/n indicates a 900LX model

C/n	Identities							
1	F-WREX	[ff 01Jun95]	F-GREX	PH-ERP	N900HG	[retro-fitted with winglets]		
2	F-WWFA	N200L	N209FJ	N970CC				
3	F-WWFG	N903FJ	JA50TH	N760				
4	F-WWJC	N204FJ	N8100E					
5	F-WWFJ	N205FJ	9M-JJS	N905EX	N500VM	N600JM		
6	F-WWFK	F-OIBL	EC-GMO	N143DL	N900FH	N711T		
7	F-WWFN	N907FJ	N45SJ	N374MV	N900SJ			
8	F-WWFB	N30LB	N500BL					
9	F-WWFE	N909FJ	N70LF					
10	F-WWFG	N910FJ	N22CS	N900Q	N910EX			
11	F-WWFI	F-GOYA	CS-DTB	N111SW	[retro-fitted with winglets]			
12	F-WWFJ	N913FJ	N900EX	(N900SB)	N912EX	F-WQBL	F-HAXA	
13	F-WWFK	VP-BRO	N127SF					
14	F-WWFN	N72WS	N7KC	[retro-fitted with winglets]				
15	F-WWFO	N915EX	N914J	N914JL	C-GOAG			
16	F-WWFA	N916EX	N67WB	N950RD	N729AD			
17	F-WWFB	N600AS	N990H	VP-BEG	N170PF	TJ-TRI	N170PF	RP-C9018
18	F-WWFE	N918EX	N18RF	N166FB	T7-ZOR			
19	F-WWFJ	N919EX	N7301	N96DS	N900CX	N88ND	[retro-fitted with winglets]	
20	F-WWFN	N920EX	N158JA	(F-OIBE)	D-AWKG			
21	F-WWFH	N330MC	N901MM					
22	F-WWFQ	N331MC	(N332MC)	(N21HJ)	N716BH			
23	F-WWFS	SE-DVE	OH-FFC	N291MJ				
24	F-WWFU	TR-LEX						
25	F-WWFV	N925EX	N55TY	N607CV	N602CV			
26	F-WWFX	N900SB						
27	F-WWFY	N927EX	N900EX	N626CC	I-FLYW	N99FG		
28	F-WWFZ	HB-IAH	G-CGPT	N328PT	VQ-BYT	T7-MJB	VQ-BYT	[retro-fitted with winglets]
29	F-WWFA	N25UD	N900MK	N17FX	N490S			
30	F-WWFB	N662P	N860FJ	N100NG	N900CQ			
31	F-WWFC	F-GSAI	HZ-OFC4	M-FALC	N940CL			
32	F-WWFE	N2425	N4425	N97NX	N794SE			
33	F-WWFF	N933EX	(N810M)	XA-TMH	XA-BEG	N903EX	N900WG	
34	F-WWFI	VP-CLB						
35	F-WWFJ	N2BD	HB-IAQ	N96NX	N913SN	N717LA		
36	F-WWFM	N326K	N826K					
37	F-WWFV	N327K	N900BZ	N900FJ				
38	F-WWFX	N328K	N68CG	N901MD	7Q-ONE	ZS-FCI		
39	F-WWFA	N939EX	VP-BID	N39NP				
40	F-WWFB	N940EX	N900EX	N606DR	N990WM			
41	F-WWFC	N5737	N81SN					
42	F-WWFD	N942EX	VP-BMS	N942CK	N909CK			
43	F-WWFE	F-GSDP	F-WQBK	EC-HOB				
44	F-WWFG	G-JCBG	N900PL	N947LF	PR-WRI	N128JL		
45	F-WWFJ	Italy MM62171						
46	F-WWFM	N946EX	XA-FEX	N40ML	N107CC	C-FGCT		
47	F-WWFO	N58CG						
48	F-WWFP	G-GPWH	G-CBHT	N627CR				
49	F-WWFR	N949EX	N404F					
50	F-WWFS	F-GPNJ						
51	F-WWFU	F-GVDP	OE-IDM					
52	F-WWFV	Italy MM62172		I-TARH				
53	F-WWFW	N953EX	PT-WQS	VP-BDZ	N53FJ			
54	F-WWFY	HB-IUX	PH-LAU					
55	F-WWFA	N498A	(N399CG)	N388GS	XA-BNM	N555ZT		
56	F-WWFC	N956EX	N404A	N909SB				
57	F-WWFD	N900MT	N900MJ	N10HZ	N10HQ	C-GXPZ		
58	F-WWFF	N958EX	N11WM					
59	F-WWFH	N959EX	N694JP	(N6940P)	N900EF			
60	F-WWFI	N960EX	PT-XSC	N60EX	YV2053			
61	F-WWFL	N961EX	N240LG					
62	F-WWFM	EC-HNU	N960SF					
63	F-WWFO	N963EX	N900EX	N435T				
64	F-WWFR	N900VM	D-AJAD	C-GBBX	N745TM	N945TM		
65	F-WWFW	N965EX	N965M	VP-CGD				
66	F-WWFA	N377SC	(N677SC)	N66FJ				
67	F-WWFB	N967EX	N312P	N312PV				
68	F-WWFC	N390DE	N271DV	N271DU	C-FSFB			
69	F-WWFD	N969EX	C-FJOI					
70	F-WWFE	N970EX	N999PM					
71	F-WWFG	N111NG	(N971EX)	N110EX				
72	F-WWFH	N2BD	N72FJ					

FALCON 900EX / 900EX EASy / 900LX

C/n	Identities
73	F-WWFI N973M VP-CGE
74	F-WWFK N315KP N811AV N600LF G-HNJC VP-CNZ N740LM N7KM
75	F-WWFL (F-GYDP) VP-BEH F-WQBK F-GXBV T7-PTL
76	F-WWFN F-GLJV F-WLJV N80F C-GMLH
77	F-WWFQ N977LP N83SV N131DS
78	F-WWFR G-DAEX D-AGSI F-GXHG D-AHER
79	F-WWFS N788CG
80	F-WWFV N881Q N900CM
81	F-WWFW N404N N404R N908SB
82	F-WWFX N982EX PR-GPA
83	F-WWFY HB-IGI N878SL
84	F-WWFA N984EX N900EX N984EX N326K (N82KK) N420KK N420PD
85	F-WWFB N985EX (N410MW) N910MW N76PW
86	F-WWFC N986EX HB-IGX VP-BEZ M-ODKZ
87	F-WWFE OE-IMA N487MA C-GGMI OE-IMI
88	F-WWFF N909MM C-GLBB (D-AHRO) N900ZM C-GWFM [retro-fitted with winglets]
89	F-WWFH N990EX N871MM (N802CB) N802CJ VT-SBK
90	F-WWFG VP-CLO
91	F-WWFJ N989EX F-WWFJ (F-OINA) F-WQBJ I-CAEX N91EX ZS-FCN [retro-fitted with winglets] N436RB
92	F-WWFK HB-IFJ N921WC N992FJ N902YP
93	F WWFL N993EX N993GT C-FPFS
94	F-WWFN N994EX N663MK N731SR
95	F-WWFO HB-IGY 9H-ALJ
96	F-WWFP N93CR N900ZA HB-JSY D-AHRN
97+	F-WNCO (F-GNCO)+ (F-GOEA)+ [+ both sets of ntu marks reserved simultaneously] CS-DFL N970RJ N963RS
98	F-WWFR N998EX N900KX N209CQ
99	F-WWFS N996EX N890FH XA-GMD N5VJ
100	F-WWFU N997EX JA55TH N550TH
101	F-WWFW N966H (N875F) N730LM
102	F-WWFX N6666P N6666R N70TT
103	F-WWFY N103EX N900EX N327K F-GYCM N103FJ N900HD
104	F-WWFA N588GS N805WM N440DM
105	F-WWFC G-LCYA (D-AHRN) N552SD [retro-fitted with winglets] N94UT
106	F-WWFD F-GSDA LX-ZAK SE-DJM N106EX
107	F-WWFE F-HBOL HB-JIN
108	F-WWFF G-JCBX N9WV N501MK N115KG
109	F-WWFG VP-BEE F-HDOM I-SLNI
110	F-WWFI N176CL N137SF
111	F-WWFJ N101EX N57EL N508PC VP-BFV OE-IEX N900VE
112	F-WWFK G-JJMX N900MF N587DZ
113	F-WWFL G-RBSG F-GYRB N121DF N497SB
114	F-WWFM N114EX N900EX (N114EX) N900YP
115	F-WWFN N720ML N720ME N44VP
116	F-WWFO Italy MM62210
117	F-WWFP N117EX (N900EX) N900SN
118	F-WWFS OH-PPR OE-IRL F-HFOX CN-RAK
119	F-WWFU N119EX N958DM N719SH
120*	F-WWFV (N120EZ) N900EX F-WWFV N900EX N106RW [w/o in hangar collapse at Washington/Dulles, VA, 06Feb10; parted out by Dodson International, Rantoul, KS]
121*	F-WWFW F-GSEF F-WWFW F-GSEF OO-FOI N793CG
122*	F-WWFX N901SB
123*	F-WWFY N990ML N990MC N80Q
124*	F-WWFZ N919SA
125*	F-WWFB N988H
126*	F-WWFC N966H N966E N889H
127*	F-WWFD N900HC N984BX
128*	F-WWFE OY-OKK (N900LK) M-ABEB N1SA
129*	F-WWFF N129EX XA-RGB XA-PGB C-GLBU C-GJPG
130*	F-WWFH VP-BEF OO-SCR
131+	F-WWFI VP-BFM N900MV N297GB
132*	F-WWFJ G-JPSX N590CL
133*	F-WWFK F-WQBJ D-AZEM
134*	F-WWFL VP-CEZ VP-CFR EI-ZMA
135*	F-WWFM N246AG
136*	F-WWFN N22LC (N22LQ) N822WW
137*	F-WWFO N88LC N50NL N50NU
138*	F-WWFP OE-IVK (OY-VIK) OY-IVK F-GNVK N538SC LV-GQK
139*	F-WWFQ N139EX N265H
140*	F-WWFR N940EX (N900EX) N54HG
141*	F-WWFS N141EX HB-JSX OE-IWG F-HMCH D-ASBG
142*	F-WWFU N142EX RA-09008
143*	F-WWFV HA-LKN
144*	F-WWFW N144EX VP-BSO N412EC
145*	F-WWFX F-GSNA (LN-SEH)
146*	F-WWFZ N146EX

FALCON 900EX EASy / 900LX

C/n	Identities									
147*	F-WWFE	N193F	N622WM							
148*	F-WWFG	5A-DCN								
149*	F-WWFH	Italy MM62244								
150*	F-WWFI	N900NS	G-SABI	F-HUBB	N15FJ	C-FXXU				
151+	F-WWFJ	VP-BSP	G-EGVO							
152*	F-WWFK	P4-SCM	UR-WIG	F-WHLV	N592CL					
153*	F-WWFL	N7818S	N1818S							
154+	F-WWFM	N47EG								
155*	F-WWFN	(F-GSMT)	N955EX	F-WQBN	F-GSMT	(LN-SEH)	LN-AOC	N852CA	G-FFFG	N91GL
	N978PW									
156*	F-WWFO	MM62245								
157*	F-WWFP	N227HD	N82HD							
158*	F-WWFQ	N15FF	N18DF							
159+	F-WWFR	N959EX	N900EX	N900SG	G-FNES	VH-MQK	VH-MQR	N6VF		
160+	F-WWFS	I-DAKO	LX-DSP	N731FJ	N615MS					
161*	F-WWFU	TC-MMG	TC-FTG							
162*	F-WWFW	N962EX	PR-CCC	N876C						
163*	F-WWFX	G-GALX	I-FLYN	N731FJ	N575JJ					
164*	F-WWFY	RA-09006								
165*	F-WWFZ	N165FJ	(N777SA)	(F-GUDA)	OE-IMC	F-HDLJ	N900LW			
166*	F-WWFM	VT-ISH								
167*	F-WWFP	N167EX	N85CL	N902SB						
168*	F-WWFQ	N900JG	(N900JF)	N900JQ	N446TD					
169+	F-WWFH	N900NF	N900NB	(N906NB)	N169FJ	N885B				
170*	F-WWFJ	N585BP	N700FL							
171*	F-WWFK	SE-DJA	N889TA	N889TD						
172*	F-WWFL	G-SIRO								
173*	F-WWFE	N7600S								
174*	F-WWFR	F-HCBM	F-WQBN	VP-BOZ	N789ZZ	N904NB				
175*	F-WWFV	N513HS								
176*	F-WWFW	N176EX	(LX-GDX)	D-AMBI	OE-IBN					
177*	F-WWFZ	N900KM	F-WQBM	VT-AKU						
178*	F-WWFA	N178EX	N900EX	N178EX	N900VG	N900VQ	N1836S			
179*	F-WWFC	SE-DJB	N718MM							
180+	F-WWFD	HZ-OFC5	M-ROWL	C-FJOA	N278RF					
181+	F-WWFH	N181EX	PR-FRU	N920JS	N13JS	N539CA				
182*	F-WWFU	N93KD	N1828S							
183*	F-WWFG	A6-MAF	A6-MMF	F-GVFL	I-SEAR					
184*	F-WWFN	G-JMMX	N512TF	F-HPAM						
185*	F-WWFV	LN-AKR								
186*	F-WWFY	N186EX	(XA-SCO)	XA-TEI						
187*	F-WWFA	N904JY								
188*	F-WWFW	N460D								
189*	F-WWFZ	OE-INB	G-RMMA							
190*	F-WWFF	N190FJ	C-GLXC	C-GLXG	N990FL					
191*	F-WWFP	N191AE								
192*	F-WWFR	I-SEAS								
193+	F-WWFU	G-REYG	N843MG	N343MG	N843MG					
194+	F-WWFK	N987AL	(PR-OLD)	N970SF						
195*	F-WWFL	C6-SZN	3A-MGA	3A-MGC	HB-JIO	Switzerland T-785*				
196*	F-WWVA	N196EX	YV2485							
197*	F-WWFC	N197EX	YV2486							
198*	F-WWFF	CS-DPF								
199*	F-WWFJ	N199FJ	N918JM							
200*	F-WWFW	F-HBDA	M-AFAJ							
201*	F-WWFY	N900EX	C-GIPX	N718AK						
202*	F-WWVC	N606SG								
203*	F-WWVD	N203FJ	XA-RET	N203FJ						
204*	F-WWVE	I-FLYI	[w/o 28Nov08 Brindisi, Italy; parted out Tarbes, France; b/u]							
205*	F-WWFB	(M-TECH)	VT-CAP	M-VGAL						
206*	F-WWFD	N206EX	N33LC							
207*	F-WWFE	N907EX	PR-PMV							
208*	F-WWFG	N286MJ								
209*	F-WWFK	N209EX	(N900RF)+	[+ntu marks worn at completion centre]				Bolivia FAB-001		
210*	F-WWFM	N210FJ	(N600US)	(N984H)						
211*	F-WWFN	G-WTOR	LX-GLD							
212*	F-WWFC	N212EX	N48CG							
213*	F-WWFI	N213EX	N28VL							
214*	F-WWFH	OE-IOE								
215*	F-WWFJ	N375SC								
216*	F-WWFQ	N44LC								
217+	F-WWFS	LX-GET	M-ROWL							
218*	(F-WWFV)	F-WWFL	N606US	P2-ANW						
219*	(F-WWFX)	F-WWFR	(TC-...)	G-ENXA	9H-LAS					
220*	(F-WWFZ)	F-WWFD	OH-FFE	OO-FFE						
221*	(F-WWVA)	F-WWFE	N221EX	N5MV						

FALCON 900EX EASy/900LX

C/n	Identities				
222*	(F-WWVF)	F-WWFF	N399EX	N63XF	
223*	(F-WWVG)	F-WWFG	N223EX	(B-MBL)	RA-09003
224+	(F-WWVH)	F-WWFC	G-JPSZ	N980SF	
225*	(F-WWVI)	F-WWFK	VP-BPW		
226*	F-WWVJ	N7600P			
227*	F-WWFI	(D-ASIE)	D-ALMS	N368FK	
228*	F-WWFJ	N228EX	N18CG		
229*	F-WWFP	N229DK			
230*	F-WWFL	F-GMDS	LN-BRG	M-MIDY	
231*	F-WWFQ	N231FJ	N720ML		
232*	F-WWFU	G-WABB	N685DC		
233*	F-WWFE	N900FJ	N707WB		
234*	F-WWFV	N432FJ	N672WM		
235*	F-WWFF	N235FJ	(PR-RJZ)	PR-ROZ	N580CB
236*	F-WWFW	TC-AZR	F-HEBO		
237*	F-WWFX	F-GZVA	M-EAGL		
238*	F-WWFG	LX-EMO			
239*	F-WWFZ	P4-GEM			
240+	F-WWFH	RA-09600			
241*	F-WWFM	9G-EXE			
242+	F-WWFN	XA-BEG			
243+	F-WWVA	N90LX	N175BC		
244+	F-WWFJ	M-ATOS	N91FE		
245+	F-WWFQ	N777QG	B-8030	M-LANG	
246+	F-WWFA	N900YG			
247+	F-WWFD	9H-GMT	D-AETD*		
248+	F-WWFE	N248LX			
249+	F-WWFB	(F-HBFL)	N63JP		
250+	F-WWFC	N250FJ	VQ-BJW	M-ATEX	
251+	F-WWFF	N311JA			
252+	F-WWFI	OH-GPE	OO-GPE		
253+	F-WWFY	I-DIEM			
254+	F-WWVB	N264C	(N264G)		
255+	F-WWVC	I-NEMO			
256+	F-WWVD	G-YCKF			
257+	F-WWVE	TC-MKR			
258+	F-WWFP	N258LX	VQ-BNH		
259+	F-WWVF	N529SG			
260+	F-WWVG	C-GTLA			
261+	F-WWVH	N261CH			
262+	F-WWVI	N577QT			
263+	F-WWVJ	F-GLYD	TC-AKE		
264+	F-WWFK	OY-SLS	ES-SLS		
265+	F-WWFV	N265LX	N993AM		
266+	F-WWFW	VP-CHG	D-AHEX*		
267+	F-WWFL	B-8208			
268+	F-WWFU	N234SA			
269+	F-WWVA	M-JPLC	N115PL	N115RL	
270+	F-WWFX	M-WING	F-HPVB		
271+	F-WWFM	(TC-IRR)	M-ISRK	M-ABGZ	F-HIBR
272+	F-WWFC	N40LB			
273+	F-WWFR	OY-MHM			
274+	F-WWFA	M-AGIK			
275+	F-WWFY	N248DV			
276+	F-WWFF	B-8212	M-TFFS		
277+	F-WWFD	F-HNLX	M-TINK	F-HDDP	N666TR
278+	F-WWVB	N278FJ			
279+	F-WWFB	HB-JTA			
280+	F-WWVC	N215EF			
281+	F-WWFQ	F-HNDO	N1130B		
282+	F-WWFH	VP-BFM			
283+	F-WWFG	TC-AOM	F-HVRO	M-PATH	F-HJMD
284+	F-WWFE	N46R			
285+	F-WWVE	OO-LMS			
286+	F-WWFN	N900VG			
287+	F-WWFI	N95BD			
288+	F-WWFP	F-HRAY			
289+	F-WWFZ	N73PS			
290+	F-WWFJ	N72PS			
291+	F-WWFY	N373RS			
292+	F-WWFX				
293+	F-WWFW	N293LX			
294+	F-WWFV	N18UD			
295+	F-WWFU				
296+	F-WWFS				
297+	F-WWFR	N960MC			

FALCON 900EX EASy / 900LX

C/n	Identities	
298+	F-WWFA	LX-LXL
299+	F-WWFB	
300+	F-WWFC	F-HVDA
301+	F-WWFD	XA-RBI
302+	F-WWFE	N1982C
303+	F-WWFF	D-ABBA
304+	F-WWFG	
305+	F-WWFH	N503Q
306+	F-WWFI	
307+	F-WWFJ	
308+		
309+		
310+		
311+		
312+		
313+		
314+		
315+		
316+		
317+		
318+		
319+		
320+		

DASSAULT FALCON 2000

C/n	Identities
1	(F-WNEW) F-WNAV [r/o 10Feb93; ff 04Mar93] (F-GMIR) F-GMOE VP-CAS F-GXJC G-YUMN M-YUMN
2	F-WNEW [rolled out Dec93; ff 11Jly94] ZS-NNF F-GJHJ N201CR
3	F-WWFA N2000A N15AS N203AF
4	F-WWMA N925AJ
5	F-WWMB N27R [parted out by Pollard Spares, Roanoke, TX]
6	F-WWMD F-GPAM F-WQBL N93GH N93GT PR-WSM N55EY N954SC M-CKSB
7	F-WWME N28R
8	F-WWMF N610AS F-WQBK VT-VLM
9	F-WWMG N435T N435TM N209FJ N783FS
10	F-WWMH N652PC N131EP
11	F-WWMK N101NS (N787RA) N721BS N248JF N48FB
12	F-WWMM I-SNAW (F-GLHJ) N105AF
13	F-WWML N2004 N722JB
14	F-WWMN N2034 N70KS N51MN N470RR
15	F-WWMO N790L N502BG
16	F-WWMB HB-IAW
17	F-WWMA N2035 N77A N88TY N89TY N659FM N658FM N62MF
18	F-WWMG F-GMPR EI-LJR VP-CJA [retro-fitted with winglets]
19	F-WWMC N790M
20	F-WWME N389GS N822TP N405ST N427GW
21	F-WWMA N390GS N11BV
22	F-WWMF N200NE N609CH N202CE N644RV
23	F-WWMH N2036 N375SC N575SC N23FJ N10JP
24	F-WWMK N2039 N376SC N876SC N18MV
25	F-WWML N2042 N96FG N122SC (N406ST) N25FJ M-NIKO T7-NIK G-TNIK
26	F-WWMN N2046 N2000A F-WQFL TC-CIN VP-BHC TC-CIN F-WQBN N112CD HB-ISF OY-ICE (F-GSAE) LX-SAM N358PR N482BC
27	F-WWMM G-JCBI F-GJSK D-BSIK F-WQBL LX-SIK F-WQBK F-GSYC B-8020 N27FJ VH-FJO
28	F-WWMO N596A N160WS N8888 [retro-fitted with winglets]
29	F-WWMA N2028 XA-TDU N700FL N889MC [retro-fitted with winglets]
30	F-WWMB HB-IAZ N480CF
31	F-WWMC N2032 N790Z
32	F-WWMD N65SD N324CL N175BC N132FJ N37MD [retro-fitted with winglets]
33	F-WWME HB-IAX N974HR
34	F-WWMF HB-IAY N234FJ
35	F-WWMG N27WP N1927G N623HD
36	F-WWMA F-GSAA (PH-WOL) PH-INJ F-GNBL VT-COT N480LP N602LP
37	F-WWMH EC-GNK F-HANC CS-IHP*
38	F-WWMI N3BM N8QM (N800BG) N710ET
39	F-WWMJ N2061 N151AE N42ST
40	F-WWMK N1C N212US N200CD
41	F-WWMD N2073 N48CG N148CG N214LD
42	F-WWMG HB-IBH F-WHLX CS-DTZ [retro-fitted with winglets]
43	F-WWMK (N2077) PT-MML N101BE N43FJ N86TW (N86TY) N775ST
44	F-WWML N2074 N2000A N49MW N37TH N623QW N303CL
45	F-WWMM N45SC N190MC
46	F-WWMN N2080 (N220JM) F-WWMN F-GMCK CS-DCM N505RR N870AR
47	F-WWMB N220JM N800BL N435JF
48	F-WWMC N2089 N701WC N701WG N48WK N888FC
49	F-WWMD (PH-EFB) VP-BEF G-GEDI F-GHGO F-WQBK VT-TBT
50	F-WWME D-BEST
51	F-WWMF N82AT N2AT N797CM
52	F-WWMI N212T N749GP N955SL
53	F-WWMJ N981 N149VB N149V N149VB N750JE
54	F-WWML D-BIRD D-BOND I-JAMY N254FJ
55	F-WWMM HB-IVM F-WQBK F-GJTG EC-JXR
56	F-WWMO TC-CYL N784BX
57	F-WWMA N2132 N18CG N918CG N122PR
58	F-WWMB N2133 N326EW N826EW
59	F-WWMC N2146 PT-WYC
60	F-WWMD N2147 XA-GNI (N260FJ) XA-TYT N524SA N898CT
61	F-WWME HB-IVN F-WQBJ F-GJTH EC-JVI N61RN N192HA*
62	F-WWMF HB-IVO CX-MBS
63	F-WWMG N2155 N2000A N804JH N800JH N806JH N302JC (N863TS) N68GL
64	F-WWMH N996AG N553GR
65	F-WWMI F-GODO (F-OIBA) VT-TAT
66	F-WWMJ N30TH N429SJ N793WF
67	F-WWMK N150BC N406NL
68	F-WWMN N200GN N629TG
69	F-WWMA N220JN (N220JM) N220EJ (N220MR) N220DF (N346SR) (N910LA)
70	F-WWMB N2168 N207QS P4-IKR D-BAMA F-WQBK VT-HDL
71	F-WWMC N92LT N811AV N811AG N811TY N811AG C-FWTF N630TS
72	F-WWMD N2169 N96LT N769JW N768JW N61JE

FALCON 2000

C/n	Identities									
73	F-WWMG	N2176	(N97LT)	N273JC	N273JE	N73FJ				
74	F-WWMH	HB-IUZ	F-GJSC	OO-VMB	N988DV	N986DV	(N829AM)	N468AM		
75	F-WWMK	N275QS	N229DA	N717FM	[retro-fitted with winglets]					
76	F-WWML	OY-CKN	F-WQBN	OY-CKN	N125GB					
77	F-WWMM	N278QS	N273TX	N888NA						
78	F-WWMJ	G-PYCO	N262PC	N78FJ	[retro-fitted with winglets]					
79	F-WWMN	N929HG	N772MC	N774MC	N79FJ	(JY-RYG)				
80	F-WWMO	N2CW	N60TC	N60TQ	N323EG					
81	F-WWVA	N281QS	N281VR							
82	F-WWVB	N752S								
83	F-WWVC	N1128B								
84	F-WWVD	N1929Y								
85	F-WWVE	N220JM	N221EJ	N344GC	XA-HHF	N127TN	N1SG*			
86	F-WWVF	N111HZ	N101HZ							
87	F-WWVG	N287QS	N4200	N910CS						
88	F-WWVH	N753S	C-FJPV	C-GSCL	C-GSMR					
89	F-WWVI	N2189	N2000A	N800GH						
90	F-WWVJ	F-GKIP	F-WQBM	N930SD	N5200					
91	F-WWVK	N46HA								
92	F-WWVL	N2191	N2000L	N850TC						
93	F-WWVM	N292QS	N292VR							
94	F-WWVN	N48HA	N517PJ	N286MG	(N94FJ)	M-IIII	N923JE			
95	F-WWVO	N628CC	[retro-fitted with winglets]							
96	F-WWVP	N88DD	N50TG	N53TG	N755FL					
97	F-WWVQ	N620AS	N922H	N922J	N12MW	N12MQ	N453SB	[retro-fitted with winglets]		
98	F-WWVR	N298QS	N289TX	M-ABCD						
99	F-WWVS	(N2099)	N111VU	N111VW	N770MP	N770MR				
100	F-WWVT	VP-CGA	N518SS							
101	F-WWVU	N2093	N399FA	OO-GFD	F-WHLX	VT-RVL				
102	F-WWVV	N515TK	N440AS	N410AS	N286CX					
103	F-WWVX	I-FLYP	F-WHLX	VT-AVH						
104	F-WWVY	N204QS								
105	F-WWVZ	N220EJ	N105LF	N711PE						
106	F-WWVA	N635E	N635F	N78LK						
107	F-WWVB	VP-CGC	N107VP	XA-RHA						
108	F-WWVC	I-FLYV								
109	F-WWVD	CS-DNP	N2218	F-WWVD	CS-DNP	N2000L				
110	F-WWVE	N2194	PP-CFF	[retro-fitted with winglets]						
111	F-WWVF	VP-BDL	F-WHLY	N132DA	G-FBJL	N925AK	N925JG	[retro-fitted with winglets]		
112	F-WWVG	N2197	N2000A	N2112L	N410GS	N112FJ				
113	F-WWVH	N213QS	N213VR*							
114	F-WWVI	ZS-PKR								
115	F-WWVK	CS-DNQ	N30AJ	N48MF						
116	F-WWVL	N2216	N52DC	N382KU						
117	F-WWVM	N2217	N54DC	N26PA						
118	F-WWVN	N218QS	N218VR*							
119	F-WWVO	F-GXDP	F-WQBN	D-BDNL	F-GESP	CS-DTR				
120	F-WWVP	CS-DNR	N120VR							
121	F-WWVQ	HZ-KSDA	F-ORAX	(F-GVDA)	VP-BNT	N78NT	M-TANA	OD-ONE	F-HFLX	M-SFOZ
122	F-WWVR	N222QS	N122VR							
123	F-WWVS	LZ-OOI								
124	F-WWVU	N224QS								
125	F-WWVV	N313GH	N813GH	N911SH	N118AD					
126	F-WWVW	N226QS								
127	F-WWVY	N227QS								
128	F-WWVZ	N228EJ	N628SA	N350M	N200JW					
129	F-WWVD	N229QS								
130	F-WWVE	N99TY	N202TH	N902MC						
131	F-WWVG	N707MM	N707MN	N317ML						
132	F-WWVH	N97NX	N905B							
133	F-WWVI	HZ-KSDB	F-WQBK	LX-SVW	F-WQBJ	B-MBK	F-WHLX	F-HKLB	TC-DGS	TC-GNC
134	F-WWVF	SX-DCF	N493S	(N493SV)	N622QW	N462ST				
135	F-WWVJ	N222BN	N196RG	N797HD						
136	F-WWVL	N236QS								
137	F-WWVM	N61KW	N510RR							
138	F-WWVN	N799BC	N856F	(N138MM)	N250DL					
139	F-WWVR	CS-DNS	N26NJ							
140	F-WWVT	N797SM	N797WC							
141	F-WWVU	N2227	N2000A	N54J						
142	F-WWVV	HZ-KSDC								
143	F-WWVW	N2230	N872EC	VT-ARF						
144	F-WWVX	F-GUJP	N317ML	N317MR	N203WB	N233EM	N233EH			
145	F-WWVZ	N245QS								
146	F-WWVA	N844AV	N866AV	N317MN	N455DX					
147	F-WWVB	N999BE	N777MN	N700CH						
148	F-WWVC	CS-DFC	N248VR	N921SA						

FALCON 2000

C/n	Identities									
149	F-WWVG	N2235	XA-MAV	XA-URK	N555GS					
150	F-WWVH	EC-HYI								
151	F-WWVI	G-IBSF	N151GR	N151CM	N10JM					
152	F-WWVJ	N98NX	N70XC	N317MQ	N246V	N243V	C-FMOS			
153	F-WWVK	N253QS								
154	F-WWVL	OY-CKI	LN-RTG							
155	F-WWVM	N255QS								
156	F-WWVN	N844UP	N844UR	N187AA						
157	F-WWVO	TC-RMK	[retro-fitted with winglets]			TC-CTN				
158	F-WWVP	N258QS								
159	F-WWVQ	N259QS								
160	F-WWVZ	VP-CGM	TC-PLM	F-WQBL	VP-BBP	N889MU				
161	F-WWVA	I-DDVF	N411YF							
162	F-WWVU	N262QS								
163	F-WWVW	N163J	OY-CKF	G-CGHI	N755BB	N991CE				
164	F-WWVY	N44JC								
165	F-WWVE	N265QS								
166	F-WWVD	(N2259)	TC-DGC	OY-CKW	F-WQBL	F-GVTC	(A6-SAF)	OY-TJF	TC-RSN	T7-RSN
167	F-WWVG	3A-MGR	3A-MGA	3A-MMA	VP-BHD	B-MAU	PR-SFB			
168	F-WWVV	N268QS								
169	F-WWVJ	N269QS								
170	F-WWVC	N220AB								
171	F-WWVK	(HZ-KSDD)	F-ORAV	N797HT	HB-JSB					
172	F-WWVN	N272EJ	N36EP							
173	F-WWVR	N673BA	OY-SIR	N988S						
174	F-WWMA	CS-DFD	N53NJ							
175	F-WWMB	N2258	XA-AVE							
176	F-WWMC	N676BA	N313AV							
177	F-WWMD	N277QS								
178	F-WWME	N279QS	N884WY	N100WY	N101NY					
179	F-WWMF	OH-FIX	N22TS							
180	F-WWMG	N2260	(N203DD)	N680DF						
181	F-WWMH	N280QS								
182	F-WWMI	N2264	N2000A	N329K	N826KR					
183	F-WWMJ	N2265	N88MX	N903GS	N460TB*					
184	F-WWMK	N2261	XA-RET	N71AX	G-MDBA	N228MN	N557PK			
185	F-WWML	N284QS								
186	F-WWMM	N2270	N551SS	N98RP						
187	F-WWMN	(F-GZAK)	LX-ZAK	F-GNDO	N87FJ	VP-BCV	N343AT	PT-SRU	N72BC	
188	F-WWMD	N2288	N317MZ	N317M						
189	F-WWMB	N2267	N2000A	N330K						
190	F-WWVA	N290QS								
191	F-WWVB	F-GUYM	TC-PRK	F-WQBJ	I-BNTN	(F-GULK)	F-GZJR	I-GEFD		
192	F-WWVC	N2289	N2000A	N515PV	N458SW	N718PM				
193	F-WWVE	N239QS	N278GS	N279GS	N247WD					
194	F-WWVF	N671WM								
195	F-WWVH	N297QS	N196KC							
196	F-WWVI	N296QS								
197	F-WWVJ	N2290	N215KH	I-KERE						
198	F-WWVL	N203QS								
199	F-WWVM	N2295	N899U	N15BY						
200	F-WWVN	I-SEAE								
201	F-WWVO	N201WR								
202	F-WWVP	N251QS								
203	F-WWVQ	I-ARIF								
204	F-WWVR	N240QS	N2317	N88DD						
205	F-WWVS	CS-DFE	N205VR	N919CH						
206	F-WWVT	N208QS	N2319	N414CC	N331DC	N831DC	N900NH			
207	F-WWVU	N207EM	OE-HEM	OM-OPF	OE-HBG					
208	F-WWVV	G-GEDY	LX-MBE							
209	F-WWVW	N209FS	N209TM	OE-HPH						
210	F-WWVX	N270QS	N2325	N850K	C-GEPG	N598WC				
211	F-WWVY	N210QS								
212	F-WWVZ	N2322	N523W	N523WC						
213	F-WWVA	N212QS	N684KF							
214	F-WWVB	N214FJ	N215QS							
215	F-WWVC	N215RE	N203CK	N215RE						
216	F-WWVD	N718KS	OE-HFA	9H-MAT	S5-CWA	VT-CLF				
217	F-WWVE	N863TM	OE-HVA	N771AT	PP-LFS					
218	F-WWVF	N218PH	N412WD							
219	F-WWVG	N219FJ	N1999	(N219FJ)	C-GOCX					
220	F-WWVH	N620BA	N306BH							
221	F-WWVI	N102MG	N1MG	N950RL						
222	F-WWVJ	N297RG	N296RG	N138FJ						
223	F-WWVK	OE-HAF	M-WING	M-WIND	OY-SNK					
224	F-WWVL	N33FJ	N33D	N40N						

FALCON 2000 / 2000DX

C/n	Identities				
225	F-WWVM	VT-AAT			
226	F-WWVN	OE-HKY	D-BSKY	VT-ARC	
227	F-WWVO	P4-IKF	ES-CKH		
228	F-WWVP	N900MC			
229	F-WWVQ	F-GXDA	TC-SNK		
230	F-WWVR	(F-HDFS)	N230FJ	N532CC	N522CC	N97FG
231	F-WWVS	VT-HGL				

Production complete, replaced by the Falcon 2000DX

DASSAULT FALCON 2000DX

C/n	Identities		
601	F-WWGY	[ff 19Jun07]	N331DC
602	F-WWMC	N30LF	[retrofitted with winglets]
603	F-WWGD	LX-ATD	N473K
604	F-WWGV	VT-VKR	

Production complete

DASSAULT FALCON 2000EX / 2000EX EASy / 2000LX

* alongside the c/n indicates a 2000EX EASy cockpit-configured aircraft
\+ alongside the c/n indicates a 2000LX aircraft

C/n		Identities								
1		F-WMEX	[r/o 19Jly01; ff 25Oct01]	(F-GMEX)	VP-BMJ	N900CH				
2		F-WWGA	N202EX							
3		F-WWGC	HB-IAJ							
4		F-WWGD	N200CH	N909CF						
5		F-WWGE	LX-DKC	F-GUDN	PH-VBG					
6	+	F-WXEY	[retrofitted with 2000LX winglets 2008]							
7		F-WWGF	D-BIRD	N40TH						
8		F-WWGG	G-JOLI	F-GUTD	OO-IAR	OE-HRA	LX-AAM	OE-HNM	S5-ADG	N1978X
9		F-WWGH	(N209EX)	HB-IGQ	OM-IGQ	EP-FSC				
10		F-WWGI	(SE-RBV)	VP-BER	OE-HKK	N992CE*				
11		F-WWGJ	I-NATS	OE-HGM	D-BGGM*					
12		F-WWGK	N313CC							
13		F-WWGL	N500R	N500FE	N71FE	(D-BJGM)	N263XF			
14		F-WWGM	HB-IAU							
15		F-WWGN	N215EX	N97GM	S5-ABR	Slovenia L1-01				
16	+	F-WWGO	PP-AAF	N16XY						
17		F-WWGP	N217EX	F-WWGP	N977CP					
18		F-WWGQ	F-GUHB	N943JB	N104MT					
19		F-WWGR	N528BD	N855TJ						
20	+	F-WWGS	N219EX	XA-GNI	XA-CDT					
21		F-WWGT	N221EX	N521CD	N801WW	N801WC				
22		F-WWGU	N218EX	PR-WQT	N218EX	VP-BDV	N122FJ	N118T		
23		F-WWGV	N223EX	N101PV						
24		F-WWGW	N224EX	N341AP						
25		F-WWGX	N225EX	N699MC	N83LT					
26		F-WWGY	N226EX	N6453	N6458	N880RJ				
27		F-WWGZ	OH-FEX	ER-KVI	N23LT					
28	*	F-WWGC	F-GUFM	N2CC	N4QG	(N28EX)	M-RONE			
29	*	F-WWGD	SX-DCA	N382CA	N12MW					
30	*	F-WWGG	D-BERT	M-PDCS	M-DUBS					
31	*	F-WWGJ	N31EX	N620MS						
32	*	F-WWGK	N666BE	N999BE	N377GM	N377AG				
33	*	F-WWGL	D-BILL	D-BOSS	N924BC	N790DC				
34	+	F-WWGM	HB-JEG	C-FJAJ	C-GJKI					
35	+	F-WWGQ	OY-CLN	N626NT						
36	*	F-WWGR	N185G	N163EB						
37	*	F-WWGS	N308U							
38	*	F-WWGT	N3BM	N8QM	N909MM					
39	*	F-WWGU	CS-TLP	9H-SFA						
40	*	F-WWGV	N240EX	PR-PPN	N888NX	PH-CHT	N131A			
41	*	F-WWGW	CS-DFF							
42	*	F-WWGX	F-GUTC	D-BMVV						
43	*	F-WWGY	N9871R							
44	*	F-WWGA	CS-DFG							
45	+	F-WWGE	VP-BVP	N205CW	N659FM					
46	*	F-WWGF	N21HE	N10EU						
47	+	F-WWGH	N711HE	N404UK	N365FJ	G-LSMB				
48	*	F-WWGI	N48NC	N1NC						
49	+	F-WWGN	F-GUDC	N50TG	N249FJ					
50	*	F-WWGO	N57MN	N133RL	N250LX	N726DC				
51	*	F-WWGP	ZS-MGD	N581GM						
52	*	F-WWMA	G-KWIN	M-ABFF	EP-TTI					
53	*	F-WWMB	N36TH	N98TH	N510CT					
54	*	F-WWMC	N221QS							
55	*	F-WWMD	N226EW	N326EW	N326LW	N57AL				
56	*	F-WWME	N56EX	N954SP	N600BL	C-FNCG				
57	*	F-WWMF	N376SC	N818BH	N707MT					
58	*	F-WWMG	N158EX	VH-CRQ	VH-CRW	VH-KRW	N37EA			
59	*	F-WWMH	N230QS							
60	*	F-WWMI	N100MB							
61	*	F-WWMJ	LX-NLK	VP-CBC	OO-FDG					
62	+	F-WWMK	N346PC							
63	+	F-WWML	OY-EJD	F-HPAD	9H-BEC					
64	*	F-WWMM	N493SF	N493S						
65	*	F-WWMN	CS-DFK							
66	+	F-WWMO	N822ST	N303QW	N318CL					
67	*	F-WWGA	OH-FOX	G-YFOX						
68	*	F-WWGC	N934ST	N360M						
69	*	F-WWGD	N56EL	N57EL	N47EL	N888WL				
70	*	F-WWGE	D-BOOK	N237BB						
71	*	F-WWGG	N71EL	N56EL	(N46EL)	N56EG	N904TF			
72	*	F-WWGH	N613GH	(N431GH)	N995GH	N172FJ				

FALCON 2000EX EASy / 2000LX

C/n		Identities					
73	*	F-WWGJ	N85MQ	N85M	N85MQ	N273SW	
74	*	F-WWGK	D-BAMM	N925BC			
75	*	F-WWGL	F-GUPH	OO-GML	F-GZLX	(D-BTIG)	M-FLCN
76	*	F-WWGM	A6-SMS	F-WQBL	(D-BBED)	D-BIKA	
77	*	F-WWGN	N377EX	XA-LFA			
78	*	F-WWGO	(F-GOTF)	I-JETF	G-JETF	OE-HCB	
79	*	F-WWGP	N88HE	N886CE			
80	*	F-WWGQ	CS-DLB				
81	*	F-WWGR	N81EX	N89CE			
82	*	F-WWGS	VP-CMD	C-GSEC			
83	+	F-WWGT	N83EX	F-WWGT	N83EX	N283SL	N669HP
84	*	F-WWGU	N522BD				
85	*	F-WWGV	N993GH	N993TN	N37HK		
86	*	F-WWGW	N223QS				
87	+	F-WWGX	N287F	C-GTPL			
88	*	F-WWGY	OE-HOT	M-ILES	G-LATE		
89	+	F-WWGZ	VP-CAM	M-XJOB	M-SNAP	N642TA	N542AP
90	*	F-WWGC	N190EX	C-GOHB	C-GOAB		
91	*	F-WWGD	N91EX	[trialled with temporary winglets Jun06-Aug06]	N233QS		
92	+	F-WWGG	N176CG				
93	*	F-WWGH	D-BFFB	N456CD	VT-RSG		
94	*	F-WWGI	N912MT	N912VV	N89RP		
95	+	F-WWGJ	N168CE	N887CE	M-ROWL	M-SNER	
96	*	F-WWGN	5B-CKO	F-WWMA	5B-CKO		
97	*	F-WWGA	N12AR	N855DG			
98	*	F-WWGP	CS-DLC				
99	*	F-WWMA	PP-MJC				
100	*	F-WWMB	N310U				
101	+	F-WWMC	N204CW	M-ORAD			
102	*	F-WWMD	G-ITIG	CS-DTF	OE-IEN		
103	*	F-WWME	(OY-FPN)	OY-PNO	F-HIKJ	B-3211	
104	*	F-WWGE	TC-DGN				
105	*	F-WWGR	N994GP	M-JETZ			
106	+	F-WWGU	N771DV	N771BV*			
107	*	F-WWGV	N367BW	N267BW	N367BW	N612HT	
108	*	F-WWGW	I-JAMJ	N560MS			
109	*	F-WWGX	CS-DLD				
110	*	F-WWMG	VP-BAK	M-STCO	N157AL		
111	*	F-WWMH	D-BASE	HB-IGU			
112	+	F-WWMI	N619SM				
113	*	F-WWMJ	VP-CMI	M-CIMO			
114	*	F-WWMK	F-GVNG	[fitted with mock Falcon 2000LX winglets 2007, later removed]	M-AMND	N671PB	N671PP
115	*	F-WWML	N232QS				
116	*	F-WWMM	N116EX	N72PS	N72PU	N80RP	
117	*	F-WWMO	VT-VLN				
118	*	F-WWGC	D-BONN				
119	*	F-WWGD	N2000A	N62YC	[w/o in hangar collapse at Washington/Dulles, VA, 06Feb10; parted out by Alliance Air Parts, Oklahoma City, OK]		
120	*	F-WWGG	N333MX				
121	+	F-WWGI	N121EX	XA-CMM			
122	*	F-WWGF	N147G				
123	+	F-WWGJ	OO-PAP	N925AK	N1933G	N1933N	
124	+	F-WWGK	N124EX	N888CE			
125	*	F-WWGM	(D-BONN)	VP-BVV	N125FJ	XA-JBT	
126	+	F-WWGO	N669PG	VP-BGI	C-FJOA	N810U	
127	*	F-WWGQ	CS-DLE				
128	+	F-WWGS	(VP-BOE)	M-CHEM			
129	+	F-WWGU	N129EX	C-GENW			
130	*	F-WWGA	N1JK				
131	+	F-WWGH	N131AG	N117AL	PT-FCS		
132	*	F-WWGN	G-OJAJ	OO-OFP	N899BC		
133	+	F-WWGP	"VP-BAH"+	[+ painted in error at completion centre]	VP-BRA		
134	*	F-WWGV	CS-DLF				
135	+	F-WWGE	N414TR	N820EC			
136	+	F-WWGF	TC-ATC	F-HLDB			
137	*	F-WWGG	N137EM	N119EM			
138	+	F-WWGI	N168AM	N880PC			
139	*	F-WWGZ	N470D	VP-CTT			
140	+	F-WWMA	OO-DFG	D-BHER*			
141	+	F-WWGK	G-WLVS	N267WB	N672WB		
142	+	F-WWGO	N100KP	N500N	N623CT		
143	+	F-WWGR	(P4-LGM)	M-LJGI	N806DB	N805DB	
144	*	F-WWGW	CS-DLG				
145	+	F-WWMB	N345EX	N47WS	C-FDBJ	N345GA	N272FC
146	+	F-WWGH	N268DM	N785AD			
147	+	F-WWGU	N278DM	N786AD	N147CJ		

FALCON 2000EX EASy / 2000LX

C/n		Identities						
148	+	F-WWGE	M-YJET	N888MX				
149	*	F-WWGJ	CS-DLH					
150	+	F-WWGL	N150FJ	N772MC				
151	+	F-WWMD	N151EX	N2000A	N151EX	M-GOLX	N257AL	N142JS
152	+	F-WWGA	OE-HMR					
153	+	F-WWGC	VT-AYV					
154	+	F-WWGG	HB-JET	N94AM	N716GC			
155	+	F-WWGZ	(CS-DLH)	N155EX	CS-DLI	N606TJ	N609TJ	N274SW
156	+	F-WWME	OY-MHA	N156FJ	N500RR			
157	+	F-WWGQ	N157EX	(PT-FLX)	PR-NXG	N107RG		
158	+	F-WWGS	N234QS	N60FK				
159	+	F-WWGT	VT-TDT					
160	+	F-WWGH	(G-CNGM)	OY-CKH	N552GR			
161	+	F-WWGX	(G-LSMB)	OY-MGO	F-HDJL			
162	+	F-WWMB	N162NS	VH-RAM	OO-PSE			
163	+	F-WWMC	N480D	N209SU	N500R			
164	+	F-WWMF	N64EX	PP-PPN				
165	+	F-WWGL	N204CE					
166	+	F-WWGN	(M-PNRE)	HS-RBR				
167	+	F-WWGP	N167EX	C-GSLU				
168	+	F-WWGU	(N168NS)	N460SJ				
169	+	F-WWGY	VT-BRK					
170	+	F-WWMG	N404UK	(N170LX)	N2000A	N515CF		
171	*	F-WWMH	N449SA					
172	+	F-WWMI	N75EK					
173	+	(F-WWMJ)	F-WWGI	M-ALRV				
174	+	(F-WWMK)	F-WWGK	N250QS	N174LX	N716CG	N716CQ	N905NB
175	+	(F-WWML)	F-WWGO	N175EX	N747RL	N747KL		
176	+	(F-WWMM)	F-WWGF	N609LS	N376SF			
177	+	(F-WWMN)	F-WWGQ	(N177NS)	M-DARA	N900FS		
178	+	(F-WWMO)	F-WWGS	N429SA	PP-AUL			
179	+	F-WWMA	N179EX	PR-OBE				
180	+	F-WWMJ	TC-SGO					
181	+	F-WWMK	(N928GC)+	[+ntu marks worn at completion centre]				LX-EVM
182	+	F-WWML	G-EDHY	ZA-EVA	N197KA	N197JK	N300FS	N883SL
183	+	F-WWGW	N183FJ	VH-WIO	N183FJ	N928WK		
184	+	F-WWMC	N9895					
185	+	F-WWMM	HB-JGF	F-HEFG	N49HT			
186	+	F-WWMN	B-MAZ					
187	+	F-WWMO	N781EX	PR-ETY				
188	+	F-WWGE	HB-JGG					
189	+	F-WWGL	N720WY					
190	+	F-WWGP	EI-TDV	N810ET				
191	+	F-WWMD	N257QS	F-GVEL	I-PBRB			
192	+	F-WWGA	(N192LX)	(OY-GLO)	(D-BSKY)	B-8025	N497DC	
193	+	F-WWGD	TC-MRK	F-HUGS				
194	+	F-WWGG	PH-CTH					
195	+	F-WWGK	F-GVFX	OY-GKJ				
196	+	F-WWGO	OY-ZWO	OO-VRO				
197	+	F-WWMF	N325B					
198	+	F-WWGR	EC-LGV					
199	+	F-WWGS	OE-HTO	M-FTHD				
200	+	F-WWME	M-ABAK	SX-MLA	F-HPKR	N501RR		
201	+	F-WWMG	D-BEKY					
202	+	F-WWMA	PP-MMF					
203	+	F-WWMH	N203LX	N801DE	N901FH			
204	+	F-WWJN	I-FEDN					
205	+	F-WWJO	N205LX	N769JW				
206	+	F-WWJP	N696SB					
207	+	F-WWJQ	(M-TANG)	N741SP	N790J			
208	+	F-WWJR	N1903W					
209	+	F-WWJS	(N209LX)	I-UCBT	PR-RNY			
210	+	F-WWJT	(D-BEKY)	N410SG				
211	+	F-WWJU	N988DV					
212	+	F-WWJV	ZS-SAB					
213	+	F-WWJX	I-MOFI					
214	+	F-WWJY	F-GZBJ	VQ-BIJ				
215	+	F-WWJZ	N215FJ	RP-C9215				
216	+	F-WWGB	N70FA	M-IKEL	N201PG			
217	+	F-WWGJ	N262MW	N58MW				
218	+	F-WWGL	N218LX	PR-JJR				
219	+	F-WWGM	N733H					
220	+	F-WWGT	M-IKAT	T7-ONE				
221	+	F-WWGD	TC-LIA					
222	+	F-WWGE	N12LX					
223	+	F-WWGH	N223LX	PR-OLD	N885FJ	PR-DLX	N223FJ	

FALCON 2000LX

C/n		Identities					
224	+	F-WWGI	N917JC				
225	+	F-WWGS	OY-SKL	N225FJ	N790R		
226	+	F-WWGV	N801WW				
227	+	F-WWGY	N377SC				
228	+	F-WWGZ	(OY-ZWO)	F-HBIP	N228BL		
229	+	F-WWJN	N1C				
230	+	F-WWJO	TC-MAA	F-HSAM			
231	+	F-WWGF	F-GTDA	F-WTDA	France 231/F-RAFC		
232	+	F-WWGX	C-GOHB				
233	+	F-WWJP	N448AS	N560US			
234	+	F-WWJR	VP-CAM	D-BLTA			
235	+	F-WWJT	(D-BOBI)	N2000A	(N235EX)	N733A	
236	+	F-WWJU	N36TH	PR-ALS			
237	+	F-WWMG	F-GTDK	F-WTDK	France 237/F-RAFD		
238	+	F-WWMC	N532CC				
239	+	F-WWMD	I-PBRP	N919BA	N1897S		
240	+	F-WWMH	M-STCO				
241	+	F-WWMJ	N688CP				
242	+	F-WWMK	N242FJ	VP-CJS	N242FJ	XA-FLC	
243	+	F-WWML	OO-GHE				
244	+	F-WWMO	HB-JKL				
245	+	F-WWMM	OE-HAM	9H-HAM			
246	+	F-WWMF	D-BOBI				
247	+	F-WWGK	PP-NPP				
248	+	F-WWJS	N326EW				
249	+	F-WWJZ	N620V				
250	+	F-WWME	N86HD				
251	+	F-WWGC	N251FJ	XA-BLZ			
252	+	F-WWGR	PP-AMK				
253	+	F-WWGO	F-HOME	M-TINK	M-FIVE	F-HLDS	B-1999
254	+	F-WWGJ	F-WWGT	PR-MDB	N80BL		
255	+	F-WWGL	N255FJ	N2000A	N544S		
256	+	F-WWJX	HB-JFI				
257	+	F-WWGB	G-WWFC	F-HJDF			
258	+	F-WWMI	N258FJ	C-FVMW			
259	+	F-WWGW	N259EX	VH-WIO			
260	+	F-WWJY	OE-HEY				
261	+	F-WWGD	G-VPCM				
262	+	F-WWGY	N383MH	N905TF			
263	+	F-WWMN	D-BVHA				
264	+	F-WWGE	P4-DBB				
265	+	F-WWJN	N885A				
266	+	F-WWJO	N409GB				
267	+	F-WWMK	N325AP				
268	+	F-WWMG	N268LX	N65NY			
269	+	F-WWGZ	F-HLXS	G-PULA			
270	+	F-WWMF	N918MJ				
271	+	F-WWJS	D-BERT				
272	+	F-WWGH	N70TF				
273	+	F-WWJP	N231TJ				
274	+	F-WWMH	N327RX				
275	+	F-WWGR	G-FLXS				
276	+	F-WWGK	OE-HTR				
277	+	F-WWGJ	D-BOOK				
278	+	F-WWGX	N881Q				
279	+	F-WWJT	N666TR	N279FJ			
280	+	F-WWMJ	PT-FKY				
281	+	F-WWMA	OY-CKK				
282	+	F-WWMI	F-HLPM				
283	+	F-WWGB	N225FD	N225DF			
284	+	F-WWGQ	(PT-FKY)	N482JC	N515AN		
285	+	F-WWJY	N58GG				
286	+	F-WWJV	C-GOFS				
287	+	F-WWMC	N844UP				
288	+	F-WWJQ	F-HJCD				
289	+	F-WWMB	XA-DFN				
290	+	F-WWGD	F-HALG				
291	+	F-WWGY	N84SV				
292	+	F-WWGV	N78KN				
293	+	F-WWGT	N1HS				
294	+	F-WWMG	TC-SMC				
295	+	F-WWGG	N812RX				
296	+	F-WWGS	F-HLPN				
297	+	F-WWMN	M-AERO				
298	+	F-WWGN	PH-PKF				
299	+	F-WWJU	N133RL				

FALCON 2000LX

C/n		Identities		
300	+	F-WWJS	N307PS	
301	+	F-WWJX	G-FLLY	N927TD
302	+	F-WWJP	LN-RTN	
303	+	F-WWGA	N84PJ	
304	+	F-WWGE	N14GD	
305	+	F-WWGF	N488GB	
306	+	F-WWGI	(N2000A)+	[+ ntu marks worn in 2015 and 2016 NBAA Convention static displays]
307	+	F-WWGJ	N87HD	
308	+	F-WWGK	XA-CHD	
309	+	F-WWGL	PR-VEN	
310	+	F-WWGR	N81SV	
311	+	F-WWGW	OY-MGA	
312	+	F-WWGB	N541Z	
313	+	F-WWGC	I-NHCO	
314	+	F-WWGQ	OY-GFS	
315	+	F-WWGX	N376SC	
316	+	F-WWGZ	TC-ASD	
317	+	F-WWMA	N9273	
318	+	F-WWMB	N100JS	
319	+	F-WWMC		
320	+	F-WWME	YU-FSS	
321	+	F-WWMF	T7-URJ	
322	+	F-WWMH	N90MC	
323	+	F-WWMJ	F-HNOA	
324	+	F-WWMK	N360SJ	
325	+	F-WWML	G-SMSM	
326	+	F-WWMO	N971MT	
327	+	F-WWMG		
328	+	F-WWJP	N897D	
329	+	F-WWJQ	N570D	
330	+	F-WWJR		
331	+	F-WWJS		
332	+	F-WWJT	N332FJ	
333	+	F-WWJV		
334	+	F-WWJX	LN-RTO*	
335				
336				
337				
338				
339				
340				
341				
342	+	F-WWGK	N342FJ	
343				
344				
345				
346				
347				
348				
349				
350				
351				
352				
353				
354				
355				
356				
357				
358				
359				
360				

DASSAULT FALCON 2000S

C/n	Identities				
701	F-WWGP	[ff 17Feb11]			
702	F-WWJV	N702FJ	N515PV		
703	F-WWJQ	F-HMCG	N957CP		
704	F-WWMA	TC-TOS			
705	F-WWGQ	G-TTJF			
706	F-WWGT	LY-GVS			
707	F-WWGG	ES-TEP	F-HCRK	M-LCFC	HS-KPA
708	F-WWGV	N748RE			
709	F-WWGS	N1824S			
710	F-WWJR	XA-KAR			
711	F-WWGN	M-ABGP	N775TM	N491N	
712	F-WWGA	PT-TRJ			
713	F-WWJU	C-GMII			
714	F-WWMC	N714RK	[cx 27Oct16 to Republic of Korea Air Force]		
715	F-WWMD	OY-GWK			
716	F-WWGF	N716FJ	HB-JGD		
717	F-WWMO	N427MJ			
718	F-WWGL	SP-ARG	SP-ARK		
719	F-WWGI	XA-GMO			
720	F-WWMM	N720NP	HK-5068X	HK-5068	
721	F-WWJX	B-8210			
722	F-WWJZ	N498DC			
723	F-WWME	TC-VGP	TC-KNK		
724	F-WWGU	N657DB			
725	F-WWGM	OY-SWO			
726	F-WWGC	N726RK	[cx 22Dec14 to Republic of Korea Air Force]		
727	F-WWML	N845UP			
728	F-WWGO	N728FJ			
729	F-WWJR	N846UP			
730	F-WWJO	N184G			
731	F-WWJN	N410GS			
732	F-WWGH	N278GS			
733	F-WWGM	N639M			
734	F-WWMD	N995G	N995GH		
735	F-WWMI	EC-MLA			
736	F-WWMM	N993GH			
737	F-WWJO	XA-HHF			
738	F-WWJU	ZS-EZY			
739	F-WWJN	N603CN			
740	F-WWGD	F-HLRX			
741					
742					
743					
744					
745					
746					
747					
748					
749					
750					

DASSAULT FALCON 7X

The Falcon 7X was originally known as the Falcon FNX.

C/n	Identities							
1	F-WFBW	[rolled out 15Feb05; ff 05May05]						
2	F-WTDA	[ff 05Jly05]	(F-HNFG)	HB-JSS				
3	F-WSKY	[ff 20Sep05]		VP-BIL	N56CL			
4	F-WWUA	[ff 08Jun06]	HB-JSZ	F-HDPO	N570RF			
5	F-WWUB	VP-BGG	F-GZLP	N705FJ	F-HFDA	9H-TOO		
6	F-WWUC	(N200L)	N607X	PR-WRM	N191ST			
7	F-WWUD	N70FL	N2016A					
8	F-WWUE	N999BE						
9	F-WWUF	(N9707X)+	[+ ntu marks worn at completion centre]				VP-BVY	TC-YHK
10	F-WWUG	XA-MAR						
11	F-WWUH	VP-BAR	M-ALMA					
12	F-WWUI	HB-JSO	N250LG					
13	F-WWUJ	N907SB	N713L					
14	F-WWUK	VP-BZE						
15	F-WWUL	CS-TLY						
16	F-WWUM	(HB-JSS)+	[+ ntu marks worn at completion centre]				N7707X	
17	F-WWUN	HB-JST						
18	F-WWUO	N273JC						
19	F-WWUP	F-GYDA	F-WWUP	F-HAKA	CS-DTS	N221HJ		
20	F-WWUQ	M-SVNX	OH-FFD	RA-09007				
21	F-WWUR	VP-BEH						
22	F-WWUS	PR-DNZ						
23	F-WWZK	N188SW						
24	F-WWZL	N171EX						
25	F-WWZM	N8000E						
26	F-WWZN	N7MR						
27	F-WWZO	VQ-BFN	N227FJ					
28	F-WWZP	TC-GMM	F-HCRM	N728GH				
29	F-WWZQ	N671WB	N675WB					
30	F-WWZR	CS-DSA	LX-DSA	M-OPDE				
31	F-WWZS	N786CS						
32	F-WWZT	XA-CXW	N564SG					
33	F-WWZU	N7X						
34	F-WWZV	(F-GVRB)	I-AFIT	9H-FCB				
35	F-WWZW	(N100HC)+	[+ ntu marks worn at completion centre]				N207TR	N82RP
36	F-WWZX	G-SRDG						
37	F-WWZY	HB-JSI	N360PZ					
38	F-WWZZ	N55LC						
39	F-WWVK	N900DW						
40	F-WWVL	M-ROLL	SE-DJL					
41	F-WWVM	N741FJ	OO-NAD					
42	F-WWVN	F-HCCX	F-WHLV	OE-IVA	M-YORK			
43	F-WWVO	CS-DSB	J2-HPV					
44	F-WWVP	HB-JLK						
45	F-WWVQ	B-8029						
46	F-WWVR	VQ-BAA						
47	F-WWVS	(CS-DSC)	RA-09009	F-HVIB				
48	F-WWVT	N748FJ	N138BT	VQ-BVS				
49	F-WWUA	VT-RGX						
50	F-WWUB	C-GMGX						
51	F-WWUC	N817X	N9997X					
52	F-WWUD	G-CNUK	N740AC					
53	F-WWVU	N12U						
54	F-WWVV	OY-JDE	F-HLIV	M-SCOT				
55	F-WWVX	OE-LLL	N54TN	PR-CSE				
56	F-WWVY	LX-ZXP						
57	F-WWVZ	OO-AAA	N157BR	C-GCUL				
58	F-WWHA	VQ-BSN						
59	F-WWHB	G-PVHT	SE-DJK					
60	F-WWHC	CS-DTD						
61	F-WWHD	B-8026						
62	F-WWHE	N62FJ	N11HD	N4VF				
63	F-WWHF	N763FJ	B-8027					
64	F-WWHH	VQ-BSO						
65	F-WWHK	C-FAWZ						
66	F-WWHL	(D-AJAB)	OH-FFF	CS-DVX				
67	F-WWUE	HB-JGI						
68	F-WWUG	F-GJLQ	France 68/F-RAFA					
69	F-WWUH	G-CGGN	OH-FFI	OY-FFI				
70	F-WWUJ	C-GRGM						
71	F-WWHM	F-HCLS	RA-09010					
72	F-WWHN	N312P	N312PY	M-HKND				
73	F-WWHO	N787AD	N144AD*					
74	F-WWHP	N906NB	N900NB					

FALCON 7X

C/n	Identities					
75	F-WWHQ	N906SB				
76	F-WWHR	HB-JSN				
77	F-WWHS	D-ACGN	D-APLC			
78	F-WWHT	SE-DJC	OY-RAB			
79	F-WWHU	HZ-SPAG				
80	F-WWUF	HB-JOB				
81	F-WWUI	I-JAMI				
82	F-WWUK	M-YNNS	M-YNNG	N317SK		
83	F-WWUL	VQ-BSP				
84	F-WWUM	VQ-BHA				
85	F-WWUN	OY-VIK				
86	F-WWUS	F-GUJC	France 86/F-RAFB			
87	F-WWUO	HZ-SPAH				
88	F-WWUP	N333KG	LX-TQJ	N887XF	N1933G	
89	F-WWUQ	N966H				
90	F-WWUR	5N-FGU				
91	F-WWZL	M-MNBB				
92	F-WWZM	HZ-OFC6	CS-DSD			
93	F-WWZN	VQ-BGG				
94	F-WWZQ	I-FFRR				
95	F-WWZT	OY-SNZ				
96	F-WWZU	M-SCMG				
97	F-WWZX	LX-MES	M-ZJBT			
98	F-WWNA	(PP-AKT)	N407KT	OY-TSS		
99	F-WWNB	N199FJ	N722AZ			
100	F-WWNC	N15FX	N714K			
101	F-WWND	N940EX	B-8028			
102	F-WWNE	PH-AJX				
103	F-WWNF	N150BC				
104	F-WWVO	A6-SMS	VP-CTG			
105	F-WWVR	G-VITA	G-DYXH	B-8213		
106	F-WWZK	PR-BTG	N106FJ	VP-CSG	M-ABGO	VP-CSG	F-HMOD
107	F-WWZR	A6-MAF	A6-MMF			
108	F-WWZS	VP-CMX	M-ABFM	XT-EBO	F-HLTI	
109	F-WWVL	SX-GRC	F-HMOM			
110	F-WWVM	M-CELT				
111	F-WWVN	SX-DCV	G-IONX	F-GKCT		
112	F-WWVK	HZ-SPAI				
113	F-WWVP	VP-CSJ	F-WHLU	F-HVON	VQ-BSF	
114	F-WWZO	G-UMKA	9H-MAK			
115	F-WWZW	N900JG				
116	F-WWZY	HB-JFN				
117	F-WWZV	EC-LLV				
118	F-WWZZ	LX-AMB				
119	F-WWHA	F-HSAS				
120	F-WWHB	OO-IDY				
121	F-WWHC	OY-EKC				
122	F-WWHE	VP-CIG				
123	F-WWHF	G-SVNX				
124	F-WWHH	OO-EJA				
125	F-WWHL	OE-ILM	D-AFSX	OE-IMF	G-OIMF	
126	F-WWHS	5N-FGV				
127	F-WWHT	V5-GON				
128	F-WWHU	G-ITIM	M-INER	OY-PGA		
129	F-WWUA	SE-DJD	OY-RAD			
130	F-WWUB	N85DN				
131	F-WWUC	N950X				
132	F-WWUD	VQ-BLP				
133	F-WWUG	N733LX	B-8023			
134	F-WWUH	F-HECD				
135	F-WWUL	VQ-BNT				
136	F-WWUM	HZ-SPAJ				
137	F-WWUN	N111HZ				
138	F-WWUS	M-OMAN				
139	F-WWVQ	P4-GIS				
140	F-WWVS	M-AKOL	N777SJ			
141	F-WWVU	VP-CDY				
142	F-WWVV	N142FJ	B-8207	N577JF		
143	F-WWVX	VP-CSW				
144	F-WWVY	F-GYBJ	B-8206			
145	F-WWVZ	N577CF				
146	F-WWHO	PR-PCT	N906TF			
147	F-WWHK	N147FJ	VP-CSX			
148	F-WWHN	G-STMT				
149	F-WWHP	B-8201	N996MS			
150	F-WWHM	N887X				

FALCON 7X

C/n	Identities					
151	F-WWHQ	N151NS	C-FLKX	C-FBNS		
152	F-WWZN	OO-LMG				
153	F-WWUO	(CS-DTT)	N66DD			
154	F-WWUF	CS-DTT				
155	F-WWHD	OY-CLS	F-HPVE			
156	F-WWUE	M-MNCC				
157	F-WWUK	B-8215				
158	F-WWZM	N747RL				
159	F-WWNC	N159FJ	B-8202			
160	F-WWUQ	D-AFPR				
161	F-WWZQ	HB-JSA				
162	F-WWUI	N771RS	PP-RFA	N17XX	N495ZC	
163	F-WWNB	N163FJ	M-OEPL			
164	F-WWZX	CS-DSC				
165	F-WWZP	(VP-CYL)	PR-YVL			
166	F-WWVR	F-HSTF	OO-ABC			
167	F-WWVO	LX-USM	HB-JUC			
168	F-WWZL	N268FJ	M-DTBP			
169	F-WWUP	N783SL				
170	F-WWUR	N889AB				
171	F-WWVT	PP-CFJ				
172	F-WWZR	N1216K	C-FMHL			
173	F-WWNE	N173CN				
174	F-WWZS	N988NW				
175	F-WWNA	(M-ALAA)	(M-LMAA)	VQ-BTV	M-OUNT	
176	F-WWVL	N76FJ	C-GLXC			
177	F-WWZT	B-8209	N166CK			
178	F-WWNF	M-LJGI				
179	F-WWVM	D-ALIL				
180	F-WWVN	N191MD				
181	F-WWVK	HB-JSM				
182	F-WWZY	LX-FDA				
183	F-WWZV	N183MK	VH-MQK	M-GMKM		
184	F-WWHC	SX-JET				
185	F-WWZZ	Ecuador FAE-052				
186	F-WWHE	M-EDIA	M-YJET			
187	F-WWHH	PP-OSM				
188	F-WWHT	F-HVBL				
189	F-WWZO	B-8218				
190	F-WWVP	TC-OIL				
191	F-WWUB	RA-09616				
192	F-WWHS	N192FJ	XA-JHS			
193	F-WW..	[test marks either F-WWHL or F-WWUD]				B-8203
194	F-WWUC	HB-JSL	D-AHGN*			
195	F-WWHU	A6-SMS	F-HZOU			
196	F-WW..	[test marks either F-WWHL or F-WWUD]				OE-IRR
197	F-WWHB	LX-TQJ	N843S*			
198	F-WWUS	OY-FWO				
199	F-WWUA	B-8216				
200	F-WWHA	M-ABFX	3A-MGA			
201	F-WWUH	(PT-YVL)	VP-CUH			
202	F-WWVX	N977GS				
203	F-WWHF	N24TH				
204	F-WWUL	VP-CBY				
205	F-WWUM	PP-VEL				
206	F-WWZU	N559AM				
207	F-WWHR	F-HGHF	(OO-AAM)	M-RTFS		
208	F-WWZK	N817X				
209	F-WWVQ	B-8205				
210	F-WWND	VP-CGS				
211	F-WWUG	N496AC				
212	F-WWVV	B-8211				
213	F-WWVZ	OO-TOI	M-MNAA	HB-JFQ		
214	F-WWHO	PR-NAK				
215	F-WWZN	N715FJ	M-WING			
216	F-WWZW	M-ARVY				
217	F-WWHD	VH-CRW				
218	F-WWUE	HB-JSE				
219	F-WWZQ	VP-CBG	T7-CBG			
220	F-WWVS	N120FJ	VP-CJS			
221	F-WWZX	N487C				
222	F-WWUF	N37TY				
223	F-WWVY	F-HEXR				
224	F-WWHN	M-FALZ				
225	F-WWZP	TC-SZA				
226	F-WWUP	VP-CLS				

FALCON 7X

C/n	Identities			
227	F-WWHK	TC-MMM		
228	F-WWUN	9H-ZSN		
229	F-WWHM	M-ISRK	LX-ISR	RA-09603
230	F-WWHQ	M-IAMI		
231	F-WWUO	OH-WIX		
232	F-WWZM	TN-ELS		
233	F-WWUI			
234	F-WWVO	(F-HLBG)	N814TP	
235	F-WWNE	N606TJ		
236	F-WWZR	OY-EJD		
237	F-WWVT	PP-DBS		
238	F-WWNC	OE-IPW		
239	F-WWHP			
240	F-WWVM	N269BK		
241	F-WWVK	N2237X		
242	F-WWUJ	LX-LMF		
243	F-WWUR			
244	F-WWVL	N1227W	N939TY	
245	F-WWHA	P4-SCM		
246	F-WWUQ			
247	F-WWVN	RA-09090		
248	F-WWVP	N347BD		
249	F-WWHC	N343MG		
250	F-WWUC	N998SS		
251	F-WWNF	B-8217		
252	F-WWZS	XA-GNI		
253	F-WWHE	RA-09601		
254	F-WWUB	TC-KMR		
255	F-WWVR	N716CG		
256	F-WWHT	RA-09602		
257	F-WWHH	(PP-CSC)	VP-CZS	
258	F-WWHU	F-HIPK		
259	F-WWVU	PH-TLP		
260	F-WWZL	N260FJ	TC-LHO	
261	F-WWZT	XA-GOR		
262	F-WWZV	N770LM		
263	F-WWUD	A6-MBS		
264	F-WWHB	RA-09009		
265	F-WWUS	N343AP		
266	F-WWUL	M-TINK		
267	F-WWUA	VP-CMW		
268	F-WWUE	VP-CRS	D-AGBE	
269	F-WWUF	VP-CDP		
270	F-WWUG	VP-CHW		
271	F-WWUH	F-HCMR	OO-GPP	
272	F-WWUJ	M-WANG		
273	F-WWUK	OO-JUK	LX-SBO*	
274	F-WWUM	F-HMAS		
275	F-WWUN	RA-09607		
276	F-WWUO	N50NL		
277	F-WWUP	G-MATO		
278	F-WWUB			
279	F-WWUC			
280	F-WWHA			
281				
282				
283				
284				
285				
286				
287				
288				
289				
290				
291				
292				
293				
294				
295				
296				
297				
298				
299				
300				

DASSAULT FALCON 8X

C/n	Identities		
401	F-WWQA	[rolled out 17Dec14; ff 6Feb15]	
402	F-WWQB	[ff 30Mar15]	
403	F-WWQC	[ff 11May15]	N8X
404	F-WWQD	F-HFSD	
405	F-WWQE	SX-CGR	
406	F-WWQF	(PR-JQF)	N406EX
407	F-WWQG	A6-SMS	
408	F-WWQH		
409	F-WWQI	G-XION	
410	F-WWQJ	VT-FCN	
411	F-WWQK	VQ-BFD	
412	F-WWQL	(PR-BVA)	D-AGBA
413	F-WWQM		
414	F-WWQN		
415	F-WWQO		
416	F-WWQP		
417	F-WWQQ		
418	F-WWQR		
419	F-WWQS		
420	F-WWQT		
421	F-WWQU		
422	F-WWQV		
423	F-WWQW		
424	F-WWQX		
425	F-WWQY		
426	F-WWQZ		
427	F-WWNA		
428	F-WWNB		
429	F-WWNC		
430			
431			
432			
433			
434			
435			
436			
437			
438			
439			
440			
441			
442			
443			
444			
445			
446			
447			
448			
449			
450			

ECLIPSE AVIATION ECLIPSE 500

C/n	Identities			
EX500-100	N500EA	[rolled out Albuquerque-Double Eagle II 13Jly02; ff 26Aug02; retired Oct03, tt 55hrs]		
EX500-101	(N502EA)	"N500EA"	[Not completed following decision to change from Williams EJ22 to P&W PWF610F engines; used as display exhibit]	
EX500-102	[Not built following decision to change from Williams EJ22 to P&W PWF610F engines]			
EX500-103	N502EA	[ff 14Apr05]		
EX500-104	[static test airframe completed 11May05]			
EX500-105	[fatigue test airframe completed 20Dec05]			
EX500-106	N505EA	[Beta test aircraft 1; ff 09Jly05]		
EX500-107	N506EA	[Beta test aircraft 2; ff 24Aug05]		
EX500-108	N503EA	[ff 31Dec04]		
EX500-109	N504EA	[ff 21Apr05; preserved at TWI Ltd headquarters, Granta Park, Cambridge, UK]		
000001	N508JA			
000002	N126DJ	N102TE	N147KN	N11PC
000003	N816KD			
000004	N229BW	N403LB	N440NE	N941CM
000005	N504RS			
000006	N109DJ	N106TE	N375KD	
000007	N110DJ	(N107TE)	TC-KEA	
000008	N941NC			
000009	N513EA	N111S*		
000010	N500VK	XB-ODY		
000011	N777VE	N80NE	N96PD	
000012	N651FC	N61HF		
000013	N317BH	N770TE	N878BW	
000014	N705PT			
000015	N515MP			
000016	N15ND	N320LA	N58KY	
000017	N17AE			
000018	N875NA	N140NE		
000019	N519EJ			
000020	N115DJ	N220TE	N312BL	
000021	N116DJ	N521TE	N800TE	
000022	N119DJ	N522TE	N22NJ	
000023	N130DJ	N223TE	2-LIFE	
000024	N561EA			
000025	N546BW			
000026	N612KB			
000027	N502LT	N563MJ		
000028	N963JG	N280NE	N984CF	
000029	N55BX			
000030	N768JF			
000031	N531EA			
000032	N80TF			
000033	N131DJ	N133TE	N51GJ	N51GQ
000034	N132DJ	N134TE	N760NE	N124KK
000035	N134DJ	N135TE	N889CM	
000036	N135DJ	N136TE		
000037	N136DJ	N37TE	PR-CCA	
000038	N112EA			
000039	N858GS			
000040	N444RL			
000041	N541LB			
000042	N168TT	[w/o Nome, AK, 01Jun11; parted out Henderson, NV]		
000043	N62RC			
000044	N489JC	N53WA		
000045	N500CD			
000046	N6100			
000047	N218JT			
000048	N570RG			
000049	N549AF			
000050	N456MF			
000051	N500UK			
000052	N502ET			
000053	N514EA	[cx 08Mar13, wfu]		
000054	N139DJ	N54TE		
000055	N141DJ	N255TE	N99XG	
000056	N142DJ	N156TE	(N868SB)	N838SB
000057	N145DJ	(N57TE)	N411VP	(AP-...)
000058	N146DJ	N158TE		
000059	N147DJ	N159TE	N322PL	
000060	N429CC			
000061	N148DJ	(N61TE)	N434MT	
000062	N150DJ	N62TE		
000063	N778VW			
000064	N717LK	N454HA		

ECLIPSE 500

C/n	Identities			
000065	N23PJ	N65TE	N384TC	
000066	N370P			
000067	N568PB			
000068	(N370P)	N615RH		
000069	N71MT			
000070	N570EA			
000071	N152DJ	N508JP		
000072	N153DJ	N94GA	N843TE	
000073	N156DJ	N173TE	N505XX	N73EJ
000074	N158DJ	(N74TE)	N179TD	
000075	N575CC			
000076	N576EA			
000077	N160DJ	N77TE		
000078	N161DJ	N78TE	N45DJ	
000079	N162DJ	(N168TE)		
000080	N580WC			
000081	N163DJ	N565FP		
000082	N382EA			
000083	N38DA			
000084	N509JA			
000085	N778TC			
000086	N990NA			
000087	N50EJ			
000088	N457TB			
000089	N44EJ	N316CP		
000090	N2486B			
000091	N54KJ			
000092	N355BM			
000093	(N457TB)	N233MT	(N7601B)	
000094	N417CG			
000095	N317DJ	N995TE	N581VC	
000096	N464PG			
000097	N502TS			
000098	N598EA			
000099	N911MX			
000100	N9922F			
000101	N539RM			
000102	N277G			
000103	N333MY	[w/o 30Jul08 West Chester/Brandywine, PA; parted out by White Inds, Bates City, MO]		
000104	N117EA			
000105	N522DK			
000106	N516EA			
000107	N706PT			
000108	N812MJ	XB-OKU		
000109	N777ZY			
000110	N501DX			
000111	N175JE			
000112	N112EJ			
000113	N717HD			
000114	N197AR			
000115	N727HD			
000116	N75EA			
000117	N117UH			
000118	N105LB			
000119	N815WT			
000120	N27052			
000121	N855MS			
000122	N164MW			
000123	N696NA	N352BB		
000124	N227G			
000125	N370EA			
000126	N953JB			
000127	N261DC			
000128	N528EA			
000129	N500DG			
000130	N322JG	N411TE	N58VL	
000131	N67NV	ZS-YTC		
000132	N964S			
000133	N21EK	N247SS		
000134	N800EJ			
000135	N3MT			
000136	N136EA	(N326LA)		
000137	N36FD			
000138	N100VA			
000139	N500MM			
000140	N100MZ	N561MJ		

ECLIPSE 500

C/n	Identities			
000141	N504TC			
000142	N2711H	ZS-DKS	[w/o nr Swellendam, South Africa, 07Dec15]	
000143	N533DK			
000144	N545MA	N90NE	2-JSEG	
000145	N145EA			
000146	N146EA			
000147	N414TW			
000148	N148LG			
000149	N149EA			
000150	N920GB			
000151	N85SM			
000152	N113EA	EC-LHC	N113EA	
000153	N800AZ			
000154	N66BX			
000155	N114EA	EC-LET	N114EA	
000156	N234EA	N562MJ		
000157	N500CE			
000158	N500ZH			
000159	N727CW			
000160	N2YU			
000161	N448HC			
000162	N224ZQ			
000163	N63AD			
000164	N884AM			
000165	N669CM	N450RB		
000166	N23FK			
000167	N800JR			
000168	N568EA	(N335LA)		
000169	N166EA			
000170	N170EA			
000171	N58EH			
000172	N964JG			
000173	N173PD			
000174	N21YP	N21YR		
000175	N512MB			
000176	N9900R			
000177	N177EA	D-ILAC		
000178	N721MA	N721NA	N48KY	
000179	N220BW	N207TB		
000180	N712WG			
000181	N99KP			
000182	N177CK			
000183	N555EJ			
000184	N118EA	EC-LII	N118EA	N776PJ
000185	N500FB	(N808KD)		
000186	N204ZQ			
000187	N187EA			
000188	N652FC			
000189	N435NF			
000190	N190CK	TC-ATS		
000191	N678PS			
000192	N61DT			
000193	N193EA	N125DB		
000194	N70EJ			
000195	N227LS			
000196	N508CP			
000197	N218G			
000198	N888DZ	T7-AEB		
000199	N165DJ	N120EA	(N477JN)	
000200	N166DJ	N119EA		
000201	N167DJ	N201EA		
000202	N169DJ	N202EA		
000203	N883LC			
000204	N607LM			
000205	N653FC	N740DM		
000206	N977VH			
000207	N207EA			
000208	N55TJ			
000209	N209EA			
000210	N140EA	N160FF		
000211	N500VH			
000212	N212EA			
000213	N888ZY			
000214	N301MK			
000215	N762DL	(N792DL)		
000216	N375ET			

ECLIPSE 500

C/n	Identities		
000217	N7FY		
000218	N142EA	N165DL	N718RB
000219	N219EA		
000220	N724ML	N18BM	
000221	N666TM		
000222	N161BB		
000223	N141EA		
000224	N722TD		
000225	N5005	N646WT	
000226	N226BR	T7-AEA	
000227	N654FC	(N227UH)	
000228	N478F		
000229	N229EA		
000230	N256DP		
000231	N619RJ		
000232	N707ES	(PR-SDD)	
000233	N869AW		
000234	N461N		
000235	N747LG		
000236	N67LP		
000237	N828PA		
000238	N989RF		
000239	N867K		
000240	N929KD		
000241	N279E		
000242	N23VA		
000243	N121G		
000244	N20KS		
000245	N853TC	N84CM	
000246	N144EA	D-INDY	
000247	N207WM	N287WM	
000248	N889BW		
000249	N29MR		
000250	N163BB	N465DG	
000251	N147EA	LV-GWT*	
000252	N214MS		
000253	N427X		
000254	N618SR	N290JP	
000255	N49PL		
000256	N375SH		
000257	N257K		
000258	N257AK		
000259	N84UR		
000260	N877PM		
000261	N159EA	N985AS	N261TD
000262	N511ED	N262DJ	
000263	(N522EA)	[aircraft not completed; components used in Eclipse 550 c/n 550-0263]	
000264	(N29SS)	[aircraft not completed; components used in Eclipse 550 c/n 550-0264]	
000265	(N767PW)	[aircraft not completed; components used in Eclipse 550 c/n 550-0265]	
000266	N143EA	N263CA	
000267	N533GT		

Production complete following the liquidation of Eclipse Aviation in February 2009. Work had begun on the following aircraft, most with N-numbers assigned, but they were not completed:

000268	(N106WH)	[components used in Eclipse 550 c/n 550-0268]
000269	(N500YD)	[components used in Eclipse 550 c/n 550-0269]
000270	(N202JG)	[components used in Eclipse 550 c/n 550-0270]
000271	[components used in Eclipse 550 c/n 550-0271]	
000272	(N444EJ)	[components used in Eclipse 550 c/n 550-0272]
000273	[components used in Eclipse 550 c/n 550-0273]	
000274	(N610PW)	[components used in Eclipse 550 c/n 550-0274]
000275	(N89RF)	[components used in Eclipse 550 c/n 550-0275]
000276	[components used in Eclipse 550 c/n 550-0276]	
000277	(N510JA)	[components used in Eclipse 550 c/n 550-0277]
000278	(N278JC)	[components used in Eclipse 550 c/n 550-0278]
000279	(N10HH)	[components used in Eclipse 550 c/n 550-0279]
000280	(N502BH)	[components used in Eclipse 550 c/n 550-0280]
000281	[components intended for Eclipse 550 c/n 550-0281 but not completed]	
000282	[components used in Eclipse 550 c/n 550-0282]	
000283	[components used in Eclipse 550 c/n 550-0283]	
000284	[components used in Eclipse 550 c/n 550-0284]	
000297	(N79EA)	[aircraft not built]

ECLIPSE AEROSPACE ECLIPSE 550

New company Eclipse Aerospace resumed Eclipse production with the model 550 in June 2012, being the Eclipse 500 airframe with uprated avionics. Fuselages, tail units and wingsets will be built by PZL Mielec in Poland and shipped to Albuquerque, NM, for final assembly.

C/n	Identities			
550-0263	(N263EJ)	N550LJ	N550AD	
550-0264	N279EJ	N264EJ	N229BW	
550-0265	N265EA	N656FP		
550-0268	N268EJ	N268EM		
550-0269	N285EA	N269EJ	D-ILAT	
550-0270	(N270EJ)	N550UZ	N260NE	N999NS
550-0271	N271EJ	N80WP		
550-0272	N272EJ			
550-0273	(N273EJ)	N771MT		
550-0274	N274EJ	N288JR		
550-0275	N275EJ	N113HX		
550-0276	N276EJ	N322BH		
550-0277	N277EJ	N317SA		
550-0278	N278EJ	N146HA		
550-0279	N279EJ			
550-0280	N280EJ	N450NE		
550-0281	(N281EJ)	[fuselage noted on production line Sep13 but not completed]		
550-0282	N282EJ	N826ES		
550-0283	N283EJ	N777VE		
550-0284	N284EJ	N284BG		
550-1001	N550F	[first Eclipse 550 built from 'scratch']		
550-1002	N150NE			
550-1003	N160NE	OE-FMO		
550-1004	N170NE	D-ILAV		
550-1005	N190NE	N484BH		
550-1006	N200NE	N550UZ		
550-1007	N210NE	N550SE		
550-1008	N230NE	N550NJ		
550-1009	N240NE	(N550NJ)	N550DM	
550-1010	N880NE			
550-1011	N610PW			
550-1012	N34WP			
550-1013	N426CB			
550-1014				
550-1015				
550-1016				
550-1017				
550-1018				
550-1019				
550-1020				
550-1021				
550-1022				
550-1023				
550-1024				
550-1025				
550-1026				
550-1027				
550-1028				
550-1029				
550-1030				

EMBRAER EMB-500 PHENOM 100

C/n	Identities				
50099801	PP-XPH	[rolled out 16Jun07; ff 26Jul07; wfu, preserved Rio de Janeiro/Jacarepagua, Brazil]			
50000001	PP-XOM	[ff 26Sep07]			
50000002	PP-XOJ	[ff 21Dec07]			
50000003	PP-XOH	[ff 26Mar08; wfu; preserved Botucatu, Brazil]]			
50000004	PP-XOG				
50000005	PP-XON	PP-SGF			
50000006	PP-XOO	N131ML	N175EW	N580JH	
50000007	PP-XOQ	PR-DDO			
50000008	PP-XOR	N82DU			
50000009	PP-XPD	N26SH	C-FLOX		
50000010	PP-XPE	N673DC			
50000011	PP-XPF	N68ER			
50000012	PP-XPG	N168FG	N6DQ	N168FG	N933MA
50000013	PT-ZYA	N76EM			
50000014	PT-ZYB	(N777SG)	Pakistan V-4102		
50000015	PT-ZYC	N100PZ	N247SK		
50000016	PT-ZYD	N484JH			
50000017	PT-ZYE	Pakistan V-4101			
50000018	PT-ZYF	N600AS	N665AS		
50000019	PT-ZYG	N458LM			
50000020	PT-ZYH	N73DB			
50000021	PT-ZYI	N300LJ			
50000022	PT-ZYT	N389MW	N522EP		
50000023	PT-ZYX	N108JA			
50000024	PT-ZYL	M-INXY	G-NUDD	N390TP	
50000025	PT-TFA	N605AS			
50000026	PT-TFB	PT-MAH	N129GD		
50000027	PT-TFC	PR-DCJ			
50000028	PT-TFD	N190BW			
50000029	PT-TFE	N200XT	VH-YYT	N899JC	N700AJ
50000030	PT-TFF	N102PA	N511WT		
50000031	PT-TFG	PP-LGT			
50000032	PT-TFH	PR-IVI			
50000033	PT-TFI	PP-CTC			
50000034	PT-TFJ	PR-DHC			
50000035	PT-TFK	SX-NSS	C-FLIX		
50000036	PT-TFL	N600HT			
50000037	PT-TFM	N100WX			
50000038	PT-TFN	N353SB			
50000039	PT-TFO	N514AF			
50000040	PT-TFP	D-IPHE	M-KELY		
50000041	PT-TFQ	N777BF	N630EE	N328MY	N685AS
50000042	PT-TFR	PR-FBS			
50000043	PT-TFS	(EI-JBA)	PR-NPP		
50000044	PT-TFT	N610AS	N639AS		
50000045	PT-TFU	N620AS	N208KB*		
50000046	PT-TFV	N574JS			
50000047	PT-TFW	Pakistan V-4103			
50000048	PT-TFX	PR-CSW			
50000049	PT-TFY	PP-AFM	[w/o 12Oct09 Angra dos Reis, Brazil; fuselage stored Sorocaba, Brazil]		
50000050	PT-TFZ	HB-VWQ	N981WA	N316BG	
50000051	PT-TGA	N575JS			
50000052	PT-TGB	N430TB			
50000053	PT-TGC	N999RN			
50000054	PT-TGD	PR-DRC			
50000055	PT-TGE	G-DRBN	SP-AVP		
50000056	PT-TGF	G-SRBN	N80EJ	(N936SM)	
50000057	PT-TGG	N576JS	N224MD	[w/o Sedona, AZ, 25May11; to scrapyard near Phoenix Sky Harbor airport, AZ]	
50000058	PT-TGH	N27WP			
50000059	PT-TGI	N206AH			
50000060	PT-TGJ	(EI-EHN)	PP-ELE		
50000061	PT-TGK	N644RM	(N644RP)		
50000062	PT-TGL	(EI-EHO)	HB-JFK	D-IHER*	
50000063	PT-TGM	N32KC			
50000064	PT-TGN	N579JS			
50000065	PT-TGO	PR-DAY			
50000066	PT-TGP	(PR-SKD)	PP-SKD	N237JA	N321VA
50000067	PT-TGQ	N629AS	N557TC	N647AS	
50000068	PT-TGR	PR-VEL			
50000069	PT-TGS	ZS-STS			
50000070	PT-TGT	N241DE			
50000071	PT-TGU	N226CP	N226KV		
50000072	PT-TGV	N777JQ			
50000073	PT-TGW	(EI-EHS)	PP-IME		

EMBRAER EMB-500 PHENOM 100

C/n	Identities			
50000074	PT-TGX	N784JP		
50000075	PT-TGY	N639AS	N876JC	
50000076	PT-TGZ	(EI-EHT)	PR-SPJ	
50000077	PT-THA	PR-PTA	N770EC	N770BR
50000078	(PT-THB)	[not built, cancelled order]		
50000079	PT-THC	N580JS		
50000080	PT-THD	YV2609		
50000081	PT-THE	N59PW		
50000082	PT-THF	N100EQ	[w/o Gaithersburg/Montgomery County apt, MD, 8Dec14]	
50000083	PT-THG	PR-JAJ		
50000084	PT-THH	N725MW	N600CS	N608CS
50000085	PT-THI	PR-IEI	N524NC	
50000086	PT-THJ	(EI-EHU)	PP-MRV	
50000087	PT-THK	N149GK		
50000088	PT-THL	N210FF		
50000089	PT-THM	N354RX		
50000090	PT-THN	N91TQ	N56SB	
50000091	PT-THO	N6745		
50000092	PT-THP	M-PHNM	OE-FOM	9H-FOM
50000093	PT-THQ	PR-UUT		
50000094	PT-THR	PR-LMP		
50000095	PT-THS	OO-NOA	PT-THS	PR-NTO
50000096	PT-THT	PR-MJD		
50000097	PT-THU	N208DX		
50000098	PT-THV	PR-DLM		
50000099	PT-THW	PT-FCC		
50000100	PT-THX	OE-FAM	9H-FAM	
50000101	PT-THY	PR-ADQ		
50000102	PT-THZ	N102EP		
50000103	PT-TIH	N511WK		
50000104	PT-TII	PP-KPL		
50000105	PT-TIJ	N67WG	N932MA	
50000106	PT-TIK	N175EM	HP-500E	N175EM
50000107	PT-TIL	N926JK		
50000108	PT-TIM	PR-OFP		
50000109	PT-TIN	PP-VDP		
50000110	PT-TIO	N581JS		
50000111	PT-TIP	N723GB		
50000112	PT-TIQ	M-YTOY	G-SVRN	
50000113	PT-TIR	Pakistan V-4104		
50000114	PT-TIS	N645AS		
50000115	PT-TIT	CS-DTC		
50000116	PT-TIU	N917LJ	N100NV	
50000117	PT-TIV	N777ZA	N636SD	N1PB*
50000118	PT-TIW	N663LS	N627DB	
50000119	(PT-TIX)	[not built, cancelled order]		
50000120	PT-TIY	(F-HDMG)	PR-DFC	
50000121	PT-TIZ	N130EC		
50000122	PT-TYA	(HB-VWS)	OE-FGR	N991CA
50000123	PT-TYB	N661EP		
50000124	PT-TYC	N190HL	N188TM	
50000125	PR-CPC			
50000126	PP-KKA			
50000127	(PT-FQA)	PT-TYD	PR-OVD	D-IAAR
50000128	PT-FQB	N43AG		
50000129	PT-FQC	N43EP		
50000130	PT-FQD	N600PB	CS-DVS	
50000131	PT-FQE	N583JS		
50000132	PT-FQF	PH-PST	(D-IAAB)	
50000133	PT-FQG	N80EJ	N637AS	
50000134	PT-FQH	PP-VIP	OK-VAN	
50000135	PT-FQI	N582JS		
50000136	PT-FQJ	N937DM	(N536EC)	C-GVJV
50000137	PT-FQK	N100FZ	(N69HT)	
50000138	PT-FQL	N585JS		
50000139	PT-FQM	N988BC		
50000140	PT-FQN	N584JS		
50000141	PT-FQO	N100FF		
50000142	PT-FQP	N893MW	N917MM	
50000143	PT-FQQ	N888PT	D-ICSH	
50000144	PT-FQR	PR-PNM		
50000145	PT-FQS	M-KICK	G-VKGO	N63007
50000146	PT-FQT	G-CGNP	N724RN	
50000147	PT-FQU	OO-GJP	D-ISTP	
50000148	PT-FQV	N623DT		
50000149	PT-FQW	N646AS		

EMBRAER EMB-500 PHENOM 100

C/n	Identities						
50000150	PT-FQX	N86DC	N427RR	N89JJ			
50000151	PT-FQY	G-RAAL	N196EC	N299PP			
50000152	PT-FQZ	PR-PCM					
50000153	PT-FUA	N121PZ					
50000154	PT-FUB	N21SB					
50000155	PT-FUC	PR-TPA					
50000156	PT-FUD	PR-JJD					
50000157	PT-FUE	N665AS	N629JJ				
50000158	PT-FUF	PR-VPJ					
50000159	PT-FUG	N525EC	N367ER				
50000160	PT-FUH	PR-PHD					
50000161	PT-FUI	PT-GCP					
50000162	PT-FUJ	M-MACH	D-IAAT				
50000163	PT-FUK	PR-BET					
50000164	PT-FUL	PP-MOR					
50000165	PT-FUM	G-PHNM					
50000166	PT-FUN	(G-COQI)	N288DX				
50000167	PT-FUO	PR-JIP					
50000168	PT-FUP	N668AS	N500TB				
50000169	PT-FUQ	(JY-AWG)	N161PA				
50000170	PT-FUR	N170AP					
50000171	PT-FUS	N625EL	C-GXMP	C-GSBJ			
50000172	PT-FUT	XA-UOB	N218RG				
50000173	PT-FUU	N173GH					
50000174	PT-FUV	PT-FLX					
50000175	PT-FUW	PR-PHE					
50000176	PT-FUX	N648DX					
50000177	PT-FUY	OO-MCV	N142TL	(N750LC)			
50000178	PT-FUZ	N88DW	N784KS				
50000179	PT-FYA	G-ROOB	OE-FHT	N646TG	N199BA	N179PH	N426FC
50000180	PT-FYB	OE-FTF	N720MV	D-IAAB			
50000181	PT-FYC	N400PZ					
50000182	PT-FYD	N669AS					
50000183	PT-FYE	N586JS					
50000184	PT-FYF	N450JF					
50000185	PT-FYG	(PP-WAJ)	G-RUBO	OE-FHO	G-ITSU		
50000186	PT-FYH	PP-WAJ	N9990M				
50000187	PT-FYI	OO-HPG	G-LGMG	9H-LGM			
50000188	PT-FYJ	N670AS	N830NF	N175EW			
50000189	(PT-FYK)	[not built, cancelled order]					
50000190	PT-FYL	OH-EPA					
50000191	(PT-FYM)	[not built, cancelled order]					
50000192	PT-FYN	VT-IAJ	N264AG				
50000193	PT-FYO	OE-FGV	9H-FGV				
50000194	PT-FYP	N649DX					
50000195	(PT-FYQ)	[not built, cancelled order]					
50000196	PT-FYR	OO-MAS	[w/o Berlin/Schoenefeld, Germany, 15Feb13]			N508ML	[parted out Denton, TX]
50000197	PT-FYS	PR-FIL					
50000198	(PT-FYT)	[not built, cancelled order]					
50000199	PR-REX						
50000200	(PT-FYU)	[not built, cancelled order]					
50000201	PT-FYV	(PR-TED)	OH-EPB				
50000202	PR-TED						
50000203	PT-FYW	VT-IAG	N524KA				
50000204	PT-FYX	VT-AVS					
50000205	PT-FYY	N4200	VT-AJI	[dbr by floodwater, Chennai, India, 01Dec15]			N963M
50000206	PT-FYZ	VH-PNM					
50000207	(PT-PYA)	[not built, cancelled order]					
50000208	(PT-PYB)	[not built, cancelled order]					
50000209	(PT-PYC)	[not built, cancelled order]					
50000210	PT-PYD	VT-SFM					
50000211	(PT-PYE)	[not built, cancelled order]					
50000212	(PT-PYF)	[not built, cancelled order]					
50000213	PT-PYG	N996LP	N996LF	N717RS			
50000214	PT-PYH	C-GYMP					
50000215	PT-PYI	D-IAAD					
50000216	PT-PYJ	N899DX					
50000217	(PT-PYK)	[not built, cancelled order]					
50000218	PT-PYL	N222GP	N387MB				
50000219	PT-PYM	PR-RHB					
50000220	PT-PYN	N100PU					
50000221	PT-PYO	PP-UBS					
50000222	PT-PYP	N101FG					
50000223	PT-PYQ	N615SM	N456RF				
50000224	(PR-ENY)	C-FSTP	N39K				
50000225	PR-ARR						

EMBRAER EMB-500 PHENOM 100

C/n	Identities					
50000226	PT-LBM	N108MG	N109LE			
50000227	PT-LBR	PP-BIO				
50000228	PT-LBS	N630AS				
50000229	PT-LBV	N85JG				
50000230	PT-LBL					
50000231	PT-LBZ	(PP-MAS)	PR-VFC			
50000232	PP-LBQ	N244MD				
50000233	PP-LBW	PP-BGG				
50000234	PP-LBX	PP-COR				
50000235	PT-TDJ	N525MN				
50000236	(PR-VBS)	PR-TLS				
50000237	PT-TDL	VH-FJP				
50000238	PT-TDM	N238KJ	VT-TSK	[dbr by floodwater, Chennai, India,01Dec15]	N964M	
50000239	PT-TDN	N225AS				
50000240	(PT-TDO)	[not built, cancelled order]				
50000241	PT-TDP	N19SG				
50000242	PT-TDQ	PR-PER				
50000243	PT-TDR	OO-OTU	D-IAAY			
50000244	PT-TDS	PR-TDV				
50000245	PT-TES	D-IAAW				
50000246	N602EE	N600AS				
50000247	PT-TGO	C-FCEX	N121PC			
50000248	PT-TGP	N917NS	(D-IAAT)			
50000249	[instructional airframe]					
50000250	PT-TJK	UR-ALB	4L-ALF	N861CB		
50000251	[instructional airframe]					
50000252	PT-TJL	N74GH	C-FMPU			
50000253	PT-TJM	UR-ALA	N860CB	N303MT		
50000254	(PT-TJN)	[not built, cancelled order]				
50000255	N255EE	C-GYMD	C-GYMT	LV-GUD		
50000256	PP-NIV					
50000257	PT-TJO	PR-IMR				
50000258	PT-TJP	N787PJ				
50000259	PT-TJQ	N161PL				
50000260	PT-TNO	(N260AL)	N888WS	N851RV		
50000261	PT-TNP	PP-JJB				
50000262	(PT-TNQ)	[not built, cancelled order]				
50000263	PT-TNR	F-HCJE				
50000264	(PT-TNS)	PT-MMP				
50000265	(PT-TNT)	C-GTLP	C-GTLG	N611EC		
50000266	(PT-TNU)	PR-REV				
50000267	(PT-TNV)	N670AS				
50000268	PT-TNW	N131BV				
50000269	PT-TNJ	N452AR				
50000270	(PT-TOA)	N60312	N999TN			
50000271	PT-TPX	XB-MRQ	XB-MUL	XA-ASS		
50000272	N60318	XA-TPA				
50000273	PT-TPY	PT-HRI				
50000274	N161CE					
50000275	PT-TPZ	PT-TAT				
50000276	PT-TRD	PT-FSF				
50000277	HP-1776	HP-1776AJQ	N88FW			
50000278	PT-TRG	PP-LMH				
50000279	PT-TSX	PT-STR				
50000280	N316N					
50000281	PT-TUA	D-IMOR				
50000282	PT-TOJ	PR-LIQ				
50000283	N6004N	N1008U	HP-1778	HP-1778AJQ	N81YA	F-HTLS
50000284	(PT-TAN)	PP-OLY				
50000285	N285GC					
50000286	N60126	N10153	HP-1779	HP-1779AJQ	LV-GQN	
50000287	PP-JLS	PR-EBK	N906KB			
50000288	PT-TAR	D-ILAP				
50000289	N289EE	N289RZ				
50000290	N6014A	N1015G	N520RB	N725TW		
50000291	N60231	N48VC				
50000292	PT-TAS	HB-VRV				
50000293	N6051D	N1015J	N221AA	YR-DDM		
50000294	N60298	N900WS	N435SC			
50000295	N60237	N10160	N100RY	D-IBSL		
50000296	N60231	C-GSAM				
50000297	PR-EAT*					
50000298	N60318	N214PC				
50000299	N6032F	N1016M	C-FGGH	N677MS	N88LV	
50000300	PT-TBO	N911YA				
50000301						

EMBRAER EMB-500 PHENOM 100

C/n	Identities		
50000302	N1018S	N6005Y	N123RX
50000303			
50000304	N1019L	N8KD	
50000305	N1019Q	N305PL	
50000306	N10200	VH-LWZ	
50000307	PR-VOG*		
50000308			
50000309	PP-EMB		
50000310	N60126	N390EE	N575JT
50000311	N1020G	N60312	N374N
50000312			
50000313	N984EP	XA-JTL	
50000314	N6051D	N5237R	
50000315	N60318	N122CR	
50000316	N823CR	N48KG	
50000317	N330XX	N44WS	
50000318	(PR-PAA)	PR-FBU	
50000319	N305PG	T7-VYT	
50000320	PR-PAO	PR-CMQ	
50000321	N6004N	N321KM	
50000322	PR-PAP	PP-JEL	
50000323	PR-PBH	N914TQ	
50000324	(PT-TJG)	PR-FYB	
50000325	PR-PBT	PP-JSZ	
50000326	PP-VRL		
50000327	(PP-AHW)	PR-HNZ	
50000328	PP-AHW		
50000329	4X-CMN		
50000330	PT-RMI		
50000331	N531EE	C-GDCC	
50000332	PR-TDM		
50000333	PR-PBM	N7913M	
50000334	N500RB		
50000335	N356N		
50000336	PR-RLM	[300th Phenom 100 delivered]	
50000337	PR-PHX		
50000338	PR-PCG	N826E	VT-ZAP
50000339	(PR-PHX)	PP-IVN	
50000340	(PP-IVN)	PR-PCH	PR-PLO
50000341	PR-PCN	PR-PLR	
50000342	PR-PCI	XA-ATT	XA-ATJ
50000343	PR-PCP	N658MB	
50000344	PR-PCQ	N589WT	
50000345	PR-PCR	PR-PMK	
50000346	PP-MKB		
50000347	PR-PCY	XA-MSO	
50000348	N548EE	N192BL	
50000349	PR-LFL	N250YB	
50000350	PR-PEI	PR-JIE	
50000351	PR-PEJ	PP-WPM	
50000352	PR-PEW	N348N	
50000353	PR-PFF	F-HSBL	
50000354	PR-PFI	F-HLRY	
50000355	PR-PFH	N914EG	
50000356	PR-PFL	B-3113	
50000357	PR-PFS	N188MR	
50000358	PR-PFT	N615DM	
50000359	N234FP		
50000360	PR-PFW	N598LG	
50000361	PR-PGE	N167ER	
50000362	PR-PGI	N100MZ	
50000363	PR-PGJ	VT-KLJ*	
50000364	(PR-PGK)	N6005Y	
50000365	PR-PAE	D-IDAS	
50000366	PR-PGK	F-HPBM*	
50000367	PR-PGP	F-HMAU	
50000368	SP-IAF		
50000369	PR-PGV	A6-EFC	
50000370	D-IUCR		
50000371	PR-PGY	A6-EFB	
50000372	(D-IUCR)	N489EE	
50000373	PR-PGZ	A6-EFA	
50000374	PR-PHF	A6-MPL	
50000375	PR-PHK		
50000376	N48KE		
50000377	N709EE	PR-ING	

EMBRAER EMB-500 PHENOM 100

C/n	Identities	
50000378	N60126	
50000379	N151GS	
50000380	N713TE	
50000381	PR-PHO	PP-CMC
50000382		
50000383		
50000384		
50000385	N600CS	
50000386		
50000387		
50000388		
50000389		
50000390		
50000391		
50000392		
50000393		
50000394		
50000395		
50000396		
50000397		
50000398		
50000399		
50000400		
50000401		
50000402		
50000403		
50000404		
50000405		
50000406		
50000407		
50000408		
50000409		
50000410		

EMBRAER EMB-505 PHENOM 300

C/n	Identities					
50599801	PP-XVI	[rolled out 12Apr08; ff 29Apr08]				
50500001	PP-XVJ					
50500002	PP-XVK					
50500003	PP-XVL					
50500004	PP-XVM	[ff 08Aug09]		PT-PVY	N914LJ	N917LJ
50500005	PT-ZXS	N454DR	(N973ME)			
50500006	PT-ZXT	N585TV				
50500007	PT-ZXW	PT-PVA	PR-DHP			
50500008	PT-ZXX	N308MJ	N999GC			
50500009	PT-ZXY	N392AS				
50500010	PT-ZXZ	PT-MLJ				
50500011	PP-ZZC	N525PC	N6DQ			
50500012	PP-ZZD	PP-OAC				
50500013	(PP-ZZE)	[not built, order cancelled]				
50500014	PP-PVB					
50500015	(PT-PVC)	[not built, order cancelled]				
50500016	PT-PVD	F-HIPE				
50500017	PT-PVE	G-MGNE	N135BC			
50500018	PT-PVF	N492BB				
50500019	PT-PVG	N117DD	N717DD			
50500020	PT-PVH					
50500021	PT-PVI	ZS-MPD	(G-....)	ZS-SYU	N521EC	ZS-SYU
50500022	PT-PVJ	PP-MCL				
50500023	PT-PVL	G-GEIR	HB-VYM			
50500024	PT-PVN	(PP-MCL)	PR-ALU			
50500025	(PT-PVN)	(PT-PVZ)	CN-MBR	[w/o 06Aug12 Altenrhein, Switzerland]	N538WS	[parted out by Dodson Int'l Parts, Rantoul KS]
50500026	PT-PVO	N69GY	PK-JCO			
50500027	PT-PVP	N300FL				
50500028	PT-PVQ	N304FL				
50500029	PT-PVK	N305FL	N833CL			
50500030	PT-PVR	N306FL				
50500031	PT-PVS	N300R	N88DW	N284PD	N428P	
50500032	PT-PVT	N307FL				
50500033	PT-PVU	N960ES	N247JK			
50500034	PT-PVV	N311FL				
50500035	PT-PVW	N394AS	N843YY			
50500036	PT-PVX	N301TG	N523DM			
50500037	PT-PVZ	(PR-PAY)	N312FL			
50500038	PT-PYR	PP-ITU	N38VC			
50500039	PT-PYW	A4O-CY	N539TA	PR-EMD	N505EC	N500AD
50500040	PT-PYS	N715MS	HZ-IBN	[w/o Blackbushe, UK, 31Jul15]		
50500041	PT-PYT	(PT-TIC)	PR-WRT	N341EC	PT-SBC	N282GS
50500042	PT-PYU	N448TM	N68TY			
50500043	PT-PYV	N300VR	N300VX*			
50500044	PT-PUB	N20T				
50500045	PT-PUC	PP-ABV	N507LJ			
50500046	PT-PUE	N300FJ				
50500047	PT-PUF	N318FL	N341FX			
50500048	PT-TDI	N898MW				
50500049	PP-OGX					
50500050	PP-TDT	N314FL				
50500051	PT-TDU	PR-STA				
50500052	(PP-PFA)	PP-LGD				
50500053	PT-TDV	N525LS	N67WG			
50500054	PT-TDW	N315FL	N918DG	N82161		
50500055	PP-OVD					
50500056	PT-THT	N697AS				
50500057	PT-TJJ	N316FL				
50500058	PT-TJR	D-CFMI				
50500059	PT-TJT	N317FL	N562TM			
50500060	(PT-TJU)	PR-ERE				
50500061	PT-TJV	N900HT				
50500062	PT-TJW	OK-PHE	OE-GDP			
50500063	PT-TKL	N505TM	N471TD			
50500064	PT-TLW	XA-LOB	(N505EC)	N364PF	XA-CAN	
50500065	PT-TNA	N14AH	N14AQ			
50500066	PT-TNB	D-CHLR				
50500067	PT-TNC	(PT-TIC)	N319FL	N116DK		
50500068	PT-TND	HB-VPG				
50500069	PT-TNF	D-CRCR	N69VK			
50500070	PT-TNH	N732AC				
50500071	PT-TNI	N896LS				
50500072	(PT-TNJ)	PP-UTI				

EMBRAER EMB-505 PHENOM 300

C/n	Identities						
50500073	PT-TNK	N583KD	N533KD	N300JK*			
50500074	PT-TNL	N322FL	(N345PY)				
50500075	PT-TNM	N324FL					
50500076	PT-TRH	N3300					
50500077	PT-TNS	PR-GCR					
50500078	PT-TRK	N330AG	PK-BSW	N578PF	HZ-SK13		
50500079	PT-TNU	N335AS					
50500080	(PT-RAB)	PK-RJD					
50500081	(PT-TVN)	N729JF	N729JE	N11TE			
50500082	PT-TRN	M-VAKE	UP-EM009				
50500083	PT-TNV	CS-DTQ					
50500084	PT-TRP	N100FG					
50500085	PT-TPM	A4O-CY					
50500086	PP-MDA						
50500087	PT-TRQ	M-APLE					
50500088	PT-TRT	N614TH	N618TH	HZ-SK14			
50500089	PT-TRR	C-GJOL					
50500090	PT-TRV	N325FL	N346FX				
50500091	PT-TRS	N300QS	CS-PHZ	N391VR	N85BZ		
50500092	PT-TRW	PP-WLP					
50500093	PT-TSS	N326FL					
50500094	PT-TST	N327FL	N347FX				
50500095	PT-TSU	N195MC					
50500096	PT-TSV	D-CHIC					
50500097	PT-TRE	N328FL	N348FX*				
50500098	PT-TSW	N175MC					
50500099	PT-TRF	TC-KEH	F-HJFG				
50500100	(PT-GPX)	N329FL	N349FX				
50500101	PT-TRJ	D-CSAG					
50500102	PT-TRO	OY-PWO	(D-CNJK)	N323EP			
50500103	PT-TRP	N65KZ					
50500104	PT-TOA	N657GF	N300GV				
50500105	PT-TRU	N330FL	N351FX				
50500106	PT-TOB	N585BC	N585PF	N443BB			
50500107	PT-TOC	PR-WIN					
50500108	PT-TOD	D-CLAM					
50500109	PT-TOG	N332FL	N352FX				
50500110	PT-TOH	PP-EMO					
50500111	PT-TOI	C-FMPN					
50500112	PT-TAU	N1505P	N347PP				
50500113	PT-TAY	PP-CGG					
50500114	PT-TAZ	PP-CMJ					
50500115	PT-TBI	N335FL	N353FX				
50500116	PT-TBM	M-MDMH					
50500117	PT-TBU	(PT-PTT)	G-CHKE	UR-ALD	N322LV		
50500118	N1039V	[ff 05Dec12 Melbourne, FL – first US-built Phenom 300]				N505EE	N43RC
50500119	PT-TBW	N301AS					
50500120	PT-TBP	N535BC					
50500121	PP-URA						
50500122	N85JE						
50500123	PT-TBX	N302QS					
50500124	PT-TCJ	N977JK					
50500125	PT-TDM	N316TA					
50500126	PP-PRP	N192DM					
50500127	PT-TDL	ZS-MPD					
50500128	(PT-TAS)	PT-TDN	N528TM				
50500129	(PT-TBT)	PT-TDO	PP-NMM				
50500130	(PT-TCU)	PT-TDQ	N302AX				
50500131	(PT-TBY)	PT-TDP	N344PL	OE-GPL			
50500132	PR-EFT						
50500133	PT-TDJ	ZS-CSB					
50500134	PR-PAE	G-JAGA					
50500135	PR-PAH	N337FL	N354FX				
50500136	PP-MPB						
50500137	(PT-TJH)	PP-SCN					
50500138	N894JH						
50500139	PR-PAL	N338FL	N355FX				
50500140	PR-HJM						
50500141	PR-PAU	N303QS					
50500142	N932DM						
50500143	PR-PBD	N304QS					
50500144	N801WZ						
50500145	PR-PAY	PP-EPH					
50500146	PR-PBG	B-9060					
50500147	PR-PBI	N310QS					
50500148	N340AS						

EMBRAER EMB-505 PHENOM 300

C/n	Identities		
50500149	C-FAJV		
50500150	PR-PBJ	(D-CAXO)	D-CHGS
50500151	N628DS		
50500152	PR-PBK	N309QS	
50500153	PR-PBL	N312QS	
50500154	N899EE		
50500155	N6032F	N342FL	N356FX
50500156	N343FL	N357FX	
50500157	PR-PBM	PP-HUC	
50500158	PR-PBN	N314QS	
50500159	N9300	VT-AJJ	
50500160	PP-BPS		
50500161	PR-PBO	N316QS	
50500162	PR-PBP	N318QS	
50500163	N862LG		
50500164	(PP-MMP)	N319QS	
50500165	PR-PBQ	N322QS	N505PJ
50500166	N440XX		
50500167	N713WD	(N589MV)	
50500168	PR-PBU	N325QS	
50500169	N800CS		
50500170	PR-PBV	N327QS	
50500171	N344FL	N358FX	
50500172	N7JW		
50500173	PR-PBX	D-CLBM	
50500174	N895JH		
50500175	PR-PBW	N328QS	
50500176	N6013X	N361CE	
50500177	PP-LMR		
50500178	PR-BJA		
50500179	N598TB	N598TP	
50500180	PR-PBD	N330QS	
50500181	HB-VYS		
50500182	PP-NRN		
50500183	PR-PBI	N331QS	
50500184	PR-PBJ	N332QS	
50500185	N585EE	C-GDJG	
50500186	PR-PBK	N333QS	
50500187	M-BEAR	N157AF	CS-LPA
50500188	N588EE	N505GP	
50500189	N340QS		
50500190	PR-NGM		
50500191	N715DE		
50500192	PR-AJN		
50500193	PP-NEF		
50500194	N343QS		
50500195	PR-PBL	HB-VPR	
50500196	PP-MCG		
50500197	M-ELON		
50500198	PR-PBN	D-CDTZ	
50500199	N377N		
50500200	(PR-HUC)	N335QS	
50500201	(PP-JBE)	N336QS	
50500202	PR-PBZ	N337QS	
50500203	CS-PHA		
50500204	PR-PCB	N300HJ	
50500205	N613R		
50500206	PR-PCD	M-KGTS	
50500207	D-COLT		
50500208	PR-PCE	N345FL	N359FX
50500209	CS-PHB		
50500210	N1887B		
50500211	PP-LJA		
50500212	N110AP	N100NG*	
50500213	PP-IBR		
50500214	CS-PHC		
50500215	N896JH		
50500216	PR-PCF	LX-MAR	F-HBDX
50500217	N865BB		
50500218	PR-PCJ	PR-DRJ	
50500219	N344QS		
50500220	PR-SAD		
50500221	N724MH		
50500222	N585PC		
50500223	PR-PCK	N969GC	
50500224	PT-PVC		

EMBRAER EMB-505 PHENOM 300

C/n	Identities			
50500225	CS-PHD			
50500226	N505FF			
50500227	(PT-PVC)	PR-DLN		
50500228	N300RZ			
50500229	PT-PCH			
50500230	N345QS			
50500231	N40ML			
50500232	PR-PCS	D-CCWM		
50500233	N360FX			
50500234	N361FX			
50500235	N235EE			
50500236	PR-PCO	PP-CTS		
50500237	N351QS			
50500238	PR-PCU	N645B		
50500239	N362FX	[dbr 26Jul16, Houston/Sugar Land, TX]		
50500240	PR-PCV	N29GS		
50500241	PR-PCW	N851AB	HZ-SK12	
50500242	N363FX			
50500243	PR-PCX	N168J		
50500244	N352QS			
50500245	PP-NBB			
50500246	N364FX	N68TJ		
50500247	PR-BEB	F-HMML		
50500248	N1505P			
50500249	PP-JDB			
50500250	N358QS			
50500251	PR-PEE	N500EC		
50500252	CS-PHE			
50500253	PR-PEF	CC-AND		
50500254	N360QS			
50500255	(PP-JDB)	PR-PEH	N73FE	
50500256	N363QS			
50500257	PR-LFH	N347QS		
50500258	N119EP			
50500259	PR-LFJ	N348QS		
50500260	CS-PHF			
50500261	PR-LFK	M-ANAP	T7-ANA	
50500262	PR-PEN	G-CRBN	N262PF	XA-VGL
50500263	PR-PEO	N353QS		
50500264	CS-PHG			
50500265	PR-PEQ	N354QS		
50500266	N566EE	G-POWO		
50500267	PR-PEU	N337AS		
50500268	N366QS			
50500269	PR-PEV	N365FX		
50500270	CS-PHH			
50500271	N571EE	N112CM		
50500272	PR-PFA	N272NR		
50500273	PR-PEK	N367QS		
50500274	PR-PEY	F-HPJL		
50500275	N373QS			
50500276	PR-PEZ	M-HPIN	G-HNPN	
50500277	N300FP			
50500278	PR-PFB	F-HJBR		
50500279	N371QS			
50500280	N317N			
50500281	PR-PFJ	N419PJ		
50500282	N974SC			
50500283	N200BF	N600GF		
50500284	PR-PFK	C-GMSO	N569EE	
50500285	N843M			
50500286	PR-PFM	LX-TAC		
50500287	N805PG			
50500288	N947AS			
50500289	N374QS			
50500290	PR-PFO	N750LC	N199BA	
50500291	PR-PFU	PP-VFV		
50500292	N48VM			
50500293	N909BK			
50500294	N379QS			
50500295	PR-PFV	N603WM		
50500296	N795W			
50500297	N588CB			
50500298	N975SC			
50500299	PR-PFY	N750SC		
50500300	(D-CHMS)	N66LD		

EMBRAER EMB-505 PHENOM 300

C/n	Identities			
50500301	PR-PFZ	N577JM		
50500302	N383QS			
50500303	PR-PGA	XA-LOB		
50500304	F-HJLM			
50500305	PR-PGB	(PP-KCB)	N217CB	N227SL
50500306	N300PH			
50500307	C-FWTF	N307PF		
50500308	PR-PGD	HB-VRW		
50500309	N386QS			
50500310	N302TG			
50500311	N9688R			
50500312	N318PT			
50500313	PR-PGG	N361AS		
50500314	N30MN			
50500315	PR-PGH	T7-ANB		
50500316	N848AM			
50500317	D-CDAS			
50500318	N897JH			
50500319	N124EK			
50500320	N10193	PR-HRO		
50500321	N995LP	(N996LP)		
50500322	N302GV			
50500323	N7DR			
50500324	N60298	D-CHMS		
50500325	PR-PGN	OE-GDF		
50500326	N6013X	N366FX		
50500327	N597TB	N598TB		
50500328	N390QS			
50500329	PR-PGO	T7-AAK		
50500330	N978PC			
50500331	N391QS			
50500332	CS-PHI			
50500333	N10139	D-CWWP		
50500334	PR-PGQ	N168JC		
50500335	N10204	XA-CSS		
50500336	CS-PHJ			
50500337	N6MG			
50500338	N505EE	N551VB		
50500339	N50WY			
50500340	XA-BRA			
50500341	PR-PGR	N368AS		
50500342	C-GEMB			
50500343	PR-PGT	D-CBBS		
50500344	N383CH			
50500345	N545EE			
50500346	PR-PGU	N804SW		
50500347	N10163	N4B		
50500348	N60126	N1873		
50500349	N392QS			
50500350	PR-PGW	PR-FVF		
50500351	N10204	N666DM		
50500352	PR-PGX	N858EE		
50500353	N152CH	N7CH		
50500354	N359AS			
50500355	N304GV			
50500356	N393QS			
50500357	N557EE			
50500358	PR-PHC	G-KRBN		
50500359	D-CCGM			
50500360	N6001M	D-CMMP		
50500361	XA-FLA			
50500362	N394QS			
50500363	N6004N	PR-LNE	B-3355	
50500364	N300YT	VT-MTV		
50500365	N395QS			
50500366	PR-PHG	(T7-ANC)	G-JMBO	
50500367	HB-VPO			
50500368	N362AS			
50500369	C-FWTF			
50500370	SP-MSG			
50500371	N398QS			
50500372	N10163	N98D		
50500373	PR-PHH	D-CMOR		
50500374	PR-PHJ	N414CB		
50500375	N6014A			
50500376	PR-PHN	D-CAGA		

EMBRAER EMB-505 PHENOM 300

C/n	Identities	
50500377	N6051D	N301AZ
50500378	N367FX	
50500379	N300QS	
50500380	N368FX	
50500381	N60NF	
50500382	N369FX	
50500383	N322QS	
50500384	N370FX	
50500385	N326QS	
50500386	N60231	N346AS
50500387	N371FX	
50500388	N372FX	
50500389	N402QS	
50500390	N1127P	
50500391	N373FX	
50500392	PR-LNF	B-3356
50500393	N374FX	
50500394	N375FX	
50500395	N1KA	
50500396	N60298	
50500397	N289FG	
50500398	D-CASH	
50500399	N165MV	
50500400	N5A	
50500401	N404QS	
50500402	N406QS	
50500403	N6A	
50500404	D-CKJE	
50500405	N407QS	
50500406	N6013X	
50500407		
50500408	N408QS	
50500409		
50500410		
50500411		
50500412		
50500413	(D-CFHZ)	
50500414		
50500415	D-CFHZ*	
50500416		
50500417		
50500418		
50500419		
50500420		
50500421		
50500422		
50500423		
50500424		
50500425		
50500426		
50500427		
50500428	N1CH	
50500429		
50500430		
50500431		
50500432		
50500433		
50500434		
50500435		
50500436		
50500437		
50500438		
50500439		
50500440		
50500441		
50500442		
50500443		
50500444		
50500445		
50500446		
50500447		
50500448		
50500449		
50500450		
50500451		
50500452		

EMBRAER EMB-550 LEGACY 500

C/n	Identities			
55000001	PT-ZEX	[rolled out 23Dec11; ff 27Nov12]		
55000002	PT-ZEY	[ff 15Feb13]?		
55000003	PT-ZFV	[ff 22Mar13]	PR-LJN	D-BJKP
55000004	PT-ZHY	PP-JJA		
55000005	PT-ZJF	PR-EUF		
55000006	PR-LFO	N762CC		
55000007	PR-LFW	N598DB	N498EE	N424ML
55000008	PR-LFQ	N878EE	PR-LFQ	N142GZ
55000009	PT-ZIJ	[prototype Legacy 450; ff 28Dec13]		
55000010	PR-LGL	HZ-A7	N510PF	
55000011	PR-LGO	N657GF	N500GX*	
55000012	PR-LGQ	N576EE	N614TH	
55000013	[believed not built due superstition over unlucky number 13]			
55000014	PR-LGW	N895EE	N550LG	
55000015	PR-LHE	Brazil 3601	[military designation IU-50]	
55000016	PR-LGY	TC-MLA		
55000017	PR-LGZ	N878EE	N886CA	
55000018	PR-LHJ	XA-TUB		
55000019	PR-LHG	PR-HIL		
55000020	PR-LGV	[second Legacy 450]	N456LG	C-FASV
55000021	PR-LHK	N725EE*		
55000022	PR-LHL	B-3385		
55000023	PR-LHM	Brazil 3602	[military designation IU-50]	
55000024	PR-LHO	N401EE	N550HD	
55000025	PR-LHS	N400FX		
55000026	PR-LHT	N298EE	N718RA	
55000027	PR-LHX	N401FX		
55000028	PR-LHY	N402FX		
55000029	PR-LIC	(N403FX)	N290EE	
55000030	PR-LIE	XA-EMB		
55000031	PR-LIJ	N729MM	D-BEER	
55000032	PR-LIK	N368EE	N446LG	
55000033	PR-LIR	N585BC		
55000034	PR-LIU	N661HS		
55000035	PR-LIW	N275EE	N306CM	
55000036	PR-LIX	N404FX		
55000037	PR-LIY	OD-CXJ		
55000038	PR-LJB	N159M		
55000039	PR-LJD	G-HARG		
55000040	PR-LJO	XA-RBG		
55000041	PR-LJU	N250LC		
55000042	PR-LJW	G-SUEJ		
55000043	PR-LJY			
55000044	PR-LKB	XA-COS		
55000045	PR-LKE	N712EA		
55000046	PR-LKF	N721EE		
55000047	PR-LKO			
55000048	PR-LKL			
55000049	PR-LKM			
55000050	PR-LKQ	N491EE	N655MC	
55000051	PR-LKP	HZ-SK11		
55000052	PR-LKT	PR-ROI		
55000053	PR-LKY			
55000054				
55000055	PR-LNI	XA-FLB		
55000056				
55000057	(PP-IUH)	PR-LNP		
55000058	PR-LNQ			
55000059				
55000060	PR-LNC	N1Y		
55000061	PR-LKZ	PP-IUH		
55000062	PR-LMI	N781MM		
55000063	PR-LMZ	RA-02788		
55000064	PR-LLZ	N859M	N459M	
55000065	PR-LMK	N782MM		
55000066	PR-LMX	N510RB*		
55000067	PR-LNR			
55000068	PR-LNS			
55000069	PR-LNT			
55000070				
55000071				
55000072				
55000073	[first US-assembled Legacy 500]			
55000074				
55000075				

EMBRAER EMB-550 LEGACY 500

C/n	Identities
55000076	
55000077	
55000078	
55000079	
55000080	
55000081	
55000082	
55000083	
55000084	
55000085	
55000086	
55000087	
55000088	
55000089	
55000090	
55000091	
55000092	
55000093	
55000094	
55000095	
55000096	
55000097	
55000098	
55000099	
55000100	

EMBRAER EMB-545 LEGACY 450

C/n	Identities			
55010001	[c/n not used, built as 55000009]			
55010002	[c/n not used, built as 55000020]			
55010003	PR-LJH	OO-NEY		
55010004	PR-LJK	N450CH		
55010005	PR-LJZ	N801EE		
55010006	PR-LKG	N460SS		
55010007	PR-LKI	N214EE	N629PT	
55010008	PR-LKN			
55010009	PR-LKU	N405FX		
55010010	PR-LKV	N450LC		
55010011	PR-LLH	N406FX		
55010012	PR-LLK	N545MB		
55010013	[believed not built due superstition over unlucky number 13]			
55010014	N6013X	[first US-assembled Legacy 450; ff 04Oct16, Melbourne, FL]		N583KD
55010015	PR-LLO	D-BFIL		
55010016	PR-LLX	N810EE	C-GASL	
55010017	PR-LMO	N407FX		
55010018	PR-LMU	N408FX		
55010019	PR-LMV			
55010020	PR-LMY	N622EE	C-FLAS	
55010021	PR-LMW			
55010022	PR-LNG	N450JE*		
55010023	PR-LNJ	N634EE		
55010024	PR-LNO	N777MC		
55010025	PR-LNU			
55010026				
55010027				
55010028				
55010029	N60237	[US-assembled airframe] N747DP		
55010030				
55010031				
55010032				
55010033				
55010034				
55010035				
55010036				
55010037				
55010038				
55010039				
55010040				

G1159 GULFSTREAM II

Notes: G1159B Gulfstream 2B conversion programme numbers have been included alongside the c/n (see also at the end of the production list)

TT indicates aircraft with tip tanks (some 2Bs were built as "TT" models and converted later)

SP indicates a specialist conversion by Aviation Partners with winglets, known as Gulfstream 2SPs; these are not 2B aircraft. The prototype was c/n 12

* in the series column indicates that engine hush kits have been fitted

C/n	Series	Identities
1	SP	N801GA [ff 02Oct66] N55RG [to Carolinas Aviation Museum, Charlotte,NC, Sep12]
2	SP	N802GA N801GA N369CS N869CS N721SW N434JW N902GT [cx Jly03; to Air Classics Museum, IL, then to Aviation Warehouse, El Mirage, CA]
3		N831GA N214GP N311JJ N555RS N300GP (N417RD) N300RD [parted out Hagerstown, MD; fuselage to private home in Urbana, MD, Dec16]
4/8	2B	N832GA N680RW N680RZ 9K-ACY VR-CAS HZ-MPM N8490P N36RR [parted out California City, CA; cx 27Jan14]
5		N100P N100PJ N65ST N655TJ N34S N3LH [parted out California City, CA]
6		N834GA N430R N122DJ N122DU [broken up Geneva, Switzerland, 2006; remains to Air Salvage Int'l, Alton, Hants, UK, for parts; removed from site by Aug08]
7	SP	CF-HOG N9300 N93QQ N118NP N701JA [parted out by Int'l Turbine Service circa Nov 03; cx Nov03]
8	SP	N833GA N18N N400SJ N400SA HB-IMV N400SA N777GG PJ-ARI N504TF N5UD N225CC N11UF N22CX S9-CRH S9-GOT ZS-TGG N267PS N225MS [parted out by Dodson International, Rantoul, KS]
9/33	2B	CF-SBR N320FE (N115RS) N209GA N343K N48EC N129WA [cx 20Jan16, wfu Dallas/Redbird, TX]
10	SP	N343K N343N N888CF XA-ROI N555LG N51TJ N667CX XB-JPL HR-AUJ N900CE [wfu; cx 15Sep08]
11		N835GA N902 N902GA N611TJ N463HK [wfu 2006; broken up; cockpit & forward fuselage preserved in Banyan Pilot Shop at Fort Lauderdale Executive]
12	SP	N500R N11UM N154X N115MR N121EA N160WC [temporarily fitted with spiroid winglets for 50hrs of test flights in 1993] N212TJ N794SB N622RR [cx 13Aug13; wfu]
13		N678RW N678RZ N98AM 5N-AMN N2GP N373LP N373LB VR-BOS N269MH N269HM N169HM [b/u Mesa/Falcon Field, AZ]
14	SP	N663P N663B N217JD N369AP N500JW XA-RBS XA-RBP
15		N375PK N77SW N416SH N125JJ N571BJ [parted out at Islip, NY, 2004 onwards]
16/13	2B	N890A N697A N711MT N38GL N24YS
17	SP	N119K N819GA N456AS N91AE N305AF N917R N217GA N1PR (N121PR) N422DV N143G N143V N202PX (N217DA) [cx 27Aug12; wfu]
18		N838GA N205M N43R (N48RA) XA-SDE XA-LZZ XC-AA70 [b/u Mexico City, Mexico]
19	SP	N839GA N1929Y N19NW N590CH (N213DC) ZS-LOG [b/u Lanseria, South Africa]
20		N2PG N755S N4SP N331P N747NB N88LN
21		N4PG N3PG N7ZX N8PG N8PQ [cx Jan93; to CIS but unable to obtain CofA] N8PQ N244DM [cx to Panama 25Jun07] "PP-EMS" [fake marks noted crudley applied to fin at Campo Grande, Brazil, Mar11]
22	SP	N862GA N5152 N145ST N22FS N683FM N206MD (N800TE) (N655JH) N217RR N216RR [instructional airframe Wilson Technological Center, Farmingdale, NY]
23		N863GA USCG 01 [VC-11A] N7TJ N890TJ [cx 05Jun13; wfu]
24		N536CS N4S (N98G) N26WP (N224TS) N800XL (N800XC) XB-KFU
25		N327K N527K N711RL N711RZ YV1681 N137GJ
26	SP	N328K N202GA PK-PJZ N975GA (N711RT) N4RT ZS-PYY
27	SP	N1807Z N121JJ N430BC N227TS (N227TJ) N227BA XB-MZK N227BA XB-NRX
28		N695ST N700ST N7004T C-GCFB N120EA N85EQ N68DM N17KW
29	SP	N869GA N930BS N919G N41RC N71TJ N941CW N188JS [cx 20Jan16, wfu Dallas/Redbird, TX]
30/4	2B	N870GA N788S N2601 N2607 N333AX N338AX N47HR XA-FHR XA-TRG N30438 XA-EHR XA-STT XB-KBO XB-KCX XC-LKN
31		N1621 N685TA N789FF N200CC N105TB [test a/c with nose probe and underwing pods]
32/2	2B	N7602 (N7601) N976B N971EC N971EQ N200AQ [cx 18May15, CofR expired]
33	SP	N1624 N1324 N217TL (N217TE) N327TL N327TC N926NY N747NB N747JX
34		N230E N130A N11SX VR-CBM N500JR N204RC [w/o 17Jun91 Caracas-Oscar Machada, Venezuela; cx Oct91]
35		N1004T N830TL N30PR
36/3	2B	N26L N26LA N5400G (N211GA) N901K N901KB N74A
37		N179AR N179AP N994JD N397RD [cx Nov02; b/u, remains to Aviation Warehouse film prop facility at El Mirage, CA]
38		N80A N880A [Quiet Spey development a/c with BAC1-11 thrust reverser on starboard engine] [cx Jun95; wfu for spares]
39	SP	N80Q N8000 N401HR (N124BN) N425A (N12BN) N1TJ N87HB N87TD [wfu at Chino, CA, 2006]
40		N1040 (N5040) N1039 VR-BLJ [w/o 20Jun96 Jos, 465m NE of Lagos, Nigeria]
41	SP	N38N (N417GA) N401GA N416K N365TC N311MG [parted out Mojave, CA]
42/12	2B	N8000J N937M N880GM VR-BMQ N1164A N36PN
43		N17583 F-BRUY N84X N33ME N691RC (N243TS) N270TS N899GA (N247LG) [impounded Toluca, Mexico, for drug-running Aug07; moved to Mexico City, Mexico; b/u]
44		N814GA N830G N585A N830G [b/u Fort Lauderdale Executive, FL circa Jan02; cx Feb02]

G1159 GULFSTREAM II

C/n	Series	Identities
45	SP	N815GA N711R PK-PJG N152RG N215RL VR-BHA N115GA N40CE US Army 89-0266 N51741 US Army 89-0266 N245GA N250MS [cx 24Mar15, CofR expired]
46	TT	N806CC N40CC N111RF C-GSLK N9272K N721CP N9BF N505JT N565KC [canx 19Jly05 aircraft b/u at, then removed from, Islip, NY]
47	SP	N803GA N35JM N553MD N809GA N809LS N800FL N800RT [cx 18Sep12; parted out California City, CA]
48/29	2B	N109G N4411 N711MC N61WH N61WE N865AA
49		N871GA N747G N74JK N830TL N830TE N830TL (N830TE) N830BH N511PA N511BA (N33EN) [cx 09Dec14, CofR expired]
50		N39N N39NX N767FL N800FL N220FL N220JR N650KA HI…
51	SP*	N2013M VR-BNE N7C N20H N20HE N20H N20HE N30HE
52		CF-FNM C-FFNM N69SF N38KM N5SJ (N52NE) "N52TJ" N711MT N211MT N52NW [canx 28Oct05 parted out]
53	SP	N107A N167A N102AB N104CD N104VV
54/36	2B	N123H CF-NOR C-FNOR N955CC N148V [wfu Houston/Hobby, TX]
55		N875GA N225SF N225SE N125DC
56	SP	N10XY N20XY N105Y N805Y N610CC N690PC N2000
57	SP	N876GA N770AC N300DK N300DL (N333ST) N33PJ N466JB N605RA [cx 25Mar13; parted out California City, CA]
58		N878GA N720Q [w/o 24Jun74 Kline, SC]
59	SP	N879GA N1823D [b/u; cx 19Nov08]
60		N892GA N500J [w/o 26Sep76 Hot Springs, VA]
61	SP	N18N N711MM N497TJ N800MC N57BG N61LH N41AV [instructional airframe, South Georgia Technical College, Americus, GA]
62		N834GA N372CM N372GM N1PG N3ZQ N7PG N7PQ Russia 62 [Black or Dark Blue] (N777TX) N20LW N262PA N128KG
63		N835GA N238U N239P N149JW N17ND (N20GP) N12GP
64/27	2B	N836GA N940BS N950BS N341NS N95SV N620K N82CK N43RJ N95SJ N351SE [impounded Bissau, Guinea-Bissau, 12Jul08]
65		N837GA N720E N1JG N500PC N58JF (N300FN)
66		N838GA N720F N165W N165U N718JS N718JA [parted out by Dodson Int'l, Rantoul, KS]
67	SP	N839GA N711S EL-WRT N10HR N400JD N67PR N568TN ZS-WHG [b/u Lanseria, South Africa, 09Jul15]
68		N308EL N308EE [cx to Panama 22Jun06, shot down over Colombia 12Aug06]
69	SP	N69NG N25JM N33CR N45JM N45Y N45YP VH-HKR N21066 N123CC N440DR N701S XA-MEM XC-LKA
70/1	2B	N711SC N711SB VR-BML N165A N451CS N451GS N908EJ N908CE N510SR N510SE N660AF [wfu at Mojave, CA; cx 25Feb2010]
71		N4CP N4CQ N711SW N907SW N48JK N47A N200AB N200EL [cx 20Jan16, wfu Dallas/Redbird, TX]
72		N397F [w/o 22Feb76 Burlington, VT]
73/9	2B	N116K N555CS N920DS N436JW 3D-TCB 7P-TCB N436JW N1B 9Q-…
74	SP	N845GA N111AC N311AC (3X-GBD) N204GA N92SV N74TJ N74HH [parted out by Dodson Int'l, Rantoul, KS; cx 26Sep16]
75/7	2B	N823GA N1000 N100AC N100CC N600CS N760U N94TJ N211SJ Venezuela 0010 [wfu Caracas/La Carlota, Venezuela]
76	SP	N711LS N227G N227GL N227GX N227G N227GA [canx 25May04; wfu]
77		N824GA N100WK N40CH N140CH N34MZ N84MZ N777JS N385M N7TJ N707SH N7TJ N700JP N125WM N994GC N994GG N277GS
78	SP*	N17585 PH-FJP CF-IOT C-FIOT N90HH HP-1A HP-1691 [parted out Fort Pierce/St Lucie, FL]
79	SP	N826GA N719GA N204A XA-SFB XA-STO XA-ARA [b/u Houston/Hobby, TX, 2008]
80	SP	N827GA N85V N85VT N500RH N510RH N82CR [structurally modified for US Navy BAMS system development]
81	SP	N828GA? N777SW N44MD N281GA N283MM N688MC N681AR XC-PGR+ N681AR (N281NW) N151SD N419MS [parted out by MTW Aerospace Inc, Montgomery, AL]
82	SP	N711DP N10LB N9040 N600B N600BT N728T N492JT [preserved Georgia Aviation Hall of Fame, Warner Robins, GA]
83		N404M N409M N409MA (N48MS) [w/o 03May95 Quito, Ecuador]
84		N5101 N5101T N27SL
85	SP	N5102 Denmark F-085 N5102 N510G N86SK N931CW N93AT N524MM N598GS ZS-MMG
86/16	2B	N880GA N179T (N179DE) [parted out Mojave, CA]
87/775/6	2B	N804GA N13GW N723J N6PC N692EB N165PA
88/21	2B	N881GA N2600 N2637M HB-IMZ N901AS N80WD N779LC
89	SP*	N882GA N100A N203A N36MW [conv to prototype "Paragon" before SP] N98WJ [cx 03May16, CofR expired]
90		N883GA N7789 N20GP N671LW
91	SP	N17586 G-AYMI VH-ASM N219GA G-OVIP VR-BRM N291GA N99ST N183SC N81FC N914MH XB-KIV XC-LKS [wfu Mexico City, Mexico]
92	SP	N884GA N300L N300U N114HC N994JD N430SA N722TP N589HM N691HM (N584DM) N629TD N374PS (N883KF). N888YZ
93	SP	N885GA N8785R TJ-AAK N215GA N62K N484TL N396BC N922MR (N159DA) [impounded Caracas, Venezuela; wfu]
94	SP	N886GA N200A N202A N623MW N420JM N420JT N18AQ N685SF N665SF YV3233

G1159 GULFSTREAM II

C/n	Series	Identities
95/39	2B	N887GA VH-ASG N427AC N836MF N836ME N113CS N118GS N889DF N2DF N608CM [wfu Mojave, CA, Feb11]
96	SP	N888GA N100KS N100WC N75WC N75SR XC-MEX XB-EBI N3005P XA-EYA N396CF [wfu Kingman, AZ]
97	SP	N889GA I-SMEG N66TF N11AL N930SD N397J (N397L) N55HY N25GJ XB-RRC [wfu 2013, stored Chino, CA]
98/38	2B	N850GA N93M N955H N988H N988DS N925DS N17MX XA-CHR XA-PSD N198AV N812RS N888CS N888ES N883ES N982B N44YS [parted out California City, CA]
99	SP	N851GA N99GA N822CA N900VL N900MP N1218C (N1273G)
100	SP	N852GA N4000X N400CX N234DB N911DB XB-FVL N400D
101	SP	N853GA N1159K (N237LM) N240CX N623CX N512JT N412JT [wfu Pachuca, Mexico; cx 11Dec14]
102/32	2B	N854GA N88AE N210GA N119CC N400CC N102CX N511PK
103	SP	N855GA N801GA G-BDMF N833GA P2-PNF P2-PNG N833GA HZ-MS4 (N103WJ) N89TJ [parted out circa Feb05 by Dodson Intl Parts, Rantoul, KS]
104/10	2B/2	N856GA N856W N858W [cvtd back to G2 standards 1989; wings to G3 c/n 303] C-FHPM N712MQ [b/u Houston/Hobby, TX]
105	SP	N807GA N23M N5997K N405GA N6060 N711TE N754JB [b/u Fort Lauderdale Executive, FL, Nov10]
106		N808GA N33M (N519TW) N397LE N226GA (N106TJ) N141JF (N473JF) [wfu Chino, CA]
107	*	N809GA N5113H N10123 [modified for aerial survey use]
108	SP	N810GA N11UC N60GG N600MB N700FS N801GA N200GH (N200GL) N900AK N183PA N189PA
109	SP	N811GA N679RW N882W N86CE N862CE N73AW N581MB [parted out]
110	SP	N814GA N5000G N200GN N200PB N21AM N21AX N92AG N417EK [cx 13May15; wfu Houston/Hobby, TX]
111		N815GA N10LB N13LB N765A N900BR N900DH [flying testbed for Snecma Silvercrest turbofan 2014]
112	SP	N816GA N102ML N102HS VR-BJG N36JK N909L N108DB N87AG N168VA N168DA XB-NXC XB-OCC [impounded Paraguana, Venezuela]
113	SP	N817GA N30RP N34RP N60CT N203GA N2S N32HC N2S N216HE (N216MF) N1BL N211BL N217JS N74RT N74RQ [dbr 19Jan05 Logan, UT; to White Inds, Bates City, MO for spares; cx 22Jan09]
114		N818GA N100PM N25BF XA-TDK (N114WJ) XB-KBE XB-KCW XC-LKL XB-NKS [destroyed by fire at clandestine airstrip nr Calabozo, Venezuela, Oct15, presumed used for drug-running]
115	SP	N819GA N677S N457SW N47JK N200BP N700BH N40AG N42PP N424GC [b/u Mojave, CA; cx 02Jul09]
116		N821GA 9M-ARR N20XY N23W (N410LR) N716TE N218SE [cx 12Apr12; wfu]
117	SP	N822GA N580RA N888SW N75CC N7500 N750RA
118		N823GA N399CB (N301FP) N399FP N650PF/NASA650 [for Prop Fan Experiments] (N651NA) N945NA [to be preserved at US Space & Rocket Center, Huntsville, AL]
119/22	2B	N824GA TU-VAF N825GA C-FHBX N2991Q N60HJ (N875E) N720G N73LP N928GF (N103EL) N305SJ N500MA XB-KKU [w/o in Venezuela 07Oct07]
120	SP	N825GA N901BM N777V N677V N20FX N393BD N392BD C-GTEW N711VL
121	SP	N200P N90EA N507JC N721RL N721PL N892TM [parted out by White Inds, Bates City, MO]
122		N832GA N429JX N4290X N61SM N84A N500RL N500RQ [parted out Mojave, CA, Aug10, then to El Mirage, CA, for film prop use]
123/25	2B	N805CC N345CP N345AA N344AA N344AB N368DS N868DS [cx 11Dec14, CofR expired]
124		N834GA HB-IEW VR-BGL VR-BGO N203GA Venezuela 0004 (N980EF) N124TV [wfu Mojave, CA circa Sep03; cx 15Jun05 as b/u; fuselage to Long Beach, CA, Nov07 for training use; tail unit still at Mojave Oct11]
125/26	2B	N870GA N367G N364G N3643 N92LA N92NA N178B
126		N43M N581WD (HB-I..) N578DF N416K N901WG [cx 13Jan10; b/u Savannah, GA, Oct10, remains to Atlanta Air Salvage, Griffin, GA]
127	TT	N17581 TR-KHB [w/o 06Feb80 Ngaoundere, Cameroun]
128		N73M N367EG N128TS N829NL [cx 25Nov14, CofR expired]
129	SP	N871GA N1H N711DS N83TE N626TC N711EV [b/u cx Nov03]
130	SP	N872GA N127V N518GS N512SD A6-PHY N666SA
131/23	2B	N17582 9M-ATT N759A N2JR
132	SP	N873GA N400M [parted out California City, CA]
133	TT	N88906 N17583 5X-UPF N44UP N444QG N442QG N930LS [wfu Mojave, CA; cx 31Mar09]
134		N806CC C-FROC N555HD N555KH N628HC (N810MY) [impounded Guatemala City/La Aurora 26Jun13]
135	SP*	N83M N113EV (N518FE) N518JT N515JT N552JT N525XL [cx 12Dec11; b/u]
136	SP	N874GA N65M ZS-JIS 3D-AAC N207GA 6V-AFL 6V-AGQ N26WB XA-ABA XA-AFP XA-FCP N95RT N190RP [parted out California City, CA; cx 26Nov14]
137	SP	N875GA N1875P N2711M VR-BJT N23AH N115MC N485GM N435GM [dbr by Hurricane Rita at Beaumont, TX, Sep05; parted out by Dodson Av'n, Rantoul, KS; cx 12Nov14]
138		N6JW YV....
139/11	2B	N880GA N18N HZ-PET HB-ITV N2UJ (N763PD) N663PD N339GA N139CF N113AR N139CF [wfu Conakry, Guinea]
140/40	2B*	N881GA C-GTWO N2667M (N101AR) N104AR N212GA VR-BJQ N189TC N730TK N159NB [parted out California City, CA; cx 13Jul16]
141		N17584 JA8431 [Mitsubishi special test aircraft]
142		N882GA N60CC N5RD N742TS N588SS [cx 04Jun13; wfu]
143		N883GA N334 N204C [w/o 04Sep91 Kota Kinabalu, Borneo; cx Nov93]

G1159 GULFSTREAM II

C/n	Series	Identities
144		N17585 HB-ITR N944NA [preserved Dryden Flight Research Center, Edwards, CA]
145	SP	N894GA N871D N871E N339H N226RM [wfu Okeechobee, FL]
146		N897GA N946NA [preserved Texas Air & Space Museum, Amarillo, TX]
147		N898GA N947NA [preserved Evergreen Aviation & Space Museum, McMinville, OR]
148/5	2B	N710MR N710MP N2615 N2815 N180AR
149		N896GA N17586 5V-TAA [w/o 26Dec74 Lome, Togo]
150	SP	N803GA N966H N988H N636MF N638MF (N631CK) N613CK N319GP N60GU ZS-TPG [parted out Lanseria, South Africa]
151/24	2B	N804GA N979RA N979GA N908JE (N988JE) N909JE YV569T
152		N17587 XA-FOU N202GA N62WB N559LC N559L
153	SP	N881GA N23A (N602CM) N111VW N110VW N132FP [parted out California City, CA; cx 18Oct16]
154/28	2B	N1625 N1JN N18JN N836MF N110GD N719SA N719SQ HI871
155/14	2B	N308A XA-GAC N477GG N471GG
156/31	2B	N806GA N400SJ N7000G N16NK N18NK N525JT N83TE N864YD (N159DJ) ZS-DJA
157		N805GA N914BS N940BS N74JK N658PC N683EC N468HW (N488HW) [parted out by Dodson Int'l, Rantoul, KS]
158	SP	N76CS N76QS N401M N2S N889JC [cx 29Sep14; wfu]
159	SP	N345UP N800DM N800DJ N880RJ N510AG [has extensive fuselage modifications]
160		N80J N801 N214GA N900TP N919TG N1123G N241MH E3-AAT
161	*	N17589 XA-ABC XC-FEZ XC-CFE Mexico TP-04/XC-UJK XB-GSN XA-RUS XA-AHM XA-AHC
162		(C-GANE) N530SW N74RV C-GTCB N74RV N666JT N668JT [cx 13Jun12; wfu]
163	SP	N17581 (YV-60CP) PJ-ABA N117JJ N117JA N117JJ [wfu Fort Pierce/St Lucie, FL]
164	SP	N17582 9K-ACX A6-HHZ N93LA N80AG XA-ESC XA-BBO XB-BBO
165/37	2B*	N810GA N7000C N788C VR-BHR N26L N965CC N183V N696MJ N945PK
166/15	2B	N811GA N515KA N66AL (N84AL) N826GA N826AG XA-SWP N776MA ZS-DGW
167	SP*	N17583 5V-TAC VR-CBC N204GA N900SF N430DP N681FM N82204 N682FM N683FM N120GS N368AG N868AG XA-UEC XA-CVS
168	SP	N812GA N10LB N26LB N193CK N635AV N168JW N317AF (N370SP) N318SP N501JV [cx 21Mar17, wfu Denton, TX]
169	SP	N17584 HB-IEX N39JK N31SY N710JL N7155P N169P N169EA N467AM N467AN XA-...
170		N991GA N14PC N502PC (N318GD) N111GD N202XT N111GD [cx Nov10; parted out Mojave, CA]
171		N17585 HZ-AFH SX-BTX [b/u Geneva, Switzerland, Nov09; fuselage to Lanseria, South Africa]
172	SP	N804GA N903G N903GA N903AG N987SA [shot down while drug-running in Mexico 24Sep07, w/o]
173	TT	N801GA XC-PET XA-SQU N98FT N173EL (N444ML) [parted out Van Nuys, CA]
174	SP	N805GA N401M N144ST N7766Z N900ES N540EA [cx 11May16, wfu Schenectady, NY]
175	SP	N17586 HZ-AFG 5T-UPR N770PA XA-FNY XC-PFT [code PF-210]
176	SP	N806GA N176P N176SB N15UC N15UG N794SB N794SC N550WP N959QP
177		N17587 5N-AGV "5N-BLV" 5N-BGV (N1513) [wfu Atlanta/Falcon-Peachtree, GA]
178	SP	N819GA N390F N104ME (N128AD) N42LC N720JW N502RG [cx 23Jul11; parted out]
179		N17588 HZ-CAD HZ-PCA [wfu Jeddah, Saudi Arabia]
180	SP	N859GA N329K N359K N37WH (N47WH) N702JA N416CG XB-MUX
181		N860GA N24DS N924DS N48CC N48CQ [wfu Tulsa, OK circa Nov02; cx 02Dec05, believed b/u]
182	TT*	N17589 CN-ANL
183	SP	N17581 A4O-AA N23AZ (N10NW) N801WC N806WC N400PJ N821PA [cx 05Jan12; wfu]
184		N861GA N80E N220GA N254CR N777RW
185	SP	N862GA N372CM N372GM N3E N3EU N511WP XA-BRE N297GB N950NA [modified for use as USAF YAL-1A (Airborne Laser) target aircraft]
186	SP	N17582 (D-ACVG) D-AFKG 5N-AML (D-AAMD) VR-BJV VP-BJV VP-BFF [parted out California City, CA]
187		N17583 N804GA HZ-ADC N202GA N802CC
188		N823GA N862G N662G N555MW N555MU N188DC [wfu Fort Pierce/St Lucie, FL; cx 29Oct14]
189/42	2B*	N333AR N512VB (N515JT) N555XL N404AC N711MQ [wfu Miami/Opa Locka, FL]
190	SP	N130K N159B N169B N900WJ N1WP N7WQ N59CD N59JR N914DZ N914CF N190CS
191	SP	N810GA N680RW N679RW N677RW N675RW N951RK [abandoned Roatan, Honduras, 22Mar13 – presumed drug-running]
192	SP	N811GA N678RW N677RW HB-ITW N273LP N192FG N192WF [wfu Toluca, Mexico; cx 10Dec14]
193	SP	N808GA N26L N26LT N54J N54JJ N227LA N117LB N227LA*
194		N17584 HB-IMW C6-BEJ C6-BFE VR-BRM N194WA N57HJ N57HE [parted out Cartersville, GA; cx 25Nov14]
195		N212K N71TP XA-ILV N195AR [parted out San Antonio, TX, 2006]
196		N400J N200BE N610MC N619MC N829GL (XA-...) N213JA
197		N800GA N5117H (N217AH) N608MD [wfu Okeechobee, FL]
198/35	2B	N825GA N365G N3652 N91LA N91NA [parted out California City, CA]
199/19	2B*	N829GA N75WC N75RP N74RP N71RP VR-BND VP-BND N900TJ N338CL N511TL [b/u Chino, CA]
200	SP	N826GA N1806P N135CP N99VA XA-AVR N17GG N281RB N17KJ (N200UJ) [cx 21Jun12; parted out California City, CA]
201	TT	N17585 HZ-AFI N105AJ [cx 26Jul12; wfu]
202	TT	N17586 A9C-BG
203	TT	N17587 HZ-AFJ [wfu circa Dec05 Geneva, Switzerland; b/u Oct07]

G1159 GULFSTREAM II

C/n	Series	Identities
204	SP	N17588 G-CXMF N806CC N937US N659PC N659WL VR-CPA VP-CPA N659WL
205	SP*	N25UG N1000 N205BL N623BM N345GL (N345GV) [cx to Mexico 03Jun16 but still wearing N345GL Oct16]
206	SP	N2PK N900BF N721CN (N609PA)
207/34	2B	N700PM (N780PM) N111UB VR-CUB VP-CUB N4UB [cx 14Oct14; parted out California City, CA]
208	SP	N808GA N62CB C-FNCG N818DA N247AD N247AB [cx 26Jun13; wfu]
209	SP*	N806GA N277T N720DR [parted out California City, CA]
210	SP	HB-IEY G-IIRR (HK-....) 8P-LAD N30FW N826GW [cx 12Aug14; instructional airframe Rome/ Griffiss, NY]
211	SP	N17581 VR-BGT VP-BGT N7079N XA-FNY XA-UTP [wfu; fuselage at football training ground nr Toluca, Mexico]
212	SP	N807GA N551MD N807CC N706TJ [parted out California City, CA]
213	SP	N1707Z N96JA (N96BK) N213X
214	SP	N17585 G-BSAL A4O-HA Oman 601 N11NZ N214NW N914KA N914KB N707KD [abandoned Roatan, Honduras, 01Apr14 still – presumed drug-running]
215	SP	N816GA N748MN
216	TT	HB-IEZ N63SD N200RG HZ-ND1 HZ-HA1
217		N88GA N81728 N880WD N880WE [cx 25Jan12; parted out California City, CA]
218		TU-VAC N218GA N187PH (N187PA) N188MR ZS-CTL [parted out California City, CA]
219/20	2B	N84V VR-BJD N307AF N923ML N505RX N575E N74RT [instructional airframe, State College of Missouri, Linn, MO]
220		N805GA N404M N307M N405MM N315TS N117GL [parted out Los Angeles/Van Nuys, CA; fuselage to Long Beach, CA, as cabin trainer]
221	SP	N575SF N575SE N2HF N600CD N827K N949NA N805NA
222		N817GA N5253A N948NA [to Pima Air & Space Museum, Tucson, AZ, for display Jul07; cx 30Apr15]
223	SP	N510US N257H N510US [wfu Mojave, CA, 23Jun09]
224	TT	N17584 N810GA N631SC N90CP N800PM N860PM [cx 02Mar15; wfu]
225	SP	N17585 G-BGLT N55922 N289K N225TR N450MH N169MM
226	SP	N1902P N1902L N5DL N448PC N355KM [parted out Fort Pierce/St Lucie, FL]
227	SP	N818GA N1841D N1841L N1BX N18XX N200LS N264CL [instructional airframe, North Valley Occupational Center, Los Angeles/Van Nuys, CA]
228	SP	N819GA (N700CQ) (N30B) N157LH N189WS [wfu Curacao; cx 03May16, CofR expired]
229		N821GA N702H N117FJ [parted out Islip, NY]
230		N17586 7T-VHB [w/o 03May82 over NW Iranian border]
231		N808GA N1102 VR-CAG VR-BHD N18RN N205K N47EC N416KD [parted out California City, CA; cx 04Jun13]
232		N806GA C-GDPB N71WS N508T N10RQ [cx 10Apr09; wfu]
233	TT	N807GA N320TR N233RS N720LH
234	TT	N808GA N910S N910R N480GA N222PV (N220GA) N500JW (N956MJ) [parted out California City, CA]
235	TT	N17581 G-HADI N5519C N16FG N256M N430RG N840RG [cx 07Aug14; wfu]
236	TT	N812GA N2998 N630PM N50PM N54BM N211DH N311DH N311BD [instructional airframe Jacqueline Cochran Discovery of Flight & Education Center, Thermal, CA]
237/43	2B	N816GA N25BH XA-MIX XA-BAL XA-SDM EC-363 EC-FRV N237RF N302DP [parted out California City, CA]
238	TT	N831GA N335H N72BP
239	TT	N17582 HZ-AFK (N239WJ) [wfu Jeddah, Saudi Arabia]
240		5A-DDR TT-AAI (N240EA)
241	SP	N830GA (N60TA) (N801GA) N90MD N902MP (N902MK) N909MK N909FK N380AC
242		5A-DDS
243		N119R N119RC N46TE [w/o 19Jan90 Little Rock, AR]
244	SP	N17584 9K-AEB N500T N509T N509TT N811DF N811DE
245/30	2B	N829GA N141GS N871D N99WJ N222NB N222NP (YV....)
246	TT*	N17587 HB-IEZ N14LT N81RR [used by NASA as High Ice Water Content research aircraft but wfu due US Gov't budget cuts; stored Chino, CA; cx 05Dec14]
247	SP*	N828GA N888MC C-GTEP N73MG N75MG N530GA
248	SP	N17589 9K-AEC N501T N510T N510TL N248TH N7WG (N70WG) N71WJ N457BE [cx 03Mar15; wfu Rome/Griffiss, NY]
249		[Gulfstream 3 airframe]
250	TT	N821GA N309EL (N94SF) N985BB [cx 16Nov12; wfu]
251		N944H N9PG N9PY N567A N36GS N251JS N933RD [cx 20May15; CofR expired]
252		[Gulfstream 3 airframe]
253	SP	N15TG N154C N915C XB-LHW XA-GEG N16YY N522HS [impounded Puerto Plata, Honduras, Nov14]
254/41	2B	N254AR N706TS N868SM
255/18	2B	N442A N4NR
256		N17581 HZ-MSD (N135WJ) N61TJ [parted out Nov04 by Dodson Av'n, Rantoul, KS]
257/17	2B	N822GA N872E N411WW N911WW N56D N1CC N1159B
258	SP	N823GA N301EC N929GV N437H N87GS N689JE
775		see c/n 87

GULFSTREAM G1159B CONVERSION PROGRAMME

No	C/n	Completion date	No	C/n	Completion date	No	C/n	Completion date
1	70	17Sep81	13	16	09May83	25	123	11Jun84
2	32	02Apr82	14	155	22Jun83	26	125	11Jly84
3	36	13Aug82	15	166	14Jly83	27	64	28Sep84
4	30	06Aug82	16	86	09Aug83	28	154	15Oct84
5	148	18Aug82	17	257	17Oct83	29	48	02Nov84
6	775	19Sep82	18	255	09Nov83	30	245	10Jan85
7	75	16Nov82	19	199	04Jan84	31	156	19Feb85
8	4	29Nov82	20	219	17Feb84	32	102	07Mar85
9	73	15Dec82	21	88	18Feb84	33	9	30Apr85
10	104	09Feb83	22	119	27Mar84	34	207	02May85
11	139	15Mar83	23	131	25Apr84	35	198	07May85
12	42	05May83	24	151	04Jun84	36	54	05Jly85

PLUS

37	165	Dec85
38	98	Jan86
39	95	Mar86
40	140	Jun86
41	254	Sep86 (rolled out as G1159B 06Oct86)
42	189	Jly87
43	237	Oct87

G1159A GULFSTREAM III

* alongside the c/n indicates fitted with engine hush kits

C/n	Identities
249	N300GA [ff 02Dec79] N901GA Denmark F-249 N163PA
252	(N777SL) N17582 (N301GA) XA-MEY N247RG N516TR
300*	N300GA N700VA N71TJ N918BG N234LR
301	N100P N21NY (N100P) N110BR N444GA N973MW (N973MV) N480RW [cx 26Feb15; parted out Mojave, CA]
302	N302GA N62GG N2610 N56L N56LA (XA-TOT) (N561ST) VP-BCT N49US N109ST N302ST N818VB [stored Okeechobee, FL] N848PF*
303	N300GA N303GA TU-VAF [rebuilt with wings from G2B c/n 104/10] N1761W N303GA [w/o 29Mar01 Aspen, CO]
304	N17583 HZ-NR2 N600YY N768J N763J (N18SL) VR-BSL N304TS [cx 26Dec13; parted out Mojave, CA]
305*	N305GA N235U N305MD N682FM PK-OCN N552JT N553JT N106KM (9M-...)
306	N306GA N777SW N72RK N72PK N862CE N863CE (N868CE) N104BK N360MB
307	N17584 C-GSBR C-GGPM N111FA
308	N717A N606PT VR-BNO N308GA N308HG N921MG
309	N18LB N1NA N2NA N803NA N992NA
310	N719A C-FYAG N6513X (N373LP) (N173LP) N982RK [cx 7Jul14; wfu]
311	N17585 HZ-AFL N311GA N721RB N711SW (N311BK) N127BK N127GK [instructional airframe, Embry-Riddle Aeronautical University, Daytona Beach, FL]
312*	N304GA N100GN N200GN N200JJ N800JH N312NW XA-RCM N116AR ZS-JGC
313	Denmark F-313 N173PA
314	N1040 N1540 N1640 N93CX N99PD (N99YD) [wfu Dallas/Redbird, TX; cx 20Jan16]
315	N315GA N2600 N2600Z N315GS N710EC N718EC N21PJ (N901JF) N90ML
316	N316GA N2601 N26018 PK-CAP PK-BND N316FA N691AC (N69EH) N300UJ [parted out by 818 Aviation, Mojave, CA]
317*	C-GKRL N344GA A6-CKZ N83D HZ-DG2 N90EP N186PA
318	N308GA N300L (N300LF) (XA-...) N70050 N150GX N150QX N150RK N500WW N17NC N184PA
319	N319Z N200SK
320*	N873E N69FF VR-BNX N320WE N624BP N624PP N410UJ N190PA
321	N30RP N94GC N321GA N100GX N100QX N313RG N310RG N9KL (N91KL) N830SU [wfu Dallas/Love Field, TX]
322	N130A N110LE (N110EE) N322GA N555NT N600ES N606ES N706JA [cx 09Jan13, wfu]
323	XA-MIC N323G XA-ERH XA-LNP
324	N17587 HZ-AFM N44200 N67JR N96MR N450CB N324JW
325	N890A N89QA N393U N155MM N55ME N59ME
326	N17582 TR-KHC N333GA (N326DD) N420JC
327	N70PS (N72PS) N57BJ N777RY N711LT N829MG N259SK ZS-LUX
328	N309GA N75RP N78RP N98RP N97AG N36WL ZS-LAH
329	N301GA N862G N1JN (N329N) N327JJ N1LW A6-ZAB N15ZA N197PA
330	Denmark F-330 [w/o 03Aug96 nr Vagar, Faroe Islands]
331	N307GA N17LB HZ-RC3 (N231WJ) [wfu Jeddah, Saudi Arabia]
332	N310GA N77TG N300BE N65BE N121JM (N121JN) N921AS N909RR N939RR
333	N600PM N50PM N901FH N901EH
334	N1PG (N1PU) N41PG N700SB N3DP
335	HB-IMX N117MS N717MS N456BE
336	N3PG N3PY (N523TX) (N523PT) (N102PT) N147X N378MB
337	N456SW N330WR
338	N862GA N372CM N372GM N87HP (N338RJ) N750SW N540EA N5408A
339	N302GA N522SB N339A N684AT N774AK N774MB [wfu Okeechobee, FL]
340	F-WDHK F-GDHK N99WJ N90WJ N340GA N4PC N2LY N57NP N557JK
341	N263C N1PR V5-PJM
342	N441A N91LJ N82A N82AE N1AQ N1JK N818SS N555XS [parted out California City, CA]
343	N305GA N664P N664S N400AL N221CM
344	N306GA N7000C 5N-IMR N344DD N344GW N804NA [NASA testbed for new wing-flap assemblies]
345*	N17585 G-BSAN VR-CCN G-GIII 5X-UOI N76TJ N454JB N550PP N918HD
346*	N17581 HZ-RH2 HZ-HR2 (N126AH) VP-BHR N103VV
347	N17583 VR-BJE N545JT N888LV N39LF
348	N756S N357PR N857PR*
349*	N89AE N89AB N1KE N6453 N6458 N711EG N111ES N911HJ [parted out California City, CA]
350	N317GA N1454H N1454 [cx May10, parted out Mojave, CA]
351	N888MC N308AF N836MF N18TM N623MS
352	N17586 HB-ITM Mexico TP-06/XC-UJN XC-LOW
353	N26619 HZ-BSA HZ-108 N212BA
354*	3D-AAC 3D-AAI N16NK N420RC N429DD N913PD [wfu Okeechobee, FL]
355	N318GA N676RW (N103HS) N876RW 8P-GAC (N105HS) N355TS ZS-TEX (N355TR)
356*	N17608 A6-HEH N356TJ N356BR
357	N303GA N340 N802GA N891MG N723MM N623NP [wfu Bournemouth, UK; last flew 30Mar12]
358*	N1761B HZ-DA1 N9711N N200DE (N1149E) N475DJ (N475CY) N358CY
359	N800J N305TC N25MT N50BH
360	N341GA N90LC (N405LM) N705JA N425SV
361	(N875E) N874RA (N361RA) (N863A) (N874RR) [wfu Okeechobee, FL]

GULFSTREAM III

C/n	Identities
362	N408M N800AR N400AA
363*	N83AL N77FK N77EK N855SA
364	N1761D HZ-AFN
365*	N1761J HZ-AFO CN-ANU
366	N2SP N90SF N222KC N333KC (N333KD) N555KC N333LX N366JA [cx 9Dec14; CofR expired]
367	(N910A) N17588 HB-ITN (N6164Z) N367GA N700FS N300FS N933PA N888SM
368	N17589 7T-VRB N368GA (N368TJ) C-GBBB (N112GS) [cx 04Dec12; parted out California City, CA]
369*	N910A N740SS N17ND N15HE (4X-CMM)
370	N319GA N100A N200A N400K N697BJ N463LM N105VS N323MK N320MK*
371	HZ-NR3 N680FM N8220F N681FM N353VA [cx 03Jan13; parted out Mojave, CA]
372	N320GA N200A N500E N500EX N724DB N724DD N523AM
373	N340GA N232HC VR-BAB VP-BAB N162JC N373GS N373RR N550RM N501BL*
374	N339GA N122DJ VR-CMF N24GA N270MC
375	N955CP VR-BOB N375GA N375NM N375NW (N75GJ) N375LT
376	N17582 A6-HHS N70AG (N5HG) N60AG N376EJ N376PJ N380AG
377*	N342GA N40CH N707RX N760AC N377RX N748JX (N377LR)
378	N343GA N955H N378HC N803CC N960DC N141MH N444KM N378SE [cx 20Feb13; parted out California City, CA]
379	N17586 HZ-MAL N379RH N282Q N28QQ N900LA N96757 [parted out California City, CA]
380	N345GA N159B N30WR
381	N304GA N277NS (N46ES) N747G N1871R N621S N221WR
382	N305GA 83-0500 US Navy 830500 [C20A] [wfu; to Southern Illinois University, Carbondale, IL, as instructional airframe]
383	N308GA 83-0501 [C20A] N65CE N30501
384	N1982C N399WW N399BH N369CS N112GS N818TJ N461AR
385	N1761K HZ-MS3 N883PA N183PA
386	N316GA N902K N902KB Mexico TP-07/XC-UJO XC-SCT
387	N26L N621JH N621JA N620JH N620JA N485GM N484GM [cx 25Jun13; wfu]
388	N309GA N902C N1C N748T N561ST N8JL N797BD N388LR
389	N310GA 83-0502 [C20A – transferred to NASA]
390*	N200SF VR-BKS VR-BLO VR-BOK VP-BOK N67TJ N1M N102AK N102AQ N124DT N303MP*
391	N349GA N29S N1S N194 (N222AP) N94BN N14SY N288KA [cx 1May14; parted out]
392	N30AH N6BX N6BZ N60GN N1GN N9WN N800WC N805WC N801WC N391SH N734TJ
393	N17587 A9C-BB HZ-MWD N33GZ XA-ABD N33GZ N519AF N200EL N300EL N200AB
394	N1761P N311GA N379XX N99WJ N888WE
395	N1761Q PK-PJA N5NW N395EJ N422TK
396	N1761S 7T-VRC N437GA N800MK N175BG
397	N351GA N59HA N978FL N692TV N767CB (N888WZ) XA-PCH N767CB
398	N315GA N88AE N827GA N827G N777RZ N610AB (N628JG) [wfu Chino, CA]
399*	N17581 7T-VRD N188TJ N528AP N399AP N818EC
400	N17585 Venezuela 0005 N990ML N500EF (N964MP)
401	N352GA N717 N400LH (N80AG) Denmark F-400 N97AG N370JL (N370J)
402	N301GA N303HB N3338 VR-BLN VP-BLN [w/o 06Feb98 Lac du Bourget, Chambery, France]
403	N347GA N39NA N39N XA-TCO (N333KC) N403NW XB-HIZ N403WJ N555GL [wfu Dubai/World Central, UAE]
404	N355GA N404M N404MM N403LM (N402LM) N8115N (N24TJ) N560SH
405	N348GA N40NB N40N N91CH N91CR N990WC N991WC (N9718P) N789TP N789TR N456AL
406	N356GA N80L N406FA XA-STT N12EN [cx 26Sep14; parted out California City, CA]
407	N17603 G-XMAF N407GA N913MK N813MK [parted out California City, CA]
408	N17608 9K-AEG YI-AKI [w/o 1991 Baghdad Airport, Iraq during Operation Desert Storm]
409*	(N353GA) N300BK N320GA N1526M N1526R N457ST N457SF N828MG N555RE N224KL
410	N350GA HZ-AFR
411	N314GA N966H N461GT N461GB [parted out by 818 Aviation, Mojave, CA]
412	N354GA N20XY N50XY N610CC N105Y N527CC N450BD
413	N357GA N77SW N778W N1 N8226M Ireland 249 N166WC N766WC N59AJ N762GS N16AJ [wfu Okeechobee, FL]
414	N358GA N165ST N165G
415	N17582 (HZ-SOG) HZ-HR4 HZ-NR2 N21NR N109DD
416*	N312GA N500AL N883A N4500X (N500XB) N19H
417	N317GA N111AC N1119C N300M N431JT N431JG [cx 4Sep14; parted out Miami/Opa Locka, FL; fuselage to Bridgewater, VA]
418*	N17583 JY-ABL JY-AMN N717TR PT-ALK N103CD [w/o Biggin Hill, UK, 24Nov14; parted out Bruntingthorpe, UK]
419	9K-AEH YI-AKJ [w/o 1991 Baghdad Airport, Iraq during Operation Desert Storm]
420	N333GA "40420" N47449 India K-2960/VT-ENR [but marks K-2960 not actually worn]
421	N318GA N99GA N421GM N721FF N921FF N711UF [parted out by Dodson Int'l, Rantoul, KS]
422	N319GA N750AC (N128AG) N407CA N903G (N903GL) N820BA N171TV N222G YV3262
423*	N1761D HZ-MIC (VR-CMC) N7134E N225SF N399RV N712AS
424	N320GA N60AC N228G N94FL N808NA
425	N344GA N425SP N492A
426	N321GA N151MZ N751MZ VR-CNJ VP-CNJ N703JA XA-ABA
427*	N327GA N44MD N42MD N87AC N300WY N308WY XA-MDC
428	N322GA N760A N760G N702DM P4-BFJ

GULFSTREAM III

C/n	Identities
429	N323GA N429SA N423SA N100HG N100HZ N77BT N77HG
430	N324GA N760C N23A N600BG N608BG
431*	N25SB (N259B) PK-CTP N99WJ P4-AEA N17LK
432	N333GA N713KM N995BC N997CM (N997HM) N704JA N469BT
433	N325GA N399CB N579TG N45KR [parted out by 818 Aviation, Mojave, CA]
434	N326GA N811JK N311JK N226G N226GC XA-SNG XB-FXD N23ET (N23SK) (N73ET) N323JH N18ZL
435	N17581 HB-ITS N435U N888PM N32KA N357KM
436	N346GA V8-HB3 V8-A11 V8-007 V8-009 N436GA N10EH N243MW
437*	N380TT N100AK N171AM
438	N302GA N1841D N911KT N473KT N30LX [modified as Airborne Multi-INT Laboratory]
439	N17586 SU-BGU
440*	N304GA N5103 (N3PY) N222BW N265A N71RP N458BE N124EP
441	N306GA N80J N214WY N467AM
442	N17587 SU-BGV
443	N315GA N5104 N21AM N813LS
444	N328GA N110MT N555HD N554HD ZS-VIP
445*	N316GA (N5103) N5105 N599DA N590DA N606DH N850PG N158PC
446	N309GA N446U N58AJ N510FR
447	N186DS N186DC N144PK N707JA N776MA [parted out Miami/Opa Locka, FL]
448	N339GA N117JJ N255SB I-MADU N123AP N178HH N710CF [testbed for Next Generation Jammer electronic warfare system]
449	N310GA XA-FOU N7C N85V N85VT [w/o 22Nov04 Houston-Hobby Airport, TX]
450	N329GA HZ-AFS N329GA PT-AAC VR-CTG N888VS N801MJ N36DA
451	(N370GA) N330GA Italy MM62022 N351FJ N500RH N5159Y N600RH N693PB N951XF [cx 31Oct12; wfu]
452	N331GA N27R N633P VR-BNZ VP-BNZ N123TL N800TD
453	N332GA HZ-109 Saudi Arabia 103 HZ-103 N213BA
454*	N334GA N60CT N1GT N273G N111G N111GX N903TC N740VC
455	N335GA N1SF (N103GA) N103GC N123CC N123MR N147MR N28YC N818DD N935DH XA-DHM
456	N336GA US Army 85-0049 [C20C] [wfu; to AMARG Davis-Monthan, AZ, 02Dec13]
457	N337GA N457H N972G N457JC
458	N338GA US Army 85-0050 [C20C] [wfu; to AMARG Davis-Monthan, AZ, 02Dec13]
459	N321GA N600B N586C N566C N54HF N555DW
460*	N322GA N500LS N500VS N500MM N500MN I-FCHI N2TQ N2TF N317ML N460PG N32MJ
461	N323GA N104AR N108AR
462	N324GA N303GA TU-VAF
463	N327GA N80AT N808T VR-BMY VP-BMY N463GE N886DT N196CC
464	N340GA N535CS N83AG N83PP N513MA N194PA
465*	N17586 86-0200 [C20B] N465GA Chile 911 N35GZ (N33GZ) N33NT N35GZ N53GL N35GZ N36JE
466*	N17583 N325GA N37HE N102AK N817MF N383MJ*
467*	N341GA JY-HAH N551AC N400WY N218MD
468	N342GA 86-0202 [C20B] [wfu; to AMARG Davis-Monthan, AZ, 03Sep15]
469*	N343GA JY-HZH N1956M N469TB N598GS N698GS YV2896
470	N344GA 86-0201 [C20B] N770GA 86-0201 [preserved National Museum of the United States Air Force, Wright-Patterson AFB, OH]
471	N347GA N888WL N583D N57TT N975RG
472*	N348GA N800CC N806CC N800CC N806CC N357H N780RH N780RA (N454BE) N353MA LV-CEG
473	N326GA US Army 86-0403 [C20C] [wfu; to AMARG Davis-Monthan, AZ, 02Dec13]
474	N311GA D2-ECB
475	N312GA 86-0203 [C20B]
476	N314GA 86-0204 [C20B]
477	N317GA 86-0205 USCG 01 [VC20B] N477SJ N477WG [parted out California City, CA; cx 15Apr15]
478	N318GA 86-0206 [C20B]
479	N319GA Italy MM62025 N50RL N556AF [parted out Miami/Opa Locka, FL; cx 25Aug15]
480	N302GA USN 163691 [C20D]
481	N304GA USN 163692 [C20D]
482	N306GA N333HK N600BL N164RJ N268RJ N111HC
483*	N309GA N66DD N766DD N19H (N483H) N343DF N343DP N794ME [parted out California City, CA]
484	N310GA N4UP N856W N506T VP-BOR N62MW N62MV
485	N315GA N721CW N777MW N80SR N5G N95NM [parted out by 818 Aviation, Mojave, CA]
486	N316GA TJ-AAW
487*	N324GA (TJ-...) TC-GAP N377GA N90005 N488SB N618KM N416WM
488	N325GA N700CN (N100BG) N800BG N446GA N401RJ N401PJ N399SC (N45PG) N500GF
489*	N328GA N272JS N888CW N388CW XA-LCA N218EE
490	N332GA N28R N388MM
491	N337GA N73RP N998JB N531JF (N531JC) N101PT N51MF N51FF A6-INF HZ-HHT [parted out California City, CA]
492	N339GA N212AT N212AD PT-WRC N492DD N188TC N848RJ N939KM
493	N322GA N400J N40QJ Ghana G540 N7513H [cx 16Nov16; CofR expired]
494	N370GA India K-2961
495	N371GA India K-2962

GULFSTREAM III

C/n	Identities
496	N372GA N310SL N21NY N89AE N89AB N99SC (N99SU) N843HS VP-CNP N384BB [parted out by 818 Aviation, Mojave, CA]
497	N373GA US Army 87-0139 N7096G US Army 87-0139 [C20E] [wfu; to AMARG Davis-Monthan, AZ, 30Jan15]
498	N374GA US Army 87-0140 N7096E US Army 87-0140 [C20E] [wfu; to AMARG Davis-Monthan, AZ, 28Jul14]
875	N333GA N333GU N210GK N290GA N728CP N845FW N298TB N416NP N300JZ

Production complete

GULFSTREAM IV/GULFSTREAM 300/350/400/450

We have been advised by Gulfstream Aerospace that the Gulfstream IV does **not** have the model number G1159C as has been quoted elsewhere.

C/n	Series	Identities
1000		N404GA [ff 19Sep85] N234DB N404DB N971EC N552WF
1001		N17581 N441GA N400GA VR-BSS VP-BSS N31001 N981SW N181CW N181CR
1002		N440GA N168WC N168WM
1003		N403GA N986AH N685TA N885TA N864YC N250RG
1004		N424GA N184CW (N199LX) N124TF N120WJ*
1005		N17582 VR-BJZ N823GA [w/o 13Jul12 Le Castellet, France]
1006		N99GM N3338 N614RD [cx 21Jun16, wfu]
1007		N420GA N100GN N100GJ N59JR N575E N710WJ
1008		N26LB N10LQ N10LB VR-BLH N412GA N119R N85WD
1009		N423GA N500LS N500VS N700LS N780LS VR-BOY Netherlands V-11
1010		N426GA N444TJ N824CA N950DM XA-AVZ
1011		N17581 A6-HHH [parted out by CAVU Aerospace, Stuttgart, AR]]
1012		N445GA N636MF N838MF N713VT (N713VL) N636GD N836MF N458BE
1013		N446GA N130B N321PT N321RT N1625 (N16251) N97FT N64AL XA-BVG N3150C (N771JG)
1014		N447GA N777SW N779SW Sweden 102001 [code 021]
1015		N17583 VR-BRF VP-BRF N450BF N772AV
1016		N427GA N95AE N29GY N880GC N21FJ
1017		N405GA N678RW (C-FNCG) VR-BHG VP-BHG N402KC N818BA
1018		N407GA N300L N43KS N418QA N113AR N25VG [parted out Dallas/Redbird, TX; fuselage to Roanoke, TX]
1019		N17584 TU-VAD
1020		N408GA N600CS N9300 N93AT
1021		N412GA N3M N3NU EC-HGH N310EL (N310EN) N21DH
1022		"N63M" [painted on a/c but not officially reg'd] N23M N23MU N663PD N955MB*
1023		N415GA N77SW N778W N85M N85MG N830EF N300JA N924MB
1024		(N130B) N412GA N96AE "N16JM" N116HM N820HB N1BB N44BB
1025		N419GA N5BK N420SZ N420SL N421SZ N928SZ N928ST N900GB N595E N250KC
1026		N17584 N151A N277RP (N277AG) N100HG N400HG
1027		N416GA TC-GAP Turkey 001 [wore dual marks TC-GAP/001] TC-GVB
1028		N428GA N712CW N712CC N605RA
1029		N429GA VR-BKI VP-BKI VP-BKH N44ZF
1030		N430GA N811JK N1WP N24JR N62JR
1031		N434GA HZ-AFU N431TL
1032		N17585 C-FSBR N315MA N315MC N888UE N432QS N254GA N2DF
1033		(HB-IMY) N69GP N173LP N1KE N6453 N6458 N711SW N711FW N76EJ (N400EE)
1034		N413GA N800BG N800BQ N841PA N388CA
1035		N435GA HZ-AFV N435TF
1036		N152A N45AC N701DB
1037		N17588 VR-BKE HZ-ADC HZ-103
1038		N17603 N438GA HZ-AFW
1039		(N431GA) N1901M N726RW
1040		N432GA N74RP N620DS N908DH N163EG N415RR
1041		N433GA N366F N888FR
1042		N17608 N400GA N22 N220GA N71TJ N68SL N217RR N889TC [parted out by Dodson Int'l Parts, Rantoul, KS]
1043		N1761B TC-ANA TC-ATA TC-GVA
1044		N423GA N1040 N1540 N154G
1045		N420GA N227G N227GH N247EM N217EM [cx 18Nov13; wfu]
1046		N1761D (HB-ITT) VR-BKU (HB-ITE) HB-ITP N119K N400CC 3B-PGF N675RW
1047		N1761J N461GA N23AC [w/o 30Oct96 Palwaukee, IL; cx Apr97]
1048		N1761K N448GA (VR-BKL) SU-BGM
1049		N402GA N372CM N372GM N113CS N829CS N136ZC N385GP N840ER
1050		N153RA N195WS N1AM N214BM N517ML
1051		N403GA N399CC N919CT (N903JF) (N903KP) N515UJ N515JA
1052		N419GA N800CC N940DC N152TS N722MM N48GL
1053		N47SL N26SL N91AE N165ST N17ND N168PK
1054		N426GA N400UP N480UP N745UP N745UR N789DK (N1DC) N860JB N220LH N254CA
1055		N1761P VR-BKV XB-EXJ XB-OEM N255GA N450MS
1056		N436GA N33M N33MX N770SC N685SF N685MF
1057		N437GA N43M N43MU N222AD N226AL N842PA
1058		N458GA N70PS VP-BSF VP-BME G-GMAC [w/o 01Dec04 Teterboro, NJ; cx 17Aug05; parted out by 818 Aviation, Mojave, CA]
1059		N17581 V8-RB1 V8-ALI V8-SR1 V8-007 N415GA N701QS N799WW N199WW N612AC N271PS
1060		N427GA N1SF VT-AMA [cx 17Jun10; parted out Mojave, CA]
1061		N17582 N457GA F-GPAK N161AK N429AL HB-IWZ N999GP
1062		N17583 N462GA N688H VR-CMF VP-CMF N104JG N619KK N619ML
1063		N17584 N54SB N333AX N720LH N745RS 9Q-CGC
1064		N439GA HB-ITT N7RP N797CM XA-AEX
1065		N442GA N584D N511C N599CN C-FCNR N835AA

GULFSTREAM IV

C/n	Series	Identities								
1066		N443GA	N118R	N466TS	N773JC	N1JR	N5JR	N63NM		
1067		N446GA	N145ST	N200LC						
1068		N17585	N95AE	N90AE	N82A	N189J	(N189WJ)			
1069		N459GA	N765A	N450AR	N1AR	N813PD				
1070		N407GA	N107A	N40KJ						
1071		N410GA	N1							
1072		N17586	N100A	N500E	N260CH	N472MM				
1073		N75RP	N75PP	N177BB						
1074		N17587	(HB-I..)	VR-BKT	VP-BKT	N740JA	N995GG			
1075		N412GA	N901K	N121JJ	N121JV	N61WH	N345DH			
1076		N17586	HZ-MNC	N338MM						
1077		N445GA	N119R	N119RC	PK-NSP	N477TS	N457DS			
1078		N17589	(G-BPJM)	G-DNVT	N211DK					
1079		N17603	XA-PUV	(N100WJ)	(N15WJ)	N479TS	N691RC	N794MH		
1080		N447GA	N20XY	N205X	M-YGIV	N108GS				
1081		N955H	(N955HC)	N777SA	N797SA	XA-RCM				
1082		N1082A	(N82BR)	M-GULF	N384MS	N555KE				
1083		N1761Q	HB-ITZ	VH-CCC	VH-CGF					
1084		(N448GA)	N1761S	HB-IMY	N41ZA					
1085		N449GA	N88GA	N864CE	N677RP	N423TT	N212JE			
1086		N460GA	N888MC	N23SY	N1086					
1087		N463GA	(N94SL)	N310SL	N1TM	N110TM	N368AG			
1088		N464GA	N4UP	N2600	N2600J	N1JN	N71JN	N93MK	N385PD	N305PB*
1089		N465GA	N53M	N53MU	Chile 911					
1090		N466GA	VR-CYM	VP-CYM	N9999M	VP-CYM	N9999M	N8989N	RP-C....	
1091		N467GA	N364G	N984JW						
1092		N468GA	N937US	N3H	N3HX	N661R	N18RF	N515PL	N515PE	N786JB
		N13SA								
1093		VR-BLC	HB-ITX	N399PA	N624BP	N100JF	N770KS			
1094		N2610	N740K	(N628NP)	N818BK					
1095		N469GA	N311EL							
1096		N17582	(G-....)	VR-CBW	VP-CBW	N167AA				
1097		N402GA	N900AL	N900AP	N4DP*					
1098		N403GA	N404CC	XA-AIS	N282CD	N7800	VP-BSF	N198GS		
1099		N489H	N299FB	(N499QS)	N199QS	N999LX	N36RR			
1100		N100AR	N100GX	B-8080	N483DJ					
1101		N404GA	N365G	N900EG						
1102		N405GA	N910B	XA-RBS	N522VR					
1103		N433GA	N90005	N103BC	VP-BIV	N3KN	C-FHPM			
1104		N600ML	N700GD	N2SA	[w/o Bakavu, Democratic Republic of Congo, 12Feb12]					
1105		N408GA	N312EL							
1106		N17608	9M-ISJ							
1107		N17581	(JA8366)	N101MU	N11FX	VH-CCO	N74TJ	N844GS	N844GF	N848GF
		N606MH								
1108		N17584	N410GA	N114AN	(N11AN)	N522AC	VH-NCP	N778MT	N463MA	
1109		N1761D	V8-ALI	V8-SR1	V8-007	N101GA	EC-IKP	G-MATF	N310EJ	N310
1110		N415GA	N404M	N404MY	N88MX	N526EE	N888MX	N721MC	N883LS	
1111		N416GA	N111JL	N111ZT	N511PA					
1112		N417GA	N12UT	N12U	N12UM	N112WJ				
1113		N423GA	N902K	N168TR	N169TT	XA-JJS				
1114		N428GA	N444LT	N555WL	XA-BAL	XA-TOO	N314GA	N44LX	N763DB	
1115		N430GA	N410M	N410MY	N440TC	VH-TXS				
1116		N431GA	N971L	N305TC						
1117		N1761J	G-HARF	N105BH	VP-CMR	N117JF	N2121	N2129		
1118		N439GA	N1526M	N2WL	N440CP	N418TT	N720CH	N269HM		
1119		N407GA	N614HF	N768J	N524AN	N716AS	N7176S			
1120		N410GA	VR-BOB	N400SA	N70AG	N20H	N888ES			
1121		N412GA	N7776	N411WW	N811WW	N214TS	N962SS	N178MH	N962SS	
1122		N40N	N226G	N317M	N317MJ	N600LY*				
1123		N457GA	I-LUBI	N529AL	N619A					
1124		N420GA	N1900W	N277GM						
1125		N432GA	N415SH	N700WB	N888LK	N888LG	N56AG	N49PP	N44CE	
1126		N426GA	5N-FGP	5N-BOD						
1127		N427GA	VR-BLR	VR-BUS	VP-BUS	N127DK	[w/o Tahiti 30Jan11]			
1128		N429GA	HZ-MFL	N428BC						
1129		N17585	EI-CAH	ZS-NMO	N1129X	N8MC	N400AJ			
1130		N436GA	N401MM	N404LM	N711GL					
1131		N437GA	N679RW	N55TD						
1132		N442GA	A6-ALI	N60NY	N604M	N80BR	N4T	N71NR	N7JM	
1133		N443GA	N700CN	N375TC	N385GP					
1134		N445GA	VR-BJD	VP-BJD	N334JC	N8796J	N990PT	(N990PJ)	N990PM	(N34S)
		N3H	N722CH*							
1135		N435GA	N500MM	N100ES	N190ES	N456BE	N85KV	N930LS	N960LS*	
1136		N401GA	N27CD	N75VB						
1137		N402GA	N299DB	N21CZ	N7RX	N37RX	N777TC	N605CM		
1138		N403GA	N200A	(N501E)	N520E	N520EP	N777SA	N501RB		

GULFSTREAM IV / IVSP

C/n	Series	Identities
1139		N404GA N99WJ N21KR N21KP N325RC N331P N134BR N572EC N630E
1140		N405GA N811JK (N827JK) N827JM N77WL
1141		N407GA N767FL N767EL N115FL N729TY
1142		N408GA I-LADA N142NW N222 N222GY
1143		N410GA HZ-AFX N143PK
1144		N415GA N100PM N250J B-HWA N114GA B-3999 N233GA B-8091
1145		N416GA N102MU N797CD N569CW LV-BYC N569CW N973MW
1146		N417GA N77SW (N778W) N777UE N776US N970SJ N970SY
1147		N419GA N200PM N820MS
1148		N427GA (JA8380) N427GA HB-IEJ N306TT
1149		N430GA N777SW N149GU N152KB N108DB N108DU
1150		N433GA V8-ALI V8-009 V8-SR1 N151G VP-BIS N386AG N900RL
1151		N375GA N80AT N109ST N151ST N109ST 9U-BKB
1152		N446GA N63M N63MU [cx 10May13; parted out California City, CA]
1153		N448GA N110LE N589HM N590HM N589HM N546MG
1154		N1761D N150PG N150GX N151GX N186DS
1155		N1761B N910S N719SA
1156		N1761K N987AC N987AR VH-TGG VH-XGG N156TS N5RD N57LQ
1157		N17581 9K-AJA N457GA OE-IJA N157FQ B-8082 N960DP
1158		N17582 N917W
1159		N17583 9K-AJB N458FA HB-IKR (D-AAGF) [cx; status?]
1160		N17584 Ireland 251 N297PJ
1161		N17585 9K-AJC N459FA N20EG N461TS N495RS
1162	C20F	N457GA US Army 91-0108 N7096B US Army 91-0108
1163		N458GA Turkey 12-003 Turkey 91-003
1164		N459GA N300GX N420CC N218KD (N103HF) [wfu Chino, CA]
1165		N460GA N780E N780N N877LC
1166		N461GA HZ-SAR HZ-AFY N166JM
1167		N17586 N1SL N49SL N1SL N275DJ
1168		N462GA A4O-AB Oman 557
1169		N463GA N500DG N600DW N600CK
1170		N464GA N711SW (N811SW) N997BC N880WD N765RM
1171		N465GA N72RK N686CG N3SA N1WE
1172		N466GA XA-SEC N472TS N85V N85VM N227SV
1173		N17587 Botswana OK1 Botswana OK2 N731AE N113WJ
1174		N467GA N174LM HB-IEQ N174SJ N4PC N6VB N41VB N10ZK N914EG N71NE
1175		N17588 HB-ITJ (N1175B) VH-CCA N18WF G-EVLN 5N-PZE
1176		N468GA V8-008 N176G VP-CRY N9253V HB-IWY N786CM
1177		N469GA N677RW N236MJ N236MY
1178		N470GA N900LS N909LS N611JM
1179		N471GA N41CP N41QR N265ST N527JC
1180		N472GA N700LS N709LS N827K XA-ASI
1181	C20H	N473GA USAF 90-0300 N473GA N906GA USAF 90-0300
1182		N475GA N200LS N202LS N75CC Chile 912
1183	SP	N476GA [ff as Gulfstream IV 23Dec91; cvtd to SP prototype and ff as such 24Jun92] VR-BDC HB-IBX N510ST N510SR N510SP
1184		N477GA N111NL (N508JM) (N805JM) N583AJ
1185	SP	N478GA N485GA N635AV N570DC
1186		N479GA 8P-MAK N345AA N344AA (N915G)
1187	C20G	N481GA US Navy 165093
1188		N482GA HL7222 N102AK
1189	C20G	N402GA US Navy 165094
1190		N403GA JA001G
1191	SP	N404GA N979RA N317M N317MR N317MB N403TB
1192	SP	N407GA N212K N180CH
1193	SP	N412GA (N980ML) N163M N620K N620KA N608CL
1194	SP	N415GA N77CP N77QR N473CW
1195	SP	N419GA XA-CHR N47HR N867CE N888PM
1196		N420GA A4O-AC Oman 558
1197		N423GA N150GX XA-CAG N969SG N4753 N771AV
1198		N425GA N99GA N68AL
1199	C20G	N428GA US Navy 165151 [code RG]
1200	C20G	N430GA US Marines 165153
1201	C20G	N431GA US Navy 165152
1202		N432GA V8-MSB V8-009 JY-RAY N369XL HB-ITF G-CFOH M-PZPZ N236CA
1203	SP	N434GA N410WW N411WW N412WW (N199PZ) (N417NK)
1204		N435GA N212AT N252CH N178PT
1205	SP	N439GA VH-ASQ N8203K N393BD N671AF
1206		N437GA N1040 N1620 N162G N315MK
1207		N441GA C-FDCS C-FJES N77SW (N77VU) N344AA (N344AB) N30LH
1208	SP	N443GA VR-BNY VP-BNY N297GB N110SN
1209		N445GA N157H N724DB N724DD N1D
1210		N448GA (N909SP) N9PC N410QS N144PK
1211		N447GA N2107Z
1212	SP	N413GA VR-BOT VP-BOT N88HP N884L (N38NZ) (N777NZ) N502JT N939PG

GULFSTREAM IV / IVSP

C/n	Series	Identities								
1213		N416GA	N56L							
1214		N405GA	N414BM	N2615	N2615B	N477JB				
1215	SP	N426GA	Sweden 102002							
1216	SP	N440GA	Sweden 102003							
1217	SP	N417GA	N981HC	N711MC	N711HE	(N711PE)	N979CB	N977CB		
1218	SP	N418SP	N5MC							
1219	SP	N446GA	PK-NZK	N50HE	N87HP	N874C				
1220	SP	N449GA	N79RP	N688TT	N688TF	N268VT				
1221	SP	N451GA								
1222	SP	N452GA	N71RP	N171JC						
1223	SP	N453GA	N935SH	N257H						
1224	SP	N454GA	N18TM	N18TD	N124TS	C-GEIV	M-IVSP	2-TRAV	2-GULF	
1225	SP	N459GA	N316GS	N816GS	N773MJ	N773AJ	N450KK	N450KD*	[parted out Miami/Opa Locka, FL, after suffering in-flight structural damage]	
1226	SP	N460GA	N41PR	N41PL	N50MG	N415WW	N96JA			
1227	SP	N463GA	(XA-VAD)	XA-DPS	N626TG	N626TC	N600VC	N958BX		
1228	SP	N464GA	N18AN	(VP-C..)	N30GD					
1229	SP	N465GA	N830EC	N270SC						
1230	SP	N467GA	9M-TRI	N101CV						
1231	SP	N470GA	N250VC	N250VZ	N255TS	VT-DLF	VT-ONE	N299MB		
1232	SP	N471GA	N232K							
1233	SP	N472GA	N575SF	VP-BFW	A6-OME	N450JE	N700MV			
1234	SP	N475GA	N924ML	I-LXGR	VP-BNB	N999NB				
1235	SP	N477GA	N100A	N500E	N500EP	N17JK	N1AZ			
1236	SP	N478GA	N100GN	N99SC	N99EJ	N869DL				
1237	SP	N480GA	N1904W	(N277GR)						
1238	SP	N483GA	N499SC	(N71LA)	N92LA	(N92LU)	N415PG	C-GCPM		
1239	SP	N484GA	N1JN	N909RX	(N105TR)	N699HH	N950DM	N121AP		
1240	SP	N486GA	N333PV	N212AW	N705PC	N789TN				
1241	SP	N487GA	N169CA	N343DF	N843DF	N117MS	N917MS			
1242	SP	N490GA	N982HC	N407GC						
1243	SP	N491GA	N404SP	VR-CBL	N39WH	N37WH	(N39WH)			
1244	SP	N404GA	JA002G							
1245	SP	N405GA	N101HC	(N7602)	N7601	N459BE	N588LS			
1246	SP	N407GA	N49RF							
1247	SP	N408GA	(N990UH)	N14UH	N477RP	N211MA	N94PC	N6PC		
1248	SP	N422GA	N62MS	N6VN	N244DS	N72RK	N700PP			
1249	SP	N423GA	N63HS	N634S	N151SD					
1250	SP	N425GA	VR-CBB	VP-CBB	N47HR	XA-CHR	N169JC	XA-JPS	XA-RUI	N169JC
		XA-KTX								
1251	SP	N429GA	(N321PT)	N60PT	N60PE	N165JF				
1252	SP	N433GA	N252C	N394TR	N707CW					
1253	SP	N435GA	N676RW	N225DC						
1254	SP	N436GA	N801CC	N930DC	N920DS	N920TB	VT-PLL	HZ-MKG	VT-PLP	N445BJ
1255	SP	N437GA	N600PM	VP-BNN	N934DF	VP-BKI	M-PBKI	N504ST		
1256	C20H	N438GA	USAF 92-0375							
1257	SP	N448GA	N4CP	N4QP	(N99PD)	N603CS	N1JN	(D-AGIV)	N603CS	N776MA
1258	SP	N416GA	N400UP	N585D	N598GS					
1259	SP	N495GA	N1PG	N4PG	N4UG	N559LC				
1260	SP	N461GA	N3PG	N810LP	(N415P)					
1261	SP	N469GA	N399CB	N57HJ						
1262	SP	N496GA	N462QS	N326AZ	N432HC					
1263	SP	N497GA	N830CB	N263S	N128TS	N147X				
1264	SP	N499GA	N464QS	N120JJ						
1265	SP	N465GA	N540W	VP-CFF	N165GD	N141CP	N450TL	VH-WXK	N370RS	
1266	SP	N412GA	N300K	N61LA	N91LA	(N91LU)	N77DY	N77D	VP-BOL	N267LG
1267	SP	N417GA	N301K	N624GJ						
1268	SP	N427GA	N990WC	N600BG	N888MF					
1269	SP	N434GA	N677SW	N677VU	N250LB	N925JS				
1270	U4	N442GA	Japan 75-3251							
1271	U4	N452GA	Japan 75-3252							
1272	SP	N454GA	N621JH	N621JA	N620JH					
1273	SP	N457GA	N372BC	N372BG	N102BG	N102BQ				
1274	SP	N458GA	"LV-WOW"	[painted in error at completion centre]				LV-WOM	Sweden 102004	
1275	SP	N459GA	N475QS	N505GF						
1276	SP	N460GA	N1955M	N1990C	N515XL	N856AF	N557WY			
1277	SP	N462GA	N5GF							
1278	SP	N464GA	VR-CTA	N98LT						
1279	SP	N466GA	N2002P	(N451C)	N925DC					
1280	SP	N468GA	N531MD	N688LS						
1281	SP	N470GA	N481QS	N129NS						
1282	SP	N471GA	(N96FL)	VR-CFL	VP-CFL	N9KN	N1925M			
1283	SP	N472GA	N401JL	N402JP	N898AW	N513MA				
1284	SP	N475GA	N1GN	N21GN	N150CM	(N577SW)	N90AM	N575CT	N707EA	N197BD*
1285	SP	N477GA	N874A	N972MS						

GULFSTREAM IVSP

C/n	Series	Identities								
1286	SP	N480GA	(N486GA)	N286GA	N464SP	N4SP	N464SP	N880G	N192NC	N192N
		N7LA	N999AA	(N620HF)						
1287	SP	N484GA	N487QS	N99GY						
1288	SP	N403GA	7T-VPR							
1289	SP	N405GA	N844HS	N802WC	N804WC	N800WC	N334MC	N202VZ	N289MU	N677FR
		N607MH	(N624MH)							
1290	SP	N408GA	N6NB	N730BA	N71VR	N988LS				
1291	SP	N412GA	7T-VPS							
1292	SP	N413GA	N1GT	N917VZ	N292MU	N492JR	N1JN	N16JN		
1293	SP	N415GA	N493QS	N429DD						
1294	SP	N416GA	HZ-MAL	N416GA	HZ-KAA	N718GM	N131SW	N294G		
1295	SP	N417GA	N495QS	N450MB						
1296	SP	N419GA	N725LB	N728LB						
1297	SP	N420GA	LV-WSS	N728JP	N710LX	N1LW*				
1298	SP	N422GA	N501PC	N961V						
1299	SP	N423GA	N499QS	N555LK						
1300	SP	N432GA	N1BN	N321BN	(N500BL)	N226MP				
1301	SP	N433GA	N92AE	N974JD						
1302	SP	N434GA	(N98AE)	N93AE	N818SS	N819SS				
1303	U4	N435GA	Japan 85-3253							
1304	SP	N436GA	N404QS	N287TX	N526EE					
1305	SP	N439GA	(N913SC)	N888SQ	N305GA	M-FMHG	N44GV			
1306	SP	N441GA	N540CH	N811DF	N89888					
1307	SP	N443GA	N94AE	N94AN	(N130WB)	N137WS				
1308	SP	N446GA	N408QS	N288TX	XA-STS					
1309	SP	N447GA	N309GA	N824CA	N56D	N992MS				
1310	SP	N448GA	(N2425)	N902	N902H	N850LG				
1311	SP	N449GA	N411QS	N271TX	N485GM					
1312	SP	N453GA	9M-ABC	N4FL	N619FL	N910AF				
1313	SP	N455GA	N94LT	N100DF	N481SC					
1314	SP	N461GA	N429SA	N427SA						
1315	SP	N413GA	N315GA	N950CM	N525KF	N580KF	N999SE			
1316	SP	N427GA	N416QS	N168RT	N40VC					
1317	SP	N417GA	N929WT	N333PY						
1318	SP	N418GA	N1624	N15Y						
1319	SP	N429GA	N878SM							
1320	SP	N437GA	N420QS	N116WJ						
1321	SP	N444GA	(N600CC)	N500CD	N905LP					
1322	SP	N445GA	N422QS	N272TX						
1323	SP	N454GA	N503PC	N565RV						
1324	SP	N457GA	N424QS	N817RA						
1325	SP	N459GA	N102FM	(N24EE)	Pakistan J-755					
1326	U4	N325GA	Japan 95-3254							
1327	SP	N327GA	TR-KHD	TR-KSP						
1328	SP	N328GA	N428QS	N450WG						
1329	SP	N329GA	SU-BNC							
1330	SP	N324GA	N400J	N40QJ	N168BB	[cx 16May17, parted out California City, CA]				
1331	SP	N331GA	N878G	EC-KEY	N74GG	(N322MG)	(N755CS)			
1332	SP	N332GA	SU-BND							
1333	SP	N333GA	N800J	N80QJ						
1334	SP	N334GA	N434QS	N626JS	N626LJ	N800CR				
1335	SP	N335GA	N720BA	N918CC	N978CC					
1336	SP	N636GA	N41CP	N235LP	C-FORB					
1337	SP	N637GA	N52MK	T7-DRM						
1338	SP	N638GA	N401WT	N100HF	XA-HNY					
1339	SP	N339GA	N327TL							
1340	SP	N340GA	N1TF	N800AL	N77D	N550GN				
1341	SP	N341GA	N441QS	N886LS						
1342	SP	N342GA	N555KC	N808T						
1343	SP	N343GA	N99SC	N2CC						
1344	SP	N344GA	N18AC	N411LL						
1345	SP	N345GA	(JY-ONE)	N457ST	N857ST	(N121PP)				
1346	SP	N346GA	N104AR	N104PR	RP-C8346	N273SF				
1347	SP	N347GA	N988H	N933JJ	N155RJ	N156WJ				
1348	SP	N348GA	N80A	PP-WJB						
1349	SP	N349GA	HZ-KS1	N349GA	N616DC	N616DG	N510MG			
1350	SP	N330GA	N396U	N1JN	N396U					
1351	SP	N351GA	N451QS	N265SJ						
1352	SP	N352GA	N452QS	N572MS						
1353	SP	N353GA	A9C-BAH	A9C-BRF						
1354	SP	N354GA	N397J	N397JJ						
1355	SP	N355GA	N66DD	N66ED	N107TD					
1356	SP	N319GA	(JY-TWO)	N600DR	N970KG					
1357	SP	N357GA	N77FK							
1358	SP	N358GA	N1625							
1359	SP	N359GA	Japan 05-3255							

GULFSTREAM IVSP

C/n	Series	Identities								
1360	SP	N360GA	N460QS	N428KS						
1361	SP	N361GA	N545CS							
1362	SP	N362GA	N888LK	(N888LF)	ZK-KFB	N662GA	VQ-BMT			
1363	SP	N363GA	N463QS	N463G	N48CC	VH-DBT	N1363G	N869MD		
1364	SP	N364GA	N143KS	N711SK	N333FG					
1365	SP	N365GA	HZ-MS04	HZ-MS4						
1366	SP	N320GA	N404M	N404XT	N445MD					
1367	SP	N367GA	HZ-KS2	N367GA	N422ML	N1EB	N618SA	N335LL	N335L	N415LT
1368	SP	N322GA	N1967M	N610MC	N411AL	N125SJ	N616RR			
1369	SP	N323GA	N469QS	N469G	N400MP	N900MP	N302SB			
1370	SP	N370GA	N240CX	N340CX						
1371	SP	N371GA	VP-CIP	N371FP	(N279AP)					
1372	SP	N372GA	N472QS	N926TT*						
1373	SP	N373GA	N373KM	N106KA	N595PE					
1374	SP	N374GA	N7PG	N1PG	N896AC	N993AC				
1375	SP	N375GA	N247KB	B-8088	N484DJ	N222RA	N888LD			
1376	SP	N376GA	N12NZ	N400CK						
1377	SP	N377GA	N477QS	N316VB						
1378	SP	N378GA	N2PG	N269WR						
1379	SP	N379GA	N60PT	VT-MST	VP-CTR	N450EF				
1380	SP	N380GA	N480QS	N480VR						
1381	SP	N381GA	VP-BZA	VP-BIV	VP-BYS	A6-NMA	PK-TWY			
1382	SP	N382GA	N1TF	(N222MC)	N1GC	N428M	C-GMRX	N65HS		
1383	SP	N383GA	N955H	N955E	(N507TE)	N707TE				
1384	SP	N384GA	(HZ-KS3)	N404AC	N945GS					
1385	SP	N485GA	N577SW	N577VU	N1818C	N4818C				
1386	SP	N486GA	N486QS	N889CG						
1387	SP	N487GA	N254SD	N854SD	N4387	N108RT				
1388	SP	N477GA	N38BG	N4SP	XA-EYA	N990EA				
1389	SP	N389GA	N489QS	N489VR						
1390	SP	N490GA	N1874M	VP-CSF	N30JE					
1391	SP	N391GA	N827GA							
1392	SP	N392GA	N492QS							
1393	SP	N393GA	N297MC	N352BH						
1394	SP	N394GA	N721RL							
1395	SP	N395GA	N961SV	N396NS						
1396	SP	N396GA	N890A	N664JN						
1397	SP	N397GA	N669BJ							
1398	SP	N398GA	N498QS							
1399	SP	N499GA	N121JM	[w/o Bedford/Hanscom Field, MA, 31May14]						
1400	SP	N478GA	N215TM	N700FS						
1401	SP	N401GA	N900LS	N300CR						
1402	SP	N479GA	N602PM	(N602AG)	(N602KF)	N602PL	VP-CLA	M-ABCT	N80AE	N799CP
1403	SP	N403GA	N403QS							
1404	SP	N404GA	N404HS	XA-FCP						
1405	SP	N310GA	N45ET							
1406	SP	N311GA	VP-BNZ	N404GA	N526EE	N104AD				
1407	SP	N312GA	N407QS	N40HB	N407NS					
1408	SP	N316GA	(N448QS)	N401QS						
1409	SP	N317GA	N67TM	N822NR						
1410	SP	N318GA	N80AT							
1411	SP	N411GA	N56MD	N56D	N303TP	N404TC	(N808TC)	N444QC		
1412	SP	N412GA	N700LS	N709LS	A6-DWD	N65CC				
1413	SP	N413GA	5X-UEF	N92SA	PP-CSW	N197SW	(N413VS)			
1414	SP	N323GA	"N819JF"	N5VS	N505VS	N333EC	(N787AF)			
1415	SP	N415GA	N71BD							
1416	SP	N416GA	N900WR							
1417	SP	N417GA	(N417QS)	N122RS	XA-RYR					
1418	SP	N418GA	7T-VPC							
1419	SP	N419GA	EI-CVT	VP-BVT	(N419GA)	N600AR	N617WM	N658DV		
1420	SP	N420GA	N72BD	N106CE	N724DB					
1421	SP	N324GA	7T-VPM							
1422	SP	N422GA	N999GP	N7UF						
1423	SP	N423GA	N621JH							
1424	SP	N328GA	SU-BNO							
1425	SP	N425GA	XA-ABA	P4-TAK	P4-DDA	P4-NMD				
1426	SP	N426GA	N426QS							
1427	SP	N427GA	SU-BNP							
1428	SP	N330GA	N512C	N990NB	N991NB					
1429	SP	N429GA	N777KK							
1430	SP	N331GA	N530JD	N14456	N913SQ	N71TV				
1431	SP	N334GA	N818ME							
1432	SP	N335GA	N211DH							
1433	SP	N433GA	N1SN							
1434	SP	N434GA	N663P	N9106						
1435	SP	N435GA	N144KK	N435GA	N994GC	N502PC				

GULFSTREAM IVSP / 300 / 400

C/n	Series	Identities							
1436	SP	N436GA	N436QS						
1437	SP	N437GA							
1438	SP	N388GA	N228RE						
1439	SP	N439GA	N586D	N505UP					
1440	SP	N391GA	N997AG	N76RP	N84HD	N40AA	N800HH		
1441	SP	N341GA	N1289M	N123LC	VH-OSW	N950LG			
1442	SP	N442GA	N481FB	N345LC	N718DW	N106TD			
1443	SP	N443GA	N305LM						
1444	SP	N344GA	(N444GV)	N400HF	N904TC	N944TC	HZ-SK1		
1445	SP	N445GA	N445QS	N474D	N474X				
1446	SP	N446GA	N317M	N317ML	N817ME				
1447	SP	N447GA	N667P	N822A					
1448	SP	N448GA	N1LB	N300LB	N808MF				
1449	SP	N449GA	N200LS	N209LS	(N4SP)	N309SG	N551CB		
1450	SP	N370GA	N809C	N435HC					
1451	SP	N351GA	N372CM	N522BP	N522BR	N244J			
1452	SP	N452GA	N603PM	(N603AG)	N603KF	N603KE	N816SP		
1453	SP	N453GA	N444QG						
1454	SP	N454GA	N454QS						
1455	SP	N455GA	N616CC						
1456	SP	N396GA	N507SA	N207AA					
1457	SP	N357GA	N234DB	N234DN	N305CF				
1458	SP	N358GA	N235KK						
1459	SP	N399GA	(D-AJJJ)	D-AJGK	N1459A				
1460	SP	N460GA	(N825LM)	HB-ILV	N331LV	(N326LM)	N326JD	N386JD	
1461	SP	N461GA	N877A						
1462	SP	N462GA	N462CS	N462CK	N457H	N1SG	N462D		
1463	SP	N463GA	N465QS						
1464	SP	N464GA	N950AV	N950HB	N119FM				
1465	SP	N465GA	RA-10201						
1466	SP	N266GA	VP-BSH	N888ZF	N466KA	N10FH			
1467	SP	N467GA	(N225BK)	N225CX	N226CX	XA-BLZ	XA-PTR		
1468	SP	N468GA	N700NY	N814RR					
1469	SP	N269GA	N5956B						
1470	SP	N470GA	N34UH	N394AK					
1471	SP	N471GA	N471CR	N923CL					
1472	SP	N372GA	N4DA	N475LC					
1473	SP	N373GA	XA-EOF	N620M	N711EG				
1474	SP	N374GA	(N948AV)	N248AB	N7799T				
1475	SP	N475GA	N24TH	N67TH	N324FP				
1476	SP	N476GA	N59AP	N52AP	N221EA				
1477	SP	N477GA	(N949AV)	N244DS	N284DS	N468AB	N100EW	N100ZW	N606PS
1478	SP	N378GA	N478GS						
1479	SP	N479GA	N1479G	N226RS					
1480	SP	N480GA	N482QS	CS-DKA	N36MW				
1481	SP	N281GA	N621SC	N691SC	4X-CPX				
1482	SP	N482GA	N13J	N121JJ					
1483	SP	N483GA	N810TM						
1484	SP	N484GA	N721FF	N717AL					
1485	SP	N485GA	N5NG						
1486	SP	N486GA	N608PM	(N608AG)	(N608KF)	M-YWAY			
1487	SP	N487GA	N428AS	N428AZ	XA-SKY	M-GFOR	VH-TSL	VP-CSH	
1488	SP	N488GA	N490QS						
1489	SP	N389GA	N142HC	N142HQ	N212WZ	N119AF			
1490	SP	N490GA	(N490QS)	N1TM					
1491	SP	N491GA	N491EC						
1492	SP	N392GA	N123MR	N500PC					
1493	SP	N493GA	N235DX	N717DX	N104DX	N154C			
1494	SP	N494GA	N400FJ						
1495	SP	N495GA	N250VC	N251MM	N33LR	N899AL			
1496	SP	N496GA	N308AB	N800AR					
1497	SP	N397GA	(N497QS)	N702GH					
1498	SP	N398GA	N780RH	N757MC					
1499	SP	N499GA	N941AM	N918TB	N918TD	N55ME	N429CK	[last a/c to bear the Gulfstream IV name]	
1500	400	N520GA	N400GA	(N55GJ)	N50EE				
1501	400	N401GA	(N402QS)	N128AB	N176MG				
1502	400	N202GA	N710EC	N710EG					
1503	300	N403GA	A6-RJA	(D-AONE)	HZ-FM2				
1504	400	N374GA	(N402QS)	N902L	N570BY				
1505	300	N405GA	A6-RJB						
1506	400	N306GA	SU-BPE						
1507	300	N307GA	N91KL	N826RP					
1508	300	N508GA	N820TM	(B-MJZ)	B-LSZ	N388AJ	N663DC		
1509	300	N509GA	N607PM	N607KF	N789RR	XA-RIN			
1510	300	N510GA	N609PM	(N609KF)	(N609RM)	N349K			

GULFSTREAM 300 / 350 / 400 / 450

C/n	Series	Identities					
1511	400	N201GA	N161MM				
1512	300	N512GA	N606PM	(N606KF)	N958TB		
1513	400	N113GA	N4UC	N928GC	N500RL		
1514	400	N314GA	N1932P	(N1931P)	LV-CAZ		
1515	400	N415GA	N851EL	N342AP			
1516	400	N516GA	N400GA	N721BS			
1517	300	N517GA	N129MH	N130MH	N900CC		
1518	400	N218GA	SU-BPF				
1519	400	N519GA	N527JG				
1520	300	N520GA	HZ-MF3				
1521	400	N221GA	N413QS				
1522	400	N522GA	N251DV	N254SD	N854SD		
1523	400	N423GA	N401FT				
1524	400	N524GA	N522AC	N522AG	XA-CHG		
1525	300	N425GA	HZ-MF4				
1526	300	N526GA	N160TM				
1527	400	N327GA	N402FT				
1528	400	N528GA	N523AC	N706VA	N702JF		
1529	400	N529GA	N477SA	(N171RH)	N702RH*		
1530	400	N330GA	N650PW	N318JW			
1531	400	N531GA	N212VZ	N531MU	A6-HHH		
1532	300	N532GA	HZ-MF5				
1533	400	N533GA	N467QS	N167TV			
1534	400	N434GA	(N650PW)	(N616KF)	N616KG	N721KJ	(N721MR)
1535	300	N435GA	N825T				

GULFSTREAM 350/450

The Gulfstream 450 was originally dubbed the GIV-X and was awarded its FAA Type certificate 13Aug04
The Gulfstream 350 is essentially a shorter-range Gulfstream 450

C/n	Series	Identities								
4001	450	N401SR								
4002	450	N442SR	N820AV	N4FC	N820AV					
4003	450	N403SR	N821AV	N704JW						
4004	450	N404SR	N450GA	N428TT	(N8875)	D-ARKK	N156WC	N4500X	N4570X	XA-AVO
4005	450	N165GA	N512JT	N512LT	(N980CM)					
4006	450	N166GA	N111CQ							
4007	450	N185GA	N142HC	N142HQ	HZ-A13	HZ-SK5				
4008	450	N608GA	N97FT	N97FL	XA-XTR					
4009	450	N909GA	N885AR	(N885RR)	(N299AJ)					
4010	450	N910GA	N425QS							
4011	350	N121GA	N502GM							
4012	450	N812GA	N80Q	N80QL	N450Z					
4013	350	N913GA	N5113	N211FZ	N931DC					
4014	450	N314GA	N415QS							
4015	350	N915GA	N117WR							
4016	350	N816GA	N5114	N551GR	XC-PFM					
4017	450	N917GA	N7RX							
4018	450	N618GA	B-KHK							
4019	350	N989GA	"N350GA"+	[+ fake marks worn in NBAA Static park Nov05 Orlando Executive, FL]						N5115
		N82CW								
4020	450	N990GA	(N450GA)+	[+ ntu marks worn in NBAA Static park Nov05 Orlando Executive, FL]						N588AT
		N326AZ								
4021	450	N621GA	N430QS							
4022	450	N622GA	N464ST	N461GT						
4023	350	N623GA	N5116							
4024	450	N624GA	N451CM	(N927EM)						
4025	450	N998GA	N440QS							
4026	350	N626GA	N5117	XA-LAA	N906JC					
4027	450	N627GA	HB-JEQ	S5-ADC	G-SADC	D-AFLY	N251HR			
4028	450	N628GA	N915BD	N881E	PK-TMI					
4029	450	N629GA	N888HH							
4030	450	N630GA	N235CG	N285CG	C-GXDN	N348RS				
4031	450	N631GA	(N450JK)	N1JK	VP-CAE	N450FK	(PT-FKK)			
4032	450	N632GA	N24XC	N82A	N823A	N809SM				
4033	450	N633GA	N989WS	N404PX						
4034	450	N634GA	N122GV	N442HM						
4035	450	N635GA	N409CC	N119AD						
4036	450	N936GA	N922H	N922N	N1MC					
4037	450	N537GA	N445QS							
4038	350	N538GA	N450RG							
4039	450	N439GA	N450GA	N760G	N539VE	N937BG				

GULFSTREAM 350 / 450

C/n	Series	Identities							
4040	350	N440GA	N350FK	VP-CAP					
4041	450	N401GA	N451DC	N121GZ					
4042	450	N442GA	N776JB	N450WC					
4043	450	N443GA	N450AB						
4044	450	N644GA	N663CP	N450KR					
4045	450	N445GA	4K-AZ888						
4046	450	N446GA	N450QS						
4047	450	N447GA	N664CP	C-GFCP					
4048	450	N448GA	N900AL	N950AV					
4049	450	N449GA	N665CP	N665P	N918E				
4050	450	N850GA	N244DS	N865R					
4051	450	N351GA	N908VZ	N405MU	N868BB				
4052	450	N452GA	N500J	N50UJ	N918CC				
4053	450	N453GA	N845G	N225FD					
4054	450	N454GA	N405QS						
4055	450	N455GA	N237GA	(N240JA)	N237GR				
4056	450	N556GA	(N450PG)	N500N	N778CR				
4057	450	N457GA	N500RP	N457GA	N2LA				
4058	450	N458GA	N218WW	N18NY					
4059	450	N459GA	N222NB	N221NB	N18S				
4060	450	N460GA	G-TAYC						
4061	450	N461GA	N450LV						
4062	450	N462GA	N450XX						
4063	450	N463GA	N930DC	N127RR*					
4064	450	N464GA	N768JJ	N763JJ	N338TZ				
4065	450	N465GA	N450GD	(N555LR)	N767DX	N767DT	PR-ETE	N450EA	N450BT*
4066	450	N466GA	OY-GVG	P4-BFL					
4067	450	N467GA	N475M	HZ-SK2					
4068	450	N468GA	N435QS						
4069	450	N469GA	N612AF						
4070	450	N470GA	N818G	N100EW					
4071	450	N471GA	N24TH	N76TH					
4072	450	N372GA	N450PG	N2194					
4073	450	N373GA	N474M	HZ-SK3					
4074	450	N374GA	N455QS						
4075	450	N375GA	N440AS	N913MK					
4076	450	N376GA	N779CS	N796MA	B-8098	N407GA	XA-ZPS		
4077	350	N377GA	N723MM						
4078	450	N378GA	N310GJ	N865JM					
4079	450	N379GA	N450NS	HZ-KSGA					
4080	450	N380GA	N555TF						
4081	450	N381GA	N926RR						
4082	450	N382GA	N451NS						
4083	450	N383GA	N251VP	N913HH*					
4084	450	N384GA	N470QS						
4085	450	N385GA	N711SW	(N711SZ)	N711FW	N88WR			
4086	350	N486GA	N722MM	N722MN	VH-NKD				
4087	450	N387GA	N800AL						
4088	450	N388GA	N450EJ	VP-CKD	B-LIS				
4089	450	N389GA	N606CH	N779AZ					
4090	450	N490GA	Pakistan J-756						
4091	450	N391GA	N450GA	(N450GQ)	D-AABB	N274TX	PR-VCO		
4092	450	N392GA	VP-BIV	VQ-BGA					
4093	450	N393GA	VP-CMG						
4094	450	N494GA	N452NS	M-ABRJ	T7-LFZ				
4095	450	N495GA	N450PU						
4096	450	N496GA	VP-BMY	B-LWX					
4097	450	N397GA	N59CF						
4098	450	N398GA	N608CH	N600AR					
4099	450	N199GA	N841WS						
4100	450	N120GA	N448QS						
4101	450	N401GA	N424PX						
4102	450	N702GA	XA-GMX						
4103	450	N603GA	VP-BTB						
4104	450	N704GA	OE-ICH	M-AAMM					
4105	450	N405GA	N450T						
4106	450	N606GA	A6-FLG	4L-GAF					
4107	450	N607GA	N717DX						
4108	450	N608GA	N227RH	N218HF*					
4109	450	N609GA	N950SW	N40AA					
4110	450	N610GA	N450WB						
4111	450	N131GA	N178SD						
4112	450	N612GA	N703LH	N3918Y					
4113	450	N913GA	D-AGVS						
4114	450	N614GA	N421QS						
4115	450	N815GA	SX-SEE	VP-BSA	T7-BSA				

GULFSTREAM 350 / 450

C/n	Series	Identities				
4116	450	N216GA	N990PT	N516VE	N483CM	
4117	450	N417GA	N450GD	N770XB	N7KV	
4118	450	N418GA	N7GU	N667LC		
4119	450	N819GA	VP-BAE	M-ARAE	OE-LAR	
4120	450	N420GA	N851GG			
4121	450	N821GA	OE-IMZ			
4122	450	N422GA	HB-JGJ	OE-ILE	N24JR	
4123	450	N423GA	A6-DJL	HB-JUS	N450PJ	VQ-BZM
4124	450	N424GA	N944AL	N512RJ		
4125	450	N425GA	N461QS			
4126	450	N426GA	N192NC			
4127	450	N427GA	N450LC	N59AP		
4128	450	N528GA	N988AL	Mexico AMT-205		XC-LMF
4129	450	N429GA	N596DC	N530PM*		
4130	450	N130GA	OE-IAG	HB-JGB		
4131	450	N531GA	N667HS			
4132	450	N532GA	N851CB	N456FX		
4133	450	N433GA	N478QS	(N478WC)	A6-ORX	
4134	450	N434GA	N9939T			
4135	450	N535GA	N499SC			
4136	450	N436GA	N65QT	A6-AZH	T7-AZH	
4137	450	N337GA	VP-CFB	M-YGLK	N519HC	
4138	450	N138GA	N458X			
4139	450	N439GA	N212LF	N212LE	N922WC	N351TP
4140	450	N740GA	N1BX	N986SP		
4141	450	N541GA	N451QS	N18CJ	N735HC	
4142	450	N742GA	N432AS	N1TT		
4143	450	N843GA	N884WT	N884WE		
4144	450	N444GA	N450GA	N72LN		
4145	450	N545GA	N9BX			
4146	450	N146GA	N468QS			
4147	450	N447GA	N10SN	N728MM	N728MN	LV-GTQ
4148	450	N448GA	VQ-BCE	N451WW		
4149	450	N449GA	N246V			
4150	450	N950GA	VP-BMV	N524JM	N523JM	
4151	450	N651GA	(N459X)	N1818C		
4152	450	N152GA	N451JC	N608D		
4153	450	N453GA	N27YA			
4154	450	N454GA	N92HL	N975GR	B-8155	
4155	450	N455GA	A6-FLH			
4156	450	N656GA	A9C-BHR			
4157	450	N657GA	N451BH			
4158	450	N458GA	N202VZ	N973MC		
4159	450	N459GA	N451C			
4160	450	N360GA	N844GF			
4161	450	N461GA	VP-BSR	T7-BSR		
4162	450	N462GA	N37JL			
4163	450	N463GA	N450GD	N450EE		
4164	450	N464GA	N718JS			
4165	450	N565GA	B-8093			
4166	450	N126GA	VP-CET			
4167	450	N467GA	N597DC	N512PM*		
4168	450	N468GA	B-8099			
4169	450	N569GA	N922CB			
4170	450	N570GA	B-8128			
4171	450	N571GA	N225CX			
4172	450	N572GA	SX-GAB			
4173	450	N175GA	N936MP			
4174	450	N574GA	N9SC			
4175	450	N475GA	TC-KHB			
4176	450	N178GA	N1DW			
4177	450	N577GA	N918LL			
4178	450	N478GA	B-8096			
4179	450	N479GA	N915AM	N919AM		
4180	450	N418GA	SX-MAW	N427MG	B-8158	
4181	450	N181GA	N123LV	M-SWAN		
4182	450	N482GA	B-LCK			
4183	450	N483GA	N903G			
4184	450	N984GA	N333SZ	B-8252		
4185	450	N985GA	VH-MBP			
4186	450	N986GA	N510AK	N511AK		
4187	450	N187GA	B-LWW			
4188	450	N188GA	N188DX	N58AJ		
4189	450	N989GA	N450GA	N555LR		
4190	450	N790GA	B-8127			
4191	450	N491GA	(N235WL)	N235PZ	N4CP	N814CP

GULFSTREAM 350 / 450

C/n	Series	Identities					
4192	450	N492GA	N1902P				
4193	450	N693GA	N77XM	B-8253			
4194	450	N494GA	N803AG				
4195	450	N495GA	N451LC	N65HD	N908CC		
4196	450	N996GA	B-8133				
4197	450	N397GA	N167AD				
4198	450	N398GA	N917VZ				
4199	450	N499GA	N804AG				
4200	450	N820GA	OE-IZK				
4201	450	N401GA	XA-CHE				
4202	450	N202GA	VP-CSH	B-LAS			
4203	450	N403GA	HB-JKF	VP-CMY			
4204	450	N904GA	N818KE				
4205	450	N452GA	(N229LS)	B-8150	N333GW	TC-TRH	
4206	450	N906GA	N236LP				
4207	450	N907GA	N807BC				
4208	450	N608GA	N888KJ	N818TS			
4209	450	N909GA	N300ES	N236KR			
4210	450	N120GA	N60TC				
4211	450	N711GA	B-8322	N8882A	N203RC		
4212	450	N922GA	TC-DYO	N451SC	OB-2017-P	N451SC	N20G
4213	450	N413GA	N450L				
4214	450	N214GA	N450BE	N835SV			
4215	450	N425GA	N847RC				
4216	450	N216GA	B-8166				
4217	450	N427GA	(N289HC)	D-ADSE	N450HE		
4218	450	N218GA	N450JR	(N450MK)	XA-ELK		
4219	450	N429GA	N213TG				
4220	450	N920GA	M-DKVL				
4221	450	N712GA	N57EL				
4222	450	N422GA	N280BC				
4223	450	N423GA	N104AR				
4224	450	N924GA	N701WC				
4225	450	N622GA	N450GD	N81GK			
4226	450	N426GA	N494EC				
4227	450	N627GA	N268ND	B-8262			
4228	450	N822GA	N85M				
4229	450	N229GA	N222NB	N220NB	N450KT		
4230	450	N730GA	N56EL				
4231	450	N931GA	N502P				
4232	450	N432GA	N129MH				
4233	450	N433GA	N175BL				
4234	450	N434GA	B-8250				
4235	450	N735GA	PR-LHW				
4236	450	N436GA	(N428TT)	N426TT	N236FS		
4237	450	N374GA	OE-LAI				
4238	450	N938GA	B-8161				
4239	450	N439GA	TC-IPK	TC-VTN			
4240	450	N940GA	I-DLGH	TC-GAP			
4241	450	N641GA	M-VICI	N224BH			
4242	450	N942GA	B-8251				
4243	450	N943GA	OH-GIV	D-AGVI			
4244	450	N444GA	(N1100A)	N125TF			
4245	450	N445GA	N7777N				
4246	450	N446GA	VP-BSQ	TC-REC			
4247	450	N647GA	P4-MVP				
4248	450	N348GA	VP-CTH				
4249	450	N249GA	TC-MZA				
4250	450	N345GA	N450CE				
4251	450	N151GA	B-8257				
4252	450	N252GA	(N383XX)	N383KK			
4253	450	N453GA	N533SR				
4254	450	N354GA	XA-ATI				
4255	450	N455GA	VP-CLI				
4256	450	N456GA	(N888JE)	N888DC			
4257	450	N457GA	N818SS				
4258	450	N258GA	B-8265				
4259	450	N459GA	N702TR				
4260	450	N460GA	OE-IOK	M-YANG			
4261	450	N261GA	N250AF				
4262	450	N462GA	M-KBBG				
4263	450	N463GA	N7GF	N721MJ			
4264	450	N964GA	B-8290				
4265	450	N465GA	OH-JVA	S5-JVA			
4266	450	N466GA	M-MNDG	N426GA	N289MH		
4267	450	N467GA	B-8267				

GULFSTREAM 350 / 450

C/n	Series	Identities				
4268	450	N468GA	N1963N			
4269	450	N469GA	HB-JKJ	VP-CMC		
4270	450	N470GA	VP-CHH	Pakistan 4270		
4271	450	N471GA	B-8271			
4272	450	N272GA	B-8291			
4273	450	N372GA	M-AVOS	T7-ZZZ		
4274	450	N274GA	B-8295			
4275	450	N275GA	N450GA	N90AE	N9ST*	
4276	450	N176GA	B-8263			
4277	450	N477GA	B-8299			
4278	450	N178GA	N278NA			
4279	450	N279GA	I-XPRA			
4280	450	N980GA	N400J			
4281	450	N281GA	N268RB			
4282	450	N282GA	VP-CQQ			
4283	450	N483GA	M-MNVN			
4284	450	N284GA	M-NELS	M-PING	VP-CPD	
4285	450	N885GA	B-8279			
4286	450	N286GA	B-8316			
4287	450	N287GA	B-8278			
4288	450	N488GA	N142HC	N142HQ	N142HC	N142HQ
4289	450	N289GA	N299SC			
4290	450	N890GA	N1Z			
4291	450	N491GA	OE-IRE	9H-SPA		
4292	450	N292GA	N440MB			
4293	450	N493GA	B-8293			
4294	450	N294GA	PT-MTP			
4295	450	N495GA	N617XT			
4296	450	N296GA	N500N			
4297	450	N297GA	B-8301			
4298	450	N998GA	N900PY			
4299	450	N299GA	N668EM			
4300	450	N400GA	B-8300			
4301	450	N901GA	B-8253			
4302	450	N902GA	N71GE			
4303	450	N303GA	M-SOBR			
4304	450	N934GA	N456SW			
4305	450	N805GA	OY-APM			
4306	450	N306GA	M-KKCO			
4307	450	N307GA	OE-IIE			
4308	450	N308GA	N450GD	C-FDBJ		
4309	450	N309GA	B-8308			
4310	450	N110GA	VP-BAK			
4311	450	N931GA	N666ZW			
4312	450	N312GA	N451PW			
4313	450	N413GA	HZ-MS4A			
4314	450	N314GA	VP-CAX	VP-CYH		
4315	450	N315GA	B-3029			
4316	450	N316GA	N238MH			
4317	450	N317GA	N229AR			
4318	450	N718GA	N154FV			
4319	450	N319GA	M-WONE			
4320	450	N820GA	N903TC			
4321	450	N432GA	N321LV	A6-VPS		
4322	450	N422GA	M-MAEE	N450VA		
4323	450	N323GA	5N-AZK	N3398A		
4324	450	N324GA	HZ-MS4B			
4325	450	N425GA	N212VZ			
4326	450	N426GA	I-BMPG			
4327	450	N427GA	N904TC			
4328	450	N328GA	HZ-MS4C			
4329	450	N429GA	N908VZ			
4330	450	N330GA	N450FX			
4331	450	N833GA	N450GA	N243PC		
4332	450	N832GA	N451FX			
4333	450	N433GA	Mexico 3915/XC-LOJ	Mexico TP-06/XC-LOJ	Mexico TP-05/XC-LOJ	
4334	450	N434GA	N452FX			
4335	450	N835GA	B-3233			
4336	450	N436GA	N453FX			
4337	450	N337GA	N169TA			
4338	450	N838GA	N899FS			
4339	450	N439GA	N454FX			
4340	450	N440GA	N455FX			
4341	450	N841GA	N584A			
4342	450	N942GA	PR-CBK			
4343	450	N443GA	N888ND			

GULFSTREAM 350 / 450

C/n	Series	Identities	
4344	450	N444GA	N450JS
4345	450	N445GA	N587DV
4346	450	N446GA	N915AM
4347	450	N447GA	N904TS
4348	450	N448GA	N222NB
4349	450	N449GA	N312JC
4350	450	N850GA	N844CB
4351	450	N351GA	N333MB
4352	450	N352GA	N817AF
4353	450	N453GA	N518GS
4354	450	N354GA	T7-SAL
4355	450	N355GA	N635E
4356	450	N356GA	OE-ITE
4357	450	N957GA	N116MK
4358	450	N458GA	N520CM*
4359	450	N459GA	G-ULFM
4360	450	N360GA	N450FJ*
4361	450	N361GA	N450ME*
4362	450	N362GA	N88999*
4363	450	N363GA	
4364	450	N964GA	
4365	450	N465GA	
4366	450	N466GA	
4367	450	N467GA	
4368	450	N468GA	
4369	450	N369GA	
4370	450	N370GA	

GULFSTREAM V / GULFSTREAM 500 / 550

We have been advised by Gulfstream Aerospace that the Gulfstream V does **not** have the model number G1159D as has been quoted elsewhere.

C/n	Series	Identities
501		N501GV [rolled out 22Sep95; ff 28Nov95] N22 N99NG [structurally modified for USAF JSTARS competition]
502		N502GV N502KA N5GV N502KA
503		N503GV N767FL
504		N504GV N313RG
F5		[Static test airframe]
505		N505GV EI-WGV N505AX N371JC
506		N506GV N158AF N500GV N33XE (N506GV) M-FISH
507		N507GA N300L N507DW N11GW
508		N508GA N777GV N899GM N777TY [w/o Palm Beach Int'l, FL, 14Feb02] N777PY [cx 10Aug04; b/u Palm Beach Int'l, FL; remains to Savannah, GA, by Oct04]
509		N509GA V8-009 V8-001 V8-009 N509GA "N61GV" N5GA VP-BNZ N509GV N855RB N888XY
510		N598GA N513MW B-8092 N194MF
511		N511GA VP-CBX N779WA
512		N512GV N636MF N838MF N863MF
513		N513GA HB-IVL N85NV
514		N514GA N777SW N304K N320K N256LK B-KDP
515		N599GA V8-007 V8-001 N55GV
516		N516GA N555CS N740BA N882WT N882WE N697PF
517		N517GA HB-IMJ
518		N518GA HZ-MIC N555GN (N36GA) N1GN N555GN N555GV N5GV (N55GV) N885G (N917ND) N17ND
519		N597GA VP-CMG N526EE N452AC N549CP
520		N596GA N17GV N450AR N818DA (N786CW) N767CW
521	C-37A	N521GA USAF 97-0400
522		N595GA (N158RA) N39PY N20H N20HN N70AG
523		N523GA N711SW N790MC N54TG
524		N524GA N400JD N674RW N1892 N474MJ
525		N594GA N252JS N40SR VT-SMI N565JT
526		N526GA N675RW N125GH
527		N527GA N5SA N25CP
528		N528GA N80RP N75RP N9UX
529		N529GA N73RP N529TA T7-TIL N677FP
530		N530GA N780F N780W
531		N531GA (N8CA) N531AF N1GT N279PH
532		N532GA N282Q (N282QT) N282QA N740SS
533		N533GA XA-CPQ
534		N534GA (N158JJ) N920DC N127GG
535		N593GA N775US (N535GV) N535V
536		N536GA N5UH N688TY N318AG
537		N537GA 8P-MAK N132SD
538		N538GA N601MD N1JN N223GA N1JN
539		N539GA N1GC N162JC
540		N640GA XA-OEM
541		N641GA N405LM N405DR N53LT N459BE
542	C-37A	N642GA USAF 97-0401
543		N643GA N91CW
544		N644GA N910DC N383LS
545		N645GA N1HC N55GV N5GV N888CW N545CC N209MG
546		N646GA XA-BAL XA-DAB
547		N647GA N73M N625TF
548		N648GA N245TT N245TJ N32BD XA-AHM
549		N649GA N317JD N718MC N718MD N123FT
550		N650GA N5101 N105CX
551		N651GA N5102 N9102
552		N652GA N9SC N189SC B-8130 N552WS N90JE
553		N653GA N516GH
554		N654GA N589HM N450BE HB-JKA N38NZ XA-AZT
555		N655GA VP-BSM VP-BSJ N813WP N102DZ
556		N656GA N556AR HB-JES
557		N657GA N83M N557E N833E
558		N658GA N750BA N600RH N500RH
559		N659GA N559GV N144KK N59JE
560		N660GA 9K-AJD
561		N661GA N108CE
562		N662GA N95AE N970SJ
563		N463GA N8CA N169CA (N169PG) (N180CH) N225EE
564		N664GA (JY-...) "N18VS" N664GA N54PR A6-DEJ N238FJ N1GN
565		N460GA N77CP N940AJ
566	C-37A	N466GA US Army 97-0049 N8VQ US Army 05-1944
567		N467GA N93M N50JE
568		N461GA N845HS N568JC HB-INQ N5HN N89HE N168CE
569		N469GA 9K-AJE

GULFSTREAM V

C/n	Series	Identities						
570		N470GA	N451CS	N521HN	N820HB			
571	C-37A	N671GA	USAF 99-0402					
572		N472GA	(N223SS)	P4-FAZ	HB-IIS	OE-IIS	D-ANTE*	
573		N673GA	9K-AJF					
574		N674GA	N1KE	N6453	N6458			
575		N475GA	N410M	N625GN				
576		N476GA	N991LF	N80PS	N80PN			
577		N577GA	HB-IVZ	VP-CAR				
578		N578GA	N1GN	N21GN	N410LM	N801AR		
579		N579GA	N23M	N866AB				
580		N580GA	N1540	N1580				
581		N581GA	N379P	N8068V	N44982	N126CH	VH-CCC	N280PH
582		N582GA	N271JG	EC-IRZ	N582GV	(N312GV)	N598KZ	
583		N583GA	HZ-MS05	HZ-MS5	HZ-MS5B			
584		N584GA	N84GV					
585		N585GA	N18NK	N16NK	N776RB			
586		N586GA	N2N	N586GV	N51VE			
587		N587GA	N300K	N416RJ				
588		N588GA	VP-BAC	N588GV	HS-WEH			
589		N589GA	N15UC	(N15UQ)				
590	C-37A	N590GA	USAF 99-0404					
591		N591GA	N301K	N25GV				
592		N592GA	N90AM	N950CM	N955CM			
593		N593GA	(I-MPUT)	I-DEAS	N977SA			
594		N594GA	N33M	N363JG				
595		N595GA	N85V	(N595GV)				
596		N596GA	(USAF 99-0405)		N383JA	N977GA	N996GA	
597		N495GA	N302K	N540M	N595E	N595B		
598		N598GA	N1SF	N598F	N808JG			
599		N496GA	N401WJ	N428WT	N800PM			
600		N650GA	N100GV					
601		N536GA	N502QS	N502VR	N588AT			
602		N538GA	N602GV	VP-BKZ	N783MB			
603		N539GA	N35CD	VH-CRQ	N881HS			
604		N551GA	LV-ZXI	N551GA	XA-EAJ	(D-AHER)	XA-JEF	XA-KUO
605		N554GA	N62MS	N62ML	N691RC	N37AL		
606		N558GA	N63HS	N53HS	N551GA	N1222P		
607		N559GA	N303K	VP-BNL	P4-SBR	N17FJ		
608		N561GA	N111LX	N608WB	N505SS			
609		N566GA	N5733	N418SG	N418SM	N101MH		
610		N567GA	(N610CM)	N253CM				
611		N568GA	N5000X					
612		N569GA	N350C	N88D	N88DZ			
613		N570GA	N504QS	N721MM	B-8097	N727PR		
614		N571GA	N614CM					
615		N572GA	N914J	N318XX	N324CX			
616		N574GA	(N457ST)	N1HC	N141HC	N5616		
617		N575GA	7T-VPG					
618		N585GA	N585JC	(N123H)				
619		N608GA	N1454H	N4377	N619GV			
620	C-37A	N535GA	USAF 01-0028					
621		N621GA	(N605M)	N605CH	N702TY			
622		N622GA	N304K	N806AC	VP-BBX	HB-JTT		
623		N623GA	N506QS	N285TX	N1AM			
624	C-37A	N624GA	USAF 01-0029					
625		N625GA	N507QS	N269TX	N100HG			
626		N626GA	N5JR	N846QM				
627		N627GA	N54KB	N54BS				
628		N628GA	N18RF	N42GX	N628BD			
629		N629GA	N711RL	N711RQ	N707GW	N188ES		
630		N630GA	N130GV					
631		N631GA	N508QS	N631VR				
632	V-SP	N632GA	N5SP	N532SP	[first GV-SP; ff 31Aug01]			
633		N633GA	N222LX					
634		N534GA	ZS-AOL	ZS-AJZ	N731AE	N700HA		
635		N522GA	N83CP	N709AA				
636		N556GA	N910V	VP-BEP	N886DT	N328MM		
637		N637GA	N509QS	(N509VR)	N176SM*			
638		N638GA	HB-IIY	N888HE	(N888HK)	US Coast Guard 02		N888HE
639		N639GA	N501CV					
640		N580GA	N752BA	N600JD	N278PH			
641		N641GA	HB-IIZ	OE-IIA	N506RD	C-GUGU		
642		N562GA	N510QS	CS-DKB	N626JS	N626JE		
643		N523GA	5N-FGS					
644		N644GA	HZ-MS5A					
645	C-37A	N645GA	USAF 01-0076					

GULFSTREAM V / 500 / 550

C/n	Series	Identities							
646		N524GA	N51FL	(N617JS)	N17JS	N856TD	N749CP		
647		N647GA	N511QS	[w/o, hit by truck while parked at San Francisco, CA, 22Sep12; parted out by AvMATS, St Louis, MO]					
648		N648GA	N85M	N85ML	VP-BSN	N626UT			
649		N649GA	N83CW	N183CW	N87WD				
650		N520GA	N1040						
651		N581GA	N651GV	N1DC					
652	C-37A	N582GA	USAF 01-0065						
653	VC-37A	N527GA	US Coast Guard 01						
654		N584GA	(N654GV)	N960AV	VP-BLA	N404M	XA-MPS		
655		N529GA	N825LM						
656		N256GA	(N218CP)	N218EC	N724AG				
657	C-37B	N587GA	USN 166375						
658		N532GA	N516QS	N150WJ*					
659		N589GA	N50KC						
660		N533GA	N130TM	N21NE	N1BB				
661		N561GA	N405HG	N900LY					
662		N662GA	N697A	N427HG					
663	C-37A	N663GA	USAF 01-0030						
664		N664GA	N564QS+ [+marks were applied but ntu]				N664GA	XA-MKI	
665		N565GA	N845HS	N223MD	N128GV	N128GB	N765SG	N999LX	
666		N566GA	(N958AV)	N699GA	[c/n changed to 699 on rereg'n to N699GA qv]				
667		N567GA	N1BN	N121BN	N123M	N168NJ	N168NB	N136ZC	
668		N568GA	N721S	HZ-SK4					
669		N569GA	N144KK	N544KK	N1UB	VP-CES	3C-LLX		
670	C-37A	N670GA	USAF 02-1863						
671		N571GA	N671LE	N671LB	N703RK				
672		N672GA	VP-BJD	N225GV	N3546	N95NA			
673		N873GA	N282QT	N673P	N169LL*				
674		N674GA	N25GV	(N26GV)	N36GV				
675		N675GA	N505RX	N1956M					
676		N676GA	Israel 676	["Nachshon Shavit" ELINT platform]					
677		N677GA	N677F						
678		N678GA	Greece 678						
679		N679GA	Israel 679	["Nachshon Shavit" ELINT platform]					
680		N680GA	(OK-ONE)	M-USBA					
681		N981GA	(N519QS)	N624N					
682		N682GA	(VP-BFD)	G-JCBV	N551M	N38BA	N919YC		
683		N683GA	JA500A	[code LAJ500]					
684		N684GA	Israel 684	["Nachshon Shavit" ELINT platform]					
685		N585GA	N685TA	N108NY					
686		N686GA	N524AC	N524AG					
687		N687GA	OE-IVY	N7160S	N716AS				
688		N688GA	(N254W)	N543H					
689		N689GA	JA501A	[code LAJ501]					
690		N690GA	N914BD	N915BD					
691		N691GA	N250DV	N525AC	N523AG	N721MC			
692		N692GA	N100TM	C-GLFV					
693		N693GA	N508P	N617EA					
694		c/n not used							
695		c/n not used							
696		c/n not used							
697		c/n not used							
698		c/n not used							
699		N566GA	(N958AV)	N699GA	N885KT	[orginally built as c/n 666]			

GULFSTREAM 500/550

5001	500	N901GA	[rolled out 19Jun02 ff 18Jly02]			N5SP	N621KD	N501ZK	N501HM
5002	550	N702GA	N550GA	N92LA					
5003	550	N703GA	N245TT						
5004	550	N904GA	HB-IGM	N145MG					
5005	550	N805GA	N4CP	N499CP	B-8152				
5006	550	N906GA	N550GW	(N345AA)	(N550AA)				
5007	550	N907GA	N754BA	N383T					
5008	550	N908GA	XA-EOF	N378L	N551GT				
5009	550	N909GA	N1HC						
5010	550	N910GA	N711RL	N711RZ	N701RH*				
5011	550	N991GA	(N522QS)	VP-BGN	N811GA	(N827DC)	VP-BNF		
5012	550	N812GA	N888LK	N918SM	N559G*				
5013	550	N913GA	N63HS						
5014	550	N914GA	Israel 514	Singapore 010		[AEW platform]			
5015	550	N915GA	N565ST	N888PX					
5016	550	N916GA	N944H	N599H					

GULFSTREAM 500 / 550

C/n	Series	Identities								
5017	550	N917GA	N62MS							
5018	550	N518GA	N818RF	N111AM						
5019	550	N919GA	SE-RDX	G-GSSO	N15019	B-8270				
5020	550	N920GA	N221DG	N243DG	N550AA					
5021	550	N921GA	N5DA	N510SR						
5022	550	N922GA	N550GV	OE-ISS	N550GV	(PR-CPD)	M-GLFV	N122TN	(PR-GFV)	PR-GMV
5023	550	N923GA	N1GN	N125N	B-8135					
5024	550	N924GA	VP-BLA	N424GA	B-8100					
5025	550	N925GA	HB-JEE	N356WW						
5026	550	N926GA	N550MT	N550TA	N921WC					
5027	550	N927GA	N91LA							
5028	550	N928GA	N55UH	HL7799	N311TK	N310TK				
5029	550	N929GA	(N550RN)	N155AN	N155AD	TU-VAR	N155AD	N550UN		
5030	550	N830GA	5H-ONE							
5031	550	N931GA	N795BA	N33LR						
5032	550	N932GA	G-HRDS	N550JD						
5033	550	N933GA	VP-BNR	N550						
5034	550	N934GA	US Army 04-1778		[C37A]					
5035	550	N935GA	N1TF	N607CV						
5036	550	N936GA	N1BN	N345KC						
5037	550	N637GA	Israel 537	["Nachshon Eitam" AEW platform]						
5038	550	N938GA	N372BG	N102BG	N192BG	N192BH	HZ-A6	HZ-SK6		
5039	550	N939GA	N401HF	N94LF						
5040	550	N940GA	N418SG	(N13J)	HB-JEV	N74VW				
5041	550	N841GA	US Navy 166376		[C37A]					
5042	550	N942GA	N528QS							
5043	550	N943GA	N550GA	N83TE	VP-BGL	N107VS				
5044	550	N944GA	Israel 544	Singapore 016		[AEW platform]				
5045	550	N945GA	N789RR	N560DM						
5046	550	N946GA	N5PG							
5047	550	N947GA	(N550YM)	(PR-NYM)	N848JA					
5048	550	N948GA	VP-CIF	VP-CIP						
5049	550	N949GA	N109ST	N89NC						
5050	550	N950GA	VP-BNO	M-SAWO						
5051	550	N851GA	VP-BNE							
5052	550	N952GA	XA-ATL							
5053	550	N953GA	N2929							
5054	550	N954GA	OE-IVV	XA-ZTK						
5055	550	N955GA	N144KK	N755VE						
5056	550	N956GA	N45ST	N556TT						
5057	550	N957GA	CS-DKC	N8228N						
5058	550	N958GA	N74RP	N2480H						
5059	550	N959GA	VP-BLR	N659GA	B-8095					
5060	550	N960GA	G-JCBC	N143G	N254SD					
5061	550	N961GA	N718MC							
5062	550	N962GA	N159JA							
5063	550	N963GA	N759WR	N411WW	N897AW	N897AT	N561CK*			
5064	550	N964GA	VP-BJD							
5065	550	N965GA	N747AE	N75CC						
5066	550	N966GA	N250DV	N280DV	N25HL					
5067	500	N967GA	N50HA							
5068	550	N968GA	EI-GDL	N407GK						
5069	550	N969GA	Israel 569	["Nachshon Eitam" AEW platform]						
5070	550	N870GA	HB-JEP	M-BJEP						
5071	550	N571GA	(N550GA)+	[+ ntu marks worn in NBAA Static display, Orlando Executive, FL, Nov05]						I-LUXO
5072	550	N572GA	(N25GV)	N572EC	N528M	N378L				
5073	550	N673GA	N800JH							
5074	550	N574GA	HZ-ARK							
5075	550	N575GA	N518QS	D-AGAZ*?						
5076	550	N576GA	N870CM	N878CM*						
5077	550	N577GA	N933H							
5078	550	N578GA	EC-JPK							
5079	550	N579GA	N860AA							
5080	550	N580GA	SE-RDY							
5081	550	N581GA	CS-DKD							
5082	550	N582GA	N550FG	N709DW	B-8136					
5083	550	N583GA	N985JC	N474D						
5084	550	N584GA	VP-BSI							
5085	550	N585GA	N235DX	N5585						
5086	550	N586GA	N609PM	N620JF						
5087	550	N587GA	US Navy 166377							
5088	550	N588GA	N5VS							
5089	550	N589GA	N771JT							
5090	550	N590GA	N282Q							
5091	550	N591GA	N3PG	N780KS*						
5092	550	N592GA	VP-CVI	VP-CVK						

GULFSTREAM 500 / 550

C/n	Series	Identities				
5093	550	N593GA	D-ADLR	[High Altitude Long-Range research aircraft]		
5094	550	N594GA	CS-DKE			
5095	550	N595GA	N550KF	N550MZ	N236MJ	
5096	550	N696GA	N3050			
5097	550	N597GA	N550GA	N806AC	N801AS	
5098	550	N598GA	US Navy 166378			
5099	550	N699GA	CS-DKF			
5100	500	N820GA	N51MF	N760CC	N760CG	N789LR
5101	550	N821GA	N550M	N904G		
5102	550	N822GA	VP-CVT	(B-HVT)	N79MA*	
5103	550	N923GA	N534QS			
5104	550	N824GA	N661CP	N314TP		
5105	500	N935GA	N500RD	PR-WQY		
5106	550	N986GA	N234DB	N888ZF*		
5107	550	N937GA	N662CP	N335LL		
5108	550	N828GA	N311CG	N611CG	N1LA	
5109	550	N829GA	VP-BIP	N818HK		
5110	550	N940GA	N585A			
5111	550	N981GA	B-KGV	VP-CKC		
5112	550	N832GA	N636MF	N363MF		
5113	550	N833GA	VP-CNR	N919PE	N175NH	
5114	550	N834GA	D-ADCA	N720JS	N196AP	
5115	550	N835GA	B-KID	N42FD	N838LM	
5116	550	N836GA	EC-JYR	XA-ALC		
5117	550	N967GA	N595A			
5118	550	N838GA	N855G			
5119	550	N519GA	RA-10202			
5120	550	N920GA	N254SD	N284SD	B-8108	
5121	550	N921GA	N550PR	N1972N		
5122	550	N522GA	N837BA			
5123	550	N523GA	VP-BBO			
5124	550	N524GA	EC-KBR			
5125	550	N295GA	N550GD	N388AC		
5126	550	N526GA	N676RW	N665JN		
5127	550	N527GA	CS-DKG			
5128	550	N928GA	N940DC	(N1759)	N1759C	
5129	550	N529GA	VP-BLW			
5130	550	N130GA	N671LE			
5131	550	N531GA	N671RW	M-GVSP		
5132	550	N432GA	Israel 532	Singapore 017		[AEW platform]
5133	550	N533GA	N531QS			
5134	550	N534GA	N712KT	N712DA	N5GV	
5135	550	N535GA	N522BP	N909AD		
5136	500	N536GA	N110ED			
5137	550	N287GA	8P-MSD			
5138	550	N638GA	N600J	N60QJ	N551RC	
5139	550	N539GA	OE-IRG	N673MM		
5140	550	N740GA	N838BA	N721L		
5141	550	N541GA	N10MZ			
5142	550	N42GA	D-ADCB	T7-ARG		
5143	550	N643GA	Singapore 018		[AEW platform]	
5144	500	N644GA	N515PL	N515PE	PR-NOC	
5145	550	N545GA	N345LC			
5146	550	N646GA	N607PM	N1852B		
5147	550	N647GA	B-LUE	VP-CEM		
5148	500	N648GA	N551KF	N650PL	VP-BCC	
5149	550	N649GA	VP-CGN	VP-CGI	N970SG	
5150	550	N43GA	CS-DKH			
5151	550	N921GA	EC-KJS	M-HOTB		
5152	550	N652GA	06-0500			
5153	550	N923GA	SE-RDZ	M-ARDI		
5154	550	N654GA	N557GA	N113CS	N113GS	N808TC
5155	550	N935GA	N550GA	EC-KUM		
5156	550	N936GA	N529QS			
5157	550	N657GA	N785QS			
5158	500	N998GA	N56UH			
5159	550	N659GA	N607CH			
5160	550	N660GA	N813QS			
5161	550	N261GA	N725MM	N725MN	N950DM	
5162	550	N662GA	EC-KLS	VT-BRS		
5163	550	N663GA	N57UH			
5164	550	N764GA	N372BG			
5165	550	N965GA	N245BD			
5166	550	N966GA	CS-DKI			
5167	550	N967GA	G-EGNS	(D-AMAN)	M-ANIE	N878DB
5168	550	N668GA	N528AP			

GULFSTREAM 500 / 550

C/n	Series	Identities				
5169	550	N569GA	N203A	N5569		
5170	550	N770GA	N105ST			
5171	550	N971GA	N550BM	D-AUTO		
5172	550	N972GA	HB-JGX	G-LGKD	N688CB	
5173	550	N673GA	N401HB	N415LM		
5174	550	N974GA	CS-DKJ			
5175	550	N975GA	HB-JGC	N887AG	N883A	
5176	550	N476GA	VP-BTC	G-CGUL	N7325	
5177	550	N977GA	VP-BCO	OE-IZM	N41PM	
5178	550	N978GA	HB-JKB	N188WR	N339JM	
5179	550	N979GA	VP-BZC	M-SQAR		
5180	550	N980GA	N108DB	N108DN	N1FS	N922WC
5181	550	N181GA	N550AN	VP-CEA	VP-CJM	
5182	550	N782GA	XA-CHR			
5183	550	N983GA	N88D	N868D	N88D	(N135RG) N35GR
5184	550	N284GA	N550GD	N550RP		
5185	550	N185GA	P4-GVV			
5186	550	N286GA	G-JCBB	N10XG		
5187	550	N187GA	N816MG			
5188	550	N188GA	N554CE			
5189	550	N189GA	D-AAAM	G-YAAZ	D-AVAR	OK-VPI
5190	550	N290GA	N546QS			
5191	550	N291GA	D-AJJK	N129KC		
5192	550	N492GA	N323BD	N990NB		
5193	550	N293GA	P4-TPS	P4-PPP	N117AL	
5194	550	N394GA	N1EB			
5195	550	N295GA	N1LB	N550SN		
5196	550	N196GA	N45ST	N385WL	N554DG	
5197	550	N597GA	SX-MFA	N888HZ		
5198	550	N298GA	LZ-FIA			
5199	550	N399GA	N443M			
5200	550	N990GA	VP-BJK	Sweden 102005		
5201	550	N991GA	CS-DKK			
5202	550	N992GA	N1SF			
5203	550	N203GA	EC-KXF	N575PK		
5204	550	N104GA	4K-MEK8			
5205	500	N405GA	(VT-ADA)	(D-ADSE)	(N51FL)	N393VF
5206	550	N806GA	N211HS	(N721V)	N169SD	N469SD
5207	550	N607GA	N101CP	N418SG	N550A	
5208	550	N908GA	5X-UGF			
5209	550	N609GA	N517QS			
5210	550	N610GA	M-ONEM			
5211	550	N711GA	N550GA	(N550JE)	N653MK	
5212	550	N512GA	TC-DAP			
5213	550	N413GA	N888HK			
5214	550	N314GA	N4PG	N550WW		
5215	550	N615GA	VQ-BLA			
5216	550	N516GA	VP-CJL	B-HVP		
5217	550	N517GA	N768JJ			
5218	550	N518GA	VQ-BGN	N550PL		
5219	550	N419GA	(N885AR)	B-KVC		
5220	550	N520GA	G-TFKR	M-TFKR	HB-JOE	
5221	550	N221GA	VQ-BLV	VQ-BLY	VP-CMD	
5222	550	N622GA	N801TM			
5223	550	N623GA	N550SG	N557H	N727TE	
5224	550	N624GA	N678SC	(N88WR)	N700MK	
5225	550	N325GA	M-VRNY			
5226	550	N526GA	N803TM			
5227	550	N217GA	M-FPIA	M-FUAD		
5228	550	N828GA	B-KCK			
5229	550	N509GA	N535QS	N55AL	N668P	
5230	550	N330GA	C-GNDN	C-GXDN	N898CE	
5231	550	N131GA	N899SR	N398TA	B-8138	N8889 N8810
5232	550	N932GA	N773MJ	N773AJ	N231CE	
5233	550	N733GA	HL8200			
5234	550	N934GA	N674RW	N897NC		
5235	550	N435GA	N589K			
5236	550	N563GA	PR-WRO			
5237	550	N937GA	N885WT			
5238	550	N838GA	B-KGP			
5239	550	N339GA	N928GC			
5240	550	N840GA	HB-JKC			
5241	550	N841GA	Turkey 09-001		TC-KOP	Turkey 09-001
5242	550	N842GA	A9C-BRN			
5243	550	N924GA	(N803TG)	B-99888		
5244	550	N744GA	N800DL			

GULFSTREAM 500 / 550

C/n	Series	Identities					
5245	550	N845GA	N802AG				
5246	550	N846GA	M-IPHS				
5247	550	N847GA	USAF 09-0501	09-0525			
5248	550	N748GA	9K-GFA				
5249	550	N849GA	N757PL				
5250	550	N952GA	"N592GA"+	[+incorrect marks worn for test-flight at Long Beach 18Nov09]	N952GA	B-LSM	
5251	550	N351GA	HZ-ALFA	N251GV			
5252	550	N552GA	N550PM				
5253	550	N523GA	PR-OGX	N1005	N446VG		
5254	550	N554GA	Turkey 10-002	TC-CBK			
5255	550	N955GA	N94924	(N94124)			
5256	550	N856GA	N1932P				
5257	550	N957GA	N253DV				
5258	550	N558GA	N780E				
5259	550	N959GA	VH-LAL	N159DE			
5260	550	N960GA	ZK-KFB	SE-RKL			
5261	550	N561GA	N780F				
5262	550	N562GA	(D-ASAF)	N315RG			
5263	550	N263GA	N605CH				
5264	550	N564GA	N551CS	N551TG			
5265	550	N965GA	N247EM				
5266	550	N926GA	VQ-BMC	N131LK			
5267	550	N867GA	XA-EAJ				
5268	550	N568GA	VQ-BHP				
5269	550	N369GA	B-8122				
5270	550	N370GA	VP-CRO				
5271	550	N971GA	CN-AMS				
5272	550	N772GA	N235PE	N77CP			
5273	550	N927GA	N273A				
5274	550	N174GA	B-8123				
5275	550	N575GA	VP-CTA				
5276	550	N276GA	B-8125				
5277	550	N527GA	4K-AI06				
5278	550	N528GA	N512JT				
5279	550	N579GA	EC-LIY				
5280	550	N508GA	(PR-EVS)	PR-FGA	N580JT		
5281	550	N581GA	XA-FEM				
5282	550	N282GA	XA-RGB	N335MC	XA-RET		
5283	550	N283GA	N332MM				
5284	550	N584GA	TC-TTC				
5285	550	N285GA	N5GV	N555GV	N4500X		
5286	550	N526GA	N235PV	N83CP			
5287	550	N587GA	VH-PFL				
5288	550	N588GA	N552GA				
5289	550	N589GA	B-8131				
5290	550	N290GA	N3M				
5291	550	N591GA	B-8132				
5292	550	N592GA	M-MOMO				
5293	550	N829GA	XA-SKY				
5294	550	N594GA	VT-TMS	N117AL	N887TM		
5295	550	N295GA	HL8288				
5296	550	N896GA	B-KEQ	N296GC	Mexico 3910		
5297	550	N792GA	USAF 11-0550				
5298	550	N598GA	B-8168				
5299	550	N529GA	N550MT	N17JS	N171DJ		
5300	550	N300GA	B-90609				
5301	550	N901GA	N550SA	M-SAJJ	M-SAAJ		
5302	550	N532GA	D-ASAF	OE-IZI			
5303	550	N303GA	B-KHJ				
5304	550	N604GA	N550GA	VP-CTE			
5305	550	N535GA	(N725AF)	N550GD	Mexico ANX-207	Mexico ANX-1207	Mexico ANX-1201
5306	550	N836GA	C-GBGC	C-GGPM			
5307	550	N507GA	N288A				
5308	550	N638GA	PR-PSE				
5309	550	N509GA	N300A				
5310	550	N510GA	5N-FGW				
5311	550	N531GA	N818LK	N818LF			
5312	550	N112GA	N415P				
5313	550	N633GA	N888VS				
5314	550	N834GA	I-ADVD				
5315	550	N835GA	G-GRZD	M-RZDC			
5316	550	N916GA	M-YBJK	N316GD	N418SG	N99SC	
5317	550	N917GA					
5318	550	N718GA	N989JC				
5319	550	N519GA	B-8137				
5320	550	N732GA	A4O-AD				

GULFSTREAM 500 / 550

C/n	Series	Identities			
5321	550	N921GA	N891E		
5322	550	N632GA	N900ES		
5323	550	N923GA	N505D		
5324	550	N524GA	VP-CJL	VP-CPY	
5325	550	N352GA	A4O-AE		
5326	550	N126GA	N510QS		
5327	550	N772GA	VP-CKG	N881WR	
5328	550	N778GA	N1911W		
5329	550	N129GA	B-8288		
5330	550	N830GA	N725AF	N550PR	
5331	550	N131GA	N53M		
5332	550	N992GA	PR-CIP		
5333	550	N833GA	N119LE		
5334	550	N934GA	N76RP		
5335	550	N853GA	B-LDL		
5336	550	N936GA	D-ABMW		
5337	550	N537GA	B-8156	N88AY	
5338	550	N988GA	N550AU		
5339	550	N339GA	N989AR	(PP-JFH)	
5340	550	N740GA	M-ATPS		
5341	550	N541GA	N200A		
5342	550	N854GA	B-8157		
5343	550	N843GA	ZS-AOL	N343AR	
5344	550	N944GA	N888XS		
5345	550	N954GA	N235DX		
5346	550	N946GA	M-JIGG	TC-ATA	
5347	550	N987GA	N79RP		
5348	550	N948GA	B-8256		
5349	550	N949GA	B-8126		
5350	550	N750GA	SX-GJJ	EI-LSY	
5351	550	N751GA	N636MF		
5352	550	N152GA	B-8255		
5353	550	N953GA	N581D		
5354	550	N454GA	D-ATIM	N535GA	
5355	550	N155GA	N625JK	HB-JKI	
5356	550	N356GA	B-KVE	RP-C8717	
5357	550	N757GA	B-8259		
5358	550	N758GA	B-8160		
5359	550	N559GA	N168NJ		
5360	550	N360GA	B-8258		
5361	550	N361GA	N616KG	N616RK	
5362	550	N562GA	N462MK		
5363	550	N763GA	N128GV		
5364	550	N764GA	B-8261		
5365	550	N565GA	N550VE		
5366	550	N566GA	N312P		
5367	550	N767GA	N96UA		
5368	550	N368GA	N550GS	XA-WOW	
5369	550	N569GA	N85JM		
5370	550	N570GA	N721MM		
5371	550	N371GA	N890A		
5372	550	N753GA	N999FH		
5373	550	N703GA	B-8260		
5374	550	N574GA	N551PM		
5375	550	N375GA	N407TR		
5376	550	N376GA	N63M		
5377	550	N577GA	B-HHI		
5378	550	N578GA	RA-10203		
5379	550	N579GA	(D-AMKA)	OE-ISN	
5380	550	N380GA	N506SA		
5381	550	N381GA	N551VL		
5382	550	N582GA	N552PM		
5383	550	N583GA	N999HZ		
5384	550	N384GA	N558GA		
5385	550	N585GA	N977HS		
5386	550	N536GA	N5092		
5387	550	N387GA	B-8268		
5388	550	N588GA	B-LMF		
5389	550	N389GA	N3788B		
5390	550	N590GA	N552X		
5391	550	N591GA	M-ALAY		
5392	550	N492GA	N504AC		
5393	550	N593GA	XA-MAV	N586MS	XA-MAV
5394	550	N494GA	M-USIC		
5395	550	N195GA	OE-LPN	N107AL	
5396	550	N596GA	N550DV	G-MRLX	

GULFSTREAM 500 / 550

C/n	Series	Identities				
5397	550	N397GA	N582D			
5398	550	N398GA	N838KE			
5399	550	N399GA	B-8273			
5400	550	N500GA	N34U	N506HG		
5401	550	N340GA	N899NC			
5402	550	N342GA				
5403	550	N983GA	N662P			
5404	550	N904GA	B-8269			
5405	550	N545GA	B-8272			
5406	550	N346GA	M-UGIC			
5407	550	N407GA	N676AS			
5408	550	N908GA	OH-GVA	D-AGVA		
5409	550	N349GA	D-AKAR	VP-CUA		
5410	550	N910GA	N284CC			
5411	550	N311GA	N523AC			
5412	550	N412GA	N721V			
5413	550	N213GA	N550DR			
5414	550	N814GA	B-8275			
5415	550	N415GA	VP-CHI			
5416	550	N516GA	N540W	N640W	US Coast Guard 02	
5417	550	N517GA	N517DW			
5418	550	N418GA	N550GA	P4-BFY		
5419	550	N219GA	N800J			
5420	550	N120GA	(G-GENT)	G-NOYA	OE-IPE	
5421	550	N142GA	N155AN	N421GD	N3546*	
5422	550	N842GA	B-8292			
5423	550	N423GA	B-8297			
5424	550	N324GA	N524VE			
5425	550	N425GA	G-ZNSF			
5426	550	N526GA	OK-KKF			
5427	550	N927GA	VT-CPA			
5428	550	N928GA	N73M			
5429	550	N849GA	Israel 429	Italy MM62293		[AEW platform; code 14-11]
5430	550	N850GA	(D-ADCL)	EC-LYO		
5431	550	N531GA	I-SEAM			
5432	550	N732GA	N1905W			
5433	550	N233GA	N524AC			
5434	550	N834GA	OE-IGO			
5435	550	N435GA	D-ADCL			
5436	550	N936GA	N568SP	N126HR		
5437	550	N537GA	B-8302			
5438	550	N938GA	N447TR			
5439	550	N539GA	N728EC			
5440	550	N940GA	N550MC			
5441	550	N541GA	N441GC			
5442	550	N424GA	N550JU			
5443	550	N443GA	N550AL			
5444	550	N344GA	N344RS			
5445	550	N445GA	B-8306			
5446	550	N146GA	N45JE			
5447	550	N147GA	B-8298			
5448	550	N148GA	N586RW			
5449	550	N944GA	B-8296	N730EA		
5450	550	N745GA	N998FA			
5451	550	N351GA	N451GV			
5452	550	N352GA	N8JK	M-TRAV	2-TRAV	
5453	550	N353GA	G-OGSE			
5454	550	N554GA	Israel 454	Italy MM62294		[AEW platform; code 14-12]
5455	550	N355GA	N169SD			
5456	550	N356GA	N456GA			
5457	550	N957GA	PR-CGI			
5458	550	N458GA	N1RP			
5459	550	N559GA	TC-KHG			
5460	550	N760GA	N75RP			
5461	550	N461GA	VP-CNP			
5462	550	N762GA	OE-LOK			
5463	550	N563GA	N514VA	N252DV		
5464	550	N464GA	XA-BUA			
5465	550	N265GA	N5465M			
5466	550	N566GA	N866BB			
5467	550	N867GA	N588PX			
5468	550	N568GA	N550XY			
5469	550	N969GA	B-3196			
5470	550	N870GA	N83M			
5471	550	N571GA	G-LSCW			
5472	550	N572GA	B-3226			

GULFSTREAM 500 / 550

C/n	Series	Identities			
5473	550	N473GA	N793CP		
5474	550	N974GA	N795CP		
5475	550	N475GA	B-8309		
5476	550	N476GA	N138GL		
5477	550	N267GA	N550GD	N550GH	
5478	550	N478GA	B-3003	N226ZH	
5479	550	N479GA	N797CP		
5480	550	N580GA	(N550KP)	HS-KPI	
5481	550	N581GA	N999LR		
5482	550	N482GA	N464GR	N464GC	VP-CAT
5483	550	N583GA	B-8373		
5484	550	N584GA	N486RW		
5485	550	N585GA	N585DW		
5486	550	N586GA	N586G		
5487	550	N587GA	N942JT		
5488	550	N588GA	N588G		
5489	550	N489GA	N559X		
5490	550	N590GA	N550AV		
5491	550	N591GA	N276A		
5492	550	N492GA	(D-ADES)	D-ADSE	N550JH
5493	550	N593GA	9M-TMJ	9M-JDT*	
5494	550	N594GA	N6HJ		
5495	550	N595GA	N550RH		
5496	550	N596GA	N500J		
5497	550	N597GA	N552AV		
5498	550	N598GA	N97FT		
5499	550	N499GA	N600J		
5500	550	N500GA	N100GA	N900AL	
5501	550	N751GA	N83CW		
5502	550	N702GA	N667P		
5503	550	N703GA	N914X		
5504	550	N904GA	N525KF		
5505	550	N305GA	PR-NZV		
5506	550	N856GA	N111		
5507	550	N807GA	N322K		
5508	550	N908GA	Mexico 3916/XC-LOK	Mexico TP-07/XC-LOK	Mexico TP-04/XC-LOK
5509	550	N909GA	N68989		
5510	550	N510GA	N70EL		
5511	550	N851GA	VP-CLK		
5512	550	N512GA	N550TY		
5513	550	N853GA	N319PP		
5514	550	N854GA	N34HS		
5515	550	N955GA	N931FL		
5516	550	N516GA	N324K		
5517	550	N517GA	N550DX		
5518	550	N518GA	I-DELO		
5519	550	N519GA	M-MNDG		
5520	550	N952GA	N587G		
5521	550	N921GA	N906FS		
5522	550	N822GA	N260Z		
5523	550	N523GA	N237GA*		
5524	550	N524GA	OE-LCY		
5525	550	N325GA	N336EB		
5526	550	N526GA	N550GA	VP-CPU	
5527	550	N527GA	N38NG		
5528	550	N528GA	N73RP		
5529	550	N529GA	N561SK		
5530	550	N830GA	N316VA		
5531	550	N531GA	(N550GD)	N63108	
5532	550	N532GA	B-3988		
5533	550	N533GA	TU-VAE		
5534	550	N534GA	N360WF		
5535	550	N535GA	N613WF		
5536	550	N536GA	A6-YMA		
5537	550	N537GA	N537BT		
5538	550	N538GA	N565JM		
5539	550	N539GA	N80AD		
5540	550	N540GA			
5541	550	N541GA	OK-JMD		
5542	550	N542GD			
5543	550	N543GD	N543RN		
5544	550	N544GD			
5545	550	N545GA	N550GU		
5546	550	N546GD	N546RN		
5547	550	N547GA			
5548	550	N548GD	N17RX		

GULFSTREAM 500 / 550

C/n	Series	Identities	
5549	550	N549GA	
5550	550	N750GA	N550RN
5551	550	N551GD	N233LT
5552	550	N552GD	
5553	550	N553GD	
5554	550	N554GD	
5555	550	N255GA	N877SB*
5556	550	N556GD	N550GA*
5557	550	N557GD	
5558	550	N558GD	
5559	550	N559GA	
5560	550	N560GD	
5561	550	N561GA	
5562	550	N562GA	
5563	550	N563GA	
5564	550	N564GA	
5565	550	N565GA	
5566	550	N566GA	
5567	550	N967GA	
5568	550	N568GA	
5569	550	N569GA	
5570	550	N570GA	
5571	550	N571GA	
5572	550	N572GA	
5573	550	N573GD	
5574	550	N574GA	
5575	550	N575GA	
5576	550	N576GA	
5577	550	N577GA	
5578	550	N578GA	
5579	550	N579GA	
5580	550	N580GA	
5581	550		
5582	550		
5583	550		
5584	550		
5585	550		
5586	550		
5587	550		
5588	550		
5589	550		
5590	550		
5591	550		
5592	550		
5593	550		
5594	550		
5595	550		
5596	550		
5597	550		
5598	550		
5599	550		
5600	550		
5601	550		
5602	550		
5603	550		
5604	550		
5605	550		
5606	550		
5607	550		
5608	550		
5609	550		
5610	550		

GULFSTREAM VI/650

Officially the Gulfstream GVI but marketed as the G650. The G650ER, an extended-range version, was made available in 2014 – including as a retro-upgrade option for existing G650s. Those known to us are indicated below.

C/n	Series	Identities				
6001		N601GD	N650GA	[r/o 29Sep09, ff 25Nov09]		N650GX
6002		N602GD	N652GD	[ff 25Feb10; w/o 02Apr11 Roswell, NM]		
6003		N603GD	N653GD	N211HS		
6004	ER	N604GD	N650GD	[ff 06Jun10]	N104GA	N650RG
6005	ER	N605GD	N655GA	[ff 24Jan11]	N914BD	
6006		N606GD	M-YGVI	OH-GVV	9H-GVI	LX-SIX
6007	ER	N607GD	N711SW	N288WR		
6008	ER	N608GD	N762MS			
6009	ER	N609GD	VQ-BNZ	N923WC		
6010	ER	N110GA	N100A			
6011		N611GD	N102BG			
6012	ER	N612GD	N524EA			
6013		N613GD	N650PH	(D-AJKI)	N871FR	
6014	ER	N614GD	N100ES			
6015		N615GD	N1AL	N515PL	N516PL	
6016		N616GA	VP-CZA			
6017		N617GA	N886WT			
6018		N618GA	N673HA			
6019		N609GA	N650RR	N650NR*		
6020		N520GA	N922H			
6021		N221GA	N305CC			
6022		N722GA	N650HC	(N650HE)	N658HC	
6023		N623GA	G-OMRE	HS-VSK		
6024		N624GA	N1KE			
6025	ER	N325GA	VP-CZZ	N988HK		
6026		N626GA	N919SB			
6027		N607GA	N521HN			
6028		N328GA	G-ULFS	N515KA		
6029		N629GA	EC-LYK			
6030		N330GA	N650MT			
6031	ER	N331GA	N606GA			
6032		N932GA	M-GSIX	N4FL		
6033		N633GA	XA-BAL			
6034		N603GA	VP-CNR			
6035		N635GA	N880MD	N712KT		
6036		N636GD	N650SS	N666KQ	N13MS	
6037		N637GA	M-USIK			
6038		N638GD	N278L			
6039	ER	N639GA	N650DX	(N650CP)	N4CP	
6040		N640GA	OY-GLF	N999NN	VP-COR	
6041	ER	N641GD	N650CK	N657AT		
6042		N604GD	N28LL	N838MF		
6043	ER	N643GA	ZK-KFB	N193LS		
6044		N604GA	N22T	N829JV		
6045	ER	N645GA	N67WB			
6046		N646GA	N788AC	N650JK		
6047		N647GD	M-KSSN	M-KSOI	VP-BJC	
6048		N648GA	N773MJ			
6049		N649GA	M-JCBB			
6050		N605GD	N650PR	N650PE		
6051		N601GA	N650TP			
6052		N602GA	N927MC			
6053		N653GA	N2N			
6054		N654GA	N650GL			
6055	ER	N655GA	N44KJ			
6056		N656GA	N374FS			
6057		N657GA	N650DA			
6058		N658GA	N511DB			
6059		N659GA	N8833			
6060	ER	N660GA	N651CH			
6061		N661GA	N221DG			
6062		N662GA	(OY-IZM)	HB-IVJ		
6063		N663GA	N451CS			
6064		N664GA	N311CG			
6065		N965GA	N1TF			
6066		N606GA	EC-LZU			
6067		N667GA	N650GU			
6068		N668GA	(N650KG)	VP-CKB		
6069	ER	N669GD	N650EW			
6070		N670GA	EI-JSK			
6071		N671GA	N650XY			
6072		N672GA	N711RL			

GULFSTREAM 650

C/n	Series	Identities			
6073		N673GA	OE-LZM	9H-LZM	
6074	ER	N674GA	N652CH		
6075		N675GA	G-REFO		
6076		N676GA	N650JH	N1F	
6077		N677GD	M-NNNN	M-NGNG	
6078		N678GA	N5GV	N6453	
6079		N679GA	(N168D)	N88D	N83DZ	N650NY
6080		N608GA	N7780	M-WIND	
6081		N681GD	A9C-BAH		
6082		N682GD	VP-CTS		
6083		N683GD	M-BADU		
6084	ER	N684GA	N650ER	N585GS	
6085		N985GA	N691LC	VP-CRZ	VP-CSG
6086		N686GD	VH-LUY	VP-BLF	
6087		N687GA	N650GA	N711SW	
6088		N688GA	N380SE		
6089		N689GA	N747SC	N650AF	
6090	ER	N690GA	N212LF	N113CS	
6091		N691GA	N1AL		
6092		N692GA	SX-GSB	EI-LSN	
6093		N693GA	N288Z		
6094		N694GA	N1777M		
6095		N695GA	LX-GVI		
6096		N696GA	M-INSK		
6097		N697GA	N650HC		
6098		N698GA	B-KEY		
6099		N699GA	M-VITA	N368GW	N333GW*
6100	ER	N601GD	N650AB		
6101		N611GA	N47TR		
6102		N612GA	VQ-BMZ		
6103		N603GD	9K-GGA		
6104	ER	N641GA	N998PB		
6105		N615GA	N1454H		
6106	ER	N616GD	N388RF	N3CP	
6107		N617GD	4K-AI88		
6108		N618GD	N761LE		
6109		N619GA	N326JD	N650TY	
6110		N610GA	VP-BBF		
6111		N611GD	N817GS		
6112		N612GD	VP-CGN		
6113		N613GD	M-PLUS		
6114		N614GD	RA-10205		
6115		N615GD	(VT-NKR)	M-SHEF	LX-LXX
6116		N616GA	9H-ZMB	N251TD	N396TC*
6117		N617GA	N650ZK	N650HF	
6118		N618GA	HB-JUF		
6119	ER	N619GD	N40D		
6120		N620GD	9H-IKO	M-YNNS	
6121		N621GD	VP-CVI		
6122	ER	N622GA	VP-CYL	VP-CCW	
6123	ER	N623GA	VP-CJJ		
6124		N624GA	N887WT		
6125	ER	N625GD	N898NC		
6126	ER	N626GA	N6D		
6127		N627GA	N650HH	N899YF	
6128		N628GD	N108DB		
6129		N629GA	VP-CZB		
6130	ER	N630GD	N652BA		
6131		N631GA	N240CX		
6132		N632GA	M-BHBH		
6133	ER	N633GA	N651AV	N271DV	
6134		N634GA	OE-IIH		
6135		N635GA	EC-MHZ		
6136		N636GA	VP-BMP		
6137	ER	N637GA	TR-KGM		
6138	ER	N638GA	N650PA	VH-LAL	
6139		N639GA	PP-WSR		
6140		N640GD	P4-LSM	LX-DLF	
6141	ER	N641GD	N651WE		
6142		N142GA	N305KN		
6143		N643GA	D-ADSK	N988DJ	
6144	ER	N644GA	N650GY		
6145	ER	N645GA	N616KG		
6146		N646GD	D-AYSM		
6147		N647GA	(M-ABIU)	P4-AZG	T7-AZG
6148	ER	N648GA	B-LHK		

GULFSTREAM 650

C/n	Series	Identities			
6149	ER	N649GA	N650GD	N1415N	
6150		N601GA	M-ABIU	N968FA	
6151		N651GA	N22T		
6152		N652GD	(N341MM)	VP-CMM	B-56789
6153	ER	N653GA	A7-CGA		
6154		N654GA	N108R	N650RH	
6155		N655GA	9K-GGB		
6156	ER	N656GD	M-YSIX		
6157	ER	N657GD	N946JB		
6158	ER	N658GD	VQ-BNZ		
6159		N659GD	VP-BCO	N277FL	
6160		N660GA	G-GSVI		
6161		N661GA	N650GA	N358V	
6162		N662GA	C-GNDN		
6163	ER	N663GA	N900KS		
6164		N664GA	N270LE		
6165	ER	N605GD	B-99988		
6166		N766GA	(N94924)		
6167	ER	N667GD	A7-CGB		
6168		N668GA	M-ABIZ	VP-CJR	
6169		N669GD	VP-BCT		
6170		N670GA	RA-10204		
6171	ER	N671GA	N2437		
6172		N672GA	N540W		
6173	ER	N673GD	N688JR	M-GAGA	
6174	ER	N674GA	N827DC	[dbr by hailstorm 28Jul16, Colorado Springs, CO]	
6175	ER	N175GA	N650FJ		
6176		N676GA	VQ-BLV		
6177	ER	N677GD	N628TS		
6178		N678GA			
6179	ER	N679GA	A7-CGC		
6180	ER	N680GD	N566NS		
6181		N681GD	B-3255		
6182	ER	N682GD	(XA-EAJ)+	[+ ntu marks worn at Long Beach completion centre]	N827DC
6183		N183GA	9K-GGC		
6184		N684GA	EC-MLR		
6185		N685GD	VP-BZF		
6186	ER	N686GD	VP-CKV		
6187		N687GD	N155AN		
6188	ER	N688GA	N82A		
6189		N689GA	9K-GGD		
6190		N690GA	PP-ADZ		
6191	ER	N691GD	VP-CKL		
6192	ER	N692GA	(D-ADSK)	N891WW	
6193	ER	N693GD	N912GG		
6194	ER	N694GA	VP-CCY		
6195		N695GA	9H-SSK		
6196	ER	N696GA	N666HD		
6197	ER	N697GA	N720LF		
6198		N698GD	M-ABJL		
6199	ER	N699GA	HL8068		
6200		N620GD	N650NB		
6201	ER	N621GD	N650XA		
6202		N622GD	VP-CPG		
6203		N623GD	A6-MAF		
6204		N624GD	N618EC	N318LS	
6205	ER	N602GA	(N67MN)	N1BN	
6206		N626GD	HB-JFP		
6207		N627GD	M-GULF		
6208		N628GD	VP-CYL		
6209	ER	N629GD	N858CG		
6210	ER	N622GA	N650ER		
6211	ER	N611GD	N651XA		
6212	ER	N612GD	HL8299		
6213	ER	N613GD	N706NR		
6214		N614GD	VP-CPM		
6215	ER	N615GA	D-AWWW		
6216	ER	N615GA	9M-ZZZ		
6217	ER	N617GA	VP-CYZ		
6218		N618GA	VQ-BAH		
6219	ER	N619GA	N515PL		
6220	ER	N620GS	N918TA		
6221	ER	N621GS	P4-GVI		
6222		N602GD	N235BH		
6223	ER	N623GA	VP-CVA		
6224	ER	N624GS	VP-CER		

GULFSTREAM 650

C/n	Series	Identities		
6225	ER	N625GD	N168NW	
6226	ER	N626GA	N500SA*	
6227		N627GA	N65FG	
6228	ER	N628GA	N200ES	
6229	ER	N629GA	VP-CZC	
6230		N630GD	N650EH	
6231	ER	N631GD	N999YY	
6232		N632GA	N464GR	
6233	ER	N633GA	PP-IZB*	
6234		N634GA	N656TT	
6235	ER	N635GA	B-88322	
6236	ER	N636GA	N805TM	
6237	ER	N637GA	VP-CMR	
6238		N638GA	N650AJ*	
6239	ER	N639GA	9M-TMJ*	
6240	ER	N640GA	N777ZH	
6241		N641GA	B-....	
6242	ER	N642GS	N671WB	
6243	ER	N643GA	N919PE*	
6244	ER	N644GA	(N687GS)	N650VC
6245	ER	N645GA	8P-ASD	
6246		N646GA	N595TG*	
6247		N647GA	M-OVIE	
6248	ER	N648GA	N1875A*	
6249		N649GA	N666FH*	
6250		N625G		
6251		N651GA		
6252		N652GS	N650GD*	
6253		N653GA		
6254		N654GA		
6255		N655GA	N66ZG*	
6256		N656GA	N312ZW*	
6257		N657GA	N1901G*	
6258		N658GA	N1948S*	
6259		N659GA		
6260	ER	N660GA	N1PG*	
6261		N661GA		
6262		N662GA		
6263		N663GA	N188W*	
6264		N664GA	N2PG*	
6265		N665GS		
6266		N606GA		
6267		N667GA		
6268		N668GA		
6269		N669GD	N846CB*	
6270		N670GA	N950CM*	
6271		N671GD		
6272		N672GA		
6273		N673GA	N67TH*	
6274		N674GA		
6275		N675GS	N650GA*	
6276		N276GA	N889LM*	
6277		N277GA		
6278		N678GD		
6279		N279GA		
6280		N680GD		
6281		N281GA		
6282		N282GA		
6283		N283GA		
6284		N284GA		
6285		N685GD		
6286		N686GD		
6287		N287GA		
6288		N288GA		
6289		N289GA		
6290		N290GA		
6291		N291GA		
6292		N292GA		
6293		N293GA		
6294		N294GA		
6295		N295GA		
6296		N296GA		
6297		N297GA		
6298		N698GA		
6299		N299GA		
6300		N630GD		

GULFSTREAM 650

C/n	Series	Identities
6301		N601GD
6302		N602GA
6303		N303GA
6304		N604GA
6305		N305GA
6306		N306GA
6307		N307GA
6308		N308GA
6309		N309GA
6310		N310GA
6311		N311GA
6312		N312GA
6313		N613GD
6314		N314GA
6315		N315GA
6316		N316GA
6317		N617GA
6318		N618GD
6319		N319GA
6320		N620GD
6321		N621GD
6322		N622GA
6323		N623GA
6324		N324GA
6325		N325GA

GULFSTREAM GVII-G500

C/n	Identities		
72001	N500GA	[ff 18May15, Savannah, GA]	
72002	N502GS	[ff 20Nov15, Savannah, GA]	
72003	N503G	[ff 20Nov15, Savannah, GA]	
72004	N504GS	[ff 20Feb16, Savannah, GA]	
72005	N505GD	[ff 04Aug16, Savannah, GA]	
72006	N506GD		
72007	N507GD		
72008	N508GD		
72009	N509GD		
72010	N510GD		
72011			
72012			
72013			
72014			
72015			
72016			
72017			
72018			
72019			
72020			
72021			
72022			
72023			
72024			
72025			
72026			
72027			
72028			
72029			
72030			

GULFSTREAM GVII-G600

C/n	Identities		
73001	N600G	[ff 27Dec16, Savannah, GA]	N601GA
73002	N720GD	[ff 24Feb17, Savannah, GA]	
73003	N730GD	[ff 05May17, Savannah, GA]	
73004	N740GD		
73005	N750GD	N600G	
73006			
73007			
73008			
73009			
73010			
73011			
73012			
73013			
73014			
73015			
73016			
73017			
73018			
73019			
73020			
73021			
73022			
73023			
73024			

HONDA HA-420 HONDAJET

C/n	Identities				
P001	N420HA	[ff 03Dec03]			
42000001	N420HJ	[ff 20Dec10]			
42000002	N420HM	[ff 18Nov11]			
42000003	N420AH	[ff 04May12]			
42000004	N420NC	[ff 16May13]			
42000005	[c/n not used]				
42000006	[c/n not used]				
42000007	[c/n not used]				
42000008	[c/n not used]				
42000009	[c/n not used]				
42000010	[c/n not used]				
42000011	N420EX	[first production aircraft, ff 27Jun14]			
42000012	N959EN				
42000013	N420KA				
42000014	N21HJ				
42000015	N420AZ				
42000016	N420HE	N420ET	N420EA		
42000017	N420TG	N420EA	N420DE	N420HE	D-ITIM
42000018	N420EU	M-HNDA			
42000019	N420MX	XA-MHU			
42000020	N774RC				
42000021	N141HJ	N557MW	N527MW		
42000022	N420BT				
42000023	N682TM				
42000024	N25HJ				
42000025	N527MW	[cx 12May16; marks reallocated to c/n 42000021]	N41JJ		
42000026	N21671				
42000027	N20ZA				
42000028	N420JB	N1MR			
42000029	N816LS	N227WP			
42000030	N421EK				
42000031	N575DM				
42000032	N71TS				
42000033	N684ST				
42000034	N515HJ				
42000035	N250SS				
42000036	N136DT				
42000037	N856WD				
42000038	N10XN				
42000039	N426HJ				
42000040	N419DB				
42000041	N718FH				
42000042	N505RP				
42000043	N742CT				
42000044	N225DB				
42000045	N1155	F-HENE			
42000046	N612PR				
42000047	N470TW				
42000048	N58JE				
42000049	N49HJ				
42000050	N120HF				
42000051	N18QB				
42000052	N368BL				
42000053	N120MM				
42000054	N110BB*				
42000055	N199HJ				
42000056	N86SG*				
42000057	N13ZM				
42000058	N819TC	I-....			
42000059	N629JT				
42000060	N526SH				
42000061	N562DB				
42000062	N814SX				
42000063	N829DL				
42000064	N420ST				
42000065	N319HJ				
42000066	N166HJ				
42000067	N316SA				
42000068	N378PM				
42000069	N707FH				
42000070	N230JL				
42000071	N422KT				
42000072	N402HJ				
42000073	N606PB				

HONDA HA-420 HONDAJET

C/n	Identities
42000074	N430HJ
42000075	N420DT
42000076	N719FH
42000077	
42000078	
42000079	
42000080	
42000081	
42000082	
42000083	
42000084	
42000085	
42000086	
42000087	
42000088	
42000089	
42000090	
42000091	
42000092	
42000093	
42000094	
42000095	
42000096	
42000097	
42000098	
42000099	
42000100	
42000101	
42000102	
42000103	
42000104	
42000105	
42000106	
42000107	
42000108	
42000109	
42000110	

IAI 1125 ASTRA / GULFSTREAM 100

Note: The SPX has model number 1125A

C/n	Series	Identities								
001		4X-WIN	[ff 19Mar84; wfu Aug86]							
002		4X-WIA								
003		[non-flying test airframe]								
004		4X-CUA	N96PC	"N425TS"	N96PC	N425TS	OB-1703			
005										
006										
007		[Aircraft not built as the owner of the first aircraft to be delivered specified that he did not want one of the first ten aircraft being built!]								
008										
009										
010										
011		4X-CUK	N450PM	N450BM	N705MA	N991RV	N500FA	N765A		
012		4X-CUL	N1125A	N25AG	N312W	N27BH	N610HC	N618HC	N939MC	(YV....)
013		4X-CUM	(N413SC)	N713SC	N112PR	N25N	N29NB			
014		4X-CUN	N400J	N400JF	N8484P	N116JC				
015		4X-CUP	N887PC	N46UF	N46UP	N14SR	N755PA	N157GA		
016		4X-CUK	N716W	N36FD	N221DT	N221PA	YV3046			
017		4X-CUD	N717WW	VR-BES	N996JP	N711JG	N711JQ	N455SH	(N800JS)	N555KE
		N565KE								
018		4X-CUR	N1188A	N500M	N500MQ	N72FL	N72EL	N1700A	YV3049	
019		4X-CUE	N30AJ	N49MW	(N499MW)	N49MN				
020		4X-CUS	N279DP	N212LD	N917SC	N15BA	[parted out by Dodson Int'l Parts, Rantoul, KS]			
021		4X-CUR	N1125A	N1125S	N1125	N200CK	N7AG	N307FT		
022		4X-CUT	PT-MBZ							
023		4X-CUG	N125GB	N23TJ	N345GC	N112EM				
024		4X-CUT	N300JJ	N999BL	N763RR	YV501T				
025		4X-CUH	N387PA	N887PA	N902AU					
026		4X-CUI	N120BJ	N120WH	N120WS	N9VL	N24PR	N1900A		
027		4X-CUJ	N199GH	N199HF	N199HE	N388WA				
028		N10MZ	N11MZ	N816HB	N800ZZ	[cx 7Jul14; wfu Wilmington, DE]				
029		N79AD	N15TW	N94TW	N154DD	N131DA	N956PP	N959PP		
030		4X-CUI	N50AJ	N90U	N90UG	N902G	N900DL	N13AD		
031		N40AJ	N125AJ	N987GK	N987G	N962A				
032		4X-CUN	N1125A	N232S	N125MG	N116PB	(N716PT)	N113PT	N514BB	
033		4X-CUP	N980ML	N922RA	N52KS	N441BC	[cx 18Jun15; wfu]			
034		4X-CUJ	N53SF	VR-CMG	N511WA	N541RL				
035		N1125K	[parted out by Marfklyn Jet Parts, TX]							
036		I-FLYL	N82RT	N195FC	N230AJ	N757BD	N727HE	YV2872		
037		N3PC	N589TB	N100SR	(N100SQ)	N400XS				
038		N803JW	N930SC	N930UC	N777AM					
039		N359V	N359VP	N359VS	N402TS	N885CA	XA-JRM	N636BC	N686BC*	
040		N279DS	N666K	N666KL	(N530CM)					
041	SP	N96AR	VR-BME	N45MS	N41AU	(N29UC)				
042	SP	N60AJ	N575ET	N575EW	EC-339	EC-GIA	N588R	N528RR		
043	SP	N56AG	(N34CE)	N90CE	N1M	N43MH	[cx 12Mar13]			
044	SP	N50AJ	N676TC	N844GA	N1UA	N334MM				
045	SP	N91FD	VH-FIS	D-CFIS	VH-FIS	N880CH	N916BG	N916CG		
046	SP	N140DR	N630S							
047	SP	N30AJ	(N134RV)	N166RM						
048	SP	N1125V	N88MF	N43RP						
049	SP	N1125Y	JA8379	N4420E	N145AS	N323P	(N1M)	N293P		
050	SP	N4EM	XA-TJF	N501JT	N45H	YV2682				
051	SP	N1125A								
052	SP	N90AJ								
053	SP	N227N	N227NL	(N315S)	N853SP	N121SG	N717CP	N419WC		
054	SP	N70AJ	N198HF	N187HF	N770FF	N770SC	YV628T			
055	SP	4X-CUI	N1125Z	N1MC	N828C	N880CA	VP-CDR	N120GA	ZS-MDA	N111EL
		N111EQ	N63XG							
056	SP	4X-CUG	N3175T	N790FH						
057	SP	4X-CUH	N3175S	YV-2199P	YV-785CP	YV-2564P	YV-785CP	N157SP	YV484T	
058	SP	N1125E	C-FDAX							
059	SP/100	N4341S	D-CCAT	HB-VNF	LX-GOL	D-CABB	[rebranded as Gulfstream 100 – but has no winglets!]			
		N666HA								
060	SP	N227AN	YV-757CP	VR-BON	VP-BON	N577AN				
061	SP	4X-CUG	N60AJ	N550M	N200ST	YV2679				
062	SP	4X-CUJ	N1125	N999GP	N9990P	N100AK	N262SP	N866G	N866Q	N874WD
		N944RS								
063	SP	4X-CUI	Eritrea 901	N74TJ	N331SK	(N60RV)				
064	SP	4X-CUG	N650GE	N650GF	N858WW					
065	SP	4X-CUJ	N75TT	N50TG	N50TQ	N30GC				
066	SP	N101NS	N419MK	C-FMHL	C-FMHB	N419MK				
067	SP	N20FE	N28NP	(N28NR)	N28NF	N267SP	N467MW	N46386	N730DF	
068	SP	N1125Z	N401WT	N46TB						
069	SP	N804JW	N247PS	[cx 21Feb13; to Savannah Technical College, GA, as instructional airframe]						

ASTRA / GULFSTREAM 100

C/n	Series	Identities								
070	SP/100	N300AJ	N805JW	N100GA	(N100GQ)	N448GR	(N149LP)	[rebranded as Gulfstream 100 – but has no winglets!]		
071	SP	4X-CUW	N60AJ	N71FS						
072	SP	N1125L	N314AD	N32TM	N365GA	[wfu; cx 06Jun13]				
073	SPX	4X-WIX	[first model SPX]		N173W	N918MJ	N24ZD			
074	SP	N500AJ	N789CA							
075	SP	4X-CUW	ZS-BCT	N75GZ	(N175SP)	N225AL	N928JA			
076	SP	4X-CUV	N1125	4X-CUV	N1125	N1125G	N699MC	N699MQ	N20YL	
077	SP	N220AJ	N771CP	YV-771CP	YV1771					
078	SP	N1125J								
079	SPX	4X-CUX	C-FCFP	N800PW	N928WG					
080	SPX	4X-CUY	(D-CCBT)	N333AJ	N333CZ	VP-CUT	C-GSSS	N411MM	C-FPSB	C-GRJP
081	SPX	N800AJ	N801G	N415BS						
082	SPX	N121GV	N882GA							
083	SPX	N383SF								
084	SPX	N795HP	N795HB	N801RS	YV....					
085	SPX	N796HP	N796HR							
086	SPX	N793A	PT-WBC	N880GP						
087	SPX	4X-CUU	C-FRJZ							
088	C-38A	N398AG	USAF 94-1569							
089	SPX	N918MK	N89HS							
090	C-38A	N399AG	USAF 94-1570							
091	SPX	N297GA	N500MZ	N500M	N91GX	N818WF				
092	SPX	N789A	VP-BMA	N92UJ	N8MC	N8MN	N100G	[crash-landed 14Sep07 Atlanta/DeKalb-Peachtree, GA; parted out]		
093	SPX	N65TD	N149TD	N707BC	N207BC					
094	SPX	N294S	N500MA							
095	SPX	N98AD	C6-JET	N98AD	N608DC					
096	SPX	N66KG	VP-CKG	N96AL	N323P					
097	SPX	N273RA	N363NH							
098	SPX	N275RA	N98FJ	N919CH	N819CH					
099	SPX	N987A	5B-CJG	N830DB	N838DB	N115BR	N34FS	N917SM		
100	SPX	N807JW	N907DP							
101	SPX	N202GA	N297GA	N711WK	(N291WK)	N610SM				
102	SPX	N525M	N359V	N359D	N877D	N858WZ	[parted out by Alliance Air Parts, OK]			
103	SPX	N755A								
104	SPX	N957P	(N104GA)	N957F	N6EL					
105	SPX	N217PT	HB-VMG	N105FN	N585RL					
106	SPX	N122GV	N876GA	N800MK	N800WS	N550HB				
107	SPX	N997GA	D-CRIS	OE-GBE						
108	SPX	N998GA	N999GP	N998GP	N302TS	N108CG				
109	SPX	N96FL	N377AC							
110	SPX	N97FL	N212T							
111	SPX	N848GA	N297GA	OE-GAM	HB-VOA	OY-YAM	N760JR			
112	SPX	N633GA	N1MC	N61JE	N81JE	N831MC				
113	SPX	N113GA	HB-VMK	N35GX	(N297GA)	N82BE	N242BG	N617RA		
114	SPX	N114GA	N114SN							
115	SPX	N526GA	HB-VMR	C-GRGE	OE-GPG	N514MM	(PH-DEQ)	(D-CENT)	B-58813	N115JJ
116	SPX	N527GA	N456PR	N12ND	N125GR					
117	SPX	N528GA	C-FTDB	C-GGHZ	C-FACG					
118	SPX	N529GA	N28NP							
119	SPX	4X-CUZ	B-20001							
120	SPX	N635GA	N770UP	C-GPDA	N100GY	N989SE				
121	SPX	N843GA	N100AK	N188AK						
122	SPX	N69GX	(N297GA)	N419TK	N110MG	N2HZ				
123	SPX	4X-CVJ	N36GX	"C-GWST"	VH-WSM	N36GX	N307JW			
124	SPX	4X-CVE	N42GX	N777FL	N777FZ					
125	SPX	4X-CVG	N44GX	N248SL	N2488L	N625MM	N625BE			
126	SPX	4X-CVJ	India L3458							
127	SPX	4X-CVG	N621KD	N327GA	N247PS	N919DS				
128	SPX	4X-CVF	N45GX	N179DC	N676TC	N314AD				
129	SPX	4X-CVG	N52GX	N424MP	N180TA	N546LS				
130	SPX	4X-CVI	N55GX	N297GA	N100GA	C-GBSW				
131	SPX	4X-CVG	N57GX	N400CP						
132	SPX	4X-CVI	N1125V	N775DF	N722AZ	N728AZ	N632BE			
133	SPX	4X-CVG	N65GX	VP-CAR	D-CGMA	OE-GBD				
134	SPX	4X-CVG	N64GX	N1125S	N666K					
135	SPX	4X-CVI	N58GX	N809JW						
136	SPX	4X-CVG	N68GX	N43RJ	(N32UC)					
137	SPX	4X-CVI	N75GX	N620KE						
138	SPX	4X-CVG	N80GX	N810JW	N10FH	N776JS				
139	100	4X-CVI	N99GX	N100GA	N420CE	N948LM	N250EX			
140	SPX	4X-CVK	N104GX	N811JW	N50MS	N404HB				
141	SPX	4X-CVI	N106GX	CC-CWK	N223GA	M-YEDT	N505PL			
142	100	4X-CVK	N109GX							
143	SPX	4X-CVH	N261GA	VT-BAV	N143FS	(YV....)	N174JF	YV....		

ASTRA / GULFSTREAM 100

C/n	Series	Identities							
144	SPX	4X-CVK	N262GA	VP-BMT	N144GX	N82HH			
145	SPX	4X-CVK	N264GA	N387PA	N3FD	(N37DE)	YV3194		
146	100	4X-CVI	N646GA	VP-BMW	N853M	C-GTLG	N590TA		
147	100	4X-CVF	N647GA	N147SW					
148	100	4X-CVI	N648GA	4X-CVI	India L3467				
149	100	N749GA							
150	100	4X-CVK	N750GA	C-FHRL	C-FIPP	OE-GKW			
151	100	4X-CVG	N751GA	C-GTDO	N907TP				
152	100	4X-CVE	N352GA	N150CT	N160CT	N900DP	N525PG	N1UA	
153	100	4X-CVJ	N353GA	OE-GBE	N133SN	N100AK			
154	100	N354GA	N221AL	XA-MEG					
155	100	4X-CVJ	N445AK						
156	100	N996GA	C-FHNS						
157	100	4X-CVK	N327GA						
158	100	4X-CVJ	N995GA	EC-JXE	ZS-SFY	EC-JXE	EC-LDS	N662EP	N158LC

Production complete

Note: Most, if not all, aircraft were first test flown with 4X- marks, some of which remain unknown to us.

The Astra was replaced by the Gulfstream 150.

IAI GULFSTREAM 150

C/n	Identities						
201	4X-TRA	[rolled out at Tel Aviv 18Jan05; ff 05May05]				N150RT	N150GV
202	4X-WID	[ff 2.9.05]	N150GA	N703HA	(N901VB)		
203	4X-CVK	N528GA	N530GP				
204	4X-WID	N373ML					
205	4X-CVK	N405GA	N715WG	N301SG	N552CB		
206	4X-WID	N806GA	N830DB	N150KM			
207	4X-CVK	N807GA	N531GP				
208	4X-WID	N208GA	N150CT				
209	4X-CVK	N409GA	N501RP	N290GA	N92AJ		
210	4X-WID	N510GA	N650GE	N428JD			
211	4X-CVK	N757GA	N248SL				
212	4X-WID	N412GA	N502RP				
213	4X-CVK	N613GA	N5950C				
214	4X-WID	N314GA	N777FL				
215	4X-CVK	N615GA	N503RP	N215GA	N247PS		
216	4X-WID	N216GA	N192SW				
217	4X-CVK	N217GA	N150GD	N217MS			
218	4X-WID	N218GA	N969WR				
219	4X-CVL	N219GA	CC-CWK				
220	4X-CVM	N220GA	N197HF				
221	4X-WID	N532GP					
222	4X-CVL	N422GA	N717EP	C-FTXX			
223	4X-CVK	N350BN	N611NC				
224	4X-CVM	N424GA	N590FA	YV3306			
225	4X-WID	N399GA	N150PU	N365GA			
226	4X-CVL	N8821C					
227	4X-CVK	N451R	OB-1951-P	N275SC	N100SR		
228	4X-CVM	N628GA	VP-BMA	N100GX			
229	4X-WID	N8841C					
230	4X-CVK	N630GA	N722SW				
231	4X-CVL	N9611Z	N787BN				
232	4X-CVM	N928ST					
233	4X-WID	N633GA	EC-KMF	N100VP	VH-PFV		
234	4X-CVK	N511CT					
235	4X-CVL	N635GA	D-CKDM	M-CKDM	N371GA	PR-FSN	N250EA
236	4X-TRA	N77709					
237	4X-CVM	N537GA	EC-KMS	CC-AOA			
238	4X-WID	N150GA	N222LR				
239	4X-CVK	N639GA	AP-MMM				
240	4X-TRA	N360AV					
241	4X-CVL	N631GA	N480JJ	[w/o Key West, FL, 31Oct11]			
242	4X-CVM	N442GA	UR-KAS	OE-GAS			
243	4X-WID	N443GA	EC-KPJ				
244	4X-CVK	N744GA	N950N	N302SG	N553CB		
245	4X-TRA	N745GA	OE-GSK	M-STEP	N162RU		
246	4X-CVL	N96AD					
247	4X-CVM	N110FS	N650DH				
248	4X-WID	N637SF					
249	4X-CVK	N191CP	N67KP				
250	4X-TRA	N850GA	N918MJ	N434JM	N581SF		
251	4X-CVL	N351GA	N22ST				
252	4X-CVK	N352GA	N769MS	N789MS	N247PS	N150GA	
253	4X-WID	N353GA	EC-KTV	N253DE	N591MB		
254	4X-CVM	N354GA	EC-KTK	N254GS	N901SS		
255	4X-TRA	N556GA	XA-PAZ	XA-UUX	N202VP		
256	4X-CVL	N262GA	N150GD	N546MM			
257	4X-WID	N457GA	XA-ADR				
258	4X-CVK	N458GA	N10RZ				
259	4X-CVM	N746GA	RP-C5168				
260	4X-TRA	N260GA	N802RR	N150GV	N150HM		
261	4X-CVL	N261GA	OE-GLF				
262	4X-WID	N272CB	N101RX				
263	4X-CVK	N263GA	(N150GV)	N802RR			
264	4X-CVM	N264GA	C-GXNW				
265	4X-CVL	N465GA	N993AC	XA-CHY			
266	4X-WID	N888YC	XA-JCZ				
267	4X-TRA	N367GA	N119KW				
268	4X-CVK	N268GA	(D-CKDN)	N365SC			
269	4X-CVM	N469GA	(D-CKDO)	N520CH	(N520SH)	XA-CPL	
270	4X-CVL	N470GA	(D-CKDP)	N110JJ	N480JJ		
271	4X-WID	N471GA	C-FTRP				
272	4X-TRA	N372GA	N399SC	N819AM	N819AB*		
273	4X-CVK	N373GA	C-GZCZ				
274	4X-CVM	N374GA	N1FC	N3FS			
275	4X-WID	N375GA	N116HW	C-GNYH	C-GWWW	C-FTIX	N719KX

GULFSTREAM 150

C/n	Identities						
276	4X-CVL	N46WY	N15PV*				
277	4X-CVK	N7FF	N1FS	N636SF			
278	4X-TRA	N700FA					
279	4X-CVM	N489GA	N935SS	N200LR			
280	4X-WID	N980GA	VP-CEP	VT-GKB			
281	4X-CVK	N631GA	N372AS	N57RG			
282	4X-TRA	N382GA	C-GPDQ	C-GZDO	N2282	N22G	
283	4X-CVL	N683GA	C-GXVK	N283GA	9H-JET	SP-TBF	
284	4X-WID	N484GA	TC-AEH				
285	4X-CVM	N485GA	C-FZCC	C-FZCG	N285GA		
286	4X-CVK	N486GA	N150GA	N1924D			
287	4X-TRA	N487GA	(D-CGPE)	D-CGEP			
288	4X-WID	N208GA	C-GWPK				
289	4X-CVL	N489GA	N650MP	N2289	N24G		
290	4X-CVM	N490GA	(XA-ATP)	XB-OMG	XA-ATZ		
291	4X-CVK	N391GA	N1920				
292	4X-TRA	N392GA	N557GA				
293	4X-WID	N393GA	PR-NTR	N935GB			
294	4X-CVL	N994GA	N565AB				
295	4X-CVM	N595GA	N194SW				
296	4X-CVK	N996GA	C-FREE				
297	4X-CVL	N217GA	N639SF				
298	4X-CVM	N298GA	N150GD	N685JF			
299	4X-TRA	N199GA	M-GASG				
300	4X-...	N300GA	OE-GKA				
301	4X-CVK	N101GA	PP-ESV				
302	4X-CVL	N702GA	N589MD	N888YV	N730GA		
303	4X-CVM	N203GA	N13WF				
304	4X-CVK	N104GA	PR-CBA				
305	4X-CVL	N305GA	N150PG				
306	4X-CVM	N806GA	N500RP				
307	4X-CVK	N907GA	N503RP				
308	4X-TRA	N208GA	N501RP				
309	4X-WID	N209GA	N116NC				
310	4X-CVL	N310GA	N151PW				
311	4X-CVK	N311GA	(N150GA)	N72AM	N150GD	N916EC	
312	4X-TRA	N112GA	YV3119				
313	4X-CVK	N913GA	Mexico 3913/XC-LOH		Mexico TP-08/XC-LOH		Mexico TP-07/XC-LOH
314	4X-TRA	N914GA	Mexico 3914/XC-LOI		Mexico TP-09/XC-LOI		Mexico TP-06/XC-LOI
315	4X-WID	N915GA	RP-C8150				
316	4X-CVL	N916GA	N963CH				
317	4X-CVM	N817GA	N622SF				
318	4X-CVK	N918GA	VT-KZN				
319	4X-CVL	N819GA	N651DH				
320	4X-CVM	N120GA	N23EW				
321	4X-CVK	N221GA	N123QU				
322	4X-CVL	N922GA	C-FWEE				
323	4X-CVM	N323GA					
324	4X-CVK	N324GA	N1ED				
325	4X-CVL	N825GA	LZ-VLZ				
326	4X-CVK	N126GA					

Production complete

IAI 1126 GALAXY / GULFSTREAM 200

Note: Some Galaxys have been re-branded as Gulfstream 200s, as shown

C/n	Series	Identities								
001		[reportedly non-flying test airframe]								
002		[reportedly non-flying test airframe]								
003		4X-IGA	[rolled out 04Sep97; ff 25Dec97; wfu Tel Aviv, Israel]							
004	200	4X-IGO	4X-CVF [not confirmed]		(N7AU)	N844GA	N711JG	(N711JU)	(N711JQ)	VP-CHW
		N789AT	PR-WTR							
005	200	4X-IGB	N505GA							
006		N7AU	N81TT	N8MF						
007		N847GA	(C-GRJZ)	HB-IUT	N844RC					
008		N998G	(N288GA)	VP-CRS	N479PR					
009	200	N849GA	N83EJ	N200AX	PR-FKK	N9889	(N173BF)			
010		N808JW	N121LS	N672PS						
011		N634GA	HB-IUU	N634GA	"HB-IGA"	HB-IUU	N56AG	(N223AM)	LZ-FIB	
012		4X-CVE	"N1TA"	N845GA	(HB-IGK)	YR-TIG	[w/o 16Jan09 Oradea, Romania]			
013	200	4X-CVG	N13GX	N200GA	"XA-MAK"	N200GA	(N13GX)	XA-MAK	N160HA	HB-IGP
		N200BH	N403SL							
014	200	N37GX	N121GV	N121GX	N467MW	N469MW	(N140GH)	N20BD		
015		4X-CVI	N38GX	N622SV	N648RR					
016		4X-CVK	N40GX	N35BP	N135BP	N35BP				
017		4X-CVF	N48GX	(N406LM)+	[+marks worn but ntu]		N415PR			
018	200	4X-CVH	N47GX	N18GZ	4X-COG	HB-JKH	N917DP			
019		4X-CVK	N39GX	N407LM	N219GA	N219AX	N612MH	N812FT		
020		4X-CVI	N46GX	N516CC	N816CC	C-FLPB				
021		4X-CVF	N321SF	(N41GX)	N321SF					
022	200	4X-CVE	N43GX	N414KD	N414KB	N200AX	N322AD	N330WJ		
023	200	4X-CVH	N50GX	N414DH	N414DK	N32TM	(N32JN)			
024		4X-CVI	N101L	N101LD	N188ML	N818CR	N251LB			
025		4X-CVK	N54GX	N2HL	N263GA	N302MC	N866G			
026		4X-CVE	N56GX	N800PJ						
027		4X-CVF	N878CS	PR-OFT						
028	200	4X-CVH	N60GX	N199HF	N139HF	N225JD				
029		4X-CVK	N61GX	VP-BLH	VP-CAS	D-BAIR	N929GA			
030	200	4X-CVF	N303MC	B-HWB	N133BA	B-8086				
031		4X-CVH	N62GX	N671PP	N671BP					
032	200	4X-CVE	N66GX	N406LM	HB-JEB	N320LV				
033		4X-CVK	N31SJ	N212MP	YV3130					
034	200	4X-CVF	N34GX	(N200GA)	N134AX	N274JC	(N216YM)	PH-YMA	N108SC	OB-2023
035	200	4X-CVE	N59GX	N110HA						
036		4X-CVK	N67GX	N144KK	N408LM	N408LN	B-KSJ	RP-C280		
037	200	4X-CVH	N337JD	N204AB	B-8083					
038		4X-CVE	N168EC	N602VC	N858DN					
039		4X-CVE	N72RK	N132JC	(N302HM)	YV3253				
040		4X-CVH	N90GX	4X-CLL						
041		4X-CVE	N101GX	YV-772CP	YV1401					
042		4X-CVF	N102GX	N701HB	N755PA					
043		4X-CVH	N103GX	N122GV	N123GV	C-FHYB				
044		4X-CVE	N105GX	N621KD	N621KB	N882LT	N882ET	N531MB		
045		4X-CVF	N107GX	N70TT	N440TT	N1221G				
046	200	4X-CVH	N108GX	PR-MEN	N889G	N878DN	C-GJFG			
047	200	4X-CVE	N110GX	N601AB	N721CJ					
048	200	4X-CVF	N112GX	N602AB	N200GA	N921TH				
049	200	4X-CVH	N290GA	N751BC	N753BC	B-8090	B-LUX	N188AJ		
050	200	4X-CVE	N291GA	N789RR	N789PR	OE-HFC	HB-JKD	N505JC	HK-4907	
051		4X-CVF	N293GA	OY-RAK	LN-SUS	N140KR	B-8089	N283DJ		
052		4X-CVG	N294GA	N700QS	N402TX	N213EP				
053	200	4X-CVE	N295GA	(N601AV)	N815JW					
054	200	4X-CVI	N296GA	N200GA	N54AX	N272JC	(N254SC)	C-FLMS		
055		4X-CVF	N255JT	N885AR	N885RR	N212SL	(HS-AAH)	HS-JAA	N979AA	
056		4X-CVE	N298GA	N929WG	N929WD	XA-PCO				
057	200	4X-CVG	N299GA	N886G						
058	200	4X-CVI	N360GA	(N702QS)+	[+marks worn but ntu]		N272MW	N726DC	N726DR	
059	200	4X-CVE	N361GA	(N602AV)	N409LM	N409BM				
060	200	4X-CVF	N270GA	N703QS	N409TX	N513RB				
061	200	4X-CVG	N271GA	N705QS	N413TX	N35RF				
062	200	4X-CVH	N362GA	N957P	XA-DRE					
063	200	4X-CVE	N363GA	N20PL	N363GA	N20PL	N363GA	SX-IFB	N810AA	HK-5154
064	200	4X-CVF	N364GA	(N706QS)	N2BG					
065	200	4X-CVG	N275GA	(N628RC)	N118KA	(SX-MAD)	SX-ONE	OE-HSG	OO-OSG	OE-HAG
066	200	4X-CVH	N276GA	N707QS	N419TX	N70HQ				
067	200	4X-CVK	N367GA	N916GR	N916GB					
068	200	4X-CVE	N368GA	N179AE	N360SJ	N860SJ				
069	200	4X-CVF	N279GA	N708QS	N403TX	N334JK				
070	200	4X-CVG	N268GA	N702QS	N415TX	N718DD				
071	200	4X-CVH	N371GA	(N706QS)	N459BN	N458BN				
072	200	4X-CVK	N272GA	N65R	N679RW	N892SB	N110WA			

GALAXY / GULFSTREAM 200

C/n	Series	Identities					
073	200	4X-CVF	N673GA	N712QS	HB-IUV		
074	200	4X-CVJ	N274GA	N80R	N889MR		
075	200	4X-CVG	N875GA	N200YB	N365CX		
076	200	4X-CVK	N376GA	N200BA			
077	200	4X-CVH	N277GA	VT-PLA			
078	200	4X-CVJ	N278GA	(HB-IUS)			
079	200	4X-CVE	N379GA	N382G	N379GA	C-FISO	
080	200	4X-CVK	N380GA	XA-MDK			
081	200	4X-CVG	N881GA	N414DH	N86CW	N186CW	
082	200	4X-CVJ	N282GA	N402LM	XA-AAN		
083	200	4X-CVE	N283GA	N403LM	N830DT		
084	200	4X-CVK	N284GA	N414KD	N1Z	N111ZD	N882SG
085	200	4X-CVJ	N285GA	N720QS	N406TX	N585DD	
086	200	4X-CVH	N286GA	XA-JHE			
087	200	4X-CVE	N287GA	(N747SG)	N707SG		
088	200	4X-CVJ	N388GA	(N721QS)	N200GA	N704JW	N179JA
089	200	4X-CVH	N289GA	OE-HTI	YR-TII		
090	200	4X-CVK	N790GA	B-KMJ	HS-LEE		
091	200	4X-CVJ	N391GA	N2HL	(N19HL)	(N918JT)	N990JT
092	200	4X-CVH	N492GA	N721QS	N417TX	N329PK	
093	200	4X-CVK	N393GA	N722QS	N422TX	N318JF	
094	200	4X-CVI	N394GA	N121GV			
095	200	4X-CVF	N595GA	N331BN	N311MK		
096	200	4X-CVG	N196GA	N600YB	N454TH		
097	200	4X-CVI	N397GA	N816JW			
098	200	4X-CVK	N398GA	ZS-PKD	VT-ARV		
099	200	4X-CVF	N499GA	N723QS	XA-MYM		
100	200	4X-CVI	N500GA	N724QS	N408TX	N483AM	
101	200	4X-CVJ	N201GA	N415SE			
102	200	4X-CVK	N702GA	N601DV	OE-HAZ	N412AP	
103	200	4X-CVH	N203GA	EC-JGN	LX-GRS	XA-POS	
104	200	4X-CVI	N104GA	N271RA			
105	200	4X-CVJ	N305GA	N725QS	N932BA	N645PM	
106	200	4X-CVG	N606GA	"N200GA"+	[+ marks worn in NBAA static display at Orlando Executive, FL, Nov05]		
		N851LE	N2G				
107	200	4X-CVF	N107GA	N707BC	N311WK		
108	200	4X-CVI	N508GA	N726QS	N324WK		
109	200	4X-CVE	N409GA	N819AP	N819VE		
110	200	4X-CVG	N510GA	N721BS	N221BS	N967PC	N489VC
111	200	4X-CVH	N995GA	N88WU	N818ER		
112	200	4X-CVI	N112GA	C-GTRL	N856T		
113	200	4X-CVK	N413GA	N727QS	N144JE		
114	200	4X-CVE	N214GA	B-LSJ	N833BA	B-8085	VP-CEK	N888NS
115	200	4X-CVF	N615GA	N200LV	N765WM		
116	200	4X-CVF	N216GA	N728QS	N921BA	N327AH	
117	200	4X-CVG	N217GA	N62GB	N162GB		
118	200	4X-CVJ	N118GA	N729QS	N620JE		
119	200	4X-CVI	N419GA	C-GWPB			
120	200	4X-CVE	N220GA	N730QS	N970BA	N200GN	
121	200	4X-CVH	N818JW				
122	200	4X-CVG	N422GA	N200GA	N173JM	(N607AW)	
123	200	4X-CVJ	N223GA	N731QS	N468JJ		
124	200	4X-CVF	N765M				
125	200	4X-CVI	N221GA	EC-JQE			
126	200	4X-CVG	N126GA	N916GR			
127	200	4X-CVH	N424GA	N737QS	N977BA	N573PT	
128	200	4X-CVE	N102FD	XA-SAN			
129	200	4X-CVF	N229GA	N711QS	N980BA	N100EK	
130	200	4X-CVG	N330GA	N565GB	PR-MMP		
131	200	4X-CVH	N771GA	N706QS	N946BA		
132	200	4X-CVI	N732GA	N751BC			
133	200	4X-CVE	N433GA	N200GX	(N202GJ)	N200VR	
134	200	4X-CVJ	N434GA	N88AY	B-8129		
135	200	4X-CVG	N435GA	B-8081			
136	200	4X-CVF	N436GA	N718QS	N299PS		
137	200	4X-CVH	N137WB				
138	200	4X-CVI	N787PR	N32BG			
139	200	4X-CVJ	N139GA	N204DD			
140	200	4X-CVE	N640GA	PR-AUR			
141	200	4X-CVG	N641GA	N701QS	N929BA	N82FB	
142	200	4X-CVF	N842GA	N235LC	SX-IRP	G-OIRP	HS-VNT
143	200	4X-CVH	N143GA	(N81TT)	C-GSQE	C-FJOJ	
144	200	4X-CVI	N217BA	N2S			
145	200	4X-CVJ	N645GA	EC-KBC			
146	200	4X-CVE	N138GA	N602RF	N333LX	N789SB	
147	200	4X-CVF	N603RF				

GALAXY / GULFSTREAM 200

C/n	Series	Identities								
148	200	4X-CVG	N844GA	N716QS	N951BA	N991RL				
149	200	4X-CVH	N404GA	(SX-IFB)	SX-IDA	N899AU	VT-EHT	[dbr by flood water Chennai, India, 01Dec15]		
150	200	4X-CVI	N698GA	EC-KCA	OE-HOP					
151	200	4X-CVJ	N651GA	N200GA	N619KS					
152	200	4X-CVE	N152GA	N752QS	N52AJ					
153	200	4X-CVF	N653GA	B-LMJ	HS-HAN					
154	200	4X-CVG	N236LC	N39ET						
155	200	4X-CVH	N136FT	N135FT						
156	200	4X-CVI	N656GA	N101L						
157	200	4X-CVJ	N557GA	N748QS						
158	200	4X-CVE	N658GA	ZK-RGB	N818TS	N500AG				
159	200	4X-CVF	N559GA	(VP-CSG)	SX-SMG	M-MSGG	N259JP	N159JH		
160	200	4X-CVG	N670RW	N452AC						
161	200	4X-CVH	(N361GA)	N49VC	N80GK	N765WS				
162	200	4X-CVI	N562GA	N719QS	N331MT					
163	200	4X-CVJ	N360GA	N35BP	SX-SEA	N680RW	G-ZZOO	M-ZZOO	G-ZZOO	N163GA
164	200	4X-CVF	N164GA	N200JB	N900GA	N212U				
165	200	4X-CVE	N565GA	N749QS	N165PB					
166	200	4X-CVG	N566GA	N631DV						
167	200	4X-CVH	N367GA	N200GV	N178TM	N888GQ	M-GULF	OK-GLF		
168	200	4X-CVI	N368GA	N755QS	N168JE					
169	200	4X-CVF	N10XQ							
170	200	4X-CVJ	N370GA	N745QS	N358TD					
171	200	4X-CVE	N671GA	EC-KLL	N636CN					
172	200	4X-CVG	N672GA	N172EX						
173	200	4X-CVI	N403GA	N200GA	N125JF					
174	200	4X-CVH	N674GA	B-8087	N148KB	N851SC	M-SBUR			
175	200	4X-CVF	N675GA	N62GB	N148MC					
176	200	4X-CVJ	N276GA	N761QS	N962MM	N176QF*				
177	200	4X-CVE	N677GA	EC-KOR	N200KN					
178	200	4X-CVG	N678GA	N758QS	N178KR					
179	200	4X-CVM	N479GA	N797M						
180	200	4X-CVF	N480GA	EC-KPF	LZ-EVL	N991EA	5N-BTF			
181	200	4X-CVJ	N461GA	N929WC						
182	200	4X-CVE	N482GA	N282CM						
183	200	4X-CVG	N636GA	EC-KPL	N636GA	PR-EST				
184	200	4X-CVF	N384GA	HB-JKG	N581JB	N322SW				
185	200	4X-CVH	N285GA	N750QS	N750NS*					
186	200	4X-CVJ	N486GA	N715WG						
187	200	N387GA	VP-BPH	N1MK						
188	200	4X-CVG	N388GA	EC-KRN						
189	200	4X-CVF	N289GA	4K-AZ88						
190	200	4X-CVH	N590GA	N369JK	N769MS					
191	200	4X-CVJ	N391GA	N819AP						
192	200	4X-CVE	N692GA	N501DV	N929AW					
193	200	4X-CVG	N493GA	HB-JGL						
194	200	4X-CVI	N494GA	N740QS	N200GQ*					
195	200	4X-CVF	N595GA	N459BN	N480BN	N441JW				
196	200	4X-CVH	N696GA	N988KD	N196X					
197	200	4X-CVJ	N116FE							
198	200	4X-CVE	N398GA	N739QS	N842SS					
199	200	4X-CVG	N139GA	LX-LAI	N401JK	N621AB				
200	200	4X-CVI	N910GA	P4-ADD						
201	200	4X-CVF	N901GA	N332TM						
202	200	4X-CVH	N682GA							
203	200	4X-CVE	N683GA	N98SP	N365GC					
204	200	4X-CVG	N804GA	N738QS	N982MM					
205	200	4X-CVJ	N805GA	M-OSPB	N205GP	B-23068	N588WH			
206	200	4X-CVI	N306GA	OE-HAS						
207	200	4X-CVE	N307GA	SX-MAJ	M-ILTD	N881HM				
208	200	4X-CVF	N94FT	N94FY						
209	200	4X-CVH	N809GA	N90FT	N878G					
210	200	4X-CVG	N510GA	N333SZ	B-LSS	N881ST				
211	200	4X-CVI	N378GA	N184TB						
212	200	4X-CVJ	N612GA	N741QS	N612GA	N104SG				
213	200	4X-CVE	N379GA	VT-JUM	N543WW					
214	200	4X-CVF	N614GA							
215	200	4X-CVH	N715GA	SX-TAJ	UR-PRM	T7-PRM				
216	200	4X-CVG	N616GA	N743QS	N440PW					
217	200	4X-CVI	N417GA	N168RR	N250HM					
218	200	4X-CVJ	N618GA	PR-BBD						
219	200	4X-CVE	N619GA	EC-LAE						
220	200	4X-CVF	N420GA	VQ-BDS						
221	200	4X-CVH	N381GA	N200BN	N408H					
222	200	4X-CVG	N722GA	EC-LBB						

GALAXY / GULFSTREAM 200

C/n	Series	Identities					
223	200	4X-CVJ	N383GA	OE-HSB	VP-CIM	M-ALIK	AP-...
224	200	4X-CVI	N824GA	M-GZOO	G-GZOO		
225	200	4X-CVE	N385GA	OE-HSN			
226	200	4X-CVF	N626GA	(N525GF)	N525AG	N831BG	
227	200	4X-CVG	N627GA	N742QS	N367GA	B-8121	VP-CDL
228	200	4X-CVH	N928GA	N488RC			
229	200	4X-CVI	N629GA	B-8120			
230	200	4X-CVJ	N630GA	N331BN	N331BD		
231	200	4X-CVG	N631GA	HB-JKE	N203GA	OE-HNG	
232	200	4X-CVE	N632GA	N262GA	B-8139	N868SC	
233	200	4X-CVF	N533GA	(ZK-VGL)	M-SWAN	M-SASS	
234	200	4X-CVH	N534GA	PR-JPP	N254JH	XA-SRD	
235	200	4X-CVG	N935GA	N244S			
236	200	4X-CVE	N536GA	N200MP			
237	200	4X-CVF	N417GA	N415VF	M-ROIL	T7-OIL	
238	200	4X-CVG	N538GA	OE-HGO	OK-GLX		
239	200	4X-CVH	N379GA	N929WG			
240	200	4X-CVE	N440GA	OE-HGE	AP-NST		
241	200	4X-CVF	N341GA	N121DX			
242	200	4X-CVE	N842GA	N688AJ			
243	200	4X-CVG	N373GA	B-8159			
244	200	4X-CVE	N264GA	VT-SNP			
245	200	4X-CVF	N945GA	B-8151	OE-HMA		
246	200	4X-CVH	N146GA	M-NICE			
247	200	4X-CVE	N472GA	B-8277			
248	200	4X-CVF	N848GA	N383AZ			
249	200	4X-CVG	N449GA	VP-CSA			
250	200	4X-CVH	N250GD	N221AE	PR-DEA		

Production complete

IAI GULFSTREAM 280

The Gulfstream 280 was originally named the Gulfstream 250 but was rebranded to improve its sales potential in China.

C/n	Identities							
1998	[static test airframe]							
1999	[fatigue test airframe]							
2001	"N250GA"+	[+ fake marks N250GA worn for roll-out ceremony at Tel Aviv, Israel, 06Oct09]	4X-WSJ	[ff 11Dec09]				
	N101GA	N280GD	(N382G)	N280LS				
2002	4X-WSM	[ff 24Mar10]		N202GA	4X-CVG	N202GA	4X-WSM	N202GA N280GU
2003	4X-WBJ	[ff 28Jun10]	"N250GA"+	[+ fake marks N250GA worn in NBAA static display, Atlanta/DeKalb-Peachtree, GA, 18-21Oct10]				
	N280GT	N280GC						
2004	4X-CVP	N280GD	N38GL					
2005	4X-CVI	N280CC						
2006	4X-CVJ	N260GA	N281CC					
2007	4X-CVE	N280FR	N280GC	XA-BAY				
2008	4X-CVF	N208GA	4K-AZ280	VP-BBI				
2009	4X-CVG	N209GA	C-FZCC	C-FZCV				
2010	4X-CVH	N310GA	M-AYBE					
2011	4X-CVI	N711GA	N280DX					
2012	4X-CVJ	N112GA	N300R					
2013	4X-CVE	N913GA	M-ASIK	OE-HPA				
2014	4X-CVF	N214GA	N282CC					
2015	4X-CVG	N215GA	N259FG					
2016	4X-CVH	N216GA	4K-AZ208	N280UK				
2017	4X-CVI	N817GA	N280PU					
2018	4X-CVJ	N918GA	N209FS					
2019	4X-CVE	N919GA	N1640					
2020	4X-CVF	N202GA	N516CC					
2021	4X-CVG	N921GA	N7HB					
2022	4X-CVH	N922GA	N28357					
2023	4X-CVI	N923GA	N158FM	N518MB				
2024	4X-CVJ	N924GA	N459BN					
2025	4X-CVE	N225GD	B-8303					
2026	4X-CVF	N226GA	N285DX					
2027	4X-CVG	N427GA	N1FC	N332BN				
2028	4X-CVH	N828GA	N1620					
2029	4X-CVI	N229GA	N1630					
2030	4X-CVJ	N830GA	B-8280					
2031	4X-CVE	N131GA	N206FS					
2032	4X-CVF	N832GA	B-8305					
2033	4X-CVG	N833GA	N711VT					
2034	4X-CVH	N534GA	N603D					
2035	4X-CVI	N835GA	N331BN					
2036	4X-CVJ	N836GA	N710BG					
2037	4X-CVE	N137GA	TC-KHD	N55AL				
2038	4X-CVF	N138GA	N92FT					
2039	4X-CVG	N139GA	N280EX					
2040	4X-CVH	N840GA	N280KR					
2041	4X-CVI	N214GA	N280GU	N62AE				
2042	4X-CVJ	N742GA	P4-NAV	N280GY				
2043	4X-CVC	N943GA	(N604D)	N927LT				
2044	4X-CVD	N744GA	N855A					
2045	4X-CVE	N845GA	B-3256					
2046	4X-CVF	N246GA	N604D					
2047	4X-CVG	N947GA	N280PF					
2048	4X-CVI	N248GA	XA-PAZ					
2049	4X-CVJ	N249GA	M-ELAS					
2050	4X-CVC	N250GA	N286RW					
2051	4X-CVD	N151GA	"N280HF"+	[+ fake marks N280HF worn at completion centre]	N199HF			
2052	4X-CVE	N252GA	N386RW					
2053	4X-CVF	N253GA	XA-FMX					
2054	4X-CVG	N254GA	N186RW	N280LM				
2055	4X-CVH	N255GA	N702BV					
2056	4X-CVI	N256GA	PR-FRT					
2057	4X-CVJ	N257GA	N977AE					
2058	4X-CVC	N258GA	N697CC					
2059	4X-CVD	N259GA	PP-MAO					
2060	4X-CVE	N260GA	N650MP					
2061	4X-CVF	N261GA	N280TD					
2062	4X-CVG	N262GA	CN-TRS					
2063	4X-CVH	N163GA	N164GD	(D-BOSA)	[ntu German marks worn at Dallas/Love Field, TX, completion centre]			
	N467MW							
2064	4X-CVI	N164GA	N456JA					
2065	4X-CVJ	N965GA	N531RC					
2066	4X-CVC	N266GA	PR-CRC					
2067	4X-CVD	N367GA	N905G					
2068	4X-CVE	N368GA	N308KB					
2069	4X-CVF	N269GA	N806JK					

GULFSTREAM 280

C/n	Series	Identities		
2070	4X-CVG	N270GA	D-BKAT	
2071	4X-CVH	N271GA	N829JC	
2072	4X-CVI	N272GA	VP-CVH	
2073	4X-CVJ	N373GA	B-66666	
2074	4X-CVC	N274GA	N28SJ	
2075	4X-CVD	N275GA	N882LT	
2076	4X-CVE	N276GA	N280FW	
2077	4X-CVF	N277GA	N280C	
2078	4X-CVG	N978GA	N696HC	
2079	4X-CVH	N279GA	N3FB	N1FC
2080	4X-CVI	N980GA	N280SD	
2081	4X-CVJ	N281GA	N98AD	
2082	4X-CVC	N282GA	N370Z	
2083	4X-CVD	N203GA	N86CW	
2084	4X-CVE	N284GA	HS-KPG	
2085	4X-CVF	N208GA	M-ISTY	
2086	4X-CVG	N286GA	M-INTY	
2087	4X-CVH	N287GA	N199SC	
2088	4X-CVI	N288GA	SP-NVM	
2089	4X-CVJ	N289GA	N283EM	
2090	4X-CVC	N209GA	N283BA	
2091	4X-CVD	N291GA	N94FT	
2092	4X-CVE	N292GA	N15TT	
2093	4X-CVF	N293GA	N1DM	
2094	4X-CVH	N294GA	N284EM	
2095	4X-CVI	N295GA	N285BA	
2096	4X-CVJ	N296GA	N960DT	
2097	4X-CVC	N297GA	N628G	
2098	4X-CVD	N998GA	N280GF	N845A
2099	4X-CVE	N299GA	N285EM	
2100	4X-CVF	N100GA	N23M	
2101	4X-CVG	N101GA	VP-BRJ	
2102	4X-CVH	N902GA	N280GD	
2103	4X-CVI	N703GA	N228BA	
2104	4X-CVJ	N214GA	N610DP	
2105	4X-CVC	N805GA	N280GL	
2106	4X-CVD	N216GA	N51EE	
2107	4X-CVE	N217GA	B-3258	
2108	4X-CVF	N718GA	N500AF	
2109	4X-CVG	N219GA	N101XT	
2110	4X-CVH	N110GA	N1540	
2111	4X-CVI	N311GA	N286BA	
2112	4X-CVJ	N112GA	N441DT	
2113	4X-CVC	N213GA	N280GF*	
2114	4X-CVD	N914GA	N357PT	
2115	4X-CVE	N815GA	N284SE	
2116	4X-CVF	N816GA	N303XT*	
2117	4X-CVG	N828FL		
2118	4X-CVH	N918GA		
2119	4X-CVI	N209GA		
2120	4X-CVJ	N120GA		
2121	4X-...	N221GA*		
2122	4X-...	N33M*		
2123	4X-...	N923GA*		
2124	4X-...	N824GA*		
2125				
2126				
2127				
2128				
2129				
2130				
2131				
2132				
2133				
2134				
2135				

JET COMMANDER / WESTWIND

C/n	Series	Identities
1	1121	N610J [ff 27Jan63; dismantled 1975]
2	1121	N611JC [test aircraft for static fatigue]
3	1121	N612J N316 N316F N400WT N409WT
4	1121	N77F N77TC N72TC N72TQ [cx 08Aug13; wfu]
5	1121	N364G N334RK N18CA C-GKFT N18CA [cx Oct86; b/u Miami, FL mid 1986; remains to Dodson Avn, Ottawa, KS]
6	1121	N5418 CF-ULG N420P N42QB [wfu; cx Dec91; b/u 1982 by White Inds, Bates City, MO]
7	1121	N112JC N1173Z N22CH N30RJ (N711VK) N77KT N77NT [b/u for spares 1989; cx Nov91]
8	1121	N157JF N31CF N749MC N749MP N101LB [wfu 1998 Tucson, AZ; b/u circa Nov00 at Tucson, AZ]
9	1121	N450JD N459JD CF-WUL N9BY N66EW N89MR (N98KK) [wfu cx Jan94; to Aviation Warehouse film prop facility at El Mirage, CA]
10	1121	N31S N31SB N600CD N5BP N9023W [wfu Jly87 to Bardufoss Videregarude Skole, Norway; TT 5322 hrs as technical airframe – circa 2002 reported b/u]
11	1121	N1172Z N1172L N111TD [parted out St. Simons Island, GA circa late 03; cx 24Jul12]
12	1121	N8300 N613J N777V N37BB N711GW N302AT N344DA LV-RDD [w/o (details unknown); wreckage noted 14May92 Moron, Argentina]
13	1121	N450RA N50VF N12CJ N1JU (N404PC) XA-SFS [wfu; b/u 1983 by White Inds, Bates City, MO]
14	1121	N350M N121BN N87DC N87DG [b/u remains with White Inds, Bates City, MO; cx Jly94]
15	1121	N365G HB-VAX N125K N320W [wfu; b/u 1983 by White Inds, Bates City, MO; cx Apr91]
16	1121	N96B N217PM N177A YV-123CP [wfu Mar93 Caracas, Venezuela; derelict Feb97]
17	1121	(HB-VAL) CF-SUA C-FSUA N91669 [wfu; to Aviation Warehouse film prop facility, El Mirage CA; cx Nov14]
18	1121	N1166Z N121HM [wfu Dec79, to Skolen for Luftfahrtsuddannel, Copenhagen-Kastrup, Denmark; scrapped 2008]
19	1121	N95B [sold May88 in Norway as technical airframe – circa 2002 reported b/u]
20	1121	N334LP N1121E [cx 11Apr13; parted out]
21	1121	N252R CF-WOA N2579E [wfu; parted out by White Inds, Bates City, MO; last allocated US marks not worn; cx Mar91]
22	1121	N148E [w/o 13Sep68 Burbank, CA]
23	1121	N2100X N349M [b/u 1983 by White Inds, Bates City, MO]
24	1121	N94B N360M N360MC N7GW N360MC N560MC [wfu 1993; cx 04Jun13]
25	1121	N555DM [to spares 1992 with Dodson Avn, Ottawa, KS; cx Aug92]
26	1121	N614J N614JC N10MC N77FV [cx Oct88; to spares Aug88 Wiley Post, OK]
27	1121	N93B N93BE [b/u for spares 1989 by White Inds, Bates City, MO; cx Apr91]
28	1121	N1190Z N77NR N234G
29	1121	N615J 4X-COJ [w/o 21Jan70 Tel Aviv, Israel]
30	1121	N401V N400CP [w/o 21Jan71 Burlington, VT]
31	1121	N399D N99GS [wfu 1994]
32	1121B	N92B N92BT N32JC N101BU N98SC [wfu Washington County A/P, PA circa 2001; canx 09Dec05 presumed b/u]
33	1121	N1180Z N151CR N104CJ VT-ERO [wfu and b/u in India, rear fuselage and some other parts to Hollister, CA]
34	1121	N1210 N1210G N102SV N102SY N329HN N777MH N130RC N111XL N500MF TG-OMF N500MF [wfu; parted out by White Inds, Bates City, MO]
35	1121	N6504V N22AC N100TH N101GS N189G N7HL N710JW [cx Nov92 as "destroyed/ scrapped"]
36	1121	N1121M N730PV N780PV [sold May88 to Norway as technical airframe; scrap late 1990]
37	1121	N967L N123JB N723JB N445 [noted derelict 11May88 Wiley Post, OK; cx 08Mar11]
38	1121	N901JL N217PM N217AL N1776F (N200WN) N106CJ N37SJ [parted out by White Inds, Bates City, MO]
39	1121	N6505V N550NM N666JD N66TS N80TF N1BC N16FP N10EA [wfu May82 to Skolen for Luftfahrtsuddannel, Copenhagen-Kastrup, Denmark; cx Apr91; to Teknisk Erhvervsskole Centre, Hvidovre, Copenhagen, 2008]
40	1121	N913HB N40JC N40AJ N40UA [wfu; remains with White Inds, Bates City, MO]
41	1121	N6510V N187G N41FL ZP- N40593 N499TR [canx 02Mar06; parted out by Dodson Av'n, Rantoul, KS]
42	1121	N6511V N599KC N3DL N6361C N111Y (N359C) N111YL [noted derelict 12Mar86 Wiley Post, OK; cx Jly94, wfu]
43	1121	N6518V N271E N186G N121CS (N385G) N386G [wfu; b/u for parts 1989; cx Oct90]
44	1121	N200M N700C N700CB N273LP N273LF N69GT N60CD [b/u for parts Rantoul, KS circa Jan01]
45	1121	N920R N340DR N340ER N121PG N910MH [wfu; to instructional airframe at Vaughn College nr.La Guardia A/P, NY, then scrapped]
46	1121	N1500C N200BP N200RM N200GT N220ST N99W [wfu for spares at Tamiami, FL; cx 03Dec14]
47	1121	N6513V HB-VBX N33GL N222GL N222HM N200LF [cx Sep87; b/u for parts by White Inds, Bates City, MO]
48	1121	N541SG N541M N400LR N444WL N8LC N486G N85MA N929GV N502U N301AJ [w/o 13Aug90 Cozumel, Mexico; cx Oct92]
49	1121	N430C N5JR [wfu; remains with White Inds, Bates City, MO]
50	1121	N612JC N133ME [in scrapyard Oct88 Wiley Post, OK; cx 27Nov12]
51	1121	N618JC SE-DCK N303LA N69WW N21BC N93JR N18JL N1EC [b/u Dodson Avn, Ottawa, KS; cx Sep94]
52	1121	N701AP N1121G N696GW N159YC N159MP N159DP [wfu; displayed Darwin Aviation Museum, Australia; some parts to Dodson Avn, Ottawa, KS]
53	1121	N1230 N1230D N10MF N103F N925HB N27BD [wfu; parted out White Inds, Bates City, MO]
54	1121	N6534V N848C [cx Aug88; b/u for spares 1989]

JET COMMANDER / WESTWIND

C/n	Series	Identities
55	1121B	(D-CHAS) D-CEAS 4X-CON N11MC N747LB [b/u; cx Jan04]
56	1121	N6550V (N53AA) N382AA XA-... N382AA Panama SAN-301 [wfu Panama City/Gelabert, Panama]
57	1121	N6544V N770WL N121AJ [wfu May82; b/u for spares]
58	1121	N90B N721AS N120GH N660W N957RC CP-2263 N580NJ [to spares; cx Dec00]
59	1121	N6538V N59JC N21AK [cx 23Aug12; parted out]
60	1121	N6545V N100RC [w/o 14Nov70 Lexington, KY]
61	1121	N1196Z N666DC N51CH N100NR N999FB N29LP N29LB [w/o 19Dec80 Many Airport, LA]
62	1121	N5415 N1777T C-GKFS N1777T [wfu circa 1995 at Tucson, AZ & b/u 9-10Dec00]
63	1121	N6546V N7784 N15G N9DM N8GA N8GE [wfu to spares White Inds, Bates City, MO]
64	1121	N6512V N500GJ N124JB N124VS [wfu Manila, Philippines circa 1999]
65	1121	N500JR [w/o 26Sep66 North Platte, SD]
66	1121	N1966J [wfu; parted out by White Inds, Bates City, MO; hulk to Salina, KS, for training use 2011]
67	1121	N650M N1121G [wfu; used for spares by Dodson Avn, Ottawa, KS]
68	1121	N196KC [w/o 01Jly68 Fayetteville, AR]
69	1121	N6527V N89B N10SN N50JP [wfu; remains with Dodson Avn, Ottawa, KS]
70	1121	N1194Z N129K [parted out by White Inds, Bates City, MO; cx 12Jun12]
71	1121	N1500M N150CM N150CT N150HR N721GB 4X-COA [preserved Israeli Air Force Museum, Hatzerim, with Mig-21 nose]
72	1121	N757AL N777WJ N7KR I-LECO N2WU VR-CAU N2WU [w/o 02Dec90 Laguna del Saule, Uruguay]
73	1121	N98SA N98S N100W N100WM [parted out at Sarasota, FL]
74	1121	N6610V N535D N47DM N300DH N93RM N74GM N274MA (N149SF)
75	1121	N6611V N1121R N212CW [parted out by White Inds, Bates City, MO]
76	1121	N6612V N1121C CF-VVX N100DG N100DR N100TR [wfu with OK Aircraft, Gilroy, CA; fuselage reported at Hollister, CA, Sep95; cx 08Sep14]
77	1121	N1121X N523AC N442WT N11BK N21JW N121JC N177JC [cx 22Dec14; CofR expired]
78	1121	N6613V N1121E N866DH N102CJ [used as spares at Opa-Locka, FL, circa Dec95]
79	1121	N454SR N100LL N36PT [reportedly scrapped; cx Jan97]
80	1121	N87B N900JL N173A N173AR N925R [wfu 1994; cx 18Mar11]
81	1121	N6617V CF-KBI C-FEYG [w/o 26May78 Winnipeg, Canada]
82	1121	N9932 N4NK N82JC N927S C-GPDH N103BW N240AA [parted out & b/u Sep03]
83	1121A	N4550E N23FF N83AL C-GHPR N503U [w/o 19Dec95 Guatemala City, Guatemala]
84	1121	N312S N600TD N600TP N600ER N16MK [wfu Dallas-Redbird, TX circa Dec05]
85	1121	N4554E N201S XC-HAD [b/u 1990 Mexico City, Mexico]
86	1121	N1100M N2JW N13TV N116MC XA-RIW XA-SHA [wfu Houston-Hobby, TX, parted out by Dodson Int'l Parts, Rantoul, KS]
87	1121	N920G N920GP N400PC N430PC N430DC N116KX [wfu; parted out at Hollister, CA]
88	1121	N963WM N70CS N751CR [b/u May87; remains to Aviation Warehouse film prop facility, El Mirage, CA; cx 08May13]
89	1121	N6B N1195N N10BK N163DC [wfu New Orleans-Lakefront A/P, LA]
90	1121	N188WP N1121E N93SC [with Dodson Int'l Parts, Rantoul, KS circa May00]
91	1121	N365RJ N1972W N73535 N711JT [w/o 13Mar75 Tullahoma, TN]
92	1121	N5420 N524X N33PS N401DE [b/u; remains at Wiley Post, OK 12May88; cx Mar89]
93	1121	N619JC N221CF N50LB (N999RA) N1PT [wfu; cx Oct94 "destroyed/scrapped" – parted out]
94	1121	N1424 N1424Z (N144JC) N1424 N94WA N64AH [wfu San Juan, PR]
95	1121B	N5412 N6412 N7090 N709Q N210FE N100CA N200MP (N3031) N200MZ N95JK N614MH CP-2259 N85JW N55HL
96	1121	N56S N56WH N59CT N7EC N1QL N1QH N10JP N10JV (N2ES) YV-2454P [wfu by Jun05 at Caracas-Charallave, Venezuela]
97	1121	N4644E N96B N3032 N3082B N34SW [parted out at Hollister, CA; cx 28Apr06]
98	1121	N1121N C-FWRN N6DB N101DE N482G N301L N333BG [parted out & b/u]
99	1121B	N4661E N922CR N922CP N22RT N22RD N63357 [cx 27Jun13; wfu]
100	1121	N4663E N605V N16GR N11WP N305AJ [wfu; still regd; remains to Aviation Warehouse film prop facility at El Mirage, CA]
101	1121	N899S N100KY N45JF N5JC N16A N16MA N16SK [sold May88 in Norway as technical airframe; later to Bodo Aviation Museum, Bodo, Norway]
102	1121	N27MD [wfu 1986; parted out by White Inds, Bates City, MO; cx 11Jun13]
103	1121	N1121S N136K N487G N10HV N13AD N77HH N998RD [parted out by Dodson Int'l Parts, Rantoul, KS]
104	1121	N4674E N87B N8RA [cx 23Aug13; wfu]
105	1121	N618JC F-BPIB N230RC C-GWPV N5094B [wfu with White Inds, Bates City, MO & b/u; cx Dec03]
106	1121B	N4690E N3711H N40AB N88AD N114HH (N114HE) N180TJ N814K N814T
107	1123	N4691E 4X-COL (4X-COK) Israel 4X-JYG/064 N2120Q Ciskei CA-01 N2120Q [b/u at Oklahoma City, OK; cx Dec90]
108	1121B	N1121Z N1WP N12JA N12JX N77ST LV-WHZ [wfu Buenos Aires/Aeroparque, Argentina, by Apr01]
109	1121	N350X N9DC N379TH N1MW TG-VWA XA-THF [wfu Guatemala City, Guatemala]
110	1121B	N4716E 4X-CPA N101SV N181SV N16GH N1121N [parted out at Hollister, CA]
111	1121	N344PS N999CA C-GDJW N1121M [cx Aug92; wfu for spares by OK Aircraft, Gilroy, CA; remains to scrapyard Long Beach, CA]
112	1121B	N4730E N91B N91WG N4WG N44WG N773WB N372Q N710DC (C-....) N710DC [instructional airframe at British Columbia Institute of Technology, Vancouver, Canada]
113	1121	N4732E 4X-CPB N8534 [b/u circa early 2003, remains at Deland, FL]

JET COMMANDER / WESTWIND

C/n	Series	Identities
114	1121	N4734E 4X-CPC N442WT N448WT N111ST N10GR N85MR N333SV [parted out at Hollister, CA, circa 1995; fuselage used as static testbed for overhauled engines for several years then to Red Barn Flea Market, Aromas, CA]
115	1121	CF-WEC C-FWEC N3252J N500VF XB-FJI [b/u Monterrey, Mexico]
116	1121	N4743E N236JP [w/o 31Oct69 Marion, VA]
117	1121	N237JF N200BP N400HC N220KP N54WC N34NW [parted out by White Inds, Bates City, MO, 1997; cx 15Nov12]
118	1121	N312S N438 N117GM (N712GM) N716BB N381DA N696RV [cx 22Dec14; wfu Cairo, Egypt]
119	1121	C-FFBC N119AC (LV-...) [reported parted out in Argentina as N119AC, after cancellation]
120	1121	N200M N203M [scrapped during 1984; cx Jan85]
121	1121A	N1121X N840AR N250JP N1121R N250UA (N121JC) [w/o 27Apr78 Flatwood, LA]
122	1121B	N4940E N801NM N122JC N666BP N122HL N122ST (XA-SCV) [cx 16Feb17, CofR expired]
123	1121A	N5410 N155VW N1121A N580WE [parted out by Dodson Int'l Parts at Rantoul, KS]
124	1121B	N1300M N300M XA-REO XA-RQT N8070U [for spares; cx Jan99]
125	1121A	N1121N N30LS N1121R
126	1121B	4X-COM N4983E N315SA N113MR N87DC N87DL LV-WEN [w/o 28Sep94 Cordoba, Argentina]
127	1121A	N6B N27X N34HD N209RR N20GB N100SR N550K N277MG [to Dodson Int'l Parts 01Apr05 for parting out]
128	1121A	N660RW N74XL N74XE N1121U N386MC (N386JM) N404WC [to Virginia Museum of Transportation, Roanoke, VA]
129	1121A	N5032E N525AW N110ST (N1121B) N102CE N121PA [to Dodson Int'l Parts Oct05 for parts use]
130	1121A	N5038E 4X-CPD N84 N44 [w/o 02Nov88 en route Westmoreland County A/P, Latrobe, PA]
131	1121A	N5039E 4X-CPE N83 N43 N7028F [at Fairmont State College, WV; canx as "possibly scrapped" Aug96]
132	1121	N200M N403M [w/o 16Dec79 Salt Lake City, UT]
133	1121B	N5041E N1172Z N56AG N56AZ N133JC N666JM N22976 N161X N122JB XA-LYM XB-GBZ N132LA [cx May13, CofR expired]
134	1121B	N111E 4X-FVN UAF1 5X-AAB 4X-COP N7638S N134N [wfu Chino, CA; cx 18May15]
135	1121B	N5043E N700HB N2DB N1KT N721GB N1121N XC-COL N900PJ P4-...
136	1121	N5044E SE-DCY [w/o 04Dec69 Stockholm, Sweden]
137	1121B	N5045E SE-DCZ N50VF N3VF N873 N500LS N300LS N5BP N700BF (N700GA) N707TE XB-FKV N47CE [cx Apr14, CofR expired]
138	1121B	N5046E 4X-COB N5BA N972TF [cx 22Aug13; wfu]
139	1121B	N5047E 4X-CPF N8535 I-ARNT N188G N481DH [parted out by White Inds, Bates City, MO. cx 09May13]
140	1121	N9040N 4X-CPG N200RC [w/o 25Sep73 Tampa, FL]
141	1121B	N9041N 4X-CPH N100CJ N160WC N177PC N177HB N163WC N163WS 5N-EZE N163WS [wfu Columbia Metropolitan, SC; cx Dec03]
142	1121C	N9042N 4X-CPI N82 N42 N50138 N51038 N1944P [instructional airframe at Pittsburgh Inst of Aeronautics]
143	1121C	N9043N 4X-CPJ N81 N41 N30AD [scrapped at Boeing Field, WA circa May98]
144	1121C	N9044N 4X-CPK N80 N45 N20K (N920KP) [wfu with White Industries, KS]
145	1121B	N9045N HB-VCC (N17DW) F-BTDA N349DA N145BW N145AJ (N805SA) N805SM [cx 28Oct13; wfu Deland, FL]
146	1121B	N9046N N99CV N99CK N923JA N926JM N444TJ [b/u for spares at Atlanta Air Salvage, Griffin, GA circa 1999]
147	1121B	N9047N N720ML N728MC N147JK N912DA (N888MP) [cx Jul13, CofR expired]
148	1121B	N9048N 4X-CPL N8536 N200DE N200DF N101NK N600K (N22LL) [cx Jun99; parted out at Hollister, CA mid 99]
149	1121B	N9049N 4X-CPM N100MC N100PC N45SL N489G N78MN N700R N1121E (N9LP) (N149BP) N606JM N666JM (N129ME) N343DA N303AJ (N308AJ) (N803AU) N149SF [wfu Kingston, Jamaica; cx Nov03]
150	1121B	N9050N 4X-CPN N1884Z N173MC N121FM N1121F [w/o 20May97 San Louis Potosi, Mexico]
151	1123	4X-CJD N1123E N88WP ZP-AGD [b/u Fort Lauderdale Executive, FL]
152	1124N	4X-CJC Israel 4X-JYF/029 4X-CJC Israel 4X-JYR/035 Israel 4X-JYR/929
153	1123	4X-CJB N773EJ N200WC N223WW XA-PUF [parted out by DK Turbines, Hollister, CA, 1998]
154	1124	4X-CJA (D-CBBE) N919JH D-CBBE N722AW N176AK N176DT
155	1123	4X-CJE N23Y N707TE N707TF
156	1123	4X-CJF N1123H N40AS N40BG (N666MP) N566MP N35D [b/u 2006]
157	1123	4X-CJG N1123Q N10MB (N820RT) [wfu; b/u c 1989-90; cx Aug92; remains with OK Aircraft, Gilroy, CA]
158	1123	4X-CJH N1123G N123DR [wfu Buenos Aires/Aeroparque, Argentina]
159	1123	4X-CJI N1123E N722W N1123Z (N12FH) N344CK N96TS [wfu to spares at Hollister, CA; cx 25Mar05]
160	1123	4X-CJJ N1123R USCG 160 4X-CJJ N1123W N221MJ N221RJ XA-AVE XA-MUI XA-RIZ
161	1123	4X-CJK D-CGLS (N653J) N185G N33WD XA-POJ [wfu after accident (no details known); remains to Dodson Av'n, Ottawa, KS, for spares]
162	1123	4X-CJL N1123S N78LB N234RC N9VC N9VQ XA-SDW (N163W) N13GW HK-.... [cx from USCAR Mar95 but still marked N13GW Feb97 at Bogota-El Dorado, Columbia]
163	1123	4X-CJM N1123T N4444U N47DC N163DL [canx Oct97, status?]
164	1123	4X-CJN D-CAAS N9114S N32WE [parted out by White Inds, Bates City, MO; cx 04Jun13]
165	1123	4X-CJO N1123R C-GWSH N102BW N22RD N30156 [wfu Deland, FL; cx 20May15]
166	1123	4X-CJP C-GDOC N360HK [b/u 1989]
167	1123	4X-CJQ N873EJ N1123H [being parted out by White Industries 1998]
168	1123	4X-CJR N973EJ N66SM N111NF [b/u Dallas-Love Field, TX circa 1998]

JET COMMANDER / WESTWIND

C/n	Series	Identities
169	1123	4X-CJS N1123U N1500C N1100D N44PR [wfu; cx 18Feb09]
170	1123	4X-CJT N1123W N112RC N150HR N90HM [wfu; cx May94]
171	1123	4X-CJU C-GJLL N223PA N89XL (ZS-ODP) [stored at Lanseria, South Africa]
172	1123	4X-CJV N1123H XB-AER N19EE YV-58CP YV-2482P [wfu]
173	1123	4X-CJW N1123Q N680K N30JM N30AN [film prop at Aviation Warehouse, El Mirage CA]
174	1124	4X-CJX N1123X N112MR N124VF N74TS N760C XA-PVR XA-UHJ N92RB [cx 18Dec12; parted out by Dodson Int'l, Rantoul, KS]
175	1123	4X-CJY N1123R N500M N500ML N51TV N523RB (N571MC) N384AT [parted out by Dodson Int'l Parts, Rantoul, KS]
176	1123	4X-CJZ N1123T C-GJCD N661MP C-FNRW N661MP N27AT N35CR
177	1123	4X-CKA N1123U N11WC N777CJ N118AF (N114ED) [cx 1991 wfu]
178	1123	4X-CKB N1123Z N999U N123CV [wfu Columbia Metropolitan, SC; cx 01Oct04]
179	1123	4X-CKC N1123Y LV-WJU N114RA [cx Apr10; parted out]
180	1123	4X-CKD HP-1A N1019K (N180JS) N72LT N72ET (N190LH) N192LH N3VL [cx May01, b/u]
181	1124	4X-CKE HK-2150X HK-2150 N107CF N325AJ N325LJ N345BS N821CN PP-...
182	1123	4X-CKF N1123Q N200HR N700EC N13KH N18BL N78BL N10122 LV-WYL [wfu Buenos Aires/San Fernando, Argentina]
183	1123	4X-CKG Honduras 318 HR-001 XB-DNY N51990 LV-WLR
184	1123	4X-CKH N1123T N666JM N866JM YV-119P CC-CRK N481MC [instructional airframe Midland College, Midland, TX]
185	1124N	4X-CKI N1123U Israel 4X-JYJ/027 Israel 4X-JYJ/927
186	1123N	4X-CKJ N1123R Israel 4X-JYO/031 Israel 4X-JYO/931
187	1124	4X-CKK N1124N N18GW (N943CL) (N715GW) (N416NL) N516AC (N789DD) N1M N280DB (N1TS) (N187TS) N241RH N187TJ
188	1124	4X-CKL N1124G C-GRDP N118RJ [parted out by Dodson Int'l Parts, Rantoul, KS]
189	1124	4X-CKM N26DS N926DS N200DL N42CM
190	1124	4X-CKN N50AL N890WW N190WW N313TW N510GT N518GT
191	1124	4X-CKO N3VF N13VF N711MR YV-777CP (N771AC) N326AJ N900FS N900JF [wfu Tamiami, FL; cx 22May16]
192	1124	4X-CKP N71M (N736US) N319BG N819RC
193	1124	4X-CKQ N60AL (YV-37CP) N101HS N420J N420JM N428JM N515LG N98BM [stored Oklahoma City/Clarence E Page, OK]
194	1124	4X-CKR N222SR N343AP N124FM N40TA N807BF
195	1124	4X-CKS N887PL N880WW (N24TE) TC-ASF (N195ML) N951DB (N920AD) [parted out]
196	1124	4X-CKT N1124E N250JP N505U N500WK (N615DM) N863AB N606MA
197	1124	4X-CKU N214CC N29GH N29CL SE-DLK [w/o 21Sep92 Umea, Sweden; cx Jan93]
198	1124	4X-CKV N800Y N744JR N600TJ N98TS N51MN N71PT N750SP (N750SB) PR-NJT
199	1124	4X-CKW N1124P N111AG N999MS D-CHDL N199WW C-FTWO
200	1124	4X-CKX N1124X N4WG
201	1124	4X-CKY N1124Q N1124N N56AG N58WW N85EQ (N85EA) N95CP N300TE (N29UF) C-FOIL N124WW [instructional airframe, Western Michigan University, Kalamazoo, MI]
202	1124	4X-CKZ D-CBAY N49968 N54MC (N254MC) N202DD (N37WC) N141LB N168DB YV-297CP N274HM N59PT N469WC PP-JJK*
203	1124	4X-CLA N1124G N124WW N880Z N22RD
204	1124	4X-CLB N221MJ N156CW N26TJ N10UJ (N100XJ) [b/u; cx Jly03]
205	1124	4X-CLC N96BA N967A N124NY N125AC SE-DLL N205AJ (N775JC) N331AP YV2032
206	1124	4X-CLD N215G N215C N215M N943LL N943JL N100ME N148H
207	1124	4X-CLE N1124P N6053C N330PC N519ME N666K D-CHAL N207WW C-FTWR [wfu; cx 24Mar16]
208	1124	4X-CLF N961JC (N961JD) N961JE N208MD N208ST N324AJ N311DB N57PT
209	1124	4X-CLG N661JB N663JB N662JB N938WH N988WH N222LH N705AC N817DK [parted out by Alliance Air Parts, Oklahoma City, OK]
210	1124	4X-CLH N662JB N69HM N661CP N662JB N23AC N38WW N444MM N59KC N337RF N425JF N428JF N2150H
211	1124	4X-CLI YV-160CP [w/o 19Feb97 near Guatemala City/La Aurora, Guatemala]
212	1124	4X-CLJ N212WW N900CS N700MD
213	1124	4X-CLK N213WW N555J N530GV N580GV N30YM (4X-NOY) 4X-CLK N27TZ
214	1124	4X-CLL N1124N N214WW N24RH (N248H) N46BK N21SF [stored Oklahoma City/Clarence E Page, OK]
215	1124	4X-CLM N215DH N500WH N946GM N238DB
216	1124	4X-CLN N216SC N1124G (N65BK) N290CA C-FAPK
217	1124	4X-CLO N8QP N8QR N217SC N217SQ N217WC N163WC
218	1124	4X-CLP N218WW N100AK C-GFAN N218DJ N74GR N218PM N425RJ N426RJ
219	1124	4X-CLQ YV-190CP N290CP
220	1124	4X-CLR N1124G C-GHBQ N9134Q N106BC N9RD
221	1124	4X-CLS N108GM N969PW N969KC (N969EG) VH-AJS [w/o 27Apr95 Alice Springs, Australia]
222	1124	4X-CLT N294W N294B N36EF N86EF N700R N3RC N598JM
223	1124	4X-CLU N1124P N124TY N303PC N20KH N518WA
224	1124	4X-CLV N898SR XA-KUG N2756T N349MC
225	1124	4X-CLW N1124U N30MR
226	1124	4X-CLX N500LS N300LS N100BC (N10BY) N124MB N120S D-CHBL N226WW C-FTWV [wfu; cx 11Mar16]
227	1124	4X-CLY N250PM N64FG N624KM

JET COMMANDER / WESTWIND

C/n	Series	Identities
228	1124	4X-CLZ N305BB N795FM [wfu Houston/Hooks, TX]
229	1124	4X-CMA N1212G N1625 N162E N40GG [parted out by Alliance Air Parts, Oklahoma City, OK]
230	1124	4X-CMB N4995N XC-HCP XC-HDA N102U N1KT [stored Oklahoma City/Clarence E Page, OK]
231	1124	4X-CMC HB-VFP N8514Y N777CF N70CA (N27TA) N331CW N331GW N600NY
232	1124	4X-CMD N1124Q N19UC N190M N773AW N4MH
233	1124	4X-CME N1124X N650GE N650G N67DF N36SF [parted out by Dodson Int'l Parts, KS]
234	1124	4X-CMF (N1124Z) HC-BGL N1124Z N161X [cx Apr13; parted out Denton, TX]
235	1124	4X-CMG N1124E (N24PP) N65A N30AB N903MM YV2978
236	1124	4X-CMH N35LH N236W N22LZ N618WA YV....
237	1124	4X-CMI N39GW N723M N28TJ N24KL
238	1124	4X-CMJ VH-AJP [wfu 2015 Nowra, Australia]
239	1124A	4X-CMK [conv to 1124A prototype] HK-2485 HK-2485W HK-2485G
240	1124	4X-CML N240WW (N400Q) N400SJ N400NE N72787 N298HM
241	1124	4X-CMM N789TE N300TC
242	1124	4X-CMN N340DR N140DR N500BJ
243	1124	4X-CMO N1124G N59WK N215SC 4X-AIP [w/o 23Jly96 Rosh-Pina/Mahanaim-I-Ben-Yaakov, Israel]
244	1124	4X-CMP N124PA N911SP N124PA N911SP
245	1124	4X-CMQ N1124P N404CB N270LC
246	1124	4X-CMR N101SV N911CU
247	1124	4X-CMS N1125G N280LM N280AZ N280AT [w/o 02Jly04 Panama City-Tocumen; dbf]
248	1124	4X-CMT N25RE VH-AJJ [wfu 2015 Wagga Wagga, Australia]
249	1124	4X-CMU N1JS [reported stolen/crashed 1985 in Mexico; cx Jul10]
250	1124	4X-CMV N250WW C-GFAO N29995 N60RV (N250KD) N914MM N418WA (N912PM)
251	1124	4X-CMW N6MJ CX-CMJ PT-LDY
252	1124	4X-CMX N1WS (N9WW) N553MC N121JD
253	1124	4X-CMY N511CC N511CQ N800WW N800WS N253MD VH-LLW [b/u Perth-Jandakot, Australia by 06Apr98]
254	1124	4X-CMZ N600TD N888R N112AB N72HB N60AV RP-C59 RP-C5988
255	1124	4X-CNA N222MW N202MW N424CS LV-CLS*
256	1124	4X-CNB VH-AJK [wfu; to fire dump at Nowra, NSW, Australia]
257	1124	4X-CNC N573P N317M N317MB N755CM N942FA N124UF N79LC N576LC [cx 30Dec15; technical airframe Delaware Technical Community College, Georgetown, DE]
258	1124	4X-CND N10MR N1857W N29AP N24DS YV-770CP N258AV (N258CF) N572M N58FB N771B [parted out by White Inds, Bates City, MO]
259	1124	4X-CNE N1124N C-GSWS N19AP N315JM VH-LLX [b/u Perth-Jandakot, Australia by 06Apr98]
260	1124	4X-CNF N401BP N525ML C-GAGP N49TA (N503RH) N80FD N525AK
261	1124	4X-CNG N167C N249E N87GS N39JN N11LN
262	1124	4X-CNH N262WW N40DG YV-393CP N262WC N79KP N150EX
263	1124	4X-CNI N29PC N918SS YV....
264	1124	4X-CNJ N351C XA-MAR N351C (N125NY) N88PV N351C N809VC N810CC
265	1124	4X-CNK N167J N7DJ [parted out by Alliance Air Parts, Oklahoma City, OK]
266	1124	4X-CNL N24KT N24KE N50DR N7HM N5HQ YV....
267	1124	4X-CNM N297W N297A N100SR N241CT N55FG
268	1124	4X-CNN (N13HH) N821H N606AB N21CX N200HR N41WH N56BP N56BN [parted out by Alliance Air Parts, Oklahoma City, OK]
269	1124	4X-CNO N3031 N50SL N21DX [parted out by Alliance Air Parts, Oklahoma City, OK]
270	1124	4X-CNP (N270WW) N270A (N27SJ) (N270DT) N501DT N475AT [w/o May06 Exuma Island, Bahamas]
271	1124	4X-CNQ N368S N102KJ N218SC C-GWKF C-FREE C-FJOJ C-GSQE
272	1124	4X-CNR N26GW N723R VH-LLY [b/u Perth-Jandakot, Australia by 06Apr98]
273	1124	4X-CNS N104RS (N566PG)
274	1124	4X-CNT N701Z N701W N274K [parted out by Alliance Air Parts, Oklahoma City, OK]
275	1124	4X-CNU N1141G N1621 N36PT N6TM N96TM
276	1124	4X-CNV VR-CAD XA-BQA N269AJ N800XL N300XL
277	1124	4X-CNW N288WW (N2AJ) N504JC D-CHCL N277WW C-GAWJ N277WW C-FTWX
278	1124	4X-CNX N505BC C-GJLK N10S C-GHYD
279	1124	4X-CNY N1126G N885DR N230TL N230JK N952HF N400TF XC-COL [w/o 24Feb05 Sapotita, Mexico]
280	1124	4X-CNZ N290W (N5BP) (N5S) N29LP N250RA N500R N508R N949CC
281	1124	4X-CQA VH-AJQ N4251H N1124F (N200XJ) VH-AJG [wfu 2015 Wagga Wagga, Australia]
282	1124	4X-CQB N711MB N186G VH-AJV
283	1124	4X-CQC N483A N666JM (N70WW) N17UC N95JK
284	1124	4X-CQD N99WH N296NW N217BL N727AT
285	1124	4X-CQE VR-CAC XA-LIJ VR-CBK XA-LIJ N85PT
286	1124	4X-CQF N1124U C-GMBH N4447T N92FE N111LP N110LP N113GH N743PB YV3327
287	1124	4X-CQG N146BF N530DL
288	1124	4X-CQH N1124Q C-GMTT N116AT N94AT N48AH N711KE
289	1124	4X-CQI N711CJ N45SJ N23SJ VR-CIL N900VP [cx 15May15; CofR expired]
290	1124	4X-CQJ N800JJ N719CC
291	1124	4X-CQK N124WK N917BE N917BF N816LC
292	1124	4X-CQL N292JC N741C N741AK
293	1124	4X-CQM N26TV N26T N26TZ
294	1124	4X-CQN D-CBBA N24DB (N73GB) HK-3884X N147A
295	1124A	4X-CQO N295WW N100AK N100AQ N555CW N730CA
296	1124	4X-CQP D-CBBB N64KT N770JJ N92WW N89TJ N710SA

JET COMMANDER / WESTWIND

C/n	Series	Identities
297	1124	4X-CQQ D-CBBC N76TG N51PD N801SM N335VB
298	1124	4X-CQR N610JA C-GESO C-GRGE N298CM N809JC [parted out]
299	1124A	4X-CQS N922CR N922CK N74JM N600TC (N288SJ) N67TJ
300	1124A	4X-CQT N500M N500MD (N20NW) N10MV PR-STJ
301	1124A	4X-CQU N500GK N815RC N815BC XB-GRN N230JS N301KF N890BA
302	1124A	4X-CQV N600J N60QJ N100AK N422BC [w/o 26Dec99 Milwaukee, WI]
303	1124A	4X-CQW N500J N50QJ N211ST
304	1124A	4X-CQX N304WW N369BG N389BG N10NL N13NL N78PT
305	1124A	4X-CQY N464EC N717LA N717EA N629WH N804CC
306	1124A	4X-CQZ YV-387CP N555BY (N9WW) (N722W) HK-3971X HK-4204X HK-4204 N306PT N123EG
307	1124A	4X-CRA YV-388CP N1124K N300HC (N301HC) N825JL N925Z N97SM N494BP N4SQ YV2908
308	1124A	4X-CRB YV-210CP YV-O-CVG-1 N308JS N308TS N628KM N639AT [parted out by Worthington Av'n Parts, MN]
309	1124A	4X-CRC (N200LH) N240S N50SK [w/o 04Apr86 nr Rosewater, TX]
310	1124	4X-CRD D-CBBD N78GJ
311	1124	4X-CRE N700MM N50XX N700MM N788MA N53LM N696RG
312	1124	4X-CRF N200LH N300LH N97HW N24FJ N316TD
313	1124	4X-CRG N146J C-FAWW N711WU N711WV N611WV C-GDSR
314	1124	4X-CRH VH-IWW N2454M N84PH N2HZ N49CT
315	1124A	4X-CRI N371H N400YM VH-BCL VH-NJW N315TR (N89TJ) N124GR YV374T
316	1124	4X-CRJ VH-ASR N93KE N33TW
317	1124	4X-CRK VH-AYI P2-BCM VH-JPW (VH-NIJ) VH-UUZ VH-KNU
318	1124	4X-CRL N298W N298A N10FG N38AE N599DP [cx 25Nov14; CofR expired]
319	1124A	4X-CRM XA-LOR N560SH N700WM (N50XX) N200KC N225N N783FS N788FS
320	1124	4X-CRN N60JP N204TM YV604T
321	1124	4X-CRO N900WW N1124N N83CT N93WW N666K N666KL N217F N810VC [wfu Fort Worth/Meacham, TX; cx 08Aug13]
322	1124A	4X-CRP N2AV N990S
323	1124	4X-CRQ N816H VH-KNS [wfu 2015 Wagga Wagga, Australia]
324	1124A	4X-CRR N3VF N90CL C-FCEJ N91MK N404HR N323MR N406HR
325	1124	4X-CRS VH-WWY N504U N124HL SE-DPT N525AJ N467MW N68PT
326	1124	4X-CRT (N88JE) N66JE [w/o 21Feb95 Denver-Stapleton Airport, CO]
327	1124	4X-CRU N50M
328	1124A	4X-CRV N816JA N819JA C-GPFC N328PC
329	1124	4X-CRW N30NS N711SE N7HM N124HS [impounded Caracas/Simon Bolivar, Venezuela]
330	1124A	4X-CRX N52GW N723K YV-332CP YV1685
331	1124	4X-CRY N556N N228N N228L LV-WOV N228L N811VC [wfu Fort Worth/Meacham, TX; cx 08Aug13]
332	1124A	4X-CRZ N24SR N332DF N43RP N43RU N913CW
333	1124	4X-CTA HR-002 HR-CEF HR-PHO
334	1124A	4X-CTB (N45MP) N40MP N325LW N42NF
335	1124A	4X-CTC N300HR N359JS N501BW EC-254 EC-GIB N21HR
336	1124	4X-CTD N245S C-FOIL N336SV N255RB N525XX N112EM [w/o Cincinnati/Lunken, OH, 18Jun13; parted out by Alliance Air Parts, Oklahoma City, OK] N497HA
337	1124A	4X-CTE N14BN N639J N900NW 4X-CTE N2518M VP-BLT N127PT
338	1124A	4X-CTF N338W N350PM N850WW N114WL N50PL [w/o 12Dec99, Gouldsboro, PA; cx Sep03]
339	1124A	4X-CTG (XC-HDA) N333CG N782PC N74AG N90KC ZK-RML ZK-PJA
340	1124A	4X-CTH 4X-CUA (XC-BDA) N1124L N212CP PT-OLN N340PM N118MP N3RC N118MP VH-KNR [wfu Wagga Wagga, Australia]
341	1124A	4X-CTI 4X-CUB N1124P N23AC N23AQ N80RE N555HD N556HD N728LW N728LM N868CP N52KS N818JH
342	1124A	4X-CTJ XA-MAK N342AJ N39RE N342TS N204AB N274HM N1VT
343	1124A	4X-CTK YV-451CP YV-O-CVG-3 YV-O-FMO-6 N343RD N999AZ N911GU
344	1124A	4X-CTL N334 N311BR N849HS N379AV N769MS N769M
345	1124A	4X-CTM N1424 (N533) N534 N534R N345TR
346	1124A	4X-CTN N100AG N1124N N610HC N610SE
347	1124	4X-CTO N347WW N30PD N21GG YV-666CP N666CP N178HH N347GA
348	1124A	4X-CTP N348WW N348SJ N960FA N16SF
349	1124A	4X-CTQ N78WW N65GW N723L N728L N123RC
350	1124A	4X-CTR VR-CBB XA-MAK N3838J N777LU N309CK [w/o 15Dec93 Orange County A/P, CA; cx Oct95]
351	1124A	4X-CTS N106WT N351TC N722AZ N728AZ N111EL N124BC
352	1124A	4X-CTT N15BN N117JW N117AH [cx 04Mar13; parted out by Dodson Av'n, Rantoul, KS]
353	1124A	4X-CTU N379JR N90CH N86UR N89UH C-GRGE EC-GSL RP-C5880
354	1124	4X-CTV N443A N512CC N506U N124LS N894TW
355	1124A	4X-CUI N355WW N355JK N241CT
356	1124A	4X-CUJ N356WW N8GA N533 N530GV N929GV N43ZZ N861GS N767AC N38TJ N993DS YV3160
357	1124	4X-CUK (N357W) C-GDUC N357EA N66FG N357BC N914DM YV....
358	1124A	4X-CUL N358CT N13UR N800MA N830MA N787RP N720MC N404PG N900DM
359	1124A	4X-CUM N8JL N86RR N500RR N500AX C-GRGE N14CN VH-IER
360	1124	4X-CUN N816S N816ST N816S N500KE
361	1124A	4X-CUO N6053C N610HC N3AV

JET COMMANDER / WESTWIND

C/n	Series	Identities
362	1124	4X-CUP N445A YV251T
363	1124	4X-CUQ N3320G N1629 N54PT (N723JM) N420JM (PR-AWB) PR-OMX
364	1124A	4X-CUR N60DG N199GH N198GH N198HF N198HE RP-C2480 N944M N67DT [cx 27Mar13; wfu]
365	1124A	4X-CUS N793JR (N185BR) N185MB N2BG N73CL
366	1124	4X-CUT VH-SQH VH-LOF N388GA N707BC N65TD N320MD
367	1124	4X-CUD N446A N511CC N455S N367WW
368	1124A	4X-CUE N28WW N368MD N83SG
369	1124A	4X-CUF N24SB (N54BC) N300JK N85WC N76ER [parted out by Alliance Air Parts, Oklahoma City, OK]
370	1124	4X-CUG N641FG N471TM N875HS N875P
371	1124	4X-CUH VH-IWJ [w/o 10Oct85 nr Sydney, Australia]
372	1124	4X-CUB N372WW N988NA N810MT (N800MT) N810ME (N5TH) N921DT N502BG N444MW N404MW N406CH N224GP N942EB N922EB
373	1124A	4X-CUK N373CM N900LM N555DH N794TK YV....
374	1124A	4X-CUL N18SF N56AG N248H N33MK N43W N30TK
375	1124	4X-CUF N79AD N79AP N66LX N66VA
376	1124A	4X-CUH 4X-CJP N1124P N110SF N376WA N376BE VH-ZYH
377	1124A	4X-CUJ N301PC
378	1124	4X-CUI N84LA N481NS C-GXKF N481NS
379	1124	4X-CUJ N52FC N62ND N302SG N851E YV588T
380	1124A	4X-CUM N50DW N380DA C-FMWW [w/o 27Jan94 Meadow Lake, Saskatchewan, Canada; cx Jly94]
381	1124	4X-CUO VH-KNJ N501U N929GV N928GV N928G N92EB N381W N50FD YV3120
382	1124A	4X-CUP N900BF N410NA (N445BL) N999BL N445BL [w/o 01May92 Waterbury, Oxford, CT; cx Mar93]
383	1124	4X-CUQ (N301PC) N82HH N20DH N84WU N84VV N942WC
384	1124A	4X-CUB N48WW N61RS (N50MF) [w/o 08Nov02, Taos, NM; cx Mar03]
385	1124A	4X-CUC N96AL YV-962CP N962MV N317JS
386	1124	4X-CUE N68WW (VH-JPL) N348DH N386RL
387	1124A	4X-CUJ N97AL VH-NGA [w/o 18Nov09 off Norfolk Island, Australia]
388	1124	4X-CUH N1124K N900H N388WW
389	1124A	4X-CUF N49WW N812M (N612M) N812G N100WP N812G N89AM YV3219
390	1124A	4X-CUB N57WW N3RL (N303E) N290RA ZS-MZM (HB-...) N59SM N122MP PR-BVB
391	1124	4X-CUG N24WW N24VH C-GMPF N155ME N303SG N59PT (N205B)
392	1124A	4X-CUA N92WW N95WC N793BG [w/o 18Jun14, Huntsville, AL; parted out by Atlanta Air Salvage, Griffin, GA]
393	1124	4X-CUK N53WW N491AN YV3291
394	1124A	4X-CUM N94WW N314AD N352TC N516CC N21RA N63PP N98HG
395	1124A	4X-CUC N95WW VH-SGY VH-APU N395SR N395TJ
396	1124	4X-CUR 8P-BAR N1124N N37BE [parted out by White Inds, Bates City, MO; cx 02Apr14]
397	1124A	4X-CUN N52SM N11CS N777HD
398	1124	4X-CUO N98WW N59AP N41C
399	1124A	4X-CUF N78WW N48SD
400	1124A	4X-CUP N200LS N300LS N900PA N900TN N917LH N917LE
401	1124	4X-CUQ N84WW N980S N30GF N936AA YV....
402	1124A	4X-CUS N87WW N999LC N51TV N325LB N63WD N224GP*
403	1124	4X-CUH N403W (N825EC) YV2981
404	1124A	4X-CUG 4X-CJR N404W N29CL
405	1124A	4X-CUJ N1124L N211DB N420TJ N420CE N424JR
406	1124	4X-CUA N406W N651E (N651ES) N100CH N830 N8QX N57KE
407	1124A	4X-CUK N407W
408	1124	4X-CUB N408W N408MJ N125HF [parted out by Alliance Air Parts, Oklahoma City, OK]
409	1124A	4X-CUM VH-JJA 4X-CUM? 4X-CUO Chile 130 N7051J N409WW XA-RET N4426Z N217RM N217BM N26KL N629WH
410	1124A	4X-CUO N1124Z (N410EL) N22BG N26VF N26VB N777DC
411	1124	4X-CUC N96WW N47LP N47LR HC-BVX N224PA
412	1124A	4X-CUP N412W N412SC N50XX N50HS N999MC N870BA
413	1124	4X-CJS 4X-CUD N413WW N35LH [parted out by Alberth Air Parts, Tomball, TX; cx 21Nov13]
414	1124A	4X-CPO 4X-CUC N86MF (N66MF) N980AW N24MN N524RH N550HB N110JD
415	1124A	4X-CUS N415EL N105BE N415EL N415TH N417PC N928HR
416	1124	4X-CUD N416W N303TS N815RK N600KE
417	1124A	4X-CUE N417EL (N417GW) N700WE N115BP (N99WF) N34FS N64FS
418	1124	4X-CUB PT-LIP N124PA N662K N317MX (N317MV) N420MP N26T N26TN
419	1124A	4X-CUF N419W N551TP N51MN N411HB N728MB
420	1124A	4X-CUH N420W N91SA N728TG
421	1124	4X-CUJ N111HN N801MS N317MQ N520MP
422	1124A	4X-COC 4X-CUI N422AW N251SP N87GS N87GJ C6-IRM
423	1124	4X-CUC N223WA N680ME
424	1124A	4X-CUJ N424W N790JR
425	1124A	4X-CUK N425WA N600LE N365CX (N365QX) N328SA N167JB
426	1124	4X-CUF N426WW N75BC
427	1124A	4X-CUN N427WW N256N N229N N229D
428	1124A	4X-CUO N428W (N92BE) N327SA N57BE
429	1124	4X-CUK (N429W) C-FROY N42FL YV3140

JET COMMANDER / WESTWIND

C/n	Series	Identities								
430	1124	4X-CUM	N430W	N821LG	N430A	N430BJ	N430PT			
431	1124	4X-CUN	N431AM	C-FGGH	N431WA					
432	1124	4X-CUH	N87NS	N317M	N62276	N317MB	(N317MT)	N320MP	N432HS	N282SM
		N60BT								
433	1124A	4X-CUH	N433WW	N433WR	N433GM	CP-2784				
434	1124A	4X-CUC	N330MG	(N346CP)	N222KC	N601DR	N187EC	N919BT	(N102AK)	N564RM
		YV606T								
435	1124	4X-CUG	(N435W)	N501CB	(N501CP)	(N669SB)	N297JS	N140VJ	N500MA	N435WW
		N99PS								
436	1124A	4X-CUE	N436WW	N50XX	N436WW	N110AF	N1904G	N100AK	N444EP	
437	1124A	4X-CUF	N437WW	N437SJ						
438	1124	4X-CUJ	(N438W)	N438AM	N100BC	(N438FS)				
439	1124A	4X-CUG	N439WW							
440	1124A	4X-CUJ	N440WW	N127SA	N220DH	PP-SDW				
441	1124	4X-CUP	PT-LPV	HK-3893X	C-FZEI	C-FPEP	N822QL			
442	1124A	4X-CUO	N406W	N830	N71WF	N830C				

Production complete

LEARJET MODELS 23 & 24

C/n	Model	Identities
001	23	N801L [ff 07Oct63; w/o 04Jun64 Wichita, KS]
002	23	N802L [ff 05May64; last flight 17Jun66; displayed at Smithsonian National Air & Space Museum Steven F Udvar-Hazy Center, Washington-Dulles, VA]
003	23	N803L N200Y N2008 N10MC N3BL
004	23	N804LJ [became c/n 23-015A]
005	23	N232R N570FT N994SA N721HW N721GB N15BE N500JW [b/u for spares around Mar87; cx Aug87 – remains to Bounty Av'n Scrapyard, Detroit-Willow Run, MI]
006	23	N505PF N578LJ N23CH N111JD N505PF [donated Oct93 to Kansas Aviation Museum]
007	23	N826L D-IHAQ [w/o 12Dec65 Zurich]
008	23	N825LJ N1203 N20S N20BD N20EP [wfu circa Mar93; exhibited outside White Inds, Bates City, MO]
009	23	N425EJ N5BL N13SN N49CK N23BY [to Arkansas Air Museum, Fayetteville, AR 2008]
010	23	N805LJ N292BC N2920C N333BF N29BF N400BF N500BF [b/u for spares Oct88 Detroit-Willow Run, MI – remains to Bounty Av'n Scrapyard, Detroit-Willow Run, MI]
011	24A	N806LJ N233VW N1966K N150WL N50JF N711PJ N711TJ N225LJ N24LG (N40TV)
012	24	N1965L N1967L N1969L N1965L
013	23	N613W N201BA N888DS N37BL N28ST [w/o 31Jul87 10km east of Guatemala City/La Aurora A/P, Guatemala; cx Dec89]
014	23	N814L N426EJ JY-AEG (HB-VEL) F-BXPT [wfu; instructional airframe Institut Aeronautique Amaury-de-la-Grange, Merville, France]
015	24	N88B [donated 28Feb92 to Pima County Air Museum, AZ; cx Mar92]
015A	23	N804LJ [w/o 21Oct65 nr Jackson, MI]
016	23	N500K N7CF N7GF N96CK [fuselage and detached wingset at compound near Davis-Monthan, AZ by Feb02; remains to Aviation Warehouse, El Mirage, CA by Oct04]
017	23	N233R N658L N32SD N30BP F-GBTA F-GDAV [w/o 30Jan89 Lisbon, Portugal; wreckage to Troyes, France, by Jun90; cx Nov92]
018	23	N807LJ N661FS D-IKAA N652J N866DB N866JS [w/o 06May80 Richmond, VA; remains with White Inds, Bates City, MO]
019	24	N4641J HB-VAI N889JF N654DN N100EA N747SC (N954SC) [cx May10; to Thakur Institute of Aviation Technology, Mumbai, India as instructional airframe]
020	23	N388R N338KK N2GP N210GP N310KR (N144WC) N388R N820L
021	23	N427EJ N427NJ N133W [w/o Burbank, CA; cx Jul81, parted out]
022	23	N428EJ N400CS N103TC N88TC N456SC N114GB [b/u; cx Feb93; remains to White Inds, Bates City, MO]
023	23	N429EJ JY-AEH HB-VEL F-GAMA [w/o after on-board fire 05Jun81 Le Bourget, France; cx 10Feb92 – to technical college at Perigueux, France]
024	23	N202Y N21U N488J N803JA (N702RK) N3ZA [b/u for spares 1982; cx Apr91; remains to White Inds, Bates City, MO]
025	23	N600G N60QG N5DM N3JL N37DM N50DM N508M N24SA [b/u for spares after accident 21Jun85; cx May89]
026	23	N706L HB-VBA F-BSTP N26008 N404AJ N222GH N404DB N540CL [parted out at Hollister, CA circa early 2000; cx 28Apr06 as b/u]
027	23	N430EJ JY-AEI HB-VES F-GAPY (N108TW) [b/u for spares 1983 Kansas City, KS; remains to White Inds, Bates City, MO; rear fuselage & tail unit used as engineering testbed for Avcom Intl ventral fin retrofit programme]
028	23	N818LJ N5DM (N56PR) (N500YY) N5QY N37CP [b/u for spares 1994 Kansas City, KS; remains to White Inds, Bates City, MO]
028A	23	N803LJ N432EJ [w/o 25Oct67 Muskegon, MI]
029	23	N7000K N715BC N1BU N66AS N61TS [wfu Sep88; b/u for spares Detroit-Willow Run, MI; cx Jan96]
030	23	N431EJ N431CA ZS-JWC N431CA ZS-JWC [sold in USA circa May02, to be used for spares for c/n 23-081; remains to Aviation Warehouse, El Mirage, CA]
031	24A	N175FS N477BL N777TF N777TE N202BA N175FS [stored dismantled at Paso Robles, CA, awaiting possible restoration – was owned by Frank Sinatra Jun65-Jun67]
032	23	N235R [w/o 23Apr66 Clarendon, TX]
033	23	N158MJ N453LJ N453JT XA-LGM XA-GAM N60DH N23TJ [wfu Sep87; cx Feb93 remains to scrapyard at Hastings-Earls Air Park, FL by Mar01]
034	23	N242WT N241BN N24FF N154AG [to Museum of Flight, Seattle WA. Displayed at Everett/Paine Field, WA] "N407V"
035	23	N100X (N10QX) N992TD [wfu; cx23Jul08]
036	23	N477K N210PC N111WM N38DM YV-278CP N123MJ
037	23	N266JP N988SA N51AJ N65LJ N41AJ N13LJ N10LJ N50AJ XA-ESS XC-UJP XC-AA28 XC-LGD [w/o 07Dec08 Lake Atlangatepec, Mexico]
038	23	N812LJ VR-BCF LN-NPE N1002B 9Q-CGM 9Q-CHB N433J N433JB N100TA N100JZ N300TA N175BA PT-LKQ [wfu Detroit-Willow Run, MI; to Detroit technical school as instructional airframe – then reportedly b/u circa 2000]
039	23	N43B N800JA N15SC N30SC N9JJ (N43CT) N121CK XA-... N121CK [b/u Niagara Falls A/P, NY, May13]
040	23	N433EJ N673WM YV-01CP N98386 (N12HJ) [b/u for spares 1989]
041	23	N205RJ N666MP C-GDDB N77VJ [b/u for spares circa 2001]
042	23	N293BC N2932C N1ZA N701RZ N69KB [b/u for spares 1982 by White Inds, Bates City, MO; cx Dec91; remains still present Nov94]
043	24	N368MJ N39T N24MW N50BA (N43AC) [sold for spares during 1987; cx Sep89]
044	23	N22B HB-VAM [w/o 28Aug72 Innsbruck, Austria]
045	23	N242F N711MR N100TA [w/o 06May82 Savannah, GA]

LEARJET 23 / 24

C/n	Model	Identities
045A	23	N803LJ HB-VBB F-BSUX N959SC [w/o 23Jly91 Detroit City, MI]
046	23	N434EJ [w/o 09May70 Pellston, MI]
047	23	N2503L N347J YV-E-GPA YV-15CP N9260A N444WC N2503L [parted out at Rantoul, KS, circa early 2000]
048	23	N805LJ N1GW N48MW N140RC [wfu at Montgomery, AL by Jul04]
049	23	NASA701 N701NA N933NA (N933N) N605NA
050	24	N828MW N828M N823M N650CA N24ET N24NJ [instructional airframe at Bombay Flying Club College of Aviation, Mumbai/Juhu, India]
050A	23	N808LJ N808JA [w/o 23May(?) 1982 in ground fire; probably at Sarasota-Bradenton, FL, where burnt fuselage was noted 25Jun82; remains to Taylorville, IL]
051	24	N1500B N1500G N100MJ (N69LL) N990TM N70JC N24VM [parted out by White Inds, Bates City, MO, 1987]
052	23	N360EJ HB-VBD N360EJ N856JB
053	23	N361EJ HB-VBC F-BTQK N23AJ [parted out by Dodson Av'n, Rantoul, KS, 1988; cx Sep92; hulk to Aviation Film Prop Warehouse, El Mirage, CA, wearing fake marks N464CL]
054	23	CF-TEL N351WB N351WC N351NR N351N [parted out by Dodson Av'n, Rantoul, KS]
055	24	N809LJ N2366Y N511WH N711CW [preserved at Tillamook Air Museum, OR]
056	23	N362EJ N332PC [w/o 06Jan77 Flint, MI; parted out by White Inds, Bates City, MO]
057	23	N448GC N448GG [parted out by Dodson Av'n, Ottawa, KS]
058	23	N363EJ N66MP N7FJ N153AG [cx 13Nov14, CofR expired]
059	23	N364EJ N31DP N331DP [b/u for spares Jun87 Detroit-Willow Run, MI – remains to Bounty Av'n Scrapyard]
060	24	N889WF N90J XA-ADJ
061	23	N316M [w/o 19Mar66 Lake Michigan, MI]
062	23	N670MF N20TA [cx 06Sep12, wfu]
063	23	N243F [w/o 14Nov65 Palm Springs, CA]
064	23	N365EJ N200G N400RB N401RB N73JT N66AM ZS-MBR 3D-AFJ ZS-MBR [wfu Oct93 Lanseria, S Africa] N259DB [parted out by Atlanta Air Salvage, Griffin, GA; cx 16May13]
065	24	N2000M N200DM N7500K (N750QK) N750WJ N957SC N707SC (XA-...) N707SC [wfu Rio Negro, Columbia]
065A	23	N388Q N28BP (N28BR) N1GZ N122M (N156AG) [fuselage and detached wingset in compound nr Davis-Monthan, AZ, by Feb02; remains to Aviation Warehouse, El Mirage, CA, by Oct04; tail unit used in 'Telle Mere Tel Fils' sculpture by Adel Abdessemed 2008]
066	23	N216RG N72MK N66MW XA-RVB XA-SDP N211TS XB-MYE
067	23	N815LJ N2ZA N703DC N720UA N331DP [w/o 18Jan90 nr Dayton, OH; cx Oct90]
068	23	N460F N902AR N902AB N575HW N9RA N400PG N152AG XA-ARG XB-GRR N73CE [to Yanks Air Museum, Chino, CA]
069	23	N814LJ N9AJ N6GJ N37BL (N34TR) [converted at some time to Model 24 standards; w/o 04Mar98 Oakland, CA, remains to White Ind's, Bates City, MO circa Oct98]
070	23	CF-ARE N1976L N197GL N111CT N101DB XA-RZM XA-TII XC-AA104 XC-JDX XB-KMY
071	23	N1001A N71LJ XA-RZC N6262T [with Dodson Avn, Rantoul, KS, for parts Jly95, still marked as XA-RZC]
072	23	N331WR N331JR N4VS N31S N2SN RP-C848
073	23	N806LJ
074	23	5A-DAC D-IATD N23TC N74MW N23AN N68WM N150AG XA-LAR XB-GRQ N83CE [sold to Maricopa County Community College, AZ]
075	23	5A-DAD [w/o 05Jun67 Damascus, Syria]
076	23	N1966W N801JA N12GP N50PJ N83LJ [cx Aug10, wfu]
077	23	N812LJ N740J N868J N500P N90658 N88EA (N611CA) N745F [w/o 30Jul88 March AFB, Riverside, CA; cx Mar90]
078	23	N690LJ [w/o 30Nov67 Orlando, FL]
079	23	N240AG N240AQ N31CK [fuselage and detached wingset in compound nr Davis-Monthan, AZ by Feb02; remains to Aviation Warehouse, El Mirage, CA by Oct04; tail unit used in 'Telle Mere Tel Fils' sculpture by Adel Abdessemed 2008]
080	23	N822LJ [w/o 09Dec67 Detroit, MI]
081	23	N369EJ N437LJ XC-JOA N418LJ (N81LJ) ZS-MDN N265DC [cx 18Apr07, wfu]
082	23	N280C N805JA N7GP (N700NP) (N216SA) [wfu Hampton – Tara Field, Atlanta GA]
082A	23	N823LJ N255ES N744CF N100TA N613BR N618BR (N118LS) [instructional airframe Blackhawk Technical College, Janesville, WI]
083	23	N824LJ [donated to the Kalamazoo Air Zoo, MI for public static display]
084	23	N788DR N101JR N119BA
085	23	N825LJ N385J N101PP [w/o 04Jun84 Windsor Locks, CT]
086	23	N1021B [w/o 06Nov69 Racine, WI]
087	24	N407V CF-UYT N7VS D-IKAB C-GEEN N998RL N24YA N24YE [parted out by Dodson Int'l Parts, Rantoul, KS cx Feb03]
088	23	N816LJ N616PS N11JK N804JA N48AS N500FM (N500LH) [w/o 02Jul91 Columbia, TN; noted dumped Oct91 Bounty Avn Scrapyard, Detroit-Willow Run, MI; cx Jun99]
089	23	N869B N969B N1968W [cx Apr01; b/u for spares by Dodson Int'l Parts, Rantoul, KS, circa 2002]
090	23	PP-FMX [w/o 30Aug69 Rio de Janeiro, Brazil]
091	23	N430JA N430J N110M N11QM [cx Dec89; b/u for spares 1989]
092	23	N415LJ N422JR N105BJ N344WC N415LJ [cx Aug10, wfu Smyrna, TN]
093	23	N416LJ N3350 N416LJ N12TA N38JD N486G N101AR N101AD N97MJ XA-SHN N80775 N7GF XA-... [still wearing N7GF at Toluca, Mexico, May11]
094	23	N417LJ N20M [w/o 15Dec72 Detroit, MI]
095	23	N366EJ N974D N5D N9RA N46452 [cx 27Oct09; to India as instructional airframe]
096	24A	N1967W N421L N527ER N33BK N1972L N1973L N1972L N464CL
097	23	N425SC N79LS N1968A N1963A [to spares 1995 remains at Hampton – Tara Field, Atlanta, GA]

LEARJET 23 / 24

C/n	Model	Identities
098	23	N112T N11111 N2DD N711 N711AE N99TC [b/u May87, Cincinnati/Lunken Field, OH; parted out by Brandis Avn, Taylorville, IL]
099	23	N7200K [cx 06May13; wfu]
100	24A	N427LJ CF-BCJ N144X N989SA N424NJ N361AA N24BA N616SC N427LJ N224SC [w/o 26Sep99 Gainsville, GA; remains to Atlanta Air Salvage, Griffin, GA]
101	24	N316M N316MF N15PL N473EJ N473 N68DM (N68FN) N24GJ XA-SGU N24WX [noted wfu at Corona Municipal apt, CA 1997; moved to Mesa/Falcon Field, AZ, by Feb08]
102	24A	N436LJ N365EJ N705NA N805NA [w/o 07Jun01 Victorville, CA; cx Sep01]
103	24	N430LJ N714X ZS-LTK N72442 ZS-LTK N90532 ZS-LTK N90532 ZS-LTK N90532 ZS-LTK N105EC XB-ADR
104	24	N433LJ N924ED N45ED
105	24	N425NJ N111EK N111EJ TR-LYB F-GDAE [cx Aug96 as wfu; reported w/o in 1989, no details]
106	24	N888NS N969J N100GP N70RL N103RB N888MC C-FNMC N888MC [cx Mar11; to India as instructional airframe]
107	24A	N48L [cx 05May15; CofR expired]
108	24	N1966L N745W N661CP N661BS N661SS C-GSIV N45811 N29LA N900JA N315AJ [b/u circa Apr04 for spares by White Industries, Bates City, MO]
109	24	HB-VAS OY-RYA SE-DCW (F-GBBV(2)) N900DL XA-NLK [wfu Toluca, Mexico]
110	24A	N388R N1969H N362AA N35JF N88JF [b/u Oct86 possibly following accident at Detroit, MI in Oct86; cx Jul89; remains with Brandis Avn, Taylorville, IL]
111	24A	N900Y N500FM N44WD N900NA
112	24	N447LJ CF-ECB N2200T N10CP (OB-....) N112DJ N104GA XA-TRQ
113	24	N438LJ (N402Y) N204Y N100SQ [to spares 1989 by Brandis Avn, Taylorville, IL]
114	24	N443LJ N999M N99DM PT-LNE [wfu at Belo Horizonte, Brazil by 2005]
115	24	N449LJ N458LJ N591D N591DL N86CC [b/u for spares during 1989 Denver, CO; remains with Brandis Avn, Taylorville, IL]
116	24A	N461F N52EN N77GH N8FM N400EP N40BP N51B N105GA (N12MB) (N1420)
117	24XR	N288VW F-BRAL N16MJ HZ-SMB N90DH N92DF N140EX N24SA
118	24	N452LJ N100GS N1008S N1919W N31SK [w/o 27Mar87 Eagle County A/P, Vail, CO]
119	24	N453LJ N453SA N605GA N994SA N110W N500PP N500P (N500PJ) N61CK N63CK [b/u for spares by Dodson Int'l Parts, Rantoul, KS circa Oct02]
120	24	N457LJ N633J N633NJ N44AJ N44NJ PT-LMF N244RD [b/u for spares by Dodson Int'l Parts, Rantoul, KS, circa Oct02]
121	24	N454LJ N454GL N454RN [w/o 26Feb73 Atlanta, GA]
122	24	N461LJ PT-CXK [w/o 04May73 Rio Galeon, Brazil]
123	24	N262HA N700C (N700ET) XA-JSC XA-JSO N35EC N25LJ N3137
124	24	N462LJ OY-EGE SE-DCU (N252DL) XA-RTV N991TD [cx 20Jul12; to Malaysia as instructional airframe]
125	24A	N651LJ [crashed 03Jan76 Anchorage, AK]
126	24	N653LJ N352WR N332FP (N345SF) N16HC [instructional airframe Craven Community College Institute of Aeronautical Technology, Havelock, NC]
127	24	N654LJ N654JC N654LD N111LJ N127LJ N37CB (N6462) N124JL [cx 19May15, CofR expired]
128	24	N655LJ HB-VBK N914BA N333X N383X N4CR HB-VBK N37594 N802W (D-CJAD) N128BJ N911KB XA-TDP (N128WD) [to spares by Dodson Int'l Parts, Rantoul, KS, circa 1999]
129	24	N656LJ D-IFUM N44GA C-GSAX N44GA [w/o 30Jan84 Santa Catalina, CA; cx Nov86]
130	24	N657LJ N420WR N1871R N1871P N130J N33CJ N330J N234MR [b/u for spares Dec87]
131	24	N659LJ N232R N282R N11FH N241JA [to Wings Over the Rockies Museum, Denver, CO]
132	24	N658LJ N233R N238R N32CA [cx Sep01; aircraft was b/u]
133	24	N660LJ N40JF N40JE N555PV N46WB N16WJ N133DF N133BL [b/u; cx Feb04]
134	24	N231R N281R N282R N215J N200GP (N202GP) N200TC N270TC N7GN N911TR N26BA [parted out at Rantoul, KS circa early 2000]
135	24	N85W N77LB LV-WMR [w/o 28Aug95 Pasadas, Argentina; fuselage at Buenos Aires-Aeroparque, for spares]
136	24	N664LJ N222RB N954S N24LW XA-JLV [wfu following flood damage; to spares Oct94 Spirit of St Louis A/P, MO]
137	24	N907CS N73HG N77RY N72FP N151AG [parted out by White Inds, Bates City, MO]
138	24	N37P N808DP N808D N575G N106CA N45JF (N106CA) N400RS N94JJ N130RS [was being converted to a 4-seat 'suborbital spaceplane' fitted with a Rocketdyne RS-88 rocket, new wings and new tail assembly. First flight was planned for Jul06, current project status unknown]
139	24	N590GA N52JH N42AJ N481EZ N96AA [b/u for spares by Dodson Int'l, Rantoul, KS circa Oct02]
140	24	N663LJ N663L N663LJ N593KR N252M N100VC N100VQ [to instructional airframe, National Aviation Academy, St Petersburg-Clearwater, FL by Oct02]
141	24	N348VL N348BJ N43AJ N141PJ XB-FJW XB-GHO [w/o 18Feb11 Pachuca, Mexico]
142	24	N591GA N200NR N777MR N723JW [instructional airframe Delaware Technical Community College, Georgetown, DE]
143	24	N592GA N145JN N778GA N49AJ N900BD N2YY (N727LG) N724LG N24WF [wfu still painted as N724LG; in compound nr Davis-Monthan, AZ, by Nov02; cx 19Jul04; hulk to Aviation Warehouse, El Mirage, CA by Oct04]
144	24	N593GA N397L N397BC N9KC N700C N303AF [parted out by White Inds, Bates City, MO, 1986; cx 11Mar05]
145	24	N690J N57ND (N57NB) N282AC (ZS-PBI) [cx 30Mar09; wfu in South Africa]
146	24	N672LJ N235Z N44CJ [w/o 02Oct81 Felt, OK]
147	24	N673LJ N595GA N16CP N444KW N33NJ N825AA (N67CK) N147KH N147CK [instructional airframe JRN Institute of Aviation Technology, India; cx 21Jan09]

LEARJET 23 / 24

C/n	Model	Identities
148	24	N406L N80CB N133TW HB-VDH N8482B N426PS (N47NR) N41MP N24ET [cx 13Aug13; impounded at Charallave, Venezuela]
149	24	N294BC N2945C N300HH N300LB N64HB N995TD [cx 09Mar06; aircraft used as instructional airframe]
150	24XR	N3807G N596GA N596HF N211HJ N211BL N24XR XA-RQB [parted out by Dodson Av'n, Rantoul, KS Oct04]
151	24	N153H N111HJ N664CL N664GL N50JF N24AJ N53GH N6177Y [cx 12Dec14, CofR expired]
152	24	N3807G N597GA N21U N98DK N9LM N48BA [wfu 1993 Kissimmee, FL; cx Aug93; parted out by Dodson Av'n, Rantoul, KS]
153	24	N524SC N1TK N159J (N53DE) N878DE (N555DH) N153BR N120RA [wfu; cx 13Jan09]
154	24	N123VW N12315 N424RD N7HA N11AK N123RE [w/o 17Oct78 Lancaster, CA]
155	24	N598GA N422U N462B N462BA N833GA N210FP N660A [parted out 1987; hulk to Aviation Film Prop Warehouse, El Mirage, CA]
156	24	N599GA N468DM N111RF N111RP N712R LZ-VTS [wfu; fire training aid at Nurnberg a/p]
157	24	N640GA N1919W N1919G N191DA N94HC N124WL N43ZP N659AT (N157BP) XA-SNZ (N650AT) N659AT N157TW [cx 15May15; CofR expired]
158	24	N642GA N392T N855GA N500MH PT-LPX N500MH N220PM PT-WEW
159	24	N647GA N855W N661JB N66MR N710TV (N269AL)
160	24	N645G N111WJ C-GTJT N4791C N989TL
161	24	N649G N224KT N24KT N24KF N222TW
162	24	N841G N338DS N91MK N919K N835AC N835AG N55NJ [w/o 07May86, Hollywood, FL; remains to Dodson Av'n, Ottawa, KS; rear fuselage & tail to Guthrie, OK]
163	24	N701AP N1AP N65339 N77AE (N777JA) N65WM N68LU [wfu, donated to mechanics school, Lewis University, IL Jul86]
164	24	N711L N464J N924BW N831RA XA-RYN N831RA XA-TKC N831RA [parted out by Dodson International, Rantoul, KS]
165	24	N844GA N469J ZS-KJY V5-KJY ZS-KJY V5-KJY ZS-KJY [parted out 2011, Lanseria, South Africa]
166	24	N993KL N500SB N124PJ N124HF N993TD [to India as instructional airframe]
167	24	N847GA N841LC N888B N664CL [instructional airframe, North Valley Occupational Center, Van Nuys, CA; cx 27Dec16]
168	24	N109JR N109JB N51CH C-GBWB N155BT N333TW
169	24	D-ICAR N9033X (N127DN) N127DM N927AA N93BP [parted out by Dodson Int'l Parts, Rantoul, KS circa Oct02]
170	24	N200DH N151WW [wfu Addison, TX]
171	24	N737FN N417WW [cx Jan11; to India as instructional airframe]
172	24	N675L N234WR N48AJ [parted out by White Inds, Bates City, MO]
173	24	N852GA N872JR N110SQ N33ST N102GP N3GL N623RC YV-824CP YV1079
174	24	N854GA N661CP N661JG N999JR N321GL N77WD N77GJ XA-LNK
175	24	N859GM N859L N288K N28BK N881FC [w/o 02Feb92 New Tamiami, FL; cx Mar93]
176	24	PT-CXJ N3034B [cx 31Jan05; b/u]
177	24	N321Q N104MB N555LB N555LA N555LB (N524DW) [fuselage and detached wing set in compound near Davis-Monthan, AZ by Feb02; to Aviation Warehouse, El Mirage, CA by Oct04; front and rear fuselage sections to children's play area, Amsterdam/Schipol, Netherlands, 2016; fuselage centre section to airport fire service, Amsterdam/Schipol, Netherlands, 2016]
178	24	N674LJ N55KS N55KX N56LB N56LS N24AJ N41BJ N723JW N11AQ [parted out at Addison, TX, circa 2005]
179	24	N920FF N300CC N111RA N111RE N410PD N410PB N412PD N717DB XC-GII XA-RQP N994TD [cx 11Jul13; wfu]
180	24	N566RB N802JA N100RA XA-SBR XA-NLA
181	24B	N234Q N1QC N651J N44PA (N144PA) N87CF N254JT N426TA
182	24B	N945GA N171L N500ZA N500ZH N155J RP-C2324 [wfu, stored at private address Quezon City, Philippines]
183	24B	N676LJ OY-AGZ F-BRNL [w/o 18Dec85 Toulouse, France]
184	24B	N950GA D-IMWZ N84J N36RS N78BH N28DL N58DM N58FN [Instructional airframe, Hampton University, Newport News, VA, then scrapped]
185	24B	N754M N44CP N144CP [parted out at Rantoul, KS circa early 2000]
186	24B	N266P N100AJ N1SS N18G (N7300G) N7300K N73PS N196CF [b/u for parts; cx Feb06]
187	24B	ZS-SGH F-GAJD N5WJ N129DM [b/u for spares Feb90]
188	24B	N230R N280R [cx 14Jan08, wfu Guthrie, OK]
189	24B	D-CJET D-IKAF D-CONA N14MJ N711DS N711DX N915US [cx 21Feb06, parted out]
190	24B	N4291G N9HM N50TC HZ-GP4 F-GBLA N190SC (N190DB) N190BP N600XJ [w/o 23Dec03 Helendale, CA]
191	24B	N855W N44LJ (N44TL) N80DH [b/u 1984 after accident; cx Mar89; remains to Dodson Av'n, Ottawa, KS]
192	24B	N1919W N12MK [w/o 06Jan77 Palm Springs, CA]
193	24B	D-IOGI N31TC N500RP N500RE N33RE N140CA N83H N83HC (N488BL) N193JF N193DB
194	24B	N952GA N77LS N851BA N62DM (N62FN) N2093A [wfu Newton, KS]
195	24B	N202BT N272GL F-BUUV N803L N555LJ (N721MD) (N46LM)
196	24B	N99SC N1125E N99ES N99E N173LP N573LP N573LR N88RD N196AF N196TB
197	24B	N953GA CF-CSS C-FCSS N52GH N87AC C-FCSS N711CN N711 N711UR N710TJ XB-SUD XA-RXA N84CT (XA-...) N24FU N89ES

LEARJET 23 / 24

C/n	Model	Identities
198	24B	N66RP N111GW N21XL N21XB N39KM [to India as instructional airframe; cx 12Nov08]
199	24B	N333CR N855W N444HC N70TJ XA-TTT
200	24B	(N24NP) N721J N721JA N246CM N119MA [being parted out at Bates City, MO circa early 2000]
201	24B	N3871J N273GL D-IDDD D-CDDD C-GTFA N100DL [w/o 23May98, Orlando Executive, FL; parted out at Bates City, MO, circa early 2000]
202	24B	N3816G N77JN F-BUFN N26MJ N999MF N123SV N814HH N814JR N333RY [parted out San Antonio, TX; cx 14Aug13]
203	24B	N515WC N3GW (N43TL) N55LJ N55MJ N203CK N203JL [to Evergreen Aviation & Space Museum, McMinnville, OR; cx 13Apr17]
204	24B	N957GA N957E N176CP N510ND N510MS [fuselage with OK Turbines, Hollister, CA by Feb05]
205	24B	N974JD N64CF N64CE (N721J) [wfu; cx 16Sep08]
206	24B	HB-VBY F-BTYV N116RM N24YA [parted out by White Inds, Bates City, MO; cx 18Apr13]
207	24XR	N851JH N878W N457JA ZS-MGJ
208	24B	D-ILDE N72335 N42HC N444AG N32MJ N444AG N444AQ N14PT XA-AAA [wfu Monterrey del Norte, Mexico]
209	24B	N970GA N16MT N14BC ZS-LWU
210	24B	ZS-LLG F-BSRL [w/o 10Jun85 over Provins nr Paris, France]
211	24B	N388P N30EH N222AP N31LB N413WF N680CJ [cx 27Aug13; wfu]
212	24B	N291BC N328TL N328JK [cx 17Apr14, wfu Charallave, Venezuela]
213	24B	N555MH N986WC N886WC N999RA N43KC N103TC N95AB N895J N24JZ XA-... N24JZ
214	24B	N192MH N192MB N666CC N668MC N214MJ N42NF N234CM [w/o 16Dec88 nr Monclova, Mexico; cx Apr91]
215	24B	N971GA N201WL N10EC N29CA (N57JR) N29CA (N57JR) N400EP [cx 9Oct14, CofR expired]
216	24B	N212LF N723LL N711DB N411SP (N821LL) N777LB N900GG XA-MMG
217	24B	N777MC N777MQ C-GPDB N8536Y C-GDKS N45824 N217AT C-FZHT N876MC
218	24B	N682LJ N101VS
219	24B	N658AT N711CE N100KK F-GECI N977GA ZS-TOY
220	24B	N292BC N248J N17FN [wfu for spares by Dodson Avn, Ottawa, KS]
221	24B	N977GA N570P (N570JG) N59JG N233TW
222	24B	N692LJ N740E N740F N740EJ [cx 19Jly05 as b/u]
223	24B	D-IOGA D-COGA D-IFVG D-CFVG N7074X [wfu for spares by Feb94]
224	24B	D-IOGE N99606 N30DH C-GPCL N102PA (N722DM) N61DM (N61FN) (N51GJ) XA-TCA [wfu Toluca, Mexico]
225	24B	N618R D-IHLZ [w/o 18Jun73 Marlensel, W Germany]
226	24B	N454LJ N335JW (N335JR) N335RY RP-C2424 [wfu]
227	24B	N244GL XA-TIP N90797 N1DD N10CB N43W N4576T N28AT N27BJ
228	24B	N245GL N4292G N7DL (D-IIDD) D-IIPD N777SA N150AB PT-OBD [wfu at Belo Horizonte, Brazil by 2005]
229	24B	N293BC N298H N551AS N864CL [w/o 08Oct84 San Francisco, CA]
230	24D	N252GL N329HN N93C N93CB N433J N433JA N18SD N477JB N482CP N819GF N67JR N7121K XA-VVI N32287 XA-SSU
231	24D	HB-VBU I-CART N693LJ N37DH N93BR [wfu; remains with Brandis Avn, Taylorville, IL; still regd]
232	24D	N123CB [w/o 17Apr71 Butte, MT]
233	24R	N253GL D-IGSO N78AF N23SG N23SQ N500RW N124TS (N56GH) N143GB N19LJ [wfu Newton, KS; cx 24Mar17]
234	24D	LV-PRA LV-JTZ [wfu wearing fake marks LV-PTA, Buenos Aires/Ezeiza, Argentina]
235	24XR	N51VL N701SC
236	24D	N26VM N48JW N25ZW N55DD N3TJ N25LJ N236TS N236WJ N93DD N990PT N890PT N47TK N59AL
237	24D	N902AR N111TT N25TA N112J N32AA N353J N889WF XA-... N25RJ N825DM N237TW
238	24D	N262GL N472EJ N49DM N48FN [to Hampton University, Newport News, VA, as instructional airframe then scrapped]
239	24D	D-ILVW D-ILHM F-GBLZ N83MJ PT-LAU [w/o 10Sep94 Brasilia A/P, Brazil]
240	24D	LV-PRB LV-JXA [possibly to spares with Dodson Int'l Parts, Olathe/New Century Air Center, KS circa Oct00]
241	24D	HB-VCT N120J N363BC (N61TJ) N63GA
242	24D	N1972G N45CP N1972G N999WA [cx 28Aug09; instructional airframe Pune Institute of Aviation Technology, India]
243	24XR	HB-VCI N2909W (N85DH) N83RG N56WS N57FL N37HT N929HF N929MC
244	24D	PT-DZU [w/o 23Aug71 Sao Paulo, Brazil]
245	24D	N275LE N275E JA8446 N275E (N44KB)
246	24D	N215Z N21NA N5SJ N35SJ N50SJ (N69SF) N61BA N184AL N600JC N444SC (N444HE) N24TE N99JB N6JM N500MS N400MS
247	24D	HB-VCN D-ICAP N23AM N42PG N247DB N997TD [w/o 10Dec01 on approach to El Paso, TX]
248	24D	OO-LFA 9Q-CBC [w/o 18Jan94 Kinshasa, Zaire]
249	24D	9J-ADF N27MJ N999M N998M XA-POS XC-AA63 N249RA N440KT [cx 19Mar13, CofR expired]
250	24D	N112C D-IMAR N122CG N2U N1U N85CA N85CD Venezuela 0006 [wfu; preserved Caracas/La Carlota, Venezuela]
251	24D	N333X N338X N251TJ N95DD XA-SBZ XA-RIC N46JA N69XW N39EL [wfu Carlsbad, CA; cx 19May15]
252	24D	N711L N711LD N972 N157AG (N252TJ) (C6-BGF) XA-... N157AG
253	24D	N123VW N999U N30FL N711DB (N30FL) N97DM N417JD N97DM [w/o 05Mar86; collided with Learjet N39DM c/n 35-040 over Pacific Ocean nr San Clemente Islands]

LEARJET 23 / 24

C/n	Model	Identities
254	24D	D-ICAY D-CCAT N13606 PT-LCV [CofA canx]
255	24D	XC-SAG XA-BBE XA-SMU N255AR [cx Jun10; to Finland as instructional airframe]
256	24D	HB-VCW N703J C-GWFG C-GWEG N256MJ N256WM [b/u Jan06 Mankato, MN; cx 04Apr06; fuselage to Guthrie, OK, by 01Oct06]
257	24D	N427JX C-GHDP N888FA [instructional airframe Southern Illinois University, Carbondale, IL]
258	24D	N75KV N25VZ N25GW N19TJ N24CK (N24DZ) (N77RS) N424RS
259	24D	N200JR N22MH (N24EA) (N22ML) I-EJIA N22MH XA-RRC [parted out by White Inds, Bates City, MO]
260	24D	N60GL C-GFJB XA-ROX XA-GBA XC-PFP XC-AGU XC-PLS
261	24D	D-IDAT D-COOL C-GBWA [b/u for spares 1993 by Global Inds; cx Jun94; remains to Bounty Av'n Scrapyard, Detroit-Willow Run, MI]
262	24D	N2GR OH-GLB N38788 N110PS OH-GLB [wfu; cx Apr03 – to RAOL Technical Vocational School, Rovaniemi, Finland, as instructional airframe]
263	24D	N3812G XB-JOY [w/o 29Jun76 Mexico City, Mexico]
264	24XR	PI-C1747 RP-C1747 [wfu Manila, Philippines]
265	24D	N2WL N32WL N456JA [w/o 24Oct85 Juneau, AK]
266	24D	N266BS VH-BSJ N266BS N266TW [cx 06Apr17, wfu Addison, TX]
267	24XR	HB-VCY N46032 N78AE N124GA VR-BHC HB-VCY N95DA VR-BMN N267MP ZS-OEA
268	24D	N53GL N111WW N123CC N92TC (N66FN) N58BL N98WJ N24TK
269	24D	XA-DIJ XA-MOV XA-DIJ XB-MZX
270	24D	XB-NAG XA-BUY N3979P PT-LEM [w/o 07Apr99 Ribeirao Preto, Brazil]
271	24D	N3818G HB-VDK F-BVEC N4305U XA-SCE [wfu Dallas/Love Field, TX]
272	24D	N51GL N117K [cx 22Jul13; wfu]
273	24D	OH-GLA N118J 5Y-GEO N51AJ XC-DOP XB-DZR
274	24D	N3871J N1U N48CT
275	24D	XB-NUR N24TC N216HB PT-LPH
276	24D	PT-JGU N25CV N56PT (N814HP)
277	24D	N131CA N181CA (N163ME) (N181RW) N106MC N57BC N277TW [instructional airframe Western Maricopa Education Center Aviation School, Glendale, AZ]
278	24D	PT-JKR N5695H N202JS
279	24D	VH-SBC N849GL N3DU N3DZ I-FREU N75CJ N101AR N955EA
280	24XR	D-ICHS N79RS ZS-NGG [b/u for spares at Nelspruit, South Africa]
281	24D	SE-DFB OY-BIZ N23MJ N281FP [to Frontiers of Flight Museum, Dallas-Love Field, TX]
282	24D	D-INKA N300JA [w/o 02Dec79 Dutch Harbor, AK]
283	24D	SE-DFA D-IEGO N51JT N20GT N31WT N47WT (N711SC) N24XR XA-UHT
284	24D	PT-JKQ
285	24D	XC-AZU XA-REK XB-GBC N995DR (N995RD) N430JW N300TJ [cx 9Dec14, CofR expired]
286	24XR	N59GL N86GC N56RD N57DB N77JL [w/o 12Nov03 St. Louis Downtown apt, IL]
287	24D	HB-VDN EC-CJA HB-VDN I-MABU N92565 PT-LCN [w/o 04Apr84 Florianapolis, Brazil]
288	24D	N288DF N7701L
289	24D	(HB-VDO) F-BRGF N131MA XA-RUJ N131MA N289SA N289G N98CG [wfu Carlsbad, CA; cx 21May15]
290	24D	N462B N23JC N934H N87AP N627ER N24TK XA-RMF N24TK N88LJ N308SM XB-AFA [b/u Toluca, Mexico]
291	24D	ZS-GLD N45862 N148J N24PJ PT-LYL N114WC (N919MA) N488DM N483DM [cx 25Apr11; instructional airframe, South Georgia Technical College; Americus, GA]
292	24D	N426NA N600PC N426NA N800PC N888TW
293	24D	XA-TIP N917BF N293MC
294	24D	N4F PT-LNK PP-EIW PT-WKL [cx; status?]
295	24D	N717HB N717HE N49TJ (N160GC) N590CH N295NW
296	24D	XA-FIW N222BN N500RK N500DJ PT-LMS
297	24D	N297EJ XA-ACC N716US (N317MR) HK-3265 N8094U N24S
298	24D	N298EJ XA-ADD N98AC N151AG N470TR N169US
299	24D	N299EJ XA-ABB XC-JCN XB-GJS N299TW [cx 22Sep14, wfu]
300	24D	N300EJ N455JA [w/o 20Aug85 Gulkana, AK]
301	24D	N137JL N111TT (N87MJ) N31BG N249HP
302	24D	N302EJ N39DM N302EJ [w/o 14Apr83 Puerta Vallarta, Mexico]
303	24D	N303EJ PT-LOJ N303EJ [to White Inds, Bates City, MO 21Jun04 for spares; cx 26Oct07]
304	24D	N304EJ N304LP N500CG N588CG [wfu Detroit-Willow Run, MI; to India as instructional airframe]
305	24D	N305EJ N98DK N305EJ (N725DM) N43DM (N43FN) N510PA N666MW N930PJ [cx 3Dec14, CofR expired]
306	24D	N306EJ N55CD N98AA N132MA XA-SAV XA-SAA N306JA (N243RK)
307	24D	N307EJ N307BJ XA-RRK [w/o 02Jan98 Tampico, Mexico; to spares by Dodson Int'l Parts, Rantoul, KS]
308	24D	N308EJ N99AA N39TT (N308LJ) N89AA XB-IRH
309	24D	N310LJ N45FC N45AJ (N4445J) N789AA N80CK N309TC [wfu Detroit/Willow Run, MI, still marked N80CK]
310	24D	HB-VDU I-AMME [w/o 06Feb76 Bari, Italy]
311	24D	N66LW N5TR N5TD N19HM N19FM N50DR N56DR N748GM N10WJ (N76PW) N311LJ [to Finland as instructional airframe May11]
312	24D	Ecuador IGM-401 N312NA N80AP [cx 25Aug15; wfu]
313	24D	Mexico MTX-01 Mexico MTX-02 [w/o 20Nov98 Mexico City, Mexico; parted out by White Inds, Bates City, MO]
314	24D	N501MH N13MJ [w/o 06Nov82 Elizabeth City, NC; cx Sep92]
315	24D	PT-KPE [wfu Sao Paulo/Congonhas, Brazil circa Sep99; fuselage to Jundiai, Brazil]
316	24D	LV-LRC Argentina T-03 LV-LRC

LEARJET 23 / 24

C/n	Model	Identities
317	24D	N133GL ZS-JJO N45AJ XA-JIQ
318	24D	N114JT N611DB
319	24XR	XC-SUP XA-SUP XC-SUP N174RD [cx Aug10; wfu in Australia] N174RD
320	24D	N3802G YU-BIH SL-BAB S5-BAB N996TD [cx Feb10; to Singapore as instructional airframe]
321	24D	N10WF N122RW N224JB C-FRNR N33TP N351MH
322	24D	XA-DAT N105GL N972H N7RL (N322TJ) N322RS [cx 01Aug12, wfu]
323	24D	N61AW N744JC N104MC N453 N27AX [wfu 2005] 'N1TL'+ [+displayed in Tulsa Air & Space Museum, Tulsa, OK, wearing fake marks N1TL 2005-2011; scrapped by Oct11]
324	24D	N107GL (possibly XA-SUY) XA-SCY N324TW
325	24D	N76RV N416G N500SW N500SQ N721SF [instructional airframe, Redstone College, Denver, CO]
326	24D	N326EJ (N400XB) N326KE N322AU XA-MMD
327	24D	N327EJ F-GGPG N327GJ N711PC [instructional airframe VARIA-Vantaa Vocational School, Helsinki, Finland Dec08; cx 10Mar09]
328	24D	D-IMMM D-CMMM [w/o Bornholm, Denmark, 15Sep12]
329	24E	N102GL N21AG N22MJ XA-RAQ XA-PFA N329TJ N24FW
330	24E	N511AT N330TW [cx 05Mar16; wfu]
331	24E	N12MJ XA-REA N32DD [instructional airframe, Lake Area Technical Institute, Watertown, SD]
332	24F	N13KL N56MM
333	24E	N76TR N32WT N75GP N75GR PT-LQK
334	24E	N6KM N66MJ N944KM [cx Dec10; to India as instructional airframe]
335	24E	N721GL N87JL N2DD N8AE N2DD N894CJ
336	24F	N3818G I-DDAE N162J N9LD N49GS
337	24F	XA-GEO XA-DET
338	24E	N729GL N30LM N30EM [b/u for spares 1989; cx Dec89; remains with Brandis Av'n, Taylorville, IL]
339	24E	N15MJ N851CC N690 N60FN N1TJ N52DD N207RG T7-SAM
340	24E	N10FU C-FHFP N54JC (N95CP) N106TJ N457GM N825AM N627JJ [cx 29Apr14, believed wfu in Venezuela]
341	24E	N22BM N22NM N3PW (N103JW) N14DM XA-...
342	24F	N40144 YV-178CP N824GA N123DG
343	24E	N102B N102C N1DK N7EJ (N602JF) [cx 11May15; CofR expired]
344	24F	N81MC [w/o 10Nov84 St Thomas, Virgin Islands]
345	24E	N500RP N500RR D-CFPD N435AS N217JS (N99UP) N217AJ
346	24E	N61SF N41TC N117AJ N117AE N69AX (HP-....) XC-LJE XB-JXZ
347	24E	N724GL N124EZ N500LL N500TS N500SR N508SR
348	24F	N725GL N4RT N4RU (N106M) N8BG N444TW [w/o Guadalajara, Mexico, 09Jan07]
349	24F	VH-FLJ N349BS XA-CAP XB-DZD XB-KJW
350	24F	N741GL N500ZA N504JV
351	24E	N19MJ N31WT N81WT N77MR (N94BD) N75NE [cx 9Dec14, CofR expired]
352	24F	N101US (N449JS) N352MD
353	24F	N740GL N711PD N411MM N63BW PT-LMA [w/o 24Feb88 Macre, Brazil]
354	24F	N678SP PT-LYE ZS-FUN [possibly w/o 14Jan06 Kinshasa, Republic of Congo]
355	24E	N7AB N7ZB N500NH N165CM
356	24F	N3283M N677SW N113JS PT-LKD
357	24F	N288J N129ME HZ-S3

Production complete

LEARJET MODEL 25

C/n	Series	Identities
001		N463LJ [used in construction of 25-002]
002		N661LJ [wfu Jly72 and used for AiResearch engine tests]
003		N594GA N11JC N4PN N97DM N97FN [Instructional airframe, Hampton University, Norfolk News, NC, then scrapped]
004		N641GA N1121 N1121C N7GJ N47MJ N251AF N225KA
005		N646GA N1969W N777RA N707TR (N707TP) (N24FN) N28FN N711SQ XA-SDQ N39CK
006		N6804L N256P N90MH N88CJ (N88GJ) N522SC N852SC N188FC (N25JX) (N857SC) N252SC N44CP XB-KQN
007		N644GA N551MD N551MB N7TJ N25NM N500JA N52JA (N58JA) N726WR [cx 15Jul16; for display at Livermore airport, CA]
008		N648GA N744W VP-BDM N744W N1976S N645L N88NJ N800GG XA-MUU
009		N843GA N670LJ 9Q-CHC N40LB [w/o 25Sep73 Omaha, NB]
010		N846GA N846HC N671WM N102PS (N10BF) (N82UH) (N121GL) N121EL [cx May03 to Kingston University, UK as instructional airframe]
011		N167J N49BA C-GHMH N108GA N525TW
012		N853GA N853DS N191DA N846YT N846YC N102AR [parted out by White Inds, Bates City, MO; cx 29Apr09]
013		N856G N515VW [w/o 17Apr69 Delemont, Switzerland]
014		N857GA N914SB N204A N316M N127AJ N8CL N14LJ N754DB [cx 07Jun04; b/u by Clay Lacy Av'n for parts]
015		N858GM CF-HMV N713US N708TR N25FN N25GJ N125U XA-LLL
016		N145JN CF-KAX N424RD N711EV N83TH N8FF N976BS (N35WE) [canx 12Sep05; b/u for parts by Jet Components Aircraft Parts, TX; hulk to Alliance Air Parts, Oklahoma City, OK]
017		N720AS N101WR N16JP N666WL N55WJ N128DM N123JS N53FL [wfu; cx 27Aug12]
018		N861GA N323WA N77SA N32PC N99ES N117CH N15MJ (N23FN) N29FN [parted out by Brandis Avn, Taylorville, IL; cx 07Jun13]
019		N591KR N88EP N88FP N100MK [w/o 21Oct78 Sandusky, OH]
020		N941GA N215Z N30TT (N90TC) N113AK N900JD N900CJ N500JS N76CK [wfu; cx 09Oct15]
021		N942GA N111LL N1JR N1LL N40SW N40SN N6NF [wfu; cx Apr95; displayed Ozark Municipal A/P, AL]
022	XR	N943GA N925WP N1ZC N99CQ (N93JH) N131MS N24BS N111WB N111WR ZS-SSM
023		N577LJ N72CD N13CR (N861L) N47AJ (N820RT) (N12RA) N850SC N767SC N147TW
024		N425RD N125ST N137BC N20HJ N20RZ
025		N920S N928S N920S N92V N49BB N242AG N225DS (N111LM) N110RA [cx Apr13; wfu Pontiac, MI]
026		N4005S N7ZA C-GMAP N283R N281R N25EC
027		N7000G N423RD N35WB N835WB (N835GM) EC-EBM N500DL N900AJ [b/u]
028		N592KR N263GL N277LE N33PF N727LJ [instructional airframe, Augusta Technical College, Thomson, GA]
029	XR	N280LC N28LA N107HF [parted out by White Inds, Bates City, MO; cx 29Apr09]
030		N951GA N999M N999MK N745W N30PS N48HM N380LC N45DM N51CA [w/o 30Mar83 Newark, NJ]
031		N294NW (N294M)
032		N373W N711DB N712DC N357HC XA-ZYZ XA-RQI [was on display in terminal at Mexico City A/P, Mexico, in 1994 but has since been removed]
033		HB-VBP N143J N786MS YV-88CP N77NJ [cx Aug03; parted out]
034		N954GA N954FA N242WT N6GC N3UC N17AR N19FN N309AJ N309LJ [cx Oct03; instructional airframe at Staverton UK then Kemble UK then City of Bristol College, UK]
035		N683LJ N33GF N33TR N616NA
036	TF	N956GA N956J N741E N741ED N15CC N15M [also carried "N25TF"] N45BK [to Singapore as instructional airframe]
037		N737EF N18JF N28AA N155AG [parted out circa Nov00; fuselage used as a cabin interior display exhibit by Best AeroNet Ltd TX; canx 18Sep03]
038		HB-VBR EC-CKD HB-VBR N738GL N36MW N444WS N83GG N400AJ N813JW N130CK [cx 2Dec14, CofR expired]
039		N959GA N959RE N17JF N66NJ N308AJ (N25VJ) N273CA [to India as instructional airframe; cx 12Nov09]
040		N687LJ HB-VBI F-BSUR (N2273G) C-GOSL N41AJ N9CZ (N98RH) N23FN N238CA [to India as instructional airframe 2009]
041		N960GA N205SC N205SA N31AA (N25RE) [parted out by White Inds, Bates City, MO]
042		N958GA N958DM (N429TJ) N50DT N800JA N797SC (N25LG) (N125WD) [derelict at Deland, FL since 2002]
043		N30LJ N808DP N300PP N234ND N473TC [instructional airframe, Tulsa Technology Center School District #18, OK]
044		N962GA N658TC [w/o 18Jan72 Victoria, TX]
045		N963GA CF-DWW N815J N33CJ N123EL N24FN N28CK [fuselage noted at MTW Aerospace's facility near Montgomery, AL in Apr02; canx 07Apr05]
046		N964GA N55KC N55KQ N33PT N345MC [w/o 09Dec12, crashed in mountains near Monterrey, Mexico]
047		N222B (N68CK) [cx 16Sep14, CofR expired]
048		N965GA N200G XA-TCY N48GR
049		N966GA N900P N900Q HP-1141P N900Q N70HJ N70SK [w/o 21Jul07 St Augustine, FL]
050		N44EL N44EE D-CONE N27MJ N55FN N999MF
051		N973GA N70MP PT-LPT N12WW N76UM (N760A)
052		N232MD N8280 N828QA N250CC (N132MA) N133MA N692FC N692FG (N69LJ) [cx 29Oct13; wfu]

LEARJET 25

C/n	Series	Identities
053		N974GA N974M N37MB N37GB N153TW [w/o 24Aug01 Lansing, NY; cx Jan02]
054		OY-AKL N12373 N500JW N509G N25MD
055		N1500B N65RC N511AJ [parted out by White Inds, Bates City, MO]
056	XR	N780A PT-LBW
057		CF-TXT C-FTXT N920EA (N225EA) N507HF [parted out by White Inds, Bates City, MO; cx 29Apr09]
058		N2366Y N273LP N273LR [parted out by Alliance Air Parts, Oklahoma City, OK]
059		N425JX N211MB [w/o 03Mar80 Port au Prince, Haiti]
060		N695LJ N564CL
061	C	N251GL PT-DUO N9CN YV-203CP (YV2365) [wfu Fort Lauderdale Executive, FL]
062		OY-AKZ N4981 N105BJ N303JJ HZ-GP4 N86MJ N27FN N25ME N21FN [Instructional airframe, Hampton University, Norfolk News, NC, then scrapped]
063		N919S C-GPDZ N184J N680J N68PJ N5DM N24LT N25FM
064		N266GL [rebuilt to Model 28 standard to act as prototype; reverted to Model 25 standards] N566NA [wfu 1998; cx 07Apr03; preserved at John C.Stennis Space Center, MS; moved to Keystone Airpark, FL, by Feb16]
065		[airframe not built]
066		[airframe not built]
067		[airframe not built]
068		[airframe not built]
069		[airframe not built]
070	C	N255GL CF-ROX C-FROX N32SM C-FZHU N911LM [parted out Griffin, GA]
071	C	N257GL YV-T-DTT YV-130P YV-132CP N97AM LV-ZTH
072	C	N256GL PT-IBR [w/o 26Sep76 Sao Paulo, Brazil]
073	XR	HB-VCM I-TAKY N3JL N3JX HZ-SMB N63SB N85FJ N888DB N45CP [w/o 30Aug02 Lexington, KY – remains with Atlanta Air Salvage, Griffin, GA]
074	B	N251GL SX-ASO [w/o 18Feb72 Antibes, France]
075	B	N241AG N241AQ N417PJ N138JB VR-CGD VR-CHT VP-CHT VP-CJF N82025 N307HF [parted out by White Inds Bates City, MO; cx 29Apr09]
076	B	HB-VCL D-CCWK N160J N711CA N831WM N222MC N222MQ N77KW XA-SJS XB-LTD [abandoned at Roatan, Honduras, 16Jul15]
077	B	PT-DVL [w/o 12Nov76 Sao Paulo, Brazil]
078	B	N258GL N64MP N64MR N276LE N188BC N778JC N778GM N229GS
079	B	D-CCAT OE-GLA N50DH N36CC (N85HR) XA-SVG XA-AVV
080	B	N1976L N1978L (N90DH) N30AP XA-POG [wfu Toluca, Mexico]
081	B	N111GL N110GL HZ-MOA HZ-AZP HZ-BB1 N66TJ N524DW
082	B	HB-VCK N30P N427RD N15AK N11AK N654 N700FC N62DM N67SY
083	C	N31CS N200Y N200MH N54FN
084	C	N2000M (C-GWUZ) N200QM N200SF F-BYAL N777TX
085	B	N8MA N8MQ [b/u for spares – fuselage in compound near Lake City, FL]
086	B	N123DM N28BP N23DB N65WH [wfu Perris, CA, by Sep09 then moved to Quartzsite, AZ]
087	C	N723LF N777LF N99XZ N25TE [dbr 09Feb03 Bethel, AK; parted out by White Inds, Bates City, MO; cx 29Apr09]
088	B	N88GC N88GQ N123SF N176G N42FE N125JL N5UJ [w/o 22Nov01 Pittsburgh, PA]
089	C	PT-IIQ (N890K)
090	B	N265GL N112CT N112CH N112ME C-GBOT N754CA C-FPUB [to India as instructional airframe]
091	B	N500CA N500CD N500MJ D-CBPD N96MJ C-FDAC N2138T (N816JA) VR-CCH N91PN
092	B	N1ED N9671A N258G N18AK N113ES N60DK N80EL N92SH N84SH YV....
093	B	N33HM N33NM PT-LEN
094	C	SX-CBM VR-BFV N97J N77RS [w/o 14Dec78 Anchorage, AK; remains to White Inds, Bates City, MO, for spares]
095	B	N200BC N303SC N303SQ C-GRCO N2094L
096	B	N742E N742Z N48FN N405RS C-GCJD N235JW N20NW XB-KPR
097	C	HB-VCS (OY-ASK) I-SFER N22NJ (N220AR) N79EV N252LJ YV3198
098	C	N7JN VR-BEM N139J VR-BGF YV-26CP N96MJ N502MH ZS-NYG
099	C	PT-IKR PT-FAF PT-LHU [w/o 28Jly92 Icuape, Brazil]
100	B	N262JE N741E N741F "N59AC"+ [+marks worn at 1988 NBAA Convention, Dallas/Love Field, TX] N25TK N829AA [cx 04Apr13, to instructional airframe, Dublin Institute of Technology, Dublin, Ireland]
101	B	N268GL N575GD N269AS N30AP N156CB N600HT N600HD N74JL N821AW N47MR [to India as instructional airframe; cx 08Jul09]
102	B	N267GL N999M N999ML N311CC N52AJ N962 N52AJ N64WH N254SC N325SJ XA-...
103	B	N428JX [dbr Richmond, VA, 03Jul75; parted out by Brandis Av'n, Taylorville, IL]
104	B	N1JR N101JR N392T XA-JAX XA-RIN N128TJ N35WJ N104WJ
105	B	N1BR N1RA N711WE N713Q N234RB N905WJ N7AT N55PD XA-SXD N55PD LY-AJB N25WJ [cx 16Nov16; CofR expired]
106	XR	N10NP N10FL N974JD N458JA N458J [w/o 01Jly91 Columbus, OH; cx Aug91]
107	B	N225CC N57DM N25NP N25NB N252BK [parted out Houston/Hobby, TX]
108	C	PT-CMY [w/o 06Apr90 Juiz de Fora, Brazil]
109	B	N888DH N333HP C-GSAS N860MX [parted out by Dodson Av'n, Rantoul, KS]
110	B	N50GL N63ET N75CA N110HA N52SD N343RK LV-... N198MA N343RK
111	B	N30TP N55ES PT-LXS N825A N45BS N25PJ
112	B	OY-BFC N173J N279LE N157G
113	C	PT-ISN [w/o 04Nov89 Belo Horizonte-Pampulha, Brazil]
114	B	N47HC (C-GLRE) N45HB N77PK N25JD N114HC XA-VMC [w/o 17.5.17, Toluca, Mexico]
115	C	PT-ISO
116	C	CF-CXY N600PC N819GY (N818GY) N666TW [w/o 19Sep03 Del Rio TX, cx Nov03]
117	B	N40AS N170GT N170RL N4402 N4405 C-FMGM N731CW N7810W [parted out by White Inds, Bates City, MO]
118	B	OO-LFZ (D-CITO) N601J N118SE (N800JA) N124MA (N79AX) VP-CMB N118MB N818CK

LEARJET 25

C/n	Series	Identities
119	B	N3810G PT-JBQ [w/o 04Sep82 Rio Branco, Brazil]
120	B	N111AF N744MC N278LE N10BD N10BU VH-OVS (N100FU) N101FU N120SL XA-AJL
121	B	N7GA HZ-MRP N39JJ N500PP N1036N [may have been XA-SAL] XA-SIO N8005Y (N821MS) [to India as instructional airframe; cx 12Nov09]
122	B	N23TA N332LS N122BS N122WC N751CA C-FSYO N751CA XB-KVX XB-LCI XB-LXL XB-MEH XB-MKO
123	B	N360AA N973JD (N914RA) N906SU N688GS
124	B	N44MJ N39JE N59BP N15CC N15CU N54H N54HU (N400DB) (N95TW) N33TW XA-ALV [to museum at Cajititlan, Mexico, Sep08]
125	B	N4MR N9AT (N85AT) N89AT N94AT N97AC (N11MC) N10VG N1VG N10VG
126	C	N12WK N114CC (N162AC) N14FN YV2465
127	B	N93C N93CE N83JM (N42BJ) N450 N450SC N222AK N425JL N225LC [cx 19May15; CofR expired]
128	B	N67PC N1MX N40BC [w/o 06Jly79 Pueblo, CO; parted out by White Inds, Bates City, MO]
129	C	N551WC N71DM (N193DR) N25MR N25MT
130	B	N111BL N25PL N26AT [instructional airframe Del Mar College, TX]
131	C	N3803G PT-JDX [w/o 26Dec78 Sao Paulo-Congonhas, Brazil; front of fuselage in use at Belo Horizonte-Pampulha, Brazil as a link trainer]
132	B	N202BT N132GL N54MC N54MQ N715JF N715MH [w/o 26Oct01 Ciudad Victoria, Mexico; cx Oct02; parted out by Dodson Av'n, Rantoul, KS]
133	B	N10RE N10RZ N51MJ N58CP XA-RZY N233CA [cx Dec10; to India as instructional airframe]
134	B	N52GL N15BH N712JA N26FN N65A [wfu; cx 06Jun11]
135	B	G-BBEE N3803G N1103R G-BBEE N7600K (N1RW) N50RW [cx 19Dec15; CofR expired]
136	B	N920CC N920US N180YA N221TC N71CE (N48WA) N753CA N48WA
137	B	N400 N37BJ N500WW N752CA N752EA
138	B	N11BU N100EP N36204 N777PD N711PD N811PD (N2HE) N73LJ N911RF [parted out by Atlanta Air Salvage, Griffin, GA]
139	XR	N618R N225AC N12MH (N14PT) N605NE N111MP [cx 10Dec14, CofR expired]
140	B	N42G N42GX N68TJ N401AC N403AC N140CA [cx Jun10; to India as instructional airframe]
141	XR	N52L N424JR N424JP N94RS N25HA ZS-BXR
142	B	N515WH N42HC (N142HC) N70CE (N70WA) N49WA
143	B	N96VF (N33VF) N111RF N113RF N143CK
144	B	N10NT N44PA [w/o 23Dec91 Carlsbad, CA; b/u Jun92]
145	B	N131GL C-GRDR N2127E N145SH LV-CFW
146	C	N146LJ N9HM N9HN C-GRQX N9HN N6KJ I-BMFE
147	B	N55KC N25KC N150WW N911JG N147BP XA-GGG
148	XR	N58GL N336WR N98RS (N98JA) YV2786
149	B	HB-VDI EC-CIM N149J N239CA [cx Jun09; instructional airframe Singapore/Seletar]
150	B	N714K N714KP N888RB (N25LP) N251JA N150CK
151	B	N366AA [w/o 31Aug74 Briggsdale, CO]
152	XR	N50L N515SC N452ET XA-POI XA-JSC N105BA N165AA
153	B	N501PS [w/o 26May77 Detroit, MI; parted out by Dodson Av'n, Ottawa, KS]
154	B	N100K N30DK N47DK N82TS N210NC N82TS [wfu Pontiac, MI]
155	B	N24TA PT-LEA
156	C	PT-KAP N613SZ N75BL N725JS
157	B	N2427F N157CA N57CK N50CK
158	B	N158GL HZ-GP3 N85MJ N334LS N71RB N924BW
159	B	Peru FAP 522/OB-1429 N24RZ [w/o 20Feb04 Fort Lauderdale Executive, FL; cx 03Feb05; parted out by Dodson Intl Parts, Rantoul, KS]
160	B	ZS-MTD VP-WKY Z-WKY ZS-MTD 3D-AEZ ZS-MTD
161	B	N4VC N61EW N236CA [cx Dec10; to India as instructional airframe]
162	XR	N62ZS N661MP N663JB N97RS N97JJ N150RS YV525T
163	B	SE-DFC N70606 N173LP N173LR C-FBEA N333AW N59SG N25RE (N65RC) N911AJ
164	B	Peru FAP 523/OB-1430 N23RZ
165	C	PT-KBC [w/o 04Jun96 Ribeirao Preto, Brazil; cx Aug97]
166	B	PT-KBD N918TD N166PC
167	B	C-GBFP
168	B	N72TP N88BT N88BY [wfu Pontiac, MI]
169	B	N471MM N743E N743F N893WA N59FL XA-KKK
170	B	N131G N711DS N170EV (N170EP) N98796 N627WS [w/o 13Jan98 Houston Intercontinental, TX; cx Oct98]
171	B	I-ELEN N1DD OY-ASP N1DD N55MF N55PT N42DG N888LR N401AJ N171WW [cx 22Mar13; to instructional airframe, Estonian Aviation Academy, Tartu, Estonia]
172	C	PT-KKV [w/o 11Jan91 nr Belo Horizonte, Brazil]
173	XR	N780AC N780AQ N777NJ N104BW XA-JSC
174	B	N74G N410SP N412SP N16KK
175	XR	N462B N462BA N96RS (N96JJ) N307AJ N75SJ N127GB
176	C	N55VL N50PE N25KV N28KV PT-LLN
177	B	N11PH N745W D-CDPD [w/o 18May83 in Atlantic approx 320 km S of Reykjavik, Iceland]
178	B	N75B N999M N999MV N999HG [w/o 08Sep77 Sanford, NC]
179	B	N659HX C-GBQC C-GSKL [parted out by White Inds, Bates City, MO; cx 02Jun08]
180	B	VH-BLJ N95BS C-FEWB N95BS VH-LJB N266BS N102VS
181	C	VH-TNN N94PK N73TW N73TA N100NB [wfu Newton, KS]
182	B	C-GLBT N4300L F-GFMZ N225JL N99MC [cx 07Apr17, CofR expired]
183	B	N66JD N5LL N83CK [cx 29Oct14, CofR expired]
184	B	EC-CKR [w/o 13Aug96 RAF Northolt, UK; to spares by White Inds, Bates City, MO 1998]

LEARJET 25

C/n	Series	Identities
185	B	N666LP N55V N988DB N988AA N988AC N606SM
186	B	YU-BJH [w/o 18Jan77 Sarajevo, Yugoslavia]
187	B	YU-BJG N187CA
188	B	G-BCSE A40-AJ N1JR [w/o 28Jly84 Waterville, ME and used for spares; remains to White Inds, Bates City, MO]
189	B	N111SF N111SZ N352SC N888DF N67HB [to Museum of Aeronautical Sciences, Tokyo/Narita, Japan 2008]
190	B	XA-DAK N190AR XA-...
191	B	N1DD N78BT N38DJ [w/o 12Jun92 Sheboygan, WI; cx Dec94; remains to Hampton/Tara Field, Atlanta, GA]
192	B	Bolivia FAB-008 Bolivia FAB-010
193	B	HB-VEF I-KISS HB-VIE I-SIMD N80GR N350DH N125RM N125TN XA-WWW
194	B	XA-COC XB-EGP XA-SXG XC-NSP XB-KYK XB-MSW
195	B	OB-M-1004 N108PA [b/u for spares 1984; cx 05May06]
196	B	N711WD N25TA [w/o 11Apr80 New Mexico]
197	B	N104GL N240AG N197WC N197CF (N96DM)
198	B	N20DK N29TS N198JA
199	XR	HB-VEI HZ-RI1 HZ-GP5 [w/o 11Jan82 Narssarssuaq, Greenland]
200	B	N2022R N680BC N350JH [parted out by White Inds, Bates City, MO]
201	B	N227RW N777SA N111AD N11TK N713B N43TS N59BL N251TS
202	B	N3807G Yugoslavia 10401 Yugoslavia 70401 YU-BRA N343CA [wfu; to Aviation Warehouse, El Mirage, CA]
203	B	N3811G Yugoslavia 10402 Yugoslavia 70402 YU-BRB N344CA N927FW (N212GW)
204	B	N376SC N373SC N472J PT-KZY [w/o 16May82 Uberaba, Brazil]
205	B	N1468B YU-BKJ Z3-BAA
206	D	N206EC N206EQ ZS-LXH
207	D	N3513F (I-GIAN) I-LEAR (N3513F) N207JC [parted out by White Industries, Bates City, MO circa 99]
208	D	N54YR N54YP C-GZIM "N500PP" N54YP N500PP N500MP N300SC N188CA
209	D	N36SC N770AC (N770PA) N770AQ N18NM N30LJ [wfu Curacao]
210	D	N133MR XA-JIN XA-RPV N97FT N75TJ N764RH XA-ULS
211	D	N3514F Bolivia FAB-010
212	D	N1450B N911MG N212NE [b/u for spares during 1989]
213	D	N551DP HZ-SS2 VR-CDH N803PF N925DW N910JB XA-CST
214	D	N30W N3UW N90BR I-AVJD N61826 N214ME N214LJ N245BS N70TF N56MD N555VH
215	D	N44FE N325JL N25UJ [cx 9Dec14, CofR expired]
216	D	N3556F N2426 (N345FJ) N80RE N80RP (N87MW) XA-PRO N216SA N767SA N68AX N724TN XA-... N724TN N77FN XA-...
217	D	N41H N217WM YV436T
218	D	N18MJ N155AU XA-RAX N14NA N251DS [parted out by Dodson Av'n, Rantoul, KS]
219	XR	N55SL XA-CCC XA-MCC
220	XR	N220HS (N419BL) (N25WL) N220NJ N99NJ N969AR
221	D	N3819G YU-BKR N147CA XA-UKH
222	XR	N1476B N726GL N4MR XA-KEY XA-MHA N4MR N225TJ N134WE XA-UNC [w/o 01Apr10 Huatulco, Mexico]
223	D	N23AM XC-DAD XA-BBA [w/o 18Jun94 Washington-Dulles A/P, VA]
224	D	N50B (N32TJ) N711NM N80AX XB-MGM XB-OZA XB-AZD XB-DDG
225	D	9J-AED N222AP N808DS N140GC [parted out by Dodson Av'n, Rantoul, KS]
226	D	N333SG N234SV N90LJ
227	D	N44BB N444PB N882SB XA-ROO (N25RE) N227EW N25RE [cx 23Jun15; CofR expired]
228	D	N228SW [parted out by Dodson International Parts Inc, Rantoul, KS]
229	D	N39415 LV-MBP CX-ECO N229WJ N890BJ
230	D	N16GT N16LJ N161AC N7RL N207HF [parted out by White Inds, Bates City, MO; cx 29Apr09]
231	D	(OO-LFW) (OO-HFW) N999M N999ME N60DK N31MJ N225HW N531CW [cx 30Sep14; to Centro Ensenanza Tecnica Aeronautica de Canaria, Tenerife, as instructional airframe]
232	D	N744LC N500EW N500LW N264TW
233	D	N55LJ N75LM N947TC
234	D	N3815G (N27GW) N234KK (N234EJ) (N28CC) XA-ESQ N234KK (N11SQ) N300JE N39BL N88DJ (N432AS) N18BL N764KF YV2681
235	XR	N400PC N400JS N400VC (N25XR) N221LV YV2675
236	D	N1466B XC-RPP
237	D	(N28BP) N137GL (N55MF) [w/o 19Jan79 Detroit, MI]
238	D	N39416 N40SW N45ZP N238MP N500TL N300TL N41NK
239	D	N192MH N45H N499EH N499BS
240	D	N78GL N83EA N33PT (N339BA)
241	D	N432SL N25TA N25TB N711WD N712BW N713RR N713LJ N213CA [cx Nov10; to India as instructional airframe]
242	D	N749GL N363HA N102RA N242GM (N242AF) N242GS YV3288
243	D	N711JT PT-LSD [w/o 02Mar96 Serra de Cantareira, near Sao Paulo, Brazil]
244	D	N7LA XA-LET N24EP N831LH N125PT [w/o 12Aug07 Farmingdale, NY; parted out by MTW Aerospace, Montgomery, AL]
245	D	N39398 LV-PAF LV-MST N245DK N60DK N606GB (N531GC)
246	XR	N40162 N51DB [w/o 21Oct86 nr Jeddah, Saudi Arabia]
247	D	N300PL [cx 05Sep12; parted out]
248	D	N80BT N80BE N500PP N900WA N95CK (N248LJ) N248CK
249	D	N20PY N249SC N211JB (N500EF) N249LJ XA-FMU N800L XA-FMU N34TN
250	D	N30LM N438DM (N60DK) N112JM N19JM N127BH [cx 27Aug12; wfu]
251	D	N752GL N78SD N290 N25FA TG-VOC N85TW
252	D	N1468B N44FH N444MK [wfu Addison, TX; cx 10May11]

LEARJET 25

C/n	Series	Identities
253	D	N253EJ N97DK (N202DR) N253J N253M N253SC N8MF N321AU YV-1049CP YV129T N69PL YV1346
254	D	N973 I-AVJE N76AX
255	D	N1433B N1ED N91ED N91MT N25GJ N717EP N219RB N219RR
256	D	N6LL N75CK
257	D	N700BJ N377C N377Q N988AS [cx 30Apr15; CofR expired]
258	D	N144FC (N54888) N54TA N888GC N333CD N258MD PT-LLL [w/o 18Mar91 Brasilia, Brazil]
259	D	LV-PAW LV-MMV [w/o 23Sep89 in Marana River, nr Posadas, Argentina – fuselage and detached wingset noted at Moron AFB Apr04, still present Oct16]
260	D	N39413 (D-CHBM) D-CHEF N43783 N74RD N80PJ N314AJ
261	D	N3802G N180MC N24JK N261WC
262	D	N23HM N440F N333CG [w/o 12Jun01 Salina A/P, KS; parted out]
263	D	N40162 N14VC N20DL N825D XA-YYY
264	D	N716NC N133JF N502JC N547JG XA-SRR [Mexican marks awaiting confirmation]
265	D	N1462B N265EJ N279TG N265LJ N31WT (N61WT) N69GF N265TW [w/o nr Nuevo Michoacan, Mexico, 19Dec14]
266	D	N3807G PT-KYR [reported w/o circa Aug89; no further details; cx during 1990]
267	D	N15ER (N400VC)
268	D	N268WC XA-SPL N268WC XA-... N268WC [wfu Pachuca, Mexico; cx 10Dec14]
269	D	N109SJ N269MD N51BL LV-PLL LV-WOC
270	D	N842GL (N123CG) N842GL N123CG (N45KB) N75AX XB-LPD N842GL N25XA
271	D	N183AP N125NE [w/o 21May80 Gulf of Mexico; cx Nov82]
272	D	N272EJ N272JM N747AN N717AN N520SR N25CY
273	D	N321AS N73DJ XA-...
274	D	N600CD D-CEPD N3131G N602NC N602N N110FP N274LJ XA-MAL XA-RZE XA-FMR
275	D	N211CD N254CL N154CL [instructional airframe Lane Community College, OR]
276	D	N188TC N188TQ N188TA XA-UUU [wfu Monterrey del Norte, Mexico]
277	D	N20MJ N34CW N283U N321GL N81MW N9RA (XA-...) N277RG XA-MME
278	D	N70JF [parted out by White Inds, Bates City, MO; cx 29Apr09]
279	D	N41ZP N81AX [wfu; cx 29Sep15]
280	D	N280LA N18TA N18RA N225AC N95EC (N510L) N280C N901PM N405SD (XA-...) N405FM
281	D	(N245KK) N45KK N45KB N555PG N800RF
282	D	N711WD XA-SKA XA-CAO
283	D	N40144 XC-DAA N45826 N312GK N444WW
284	D	XC-CFM N284TJ
285	D	N6666R (N28RW) N6666K N666KK N422G I-COTO [w/o Feb86 Paris-Le Bourget, France]
286	D	N28MJ XA-ROZ N6596R XA-RVI XC-AA83+ XA-TAQ N850MX N9QM [cx 01Mar07, wfu][+ marks not confirmed]
287	D	N39416 RP-C4121 N63KH N287MF XA-ZYZ N20AD XA-ZZZ [parted out by White Inds, Bates City, MO, circa 2001]
288	D	N31WT N61WT N40BC N100WN (N40BC) [instructional airframe Columbus/Bolton, OH]
289	D	N1087T RP-C6610 RP-C400 N389GA N321GL N321GE XA-TWH
290	D	N221AP XA-ELR N221EL N321RB N600GM
291	D	N1088D N666RB N952 N600JT N530DC (N477MM) N453MA XB-MCW
292	D	N1088C N92MJ N92CS N711VT N711VK N604AS
293	D	N999TH N97JP XA-PIU
294	D	N27K N419GL N125TJ N161RB N88NJ N881J [parted out by Dodson Av'n, Rantoul, KS; cx 20Apr06]
295	D	N229AP N137K ZS-LUD OE-GHL N295DJ (N298GS) N45ES XC-AGR N25HF XB-MYG
296	D	N712RW N712SJ N55DD N55MJ PT-OHD [destroyed by Venezuelan armed forces 10Apr14 on suspicion of drug-running]?
297	D	N297EJ N36NW N297EJ N24KW N389AT
298	D	N923GL N711TG N711TQ (N712CB) XA-ABH N298DR N242PF YV448T
299	D	N222LW I-KIOV (N8217W) N299MW (N5B) N117SH [wfu; cx 07Jul15]
300	D	(N46BA) N659HX N108FL
301	D	N416RM N610LM (N888JA) N25CZ N82AX N301MT HI980
302	D	N521JP N28BP N740K N700DA N702DA N25CY N881P YV592T YV3116
303	D	XA-JOC XA-UTV
304	D	N25NY
305	D	N88JA N53TC N188R XA-AAS XA-TAK XA-TAQ XA-MET
306	D	XA-DUB XC-GUB
307	D	LV-PEU LV-OEL [preserved Museo Nacional de Aeronautica, Moron AFB, Argentina]
308	D	N23AM XA-RMF N2721U XB-GDR XA-SXY N102RR N727LM
309	D	XA-GRB XB-DKS XA-DAZ XA-PAZ XB-KWN
310	D	N1088C N211PD N211JC (N211JE) YV2611 YV2699
311	D	N39391 N199BT ZS-NJF N199BT N502JV
312	D	N94MJ XC-HIS
313	D	N31MJ N31GS N37RR N727AW N727CS N631CW N727CS N251AL
314	D	N1466B I-DEAN HB-VHM N38328 N30AD N40AD XA-LUZ XA-REE N42825 N95BP N305AR
315	D	N10873 N3798A N83TC N273KH N273M XA-TSL N315FW XA-ASP XA-MMI
316	D	N3793X N1AH (N782JR) N17AH [fitted with Williams-Rolls FJ44 engines ff 09Jan03 at Guthrie, OK]
317	D	N821LM N660TC N969SS (N96DC) N317TS N317VS N25CY N35DL XB-OAC
318	D	N522JP N522TA N999BH [w/o 05Sep93 Rowe Mera, 30m from Santa Fe Municipal A/P, NM; cx May94]
319	D	N319EJ N911EM N680JC N712DP [instructional airframe at Savo Vocational College, Finland; cx 23Nov09]

LEARJET 25

C/n	Series	Identities									
320	D	N320EJ	OO-LFR	N690JC							
321	D	N25AM	YV....								
322	D	5N-AOC	N19GE								
323	D	N323EJ	N70SE	N6YY	PT-LMM						
324	D	N711BF	XA-POP	N970WJ	[cx 24Mar17; CofR expired]						
325	D	N123NC	N523SA	N1411S	XA-RXB	N1411S	N2U	XA-TBV	N325JB	XB-HGE	XB-GCP
326	D	N771CB	N25NB								
327	D	N54GP	N52DA	(N54JC)	(N327BC)	N444TG					
328	D	N7LC	(N12FS)	OB-R-1313	OB-1313	N58DJ	N200NR	N725DM	N328JW	N518JG	XB-JLU
		XB-MBW									
329	D	N3799B	XC-GNL	XA-GNL	N613GL	N83TE	N401DP				
330	D	(N523JP)	N521JP	XA-RZT	XA-RCG	XC-AA84	N330LJ	N330L			
331	D	N462B	N422B	N462B	N482CP	N657BM					
332	D	XC-FIF	XB-DZQ	XA-AFH	[cx; status?]						
333	D	N34MJ	N555SD	[cx 8Jul14, CofR expired]							
334	D	N20RD	N57DL	N334MD	XA-RYH	N23W	XB-JKK	XA-ULG			
335	D	N27KG	PT-LUZ								
336	D	XA-LAP	N6354N	XA-VYA	XA-JYL						
337	G	N3810G	N937GL	N337GL	LV-P...	LV-WBP	N14CK	XA-UKK			
338	D	XA-LOF	N4447P	[wfu Fort Pierce/St Lucie, FL]							
339	D	N3798D	HK-2624X	HK-2624P	N21HR	Mexico MTX-03		Mexico AMT-202			
340	D	N980A	N625AU	N891P							
341	D	N341FW	N101DL	XA-TAM	(N.....)	XA-SAE	N58HC				
342	D	N820M	N984JD	(N187DY)	I-RJVA	N707CA	XA-RXQ	N342AA	N342GG	N25PW	
343	D	N3797L	N456CG	(N458CG)							
344	D	N3798L	N37943	5N-ASQ	[w/o 22Jly83 Lagos, Nigeria]						
345	D	N345EJ	N345KB	N711SC	LV-PHU	LV-WLG					
346	D	N39412	N3798V	N300WG	N41TC	N72AX	XA-ZZZ	N181PA	YV....		
347	D	N39415	N347EJ	D-CHIC	N25NM	N347MD	N347AC	N202JW	N347AC	(N347JW)	N347JV
		N203VS									
348	D	N37949	N440DM	N522GS	N522JS	N988AA					
349	D	N40146	N349EJ	N20GT	XA-NOG	[w/o 02Sep93 Tijuana, Mexico]					
350	D	N350AG	(N428CH)	N648JW	LV-BZC						
351	D	N878ME	XA-POQ	N837CS	N302PC	N402DP	N425RH	N425RA	N21NW		
352	D	N3794P	RP-C1261	N7035C	XA-MMO	(N352XR)	N25FN	N125JW			
353	D	N353EJ	N800DR	(N50MT)	XA-RKP	XA-RLI	N510TP	N71AX	N43DR		
354	D	N3795U	N515TC	N304VS							
355	D	(N830WM)	N202WM	N7801L	N713DJ	XA-SNO	XA-EAS	N355AM	LV-WRE		
356	D	N78DT	N100NR	N108NR	N25PT	N251MD	N62DK	YV544T			
357	D	N40149	N3797U	N148JW	N812MM	XA-ROC	N250LB	N27KG	LV-WXY		
358	D	N1461B	N37971								
359	D	N6307H	N37973	N359SK	N666RE	N666PE	N116JR	XA-LRJ	XB-MXZ		
360	D	N6340T	N8563B	N618R	N618P	N360JG	XA-...				
361	D	N4291K	N218NB	N218NR	N804PH	N804RH	XA-TYW				
362	D	N39398	N25GL	N52CT	N717CW	(N107MS)	N107RM				
363	D	N39416	N85654	N91MT	N2PW	XA-RSU	N197LS	YV1738			
364	D	N10873	N8565Y	N25TZ	XA-TIE	XB-LYG	N25TZ	YV....			
365	D	N1473B	N7260C	N218R	N365CM	XA-SJN	XB-KDQ				
366	D	N1088D	N7261B	(ZS-LRI)	XA-SWX	N366LJ	ZS-CAT	N366LJ	XB-IFW	XA-SOH	
367	D	N7262A	N51DT	VT-SWP	N4488W	N25HF	XA-...				
368	D	N1088A	N8567J	XA-PIM	N8567J	N368D	YV3191				
369	D	N10872	N8566Z	N369MJ	N2213T	N369D	XB-JJS				
370	D	N39399	N72600	N610JR	N610JB	N220TG	N223TG	C-GSWS	XA-SJO	N370LJ	N252HS
		N972H	N888DV	[parted out by Dodson Av'n, Rantoul, KS]							
371	D	N1468B	N72603	N125DB	N44SK	N1WT	N1U	(N102U)	N4ZB	N72WC	N188PR
		LV-FDB*									
372	D	N40149	N72606	N5NC	N722EM	N418KS	YV2873				
373	D	N3819G	N29EW	EC-EGY	XA-ACX	XA-RCH	XB-OGU				

Production complete

LEARJET MODEL 28

C/n	Identities								
28-001	N9RS	N9KH	N128MA	N3AS	N128LR				
28-002	N39404	N511DB	XC-VSA						
28-003	N157CB	N42ZP	N555JK	N44QG	N14QG	N28LR	N25GW	N800GA	
28-004	N39394	N125NE	HB-VGB	XA-KAJ	N225MS	XA-KAJ	N28AY	N43PJ	N769CA
28-005	(N31WT)	N8LL	N500LG						

Production complete

LEARJET MODEL 29

C/n	Identities					
29-001	N929GL	HB-VFY	N929GL	XC-IST		
29-002	N723LL	N920GL	XC-DFS	XC-HIE/PF-201		XB-JHV
29-003	N289CA	VT-EHS	India K-2995		[wfu]	
29-004	N39412	N294CA	VT-EIH	India K-2996		[wfu]

Production complete

LEARJET MODEL 31

C/n	Series	Identities									
001		N311DF	N984JD	[w/o 23Feb90 Taiyuan, China; cx Mar90; to spares by Dodson Avn, Ottawa, KS]							
002		N7262Y	PT-LVO	N102NW	N350DS	N322TS	N386MM				
003		N10873	N31CG	N331CC	N888CP						
004		N1088D	XA-ZTH	N314SC	LV-CNQ						
005		N39415	XA-GMD	XA-RFS	N942BY	(N963Y)	N431BC	PR-AVM	(PR-OXY)	N77779	
006		N6331V	N26LC	C-GKMS	N103TD						
007		N3819G	PT-LXX								
008		N71JC	[w/o 02Sep97 Aberdeen, MS; to Atlanta Air Salvage, GA Nov97 for spares]								
009		OO-JBA	N173PS	N727CP	N38MG						
010		N31LJ	N446	PT-LLK	N311TS	N89HB	PP-LFV				
011		N3803G	HB-VJI	D-CTWO	M-LEAR	D-CFST	[cx; wfu]				
012		N917MC	XA-RUU	XA-TUL	XA-LMS	(N510TL)					
013		PT-LVR	N213PA	PT-XTA							
014		N1468B	N5VG	PT-OFJ	N5VG						
015		N111TT	N260LF								
016		N4291K	N666RE	N92LJ	N1DE						
017		N4289U	N17VG	PT-OFK	[crashed 26Feb93 Rio de Janeiro-Santos Dumont, Brazil; rebuilt with new wingset]						
		N17VG	N600AW	N801CT	PR-LRR						
018		N40144	HB-VIM	N19TJ	(N20LL)	N90BA					
019		(N19LT)	PT-OFL	N19LT	N818LJ	(N631LA)					
020		N42905	N31LJ	N337FP	XA-UJQ						
021		N3802G	XA-RNK	XA-CYA	N31YA						
022		N331N									
023		N111VV	PR-SFA								
024		N30LJ	LV-PFK	LV-RBV	N90PB	N92EC	N912TB	XA-MRS	N731GA		
025		N39399	I-AIRW	N50AN	[stored Milan/Linate still wearing I-AIRW]						
026		N91164	XA-HRM	XA-HGF	XA-DIN	N39TJ	N45HG	N706SA	(N184RM)	N103JL	
027		N91201	N30LJ	N2FU							
028		N90WA									
029		N9173L	(XB-ZRB)	XB-FKT							
030		N525AC	N255DV	N255DY	XA-JYC	[impounded at Houston/Hobby, TX, Apr11]					
031		N5000E	N9132Z	N31HA	ZS-OFW	N878MA	ZS-OFW	N878MA	N93SK	N111YA	N264HA
032		N5010U	XA-AAP	XA-BRG	XB-KDK						
033		N5012H	9V-ATA	N603LJ	N632PB	(N638PB)	N407BS				
033A		N2603S	9V-ATC	N311LJ	N156JS	N990GC					
033B		N2600S	9V-ATD	[w/o 21Jly97 30m S of Ranong, Thailand]							
033C		N5013L	9V-ATE	N310LJ	N158JS	N555VR	N55VR	VH-OVX			
033D		N5023D	9V-ATF	N312LJ	N157JS	N539BA	(N777YL)				
034		N5015U	9V-ATB	N604LJ	N45PK	N394SA	CS-DDZ				
035	A	N50111	N618R	N618RF	N3VJ						
036	A	N31LJ	N88MM	D-CVGP	N316LJ	N127V	N127VL	(N127V)			
037	A	N31TF	PT-OVZ								
038	A	N5016V	N4	N131NA	N500WR	N2RW	N338CW				
039	A	N90LJ	N10ST	N16ST	N22AX	N23AX	N71AL				
040	A	VR-CHJ	N9HJ	VR-CHJ	VR-CGS	N340LJ	N314MK	N55VY	N613SZ	N2SM	
041	A	N131TA	N9CH	N319CH	RP-C8822						
042	A	D-CGGG	D-CURT								
043	A	N5009V	C-GLRJ	N43LJ	N531SK						
044	A	N50163	XA-MJG	XA-HRM	XA-OLE						
045	A	N50159	N67SB	YU-BRZ							
046	A	D-CCKV	N131PT	N352EF							
047	A	N31UK	N39TW	LV-CNF							
048	A	N43SF	N43SE	N314XS	N864KB	N864KV					
049	A	D-CDEN	D-CADC	N107GM	N131TT	N61VW					
050	A	N92UG	N38SK	(N166AA)	N548LM						
051	A	N9152R	N1905H	N351AC							
052	A	N50LJ	N301AS	N75MC	N899CS	XA-TGM					
053	A	N9173Q	N44QG	(N44ZG)	N31FF	(N555JS)	N163AL				
054	A	N2603G	N92FD	N82KK	N82KL	N54TN	LV-BFG				
055	A	N9143F	N666RE	N425M							
056	A	N25685	N303WB	N56LF	XA-UUQ						
057	A	N9147Q	D-CSAP	D-CJPD							
058	A	N5017J	N26018	N770CC	"ZS-OJO"	(N258SC)	N590MH	N298CH	N825AC	LV-BRC	
059	A	N25999	(N31LJ)	N31TK	(N67MP)						
060	A	N2600Z	N156SC	N156EC	N696PA	N699CP	N52SY				
061	A	N51057	(N740E)	N9152X	N740E	N740F	N261SC	XA-RCF			
062	A	N25997	AP-BEK								
063	A	(N27)	N2	N995AW	N707NV	(N31AX)	N131LJ	N510AB			
064	A	N142GT	N444HC								
065	A	N50153	N26005	N44SF	N44SU	N64NB					
066	A	N5009V	N26006	PK-CAH							
067	A	N9173M	TG-AIR	TG-MYS							
068	A	N2603X	N743E	N743F	N500CG	(N500CQ)	N500EW	C-GWXK	N680AF	N131GR	
069	A	N9173V	N744E	N744N	(N169SC)						
070	A	N2602Y	N741E	N741F	(N270SC)	N370SC	XA-CTL				

LEARJET 31

C/n	Series	Identities									
071	A	N9173N	N742E	N742F	N271SC	XA-MCA					
072	A	N31LJ	N45UF	(N14WT)	N211RN						
073	A	N46UF	XA-ZYZ								
074	A	N999AU	(VP-B..)	N999AU	N128GB	N174TS	N131BR				
075	A	N418R	N418RT	N631SF	N636SF	N636SE					
076	A	N40339	XA-SPR	XA-PIC	N518SA	N215TT	N456JN				
077	A	N26002	PK-CAJ								
078	A	N40280	N31LJ	XA-SNM	N112CM	N539LB	XA-RDL	XC-LNF	XA-RDL		
079	A	N40349	N41DP	N91DP							
080	A	N2601K	N80LJ	N986MA							
081	A	N31LJ	N81LJ	N83WM	N83WN	LV-YMB					
082	A	N5014F	N4022X	PT-MVI	N727BT	XA-CCC					
083	A	N5012Z	N40363	N789SR							
084	A	N4034H	N196HA	N840SW							
085	A	N5013Y	N4005G	XA-PEN	N531AT	N321GL	N480ME				
086	A	N2603Q	N867JS	N105FX	OY-LJB	N166BA	N969	N1BR	N11BR	XB-ORM	N11BR
087	A	N9173T	N868JS	N106FX	OY-LJC	N167BA	N535PS				
088	A	N50088	N31LJ	N500JE	N508J	N500JE					
089	A	N5009L	N77PH	N77PY							
090	A	N9173X	N78PH	N78PR	N557PK	N557BK					
091	A	N5019Y	V5-NAG								
092	A	N50302	N711FG								
093	A	N4031K	(N917BD)	N916BD	N716BD						
094	A	N4027K	N31AX	(N916BD)	N917BD	N817BD	N36BL				
095	A	N50459	N163JD	OK-AJD	N395LJ						
096	A	N5009V	N4006G	N30LX	N30TK	(N31TK)	N37BM				
097	A	N50207	N31LJ								
098	A	N5012H	N50378	N148C	N721MJ	(N521MJ)	N797KB	N200KB			
099	A	N5049J	N1932P	N1932K							
100	A	N5001X	N31LR	PT-MCB	N31LK	PR-SCB	N342JP				
101	A	N5010J	N293SA	N900R	N79BJ	XA-MGM	ZS-LJC	V5-TUC			
102	A	N5002D	N107FX	N731RA	C-GWXP	N681AF	C-GHJJ	N102WG	N25BB		
103	A	N5003F	(N31AZ)	PT-TOF	N766AJ	N407RA	PT-BBB	N213BR	LV-FKB		
104	A	N4010N	N108FX	OY-LJI	N104BX	N631CC					
105	A	N51054	N5005K	N109FX	N109HV	N109FX	N109HV	PR-PLM			
106	A	N29RE	N531RA	N581RA	N531TS	N784AM					
107	A	N5012H	N31HY	C-GHCY	N107TS	N107LP	N213AR	N942RC			
108	A	N110FX	(N110BX)	(N288BF)	N288FF						
109	A	N5029F	N261PC	N261PQ	N722JS	N882JD	N728CL				
110	A	N40130	PT-WIV								
111	A	N50114	C-GRVJ	N113AF	N111AF	N420LJ	LV-BTF				
112	A	N5082S	LX-PCT	N359RA	(PT-PPP)	(N190MM)					
113	A	N31LJ	N331SJ	(N642GG)	N131GG						
114	A	N524HC									
115	A	(N5005M)	N112FX	N31NR	ZS-NYV	(PP-NYV)	PR-NYV				
116	A	N113FX	N112FX	N112HV	N31UJ	LV-CLK					
117	A	N317LJ	N517CC								
118	A	N318LJ	N815A	N815E	PP-JNY						
119	A	N114FX	N114HY	N996JS							
120	A	N5020Y	I-TYKE	N200TJ	C-GHJU						
121	A	N121LJ									
122	A	(N112FX)	N122LJ	PT-WLO							
123	A	N323LJ	N48AM	N23NP	N23VG	N85KH	HK-4891				
124	A	N124LJ	N931FD	N931ED							
125	A	N125LJ	N527JG	N125FS							
126	A	N8066P	N22SF	N22UF	N18BL	N100BL	N239CA				
127	A	N80727	HB-VLR	N54HT							
128	A	N8082J	N400	(N469)	N365GL						
129	A	N8079Q	N115FX	N115BX	N645HA						
130	A	N5013N	N31PV	TG-SHV							
131	A	N80631	N31LR	N319SC	PR-WMA						
132	A	N116FX	N116BX	N929JH							
133	A	N8073Y	N117FX	OY-LJL	N331ZX	N314SG	(N820AT)				
134	A	N5014E	N118FX	N118BX	N977AR	N134LJ	N164AL				
135	A	N80645	PT-WSB								
136	A	N119FX	N119BX	N119FX	N131DA	N47TR	N509AB				
137	A	N120FX	N120RV	N459A	N165AL						
138	A	N138LJ	V5-NPC								
139	A	N139LJ	N131AR	N229KD	N29KD	XA-...					
140	A	N140LJ	N96LF	VP-BML	N314AC	N45HG	N95HG	N977JP			
141	A	N121FX	(N121HV)	N121PX	XA-ARQ						
142	A	N142LJ	ZS-EAG	N698MM	N382AL	N372JL					
143	A	N122FX	N122BX	XA-EGU							
144	A	N144LJ	JA01CP								
145	A	N124FX	N145LJ	N29RE	N89RF	(N696RB)	LV-BDM				
146	A	N30046	N218NB	(ZS-DCT)	ZS-AGT	N218NB					

LEARJET 31

C/n	Series	Identities							
147	A	N198KF	N202LC	N157EC	N45KK	N31GQ			
148	A	N148LJ	(PT-XIT)	PT-XPP					
149	A	N1904S	N685RC	PR-JJV					
150	A	N31NR	N6666R	N6666A	N316RS	N316AS	N595PA	N381AL	N31LR
151	A	N3019S	N583PS	N583LJ	N31NF	PR-ENE			
152	A	N517GP	N989CG						
153	A	N6666R	N30111	RP-C6153	(N37RA)	N153NP	N349HP	N153RB	
154	A	N337RB	N154RT						
155	A	N525GP	D-CPRO	D-CAMB					
156	A	N124FX	(N29RE)	N181PA	N5007	N484BA			
157	A	N125FX	N800CK	LV-CXE	N800CK				
158	A	N126FX	N126BX	PR-LRJ					
159	A	N127FX	N127BX	XA-AFX					
160	A	N31LR	VP-BMX	LX-EAR	(D-CPRO)	N160CF			
161	A	N3016X	N177JB						
162	A	N525GP	N162LJ	N125GP	ES-PVH				
163	A	N128FX	N431DA						
164	A	N131GM	N164SB	XA-USF					
165	A	N31TD	N885TW	N808W	N608W	XA-...			
166	A	N166DT	N811PS	N366TS	PR-GBN	N296SF	XB-GYB	[w/o Apaseo del Alto, Mexico, 22Oct15]	
167	A	N167LJ	I-ERJB	N613SA	D-CGOM	LX-OMC	I-CFLY		
168	A	N168LJ	N811CP	N31CV	YV-952CP	N952VS	PP-CTA	N127NS	
169	A	N197PH	N659BX						
170	A	N31NR	(ZS-DHL)	ZS-OML	(OY-LJN)				
171	A	N50157	N129FX	N31MW	N820MT	N31NV	N171AR		
172	A	N197PH	N130FX	N312CC	N312TL				
173	A	N173LC	N31KH						
174	A	N9VL	Mexico MTX-02		Mexico AMT-201		Mexico ANX-1201		ANX-1204
175	A	N131FX	N175FF	N27AL	N31WU	N240B			
176	A	N176WS	XA-LRD						
177	A	N132FX	N569SC						
178	A	N50145	RP-C6178	N178NP	PR-MKB				
179	A	N133FX	N133BG	XA-RAN					
180	A	N1926S							
181	A	N134FX	N526GP	N418DL					
182	A	N136FX	N527GP	N399RW	N699GG				
183	A	N183DT	N183ML	LV-BFE					
184	A	N931RS							
185	A	N31LR	N110SC	N31MJ	N515CS				
186	A	N137FX	N45PK	N45PD	RP-C1432				
187	A	N932FD	N932ED	C-FVNC					
188	A	N70AE	N70AY						
189	A	N138FX	N316RS	N158R	N239AY	N189RM*			
190	A	N316AC	N8TG						
191	A	N631AT	OE-GTA	Mexico AMT-206		Mexico ANX-1206			
192	A	N50088	N531RA	N382AL	N552LM				
193	A	N44SF	N44SZ	N129JD	N553LM				
194	A	N29SM	N29SN						
195	A	N134FX	N134CG	XA-NTR					
196	A	N136FX	N136BX	N1JM	N54CH	N331US			
197	A	N20XP							
198	A	N500MP							
199	A	N900P	N901P	N895DM					
200	A	N31NR	N797WB	N599CT	N900EL				
201	A	N4003K	N137FX	N776PH	N32HH				
202	A	N4003L	ZS-PNP	ZS-AJD	OO-ENZ	D-CAAY	N99AT		
203	A	N63SE	VP-BAW	OD-PWC	N595SA	PR-GJC	N221EJ		
204	A	N204RT							
205	A	N50153	VP-CFB	N71FB	YR-TYC	D-CGFK	D-CKUM		
206	A	N5000E	N79SE						
207	A	N50126	D-CSIE	D-CGFM					
208	A	N138FX	N138FY	N751BP	N518JG	N518JC	N227KT	N131AR	XB-NZS
209	A	N139FX	N139FY	N209HR	N428BB	XA-ARD			
210	A	N927DJ	(N928DJ)	N631SF					
211	A	N5013Y	N574DA	N574BA	N5NC	N276PS			
212	A	N31KJ	N480JJ	N481JJ	N128BG				
213	A	N5009V	D-CMRM	N213MF	PR-MVF	N213NU	PK-JKI		
214	A	N5000E	N124DF	PT-FZA	N125DF	PR-PJD			
215	A	N40075	N30051	N786YA	(N784LB)	N31MC			
216	A	N40077	N999GH	N321GL	N311JS				
217	A	N40078	N10SE	N110SE					
218	A	N30050	N1ED	N41ED					
219	A	N214RW	N214PW	N518JG	N638SF				
220	A	N5009T	N220LJ	N521CH	N521WH	N54AP			
221	A	N68ES	N278JM	XB-MBP					
222	A	N5013U	N200CH	N770CH	N14T	LV-BSO			

LEARJET 31

C/n	Series	Identities								
223	A	N40012	N8064K	N800CH	N501RS					
224	A	N3001H	(XA-VMX)	N224LJ	N411DJ					
225	A	N3003S	N334AF	N834AF						
226	A	N138FX	N226LJ	N7SN	N32PF					
227	A	N30054	N40073	D-CGGG						
228	A	N3018P	N955JS							
229	A	N50005	(N11TK)	N229LJ						
230	A	N5004Z	N295PS	N556HD	N558HD	XA-GCM	N558HD	XA-JMB		
231	A	N5005Q	XA-VTR	N712EJ	(N759FS)	N724FS				
232	A	N5008S	N668VP	N68VP						
233	A	N5005X	LX-PAT	N233BX	EI-MAX	N726MP	PR-MUR			
234	A	N5028E	N376MB	XA-EFX	XA-UMV					
235	A	N31NR	N317K	XA-UBI						
236	A	N314DT	N57TS							
237	A	N23UP	N19UP	N84MJ	N44LG	N37LG	N962FM			
238	A	N36UP								
239	A	N686AB								
240	A	N998AL	N990AE	N440SC	N48VP					
241	A	N335AF	N633SF							
242	A	N40043	(PR-BOI)+	[+ ntu marks worn at Tucson completion centre Apr03]				N40031	N903LJ	N600AW
		N600AN	N680SW	N132PH	N132RH*					

Production complete

LEARJET MODEL 35

* after the series letter or in the series column indicates the aircraft has been fitted with Avcom delta fins.

C/n	Series	Identities
001		N731GA [ff 22Aug73] N351GL [on display at entrance to Learjet factory, Wichita, KS]
002		N352GL N35SC C-GVVA N11382 [parted out by Alliance Air Parts, Oklahoma City, OK]
003		N731GA N931BA N263GL N370EC N4RT N960AA N700WL N703MA N111WB
004		N74MP N74MB N74MJ C-GIRE [cx Feb15; to Algonquin College, Rockcliffe, Canada, as instructional airframe]
005		EC-CLS TR-LXP EC-CLS N175J N178CP
006		N356P N39DM N39FN
007		D-CONI N75DH N47JR (N65FN) N35UJ N357RM N110UN [cx 25Jun12; to Singapore as instructional airframe]
008		N673M PT-LFS PP-ERR
009		N44EL N14EL N275J N263GL PT-LGR N335AT
010		N888DH N888DE N35AJ
011		N3816G N400RB N408RB N531AJ XA-RJT XB-WID
012		N711 N71LA C-GVCB N2242P N95SC N975AA N975AD N97TJ XA-SVX [dbr Magdalena de Kino, Mexico, 12Jun95]
013	*	N1DA N7TJ N304AF N35JN N35BN N535TA N913CK
014		N71TP N73TP (N72TB) N98VA N69PS N77LJ N190GC N844L [wfu El Paso, TX]
015		N291BC N57FF N58FF N58CW N335JL (N335SS) N354PM [parted out by Alliance Air Parts, Oklahoma City, OK]
016		N136GL N5867 N9CN N1SC N18CV VP-CLT N31HK
017		N119GS N551CC N456MS N600DT N635RJ*
018		D-CORA F-GBMB N696SC N435JL N696SC N435JL (N435EC) [Parted out by White Inds, Bates City, MO; cx 29Apr09]
019	*	N959AT PT-LGF N19NW N71LG N1AK N157AK N750RM YV1828
020		XA-BUX N95TC [w/o 20Dec84 Waco Airport, TX; remains to White Inds, Bates City, MO]
021	A	N101GP N91CH N33TS N442JT N4415S N53FN N220NJ N535LC
022		OY-BLG N90WR [cx 05May15; CofR expired]
023		N986WC N886WC N886CS N443RK [cx 08Aug13; wfu]
024		N316 N24GA N528JD N528EA N241RT N411BA N159RA
025		9K-ACT N40TF N135TX N510LJ N185BA (N188JA) N435UJ [parted out by Dodson Int'l, Rantoul, KS]
026		D-CDHS D-CBRK N54754 N89TC
027		N31WS
028		N135GL N20BG XC-IPP [carried dual marks XC-IPP/TP104] Mexico TP104
029		N711AF [w/o Katab, Egypt 11Aug79 en route Athens-Jeddah]
030	*	N816M N16FN N542PA [code "TX"] (N30TK) C-GKPE N542PA [cx 30Nov2016, wfu]
031		N77FC N77U N77TE N160AT N233CC N19WG
032		N711CH (N711QH) N711MA N235JW N711MA N710GS N91GJ
033		N7KA HZ-KA1 N2297B N31FN N524PA
034		N37TA
035		N711R (N711RQ) N7125 N350TS N92TS YV....
036		N134GL N76GL N76GP N90AH N351AJ N135AJ
037	*	N1462B N100GL N58M N35GQ N600WT N520PA N45TK N333KC N24NW
038		(VH-UDC) VH-ELJ C-FBFP N10972 [parted out by Alliance Air Parts, Oklahoma City,OK]
039		N1HP N382TC
040		C-GGYV N39DM [w/o 05Mar86 over Pacific Ocean nr San Clemente Island; collided with Learjet 24D-253 N97DM qv]
041		N202BT N202BD N711BH N41PJ (N433JW) N41NW (N694PG) [parted out by Alliance Air Parts, Oklahoma City, OK]
042		N221UE N73TJ N270CS XA-FFF XB-RYT
043		C-GVCA N575WW [parted out at Scottsdale, AZ]
044		N38TA N44MW N44VW N130F [parted out by Alliance Air Parts, Oklahoma City,OK]
045	*	N1461B HB-VEN N35HB N99786 N999M XA-HOS N45MJ N117CH N304TZ N304AT N1140A (N40AN) [parted out by Alliance Air Parts, Oklahoma City, OK]
046		VH-SLJ VH-FSX VH-LJL N58EM
047	A	XA-ALE N13MJ N701AS [parted out by Alliance Air Parts, Oklahoma City, OK]
048	*	N233R N64MH F-GHMP N8040A [parted out by Alliance Air Parts, Oklahoma City,OK]
049		JY-AEV N3759C C-GBWL N235JL N899WA LV-ZZF [wfu Buenos Aires/Aeroparque, Argentina]
050		CC-ECO Chile 351
051		SE-DEA N2BA (N123MJ)
052		JY-AEW [w/o 28Apr77 Riyadh, Saudi Arabia]
053		N1976L N53FN N541PA [cx 30Nov16, wfu]
054		VR-BFX N53650 N54PR N109MC N435MS
055		D-CONO N70WW I-NIKJ N255RG N255JH C-GCJD N354LQ
056		(JY-AEX) N106GL N645G
057		N551MD N57GL C-GHOO N57GL N35MR C-GTDE
058		C-GPUN [w/o 11Jan95 Massett, Queen Charlotte Islands, BC, Canada]
059		N221Z N51FN [w/o 02Apr90 Carlsbad, CA; remains to White Inds, Bates City, MO]
060		N64MP N64MR N47BA (N590CH) [w/o 25Oct99 near Mina, SD]
061		N424DN N4246N N238RC N235EA
062		N217CS ZS-LII TL-ABD N701US N310BA N31DP
063		N828M N663CA N80PG
064		N290BC N291BC N100GP (N257DP) N257SD N622RB N921TM
065		N425DN N4358N [parted out by Alliance Air Parts, Oklahoma City, OK]
066		CC-ECP Chile 352

LEARJET 35

C/n	Series	Identities
067	A	N118K N888DJ (N66FN) N32FN (N52FL) N135FA
068	A	HB-VEM Switzerland T-781 N168TR
069	A	N103GL N591D N1CA N10AQ N35NW N48GP N51FN
070	A	D-CITA N3GL N503RP N50FN N543PA N50FN
071	A	JY-AFD F-WDCP F-GDCP N82GA N199CJ N99FN VH-ESW
072	A	N2015M N4415M PR-MLA
073	A	N108GL N163A (N64FN) N352TX N610GA N536KN
074	A	N5000B N530J N666JR N100T N198T N351PJ
075	A	N3503F HB-VEV JY-AFE N3503F (N117DA) N48RW N30FN SE-DHP
076	A	N959SA N76CK
077	A	N814M N819JE (N707BJ) N46TJ (XA-...) ZS-NRZ N98LC [parted out by Alliance Air Parts, Oklahoma City, OK]
078	A	N95BA N95BH N711SW N711SD N440JB N112EL N45AW N145AM
079	A	N6000J N660CJ N560KC N7777B N500DS N68QB YV....
080	A	N109GL N23HB N10AZ N17AZ
081	A	N3523F JY-AFF N3523F N118DA N81FR N353CK
082	A	N235HR N285HR N700GB N700SJ [parted out by Alliance Air Parts, Oklahoma City,OK]
083	A	(N600CC) N400CC (N400MJ) (N45SL) N500CD N121CL YV-100CP N400LV N581CC N581PH
084	A	N111GL N56HF N135WB N184TS (N696JH) N903AL D-CFAY [parted out Nurnberg, Germany]
085	A	N15WH (N353CK)
086	A	N435M N26DA N98MD N86CS N860S [parted out by Alliance Air Parts, Oklahoma City, OK]
087	A	N720GL N835GA N862PD (N862BD) N18AX N48ES
088	A	N3545F HB-VEW N35GE OE-GBR N72JF [parted out by Alliance Air Parts, Oklahoma City, OK]
089	A	N3547F D-CCHB
090	A	HB-VEY I-FIMI N88BG N290CK
091	A	VH-TLJ C-GBLF N8GA D-CIRS N37FA (N900JV) XB-LWW
092	A	N722GL N424JR C-GPFC N46931 N92NE N92EJ N39WA N73CK
093	A	N804CC C-GFRK N5474G N44PT PT-LOT
094	A	N506C N935BD N200EC N92EC N94GP (N65PF) (N35PF) N94AF
095	A*	N971H N971F N68UW N66KK N500LL
096	A	N214LS (N11JV) N87AT (D-CHRC) N96FA N94RL
097	A	N135J N108RB
098	A*	N20CR N21GL N44UC (N998DJ) (N998M) N72DA [cx 23Jan12; preserved Duncan Aviation facility, Lincoln, NE]
099	A	N40146 HB-VFC I-MCSA [w/o 22Feb78 Palermo, Sicily]
100	A	N550E N558E C-GRFO [cx 29Nov12, wfu]
101	A	N40149 N109JR N109JU N721AS N751AC N540PA
102	A	N1451B N232R PT-OEF [w/o 02May92 Morelia, Mexico; remains to Dodson Int'l for spares]
103	A	N96RE N50MJ PT-LCD
104	A	N87W N873LP [w/o 22Sep85 Auburn, AL]
105	A	(N720GH) N102GH N102GP N612KC N18FN N444WB
106	A	N101BG N15TW [w/o 08Dec85 Minneapolis, MN; remains to Brandis Avn, Taylorville, IL]
107	A	N723GL [w/o 12Dec85 Esterwood, TX]
108	A*	D-COCO F-GCLE N86PC (N86PQ) D-CJPG
109	A	N506GP N911AE [parted out by White Inds, Bates City, MO]
110	A	(N12EP) N4J [parted out by Alliance Air Parts, Oklahoma City, OK]
111	A	N3815G (HB-VFE) (I-SIDU) OE-GMA I-LIAD D-CONE
112	A	N3810G D-CCAY N247TA N299LR N999ND N20HJ (N120WH) N354JC (N354DT) N354SS
113	A	N763GL N35CL N35RN N14M N684LA N684HA (N113AN) [cx 19May15; CofR expired]
114	A	N3807G D-CONA N18G N851L D-CATY [w/o 14Dec94 Moscow-Sheremetyevo A/P, Russia; to Dodson Int'l, Rantoul, KS, for parts use] N851L
115	A	Argentina T-21 [w/o 09Mar06 La Paz, Bolivia]
116	A	I-MMAE N116AM N58CW
117	A	N3155B N78MC YV499T YV3027
118	A	N39391 HB-VFK N115MA N50MT N88JA N118FN
119	A	HB-VFG D-CHER N93MJ OY-ASO N93MJ N36FN (N64DH) N549PA [code "GA"]
120	A*	N400JE (N400RV) N220CK
121	A	N43EL (D-CFVG) N43TJ N752AC VH-LJG
122	A	D-CCHS OE-GMP N27TT [parted out by Alliance Air Parts, Oklahoma City, OK]
123	A	N3802G N900JE N900BJ
124	A	N1500E N35WG N8LA C-GTJL
125	A	N3803G N777MC N777NQ N111MZ N125GA N351EF
126	A	N744GL N15EH
127	A	N727GL N351TX (N800VL)
128	A	N231R N257AL N39PJ [parted out by White Inds, Bates City, MO; cx 07Apr17]
129	A	N22BX N229X XA-ZAP
130	A	N230R (N44KW) N757AL (N116PR) [cx Apr11; wfu]
131	A	N3812G N26GB N26GD N155AM
132	A	N431M N420PC N37TJ N135AG
133	A	N728GL N35NB N58RW I-ALPM N133GJ N133EJ
134	A	N1473B N88EP N235DH N238JA [parted out by White Inds, Bates City, MO; cx 29Apr10]
135	A*	(OO-LFX) N22MJ D-CDAX N719US N11AK I-ZOOM N135GJ D-CFAX [w/o 26Oct14, Tamanrasset, Algeria]
136	A	Argentina T-22
137	A	N3819G HB-VFL EC-DEB N41FN N35TJ [wfu; cx 10May11]

LEARJET 35

C/n	Series	Identities
138	A	N7735A N31FB N3RA N83TJ N35WH N100MS N138NA N124ZT [parted out by Alliance Air Parts, Oklahoma City, OK]
139	A*	N15SC D-CGFD
140	A	N742GL N888BL N72TP N40BD N76RA
141	A	N743GL N66WM N553M N553V
142	A	N815A N815L N241CA
143	A*	N3811G N301SC OE-GER N20DK LV-BPA
144	A	N39398 D-CCAP N705US N35KC OY-CCT N118MA N135JW (N118MA) N56HF N56EM [parted out by White Inds, Bates City, MO]
145	A	N39394 HB-VFB Switzerland T-782 N145GJ (N166AG) VH-SLD
146	A	N55AS N351AS
147	A	N717W HZ-KTC N499G N717W N55F [parted out by Alliance Air Parts, Oklahoma City, OK]
148	A	N103GH N103GP N333RP N500RW [w/o 24May88 Teterboro, NJ]
149	A	OO-KJG HB-VGN N85351 N273MC N273MG N600LE N600AE N600AW N800AW (N40AN) [w/o 19Mar04 Utica-Oneida County, NY; parted out by Dodson Int'l, KS, circa Dec05]
150	A	N100EP [w/o 12May87 West Mifflin, PA; cx 01May90]
151	A	N39399 N711L N813M [aircaft stolen 13Apr85; fate unknown]
152	A*	N101HB N964CL [confiscated in Bolivia and donated post 12Jun90 to AF] Bolivia FAB-009 N964CL XA-RIN XA-WIN
153	A	C-GZVV N573LP N573LR N647MP*
154	A	N650NL N117RB N244RG
155	A	N760LP N760DL N110KG "N1001L" N110AE N70AX (N892AC) N703DJ
156	A	N170L N190EB N190DA N35WE N720RA [crashed on approach to PalWaukee, IL, 05Jan10, w/o]
157	A	N746GL YV-01CP N57FF N57FP N157DJ ZS-MWW N26GP N389AW
158	A	N835AC N158MJ N158NE N800GP [w/o Springfield, IL, 06Jan11; cx 05Dec11]
159	A	N93C N93CK (N135CK) D-CAPO
160	A*	D-CCCA
161	A	N39415 YV-65CP N433DD
162	A	N751GL (HB-VFO) N711HH N1978L N222SL XA-CZG
163	A	YV-173CP N27BL N163CK
164	A	N1473B N248HM N50MJ [cx Apr11; wfu]
165	A	N40144 A4O-CA VH-HOF N16BJ N72CK
166	A	N831CJ N831J N719JB N10UF
167	A*	N725P N813AS [parted out by Alliance Air Parts, Oklahoma City, OK]
168	A	N22SF N22SY N36TJ N75RJ N68TJ C-GPDO C-FZQP [cx 29Nov12, wfu]
169	A	N135ST N48CN N500JS N707RG
170	A	N100K N354RZ C-GPDQ C-GFEH N335NA N335AS N88NJ N870CK
171	A*	N747GL C-GNSA N823J N1968A N1968T N196DT N455RM (N48DK) N40DK N171WH XA-ICU
172	A	N748GL SE-DDG N72TJ N32JA SX-BFJ (N32JA) N50AK (ZS-ZZZ)
173	A	N750GL HZ-MIB N750GL (HZ-NCI) N100GU N116EL (N83DM) YU-BPY N326DD
174	A	TR-LYC N65DH D-CAVI (F-GGRG) N130TA D-CAMB N82283 N38AM N773DL N474KA
175	A	D-CDWN SE-RCA
176	A	N317MR XA-ACC N176JE (N67GA) XA-BUX
177	A	N1461B N77CP N77CQ N174CP D-CITY
178	A	N40146 N22CP N22CQ N35GG N900JC (N104AA) [parted out by Alliance Air Parts, Oklahoma City, OK]
179	A*	N39412 D-CCAR D-CAPD N718SW (N696SC) C-FHLO N801PF D-CGFA
180	A	N3819G N222BE N222BK N35CX N44HG N701DA
181	A	N35LJ N35PR N35PD N5114G PT-LSJ
182	A	N1450B N33HB N3HB N3HA N221SG [cx 30Jan14; wfu]
183	A	N3802G N720M N72JM N106XX N51TJ N137RS (N137TS) N183FD N717AJ
184	A	N1462B HB-VFO [damaged 06Dec82 Paris-Le Bourget, France; believed repaired] N7092C [cx 04Nov13; parted out]
185	A	N99ME N99VA N10BF N99VA N900EM TC-GEM OE-GAV ZS-SES RP-C5354
186	A	N753GL N590 N96DM (N317JD) N96FN [cx 10Oct14; wfu]
187	A	N755GL N32HM (N888DT) N799TD
188	A	VH-AJS N39293 N20RT (N38FN) N3MJ N343MG N135AC N35TK N88TJ N999JF N924AM CX-JYE N352RJ
189	A	N3811G VH-AJV N39292 (N189TC) N32TC N32FN N35KC N18NM N727JP I-AVJG [w/o 24Oct99 on approach to Genoa A/P, Italy]
190	A	N32BA N202VS N202WR (N208WR) N181EF
191	A	N3810G (YV-15CP) HB-VFX N75TF N35NP N35SE N535AF
192	A	N4995A N225CC N225QC N49PE N49BE VH-LRX
193	A	N1465B (YV-131CP) VH-SBJ N620J VH-SBJ N2743T N9EE N359EF
194	A	N91W N86BL N86BE [w/o 5Apr00 Marianna Municipal apt, FL]
195	A	N1471B D-CONY N555JE SE-DHO
196	A	HB-VFU EC-DFA [w/o 13Aug80 Palma, Spain]
197	A	N754GL N754WS HK-4982
198	A	N25FS I-ALPT N198GJ
199	A	N40144 N9HM (N9HV) N30DH N34TC N444HC N235JS
200	A	N3818G D-CCAR OO-LFY N200LJ N606 N80UT N200LJ P4-TID
201	A	N39415 N79MJ N35RT N35RF XA-PIN N35AZ N136WE N135AV N234MR
202	A	VH-MIQ N499G D-CGPD N55FN
203	A	N744E N744P VR-CUC N203RW N97CE
204	A	N1466B D-COSY N87MJ N99ME N7PE (N277AM) D-CFTG

LEARJET 35

C/n	Series	Identities
205	A	N39418 N80SM N59DM N59FN N568PA
206	A	N760GL (N66HM) HB-VGH N189TC N123CC N38PS (N46KB)
207	A	N40146 N711 N3PW N620JM [w/o 15Jul05 Vail/Eagle County, CO]
208	A	N40149 N40TA (N691NS) N39DK (N39DJ) N67PA
209	A	N399W N339W N711DS N22MS [w/o McMinnville, OR, 13May13]
210	A	N840GL (N35HM) N42HM N721CM XB-FNF N210WL N770JP
211	A	N1461B D-CATY N15MJ N600LC N500KK N500GM N998JP N44TT N621RB N920TM
212	A	N3803G N180MC N291A N989AL
213	A	N800RD (N935NA) XC-CUZ
214	A	N279DM [parted out by White Inds, Bates City, MO]
215	A	VH-UPB N2951P N80CD N80GD N35ED N41RA
216	A	N3819G D-CATE N24MJ N39MB N142LG N335RD N991AL
217	A*	N39412 N111RF N122JW N217CK
218	A	N256TW N481FM (N601WT) (N83TE) N781RS [w/o 28Dec05 Truckee-Tahoe, CA]
219	A	N39416 VH-BJQ N502G N350JF [shot down 29Aug99 Ethiopia/Eritrea Border]
220	A	N79BH N333RB N220GH N873LP N873LR (N373LP) N220GS
221	A	N1462B N845GL VH-WFE VH-FSY N221TR XA-MMN
222	A*	N1468B HB-VFZ I-EJID N90AL HB-VFZ N789KW D-CGFG
223	A	N215JW D-CGRC
224	A*	N96AC N56PB N40RW N28MJ N269JR
225	A	N225MC TG-JAY N34TJ N225CF [wfu Houston Intercontinental Sep06]
226	A	N1127M N30HJ [parted out by White Industries Inc, Bates City, MO; cx 29Apr09]
227	A	N211BY N25RF N88NE N85GW (N227MJ) N902JC N366TT [parted out by Alliance Air Parts, Oklahoma City, OK]
228	A	N101PG N4GB SX-BNT N100NW N72LG N921CH
229	A	N1476B N8MA N717JB N718EA N41WT N31WT (N214LS) N415LS N4415W [parted out by Dodson Int'l, Rantoul, KS]
230	A	N39418 N714K PT-WAR N81458 N356AC N37HJ N595BA
231	A*	(N10AB) (N712DM) N911DB N62DK VH-JCR
232	A	N8281 N4415S N503LB
233	A	N35SL N35AW (N442HC) N23A
234	A	N35WR
235	A	N841GL N600CN N256MA (N256MB) N166HL N166HE LV-ZSZ [w/o Buenos Aires/San Fernando, Argentina, 19Oct15]
236	A	G-ZOOM N8537B N90LP N4XL N900EC N600GP (N415RD) EC-HLB N65RZ
237	A	N843GL N78MN I-KUSS (N37DJ) N72LE N237TJ (N36BP) N300TW N300TE N11UF N237CK
238	A	N844GL N80HK ZS-INS 3D-ACZ ZS-INS N248DA N500CG N500HG N500HZ N32RZ [dismantled at Boca Raton, FL while still painted as N500HZ circa Jan04; to White Inds, Bates City, MO for spares use]
239	A	N1473B N847GL (HB-VGC) VH-KTI VH-LEQ N239GJ N521PA [w/o 14Dec94 Fresno, CA; cx Jun95]
240	A	N240B N249B N135WE N35LJ
241	A	N42FE N500GP N500FD N240JS N500EX N500ED
242	A	N846GL VH-WFJ VH-FSZ N242DR
243	A	N3812G HZ-ABM N81863 I-AGEB N2217Q XA-HYS N152TJ XA-THD N747RY
244	A	N1451B RP-57 RP-C57 N244TS N244LJ (N116KV)
245	A	N2WL N1526L N30PA
246	A	N50PH N50PL N555GB N1DC N628DB YV543T
247	A	YV-265CP N110JD N38FN N523PA N544PA
248	A	N3811G C-GBFA N128CA
249	A	N107JM I-KALI N249DJ N300DA C-FICU [parted out in USA; cx 16Feb09] (N374LJ)
250	A	N3250 (N87RS) N63LE N63LF N947GS
251	A	N27NB N27HF N251CT N387HA
252	A	N28CR PT-KZR
253	A	N40144 N211DH N611CM N611SH N129TS N129TK
254	A	N666CC N34FN N522PA (N54TK) N254US N720WW
255	A	N44EL N44ET N610HC N616HC XB-LHS XB-FNW XB-USD XA-USD [w/o 19Nov13, crashed into sea on departure from Fort Lauderdale International, FL; wreckage parted out by Atlanta Air Salvage, Griffin, GA]
256	A	N712L N6GG N50DD N911ML (N402FW) (N811ML) (N66PJ) N335RC
257	A	F-GCMS N257DJ N417BA
258	A	(N1700) N28BG N35MH N583PS N583BS (N218CR) N17UF [w/o 10Nov14 Grand Bahama, Bahamas]
259	A	N39413 HB-VGC N9113F N259HA (N259JC) HK-3983X N25AN [parted out by Alliance Air Parts, Oklahoma City, OK]
260	A	N40PK
261	A	N900RD XA-ELU N35SJ N35FN N63DH N58MM
262	A	N237GA N237AF
263	A	D-CCAD N4577Q N37FN EC-GXX N8228P EC-GXX (N2422J) (ZS-PBA) [dbr Olbia, Italy, as EC-GXX 25Aug02; ntu reservations made later, for parts use]
264	A*	XA-ATA N35GX N40DK N3056R VR-CDI N64CP N264CK
265	A	N1462B (G-ZEST) G-LEAR United Arab Emirates 801 A6-RJI G-LEAR SX-SEM
266	A	N3904 SE-DDI N922GL N35GC
267	A	N39418 XA-LAN [w/o 08Jan93 nr Hermosillo, Mexico]
268	A*	N10870 YV-286CP N3857N (N286CP) N510SG N2U D-CGFB
269	A	N881W N225F N211WH N886R
270	A	N10871 (YV-15CP) YV-O-MRI-1 Venezuela FAV0013 N31MC [w/o 17Oct07, Goodland, KS; parted out by Alliance Air Parts, Oklahoma City, OK]

LEARJET 35

C/n	Series	Identities
271	A*	N1088A LV-PET LV-OAS N40AN [w/o 10Jan07 Columbus, OH; parted out by Alliance Air Parts, Oklahoma City, OK]
272	A	N39398 N272HS N500EF N321AN N89TB
273	A	N1465B N35FH N103C N103CL N273LJ
274	A	N1087Y N274JS N274JH N83CP N711BE (N35WG) N274FD N274JS N53G [parted out by Alliance Air Parts, Oklahoma City, OK]
275	A	N10872 G-ZEAL (N43PE) N43FE (N65WH) N235SC N72LL ZS-SFV
276	A	N44LJ N613RR N69BH [cx 04Nov14; wfu]
277	A	N925GL N723LL N70CN N127HC XA-PUI N350MD (N9876S) N27TJ N42B (N6362D) (N489) N2WQ N999JS
278	A	N1476B HB-VGL ECT-028 EC-DJC N300ES N17GL N12RP
279	A	N19LH [w/o 15Jly97 Avon Park, FL]
280	A(C21A)	N80MJ HP-912 YN-BVO US Army 87-0026 N35AX N142LM N542LM
281	A	N80WG N425M N425AS
282	A	N504Y N80CD N80GD N9CH N444CM N62MB
283	A	N920C N205EL N205FL N386CM
284	A	(D-CEFL) D-CCAX OO-GBL N43MF
285	A	N777RA N75KV N34TB VH-MZL N818WS N42PJ (N528VP) N725ST CX-PYB
286	A	N333X (N333XX) N200SX PT-LSW N286WL N286SD
287	A	N17EM N71HS N929SR N929SL N156BA N170LD N177LD
288	A	N1476B HB-VGM N43DD N288NE N288JE N288JP N1441M
289	A	N3JL N802CC N289MJ N289NE N289LJ N36TJ N217TA
290	A	N2022L XA-RAV XA-ORO
291	A	N7US N535PC [w/o 14Feb91 2 miles N of Aspen Airport, CO; cx Jly91]
292	A	N634H N292ME
293	A	N182K [w/o Groton, CT, 02Jun06]
294	A	N745E N745F N35VP N440HM [w/o 27Feb97 Greenville, SC; remains to White Inds, Bates City, MO]
295	A	PT-LAA N94AA N474AN N295CK
296	A	N296BS XA-LML N51JA N66NJ [cx 14Oct15; parted out by DK Turbines, CA]
297	A	N746E N746F N38US N777DM N3313C N235LJ [parted out by Mango Aviation Parts, FL]
298	A	I-FLYC N298NW N298CK
299	A	N244FC PT-LGS N148X (PT-PMV) PT-XLI [cx, CofA suspended]
300	A	N365N N104PH
301	A	N301TP N999RB N102ST N102BT N190VE N98AC N945W
302	A	N717DS N780A N78QA N41ST N631CW N51LC [parted out by Alliance Air Parts, Oklahoma City, OK]
303	A	N771A PT-LLS
304	A	N464HA N112PG N534H N534A N53GH N53GL (N97QA) N995CR ZS-BLE
305	A	N3VG N33NJ N519GE [parted out by Alliance Air Parts, Oklahoma City, OK]
306	A	N926GL N66LM N601MC N77LN N111US N1110S N71E (N63602) (N485) N9ZD
307	A	N120MB (N119HB) N677CT N623KM
308	A	N99MJ N747GM (N7LA) (N747RL) XA-UPR
309	A	(YV-328CP) HB-VGT OE-GAR N8216Z N100MN D-CHPD C-GUAC
310	A	N97JL N13HB (N13HQ) N8280 N310ME N310PJ
311	A	D-CDHS N723US N35BG OE-GPN N311BP HC-BSZ N121JT N581AS N711EC
312	A	LV-PHX LV-OFV N369BA N62RA
313	A	N39413 (F-GCLT) TR-LZI N31WR N352CK
314	A	N35AK (N118GM) N777LD
315	A	N927GL N662AA D-CCAA (N121JT)
316	A	N39398 N1503 N1507 N35AH N18ST N99GK N89GK N384JW N884JW XA-UKF
317	A	N10871 SE-DEM N98TE N317TT
318	A	N444WB N103CF N318NW (N35WU)
319	A	Argentina T-23
320	A	N905LC N905LD N35FS N320M N30GJ N393JP N32PJ N727MG N35RT
321	A	N14TX (N19LM) N77LP XA-RVB XC-AA60 (N321WJ) Mexico TP-106 Mexico 3909/XC-UJG
322	A	N305SC PT-WGF
323	A*	N735A N357EF
324	A	G-JJSG G-JETN G-JETG N8064A VH-LJJ
325	A	D-CARO I-FFLY N325NW
326	A	PT-LAS N155WL N255JC N612DG N35SA XA-OEC
327	A	N3797N N135UT N327F N32PF N32PE YV....
328	A	N3807G N1502 N35NY N35NX N392JP N408MG N731RA
329	A	N39412 N53DM N261PC N261PG XA-...
330	A	N930GL [partially destroyed Dec89 during US invasion of Panama; b/u for spares; cx Jly91]
331	A*	N10870 HB-VGU I-EJIB N700NW N435JW D-CGFC
332	A	N600LN N332FG (N598WW) N543WW N827CR XA-LBS
333	A	Argentina T-24 [w/o 07Jun82 S Atlantic]
334	A	N2815 N350RB N334SP (N334AB) N235MC
335	A	N25MJ N155TD N8YY N15Y N335DJ N335NE N335EE N800CD N800CH N880CH N3MB N135SH
336	A	HB-VGW N590J N166RM N782JR XA-PYC (N336EA) XA-BNO XC-DGO
337	A	N80ED N337WC N710AT N39HJ
338	A	N1473B RP-C7272 N610GE RP-C610 [cx, wfu Manilla, Philippines]
339	A	N24JK N24CK N15CC N1500 PT-LZP
340	A*	N11AM N11YM N504F XA-DAZ XC-LNE XA-DAZ
341	A	N3802G D-CARE XA-HOS N259WJ ZS-CEW P4-KIS OE-GMS OE-GPI M-EASY

LEARJET 35

C/n	Series	Identities
342	A	N1088D N37931 VH-SDN VH-LGH N678S YV-15CP N56JA [parted out by Alliance Air Parts, Oklahoma City, OK]
343	A	N135MB N80BT N21NA N21NG N998GC LV-BPO
344	A	N40149 YV-327CP N344MC N630SJ (N111BJ) N45MF
345	A	N3818G N10RE VH-EMP N345LJ N30DK [w/o 24Oct04 San Diego-Brown Field, CA]
346	A	N3803G C-GMGA N35AJ I-DLON (N34LZ) EC-IIC D-CTRI
347	A	OE-GNP N85SV
348	A	(N17ND) N3798B N600BE N500MJ N35TL N35DL (N8JA) N7ZH
349	A	N272T XA-TCI N252WJ (N349TS) ZS-ARA
350	A	N88NE N35WB
351	A	N500RP N500DD N500ND [w/o 11Aug07 Melville Hall, Dominica; parted out by Alliance Air Parts, Oklahoma City, OK; cx 12Jan10]
352	A	YV-326CP N30GD N600G N71A (N999JA) N35CZ N800GJ N47RA
353	A	N3819G C-GDJH
354	A	N1450B D-CART N212GA N405GJ
355	A	N1468B LV-PJZ LV-ONN N64RV N345 N351WB N721EC
356	A	N54YR N54YP N800WJ (VR-C..) PT-LUG
357	A	N3797S N1001L (N289GA) ZS-MGK (N100L) N104SB N357LJ
358	A	N524HC N358PG N108JN
359	A	(N127RM) HB-VHB N136JP
360	A	N185FP N1129M (N360GL) N360LJ (N901MS) (N987DK) YV2661
361	A	N924GL PT-LBS PT-FAT PT-OCZ
362	A	N3794M N888MV N399KL N773LP N633DS N362FW
363	A	N52MJ N183JC N19RP PP-CRT
364	A	N3794Z (N65TA) N981TH N950CS N490BC N353EF HK-4826
365	A	G-ZONE (N4564S) G-ZIPS G-SEBE G-CJET G-GJET D-CFAI [w/o 12Jun08 Kinsangani, DR Congo]
366	A	N411LC N49AT (N94AA) N119CP N350DA HS-CFS VH-YPT VH-LJU
367	A	N714S (N67TJ) N97RJ N232CC N360AX N315DG*
368	A	N35FM SE-DHE N368BG N99KW N450MC N351TV
369	A	Argentina VR-17 Argentina T-24 Argentina T-26
370	A	HB-VGY N11MY N1MY (N56PR) VR-BKB N8216Q XA-RKY XA-OFA XA-CVD N87GA XA-CVD XB-JOA
371	A	LV-PLY LV-ALF N399BA
372	A	HB-VGX N372AS PT-LJK
373	A	SE-DER XA-BRE XA-RUY N97AN N971K LV-BNR
374	A	HZ-106 HZ-MS1A [parted out by Atlanta Air Salvage, Griffin, GA, 2009]
375	A	(YV-270CP) HZ-107 HZ-MS1B [parted out by Atlanta Air Salvage, Griffin, GA, 2009]
376	A	N458JA N77FK N33WB XA-SBF N979RF
377	A	(N711EV) N933GL N10WF N18WE N46MF
378	A	CX-BOI/FAU 500 (N900DG) N354ME N354EF
379	A	N23VG N18LH N217RT XB-IWL XB-KPB [damaged at Guadalajara 02Aug08]
380	A	N82JL N291BX N291BC N281BC XA-SBA N11SQ XA-SGK XA-MSH N903WJ C-GAJS
381	A	D-CORA N65DH (N40TM) N300CM N335K N35NA N131AJ
382	A	N382BL N382BP OE-GAF N60WL
383	A	N66FE N364CL
384	A	N37984 N811DF N811DD N384CF
385	A	N535MC N350EF D-CFIV
386	A	N13VG N999FA LV-BAW
387	A*	D-CARL
388	A	N1929S N388PD N388LS [w/o 24Dec96 Smarts Mountain on approach to Lebanon-Municipal, NH; cx May98]
389	A	N59MJ N377C N31WT N31WE VR-BLU N436DM N79AX N389KA
390	A	N500PP N508P N831CW C-FJEF C-FPRP [parted out by Alliance Air Parts Inc, Oklahoma City, OK] N831CW
391	A	N3793D N444BF N813RR N89AT I-RYVA N888PT XA-SWF [w/o 23Jun95 Tepico, Mexico]
392	A	N931GL N1ED N18DY N1XL [parted out by Precision Jet Service, Stuart, FL; cx 10Apr14]
393	A	N932GL N666RB N700WJ PT-LOE
394	A	N1466K N816JA N94MJ N60DK N626JS N232PR N238PR C-GLNL
395	A	HB-VHD N3261L N30GL N246CM N395MY C-GVGH Argentina VR-24
396	A	N2000M N938GL N5139W VR-CBU N5FF N74JL PT-OPJ
397	A	N33PT D-CLAN N200TW (N335JD)
398	A	N3797A N1AH [w/o 16May97 Great Falls, MT; cx Nov97; to spares by White Inds, Bates City, MO, 1998]
399	A	N37965 N540HP (N399DJ) N399AZ PT-OVC (N399AZ) [w/o 04Nov07 Sao Paulo, Brazil]
400	A	VH-CPH (VH-CPQ) VH-TPR VH-JIG VH-RHQ VH-OVB
401	A	N66LJ (N177SB) N771SB N535JM XC-LNH XA-USI XA-DIJ
402	A	N3402 N610JR N7AB N35BG
403	A	N37966 N312CT N312CF N312CE N100NR N101HW N100HW N403FW [parted out by Alliance Air Parts, Oklahoma City, OK]
404	A	N500JS N404BB N404KA N404DP N804TF
405	A	N41MJ (N181GL) N35AS N35FS N442DM N135DA D-CVFL*
406	A	N764G N35Q I-KELM ER-LGA HS-EMS [cx, wfu Bangkok/Don Mueang, Thailand]
407	A	N3793P N234DT N221MC N407MR C-GIWD C-GIWO
408	A	(N33VG) N3798P LV-POG LV-AIT
409	A	N50PD N858TM N123LC N888BS N35FE N351AM
410	A	N12109 N1210M C-FHDM N441CW (N21WS) N820RP N89RP N352TV
411	A	PT-LBY N94GP

LEARJET 35

C/n	Series	Identities
412	A	N37980 N6666R N412GL (N31LM) N314C XA-RGH
413	A	HB-VHE N2637Z F-GHAE N413MA N27KG D-CFCF
414	A	(N135AB) N39MW PT-SMO N414TJ N196SD N196SP N815DD XA-...
415	A	N125AX N19GL N415DJ D-COSY SE-DZZ
416	A	N306M N35MV N40GG N841TT N841TF
417	A	N934GL N117FJ (N117RJ) D-CONO N97D N90RK HC-BTN (N37HR) N281CD LX-ONE C-GXCB
418	A	XA-KCM XA-SCA N366AC LV-BPL
419	A	N935GL N25EL N53JM N35SM N72AX
420	A	N35RT N35PT N100KK N100KZ N181CA
421	A	N44MJ N85CA N85QA (N88AH) N3AH N413JP I-VULC D-CDSF D-CQAJ
422	A	YV-434CP N86BL N45AE
423	A	N369XL N200TC (N335GA) D-CAVE [cx, wfu Karlsruhe]
424	A	N2844 N508GP N52FN
425	A	N111KK N111KZ N425SA
426	A*	D-CARD N43W N43H ZS-NID N1128J RP-C1426 N143LG N543LM
427	A	N1087Z VH-FOX N42LL N358AC N36HJ [parted out by MTW Aerospace, AL]
428	A	N1465B VH-ELC N17LH VH-SLE [wfu 2015 Wagga Wagga, Australia]
429	A	G-ZING G-GAYL G-ZENO United Arab Emirates 800 A6-RJH G-ZING (D-CSOS) (SX-SEN) 9H-MRQ
430	A	N10870 Finland LJ-1
431	A	N1088A YV-433CP N34FD N431CW N431AS N355PC N431CK
432	A	F-GDCN N4445Y N330BC VR-CAD G-HUGG VH-VLJ
433	A	N39416 D-CARG HB-VCZ N26583 N95AC (N93RC) PT-LIH [w/o 15Mar91 Uberlandia, Brazil]
434	A	N4401 N469BB (N434CJ)
435	A	N435N XC-HHJ
436	A	N37988 PT-LDN N436BL N100AT LV-CMO
437	A	N3803G YV-432CP YV2044
438	A	N17ND N600LL N12GJ N300R N308R N308BW N35WL
439	A	N439ME HK-3121X HK-3121 N55RZ N35LW (N35FT) N402DP N911WX N611TA
440	A	N101HK N101PK N903HC N908HC (N354EM) N917SC N300SC D-CTOP
441	A	N1471B N551WC TC-MEK N441PC N441PG N74SP N404JS RP-C1404 N699ST N922TM
442	A	N40149 N3799C N35BK N442NE [w/o 26Jul88 Morristown, NJ; parted out by White Inds, Bates City, MO]
443	A	N135RJ N258G N335MR (N335SJ)
444	A	N3818G D-CARH N44695 N444MJ N144WB N1U N44SK N615HP N615HB VH-LFA
445	A	N3802G HB-VHG I-MOCO [w/o 08Feb01 Nurnberg, Germany]
446	A	N37962 N80AS N96CP N96CR N794GC N403DP
447	A	N127K N300FN D-COKE XA-DOC
448	A	N48MJ N222BG N595PL N577AC
449	A	N37947 N777LF N449QS XA-GDO XB-GDO
450	A	N450KK N950SP
451	A	N1462B Finland LJ-2
452	A	N25MJ N279SP N452DA [w/o 15May17, Carlstadt, NJ]
453	A	N124MC N802JW (N802EC) N453AM
454	A	N3794W (N379BW) N80AR (N80KR) N661MS
455	A	N3794U N455NE N988QC
456	A	N711CD N456CL
457	A	N1451B N900P N974JD (N113LB) N874JD N113LB N49WL
458	A	N276JS YV-997CP N86RX N4EA
459	A	VH-MIE N306SP N80BL N969MT N829CA [w/o 13Jul04 Charlestown, St. Kitts & Nevis; to Dodson Av'n, Rantoul, KS for spares]
460	A	XC-PGR XA-MPS XA-JJJ N994EA
461	A	N64CF
462	A	N3811G N8562W N147K N801K N7117 N135TP N394PA LV-BXU
463	A	N1088D VH-ULT VH-FSW VH-FSU N68LL N32HJ N699BA C-GTWX
464	A	(N75PK) N1DC PT-LHX N464WL VP-BJS N111KR
465	A	N465NW
466	A	VH-WFP N39SA (N700WJ) N600WJ D-COCO [w/o 08Jun93 Cologne-Bonn, Germany; remains to Dodson Av'n, Rantoul, KS for spares]
467	A	N3796Q HZ-MS1 HZ-MS1C [parted out by Atlanta Air Salvage, Griffin, GA, 2009]
468	A*	VH-ANI N468LM OY-CCJ
469	A	N39416 N3202A N660SA N444TG N71MH N35JN N35EG
470	A	N3810G Finland LJ-3
471	A	VH-BQR N95AP N110FT N529BC
472	A	N1468B N448GC N448WC N448WG PT-ONK (N472AS) N54HF N35TN N335MW N138WE N612SQ N81RA
473	A	N3796P PT-LFT N3UJ N44AB N35TH N777LB N35CY
474	A	N39413 N37975 PT-LEB [wfu Jundiai, Brazil]
475	A	N10873 N3797K 3D-ADC ZS-TOW (N42AJ)
476	A	N3818G N476VC N777LB N776JS N1TW
477	A	N40162 N3797B N82GL N80CD N95EC N477WB (N477MS) N24JG N235UJ N155RD N608GF N376HA N480YA [parted out by Alliance Air Parts, Oklahoma City,OK]
478	A	N3815G LV-TDF [w/o 15May84 Ushuaia, Argentina]
479	A	N3816G N8565J N31WT N30SA PT-LHT
480	A*	N3819G (VH-ALH) N8563A N35CK (N484) (N35FH) N39DK [parted out by Alliance Air Parts, Oklahoma City, OK]

LEARJET 35

C/n	Series	Identities
481	A	N1466B N6666K N666KK N728MP N729HS HK-3122X HK-3122 N729HS N27NR OO-LFV N99NJ [cx 30Jun14; wfu]
482	A	N482U [w/o 13Feb83 en route Kuala Lumpur-Colombo] N2286D [reason for new N-number not yet known; cx 07Nov13; CofR expired]
483	A	N40144 N8562Y N202BT (N203AL) N327CB N990LC
484	A	N4289U Argentina VR-18 Argentina T-25
485	A	N4290C N485S XA-RZZ N710WL N485AC N90J
486	A	N4291G N821PC N117EL N810CC N925DM N817EM
487	A*	N4289Y N206FC N206EC N400MC N391JP N391JR N487FW N890LR N890LJ
488	A	N8563G N848GL N30W N30WY N900R N907R XA-UGK N61SJ XC-OAH XB-NKR XA-SKI
489	A	N1473B N222BE N312LG
490	A	N1087Z N64MP N502JF C-GTWL
491	A	N1087Y N8563N N491HS N241AG N485 I-AGEN N135PG N394JP N35NK N491RV
492	A	N39399 N8566B N35NP N37SV N335UJ N492RM N994CR N492RM N490JP
493	A	N3811G N8564M N482SG I-FFRI N493NW N493CH N354CL
494	A	N1476B PT-LDM
495	A	N1088D N440MC N383AL N47MF
496	A	N3803G N8564K N856RR N496SW N39TH N496SW (N496LJ) N825LJ
497	A	N1450B N8565N N50PH N21DA N15RH N518PR N758JA XA-...
498	A	N3815G N8564P I-FLYH N498JR N400FF C-GTDM
499	A	N3818G N85645 N84AD PT-LII HK-3921 N38AL N499WJ N1TS N911DX N32HM
500	A*	N1465B N8566X N66LN N101US N81CH N81QH N144LG N544LM
501	A*	N3816G HB-VHR N711PR N35HW N326HG N565GG D-....
502	A	N1476B N8565X N747CP
503	A	N1087Z N8567A HB-VII HK-3646X N8567A N77NR N542SA
504	A*	N10871 N8568B G-RAFF N505DH OE-GMJ D-CTWO
505	A	N1471B N7259J N505EE N494PA N60DK N90PN C-GJDA N505GJ
506	A	N3819G N317BG N10BD [on display in the terminal at Denver Int'l by May03 having been the first aircraft to land at the new airport in 1993]
507	A	N3802G N35GJ N35HP N42HP N42HN
508	A	N40144 N741E N741F N7777B N881CA N508TF N452AC LV-BOX
509	C21A	N6317V N7263C 84-0063 N35AL N826RD N135PT [w/o 04Aug03 Poquonock River, Groton, CT]
510	C21A	N6331V N7263D 84-0064 [preserved Wright-Patterson AFB USAF museum, OH]
511	C21A	N4289X N7263E 84-0065 [preserved Scott AFB Heritage Air Park, IL]
512	C21A	N4290J N7263F 84-0066 [w/o Decatur, IL, 02Oct06]
513	C21A	N4291G N7263H 84-0067 N35AQ N117PK HK-4662
514	C21A	N4289Z N7263K 84-0068 [wfu AMARC 26Jan07, park code AACJ0020]
515	C21A	N4290K N7263L 84-0069 [to Embry-Riddle Aeronautical University, Daytona Beach, FL]
516	C21A	N4291K N7263N 84-0070
517	C21A	N6340T N7263R 84-0071
518	C21A	N4289Y N7263X 84-0072
519	C21A	N6307H N400AD 84-0073 [wfu AMARC 16Jan07, park code AACJ0011]
520	C21A	N42905 N400AK 84-0074 [wfu AMARC 08Jan07, park code AACJ0005]
521	C21A	N4291N N400AN 84-0075 [wfu]
522	C21A	N4290Y N400AP 84-0076 N506HL
523	C21A	N4289U N400AQ 84-0077 [parted out by Alliance Air Parts, Oklahoma City, OK]
524	C21A	N6317V N400AS 84-0078 [wfu AMARC 08Jan07, park code AACJ0006]
525	C21A	N6331V N400AT 84-0079
526	C21A	N4289X N400AU 84-0080 [wfu AMARC 10Jan07, park code AACJ0007]
527	C21A	N4290J N400AX 84-0081 N527Z [wfu]
528	C21A	N4289Z N400AY 84-0082 N528L [wfu; stored Springfield, OH]
529	C21A	N4291G N400AZ 84-0083
530	C21A	N4290K N400BA 84-0084 N352PJ
531	C21A	N4291K N400FY 84-0085
532	C21A	N6340T N400BN 84-0086 [wfu AMARC 18Jan07, park code AACJ0013]
533	C21A	N4289Y N400BQ 84-0087
534	C21A	N6307H N400BU 84-0088 [wfu AMARC 22Jan07, park code AACJ0015]
535	C21A	N4290C N400BY 84-0089 (N61905) [wfu AMARC 10Jan07 park code AACJ0008]
536	C21A	N42905 N400BZ 84-0090 [wfu]
537	C21A	N4290Y N400CD 84-0091 N506LG
538	C21A	N400CG 84-0092 [wfu AMARC 27Sep11]
539	C21A	N400CJ 84-0093 [parted out by Alliance Air Parts, Oklahoma City, OK]
540	C21A	N400CK 84-0094
541	C21A	N400CQ 84-0095
542	C21A	N400CR 84-0096
543	C21A	N400CU 84-0097 [w/o 02Feb02 Ellsworth AFB, SD]
544	C21A	N400CV 84-0098 N865SP
545	C21A	N400CX 84-0099
546	C21A	N400CY 84-0100 N400CY [wfu; instructional airframe Eastern Florida State College, Cocoa, FL]
547	C21A	N400CZ 84-0101 N400CZ [parted out by Dodson Int'l, Rantoul, KS]
548	C21A	N400DD 84-0102 N400FQ [parted out by Dodson Int'l, Rantoul, KS]
549	C21A	N400DJ 84-0103
550	C21A	N400DL 84-0104 [wfu AMARC 16Jan07, park code AACJ0012]
551	C21A	N400DN 84-0105 [wfu AMARC 08Jan07, park code AACJ0004]
552	C21A	N400DQ 84-0106 [instructional airframe, Keesler AFB, MS]

LEARJET 35

C/n	Series	Identities
553	C21A	N400DR 84-0107 [wfu AMARC 28Sep11]
554	C21A	N400DU 84-0108 [wfu AMARC 12Jan07, park code AACJ0010]
555	C21A	N400DV 84-0109 [parted out by Alliance Air Parts, Oklahoma City, OK]
556	C21A	N400DX 84-0110 [parted out by Alliance Air Parts, Oklahoma City, OK]
557	C21A	N400DY 84-0111 N38VM N400DY
558	C21A	N400DZ 84-0112 [wfu AMARC 27Sep11]
559	C21A	N400EC 84-0113 [wfu AMARC 24Jan07, park code AACJ0018]
560	C21A	N400EE 84-0114 N21VN
561	C21A	N400EF 84-0115 [wfu AMARC 12Jan07, park code AACJ0009]
562	C21A	N400EG 84-0116 [wfu AMARC 24Jan07, park code AACJ0017]
563	C21A	N400EJ 84-0117 [wfu AMARC 22Jan07, park code AACJ0016]
564	C21A	N400EK 84-0118 [parted out by Alliance Air Parts, Oklahoma City, OK]
565	C21A	N400EL 84-0119 N400EL [parted out by Dodson Int'l, Rantoul, KS]
566	C21A	N400EM 84-0120
567	C21A	N400EN 84-0121 [w/o 15Jan87 Alabama, LA]
568	C21A	N400EQ 84-0122 [wfu AMARC 18Jan07, park code AACJ0014]
569	C21A	N400ER 84-0123 N118MD N879TC
570	C21A	N400ES 84-0124
571	C21A	N400ET 84-0125
572	C21A	N400EU 84-0126
573	C21A	N400EV 84-0127 N508YV [parted out by Dodson Int'l, Rantoul, KS]
574	C21A	N400EX 84-0138 [wfu AMARC, park code AACJ0001]
575	C21A	N400EY 84-0128 N499UM [instructional airframe Seattle, WA]
576	C21A	N400EZ 84-0129
577	C21A	N400FE 84-0130 (N499YK) N36SP
578	C21A	N400FG 84-0131 [parted out by Alliance Air Parts, Oklahoma City, OK]
579	C21A	N400FH 84-0132 [wfu AMARC 26Jan07, park code AACJ0019]
580	C21A	N400FK 84-0133 [wfu AMARC 08Jan07, park code AACJ0002]
581	C21A	N400FM 84-0134 N72GH [instructional airframe, Pittsburgh Institute of Aeronautics, PA]
582	C21A	N400FN 84-0135
583	C21A	N400FP 84-0136 [w/o 17Apr95 Alexandra City, AL]
584	C21A	N400FQ 84-0141 [wfu AMARC 03Jan07, park code AACJ0003] N400FQ [reg'd 21Feb14, believed in error; cx 12Mar14]
585	C21A	N400FR 84-0137
586	C21A	N400FT 84-0142
587	C21A	N400FU 84-0139
588	C21A	N400FV 84-0140 N335KB
589	A	N1087T N8567K PT-GAP (N3215K) [cx, CofA expired; wfu Sorocoba, Brazil]
590	A	N1451B N35GA N35KT N969MC N827CA (N822SF) N882SC
591	A	N3803G N8567Z N72626 N500EX N822CA N822CP N9ZM N9ZB N880Z
592	A	N3810G N952GL N45KK N93LE
593	A*	N40146 N32B I-FLYG N593LR N593PN VH-PPF VH-LPJ
594	A	N1088C N72596 N7007V (ZS-PTL) (ZS-EFD) OY-LJA N410BD N747BW
595	A	N3815G N85PM N414KL N95JN
596	A	N1473B N72612 N62WM YV-850CP N850MM N826CA N826CP N352HS
597	A	N39394 N8567R N54GL N597BL N597JT N355CA N604S
598	A	N39415 N8567T PT-LGW
599	A	N40144 N58GL N367DA
600	A	N823CA N823CP N995DP
601	A	N3818G China HY986 B-4186
602	A	N10873 China HY987 B-4187
603	A	N1471B China HY988 B-4188
604	A	N1462B N59GL N604BL N73LP N604GS
605	A	N1088D N185HA N35AS N825CA N925CA YV526T N925CA
606	A	N3803G N1735J N35PD N3WP N96GS
607	A	N39399 N72614 PT-LIJ N68MJ D-CGFH
608	A	N40162 N8567Z N111SF N14T N96AX ZS-IGP VH-ZSX VH-IJG
609	A	N4290J N36NW N788QC XA-JRH N609TF N986SA
610	A	N1473B N101AR N161MA N610LJ (N354GG) (N354GE)
611	A*	N39413 N622WG N611TW VH-ESM
612	A	N3812G N8568D N2FU N501TW N551TW N551HM N36BP D-CGFI [w/o near Olsberg, Germany, 23Jun14 after mid-air collision with Luftwaffe Eurofighter]
613	R-35A	N4289X Brazil 6000
614	A	N3815G G-PJET HB-VJC G-SOVN G-VIPS G-OCFR N335EA N683EL N683EF D-CFOR D-CGFO
615	R-35A	N1466B N7260E Brazil 6001
616	A	N3807G N8568Q PT-LQF N616LJ N876CS N876C D-CEXP
617	R-35A	N4289Z Brazil 6002
618	A	N10871 YU-BOL SL-BAA S5-BAA N618DM N618CF N9099
619	A	N4290K N8568V PT-POK [wfu in grounds of owner's home, Lago Sul, Brasilia, Brazil]
620	A*	N1451B I-KODM VR-BNI N232FX XA-COI N620EM N500CG N500CQ XA-ODW
621	A	N1468B N999TH N999TN PT-OFW N242MT PR-ABP
622	A	N4290C N7260H N610R N81MR
623	A	N40149 N7260Q Thailand B.TL12-1/30 60504 Thailand B.TL12-1/30 40207
624	C21A	N39404 86-0374
625	C21A	N4289Y 86-0375 N625BL (N522AG) N625CY

LEARJET 35

C/n	Series	Identities
626	A	N39398 N7261R N35AJ N711NF C-GNPT N335MG (N385MG) N21BK
627	A	N4289U N7260T PT-LMY
628	C21A	N3810G 86-0376 N628BL N628WJ CX-VRH N628DC N628GZ LX-TWO N289AW
629	C21A	N40144 86-0377
630	A	N42905 N72630 N742E N742P N388PD
631	VU-35A	N3818G Brazil 2710 [converted to R-35AM aerial reconnaissance platform 2010/2011] Brazil 6003
632	VU-35A	N1461B Brazil 2711 [converted to R-35AM aerial reconnaissance platform 2010/2011] Brazil 6004
633	VU-35A	N39416 Brazil 2712 [converted to R-35AM aerial reconnaissance platform 2010/2011] Brazil 6005
634	ZR	N1462B I-EAMM N626BM [has Raisbeck modified wing set]
635	A	N1471B Thailand B.TL12-2/31 60505 Thailand B.TL12-2/31 40208 [w/o 08Non06 Nakhon Sawan, Thailand]
636	VU-35A	N1476B Brazil 2713
637		[airframe not built]
638	A/VU35A	N39412 Brazil 2714
639	A/VU35A	N6317V Brazil 2715
640	A/VU35A	N3816G N8568Y Brazil 2716
641	A/VU35A	N1087Y N7261H Brazil 2717
642	A/VU35A	N1465B N7262X Brazil 2718
643	A	N39418 G-LJET (N35NK) N643MJ D-CGFJ
644	A	N1088C N1043B PT-LLF (N54SB) C-GMMY N893AC C-GYFB
645	A*	N43TR N645AM
646	A	N3812G XA-UMA N646EA N717JB N712JB G-MURI [w/o 2May00 Lyon-Satolas A/P, France; crash remains to Fort Lauderdale Executive, FL]
647	A	N410RD N915RB N815RB (N647TJ) ZS-DJB N335PR
648	A	N1045J N974JD XB-LHS N648JW RP-C648 N648J N97LE
649	A*	N10870 HB-VJJ N35QB ZK-XVL VH-LJA
650	A*	N1022G PT-LYF N135MW N650LR N393SC
651	A	HB-VJK N405PC N9RA
652	A	N6307H N99FN D-CURE N652SA N49AZ N2KZ N652KZ
653	A	HB-VJL LX-LAR VH-LPF
654	A	N4290K N633WW N600LF (N95EC) (B-98183) ZS-NSB B-98183 N8189 N770BM D-CGFN*
655	A	N1088A N16FG PT-MFR N785JM C-GMMA N355GA N655JH YV523T N655JH
656	A*	N3810G G-JETL N335SB N356JW G-ZMED D-CFOR
657	A	N1473B N1CA N10AH
658	A*	N39404 N573LP N162EM N77NJ N592UA [parted out by Alliance Air Parts, Oklahoma City, OK]
659	A	N4290Y N873LP (N878LP) N413LC N776BG
660	A	N1087Z C-GLJQ N660L C-GLJQ N421SV
661	A	(N8888D) N1268G VH-PFA [operated by Singapore AF as a target towing aircraft]
662	A	G-NEVL G-BUSX N35UK N27AX N663TW
663	A	N91480 D-CCCB
664	A	N9130F N117RJ C-GRMJ N640BA D-CMIM*
665	A	N5009T N291K N35UA LV-BRT
666		[airframe not built as this number is considered unlucky in the USA]
667	A	N5018G N91566 N135DE
668	A	N5011L N9168Q N441PC
669	A*	N5014F N91452 OO-JBS N7XJ (N487LP) A6-FAJ N669LJ N393CF N893CF C-GWFG
670	A	N5012K N35UK N599SC OY-CCO (HP-....) HK-3949X (N670WJ) OY-CCO N787LP N987LP N460SB
671	A*	N9141N (ZS-NEX) (ZS-NFS) ZS-NFK N671BA LV-PLV LV-WPZ N671BX N671TS G-JMED D-CTIL
672	A	N9140Y N672DK N45KK XA-FMT XB-GSM
673	A	N5014F N9173G C-FBDH C-GPDO N835MC 9M-NOR Malaysia M102-01
674	A	N2601G N22SF N22SN N900JE N674LJ LV-BIE N674LJ D-CGFP*
675	A	N2602M B-98181 [w/o 17Sep94, shot down in error while target-towing off coast of Taiwan]
676	A	N5012Z N35LJ N235AC N620MJ D-CYES D-CGFQ*

Production complete

LEARJET MODEL 36

* after the series letter or in the series column indicates the aircraft has been fitted with Avcom delta fins.

C/n	Series	Identities
001		N26GL [ff 09Jan73 as a model 26 c/n 26-001; used as development airframe for both the model 35 and 36] C-GBRW-X C-GBRW [has winglets in place of tip tanks; cx Apr97 to Montreal/St Hubert Aeronautical College painted as C-XPWC to celebrate its active life as a flying test bed with Pratt & Whitney Canada]
002		N362GL D-CMAR YV-T-ASG YV-161P YV-89CP (N2297G) N18AT D-CELA N3239A N84DM N84FN
003	*	N363GL N36TA N55CJ N361PJ
004	*	N1918W (D-CCAC) D-CCPD N50DT N180GC N54PA
005	*	LV-LOG N9108Z N905CK
006		(I-CRYS) HB-VEA D-CAFO D-CDFA [w/o 25Mar80 Libya]
007	*	N138GL N173JA N226CC SX-AHF VR-BHB N83DM N83FN
008	*	N20JA VR-BJD VR-BJO N84MJ N101AR (N701AR) N101AJ (N43A)
009		N2000M N704J N44GL N25CL N15CC N505RA N505HG
010	*	N50SF N45FG
011		PT-KQT N26MJ N26FN
012		N139GL N215RL VR-BFR N2267Z C-GBWD N666TB N36CW N222AW N55GH N712JE N547PA [code "AK"]
013	*	N352WC (N852WC) SE-DDH N3280E N3PC N13JE D-CBRD N71PG
014		N900Y N200Y VH-SLJ [wfu2015, Wagga Wagga, Australia]
015	*	N14CF N10FN
016	*	HB-VEE JY-AET F-GBGD N616DJ N12FN
017	*	N1010A N17LJ (N32JA) (N361PJ) N362PJ
018	A*	PT-KTU N418CA PT-ACC (N7379M) N418CA N779CM
019	A	N300CC N89MJ C-GLMK N718US N300DK N300DL C-GLAL N719JE N540PA N527PA
020	A	JY-AFC [w/o 21Sep77 Amman, Jordan]
021	A	N3524F I-AIFA [w/o 10Dec79 Forli, Italy]
022	A*	N761A N38WC N36PD N44EV N31GJ
023	A	N1871R N1871P N187MZ (N64FN) N767RA N6YY N56PA
024	A	N38D N978E C-FEMT
025	A	N774AB N730GL OE-GLP C-GVVB N500MJ (N98A) N800BL N32PA
026	A	(N762L) N762GL N23G C-GGPF N6617B N8U (N888TN) (N8UB) N1U N8UA N86BL
027	A*	N836GA N484HB N27MJ N16FN
028	A	N731GA N75TD N545PA [code "HI"]
029	A	(N79JS) HB-VFD N116MA
030	A	N71TP N74TP N360LS N36PJ (N36AX) N160GC
031	A	N20UC N20UG D-CFOX N20UG N62PG
032	A*	N40146 N745GL N22BM N36BP HB-VLK N950G (N16AJ) VH-CMS N132LJ
033	A	N762L N14TX [w/o 06Dec96 Stephenville, Newfoundland, Canada. Parted out by White Industries Inc, Bates City, MO]
034	A	N763R China HY985 B-4599
035	A	N3807G VH-BIB N266BS VH-BIB N71CK
036	A*	N1462B N610GE N36MJ N136DH
037	A	RP-C5128 N555WH C-GRJL C-FCLJ
038	A	N304E N15FN N548PA N700GG N363PJ
039	A	N217CS C-GSRN N4998Z N25PK N99RS
040	A	HB-VFV N902WJ N110PA N70UT N70UP (N444SC) (N442SC) N500SV N72AV N82GG
041	A	N79SF [w/o 08Jan88 Monroe, LA]
042	A	N39391 HB-VFS [w/o 23Sep95 Zarzaitine, Algeria]
043	A	N1010G N43LJ N53JA (N143JW) N432JW (N521JW) XB-JPX
044	A	N1010H N44LJ N54JA (N77JW) N286AB N70LJ
045	A	(N700MD) N900MD N13FN N546PA [w/o 03Dec02, Astoria, WA; parted out; cx Jun03]
046	A*	F-BKFB N4448Y N146MJ N17A
047	A	G-ZEIZ N2972Q N14CN N36SK OE-GMD N36PJ
048	A*	HB-VHF N3999B (N14FU) N2FU N24PT N3NP PT-WGM N32AJ D-CFGG
049	A	N661AA N136ST VH-SLF [wfu 2015, Wagga Wagga, Australia]
050	A	N3456L XA-RIA Mexico TP-105/XC-AA24 Mexico TP-105/XC-UJP
051	A	N4290J Peru 524/OB-1431
052	A	N1087T Peru 525/OB-1432
053	A	N39418 China HY984 B-4184
054	A/U36A	(N54GL) N1087Z Japan 9201
055	A	N10871 OE-GNL N365AS PP-JAA S9-CRH ZS-CRH N41GJ
056	A/U36A	N3802G Japan 9202 [w/o 21May03 Iwakuni AFB, Japan]
057	A	N39394 HB-VIF VH-JCX
058	A/U36A	N4290J Japan 9203 [w/o 28Feb91 Shikoku Island, Japan]
059	A/U36A	N1087Z Japan 9204
060	A/U36A	N1088A Japan 9205
061	A/U36A	N50154 N2601B Japan 9206
062	A*	N4291N D-CGFE
063	A*	N6340T N1048X D-CGFF

Production complete

LEARJET MODEL 40

C/n	Identities						
45-001	N45XL	N40LX	[converted from model 45 circa 2002 and ff as such on 31Aug02]				
2001	N40LJ	[ff 05Sep02]		N401LJ			
2002	N40KJ	N789AH	N482ES	PR-JOF			
2003	N404MK	LQ-BFS					
2004	N40082	N605FX	N605BX				
2005	N40083	N606FX	M-LRJT	N657MP	N302CR*		
2006	N50111	D-CNIK	PR-WSB				
2007	N50126	N40PX	G-MOOO	N990JT	N64HT	LV-GVR	
2008	N5013U	N2408	N99GK				
2009	N40LJ	CC-CMS					
2010	N50163	N46E	N46FE				
2011	N4001G	N51001	N411AJ				
2012	N607FX	N479JS					
2013	N5018G	XA-GRR					
2014	N608FX	N499GS					
2015	N40077	I-ERJG	OE-GGC				
2016	N40078	I-ELYS					
2017	N5009T	N502JM	N700KG				
2018	N5018G	OE-GGB	D-CGGB	N118AV	PP-ASV		
2019	N50111	G-FORN	I-FORR				
2020	N50153	PR-ONE					
2021	N5013U	N401EG					
2022	N5013Y	N609FX	N510GW	N537XX			
2023	N50163	N521CH					
2024	N424LF	N40ML	I-YLFC	9H-CFL			
2025	N225LJ	N240RP					
2026	N5014E	OE-GVI	EC-JYY	N77CJ	(XA-...)		
2027	N50154	N40LJ	N610FX	N684JB	N116DJ		
2028	N40XR						
2029	N40073	N996AL	N998AL	[w/o 18Jun09 Fort Worth/Meacham, TX; parted out by Alliance Air Parts, Oklahoma City, OK]			
	N998AQ						
2030	N40076	XA-SNI					
2031	N40085	RP-C3110					
2032	N5015U	N10SE					
2033	N404EL	N77ZE					
2034	N5018G	I-PARS	N151VA	PT-FRD			
2035	N40050	N1848T	N1348T	PR-PPG			
2036	N100HW						
2037	N237LJ	N611FX	N689JB	N119DJ			
2038	N22GM	N290GS					
2039	N612FX	N256MH	N120DJ				
2040	N5009V	(XA-GPE)	XA-CGF	N112DJ	PR-WNA		
2041	N614FX						
2042	N256AH	N258AH	XA-PAR				
2043	N4001G	C-FMHA					
2044	N5016V	N140LJ	N232PH				
2045	N176CA	N88LJ					
2046	N4004Q	N40LJ	N773RS	XC-TJN			
2047	N616FX	N473BD	XA-RAB				
2048	N40077	N80169	PR-JBS	N586CC	PP-NRV		
2049	N5012K	N140WW	N422KS	N239SR			
2050	N5015U	VP-BHT	N609CR				
2051	N615FX	PR-LOU					
2052	N784CC						
2053	N5018G	I-ERJJ	N253EC	N253RM			
2054	N50111	G-MEET	XA-USP				
2055	N5010U	N55XR	N506KS				
2056	N411HC						
2057	N616FX	N200KJ					
2058	N71NF	N71NX	N219RB				
2059	N619FX	N695BD	I-GURU				
2060	N999EK	N133VS					
2061	N5016Z	D-CLUX	N108JE				
2062	N4005Q	PT-XDN					
2063	N240WG	N740KG					
2064	N5000E	(OY-KVP)	"OY-KPV"	"N34AG"	N540LH	OY-KVP	
2065	N617FX	N356RR					
2066	N50154	N2758W					
2067	N618FX	XA-NJM					
2068	N5012G	PP-FMW	N286KR	N137BR			
2069	N24VP	N29RN	N29RE				
2070	N77HN	N711BH					
2071	N40077	OY-ZAN	D-CLUZ	(D-CFAF)	D-CLOZ	N550VT	N301RJ
2072	N4003K	N83JJ	N15UB	N25UB			

LEARJET 40

C/n	Identities					
2073	N40083	N975DM				
2074	N40012	G-STUF	N268KR	N41UA		
2075	N75XR	N484CH	PR-MFX			
2076	N618FX	N618PJ				
2077	N5015U	XA-VFV	N951FM			
2078	N40079	I-GOCO				
2079	N40082	D-CVJP	OE-GVA	N427DC	PP-LRJ	
2080	N40076	D-CPDR	F-HPEB			
2081	N24VP	PR-DIB	(N288KR)			
2082	N619FX	N338VT				
2083	N51054	N419ET	N412ET	N740KD		
2084	N40LJ	N65TP				
2085	N620FX					
2086	N4003W	PR-PTR				
2087	N40NB	N779CF				
2088	N288AS					
2089	N621FX	N450LJ				
2090	N4003K	N90XR				
2091	N5009T	D-CVJN	N431DC	OE-GHF		
2092	N426JK	N173DS	C-FIPP			
2093	N5016Z	D-CAHB	N880MS	PR-BCC		
2094	N40079	CS-TFO				
2095	N622FX	N803EA	N27AX			
2096	N40083	OY-RED	LV-CJY			
2097	N40078	(D-CVJT)	OE-GVX	N480ES		
2098	N40043	N346CN	N346CM	N810JK		
2099	N623FX	N627SC				
2100	N959RP	(N959RB)	N901FP			
2101	N152UT	VT-VSA	N152UT	N725BH		
2102	N4003K	G-HPPY	C-GLRP	PR-LJG*		
2103	N140HM					
2104	N624FX	N550DN	C-GSJV			
2105	N40085	N295SG	N296SG	(N998AL)	N4003L	PR-JEC
2106	N700MB					
2107	N50145	D-CGGC	N204PG	PP-CRV		
2108	N5009T	(G-RMPI)	N718EJ	N945EJ		
2109	N625FX	N77NR	N905ST			
2110	N50157	N556HD	N554HD	LV-GQW		
2111	N40PD					
2112	N40050	OE-GXX				
2113	N40075	N477XR	N123AC			
2114	N40083	N663LB	PR-PVI			
2115	N5012Z	N115LJ				
2116	N625FX					
2117	N4004Q	(XA-LOA)	PP-CRC			
2118	N4008G	N289JP	N57MC			
2119	N40082	N119NJ	N300GF			
2120	(D-COIN)	N626FX				
2121	N40081	(D-COIN)	N140EP	N24QT	N124QT	N18AX
2122	N40162	N990WA				
2123	N4003W	N255AH	N256AH			
2124	N50126	(N627FX)	N403LS			
2125	N5016Z	N44LG				
2126	N5017J	N46MW				
2127	N5016V	N209MD				
2128	N5012H	N802AK				
2129	N785BC	[prototype Learjet 70]		N616KK		
2130	N50185	N998AL	(N998AB)	N998NJ		
2131	N40075	N25TQ	N25QT	N125QT	N70AX	PP-CPR*
2132	N51053	N641K	N341K			
2133	N40079	N49HM	PR-RNF	M-DMBP		

LEARJET 70

Although officially registered as Learjet 40s with c/ns following that model's sequence, Learjet 70s have also been allocated secondary c/ns by Learjet Inc as listed below. This second c/n has been painted on many (if not all) of the Learjet 70s built so far.

C/n		Identities			
2134	70-001	N40085	N9CH		
2135	70-002	N4001G	N356K		
2136	70-003	N50185	N959RC	N959RP	
2137	70-004	N40162	N137LJ	N444KM	N31PF
2138	70-005	N4002P	(N359K)	N352K	
2139	70-006	N70NJ			
2140	70-007	N10870	N359H	N359K	
2141	70-008	N5012H	N15UB		
2142	70-009	N4004Q	C-GTLP		
2143	70-010	N40050	N342K		
2144	70-011	N4001G	N998AB	N998AL	
2145	70-012	N50153	C-GFFT		
2146	70-013	N98QC			
2147	70-014				
2148	70-015				
2149	70-016				

LEARJET MODEL 45

C/n	Identities							
001	N45XL	[ff 07Oct95]	N40LX	[converted to Model 40 circa 2002 qv]				
002	N45LJ	N452LJ	[instructional airframe, Wichita Area Technical College National Center for Aviation Training, KS]					
003	N453LJ	(N789H)	[to ground instruction airframe, Pima Community College, Tucson, AZ]					
004	N454LJ	[w/o 27Oct98 Wallops Island, VA]						
005	N455LJ	G-ZXZX	OE-GIQ					
006	N456LJ	ZS-OIZ	N456LM	N721CP	YV351T	N445BH	N45YF	
007	N457LJ	(ZS-JBR)	(ZS-BAR)	ZS-OPD	VH-EJK	(ZS-ITT)	TC-CMB	
008	N745E	N80RP	N458DP					
009	N984GC	N459LJ	N500CG	N395WB				
010	(D-CWER)	N41DP	N903HC	N311BP	N811BP	N556JP		
011	N741E	N741F	N89RP	N459DP				
012	N5009V	N412LJ	(OE-...)	D-COMM	D-CMLP	N450TJ		
013	N5010U	N413LJ	D-CEWR	D-CFWR	N45LR			
014	N708SP	(N202JR)						
015	N31V	N30AB	N781RX					
016	N743E	N743F	N74SG	XA-WNG	N797CH	XA-UVA	N716SC	N607BF
017	(D-CWER)	N417LJ	D-CESH	D-CSMS	M-CSMS			
018	N418LJ	OO-LFS	D-CDOC					
019	N56WD	N45LJ	C-GCMP	(N.....)	C-GLRJ	N442LF	VT-CRA	
020	N5000E	HB-VMA	N45NP	C-GVVZ				
021	N5009T	HB-VMB	CS-TFI	N440JJ				
022	N5012G	PT-TJB	N453BL	N345RL	N845RL	C-GSWQ		
023	N740E	(N740SG)	N353AP	N45HM				
024	N145ST	C-FBCL	C-FVSL	D-CNMB				
025	N742E	N742F	(N354AP)	(N909DD)	N200KP	N300AN		
026	N405FX	N405BX	XC-HIE					
027	N156PH	N156PB	N445SB	N838TH	N1250			
028	N5014E	HB-VMC	XC-VMC	[w/o 04Nov08 Mexico City, Mexico]				
029	N5013Y	9V-ATG	N290LJ	N170LS				
030	N5012H	N157PH	N157PB					
031	N5016V	9V-ATH	N310LJ					
032	N4FE	N932JC	N774MC	N621VS*				
033	N50162	9V-ATI	VH-SQD	T7-SCI				
034	N45FE	N454LP	XA-VYC					
035	N5013U	9V-ATJ	VH-SQM	A4O-..				
036	N345WB	I-FORU						
037	N50145	OE-GDI	G-CPRI	ZS-CJB				
038	N454AS	(N454RR)	N14FE	N14BX	XA-RIU			
039	N456AS	N15FE	(N390AB)	N45FE	N238LM			
040	(N145MC)	N68PC	N68PQ	N501CG	N930TC			
041	N541LJ	C-GPDQ	C-GPDB					
042	N10R	N917LH	XA-JAO					
043	D-CRAN	N45VB						
044	D-CLUB	N888CX	4O-MNE					
045	N4545	PR-SZA						
046	ZS-PTL	ZS-OLJ	ZS-BAR	ZS-OXB	N136MA	N336UB	XB-RMT	XA-RMT
047	N158PH	N158PD	N206CK	[2000th Learjet built]				
048	PT-XLR							
049	N711R							
050	N16PC	N16PQ	LV-BOU					
051	N145KC	N927SK						
052	N5011L	ZS-DCT	N745SA	N233MK				
053	N685RC	N3211Q	N1904S					
054	N345MA							
055	N63MJ	N45LR	G-JRJR	G-OLDF	G-GOMO	G-PFCT	G-UJET	
056	N196PH	VH-LJX						
057	N75TE	N83TN	N83TZ	XA-SUK	XA-UVW			
058	N50111	RP-C1944	N660HC	N237DM	N55DG			
059	N50153	VP-CVL	N590JC	ZS-PNP				
060	N1MG	N459LC						
061	N111KK	N443SL						
062	N512RB	N543CM						
063	N10J	N10JY						
064	N800MA	N800UA	EC-ILK	I-AVND				
065	N100KK	N100KZ						
066	N94CK	D2-FFX						
067	N5087B	XA-LRX	XA-QUE	N220AR	XA-PRA			
068	I-ERJD	OE-GJC	N145RG	N126BK				
069	N50157	SU-MSG	D2-EBN					
070	N50163	LX-IMS	N450JC	LV-GVX				
071	N145K	N145KL	N989PA	N103EZ	N109EZ			
072	N5016Z	I-ERJC	N720CC	N720GB				
073	N65U	N66SG						
074	N815A	N740TF						

LEARJET 45

C/n	Identities					
075	N450BC					
076	N245K	N2451Y	N988PA	N881MJ		
077	N5018G	PT-XVA	N770DS	XA-AIM	N273LM	N476CA
078	N5016Z	N116AS				
079	N5FE	N100GY				
080	N42HP	N45UJ	N451DJ	(N451DZ)	N45EJ	
081	N76TE	N145GM	N30TL	PT-FLE		
082	N40082	N1HP	N473YH	N184R	N95VS	
083	N5013Y	OY-LJG	ZS-TJS			
084	N5009V	HB-VML	OE-GVM	HB-VML	N845SC	[dbr in refuelling incident at Bangor, ME, 23Dec14; parted out by Alliance Air Parts, Oklahoma City, OK]
085	N454CG	C-FPBX				
086	N4001G	N386K	C-GMRO			
087	N645HJ	N64HH				
088	N454MK	C-FMGL	C-FLLH	N484VL	N910LJ	
089	N406FX	N406BX	XA-EFM			
090	N407FX	N452CJ				
091	N408FX	(N408BX)	N451WM	[parted out by Deer Valley Aviation Parts, Wilmington, DE]		
092	N5016V	ZS-LOW	(ZS-PPR)	ZS-PDG	D2-SRR	
093	N5014F	N450TR	(PT-XLF)	I-ERJC	[w/o 01Jun03 Milan-Linate, Italy]	
094	N300JE	N800WC	N49CJ	LQ-CPS		
095	N409FX	N409F	N786CC			
096	N5009T	C-GDMI	N450JG	C-FNJT		
097	N5017J	D-CMSC	LX-LAR			
098	N6FE	N450HA				
099	(N545RS)	N7FE	N745TT			
100	N50145	N45LJ	RP-C1958	N345BH		
101	N410FX	N410BX	N22AX			
102	N411FX	N411BX	N810YS	XA-EEA	XA-UUB	N102ES
103	N412FX	(N412F)	N720MC	N45XT		
104	N40012	OH-IPJ	N450BK	3D-BIS	4O-SEV	
105	N105LJ	N397AT	(N17LJ)	N89ZZ	N99NJ	
106	N145XL					
107	N145CG	(N145CM)	N762EL			
108	N50154	N313BW	N313BH			
109	N60PC	N451CF	N945HC			
110	N4002P	N222MW				
111	N414FX	N414BX	XA-BFX	XC-HIF		
112	N415FX	CN-TJB				
113	N416FX	N124BP	N869DL	N1245L		
114	N417FX	N318SA				
115	N90UG	(N405MW)	N45MW			
116	N50111	OY-LJJ	A6-MED	OY-LJJ	N116WE	PP-CPN
117	N40081	ZS-DCA				
118	N50163	N5XP	N75XP			
119	N5016V	N316SR	N1RB	N145LR		
120	N418FX	N418FA	N45TU			
121	N316SR	(N666BG)	N45HF			
122	N945FD	D-....				
123	N454LC	N484LC	N21AX	N750CR		
124	N4003Q	G-OLDL	N124AV	G-JANV	N526CF	
125	N419FX	N145MW	N145MN	PP-JAW		
126	N420FX	C-FXHN	C-GMCP			
127	N421FX	N421FY	XA-ALF			
128	N10NL					
129	N4003W	N9CH	N455DG			
130	N583FH	N4001G	(ZS-OSP)	N418MN		
131	N444MW	N218JL				
132	N132LJ	N889CA				
133	N645KM	N183CM				
134	N4004Q	N423FX	N423FA	N751JC		
135	N4004Y	N422FX	N423DC	XA-UJR		
136	N45BA	(N136LJ)	N583PS	N883BS	N654AT	N659AT
137	N45AJ	N800AB				
138	N5018G	G-OLDJ	N138AX	G-SOVB		
139	N45VL	XA-UAG	XA-EMM			
140	N40050	XA-AED	N345SV			
141	N142HC	N142HQ	N858MK	N910JK		
142	N145SB	(N450DS)	CC-ADC	N129FS	N188SG	
143	N4005Q	N145GS	N334AF	N384AF	N917BE	
144	N5011L	D-CEMM	CS-TLW			
145	N50145	N421FX	N942FK			
146	N424FX	N460DC	PR-OPF			
147	N425FX	N425LW	N44NJ			
148	N40075	N8084R	D-CDEN	OE-GAR	M-ROMA	N148LJ N33NJ

LEARJET 45

C/n	Identities						
149	N451CL	N451GL	N904HD				
150	N245KC	N348K	(N848K)	N546DH			
151	N345K	N345FM					
152	N3013Q	N5014E	VH-CXJ				
153	N30137	C-GCMP	N302KR	N345FF			
154	N3008P	N886CA	N918EG				
155	N145MC	N882CA					
156	N3017F	G-OLDC	N156AV	C-FLRJ	N495EC		
157	N545RA	N341K	N371K	PR-LEB			
158	N3019T	LX-DSL	I-DFSL	D-CPSG	N523BM	N979DR	
159	N5001J	N828CA	N696KT				
160	N455PM	N455DE	N863CA	N863LB			
161	N3000S	G-OLDR	N161AV	G-SOVC	SE-RKY	D-CSOS	
162	N426FX	N426LW	PR-BFM	N455EA			
163	N427FX	N427BX	5N-BGR	C-FZAU	N45NY		
164	N428FX	PR-OSF					
165	N429FX	XA-SEG					
166	N430FX	(N430BX)	(PR-MIS)	C-GEJD			
167	N5012V	G-GMAA					
168	N50088	VH-PFS					
169	N5013D	N77HN	N332K	N424TG			
170	N5013E	(XA-SKY)	N50154	N45UP	N45VS		
171	N171DP	N342K	(N322K)	XA-PBX			
172	N70PC	N1893N					
173	N900P	N906P					
174	N45HC	N887SG					
175	N328RR	N30SF	N41TF				
176	N5016S	N45TK	N176TK	XA-IKE			
177	N431FX	N695GL	PP-MPJ				
178	N50207	XA-JMF	N317GS				
179	N5023U	N863CA	N541AL	N45MR	N179MR	N942MB	
180	N880LJ	N345RL					
181	N5024E	ZS-PTL	(ZS-FUL)	(ZS-AJN)	V5-TTO		
182	N50248	N345AW					
183	N5025K	N511WP	C-GHMP				
184	N45VP	N866CA					
185	N273LP						
186	N158EC						
187	N5030J	N146XL	N451KG*				
188	N5018G	N21BD	XA-UJZ				
189	N5030N	N800MA	D-CSUL	XA-CMA			
190	N41PC	N41PQ	N787EJ	N988RC			
191	N158EC	N191LJ	XA-LVS				
192	N433FX	PP-MMX					
193	N434FX	N865CA					
194	N5040W	ZS-YES	ZS-ULT				
195	N5040Y	VH-SQR	N113RX	(N713RX)	N508RX		
196	N50353	N473LP	N531AC				
197	N432FX	PP-JLY	N197EC				
198	N5048K	N45UG	N229BK				
199	N545EC	N1925P	N1925B				
200	N451ST	HK-5107					
201	N473LP	N452ST	(N451SC)	N617RX			
202	N5048Q	N445N					
203	N145AR						
204	N5010U	N204MK	VH-ZZH	N45NP			
205	N5011L	N5052K	N88AF				
206	N45UG	N5042A	N45AX	N445AX	N445RM		
207	N5000E	VH-SQV	N131RX	(N431RX)	N164RX		
208	N5009V	N5050G	N715CG	N719CG	N615CG		
209	N435FX	(N435FA)	N300JC	N209KM	XA-CFX		
210	N5009V	N866RA	N29RE	N29ZE	XA-ALA	N233TM	N1TK
211	N50145	N50490	N300AA	N300AQ	(N299BB)	M-MRBB	
212	N50111	N434FX	N599TA				
213	N50126	D-CEWR	G-MUTD	G-RWGW	M-RWGW	C-FHCW	
214	N214LF	N29SM	N555CK				
215	N5018G	N822CA	N352K	N852K			
216	N5016V	C-GHCY	N359K	(N559K)	N777QL		
217	N5016Z	N1RL	N400	N401Q	N217MJ	(N977AR)	
218	N50163	N310ZM	N451JC	ZS-OPY			
219	N4003K	ZS-BAR	ZS-OPR				
220	N40077	N825CA					
221	N823CA						
222	N673LP	N673LB	N826CA				
223	N40081	(D-CTAN)	C-FNRG	C-GPKS	N338K	ZS-LRJ	

LEARJET 45

C/n	Identities						
224	N822CA	N822GA	N77702	C-GQPM			
225	N436FX	N518GS	N558GS	N90GS	N330GS	N456GS	
226	N40085	I-ERJE	N126EC				
227	N437FX	N721BS	N821BS	N903RL	N70AE	N645FD	
228	N5012Z	ZS-LOW	V5-LRJ				
229	N40079	N159EC					
230	N4008G	N451N					
231	N40073	N30PC	N30PF	N145HC	N145GP	XA-ALN	
232	N40076	N45XR	LV-ARD				
233	N5000E	N45KX					
234	N5009T	Ireland 258					
235	N50145	N30PC	N30PQ	XA-JPG			
236	N5018G	N125GW	N66DN	G-LLOD	XA-SAA		
237	N5017J	N45QG	N44QG	N43QG	PP-HSI	N556CG	
238	N570AM	(N577CC)					
239	N45LJ	C-GJCY					
240	N5016Z	(D-CTAN)	N50579	N9FE	N45ZR		
241	N241LJ	N820KD*					
242	N4003W	N45SY	PR-OTA				
243	N4004Q	G-IOOX	OE-GFF	XA-ZZZ			
244	N5009V	N545K					
245	N5010U	N745K					
246	N5012G	XA-HFM	N1019K	XA-SAP			
247	N50154	N3AS	N401SF				
248	N4004Y	N48TF	(N83TR)	N48TE	LV-CAR		
249	N40075	C-GLRS	M-GLRS	N435DC			
250	N40050	OO-LFN	ZS-CVU				
251	N40073	N145XR	XA-MVG	N45VG	N918DG		
252	N40076	N272BC	N876BC	N272BC	N876BC	XA-UXS	
253	N4008G	N45NM					
254	N729SB	N728SB	LV-BXD				
255	N40081	C-FSDL	C-GUSM				
256	N5011L	B-3988	N97XR	XA-GTP			
257	N5012H	N555VR					
258	N5015U	N45LJ	N395BC				
259	N40PC	N451LJ	(N778T)				
260	N745TC						
261	N5010U	N451BW					
262	N50126	VH-VVI	N45AU	VH-VVI			
263	N50157	N263RA	N263MR	LV-GOM			
264	N5016V	N910BD	N916BD	N816BD	N1899	N189PP	
265	N5017J	G-OLDT	N630BB	P4-BFS			
266	N40012	"LX-IMS"	[wrongly painted at completion centre]	LX-IMZ	(D-CLHM)	D-CHLM	N787CH
267	N4002P	N451HC	N219JL				
268	N5009V	N145K					
269	N4003W	N245K					
270	N4004Q	(ZS-FUL)	C-FBLJ	C-FXYN	N820AT		
271	N4004Y	N45XR	N435FX	XB-NHM	XA-EXE	XA-QLO	
272	N40043	N288CB					
273	N4005Q	N183TS					
274	N40075	N274CZ	N728VG	N274RM*			
275	N40082	C-FRYS					
276	N40084	N88WV					
277	N40086	N912BD	N918BD	N818BD			
278	N63WR	(N63WL)	N63WJ				
279	N4008G	N45LJ	N279AJ	[w/o 03Jan09 Telluride, CO; parted out by Alliance Air Parts Oklahoma City, OK]			
280	N40079	G-CDNK	CS-DTL	N145JP	M-RBIG		
281	N5012H	N617BD	N917BD	N817BD	XA-JRS		
282	N456Q	N45QQ					
283	N4DA						
284	N40078	XA-ARB					
285	N5012Z	N300AA					
286	N50126	G-CDSR	CS-DTM	VH-LJQ			
287	N5013Y	CS-TLT	F-HACP	(D-CBCP)	9H-BCP		
288	N5014F	C-FBCL	C-GKDT	N547LF	N651AY		
289	N5013U	N68PC	N68PQ	N840JM			
290	N45BZ	VT-TRI					
291	N4002P	OO-EPU	N291LJ				
292	N4003W	JA01GW	N98XR	N273TA	N852BA	N95AX	N155ME
293	N45XR	(N694SC)	TG-ABY	N45HD			
294	N5014E	G-OLDW	G-IZIP	N595LA	TC-RSB		
295	N4004Y	XA-UFB					
296	N4003K	N454LC	N484LC	N118RK			
297	N50154	(N145CG)	N145CM				
298	N5000E	N191TD					

LEARJET 45

C/n	Identities					
299	N453ST	N445WF				
300	N145AP					
301	N45KJ	N996BP	N45VA			
302	N4008G	JA02GW	N99XR	CS-TFQ		
303	N40043	C-FANS	N303LJ			
304	N40086	N400	N4009	N90RZ	(N473AC)	N117WH
305	N40073	N45XR	N808KS	ZS-KAA	T7-KAA	
306	N5009T	OY-OCV	M-EOCV	N306AV	(N245LH)	N796JH
307	N425G					
308	N436FX	N415CL	ZS-OPM	LX-LAA		
309	N436FX	LV-BXV				
310	N5014F	N345K				
311	N40078	G-OLDK	G-IZAP	G-XJET		
312	N575AG	N808AK	PR-PAK	N808AK		
313	N45KH					
314	N74PT					
315	N437FX					
316	N50145	AP-BHY				
317	N438FX	N605SE	N87SK			
318	N45LJ	(N45XR)	N196CT	N797ES	N793ES	
319	N16PC	N451XR	YV3193			
320	N452A	PR-CAO				
321	N4002P	ZS-OPN	LX-EAA			
322	N5011L	N313BW				
323	N50157	N125BW				
324	N50126	N12VU				
325	N40085	N390GG	Mexico 3912			
326	N50126	N507FG	XB-GTH			
327	N50153	N726EL	N816LP	N526EL	5N-LDM	
328	N40081	F-HCGD	G-HCGD	N87AX	N214TG	
329	N5012K	N454JF	PR-CSM			
330	N5009V	N45XT	N2HP	N36GL		
331	N40084	N583PS				
332	N45XR	N445TG				
333	N438FX					
334	N4003Q	N445SE				
335	N435HH					
336	N40073	N45YH	4X-CYH	M-EANS	N55EP	(N54EC)
337	N10J					
338	N45TK	N46TK	N45TQ	N45KV	XA-ABD	
339	N454N					
340	N5014F	N300JQ	N300JC	N922KM	N657PP	
341	N439FX					
342	N5011L	ZS-OPO	D-CDRF	LX-ONE		
343	N45HG					
344	N607FG	N196AT				
345	N5017J	N45MR	(N45MX)	Peru 526		
346	N440FX					
347	N40050	D-CINS				
348	N4005Q	N744E	N66MT			
349	N45HK					
350	N50153	5N-BLW				
351	N60PC	N351XR	N392DL			
352	N988MC					
353	N903BT	PP-SCE	N903BT	LV-GQM		
354	N40077	N135CG				
355	N4008G	N45XP				
356	N745E	N961MM				
357	N441FX					
358	N40081	5N-DAL				
359	N710R					
360	N5012H	C-FMGL	N249TX	N80AE		
361	N45LJ	N44QG	N547LF	N505BC		
362	N40075	C-GLYS	N251TX	N119GM		
363	N453A					
364	N442FX	N442FP				
365	N5XP	ZS-SGU				
366	N20FE	N301KR	N366LV			
367	N741E					
368	N4003W	EI-WFO	N350AP	[prototype Learjet 75]		
369	N40082	ZS-AJD				
370	N4005Q	N743E				
371	N443FX	N21AX	N31AX	N654AT		
372	N5009V	4O-BBB	D-CRBE	SE-RMO		
373	N5013U	N984XR				

LEARJET 45

C/n	Identities					
374	N5014F	VP-BSF	M-ABEU			
375	N4003L	G-SNZY	N24AX	N256TT		
376	N4002P	N145GR	N145GM	N15CF		
377	N50163	N54AX	N45AX			
378	N444FX					
379	N50154	N379LJ				
380	N45XR	N774CC	N729JM	N729JV	N818AF	N317MC*
381	N5010U	N45XR	RP-C8338	N296JA		
382	N40073	CS-TFR				
383	N5016V	N176MG	PR-VPO	N91FG	N145PJ	
384	N5012H	N694LP	N745KD			
385	N5015U	XA-HUR				
386	N545CG					
387	N41PC	N325PT				
388	N40078	LV-BTO				
389	N389CG	YV2565				
390	N390CG	YV2567				
391	N40086	G-OSRL				
392	N40144	N45LJ	N81FJ			
393	N40146	N93XR	N504WV	N245FH		
394	N40043	(N45LJ)	N818CH	N918DG	N145VG	
395	N40149	D-CLMS				
396	N396GC	YV1118				
397	N40079	(N445FX)	N458A	N192TD		
398	N398CG	N818CH	N694SH	N5014E	LX-JAG	LX-RSQ
399	N50145	(N545K)	N545KS	N32AA		
400	N40085	N145MW				
401	N50111	N848CA	N848AG			
402	N10873	(N745K)	N26QT	N945K		
403	N40012	N245CM				
404	N4001G	OO-KJD	G-DDDJ	N961AS		
405	N5015U	(N451K)	N474TC			
406	N40149	(N452K)	N624EC	N821LC		
407	N5011L	N359JR	YV2670	YV2734		
408	N4005Q	C-FVSL	N286KR	N960AS		
409	N40077	(N453K)	N667MC			
410	N940K	N94CK				
411	N40082	N411VE	N45TK	N451SD		
412	N5010U	N309KC	PT-SAF			
413	N40012	"N45XR"+	[+ fake marks N45XR worn in NBAA static display Atlanta/DeKalb-Peachtree, GA, 19-21Oct10]			
	N451A					
414	N4001G	N414VE	N414VF	N45RR		
415	N40162	N415VE	YV2716			
416	N5012G	C-FBCL	N590CH	N450FC		
417	N5014E	N30PC				
418	N4002P	N411FG	N103EZ*			
419	N4003K	N454LC				
420	N50157	N511FG				
421	N5009V	C-FSDL	N589CH	N5015U	M-ABGV	
422	N40073	PR-HVN				
423	N40144	N70GM	N45XR	N545AR	N808W	
424	N5018L	N424VE	YV2738			
425	N10872	N425VE	YV2739			
426	N5012H	N681P				
427	N5016V	N98AS	N3AS			
428	N4003L	N46TQ	N46TK	N452SD		
429	N4004Q	N999LB	N399LB	N121GZ	N551MM	
430	N5012K	N618CW				
431	N5015U	N28QT	N128QT	N780BH		
432	N50154	N70PC				
433	N5010U	LV-CVQ				
434	N50157	N34XR	C-GCMP			
435	N5016Z	N45LD	N916BD	N845BA	N501KT	
436	N5017J	N45MX	N528JJ			
437	N4002P	N437LJ	N422AJ	N455NJ		
438	N4003K	HB-VDW				
439	N50111	N826EP				
440	N40050	LV-CYQ				
441	N40076	N2476	N2426			
442	N40078	N104DN	N925ST			
443	N40082	N443LJ	N21AX	XA-...		
444	N40144	AP-BKP				
445	N40149	N445FD	N483SC			
446	N10871	[Learjet 75 development a/c]			N446LJ	N446DJ
447	N50185	N45GH				

LEARJET 45

C/n	Identities				
448	N40084	N365LP			
449	N5009V	N986BL			
450	N5011L	N917BD	N846BA	N131JX	
451	N5012H	N925MW			
452	N50126	N247MX			
453	N5016V	N68PC			
454	N5009T	N918BD	N849BA	N5015U	M-ABJA
455	N5012Z	N445FD			

LEARJET 75

Although officially registered as Learjet 45s with c/ns following that model's sequence, Learjet 75s have also been allocated secondary c/ns by Learjet Inc as listed below. This second c/n has been painted on many (if not all) of the Learjet 75s built so far.

C/n	Identities					
456	75-001	N50145	N157MW			
457	75-002	N5013Y	N457LJ	XA-MBU		
458	75-003	N575AR				
459	75-004	N5015U	N353K			
460	75-005	N40043	N999LB			
461	75-006	N40081	N461LJ	N75FP		
462	75-007	N5014F	N354K			
463	75-008	N5017J	C-FMGL			
464	75-009	N5013U	N1845T	N1848T		
465	75-010	N40012	C-GLYS			
466	75-011	N40073	C-FVSL			
467	75-012	N5012G	C-FBCL			
468	75-013	N10872	C-FSDL			
469	75-014	N40079	N984BH			
470	75-015	N5016Z	N19GR			
471	75-016	N5000E	N366CM	N346CM		
472	75-017	N5009T	N228H	N2HP		
473	75-018	N5009V	N475JT			
474	75-019	N50111	N455SC			
475	75-020	N5012Z	N275DE	N1850M*		
476	75-021	N50126	V5-RON			
477	75-022	N5014E	N60PL	N60PC		
478	75-023	N5010U	N977RJ			
479	75-024	N5016V	(N445FX)	N470FX		
480	75-025	N10873	N495RJ			
481	75-026	N5011L	N26QT			
482	75-027	N50157	N482LJ	XA-MBD		
483	75-028	N4003K	N101KK			
484	75-029	N4003W	N342SP			
485	75-030	N4005Q	N752R			
486	75-031	N40076	N63WG	N63WR		
487	75-032	N40082	N178TM			
488	75-033	N40077	F-HINC			
489	75-034	N40078	N100SA	N991GS	N800CH	
490	75-035	N4008G	SP-AAW			
491	75-036	N50163	OE-GEC			
492	75-037	N5016Z	N492LJ	XA-MBT		
493	75-038	N5009V	XA-SKA			
494	75-039	N5009T	9H-DDJ			
495	75-040	N5000E	N16PC			
496	75-041	N5018G	N877W			
497	75-042	N5012K	N175MX			
498	75-043	N50145	N333KK	N111KK		
499	75-044	N50111	N504CR			
500	75-045	N5012Z	N471FX			
501	75-046	N5013U	N472FX			
502	75-047	N4002P	N473FX			
503	75-048	N5013Y	N751LJ			
504	75-049	N5014E	N75LY			
505	75-050	N5014F	N812BR			
506	75-051	N50154	N474FX			
507	75-052	N40083	N45HC	N46F		
508	75-053	N5011L	N475FX			
509	75-054	N5010U	(XA-RAN)+	[+ ntu marks worn at the factory]		XA-VRM
510	75-055	N40079	N300JC			
511	75-056	N4003K	N476FX	N536MG		
512	75-057	N4003Q	N234TG	N176TG		
513	75-058	N4003L	RP-C629			
514	75-059	N50126	N477FX	N649JP		
515	75-060	N5017J	N40PC			
516	75-061	N5012H	N478FX	PP-MVH		
517	75-062	N50157	N912BD	N917BD		
518	75-063	N4003W	N918DD	N918BD		
519	75-064	N5016V	N1878C			
520	75-065	N4004Q	N916DD			
521	75-066	N4004Y	XA-MBC			
522	75-067	N40043	XA-MBS			
523	75-068	N4005Q	N72NF	N71NF		
524	75-069	N40075	XA-MBO			
525	75-070	N5021G	N282TA	N273TA		
526	75-071	N40076	XA-UXC			
527	75-072	N40050	XA-UXD			

LEARJET 75

C/n	Identities				
528	75-073	N40073	N753A		
529	75-074	N40012	N800KD		
530	75-075	N40078	C-GAJG		
531	75-076	N4008G	N769ST		
532	75-077	N40081	N786HD		
533	75-078	N40082	N173DX	N173DS	
534	75-079	N40084	N106GS	N90GS	
535	75-080	N40085	G-USHA		
536	75-081	N40086	N75LJ	N422JA	N422AJ
537	75-082	N10870	N418AB		
538	75-083	N10871	C-GYMD		
539	75-084	N40077	N574SF		
540	75-085	N10872	G-ZNTH		
541	75-086	N10873	N175HG		
542	75-087	N40144	N918PT		
543	75-088	N40146	N823LF	N6DA	
544	75-089	N40149	N751LP		
545	75-090	N40162	XA-EMA		
546	75-091	N5018L	N25QT		
547	75-092	N50185	N24QT		
548	75-093	N5000E	N28QT		
549	75-094	N5009T	N716FG		
550	75-095	N5009V	N816FG		
551	75-096	N5011L	N24AX		
552	75-097	N5012K	N754A		
553	75-098	N50145	N758A		
554	75-099	N5018G	N752LP		
555	75-100	N50111	TG-CCH*		
556	75-101	N5012G	N72HL		
557	75-102	N5012Z			
558	75-103	N50126	N272HL^		
559	75-104	N5013U			
560	75-105	N5010U			
561	75-106	N5012H			
562	75-107	N5013Y			
563	75-108	N5014E			
564	75-109				
565	75-110				
566	75-111				
567	75-112				
568	75-113				
569	75-114				
570	75-115				
571	75-116				
572	75-117				
573	75-118				
574	75-119				
575	75-120				
576	75-121				
577	75-122				
578	75-123				
579	75-124				
580	75-125				

LEARJET MODEL 55

C/n	Series	Identities
001	60	N551GL [model 55 prototype converted to 55C prototype] N551DF [converted to Model 60 prototype] N60XL [cx Sep96; wfu]
002		N552GL [given new c/n 55-139A on conversion to 55C standards (qv); cx Apr91]
003		N553GP N162GA N553DJ (N553GJ) N612EQ YV487T YV2904
004		N90E N50L N24JK N24CK D-CLIP (N500FA) N155DD N155PJ N728MG YV2868
005		N40ES N128VM N550CS (N94TJ) N440DM N440BM N999CM
006		N113EL N212JP N126EL N355DB N228PK N427TL N655TR
007		N41ES I-KILO [w/o 04Apr94 San Pablo Airport, Seville, Spain; remains to Atlanta Air Salvage, Griffin, GA]
008		N551SC N322GC
009		N42ES N55SJ HB-VIB N955FD N955MD N955LS N559BC N800LJ
010		N57TA [w/o 13Nov81 Waterkloof AFB, S Africa]
011		N37951 (N57TA) N411GL N574W D-CREW N200BA ES-PVV LY-LRJ SE-RCK D-CMAX [b/u May16, Nurnberg, Germany]
012		N55GH N23G N104BS N48HC N85XL N666TV N135GL
013		N10872 (D-CCHS) OE-GNK N3238K PT-LEL N82679 (N519AC) (N155AJ) (D-CEWR) D-CUTE N82679 D-CUTE N155SB N550JB YV598T
014		N40144 N90BS N55KC XA-PIL N550RH N155MP (N554EM) N455EM N551CG N1CG N441CG N303PM N308PM N52LJ YV591T
015		(YV-41CP) N39413 HB-VGV N515DJ N550LJ D-CION N27DD N551MF
016		N646G N717EP N717EB (N116GL)
017		N760AC N760AQ D-CCGN
018		N39E N599EC N797CS N822MC N805PC
019		YV-41CP N141SM C-GSWP
020		N720M N20DL N57B N8GT N123LC N35PF N55NY
021		N3794B N700TG EI-BSA I-LOOK N619MJ (N721GS) N211GS
022		N64WM VR-BOL VP-BOL N155GM N712MC N414TB
023		N3796B N7784 N110ET (N236PJ) [parted out by Alliance Air Parts, OK]
024		HB-VGZ N224DJ HB-VGZ N900FA (N54NW) N824CC
025		N236R N57PM N57FM N92MG N979RD YV3238
026		N8565H N55HD N21VB D-CILY (N96AF) N421QL (N321GL) N318JH N1324B N285DH
027		N3796X OE-GKN N3796X N123LC B-3980 N227A B-3980 N59HJ [parted out by Florida Jet Parts, Fort Lauderdale, FL]
028		N3794C PT-LDR N3794C PT-LOF N7244W (N53HJ) N556GA N556HJ N515CY
029		N4CP D-CLIP N29DJ N10CP PT-OHU N10CP N82JA N100VA N29NW (N55PJ) N915RT
030		N986WC N959WC N117WC N55LJ (N155CD) N122LX N238AX
031		YV-12CP YV1794
032		N75TP (N72TP) N71TP N81CH N11TS N83SD N183SD N255UJ N125LR XA-UCI
033		N96CE N960E N917S N414RF N155CS (VR-CJA) VR-CML PT-OOW N38JA (N377JW) (N77JW) N971EC N398AC N355UJ N355RM
034		N3795Y D-CARX N84DJ D-CLUB N77JW N37JA (N234LC) (N334JW) N123LC N550TC
035		N115EL (N100GU) N1968A N127EL D-CVIP N97AF C-GPCS VP-CUC N816MC VP-CTY N60GD
036		N3803G N555GL N81CH N76AW N81CH N236JW N155HM N723CC
037		N41CP N86AJ PT-OBR N53HJ
038		N551HB N50AF N666TK
039		N39418 N770JM N97J VR-BQF N339BC N539JM N399RL
040		N3802G HZ-AM11 HZ-AM2 N426EM N55HK N554CL
041		N401JE N155PJ N41EA N550RH (HP-....) HK-4016X N141FM N550LJ N802GJ N17LJ N923AL N928AL
042		N1462B N3796U N160TL D-CMTM N575GH
043		N5543G N785B (N500JC) N500JW N30AF N430HM (N455EC) N83WM YV3250
044		N3797C PT-LHR
045		N1451B HB-VHK EC-DSI VR-BHV EC-DSI (N90583) N49PE (N49PD) I-AGER N550AK (N123LC) [cx 15Nov14, CofR expired]
046		N23HB (N13HB) N3HB N55HL N855PT
047		N600C
048		(N734) N3796Z VH-LGH N73TP N67RW PT-OBS N558AC N558HJ N831JP
049		N6317V N3796C D-CCHS N150MS
050		N4289X D-CARP (HB-...) (N122JD) OY-FLK N220JC (N552BA) (N55UJ) [w/o 23Jun00 Boca Raton, FL]
051		N734 N22G N22GH N55KS N55KD D-CATL [United Nations code UN-453] N832JP HI929
052		N4289Z YV-292CP N55GF N551DB D-COOL
053		N4290Z N85653 YV-374CP (N1450B) N500RP N501RP N205EL (N205EF) N253S N531K
054		N42905 N54GL HB-VHL N54NW (N54LZ) (N54JZ)
055		(N155JC) N155LP N970H N970F N825MG N852PA N1JG N5QG YV3164
056		N8563E (N854GA) N946FP N59GS N272TB N270AS OH-IPP N156JC N607BF N607BR N62LJ
057		N4290Y N10CR N733EY N733E
058		(N55BE) N500BE N200PC N129SP N58SR YV2961
059		(N211BY) D-CAEP N50AF N59LJ OE-GRR M-KRRR D-CMED
060		N6331V N60MJ N53JL N86AJ N8YY N60LT PT-OUG N6364U N255TS N996CR N24NV
061		N117EL N222MC N132EL D-CFUX ES-PVT D-CFAI N655NC

LEARJET 55

C/n	Series	Identities
062		N62GL N24G N316 N292RC N855DB (N107MC) N69VH
063		N40146 N8563P N1744P N74RY N63AX N5XR
064		N255ST N121LT N900PJ N912MM (N17LZ) N400AT
065		N1088C N8565K N555GL N1125M (N565B) N75LJ N477YP
066		N237R (N550DD) N50DD N717HB
067		N39412 N120EL N127GT N505EH
068		N1088A N38D N135LR
069		N551UT N102ST N817AM
070		N1471B F-GDHR [w/o 05Feb87 over Cameroons nr Nigerian border]
071		N3807G (N155UT) N155JC N113YS
072		N58AS N55AS N55AQ PT-MSM N72ET SX-BNS N5572
073		N1087Z HB-VHN I-VIKY D-CARE N355DH N73WE N357PR N857PR N155V N667MB
074		N5574 N74GL N151PJ N701DB N155LR N905RL N755CL [parted out by Alliance Air Parts, Oklahoma City, OK]
075		N39415 N8563Z N675M N55GM N55GH N90NE N117LR
076		N155JC N2855 N30GL C-GKTM N551RA
077		N3812G N8563M N58M N85NC N245MS (N99YB)
078		N39391 (N55GJ) N55GV N56TG (N120GR) I-ALPR N55VK N345RJ N270JP
079		N39404 (N2855) N1983Y N700SR
080		N1465B N85632 PT-LET
081		N1468B N85631 N777MC N777MQ N903JC N61SJ
082		N39394 N1075X N33GL N68LP N817AM N139SK N599TC
083		N40149 N55GZ N6789 (N6780) N551AS (N500HG) N550HG (N550CK)
084		N39413 N85643 N740AC I-FLYJ D-CWDL ZS-ELI
085		N238R N58PM N58FM N55NM (N551MD) (N146PA) N225MD YV618T
086		N40162 D-CACP N8227P PT-LUK N558RA
087	ER	N1451B N8564Z N103C N520SC N520SQ N554PF N902RL SE-RGU N1852 M-TNTJ N955NC D-CAAY
088		N1461B N55GJ N155GS N900JB N901JC N522WK N60ND
089		N4289U N8564X N170VE N555CJ N789PF N628PT N312AL C-GLRJ C-GCIL
090		N40146 N723H D-CGIN N181EF N55UJ XA-BZA N86BR
091		N3810G N8566F N91CH N991CH N91PR (N69B) N700JE (N567SC) N591SC N30TK N911FC N429FC
092		N1462B N724J N400JT D-CLUB N500FA N40DK N890AC
093		N725K N32KJ N531P
094		N1088C N235HR (N236HR)
095		N39398 N8565Z N55RT D-CAAE
096		N1087T N1045X N8010X N126KD N126KL
097		N4290C N8566Q N40CR N20CR
098	ER	N726L D-CCON N550SC (N455UJ) N1324P (N132TP) N155ER
099		(N5599) N2992 N17GL N95WK
100		N3807G N552UT N552SQ N500NH (N500NB) N717AM
101	ER	N39415 N101HK N101PK N101HK N211EF N501TW N251VG (C-FNRG) N251NG C-FNRG N1129M N112WQ N307JA YV615T
102	ER	N1087Y N55DG I-OSUA N44GA PT-WSS N112FK N604FK N155TS N155SJ
103	ER	N10870 N921FP [w/o 06Aug86 Rutland, VT]
104		N39404 N18CG N18CQ (N95TJ) N277AL
105		N39391 N55GK N22G N274 C-GQBR N55AR
106		N3812G N60E N90AM N318JH N824MG (N850PA)
107	ER	N1466B N760G N155JT N304AT D-CWAY PH-ABU D-CWAY
108		(N888FK) N77FK N78FK N222MC N220VE (N551AM) N517AM (D-CMAX) D-CUNO N855NC
109		N348HM D-CVIP ZS-ELJ
110		N39412 N55GY (N24RH) N455RH
111		N1461B N7260G PT-LIG [w/o 09Nov94 Guanabara Bay, Rio de Janeiro, Brazil; parted out by Dodson Avn, Ottawa, KS]
112		N3802G (YV-325CP) N325CP LN-VIP N7AU EC-HAI N55LF [w/o 19Jul04 Fort Lauderdale Executive, FL; canx 17Mar05]
113		N1450B N7262M N713M N236HR N57MH N57MV
114		N39398 N72608 N34GB N355UA
115		N1476B N6666R N6666K N633AC N155BC N803GJ
116		N1087Y N85GL N116DA N51V N51VL N801GJ
117		N3807G N8567X N255MB N155RB N385RC
118		N39416 C-FCLJ N257SJ
119		N3816G N72613 N273MC N273MG N237PJ
120		N39418 N72629 N55LK (N486) N1127M N120LJ N777YC N329TJ
121		N3811G N8568J N65Y N155SC N747AN N1VG
122		N10870 N8568P N18ZD N99KW N99KV C-FHJB OE-GRO D-CGBR
123		N6331V N44EL N121US N150NE N417AM N420BG
124		N39391 N58CG N58CQ SX-BTV D-CONU
125	ER	N6307H N610JR
126		N4291G N7260J YV-125CP N7260J N16LJ (N162JG)
127	B	N6340T HZ-AM2 N73GP
128	B	N1087T N255BL N7US N7UA N10BF N717JB N8MF N655GP N787GT
129	B	N4290Y N75GP N655AL N60WA N72LJ N919AY
130	B	N4291N N55VC
131	B	N1088A N7260K N52CT YV2770

LEARJET 55

C/n	Series	Identities									
132	B	N4291K	N67WM	N133WB	(N333GJ)	(N133SU)	N122SU	N242RB	N795HA	[parted out by MTW Aerospace, Montgomery, AL]	
133	B	N155PL	N155LJ	N55LF	N700R	N810V	EC-INS				
134	B	N39399	N7261D	PT-LDR							
135	C	N1055C	PT-LXO	[w/o Rio de Janeiro/Santos Dumont, Brazil, 12Aug10]							
136	C	N3811G	N767AZ	N767NY	N155PS	OE-GCF	PH-MED	OE-GCF	D-CFAZ	N990CH	
137	C	N39413	N95SC	N155SP	PR-ERR						
138	C	N4291G	TC-MEK	TC-FBS	VR-CDK	N9LR	N338FP	N270WS	N234ES	YV3102	
139	C	N39391	N1039L	PT-LZS	PT-GMN	N139ST	N552TL				
139A	C	[converted from 55-002 (qv)]			N4289X	N994JD	N984JD	N55GM	(N55ZT)	N518SA	N518SB
140	C	N72616	PT-OCA	Brazil FAB6100							
141	C	N155DB									
142	C	N555MX	N755VT								
143	C	N10871	D-CMAD	ES-PVD	N143LJ						
144	C	N144LT	PT-OJH	N40CR	N178AM						
145	C	N66WM	N10CR	N211BC	N721AH	YV3304					
146	C	N9125M	PT-ORA	N559RA							
147	C	N55UK	N499SC	N111US	N160NE	N177AM	YV3179				

Production complete

LEARJET MODEL 60

C/n	Identities
55-001	N551GL N551DF N60XL [prototype Model 55 converted to Model 60 standards]
001	N601LJ [rolled out 05May92; ff 15Jun92; to instructional airframe, Ecole Nationale d'Aerotechnique, Montreal/St Hubert, Canada, Jan17; cx 21Apr17]
002	N602LJ C-GLRS C-GLRL N602LJ N190AS N1940 (N602DM) N170MK N32SW
003	N60LJ N961MR N808ML N60FE N48KZ N117KB
004	N60UK N194AL N600PJ N863PA N44RM
005	N5011L N610TM N869JS N205FX OY-LJD N104SD N60KJ VP-BGB N60KJ N160AJ [parted out by Bizav Support LLC, FL]
006	N60VE N60VL N606TS N606BR N8783 [parted out by MTW Aerospace, Montgomery, AL]
007	N448HM (N212FX) N219FX N204FX (N204BX) N60UJ N760CF N733SW N457UT
008	N608LJ PT-OVI N608LJ N222FX N222HV N260UJ (N359RM) N808SK
009	N26029 N54
010	N5012H N477DM N477BM HB-VLU N525CF N928CD N928GD C-FBDR N610TS N561TC N610TS N692PC N212JA
011	N5013U N60T OY-LJE N61YC N611TS N843CP
012	N5014H N123CC N147CC N626KM N80DX N25MX
013	(N960H) N26011 N55
014	N7US N862PA [parted out by Florida Jet Parts, Fort Lauderdale, FL]
015	N960H (N960HL) N826SS N861PA N711SE N711SZ
016	N50153 TC-MEK N788MM UR-CHH UR-NAC N60HM
017	N50157 N9173R N760AC N660AH (N860AH) N60GG N864PA N498SW N500SW [w/o Aspen A/P, CO, 07Jun12] N794AA [parted out by Alliance Air Parts, Oklahoma City, OK, still wearing marks N500SW]
018	N5009T N4016G N24G N24GU
019	N50153 N40366 HB-VKI D-CRAN D-CFAN
020	N600L N606L [parted out by Alliance Air Parts, Oklahoma City, OK]
021	N600LC N600LG N600GA N732LH N260AJ
022	N2602Z N22G N22GU
023	N40323 N60SB N60SR N588BA N440HA
024	N2601V LV-PGX LV-WFM N415NP
025	N9155Z N299SC N299SG N919RS N479PF
026	N4026Z N60LJ N700GS N60LJ N347GS N14T N14TU
027	N4027S XA-ICA N4230S N12FU N69LJ M-AUTO N271SC N878RG
028	N50298 N870JS N206FX N206HY
029	N4029P N55KS C-FBLU C-GFAX N296TS N64SL N119FD [w/o Valencia, Venezuela 05May13]
030	N4030W N164PA TC-ELL YR-RPB 9H-AFJ D-CFAZ
031	N4031L N228N N841TT N841TP
032	N5013D OE-GNL D-CPMU D-CIFA*
033	N4031A N56
034	N5034Z 9M-CAL
035	N50353 VR-BST N116AS N1DC [w/o 14Jan01 Troy, AL] N1498G N68563
036	N5014E N60LR N44EL
037	N5017J N4037A N637LJ N101HW N101ND
038	N4007J N638LJ C-FJGG
039	N50154 N5003X N57 N8071J N57
040	N399SC N899SC N660AS N600AS N600CN
041	N5004Y N699SC N166HL
042	N4010K N90AG N90AQ N60MG N821DF
043	N5043D C-GHKY N43NR
044	N5044N N618R (N618P) (N1618R) N613R N668RC LV-CPL
045	N5045S N60WM N711VT N711VJ N903AG N454AN
046	N50157 N5006G (PT-WGB) N214FX N214BX N239RC N710TP (N710TF) N137RH
047	N5007P N418R N50DS N850DS N647TS N647EF N600LJ
048	N5008Z N648LJ N730M N551ST
049	N50298 N227N N247N N126CX N459SF
050	N50450 N207FX N207BX N923SK N924PS
051	N5051X N63BL OY-LJH D-CHER ES-PVC N247MH
052	N5022C ZS-NTV (N42AJ) N120HV N247CP N900KK N769DS XA-MGM N60LJ
053	N5012Z N5053Y B-3981 N91772 N360UJ N744DB N744RD
054	N65BL VP-BMM N301RJ N777YY
055	N5014E N5055F N1CA (N143CA) N660CB N574DA (N574BA) B-3925
056	N5013Y N60LR N117RJ N700CH (N556SA) N92FG LV-GQR
057	(N5010U) N50050 N58
058	N5016V N92BL XA-BRE XA-IRE
059	N5059J N208FX N208BX N60KF N159SC LV-BFR
060	N50602 N209FX OY-LJM N209FX OY-LJM N175BA N909SK N604SL
061	N50162 N98BL N219DC C-FRGY
062	N5012H N5006T (N510SG) N707SG N707SQ C-GLRS N62BX N551BD LV-CPC
063	N5015U N5003U N8270 N660BC N496WH
064	N210FX N210HV N529KF N529KE N405DC
065	N5006V N30W N718AN N654AN
066	N5006K N8271 N176KS Colombia FAC1214
067	N799SC N118HC N60HM N504AB
068	(N96ZC) N95ZC N823TR N64LE N160JD LV-CKK
069	N50324 N60CE D-CITA

LEARJET 60

C/n	Identities					
070	N5035R	N21AC				
071	N60LJ	N940P	N658KS			
072	N5072L	9M-FCL				
073	N50761	N256M	N860PD			
074	N8074W	N620JF	N674BP	N600PH		
075	N675LJ	N9CU	(N609LC)	N233VR	N696RB	
076	N211FX	N211BX	N494PA	LV-CCO		
077	N212FX	N677LJ	C-GLRS	N227FX	N227BX	N60GF
078	N5068F	N188TC	N188TG	N168ZZ		
079	N319LJ	N95AG	LV-FDQ			
080	N8080W	N59				
081	N681LJ	N60LJ	N180CP			
082	N682LJ	N600LN	N534TP	[parted out by Alliance Air Parts, Oklahoma City, OK]		
083	N683LJ	N383MB	N255RK	N725SC	N512TB	LV-GCK
084	N684LJ	N59FD	N100R	N306R	N8JR	N600TD
085	N685LJ	N99KW	N89KW	N814GF	D-CFAJ	
086	(N213FX)	N686LJ	(N777CB)	N797CB	N797CP	N607SB
087	N687LJ	N411ST	N410ST	N787LP	N601CN	
088	N688LJ	XA-TZF	XA-TZI			
089	N8089Y	XA-MDM				
090	N8090P	PT-WMO	N460BG	N85NC	N255SP	N143LP
091	N8071L	N896R	N91LE	N156DH		
092	N5092R	C-FBLJ	C-FBLO	N907SK	N226SF	N92NS
093	N80683	RP-C648	N109JE	N109JR	N129JR	N717JB	N160EE
094	N60LR	A6-SMS	(N511CL)	N93BA	TC-ARC	N789MS
095	N5005X	N602SC	N82KK	(N82KD)		
096	N8086L	N603SC	N269GJ*			
097	N8067Y	N897R	N60TX	N688DB		
098	N50758	N218FX	N218BX	N797PA	N16CS	VP-C..
099	N212FX	N212BX	N60AN	N173KR		
100	N6100	N60MN	N876SF			
101	N215FX	N215BX	N179LF			
102	N8082B	LV-WXN	N102LJ			
103	N216FX	N216BX	N298EF	(N399JR)		
104	N104LJ	N83WM	N903AM	N614TS	N160BL	N60VV
105	N217FX	N217BX	N60BC			
106	N106LJ	N140JC	N945GS	N945G		
107	N107LJ	D-CFFB	D-CFAF			
108	N220FX	(N220PX)	N60RY	N38CP		
109	N109LJ	N707SG	N747SG	N177KS	N215KM	N78FR
110	N60LJ	N928CD	N600CL			
111	N221FX	N898PA	(N898PR)			
112	N299SC	N808WG	N160BS			
113	N599SC	N60LH	N700R	N702R	N160GG	
114	N3014R	N199SC	N114PJ	N154AK		
115	N3015F	N500	N500ZH	N600GG		
116	N116LJ	XA-VIG				
117	N889DW					
118	N3018C	N11AM				
119	N119LJ	N626LJ	N8811A			
120	N120LJ	D-CSIX	(N141MB)			
121	N621LJ	PT-XFS				
122	N622LJ	N61DP	A6-IAS	A6-ASM		
123	N356WA	N97LJ				
124	N223FX	(N223BX)	N260AN	XA-IBC		
125	N60LR	VP-CRB	N917SC			
126	N224FX	N160AN	N660CJ			
127	N225FX	(N225BX)	N460AN	XA-ONE		
128	N226FX	(N660AN)	N61ZZ	N8888	N8889	N975LV
129	N629LJ	D-CBAD	N45US	N160GH	N717BK	
130	N630LJ	N90MC	N384JW			
131	N631LJ	XA-JJS	XB-JCG	XA-MHP	N841SC	
132	N228FX	N9200M	XA-UUP			
133	N133LJ	C-FIDO	C-FBCD	C-FCMG	N500CW	
134	N134LJ	XA-ZTA				
135	N135LJ	N98JV				
136	N136LJ	N60RL	N60RU			
137	N229FX	N360AN	N240JK			
138	N230FX	(N230BX)	N560AN	N160BP		
139	N233FX	N139XX	EI-IAT	N370AT	N7734T	(N77511)
140	N98JV	N140LJ	Argentina T-10			
141	N234FX	N141LJ	OY-JKH	N163BA	N655TH	N888KL
142	(N642LJ)	N426JN	(N940RL)	N116LM		
143	N235FX	N6666R	N6666A	N393TA	N143FA	N143AA	N759SH
144	N60144	D-CKKK	N94BA	N929SR		
145	N145LJ	LX-PRA	I-PRAD	N960TT	N826LJ	

LEARJET 60

C/n	Identities									
146	N50776	N261PC	N800R	N809R	N790SU					
147	N138SP	N133SR	N160RM	(N158JP)	N420JP	(N42JP)	N727SJ	N69ZJ	N61GD	
148	N80701	D-CETV	N648TS	HB-VOZ	D-CHER					
149	N149LJ	(ZS-JRM)	SU-BNL	SU-EZI	VP-BEZ	N260CA	EI-REX	N160EM		
150	N80667	A6-SMS	N150BX	N200MT						
151	N234FX	N9ZM	N11TS	(N11TR)						
152	N50126	Mexico MTX-01		Mexico AMT-200		Mexico ANX-1200		Mexico ANX-1203		
153	N235FX	(N235BX)	N424KW							
154	N233FX	N969JD	N523MV	N313AR	N225GP*					
155	N88V									
156	N76SF	N76QF	N605SB							
157	N236FX	N114LJ	YV3146							
158	N237FX	N50EL	N460JD	HB-VWN	N838MA	VH-NPP				
159	N43SF	N43QF	N721MJ	PP-WIN						
160	D-CDNY	D-CGEO	T7-SOV	N612JC						
161	D-CDNZ	EC-JVM								
162	N99ZC									
163	N238FX	N238BX	N326HG							
164	N60LJ	PT-XGS								
165	N929GW	N929GV	LV-FUF							
166	N239FX	N60ZD	N114BD							
167	N240FX	N240BX	OE-GVB	N167XX	LZ-AXA	(D-CHRN)	M-WISO	LV-CZX		
168	N706CJ	N706CR	N724JS	N721SE						
169	N5014F	OE-GII	D-COMO							
170	N50154	D-COWS	9H-AEE	F-HAVB	D-CNUE					
171	N422CP	N422CR	N424MW	N422CR	N424MW	N614SG*				
172	N241FX	N241BX	XA-DGO	XA-RIN	XA-URG	N121TN	N743LG			
173	OY-LJF	D-CEJA	ZS-TEJ							
174	N242FX	N242ZX	XA-COI	N174BL	N252VR					
175	N243FX	N243F	XB-KYZ	XB-LBO	XB-LEJ	XB-LLT	N175PC	XA-JKM		
176	N176MB	N10MB								
177	N60LR	N991DB								
178	N244FX	N178MM								
179	N9012H	C-FCNR	HB-VNV	D-CIII	N17XL	LV-FUT				
180	N777MC	N377MC								
181	N273MC	N278MC*								
182	N245FX	N600NM	N600EF							
183	N246FX	N810Y	XB-SLL	XA-GSL						
184	TC-DHF	N184LJ	N752BP	N606SB						
185	N464TF	N604GJ								
186	N186ST	N58ST	N294DD							
187	N247FX	N27ZH	N470MD							
188	N248FX	N255SL								
189	N189LJ	PR-XJS								
190	N5012K	N190LJ	EI-IAU	ES-PVS	N812RP					
191	N40073	N30154	N660AS	N710SG						
192	N601GG									
193	N249FX	N627AF	N193AF	N876MA						
194	N250FX	N250SG	(N96FF)	LV-CIO						
195	N251FX	N251SD								
196	N252FX	(N252RD)	(XA-XOX)	N358AP	(D-CHRO)	LV-CUE				
197	N5010U	N23PZ	P4-AVM	OE-GYG	N420KM	N420KV				
198	N198HB									
199	N253FX	N502RP	N502RB	N600AJ	[parted out by Dodson Int'l, Rantoul, KS]					
200	N254FX	N254FY	(OY-TCG)	(OY-LJK)	A6-EJA	D-CSLT				
201	N411ST	N411SK	N614JH	N269JH						
202	N1RB	N202LJ	XA-TSA	N202LJ	XA-UQP					
203	N770BC	N770BG	LZ-BVV	(D-CFAG)						
204	N4008G	I-NATZ	N30GJ	(N90GJ)	N50GJ					
205	N40043	N205ST	N12ST	N64HA	(N64HX)	N358P	(N358PP)	N358F		
206	N40076	(N254FX)	N500RP	N916BG	N909JS	N448GL				
207	N777VC	(N207VC)	N777VQ	N706CJ	N207LJ					
208	N40084	(N235HR)	N821CC	(N112MT)	N208BH					
209	N40085	N1221J								
210	N40086	ZS-NVP+	[+marks worn for at least 16 months at the Tucson, AZ, completion centre but ntu]							N700JE
	C-FGJC	C-FCTK	N427PM	N512CZ						
211	N5012Z	D-CHLE	I-MRGC	N849WC						
212	N5012H	LX-RPL	I-RPLY	N295KR	N708CF					
213	N40079	N65T	N14T	N717FF						
214	N5016Z	D-CIMM	OE-GFA	C6-ZIP						
215	N40083	N44SF	N44QF	VP-BCY	N275HZ					
216	N131TR	N888LJ								
217	N5012G	N60LJ	N600ML	XA-VLA						
218	N50157	N8084J	EI-IAW	C-GRBZ	N727BG	N216DY*				
219	N660KS	N552SK								
220	N80857	N254FX	N254FZ	N255FX	(N447FA)	(XA-ONE)	N359AP	VP-BOD	N260GD	

LEARJET 60 / 60XR

C/n	Identities
221	N255BD XA-JWM XA-FGP
222	N8088U N60VE N1128M
223	N3006J N109JR N109JZ N309MG N375BW
224	N61VE N64MG
225	N30170 N22SF N22QF N60HS N60TG (N770JB) N312AL
226	N3011F N128V N596MC N596MG N229TS
227	N253FX N503RP N503RE N582MM
228	N255FX N10ST N65HA N65HU
229	N23SR N38SV
230	N50031 N826SR N235CG N356CG N600LG
231	N3015M N40012 D-CDNX SX-BNR
232	N5004J LV-ZYF N232LJ N95BD N95BQ N211BD
233	N5008F N33DC N520SC N520S N405TK
234	N5013J N24SR LV-CAY
235	N5013N N252RP
236	N5015T I-IINL OE-GNI N716BG N916BG N555EH
237	N699DA PR-WBW
238	N5018U N753BP (N140CT) N260BS
239	N5019R (ZS-SCT) N503BC
240	N5019V N29LJ
241	N5026Q N253FX N603GP N603GR
242	N5027Q PR-LDF N5027Q [w/o 07Oct02 Santa Cruz do Sul, Brazil]
243	N50287 OY-LGI EC-JVB N65LJ
244	N5031R N884TW N335AF N835AF N160MG
245	N50330 XA-ORA N290KR N474PT
246	N5035F D-CWHS N64JP
247	N254FX N645MD LV-FVZ
248	N5038N OE-GMR N248L N787LP N787LD N248LA
249	N50422 N4004Q D-CLUB EC-JYQ (D-CFAK) D-CFAX
250	N50433 XA-FLY N50433 XA-FLY
251	N50458 N747DP N847DP N220MD
252	N5012H N5051X N749SS
253	N5012K C-GIIT C-FBLU N1127M
254	N5015U RP-C6003 N773SW
255	N5013U OO-TME ER-LGB N166MS N160RJ
256	N5013Y OY-LJK D-CCGG N401SY
257	N50157 N256FX N977SS N671CB N772EC*
258	N202N
259	N40075 N600L
260	N40050 N257FX N973HR
261	N4003Q D-CROB N397JK
262	N4003W N5051A N126KD N440DM N440DN N604BK
263	N258FX N876CS
264	N40084 N214RW N214PW N811RA
265	N40086 N600LC [parted out by Alliance Air Parts, Oklahoma City, OK]
266	N259FX N266LJ N156BF (N156BE) N506AB
267	N5009V N50558 N60YC N60SN PP-LRR N166MS N618L
268	N5011L N268WS N21NV
269	N5012H N100NR N903AM
270	N5012K VH-MZL LV-BDX N247SC A6-MAJ OE-GMA [stored Dubai]
271	N271L N954WS
272	N50157 N60KH P4-BAZ N272DJ LV-CBI
273	N4002P VH-OCV RP-C2956 VH-EXJ N60SE N52JT
274	N4003K D-CSIM
275	N101UD ES-PVI LV-GVT
276	N5000E N838RC OE-GDF D-CDSM M-AIRS N276BG
277	N40079 LX-LOU N404CD
278	N5012K N60RL
279	N50145 Z3-MKD
280	"N50127"+ [+marks as reported but not a recognized Learjet test reg'n] OE-GKP G-SXTY [cx to USA 15Jan17 but no N-number allocated]
281	N5013U "OE-GTS"+ [+marks painted in error at Wichita, KS in Feb05] OE-GTF D-CGTF OH-GVE ES-LVC D-CFAG VH-AND
282	N5013Y TC-RKS N207AW
283	N5009T N60LJ PR-GCL N160JA N415SG
284	N5000E EC-JIE N284L N461MC
285	N5009T N72CE N183BX
286	N4003K (D-CSIS) N262DB G-LGAR N875CA
287	N4003L OE-GGL M-ALEX ES-PVJ
288	N40077 N103LS N719JB
289	N40083 N785DR VP-BGS M-ABGI N770BM
290	N5012K N260DB D-CFLG (D-CHRN) N60FZ PP-BIN N548WC VH-XPN
291	N4003Q XA-KCM
292	N5011L N380BA N580BA N372EX*
293	N60SE N772PP
294	N50163 [first LJ60XR, ff 03Apr06] N60XR N160BG D2-EPC

LEARJET 60XR

C/n	Identities								
295	N259FX	N314CM							
296	N5016Z	EC-JPV	N296L						
297	N5012G	XA-KLZ							
298	N40012	N729LJ	N812GR						
299	N50153	N75CT							
300	N40081	OH-AEM	G-CJMC	EI-DXW	YL-ABA	OE-GSV	(D-CFAX)	D-CFAK*	
301	N50157	ZS-GSG	N301LJ	N440MC					
302	N5012H	(OE-GJA)	ES-PVP						
303	N40075	(OE-GJA)	(OH-GVI)	OE-GTO	OH-III	ES-III			
304	N40076	(D-CGNF)	OE-GNF	N355AP	VH-SBU	N604ED	N605QR*		
305	N40050	OH-VIV	EI-VIV	M-IGOR	OE-GMD	TC-SHY			
306	N5013Y	N80177	N500	N5009	N869AV				
307	N260FX								
308	N115AN	N115AD							
309	N460MC								
310	N222BR	PP-BED							
311	N710SG	N202SJ	VP-BLC	N327AR	XA-JGC				
312	N5013U	OH-VMF	VP-CCD	HZ-OSR	VP-CCD				
313	N4003L	N613H	G-HOIL	M-HOIL	N61WF				
314	N999LJ	[w/o 19Sep08 Columbia Metropolitan, SC; parted out by Atlanta Air Salvage, Griffin, GA]							
315	N604KT								
316	N5017J	N50LK	N923AL						
317	N5012Z	(OH-GVI)	OE-GSU	N292KR	Colombia FAC1216				
318	N777VC	N770PC							
319	N261FX	(D-CVIP)	N814TS	D-CVIP*					
320	N60LJ	N229BP	N229RP	(C-....)					
321	N5010U	N675BP	N574DA	(PP-BRP)	XA-MES				
322	N710SG	N724CJ	N5014F	OY-MIR	OE-GSC	N924KW	N528WG*		
323	N50157	N262FX	N98UF						
324	N50126	N707CS	N797CS						
325	N5013Y	P4-SSV	M-SSSV	N608JA	PP-JAE	N325LJ			
326	N5018G	N80172	OD-MHA	M-APWC	M-MHAC	N362SC	TC-...		
327	N5016Z	9H-AFB	N545LF	LV-CKA					
328	N5000E	VP-BBZ	G-XXZZ	M-URAL	YL-BJA				
329	N50111	LZ-BVE							
330	N5102G	OK-JDM							
331	N4001G	(D-CDEF)	N331PL	HK-4565	N337SC				
332	N5013U	OE-GLX	N804JD	LV-FPM	N632SC	N699TL*			
333	N4003L	OE-GLY	N805JD	N943RM	YV3065	YV3167			
334	N263FX	(N334BG)	XA-ORI						
335	N5014E	TC-MEN							
336	N4004Y	A6-NGN	HZ-NGN	N781SC	N770X				
337	N60LJ	N337BG	XA-FMT						
338	N5016V	N338PR	A6-SBF	CS-EAE	A9C-BXK	A6-SBF	N398AA	N121EL	N111EL
339	N5010U	N160TG	N610CR						
340	N264FX	N714TS							
341	N5012K	A6-CYS	M-YCYS						
342	N40073	SP-CEZ							
343	N5015U	C-FEDG	C-FEDU	N60XA	PP-CTP	N343EC			
344	N40076	OO-ADH	LV-BZJ						
345	N265FX								
346	N724EH	N724EB	AP-BKB						
347	N5012Z	P4-EXG	UP-LJ001	N786SC	XA-RYO				
348	N266FX	N550DG							
349	N40012	C-GJLN	N220EJ						
350	N5011L	D-COMO	VP-COO	VP-CBO	VP-CIO				
351	N5013Y	D-CJAF							
352	N4003Q	(G-DOKK)	VH-THG	N352XR					
353	N5017J	N999YC	LV-BTA						
354	N5000E	(PP-ONE)	N60LE	PP-ONE					
355	N40077	OH-IVS	N483VL						
356	N267FX	N356JH							
357	N50111	PR-MLR							
358	N60XR	N358JA							
359	N5018G	OE-GVJ	N806JD	LV-FPN	N359LW	N317EC			
360	N5012G	OE-GVT	N809SD	LV-CRC	N360SN				
361	N5014E	N361TS	N487LP						
362	N10870	N62XR	CS-DTH	N306KR	9H-LJE				
363	N50145	N1JB							
364	N40076	OE-GVV	N810SD	N604WC					
365	N4004Y	N65LR	(C-....)	(N53LV)					
366	(N268FX)	N988P	N900P	N60AX					
367	N5012K	"N60XR"+	[+fake marks N60XR worn in NBAA static displays at Orlando Executive, FL, Oct09 and Atlanta/DeKalb-Peachtree Oct10]	N5012K	N367LJ	(N437JL)			
368	N10872	(N420JP)	N42JP	N468JM	N368XR	N365KM			
369	N10873	OY-KYS	M-MARI	UR-ISH	T7-ISH				

LEARJET 60XR

C/n	Identities							
370	N326SM	HZ-MS1A						
371	N4003K	HZ-MS1B						
372	N50153	(N269FX)	ES-LVA					
373	N5018L	(D-CGVD)	OE-GVD	N811SD	M-ELHI			
374	N5000E	N60LJ	N83TR	N358P				
375	N3099	N106FF						
376	N50157	(OK-YXY)	N76XR	N40149	XA-TCO	N561CT	N711SE	
377	N4002P	C-FLTB	N357AP	TG-AIR				
378	N50163	(D-CBOB)	N984BD	N60HJ				
379	N50154	(CS-DJA)	N79XR	N51054	I-SDAG	(D-CFAS)	D-CURE	
380	N4003L	N380L	XB-RGB					
381	N4003Q	B 3926						
382	N5013U	M-IGHT	ZK-JAK					
383	N5009V	N383LJ	A6-RJE	A6-VGG				
384	N5013Y	VT-DBC	M-INNI					
385	N694HC	N10871	5A-UAE					
386	N40076	N60SJ	OE-GVE	N812SD	D-CFAD	D-CLUZ		
387	N40078	N201UD	C-FJOL					
388	N60LJ	N724EH	N724EF					
389	N50153	N883RA						
390	N5018G	N649SP						
391	N50111	B-3935						
392	N5016Z	N90CE						
393	N5017J	N393AC	N668JH	VP-CHU	N60AJ			
394	N40084	VT-MAM						
395	N5000E	N168KS	TC-KLC					
396	N50126	N396LJ	LV-CRB	N695SC	XA-VIT	XA-VTO		
397	N50145	N810YS						
398	N40086	N787LC	N787LP					
399	N5013U	LZ-TRH						
400	N40043	N80170	XA-RAV					
401	N40146	OE-GVF	N60AJ	TC-AEK				
402	N40083	N93EW						
403	N40085	OE-GVG	N716RJ	XA-AIG				
404	N5009T	N901PM						
405	N5011L	OE-GVH	N718RJ	XA-MGM				
406	N5012Z	OE-GVN	N731RJ	"XA-UOC"	[incorrect marks worn at Tucson service centre Oct15]			XB-UOC
407	N50163	OE-GVP	N732RJ	(N956RS)				
408	N4003Q	N95CE						
409	N5014F	(D-CAEX)	OE-GVQ	N738RJ				
410	N10870	N717EL	N717EP					
411	N5014E	N88MZ						
412	N5018G	VT-UNO						
413	N4001G	N27LJ						
414	N40012	I-GSIN	OE-GLJ					
415	N4005Q	N81GD						
416	N5012G	N603GP	N803GP	N416GP				
417	N4003W	N249S	N844S					
418	N40077	N220AZ						
419	N4008G	N20GJ	N30GJ					
420	N10873	N723HC						
421	N40162	N268FX	N421XR	M-GLFZ	M-YETD	D-CETD	N588BF	
422	N40086	N269FX	N422XR	N104RJ				
423	N5018L	N270FX	(N423XR)	N760AA	N1972H			
424	N50163	N271FX	(N424XR)	N424LJ	N600LN			
425	N5012K	N425GS						
426	N4003Q	C-GJDR	N377PT	N357PT	N857PT			
427	N4004Y	N929GX	N929GW					
428	N50154	N60FP						
429	N50153	XA-USZ						
430	N40146	XA-JWM	[dbr Fort Lauderdale International, date nyk; parted out by Dodson Int'l, Rantoul, KS]					
431	(N40075)	[test marks allocated but aircraft not built]						
432	(N40083)	[test marks allocated but aircraft not built]						

Production complete

LOCKHEED JETSTAR

Aircraft which were converted to -731s by Garrett AiResearch were given a sequential conversion number by that company; these numbers appear alongside the c/n in the production list.

C/n	Series	Identities
1001		N329J [ff 04Sep57; last flight 16Aug82; donated to Pacific Vocational Inst, Vancouver, Canada; to Seattle Museum of Flight, WA, circa Aug04]
1002		N329K N711Z [displayed Andrews AFB, MD, in USAF colours, code 89001]
5001/53	731	N9201R [ff 21Oct60] N1 N21 N1 N11 N7145V [wfu; to Pratt Community College, KS; to White Ind's, Bates City, MO, for spares 1998]
5002	6	N9202R EP-VRP N106GM N69TP N81JJ N148PE [b/u for spares Mar85, Minneapolis/St Paul, MN. Fuselage still in nearby scrapyard Feb07]
5003	6	N9203R NASA14 N814NA [cx Dec89; for disp Plant 42 Heritage Airpark, Palmdale, CA]
5004	6	N9204R N13304 N524AC N777EP N69HM N777EP [displayed Graceland Estate, Memphis, TN]
5005	6	N161LM N176LG N12121 N716RD N712RD N70TP XA-SIN XB-DLV (N22265) [wfu as XB-DLV Van Nuys, CA and scrapped]
5006/40	731	N9280R N12R N227K N731JS N222Y N6NE (VR-CCC) [wfu Southampton, UK, after landing accident; was on fire dump; remains to Florida]
5007/45	731	N9205R N110G N72CT N971AS [impounded 1992 Atlanta-Peachtree, GA; b/u for spares 1993; fuselage dumped in field adjacent to Atlanta-Peachtree]
5008	6	N500Z N400M [w/o 27Dec72 Saranac Lake, NY]
5009	6	N9206R N540G N767Z N717X N717 (HB-VET) N717JM [cx Sep84; b/u for spares]
5010	6/C140A	59-5958 [preserved Travis AFB, CA, originally in museum then elsewhere on base]
5011/1	731	N9282R Indonesia T17845 PK-PJS 9V-BEE PK-PJH N731A C-GKRS N10461 N159B N88JM [b/u for spares late 1985; fuselage at Lincoln, NE 1988]
5012	6	N9283R D-BABE N10123 N1012B N500SJ N501AL [wfu Opa-Locka, FL; cx Jan94; derelict Mar94]
5013	8	N9284R N322K N523AC N11JC HZ-MAC N11JC N8AD N158DP (N5AX) [b/u for spares Mar88 by White Inds, Bates City, MO]
5014	6	N58CG N158CG N9MD N54BW N95GS [b/u for spares 1989 Miami, FL; cx 17Mar03]
5015	6	NASA4 N172L N103KC N505T N9046F N66MP [wfu; to South Seattle Community College, WA, as instructional airframe; cx Oct00]
5016	6	N9210R N2222R (N222R) N20TF HZ-AFS HZ-SH2 N4258P N712GW N440RM [open storage Roswell, NM circa Oct97]
5017	6/VC140B	N9286R 61-2488 [AMARC park code CL001] [preserved Warner-Robins AFB, GA]
5018	6	N9287R (CF-DTX) C-FDTX [preserved National Aviation Museum, Rockcliffe, Canada]
5019	6	N9288R N105GM N105GN (N70TP) N5UD N50UD [b/u 1986; tail section at North Perry, FL 1989; fuselage converted into mobile home, derelict at Big Guy's Auto facility nr Gainesville, GA]
5020	6	N9207R N371H N300CR N308WC [cx Sep88; b/u for spares]
5021	6	CF-ETN C-FETN N564MG [b/u for spares Memphis, TN]
5022	6/VC140B	61-2489 [AMARC park code CL006] [preserved Pima County Museum, Tucson, AZ]
5023	6	N9221R I-SNAL N711Z N1107Z N767Z N979RA N879RA N723ST N20PY N2ES (N6ES) [b/u for spares Mar88 by White Inds, Bates City, MO]
5024	6/VC140B	61-2490 [stored AMARC Davis-Monthan AFB, AZ with park code CL004 then preserved Lyndon B Johnson National Historical Park, TX, Aug10]
5025	6	(62-12166) W Germany CA101 W Germany 1101 SU-DAF ST-JRM [not confirmed if marks have been taken up]
5026	6/C140A	59-5959 [noted preserved 29Sep92 Scott AFB]
5027	6/VC140B	61-2491 [displayed Rhein-Main AFB, Germany]
5028	6/C140A	59-5960 [wfu; stored Greenville, TX, then auctioned for scrap 2010]
5029/38	731	N3E N3EK N340 N39BL N1BL N166AC N112TJ (N25TX) (N1406) [to Aviation Warehouse, El Mirage, CA by Oct04]
5030	6/C140A	59-5961 [w/o 07Nov62 Warner-Robins AFB, GA]
5031	6/VC140B	61-2492 [preserved USAF Museum, Wright Patterson AFB, OH]
5032	6/C140A	59-5962 [at Edwards AFB, CA, for Museum]
5033/56	731	N1620 N16200 N33EA N100CC N100AC N200CC N200CG XB-FIS N25WA N50EC (N890MC) N500MA [cx Oct02, b/u; fuselage at Conroe, TX, in 2005 but removed by Feb08]
5034	6/VC140B	61-2493 [stored AMARC Davis-Monthan AFB, AZ with park code CL003; to Western Air Parts]
5035	6	(62-12167) W Germany CA102 [w/o 16Jan68 Bremen, W Germany; reported stored Bremen]
5036/42	731	N1622 N1622D N41TC N776JM N444JH N90KR N900CR [b/u circa 2001; cx Oct01]
5037/24	731	N9211R N2600 [damaged in pressurisation tests; rebuilt as c/n 5128, but still known as c/n 5037] N519L N3060 N60CN N60CH N11UF (N71UF) N90TC N10DR N6JL N552JH N770JR [cx Jun08, wfu Palm Beach International, FL]
5038	6	N9212R N341NS N341N N22CH N11UF N11UE (N44KF) [b/u; cx Dec92; remains to Aviation Warehouse film prop yard at El Mirage, CA]
5039	6	N600J N60QJ N81MR N86HM N200CK [cx Sep90; was stored Spirit of St Louis A/P, MO; presumed since scrapped]
5040	6	N505C N518L N7SZ N888RW [cx May88; spares May88; remains blown up Fort Lauderdale, FL for film]
5041	6/C140B	62-4197 [stored AMARC Davis-Monthan AFB, AZ with park code CL007; parted out; used in artwork at Pima Air & Space Museum, Tucson, AZ]
5042	6/C140B	62-4198 [to Battle Damage Repair Unit, Mildenhall AFB, UK; b/u by 22Jan92 Mildenhall]
5043	6/C140B	62-4199 [stored AMARC Davis-Monthan AFB, AZ, park code CL002, then to Western Air Parts]
5044	6/C140B	62-4200 [stored AMARC Davis-Monthan AFB, AZ, park code CL005, then to Western Air Parts; used in artwork at Pima Air & Space Museum, Tucson, AZ]
5045	6/C140B	62-4201 [stored AMARC Davis-Monthan AFB, AZ, park code CL008, then to Hill AFB Museum, UT]
5046	6	N9282R PK-IJS Indonesia T-9446 Indonesia A-9446 [wfu Jakarta-Halim AFB, Indonesia; later put on display at Garuda's training centre at Kushadasi, Indonesia]
5047	6	N9214R N409M N409MA N555PB [cx Oct90; scrapped]

LOCKHEED JETSTAR

C/n	Series	Identities
5048	6	N9215R N40N N40NC N98KR N98MD N500WN N500WZ N428DA (N130LW) [preserved Marietta Aviation Museum, GA; cx 15Aug13]
5049	6	N9216R N1230R N96B N96BB [wfu at South Seattle Community College, WA]
5050/34	731	N207L N208L N141TC HZ-THZ N434AN [b/u Apr94 by Atlanta Air Salvage, Griffin, GA]
5051	6	N9217R N400KC N44MF N31S N310AD N555BS N488JS N488GR [part of 'Disaster' attraction at Universal Studios, Orlando, FL, since Jan08]
5052	6	N9218R N300P N66CR CF-DTM C-FDTM N9739B [b/u for spares early 1989 Bi-States Park, St Louis, MO; cx Jun92]
5053/2	731	N9219R N12R N121CN N69CN N14WJ XA-POU XC-JCC XA-BCE XC-JCC [wfu Topeka/Forbes Field, KS by 2007]
5054/59	731	N9220R N7600J N7600 N20AP N354CA N721PA [parted out by White Inds, Bates City, MO]
5055/21	731	N9222R N296AR N303H N90ZP N85BP (N43JK) (N86BP) (N79MB) N304CK N707EZ N99FT [wfu at Chino, CA, circa Sep95; cx Mar96; parted out remains to scrapyard at Long Beach, CA]
5056	6	N9223R N105G N105GH N300AG HZ-FNA [b/u Spirit of St Louis A/P, MO]
5057	6	N1007 N90U N90ME [cx Mar87; b/u Memphis, TN during 1988]
5058/4	731	N100A N100AL N1500M N50AS N600TT (N600DT) N600TP N381AA N131EL N200DW XA-TTE XB-JIZ [wfu circa 2006 Toluca. Mexico]
5059	6	Indonesia T-1645 Indonesia A-1645 [preserved in museum Yogjakarta-Adisutjipto, Indonesia painted as A-9446]
5060	6	N9225R N31F N55NC [cx May88; b/u Jun88 Fort Lauderdale International, FL]
5061/48	731	N9226R N506T N506D N47BA N67GT N152GS N161GS N123GA (N888WW) N488MR N488EC N333EC N338EC [b/u Palm Beach Int'l, FL, 2006]
5062/12	731	N679RW N2200M RP-57 N111G VR-BHF EC-697 EC-FGX [reported parted out in US circa 2005]
5063	6	N9228R N420L N420A N420G N499PB XC-LIT
5064/51	731	N184GP N3QS N3QL [parted out Rantoul, KS circa early 2000]
5065	6	N9229R N1966G S9-NAD [wfu 1989; used as spares for c/n 5085]
5066/46	731	N9230R N228Y N7782 XA-HRM XA-JHR XA-SAE XA-MIK [reported w/o 16Nov95, no other details]
5067	6	N871D N711Z N207L (N267AD) N267L [w/o 29Mar81 Luton, UK]
5068/27	731	N9231R N96GS [w/o 06Jan90 Miami A/P, FL; used as spares; cx Jan91]
5069/20	731	N910M N918MM XA-PGO N197JS [reported for spares; cx Feb99]
5070/52	731	N992 N9921 C-GAZU N9921 N177NC N731AG N114CL N888CF N888WT N712TE N731WL [cx 26Jan05; parted out]
5071	6	(62-12845) W Germany CA103 1103 SU-DAH ST-PRE [wfu Khartoum, Sudan]
5072/23	731	N9233R N500Z N74AG [b/u; cx Dec99]
5073	6	N7775 [fuselage used as interior mock-up by KC Avn, Dallas, TX]
5074/22	731	N9234R N67B N267P N267GF N168DB N777SG N171JL [parted out circa 2001; cx Oct01 fuselage at City Museum, St.Louis, MO]
5075/19	731	N397B N540G N2345M N1DB N500ES [b/u Rockford, IL, Apr06]
5076/17	731	N9235R N100C N3E N3EK N69ME N76HG [b/u Rockford, IL, May06]
5077	6	N9236R N1924V N1EM [w/o 25Mar76 Chicago, IL]
5078/3	731	N711Z N7105 N472SP N52TJ N916RC (N916RG) N515AJ N124RM [cx 19Apr04; preserved at Aviation Institute of Maintenance, Houston/Hobby, TX]
5079/33	731	N9238R XA-RGB XA-MAZ N58TS [parted out by Alliance Air Parts, Oklahoma City, OK]
5080	6	N914X N914P N77HW [wfu & scrapped – details not known]
5081	8	N200A N200AL N4SP N4SX [cx Sep87; b/u for spares during 1987]
5082/36	731	N320S N917J N82SR TC-OMR P4-CBJ 3C-QQU
5083/49	731	N208L N141LM N161LM N257H N257HA C-GAZU N27FW N817BD N198DL [cx 09Nov15; wfu Wilmington, DE]
5084/8	731	N9240R N83M N732M N910E N520S [w/o 11Feb81 Westchester, NY]
5085	6	N9241R N586 N5861 S9-NAE VR-CCY [to Abu Dhabi Higher College of Technology, marked as "HCT"]
5086/44	731	N9242R N27R N27RL N600J N60UJ HZ-FBT N711AG N27RC (N65JW) N313JS
5087/55	731	N9243R N41N N800J N31LJ N31WG N75MG N33SJ [cx 25Apr13; CofR expired. Fuselage to Planes of Fame museum, Chino, CA]
5088	6	N9244R CF-DTF C-FDTF [cx late 1986; preserved in Atlantic Canada Aviation Museum, Halifax, Canada]
5089	8	N9245R N324K N120AR (N85DL) (XA-...) N120AR [used for spares Jan94 by TAESA Mexico City, Mexico]
5090	8	N9246R N106G N10MJ N55CJ N555SG [wfu 1989 Fort Lauderdale Executive, FL (cf c/n 5094)]
5091	6	N9247R N107G N107GH N118B N118BA [wfu; remains to White Inds, Bates City, MO; cx May93]
5092/58	731	N9248R N372H N901H N110AN N110DD VR-CSM VP-CSM [wfu Toulouse, France]
5093	6	N9249R N711Z N5000C N5000B N76EB N22RB [cx Oct90; b/u for spares circa Sep90]
5094	6	N9250R N3030 N3080 [rebuilt with tail section from c/n 5090; wfu Opa-Locka, FL; derelict there Feb94; cx 09Dec14]
5095/30	731	N9251R N78MP N780RH N731L [b/u; cx Jan04]
5096/10	731	N9252R N530G [cx 17Jun04; b/u; fuselage at Conroe, TX in 2005 but removed by Feb08]
5097/60	731	N9253R N300L N306L N77D N81366 N1BL N922MS [parted out by Dodson Int'l Parts, Rantoul, KS; fuselage to Sir Sandford Fleming College, Peterboro, Canada, by Sep08, instructional airframe painted as 'C-FCCC']
5098/28	731	N9254R N1967G N5098G (N98MD) N417PJ N199LA N792AA N942Y (N963Y) XA-TVK
5099/5	731	N9255R N533EJ N594KR N277NS N323P N62K N62KK N18BH (N117J) [wfu Fort Pierce/St Lucie, FL; cx 24Jun11]
5100/41	731	N9256R N207L XA-FIU N35JJ XA-GZA N510TS N800GD [wfu Conroe, TX]

LOCKHEED JETSTAR

C/n	Series	Identities
5101/15	731	N9208R N7008 N7008J N760DL N760DE XA-JJS N26MJ N800AF N511TS [wfu Aug05 Guthrie, OK; cx to Australia, but only engines went – fuselage remained in USA]
5102	8	N9235R N326K N500ZB N75CC N7500 N85CC N601JJ [wfu Oct94 Spirit of St Louis A/P, MO & scrapped cx Feb00]
5103	8	N23M N672M N176BN N176AN N101AW XA-TAZ (N101AW) XA-TAV [used for fire training at Aruba wearing its previous US marks N101AW]
5104/6	731	N902K N902KB N155AV N155TJ [parted out; cx 22May13]
5105	8	N277T N2277T N7005 N17005 HZ-MA1 [to Lycee Saint-Exupery Blagnac, Toulouse, France, for training use]
5106/9	731	N238U N288U CF-GWI N8SC N1329K YV-03CP [wfu Maracaibo, Venezuela]
5107	8	N118K N337US N7788 YV-187CP N7788 N69MT [parted out Jun93 Hollister, CA]
5108	8	N7953S N1207Z N24UG N68CT N680TT XA-SWD N104CE [cx 11Aug16; CofR expired]
5109/13	731	N7954S N968GN N968BN N678BC [b/u for spares 1992 Chandler Municipal A/P, AZ; fuselage noted Apr94 on fire dump Phoenix-Skyharbor A/P, AZ; gone by Oct98]
5110/47	731	N7955S N2600 N2601 N788S N49UC [b/u for spares during 1990; cx Dec93]
5111	8	N7956S N5111H N11SX N115MR N115DX [b/u circa Aug91 Addison, TX; wings to Spirit of St Louis A/P, MO]
5112/7	731	N7957S N910G N99MR N499PC N728PX N475MD [parted out by White Inds, Bates City, MO]
5113/25	731	N7958S N505C N124RP N303LE (N1967J) (N65JW) N1962J N77BT N542TW [parted out by White Inds, Bates City, MO, Nov05; cx 29Apr09]
5114/18	731	N7959S N930MT N930M N94K N111GU N26GL 5B-CHE 5A-DBZ
5115/39	731	N933LC N933CY N26TR N40XY N8300E N1151K [b/u Willard A/P, Champaign, IL Aug95]
5116	8	N7961S N222QA N3HB N60BC [wfu 29Sep92 Spirit of St Louis A/P, MO; fuselage still present circa Apr96]
5117/35	731	N7962S N210EK N310CK VR-BSH VP-BSH (N858SH) VP-BLD [wfu Toulouse, France]
5118	8	N7963S N333QA N333KN N222KN [b/u 1987 Memphis, TN]
5119/29	731	N7964S N11HM N508T N508TA N500AG N1DB N9GU [parted out by White Inds, Bates City, MO]
5120/26	731	N7965S N40DC HZ-TNA [wfu Geneva, Switzerland by mid 2004; b/u 22-25Mar11]
5121	8	N7966S W Germany 1102 SU-DAG ST-PRM [still at Cairo, Egypt as SU-DAG Oct02]
5122	8	N7967S N1107Z N1107M N213AP [cx Mar89; b/u during 1989]
5123/14	731	N7968S N1844S N559GP N441A N47UC N123GN N57NP N57NR (N425MK) N725MK [wfu Hayward, CA]
5124	8	N7969S N46F N7SZ XA-SBQ XA-SKI XC-SKI
5125/31	731	N7970S N47UC N48UC N31BP [parted out by Aerovision International, OK]
5126	8	N7971S N955H N955HL N20S N39E N39Q [b/u for spares Aug83]
5127	8	N7972S N42G N42GB N3GR N636C (N636MC) N636 N171CC [derelict 1991 Van Nuys, CA; cx Jun92 to Aviation Warehouse film prop yard, El Mirage, CA, wearing marks "N171SG"; cockpit section used in 'Telle Mere Tel Fils' sculpture by Adel Abdessemed 2008]
5128/16	731	N7973S N26S 5B-CGP N128BP N777PZ [parted out Houston-Hobby, TX]
5128S		[see c/n 5037/24]
5129	8	N7974S Saudi Arabia 101 XA-TJW XA-TZW [parted out Toluca, Mexico]
5130	8	N7975S Saudi Arabia 103 Saudi Arabia 102 XA-TJV XA-TZV XA-PES [wfu Toluca, Mexico]
5131	8/Fanstar	N7976S N30RP N31RP N64C N212JW N380AA [derelict 1991 Van Nuys, CA; cx Mar92]
5132/57	731	N7977S N1620 N1620N N100GL N801 N1JN N989JN XA-PSD XA-BEB
5133	8	N7978S N329K N322K C-GPGD VR-CAW HZ-WBT HZ-WT1 HZ-FK1 XA-ROF XA-ROK [wfu Jan95 Mexico City A/P, Mexico, used as ticket office in car park of Wal-Mart store in eastern Mexico City]
5134/50	731	N7979S N295AR N500S N50PS N72HT N136MA XA-JMN XA-TPD [wfu Addison, TX, by Sep03; removed from airport by road March14]
5135	8	N7980S N636 N900H N500WN N500FG [parted out Spirit of St.Louis, MO, still marked N500WN; cx 28Aug09]
5136	8	N5500L Libya 001 5A-DAJ [wfu]
5137	8	N5501L EP-VRP Iran 1004 Iran 5-9001
5138	8	N5502L N1301P N333RW N31DK N801 (N700MJ) [wfu at Greenville Technical College, SC; used as an instructional airframe]
5139/54	731	N5503L N991 N991F N10DR XA-RVG N1189A [to Atlanta Air Salvage, Griffin, GA, Apr97 still marked as XA-RVG; US marks cx Apr97]
5140	8	N5504L XB-VIW XA-JCG XA-EMO [wfu Jan06 Toluca, Mexico]
5141	8	N5505L N711Z N7967S N12241 N244 N4436S HZ-SH1 N4493S XB-CXO N3982A N747GB [derelict at Lagos, Nigeria, circa Jan98]
5142	8	N5506L N5113H N1UP N20SH HZ-SH3 N90658 N86TP N91LJ N91UJ N86TP N39LG N23FE XA-SOY [wfu by 2006 Toluca, Mexico]
5143	8	N5507L N100UA N31UT N5070L N5878D C-GATU N620JB N326CB [b/u; cx Jan00]
5144	8	N5508L Mexico JS10201 Mexico DN-01 Mexico JS10201 Mexico 3908 [wfu 2013; preserved in Mexican Air Force museum, Santa Lucia, Mexico]
5145	8	N5509L N46K XB-DBJ XB-JFE XA-JFE N511TD [to Greater St Louis Air & Space Museum, IL; cx 27Aug12]
5146	8	N5510L N80GM C-GWSA N4990D N499AS N545BF [b/u for spares Jan87]
5147	8	N5511L N744UT N718R N212AP [wfu for spares Jan93 Greenwood, LA]
5148	8	N5512L N964M N21SH HZ-SH4 N900SA XA-ROK XA-ROF XA-OLI [cx]
5149/11	731	N5513L N711Z N157JF N157QP N524AC N110MN N110MT N100MZ VR-BJI [b/u for spares Feb91]
5150/37	731	N5514L N516WC N200CC N200CG N42C N312CK N100TM (N345CK) (N710JA) N721CR N911CR [parted out by White Inds, Bates City, MO]
5151	8	N5515L N711Z N46KJ N45K XA-PUL [wfu Jan94 for spares by TAESA Mexico City, Mexico, used as ticket office in car park of Wal-Mart store in southern Mexico City]

LOCKHEED JETSTAR

C/n	Series	Identities
5152	8	N5516L N500JD N113KH XA-SOC [b/u for spares Toluca, Mexico circa Jan03]
5153/61	731	N5517L N711JS N500PG N430MB N416KD N416SJ
5154	8	N5518L N3031 N756 N766 XC-SRH N43AR [parted out Fort Lauderdale Executive, FL circa Jly00]
5155/32	731	N5519L N711Z XA-FES N4248Z N55NE N10PN N79AE N59CD N1DB (VR-BQG) (N120RL) VR-BRL VP-BRL N84GA N116DD [w/o Dallas/Love Field, TX, 10Mar06, cx]
5156	8	N5520L 9K-ACO N70TP XB-DBT N16AZ [wfu] N1B
5157	8	N5521L N9WP N29WP XB-DUH [displayed at entrance to Dodson Av'n at Rantoul, KS painted as "N001DT"]
5158	8	N5522L N516DM C-GTCP N1DT XA-POO XA-FHR XA-TDG
5159	8	N5523L N520M XB-DBS [wfu]
5160	8	N5524L C-FRBC (N60EE) [b/u late 1988 Memphis, TN]
5161/43	731	N5525L N22ES N60SM N119SE N1329L N200PB N99VR LY-AMB N5161R XB-KCV XB-KFR [impounded at Valencia, Venezuela, 07Sep07 for drug-running]
5162	8	N5526L N10CX N10JJ XA-HNY XB-KLV

One of 5A-DAJ c/n 5136 or 5A-DBZ c/n 5114 was dbr by munitions fire at Tripoli in July 2014.

C/n	Series	Identities
5201	2	N5527L N711Z N711DZ (N93JD) N93JM N745DM N777AY [cx 14May14, wfu Miami/Opa Locka, FL]
5202	2	N5528L N717 N717X N333KN N20GB EC-232 EC-FQX VP-CBH P4-CBG 3C-QRK N25AG [b/u Kemble, UK, 2006; remains to Air Salvage Int'l, Alton, Hants, UK; fuselage to Apple Camping campsite, Redberth, Wales]
5203	2	N5529L EP-VLP Iran 1003 [reported w/o 05Jan95 Isfahan, Iran]
5204	2	N5530L N19ES N59AC N500PR N167R N25WZ (N220ES) N202ES N814K [parted out 2008; to Cavanaugh Flight Museum, Addison, TX]
5205	2	N5531L N5000C N500QC N718R N713R YV-826CP N16BL N454JB N72GW
5206	2	N5532L N107GM XA-STG XA-JML N329JS [to White Inds, Bates City, MO Dec04 for parts]
5207	2	N5533L N176BN N34WR
5208	2	N5534L N322CS N123CC (N29TC) N38BG N95BD N95BK [cx 13Aug12, wfu]
5209	2	N5535L N500S N297AP N529TS N375MD [damaged 24Oct05 by Hurricane Wilma at Fort Lauderdale Executive, FL; parted out by Dodson Int'l Parts, KS]
5210	2	N5536L N400KC N707WB N787WB [parted out; fuselage at Aircraft Support Group facility at Conroe, TX in 2005 but removed by Feb08]
5211	2	N5537L N500T (N500YY) N56PR N821MD N118B XA-PWR N261US [wfu Fort Pierce/St Lucie, FL, still wearing XA-PWR]
5212	2	N5538L N3030 N5030 N167G XA-ACC N167G (N95SR) [b/u; cx Aug03; fuselage at Aircraft Support Group facility at Conroe, TX in 2005 but removed by Feb08]
5213	2	N5539L N501T N501J N60JM (N600JT) N65JT N710RM
5214	2	N5540L N530M N601CM N760DL N760DE (N9366Q) N106JL N848AB N221CR N3RC N50KP XA-CVE N50127 XA-RCR [parted out by Alliance Air Parts, Oklahoma City, OK, still wearing marks N50127]
5215	2	N5541L (N215HZ) VR-BJH N329MD N777WJ XA-FHS N215DL N215TS (N1X) N1TS N1X N800TS N80TS N808RP N175MD [cx 27Jan12, wfu; engines sold, airframe to private museum]
5216	2	N5542L N95BA N99E N797WC N797WQ [cx 22Nov16, wfu]
5217	2	N5543L N106G N814CE N500EX N504EX N1MJ N486MJ N1MJ 9G-ABF
5218	2	N5544L N716RD N816RD N901C [cx 20Dec05; presumed wfu]
5219	2	N5545L N107G N21VB C-GBDX N219MF N104BK N770DR 5H-APH LY-EWC N522AG N500DB (N5VN) N800GD
5220	2	N5546L N32KR A6-KAH TC-NOA VP-CGH [cx; wfu]
5221	2	N5547L 5A-DAR [w/o 16Jan83 en route Libya-Algeria]
5222	2	N5548L N509T (N509TF) N509J C-GAZU VP-BCP A6-CPC N813P N311RS
5223	2	N5549L N105G N341K N1DB N644JW N1MJ N886DT N887DT ZS-ICC [parted out Lanseria, South Africa]
5224	2	N4016M N1924G N285LM N3QS N6QZ N116DD N700RM
5225	2	N4021M N746UT N990CH N42KR TC-IHS N900DB (N9KE)
5226	2	N4026M N2MK N815RC N308SG TC-SSS
5227	2	N4033M N211PA N23SB N30Y (N811) N110AN N171SG N117AJ N375MD [cx 14May14, wfu Miami/Opa Locka, FL]
5228	2	N4034M N372H XA-RMD N400MP N400MR XA-CON
5229	2	N4038M N7NP N351WC N851WC (N50NM) N500NM VR-CNM N222MF XA-TCN N224MF N377SA [cx 21Feb17; wfu]
5230	2	N4042M N257H N901FH N901EH N701JH N275MD [cx 14May14, wfu Miami/Opa Locka, FL]
5231	2	N4043M N196KC (N788JS) N988MW N112MC XA-FHR XA-TPJ XA-AAL [wfu Toluca, Mexico]
5232	2	N4046M N90CP N90QP N77C [preserved TWA Museum, Kansas City/Downtown, MO]
5233	2	N4048M YI-AKA 7T-VHP OD-KMI HB-JGK
5234	2	N4049M N357H N920DY N920DG "N234TS" XA-EKT XB-NZJ
5235	2	N4055M YI-AKB [destroyed at Quadisiya Air Base, Iraq, during Gulf War Jan91]
5236	2	N4056M N531M N2JR N34TR N741AM (A6-...) ST-FSA
5237	2	N4058M YI-AKC Iran 5-9003
5238	2	N4062M YI-AKD [destroyed at Quadisiya Air Base, Iraq, during Gulf War Jan91]
5239	2	N4063M YI-AKE [destroyed at Quadisiya Air Base, Iraq, during Gulf War Jan91]
5240	2	N4065M YI-AKF [destroyed at Al Muthana Air Base, Iraq, during Gulf War Jan91]

Production complete

MBB HFB 320 HANSA JET

C/n	Series	Identities
V1/1001		D-CHFB [ff 21Apr64; w/o 12May65 Torrejon, Spain]
V2/1002		D-CLOU (D-CASE) [wfu 24Sep70; preserved Deutsches Museum, Munich, Germany, but removed to Flugwerft Schleissheim museum at Oberschleissheim until 2019 to allow Deutches Museum refurbishment]
1021		D-CARA [wfu Braunschweig 25May84; on static display at Finkenwerder, Germany]
1022		D-CARE [CofA exp 28Apr72; under restoration Berlin/Gatow, Germany]
1023		D-CARI N320J N1320U N320AF N103F [b/u for spares]
1024		D-CARO W Germany (YA111) W Germany (CA111) W Germany D9536 W Germany 1607 F-WZIH [preserved Musee de l'Air, Paris, France]
1025		D-CARU W Germany (YA112) W Germany (CA112) W Germany D9537 W Germany 1608[in open storage at Manching, Germany by 2001; to Finkenwerder, Germany, by road Aug07 for restoration to flying condition]
1026		D-CARY N890HJ N71CW (N1026) N71DL TC-FNS [cx 1991; wfu Hannover, Germany circa Sep88; to Museum Hannover Laatzen marked "D-CARY"]
1027		D-CASO I-TALC (D-CASO) D-CITO N905MW N127MW [w/o 05Oct84 Aberdeen, SD]
1028		D-CASU 5N-AMF [w/o 25Jly77 Abidjan, Ivory Coast]
1029		D-CASY [w/o 29Jun72 Blackpool, UK]
1030		D-CATE N247GW N111DC [wfu; noted dismantled at Monroe, MI Aug95; cx 28Aug14]
1031		D-CERA N300SB N750SB [cx Dec90; wfu Fort Lauderdale Executive, FL; hulk stored Opa-Locka, FL for spares]
1032		D-CERE PH-HFA N130MW N132MW [wfu; b/u]
1033		D-CERI PH-HFB N132MW N130MW [b/u 1989]
1034		D-CERO N320J N320MC [w/o 09Mar73 Phoenix, AZ and b/u; cx Oct90]
1035		D-CERU PH-HFC N128SD [wfu for spares use Monroe, MI circa Aug97]
1036		D-CESA N891HJ N380EX N2MK N136MW (N92047) [cx 22Aug13; wfu]
1037		D-CESE N892HJ N5ZA N6MK N6ML N555JM YV-999P N604GA [w/o 30Nov04 Spirit of St. Louis Airport, MO]
1038		D-CESI N110WS N5627 (N18RA) N192AT N301AT N605GA [instructional airframe at Jefferson County Technical College/Bowman Field, KY]
1039		D-CESO N118RA N893HJ CF-WDU N666LC N666LQ N205MM N208MM N171GA [submerged into Portage Quarry nr Bowling Green, OH, 2006 for diver training]
1040		D-CESU I-ITAL N7158Q [b/u for spares Mojave, CA; remains to Aviation Warehouse film prop facility at El Mirage, CA; canx 27Jan06 as wfu]
1041		D-CIRA W Germany 1601 (D-CIRA) N92045 (N62452) N602GA [wfu Toledo, OH noted Mar00 devoid of marks]
1042		D-CIRE W Germany 1602 TC-LEY TC-SEN TC-GSB (N7684X) N106TF (N603GA) [b/u circa 2000 – remains being used by Fire Department at Louisville, KY]
1043		D-CIRI W Germany 1603 TC-KHE TC-LEY (D-CHFB) [to M.Rahmi Koc Museum, Istanbul, Turkey, 14Dec12 for public display]
1044		D-CIRO [w/o 18Dec70 Texel Is, Netherlands]
1045		D-CIRU N5602 N894HJ N4ZA N7ES [wfu Fort Lauderdale Executive, FL, for spares; remains to Opa-Locka, FL; scrapped]
1046		D-CISA W Germany 1604 TC-NSU [cx 1991; wfu]
1047		D-CISE W Germany 1605 TC-OMR [cx 1991; wfu]
1048		D-CISI W Germany 1606 [preserved GAF Museum, Gatow, Berlin]
1049		D-CISO XC-DGA XC-TIJ [b/u 1991, possibly following accident at San Diego, CA 11Jun84; remains to Mojave, CA]
1050		D-CISU LV-POP LQ-JRH (N1184L) N2675W N777PV N777PS N777PZ N777PQ [wfu for spares use Monroe, MI circa Aug97]
1051		D-CORE N895HJ N6ZA N888DL [b/u Jly 90 for spares – remains to Aviation Warehouse film prop yard at El Mirage, CA]
1052		D-CORI PT-IDW N173GA [instructional airframe at Jefferson County Technical College/Bowman Field, KY]
1053		D-CORO PT-IOB N176GA [wfu, cx Feb07]
1054		D-CORU N896HJ N480LR [cx Feb87; to spares use Monroe, MI circa Aug97]
1055		D-CORY N897HJ N11NT N87950 N30AV (N21SU) TC-GSA (N7685T) N105TF [cx 27Feb13, b/u]
1056		D-COSA [to instructional airframe at Manching, Germany; later to museum at Niederaltaich, Germany (minus engines & wings)]
1057		D-CLMA D-COSE (N107TW) VR-CYR YV-388CP [impounded for drug-smuggling Venezuela Aug2004]
1058	ECM	D-COSI Germany 1621 N322AF [b/u at Hollister, CA circa Jly98]
1059	ECM	D-COSO W Germany 9825 W Germany 1622 [w/o 27Nov76 Schwabmuenchen, W Germany]
1060	ECM	D-COSU W Germany 9826 Germany 1623 (D-CCCH) N321AF [b/u at Hollister, CA, circa Jly98]
1061	ECM	(D-CUNA) D-CANI Germany 1624 (D-CEDL) N320AF [cx 05Sep12, b/u]
1062	ECM	(D-CURE) D-CANO Germany 1625 N323AF [b/u at Hollister, CA circa Jly98]
1063	ECM	(D-CURI) D-CANU Germany 1626 [preserved GAF Museum, Gatow, Berlin]
1064	ECM	(D-CURO) D-CAMA Germany 1627 N324AF [b/u at Hollister, CA circa Jly98]
1065	ECM	(D-CURU) D-CAME Germany 1628 N325AF [b/u at Hollister, CA circa Jly98]
1066		(D-CURY) (D-CAMO)
1067		(D-CUSA) (D-CAMU)
1068		(D-CUSE) (D-CALA)
1069		(D-CUSI) (D-CALE)
1070		(D-CUSO) (D-CALI)
1071		(D-CUSU) (D-CALO)
1072		(D-CUSY) (D-CALU)
1073		(D-CADA)
1074		(D-CADE)
1075		(D-CADI)
1076		(D-CADO)
1077		(D-CADU)

HFB 320 HANSA JET

C/n	Series	Identities			
1078		(D-CATI)			
1079		(D-CANA)			
1080		(D-CANE)	(D-CINA)	(D-CCVW)	(D-CDVW)

Notes: 1021 to 1065 above also have a secondary c/n (S1 to S45)
1066 to 1080 not completed; used for spares

MU300 DIAMOND

C/n	Series	Identities
001SA	2	JQ8001 N181MA [to Beech Field, Wichita, KS fire department for training; cx 18Feb09]
002	1	JQ8002 N81DM JQ8003 JA8248 [cx, wfu]
A003SA	1A	N300DM N300TS (N300TJ) (N303JH)
A004SA	1A	JQ8004 N302DM (N40BK) N59TJ N102WR (N88TJ) N541CW (N484CW) (N541TM) [parted out by White Industries, Bates City, MO; cx 04Feb09]
A005SA	1A	JQ8005 N304DM N450TJ N15AR N40GC N700LP N30HD N110DS [parted out by White Industries, Bates City, MO]
A006SA	1	N325DM C-FPAW N400TJ N777JJ N750TJ N200LP [parted out by Alliance Air Parts, Oklahoma City, OK]
A007SA	1A	N301DM N707CW N507CW N485CW N507CW N24HD N567JK [parted out by Alliance Air Parts, Oklahoma City, OK]
A008SA	1A	N303DM (N56SK) N399DM (N442JC)
A009SA	1A	N305DM N909GA N306P N318RS N360CA [parted out by White Inds, Bates City, MO]
A010SA	1A	N306DM N69PC (N9FC) N300DH N703JH N931MA
A011SA	1A	N307DM (N77GA) N114DM N211GA
A012SA	1A	N308DM N82CT N7RC N107T I-GIRL N112GA N316LP [cx 2Oct14, CofR expired]
A013SA	1	N81HH I-VIGI [w/o 15Oct99 Parma, Italy]
A014SA	1	N15TW N339DM OH-KNE OY-FYN (N517KR)
A015SA	1A	N315DM N415RC N271MB N870P N789DD N789DJ
A016SA	1A	N133RC N100DE N208F N530RD N10NM N706JH N411RE
A017SA	1A	N14DM N75BL (N33MM) N399MM
A018SA	1A	N900LH C-GRDS N138DM N118GA N83BG (N831TJ)
A019SA	1	N311DM N9LP N6PA N319DM N400GK (N438AM)
A020SA	1A	N399RP (N911JJ) [parted out by White Inds, Bates City MO; cx 29Apr09]
A021SA	1	N222Q N4LK N678PC N405MG
A022SA	1A	N313DM N18KE (N816S) N322MD N322BE N800TJ N811DJ (N397SL) N400UF
A023SA	1A	N314DM OY-BPC SE-DDW OY-BPC N79GA N17TJ N22BN N150CA [parted out by White Inds, Bates City, MO]
A024SA	1A	N316DM N320CH N95TJ N450PC N674AC XB-CTC
A025SA	1	N317DM N63GH N1843S N1843A N400HH
A026SA	1	N5UE N55JM N900DW N140AK N526CW N326CW N486CW (N426TM) (N26FA) N28FM [cx11Jun13; wfu]
A027SA	1	N319DM N237CC N800RD N27TJ N7PW [cx13May13; wfu]
A028SA	1A	N320DM N331DC N900WJ [to Dodson Int'l Parts, Rantoul, KS; parted out]
A029SA	1A	N321DM N1UT N10TE N89TJ N100RS (N22CX) [cx 14Mar13, wfu]
A030SA	1A	N322DM N191GS N41UT N58TJ N301P N83SA (N800GC)
A031SA	1A	N174B N2220G N956PP N958PP [parted out by White Inds, Bates City, MO]
A032SA	1A	N323DM N132GA N320T N929WG N83CG (N996DR)
A033SA	1A	N312DM N520TT N223S N5EJ N717CF N717DF N148J [parted out by White Inds, Bates City, MO]
A034SA	1A	N318DM N303P N334KC PR-WTZ
A035SA	1A	N300HH HB-VHX N135GA N702JH N37CB
A036SA	1	N326DM N18BA N997MX
A037SA	1A	N327DM OY-CCB LN-SJA N109TW N134RG [parted out by White Inds, Bates City MO;cx 29Apr09]
A038SA	1	N338DM N147DA N147WC N42SR (N212PA) [Parted out by White Inds, Bates City, MO]
A039SA	1A	N328DM C-GRDX N139DM N399MJ PT-OXT
A040SA	1A	(N329DM) N82CS N188ST N40GA [cx 18Jul13; wfu]
A041SA	1A	N330DM (N444SL) N45GL N83AE N300AA N300AR N104GB
A042SA	1A	N331DM N420TJ N8LE (N420FA)
A043SA	1A	N332DM N19R
A044SA	1A	N334DM N309DM N110DK N146GA N606JM N600GW
A045SA	1A	N335DM N334DM N99FF N154GA N60B N61GA N777DC N545TP N395WB N393WB
A046SA	1A	N346DM (YV-274CP) (N146GA) N151SP N272BC N272BG N900BT N109PW HA-YFE
A047SA	1	N347DM N138RC N76LE N47TJ N45NP N47PB N333TS N2WC
A048SA	1A	N335DM (OO-EBA) VH-JEP N335DM PT-LNN [w/o 23Mar03 Santos Air Base, Brazil]
A049SA	1A	N336DM N300LA YV-309P YV-29CP N40MF XA-SOD N411SP PP-JCP
A050SA	1A	N350DM N257CB N826JH N528LG
A051SA	1A	(N357DM) N351DM N550HS (N35P) D-CGFV TC-YIB [w/o in ground accident; to Dodson Avn, Rantoul, KS, for spares] (N550HS)
A052SA	1	N352DM HB-VHT I-FRAB N70XX [Oct05 to White Industries, Bates City MO for parts]
A053SA	1	N353DM D-CDRB JA30DA
A054SA	1A	N354DM N850TJ N141H N491BT
A055SA	1A	N877S N877T N89EM N600MS N600CG XA-UIC [wfu Monterrey del Norte, Mexico]
A056SA	1A	N341DM N101AD N156GA I-FRTT N255DG
A057SA	1A	N342DM N119MH N334WM N510BC
A058SA	1A	N343DM N384DM VR-BKA N7050V N442EA
A059SA	1A	N345DM N344DM I-DOCA N126GA N1JC (N259JM)
A060SA	1A	N345DM (N300SJ) N585TC [parted out by White Inds, Bates City, MO; cx 29Apr09]
A061SA	1A	N348DM N18T N500PP
A062SA	1A	N349DM G-JMSO N362MD 3D-AFH N426DA TG-LAR N64EZ N616MM N817GR
A063SA	1A	N363DM N54BE N51B N51BE N984SA [parted out by Atlanta Air Salvage, Griffin, GA]
A064SA	1A	N364DM N246GA I-SELM N800LE HI-646SP N2225J N400ML YV195T YV2347
A065SA	1A	N361DM N65JN N165GA OY-CDK I-GENC N54RM N16MF N925MJ
A066SA	1A	N366DM N1TX (N185GA) "N66FG" N88MF N88ME PR-JTS

DIAMOND 1

C/n	Series	Identities
A067SA	1A	N367DM N123VJ I-ALGU N184SC N65SA N63DR N617BG [parted out by White Industries, Bates City, MO; cx 04Feb09]
A068SA	1A	N368DM N368PU N103HC
A069SA	1A	N355DM N56MC N250GP (N197SL) (N501EZ)
A070SA	1A	N370DM D-CNEX OY-BPI N84GA N60EF
A071SA	1A	N371DM (N106GA) N70GA N71GH
A072SA	1A	N372DM PT-LGD N174SA N777DC N779DC
A073SA	1A	N356DM N717VL N1715G N94LH N94LD
A074SA	1A	N374DM N22WJ JA8298 N19GA N32HP [parted out by Dodson Int'l, Rantoul, KS]
A075SA	1A	N375DM N11WF N824DW [wfu; cx 14May11]
A076SA	1A	N376DM N76LE C-GLIG [w/o 01Mar95 Jasper-Hinton A/P, Alberta, Canada] N8221M [parted out by White Inds, Bates City, MO; regn cx Aug01 a/c b/u]
A077SA	1A	N377DM N68PL N66PL N975GR N851C
A078SA	1A	N378DM N710MB [w/o 15Dec93 nr Goodland, KS. Parted out by White Industries, Bates City, MO]
A079SA	1A	N379DM (N574U) N574CF N213LG N765KC
A080SA	1A	N380DM N380CM N770PC N925WC N275HS N44MM
A081SA	1A	N381DM N381MG N81TJ N317CC N317GC N750TJ N50EF XA-...
A082SA	1A	N382DM N105HS N555FA N62CH N214PG [wfu Chino, CA]
A083SA	1A	N383DM N12WF N83TK N417KT [Parted out by White Inds, Bates City, MO]
A084SA	1A	N484DM (N484VS) (N84DT) N840TJ N160S N160H EC-JKL
A085SA	1A	N485DM I-TORA N485DM N777MJ (N911JJ) N70VT N87DY [cx 21May12, wfu]
A086SA	1A	N486DM N515KK N428NG
A087SA	1A	N487DM HB-VIA (PH-JSL) N870AM I-AVEB
A088SA	1A	N482DM
A089SA	1A	N483DM N100EA N89SC N88CR N20PA PP-ELT
A090SA	1A	N312DM G-TOMY N300LG (N64EZ) C-GLIG N464AM
A091SA	1A	N357DM (N357MD) PT-OVM (N485DM) N611AG N400HG N400NF N301AE
A092SA	1A	JA8246 [w/o 23Jly86 Sado Island, Japan]

Production complete

Note: Diamond 2s are included under Beechjet 400s.

MS760 PARIS

C/n	Series	Identities
01		F-WGVO [ff 29Jly54] F-BGVO EP-GVO+ [+ temporary marks used for demonstration flight from 1957 Paris Air Show] F-BGVO [w/o 01May58 Lisbon, Portugal]
02		[used as static test airframe and b/u]
03		F-BHOK France 03 F-SDIA (F-Z...) F-SDIA [w/o 24Dec64 Mont de Marsan, France]
001		F-WIET France 1 F-ZADS F-SDIB F-ZADS F-SDIB 330-DB/F-SDDB [to Musee de l'Air et de l'Espace, Le Bourget, France, Oct09]
002		EP-HIM F-BOJO N760MM N1EP N207MJ
003		Argentina A-01/E-201 [wfu 1994; to IV Brigada Museum, Mendoza, Argentina]
004	2	Argentina A-02/E-202 [wfu 2007; stored Mendoza, Argentina]
005	1A	F-WJAA N760H N2NC N2TE XB-FJO N2TE (N760LB) [w/o 30Nov96 Santa Ana/Orange County, CA; cx Mar97]
006		F-WJAB N84J N760J [b/u 05Apr81; cx May81]
007		Argentina A-03/E-203 [w/o 27Jan61 Mendoza, Argentina]
008		F-WJAC G-36-2 G-APRU N60GT
009		F-WJAD N300ND N722Q
010		Argentina A-04/E-204 [wfu 1998; stored Mendoza, Argentina]
011		Argentina A-05/E-205 [wfu 2006; stored Mendoza, Argentina]
012		France 12/F-YDJ? [w/o 13Apr59 Hyeres, France]
013		Argentina A-06/E-206 [w/o 11Mar88 Mendoza, Argentina; rebuilt with tail unit and fuselage parts from c/n 016 for display at Ezeiza, Argentina]
014		France 14 France 312-DF/F-RHDF [dismantled at Long Beach, CA circa Dec97; fuselage at San Luis Obispo, CA circa May01; to Estrella Warbirds Museum, Paso Robles, CA]
015		Argentina A-07/E-207 [wfu 2007; to Museo Aeronautico, Moron, Argentina]
016		Argentina A-08/E-208 [wfu 2001; parts used in rebuild of c/n 013 for display purposes]
017		Argentina A-09/E-209 [wfu 1995; preserved Rio Gallegas, Argentina]
018		Argentina A-10/E-210 [w/o 09Nov59 Cordoba, Argentina]
019		France 19 France 41-AR/F-SCAR [stored Chateaudun, France Apr97]
020		France 20 F-SDIC 20-Q/F-RABQ [w/o 26Oct62 Bernay en Brie, France]
021		Argentina A-11/E-211 [w/o 06Oct89 Mendoza, Argentina]
022		Argentina A-12/E-212 [wfu 2007]
023		France 23 330-DO/F-SDDO [stored Chateaudun, France Apr97]
024		France 24 65-KW/F-FBLW [to Ailes Anciennes Toulouse for restoration Nov03; preserved wearing code 330-DB in Aeroscopia museum, Toulouse/Blagnac, France]
025		France 25 42-AP/F-SCAP 116-CB [stored Chateaudun, France circa Mar01]
026		F-WJAA France 26 ...-LN/F-RBLN [stored Chateaudun, France circa Sep99]
027		France 27 ...-DE/F-RHDE N760PJ
028		F-WJAE I-SNAI N760X
029		France 29 65-LC/F-RBLC [stored Chateaudun, France Apr97]
030		France 30 65-LI/F-RBLW N370AS N761X
031		France 31/F-YCB. [wfu 23Jly72; instructional airframe Rochefort, France]
032		32 Aeronavale/Marine F-AZLT
033		33 Aeronavale/Marine [preserved Musee de Tradition de l'Aeronautique Navale, Rochefort, France]
034		France 34 43-BB/F-SCBB 113-CG N371AS
035		France 35 43-BL/F-SCBC
036		France 36 44-CC/F-SCCC 316-DH N373AS [cx 16Sep13; CofR expired]
037		France 37 34-Z/F-RABZ [w/o 07Dec67 Les Loges, France]
038		France 38 41-A/F-SCAS 115-ME N374AS [cx 24Mar17; CofR expired]
039	1A	F-WJAA F-BJET [stored Reims-Prunay, France circa Jly99; to USA for spares 2007]
040		40 Aeronavale/Marine [instructional airframe at Lycee Professionel Robert & Nelly de Rothschild, St Maxim, France]
041		41 Aeronavale/Marine N41NY [parted out]
042		42 Aeronavale/Marine [instructional airframe at Morlaix-Ploujean May03]
043		(N888JK) (N776JK) N776K N760C N760S
044		France 44 4D-L/F-RBLD N375AS
045		France 45 43-B./F-SCB. 316-DI N378AS [cx 18Apr17, CofR expired]
046		46 Aeronavale/Marine [in Ailes Anciennes Pays Beaunois collection at Chateau de Savigny les Beaunois]
047		47 Aeronavale/Marine [wfu]
048		France 48 Aeronavale/Marine [w/o 04Jan68]
049		N760M [w/o 03May69 Evadale, TX]
050	2	CN-MAJ CF-MAJ N6068 N111ER N42BL N23ST [w/o 11Sep90 Albuquerque, NM; cx Jun91]
051		Brazil C41-2912 France 51 330-DC/F-SDDC N751PJ [to Den Helder, Netherlands 16Apr04 for restoration towards flying condition]
052		Brazil C41-2911 [wfu]
053		Brazil C41-2910 France 53 OD/F-RHDD N53PJ [to China Jan16 for refurbishment and resale]
054		Brazil C41-2913 France 54 41-A./F-SCA. N354AS [cx 24Sep13; CofR expired]
055		Brazil C41-2914 [wfu]
056		Brazil C41-2915 France 56 65-LG/F-RBLG 133-CM N956P [cx 24Sep13; CofR expired]
057		Brazil C41-2918 France 57 41-AC/F-SCAC N657P [cx 24Sep13; CofR expired]
058		Brazil C41-2920 France 58 65-LB/F-RBLB 312-DG N760F [cx 18Apr17, CofR expired]
059		Brazil C41-2916 France 59 41-A./F-SCA. 133-CF N959P [cx 18Mar13, CofR expired]
060		Brazil C41-2917 France 60 41-AT/F-SCAT N7601R [to China Jan16 for refurbishment and resale]
061		Brazil C41-2919 France 61 ...-LY/F-RBLY N961P [cx 18Mar13, CofR expired]
062		Brazil C41-2921 France 62 65-LV/F-RBLV 314-DO [stored Chateaudun, France circa Mar01]
063		Brazil C41-2923 [wfu]
064		Brazil C41-2922 [stored Santa Cruz, Brazil]
065		Brazil C41-2924 France 65 65-LF/F-RBLF 330-DP

PARIS

C/n	Series	Identities
066		Brazil C41-2925 [wfu]
067		Brazil C41-2926 [w/o 29Oct62 Nova Lima, Brazil]
068		Brazil C41-2927 France 68 NB/F-ZJNB
069		HB-PAA Switzerland J-4117 HB-PAA [cx Jun84; to Musee Europeen de l'Aviation de Chasse Montelimar-Ancone, France] N760FB
070		Brazil C41-2928 France 70 65-LF/F-RBLF [displayed at Tarbes-Lourdes, France marked as "F-MSAD"]
071		Brazil C41-2929 France 71 65-LE/F-RBLE N571P [cx 19Mar13, CofR expired]
072	1A	F-BJLV N760FR [parted out Mojave, CA; hulk stored Santa Rosa, CA]
073		France 73
074		Brazil C41-2930 France 74 [w/o 02Dec80 Natal, Brazil]
075		Brazil C41-2931 France 75 65-LZ/F-RBLZ N975P
076		Brazil C41-2932 [preserved Brazilian AF Museum, Camp de Abonsas, nr Rio de Janeiro, Brazil]
077		Brazil C41-2933 France 77 65-LP/F-RBLP [to Estrella Warbirds Museum, Paso Robles, CA, by Feb10]
078		Brazil C41-2934 France 78 65-LY/F-RBLY 115-ME [stored Chateaudun, France Apr97]
079		Brazil C41-2935 France 79 [wfu 15Apr79; to SOPEMEA Villacoublay, France 31Jan89 for stress tests]
080		Brazil C41-2936 France 80 314-D/F-RHD. GE-316 80/DE [wfu Chateaudun, France – on dump by 20Jun98]
081		Brazil C41-2937 France 81 41-A./F-RBLL ELA61 N81PJ
082		Brazil C41-2938 France 82 65-L./F-RBL. N761JS [cx 21Oct10, wfu]
083		Brazil C41-2939 France 83 NC/F-ZJNC [code 316-DB] [stored Chateudun, France circa Jly00]
084		84 Aeronavale/Marine [w/o 23Dec70 Le Bourget, Paris, France]
085		85 Aeronavale/Marine F-AZTL*
086	1A	F-BJLX N9035Y [b/u Mojave, CA; hulk stored Santa Rosa, CA]
087		87 Aeronavale/Marine N87NY
088		88 Aeronavale/Marine N88NY N626TC N760JS
089	2	F-BJLY N999PJ
090		D-INGE N334RK N454HC N69X
091		France 91 65-LU/F-RBLU [to Musee d'Aeronautique, Orange, France, by Apr07]
092		France 92 118-DA/F-RHDA 316-DL N763JS
093		France 93 65-LD/F-RBLD N764JS [cx 30Nov10, wfu]
094		France 94 65-L./F-RBL. N765JS [cx 17Dec10, wfu]
095		France 95 .../F-RBL. [w/o 03Aug67 Melun, France]
096		France 96 65-LU/F-RBLU [w/o 29May82 Villacoublay, France]
097		France 97 65-LH/F-RBLH [reported as G1-330 "330 DC"] N97PJ PP-XUM
098	2	D-INGA F-BOHN HB-VEP 3A-MPP F-GKPP [w/o Oct91 Calvi, Corsica; [used for spares for c/n 111]
099		I-SNAP [w/o 27Oct62 Milan, Italy]
100		F-ZJNJ France 100
101	2	France 101 F-BNRG (N7038Z) N760PJ N444ET (N760PJ) N520DB [cx 24Mar17; CofR expired]
102	2B	F-BJZQ PH-MSR N760E HB-VEU N99HB N20DA
103	2B	F-BJZR PH-MSS N760N YV-163CP N760N N760T [wfu Oct94 Mojave, CA; hulk stored Santa Rosa, CA]
104	2B	F-BJZS PH-MST N760P N760R [stored Santa Maria, CA]
105	2B	F-BJZT PH-MSU N760Q F-BXQL [stored Reims-Prunay, France circa Jly99; to USA for spares 2007]
106	2B	F-BJZU PH-MSV N5878 [used as a source of spare parts for c/n 008 N60GT]
107	2B	F-BJZV PH-MSW N5879
108	2B	F-BJZX PH-MSX N760AR
109		(F-BJZY) [airframe not built; RLS, Netherlands, option cx]
110		(F-BJZZ) [airframe not built; RLS, Netherlands, option cx]
111	2	I-FINR C6-BEV N760FM [cx 31Jan13, CofR expired]
112		F-EXAA HB-PAC F-BOJY N65218 N7277X N710K [b/u Mojave, CA; cx10May13; hulk stored Santa Rosa, CA]
113		France 113 F-ZJNI
114		France 114 F-ZJNJ [preserved Villacoublay, France]
115		France 115 F-ZJOV [instructional airframe Toussus-le-Noble, France]
116		France 116 F-ZJON
117		France 117 F-ZJAZ
118		France 118 F-ZJNQ
119		France 119 F-ZLNL [wfu by 05Jun05 Istres, France; to museum at Saint Victoret, Marseille, France, 27Feb06]
01	3	F-WLKL F-BLKL [being refurbished at Le Bourget, France, 2011, after over 10 years stored at Reims-Prunay, France]

Production complete

Production by FMA in Argentina

C/n	Series	Identities
A-1		Argentina E-213 [w/o 29Mar73; collided with E-217 c/n A-5 Santa Luis, Argentina]
A-2		Argentina E-214 [w/o 30Dec74 Cordoba, Argentina]
A-3		Argentina E-215 [wfu 1998; preserved Ameghino, Argentina]
A-4		Argentina E-216 [w/o 26Apr62 Moron, Argentina]
A-5		Argentina E-217 [w/o 29Mar73; collided with E-213 c/n A-1 Santa Luis, Argentina]
A-6		Argentina E-218 [w/o 11Feb81 Mendoza, Argentina – but see A-35]
A-7		Argentina E-219 [wfu 1998 and by 2005 displayed on a roundabout near Mendoza apt, Argentina]
A-8		Argentina E-220 [wfu 2005; stored Mendoza, Argentina]

PARIS

C/n	Series	Identities	
A-9		Argentina E-221	[wfu 1994; preserved Mendoza, Argentina]
A-10		Argentina E-222	[wfu 1994 and stored by Lockheed Martin Aircraft Argentina SA]
A-11		Argentina E-223 [code 23]	[wfu 1994 and std by Escuela de Suboficiales de la Fuerza Aerea (ESFA)]
A-12		Argentina E-224	[wfu 1998; to museum at Santa Romana, Argentina]
A-13		Argentina E-225	[wfu 1994; stored with Area Material Quilmes (AMQ), Argentina]
A-14		Argentina E-226	[wfu 1994; preserved Cordoba, Argentina]
A-15		Argentina E-227	[wfu 2006; dismantled at Mendoza, Argentina]
A-16		Argentina E-228 [code 28]	[w/o 16Aug65 Formosa, Argentina]
A-17		Argentina E-229 [code 29]	[wfu 1994 and stored by Lockheed Martin Aircraft Argentina SA]
A-18		Argentina E-230	[wfu 1994; to Escuela Nacional Education Tecnica, Mendoza, Argentina as instructional airframe]
A-19		Argentina E-231	[w/o 09Dec64 "EAM"?]
A-20		Argentina E-232	[wfu 2002; to instructional airframe, Mendoza, Argentina]
A-21		Argentina E-233	[wfu 1995; preserved Mendoza, Argentina]
A-22		Argentina E-234	[w/o 1990 Mendoza, Argentina]
A-23		Argentina E-235	[wfu 1998; stored Mendoza, Argentina; an FMA Paris painted as E-235 is displayed at Museo de Aera de Material, Rio Cuarto but is believd not to be c/n A-23]
A-24		Argentina E-236	[wfu 2005; stored Mendoza, Argentina]
A-25		Argentina E-237	[w/o 04Nov83 San Luis, Argentina]
A-26		Argentina E-238	[w/o 30Dec78 Mendoza, Argentina]
A-27		Argentina E-239	[w/o Jun78 Mendoza, Argentina]
A-28		Argentina E-240	[w/o 20Mar85 San Juan, Argentina]
A-29		Argentina E-241	[wfu 2006]
A-30		Argentina E-242	[wfu 2007]
A-31		Argentina E-243	[wfu 1998; by 2005 displayed by San Justo Aero Club, San Justo, Argentina]
A-32		Argentina E-244	[wfu 1998; preserved San Juan, Argentina, wearing marks E-245]
A-33		Argentina E-245	[wfu 1998; stored Bahia Blanca, Argentina]
A-34		Argentina E-246	[w/o 09Feb77 Cordoba, Argentina]
A-35		Argentina E-247	[wfu 1993 to Museo Nactional de Aeronautica, by Apr04 displayed on a pole at Moron, Argentina painted as E-218]
A-36		Argentina E-248	[w/o 08Nov77 Cordoba, Argentina]

Production complete

PIAGGIO PD808

C/n	Series	Identities	
501	TA	MM577	[wfu by 1996, on dump at Pratica di Mare by Mar98]
502	TA	MM578	[on dump at Pratica di Mare by Mar98; b/u]
503	VIP	I-PIAI	[w/o 18Jun68 San Sebastian, Spain]
504	VIP	I-PIAL	[wfu 1998]
505	GE1	MM61958	[wfu at Pratica di Mare by Nov97]
506	VIP	MM61948	[wfu; preserved at Cadimare former seaplane base, La Spezia,Italy]
507	VIP	MM61949	[wfu mid-1990s; to Ditellandia Air Park, Castel Volturno by Jul99]
508	VIP	MM61950	[wfu Rome/Ciampino 2006]
509	VIP	MM61951	[wfu at Pratica di Mare by Mar98]
510	TP	MM61952	[converted to PD808 GE2; wfu at Pratica di Mare by Aug04; preserved at ITISM, Faraday college, Ostia, Rome, Italy by May09]
511	TP	MM61953	[w/o 15Sep93 Venice, Italy]
512	TP	MM61954	[wfu at Pratica di Mare by Aug98]
513	TP	MM61955	[converted to PD808 GE2; wfu by May05; preserved as gate guardian at Parma, Italy]
514	TP	MM61956	[wfu to dump at Pratica di Mare by Mar98; b/u]
515	TP	MM61957	[wfu at Pratica di Mare by Mar98]
516	GE1	MM61959	[wfu by Mar98; preserved near Ciampino airport, Rome, Italy]
517	GE1	MM61960	[wfu at Pratica di Mare by Aug04; b/u]
518	GE1	MM61961	[wfu; preserved at Italian Air Force Museum, Vigna di Valle, Italy]
519	GE1	MM61962	[wfu by Aug04; stored at Naples airport, Italy]
520	GE1	MM61963	[wfu before Jun93 Pisa, Italy; dismantled at Pratica di Mare by Nov97; remains to Ditellandia Air Park, Castel Volturno by Nov99]
521	RM	MM62014	[wfu; preserved Vialo Europa, Lucca, Italy]
522	RM	I-PIAY	MM62015 [wfu at Pratica di Mare by Mar98; b/u]
523	RM	MM62016	[wfu at Pratica di Mare by Nov97]
524	RM	MM62017	[wfu at Pratica di Mare by Feb98; b/u]

Production complete

NORTH AMERICAN/ROCKWELL SABRE MODELS

T-39 SERIES

C/n	Series	Identities
265-1	CT-39A	59-2868 N2259V [displayed Kirtland AFB, NM as 59-2868]
265-2	CT-39A	59-2869 N4999G 59-2869 [AMARC park code TG033; std wfu Sep93 Memphis Airport, TN]
265-3	NT-39A	59-2870 [to AMARC 21Aug03, park code AATG0105]
265-4	T-39A	59-2871 [w/o 13Nov69 Eglin AFB, FL]
265-5	CT-39A	59-2872 N2296C 59-2872 [AMARC park code TG015]
265-6	T-39A	60-3478 [to AMARC 22Aug03, park code AATG0106]
265-7	CT-39A	60-3479 [AMARC park code TG082]
265-8	CT-39A	60-3480 [AMARC park code TG013]
265-9	CT-39A	60-3481 [AMARC park code TG085] [to Lane Community College, Eugene, OR; to Evergreen Aviation & Space Museum,Mcminnville, OR; to Classic Aircraft Aviation Museum, Hillsboro, OR]
265-10	CT-39A	60-3482 [AMARC park code TG016] N510TA XA-TFD [w/o 4Feb00 Merida, Mexico]
265-11	T-39A	60-3483 [preserved Travis AFB, CA]
265-12	CT-39A	60-3484 [AMARC park code TG024] N7043U XB-GDU XA-TFC [w/o 16May97 20km S of Monterrey-Del Norte, Mexico]
265-13	CT-39A	60-3485 [AMARC park code TG003] [West Intl Aviation, Tucson, AZ]
265-14	CT-39A	60-3486 [AMARC park code TG008] XA-TIY [wfu; stored Laredo, TX]
265-15	CT-39A	60-3487 [AMARC park code TG021] N510TD [cx Sep98 still in AMARC as 60-3486]
265-16	CT-39A	60-3488 N431NA [instructional airframe at Des Moines Educational Resource Center, IA; cx 21May13]
265-17	CT-39A	60-3489 [AMARC park code TG058] [to Houston Community College, TX]
265-18	CT-39A	60-3490 [AMARC park code TG062] N8052V [South Seattle Community College, WA]
265-19	CT-39A	60-3491 [AMARC park code TG009]
265-20	CT-39A	60-3492 [AMARC park code TG007] [to Thief River Falls Tech College, MN]
265-21	CT-39A	60-3493 [AMARC park code TG057] [to Moses Lake, WA for instructional use]
265-22	CT-39A	60-3494 [AMARC park code TG094]
265-23	CT-39A	60-3495 [displayed Scott AFB, IL]
265-24	CT-39A	60-3496 [AMARC park code TG072] [to Cochise College, Douglas, AZ]
265-25	CT-39A	60-3497 [AMARC park code TG066]
265-26	CT-39A	60-3498 [AMARC park code TG077] [at Chandler Williams Gateway, AZ, Apr94]
265-27	CT-39A	60-3499 [AMARC park code TG037]
265-28	CT-39A	60-3500 [AMARC park code TG030] [to Letourneau College, Longview, TX]
265-29	CT-39A	60-3501 [AMARC park code TG093]
265-30	CT-39A	60-3502 [AMARC park code TG095] [to Dr Robert Smirnow, E Northport, NY]
265-31	GCT-39A	60-3503 [preserved Air Classics Museum, Aurora, IL]
265-32	CT-39A	60-3504 [to Bi-States College, St Louis, MO, then to Wyoming Technical College, Oakland, CA; to Oakland Aviation Museum, Oakland, CA] (N3504)
265-33	T-39A	60-3505 [displayed Edwards Flight Test Museum, CA]
265-34	T-39A	60-3506 [w/o 09Feb74 Colorado, CO]
265-35	CT-39A	60-3507 [AMARC park code TG061] [West LA College, Los Angeles, CA marked as "0350" – painted as N3507W (these marks used on a PA-32)]
265-36	CT-39A	60-3508 [AMARC park code TG042] [believed b/u]
265-37	CT-39A	61-0634 [displayed Dyess AFB, TX]
265-38	CT-39A	61-0635 [AMARC park code TG054] [to Lafayette Regional A/P, LA]
265-39	CT-39A	61-0636 [AMARC park code TG089]
265-40	CT-39A	61-0637 [AMARC park code TG035]
265-41	CT-39A	61-0638 [AMARC park code TG096] [to Jett Paqueteria S.A. for parts use circa 2006 noted 14Apr06 Laredo TX]
265-42	CT-39A	61-0639 [AMARC park code TG086] N21092 [instructional airframe at Blackhawk Technical College, Janesville, WI, then disposed of]
265-43	T-39A	61-0640 [w/o 16Apr70 Halifax County A/P, NC (midair collision with a TA-4F)]
265-44	CT-39A	61-0641 [AMARC park code TG036] [to Rock Valley College, Rockford, IL]
265-45	CT-39A	61-0642 [AMARC park code TG045]
265-46	CT-39A	61-0643 [AMARC park code TG022]
265-47	T-39A	61-0644 [w/o 07May63 Andrews AFB, VA]
265-48	CT-39A	61-0645 [AMARC park code TG091] N6CF XA-TFL [w/o Culiacan, Mexico 05Jul07]
265-49	T-39A	61-0646 [w/o 14May75 10 miles north of Richmond, VA]
265-50	CT-39A	61-0647 [AMARC park code TG078] [to Coast Community College, Costa Mesa, CA]
265-51	CT-39A	61-0648 [AMARC park code TG017] [to scrapyard of West Intl Aviation,in 1993]
265-52	T-39A	61-0649 N1064 [AMARC park code TG047; to Portland A/P fire service, OR, still wearing 61-0649; no longer present Oct10]
265-53	CT-39A	61-0650 [AMARC park code TG043] [instructional airframe, Everett Community College, WA]
265-54	CT-39A	61-0651 [AMARC park code TG040] [instructional airframe, Trident Technical College, Moncks Corner, SC]
265-55	CT-39A	61-0652 N4999H 61-0652 [AMARC park code TG087]
265-56	CT-39A	61-0653 [AMARC park code TG071] [to Community College of San Francisco, CA]
265-57	CT-39A	61-0654 [AMARC park code TG044] "N1ERAU" [to Jett Paqueteria S.A. for parts use circa 2006 noted 14Apr06 Laredo TX]
265-58	CT-39A	61-0655 [AMARC park code TG005] [sold 1992 to Av-mats, St Louis, MO; ex storage]
265-59	CT-39A	61-0656 [AMARC park code TG010]
265-60	CT-39A	61-0657 [AMARC park code TG023] [to Rice Aviation, Houston-Hobby, TX]
265-61	CT-39A	61-0658 [AMARC park code TG034] [to Frederick Community College, Frederick, MD; removed by road 15Aug00, reportedly to Texas]
265-62	CT-39A	61-0659 [AMARC park code TG026] XA-TNP [w/o Culiacan, Mexico, 30Dec06]
265-63	T-39A	61-0660 [displayed McClellan AFB, CA]
265-64	T-39A	61-0661 [w/o 29Jul62 Paine Field-Seattle, WA]

SABRE T-39 SERIES

C/n	Series	Identities
265-65	CT-39A	61-0662 [AMARC park code TG032] [b/u Spirit of St Louis, MO; remains to Clarkesville, MO, by 1993]
265-66	CT-39A	61-0663 [AMARC park code TG067] [b/u nose/forward fuselage by firestation at New Orleans/Lakefront A/P, LA; removed by road late Apr01]
265-67	T-39A	61-0664 [AMARC park code TG063] [to Deuel Vo-Tech Inst, Tracy, CA, 08Jun90; to Castle Air Museum, Atwater, CA, 05Dec07]
265-68	CT-39A	61-0665 [AMARC park code TG028]
265-69	CT-39A	61-0666 [AMARC park code TG014]
265-70	CT-39A	61-0667 [AMARC park code TG088] N7143N [w/o Khartoum A/P, Sudan in either 1993 or 1994; to Fujairah, UAE minus wings & engines; noted Jan04]
265-71	CT-39A	61-0668 [AMARC park code TG051] [believed b/u]
265-72	CT-39A	61-0669 [AMARC park code TG075] [to Metro Tech Aviation Career Center, Oklahoma City, OK]
265-73	CT-39A	61-0670 [operational Maxwell AFB, AL]
265-74	CT-39A	61-0671 [AMARC park code TG090] [to ground trainer Keesler AFB, MS]
265-75	T-39A	61-0672 [w/o 13Mar79 S Korea]
265-76	CT-39A	61-0673 [AMARC park code TG038] N4313V XA-TJZ [wfu; stored Laredo, TX]
265-77	CT-39A	61-0674 [displayed Hill AFB, UT]
265-78	CT-39A	61-0675 [displayed Yokota AFB, Japan; reported b/u circa 1998]
265-79	CT-39A	61-0676 [AMARC park code TG049]
265-80	T-39A	61-0677 N9166Y [at Helena Vocational Technical Center, Helena ND]
265-81	CT-39A	61-0678 [AMARC park code TG012]
265-82	T-39A	61-0679 [AMARC park code TG069] N6581E [at Spokane Community College, WA]
265-83	CT-39A	61-0680 [AMARC park code TG039] N32010 [Central Missouri State University, MO; at Warrensburg, MO marked "1068"]
265-84	CT-39A	61-0681 [instructional airframe at Michigan Institute of Aeronautics, Canton, MI]
265-85	CT-39A	61-0682 [AMARC park code TG031] [to Southwest Michigan College, Dowagiac, MI]
265-86	CT-39A	61-0683 [AMARC park code TG025] N510TB XB-GDW XA-GDW [wfu; stored Laredo, TX]
265-87	T-39A	61-0684 [scrapyard Davis-Monthan, AZ/"Bob's Air Park"; believed b/u]
265-88	T-39A	61-0685 [preserved US Army Aviation Museum, Fort Rucker, AL]
270-1	T-39B	59-2873 [preserved Wright-Patterson AFB, OH, until 1986 then stored at China Lake NWC, CA]
270-2	T-39B	59-2874 [AMARC park code TG103]
270-3	T-39B	60-3474 [operational Edwards AFB, CA]
270-4	T-39B	60-3475 [AMARC park code TG098]
270-5	T-39B	60-3476 [AMARC park code TG102]
270-6	T-39B	60-3477 [AMARC park code TG101]
276-1	T-39A	62-4448 [w/o 28Jan64, Erfurt, East Germany – shot down by Soviet Air Force]
276-2	CT-39A	62-4449 [AMARC park code TG092] [preserved Pima County Museum, Tucson, AZ]
276-3	CT-39A	62-4450 [AMARC park code TG006] [to Jett Paqueteria S.A. for parts use circa 2006 noted 14Apr06 Laredo TX]
276-4	CT-39A	62-4451 [AMARC park code TG060] N31403 XA-TQR [wfu; stored Laredo, TX]
276-5	T-39A	62-4452 [preserved Travis AFB, CA]
276-6	T-39A	62-4453 N6552R XA-TGO [wfu; stored Laredo, TX]
276-7	CT-39A	62-4454 [AMARC park code TG018]
276-8	CT-39A	62-4455 [AMARC park code TG065] N4314B XA-TJU [w/o Monterrey, Mexico, 19Dec06]
276-9	CT-39A	62-4456 [AMARC park code TG056] [at Westwood College of Aviation Technology, Los Angeles, CA painted as N1965W]
276-10	CT-39A	62-4457 [AMARC park code TG002]
276-11	T-39A	62-4458 [w/o 25Mar65 Clark AFB, Philippines]
276-12	CT-39A	62-4459 [AMARC park code TG041] [to Clover Park Vo-Tech, Tacoma, WA]
276-13	T-39A	62-4460 [w/o 28Feb70 Torrejon AFB, Spain]
276-14	T-39A	62-4461 [displayed Warner-Robins AFB, GA, until 2013, then disposed of]
276-15	CT-39A	62-4462 [AMARC park code TG046] [instructional airframe at Trident Technical College, Moncks Corner, SC, wearing fake marks N24462]
276-16	CT-39A	62-4463 [AMARC park code TG100]
276-17	CT-39A	62-4464 [AMARC park code TG004] [to Utah State University, Salt Lake City, UT]
276-18	T-39A	62-4465 [preserved March AFB, CA]
276-19	CT-39A	62-4466 [AMARC park code TG019] [to technical school at Detroit City airport, MI]
276-20	CT-39A	62-4467 [AMARC park code TG083] [at GTCC Aviation Center, Greensboro, NC; wears fake marks 66866]
276-21	CT-39A	62-4468 [AMARC park code TG020] N63611 XA-TIX [wfu; stored Laredo, TX]
276-22	CT-39A	62-4469 [AMARC park code TG064] [to Wyotech, Bedford, MA. Scrapped 2007]
276-23	CT-39A	62-4470 [displayed Maxwell AFB, AL]
276-24	CT-39A	62-4471 [displayed Ramstein AFB, W Germany]
276-25	CT-39A	62-4472 [AMARC park code TG011] N39RG XA-...
276-26	CT-39A	62-4473 [AMARC park code TG029] [forward fuselage at Greater St Louis Aviation Museum, St Louis, MO]
276-27	CT-39A	62-4474 [AMARC park code TG027] XB-GDV N510TC XA-TDX [wfu; stored Laredo, TX]
276-28	CT-39A	62-4475 [AMARC] [noted flying during 1991 ex storage at AMARC; to Milwaukee Area Technical College, WI, by Sep92]
276-29	T-39A	62-4476 [AMARC park code TG099]
276-30	CT-39A	62-4477 [AMARC park code TG048; to Milwaukee Area Technical College, WI] "N269Y" [fake marks]
276-31	T-39A	62-4478 [preserved USAF Museum Wright-Patterson AFB, OH]
276-32	CT-39A	62-4479 [AMARC park code TG052] N988MT [to Metro-Tech Aviation Center, Oklahoma, OK]
276-33	CT-39A	62-4480 [AMARC park code TG068] N24480 N39FS
276-34	CT-39A	62-4481 N33UT [to University of Tennessee, Tullahoma, TN] N741MT [to Middle Tennessee State University, Murfreesboro, TN, 2006]
276-35	CT-39A	62-4482 [displayed Kelly AFB, TX, then to AMARC 30Jan04, park code AATG0107]

SABRE T-39 SERIES

C/n	Series	Identities
276-36	CT-39A	62-4483 [AMARC park code TG055] [to Indian Hills Community College, IA]
276-37	T-39A	62-4484 [displayed Kadena AFB, Japan]
276-38	CT-39A	62-4485 [displayed Yokota AFB, Japan]
276-39	CT-39A	62-4486 [AMARC park code TG050] N265WB XA-TJY [wfu; stored Laredo, TX]
276-40	CT-39A	62-4487 [displayed SAC Museum, Ashland, NE]
276-41	CT-39A	62-4488 [operational Andrews AFB, MD]
276-42	CT-39A	62-4489 [AMARC park code TG074] N65618 [to Colorado Northwestern Community College, Rangely, CO; cx Sep95; status?]
276-43	CT-39A	62-4490 [AMARC park code TG079] [to Jett Paqueteria S.A. for parts use circa 2006, noted 14Apr06 Laredo TX]
276-44	CT-39A	62-4491 [AMARC park code TG081] N63811 XA-TIW [wfu; stored Laredo, TX]
276-45	CT-39A	62-4492 [painted as N1SJ with San Jose University's Avn Dept, San Jose Airport, CA (the real N1SJ used by Cessna 310 (U-3) s/n 57-5856)]
276-46	CT-39A	62-4493 [AMARC park code TG076] [to instructional airframe, Penn College, Williamsport, PA, wearing fake marks N1PC]
276-47	CT-39A	62-4494 [displayed Chanute Air Museum, Rantoul, IL]
276-48	CT-39A	62-4495 [AMARC park code TG059] N6612S N1929P [to college in Yunlin, Taiwan, as instructional airframe]
276-49	CT-39A	62-4496 [w/o 20Apr85 Scranton/Wilkes Barre, PA]
276-50	CT-39A	62-4497 [AMARC park code TG053] [to Wyotech, Bedford, MA] "N15EC"
276-51	CT-39A	62-4498 [AMARC park code TG080] [to Salt Lake City Community College, UT]
276-52	CT-39A	62-4499 [w/o 24Jun69 McCook, NB]
276-53	CT-39A	62-4500 [AMARC park code TG070] [to Milwaukee Area Technical College, WI]
276-54	CT-39A	62-4501 [AMARC park code TG073] [to O'Fallon Technical College, St Louis, MO]
276-55	T-39A	62-4502 [w/o 31Dec68 Langley AFB, VA]
277-1	T-39D	150542 [stored China Lake NWC, CA]
277-2	T-39D	150543 [AMARC park code 7T-027] (N960M) (XA-AAG)
277-3	T-39D	150544 [code F18] [AMARC park code 7T-006]
277-4	T-39D	150545 [wfu and b/u]
277-5	T-39D	150546 [code F201] [AMARC park code 7T-014]
277-6	T-39D	150547 [code F211] [AMARC park code 7T-021] (N959M) (XA-AAI)
277-7	T-39D	150548 [code F10] [AMARC park code 7T-008] (N956M) (XA-AAF)
277-8	T-39D	150549 [code F11] [AMARC park code 7T-011]
277-9	T-39D	150550 [at Pensacola NAS, FL]
277-10	T-39D	150551 [AMARC park code 7T-002] [believed b/u]
285-1	T-39D	150969 [AMARC park code 7T-026] (N957M) (XA-AAJ)
285-2	T-39D	150970 N431NA [cx Dec91; wfu and b/u]
285-3	T-39D	150971 [AMARC park code 7T-001] [believed b/u]
285-4	T-39D	150972 [at Pensacola NAS, FL]
285-5	T-39D	150973 [code F203] [AMARC park code 7T-013]
285-6	T-39D	150974 [code F204] [AMARC park code 7T-015]
285-7	T-39D	150975 [code F12] [AMARC park code 7T-007]
285-8	T-39D	150976 [code F205] [AMARC park code 7T-016]
285-9	T-39D	150977 [at Pensacola NAS, FL]
285-10	T-39D	150978 [code F218] [AMARC park code 7T-009]
285-11	T-39D	150979 [code F206] [AMARC park code 7T-017]
285-12	T-39D	150980 [code F14] [AMARC park code 7T-004]
285-13	T-39D	150981 [AMARC park code 7T-012] [believed b/u]
285-14	T-39D	150982 [code F219] [AMARC park code 7T-022]
285-15	T-39D	150983 [code F212] [AMARC park code 7T-023]
285-16	T-39D	150984 [code F208] [AMARC park code 7T-010]
285-17	T-39D	150985 N32508 [preserved Pensacola, FL]
285-18	T-39D	150986 [displayed Warner-Robins AFB, GA]
285-19	T-39D	150987 [preserved NAS Patuxent River, MD]
285-20	T-39D	150988 [code F209] [AMARC park code 7T-005]
285-21	T-39D	150989 [stored China Lake NWC, CA]
285-22	T-39D	150990 [code F213] [AMARC park code 7T-024]
285-23	T-39D	150991 [code F17] [AMARC park code 7T-003]
285-24	T-39D	150992 [active at China Lake NWC, CA circa May97]
285-25	T-39D	151336 [code F214] [AMARC park code 7T-025] (N961M) (XA-AAH)
285-26	T-39D	151337 [at Pensacola NAS, FL]
285-27	T-39D	151338 [preserved Southern Museum of Flight, Birmingham, AL]
285-28	T-39D	151339 [preserved US Naval Aviation Museum, NAS Pensacola, FL]
285-29	T-39D	151340 [code F216] [AMARC park code 7T-018] [wfu to DMI scrapyard at AMARC]
285-30	T-39D	151341 [code F217] [AMARC park code 7T-019]
285-31	T-39D	151342 [AMARC park code TG-097] [to Milwaukee Area Technical College, WI]
285-32	T-39D	151343 [dumped NAS Pensacola, FL; believed b/u]

Production complete

AMARC or AMARG indicates aircraft at Aerospace Maintenance and Regeneration Center, Davis-Monthan, AZ

SABRE 40

C/n	Series	Identities
282-1	R	N7820C N177A N766R XC-OAH XC-JCK (N351JM) N116SC [cx Jul10; wfu]
282-1	R	N7820C N177A N766R XC-OAH XC-JCK (N351JM) N116SC [cx Jul10; wfu]
282-2	T-39N	N577R N577PM N100WF N108W N108U N57GS N67WW N16TA N304NT US Navy 165512 [wfu; to AMARG Davis Monthan, AZ, 23May14]
282-3		N570R (N57QR) N467H [wfu Van Nuys A/P, CA, circa 2002; parted out; cx Jun11]
282-4		N6358C N14M N75JD N111MS N408TR [cx Sep03; in use as instructional airframe by Toledo Public Schools, OH]
282-5		N30W [w/o 21Dec67 Perryville, MO]
282-6		N6360C N600R XB-HHF XA-SBS XA-GYR XA-UCS [w/o Mexico City 05Jul06]
282-7		N6361C N360J N576R N1102D N43NR N101US N43NR N122RP XA-SEN XB-EZV XA-STU N706A [wfu; b/u Opa-Locka, FL]
282-8		N6362C N520S N366N N369N N140MM [wfu Sep93 and parted out; cx Nov96]
282-9	T-39N	N6363C N620M N620K N327JB (N327RH) N329SS N301NT US Navy 165509 [wfu; to instructional airframe, NAS Pensacola, FL]
282-10		N6364C N525N N9503Z [w/o 07Mar73 Blaine, MN]
282-11		N6365C N167H N167G N73PC N10SL [wfu for spares & b/u Fort Lauderdale Executive, FL; cx Jun03]
282-12		N6366C N905M N888PM N368DA N107CJ [wfu Opa-Locka, FL; cx Mar97]
282-13		N6367C N899TG N408S N408CS N408CC XA-SMP N502RR XA-TKW
282-14		N6368C N2009 N31BC N31BQ N30BE (N30PN) [b/u during 1986; remains at Clarkesville, MO]
282-15		N6369C N106G N1062 N32BC N32BQ (N19MS) N40SE N21PF N43W N43WL [cx 02Dec14; wfu]
282-16		N6370C N227SW N227S N40GP N41GS [b/u for spares Miami A/P, FL during 1989]
282-17		N6371C N911Q N382RF N392F N900CS XA-HOK [wfu; remains at Clarkesville, MO]
282-18		N6372C N107G N1072 N113SC N15TS N131BH [cx 02May07; b/u]
282-19	R/T-39N	N6373C N881MC N881MD N100CE N1000E (N40R) N311NT US Navy 165519
282-20	T-39N	N6374C N265R N3298D N40YA (N282AM) N315NT/US Navy 165523 [wore dual marks] [wfu; to AMARG Davis Monthan, AZ, 22May14]
282-21		N6375C N168H N168D N87CM [wfu Clarkesville, MO; parted out; cx 30Apr15]
282-22		N6376C N747 N747E [w/o 21Dec94 Buenos Aires-Aeroparque, Argentina; parted out Buenos Aires-Don Torcuato]
282-23		N6377C N282NA N8400B N800M N80QM N301HA N50TX (N265AC) N123CD (N55ME)
282-24		N6378C N720J N360Q N40DW N8AF XA-JDN
282-25		N6379C HB-VAK I-SNAK N40SJ I-NICK [wfu; to White Inds, Bates City, MO, for spares Oct98]
282-26		N6380C N60Y N6087 N737E N153G N300CH XA-RED XA-DAN XA-RED [cx; fate?]
282-27		N6381C N720R N129GP N129GB N111EA N61RH [wfu Oct93 to Spartan College of Aeronautics & Technology, Tulsa Int'l A/P, OK]
282-28	T-39N	N6382C N6565A N6565K N524AC N524AG N27DA N197DA N40CD N482HC N314NT US Navy 165522 [w/o Gulf of Mexico 08May02 in mid-air collision with 165525 c/n 282-100]
282-29	T-39N	N6383C N910E N170JL N170AL N170DD N303NT US Navy 165511 [wfu; to AMARG, Davis-Monthan, AZ, 22May13]
282-30	T-39N	N6384C N526N N7090 N709Q N801MS N306NT US Navy 165514 [wfu; to AMARG Davis Monthan, AZ, 03Sep14]
282-31		N23G N236Y N800Y N700R N577VM N34AM [wfu; to spares 1993 Spirit of St Louis, MO; remains with Fire Service at Springfield Airport, IL]
282-32	T-39N	N100Y N100HC N711UC N40SL N40WP N8GA N456JP N312NT US Navy 165520 [wfu; to George Stone Technical Center, Pensacola, FL, as instructional airframe 20Oct14]
282-33		N737R N903K N903KB N168W
282-34		N6389C N575R N5PC N5PQ N400CS N940CC [cx 15Nov12, wfu]
282-35		N6390C N341AP N341AR N567DW [b/u circa 1985; remains to Clarkesville, MO]
282-36		N6391C N1903W N1908W N22BN N59PK N59K N59KQ N63A N88JM N200MP N40LB [cx 30Aug12, wfu Fort Lauderdale Executive A/P, FL]
282-37		N6392C N265W N77AP [w/o 07Nov77 New Orleans, LA]
282-38		N6393C N2997 N299LR N100FS (N68AA) N999VT N921JG N339PM [parted out by AvMATS, St Louis, MO; cx Jun11]
282-39	R	N6394C N442A N947R N333B XA-BAF (N4492V) XA-RGC XA-RTM XA-PIC [wfu Toluca, Mexico]
282-40		N6395C N738R N715MR N40BP [wfu Oct93; parted out Clarkesville, MO; remains form part of MonstroCity exhibit at City Museum, St Louis, MO]
282-41		N6396C N661P N300RC N300RG N707JM N57RM (N300TK) (N116AC) N240AC XB-AYJ [impounded Panama City Balboa/Paitilla, Panama, Dec01]
282-42		N6397C N727R N904K N904KB (N61FC) N40EL N500RK N50CD [w/o 03Feb90 Detroit, MI; cx Oct91; remains to Spirit of St Louis A/P, MO 1995]
282-43	R	N6398C N730R XA-JUD N4469F Ecuador 043
282-44		N6399C N4567 N1DC N1QC N44NP N600JS N64MA [instructional airframe, Middle Georgia College Aviation Campus, Eastman, GA]
282-45		N6552C N747UP N344UP N255GM N333GM N333NM
282-46	CT-39E	N6553C N339NA 157352 [w/o 21Dec75 Alameda AFB, CA]
282-47		N740R N34W [w/o 04Jan74 Midland, TX]
282-48	R	N6555C N747R N90GM (N153G) XA-JUE N4469M XA-CPQ N4469M XA-RGC N47VL [parted out Perryville, MO]
282-49		N6556C N757R N905K N905KB Sweden 86001
282-50		N6557C N757E N956 N956CC XA-SMQ N282CA [wfu Spirit of St Louis, MO, still wearing previous identity XA-SMQ; b/u; cx 24Jul08]

SABRE 40

C/n	Series	Identities
282-51		N733R N108G N108X N227LS N225LS (N51MN) [noted 31Aug91 wfu Spirit of St Louis A/P, MO; remains to Elsberry, MO]
282-52	R	N7502V N200A N2000 N2004 N40R N77MR (N77MK) N303A N282MC N64DH
282-53		N7503V N999BS N123MS N101T N62K N62Q (ZS-GSB) ZS-PTJ N67201 N600BP N555PT [cx Jan91; parted out Spirit of St.Louis, MO]
282-54		N7504V N255CT N256CT XA-EEU [w/o 1980 ground accident in Mexico]
282-55		N7505V N2007 N353WB N353WC N68HC N68HQ N221PH (N221PX) [b/u during 1986; cx Feb91; fuselage to Spirit of St.Louis A/P, MO circa Aug00]
282-56		N7506V N322CS N10CC N722ST N722FD (N722ED) N204TM N85DA XA-RPS [reported wfu]
282-57		N7507V N27C N545C N1909R N1909D [to spares at Spirit of St Louis A/P, MO circa May97]
282-58		N7508V N1101G N110FS [wfu; remains at Spirit of St.Louis A/P, MO circa Oct00; cx Sep01]
282-59		N7509V N48WS N48WP (N2SN) N17LT XA-ESR N465S N40SE N43CF [parted out Perryville, MO; cx Aug95]
282-60	T-39N	N7510V N903G N66TP N22TP N256MA N256EN N256EA N555AE N555AB N141H N316NT US Navy 165524 [w/o northwest Georgia, USA, 10Jan06]
282-61	T-39N	N550L N550LL N231A XA-RGC XA-EGC N2568S (N60WL) N33TW N309NT US Navy 165517 [wfu; to AMARG Davis Monthan, AZ,03Sep14]
282-62		N1863T [cx Sep87, wfu]
282-63		N325K XA-AFW XB-IHB
282-64		N7514V N9000V N9000S N800CS [b/u 1986; cx Feb90]
282-65		N2232B N145G XA-GGR XA-MJE
282-66	T-39N	N2233B N355MJ N4943A N737R N40NR N40HC N48TC N54CF N98CF N305NT US Navy 165513 [w/o 12Apr10 nr Morgantown, GA]
282-67	A	N2234B N711T N140RF [cx Aug10; parted out by AvMATS, St Louis, MO]
282-68	R	N2235B N788R N801NC N22MY N22MV N60RB XA-LEL N4469N Ecuador 068 [w/o 03Jun88 Quito A/P, Ecuador]
282-69		N2236B N125N N256MA N125NL N1MN N43NR N777V N777VZ N49RJ [canx 09Dec04; b/u]
282-70		N2236C N377P N874AJ N111AB N654E N22CH N70SL N17LT N34LP N3280G [impounded Mexico City, Mexico; cx 06Jul13, CofR expired; current status not known]
282-71		N2239B N957 N957CC XA-SMR [dbr Saltillo, Mexico, 30Jun07]
282-72	T-39N	N744R (N880HL) (N69CG) N78GP N986JB N307NT US Navy 165515 [wfu; to AMARG Davis Monthan, AZ, 28Aug14]
282-73		N630M N630N [cx Jun85; b/u for spares; remains at Spirit of St.Louis A/P, MO, circa Oct00]
282-74		N2241B N572R N707TG N707FH [b/u and cx Nov02]
282-75		N2241C N48CG (N48CE) [b/u 1983; remains to Clarkesville, MO]
282-76		N2242B N474VW D-CAVW N787R N124H N415CS N415GS N350E N58025 N8345K N265CM N257TM [b/u circa May02, cx Jun02]
282-77	T-39N	N2244B N608S N608AR N189AR N96CM N27KG N310NT US Navy 165518 [wfu; to AMARG Davis Monthan, AZ, 20Feb14]
282-78		N739R [w/o 16May67 Ventura, CA]
282-79		N2248C N797R N701NC N35CC N111AC XA-CYS
282-80		N2249B N36050 N360E N40JF N40WH XA-FTN XB-JGI [parted out Perryville, MO]
282-81	T-39N	N2250B N36065 N360N N99CR N416CS N1GY N302NT US Marines 165510 [wfu; to AMARG Davis Monthan, AZ, 23Jul14]
282-82		N574R N736R N713MR (N777ST) N19MS N366DA XB-EQR N39RG [to Tulsa Technology Center, Tulsa, OK, as instructional airframe 2006]
282-83		N726R N642LR N232T N160TC N82ML [wfu for spares c Oct94 Clarkesville, MO; cx Mar95]
282-84	CT-39E	N2254B 157353 [code 353RW] [AMARC park code 7T-028]
282-85	CT-39E	N2255B 157354 N958M XA-AAW [substantial damage 02Jun03 in hanger collapse at Laredo, TX still wearing 157354]
282-86		N86 [cx Sep92; wfu; stored in bare metal Oklahoma City, OK, no marks visible]
282-87		N87 N36P N399P [at Pittsburgh Inst of Aeronautics, PA]
282-88		N88 [cx Dec93; instructional airframe Hampton University/Hughes Training Inc Aero Science Center, Newport News, VA, then scrapped]
282-89		N89 [cx Oct91; b/u for spares]
282-90	T-39N	N2569B N928R CF-NCG C-FNCG N3831C N155GM N362DA N308NT US Navy 165516 [wfu; to AMARG Davis Monthan, AZ, 28Aug14]
282-91		N9500B N5511A N5511Z N66ES N40NR Sweden 86002
282-92	CT-39E	N2676B 158382 N825SB [to Tulsa Technology Center, Tulsa, OK, as instructional airframe 2005]
282-93	CT-39E	N4701N 158381 [w/o during 1991 nr Spratley Islands, S China Sea]
282-94	T-39N	N4703N N16R N216R N6TE N147CF N40TA N313NT US Navy 165521
282-95	CT-39E	N4704N 158380 N425NA 158380
282-96	CT-39E	N4705N 158383 [wfu; to Dodson International Parts, KS circa 2004]
282-97		N4706N N85 [w/o 14Jan76 Recife, Brazil]
282-98	A	N4707N N40SC N516WP N516LW N767JH YV416T YV2871
282-99	A	N7594N N78TC N22CH N400GM N100FG N12BW N211BR
282-100	A/T-39N	N19HF N82CF XA-LEG N71325 (N302NT) N317NT US Navy 165525 [w/o Gulf of Mexico 08May02 in mid-air collision with 165522 c/n 282-28]
282-101	A	N7596N N1BX N111XB N101RR N160W
282-102	A	N7597N N2WR N800DC N74MG N74MJ (N157AT) XA-PIH XB-JKV XA-UGB
282-103	A	N7598N N44P N9MS N217A N217TE N217E N730CA N730CP [cx 21Oct13; wfu]
282-104	A	N40CH N78BC N99XR N100KS N26SC N26SE N925BL XA-SEU N104SL [b/u; cx 24Jul08]

SABRE 40 / SABRE 60

C/n	Series	Identities
282-105	A	N2HW N2QW N22BJ N312K N921JG XA-SCN XC-AA73 [noted derelict at Mexico City, Mexico in Jan03]
282-106	A	N7595N XB-DUS XA-RKG (N22NB) N333GM N854RB YV-1144CP YV120T [wfu Caracas/Simon Bolivar, Venezuela]
282-107	A	N7584N N40NR CF-BRL [w/o 27Feb74 Frobisher Bay, Canada]
282-108	A	N7596N N442WT N442WP N306CW N85CC N8500 [cx 27Feb17, wfu]
282-109	A	N4NP N700CF N93AC N77AT Ecuador 047
282-110	A	N7597N N477X N477A N250EC [wfu Entebbe, Uganda after suffering gunfire damage in Democratic Republic of Congo circa May03; cx 04Jun04, w/o]
282-111	A	N7662N N9NR XA-SAG N32654 N213BM (N200CK) (N431DA) (N246GS) N7KG [to Tulsa Technology Center, Tulsa, OK, as instructional airframe 2006]
282-112	A	N7667N N6789 N6789D N301PC N306PC N55MT N164DA N74MB N164DA N164DN N40ZA XA-UBG XA-UEY
282-113	A	N8311N N40SC N40BT N30AF N430MB N430MP
282-114	A	N64MC N64MG XA-ATC XC-SUB XA-ATC (N7SL) XB-RGS XB-RGO XB-MDG XA-UNV
282-115	A	N8333N N376D N376DD N376RP XA-MNA XA-GCH XA-LML
282-116	A	N4PH XB-BBL [wfu Toluca, Mexico]
282-117	A	N8338N (HB-VCZ) I-MORA N1WZ Mexico TP108/XC-UJH N3159U N265SC (N298AS)
282-118	A	N8339N PT-JNJ N19BG [wfu Aug93 still as PT-JNJ; to spares cOct94 Clarkesville,MO; cx Aug95]
282-119	A	N8341N N5565 [w/o 15Jan74 Oklahoma City, OK]
282-120	A	N73HP N73DR YV225T
282-121	A	N8349N PP-SED [fuselage to Spirit of St.Louis A/p, MO circa Sep97]
282-122	A	N40JW N188PS "N409GL" N188PS N409GL [parted out by AvMATS, St Louis, MO]
282-123	A	N8350N XA-APD XB-ESS
282-124	A	N193AT N200E N2006 N40JE N20ES N70ES XA-TYZ XB-EGO [wfu; stored at Global Park industrial estate, Queretaro, Mexico]
282-125	A	N8356N XB-NIB XA-SQA
282-126	A	N40NS XA-SNI N40GT
282-127	A	N110PM N183AR N63SL OB-T-1319 OB-1319 [w/o 03Sep93 Buenos Aires, Argentina; remains to Opa-Locka, FL]
282-128	A	N99AP XA-LIX N99114 XB-JPS
282-129	A	N75W N75WA N75MD (N99FF) XA-RLH [b/u Monterrey del Norte, Mexico]
282-130	A	N33LB N44NR XC-SRA Mexico TP107 Mexico TP105/XC-UJG XC-HEY Mexico TP105/XC-UJI XC-PGE XA-REG XC-AA51
282-131	A	N9251N N3BM N3QM N82R LV-WND
282-132	A	N9252N N28TP N70BC N240CF N240JR [cx 15Apr13; CofR expired]
282-133	A	N65740 N41NR I-RELT
282-134	A	N40NR N60RC (YV-64CP) N66CD XA-MVG XB-MVG N134JJ N40NJ
282-135	A	N4GV N777SL N7778L N55PP N820JR N200E N2006 (N67BK) [cx 06Jun13; wfu]
282-136	A	N44PH N211SF N112ML CP-2317 (N68ML)
282-137	A	N65763 N5511A N5512A N53WC N9NR N87CR N870R N881DM XA-LMA [wfu Mexico City, Mexico]

Production complete

Note: The following T-39N aircraft "converted" by Sabreliner Corp for use in US Navy training contract had the serials applied as shown above, while still current on the USCAR
282-2, 282-9, 282-19, 282-20, 282-28, 282-29, 282-30, 282-32, 282-60, 282-61, 282-66, 282-72, 282-77, 282-81, 282-90, 282-94 and 282-100

SABRE 60

C/n	Series	Identities
306-1		N306NA N978R N521N N571NC XA-REC N359WJ
306-2		N307NA N968R N22MA N277CT N2710T N666BR XA-PUR N36RZ [cx 08Aug13; wfu]
306-3		N177A N1001G N925Z N61MD N424R N160CF LV-WPO [w/o 16Jly98 Cordoba, Argentina]
306-4		N4709N N178W N1210 N121JE [cx 29Jul16, CofR expired]
306-5	A	N365N N302H N7090 OO-IBS N7090 (N477JM) N161CM [parted out by White Inds, Bates City, MO; cx 29Apr09]
306-6	A	N4712N N662P N662F N311RM XA-HHR XA-ADC XA-SMF XB-IYS
306-7		N4715N N523N N63NC N531NC N30PY N60GH N60EX N60CR N64AM XA-SND XB-HDL XB-KPC XA-UOO
306-8		N4716N N73G N73GR N361DA N84LP N613BR N813BR [instructional airframe, Middle Georgia College Aviation Campous, Eastman, GA]
306-9		N4717N N47MN N998R N958R N1298 N32UT N5071L N4LG [to Greenville Technical College, SC, as instructional airframe]
306-10		N4720N N30W N9000V N9001V N19CM N125MC N946JR [parted out at Paynesville, MO circa early 2000]
306-11		N4721N N723R N743R [w/o 13Apr73 Montrose, CO]
306-12		N4722R N90N N9QN N18N N900P XA-ACE XA-CCB XC-HHL XC-AA26 [parted out following flood damage reportedly in 1994; fuselage at Festus, MO, circa Apr96]
306-13		N4723N N60Y N555SL N33BC N33BQ (N256MT) N60EL N306CF RA-3077K RF-14423

SABRE 60

C/n	Series	Identities
306-14		N4724N N24G N24GB (N60AG) N24GB N1JN N43GB N60JN [wfu; fuselage at Festus, MO, circa Apr96]
306-15		N4725N N101L N60BK N360CH N221PH N221PF XA-RUQ N604MK N600SJ [rebuilt with parts from c/n 306-16; canx 06Apr06 as b/u]
306-16	A	N4726N N787R N5415 (N542S) N7090 N967R N100PW N160RW N105UA N33UT N38UT N5075L [parted out Sep92 Spirit of St Louis, MO; remains to Clarkesville, MO; cx May95]
306-17		N4727N (D-COUP) N988R N2UP N2UR N13SL N401MS [has been parted out]
306-18		N4728N N908R N339GW N18HH N36HH (N60RL) N11AQ N12PB N29PB XB-LOA
306-19		N4729N N918R N8000U N50DG [to spares Perryville, MO; cx Jan99]
306-20		N4730N N938R N330U N22JW N44SB N78JP N55BP N155EC XA-PEI N155EC XA-REI XA-TLL XC-AAJ XA-UJW
306-21		N4731N N948R N442A N60HC XB-LRD XB-QND XC-AAC
306-22		N4732N N746UP N743UP (N450CE) XA-CHP [wfu Toluca, Mexico]
306-23		N4733N N908R CF-BLT C-FBLT N15RF N77AT N68MA N85HS N616TR
306-24	A	N4734N N958R N5419 N300TB N58JM N990AC (N995RD) N600GL (N600GE) [cx 08Jul13; wfu]
306-25		N4735N N210F N212F N47MM (N613E) N60DL N60DE OB-1550 N60DE LV-WOF [derelict at San Fernando, Argentina by Nov01]
306-26		N4736N N644X N323R N71CD N31CJ (N377EM) XA-CEN [wfu Toluca, Mexico]
306-27		N4737N N978R I-SNAD N11AL N888WL N105DM (N777CR) (N55ME) (N105SS) N103TA [wfu Banjul, Gambia, after taxying accident 22Apr09]
306-28		N741R N741RL N353CA [wfu]
306-29		N4741N N3000 N3008 N995 N3008 N771WW [cx Jan95 as destroyed reportedly on 10Jan95 – cabin fire at Lexington-Blue Grass Airport, KY; to White Inds, Bates City, MO] N771WB [cx Aug98; parted out]
306-30		N4742N N905R N905BG N2440G N2440C N1116A N104SS [wfu Fort Lauderdale, FL; parted out by White Inds, Bates City, MO]
306-31		N307D N274CA [cx Jun11; parted out]
306-32		N4743N N3278 [parted out at Spirit of St Louis, MO circa early 2000; cx Sep01]
306-33		N4745N N600B XB-APD XA-APD N3FC N30TC N711TW N60JF (N660BW) N78RR N500RR N399SR HC-BQT CC-CGT N633SL
306-34		N4746N N3533 N747RC XA-VIO Mexico MTX-02 Mexico MTX-01 Mexico MTX-04 Mexico AMT-203 XB-RGO
306-35		N4748N N3456B XB-JMR
306-36		N4749N N918R N18N N90R N436CC XA-RIR [wfu by 2006 Toluca, Mexico]
306-37		N4750N N4S N4SE (N60EX) N562R [canx 23May05 as b/u]
306-38		N4751N N253MZ N251MA N229LS N230A XA-PEK XA-DCO XC-HGY [preserved Plaza Estado de Mexico, Ciudad de Toluca, Mexico]
306-39		N4752N N10PF N888MC N507TF N747UP N745UP XA-RTH XA-SLH N82197 (N39SL) [to spares Sep97 at Spirit of St.Louis, MO still as XA-SLH; marks N82197 cx Jun00 as b/u]
306-40		N4753N N907R N711WK N1UP N1UT N997ME XA-SBX N306SA [wfu]
306-41		N4754N N925R N173A N1909R (N8909R) N614MM LV-WLX (N62DW) N856MA [reported destroyed in unknown circumstances in early 2003 in Democratic Republic of Congo; cx Aug03]
306-42		N4755N N915R N80L N58CG N60EL N120JC N128JC XA-VEL XB-IZR
306-43		N4757N N5420 N6NR N6NP N6NE N60AH N10UM N115CR
306-44		N4760N D-CEVW N111VW N45RS N86Y N60RS (N83RH) N129KH HC-BQU N562MS [parted out by AvMATS, St Louis, MO; cx Jun11]
306-45		N4763N N742R N742K N169RF [w/o 07Nov92 Phoenix-Sky Harbor A/P, AZ; cx Jan95]
306-46		N4764N N3600X N100FL N100FN N642RP [cx Jun11; parted out]
306-47	A	N4765N N927R XB-ZUM XA-ZUM XA-ZOM XB-ESX XB-CVS
306-48		N7519N N938R N234U N284U N60AG N75HP N86HP N4228A N4NT [cx 04Aug14; wfu]
306-49		N7522N N29S N29SX N645CC XA-POR XA-RNR [reported wfu 1991]
306-50		N7529N N948R N100Y XA-VIT XA-MUL XB-FSZ N601GL [cx 19Nov14, CofR expired]
306-51		N7531N N928R C-GDCC N141JA N60JC
306-52	CT-39G	N7571N N955R 158843 [AMARC park code 7T031]
306-53		N7573N N957R N99AA N963WL N963WA N624FA N48MG N68TA N999KG (N999LG) N699RD [canx 26Jly05 as b/u]
306-54		N7574N N370VS N1020P N38JM N100EU N38JM N33TR N97SC N610RA [cx 27Aug13; wfu Toluca, Mexico]
306-55	CT-39G	N7575N N908R N5419 158844 [AMARC park code 7T034] [returned to service] 158844 [wfu; to AMARG, Davis-Monthan, AZ, 22May13]
306-56		N7576N N935R N14M N19M N19U XA-CMN XA-RXP XA-DSC [wfu Toluca, Mexico]
306-57		N7577N N937R N7NR N53G N22EH N122EH N701FW N465JH XA-RLS [noted wfu at Toluca, Mexico, Jan02]
306-58		N7578N N80E N80ER N1MN N1PN N529SC N529SQ N529CF XA-AGT [wfu Toluca, Mexico]
306-59		N945R N20G N20GX N10LX [cx 26Feb16; b/u Goodyear, AZ]
306-60		N947R N115L N31BC N555RR N15H N15HF [modified to act as flying testbed for Williams EJ22 engine, 2002; to instructional airframe, Michigan Institute of Aviation & Technology, Canton, MI]
306-61		N965R N961R (N1VC) N76GT N1JN N1JX [instructional airframe at Battle Creek, MI, since Nov04]
306-62		N967R N66NR N7090 N905R N905P N32BC N62CF N162JB [b/u circa 2001]
306-63		N978R XB-BIP XA-CIS XA-ABC XA-LRA XB-FST XB-FUZ XA-FNP XB-ZNP XA-TSS XB-MBV

SABRE 60

C/n	Series	Identities
306-64		N8357N N21BM N370L N1024G (N500RK) N96CP N74BS [a/c dismantled, fuselage noted at Spirit of St Louis, MO 08Dec02]
306-65	CT-39G	N8364N 159361 [reported wfu Sigonella, Italy 1992]
306-66	CT-39G	N8365N 159362 [AMARC park code 7T032]
306-67	CT-39G	159363 [wfu; dumped Jan97 Edwards AFB, CA circa 1996]
306-68		N8000 N2HW N2HX N265DP Ecuador 049
306-69	CT-39G	159364 [AMARC park code 7T-030] [returned to service circa 2000] 159364 [wfu; to AMARG, Davis-Monthan, AZ, 31Jan14]
306-70	CT-39G	159365 [wfu; to AMARG, Davis-Monthan, AZ, 21Nov13]
306-71	A	N31BM N370M N1028Y N71CC
306-72		N231CA N231A N550SL N6TM N60TM XA-RYD N97SC XA-GIH XA-PRO XB-MMN
306-73		N65745 N7NR N601MG N90EC XC-OAH XA-TNW N442RM [w/o in mid-air collison on approach to San Diego/Brown Field, CA, 16Aug15; cx 05Nov15]
306-74		N920G [w/o 27Dec74 Lancaster, PA]
306-75		N110G N666WL N709AB N509AB N11LX
306-76		N65750 N67NR N333PC N333NC N82MW N86CP (N760SA) [cx 23Mar15, wfu]
306-77		N65751 N180AR N787R [wfu; to spares 1994 Spirit of St Louis A/P, MO; cx Apr95]
306-78		N65752 C-GRRS N140JA N477X [b/u; cx 24Jul08]
306-79		N4NR N4NE N768DV (N7682V) N43JG N539PG [parted out by White Inds, Bates City, MO; cx 08Nov12]
306-80		N65756 PT-KOT N61FB [cx 28Feb17; CofR expired]]
306-81	A	N6NR N6ND N30CC [wfu; to spares circa Oct94; remains to Av-Mats Clarkville, MO; cx Jan96]
306-82		N65759 N60SL N59K
306-83		N14CG N14CQ N411MD N300YM N99FF XA-RLL XB-KQY
306-84		N65762 PT-KOU N8025X N383TS N55ZM N265GM [wfu; cx 19Jun09]
306-85		N65764 N217A N500RK N355CD N855CD N211BR [dbr by fire-suppressant foam Mojave, CA, 2007; parted out by AvMATS, St Louis, MO; cx Jul10]
306-86		N65765 N60SL N60TG XA-ICK XB-KSL XB-MRU
306-87		N65767 N100CE N60RS N100MA N400CE N200CE XA-RFB XB-PCJ
306-88		N65769 N992 N22CG XA-RAP
306-89		N65770 N23DS N86RM XA-ECM N86RM XA-STI [wfu by 2006 Toluca, Mexico]
306-90		N65772 N181AR N13SL N148JP N123FG N265MK XB-FMB
306-91		N65774 N204R N204G N60BP N660RM (N45MM) LV-WXX
306-92		N65775 N711S N328JS N74AB N33JW
306-93		N65777 N366N N182AR N200CX N507U XA-JCE XB-IXJ XB-MXG
306-94		N65778 HZ-MA1 HZ-NCB N75JT N217RM N217RN N348W [cx 14Aug12, parted out by AvMATS, St Louis, MO]
306-95		N65783 N999DC N124DC N124VC
306-96		N65784? N54784 N68HC N48HC (N1318E) N315JM XB-ETV
306-97		N65785 I-FBCA N3WQ N344K N85DB N707DB N98LB XA-RWY XA-SVH N90TT N97NL N15DJ XA-SVG
306-98		N65786 N6MK N169AC N531AB XA-GUR XB-MXU
306-99		N65789 N905R N16PN N66GE N66GZ [parted out]
306-100		N65790 N881MC N81HP N5379W N60SE XA-RLR XB-LAW XA-TMF
306-101	A	N65791 N68NR N376D N60FS N376D N378D
306-102		N65792 N108G N555AE N444MA N265TJ N70HL
306-103		N65794 N11UL N40TL N234DC [cx 11May15; b/u Fort Myers/Page Field, FL, Feb17]
306-104	CT-39G	N65795 160053 [wfu; to AMARG, Davis-Monthan, AZ, 24Sep13]
306-105	CT-39G	N65796 160054 [wfu; preserved NAS Pensacola]
306-106	CT-39G	N65797 160055 [wfu; to AMARG, Davis Monthan, AZ, 06Mar13]
306-107	CT-39G	N65798 160056 [AMARC park code 7T-029] [to museum at Pensacola NAS, FL, by Feb09]
306-108	CT-39G	N65799 160057 [w/o 03Mar91 approx 1.5 miles from Glenview NAS, IL]
306-109	A	N2101J N522N N64NC N521NC N602KB XA-SBV N60SQ XA-...
306-110		N2103J N60RS HZ-MA1 N13SL XA-RTP N75GM XB-HJS
306-111		N2106J N300RC XA-SKB XC-PFN [code PF-213] [w/o 28Jly04 Mexicali, Mexico]
306-112		N2107J N740R N740RC CC-CTC N700AU
306-113		N2108J N712MR N2626M N113T XA-TVZ XC-LMP
306-114	65	N2109J N65R N60TF N65R N65RN N990PT N990PA
306-115		N2118J (XA-LEI) Bolivia FAB-001 Bolivia FAB-002 [cx; wfu 2013]
306-116	A	N2119J N605RG N44WD N39CB
306-117		N2120J N22MY Ecuador FAE-001A [reported wfu]
306-118		N2122J N65NR N711MR N2635M N607SR N607CF
306-119	A	N2123J N167H N110MH XA-JMD N109MC N41RG
306-120		N2124J N265C N265SR N1GM [cx 20May13; parted out Perryville, MO]
306-121		N2130J N880KC (N15CK) N880CK XA-SYS N789SG XA-LED
306-122	A	N2131J N168H N56RN XA-GUR N110JG [cx Jun11; parted out]
306-123		N2132J N710MR N2627M N128VM (N213BE) N28VM XA-PAX N97SC XA-ATE
306-124	A	N2133J N65NR N60RS N48WS XB-MDO
306-125		N2134J N32PC XA-RGC N265RW N261T XA-SLJ N28HH XA-AEV XA-JML
306-126		N2141J N60SL N7NR N7NF N1CH N85HP N4227N HC-BUN N111F XA-TGA XB-MQN
306-127		N2142J N5NE N60DD XA-CUR XB-JTG
306-128		N2143J N80CR N100CE N117JL "N24TK" N117JL XA-SJM XB-SOL XA-CUN XB-NOA
306-129		N2144J N711ST N749UP N95RC N60ML XB-ULF

SABRE 60

C/n	Series	Identities
306-130		N2145J XA-OVR XA-JIK XB-JMM XA-AFG XA-UFQ [dbf Calaya, Mexico, 18Dec08, w/o]
306-131		N2149J N5DL N35DL N61DF N131JR (N131SE) XA-GUR [w/o Nov04 Toluca, Mexico]
306-132		N2150J N60RS N108W (N994W) N60AG N265U XB-MMW XB-KLQ [w/o 09Dec14; shot down over Venezuela on drug-running flight]
306-133		N2151J N6NE N9NP N700WS I-PATY N360CF N400JH N468RB
306-134		N2152J N323EC N282WW [cx 08May15; wfu Guatemala City/La Aurora, Guatemala]
306-135		N2535E N9NR N9NT N64CM N59JM N60AM N921MB HC-...
306-136	65	N2501E N465S N65RS [redesignated c/n 465-1 1981 as first Sabre 65 (qv)]
306-137		N2506E N60SL N650C N18X XA-SAH
306-138		N2508E N22BX N800RM N700JR N702JR XA-RVT
306-139		Mexico TP105 Mexico TP103/XC-UJE XC-UJS
306-140		N636 N636MC N60AF N26SC N26SQ XA-SSV
306-141		N8NR (N89N) (N8NF) N141SL (N707GP)
306-142		N60RS N80CR N742R N742RC N190MD N40KJ (N70LW) N700MH (N700DA) N143DZ
306-143		N800M N80QM N741R N741RC XA-SIM XA-SUN XA-TPU XA-URI
306-144		N2519E Mexico TP106 Mexico TP104/XC-UJF Mexico AMT-204
306-145		N60SL N730CA XA-LOQ XC-JDC XC-CAM
306-146		N301MC N301MG N360CH XA-ARE (N146BJ) N31CR N44DD

Production complete

SABRE 65

C/n	Series	Identities
465-1		N2501E N465S N65RS N77A N65KJ N117MB (N117MN) N65HH [originally Sabre 60 c/n 306-136]
465-2		N465T N251JE N45H N624DS N124SD
465-3		N65RS N6K N170JL N170CC N1CF N65BT
465-4		N1058X N14M N141PB N800TW N804PA
465-5		N24G N55KS N52GG N60CE N241H [w/o 11May00 Molokai, HI]
465-6		N65NC N511NC N65SR N1CC N41CQ (N652CC) N2CC N432CC
465-7		N10580 N2000 N2800 N2000 N2700
465-8		N10581 XA-GAP XB-UNA
465-9		N6NP N769KC (N769EG) N6GV
465-10		N65SL N77TC N336RJ
465-11		N3000 N3030 N25UG N5739 N57MQ XA-...
465-12		XA-OVR XA-PVR XB-GMD N112PR N112PV N529SC N73TJ N77GU
465-13		N7HF N13MF N945CC N95TL [wfu Chino, CA]
465-14		N651S N301MC N67SC N71RB N740R N25SR XA-SPM
465-15		N2513E XA-ZUM N465TS N25VC
465-16		N31BC N7000G N700QG N65SR N112CF N920CC N603MA N75HL N75HE XA-APC XC-LNI XA-APC XB-GCU
465-17		N2537E N905K N4MB N32290 (N322TW) N74VC
465-18		N4M N696US XA-XPA XB-XPA
465-19		N65RC N91BZ [parted out by AvMATS, St Louis, MO]
465-20		N2544E N173A
465-21		N2586E (N65HM) N465LC (N265CA) N701FW
465-22		N996W N678AM 9H-ABO VR-CEE N927AA N883RA N889RA XB-RSH XA-UUS
465-23		N904K (N904KB) N223LB XB-MMZ N65JR
465-24		N65NR N2545E N8000U N800CU N65JR N265PC N741R N777SK N271MB N22CS XA-INM
465-25		N9000F N25MF N125BP N324ZR N812WN N42DC
465-26		N465SL N2548E N65DD N31SJ N488DM N770MD
465-27		XA-ARE XA-AVR XA-FVK N351AF N111AD N39TR N4CS N247CS
465-28		N2549E N333PC N742R N24RF (N129BA) N66GE
465-29		N6NR N976SR N779CS
465-30		N25ZC (N25ZG) N89MM N65TC N465SC
465-31		N2550E N65FC N265M N670AC
465-32		N97RE N303A HB-VCN N329Z
465-33		N994 N869KC (N869EG) (N271MB) N465SR N265C VP-CBG N265VP N70SK
465-34		(N50DG) N112KM N80FH N65TS N47SE
465-35		N2590E N65AK
465-36		N651GL N652MK N424JM N65MC
465-37		N750CS N750CC YV415T N465NH N465PD
465-38		N850CS N850CC (N4LQ)
465-39		N2551E N5511A N551FA N203JK N41LV N901CD [b/u Fort Lauderdale Executive, FL, Aug13]
465-40		N341AP N465RM N465PM N801SS N861SS [parted out by White Inds, Bates City, MO]
465-41		N2556E N800M
465-42		N2561E N415CS N41TC N15CC N150HN N15CC N64SL N45NP N875CA N799MW
465-43		N950CS N228LS N83TF N955PR N65T

SABRE 65 / 75 / 75A

C/n	Series	Identities
465-44		N7NR N74BJ
465-45		N442WT N448WT N65TJ (N265DR) N65DR N265DS
465-46		N20UC N79CD N65FF N65CC N307ST N265FT
465-47		N265A N33TR
465-48		N2539E XA-MLG N500WD N265SP N265CP [canx 15Jun15; CofR expired]
465-49		N455SF N455LB N500RR N82CR N697US
465-50		N2570E N129GP N959C N920DY (N920DG) XB-MYP
465-51		N3BM N3QM N114LG N69WU
465-52		N500E N96RE
465-53		N76NX N80R N80RN N465BC
465-54		N2579E N6000J N600QJ N1909R N65SR [cx 28Mar15, wfu]
465-55		N2574E XA-LUC XA-RYO XB-RYO XA-TOM XB-RSC [w/o Las Vegas/McCarran, NV, 05Jul13; to scrapyard nr Phoenix Sky Harbor, AZ]
465-56		N544PH N265JS N65TL N499NH
465-57		N903K N355CD
465-58		N65AM N670AS N670H
465-59		N65AN HB-VJF N59SR N61DF N8500 N35CC N35CQ
465-60		N2580E N88BF (N688WS) N654YS
465-61		N23BX N117JW N92VC
465-62		N56NW N65AF N265WS
465-63		N2N N605Y N2N N2NL
465-64		N99S [w/o 11Jan83 Toronto, Canada; cx Aug91]
465-65		N29S N29SZ N65AD (N925WL) N963WL XA-SCR N600TG N395GA
465-66		N964C
465-67		N65AR N921CC
465-68		N65AH OO-IBC N68LX N165NA N930RA N6NR N888UP
465-69		N33BC (N31BC) N400KV N25KL N65ML
465-70		N15AK N15EN N58CM N58HT
465-71		N728C N75G N75GL N75VC
465-72		N857W (OO-RSA) (OO-RSB) OO-RSE N465SP XB-PTC
465-73		N64MC N64MQ N651MK
465-74		N700JC
465-75		N2581E N570R
465-76		N65L N376D

Production complete

SABRE 75

C/n	Series	Identities
370-1		N7572N [used as parts for other test aircraft]
370-2		N7585N N75NR N8NR N80K N10M [wfu; cx 08Sep06]
370-3		N7586N N70NR N125N N125NX [wfu; cx 19May09]
370-4		N7587N N75U N75UA N37GF N370BH N400DB (N404DB) N726JR [dbr San Jose, Costa Rica, 03Sep07]
370-5		N7588N N75NR N23G N55KS N55KZ N58KS N250BC N265SR XA-RYJ
370-6		N7589N N2TE XA-SGR N29019 (N30EV) [wfu; cx Sep91; remains to Clarkesville, MO]
370-7	A	N7590N N75NR N60PM N60PT N75DE XB-ERU N670C (N26TJ) (N272HS) [cx 03Dec14; CofR expired]
370-8		N7591N N3TE N70HC [b/u for spares Sep90 Little Rock, AR; canx Jun96; remains to Paynesville, MO]
370-9		N7592N N8NR N8NB N55CR XA-RZW XB-GJO N370SL [parted out at Spirit of St Louis, MO circa early 2000 still wearing its previous identity XB-GJO; cx Jan01, scrapped]

Production complete

SABRE 75A

C/n	Series	Identities
380-1		N7593N N6K N87Y N30GB N100EJ (N200UN)
380-2		N8445N N2440G N2440C N19PC N380SR N9GN N642TS N406PW YV265T
380-3		N8467N Argentina T-10 Argentina T-11 [wfu Cordoba/Rio Cuarto, Argentina]
380-4	80A	N65733 N5105 N510AA N75SE XA-RLP N11887 (LV-...) N11887
380-5		N51 N125MS N223LP N71460 XA-TUD [wfu Toluca, Mexico]
380-6	80A	N65741 N5106 N50GG N75TJ N711GL N711GD N184PC [preserved on barge at Fort Lauderdale, FL]
380-7		N65744 N67KM [w/o 14Jun75 Watertown, SD]
380-8		N65749 N5107 N500NL [wfu; parted out Feb93 – possibly following an accident on 23Feb75 at Oakland-Pontiac, MI]
380-9	80A	N5108 N510BB N6SP N383CF N995RD
380-10		N52 [cx Sep95 wfu; in use as an instructional airframe at Burlington, VT]

SABRE 75A

C/n	Series	Identities
380-11	80A	N5109 N5109T N265SR N151TB [cx 11Jan05; parted out by White Industries, Bates City, MO]
380-12		N65758 (N335K) HB-VEC D-CLAN N75SL D-CLAN N120YB (N4WJ) N75BS [b/u; cx 24Jul08]
380-13		N65761 Argentina AE-175
380-14		N53 N72028 [being parted out at Rantoul, KS circa early 2000]
380-15		N65766 (N338K) N80NR N1841D N1841F N15PN N18TF N18TZ XA-LEG N22JW N424R
380-16		N54 N126MS N12659 N801FT
380-17	80A	N65768 (N339K) N80RS 5N-AMM N70TF N15RF N111Y N1115 N380BC [parted out]
380-18		N55 N127MS [wfu; parted out Perryville, MO; cx Jly95]
380-19		N65771 D-CLUB N500TF N100RS XB-EPM XA-EPM N54HH N80HG N80TN [b/u and cx Jun02]
380-20		N56 N773W N109SB
380-21	80A	N65773 N711A N75A N22NT N25AT N577SW N111AG N840MA N647JP N82AF N380MS XA-...
380-22		N57 N132MS N131MS [wfu; parted out Perryville, MO; cx Jly95]
380-23		N65776 N68KM N102RD N800CD [cx 24Mar17, CofR expired]
380-24	80	N58 N219TT [parted out by AvMATS, St Louis, MO]
380-25		N50PM N90AM N16LF N13NH N400RS
380-26		N59 N128MS N2200A [parted out circa Jan02 Spirit of St Louis A/P, MO; cx Jun11]
380-27		N65787 N8NR N8NB N10CN N6NR N6NG N90GM N90GW N85DW [w/o 14Aug00 near Ironwood, MI]
380-28		N60 [cx Jun96; wfu]
380-29		N61 N131MS N58966 N132MS N71543 [used for fire training by University of Illinois, Champaign, IL and destroyed as a result]
380-30		N65793 N69KM N265CH N265DP N818DW N818LD N42799 [cx Jun11; parted out]
380-31		N62 N75CN [parted out at Rantoul, KS circa early 2000]
380-32	80A	N2100J N75RS N64MP N64MQ N66ES N66ED (N86SH) N380DJ N198GB XA-JRF
380-33		N63 N129MS N7148J N802FT
380-34		N2104J N6LG (N112KH) N382MC Ecuador FAE-034 Ecuador AEE-403 N97SC XC-DDA
380-35		N64 [w/o 29Sep86 Liberal, KS; cx Aug88]
380-36		N2105J N75A JY-AFM N75HL (N835MA) XA-MCB N377HS [canx 22Feb05 as b/u]
380-37		N65 N774W [cx 06May15; CofR expired]
380-38		N2102J D-CAVW N85031 N3RN HZ-AMN N95TJ N75AK N316EC N316EQ [cx 11Dec14; CofR expired]
380-39		N2110J N7NR N102MJ N88JM N38JM (N60WP) N40WP XA-PON N2093P XA-SXK XC-ONA N354SH (N805HD) (N55HD) N105HD [cx 07Apr17, CofR expired]
380-40		N2112J N4NR N4NB N75NL N920DY N820DY N14TN XA-UBH XA-UEK [wfu Toluca, Mexico]
380-41		N2113J N33NT N400N N400NR [parted out by White Inds, Bates City, MO]
380-42		N2114J N75RS D-CHIC N75AG XA-MVT N6YL N3RP N80KR [parted out by MTW Aerospace, Montgomery, AL]
380-43		N2115J N6NR N2265Z [wfu prior Sep90 Clarkesville, MO]
380-44	80A	N2116J N2440G N380GK YV338T
380-45		N2117J D-CCVW N218US (N218UB) N753TW Ecuador FAE-045 Ecuador AEE-402 [not confirmed] [AEE-402 was w/o 10Dec92 nr Quito A/P, Ecuador]
380-46		N2125J (N50K) N90C XA-RIH XC-HFY XC-AA89 [b/u Mexico City, Mexico]
380-47		N2126J N25BH N25BX N33RZ XA-...
380-48	80A	N2127J N8NR N8NG N805RG N6PG N27TS N132DB N100BP XB-JYZ
380-49	80A	N2128J N4PG (N41B) N4PQ N4PG N673SH N673FH N221PH N265KC
380-50	80A	N2129J N5PG N5EQ N5PG N179S XA-ROD XA-RLR XA-TDQ XA-ACD XB-ACD
380-51		N2135J N43R N4343 N711BY (N12GP) N808EB N80LX N180NA N382LS N380CF [cx to Mexico 28Jul10 but w/o Queretaro, Mexico, 30Jan16 still as N380CF]
380-52		N2136J N75A N177NC N177NQ N70KM N84NG N34NG N929GC N929CG [dbr Guyana, Venezuela; cx 25Aug16]
380-53		N2137J N75NR JY-AFN HZ-THZ N8526A N75HZ XC-FIA XB-DVP N380SR N827SL XB-CYA
380-54		N2138J N6NR N62NR N10CN N350MT N81GD N999M N176DC N380CF N910BH N380FP XA-... [although cx to Mexico 28Oct13, still flying as N380CF]
380-55		N2139J N33KA HZ-CA1 N120KC XA-OAF XB-RDB XB-GSP
380-56		N2146J JY-AFL N14JD (N914JC) N22NB [cx 10Jul14, wfu]
380-57		N2147J N80RS N75A HZ-RBH JY-AFH [wfu]
380-58		N2148J N75RS N380T XA-CHA XA-SEB XA-GHR N8267D XA-UEQ XC-LKB
380-59		N80AB (N935PC) N83AB N911CR N27LT N1LT [parted out Tulsa, OK; cx 31Jul08]
380-60		N2521E D-CBVW N4260K N100TM XB-RSG XB-SHA XA-RDY N60SL XA-AOV
380-61		N2522E JY-AFO 9L-LAW N727US [parted out at Spirit of St.Louis, MO circa 1996 cx Jan00]
380-62		JY-AFP [wfu]
380-63		N75RS N448W
380-64		N75NR N75Y N942CC JY-JAS [w/o Alexandria, Egypt, May06]
380-65		YU-BLY RC-BLY 9A-BLY N88JJ N69JN N972NR
380-66		N2536E N6PG N6VL N6PG N75L N943CC N819GY [parted out by AvMATS, St Louis, MO]

SABRE 75A

C/n	Series	Identities						
380-67		N2528E	Mexico TP 103		Mexico TP 101/XC-UJC		[w/o 26Oct89 Saltillo, Mexico; fuselage to Spirit of St.Louis A/P, MO]	
380-68		N2538E	Mexico TP 104		Mexico TP 102/XC-UJD		XC-UJU	[preserved at military base near Mexico City]
380-69		N2542E	N111VW	(N111VS)	N111VX	N547JL	[w/o 18Jly98 near Marion, KS]	
380-70		(N13ME)	(N15ME)	N101ME	N1NR	(N380RS)	N110AJ	[wfu Fort Lauderdale Executive, FL]
380-71		HZ-NR1	N80HK	XA-TSZ				
380-72		HZ-SOG	N380N	N90N	N555JR	N933JC	[cx 21May15; wfu Pontiac, MI]	

Production complete

SN601 CORVETTE

C/n	Identities
01	F-WRSN [ff 16Jly70; w/o 23Mar71 Marseille, France (model SN600)]
1	F-WUAS [ff 20Dec72] F-BUAS F-WUAS F-BUAS France (CEV) 1/F-ZVMV coded MV [wfu by Jun05 at Istres, France]
2	F-WRNZ F-BRNZ France (CEV) 2/F-ZVMW coded MW [to Vitrolles Engineering College nr Marseille, France]
3	F-WUQN F-BUQN F-WUQN F-BUQN [w/o 16Oct00 Toulouse-Blagnac, France; repaired to non-flying condition and painted as "F-WUQN" on display at entrance to Airbus facility St. Nazaire, France]
4	F-WUQP F-BUQP [wfu Toulouse, France; instructional airframe at Vitrolles, France]
5	F-BVPA F-ODJX F-BVPA CN-TDE [instructional airframe, Institut Mecanique Aeronautique et Automobile, Annecy, France]
6	F-WUQR F-BVPB F-OGJL F-BVPB [regn cx circa 2000; CofA expired; instructional airframe at St.Yan, France; moved to Le Bourget by 10Apr03]
7	F-OBZR N611AC F-BVPK
8	F-WPTT 6V-AEA F-GJAS
9	F-WRQK F-BRQK N612AC F-BTTR F-OCRN TN-ADI [reported wfu South of France]
10	F-BVPO N600AN F-GFEJ France (CEV) 10/F-ZVMX coded MX [instructional airframe at Lycee Stella, Reunion]
11	(F-WIFU) N613AC F-BTTS TR-LWY F-ODKS F-BTTV EI-BNY F-WFPD (F-GFPD) F-GKGA [wfu; cx 08Dec09; preserved in Aeroscopia museum, Toulouse/Blagnac, France]
12	F-BVPC TR-LYM TJ-AHR F-GMOF [parted out; broken up at Le Bourget, France, by Mar12]
13	F-BVPD N601AN F-GFDH [wfu; cx 08Dec09]
14	F-BVPS SP-FOA (F-GIRH) [last noted 29Mar06 dismantled on a low-loader at Le Bourget, France]
15	F-WIFA SE-DEN OO-MRA OO-MRE F-GDUB SE-DEN N17AJ F-GEQF D6-ECB F-GNAF EC-HHZ [wfu]
16	F-BVPT 5R-MVN 5R-MBR [wfu Antananarivo, Madagascar]
17	F-WNGQ N614AC F-BTTM F-ODTM YV-572CP [w/o 21Jun91 Las Delicias A/P, Santa Barbara del Zulia, Venezuela]
18	F-WNGR N615AC F-BTTO N604AN [cx Dec90; sold to Drenair, Spain, for spares use]
19	F-BVPL F-OCJL F-BVPL TZ-PBF (F-GDRC) F-SEBH F-GEPQ EC-HIA [wfu; cx 2006]
20	F-WNGS N616AC F-BTTN TR-LZT F-GKJB [wfu 31Mar93 for spares at Toulouse, France; wings used in rebuild of c/n 28; forward fuselage to cabin trainer use]
21	F-BVPE OY-SBS [w/o 03Sep79 Nice, France]
22	F-WNGT N617AC F-BTTU F-ODFE TN-ADB [w/o 30Mar79 Nkayi, Congo Republic]
23	F-BVPF OY-SBR [wfu Aalborg, Denmark circa Feb05; last flight 26Dec04; to Danmarks Flymuseum, Stauning, Denmark]
24	F-BVPI EC-DQC [sold in USA for scrap/spares and b/u Mar92 Toulouse, France]
25	F-WNGU F-BVPG F-OBZV F-BVPG [cx Oct06, C of A expired]
26	F-WNGV N618AC F-ODFQ PH-JSB F-GDAY EC-DQE [noted dismantled 2000 at Dieupentule, France; intended as a museum exhibit but cut up by local gypsies]
27	F-BVPH N26674+ [+ marks not confirmed] EC-DQG [w/o 25Nov00 Cordoba, Spain]
28	F-WNGX F-BTTL (OO-TTL) F-GPLA
29	F-WNGY F-BVPJ F-OBZP F-BVPJ F-OBZP TY-BBK [w/o 16Nov81 Lagos, Nigeria]
30	F-WNGQ F-BTTP OO-MRC TR-LAH OO-MRC EC-DUE (F-GKGB) F-GLEC [wfu; cx 27Oct09]
31	F-WNGZ F-BTTK N602AN F-WZSB EC-DYE F-GJAP [to Musee de l'Air et de l'Espace, Le Bourget, France 17Oct09; cx 08Dec09]
32	F-WNGR F-BTTQ OY-ARA SE-DED OY-ARA EC-DUF F-GILM [wfu 08Dec09; preserved at entrance to Airbus factory, Meaulte, France]
33	F-BTTT OY-SBT [wfu]
34	F-WNGS F-BYCR OY-ARB SE-DEE OY-ARB SE-DEE F-GKGD CN-TCS 5R-MHK [preserved in grounds of Air Formation facility nr Toulouse/Blagnac airport, France]
35	PH-JSC F-GDAZ YV-589CP YV-01CP F-ODSR 5R-MVD F-ODSR [wfu]
36	F-BTTS PH-JSD F-OCDE XB-CYA XB-EWF XA-BCC N601RC N600RA [parted out by Atlanta Air Salvage, Griffin, GA]
37	F-BTTU [w/o 31Jul90 St Yan, France; cx 12Feb91 as "reformed" 04Dec90]
38	F-ODIF 5A-DCK
39	F-WNGY F-OBYG TL-SMI TL-RCA F-GJLB CN-THL
40	F-WNGZ F-ODJS XB-CYI N601CV N200MT N220MT [parted out by Atlanta Air Salvage, Griffin, GA circa Feb05]

Production complete

SYBERJET SJ30

Originally called the Swearingen SA-30 Gulfjet, then the Swearingen SJ-30 and SJ30-1, then the Sino Swearingen SJ30-2, then the Emivest SJ30.

C/n	Identities		
001	N30SJ	[ff 13Feb91 Stinson Field, TX. Stretched to become SJ30-2 prototype and ff 8Nov96; cx Oct99, wfu. To Lone Star Flight Museum, Galveston, TX, Dec06. Scrapped following storm damage sustained in Sep08]	
002	N138BF	[rolled out 17Jly00; ff 30Nov00; crashed near Del Rio, TX, 26Apr03 during high-speed test-flight, killing Sino-Swearingen's chief test pilot; w/o]	
003	N30SJ	N110SJ	
004	N709JB	N404SJ	
005	N50SJ	[ff Jan05]	
006	N60SJ	N901HB	N30SJ
007	N70SJ	N7SJ	
008	(N80SJ)	N200DV	
009	[in production, not yet completed]		
010	N30GZ		
011			
012			
TF-2	[static test frame]		
TF-3	[static test frame]		

EXPERIMENTAL & NON-PRODUCTION TYPES

ADAM AIRCRAFT A700

A 6-8 seat very light jet powered by 2 Williams FJ-33 engines

C/n	Identities		
0001	N700JJ	N700AJ	[ff 27Jly03; cx 08Jun07, wfu]
0002	N700LJ	[ff 06Feb06; cx 02Oct12, wfu]	
0003	N703AJ	[cx 29May09, wfu]	
0004	N700AJ	[cx 06May09, wfu]	

Company filed for bankruptcy February 2008, production ceased.

CHICHESTER-MILES LEOPARD

C/n	Identities	
001	G-BKRL	[first flight late 1988; cx 25Jan99, wfu; to Bournemouth Aviation Museum, UK, in dismantled state circa Feb05]
002	G-BRNM	[preserved Bournemouth Aviation Museum, UK 2003-2008 then Midland Air Museum, Coventry, UK]

DASSAULT FALCON 30

C/n	Identities	
01	F-WAMD	[wfu Bordeaux, France; never entered production; fuselage at Vitrolles Engineering University, nr Marseille, France, 1990]

DASSAULT FALCON 5X

A new long-range super-midsize twin-jet under development but subject to a 2-year delay due to problems with the new Snecma Silvercrest engines selected to power it. First flight is currently scheduled for 2017 with customer deliveries following in 2020.

C/n	Identities	
1	F-WIDE	[r/o 02Jun15, Bordeaux, France]

DIAMOND D-JET

A 4-passenger, single pilot "personal" jet powered by a single Williams FJ-33 engine giving a range of 1350NM at an operating altitude of 25,000 ft.

C/n	Identities	
10-0001	C-GVLJ	[ff 18Apr06 London, ONT, Canada; cx 31Oct08, wfu]
DJ1-0002	C-FPTM	[ff 14Sep07; CofR canx 31Aug12 but not deleted from Canadian register]
DJ1-0003	C-GUPJ	[ff 14Apr08; CofR canx 31Aug13 but not deleted from Canadian register]

ECLIPSE 400 CONCEPT JET

A 4-seat, single-engined "personal jet" built to test the single-engined jet market. Officially registered as a Swift Engineering Inc Mark 400.

C/n	Identities	
SE-400-001	N5184U	[ff 02Jul07]

EPIC ELITE

A 6-seat very light jet powered by two Williams FJ-33-4A engines.

C/n	Identities	
001J	C-GROL	[ff 07Jun07]

EXPERIMENTAL & NON-PRODUCTION TYPES

EPIC VICTORY

A 4-seat "personal jet" powered by a single Williams FJ-33-4A engine.

C/n	Identities		
001	N370EJ	[ff 06Jul07]	
002	N975AR	N952R	[converted to turboprop]

GROB G180 SPn Utility Jet

Grob Aerospace unveiled its ten-seat (including crew), carbon-fibre SPn Utility jet at the 2005 Paris Air Show. Development of the type drove the company into insolvency. H3 Aerospace purchased the company in January 2009 but decided not to continue the SPn programme.

C/n	Identities			
90001	D-ISPN	[ff 20Jly05]	D-CSPN	[to Deutsches Museum Flugwerft Schleissheim, Munich, Germany, 2012]
90002	D-CGSP	[ff 29Sep06, w/o Tussenhausen-Mattsies 29Nov06]		
90003	D-CSPJ	[ff 29Oct07]	F-WINT	
90004	D-CSPG	[ff 07Aug08]		
90005	[assembly commenced but not completed]			

GULFSTREAM 550 PEREGRINE

C/n	Identities			
551	N9881S	N550GA	N84GP	[wfu Mar92; to Oklahoma Air & Space Museum, Oklahoma City, OK]

HONDA MH02

C/n	Identities	
001	N3097N	[ff 05Mar93 – undertook 170 hours of test flying which ended in Aug96, displayed in the Honda Hall, Motegi, Japan]

LEARJET MODEL 85

Official Bombardier designation was LJ-200-1A10. Development was ceased in 2014 due to weak demand and Bombardier management's desire to focus resources on the new Global 7000 and 8000.

C/n	Identities	
3001	N851LJ	[r/o 07Sep13; ff 09Apr14; stored Wichita/Mid-Continent, KS]
3002	(N852LJ)	[marks requested but aircraft not completed; stored Wichita/Mid-Continent, unmarked]
3003	(N853LJ)	[marks requested but aircraft not built]
3004	(N854LJ)	[marks requested but aircraft not built]
3005	(N855LJ)	[marks requested but aircraft not built]
3006	(N856LJ)	[marks requested but aircraft not built]

McDONNELL MD220

C/n	Identities			
1	N119M	N220N	N4AZ	[never entered production; ferried Albuquerque, NM, to El Paso, TX 21Dec85 – where it is wfu]

NORTH AMERICAN UTX

C/n	Identities	
246-1	N4060K	[b/u circa 1967]

EXPERIMENTAL & NON-PRODUCTION TYPES

PILATUS PC-24

C/n	Identities	
P01	HB-VXA	[rolled out 1Aug14, Stans, Switzerland; ff 11May15]
P02	HB-VXB	[rolled out Feb15, Stans, Switzerland; ff 16Nov15]
P03	HB-VSA	[ff 06Mar17, Stans, Switzerland]

PIPER PA-47 PIPERJET/ALTAIRE

A 6-seat "personal" jet powered by a single Williams FJ44 engine, development work on which was suspended in 2011.

C/n	Identities
4798E001	N360PJ [ff 30Jul08 Vero Beach, FL; to Florida Air Museum, Lakeland, FL, Dec11; cx 15Feb12]

SABRE 50

C/n	Identities		
287-1	N287NA	N50CR	[did not enter production; preserved Evergreen Aviation & Space Museum, McMinnville, OR]

SCALED COMPOSITES 143 TRIUMPH

C/n	Identities	
C/n	Identities	
001	N143SC	[ff 12Jly88; further development abandoned; wfu Sep92 Mojave, CA; placed on display outside Scaled Composites premises at Mojave, CA]

SPECTRUM 33

C/n	Identities	
0001	N322LA	[ff 07Jan06, w/o 25Jly06 Spanish Fork, UT. Powered by 2 rear-mounted Williams FJ33 engines giving a range of 2000nm, the aircraft had a cabin slightly larger than that of the CitationJet CJ2. Current project status uncertain]

VISIONAIRE VANTAGE/EVIATION EV-20

C/n	Identities	
001	N247VA	[ferried to Brazil Nov04 for conversion to EV-20 powered by 2 Williams FJ44 turbofans; project abandoned, returned to Ames, IA, 18Feb06 and wfu; subsequently moved to Hickory, NC]

WILLIAMS V-JET II

Officially registered as a Scale Composites 271. The V-Jet II is a small, all-composite 6-seat jet powered by a single Williams FJX-2 engine. It was built primarily as a test-bed for the FJX-2 engine rather than for series production.

C/n	Identities	
001	N222FJ	[wfu and presented to the EAA AirVenture Museum, Oshkosh, WI on 27Jly00]